SHAMAN KING

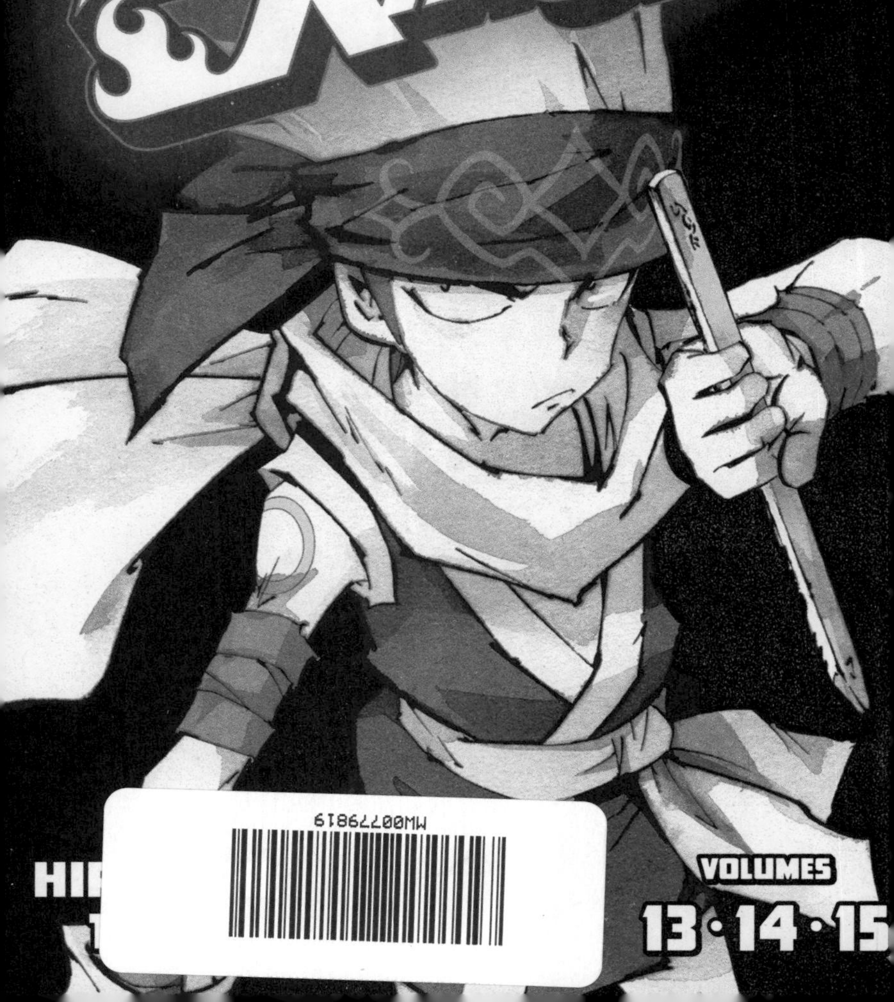

VOLUMES

13 · 14 · 15

SHAMAN KING

VOLUMES
13·14·15

TABLE OF CONTENTS

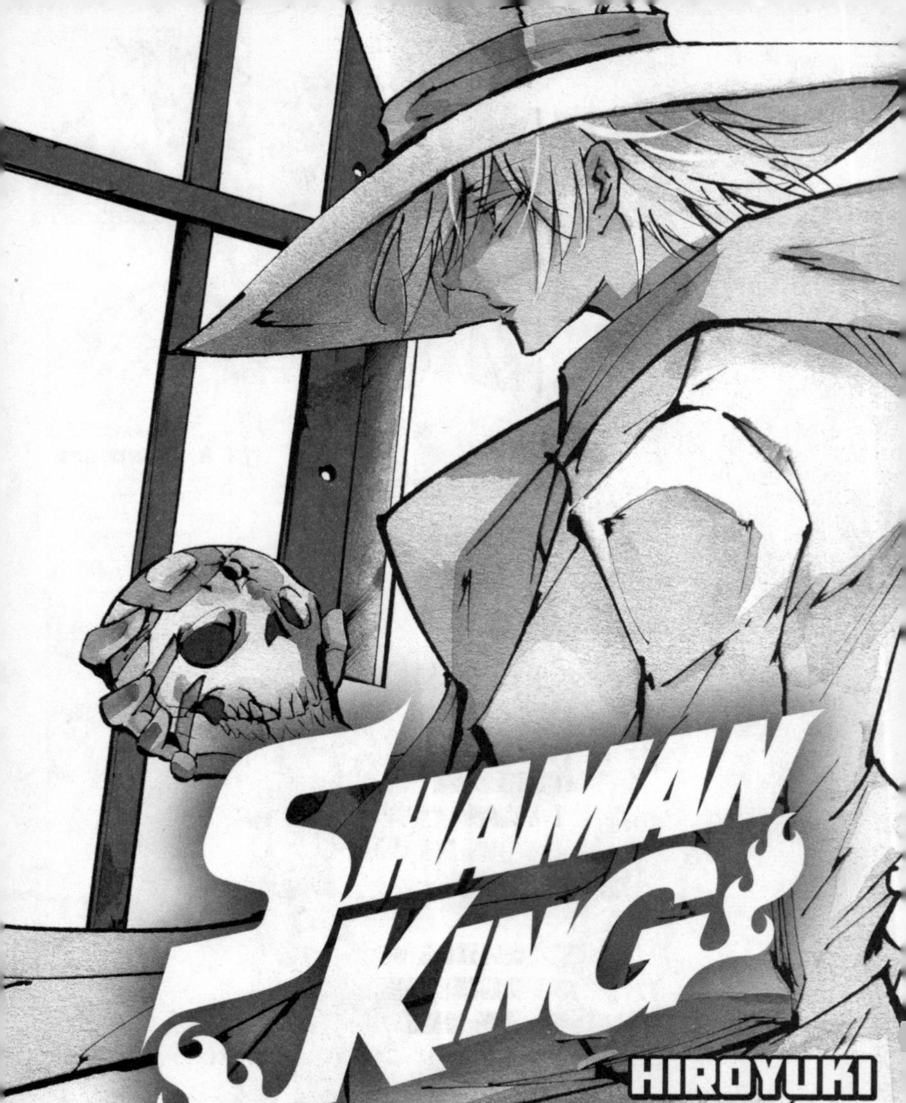
SHAMAN KING
HIROYUKI TAKEI

13 The Return of Faust

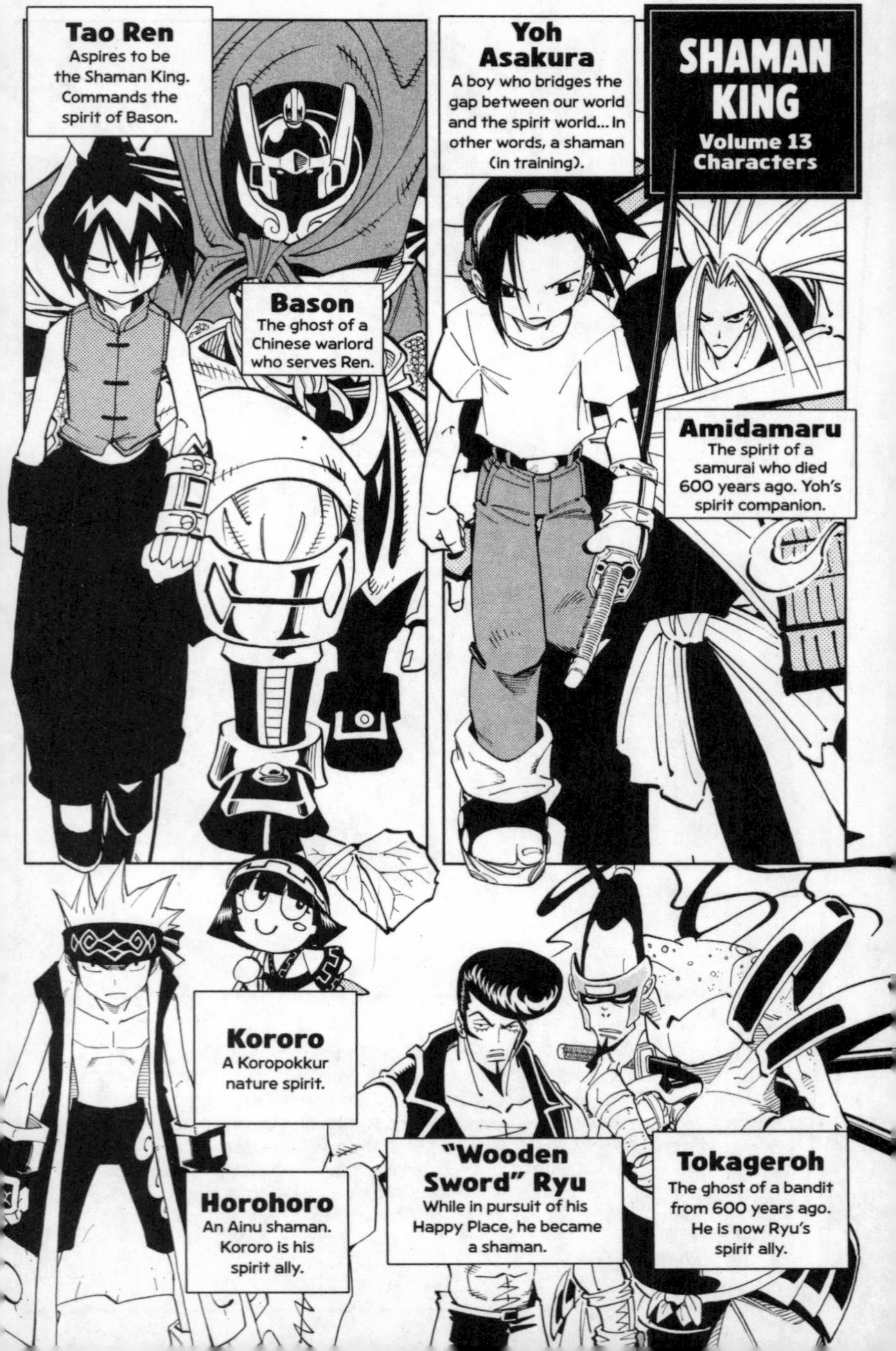
SHAMAN KING
Volume 13 Characters
Yoh Asakura
A boy who bridges the gap between our world and the spirit world... In other words, a shaman (in training).
Amidamaru
The spirit of a samurai who died 600 years ago. Yoh's spirit companion.
Tao Ren
Aspires to be the Shaman King. Commands the spirit of Bason.
Bason
The ghost of a Chinese warlord who serves Ren.
Tokageroh
The ghost of a bandit from 600 years ago. He is now Ryu's spirit ally.
"Wooden Sword" Ryu
While in pursuit of his Happy Place, he became a shaman.
Kororo
A Koropokkur nature spirit.
Horohoro
An Ainu shaman. Kororo is his spirit ally.

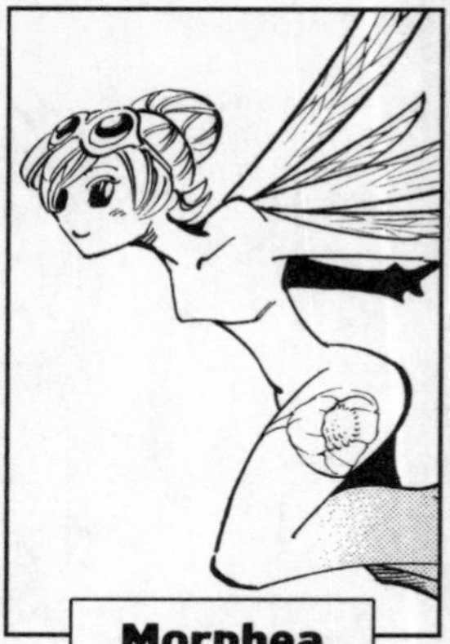

Morphea
Lyserg's spirit ally.
A poppy flower fairy.

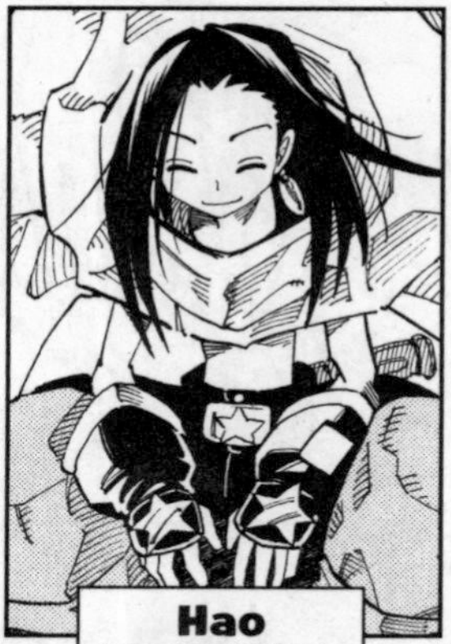

Hao
An enigmatic figure
who calls himself
the "Future King."

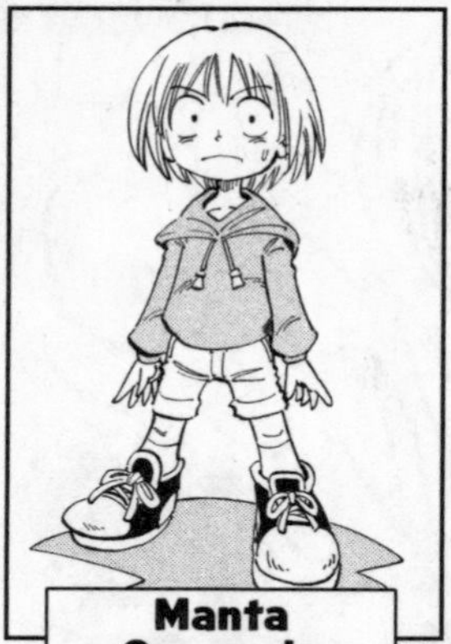

Manta Oyamada
Yoh's friend. Always
carrying his trusty
dictionary.

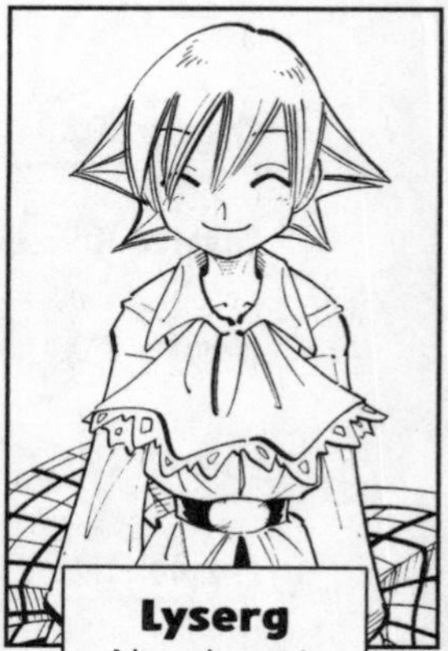

Lyserg
A boy who wants
revenge against Hao.

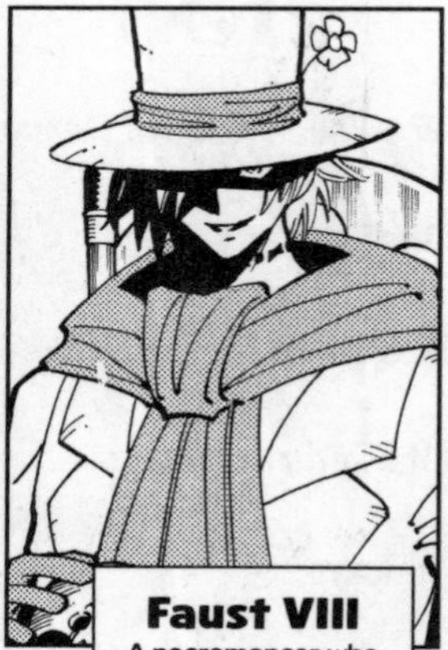

Faust VIII
A necromancer who
fought Yoh in the
preliminaries.

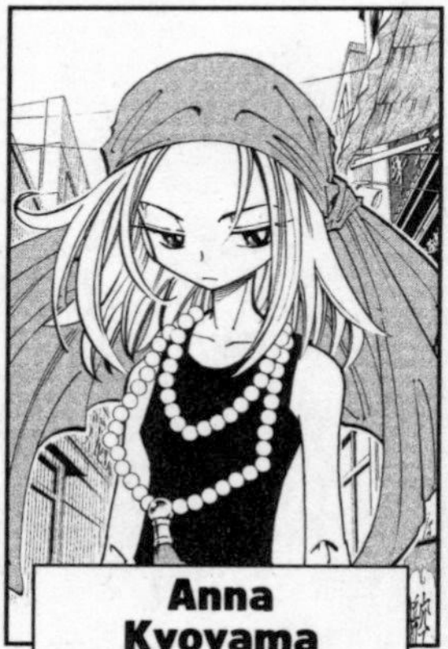

Anna Kyoyama
An *itako* from Mt. Osore.
Yoh's arranged fiancée.

THE STORY SO FAR

This kid named Yoh Asakura-kun transferred to my class from Izumo... and it turns out he's a shaman! He made it into the Shaman Fight, which takes place once every 500 years, and the Patch dumped him and his fellow competitors in North America for their first challenge—to find their way to the Patch Village. Newly teamed up with Lyserg, Yoh-kun and friends arrived at the village. However, they were confronted by Hao's minions. Then along came the X-Laws, sworn enemies in hot pursuit of Hao. The village is just within reach! And who is this Great Spirit that awaits on that land...?!

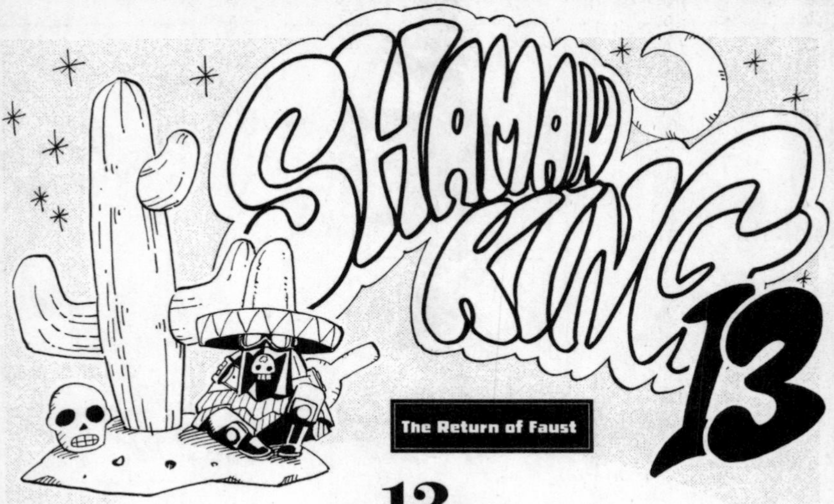
SHAMAN KING
13
The Return of Faust

13

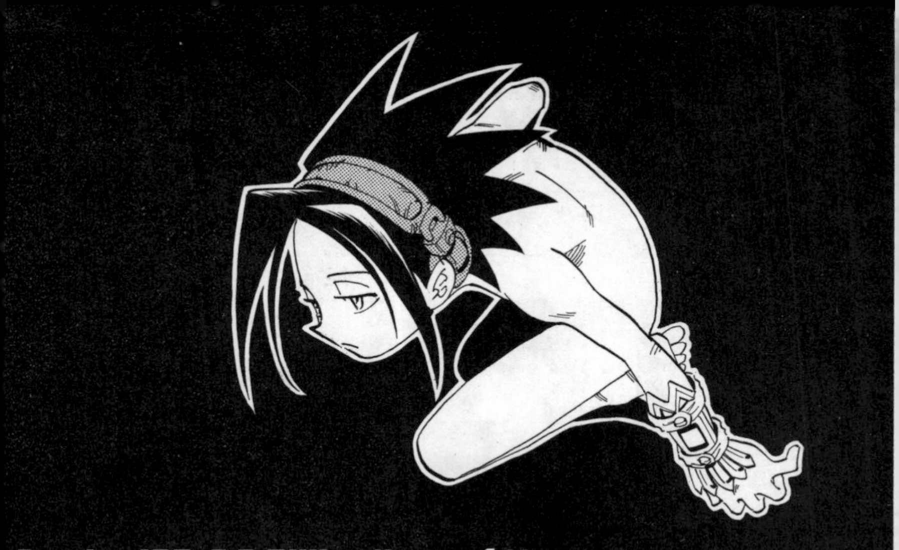

Chapter 108: 5.6 Billion Years of Memories

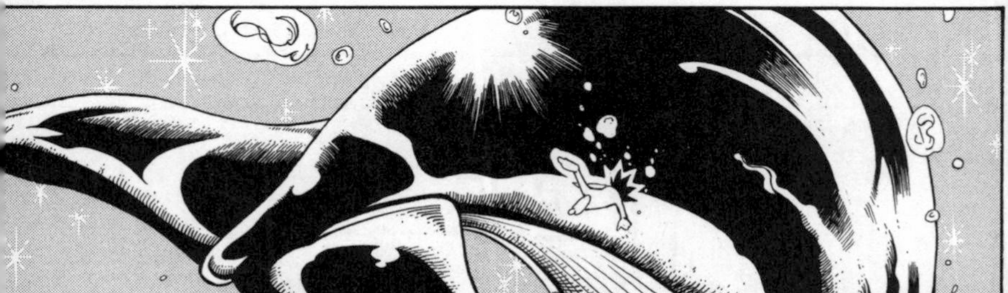

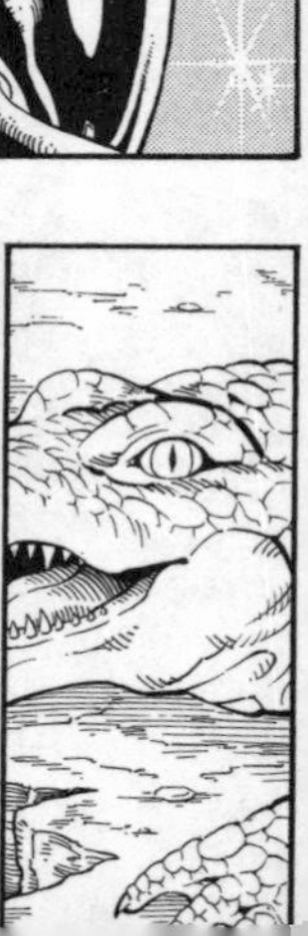

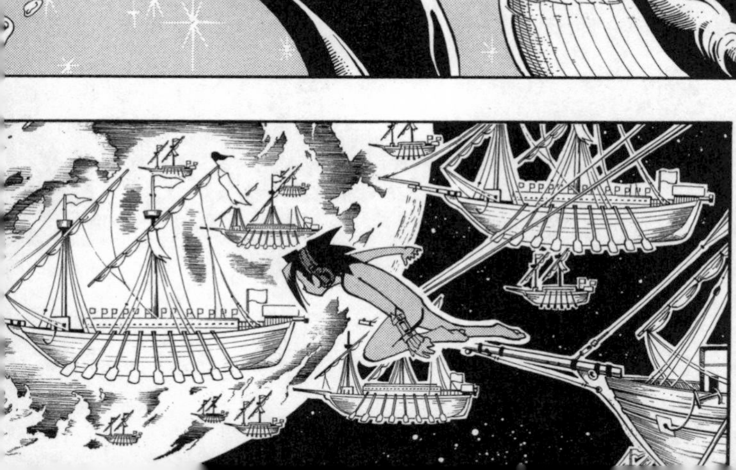

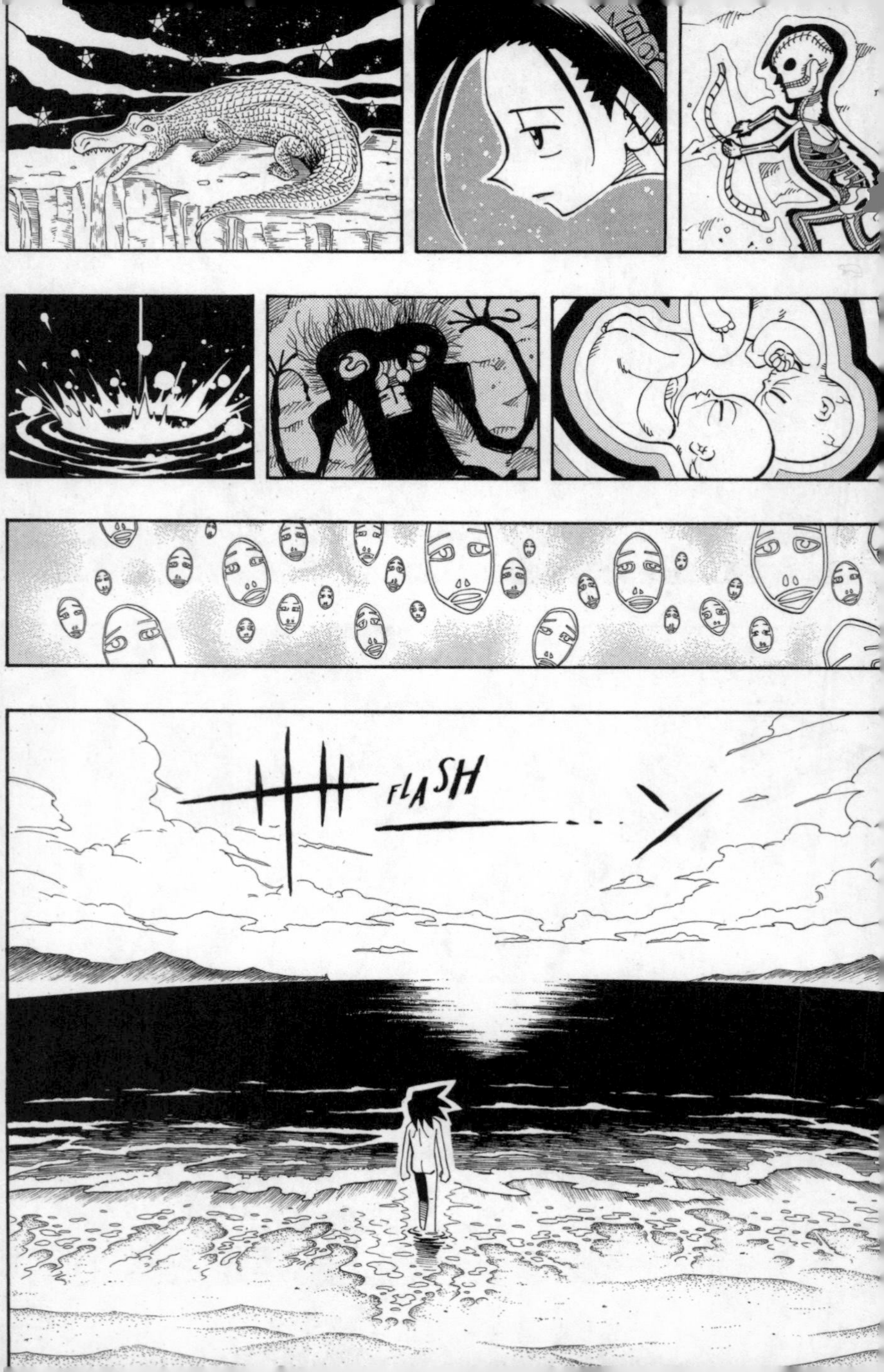
FLASH

Chapter 108:

5.6 Billion Years of Memories

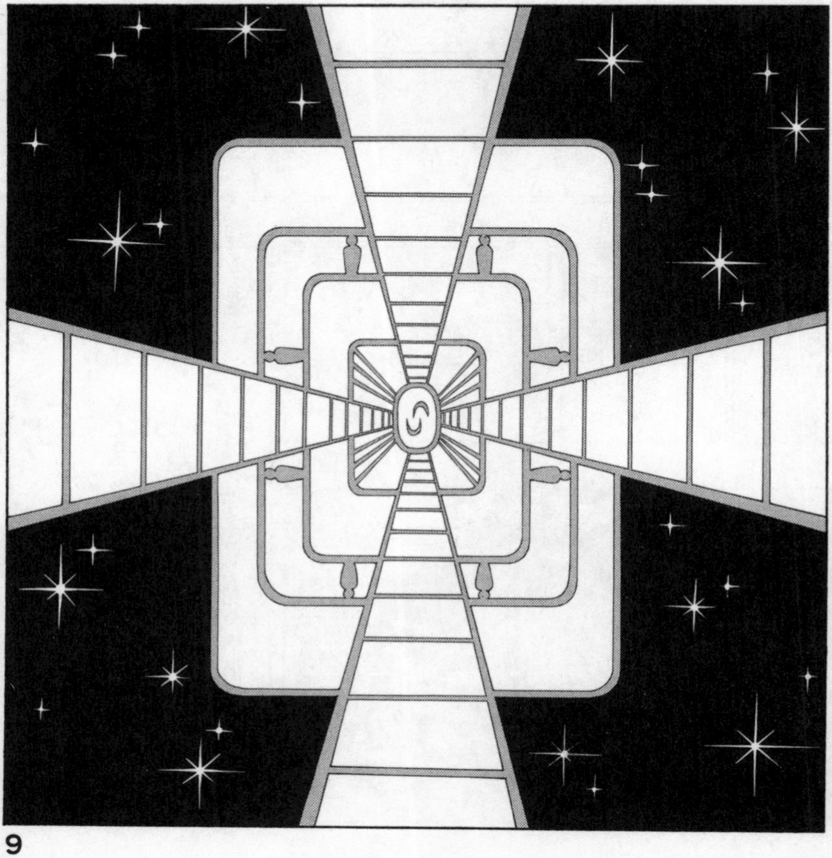

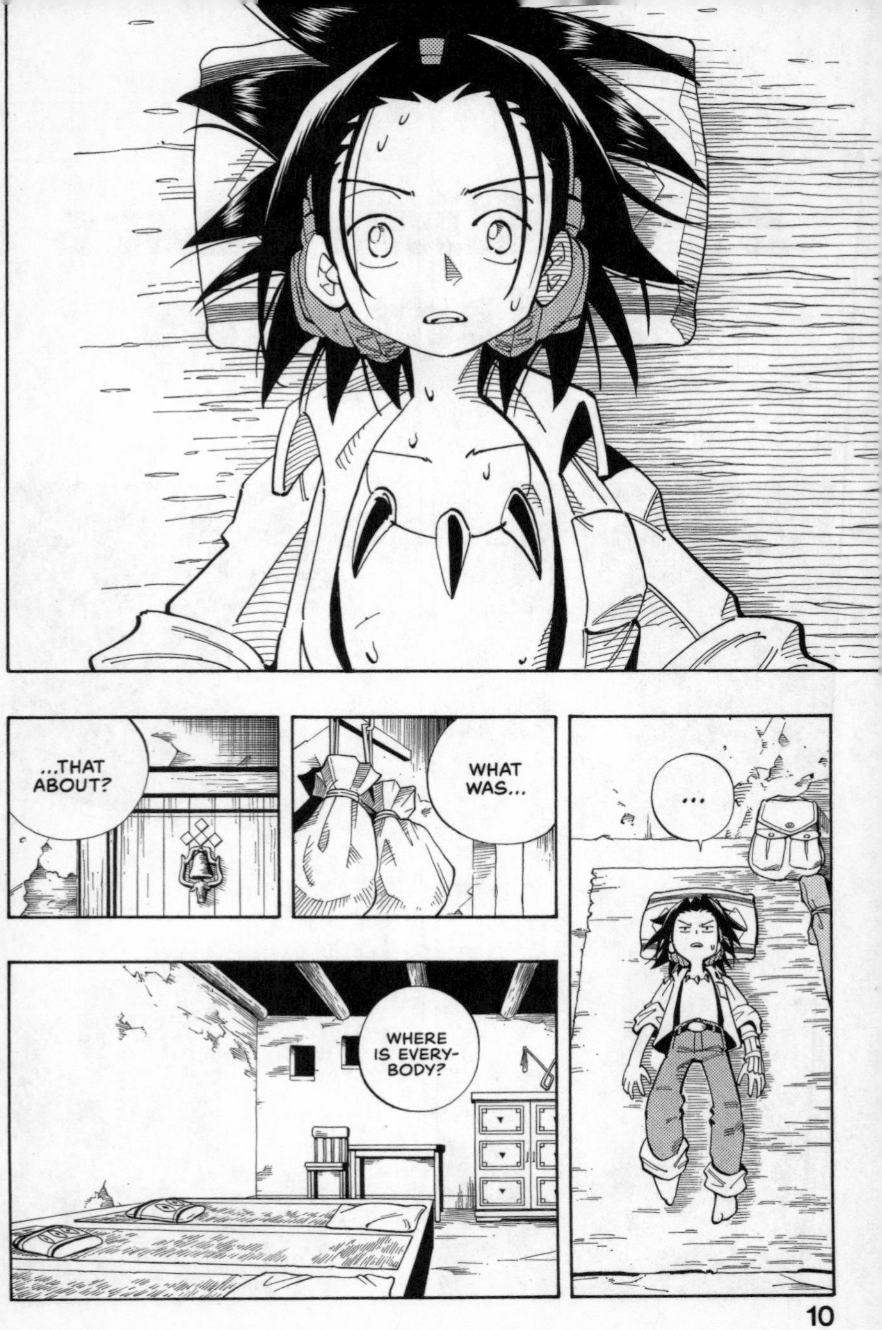
...
WHAT WAS...
...THAT ABOUT?
WHERE IS EVERY-BODY?

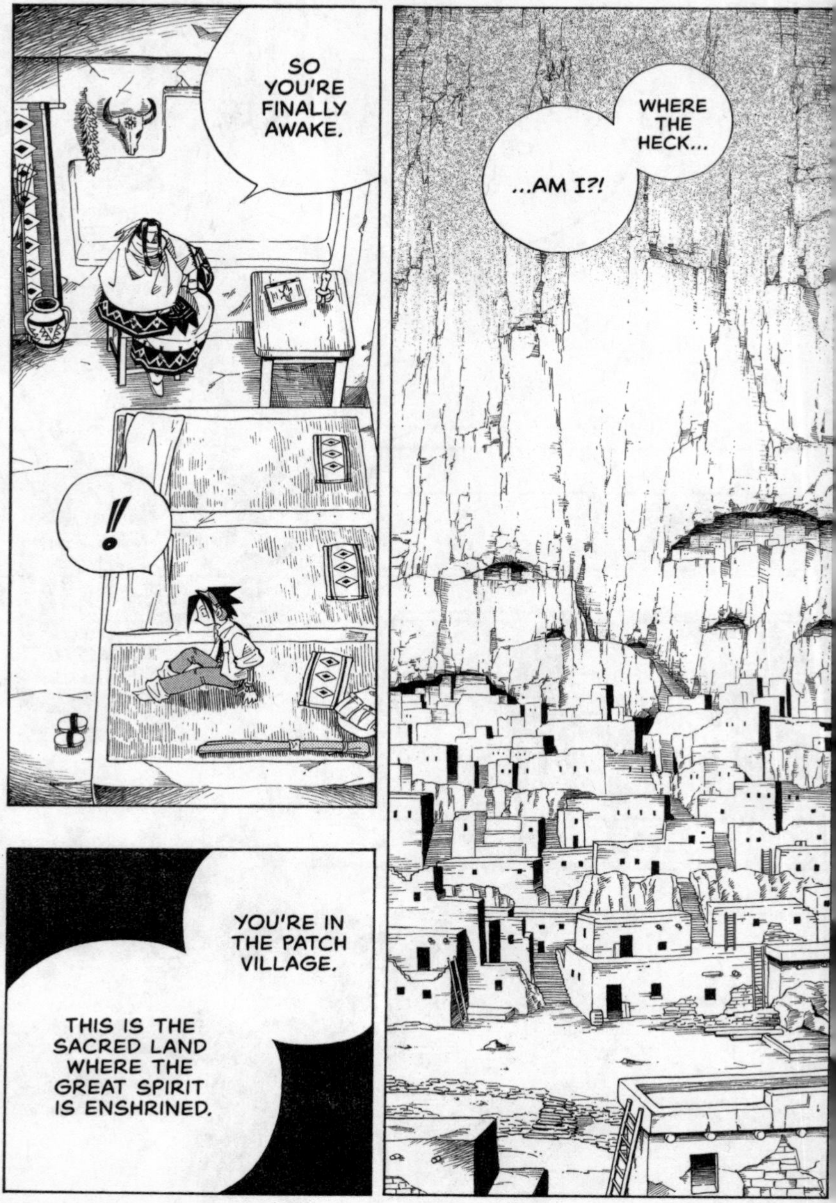
WHERE THE HECK...
...AM I?!
SO YOU'RE FINALLY AWAKE.
!
YOU'RE IN THE PATCH VILLAGE.
THIS IS THE SACRED LAND WHERE THE GREAT SPIRIT IS ENSHRINED.

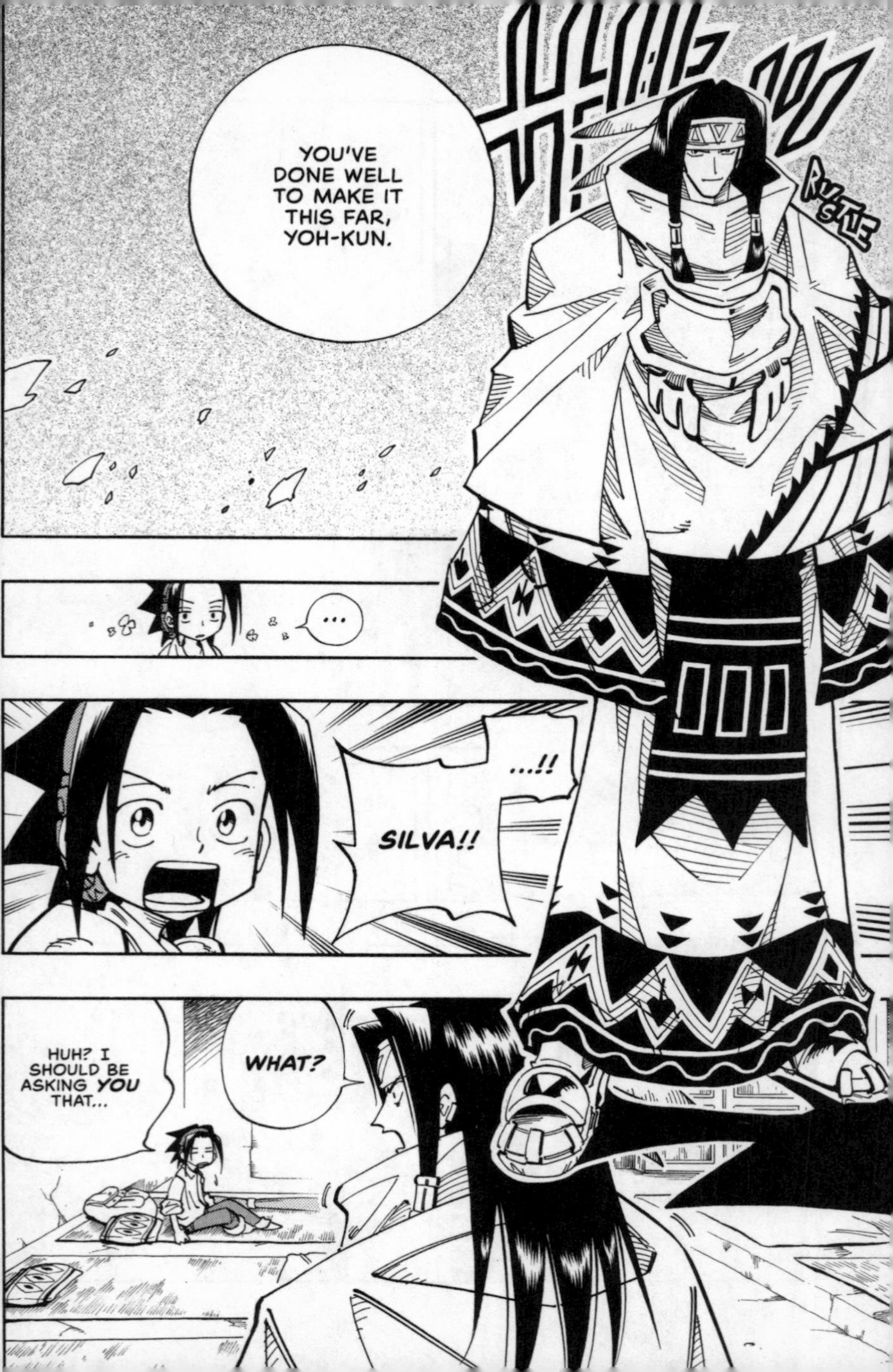
RUSTLE
YOU'VE DONE WELL TO MAKE IT THIS FAR, YOH-KUN.
...
...!!
SILVA!!
WHAT?
HUH? I SHOULD BE ASKING YOU THAT...

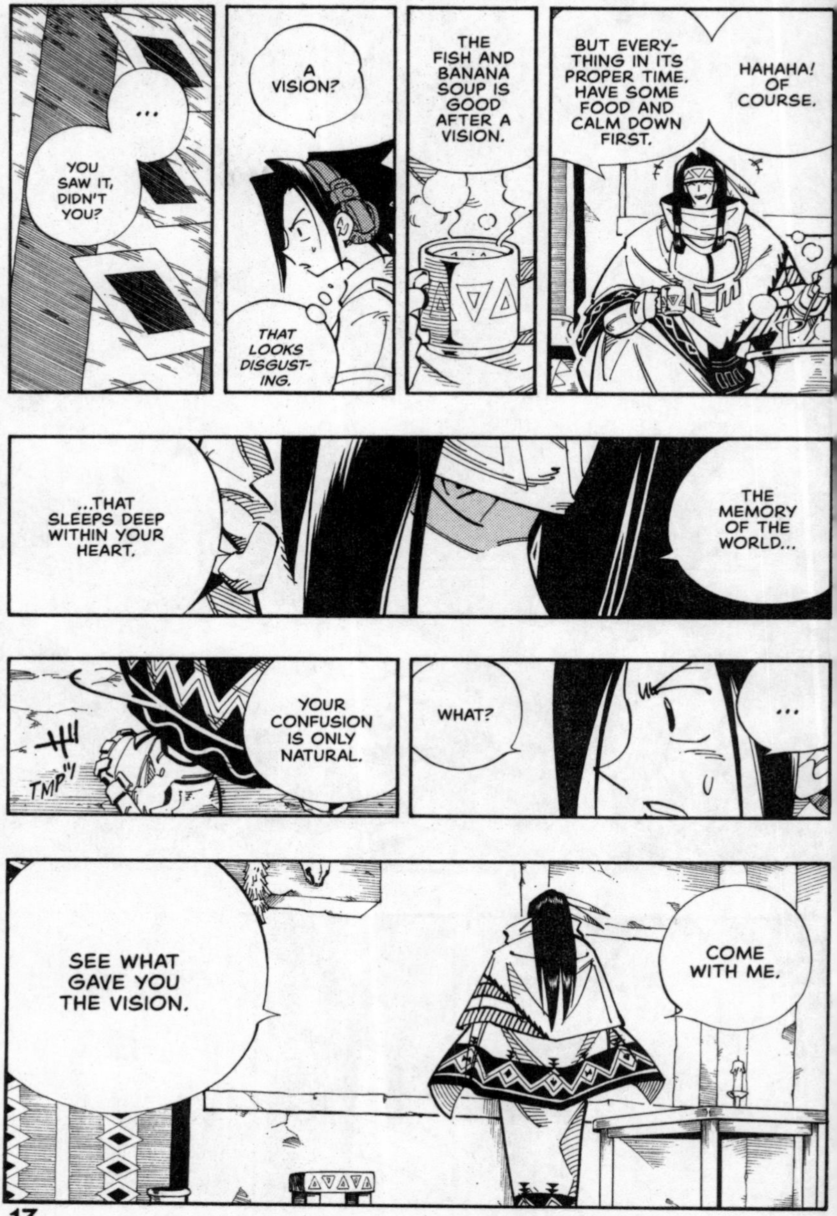
HAHAHA! OF COURSE.
BUT EVERYTHING IN ITS PROPER TIME. HAVE SOME FOOD AND CALM DOWN FIRST.
THE FISH AND BANANA SOUP IS GOOD AFTER A VISION.
A VISION?
THAT LOOKS DISGUSTING.
...
YOU SAW IT, DIDN'T YOU?
THE MEMORY OF THE WORLD...
...THAT SLEEPS DEEP WITHIN YOUR HEART.
...
WHAT?
YOUR CONFUSION IS ONLY NATURAL.
TMP
COME WITH ME.
SEE WHAT GAVE YOU THE VISION.

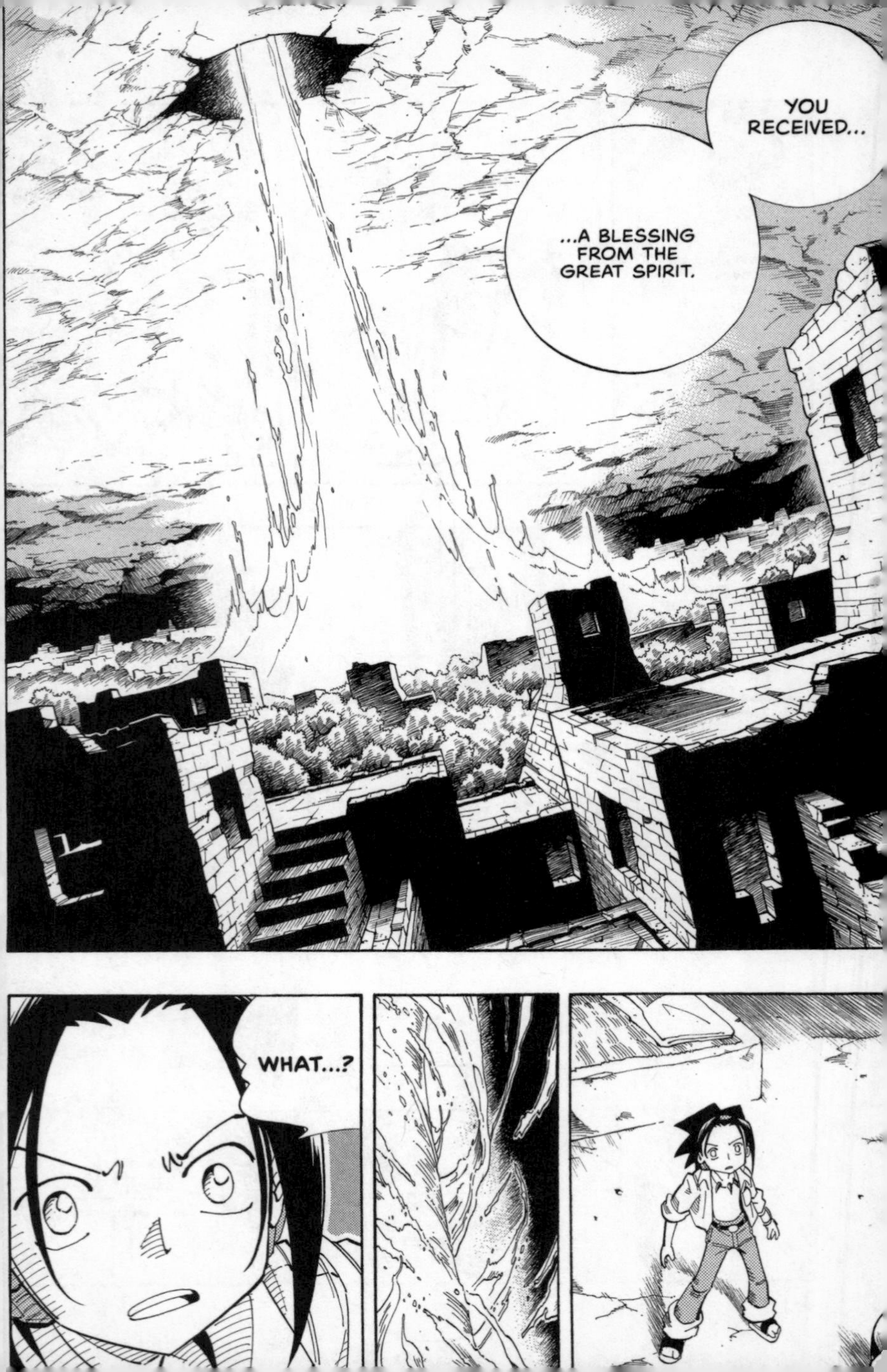
YOU RECEIVED...
...A BLESSING FROM THE GREAT SPIRIT.
WHAT...?

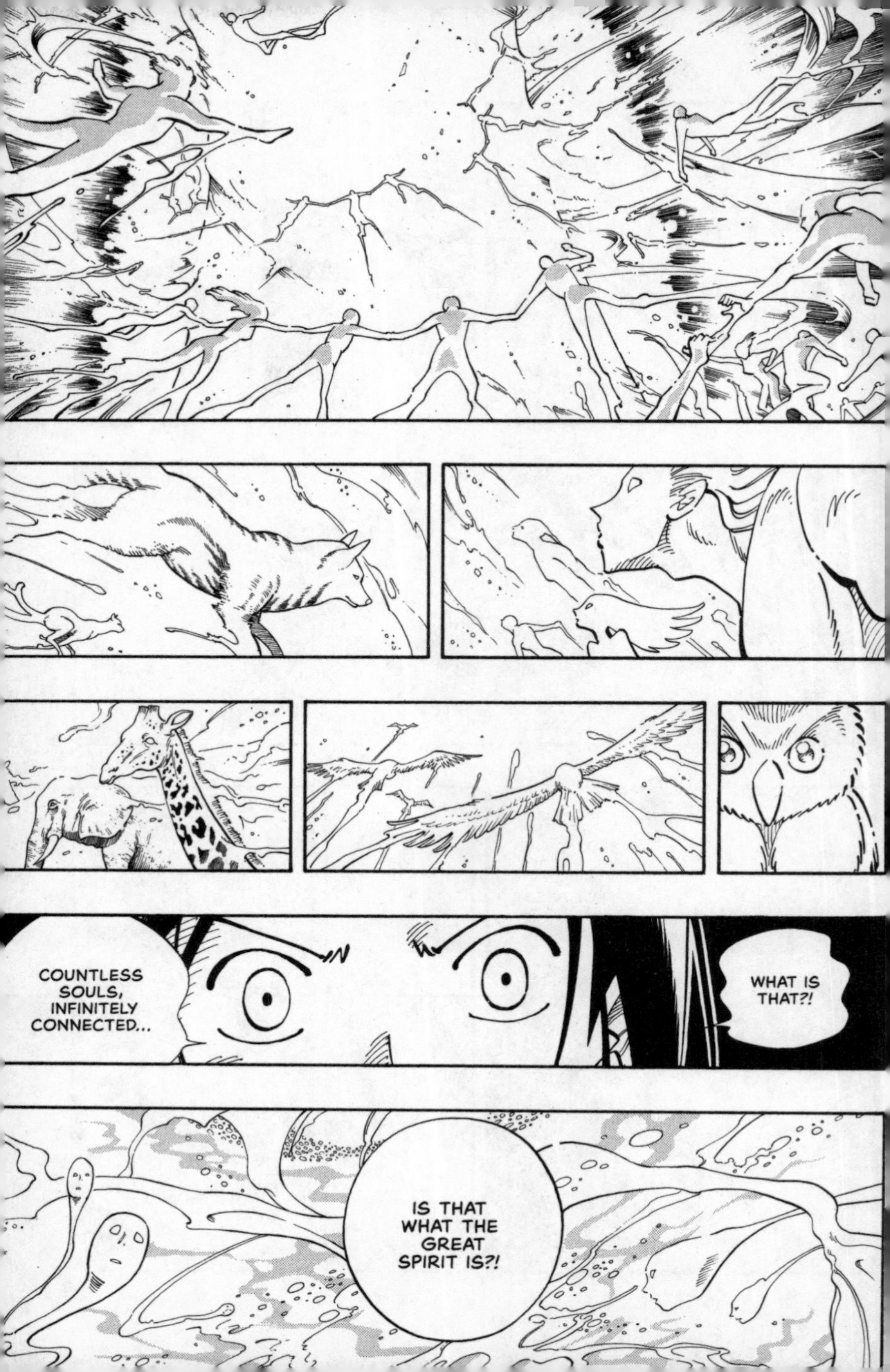
WHAT IS THAT?!
COUNTLESS SOULS, INFINITELY CONNECTED...
IS THAT WHAT THE GREAT SPIRIT IS?!

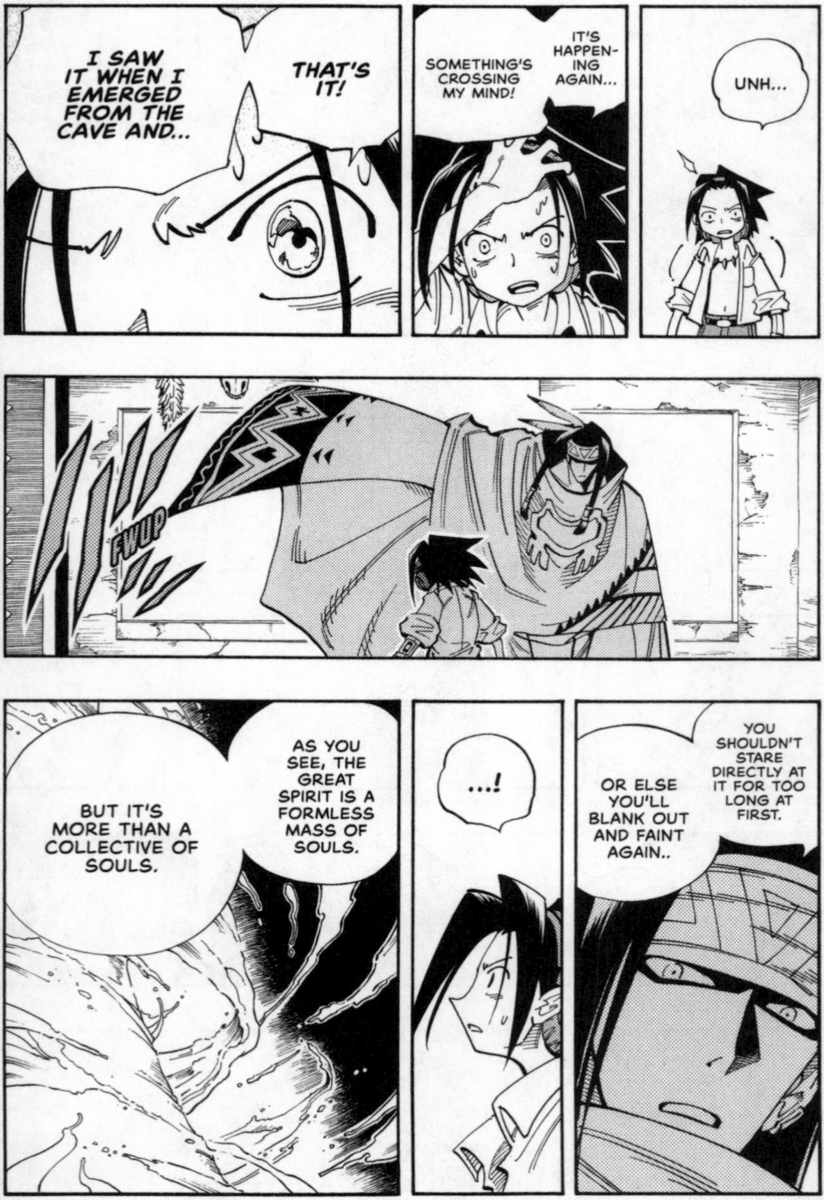
UNH...
IT'S HAPPENING AGAIN...
SOMETHING'S CROSSING MY MIND!
THAT'S IT!
I SAW IT WHEN I EMERGED FROM THE CAVE AND...
FWUP
YOU SHOULDN'T STARE DIRECTLY AT IT FOR TOO LONG AT FIRST.
OR ELSE YOU'LL BLANK OUT AND FAINT AGAIN..
...!
AS YOU SEE, THE GREAT SPIRIT IS A FORMLESS MASS OF SOULS.
BUT IT'S MORE THAN A COLLECTIVE OF SOULS.

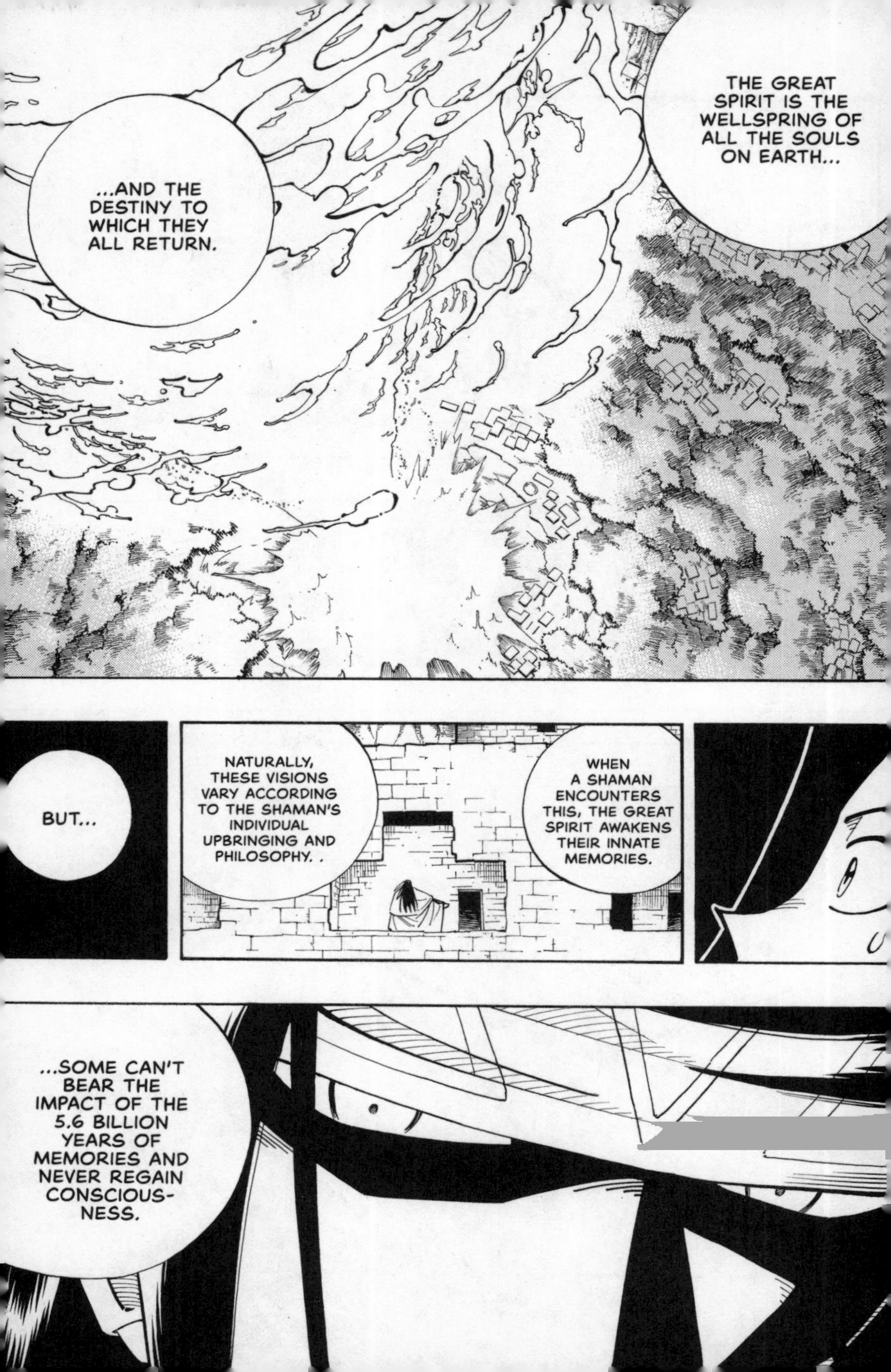
THE GREAT SPIRIT IS THE WELLSPRING OF ALL THE SOULS ON EARTH...
...AND THE DESTINY TO WHICH THEY ALL RETURN.
WHEN A SHAMAN ENCOUNTERS THIS, THE GREAT SPIRIT AWAKENS THEIR INNATE MEMORIES.
NATURALLY, THESE VISIONS VARY ACCORDING TO THE SHAMAN'S INDIVIDUAL UPBRINGING AND PHILOSOPHY. .
BUT...
...SOME CAN'T BEAR THE IMPACT OF THE 5.6 BILLION YEARS OF MEMORIES AND NEVER REGAIN CONSCIOUS-NESS.

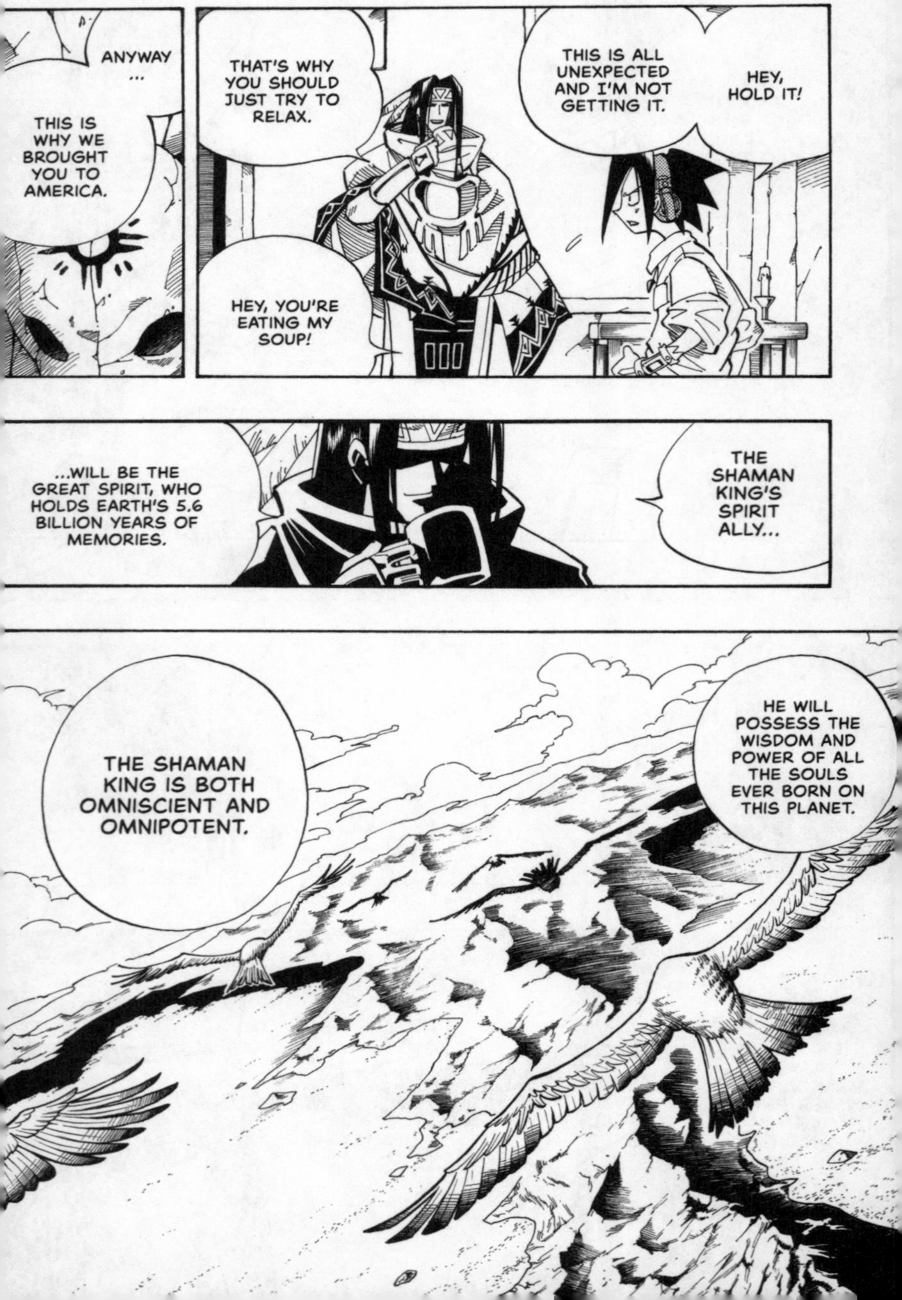
HEY, HOLD IT!
THIS IS ALL UNEXPECTED AND I'M NOT GETTING IT.
THAT'S WHY YOU SHOULD JUST TRY TO RELAX.
HEY, YOU'RE EATING MY SOUP!
ANYWAY ...
THIS IS WHY WE BROUGHT YOU TO AMERICA.
THE SHAMAN KING'S SPIRIT ALLY...
...WILL BE THE GREAT SPIRIT, WHO HOLDS EARTH'S 5.6 BILLION YEARS OF MEMORIES.
HE WILL POSSESS THE WISDOM AND POWER OF ALL THE SOULS EVER BORN ON THIS PLANET.
THE SHAMAN KING IS BOTH OMNISCIENT AND OMNIPOTENT.

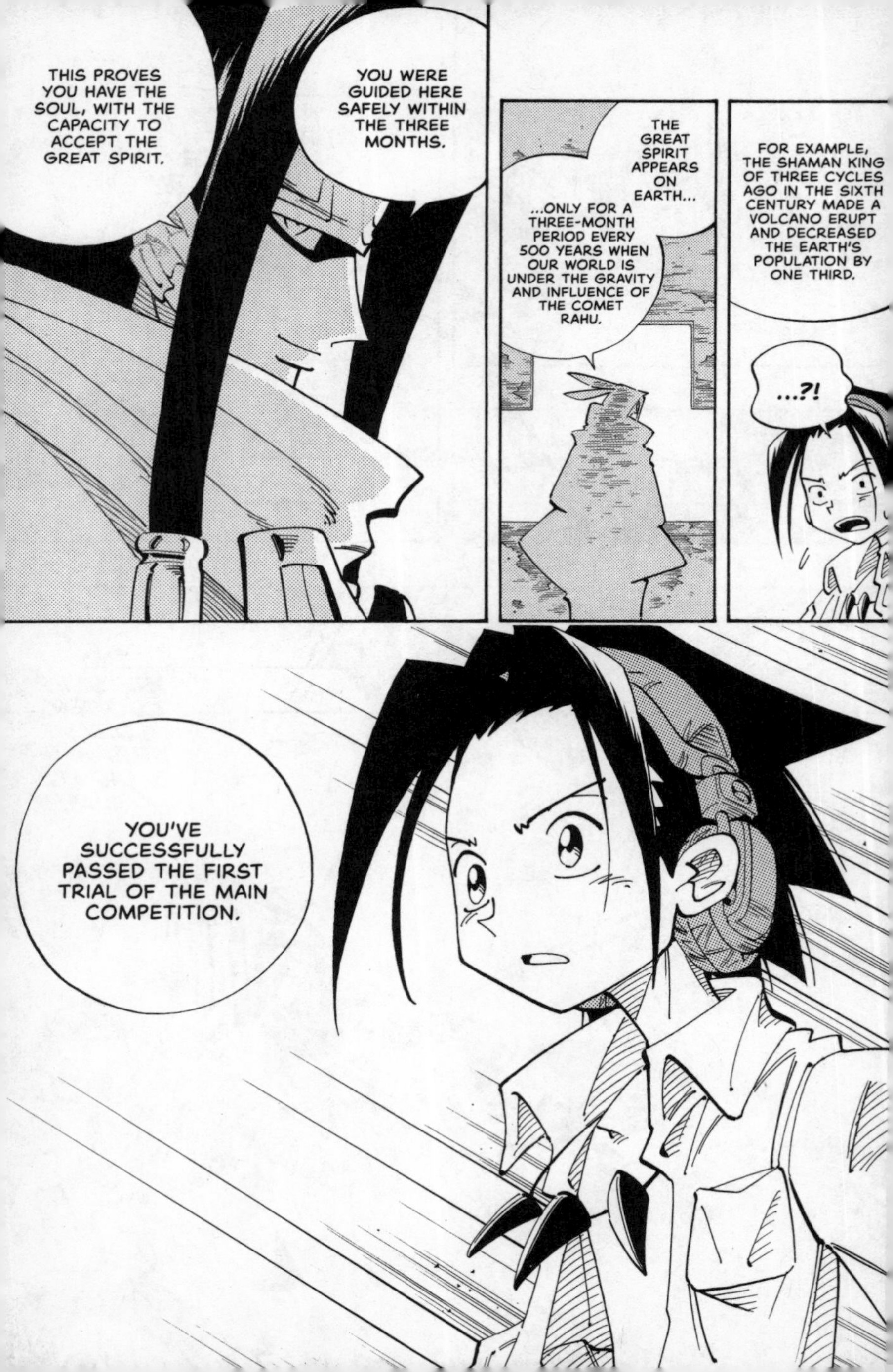
FOR EXAMPLE, THE SHAMAN KING OF THREE CYCLES AGO IN THE SIXTH CENTURY MADE A VOLCANO ERUPT AND DECREASED THE EARTH'S POPULATION BY ONE THIRD.
...?!
THE GREAT SPIRIT APPEARS ON EARTH...
...ONLY FOR A THREE-MONTH PERIOD EVERY 500 YEARS WHEN OUR WORLD IS UNDER THE GRAVITY AND INFLUENCE OF THE COMET RAHU.
YOU WERE GUIDED HERE SAFELY WITHIN THE THREE MONTHS.
THIS PROVES YOU HAVE THE SOUL, WITH THE CAPACITY TO ACCEPT THE GREAT SPIRIT.
YOU'VE SUCCESSFULLY PASSED THE FIRST TRIAL OF THE MAIN COMPETITION.

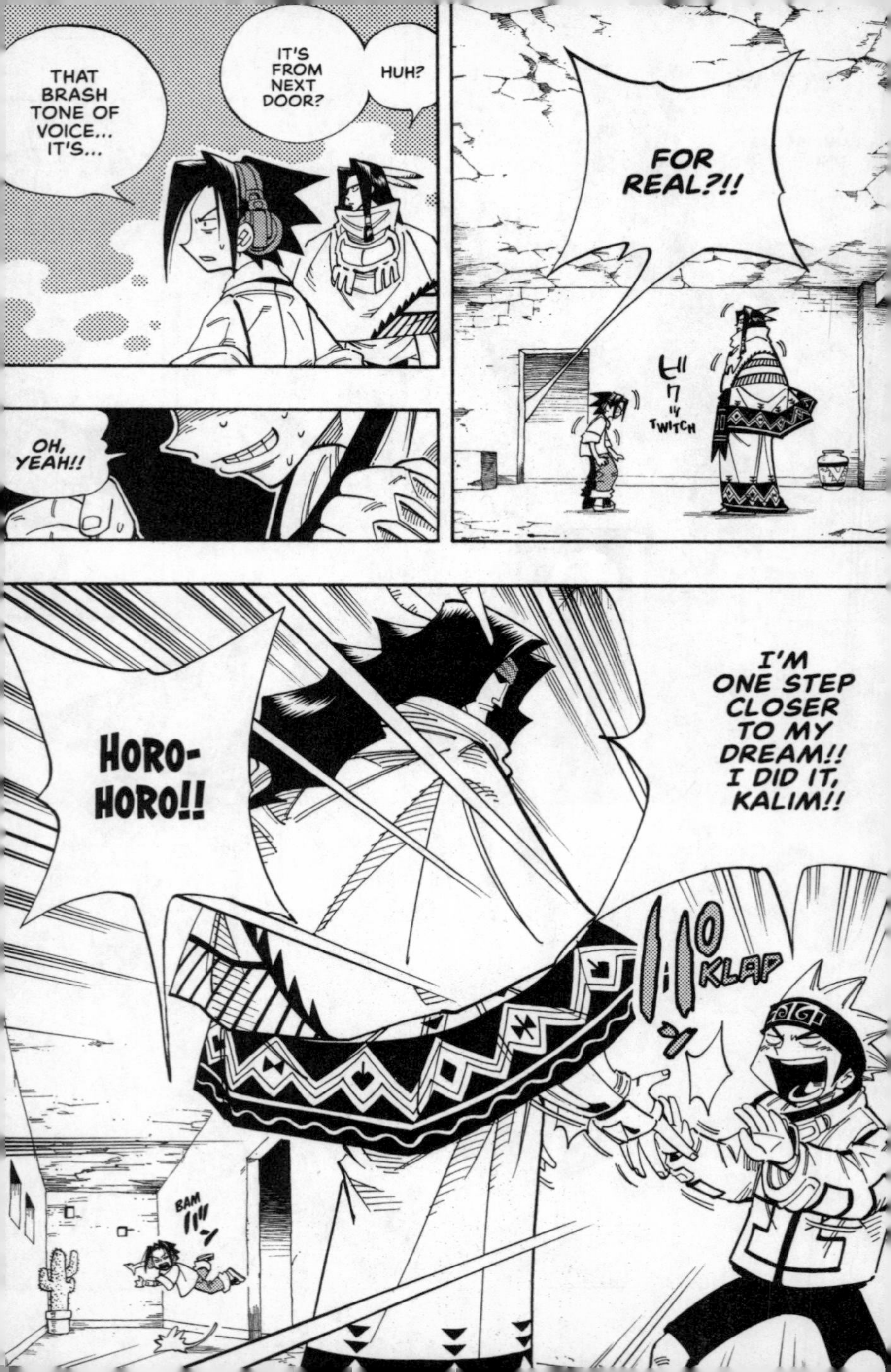
FOR REAL?!!
ビク
TWITCH
HUH?
IT'S FROM NEXT DOOR?
THAT BRASH TONE OF VOICE... IT'S...
OH, YEAH!!
I'M ONE STEP CLOSER TO MY DREAM!! I DID IT, KALIM!!
HORO-HORO!!
KLAP
BAM

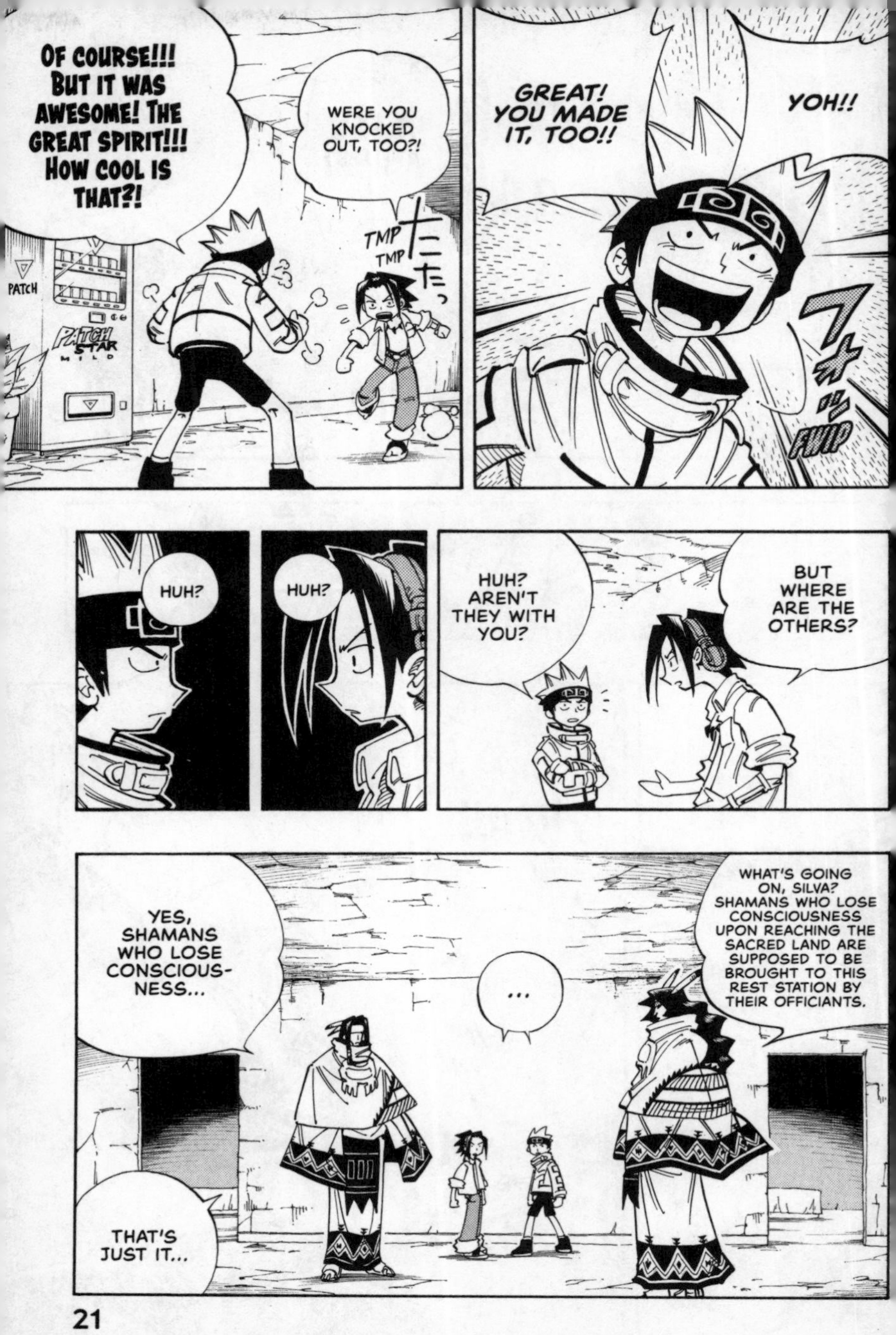
YOH!!
GREAT! YOU MADE IT, TOO!!
FWIP
WERE YOU KNOCKED OUT, TOO?!
TMP TMP
OF COURSE!!! BUT IT WAS AWESOME! THE GREAT SPIRIT!!! HOW COOL IS THAT?!
PATCH
PATCH STAR MILD
BUT WHERE ARE THE OTHERS?
HUH? AREN'T THEY WITH YOU?
HUH?
HUH?
WHAT'S GOING ON, SILVA? SHAMANS WHO LOSE CONSCIOUSNESS UPON REACHING THE SACRED LAND ARE SUPPOSED TO BE BROUGHT TO THIS REST STATION BY THEIR OFFICIANTS.
...
YES, SHAMANS WHO LOSE CONSCIOUS-NESS...
THAT'S JUST IT...

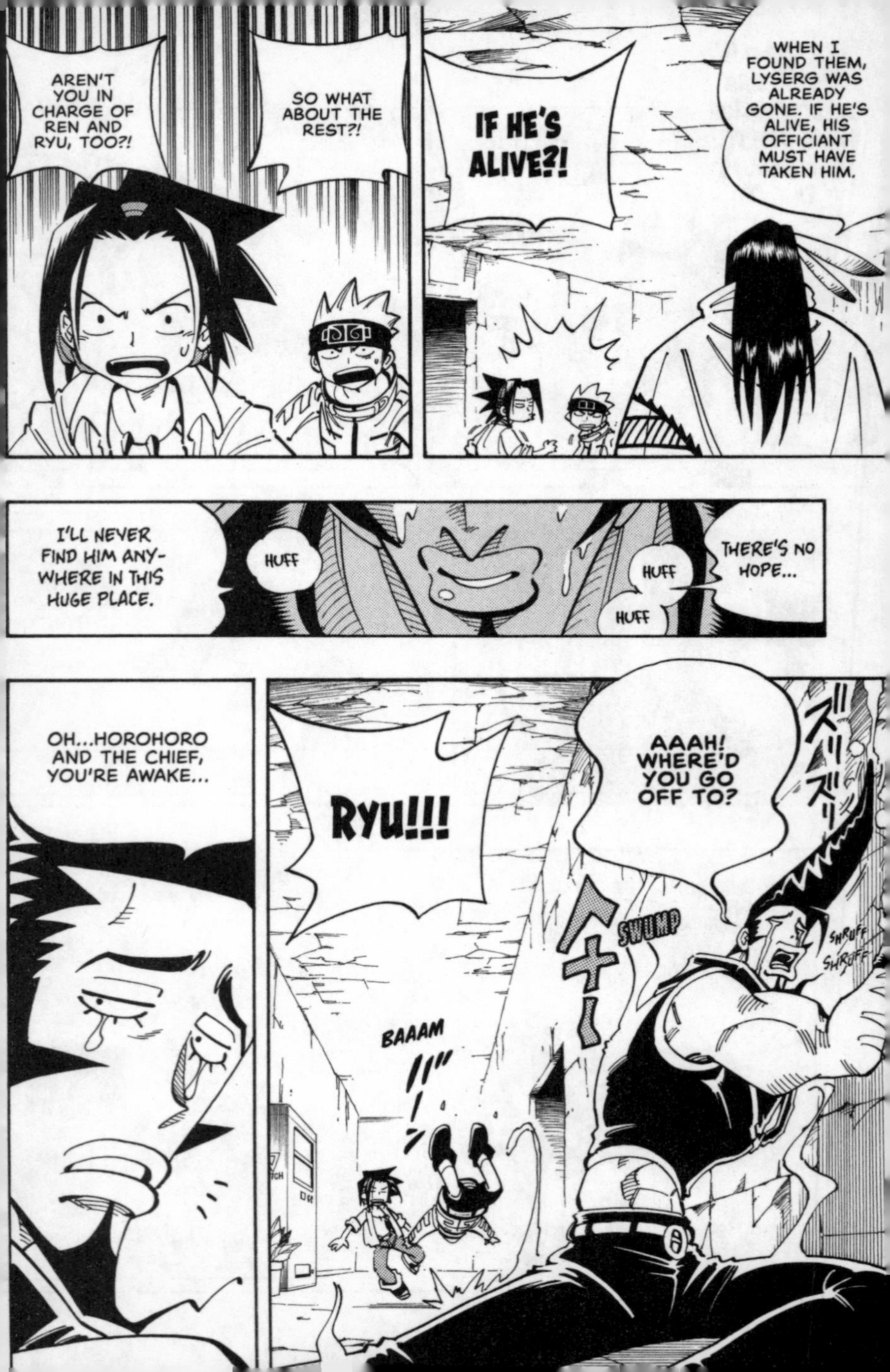
WHEN I FOUND THEM, LYSERG WAS ALREADY GONE. IF HE'S ALIVE, HIS OFFICIANT MUST HAVE TAKEN HIM.
IF HE'S ALIVE?!
SO WHAT ABOUT THE REST?!
AREN'T YOU IN CHARGE OF REN AND RYU, TOO?!
THERE'S NO HOPE...
HUFF
HUFF
HUFF
I'LL NEVER FIND HIM ANY-WHERE IN THIS HUGE PLACE.
AAAH! WHERE'D YOU GO OFF TO?
SHRUFF
SHRUFF
RYU!!!
SWUMP
BAAAM
OH...HOROHORO AND THE CHIEF, YOU'RE AWAKE...

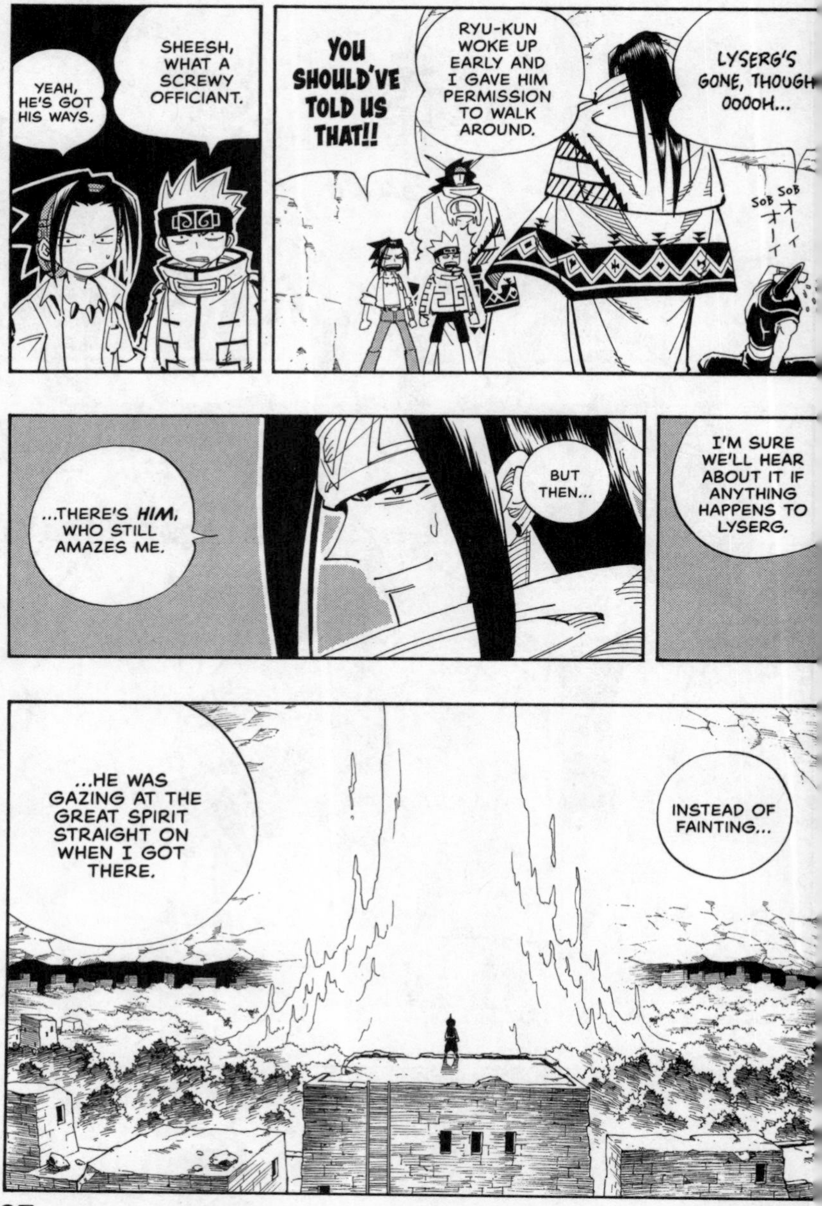
LYSERG'S GONE, THOUGH
OOOOH...
SOB SOB
オーイオーイ
RYU-KUN WOKE UP EARLY AND I GAVE HIM PERMISSION TO WALK AROUND.
YOU SHOULD'VE TOLD US THAT!!
SHEESH, WHAT A SCREWY OFFICIANT.
YEAH, HE'S GOT HIS WAYS.
I'M SURE WE'LL HEAR ABOUT IT IF ANYTHING HAPPENS TO LYSERG.
BUT THEN...
...THERE'S *HIM*, WHO STILL AMAZES ME.
INSTEAD OF FAINTING...
...HE WAS GAZING AT THE GREAT SPIRIT STRAIGHT ON WHEN I GOT THERE.

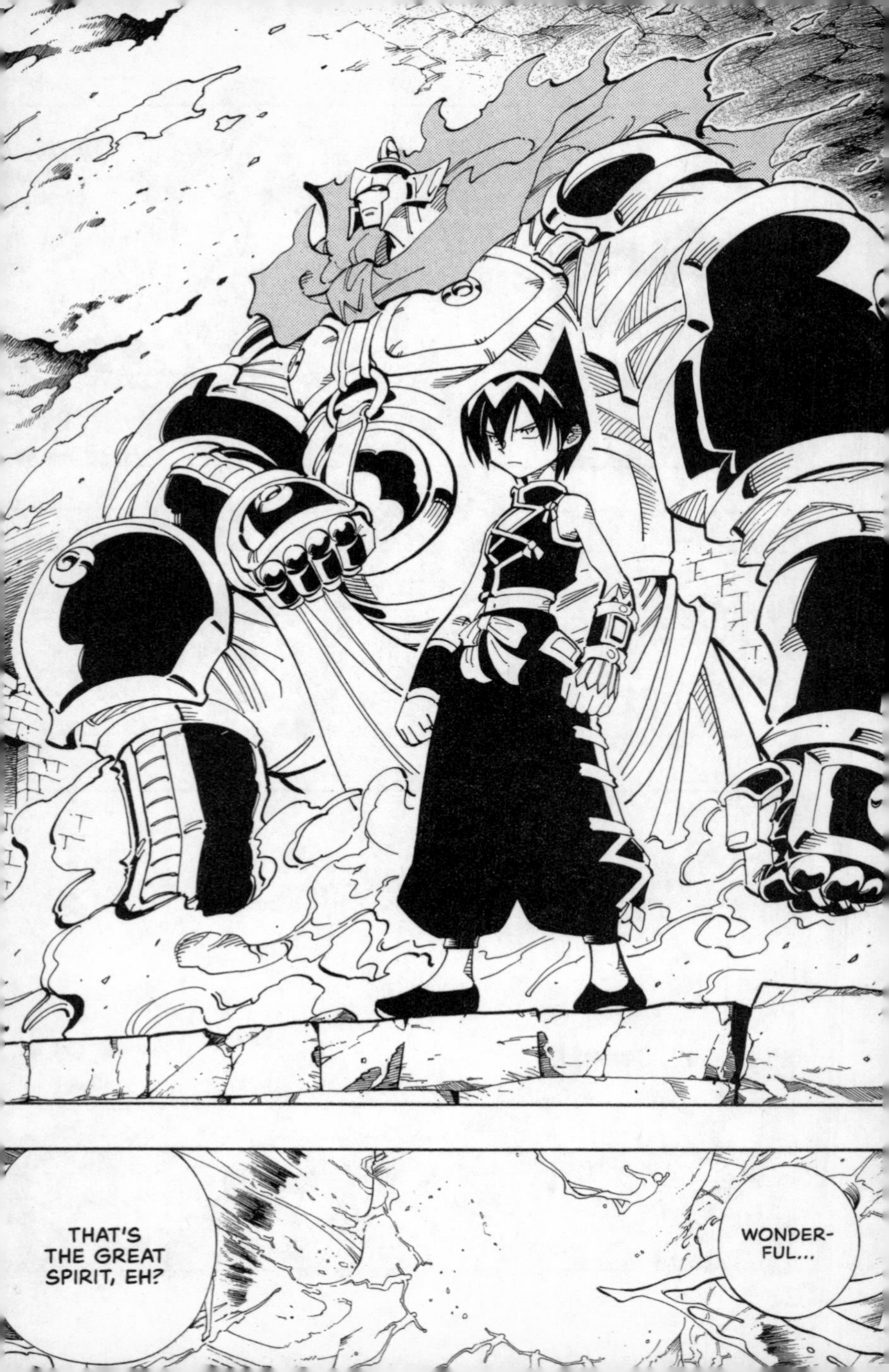
WONDER-FUL...
THAT'S THE GREAT SPIRIT, EH?

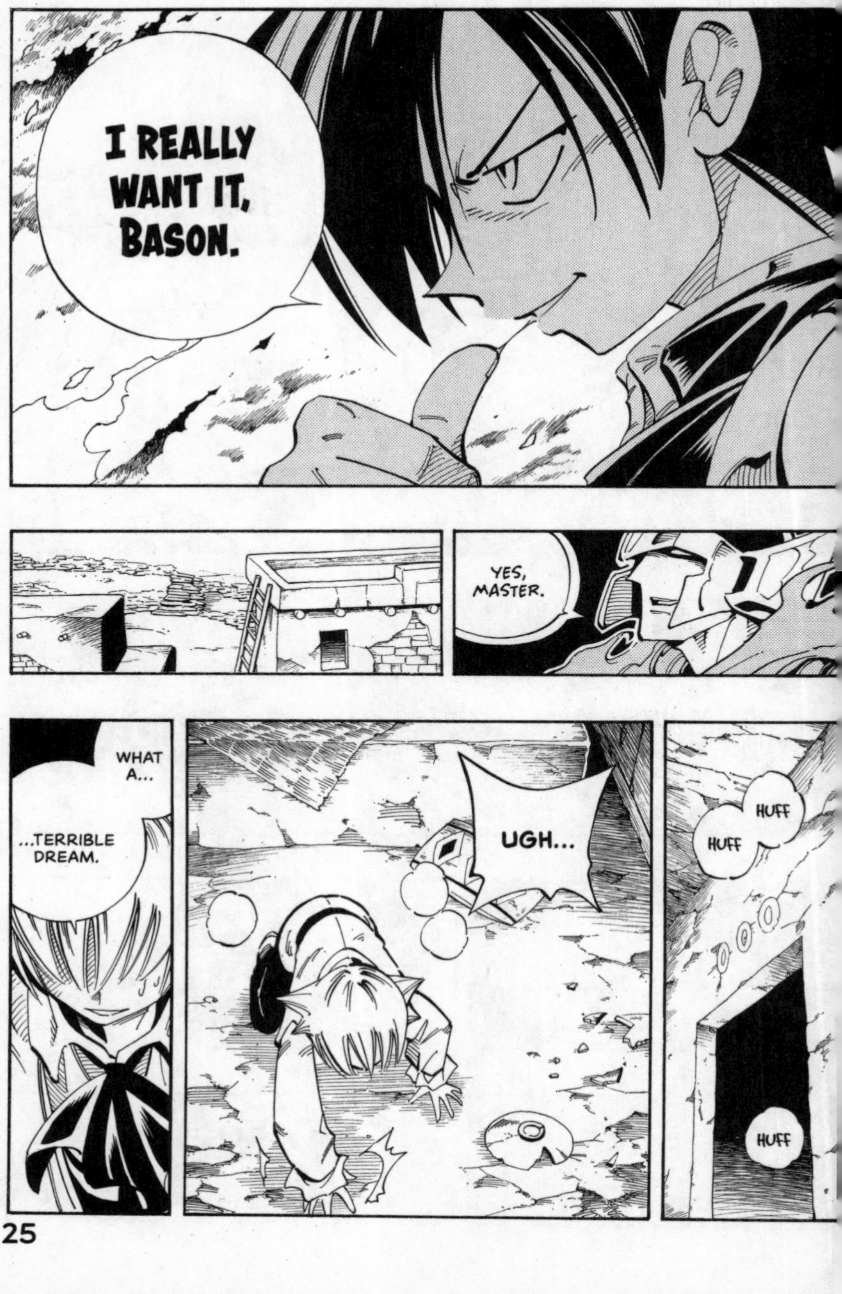
I REALLY WANT IT, BASON.
YES, MASTER.
HUFF
HUFF
HUFF
UGH...
WHAT A...
...TERRIBLE DREAM.

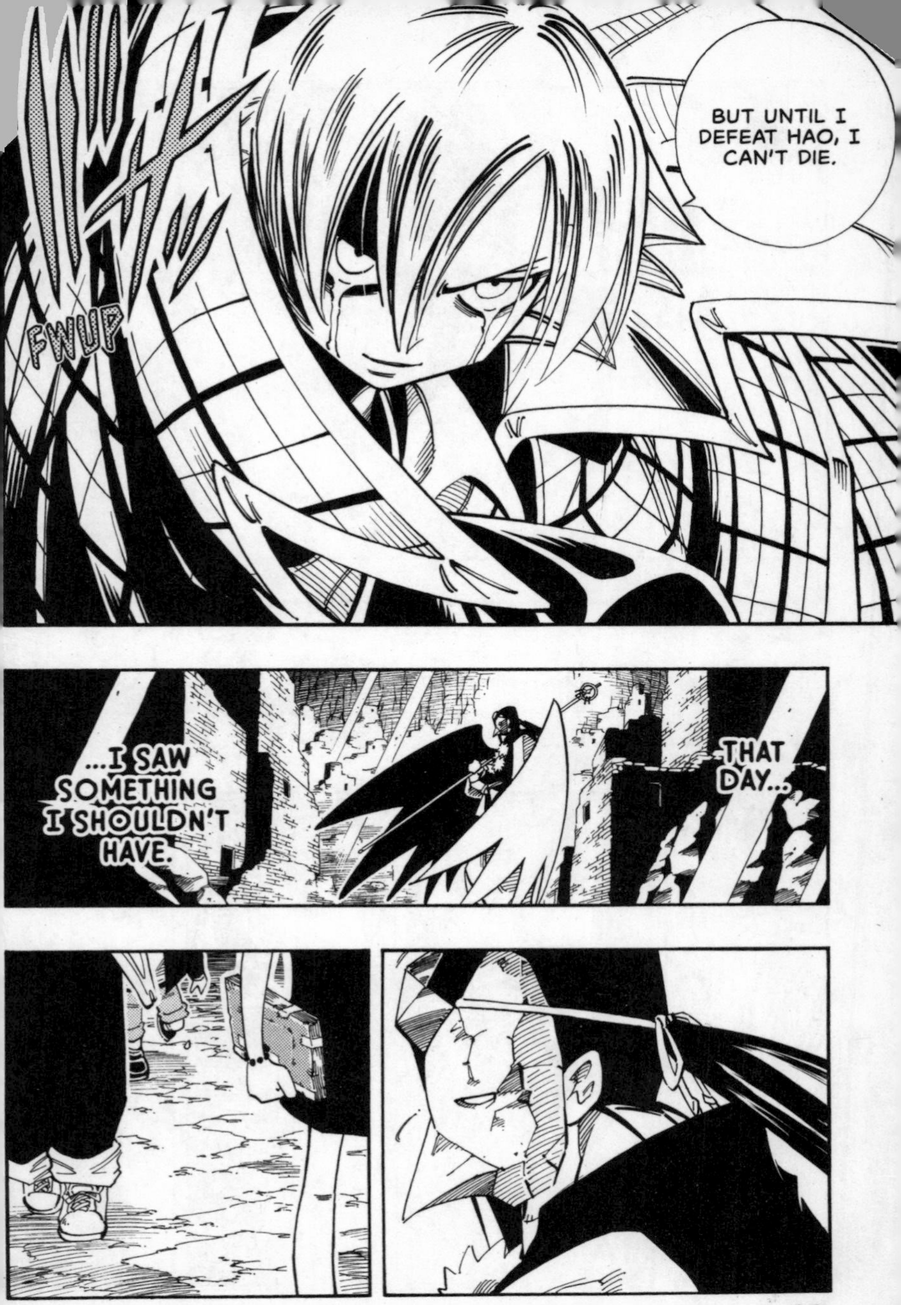
BUT UNTIL I DEFEAT HAO, I CAN'T DIE.
FWUP
THAT DAY...
...I SAW SOMETHING I SHOULDN'T HAVE.

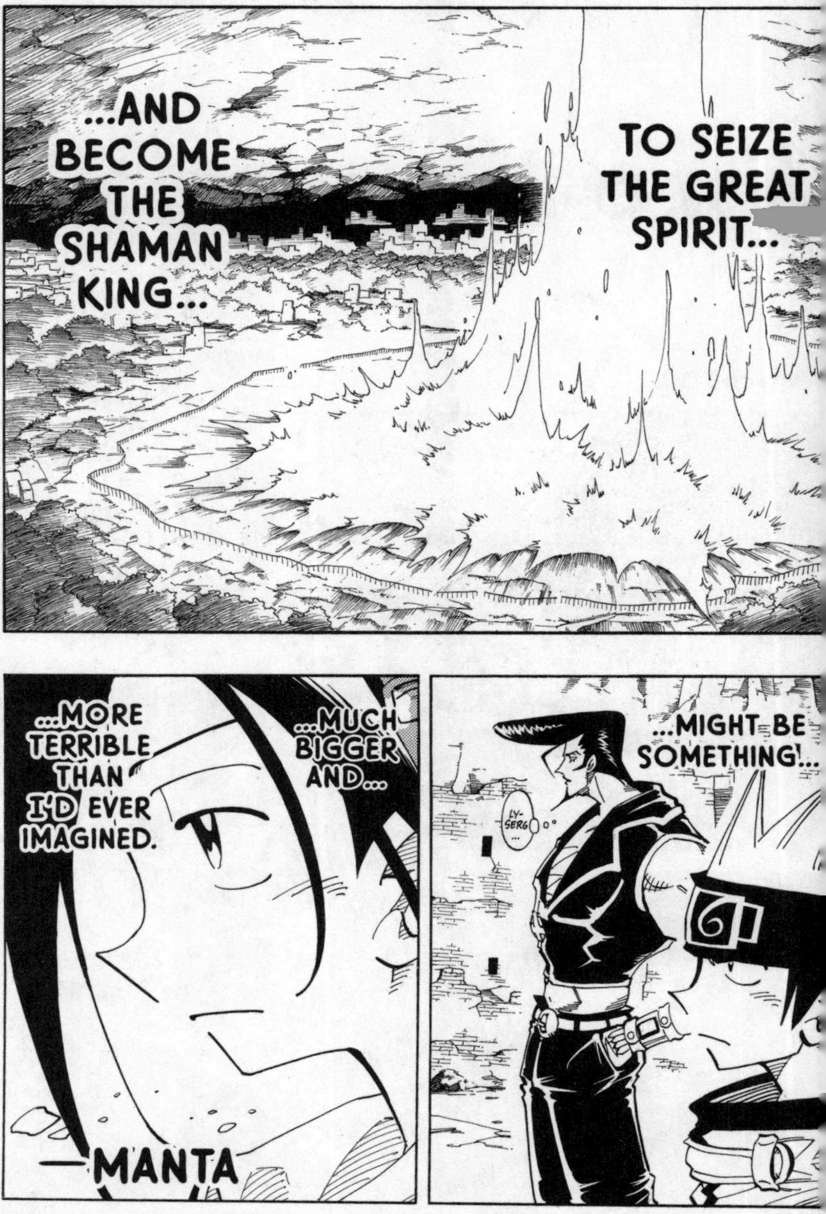
TO SEIZE THE GREAT SPIRIT...
...AND BECOME THE SHAMAN KING...
...MIGHT BE SOMETHING...
LY-SERG ...
...MUCH BIGGER AND...
...MORE TERRIBLE THAN I'D EVER IMAGINED.
—MANTA

SHAMAN KING CHARACTER FILE No.59

Joco

March 2001

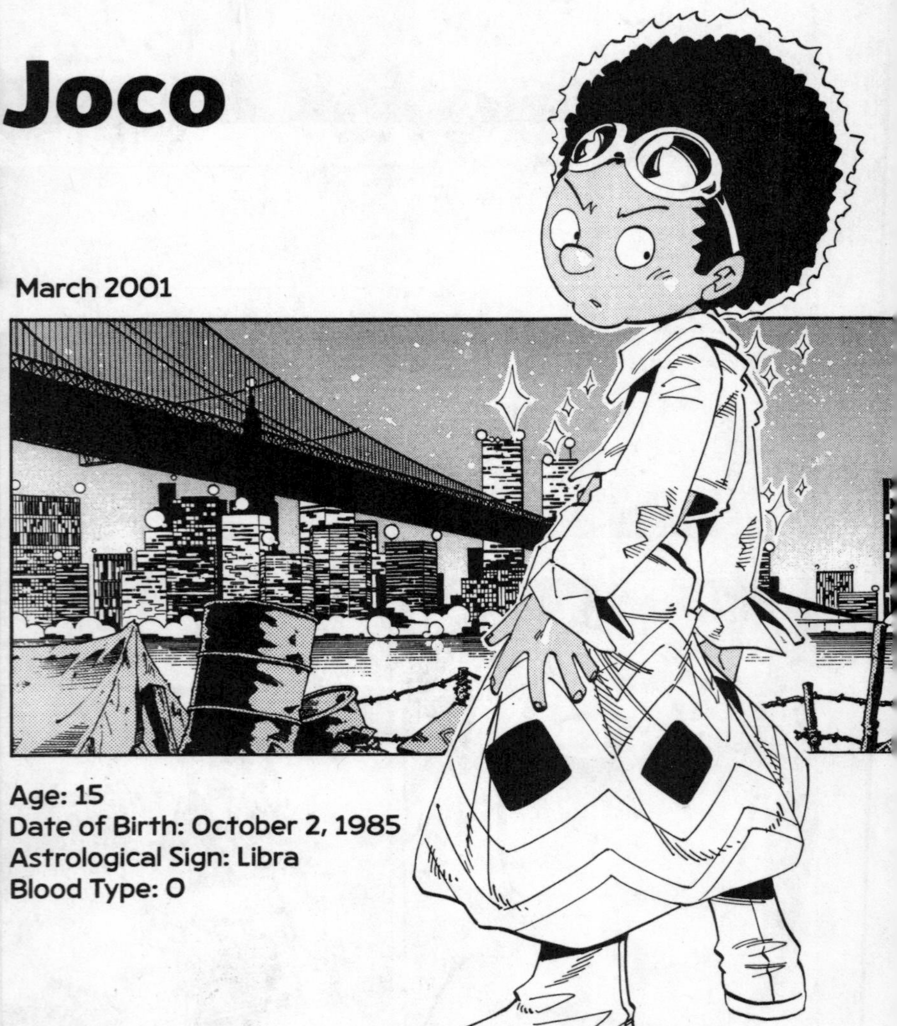

Age: 15
Date of Birth: October 2, 1985
Astrological Sign: Libra
Blood Type: O

Chapter 109: The Shaman Village

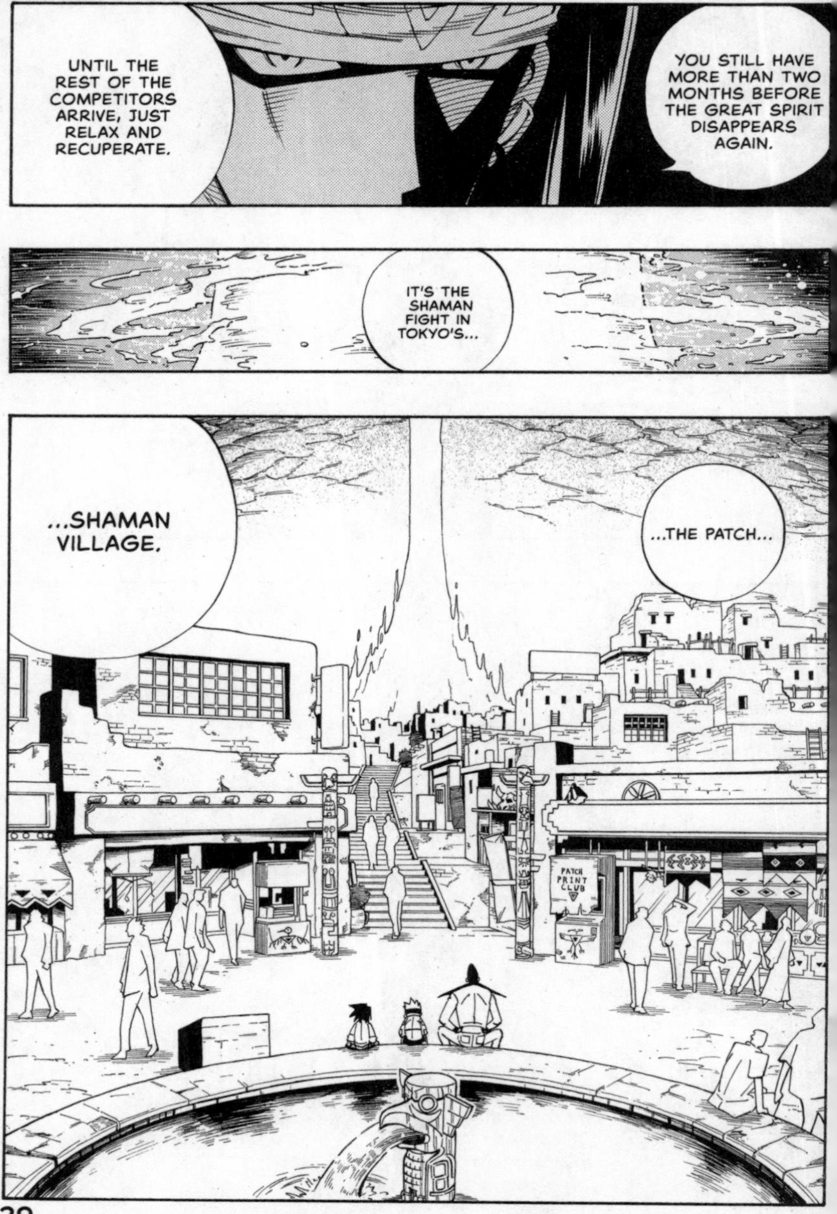
YOU STILL HAVE MORE THAN TWO MONTHS BEFORE THE GREAT SPIRIT DISAPPEARS AGAIN.
UNTIL THE REST OF THE COMPETITORS ARRIVE, JUST RELAX AND RECUPERATE.
IT'S THE SHAMAN FIGHT IN TOKYO'S...
...THE PATCH...
...SHAMAN VILLAGE.
PATCH PRINT CLUB

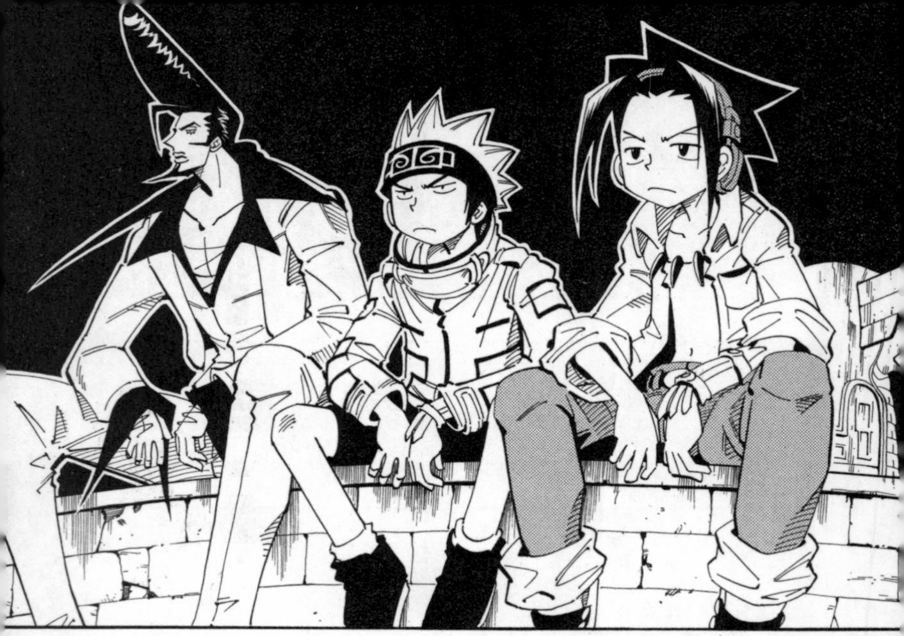

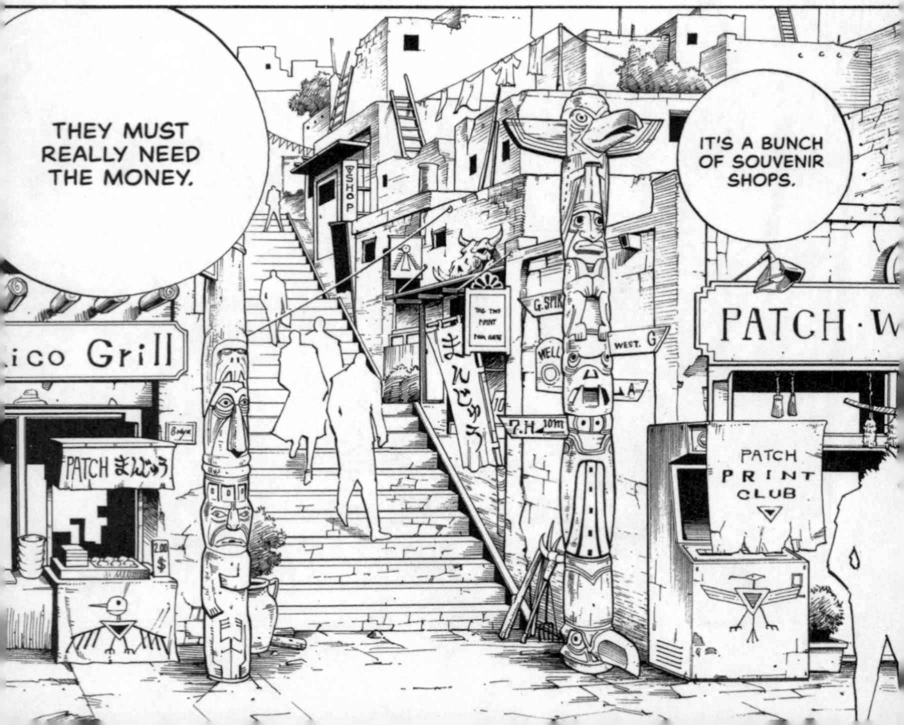
IT'S A BUNCH OF SOUVENIR SHOPS.
THEY MUST REALLY NEED THE MONEY.
PATCH · W
PATCH PRINT CLUB
SHOP
WEST. G
ico Grill
PATCH まんじゅう

Chapter 109:

The Shaman Village

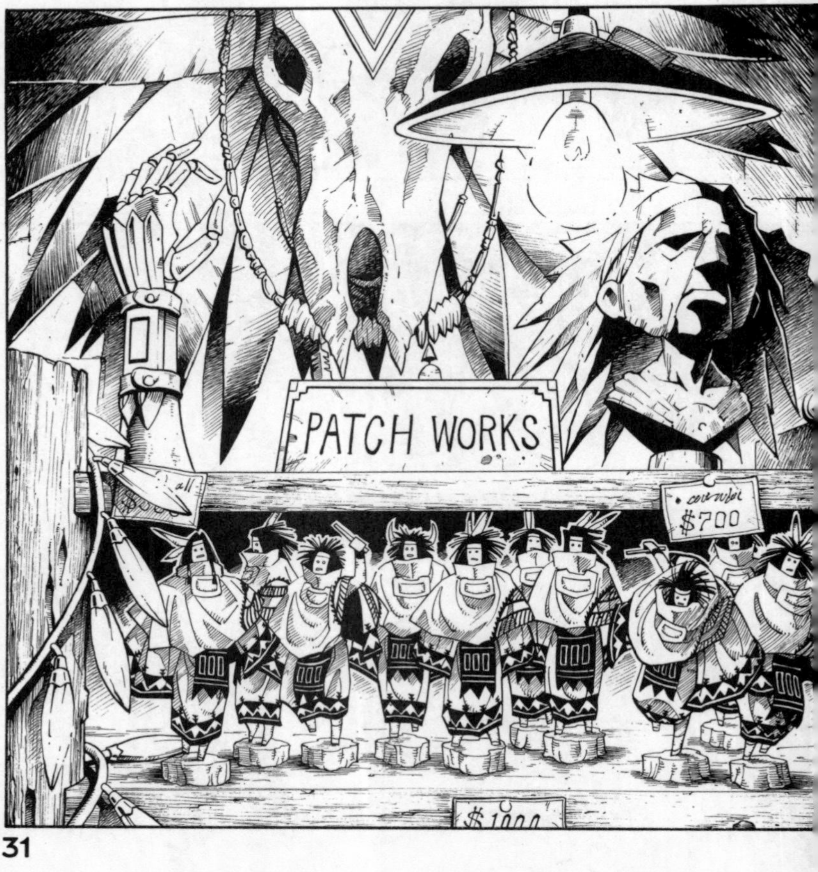
PATCH WORKS
$700
$1000

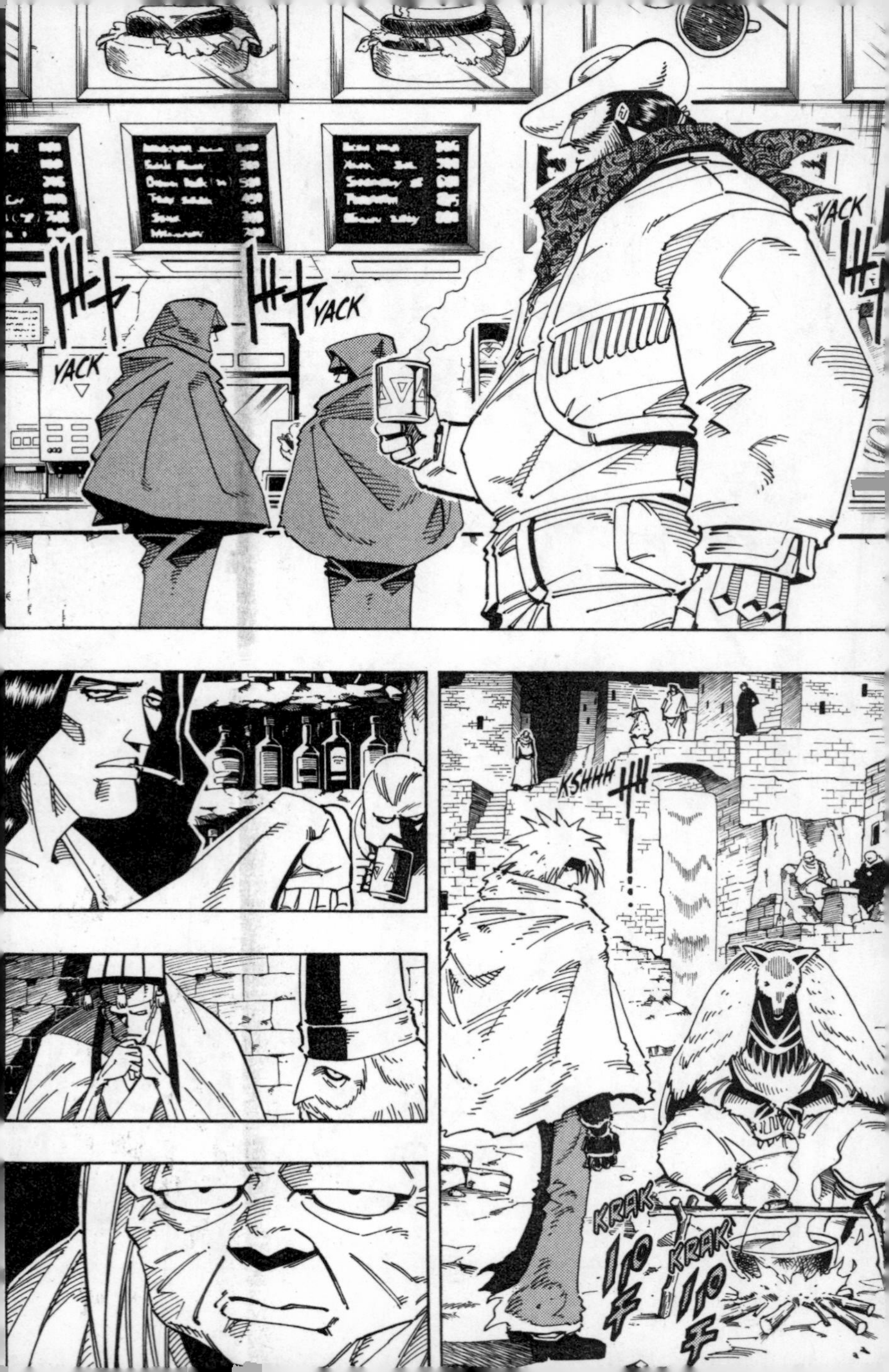
YACK
YACK
YACK
KSHHH
KRAK
KRAK

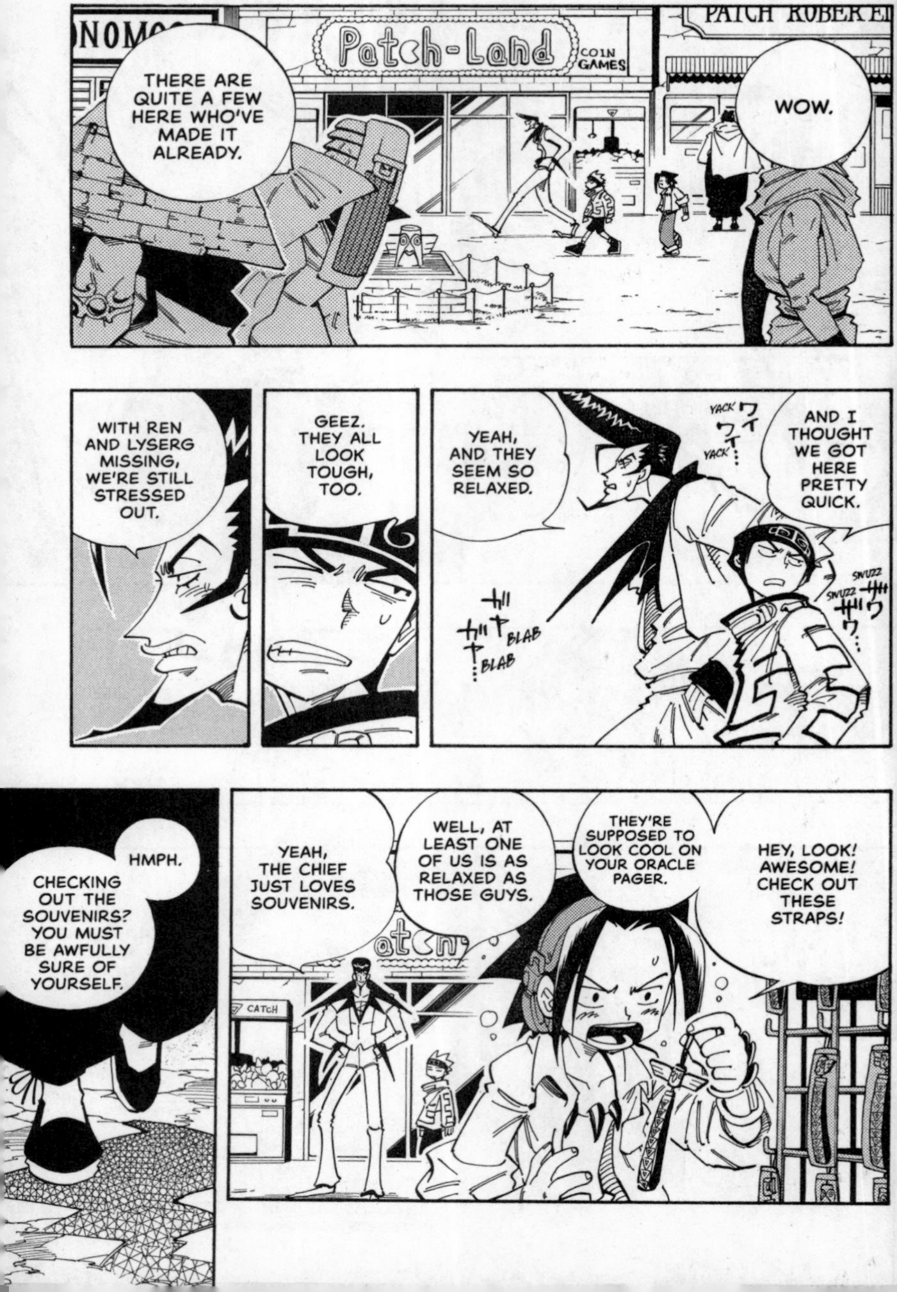
Patch-Land
COIN GAMES
WOW.
THERE ARE QUITE A FEW HERE WHO'VE MADE IT ALREADY.
AND I THOUGHT WE GOT HERE PRETTY QUICK.
ワイワイ… YACK YACK…
ザワザワ… SNUZZ SNUZZ
YEAH, AND THEY SEEM SO RELAXED.
ガヤガヤ… BLAB BLAB
GEEZ. THEY ALL LOOK TOUGH, TOO.
WITH REN AND LYSERG MISSING, WE'RE STILL STRESSED OUT.
HEY, LOOK! AWESOME! CHECK OUT THESE STRAPS!
THEY'RE SUPPOSED TO LOOK COOL ON YOUR ORACLE PAGER.
WELL, AT LEAST ONE OF US IS AS RELAXED AS THOSE GUYS.
YEAH, THE CHIEF JUST LOVES SOUVENIRS.
CATCH
HMPH.
CHECKING OUT THE SOUVENIRS? YOU MUST BE AWFULLY SURE OF YOURSELF.

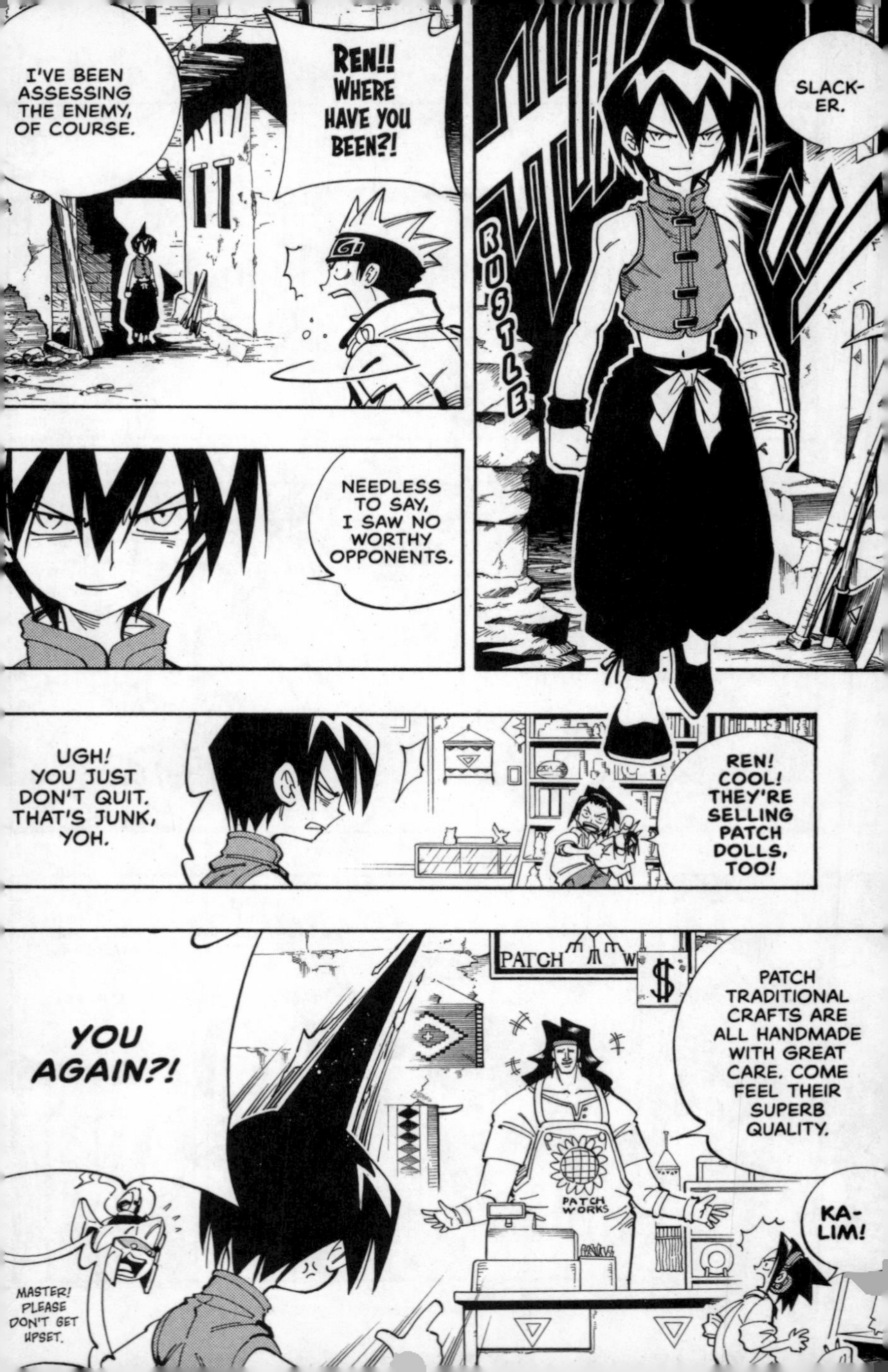
SLACKER.
RUSTLE
REN!! WHERE HAVE YOU BEEN?!
I'VE BEEN ASSESSING THE ENEMY, OF COURSE.
NEEDLESS TO SAY, I SAW NO WORTHY OPPONENTS.
REN! COOL! THEY'RE SELLING PATCH DOLLS, TOO!
UGH! YOU JUST DON'T QUIT. THAT'S JUNK, YOH.
PATCH TRADITIONAL CRAFTS ARE ALL HANDMADE WITH GREAT CARE. COME FEEL THEIR SUPERB QUALITY.
PATCH W
$
KA-LIM!
PATCH WORKS
YOU AGAIN?!
MASTER! PLEASE DON'T GET UPSET.

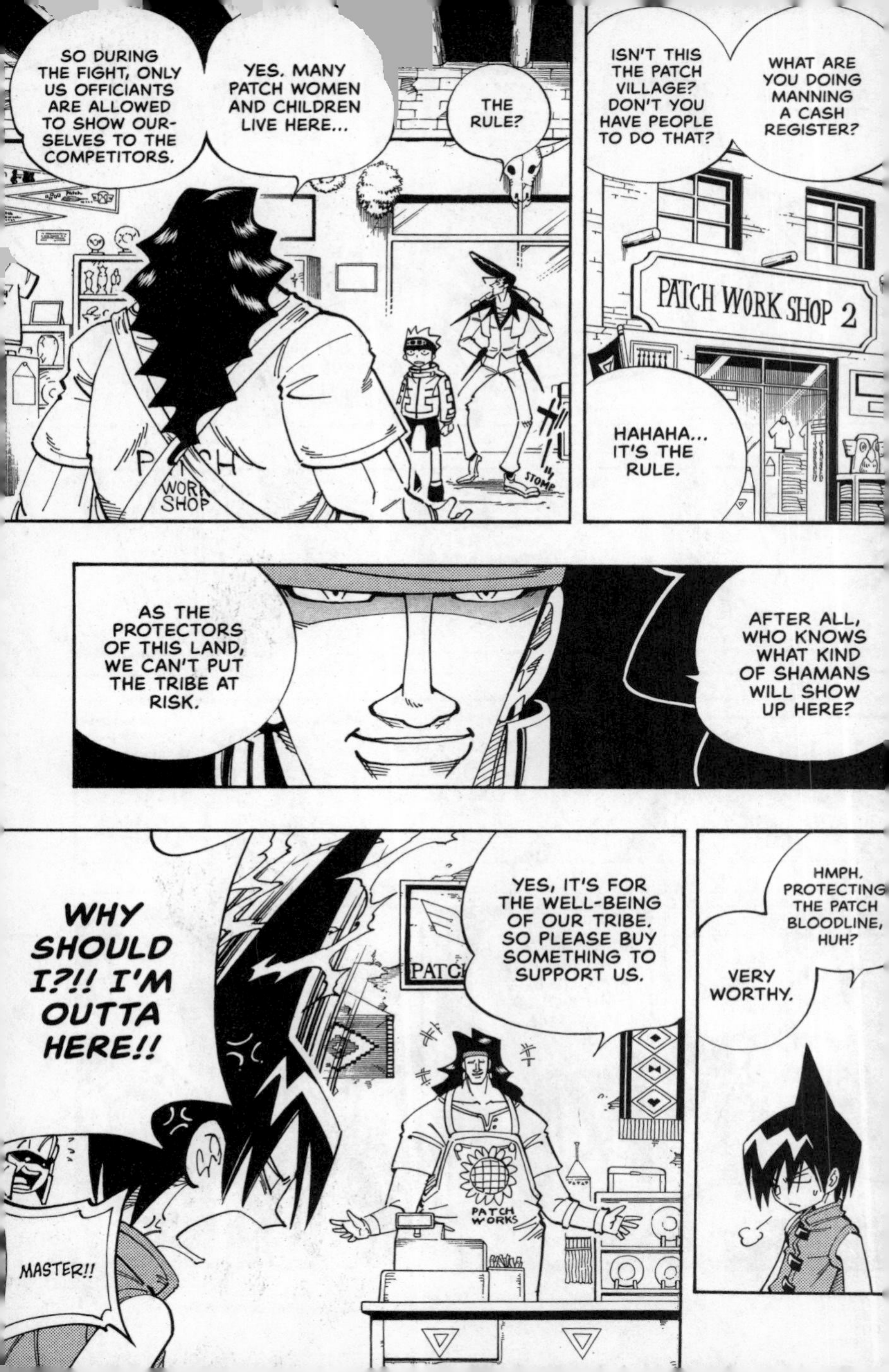
WHAT ARE YOU DOING MANNING A CASH REGISTER?
ISN'T THIS THE PATCH VILLAGE? DON'T YOU HAVE PEOPLE TO DO THAT?
PATCH WORK SHOP 2
HAHAHA... IT'S THE RULE.
THE RULE?
YES. MANY PATCH WOMEN AND CHILDREN LIVE HERE...
SO DURING THE FIGHT, ONLY US OFFICIANTS ARE ALLOWED TO SHOW OURSELVES TO THE COMPETITORS.
STOMP
PATCH WORK SHOP
AFTER ALL, WHO KNOWS WHAT KIND OF SHAMANS WILL SHOW UP HERE?
AS THE PROTECTORS OF THIS LAND, WE CAN'T PUT THE TRIBE AT RISK.
HMPH. PROTECTING THE PATCH BLOODLINE, HUH?
VERY WORTHY.
YES, IT'S FOR THE WELL-BEING OF OUR TRIBE. SO PLEASE BUY SOMETHING TO SUPPORT US.
PATCH WORKS
WHY SHOULD I?!! I'M OUTTA HERE!!
MASTER!!

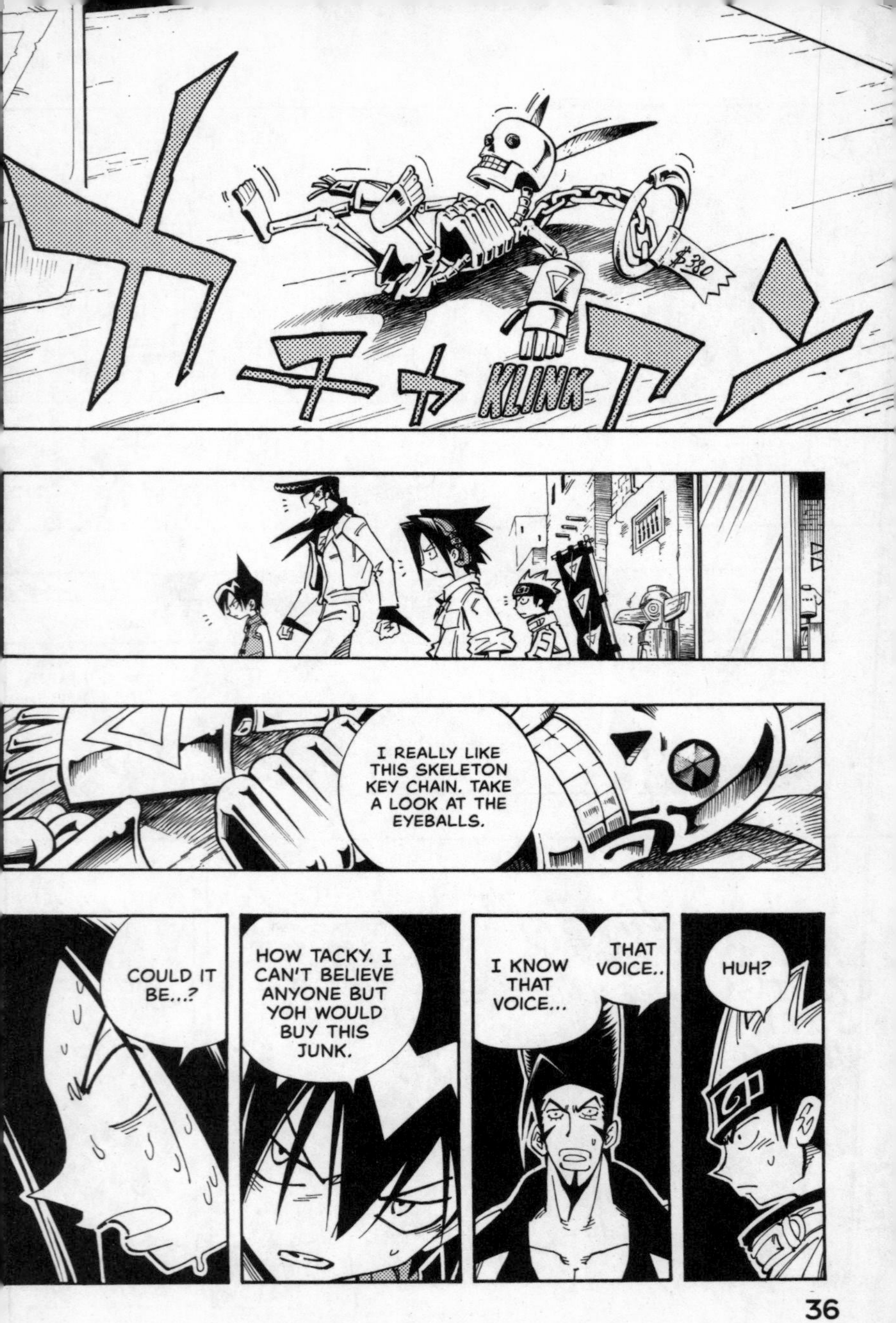

$380
KLINK
I REALLY LIKE THIS SKELETON KEY CHAIN. TAKE A LOOK AT THE EYEBALLS.
HUH?
THAT VOICE..
I KNOW THAT VOICE...
HOW TACKY. I CAN'T BELIEVE ANYONE BUT YOH WOULD BUY THIS JUNK.
COULD IT BE...?

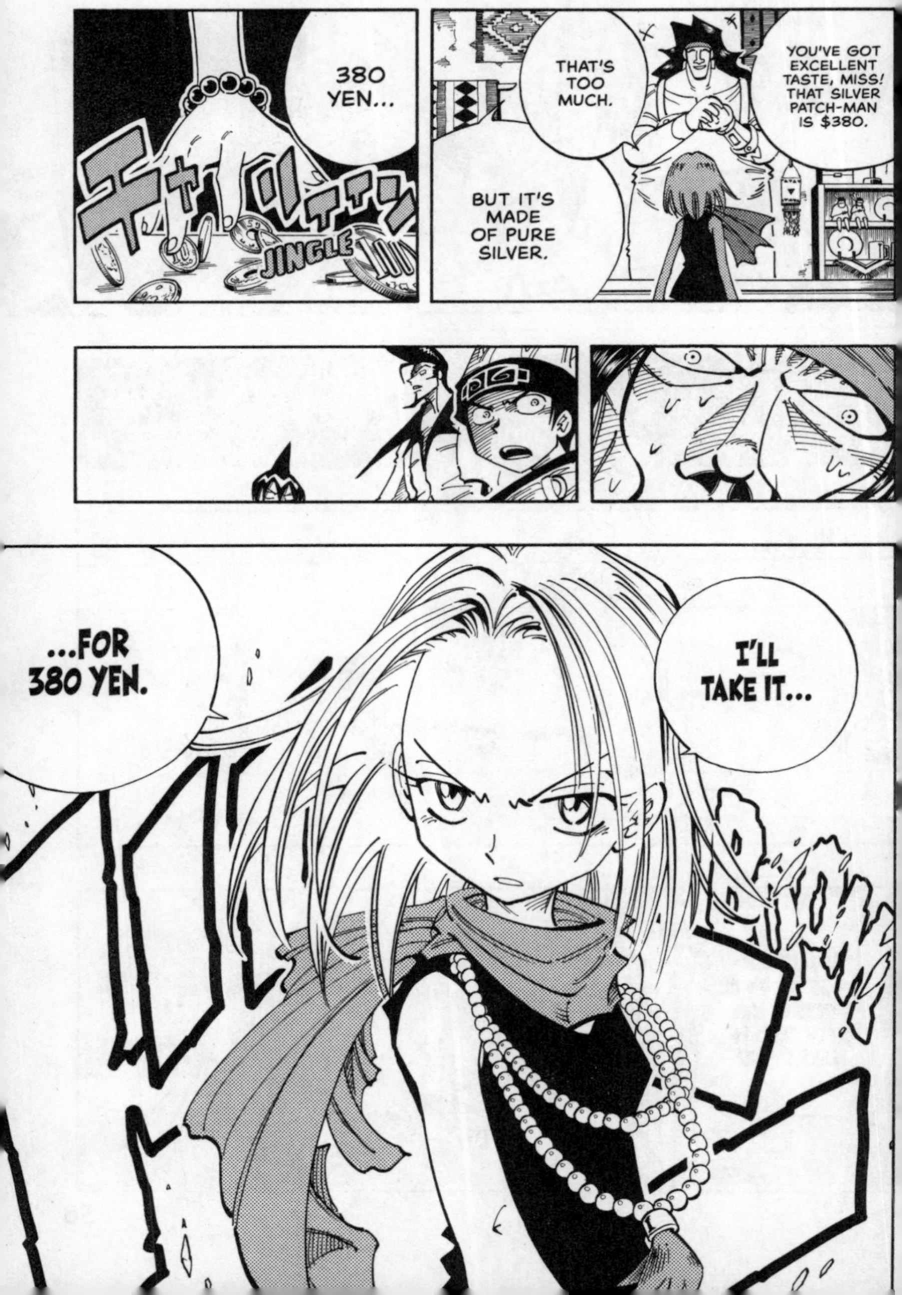
YOU'VE GOT EXCELLENT TASTE, MISS! THAT SILVER PATCH-MAN IS $380.
THAT'S TOO MUCH.
BUT IT'S MADE OF PURE SILVER.
380 YEN...
JINGLE
I'LL TAKE IT...
...FOR 380 YEN.

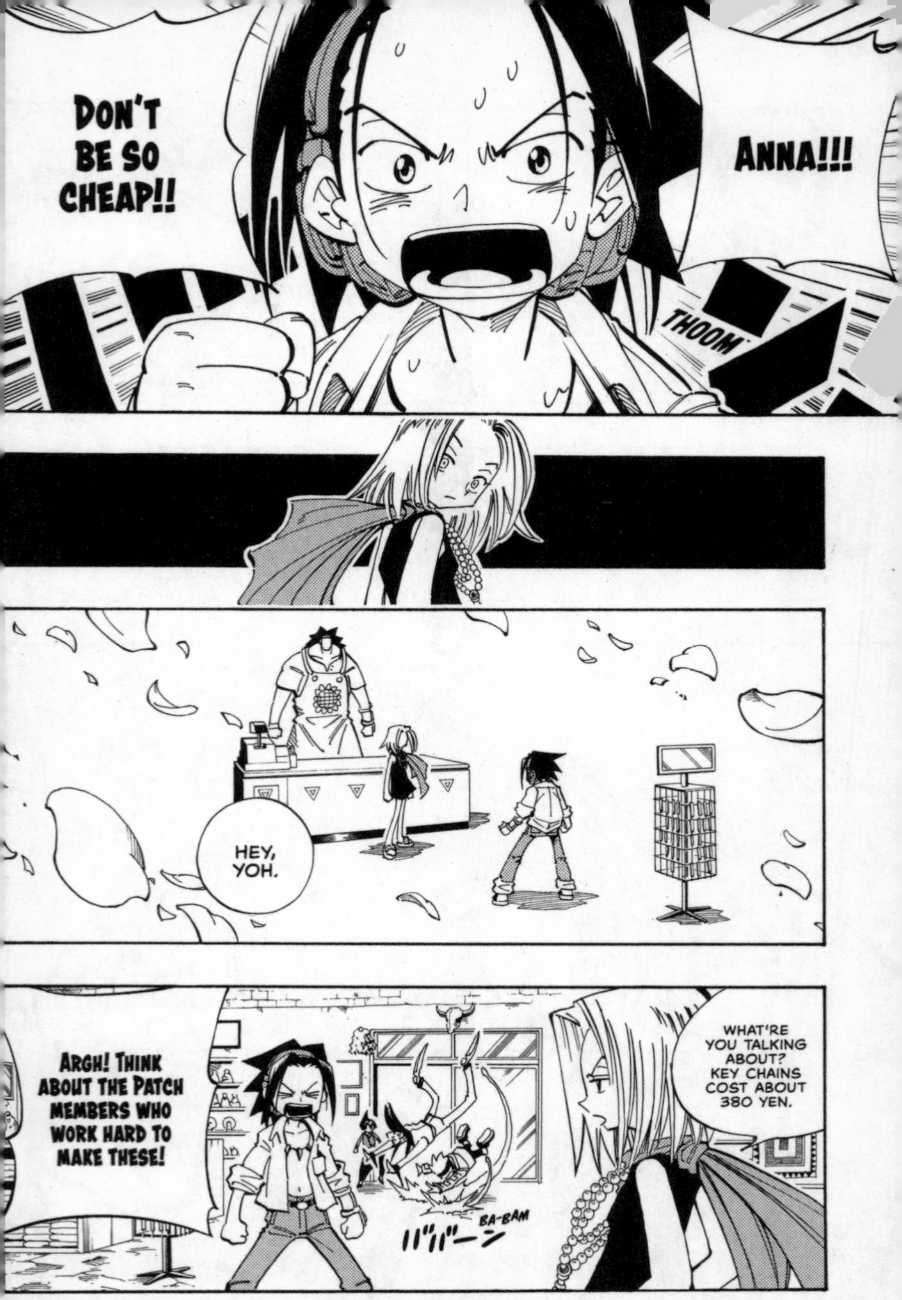
DON'T BE SO CHEAP!!
ANNA!!!
THOOM
HEY, YOH.
WHAT'RE YOU TALKING ABOUT? KEY CHAINS COST ABOUT 380 YEN.
ARGH! THINK ABOUT THE PATCH MEMBERS WHO WORK HARD TO MAKE THESE!
BA-BAM

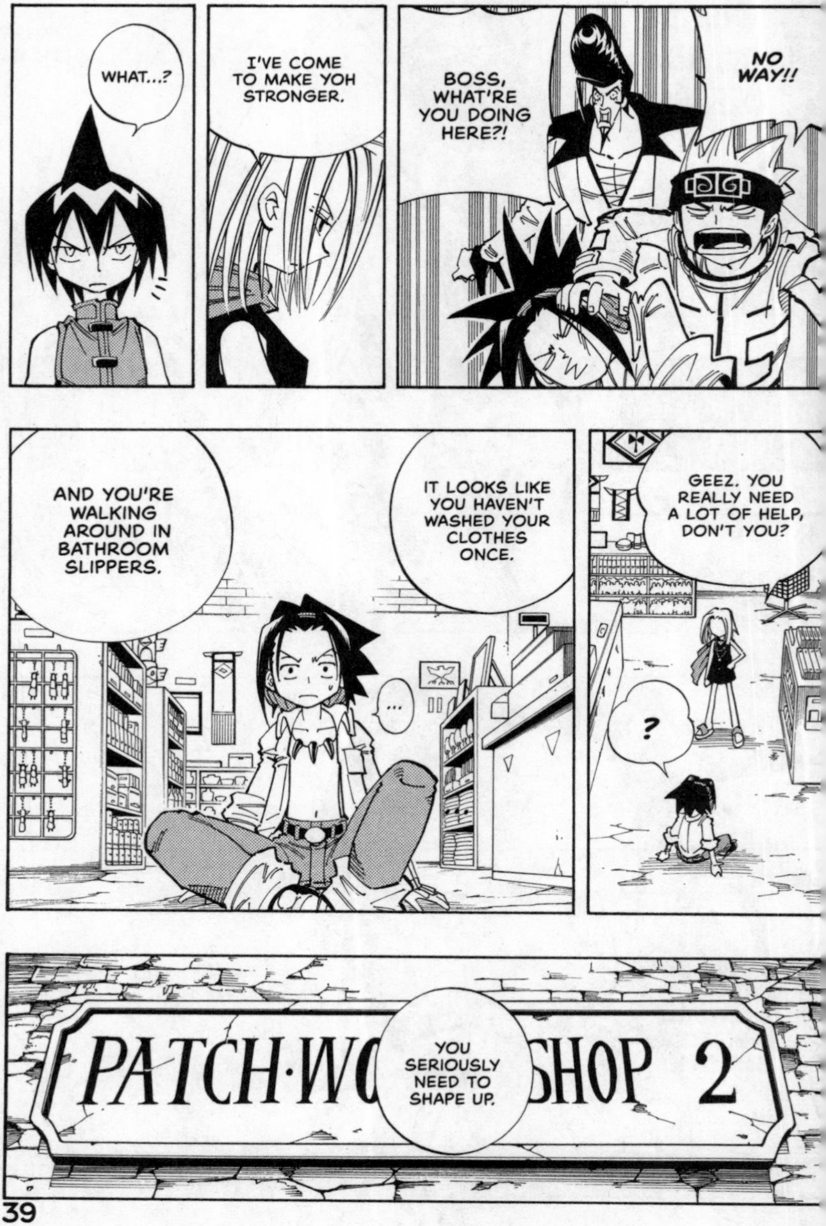
NO WAY!!
BOSS, WHAT'RE YOU DOING HERE?!
I'VE COME TO MAKE YOH STRONGER.
WHAT...?
GEEZ. YOU REALLY NEED A LOT OF HELP, DON'T YOU?
?
IT LOOKS LIKE YOU HAVEN'T WASHED YOUR CLOTHES ONCE.
AND YOU'RE WALKING AROUND IN BATHROOM SLIPPERS.
...
PATCH·WO
SHOP 2
YOU SERIOUSLY NEED TO SHAPE UP.

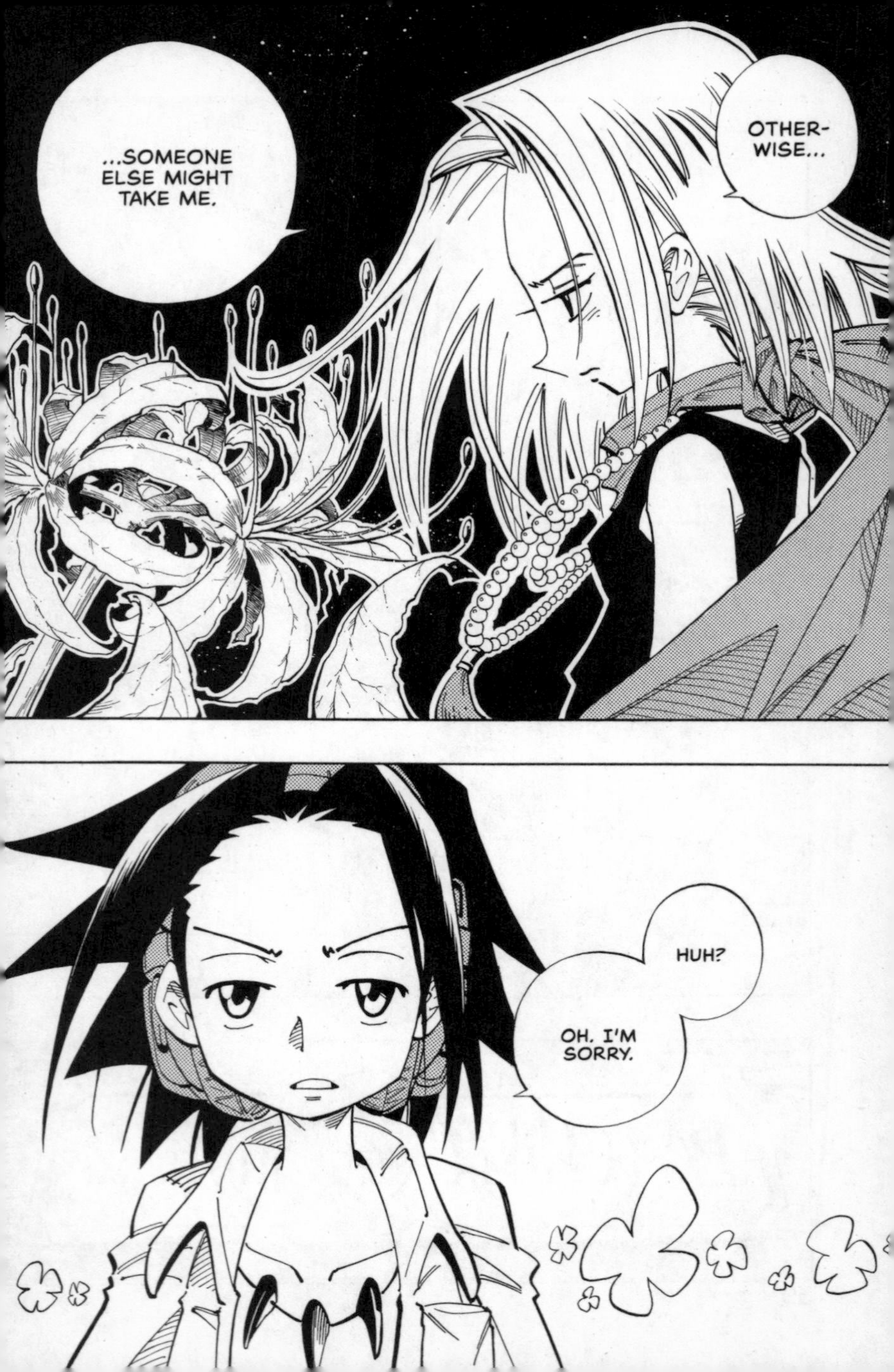
OTHER-WISE...
...SOMEONE ELSE MIGHT TAKE ME.
HUH?
OH. I'M SORRY.

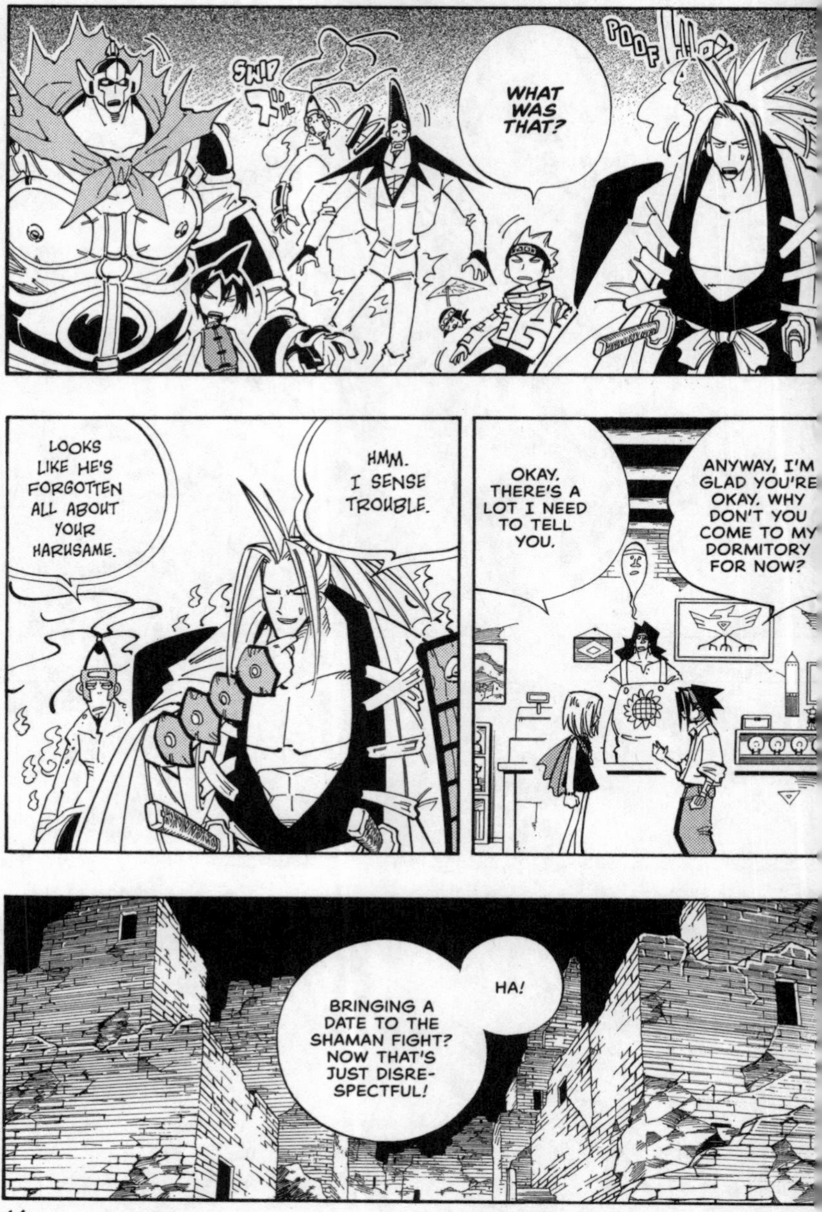
POOF
WHAT WAS THAT?
SWIP
ANYWAY, I'M GLAD YOU'RE OKAY. WHY DON'T YOU COME TO MY DORMITORY FOR NOW?
OKAY. THERE'S A LOT I NEED TO TELL YOU.
HMM. I SENSE TROUBLE.
LOOKS LIKE HE'S FORGOTTEN ALL ABOUT YOUR HARUSAME.
HA!
BRINGING A DATE TO THE SHAMAN FIGHT? NOW THAT'S JUST DISRESPECTFUL!

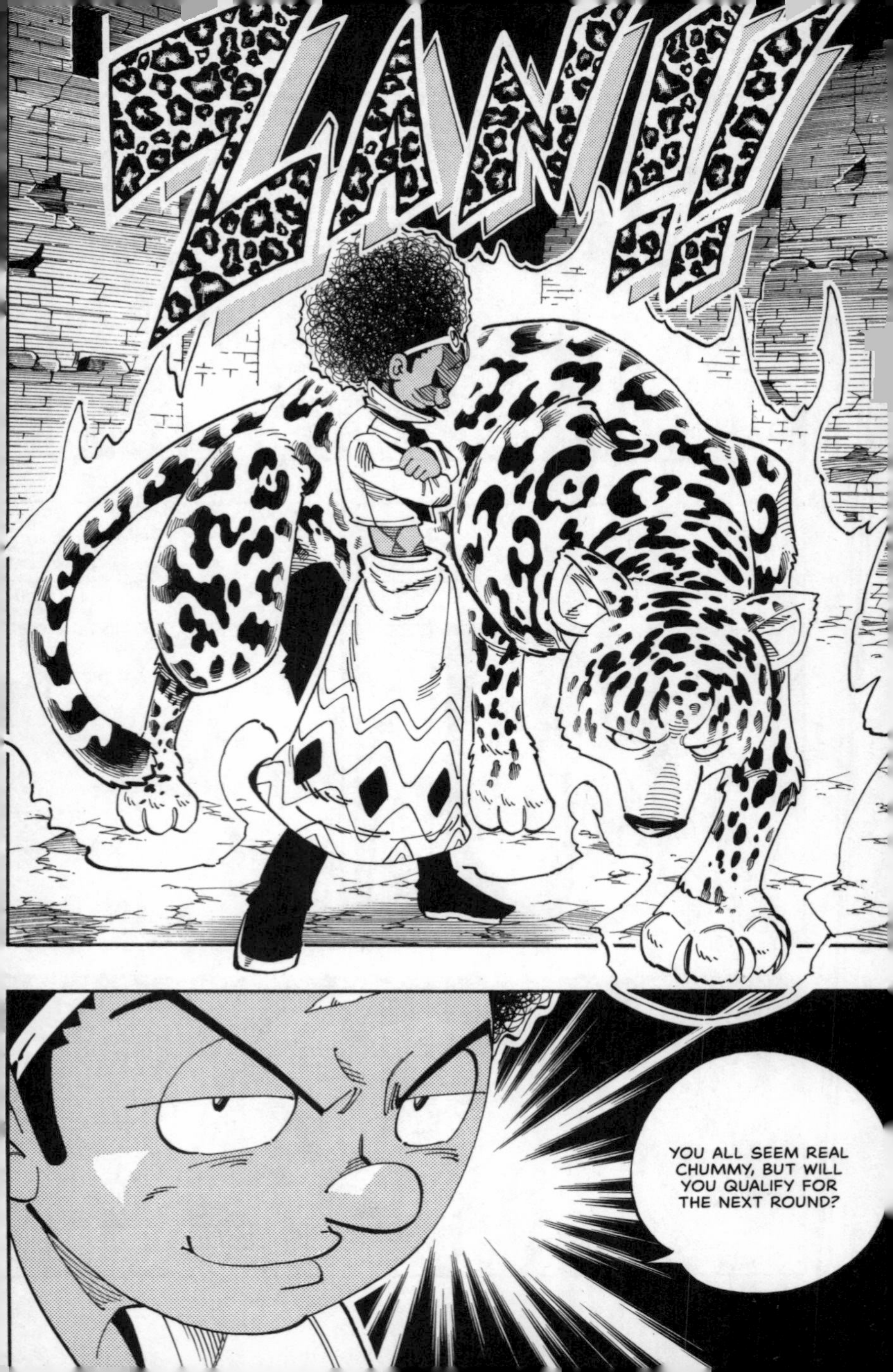
ZLAM!!
YOU ALL SEEM REAL CHUMMY, BUT WILL YOU QUALIFY FOR THE NEXT ROUND?

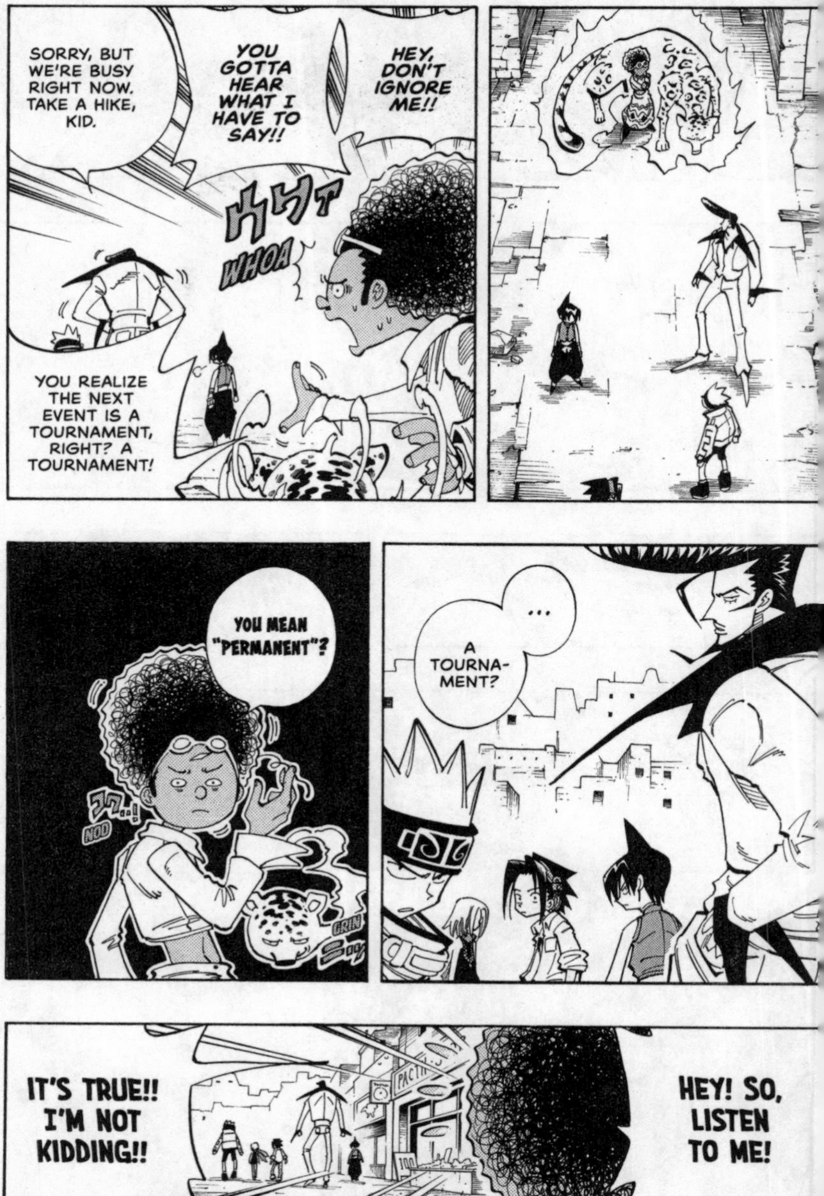
HEY, DON'T IGNORE ME!!
YOU GOTTA HEAR WHAT I HAVE TO SAY!!
SORRY, BUT WE'RE BUSY RIGHT NOW. TAKE A HIKE, KID.
WHOA
YOU REALIZE THE NEXT EVENT IS A TOURNAMENT, RIGHT? A TOURNAMENT!
...
A TOURNAMENT?
YOU MEAN "PERMANENT"?
NOD
GRIN
HEY! SO, LISTEN TO ME!
IT'S TRUE!! I'M NOT KIDDING!!

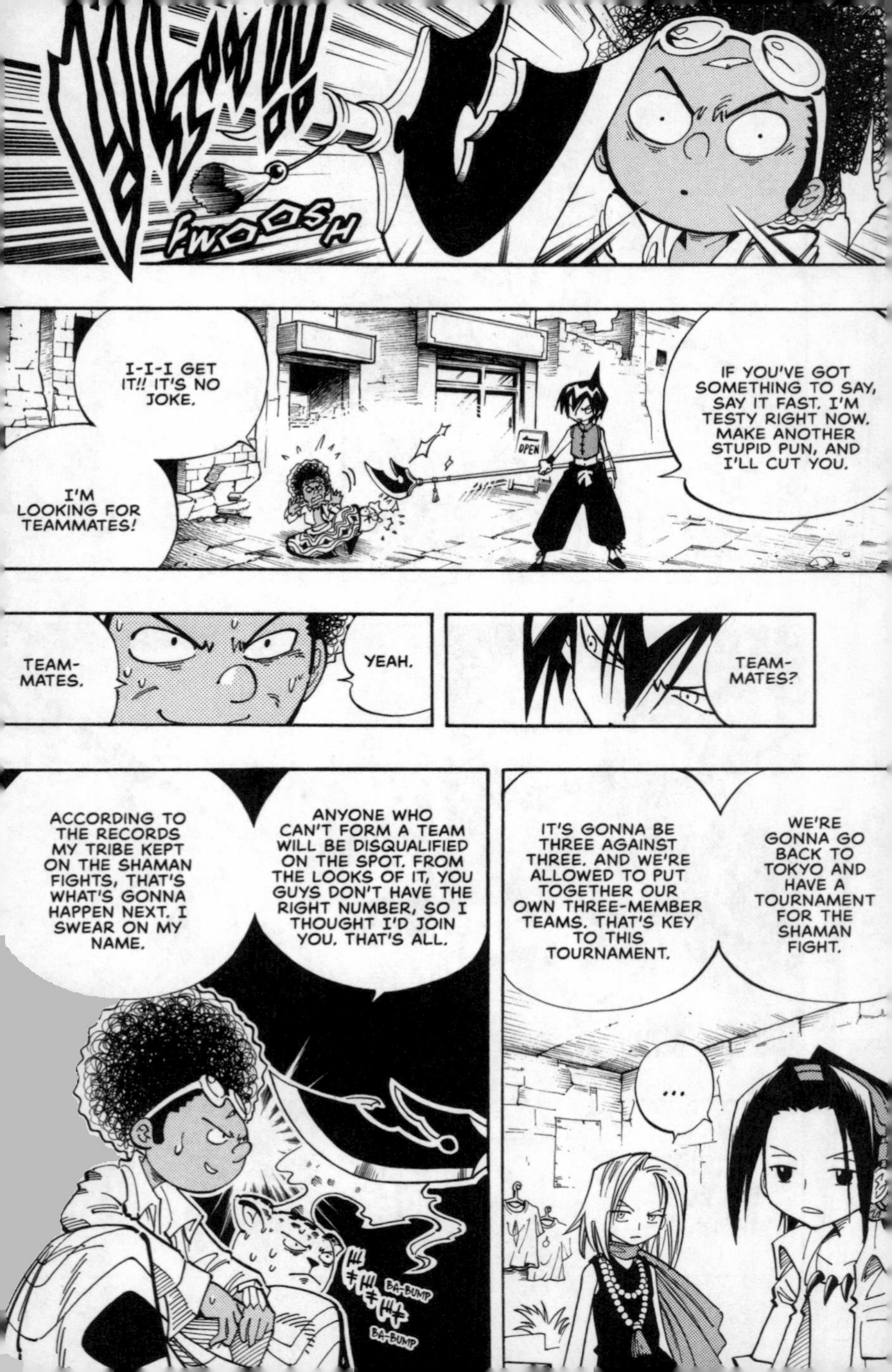
FWOOSH
IF YOU'VE GOT SOMETHING TO SAY, SAY IT FAST. I'M TESTY RIGHT NOW. MAKE ANOTHER STUPID PUN, AND I'LL CUT YOU.
I-I-I GET IT!! IT'S NO JOKE.
I'M LOOKING FOR TEAMMATES!
TEAM-MATES?
YEAH.
TEAM-MATES.
WE'RE GONNA GO BACK TO TOKYO AND HAVE A TOURNAMENT FOR THE SHAMAN FIGHT.
IT'S GONNA BE THREE AGAINST THREE. AND WE'RE ALLOWED TO PUT TOGETHER OUR OWN THREE-MEMBER TEAMS. THAT'S KEY TO THIS TOURNAMENT.
...
ANYONE WHO CAN'T FORM A TEAM WILL BE DISQUALIFIED ON THE SPOT. FROM THE LOOKS OF IT, YOU GUYS DON'T HAVE THE RIGHT NUMBER, SO I THOUGHT I'D JOIN YOU. THAT'S ALL.
ACCORDING TO THE RECORDS MY TRIBE KEPT ON THE SHAMAN FIGHTS, THAT'S WHAT'S GONNA HAPPEN NEXT. I SWEAR ON MY NAME.
BA-BUMP
BA-BUMP

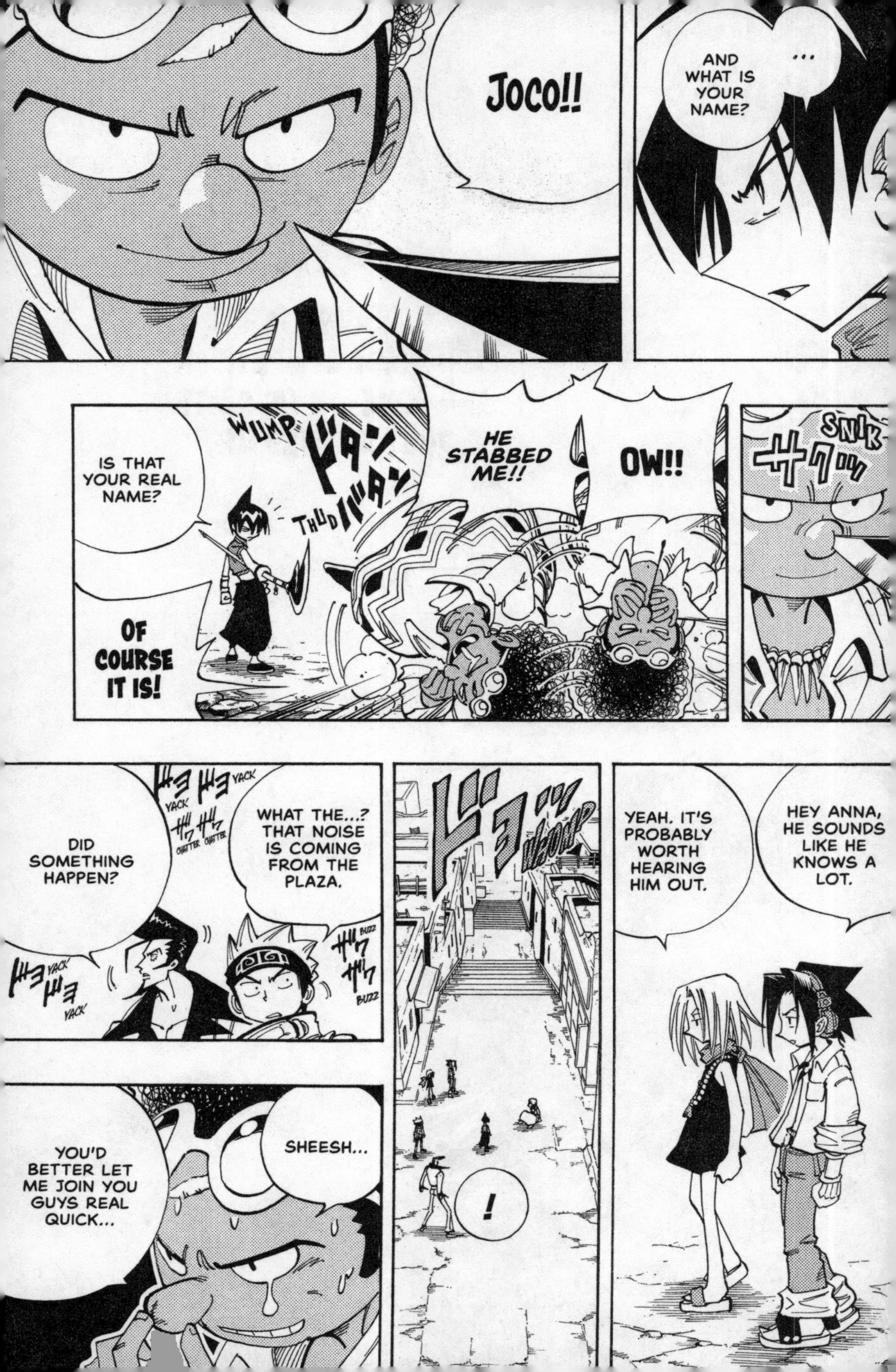
AND WHAT IS YOUR NAME?
...
JOCO!!
SNIK
OW!!
HE STABBED ME!!
WUMP
IS THAT YOUR REAL NAME?
THUD
OF COURSE IT IS!
HEY ANNA, HE SOUNDS LIKE HE KNOWS A LOT.
YEAH. IT'S PROBABLY WORTH HEARING HIM OUT.
WHOMP
!
YACK YACK
BUZZ BUZZ
WHAT THE...? THAT NOISE IS COMING FROM THE PLAZA.
CHATTER CHATTER
DID SOMETHING HAPPEN?
YACK YACK
SHEESH...
YOU'D BETTER LET ME JOIN YOU GUYS REAL QUICK...

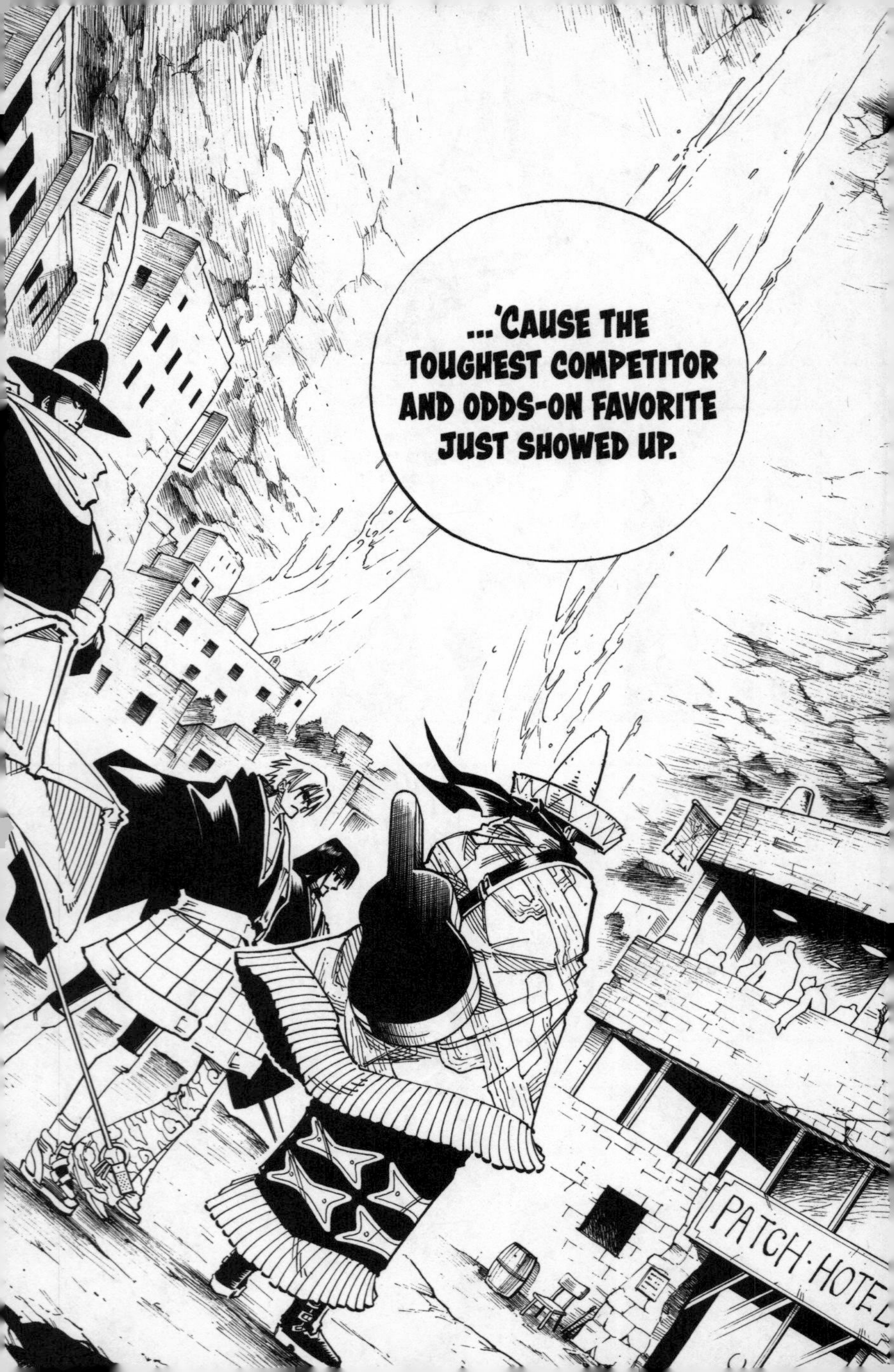
...'CAUSE THE TOUGHEST COMPETITOR AND ODDS-ON FAVORITE JUST SHOWED UP.
PATCH·HOTEL

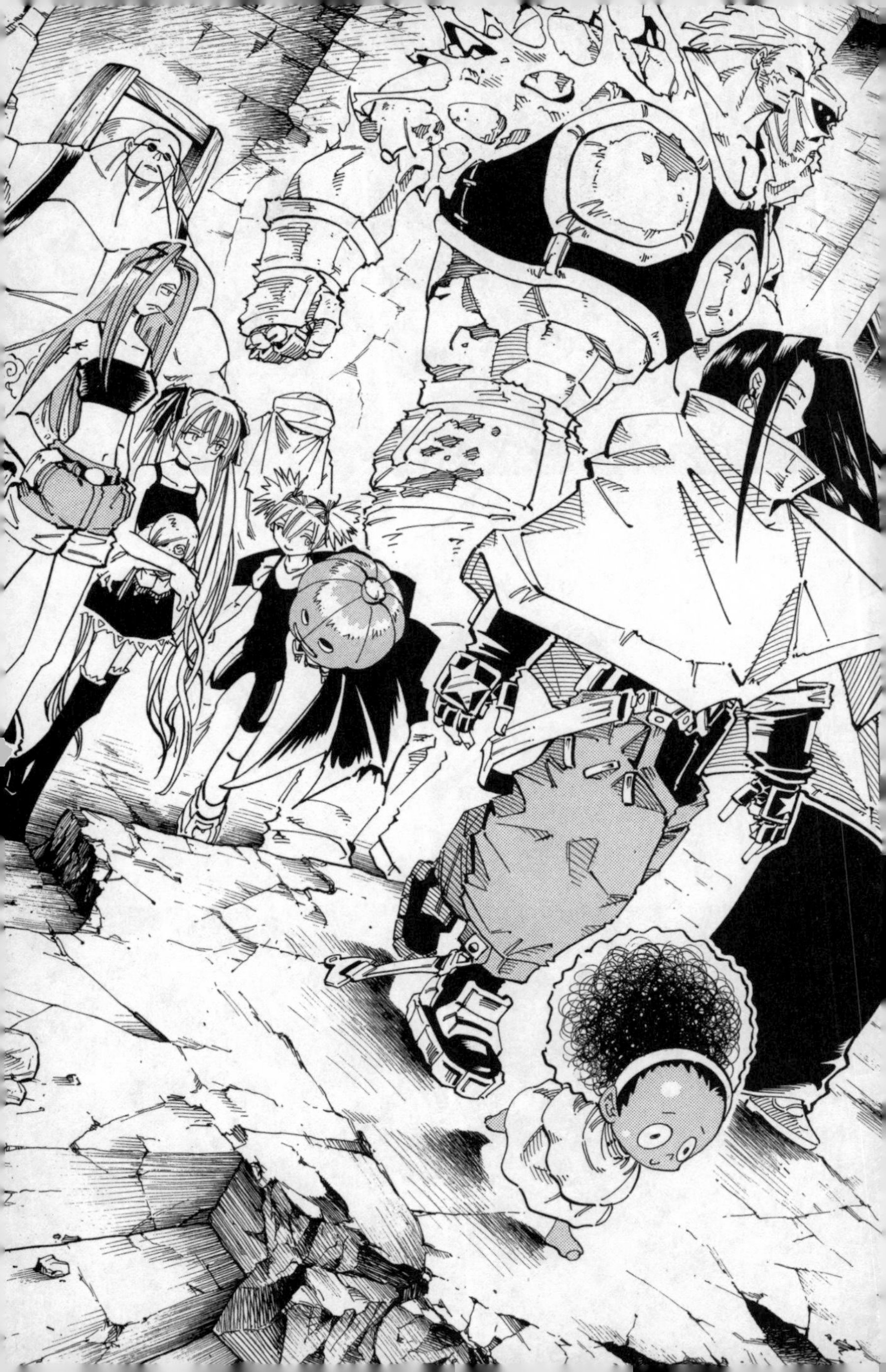

SHAMAN
KING
13

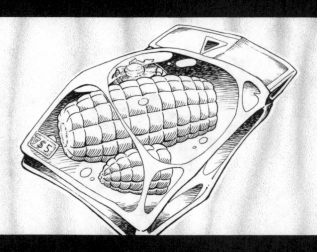

Patch Mini Pickles
(Local Specialty)

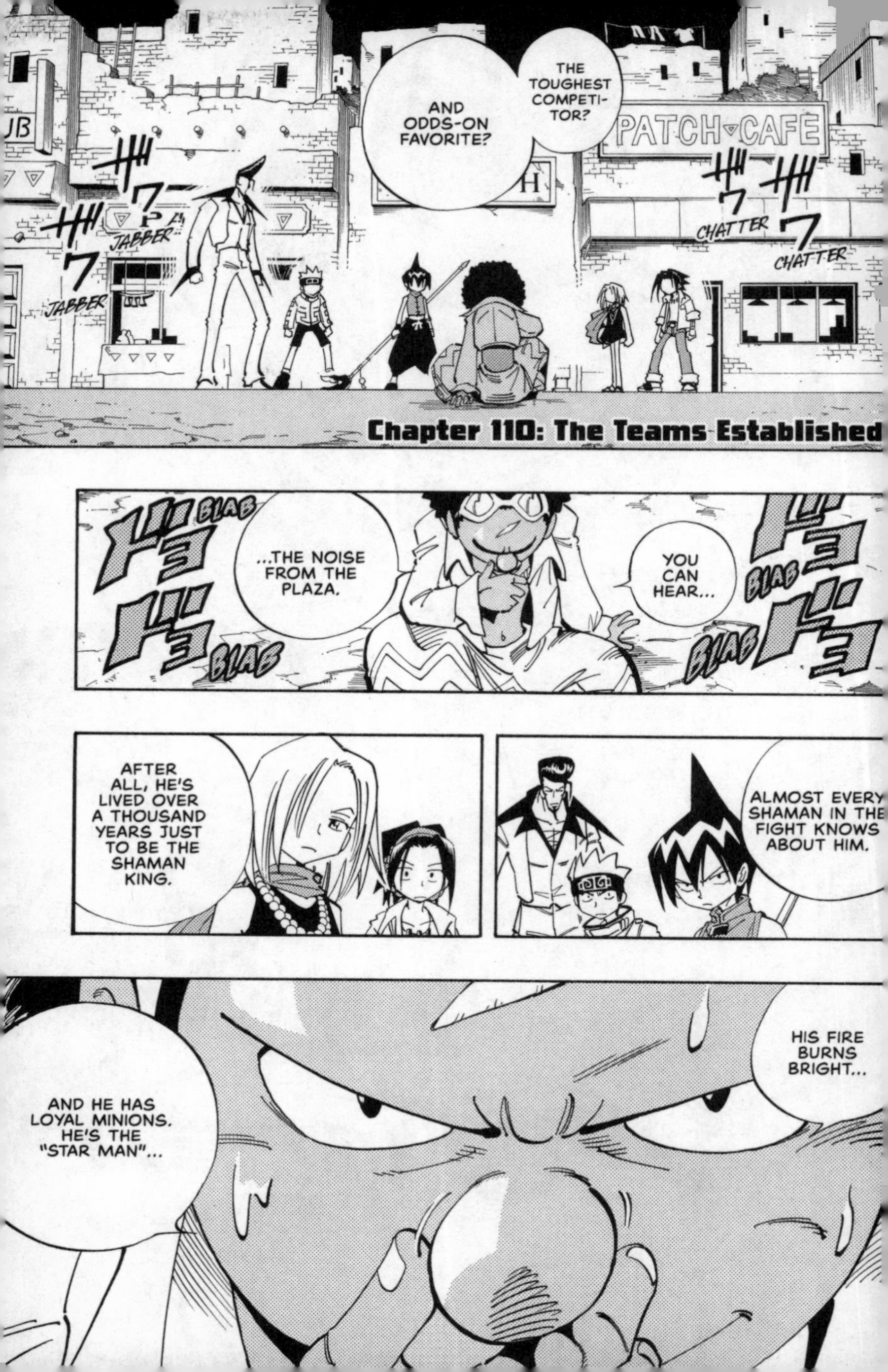
CHATTER
CHATTER
THE TOUGHEST COMPETI-TOR?
AND ODDS-ON FAVORITE?
JABBER
JABBER
PATCH CAFE
Chapter 110: The Teams Established
BLAB
BLAB
YOU CAN HEAR...
...THE NOISE FROM THE PLAZA.
BLAB
BLAB
ALMOST EVERY SHAMAN IN THE FIGHT KNOWS ABOUT HIM.
AFTER ALL, HE'S LIVED OVER A THOUSAND YEARS JUST TO BE THE SHAMAN KING.
HIS FIRE BURNS BRIGHT...
AND HE HAS LOYAL MINIONS. HE'S THE "STAR MAN"...

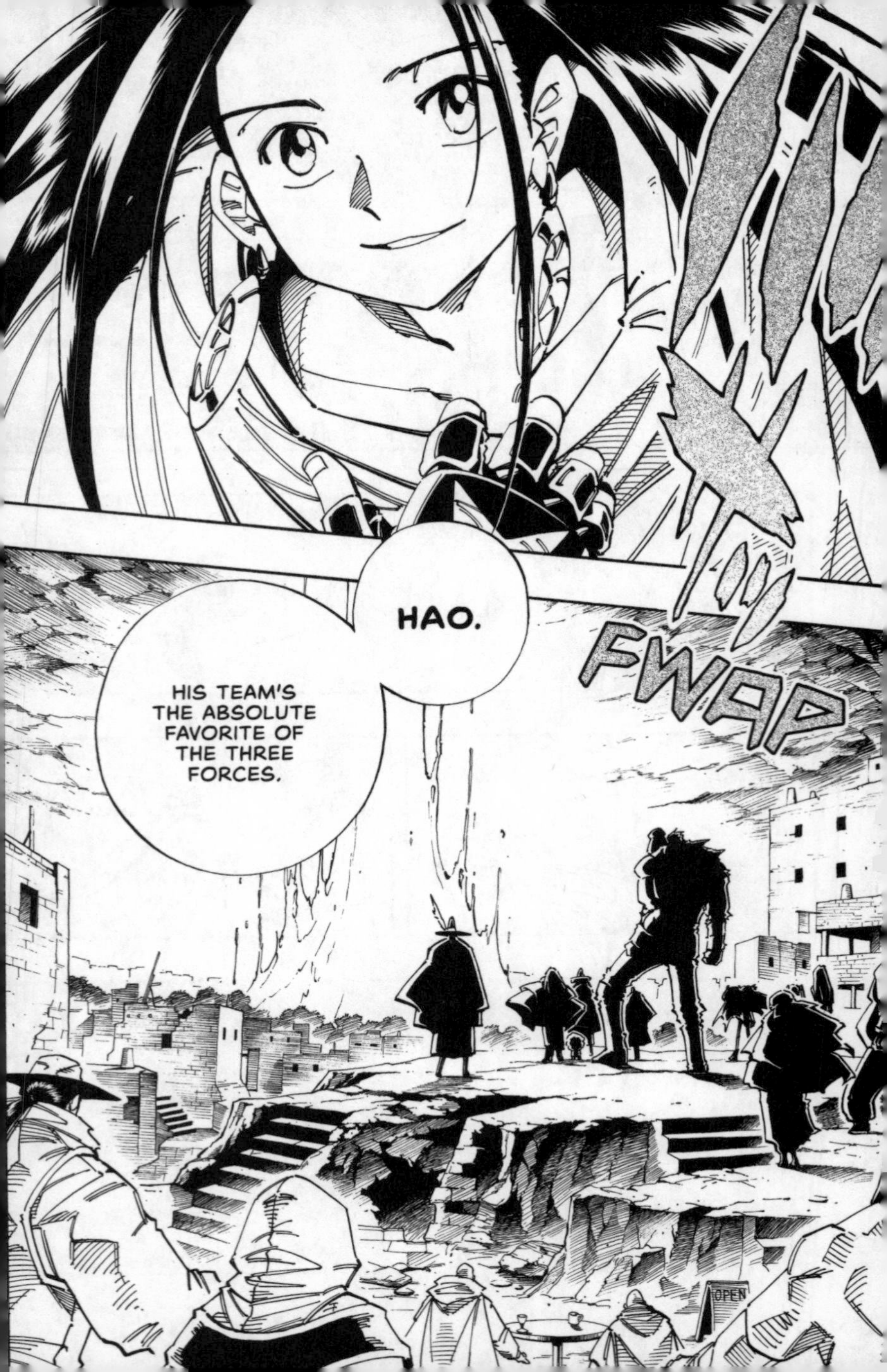
FWAP
HAO.
HIS TEAM'S THE ABSOLUTE FAVORITE OF THE THREE FORCES.
OPEN

Chapter 110:

The Teams Established

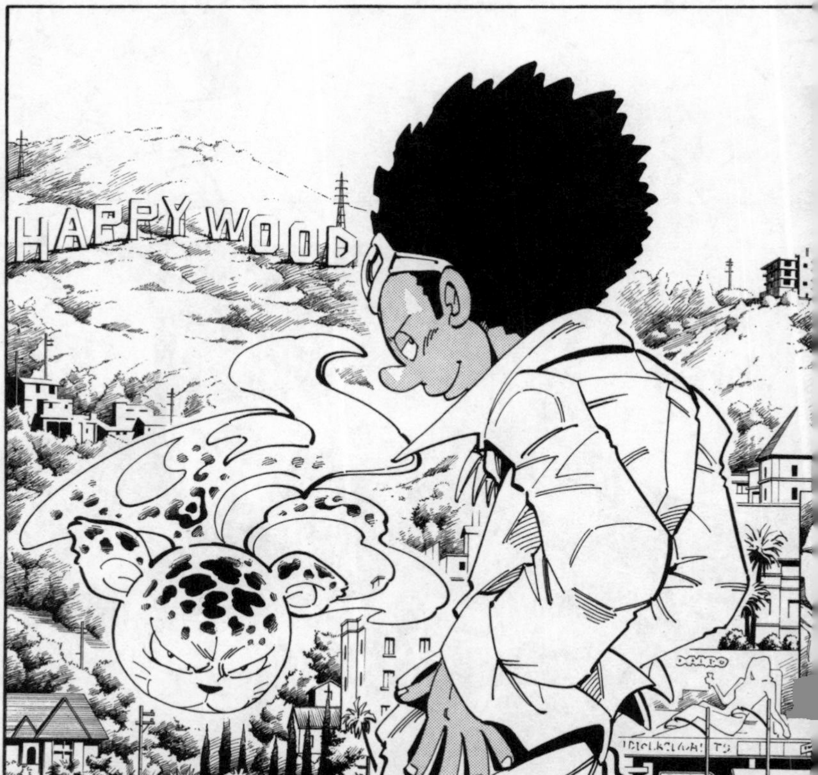
HAPPY WOOD

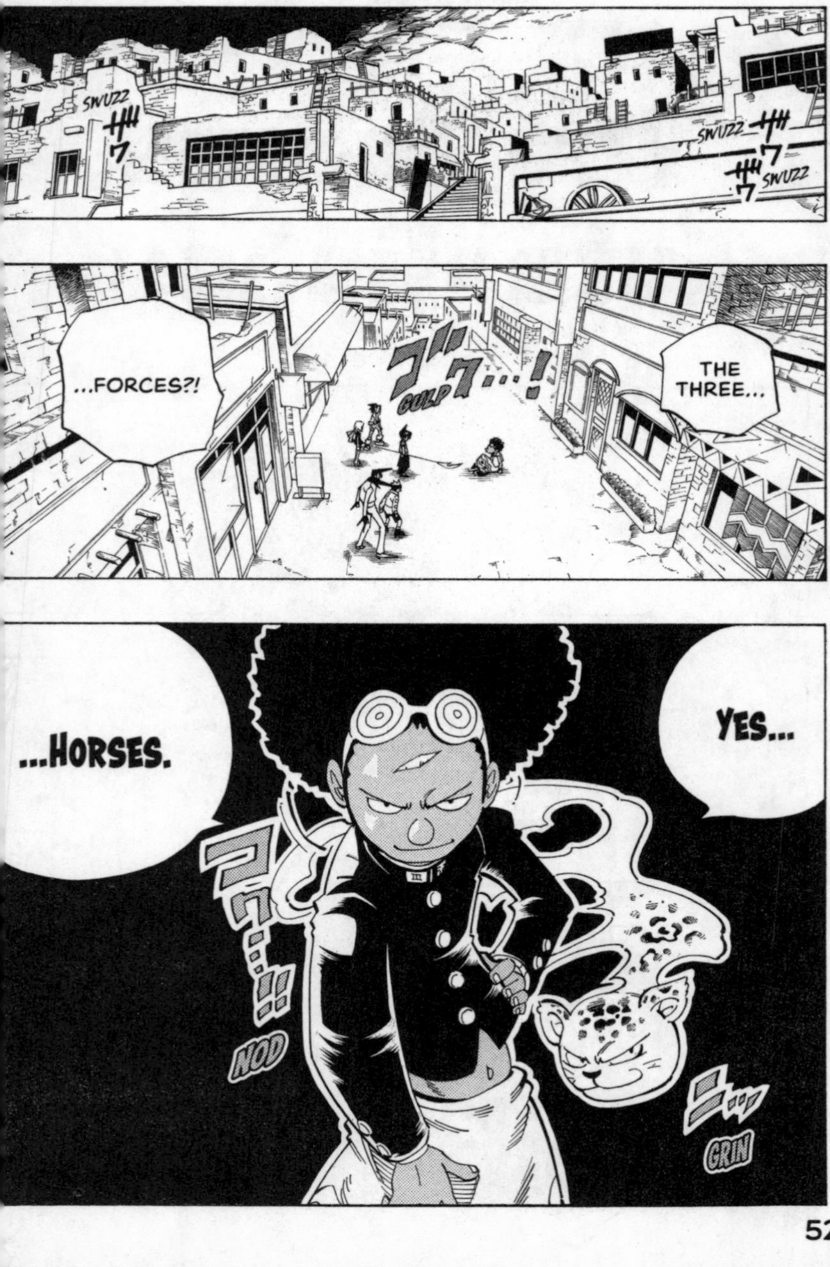
SWUZZ
SWUZZ
SWUZZ
THE THREE...
GULP
...FORCES?!
YES...
...HORSES.
NOD
GRIN

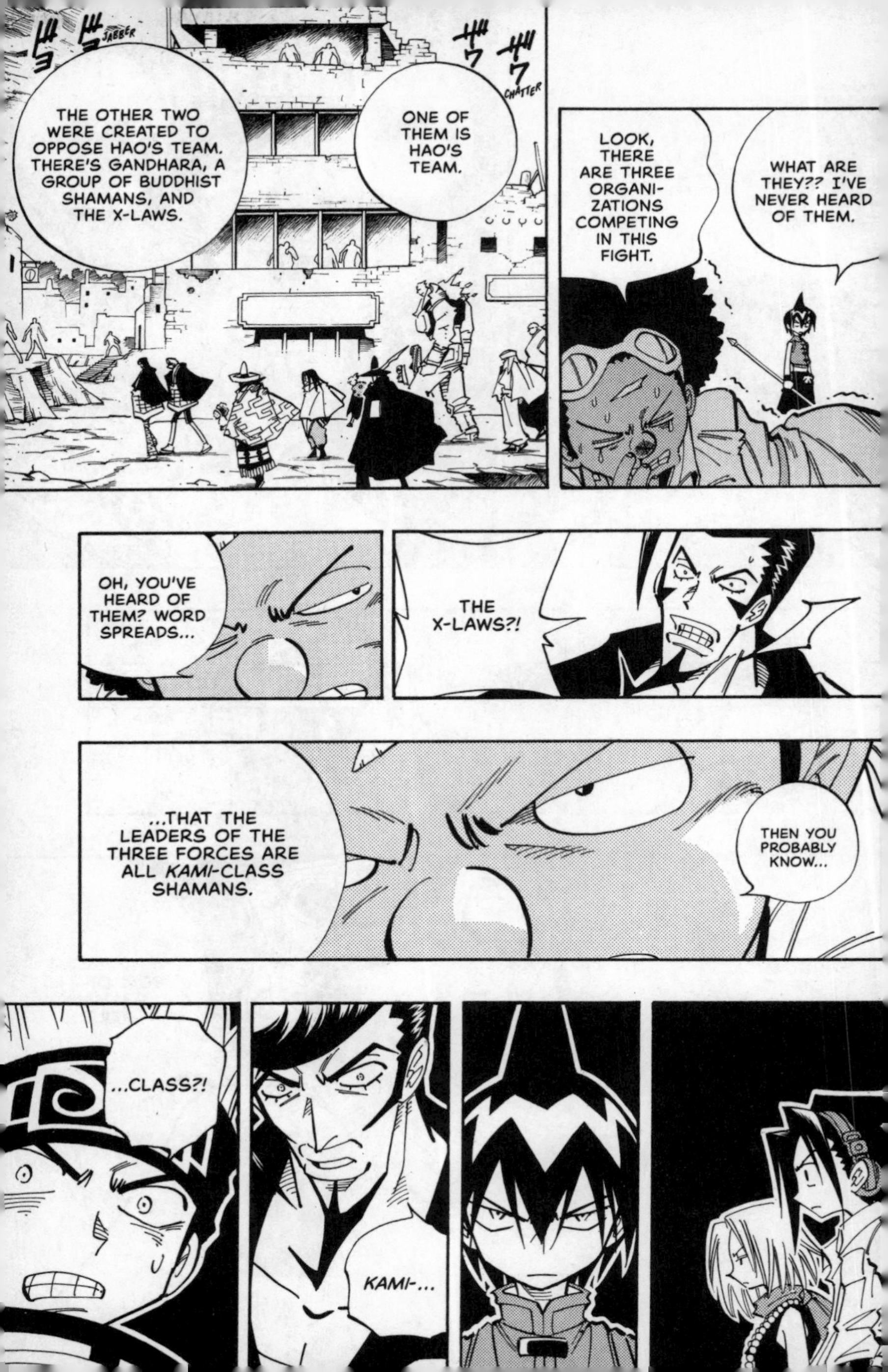
WHAT ARE THEY?? I'VE NEVER HEARD OF THEM.
LOOK, THERE ARE THREE ORGANI-ZATIONS COMPETING IN THIS FIGHT.
CHATTER
ONE OF THEM IS HAO'S TEAM.
THE OTHER TWO WERE CREATED TO OPPOSE HAO'S TEAM. THERE'S GANDHARA, A GROUP OF BUDDHIST SHAMANS, AND THE X-LAWS.
JABBER
THE X-LAWS?!
OH, YOU'VE HEARD OF THEM? WORD SPREADS...
THEN YOU PROBABLY KNOW...
...THAT THE LEADERS OF THE THREE FORCES ARE ALL *KAMI*-CLASS SHAMANS.
KAMI-...
...CLASS?!

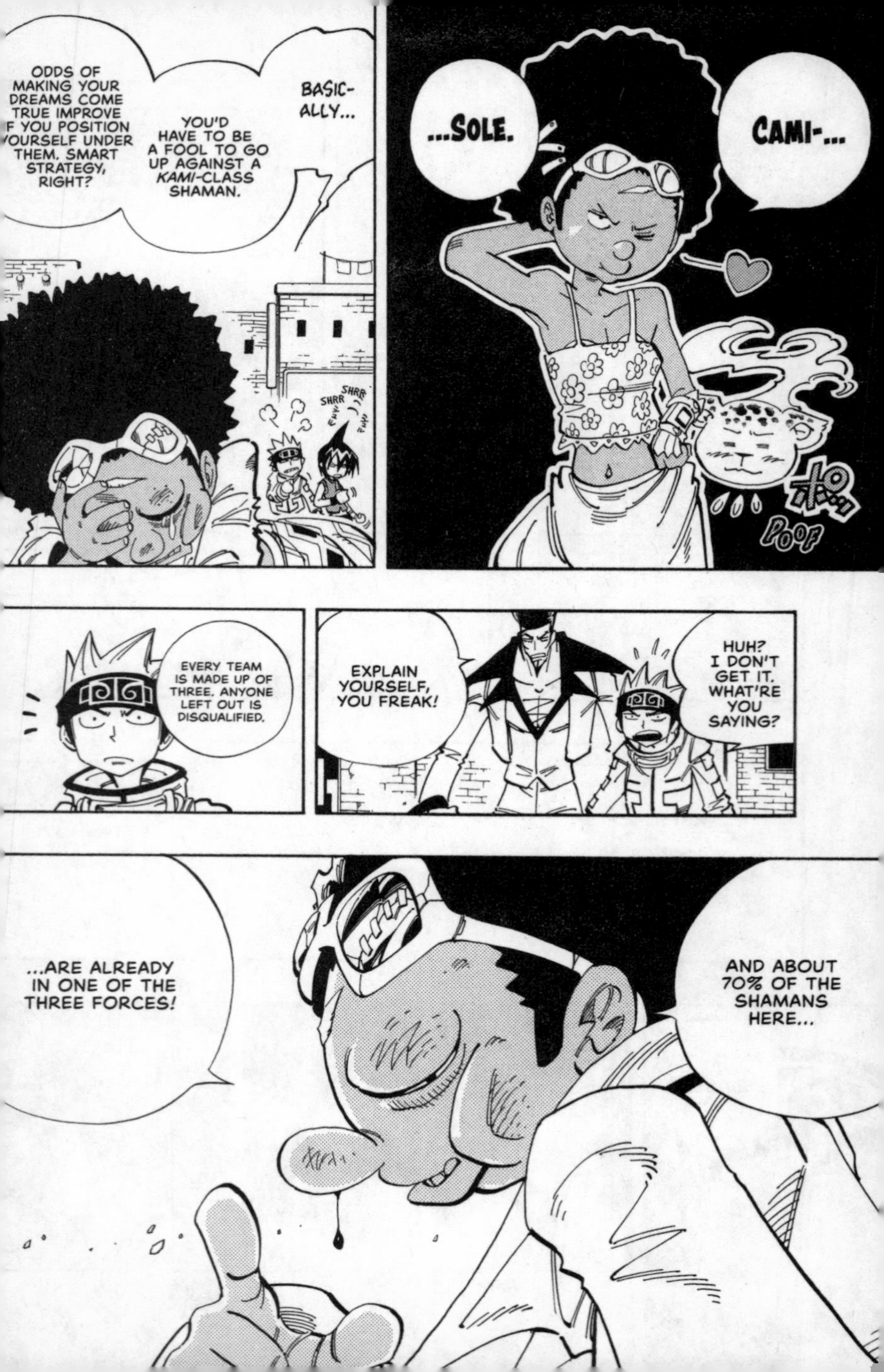
CAMI-...
...SOLE.
POOF
BASIC-ALLY...
YOU'D HAVE TO BE A FOOL TO GO UP AGAINST A *KAMI*-CLASS SHAMAN.
ODDS OF MAKING YOUR DREAMS COME TRUE IMPROVE F YOU POSITION OURSELF UNDER THEM. SMART STRATEGY, RIGHT?
HUH? I DON'T GET IT. WHAT'RE YOU SAYING?
EXPLAIN YOURSELF, YOU FREAK!
EVERY TEAM IS MADE UP OF THREE. ANYONE LEFT OUT IS DISQUALIFIED.
AND ABOUT 70% OF THE SHAMANS HERE...
...ARE ALREADY IN ONE OF THE THREE FORCES!

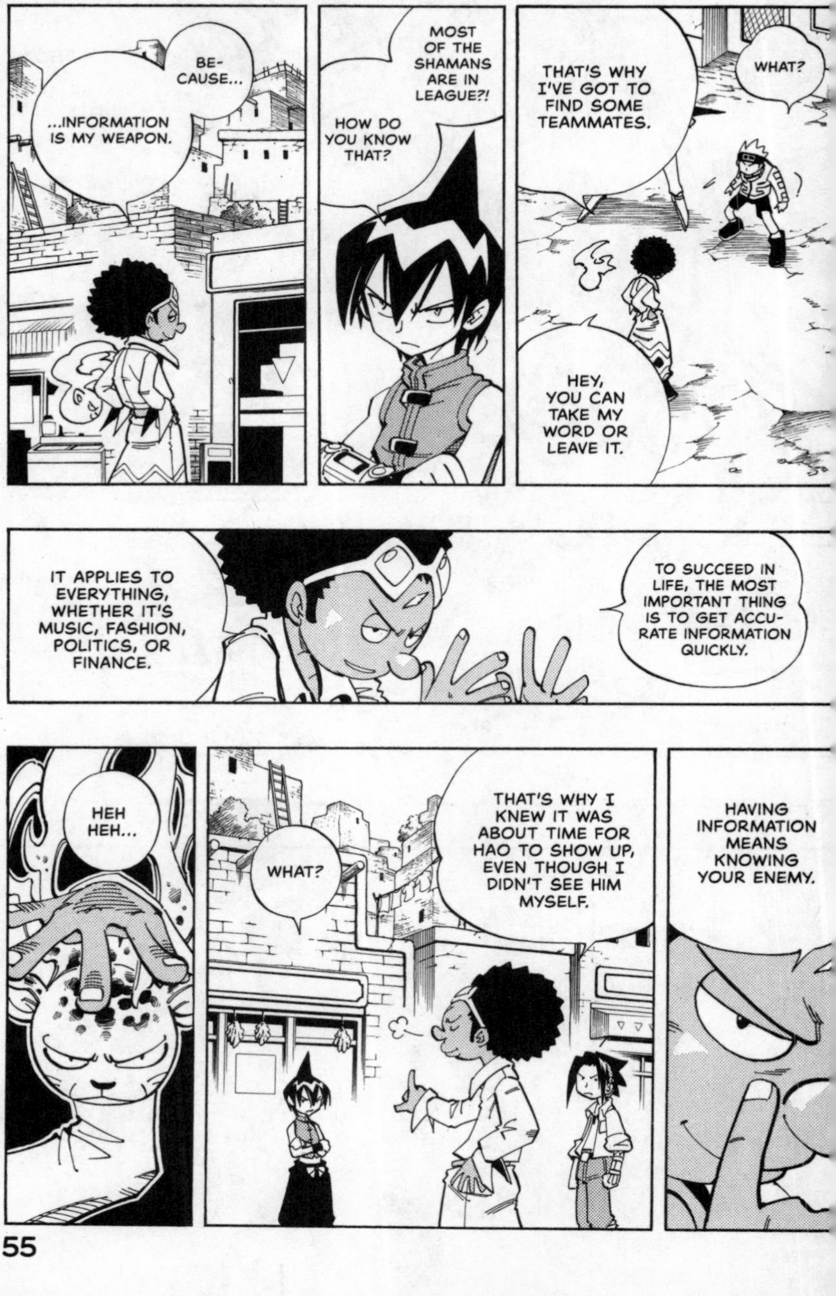
WHAT?
THAT'S WHY I'VE GOT TO FIND SOME TEAMMATES.
HEY, YOU CAN TAKE MY WORD OR LEAVE IT.
MOST OF THE SHAMANS ARE IN LEAGUE?!
HOW DO YOU KNOW THAT?
BE-CAUSE...
...INFORMATION IS MY WEAPON.
TO SUCCEED IN LIFE, THE MOST IMPORTANT THING IS TO GET ACCU-RATE INFORMATION QUICKLY.
IT APPLIES TO EVERYTHING, WHETHER IT'S MUSIC, FASHION, POLITICS, OR FINANCE.
HAVING INFORMATION MEANS KNOWING YOUR ENEMY.
THAT'S WHY I KNEW IT WAS ABOUT TIME FOR HAO TO SHOW UP, EVEN THOUGH I DIDN'T SEE HIM MYSELF.
WHAT?
HEH HEH...

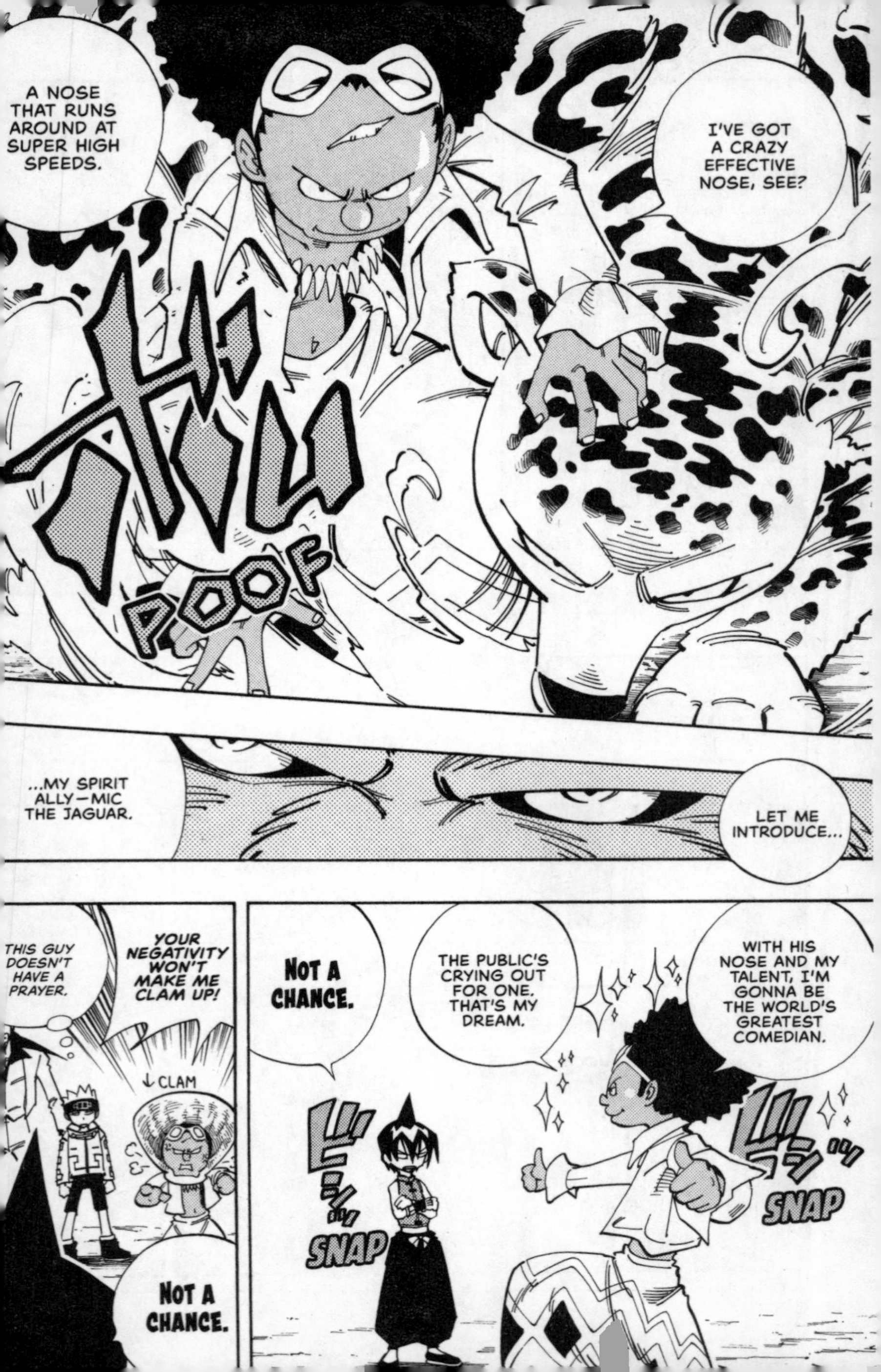
I'VE GOT A CRAZY EFFECTIVE NOSE, SEE?
A NOSE THAT RUNS AROUND AT SUPER HIGH SPEEDS.
POOF
LET ME INTRODUCE...
...MY SPIRIT ALLY—MIC THE JAGUAR.
WITH HIS NOSE AND MY TALENT, I'M GONNA BE THE WORLD'S GREATEST COMEDIAN.
SNAP
THE PUBLIC'S CRYING OUT FOR ONE. THAT'S MY DREAM.
NOT A CHANCE.
SNAP
YOUR NEGATIVITY WON'T MAKE ME CLAM UP!
THIS GUY DOESN'T HAVE A PRAYER.
↓CLAM
NOT A CHANCE.

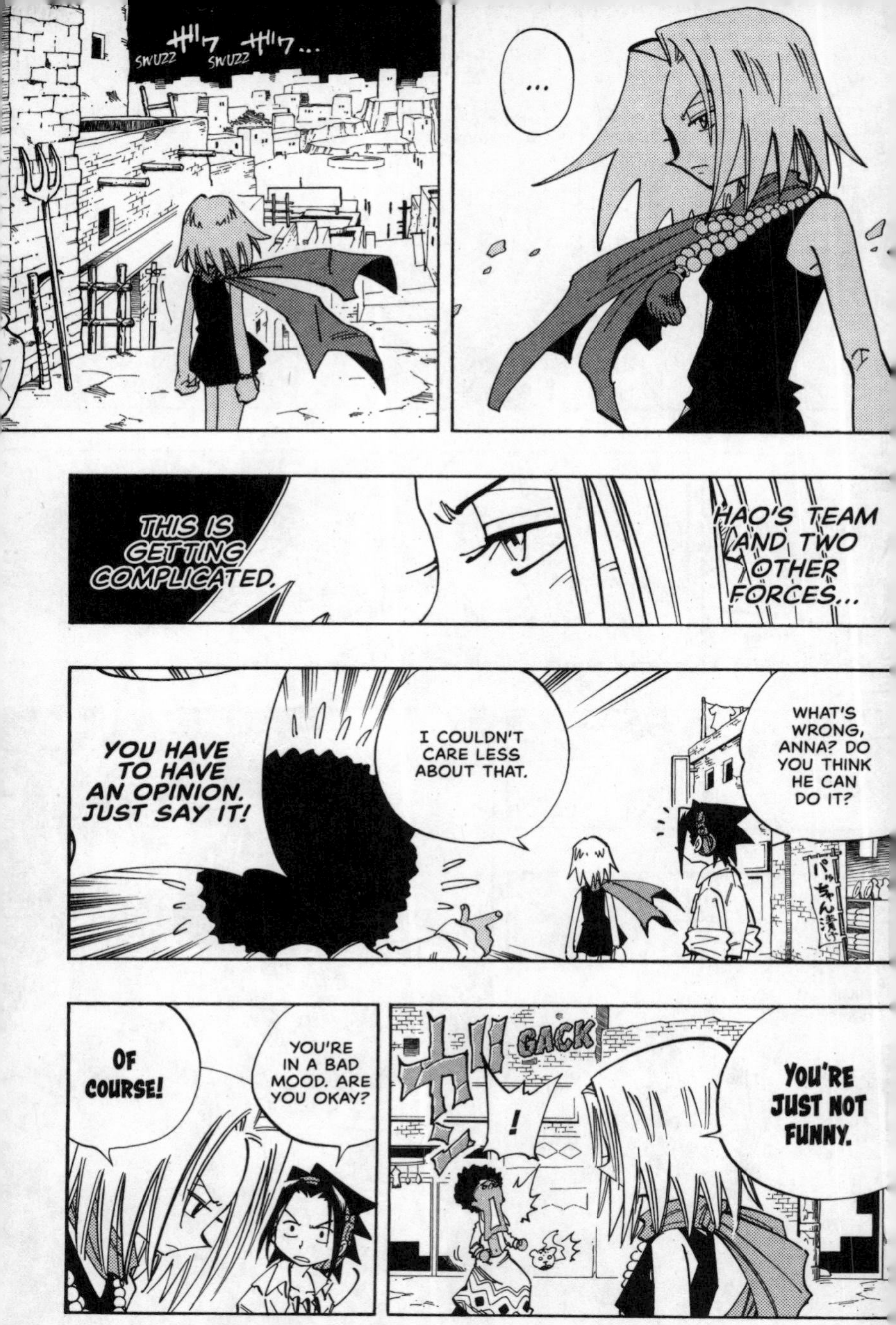
...
ザワ SWUZZ ザワ SWUZZ...
HAO'S TEAM AND TWO OTHER FORCES...
THIS IS GETTING COMPLICATED.
WHAT'S WRONG, ANNA? DO YOU THINK HE CAN DO IT?
I COULDN'T CARE LESS ABOUT THAT.
YOU HAVE TO HAVE AN OPINION. JUST SAY IT!
YOU'RE JUST NOT FUNNY.
ガッ GACK
!
YOU'RE IN A BAD MOOD. ARE YOU OKAY?
OF COURSE!

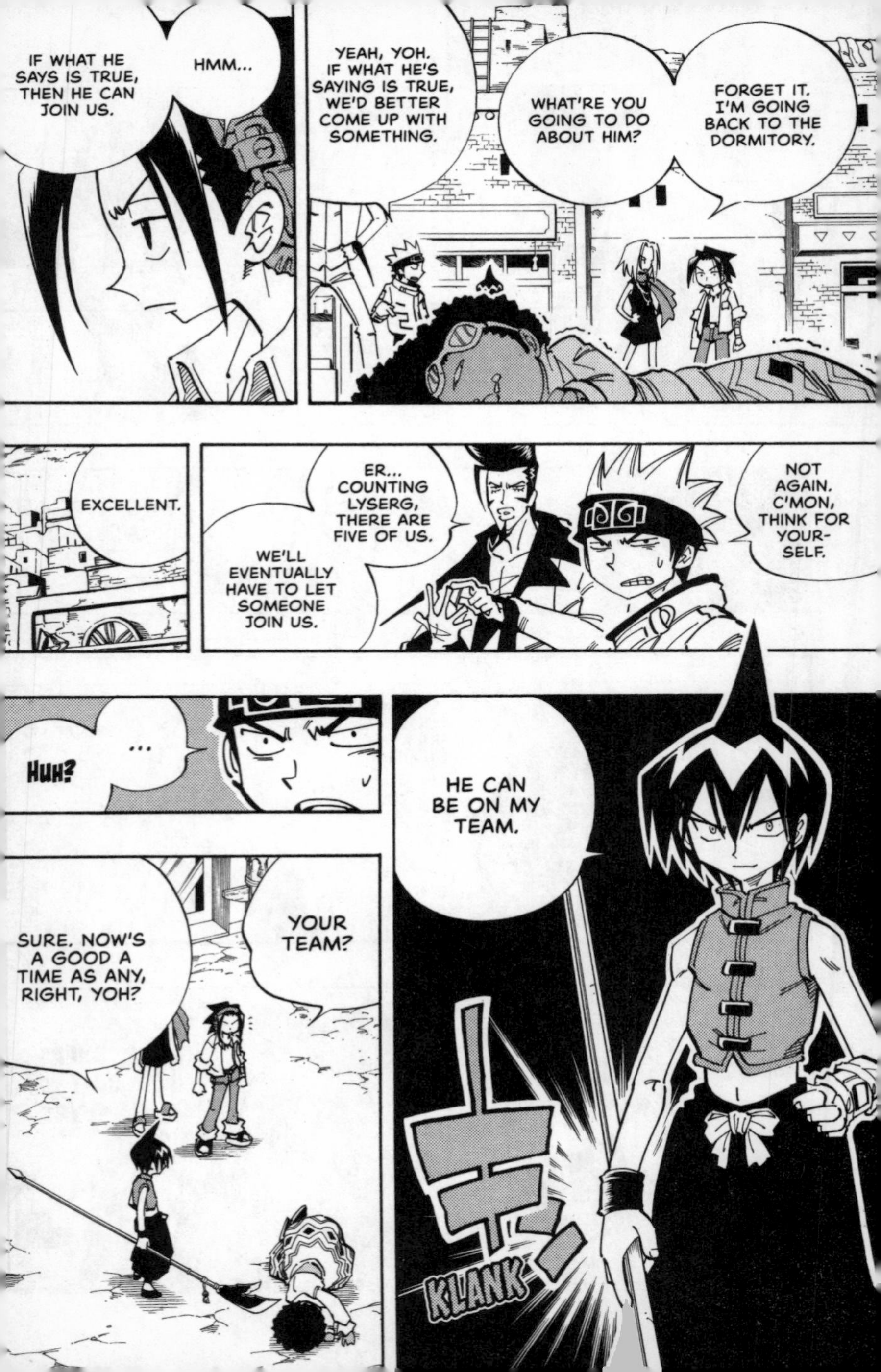
FORGET IT. I'M GOING BACK TO THE DORMITORY.
WHAT'RE YOU GOING TO DO ABOUT HIM?
YEAH, YOH. IF WHAT HE'S SAYING IS TRUE, WE'D BETTER COME UP WITH SOMETHING.
HMM...
IF WHAT HE SAYS IS TRUE, THEN HE CAN JOIN US.
NOT AGAIN. C'MON, THINK FOR YOUR-SELF.
ER... COUNTING LYSERG, THERE ARE FIVE OF US.
WE'LL EVENTUALLY HAVE TO LET SOMEONE JOIN US.
EXCELLENT.
HE CAN BE ON MY TEAM.
KLANK
...
HUH?
YOUR TEAM?
SURE. NOW'S A GOOD A TIME AS ANY, RIGHT, YOH?

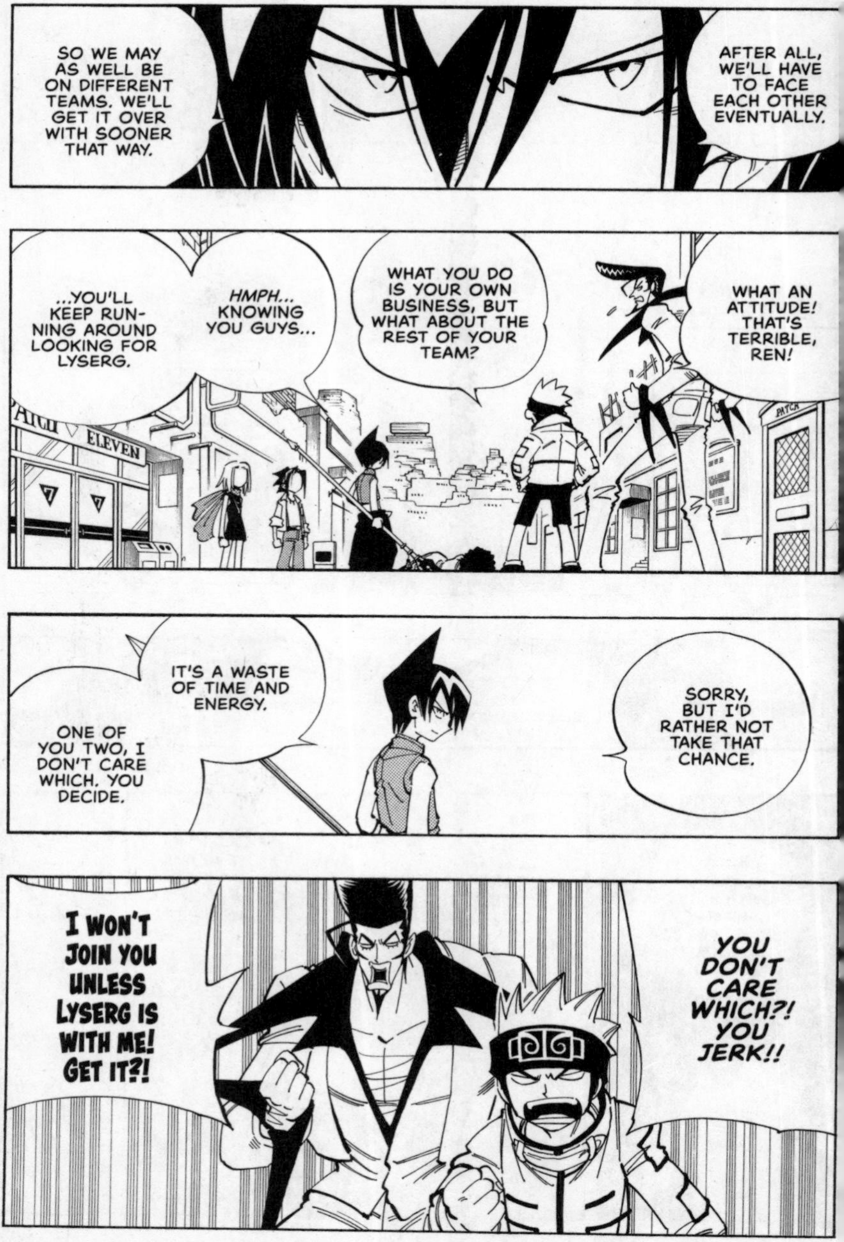
AFTER ALL, WE'LL HAVE TO FACE EACH OTHER EVENTUALLY.
SO WE MAY AS WELL BE ON DIFFERENT TEAMS. WE'LL GET IT OVER WITH SOONER THAT WAY.
WHAT AN ATTITUDE! THAT'S TERRIBLE, REN!
WHAT YOU DO IS YOUR OWN BUSINESS, BUT WHAT ABOUT THE REST OF YOUR TEAM?
HMPH... KNOWING YOU GUYS...
...YOU'LL KEEP RUN-NING AROUND LOOKING FOR LYSERG.
SORRY, BUT I'D RATHER NOT TAKE THAT CHANCE.
IT'S A WASTE OF TIME AND ENERGY.
ONE OF YOU TWO, I DON'T CARE WHICH. YOU DECIDE.
YOU DON'T CARE WHICH?! YOU JERK!!
I WON'T JOIN YOU UNLESS LYSERG IS WITH ME! GET IT?!

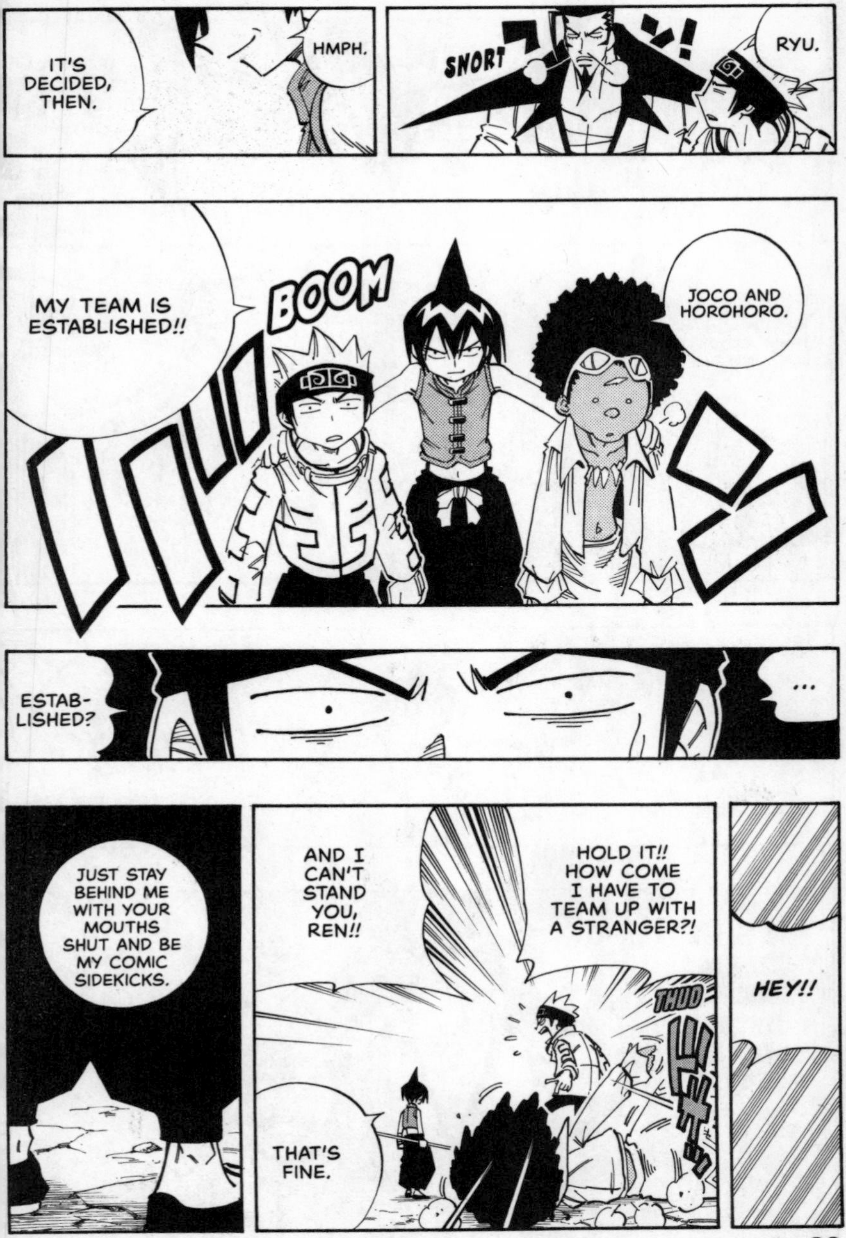
RYU.
SNORT
HMPH.
IT'S DECIDED, THEN.
JOCO AND HOROHORO.
BOOM
MY TEAM IS ESTABLISHED!!
...
ESTAB-LISHED?
HEY!!
HOLD IT!! HOW COME I HAVE TO TEAM UP WITH A STRANGER?!
AND I CAN'T STAND YOU, REN!!
THUD
THAT'S FINE.
JUST STAY BEHIND ME WITH YOUR MOUTHS SHUT AND BE MY COMIC SIDEKICKS.

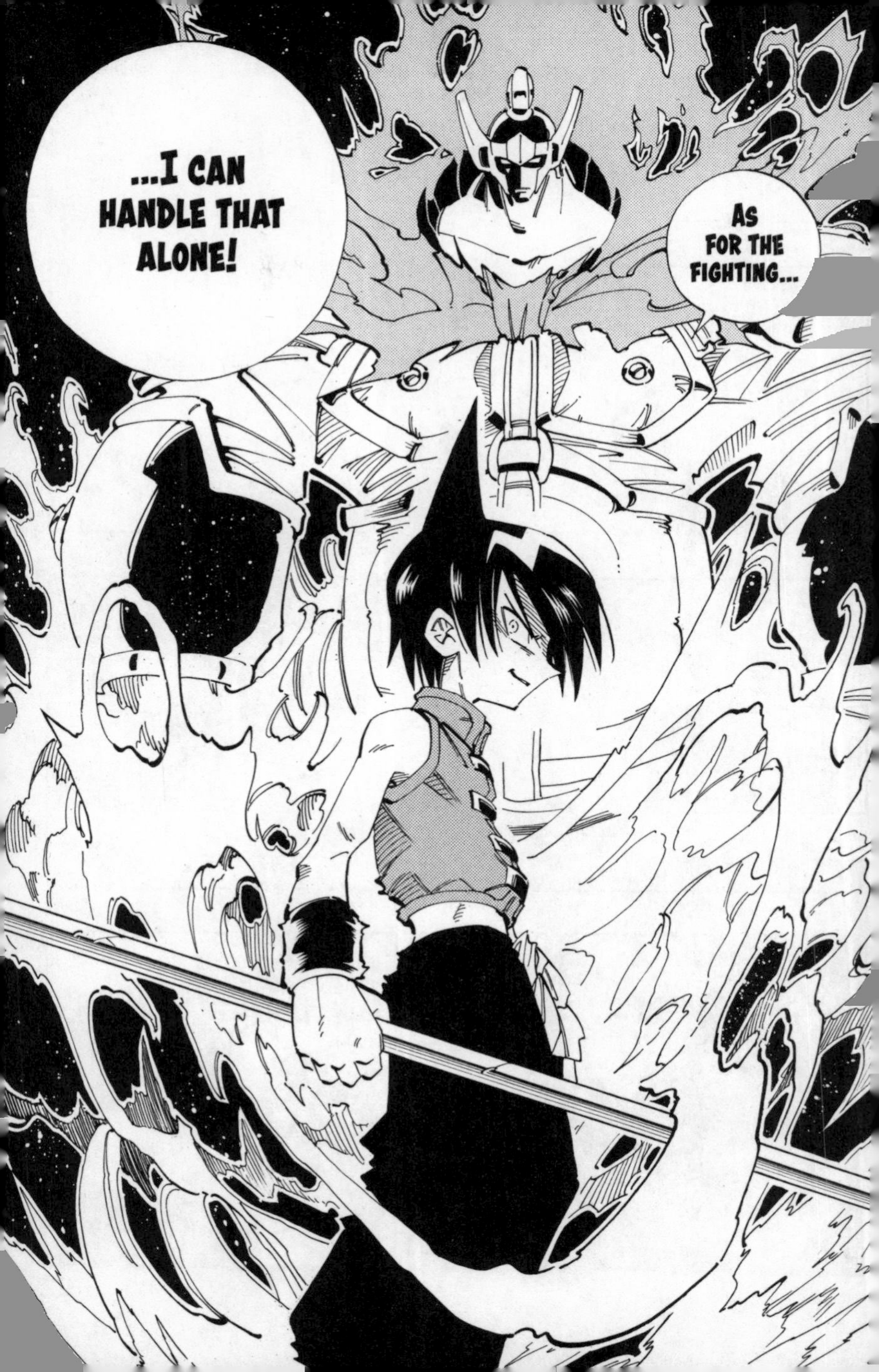
AS FOR THE FIGHTING...
...I CAN HANDLE THAT ALONE!

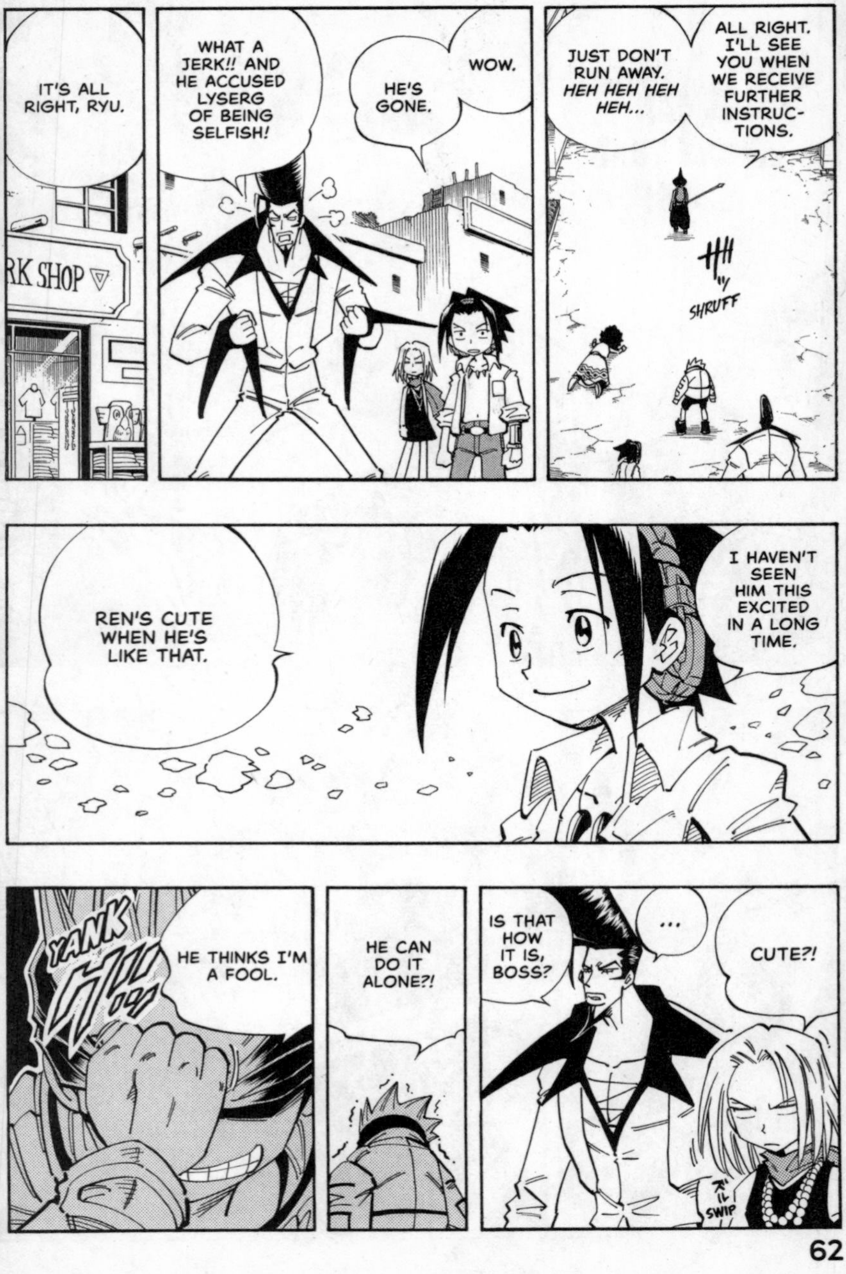
ALL RIGHT. I'LL SEE YOU WHEN WE RECEIVE FURTHER INSTRUC- TIONS.
JUST DON'T RUN AWAY. *HEH HEH HEH HEH...*
SHRUFF
WOW.
HE'S GONE.
WHAT A JERK!! AND HE ACCUSED LYSERG OF BEING SELFISH!
IT'S ALL RIGHT, RYU.
RK SHOP
I HAVEN'T SEEN HIM THIS EXCITED IN A LONG TIME.
REN'S CUTE WHEN HE'S LIKE THAT.
CUTE?!
...
IS THAT HOW IT IS, BOSS?
SWIP
HE CAN DO IT ALONE?!
HE THINKS I'M A FOOL.
YANK

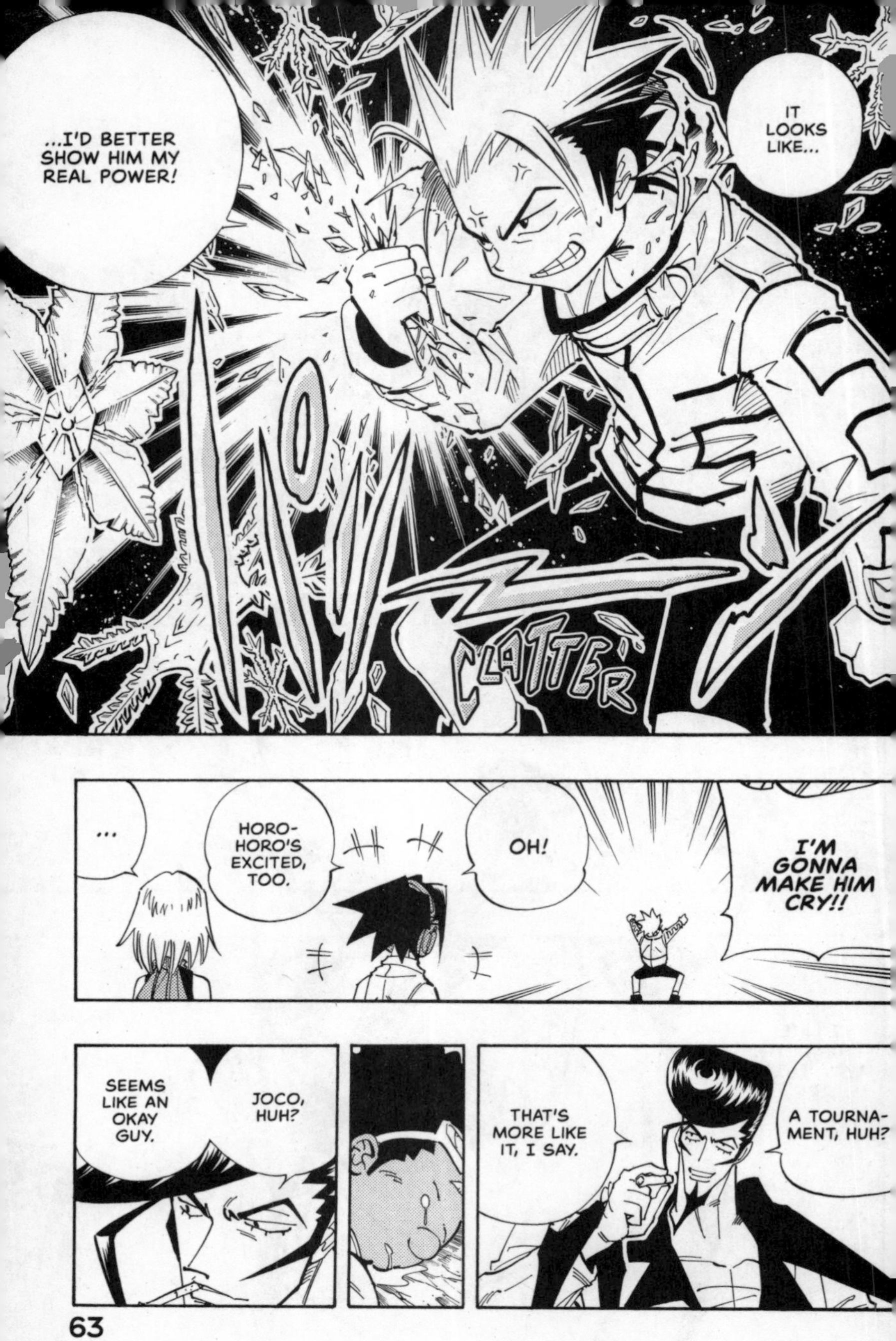
IT LOOKS LIKE...
...I'D BETTER SHOW HIM MY REAL POWER!
CLATTER
I'M GONNA MAKE HIM CRY!!
OH!
HORO-HORO'S EXCITED, TOO.
...
A TOURNA-MENT, HUH?
THAT'S MORE LIKE IT, I SAY.
JOCO, HUH?
SEEMS LIKE AN OKAY GUY.

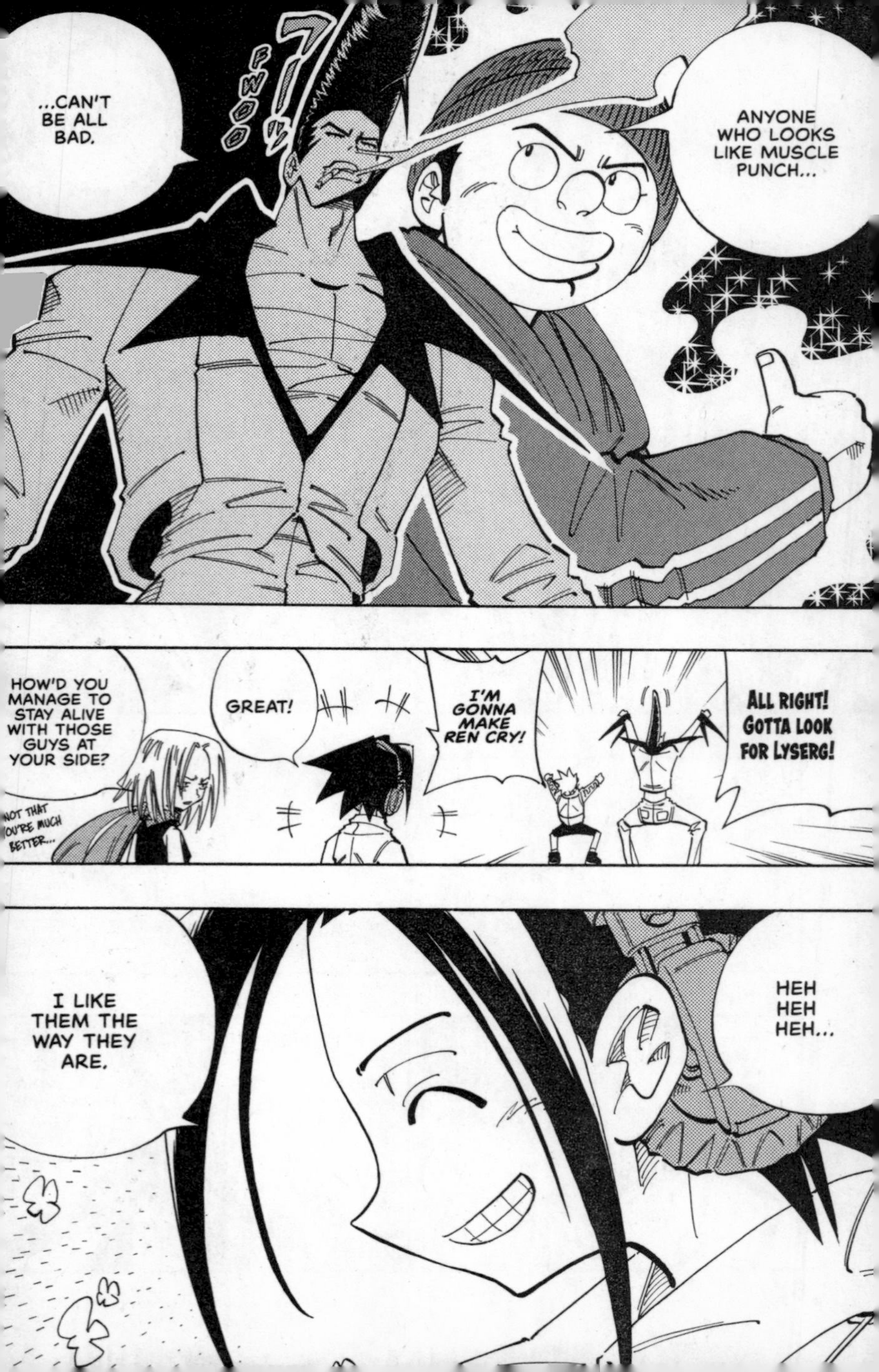
ANYONE WHO LOOKS LIKE MUSCLE PUNCH...
FWOO
...CAN'T BE ALL BAD.
ALL RIGHT! GOTTA LOOK FOR LYSERG!
I'M GONNA MAKE REN CRY!
GREAT!
HOW'D YOU MANAGE TO STAY ALIVE WITH THOSE GUYS AT YOUR SIDE?
NOT THAT YOU'RE MUCH BETTER...
HEH HEH HEH...
I LIKE THEM THE WAY THEY ARE.

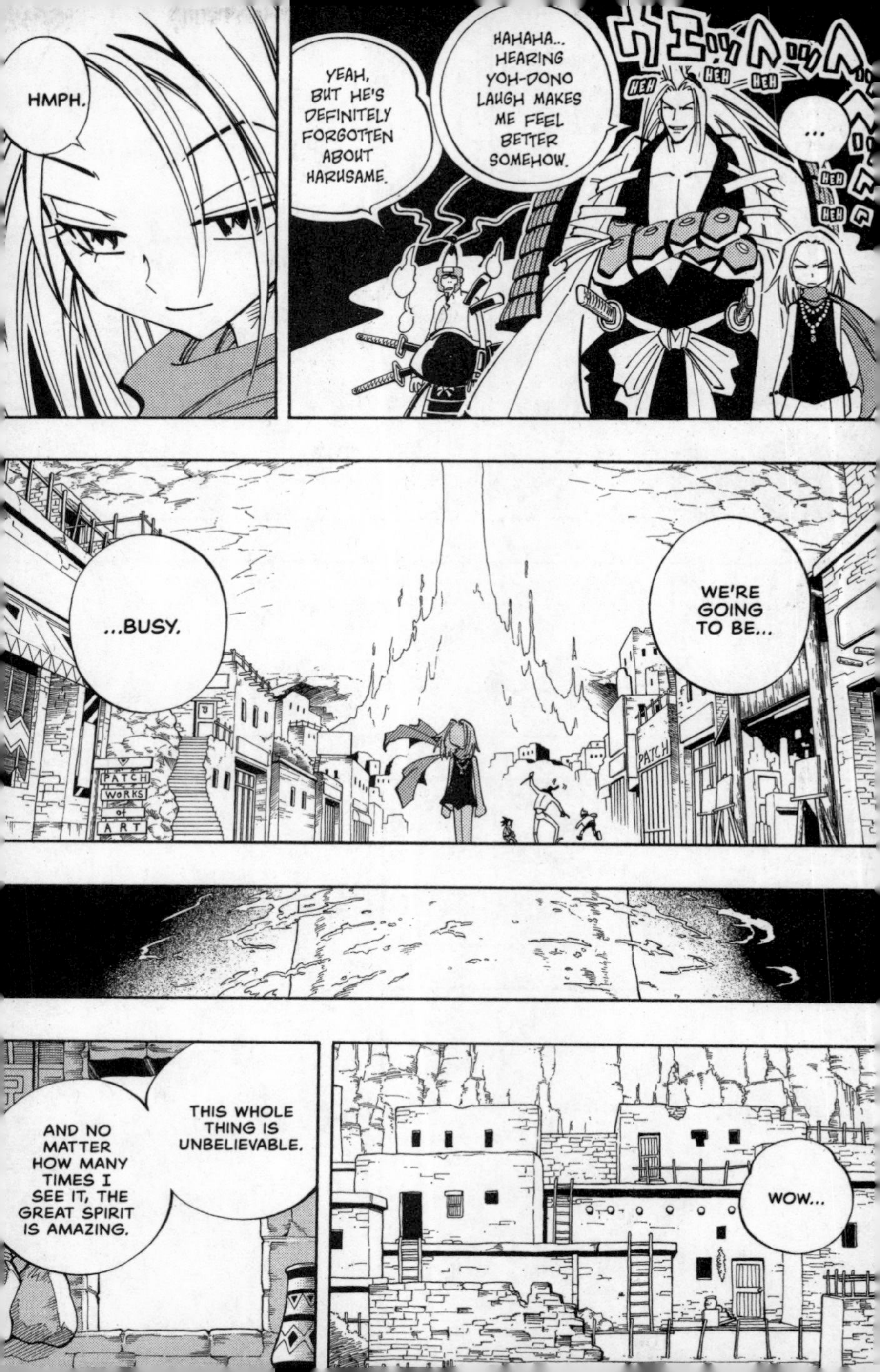
HEH HEH HEH HEH HEH
...
HAHAHA... HEARING YOH-DONO LAUGH MAKES ME FEEL BETTER SOMEHOW.
YEAH, BUT HE'S DEFINITELY FORGOTTEN ABOUT HARUSAME.
HMPH.
WE'RE GOING TO BE...
...BUSY.
PATCH
PATCH WORKS of ART
WOW...
THIS WHOLE THING IS UNBELIEVABLE.
AND NO MATTER HOW MANY TIMES I SEE IT, THE GREAT SPIRIT IS AMAZING.

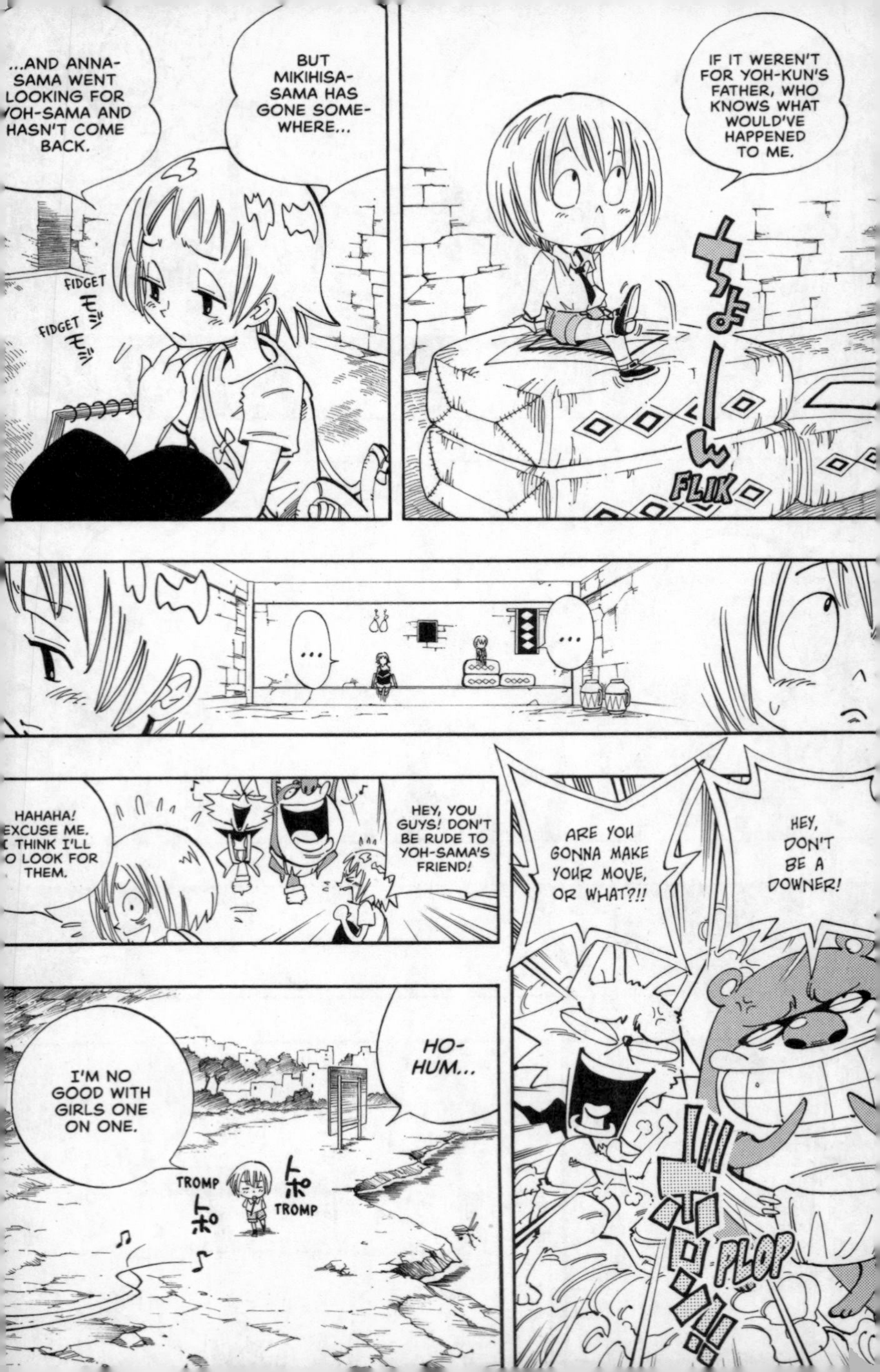

IF IT WEREN'T FOR YOH-KUN'S FATHER, WHO KNOWS WHAT WOULD'VE HAPPENED TO ME.
ちょーん
FLIK
BUT MIKIHISA-SAMA HAS GONE SOMEWHERE...
...AND ANNA-SAMA WENT LOOKING FOR OH-SAMA AND HASN'T COME BACK.
FIDGET モジ
FIDGET モジ
...
...
HEY, DON'T BE A DOWNER!
ARE YOU GONNA MAKE YOUR MOVE, OR WHAT?!!
ボロン!!
PLOP
HEY, YOU GUYS! DON'T BE RUDE TO YOH-SAMA'S FRIEND!
HAHAHA! EXCUSE ME. THINK I'LL O LOOK FOR THEM.
HO-HUM...
I'M NO GOOD WITH GIRLS ONE ON ONE.
トポ
TROMP
TROMP
トポ

Along the highway...

A SONG?

...?

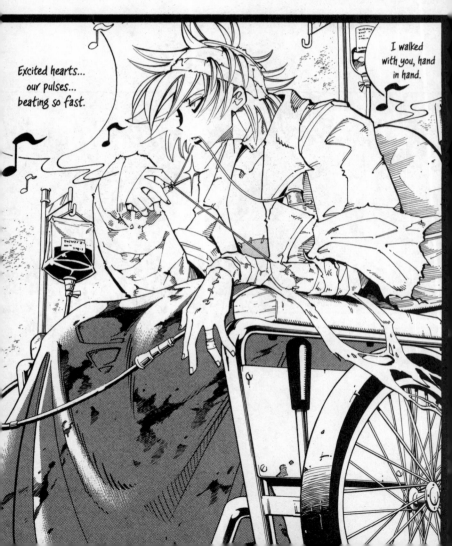

Excited hearts... our pulses... beating so fast.

I walked with you, hand in hand.

Mic

March 2001

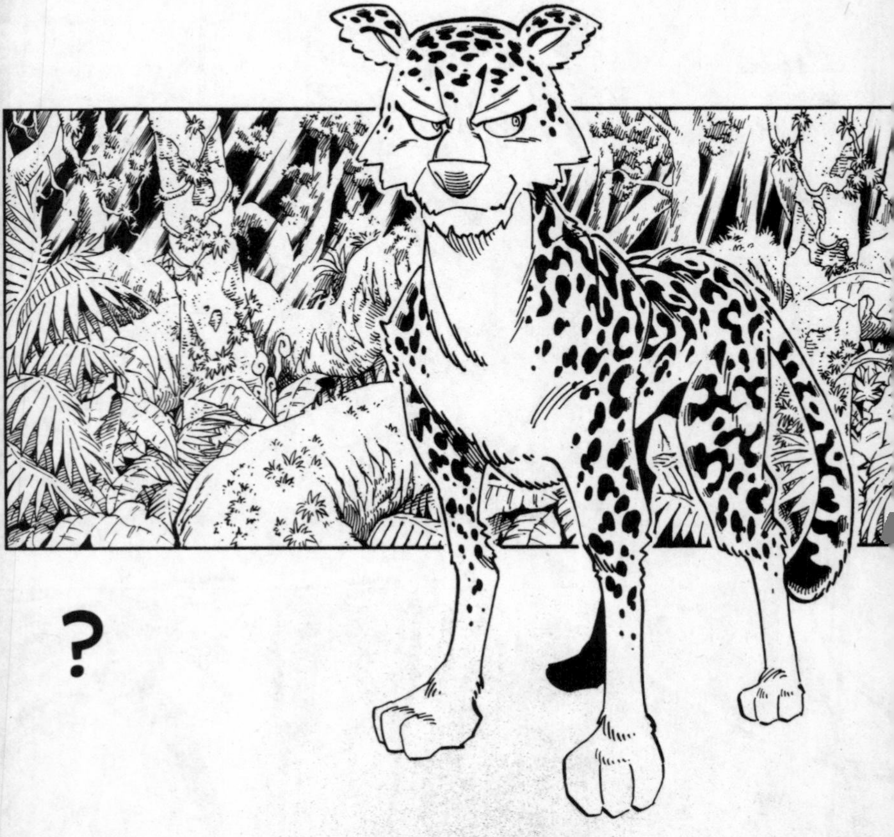

?

Chapter 111: The Return of Faust

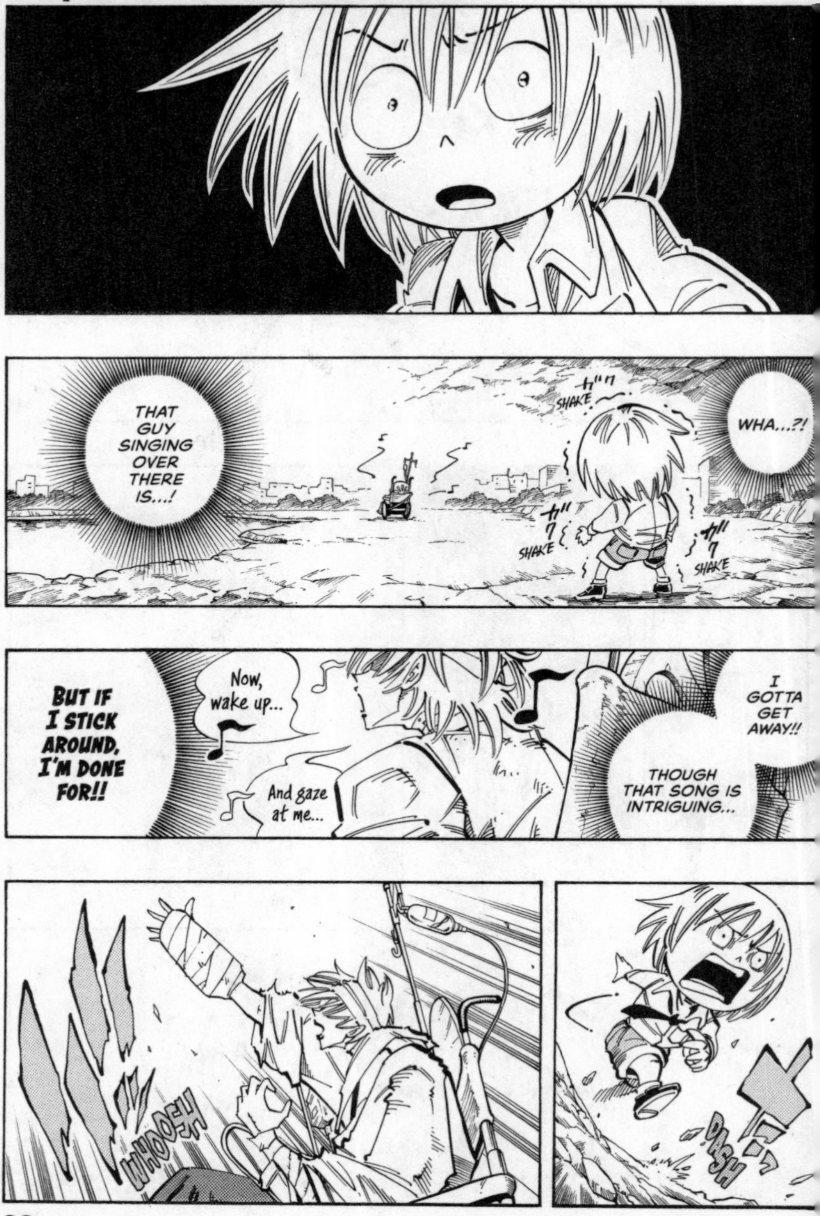
WHA...?!
SHAKE
THAT GUY SINGING OVER THERE IS...!
SHAKE
SHAKE
I GOTTA GET AWAY!!
THOUGH THAT SONG IS INTRIGUING...
Now, wake up...
And gaze at me...
BUT IF I STICK AROUND, I'M DONE FOR!!
DASH
WHOOSH

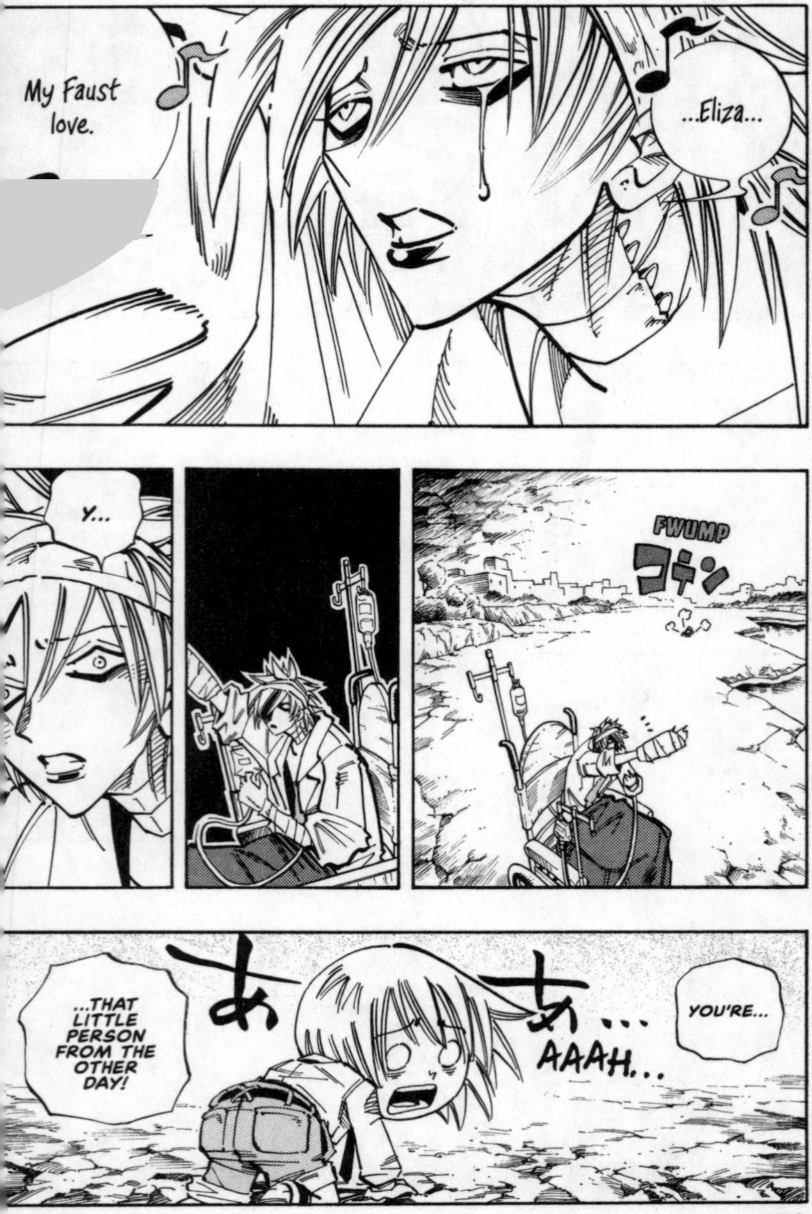
...Eliza...
My Faust love.
FWUMP
コテン
Y...
YOU'RE...
ああ...
AAAH...
...THAT LITTLE PERSON FROM THE OTHER DAY!

The Return of Faust

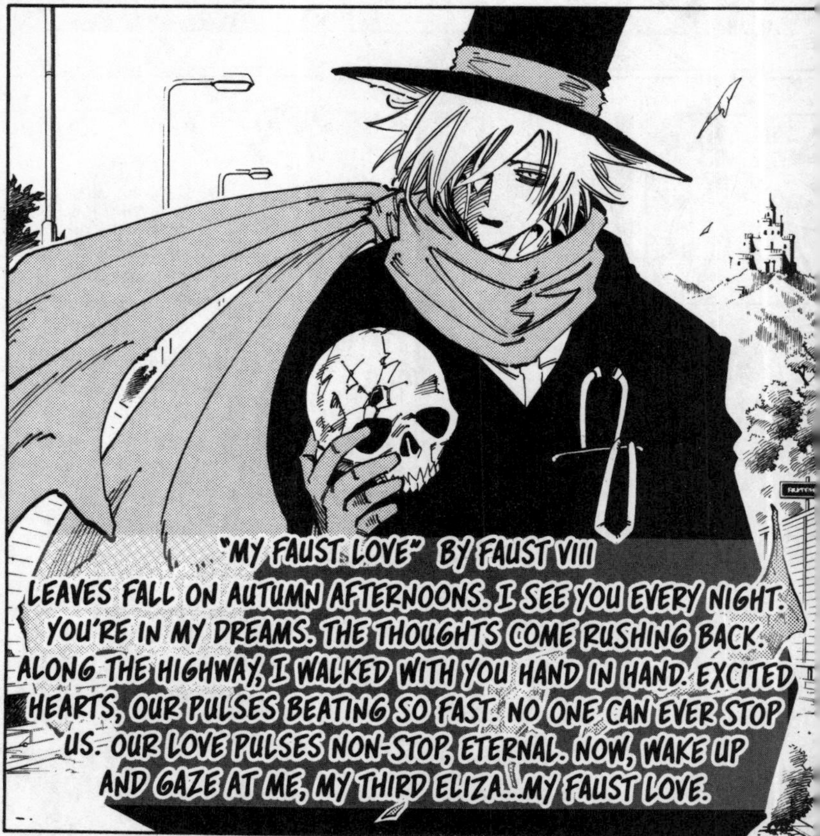
"MY FAUST LOVE" BY FAUST VIII
LEAVES FALL ON AUTUMN AFTERNOONS. I SEE YOU EVERY NIGHT. YOU'RE IN MY DREAMS. THE THOUGHTS COME RUSHING BACK. ALONG THE HIGHWAY, I WALKED WITH YOU HAND IN HAND. EXCITED HEARTS, OUR PULSES BEATING SO FAST. NO ONE CAN EVER STOP US. OUR LOVE PULSES NON-STOP, ETERNAL. NOW, WAKE UP AND GAZE AT ME, MY THIRD ELIZA...MY FAUST LOVE.

Chapter 111:

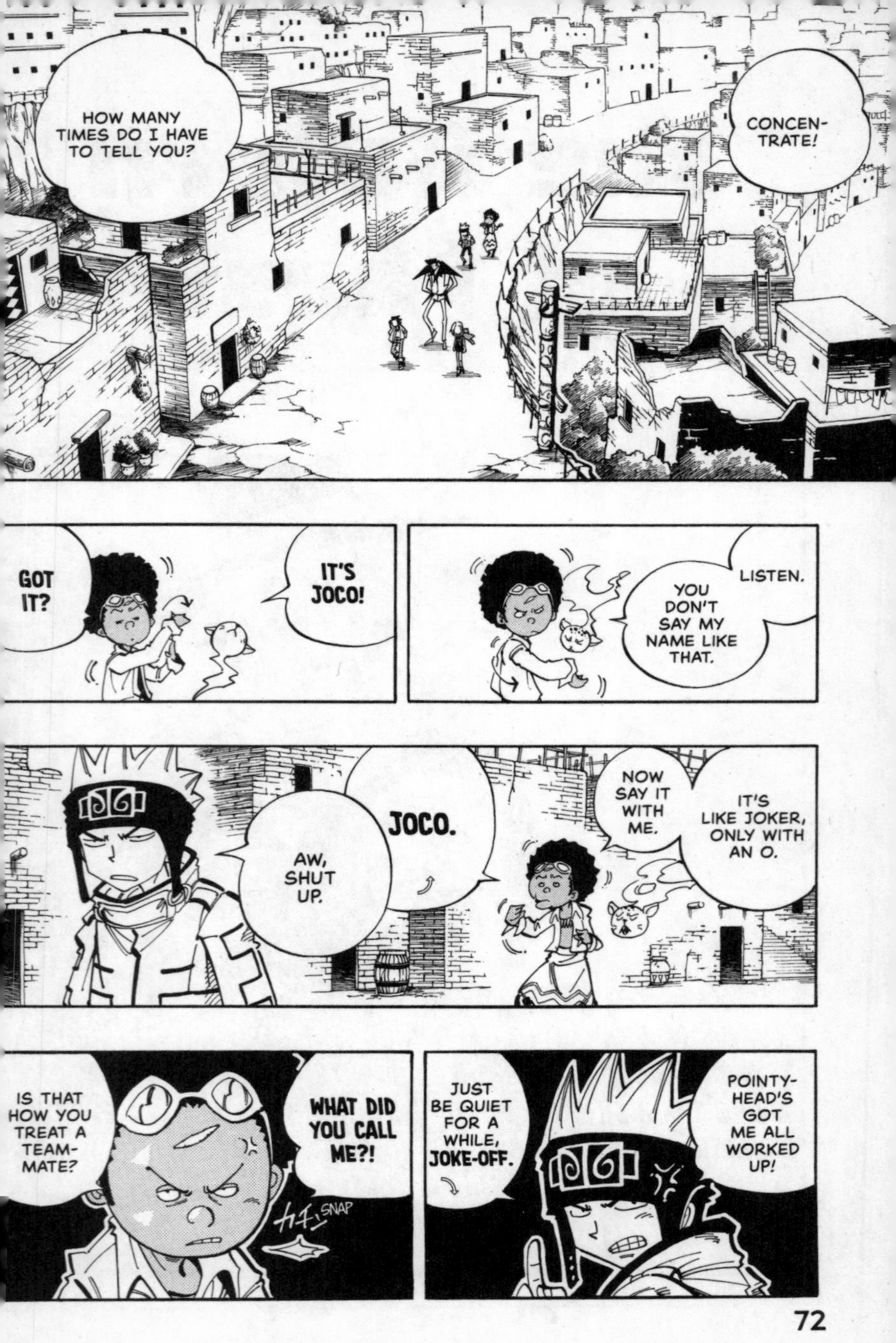
CONCENTRATE!
HOW MANY TIMES DO I HAVE TO TELL YOU?
LISTEN.
YOU DON'T SAY MY NAME LIKE THAT.
IT'S JOCO!
GOT IT?
IT'S LIKE JOKER, ONLY WITH AN O.
NOW SAY IT WITH ME.
JOCO.
AW, SHUT UP.
POINTY-HEAD'S GOT ME ALL WORKED UP!
JUST BE QUIET FOR A WHILE, JOKE-OFF.
WHAT DID YOU CALL ME?!
SNAP
IS THAT HOW YOU TREAT A TEAM-MATE?

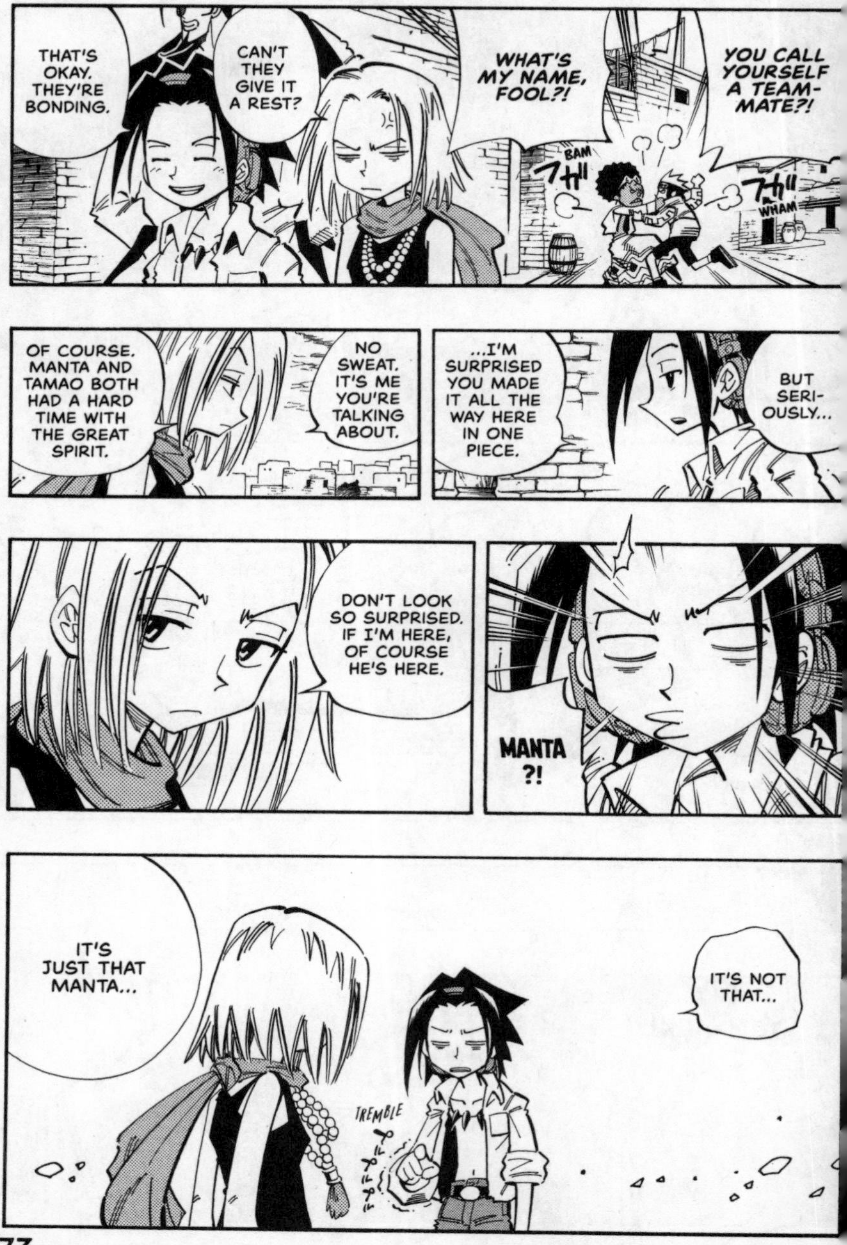
YOU CALL YOURSELF A TEAM-MATE?!
WHAT'S MY NAME, FOOL?!
WHAM
BAM
CAN'T THEY GIVE IT A REST?
THAT'S OKAY. THEY'RE BONDING.
BUT SERIOUSLY...
...I'M SURPRISED YOU MADE IT ALL THE WAY HERE IN ONE PIECE.
NO SWEAT. IT'S ME YOU'RE TALKING ABOUT.
OF COURSE. MANTA AND TAMAO BOTH HAD A HARD TIME WITH THE GREAT SPIRIT.
MANTA ?!
DON'T LOOK SO SURPRISED. IF I'M HERE, OF COURSE HE'S HERE.
IT'S NOT THAT...
TREMBLE
IT'S JUST THAT MANTA...

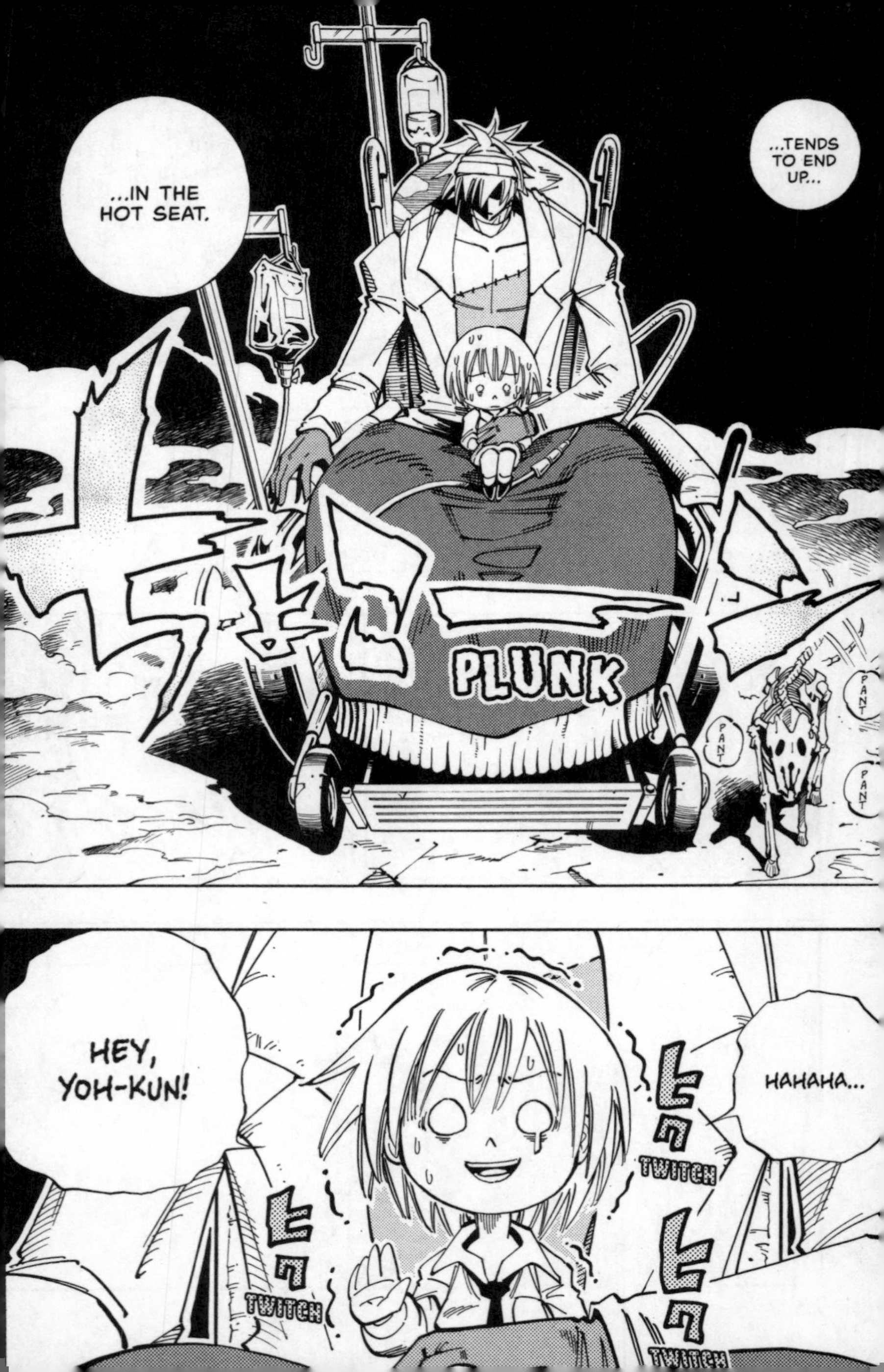
...TENDS TO END UP...
...IN THE HOT SEAT.
PLUNK
PANT
PANT
PANT
HAHAHA...
HEY, YOH-KUN!
TWITCH
TWITCH
TWITCH

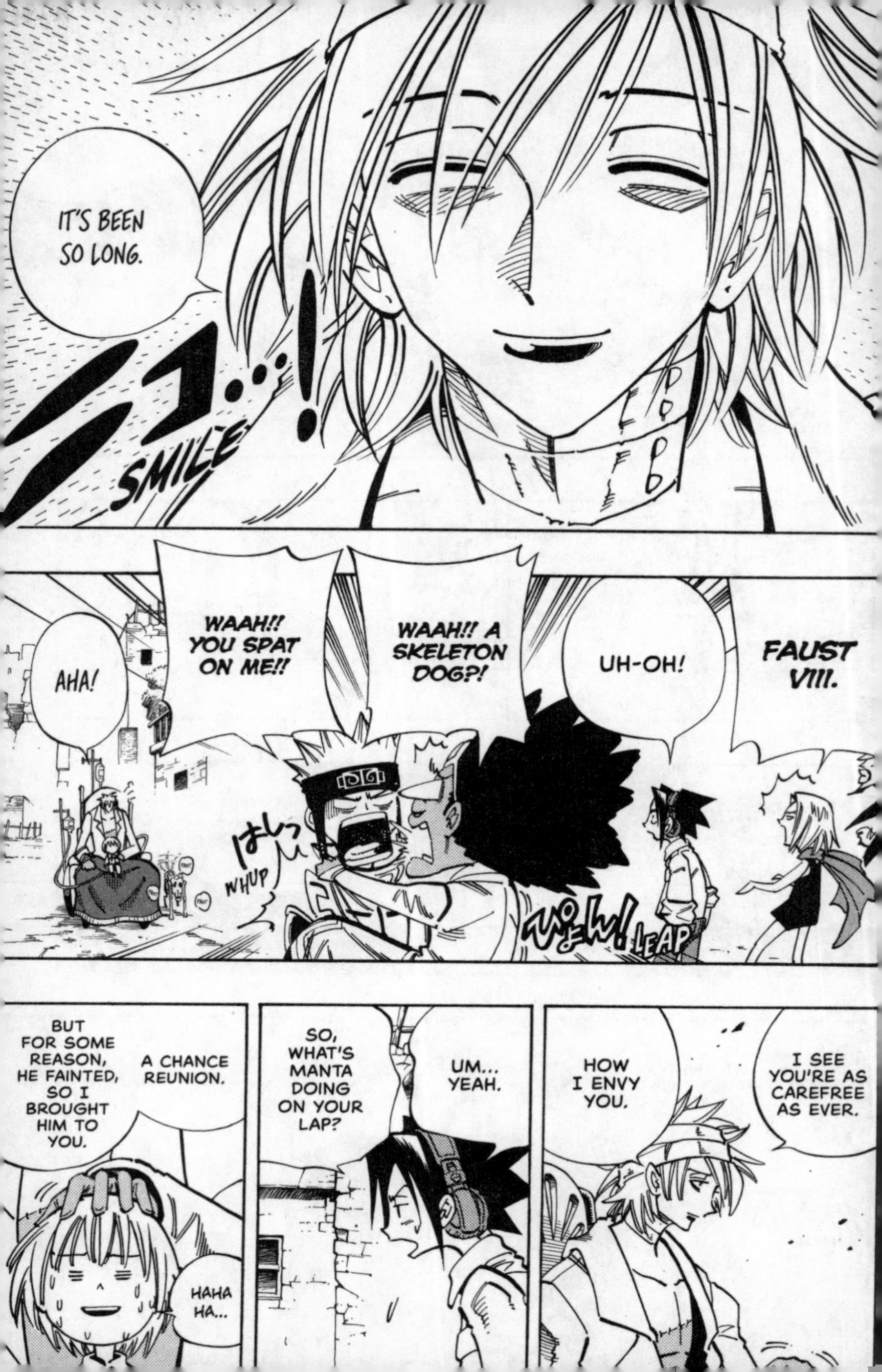
IT'S BEEN SO LONG.
ニコ…!
SMILE
FAUST VIII.
UH-OH!
WAAH!! A SKELETON DOG?!
WAAH!! YOU SPAT ON ME!!
AHA!
ぴょん! LEAP
はしっ WHUP
I SEE YOU'RE AS CAREFREE AS EVER.
HOW I ENVY YOU.
UM... YEAH.
SO, WHAT'S MANTA DOING ON YOUR LAP?
A CHANCE REUNION.
BUT FOR SOME REASON, HE FAINTED, SO I BROUGHT HIM TO YOU.
HAHA HA...

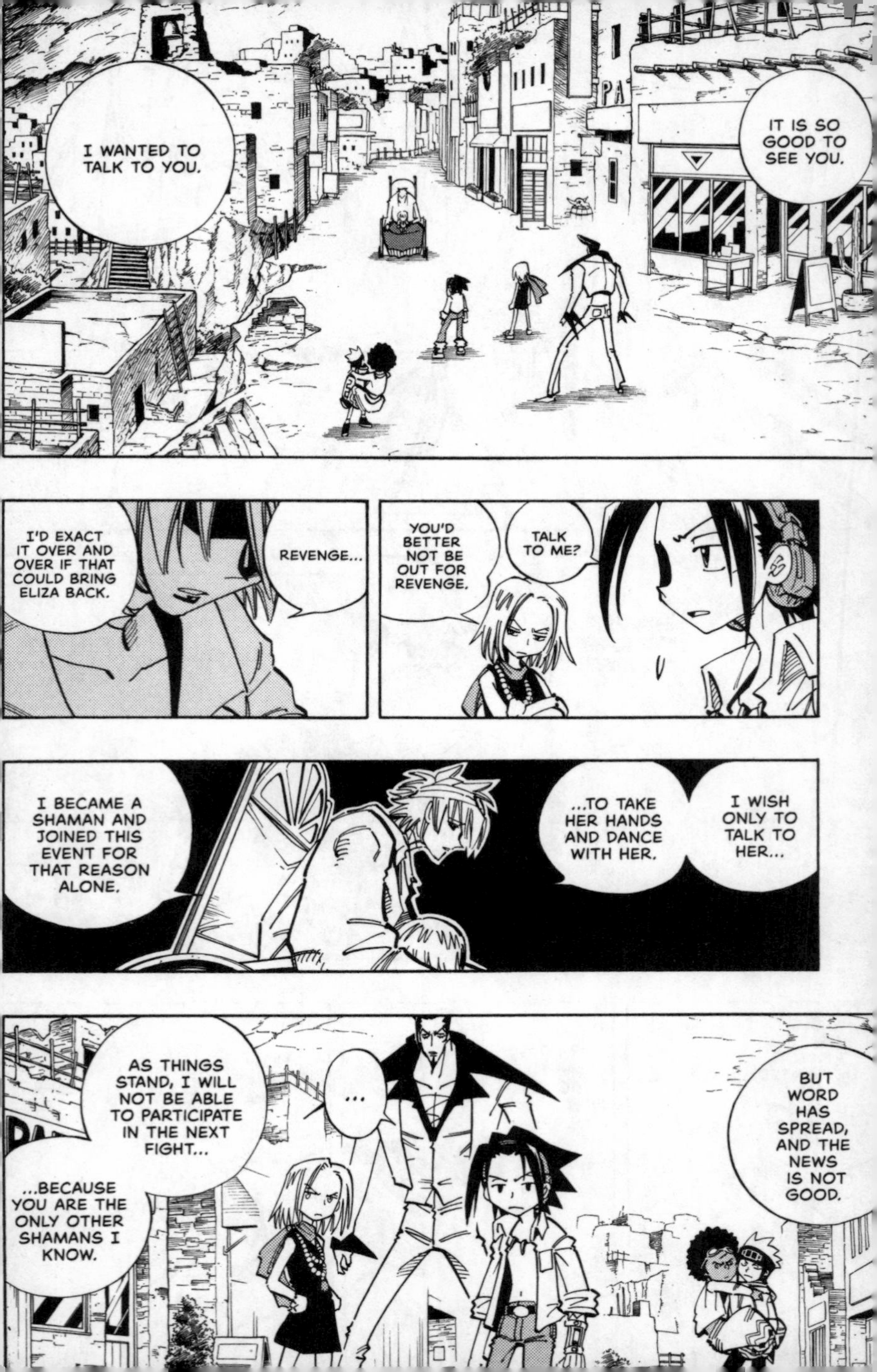
IT IS SO GOOD TO SEE YOU.
I WANTED TO TALK TO YOU.
TALK TO ME?
YOU'D BETTER NOT BE OUT FOR REVENGE.
REVENGE...
I'D EXACT IT OVER AND OVER IF THAT COULD BRING ELIZA BACK.
I WISH ONLY TO TALK TO HER...
...TO TAKE HER HANDS AND DANCE WITH HER.
I BECAME A SHAMAN AND JOINED THIS EVENT FOR THAT REASON ALONE.
BUT WORD HAS SPREAD, AND THE NEWS IS NOT GOOD.
...
AS THINGS STAND, I WILL NOT BE ABLE TO PARTICIPATE IN THE NEXT FIGHT...
...BECAUSE YOU ARE THE ONLY OTHER SHAMANS I KNOW.

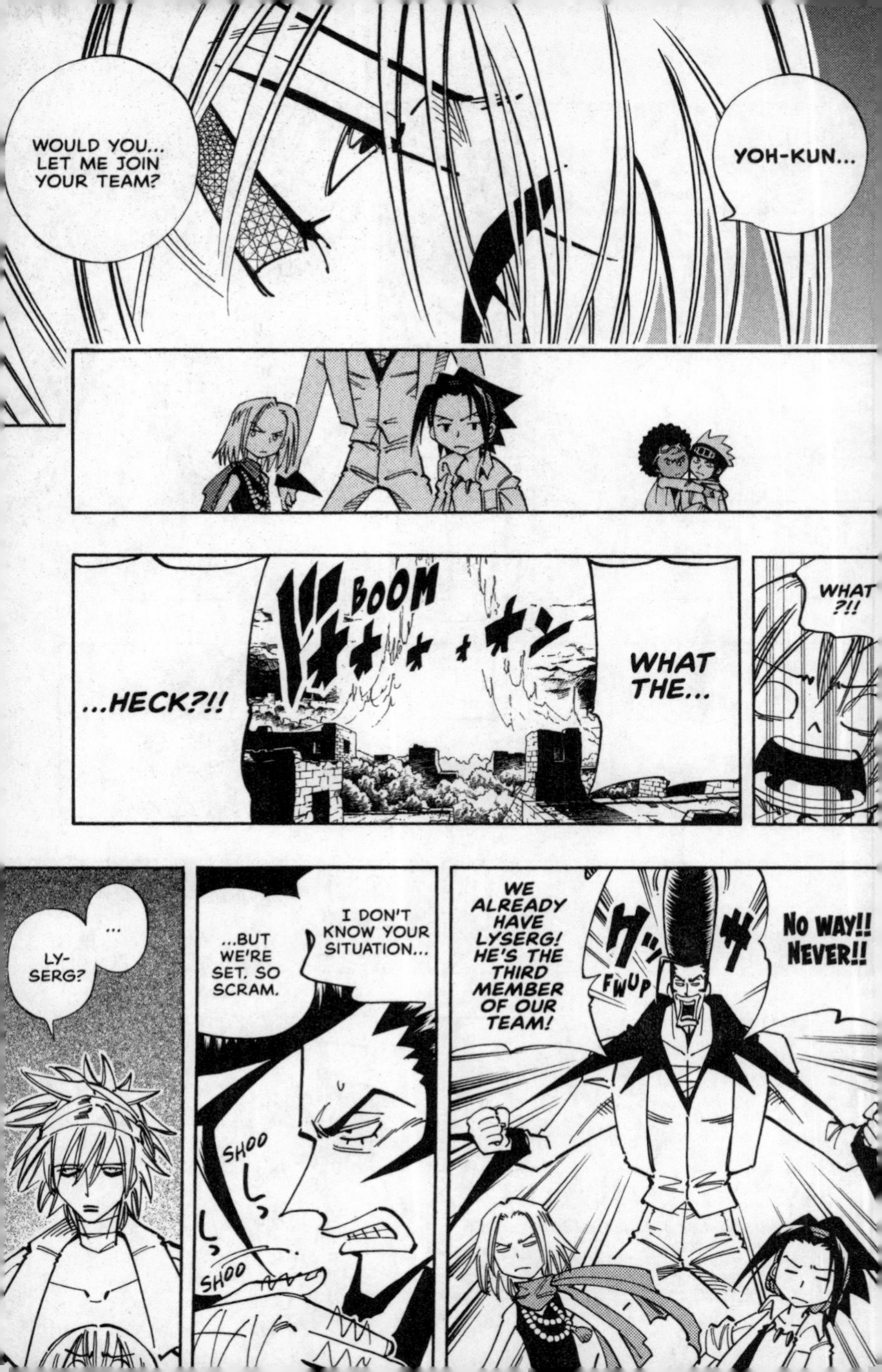
YOH-KUN...
WOULD YOU... LET ME JOIN YOUR TEAM?
WHAT ?!!
WHAT THE...
BOOM
...HECK?!!
NO WAY!! NEVER!!
WE ALREADY HAVE LYSERG! HE'S THE THIRD MEMBER OF OUR TEAM!
FWUP
I DON'T KNOW YOUR SITUATION...
...BUT WE'RE SET. SO SCRAM.
SHOO
SHOO
...
LY-SERG?

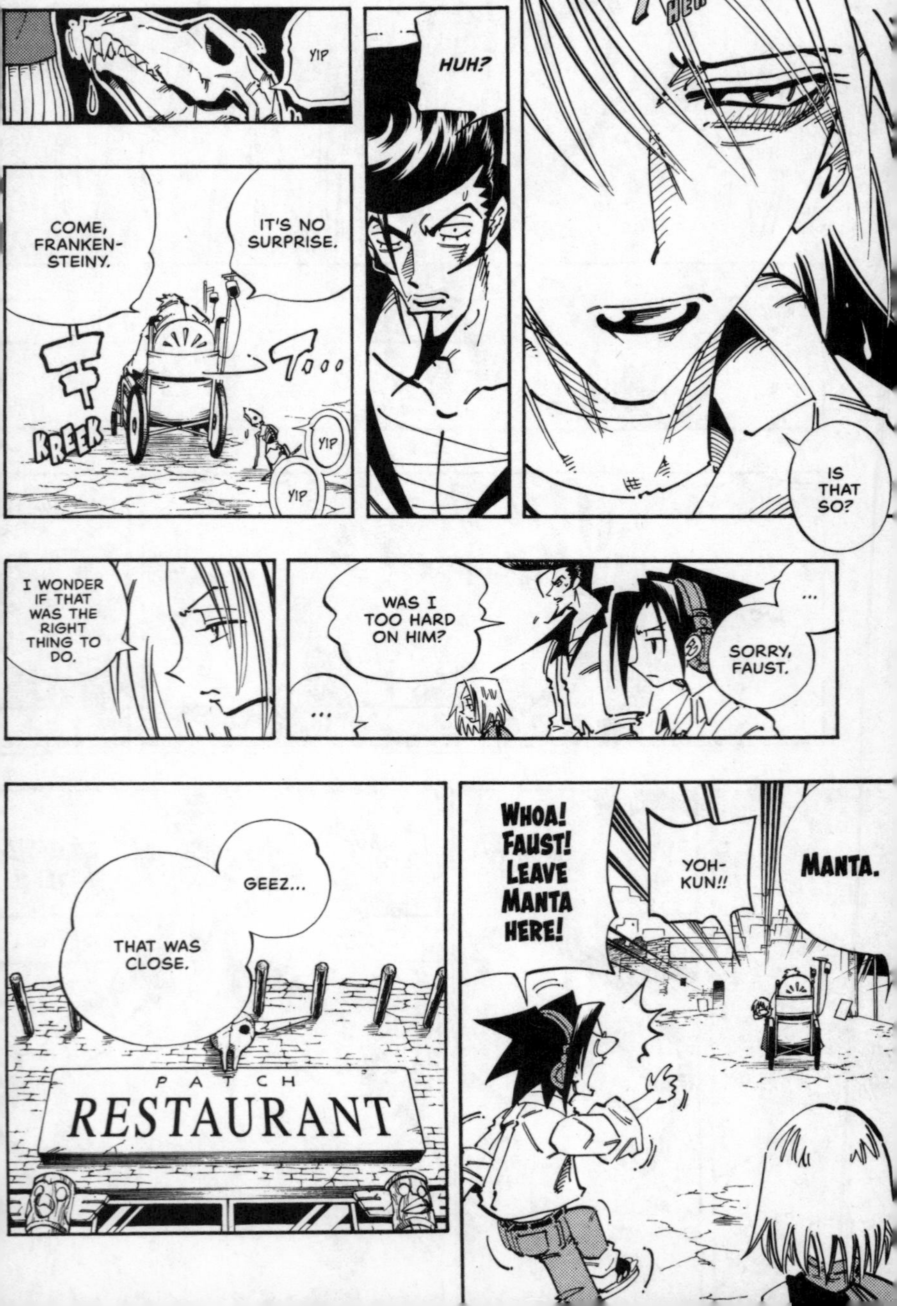

7...
HEH
IS THAT SO?
HUH?
YIP
IT'S NO SURPRISE.
COME, FRANKEN-STEINY.
KREEK
YIP
YIP
...
SORRY, FAUST.
WAS I TOO HARD ON HIM?
...
I WONDER IF THAT WAS THE RIGHT THING TO DO.
MANTA.
YOH-KUN!!
WHOA! FAUST! LEAVE MANTA HERE!
GEEZ...
THAT WAS CLOSE.
PATCH
RESTAURANT

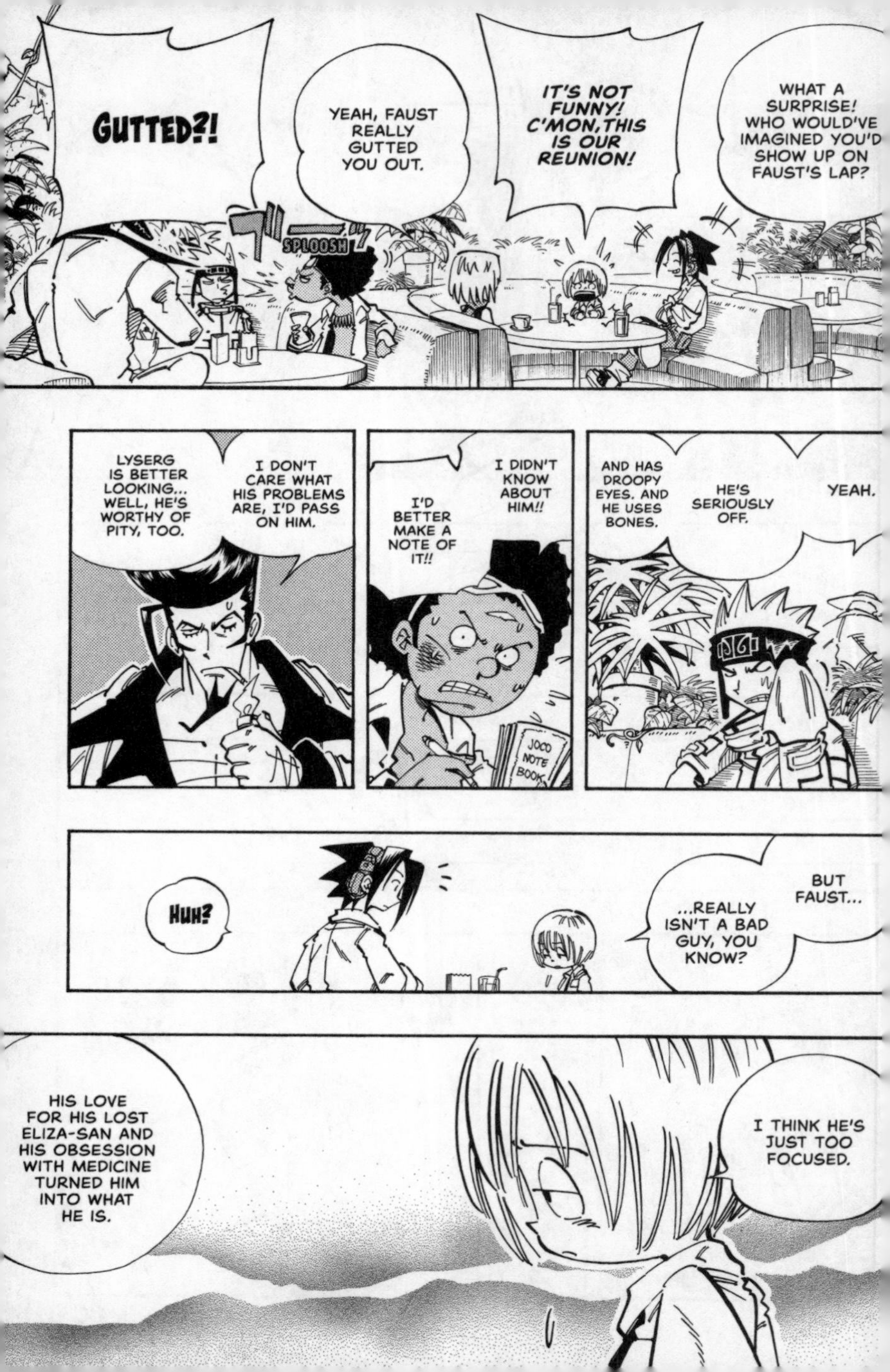

WHAT A SURPRISE! WHO WOULD'VE IMAGINED YOU'D SHOW UP ON FAUST'S LAP?
IT'S NOT FUNNY! C'MON, THIS IS OUR REUNION!
YEAH, FAUST REALLY GUTTED YOU OUT.
SPLOOSH
GUTTED?!
YEAH.
HE'S SERIOUSLY OFF.
AND HAS DROOPY EYES. AND HE USES BONES.
I DIDN'T KNOW ABOUT HIM!!
I'D BETTER MAKE A NOTE OF IT!!
JOCO NOTE BOOK
I DON'T CARE WHAT HIS PROBLEMS ARE, I'D PASS ON HIM.
LYSERG IS BETTER LOOKING... WELL, HE'S WORTHY OF PITY, TOO.
BUT FAUST...
...REALLY ISN'T A BAD GUY, YOU KNOW?
HUH?
I THINK HE'S JUST TOO FOCUSED.
HIS LOVE FOR HIS LOST ELIZA-SAN AND HIS OBSESSION WITH MEDICINE TURNED HIM INTO WHAT HE IS.

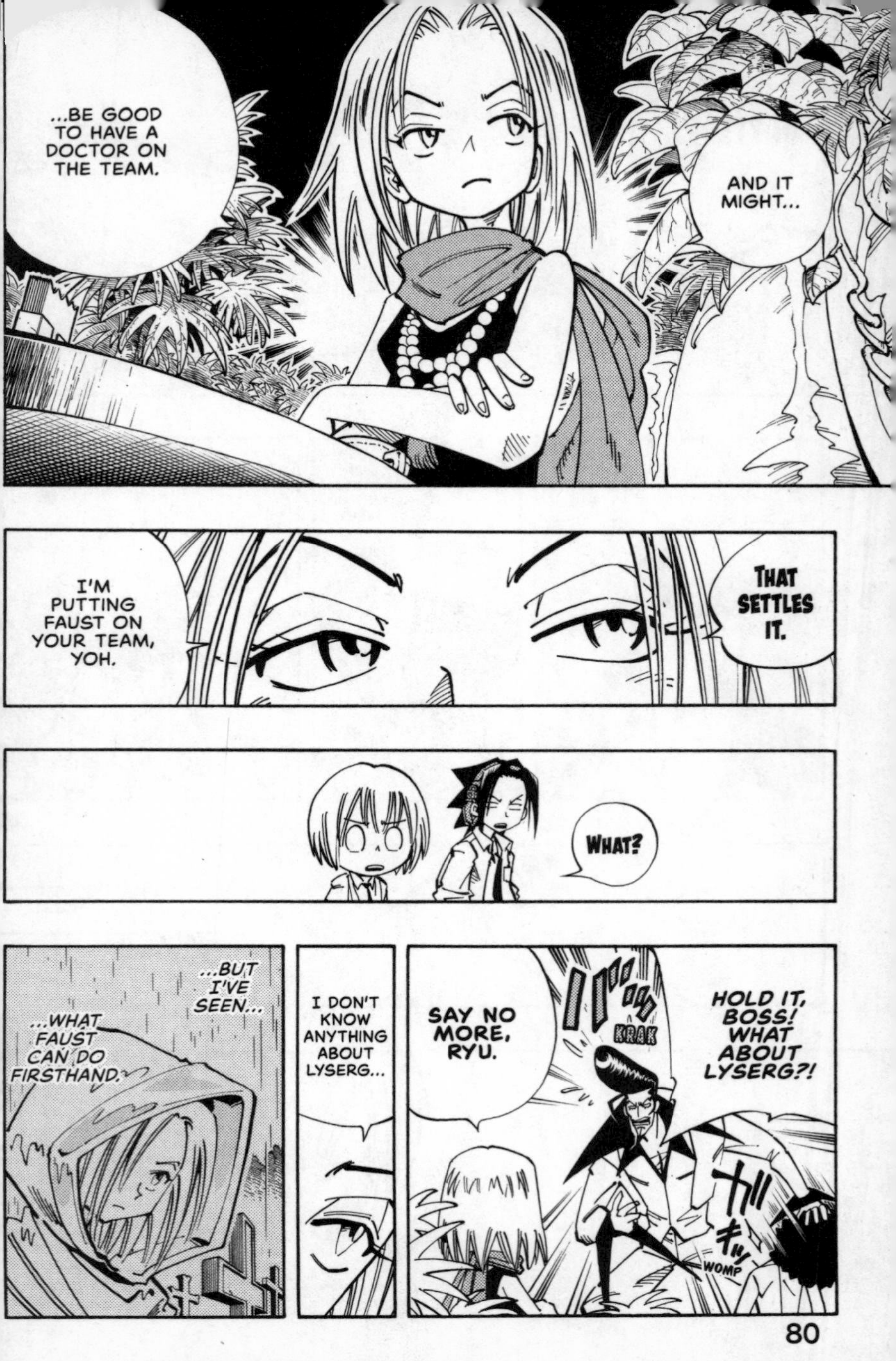
AND IT MIGHT...
...BE GOOD TO HAVE A DOCTOR ON THE TEAM.
THAT SETTLES IT.
I'M PUTTING FAUST ON YOUR TEAM, YOH.
WHAT?
HOLD IT, BOSS! WHAT ABOUT LYSERG?!
KRAK
SAY NO MORE, RYU.
WOMP
I DON'T KNOW ANYTHING ABOUT LYSERG...
...BUT I'VE SEEN...
...WHAT FAUST CAN DO FIRSTHAND.

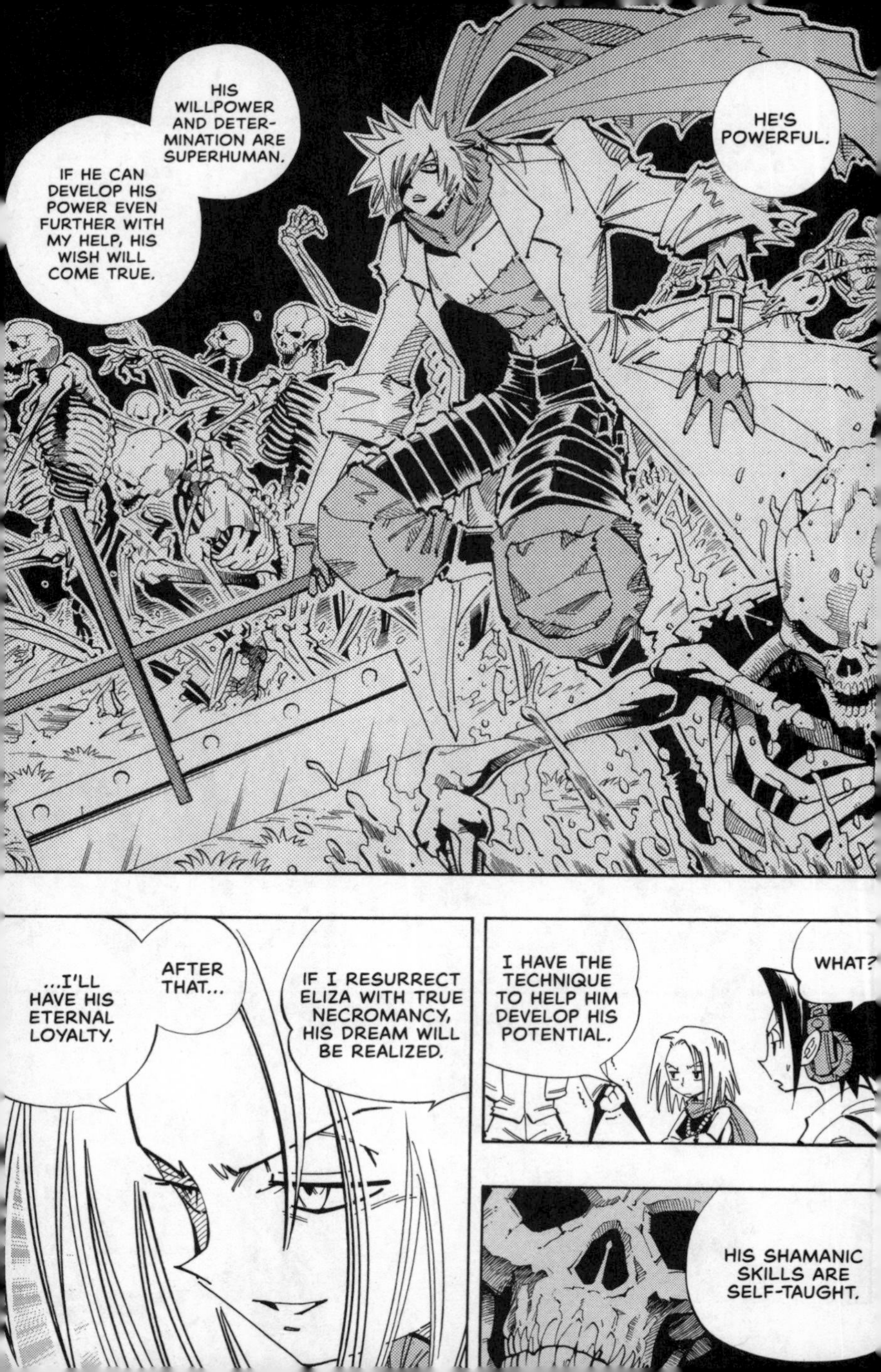
HE'S POWERFUL.
HIS WILLPOWER AND DETERMINATION ARE SUPERHUMAN.
IF HE CAN DEVELOP HIS POWER EVEN FURTHER WITH MY HELP, HIS WISH WILL COME TRUE.
WHAT?
I HAVE THE TECHNIQUE TO HELP HIM DEVELOP HIS POTENTIAL.
HIS SHAMANIC SKILLS ARE SELF-TAUGHT.
IF I RESURRECT ELIZA WITH TRUE NECROMANCY, HIS DREAM WILL BE REALIZED.
AFTER THAT...
...I'LL HAVE HIS ETERNAL LOYALTY.

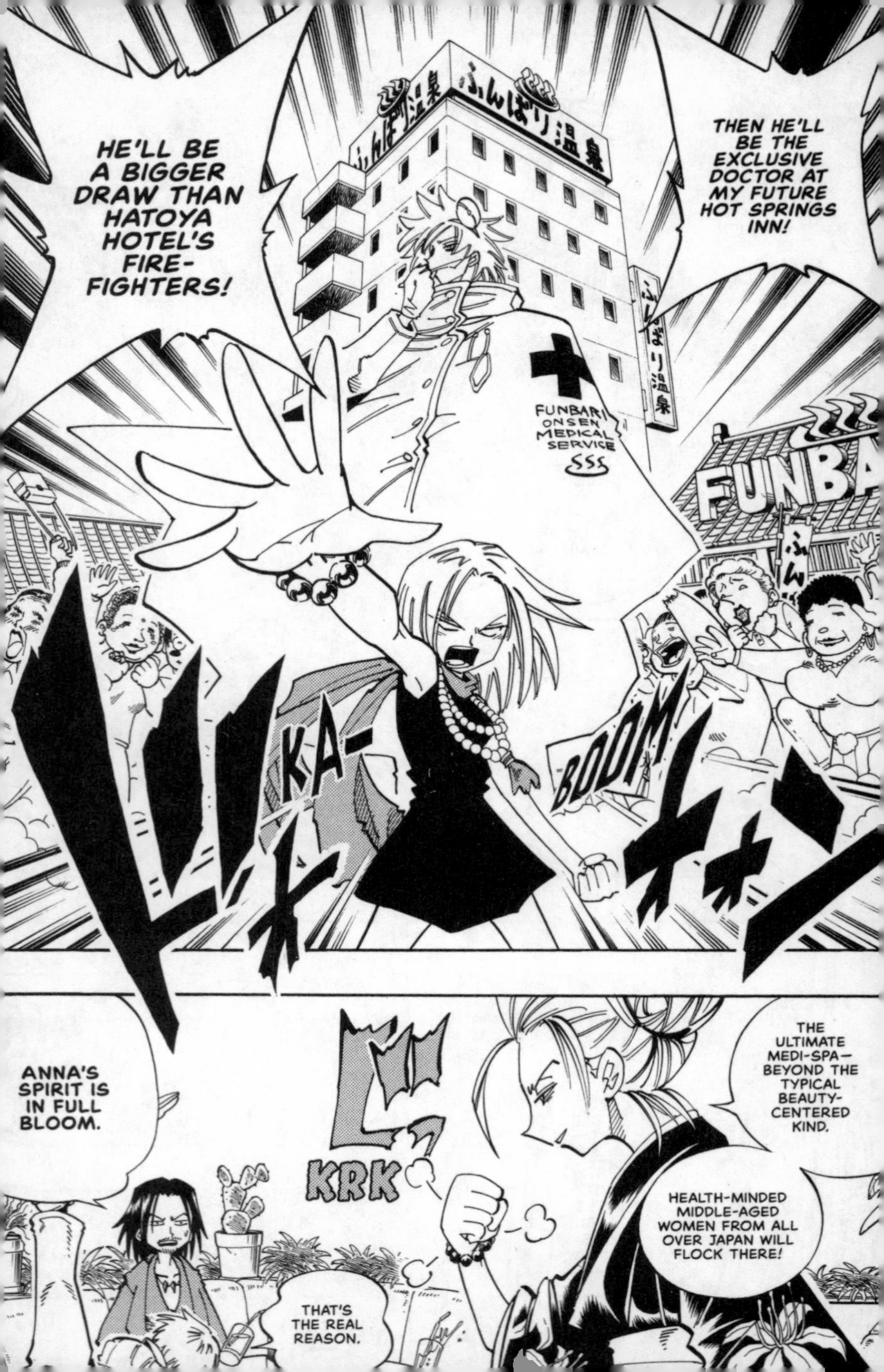
THEN HE'LL BE THE EXCLUSIVE DOCTOR AT MY FUTURE HOT SPRINGS INN!
HE'LL BE A BIGGER DRAW THAN HATOYA HOTEL'S FIRE-FIGHTERS!
ふんばり温泉
ふんばり温泉
FUNBARI ONSEN MEDICAL SERVICE
FUNBA
KA-
BOOM
THE ULTIMATE MEDI-SPA—BEYOND THE TYPICAL BEAUTY-CENTERED KIND.
HEALTH-MINDED MIDDLE-AGED WOMEN FROM ALL OVER JAPAN WILL FLOCK THERE!
KRK
ANNA'S SPIRIT IS IN FULL BLOOM.
THAT'S THE REAL REASON.

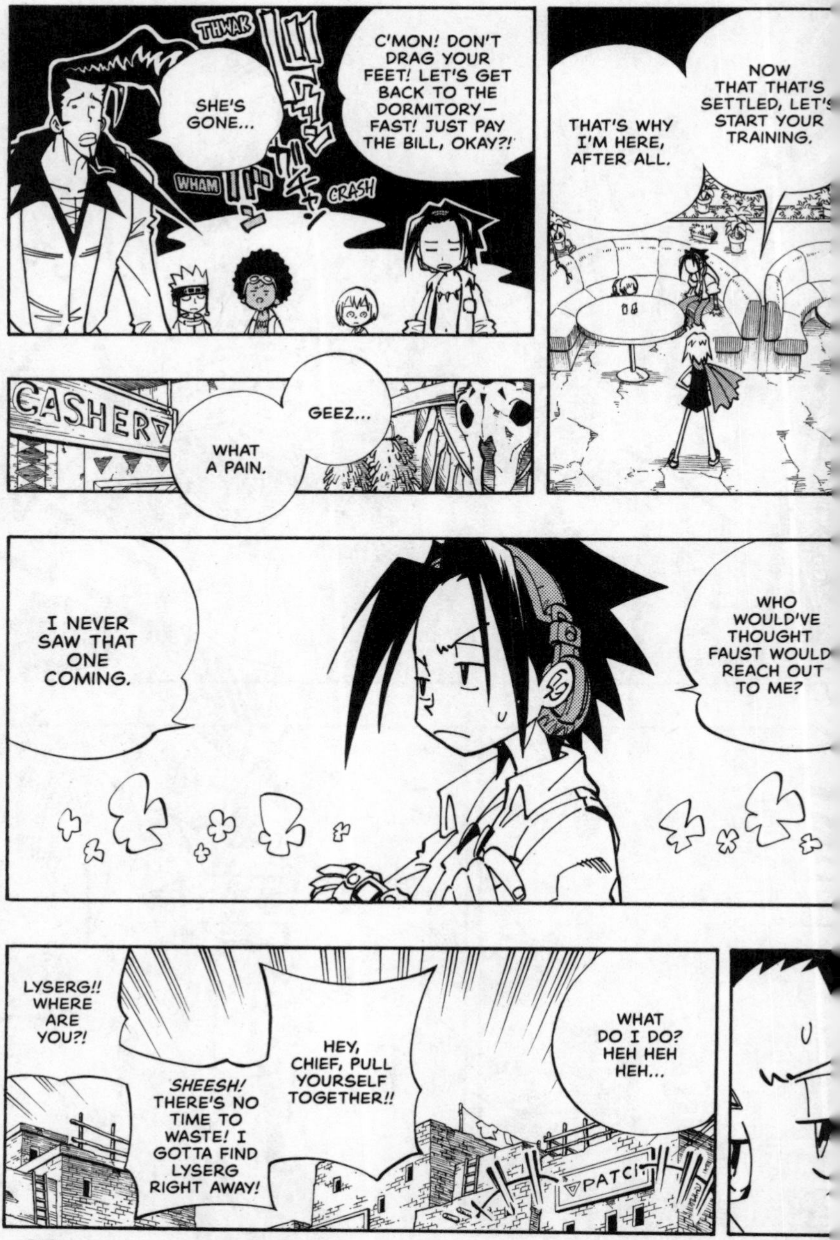
NOW THAT THAT'S SETTLED, LET'S START YOUR TRAINING.
THAT'S WHY I'M HERE, AFTER ALL.
C'MON! DON'T DRAG YOUR FEET! LET'S GET BACK TO THE DORMITORY— FAST! JUST PAY THE BILL, OKAY?!
THWAK
WHAM
CRASH
SHE'S GONE...
GEEZ...
WHAT A PAIN.
CASHER
WHO WOULD'VE THOUGHT FAUST WOULD REACH OUT TO ME?
I NEVER SAW THAT ONE COMING.
WHAT DO I DO? HEH HEH HEH...
HEY, CHIEF, PULL YOURSELF TOGETHER!!
LYSERG!! WHERE ARE YOU?!
SHEESH! THERE'S NO TIME TO WASTE! I GOTTA FIND LYSERG RIGHT AWAY!
PATCI

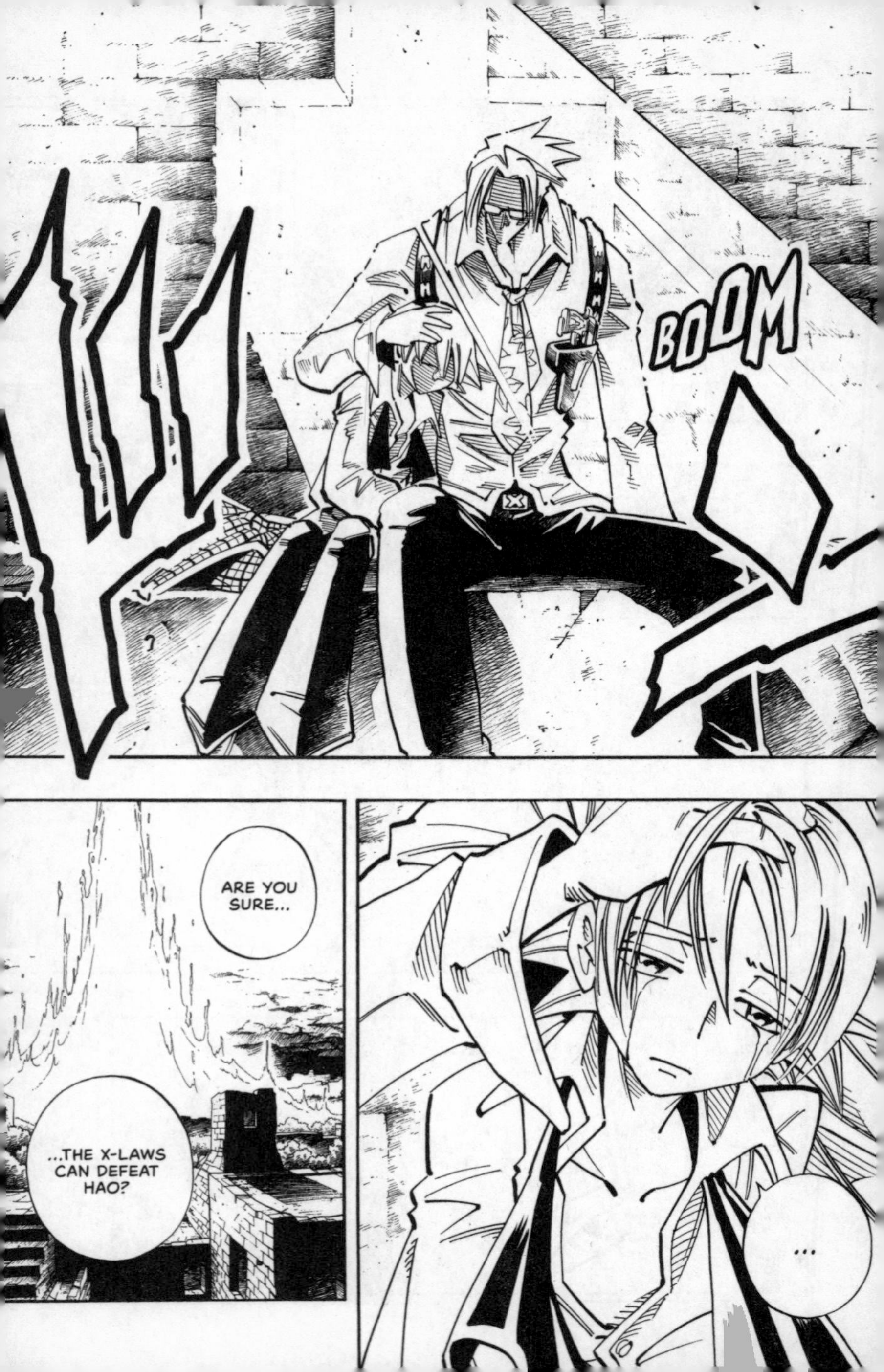
BOOM
...
ARE YOU SURE...
...THE X-LAWS CAN DEFEAT HAO?

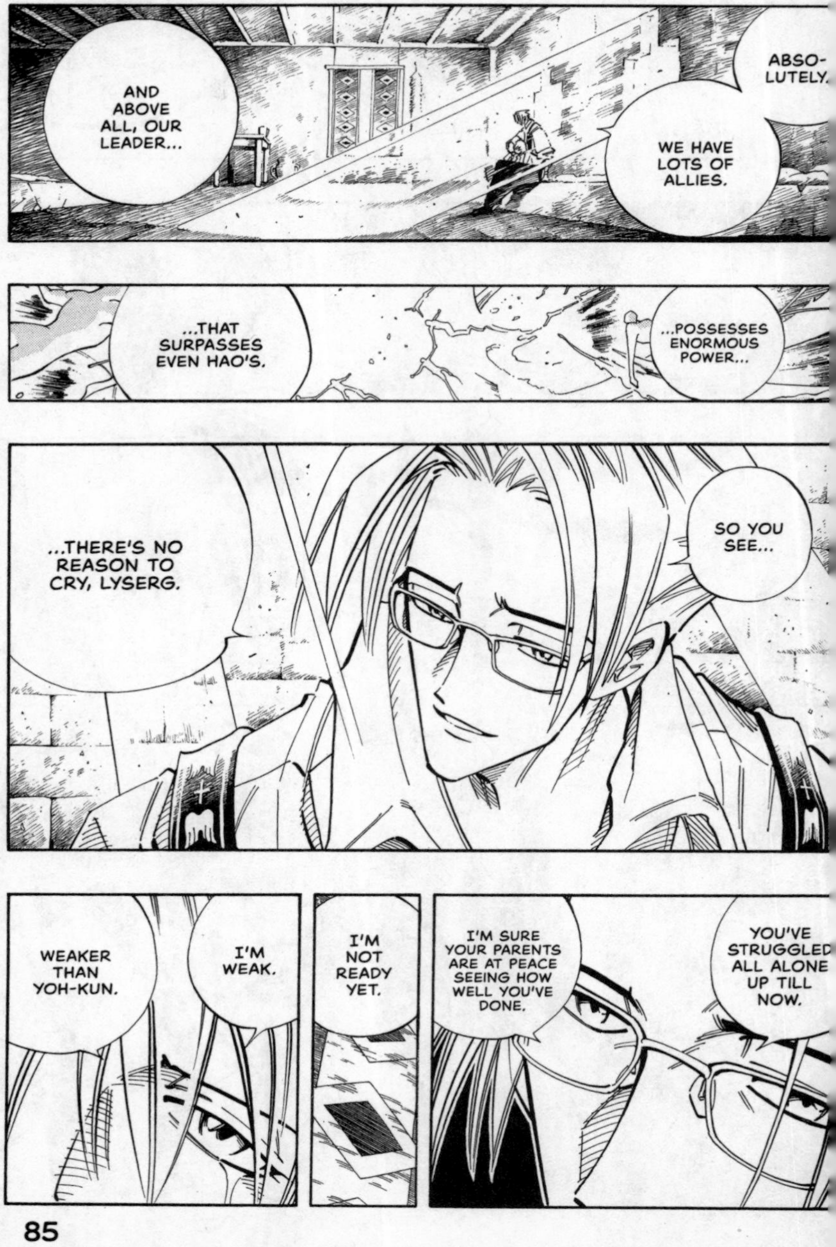
ABSO-LUTELY.
WE HAVE LOTS OF ALLIES.
AND ABOVE ALL, OUR LEADER...
...POSSESSES ENORMOUS POWER...
...THAT SURPASSES EVEN HAO'S.
SO YOU SEE...
...THERE'S NO REASON TO CRY, LYSERG.
YOU'VE STRUGGLED ALL ALONE UP TILL NOW.
I'M SURE YOUR PARENTS ARE AT PEACE SEEING HOW WELL YOU'VE DONE.
I'M NOT READY YET.
I'M WEAK.
WEAKER THAN YOH-KUN.

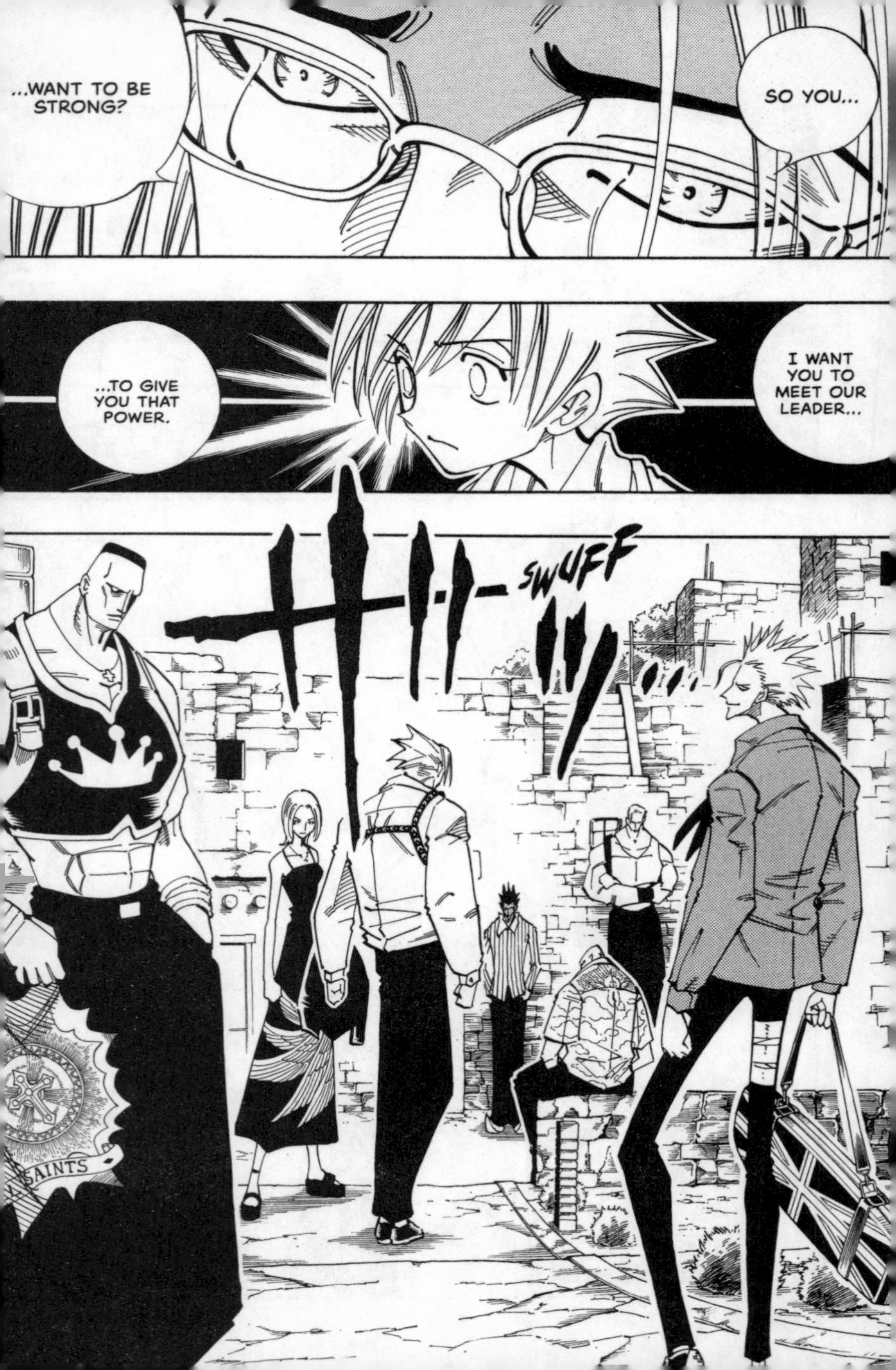
SO YOU...
...WANT TO BE STRONG?
I WANT YOU TO MEET OUR LEADER...
...TO GIVE YOU THAT POWER.
SWUFF
SAINTS

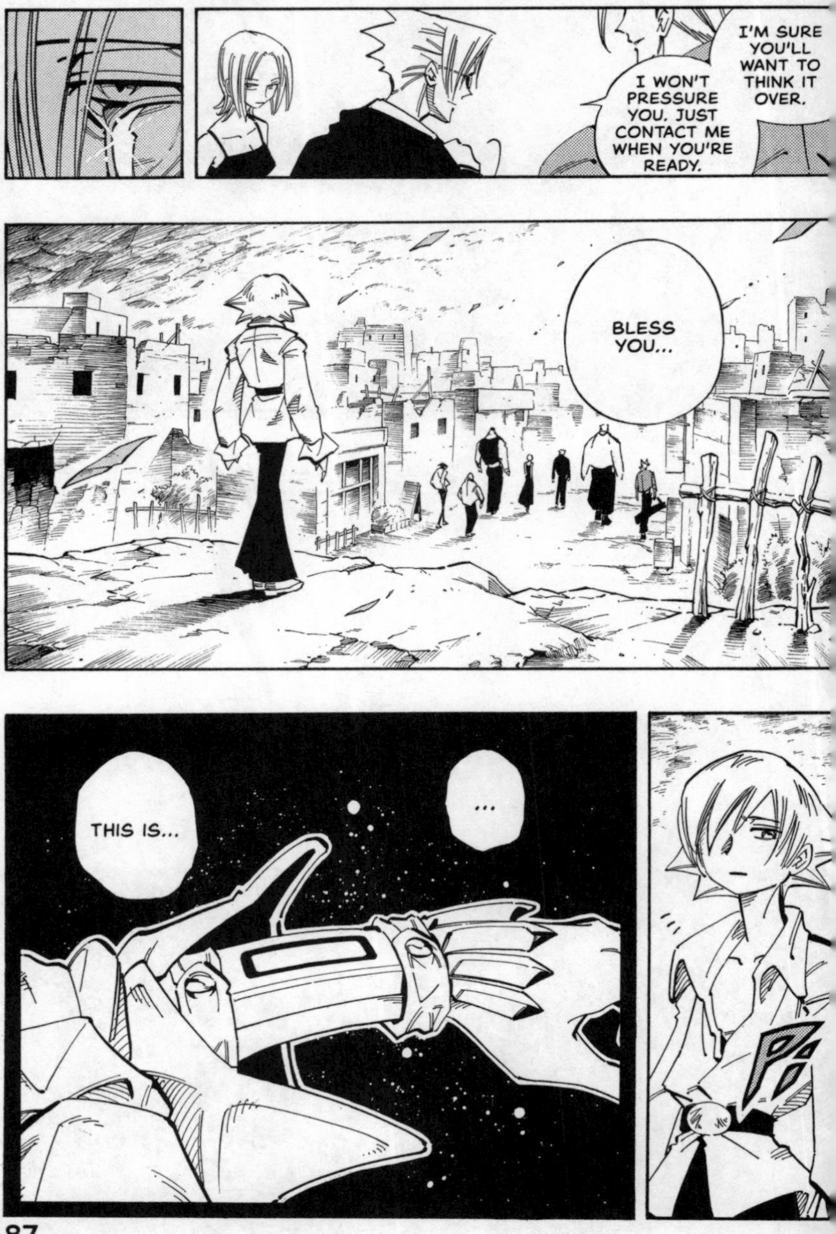
I'M SURE YOU'LL WANT TO THINK IT OVER.
I WON'T PRESSURE YOU. JUST CONTACT ME WHEN YOU'RE READY.
BLESS YOU...
...
THIS IS...

SHAMAN
KING
13

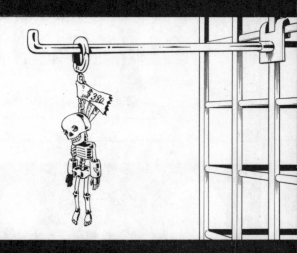

That Token
(Silver Patch-Man)

Chapter 112: In Tokyo

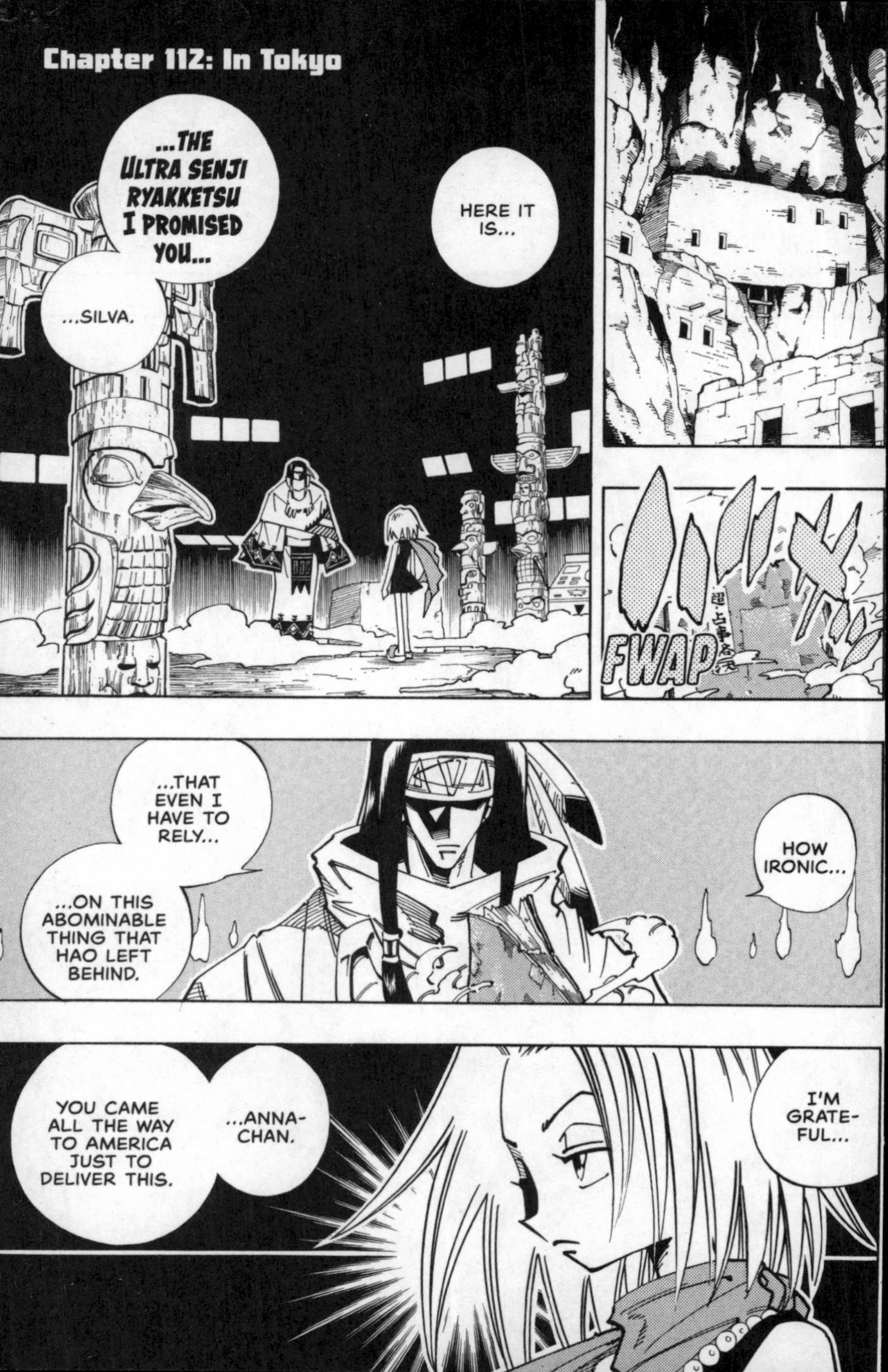
FWAP
HERE IT IS...
...THE ULTRA SENJI RYAKKETSU I PROMISED YOU...
...SILVA.
HOW IRONIC...
...THAT EVEN I HAVE TO RELY...
...ON THIS ABOMINABLE THING THAT HAO LEFT BEHIND.
I'M GRATE-FUL...
...ANNA-CHAN.
YOU CAME ALL THE WAY TO AMERICA JUST TO DELIVER THIS.

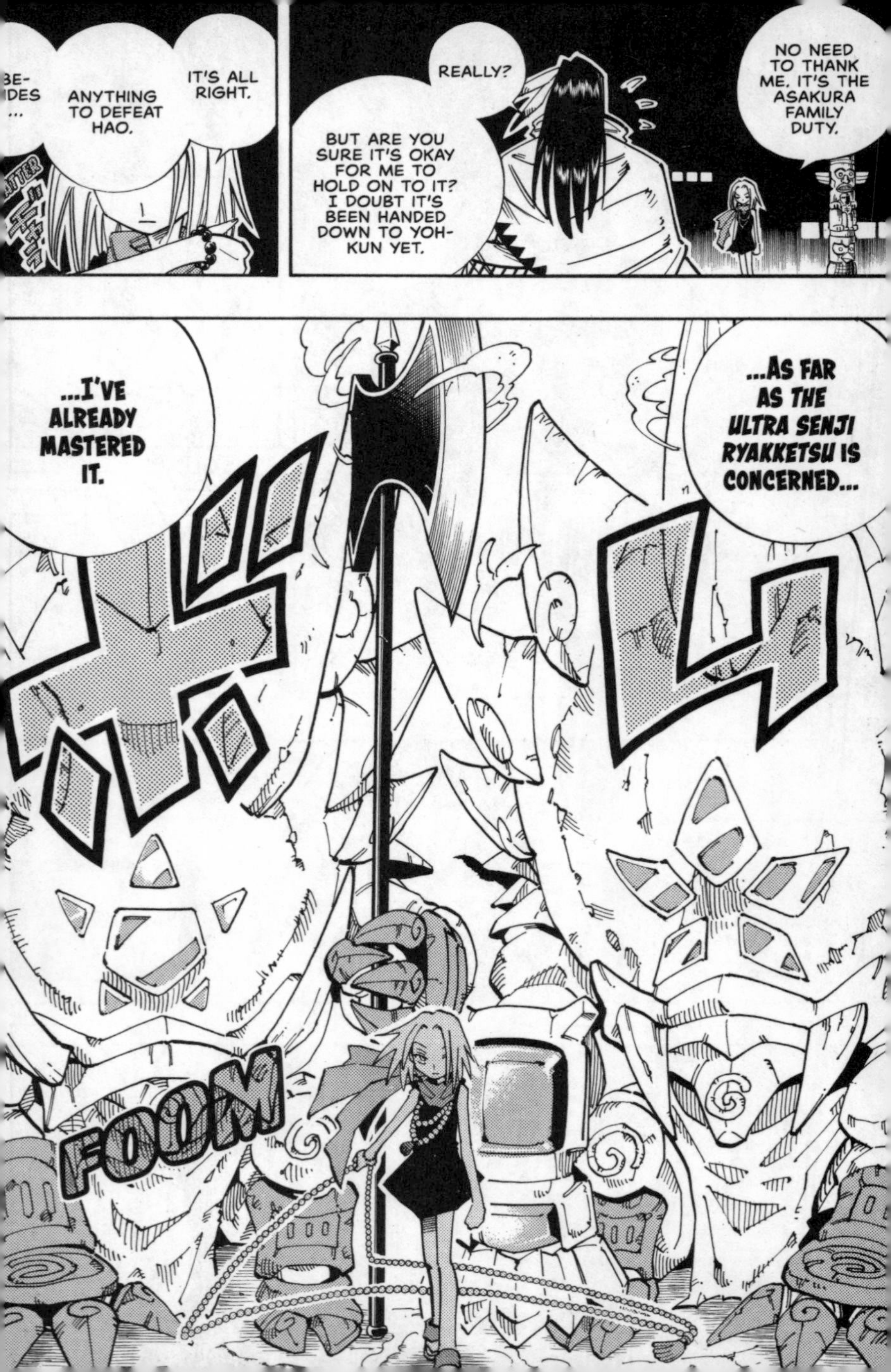
NO NEED TO THANK ME. IT'S THE ASAKURA FAMILY DUTY.
REALLY?
BUT ARE YOU SURE IT'S OKAY FOR ME TO HOLD ON TO IT? I DOUBT IT'S BEEN HANDED DOWN TO YOH-KUN YET.
...
IT'S ALL RIGHT.
ANYTHING TO DEFEAT HAO.
BE-
...AS FAR AS THE ULTRA SENJI RYAKKETSU IS CONCERNED...
...I'VE ALREADY MASTERED IT.
FOOM

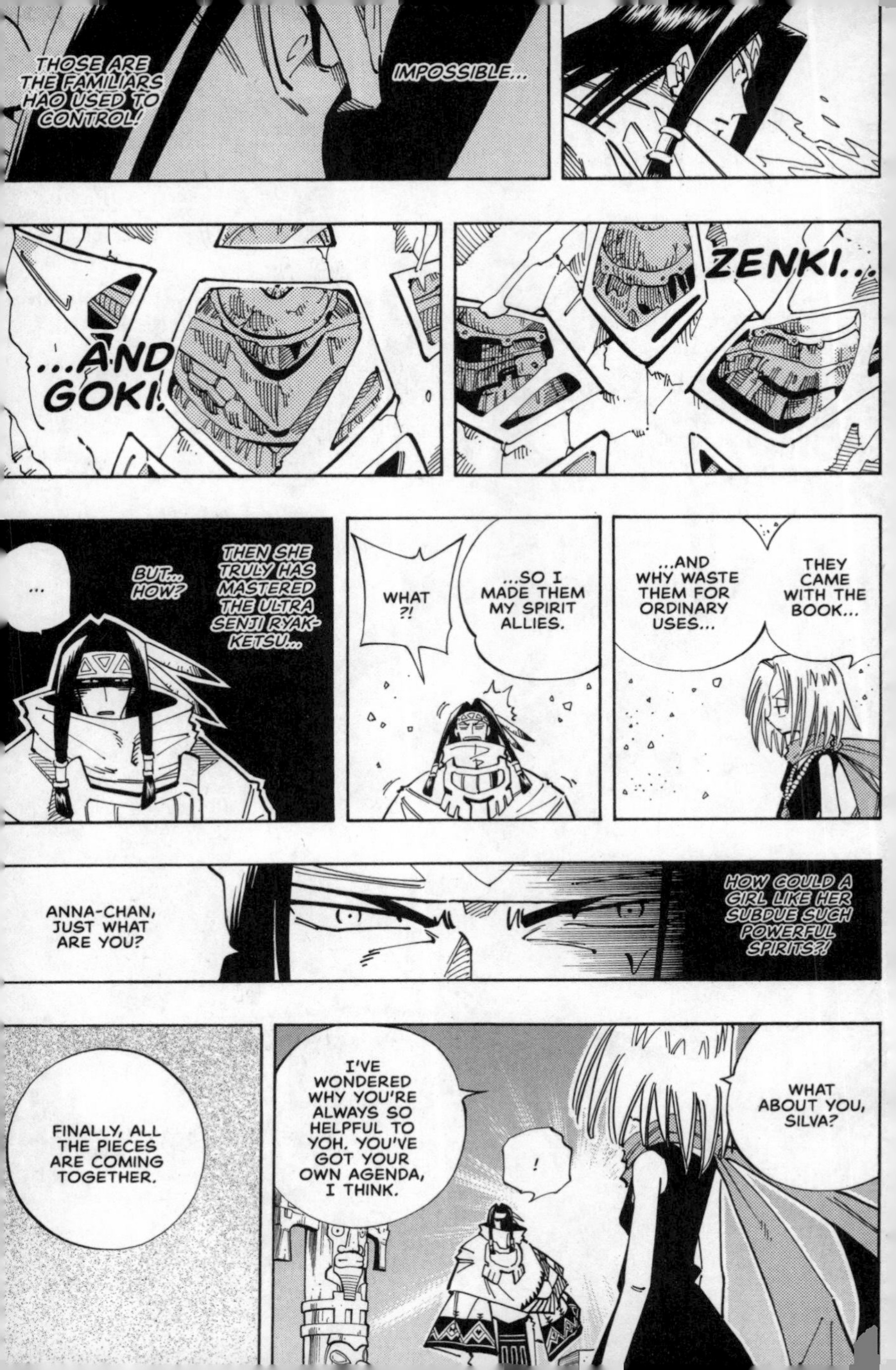
IMPOSSIBLE...
THOSE ARE THE FAMILIARS HAO USED TO CONTROL!
ZENKI...
...AND GOKI!
THEY CAME WITH THE BOOK...
...AND WHY WASTE THEM FOR ORDINARY USES...
...SO I MADE THEM MY SPIRIT ALLIES.
WHAT ?!
THEN SHE TRULY HAS MASTERED THE ULTRA SENJI RYAKKETSU...
BUT... HOW?
...
HOW COULD A GIRL LIKE HER SUBDUE SUCH POWERFUL SPIRITS?!
ANNA-CHAN, JUST WHAT ARE YOU?
WHAT ABOUT YOU, SILVA?
I'VE WONDERED WHY YOU'RE ALWAYS SO HELPFUL TO YOH. YOU'VE GOT YOUR OWN AGENDA, I THINK.
!
FINALLY, ALL THE PIECES ARE COMING TOGETHER.

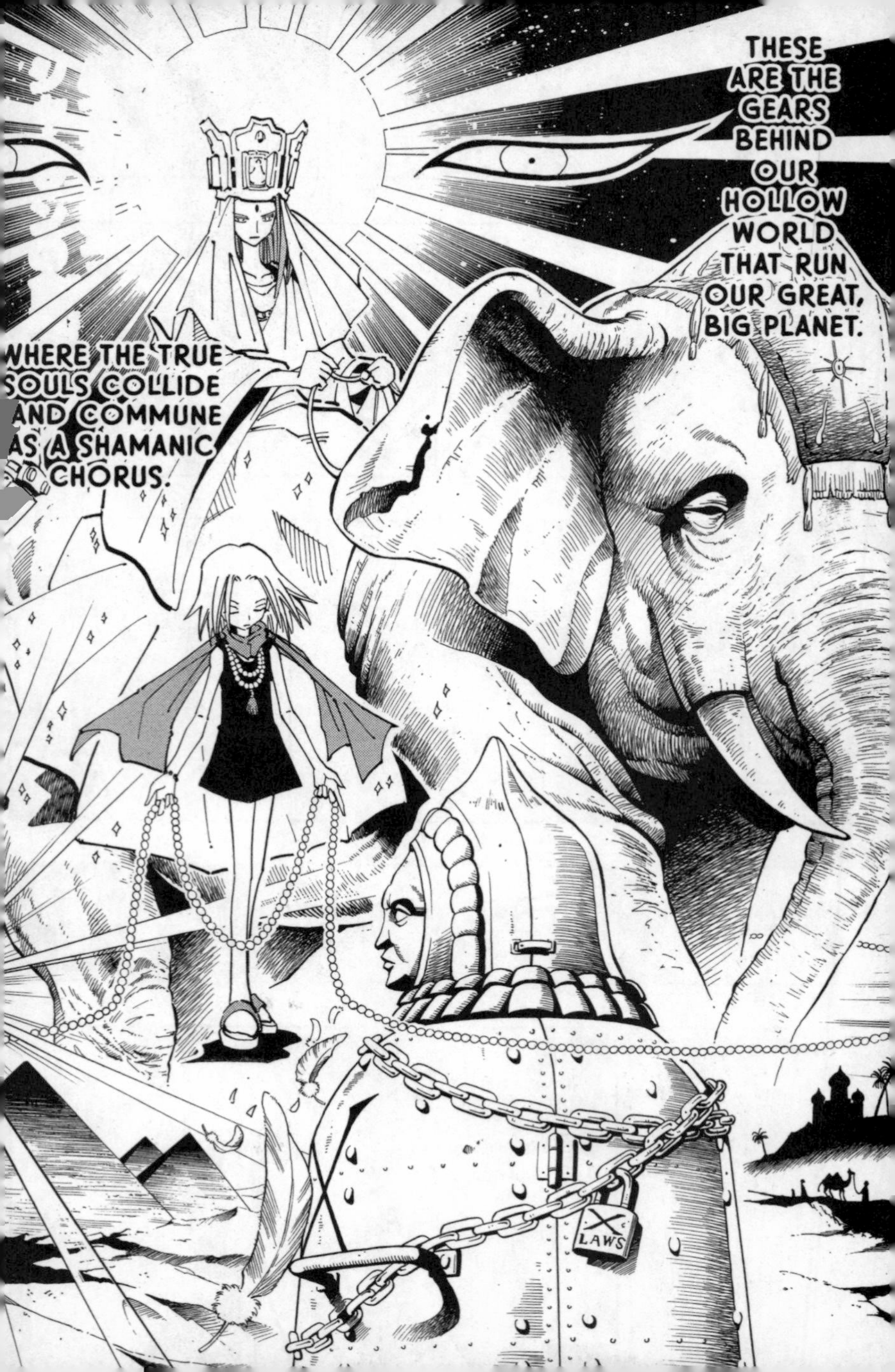
THESE ARE THE GEARS BEHIND OUR HOLLOW WORLD THAT RUN OUR GREAT, BIG PLANET.
WHERE THE TRUE SOULS COLLIDE AND COMMUNE AS A SHAMANIC CHORUS.
LAWS

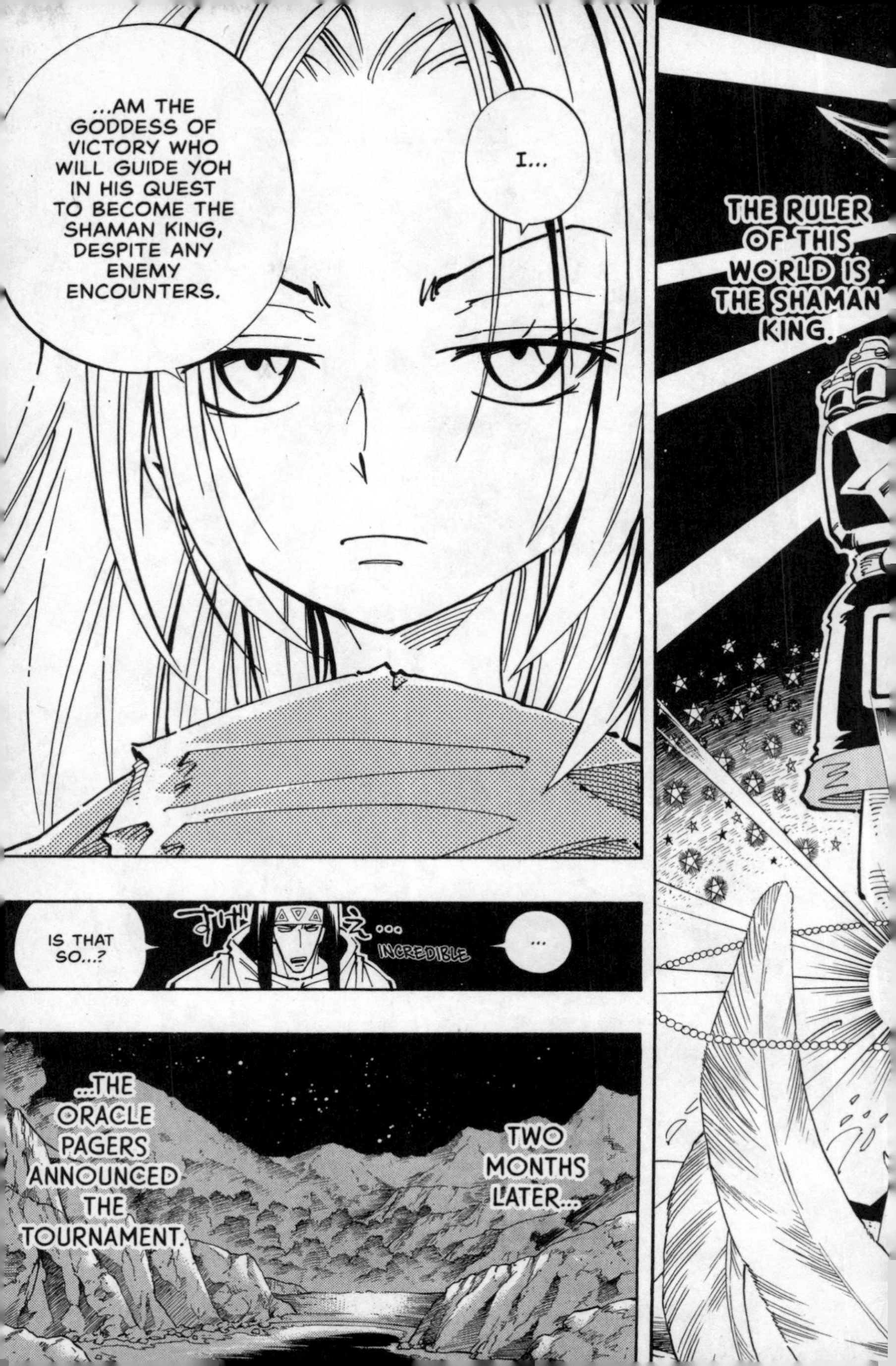
THE RULER OF THIS WORLD IS THE SHAMAN KING.
I...
...AM THE GODDESS OF VICTORY WHO WILL GUIDE YOH IN HIS QUEST TO BECOME THE SHAMAN KING, DESPITE ANY ENEMY ENCOUNTERS.
...
INCREDIBLE
IS THAT SO...?
TWO MONTHS LATER...
...THE ORACLE PAGERS ANNOUNCED THE TOURNAMENT.

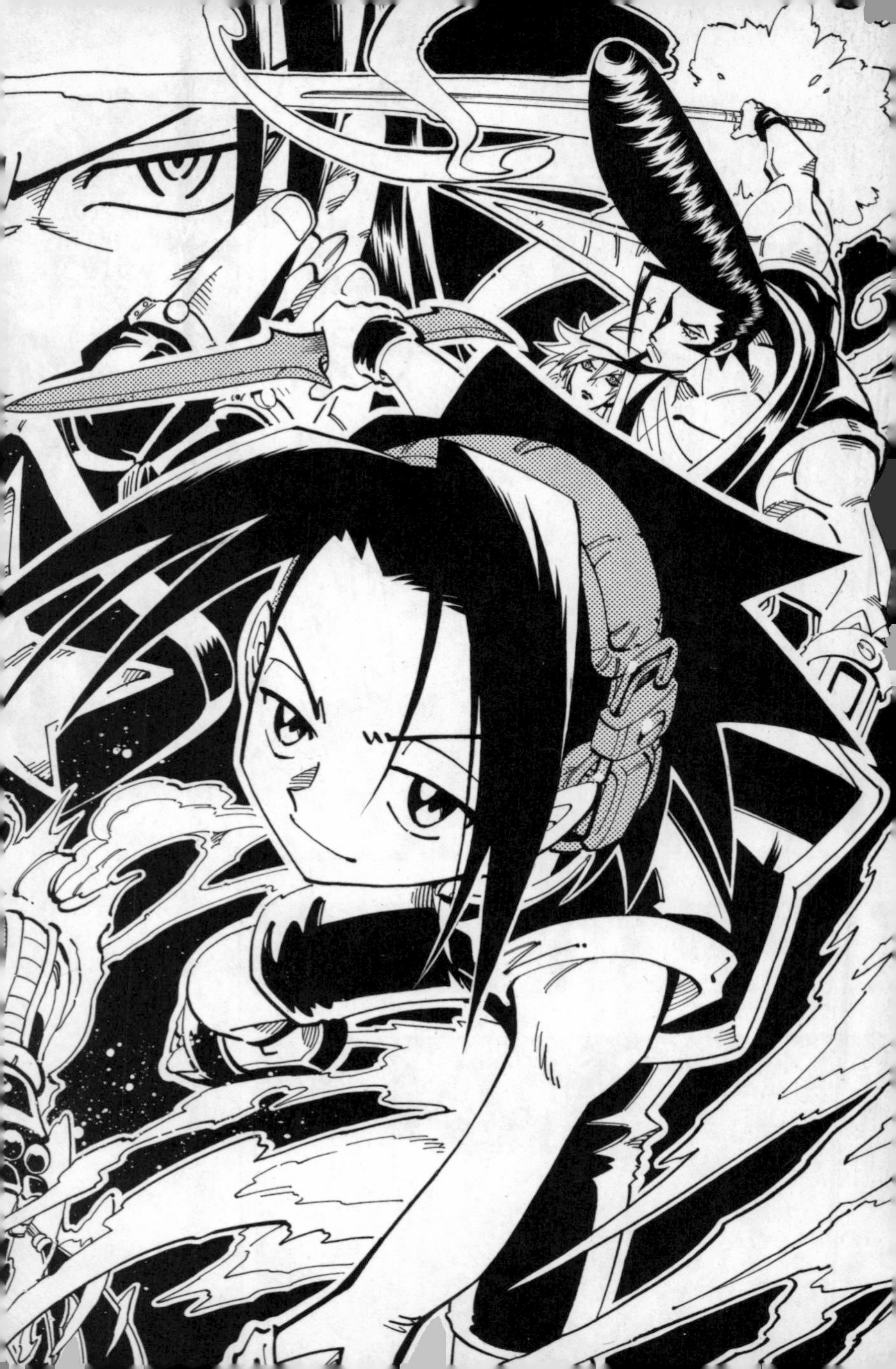

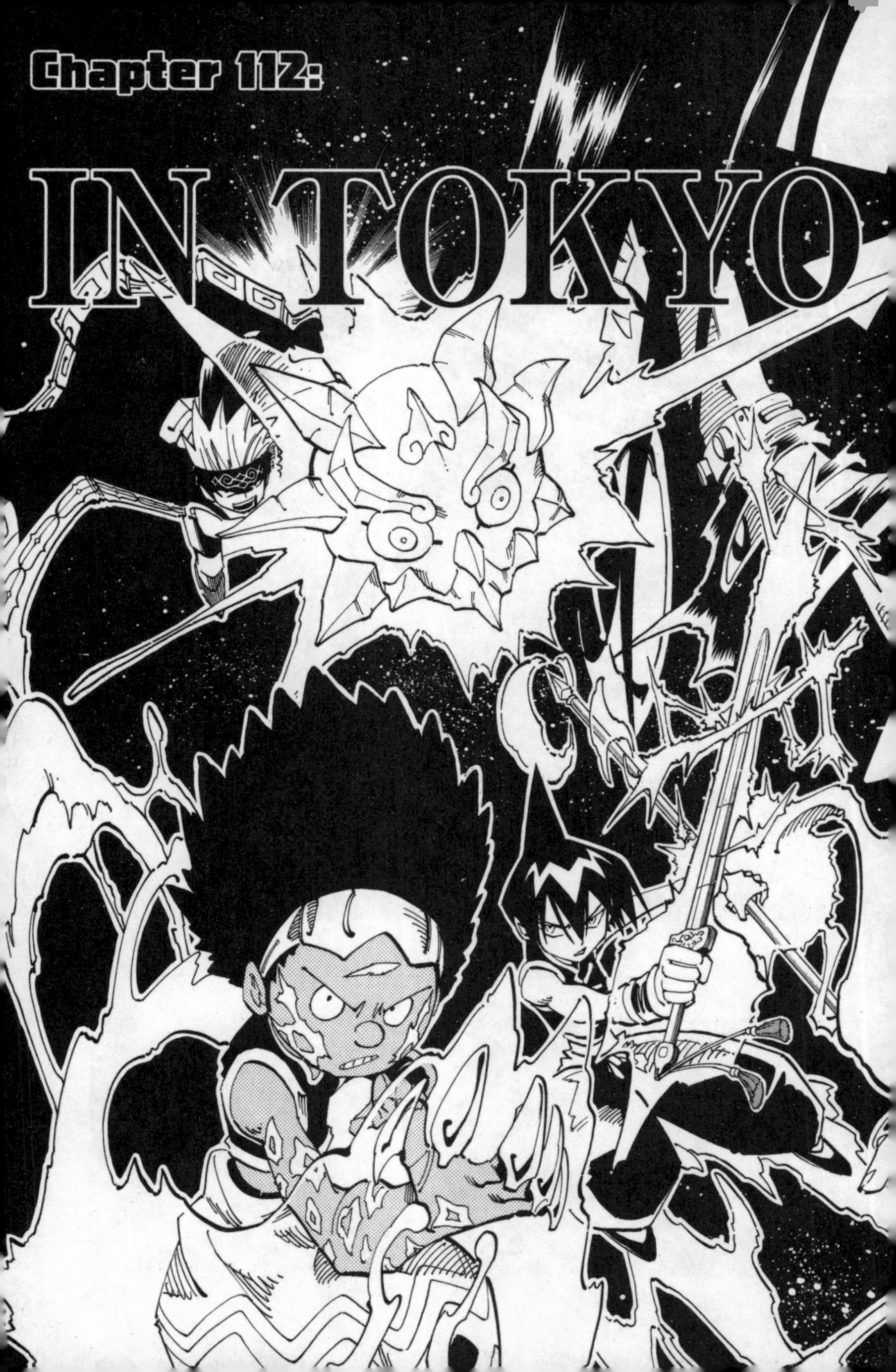
Chapter 112:
IN TOKYO

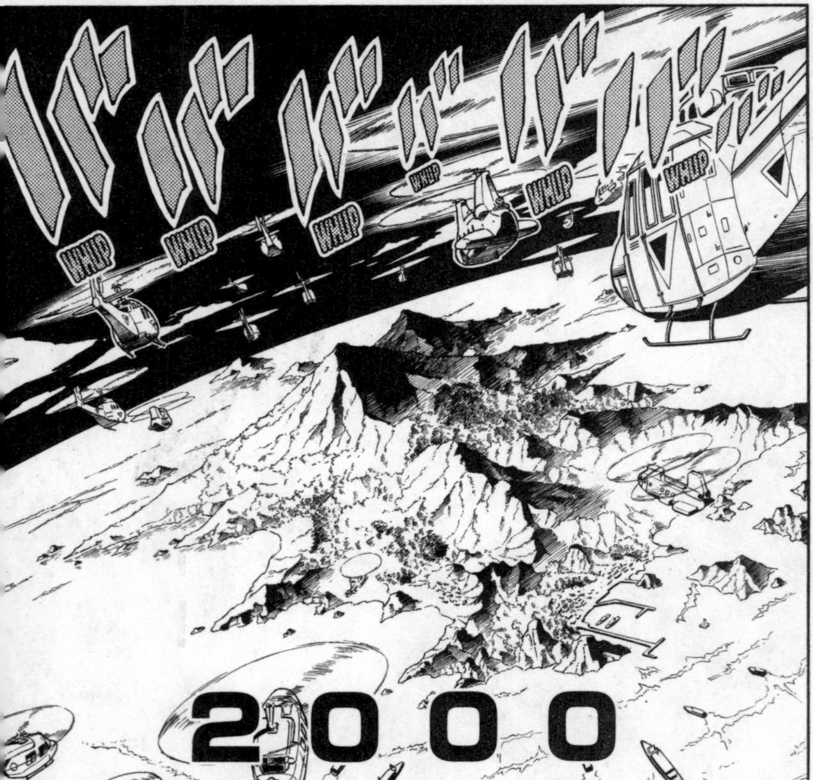
WHIP
WHIP
WHIP
WHIP
WHIP
WHIP
2000
THE UNINHABITED ISLAND OF TOKYO

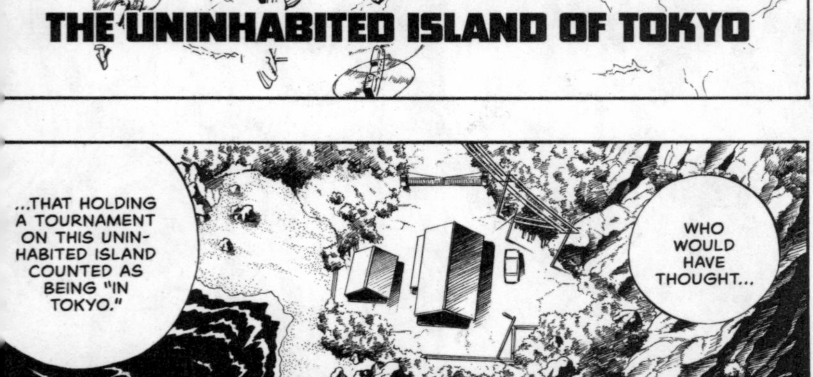
WHO WOULD HAVE THOUGHT...
...THAT HOLDING A TOURNAMENT ON THIS UNINHABITED ISLAND COUNTED AS BEING "IN TOKYO."

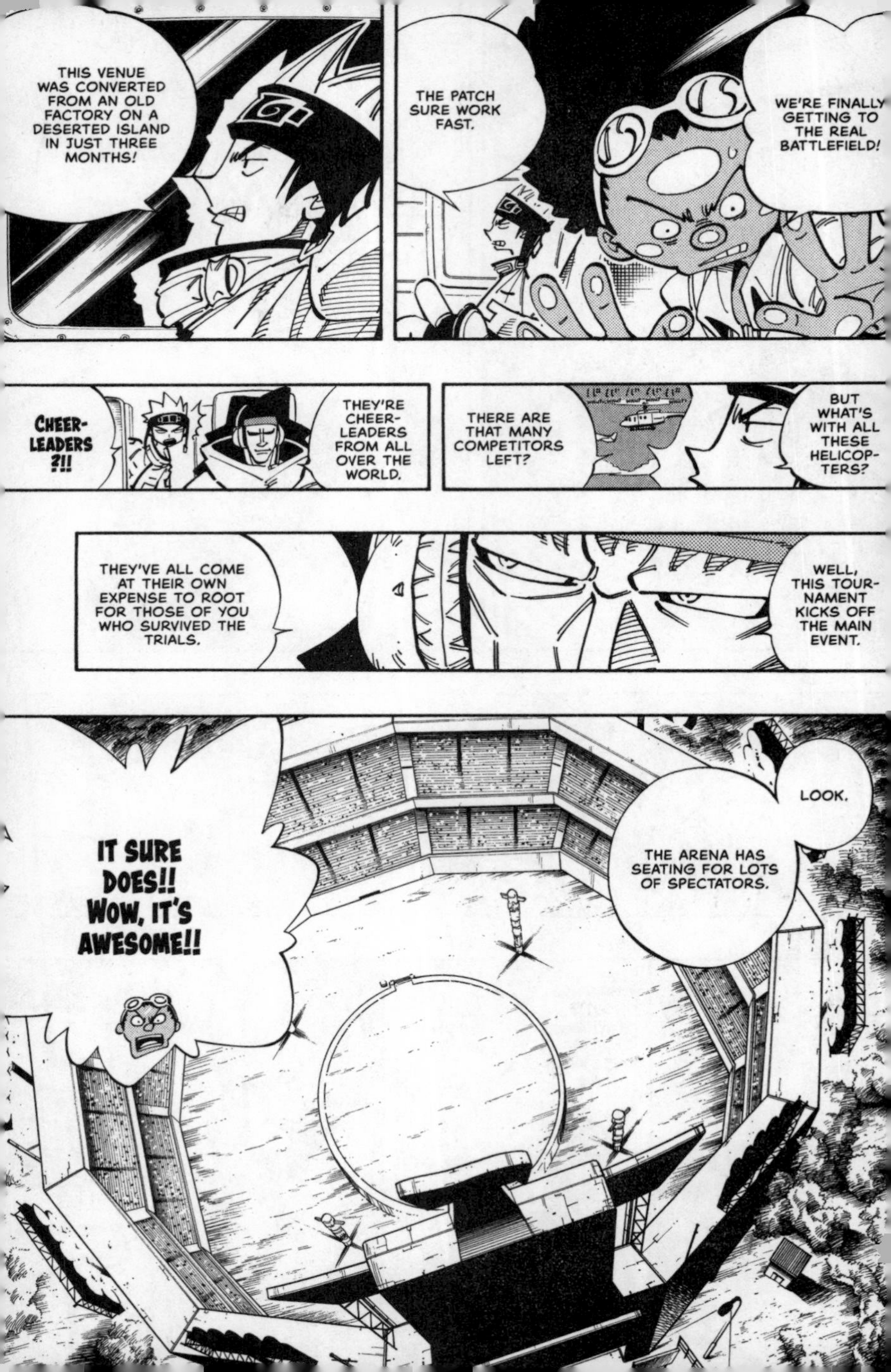
WE'RE FINALLY GETTING TO THE REAL BATTLEFIELD!
THE PATCH SURE WORK FAST.
THIS VENUE WAS CONVERTED FROM AN OLD FACTORY ON A DESERTED ISLAND IN JUST THREE MONTHS!
BUT WHAT'S WITH ALL THESE HELICOP-TERS?
THERE ARE THAT MANY COMPETITORS LEFT?
THEY'RE CHEER-LEADERS FROM ALL OVER THE WORLD.
CHEER-LEADERS ?!!
WELL, THIS TOUR-NAMENT KICKS OFF THE MAIN EVENT.
THEY'VE ALL COME AT THEIR OWN EXPENSE TO ROOT FOR THOSE OF YOU WHO SURVIVED THE TRIALS.
LOOK.
THE ARENA HAS SEATING FOR LOTS OF SPECTATORS.
IT SURE DOES!! WOW, IT'S AWESOME!!

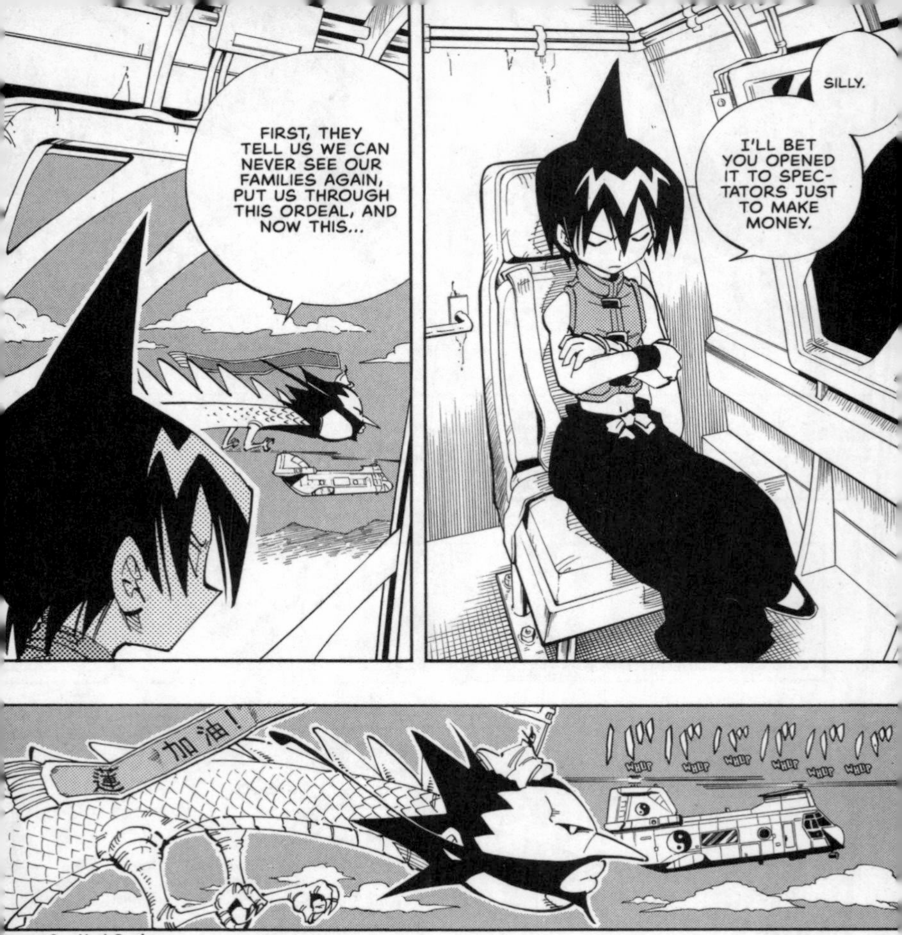
SILLY.
I'LL BET YOU OPENED IT TO SPECTATORS JUST TO MAKE MONEY.
FIRST, THEY TELL US WE CAN NEVER SEE OUR FAMILIES AGAIN, PUT US THROUGH THIS ORDEAL, AND NOW THIS...
WHUP WHUP WHUP WHUP WHUP WHUP
蓮 加油!

anner: Good luck Ren!

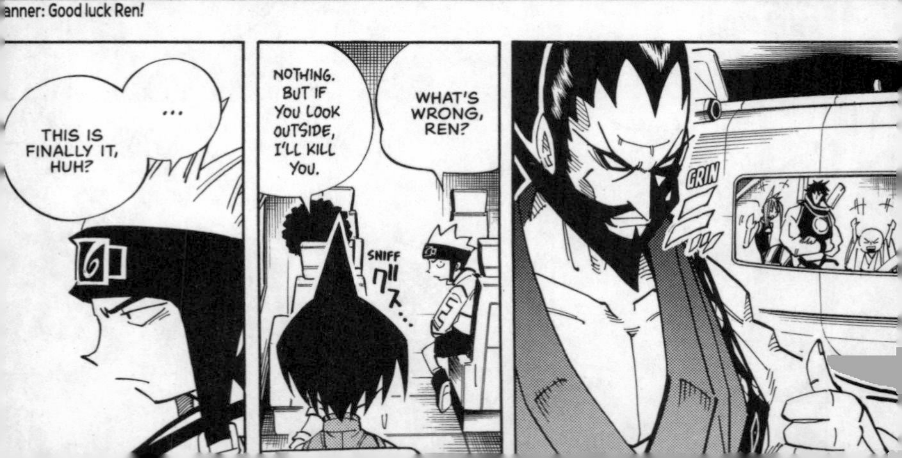
GRIN
WHAT'S WRONG, REN?
NOTHING. BUT IF YOU LOOK OUTSIDE, I'LL KILL YOU.
SNIFF
グス...
...
THIS IS FINALLY IT, HUH?

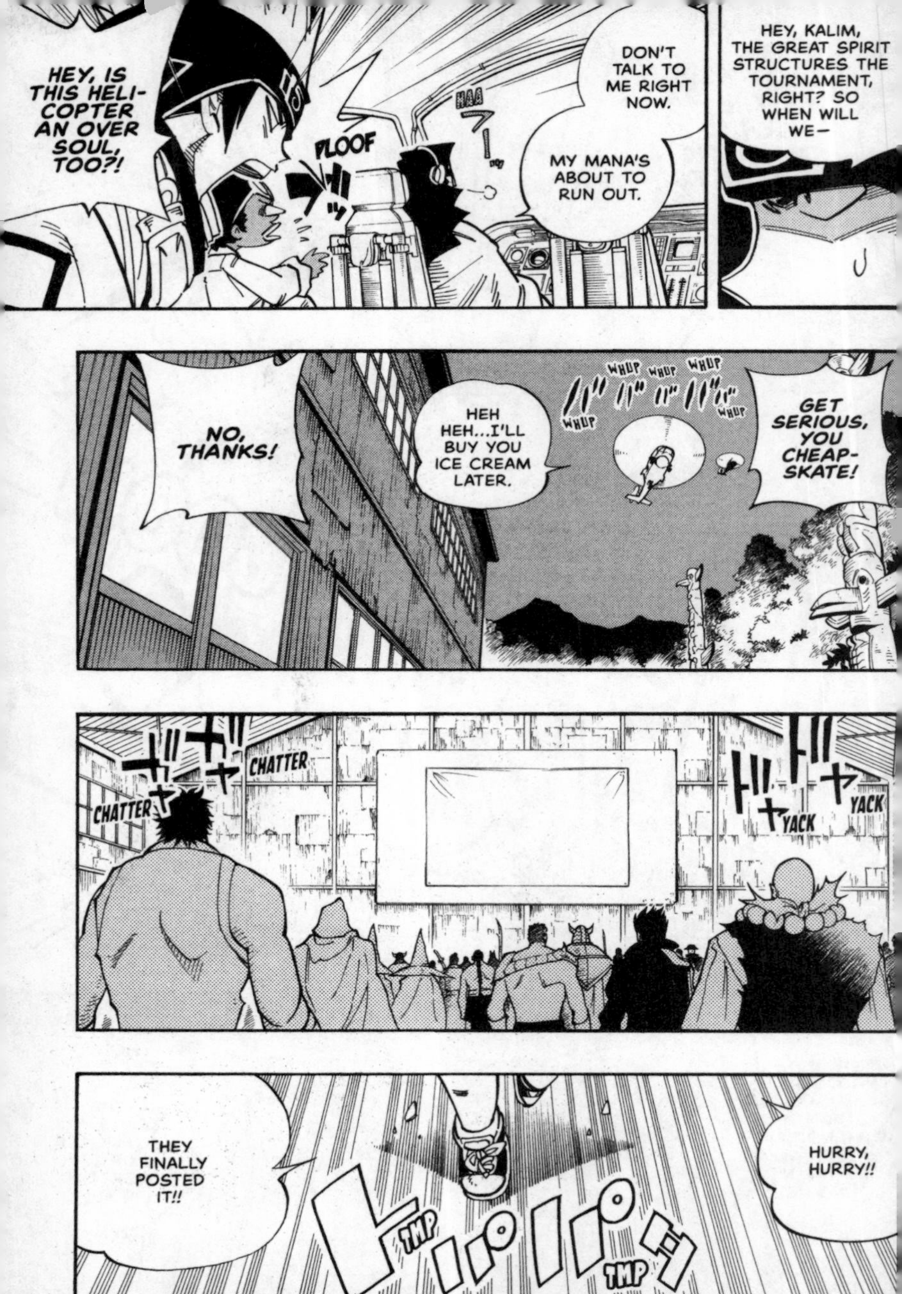
HEY, KALIM, THE GREAT SPIRIT STRUCTURES THE TOURNAMENT, RIGHT? SO WHEN WILL WE—
DON'T TALK TO ME RIGHT NOW.
HAA
MY MANA'S ABOUT TO RUN OUT.
PLOOF
HEY, IS THIS HELICOPTER AN OVER SOUL, TOO?!
GET SERIOUS, YOU CHEAPSKATE!
WHUP WHUP WHUP WHUP WHUP
HEH HEH...I'LL BUY YOU ICE CREAM LATER.
NO, THANKS!
YACK YACK
CHATTER CHATTER
HURRY, HURRY!!
TMP TMP
THEY FINALLY POSTED IT!!

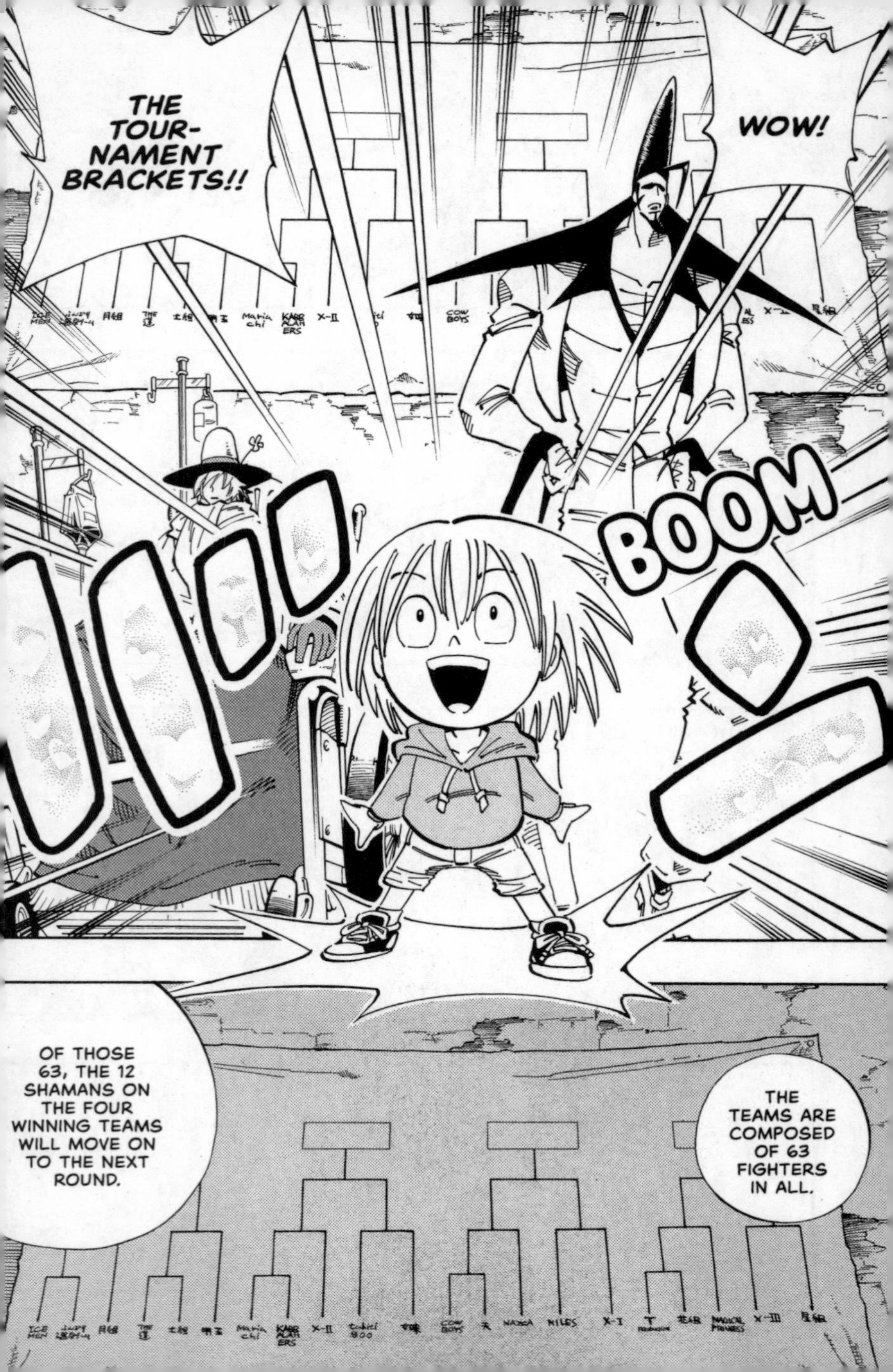
WOW!
THE TOUR-NAMENT BRACKETS!!
BOOM
THE TEAMS ARE COMPOSED OF 63 FIGHTERS IN ALL.
OF THOSE 63, THE 12 SHAMANS ON THE FOUR WINNING TEAMS WILL MOVE ON TO THE NEXT ROUND.

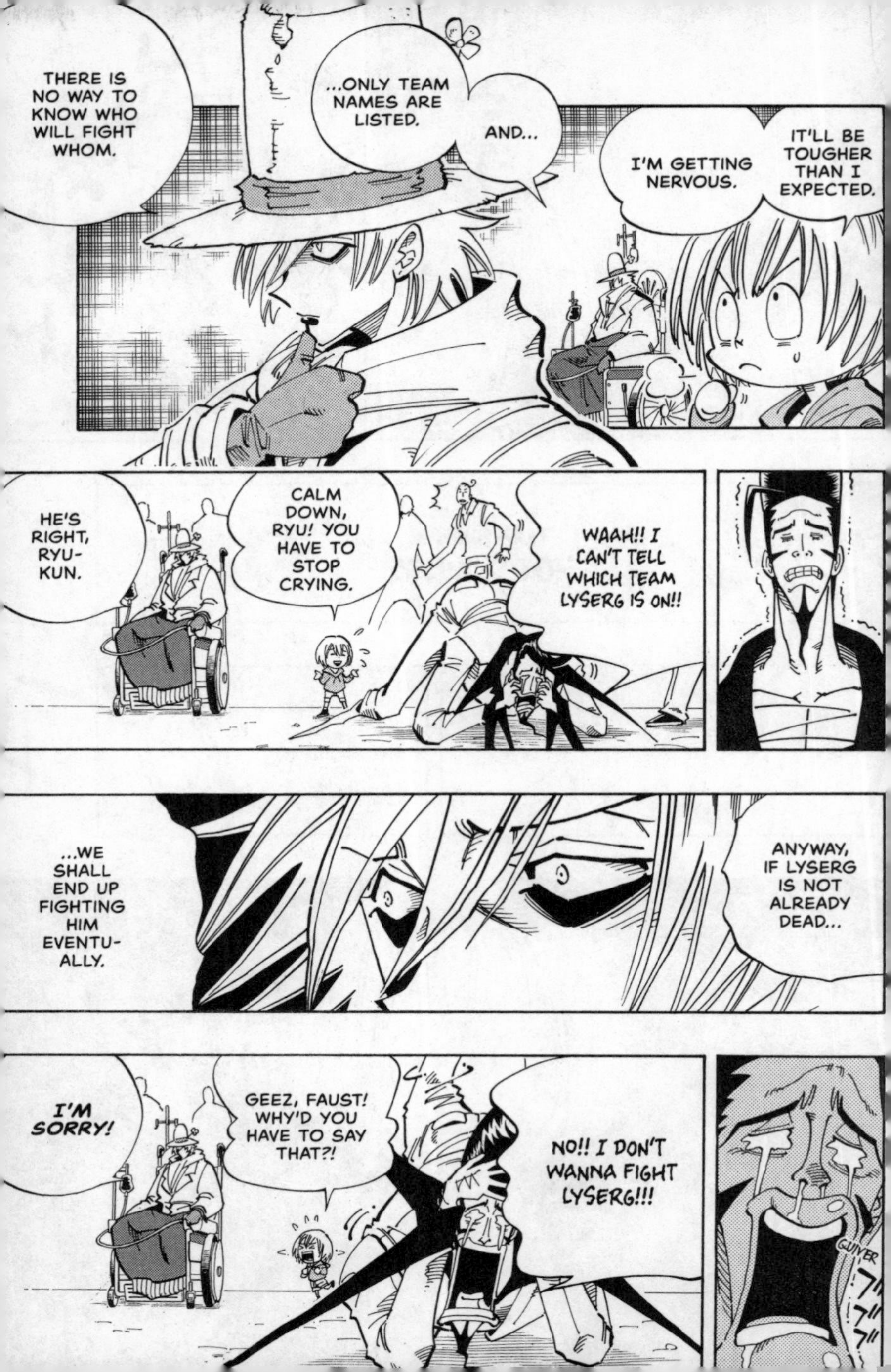
IT'LL BE TOUGHER THAN I EXPECTED.
I'M GETTING NERVOUS.
AND...
...ONLY TEAM NAMES ARE LISTED.
THERE IS NO WAY TO KNOW WHO WILL FIGHT WHOM.
WAAH!! I CAN'T TELL WHICH TEAM LYSERG IS ON!!
CALM DOWN, RYU! YOU HAVE TO STOP CRYING.
HE'S RIGHT, RYU-KUN.
ANYWAY, IF LYSERG IS NOT ALREADY DEAD...
...WE SHALL END UP FIGHTING HIM EVENTUALLY.
QUIVER
NO!! I DON'T WANNA FIGHT LYSERG!!!
GEEZ, FAUST! WHY'D YOU HAVE TO SAY THAT?!
I'M SORRY!

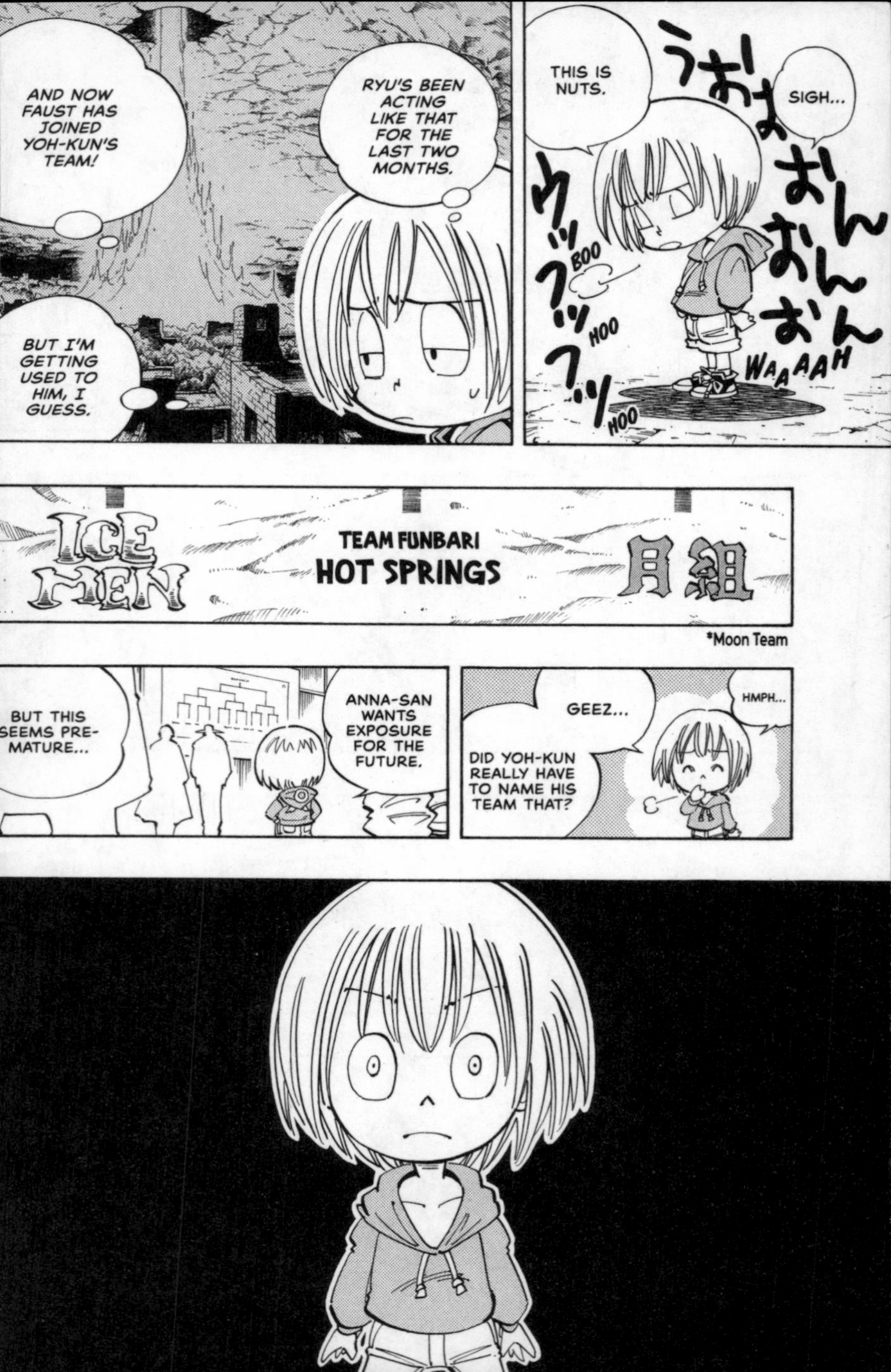

SIGH...
THIS IS NUTS.
うおぉおんおんおん
WAAAAH
ウッフッフッ
BOO HOO HOO
RYU'S BEEN ACTING LIKE THAT FOR THE LAST TWO MONTHS.
AND NOW FAUST HAS JOINED YOH-KUN'S TEAM!
BUT I'M GETTING USED TO HIM, I GUESS.
月組
TEAM FUNBARI HOT SPRINGS
ICE MEN
*Moon Team
HMPH...
GEEZ...
DID YOH-KUN REALLY HAVE TO NAME HIS TEAM THAT?
ANNA-SAN WANTS EXPOSURE FOR THE FUTURE.
BUT THIS SEEMS PREMATURE...

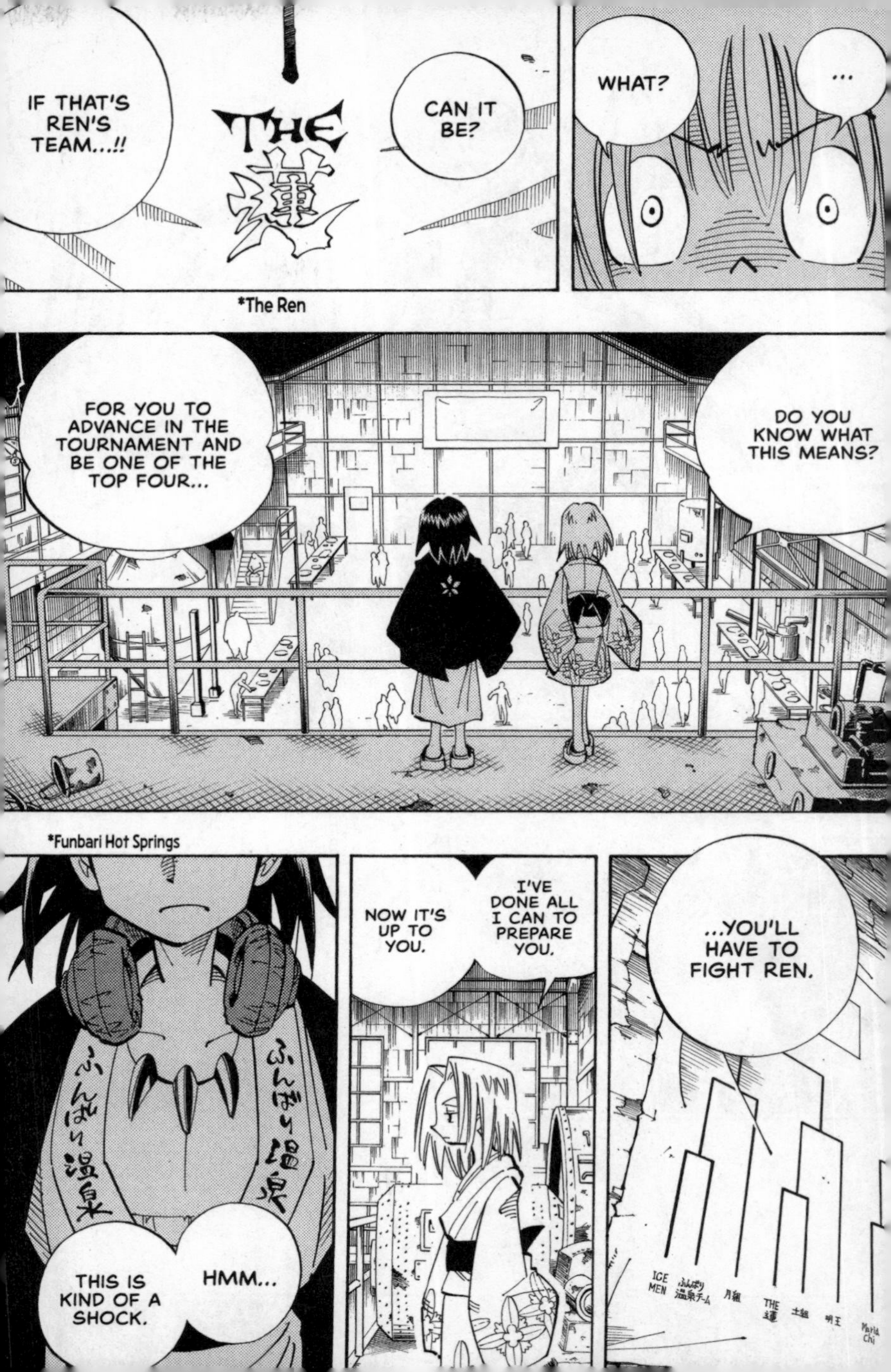
...
WHAT?
CAN IT BE?
THE 蓮
IF THAT'S REN'S TEAM...!!
*The Ren
DO YOU KNOW WHAT THIS MEANS?
FOR YOU TO ADVANCE IN THE TOURNAMENT AND BE ONE OF THE TOP FOUR...
*Funbari Hot Springs
...YOU'LL HAVE TO FIGHT REN.
ICE MEN
ふんばり温泉チーム
月組
THE 蓮
土組
明王
Maria Chi
I'VE DONE ALL I CAN TO PREPARE YOU.
NOW IT'S UP TO YOU.
ふんばり温泉
ふんばり温泉
HMM...
THIS IS KIND OF A SHOCK.

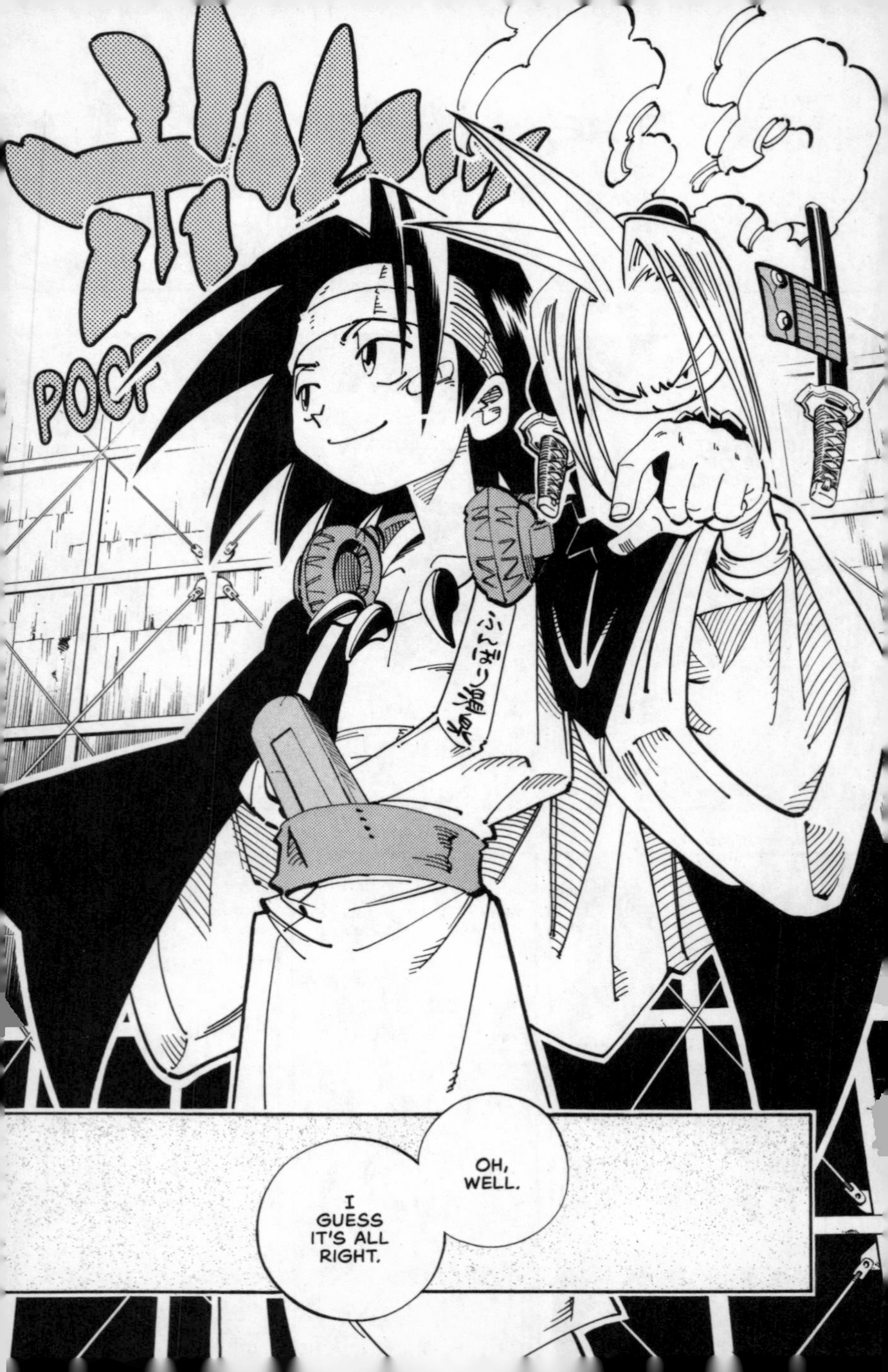
POCK
ふんばり温泉
OH, WELL.
I GUESS IT'S ALL RIGHT.

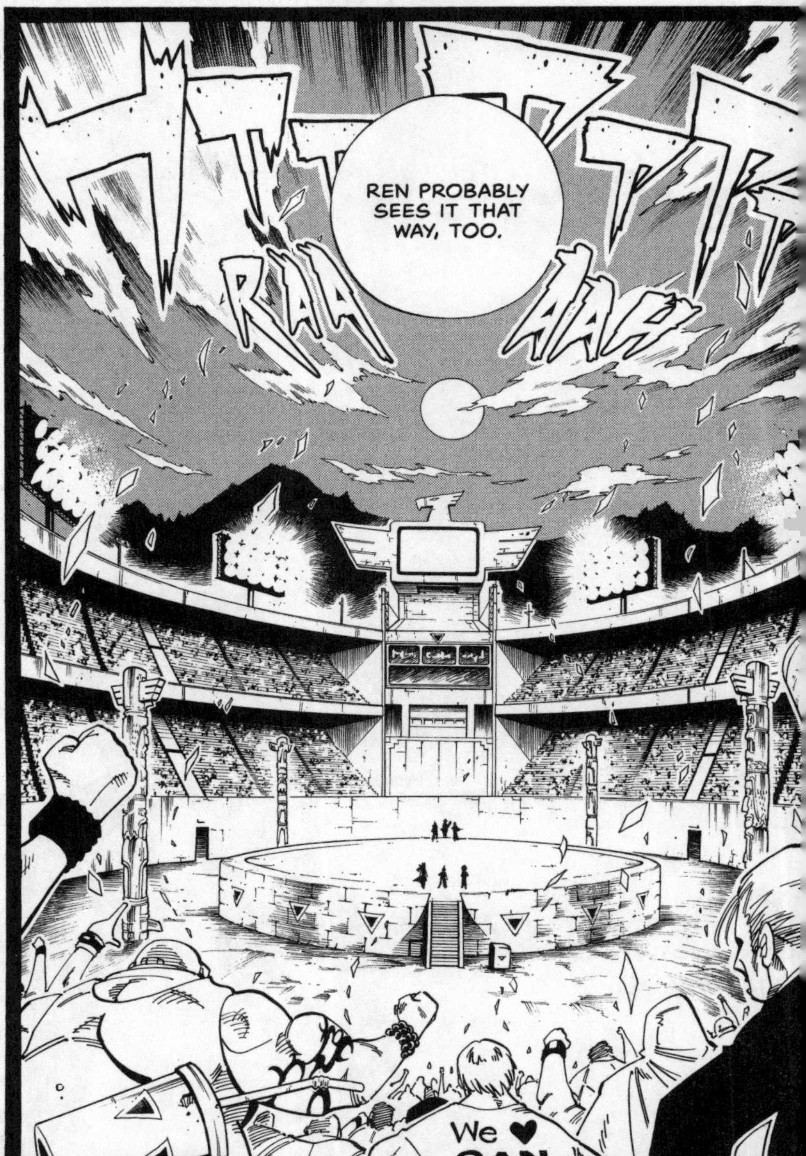

REN PROBABLY SEES IT THAT WAY, TOO.
RAA
AAA
We ♥ GAN

Radim

March 2001

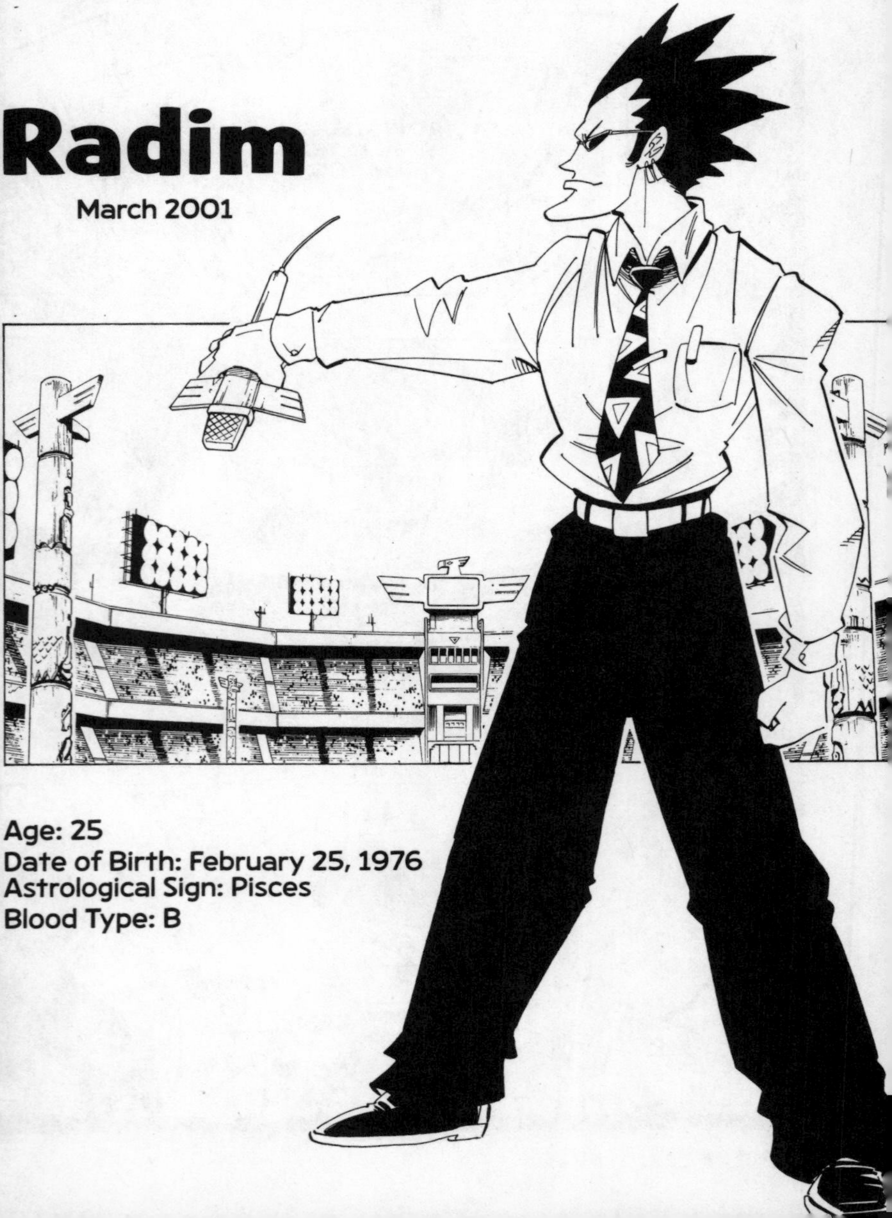

Age: 25
Date of Birth: February 25, 1976
Astrological Sign: Pisces
Blood Type: B

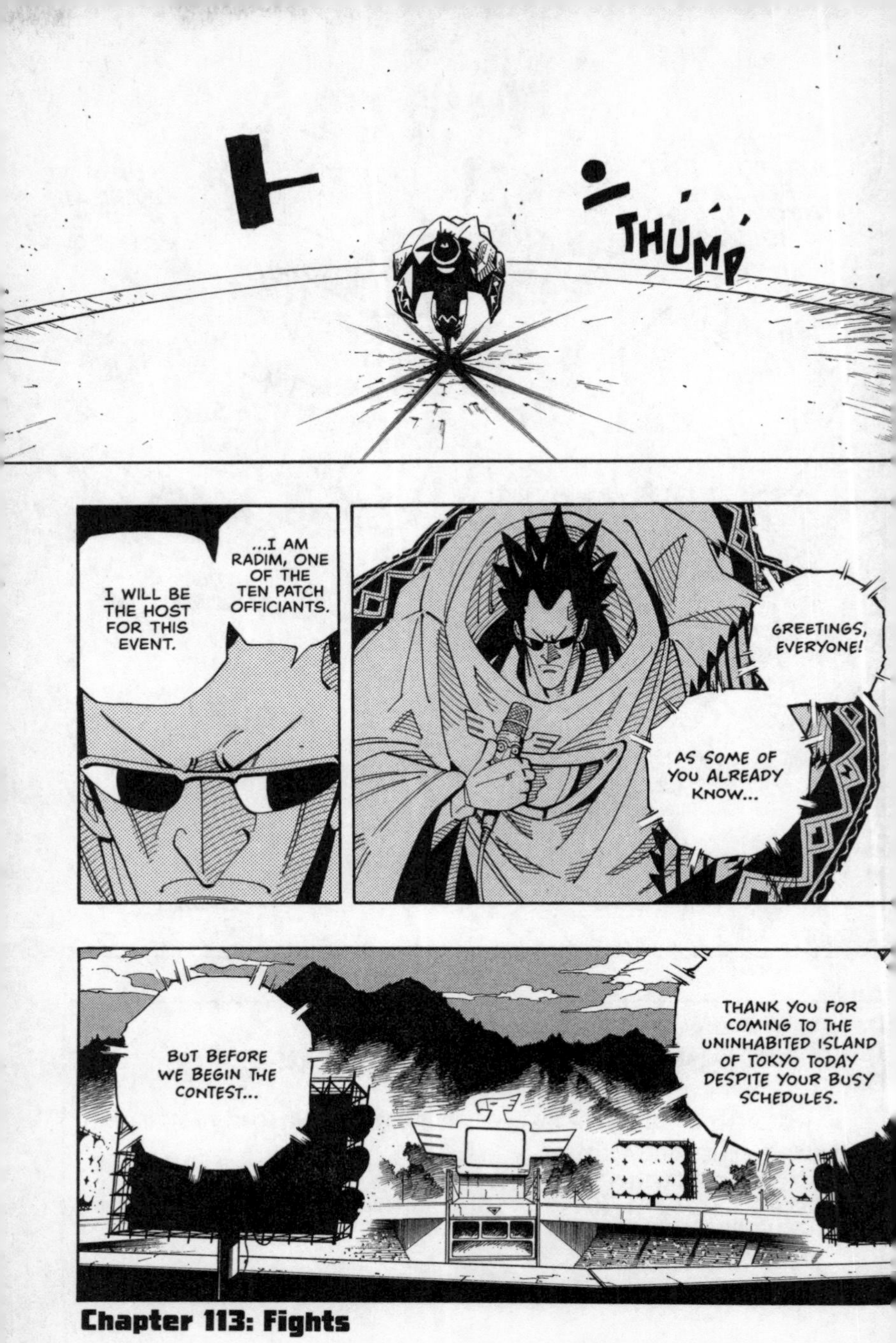
THUMP
GREETINGS, EVERYONE!
AS SOME OF YOU ALREADY KNOW...
...I AM RADIM, ONE OF THE TEN PATCH OFFICIANTS.
I WILL BE THE HOST FOR THIS EVENT.
THANK YOU FOR COMING TO THE UNINHABITED ISLAND OF TOKYO TODAY DESPITE YOUR BUSY SCHEDULES.
BUT BEFORE WE BEGIN THE CONTEST...

Chapter 113: Fights

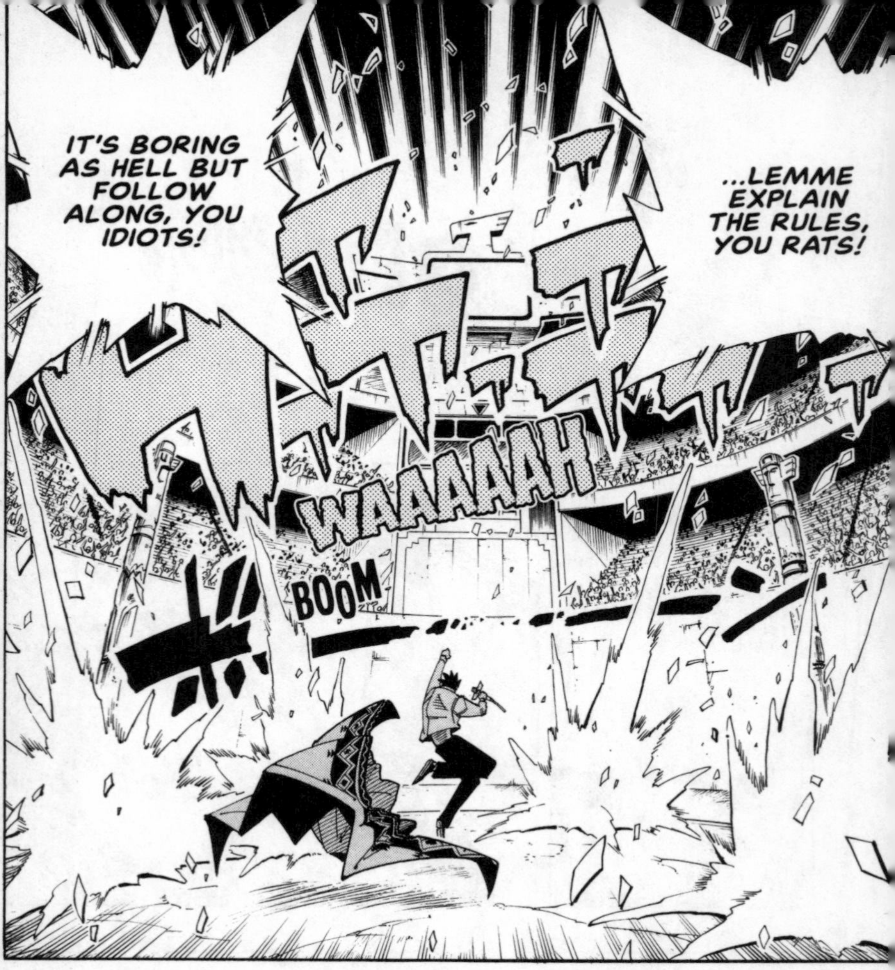
...LEMME EXPLAIN THE RULES, YOU RATS!
IT'S BORING AS HELL BUT FOLLOW ALONG, YOU IDIOTS!
WAAAAAH
BOOM

SHAMAN FIGHT IN TOKYO

RULES FOR TOURNAMENT ONE:

* THIS EVENT INVOLVES THREE-ON-THREE BATTLES WITH NO TIME LIMITS.
* SPIRIT ALLIES ARE ALLOWED.
* A TEAM LOSES WHEN NONE OF ITS MEMBERS CAN ENGAGE THEIR OVER SOULS, A MEMBER LEAVES THE FIGHTING AREA (I.E., GOES OUTSIDE THE TOTEM POLES), OR THE TEAM DECIDES NOT TO CONTINUE.

Chapter 113:

Fights

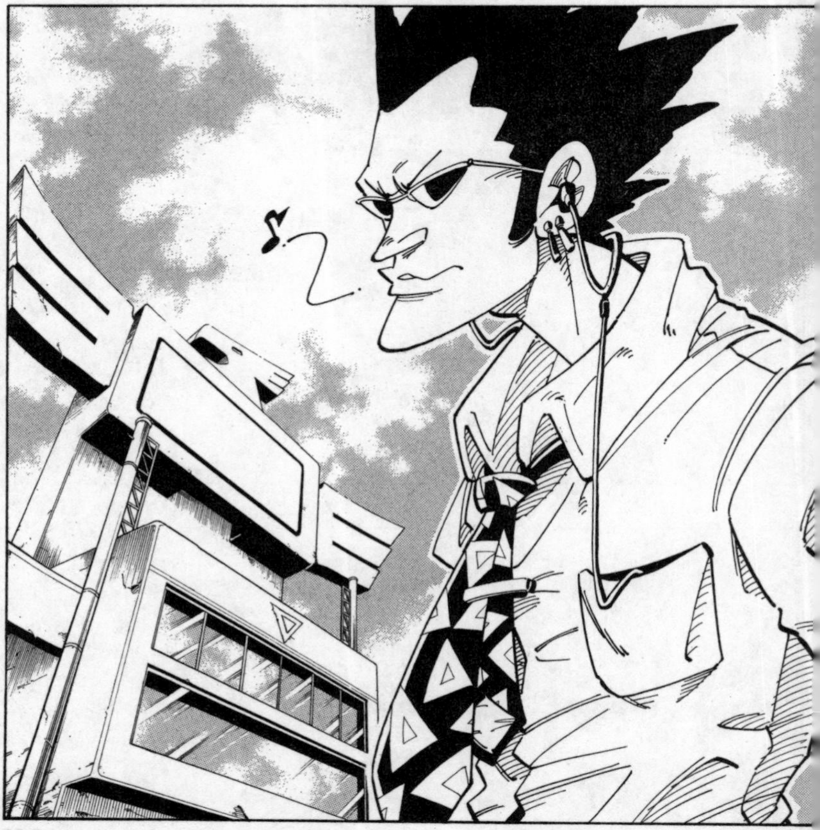

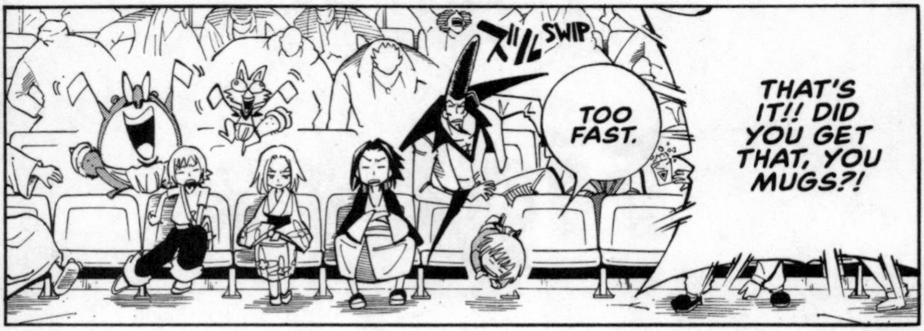
THAT'S IT!! DID YOU GET THAT, YOU MUGS?!
SWIP
TOO FAST.

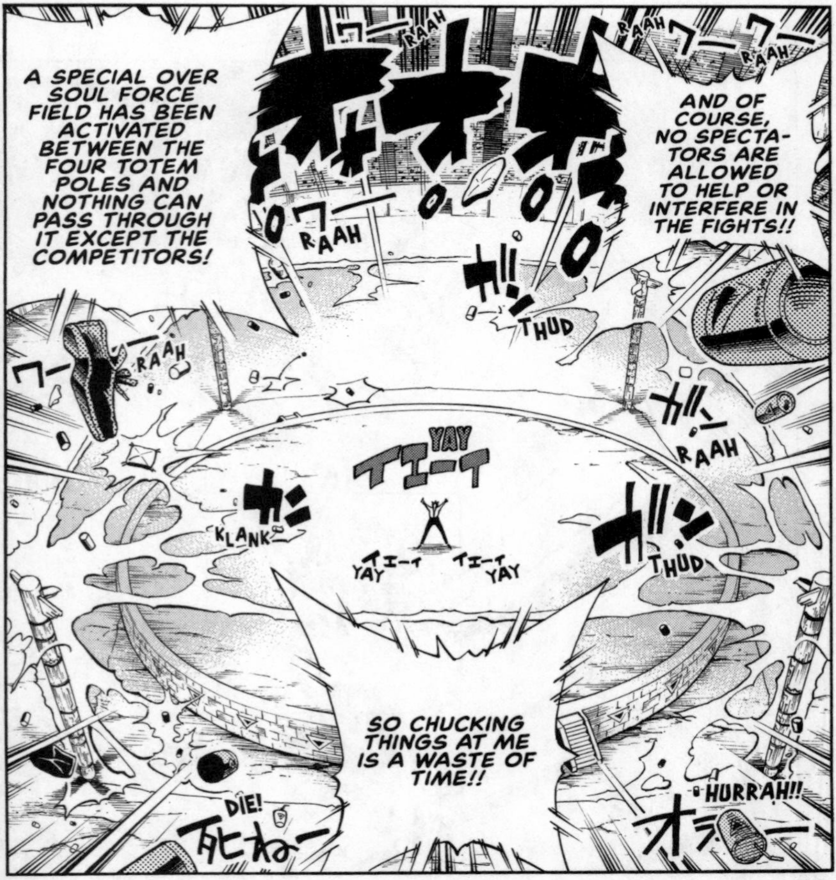
RAAH
RAAH
RAAH
A SPECIAL OVER SOUL FORCE FIELD HAS BEEN ACTIVATED BETWEEN THE FOUR TOTEM POLES AND NOTHING CAN PASS THROUGH IT EXCEPT THE COMPETITORS!
AND OF COURSE, NO SPECTATORS ARE ALLOWED TO HELP OR INTERFERE IN THE FIGHTS!!
RAAH
THUD
RAAH
RAAH
YAY
KLANK
THUD
YAY
YAY
SO CHUCKING THINGS AT ME IS A WASTE OF TIME!!
HURRAH!!
DIE!

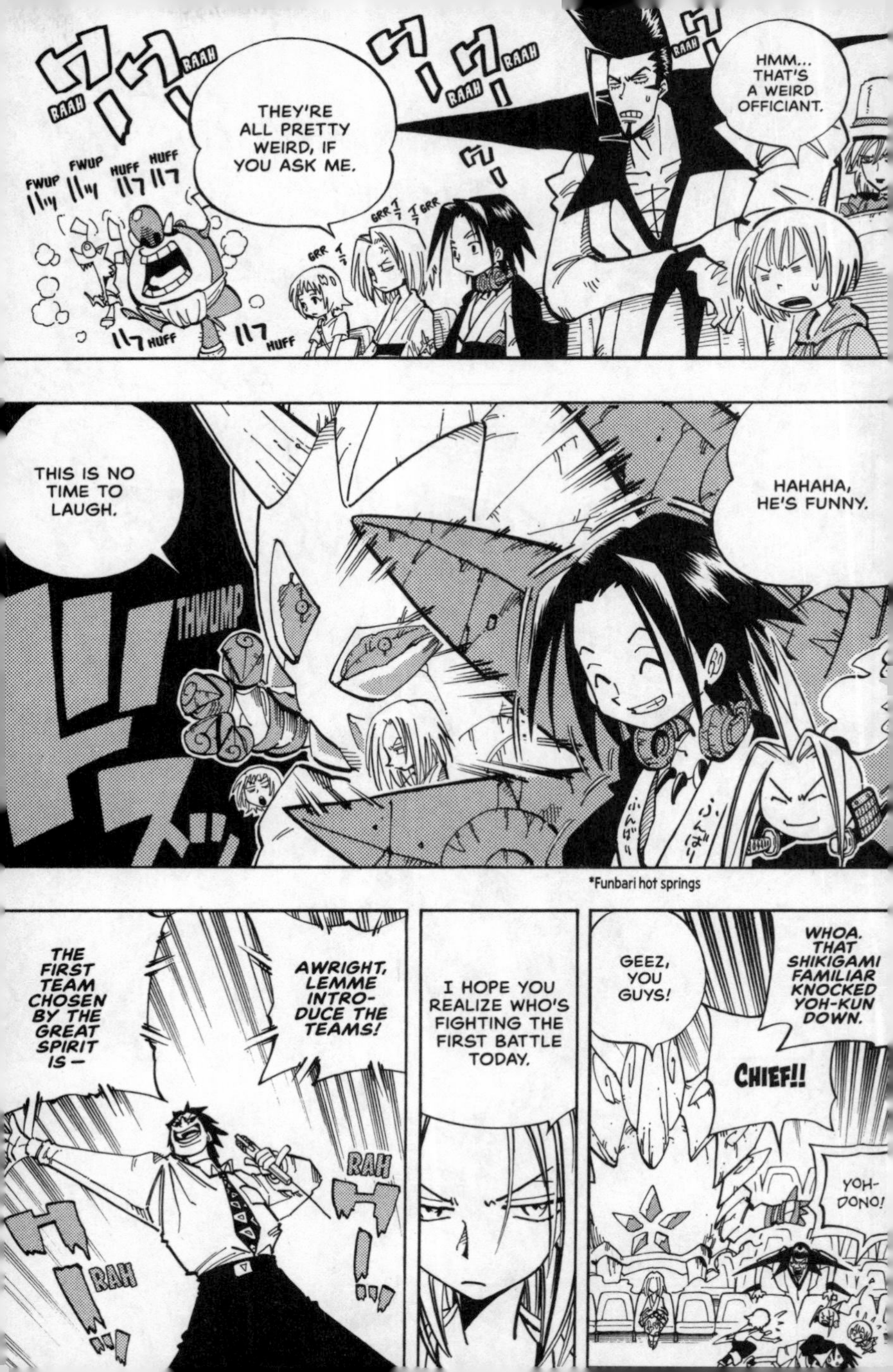
RAAH
HMM... THAT'S A WEIRD OFFICIANT.
RAAH
RAAH
RAAH
THEY'RE ALL PRETTY WEIRD, IF YOU ASK ME.
RAAH
RAAH
GRR
GRR
GRR
HUFF
HUFF
FWUP
FWUP
HUFF
HUFF
HAHAHA, HE'S FUNNY.
THWUMP
THIS IS NO TIME TO LAUGH.
WHOA. THAT SHIKIGAMI FAMILIAR KNOCKED YOH-KUN DOWN.
GEEZ, YOU GUYS!
CHIEF!!
YOH-DONO!
I HOPE YOU REALIZE WHO'S FIGHTING THE FIRST BATTLE TODAY.
RAH
AWRIGHT, LEMME INTRO-DUCE THE TEAMS!
THE FIRST TEAM CHOSEN BY THE GREAT SPIRIT IS—
RAH

*Funbari hot springs

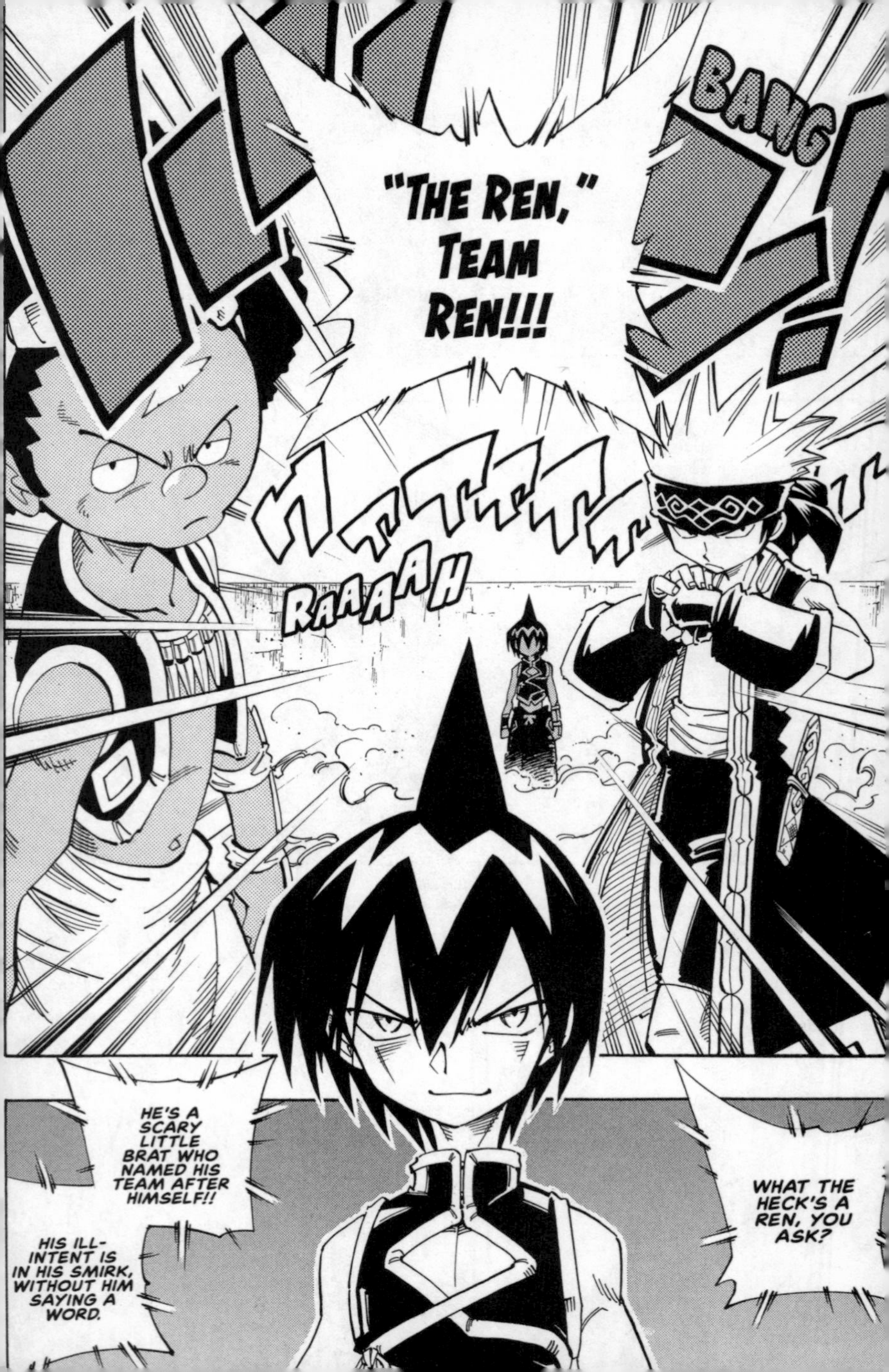
BANG
"THE REN," TEAM REN!!!
RAAAAH
WHAT THE HECK'S A REN, YOU ASK?
HE'S A SCARY LITTLE BRAT WHO NAMED HIS TEAM AFTER HIMSELF!!
HIS ILL-INTENT IS IN HIS SMIRK, WITHOUT HIM SAYING A WORD.

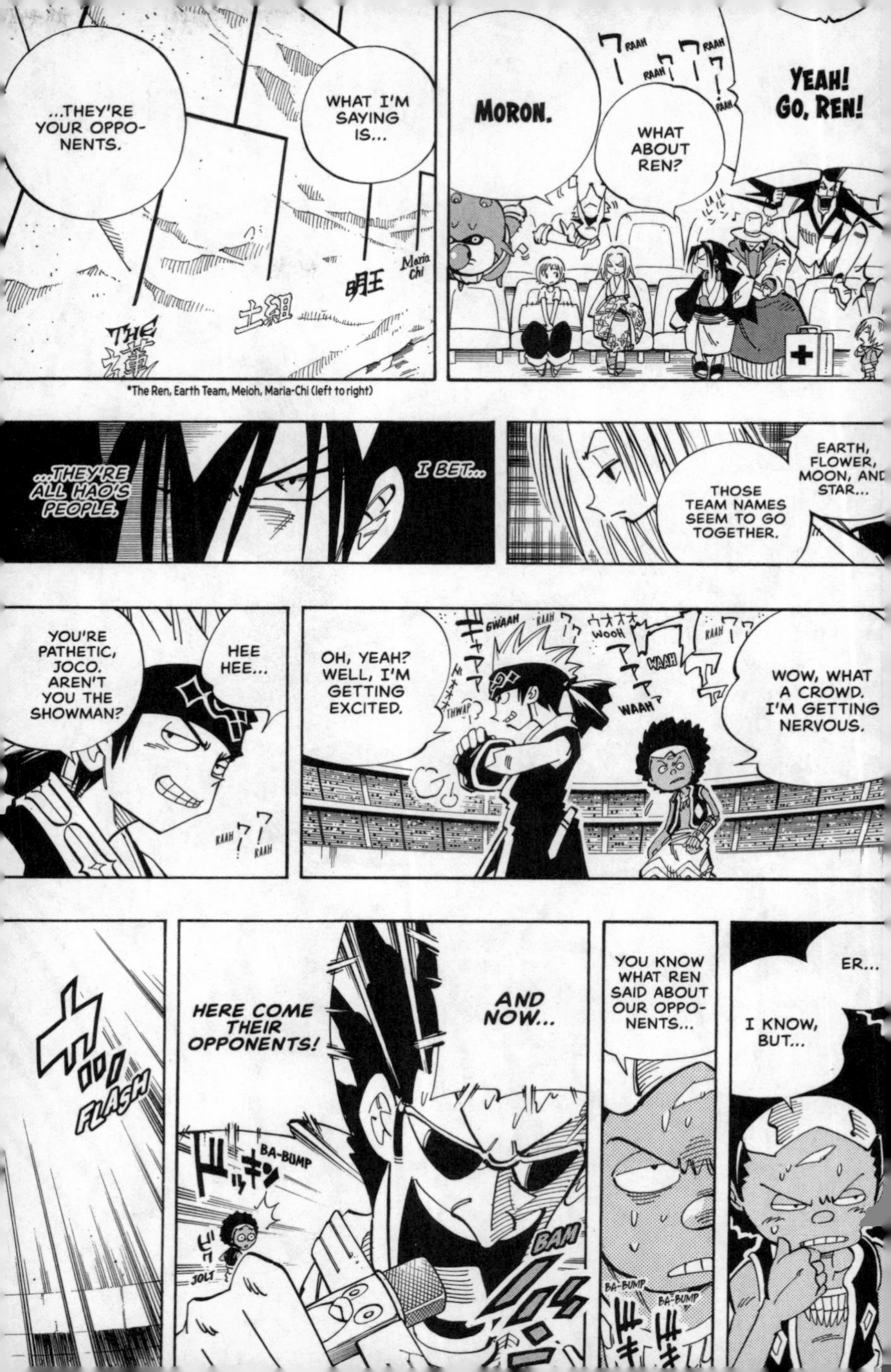
YEAH! GO, REN!
RAAH RAAH RAAH RAAH
WHAT ABOUT REN?
LA LA
MORON.
WHAT I'M SAYING IS...
...THEY'RE YOUR OPPONENTS.
Maria Chi
明王
土組
THE
*The Ren, Earth Team, Meioh, Maria-Chi (left to right)
EARTH, FLOWER, MOON, AND STAR...
THOSE TEAM NAMES SEEM TO GO TOGETHER.
I BET...
...THEY'RE ALL HAO'S PEOPLE.
RAAH
WOW, WHAT A CROWD. I'M GETTING NERVOUS.
WAAH
WAAH
WOOH
RAAH
GWAAH
OH, YEAH? WELL, I'M GETTING EXCITED.
THWAP
HEE HEE...
YOU'RE PATHETIC, JOCO. AREN'T YOU THE SHOWMAN?
RAAH RAAH
ER...
I KNOW, BUT...
YOU KNOW WHAT REN SAID ABOUT OUR OPPONENTS...
BA-BUMP
BA-BUMP
AND NOW...
HERE COME THEIR OPPONENTS!
BA-BUMP
BAM
JOLT
FLASH

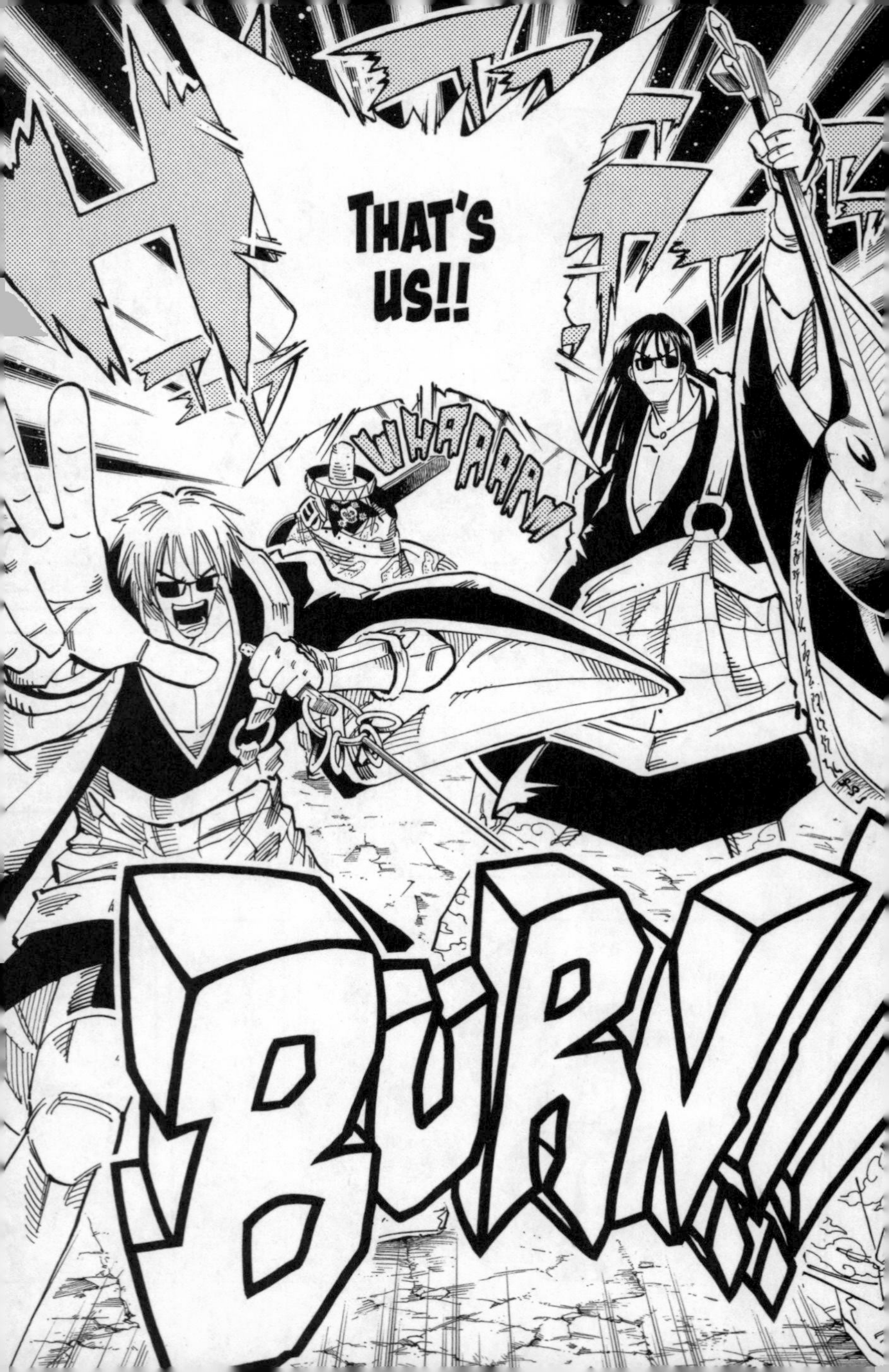
THAT'S US!!
WHAAAAW
BURN!!

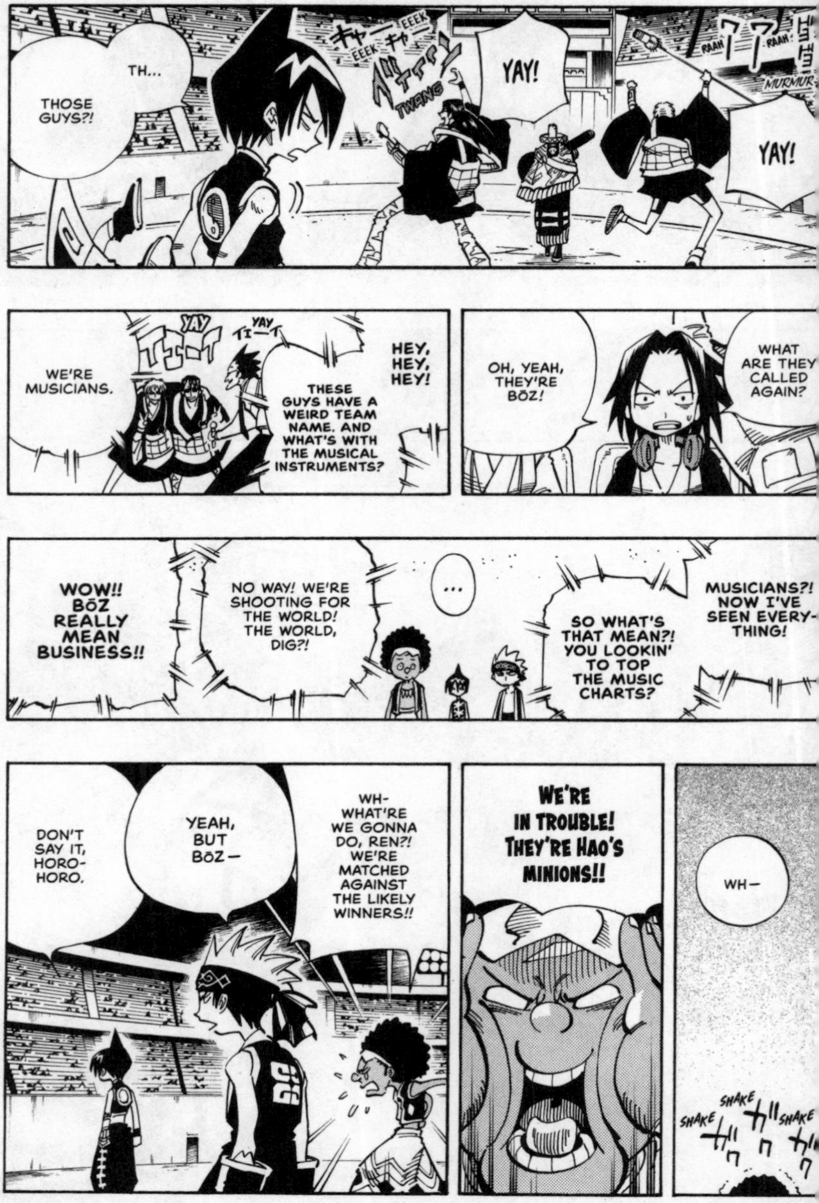
RAAH
RAAH
MURMUR
YAY!
YAY!
EEEK
EEEK
TWANG
TH...
THOSE GUYS?!
WHAT ARE THEY CALLED AGAIN?
OH, YEAH, THEY'RE BŌZ!
HEY, HEY, HEY!
YAY
YAY
THESE GUYS HAVE A WEIRD TEAM NAME. AND WHAT'S WITH THE MUSICAL INSTRUMENTS?
WE'RE MUSICIANS.
MUSICIANS?! NOW I'VE SEEN EVERY-THING!
SO WHAT'S THAT MEAN?! YOU LOOKIN' TO TOP THE MUSIC CHARTS?
...
NO WAY! WE'RE SHOOTING FOR THE WORLD! THE WORLD, DIG?!
WOW!! BŌZ REALLY MEAN BUSINESS!!
WH—
SHAKE
SHAKE
SHAKE
WE'RE IN TROUBLE! THEY'RE HAO'S MINIONS!!
WH-WHAT'RE WE GONNA DO, REN?! WE'RE MATCHED AGAINST THE LIKELY WINNERS!!
YEAH, BUT BŌZ—
DON'T SAY IT, HORO-HORO.

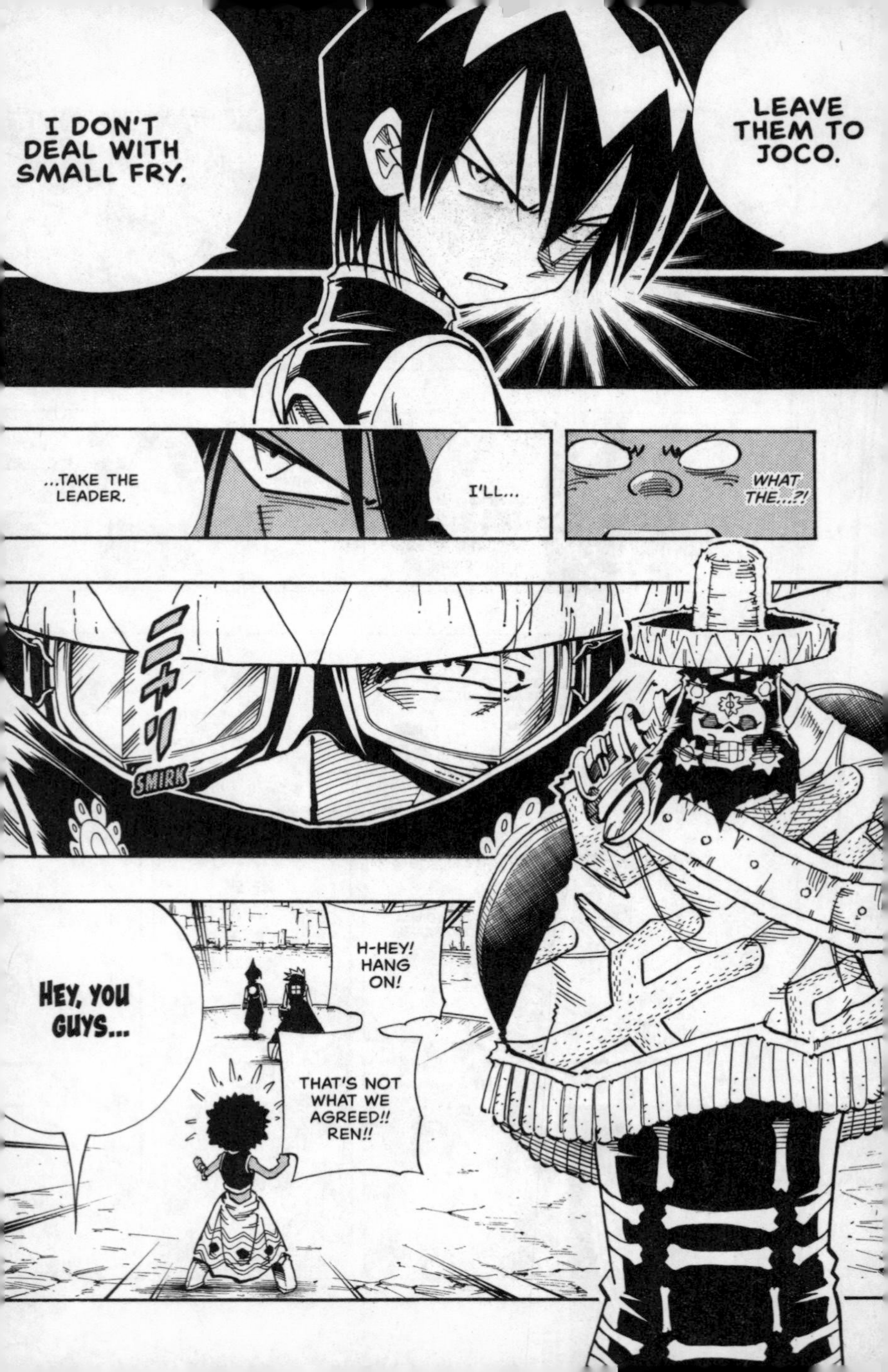
LEAVE THEM TO JOCO.
I DON'T DEAL WITH SMALL FRY.
WHAT THE...?!
I'LL...
...TAKE THE LEADER.
SMIRK
H-HEY! HANG ON!
THAT'S NOT WHAT WE AGREED!! REN!!
HEY, YOU GUYS...

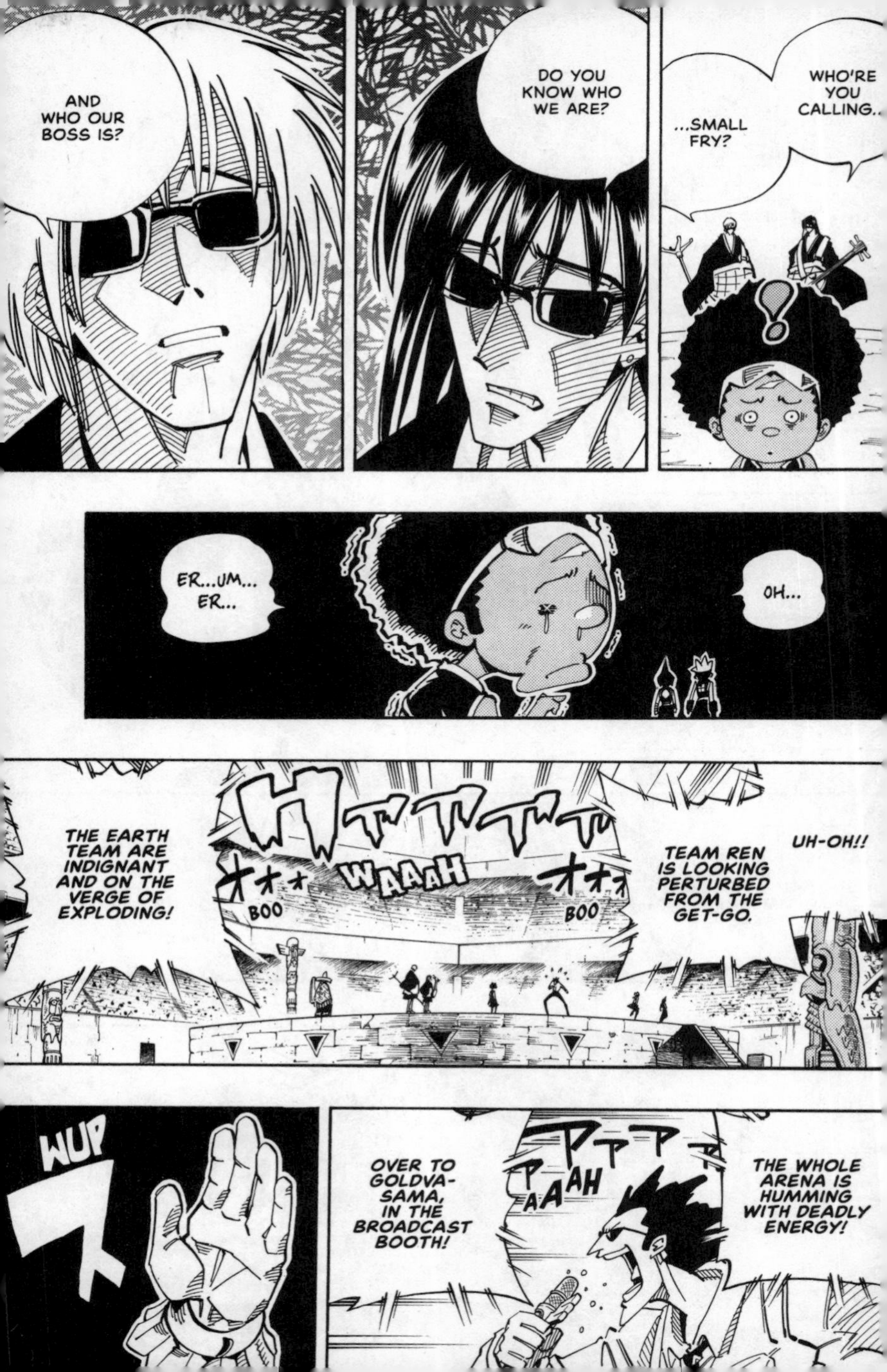
WHO'RE YOU CALLING...
...SMALL FRY?
DO YOU KNOW WHO WE ARE?
AND WHO OUR BOSS IS?
OH...
ER...UM... ER...
UH-OH!!
TEAM REN IS LOOKING PERTURBED FROM THE GET-GO.
BOO
WAAAH
BOO
THE EARTH TEAM ARE INDIGNANT AND ON THE VERGE OF EXPLODING!
THE WHOLE ARENA IS HUMMING WITH DEADLY ENERGY!
AAAH
OVER TO GOLDVA-SAMA, IN THE BROADCAST BOOTH!
WUP

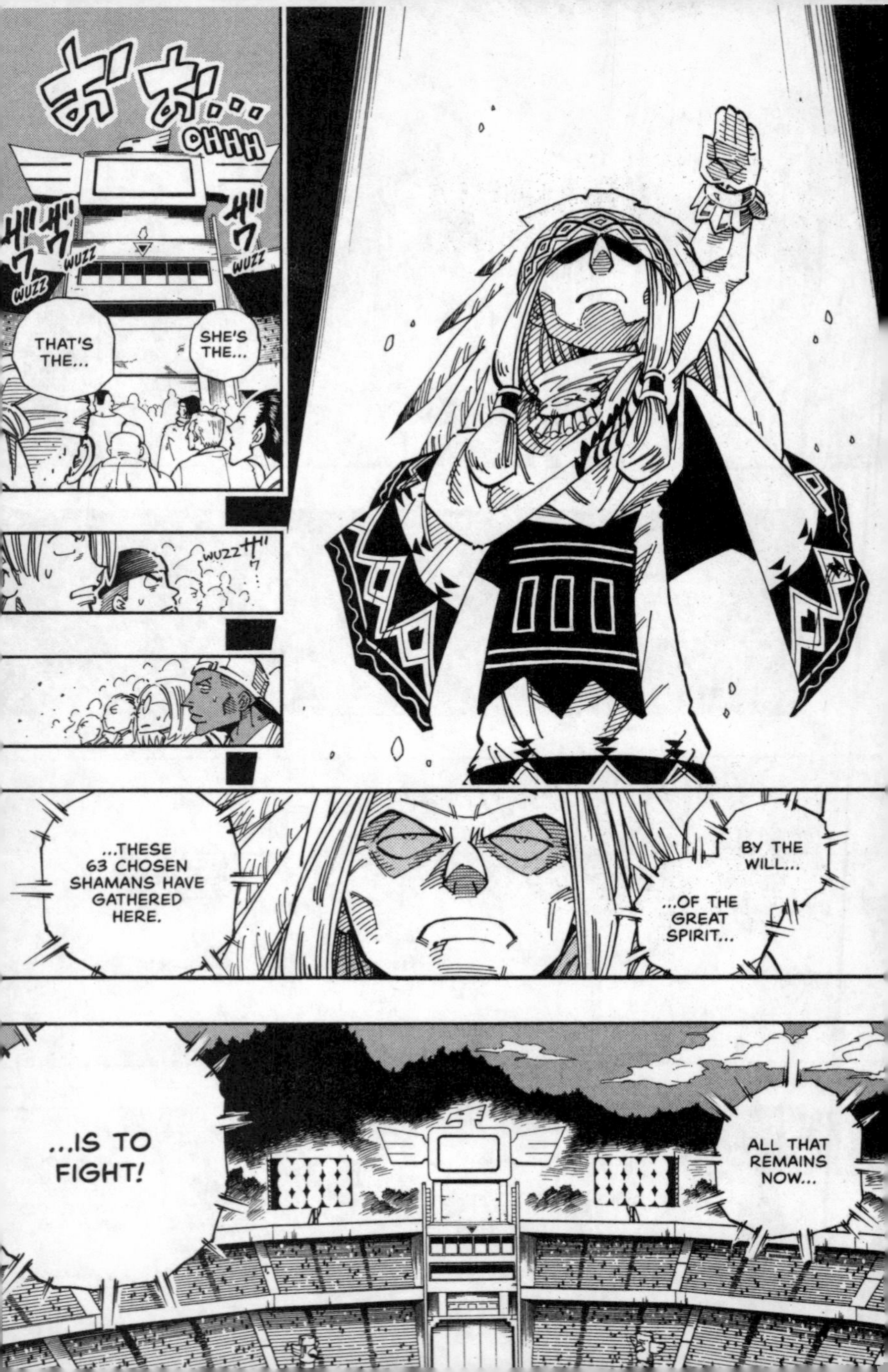
おお...
OHHH
ザワ
WUZZ
ザワ
WUZZ
SHE'S THE...
THAT'S THE...
ザワ
WUZZ
WUZZ ザワ
BY THE WILL...
...OF THE GREAT SPIRIT...
...THESE 63 CHOSEN SHAMANS HAVE GATHERED HERE.
ALL THAT REMAINS NOW...
...IS TO FIGHT!

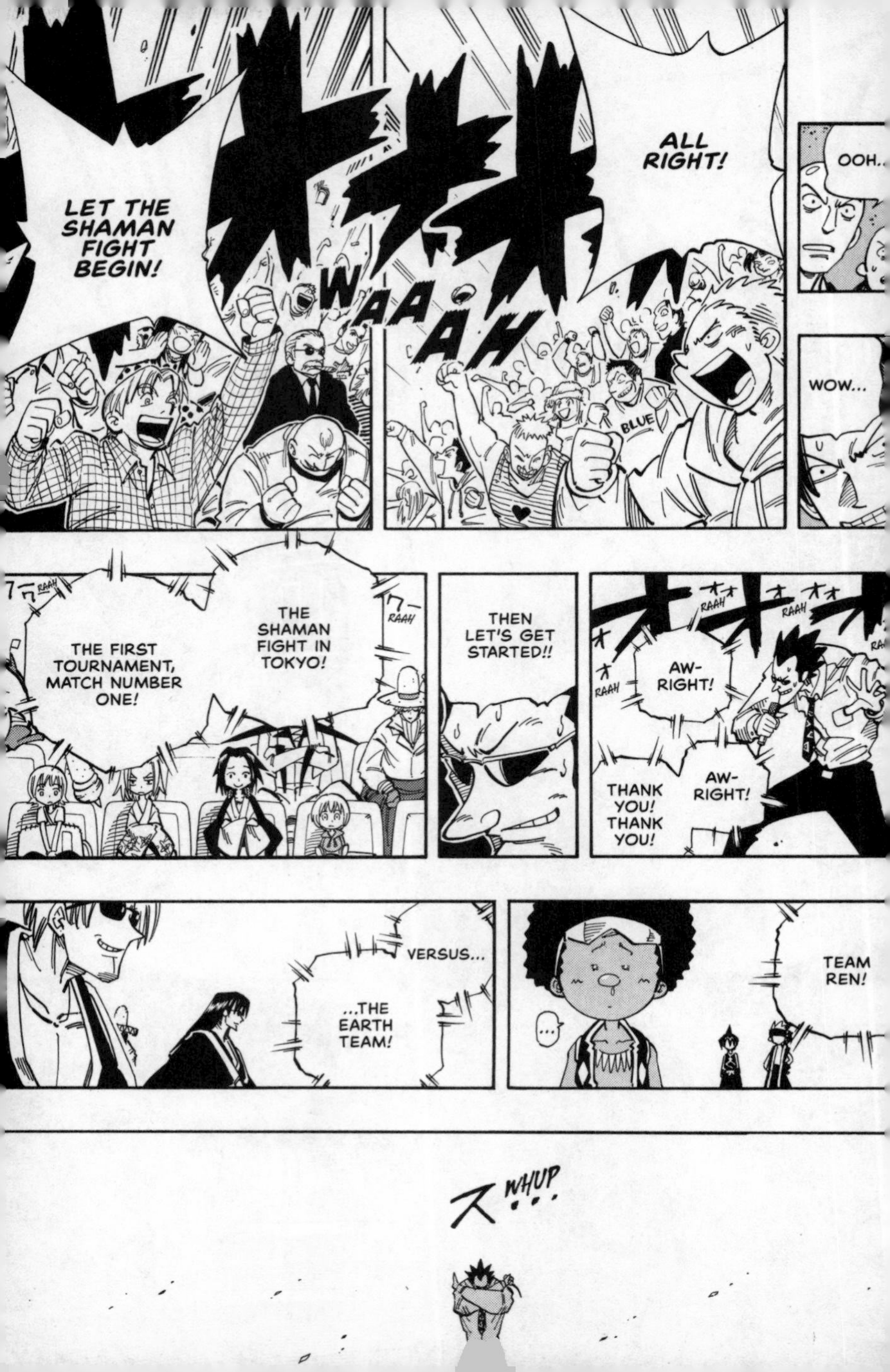

OOH...
WOW...
ALL RIGHT!
WAAAAH
LET THE SHAMAN FIGHT BEGIN!
RAAH
AW-RIGHT!
AW-RIGHT!
THANK YOU! THANK YOU!
THEN LET'S GET STARTED!!
RAAH
THE SHAMAN FIGHT IN TOKYO!
THE FIRST TOURNAMENT, MATCH NUMBER ONE!
TEAM REN!
...
VERSUS...
...THE EARTH TEAM!
WHUP...

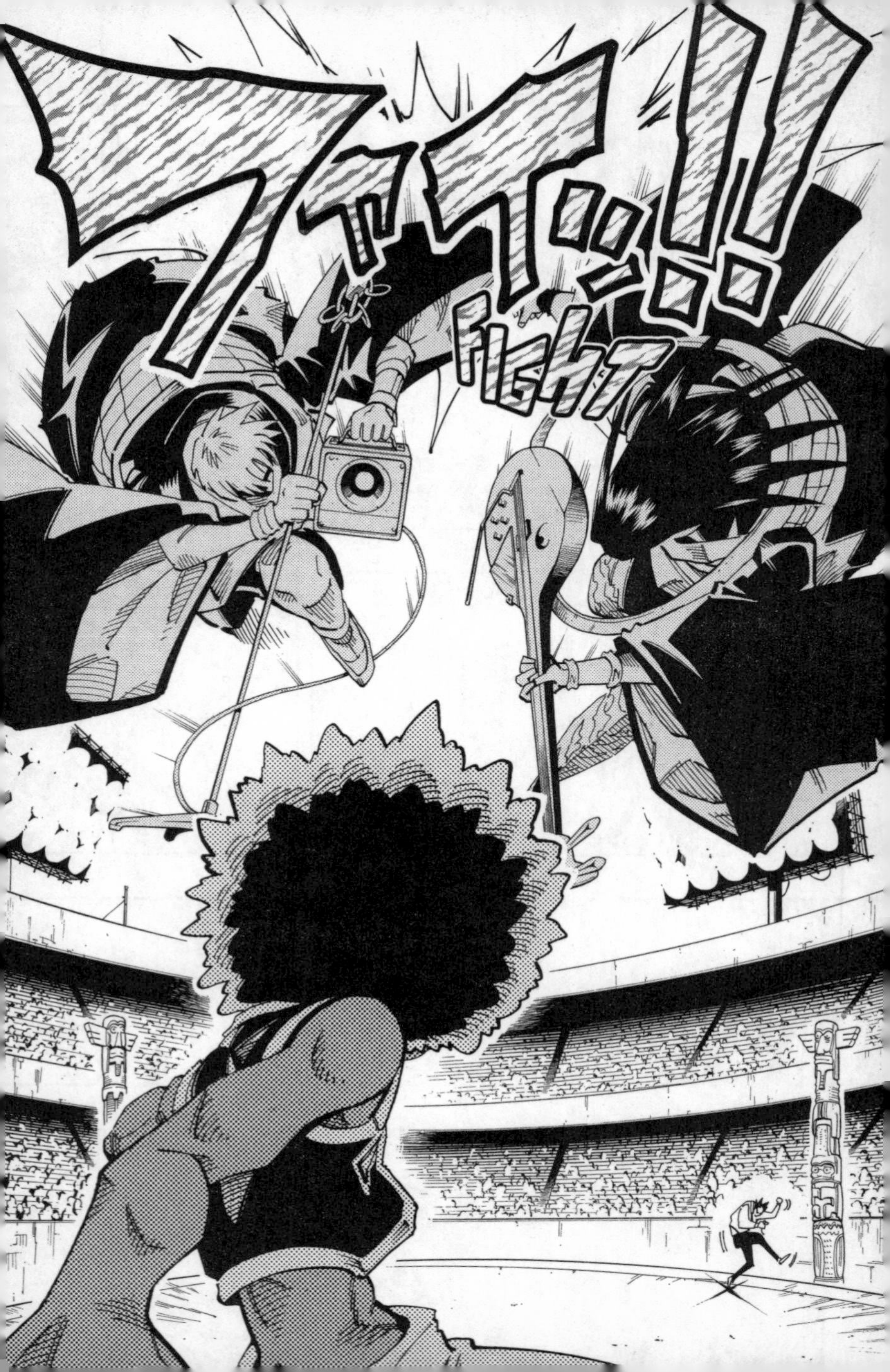
ファイッ!!
FIGHT

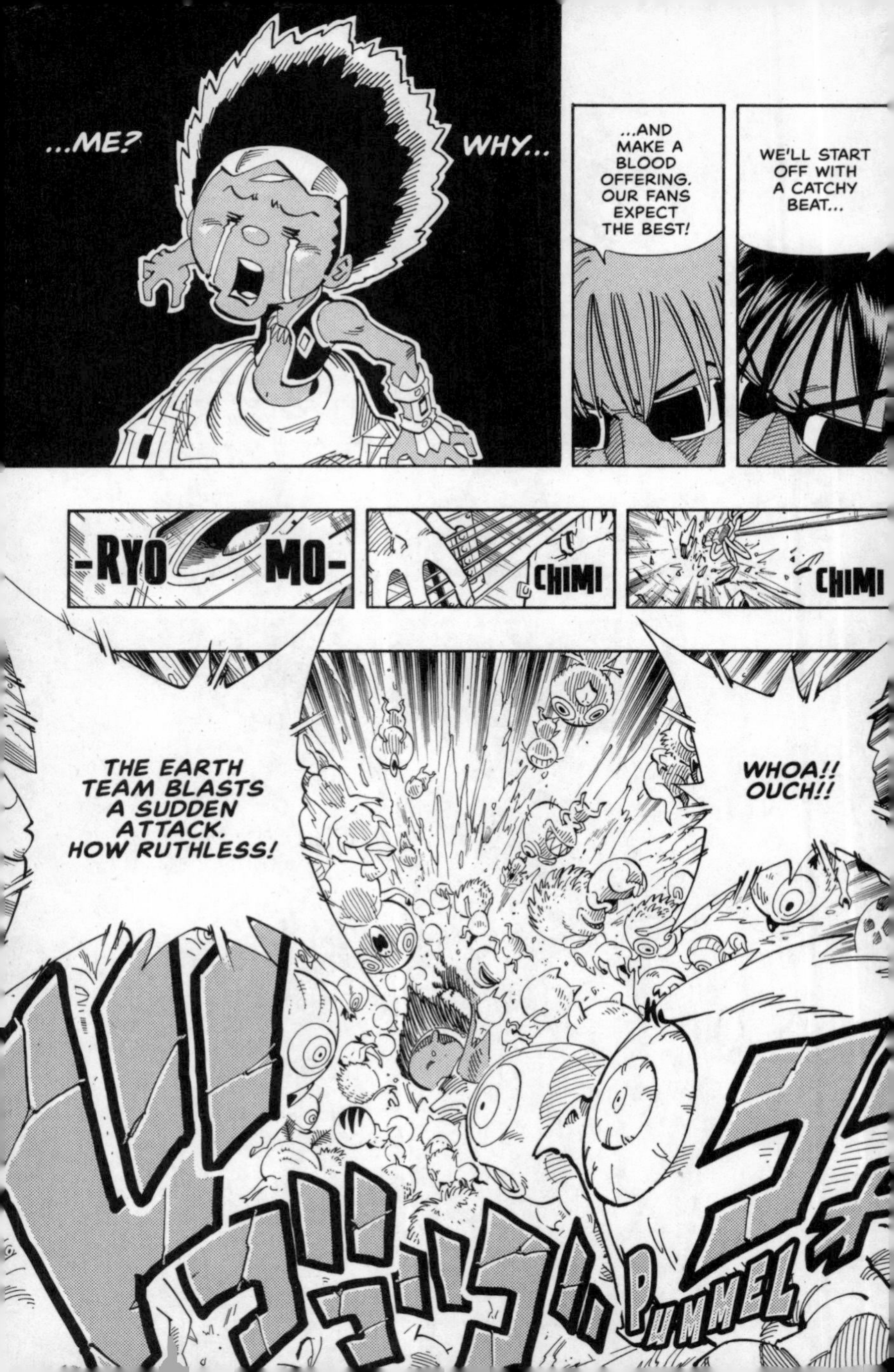
WE'LL START OFF WITH A CATCHY BEAT...
...AND MAKE A BLOOD OFFERING. OUR FANS EXPECT THE BEST!
WHY...
...ME?
CHIMI
CHIMI
-RYO
MO-
WHOA!! OUCH!!
THE EARTH TEAM BLASTS A SUDDEN ATTACK. HOW RUTHLESS!
PUMMEL

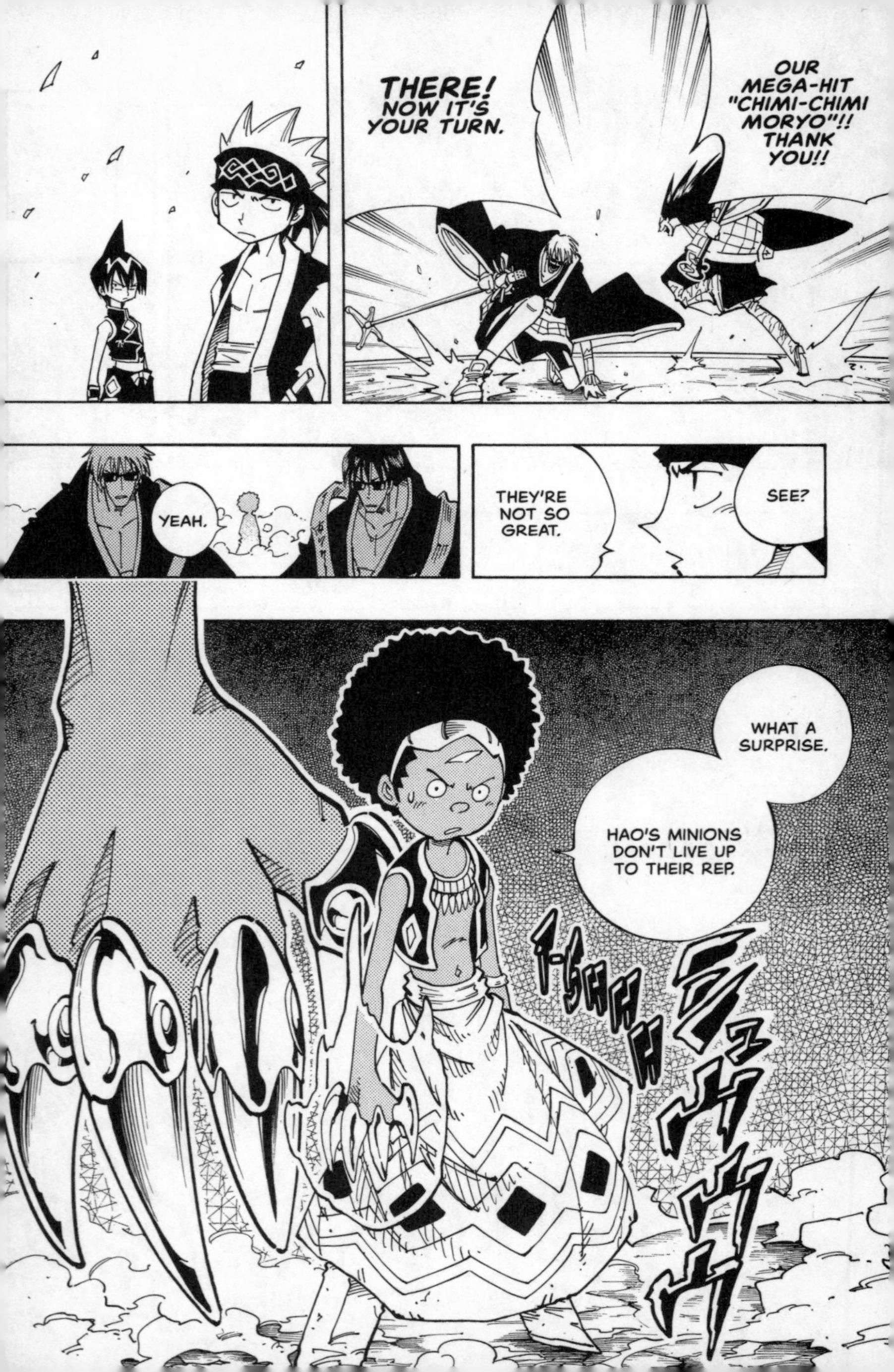
OUR MEGA-HIT "CHIMI-CHIMI MORYO"!! THANK YOU!!
THERE! NOW IT'S YOUR TURN.
SEE?
THEY'RE NOT SO GREAT.
YEAH.
WHAT A SURPRISE.
HAO'S MINIONS DON'T LIVE UP TO THEIR REP.

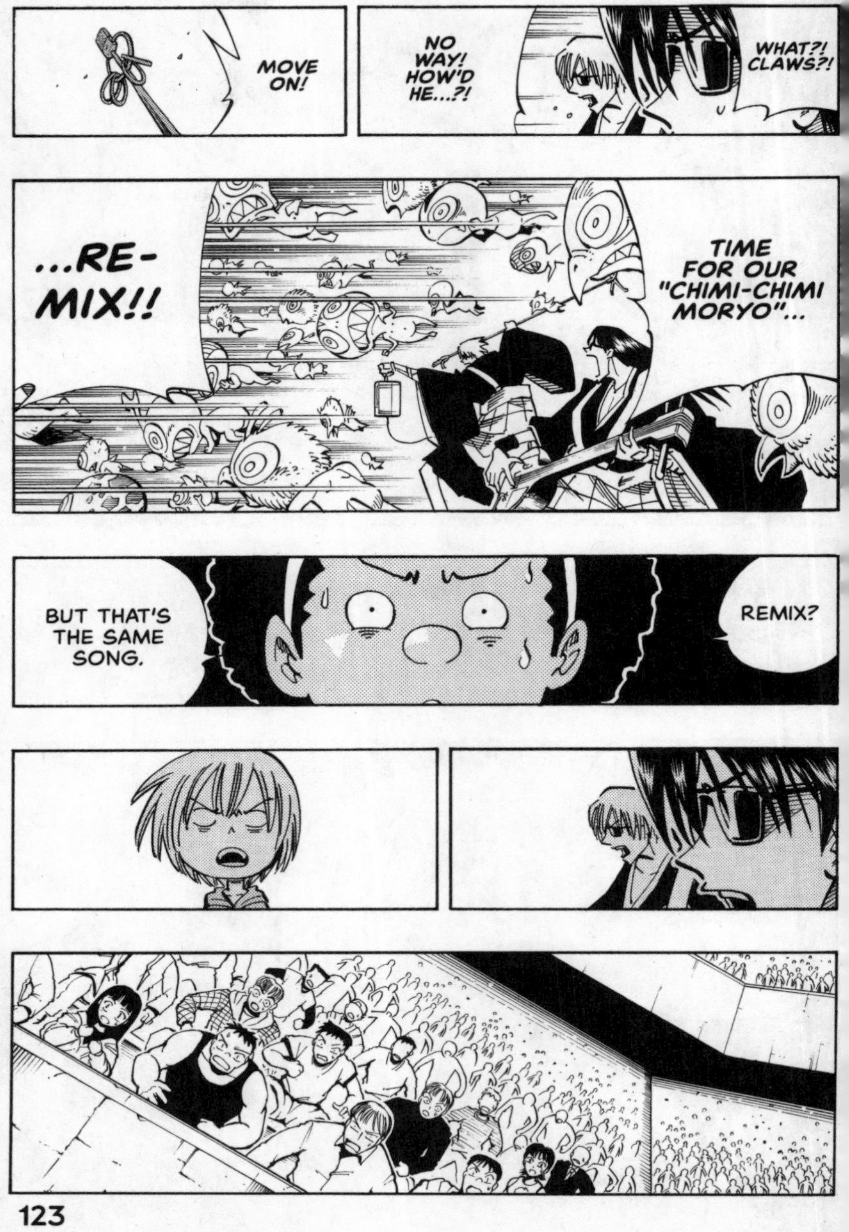
WHAT?! CLAWS?!
NO WAY! HOW'D HE...?!
MOVE ON!
TIME FOR OUR "CHIMI-CHIMI MORYO"...
...RE-MIX!!
REMIX?
BUT THAT'S THE SAME SONG.

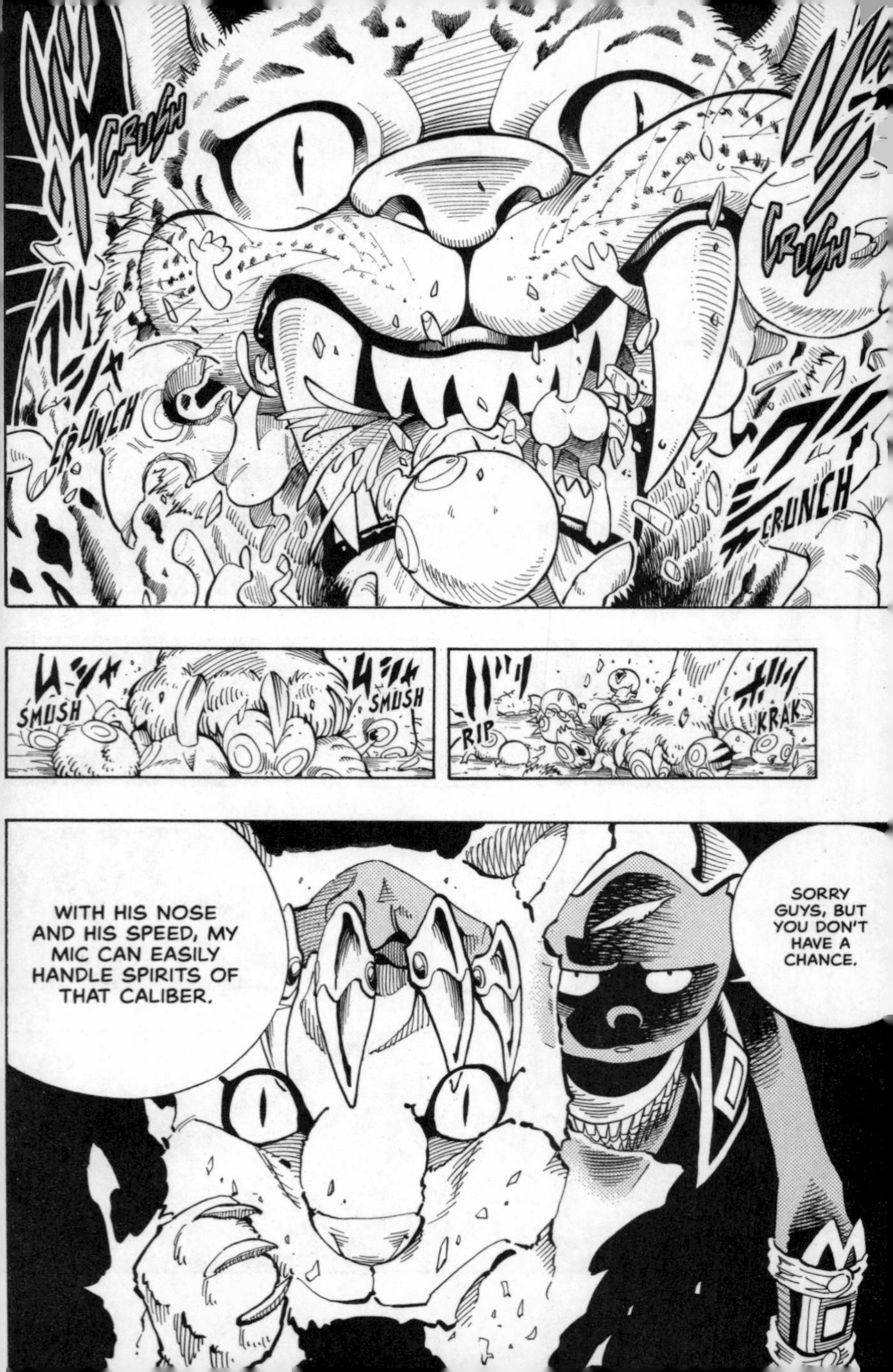
CRUSH
CRUNCH
CRUSH
CRUNCH
RIP
KRAK
SMUSH
SMUSH
SORRY GUYS, BUT YOU DON'T HAVE A CHANCE.
WITH HIS NOSE AND HIS SPEED, MY MIC CAN EASILY HANDLE SPIRITS OF THAT CALIBER.

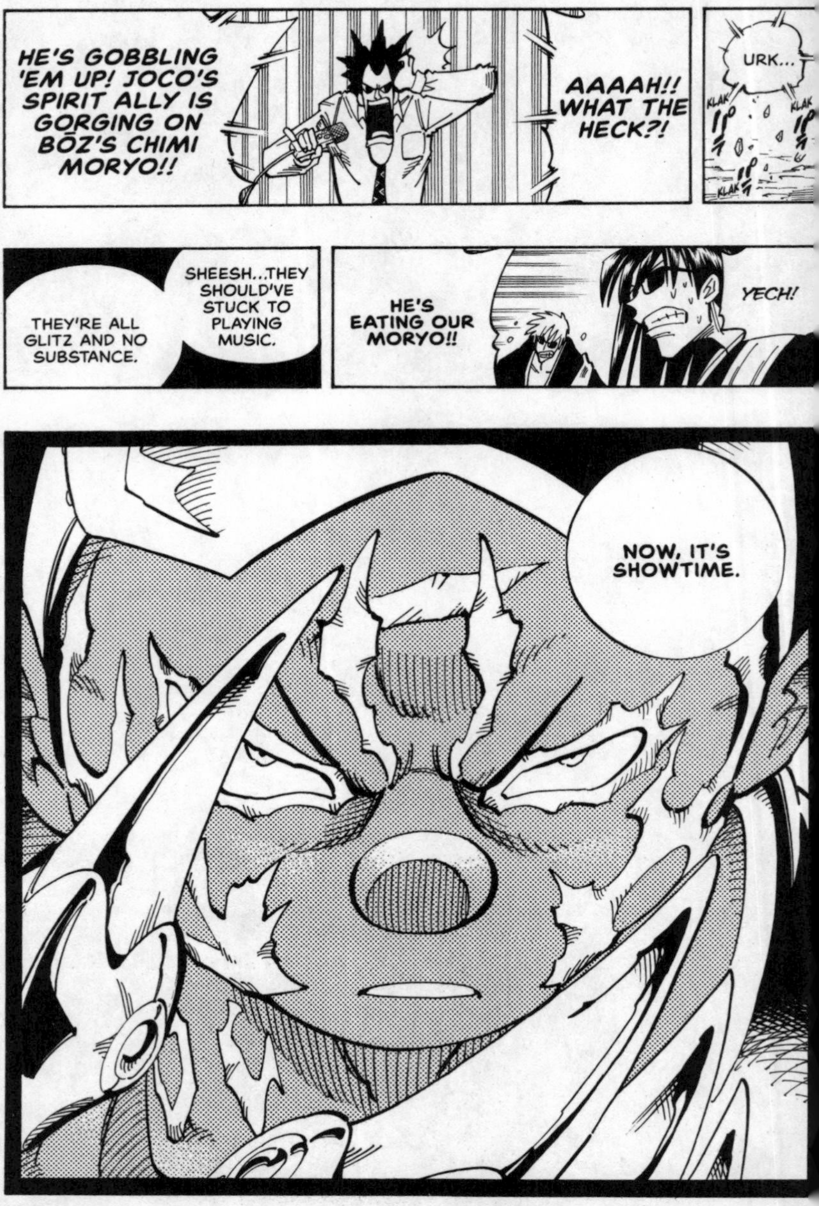
URK...
KLAK
KLAK
KLAK
AAAAH!! WHAT THE HECK?!
HE'S GOBBLING 'EM UP! JOCO'S SPIRIT ALLY IS GORGING ON BŌZ'S CHIMI MORYO!!
YECH!
HE'S EATING OUR MORYO!!
SHEESH...THEY SHOULD'VE STUCK TO PLAYING MUSIC.
THEY'RE ALL GLITZ AND NO SUBSTANCE.
NOW, IT'S SHOWTIME.

SHAMAN
KING
13

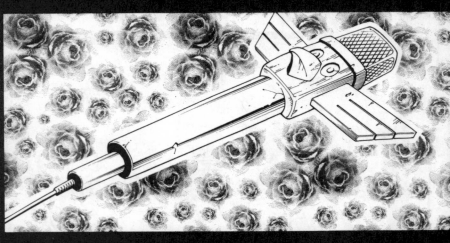

Radim's Favorite Microphone!
(Traditionally Handcrafted)

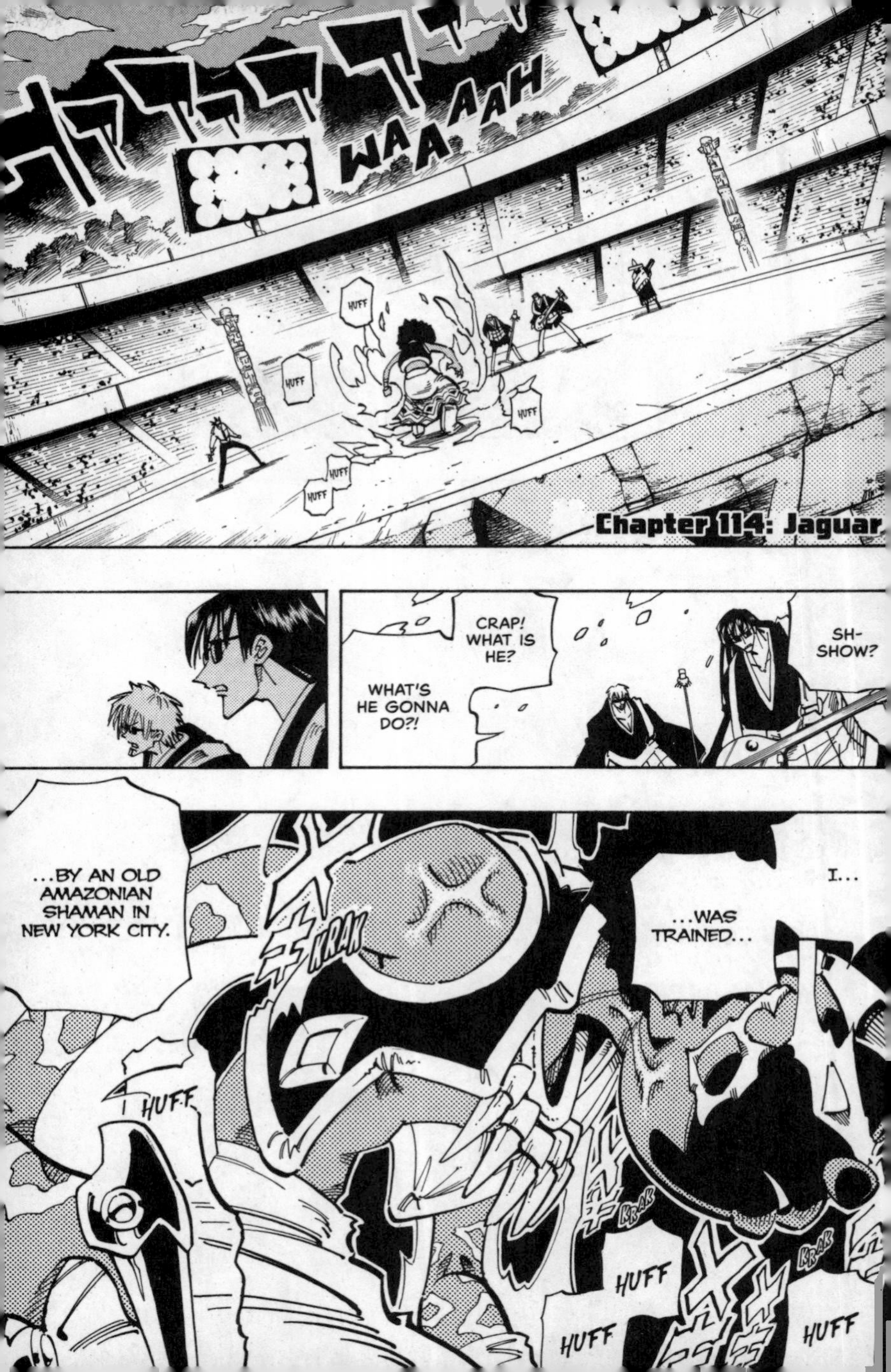
WAAAAH
HUFF
HUFF
HUFF
HUFF
HUFF
Chapter 114: Jaguar
SH- SHOW?
CRAP! WHAT IS HE?
WHAT'S HE GONNA DO?!
I...
...WAS TRAINED...
...BY AN OLD AMAZONIAN SHAMAN IN NEW YORK CITY.
KRAK
HUFF
KRAK
KRAK
HUFF
HUFF
HUFF

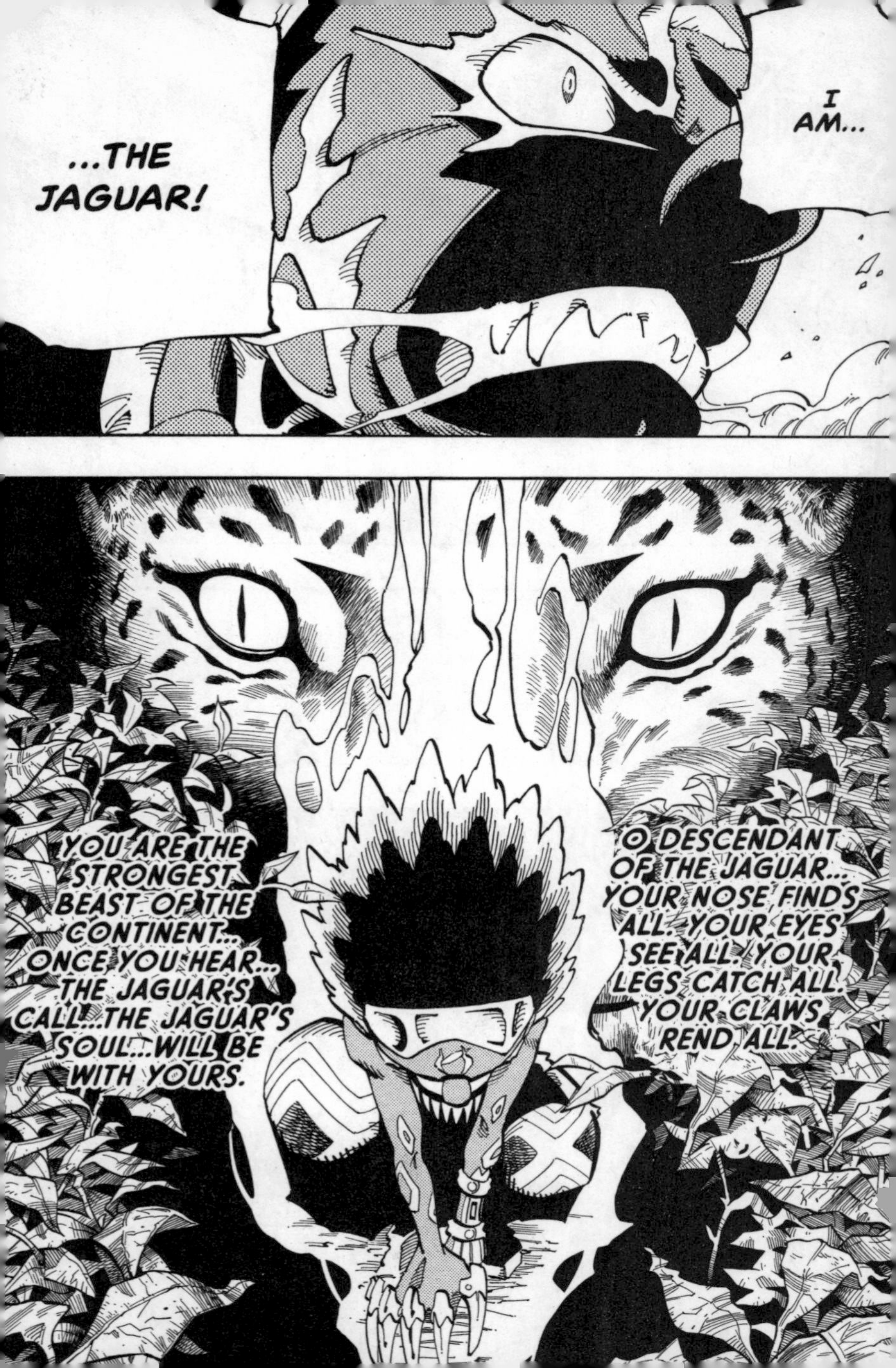
I AM...
...THE JAGUAR!
O DESCENDANT OF THE JAGUAR... YOUR NOSE FINDS ALL. YOUR EYES SEE ALL. YOUR LEGS CATCH ALL. YOUR CLAWS REND ALL.
YOU ARE THE STRONGEST BEAST OF THE CONTINENT... ONCE YOU HEAR... THE JAGUAR'S CALL...THE JAGUAR'S SOUL...WILL BE WITH YOURS.

Chapter 114:

Jaguar

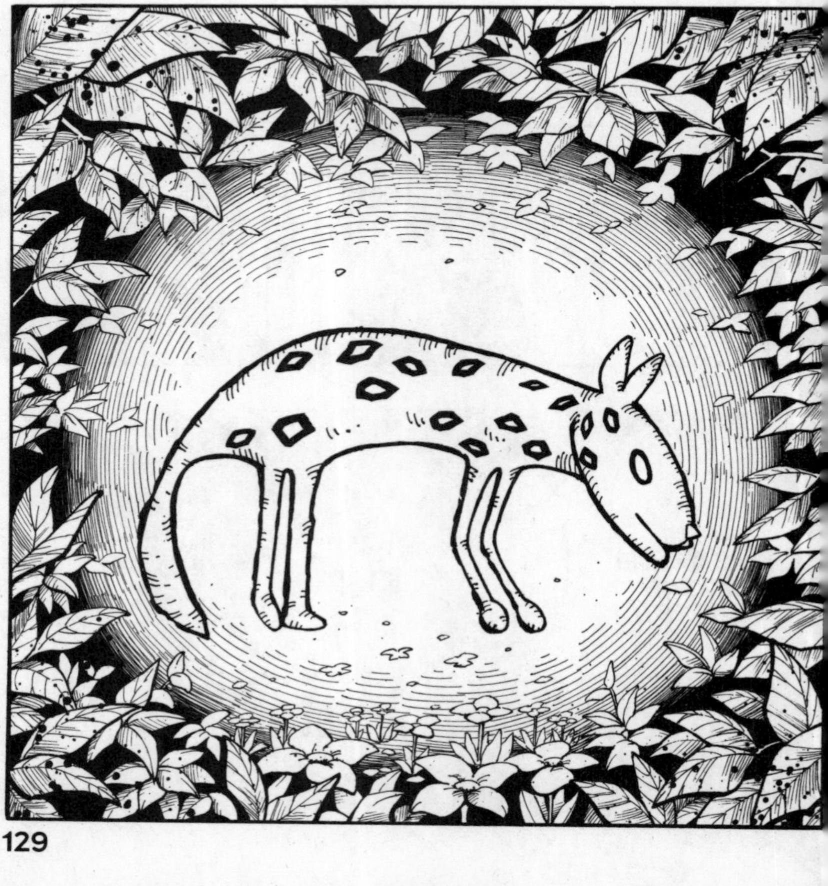

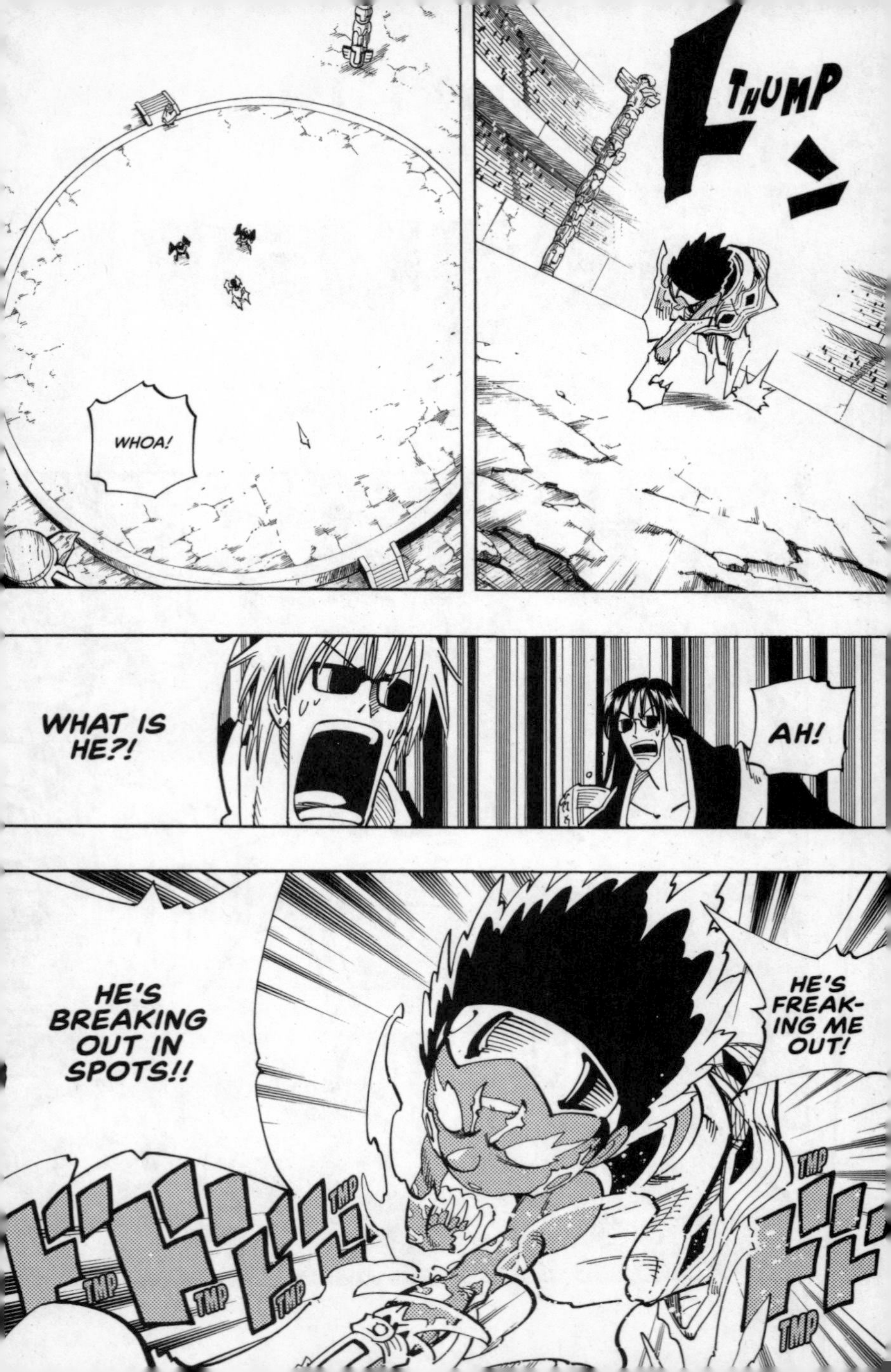
THUMP
WHOA!
AH!
WHAT IS HE?!
HE'S FREAKING ME OUT!
HE'S BREAKING OUT IN SPOTS!!
TMP TMP
TMP TMP TMP TMP

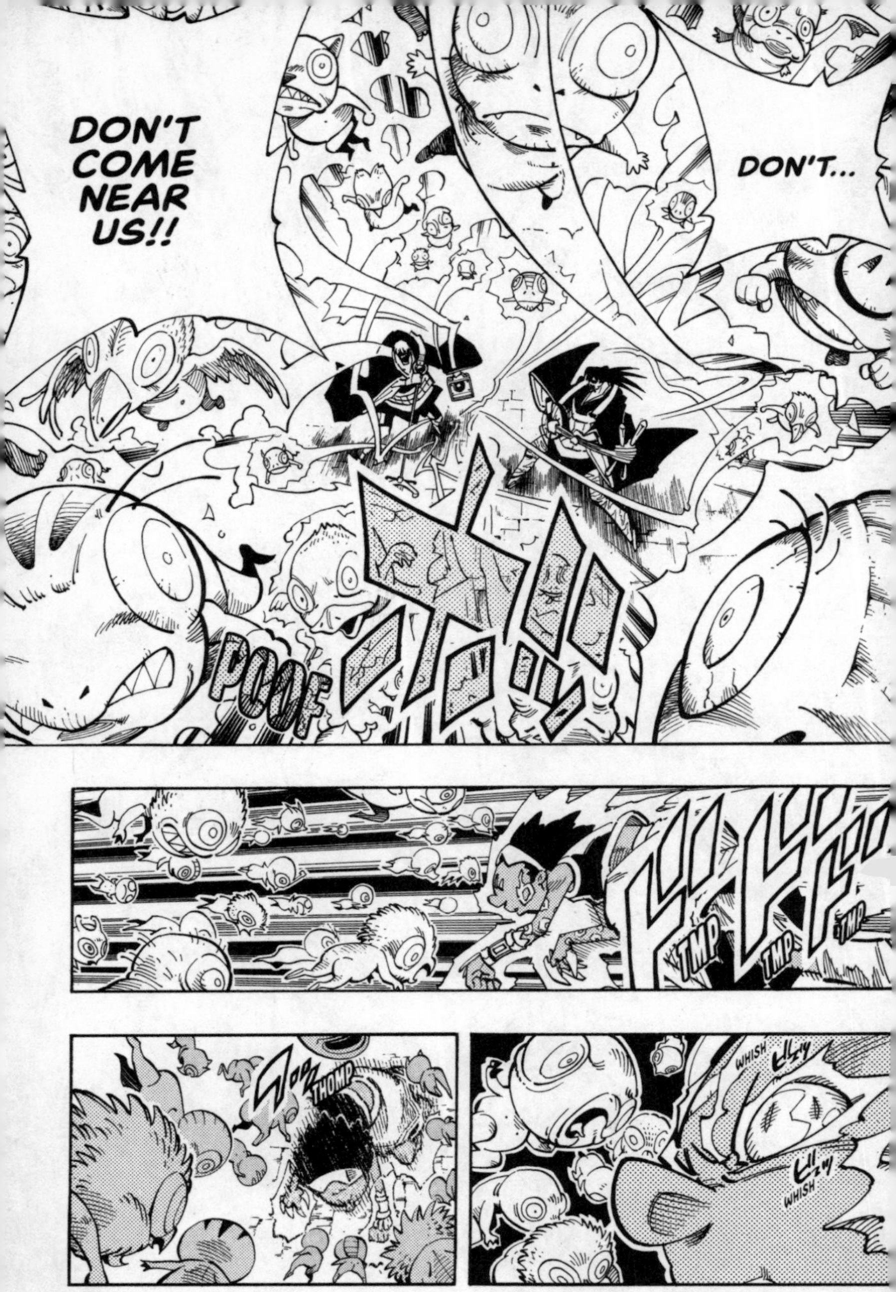
DON'T...
DON'T COME NEAR US!!
POOF
TMP
TMP
TMP
WHISH
WHISH
THOMP

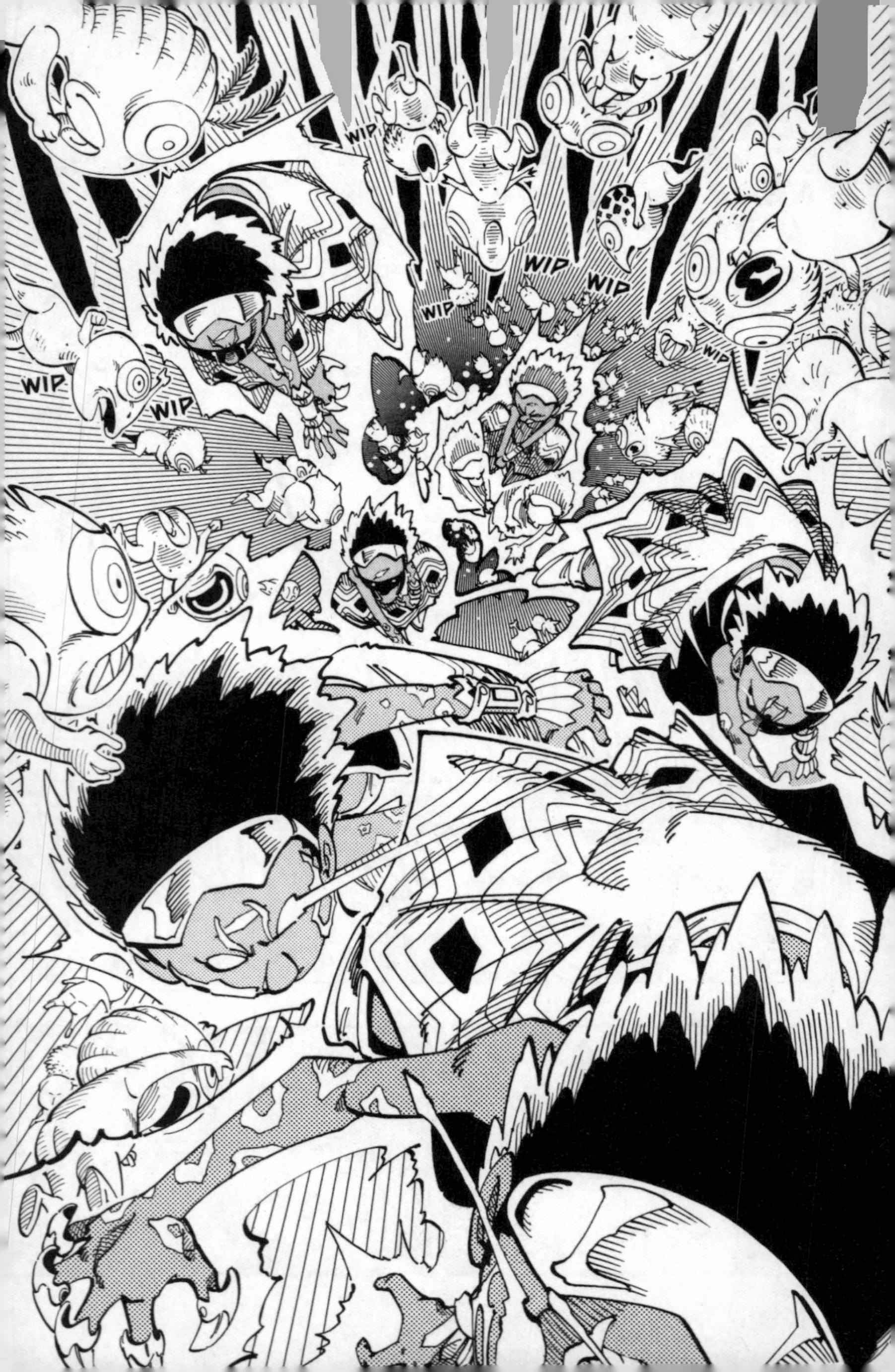
WIP
WIP
WIP
WIP
WIP
WIP
WIP

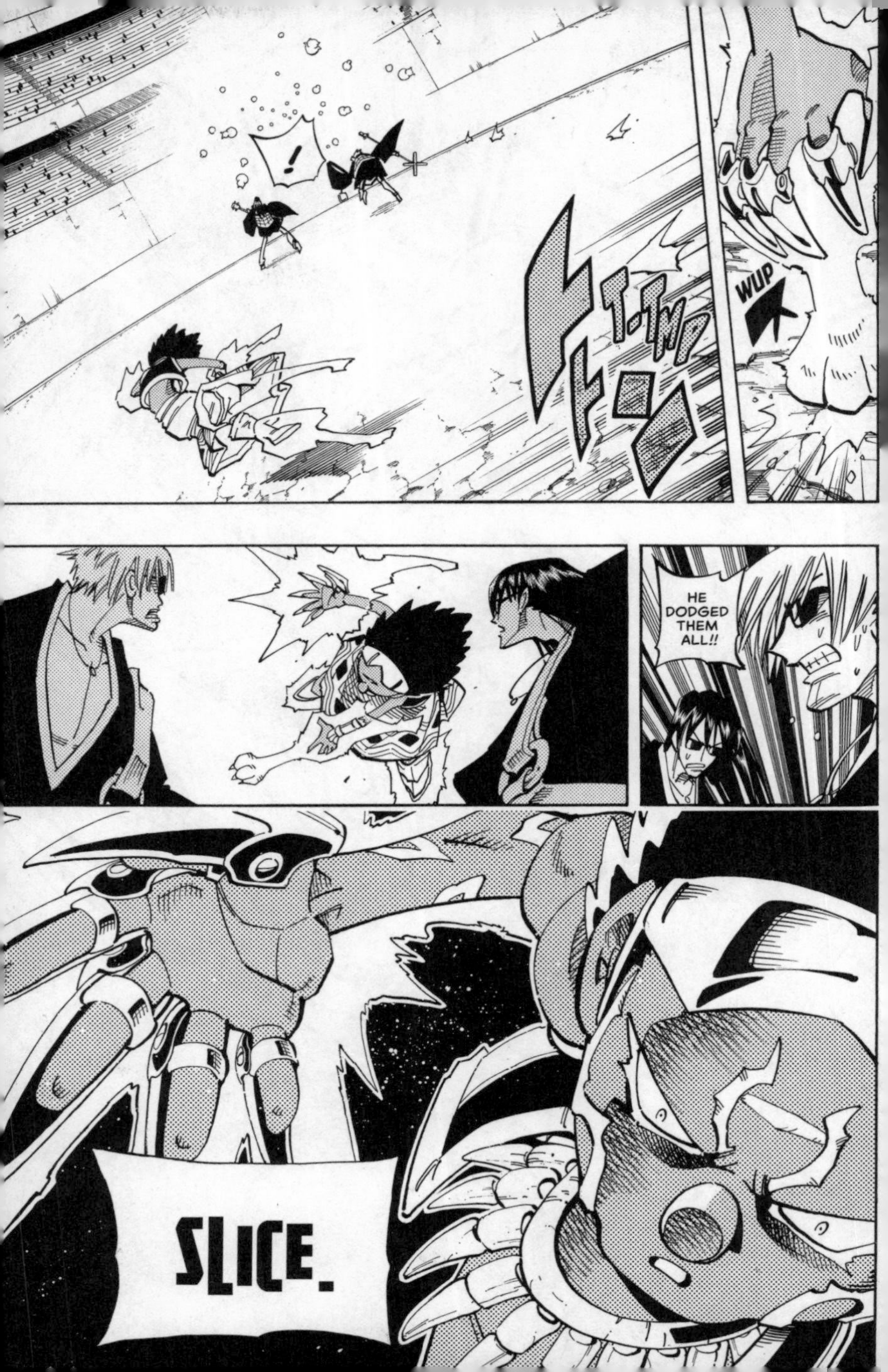
WUP
!
T-TMP
HE DODGED THEM ALL!!
SLICE.

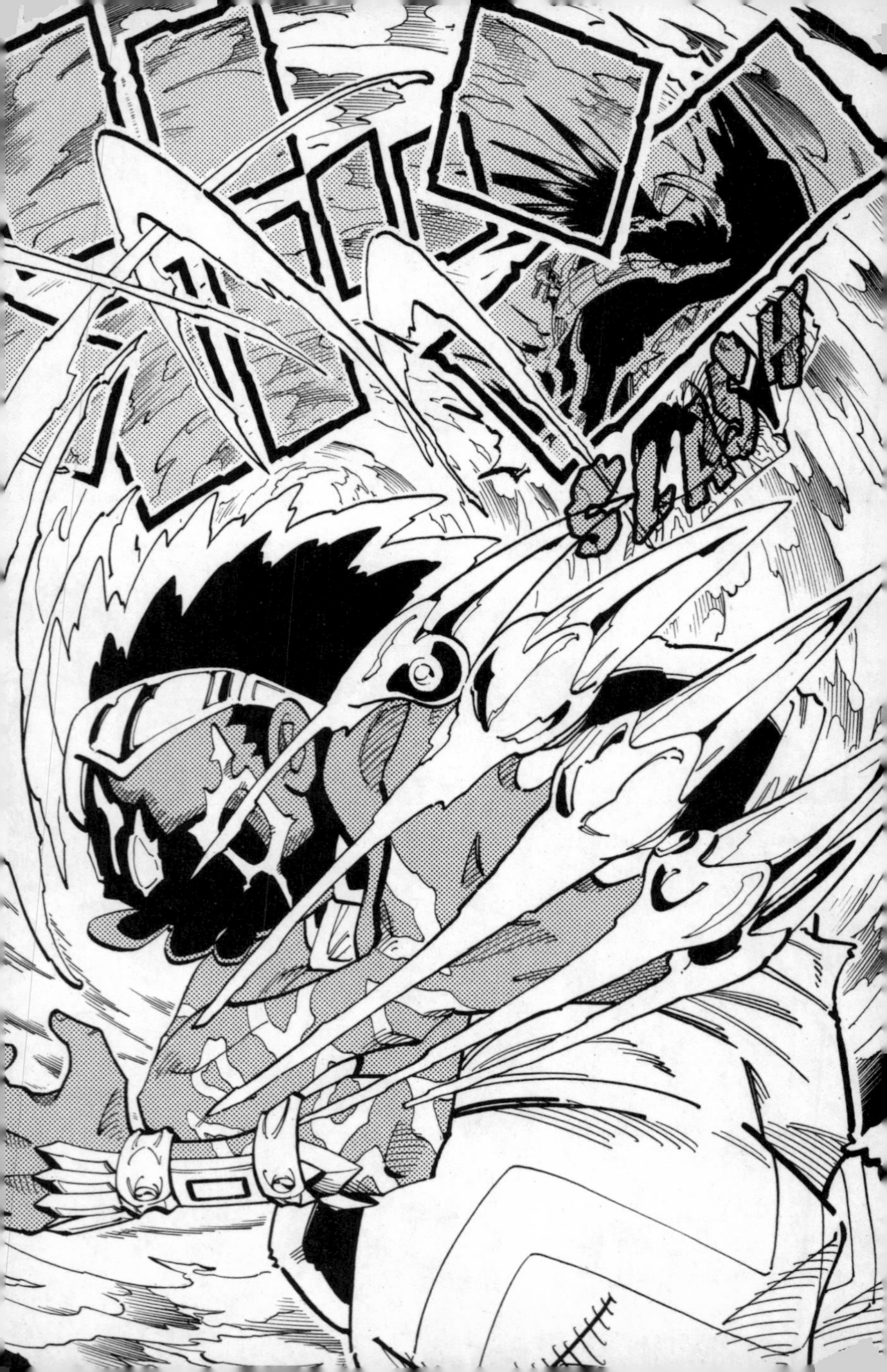
SLASH

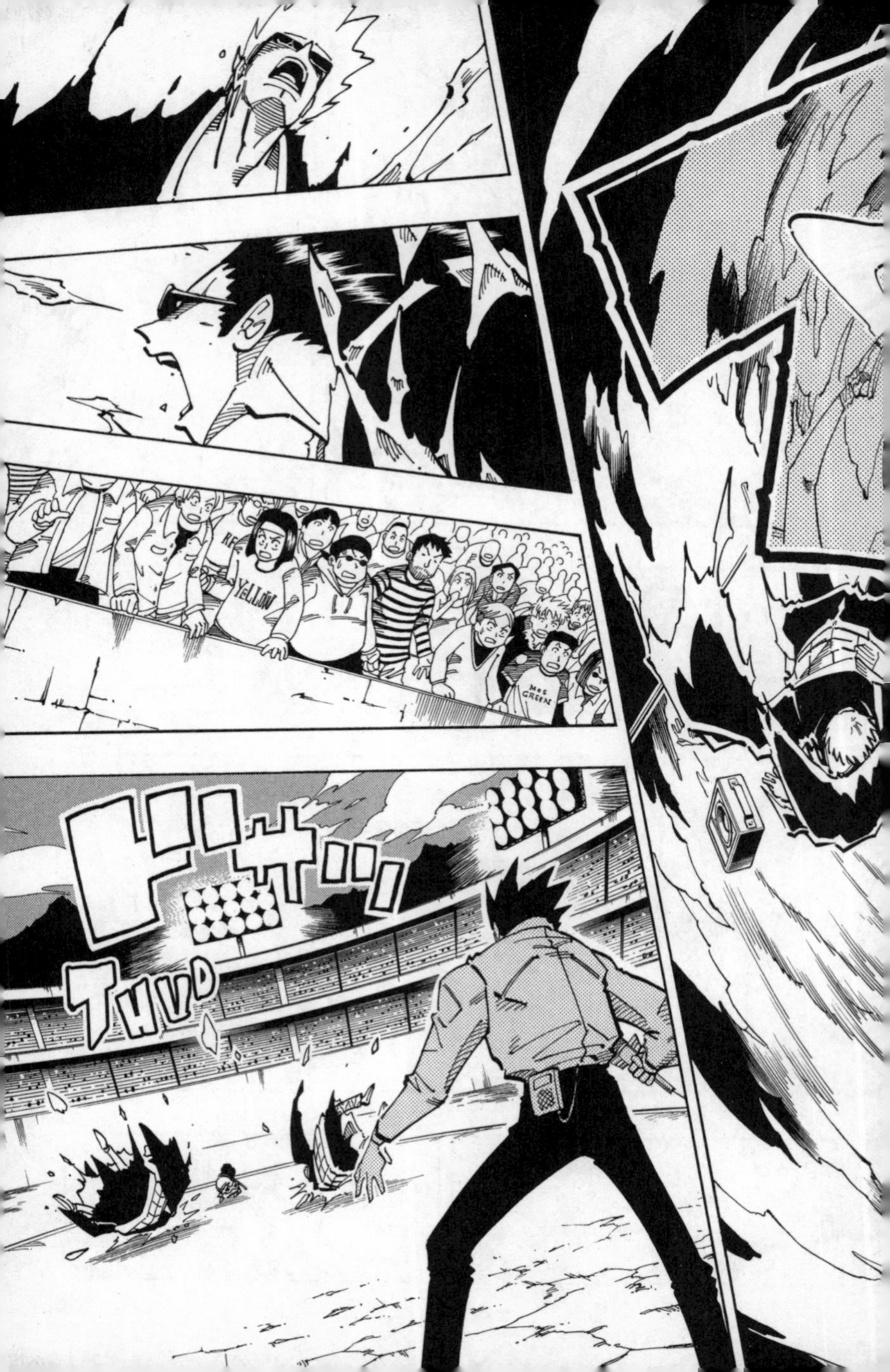
THUD

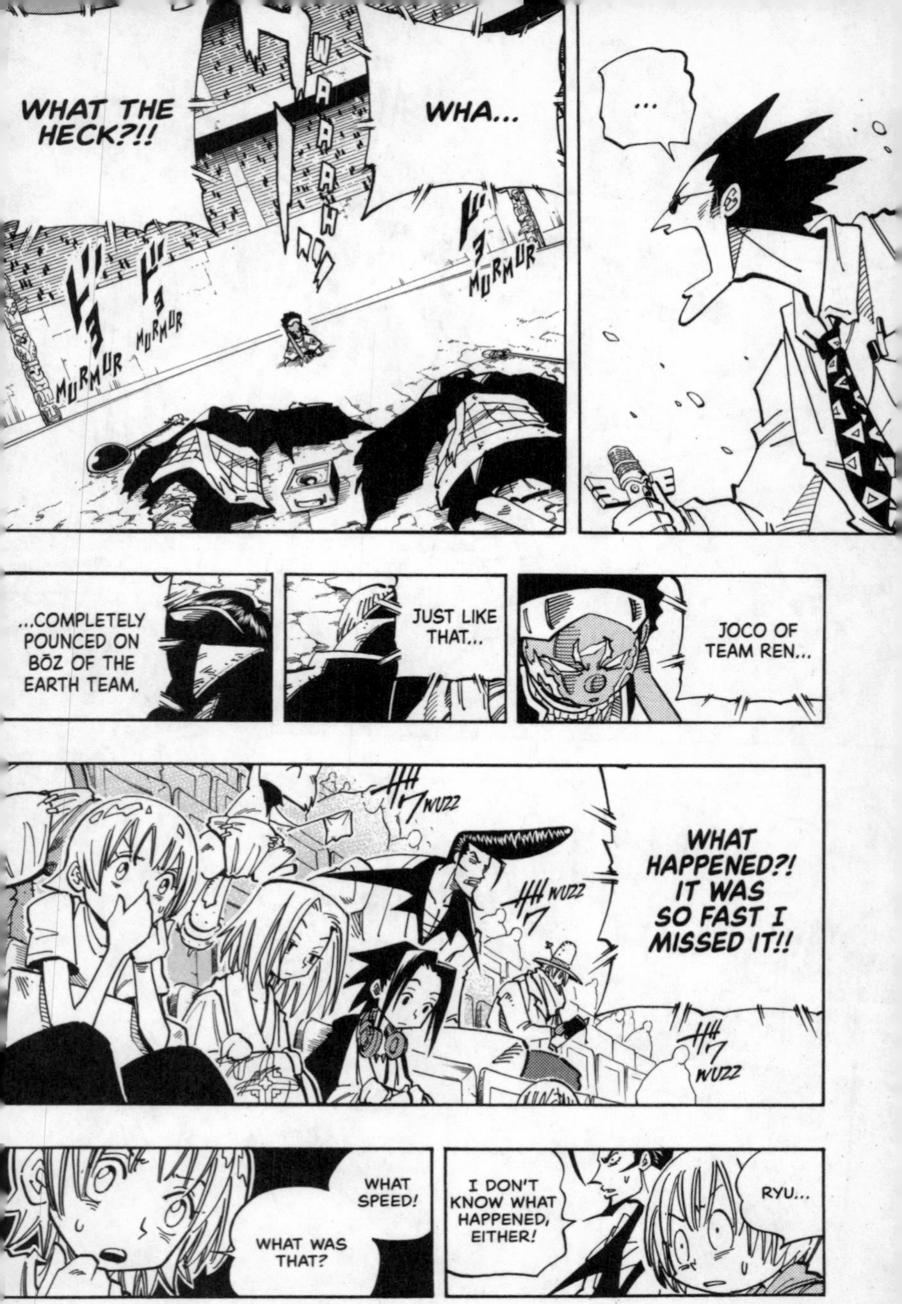
...
WHA...
WHAT THE HECK?!!
MURMUR
MURMUR
MURMUR
JOCO OF TEAM REN...
JUST LIKE THAT...
...COMPLETELY POUNCED ON BŌZ OF THE EARTH TEAM.
WUZZ
WHAT HAPPENED?! IT WAS SO FAST I MISSED IT!!
WUZZ
WUZZ
RYU...
I DON'T KNOW WHAT HAPPENED, EITHER!
WHAT SPEED!
WHAT WAS THAT?

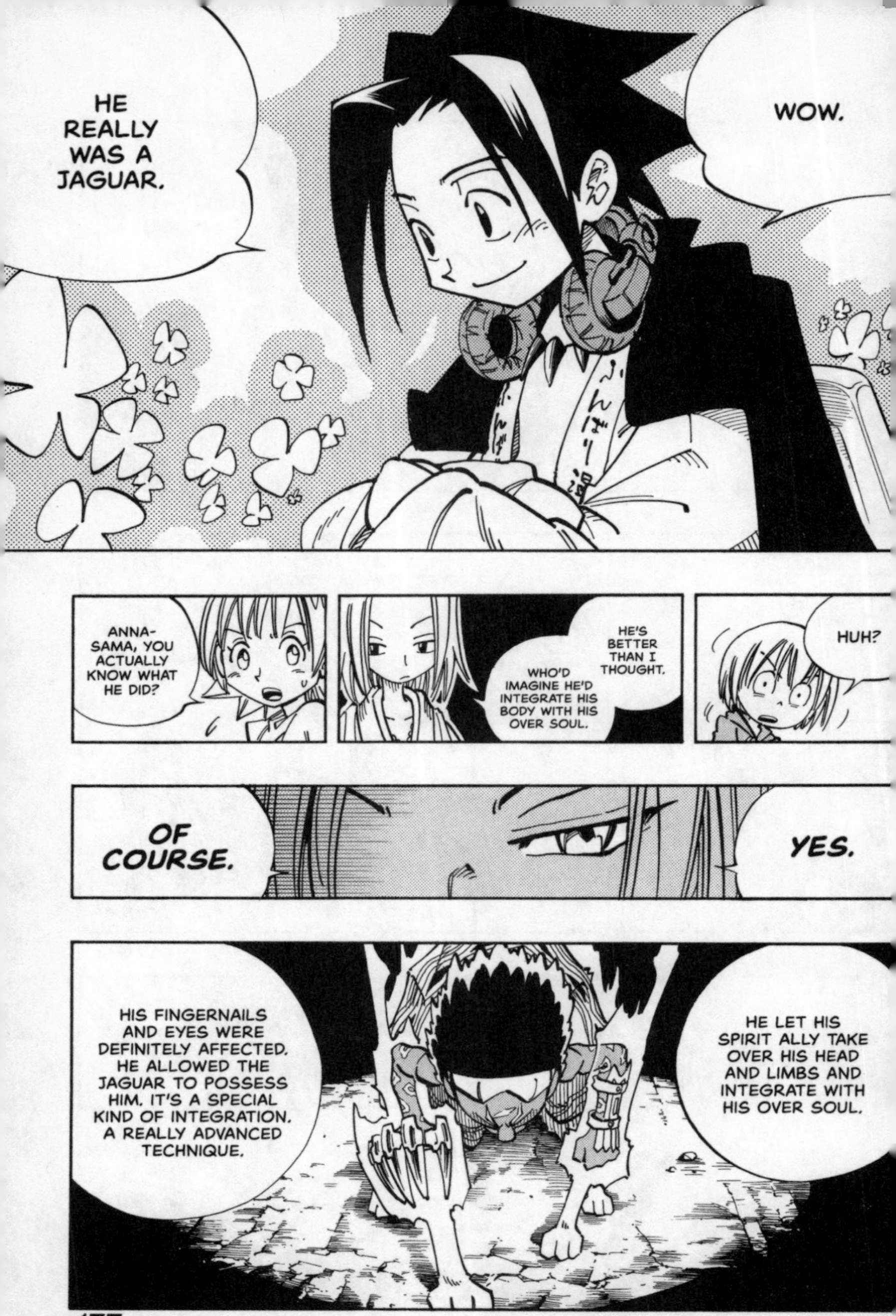
WOW.
HE REALLY WAS A JAGUAR.
HUH?
HE'S BETTER THAN I THOUGHT.
WHO'D IMAGINE HE'D INTEGRATE HIS BODY WITH HIS OVER SOUL.
ANNA-SAMA, YOU ACTUALLY KNOW WHAT HE DID?
YES.
OF COURSE.
HE LET HIS SPIRIT ALLY TAKE OVER HIS HEAD AND LIMBS AND INTEGRATE WITH HIS OVER SOUL.
HIS FINGERNAILS AND EYES WERE DEFINITELY AFFECTED. HE ALLOWED THE JAGUAR TO POSSESS HIM. IT'S A SPECIAL KIND OF INTEGRATION. A REALLY ADVANCED TECHNIQUE.

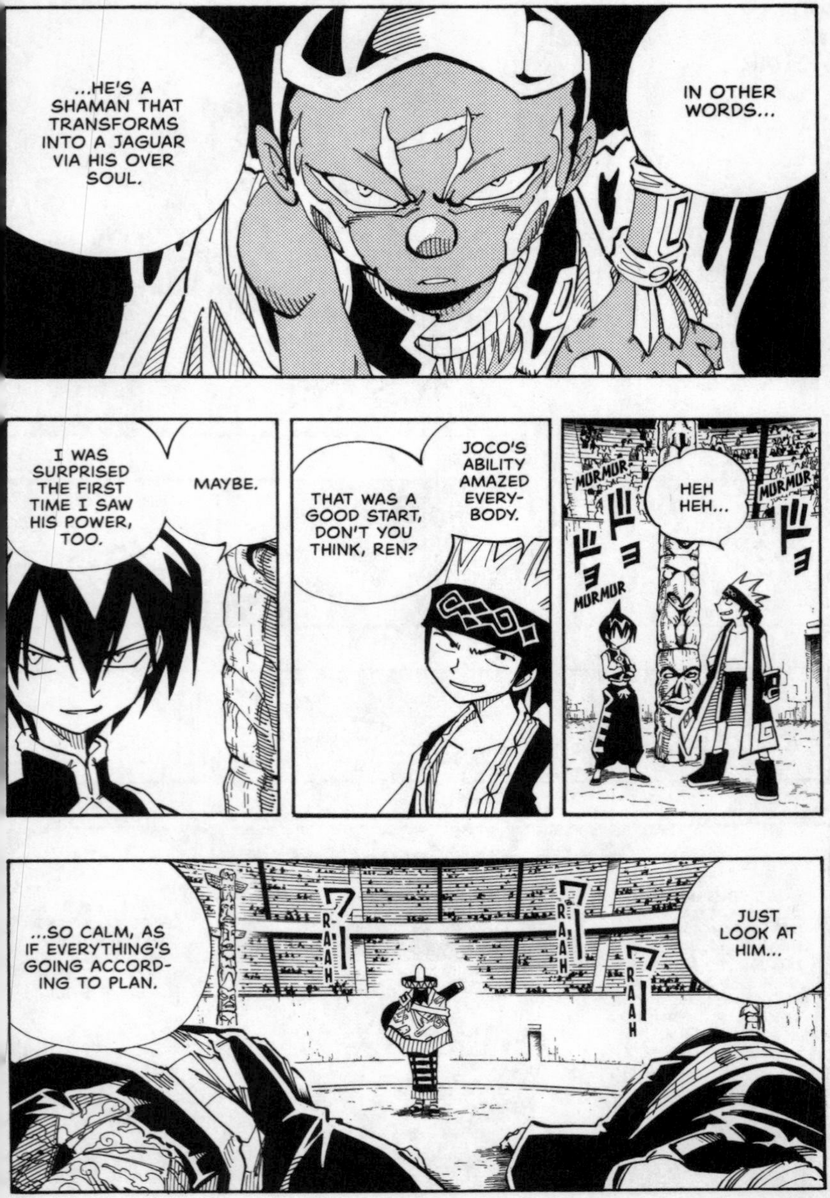
IN OTHER WORDS...
...HE'S A SHAMAN THAT TRANSFORMS INTO A JAGUAR VIA HIS OVER SOUL.
MURMUR
ドョ
MURMUR
HEH HEH...
ドョ
MURMUR
ドョ
JOCO'S ABILITY AMAZED EVERY-BODY.
THAT WAS A GOOD START, DON'T YOU THINK, REN?
MAYBE.
I WAS SURPRISED THE FIRST TIME I SAW HIS POWER, TOO.
JUST LOOK AT HIM...
ワー RAAH
ワー RAAH
ワー RAAH
...SO CALM, AS IF EVERYTHING'S GOING ACCORD-ING TO PLAN.

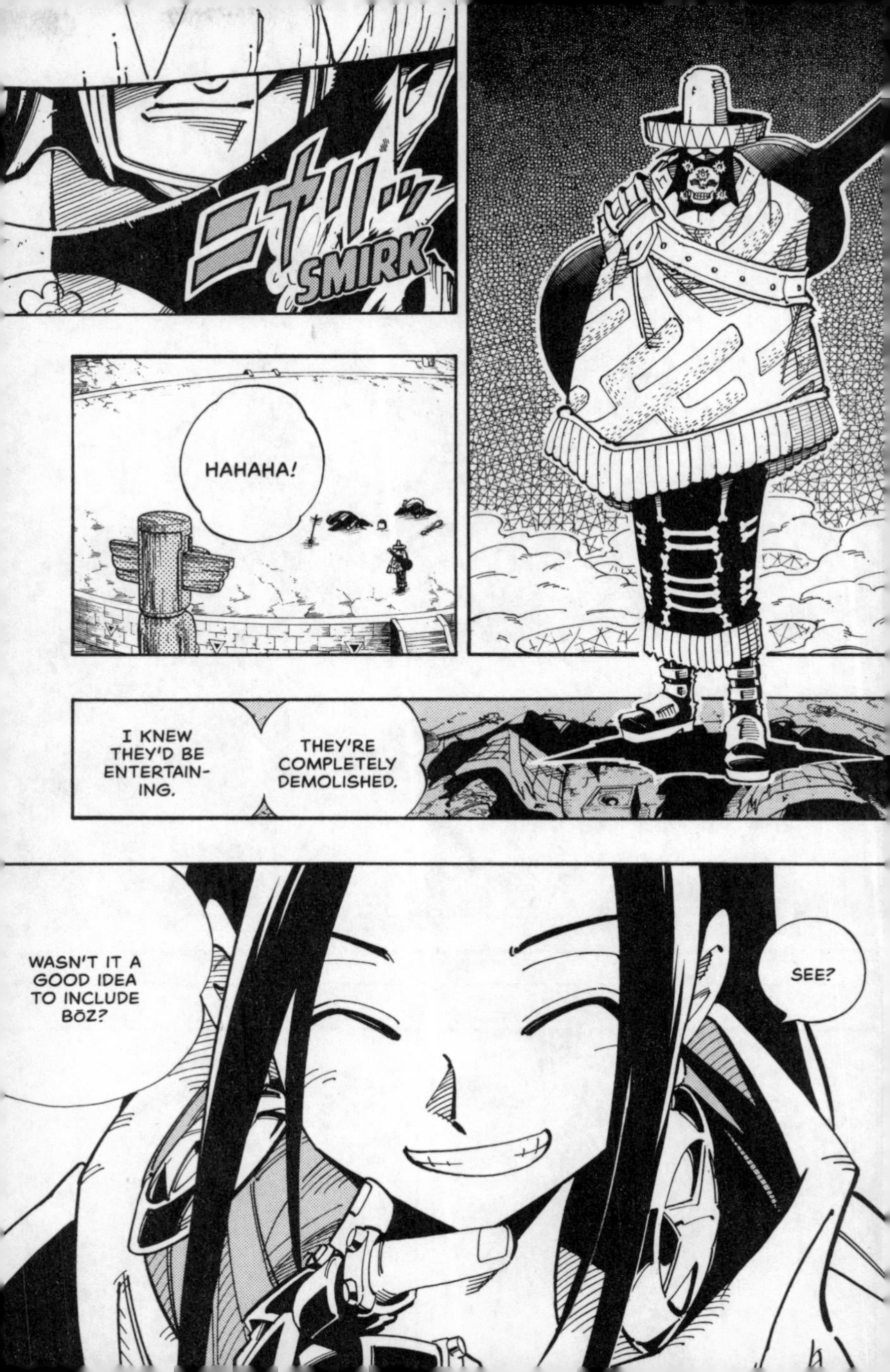

ニヤリッ
SMIRK
HAHAHA!
THEY'RE COMPLETELY DEMOLISHED.
I KNEW THEY'D BE ENTERTAIN-ING.
SEE?
WASN'T IT A GOOD IDEA TO INCLUDE BŌZ?

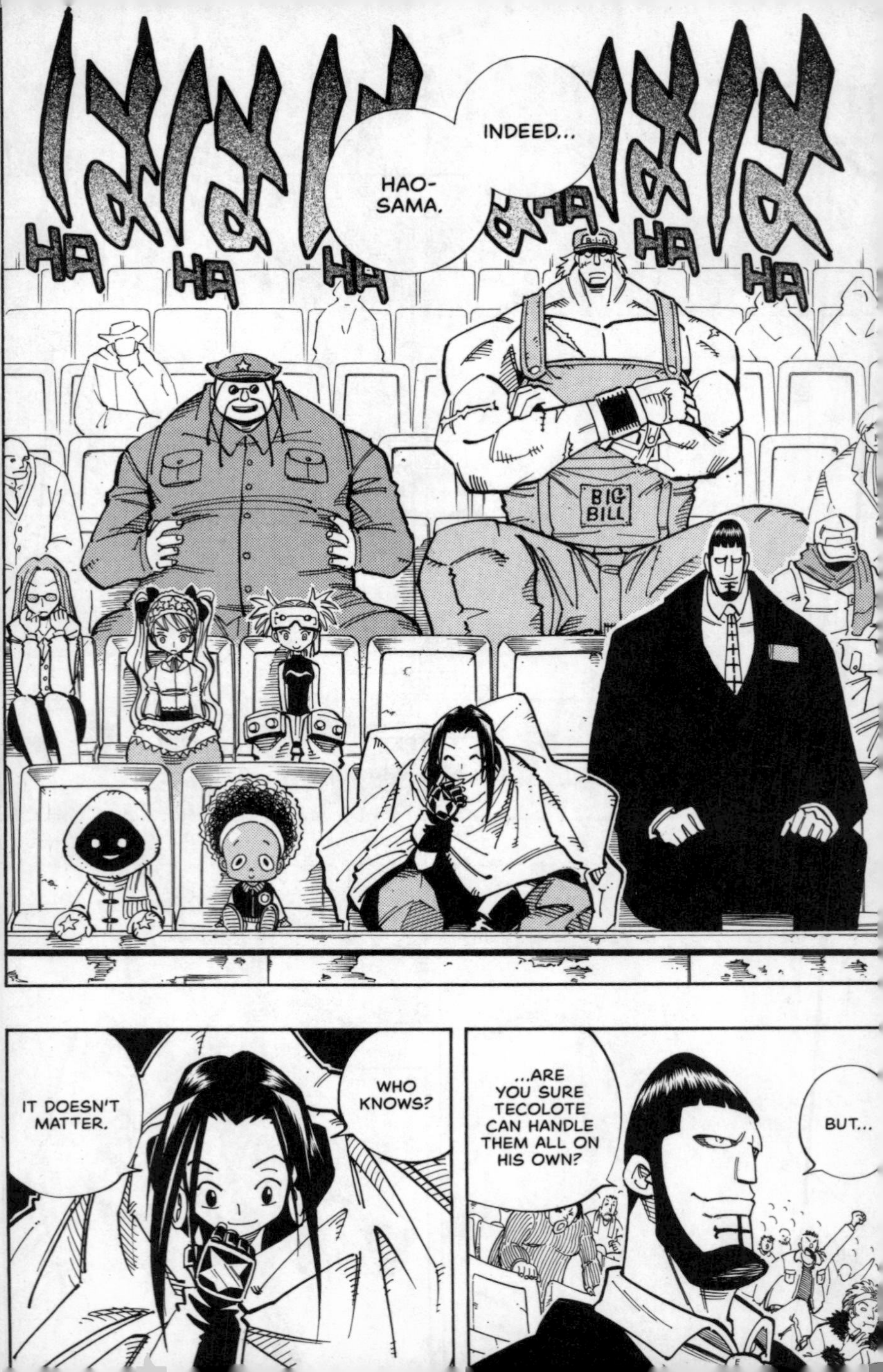

HA HA HA HA HA HA
INDEED...
HAO-SAMA.
BIG BILL
BUT...
...ARE YOU SURE TECOLOTE CAN HANDLE THEM ALL ON HIS OWN?
WHO KNOWS?
IT DOESN'T MATTER.

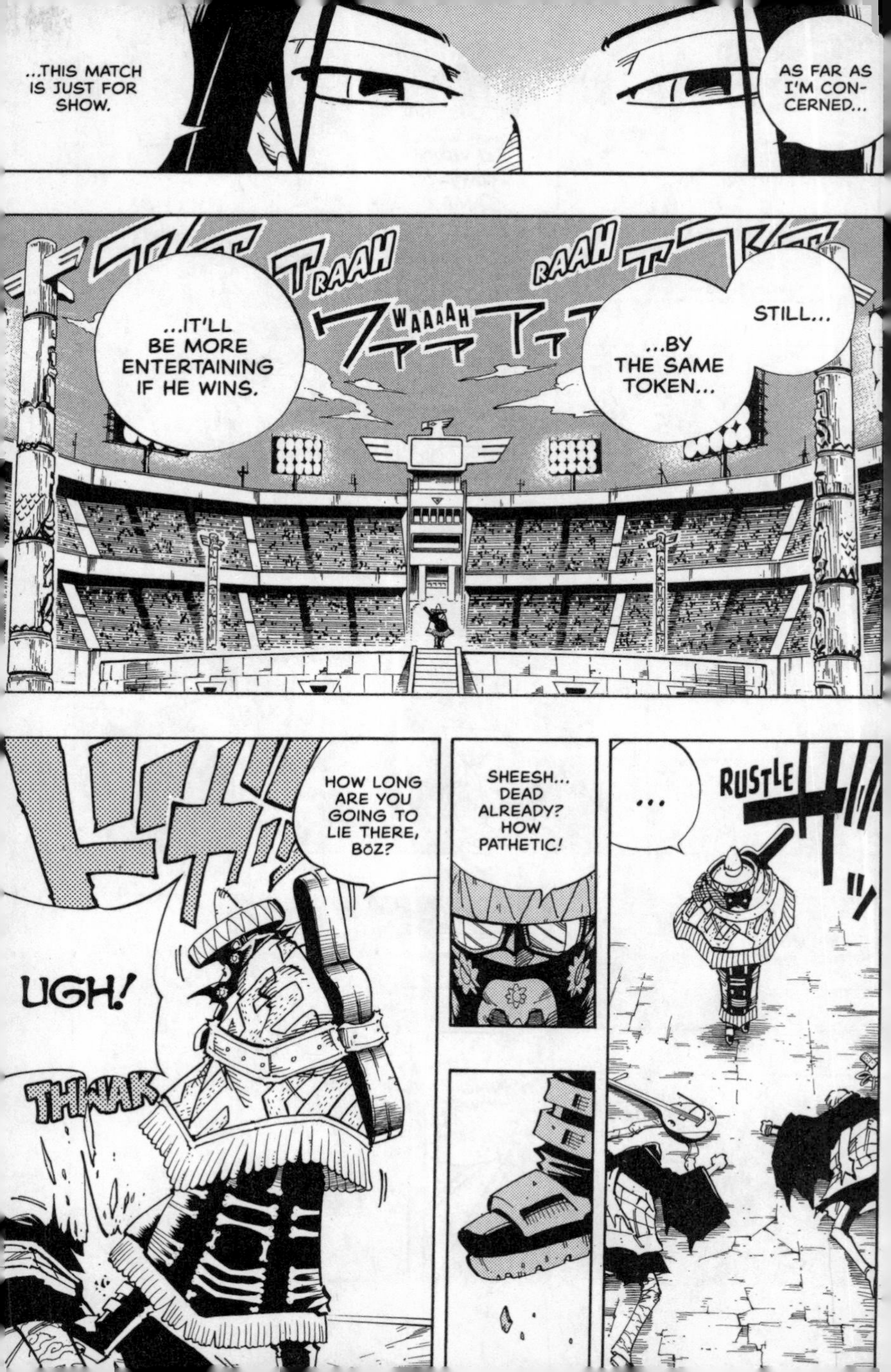
AS FAR AS I'M CON-CERNED...
...THIS MATCH IS JUST FOR SHOW.
RAAH
STILL...
...BY THE SAME TOKEN...
WAAAAH
TRAAH
...IT'LL BE MORE ENTERTAINING IF HE WINS.
...
RUSTLE
SHEESH... DEAD ALREADY? HOW PATHETIC!
HOW LONG ARE YOU GOING TO LIE THERE, BŌZ?
UGH!
THWAK

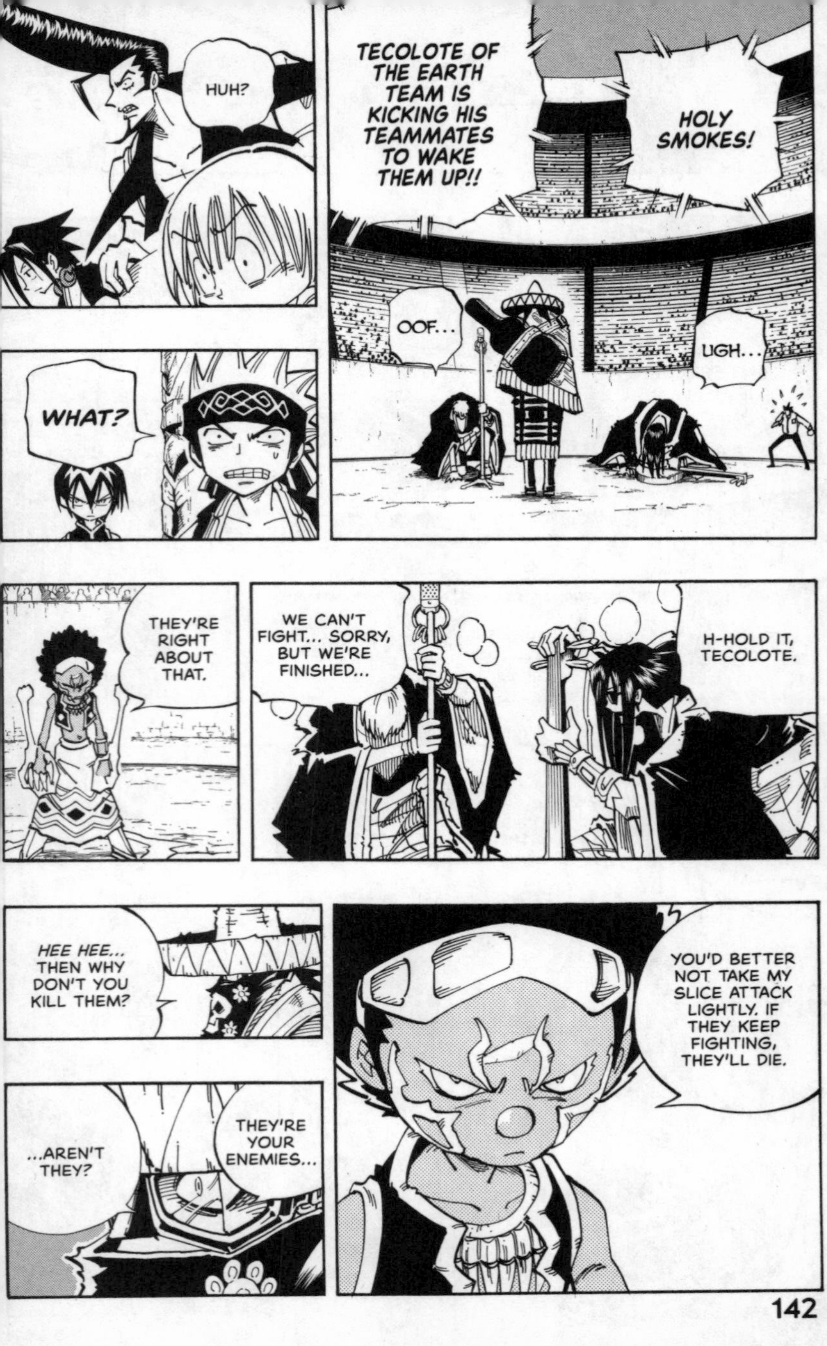
HOLY SMOKES!
TECOLOTE OF THE EARTH TEAM IS KICKING HIS TEAMMATES TO WAKE THEM UP!!
UGH...
OOF...
HUH?
WHAT?
H-HOLD IT, TECOLOTE.
WE CAN'T FIGHT... SORRY, BUT WE'RE FINISHED...
THEY'RE RIGHT ABOUT THAT.
YOU'D BETTER NOT TAKE MY SLICE ATTACK LIGHTLY. IF THEY KEEP FIGHTING, THEY'LL DIE.
HEE HEE... THEN WHY DON'T YOU KILL THEM?
THEY'RE YOUR ENEMIES...
...AREN'T THEY?

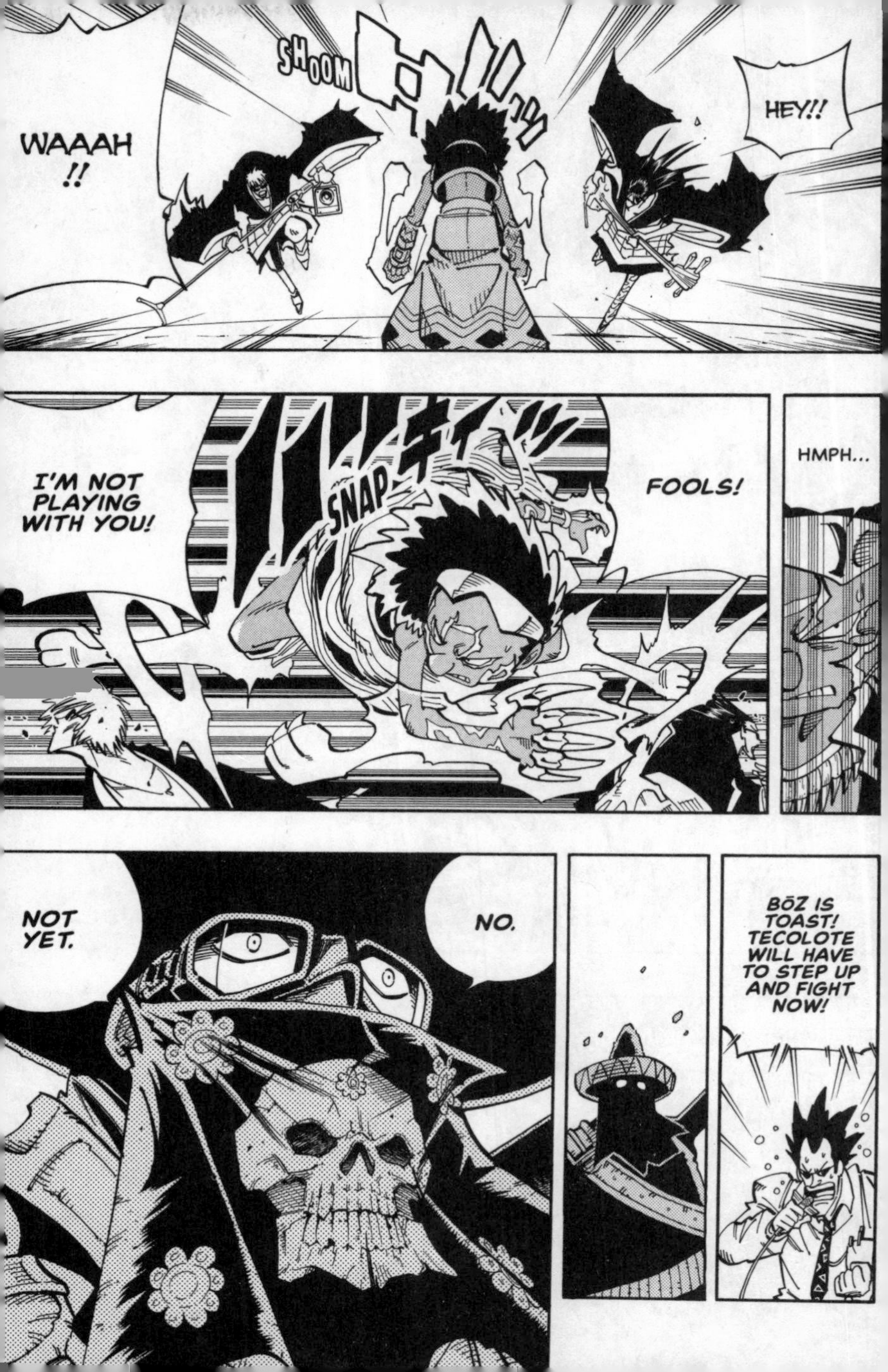
HEY!!
SHOOM
WAAAH !!
HMPH...
FOOLS!
SNAP
I'M NOT PLAYING WITH YOU!
BŌZ IS TOAST! TECOLOTE WILL HAVE TO STEP UP AND FIGHT NOW!
NO.
NOT YET.

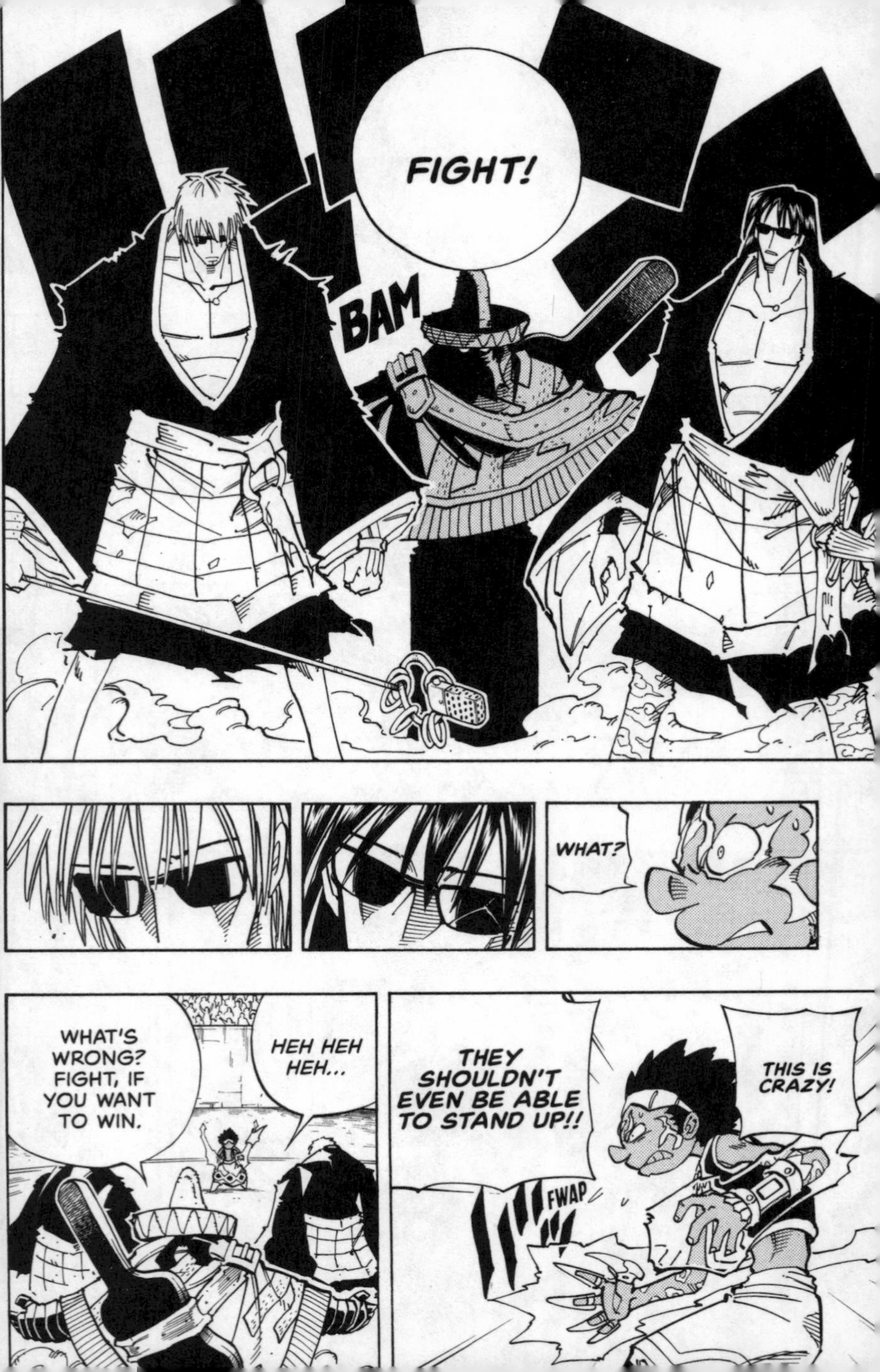
FIGHT!
BAM
WHAT?
THIS IS CRAZY!
THEY SHOULDN'T EVEN BE ABLE TO STAND UP!!
FWAP
HEH HEH HEH...
WHAT'S WRONG? FIGHT, IF YOU WANT TO WIN.

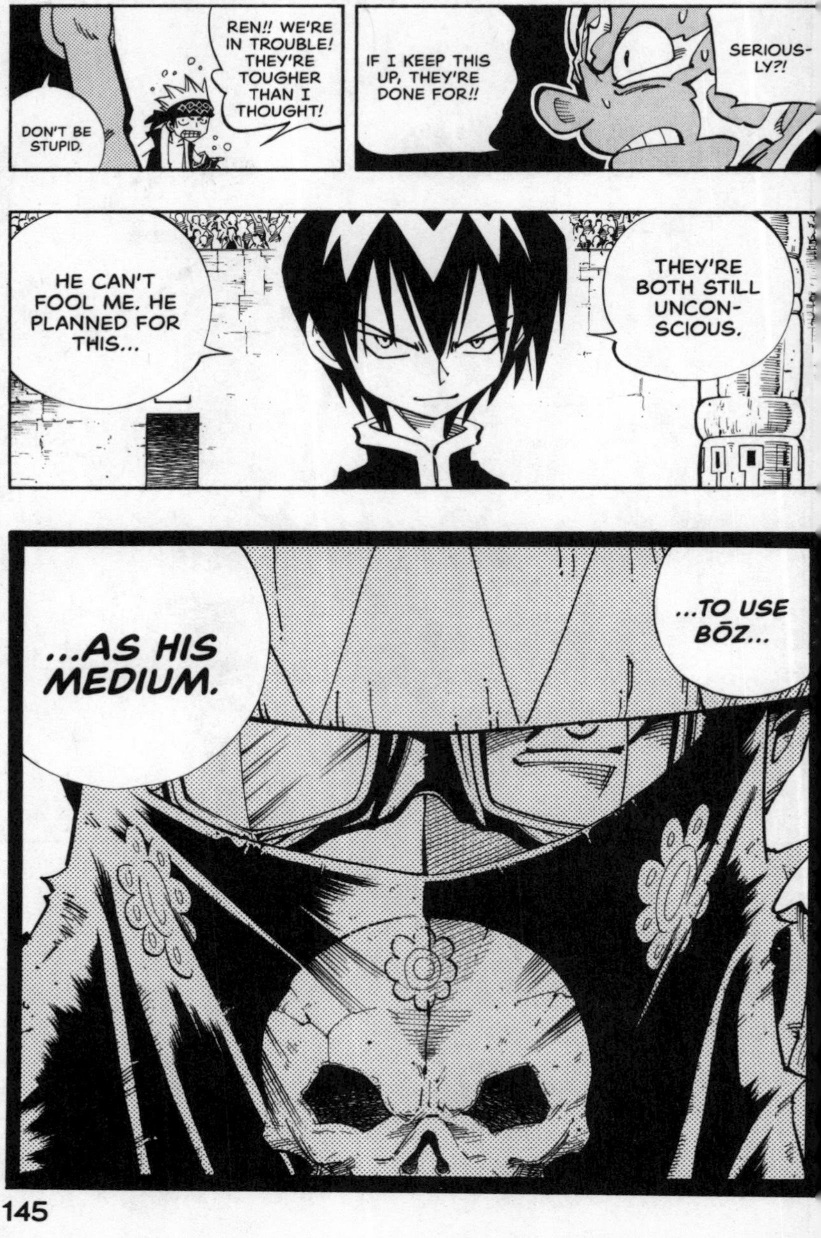
SERIOUS-LY?!
IF I KEEP THIS UP, THEY'RE DONE FOR!!
REN!! WE'RE IN TROUBLE! THEY'RE TOUGHER THAN I THOUGHT!
DON'T BE STUPID.
THEY'RE BOTH STILL UNCON-SCIOUS.
HE CAN'T FOOL ME. HE PLANNED FOR THIS...
...TO USE BŌZ...
...AS HIS MEDIUM.

SHAMAN KING CHARACTER FILE No.62

Tecolote

March 2001

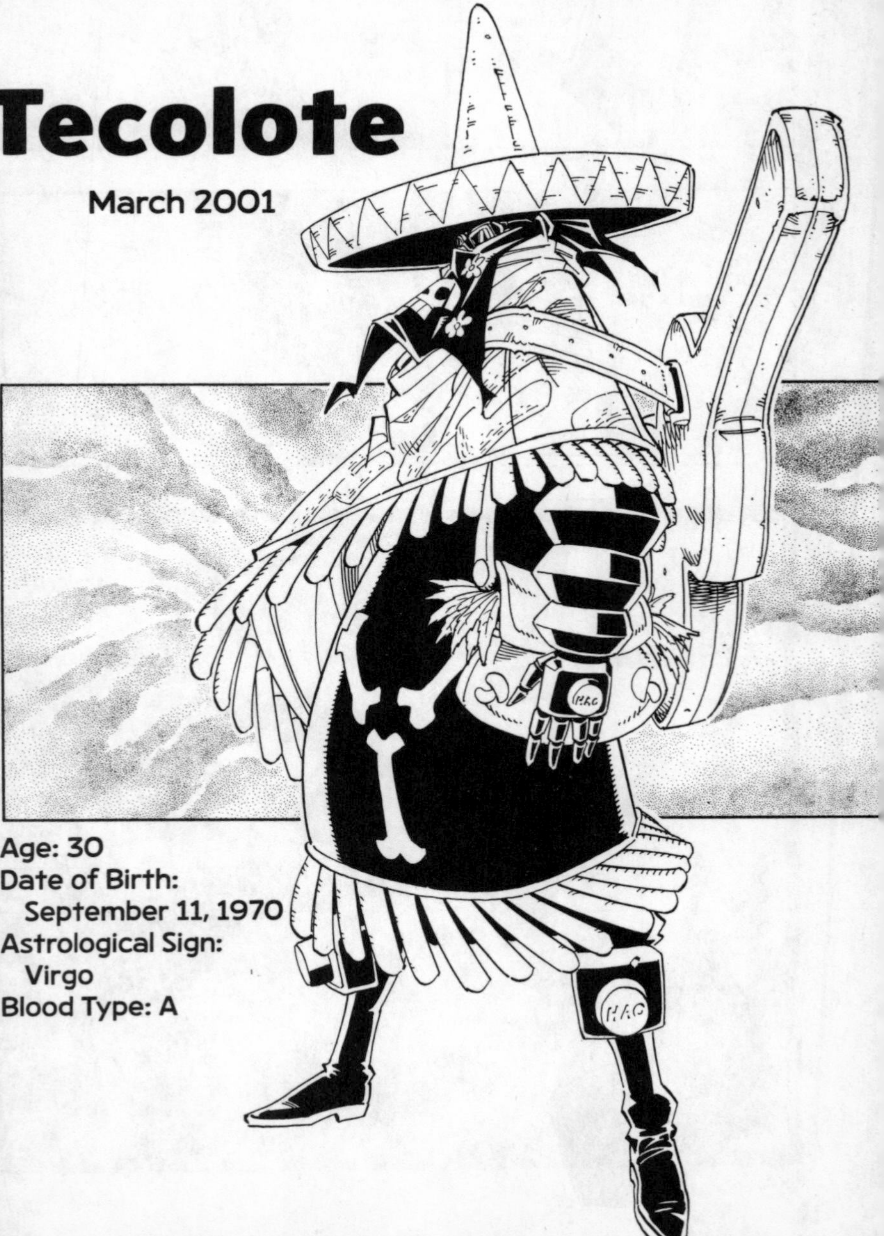

Age: 30
Date of Birth:
September 11, 1970
Astrological Sign:
Virgo
Blood Type: A

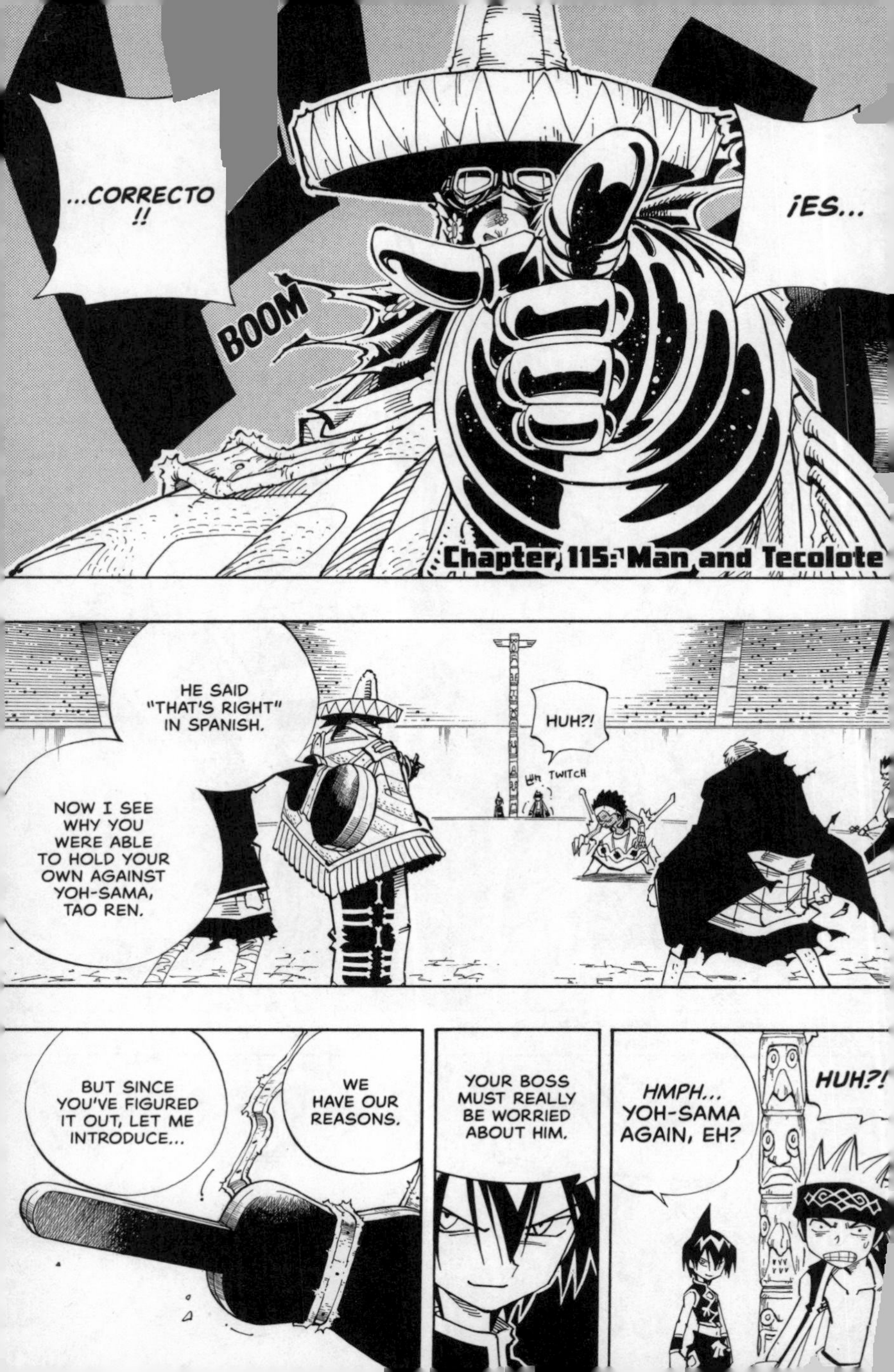
¡ES...
...CORRECTO!!
BOOM
Chapter 115: Man and Tecolote
HE SAID "THAT'S RIGHT" IN SPANISH.
NOW I SEE WHY YOU WERE ABLE TO HOLD YOUR OWN AGAINST YOH-SAMA, TAO REN.
HUH?!
TWITCH
HUH?!
HMPH... YOH-SAMA AGAIN, EH?
YOUR BOSS MUST REALLY BE WORRIED ABOUT HIM.
WE HAVE OUR REASONS.
BUT SINCE YOU'VE FIGURED IT OUT, LET ME INTRODUCE...

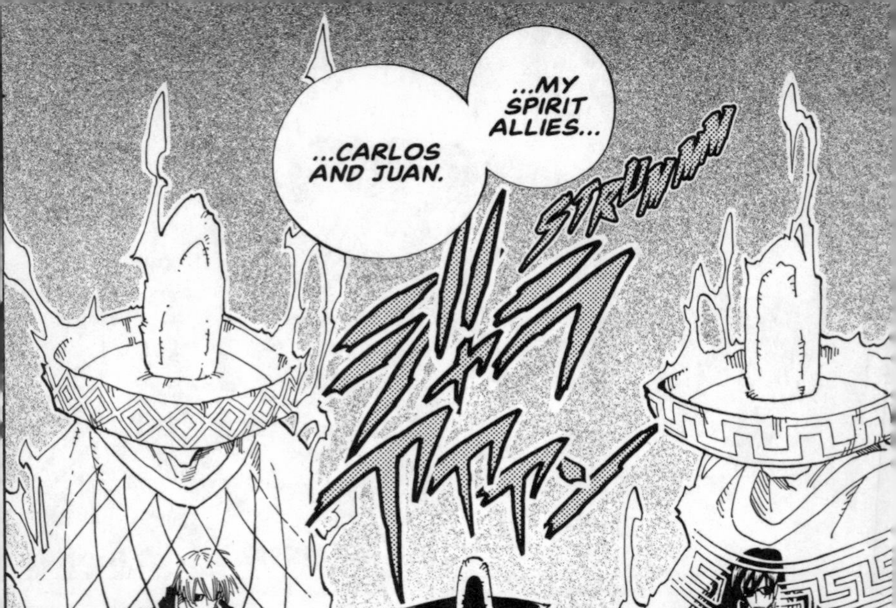
...MY SPIRIT ALLIES...
...CARLOS AND JUAN.
STRUMMMM

*Mariachi: A band or musicians typical of Mexico. It includes violins, trumpets, and various guitars with 7-8 musicians.

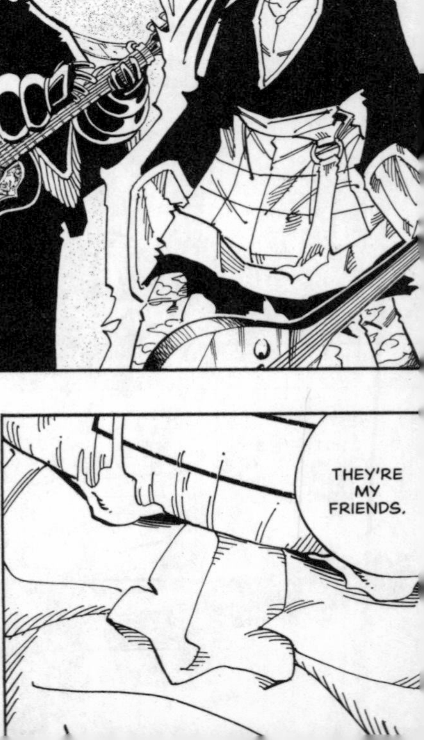
THEY'RE MY FRIENDS.

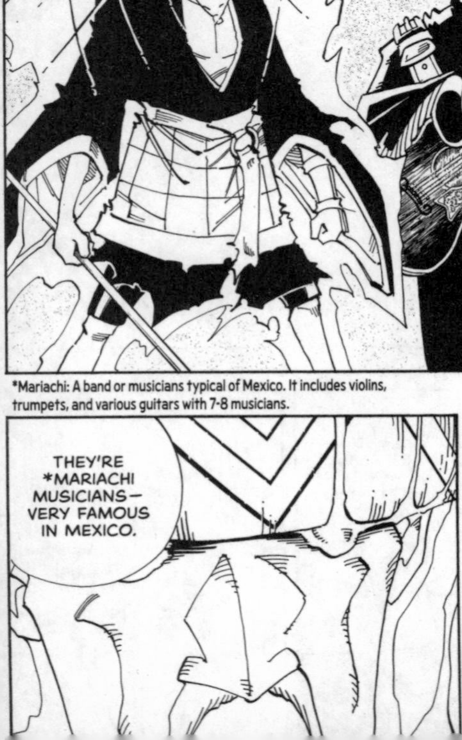
THEY'RE *MARIACHI MUSICIANS— VERY FAMOUS IN MEXICO.

Chapter 115:

Man and Tecolote

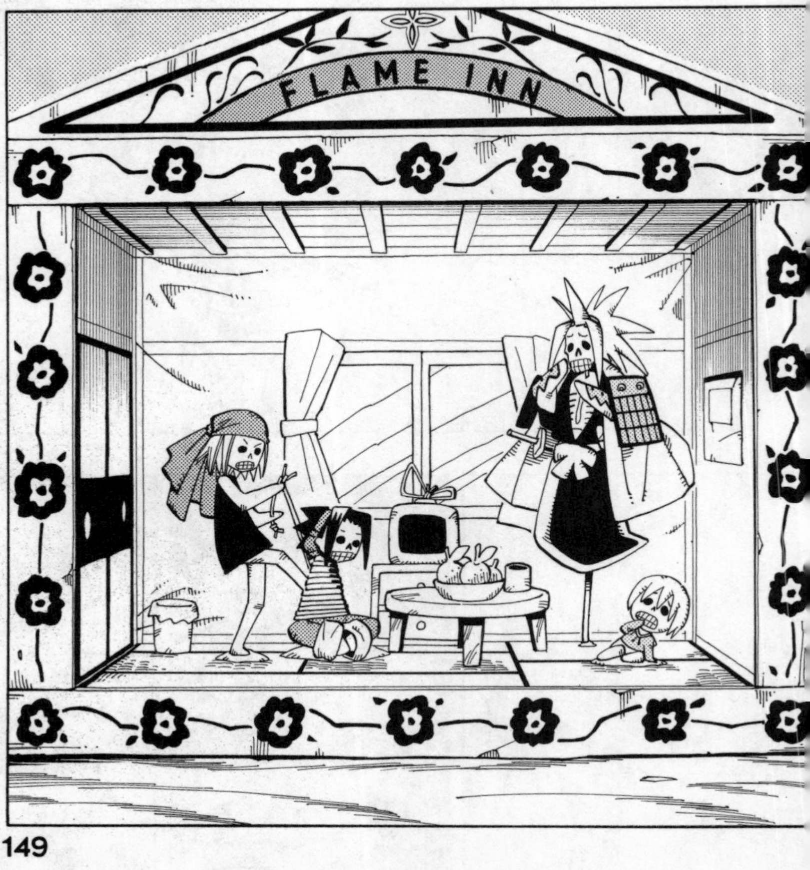
FLAME INN

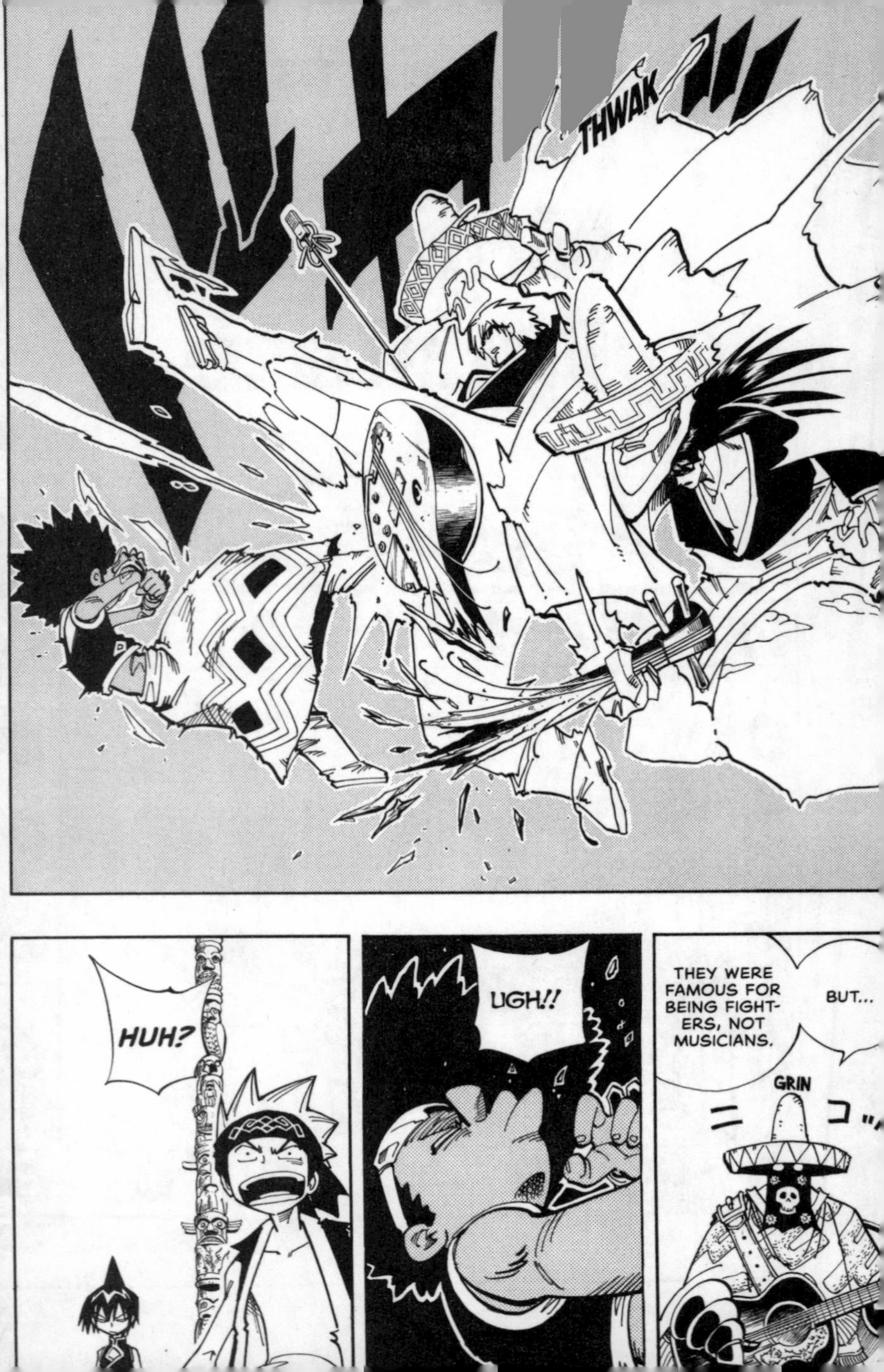
THWAK
THEY WERE FAMOUS FOR BEING FIGHTERS, NOT MUSICIANS.
BUT...
GRIN
ニコッ
UGH!!
HUH?

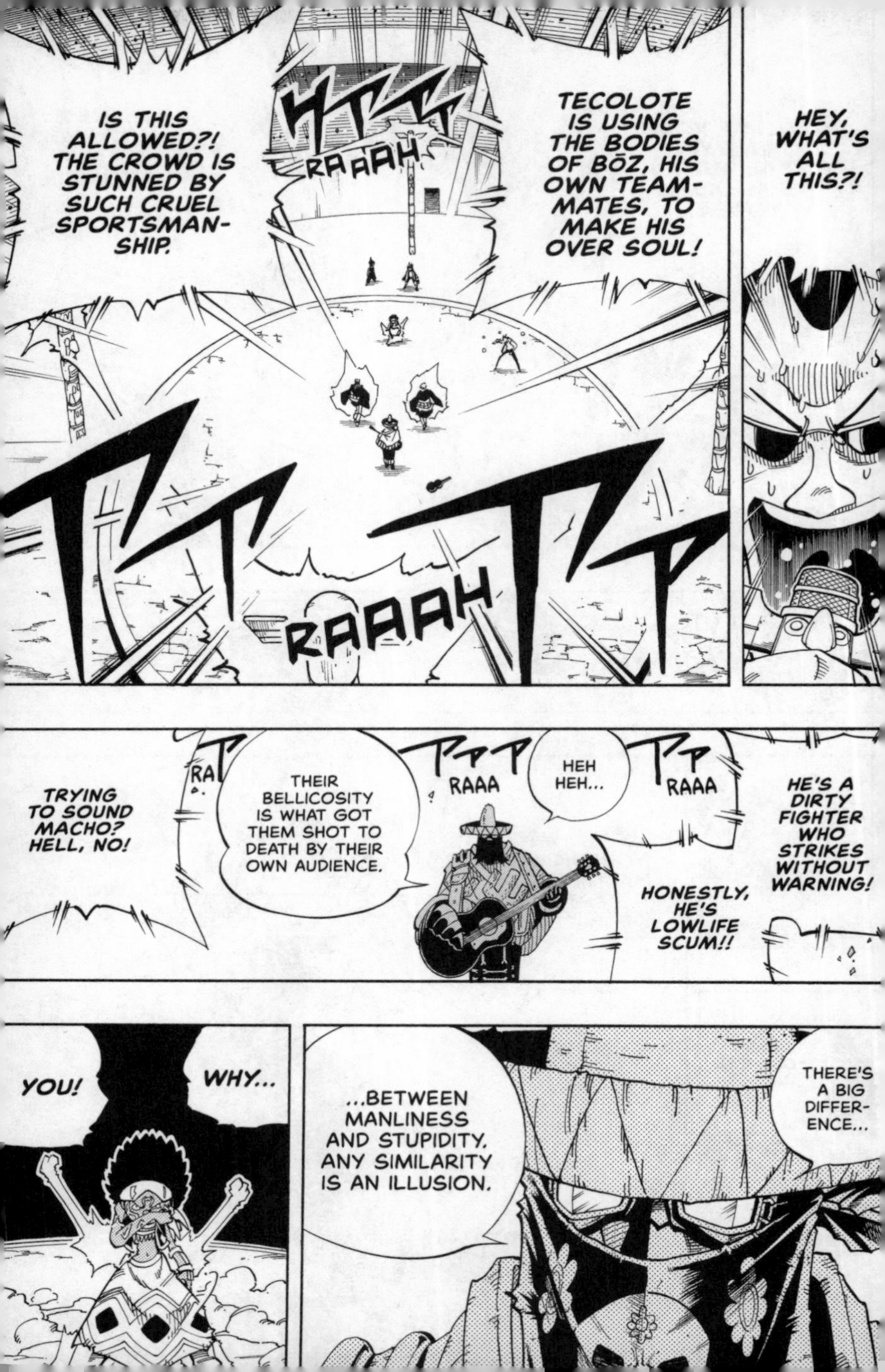
HEY, WHAT'S ALL THIS?!
TECOLOTE IS USING THE BODIES OF BŌZ, HIS OWN TEAM-MATES, TO MAKE HIS OVER SOUL!
RAAAH
IS THIS ALLOWED?! THE CROWD IS STUNNED BY SUCH CRUEL SPORTSMAN-SHIP.
RAAAH
HE'S A DIRTY FIGHTER WHO STRIKES WITHOUT WARNING!
HONESTLY, HE'S LOWLIFE SCUM!!
RAAA
HEH HEH...
RAAA
THEIR BELLICOSITY IS WHAT GOT THEM SHOT TO DEATH BY THEIR OWN AUDIENCE.
RA
TRYING TO SOUND MACHO? HELL, NO!
THERE'S A BIG DIFFER-ENCE...
...BETWEEN MANLINESS AND STUPIDITY. ANY SIMILARITY IS AN ILLUSION.
WHY...
YOU!

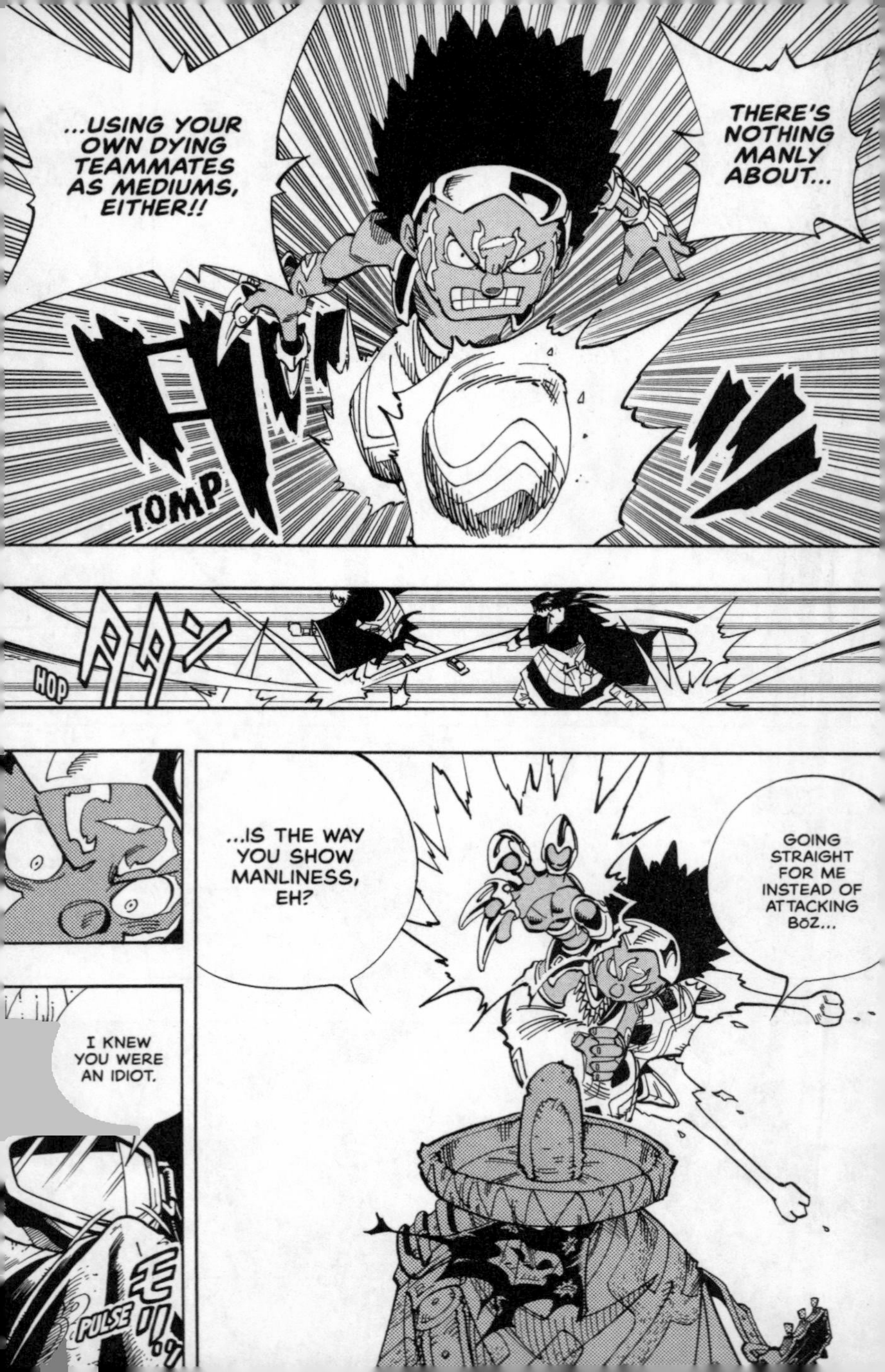
THERE'S NOTHING MANLY ABOUT...
...USING YOUR OWN DYING TEAMMATES AS MEDIUMS, EITHER!!
TOMP
HOP
GOING STRAIGHT FOR ME INSTEAD OF ATTACKING BŌZ...
...IS THE WAY YOU SHOW MANLINESS, EH?
I KNEW YOU WERE AN IDIOT.
PULSE

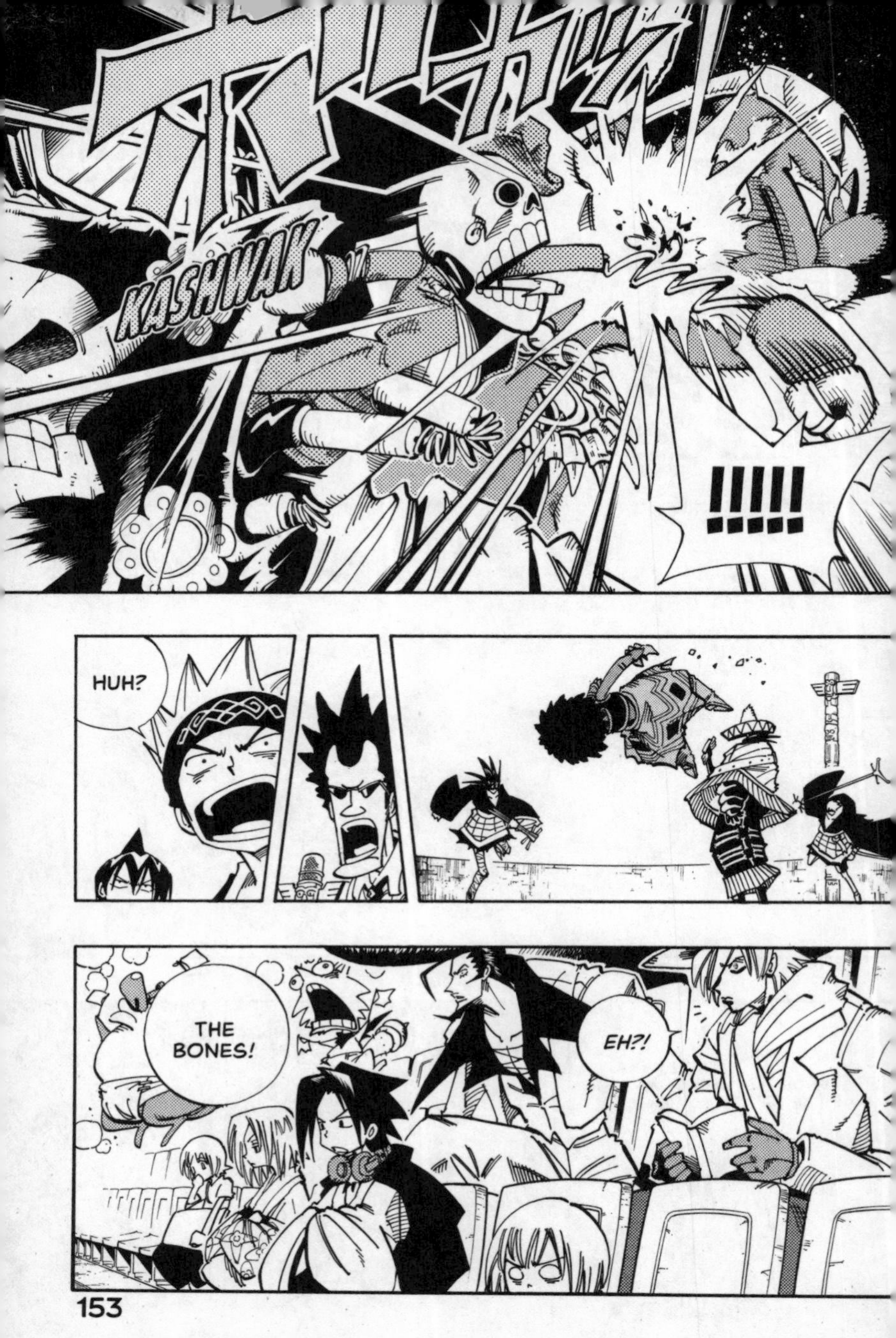
KASHWAK
!!!!!
HUH?
EH?!
THE BONES!

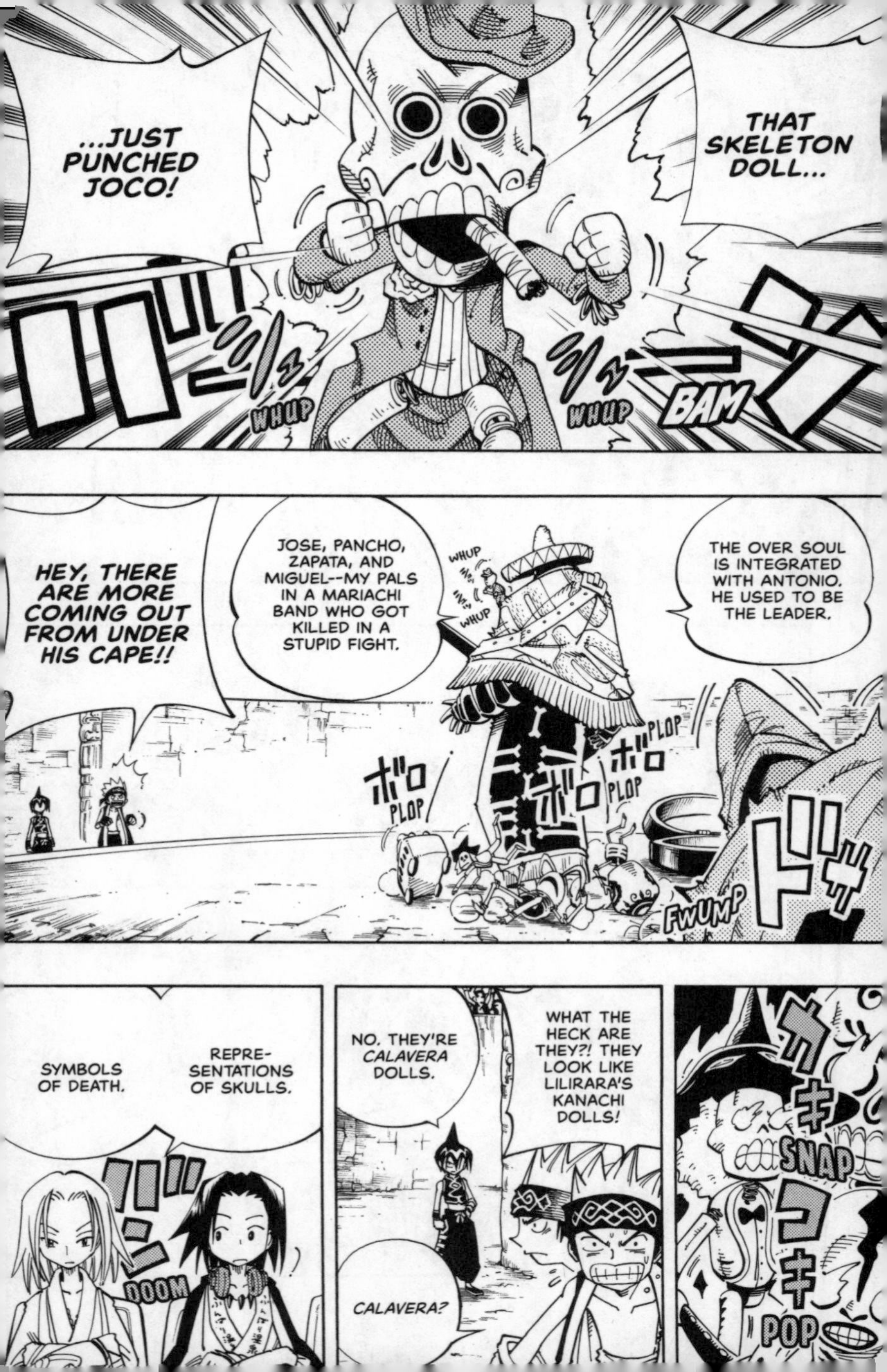
THAT SKELETON DOLL...
...JUST PUNCHED JOCO!
BAM
WHUP
WHUP
THE OVER SOUL IS INTEGRATED WITH ANTONIO. HE USED TO BE THE LEADER.
JOSE, PANCHO, ZAPATA, AND MIGUEL--MY PALS IN A MARIACHI BAND WHO GOT KILLED IN A STUPID FIGHT.
WHUP
WHUP
HEY, THERE ARE MORE COMING OUT FROM UNDER HIS CAPE!!
FWUMP
ボロ
PLOP
ボロ
PLOP
ボロ
PLOP
SNAP
POP
WHAT THE HECK ARE THEY?! THEY LOOK LIKE LILIRARA'S KANACHI DOLLS!
NO, THEY'RE *CALAVERA* DOLLS.
CALAVERA?
REPRE-SENTATIONS OF SKULLS.
SYMBOLS OF DEATH.
DOOM

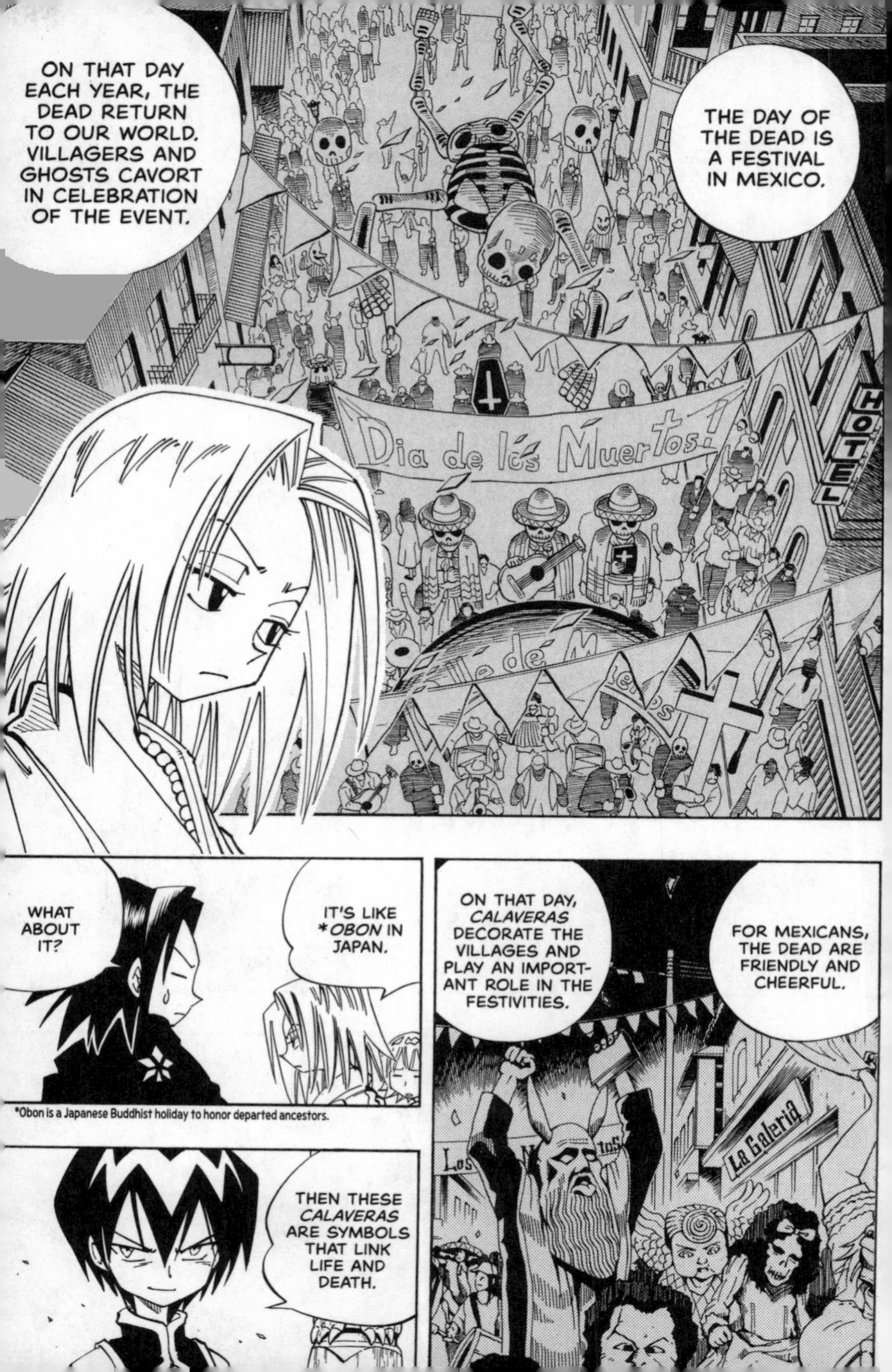
THE DAY OF THE DEAD IS A FESTIVAL IN MEXICO.
ON THAT DAY EACH YEAR, THE DEAD RETURN TO OUR WORLD. VILLAGERS AND GHOSTS CAVORT IN CELEBRATION OF THE EVENT.
HOTEL
Dia de los Muertos!
FOR MEXICANS, THE DEAD ARE FRIENDLY AND CHEERFUL.
ON THAT DAY, *CALAVERAS* DECORATE THE VILLAGES AND PLAY AN IMPORTANT ROLE IN THE FESTIVITIES.
La Galeria
IT'S LIKE *OBON IN JAPAN.
WHAT ABOUT IT?
THEN THESE *CALAVERAS* ARE SYMBOLS THAT LINK LIFE AND DEATH.

*Obon is a Japanese Buddhist holiday to honor departed ancestors.

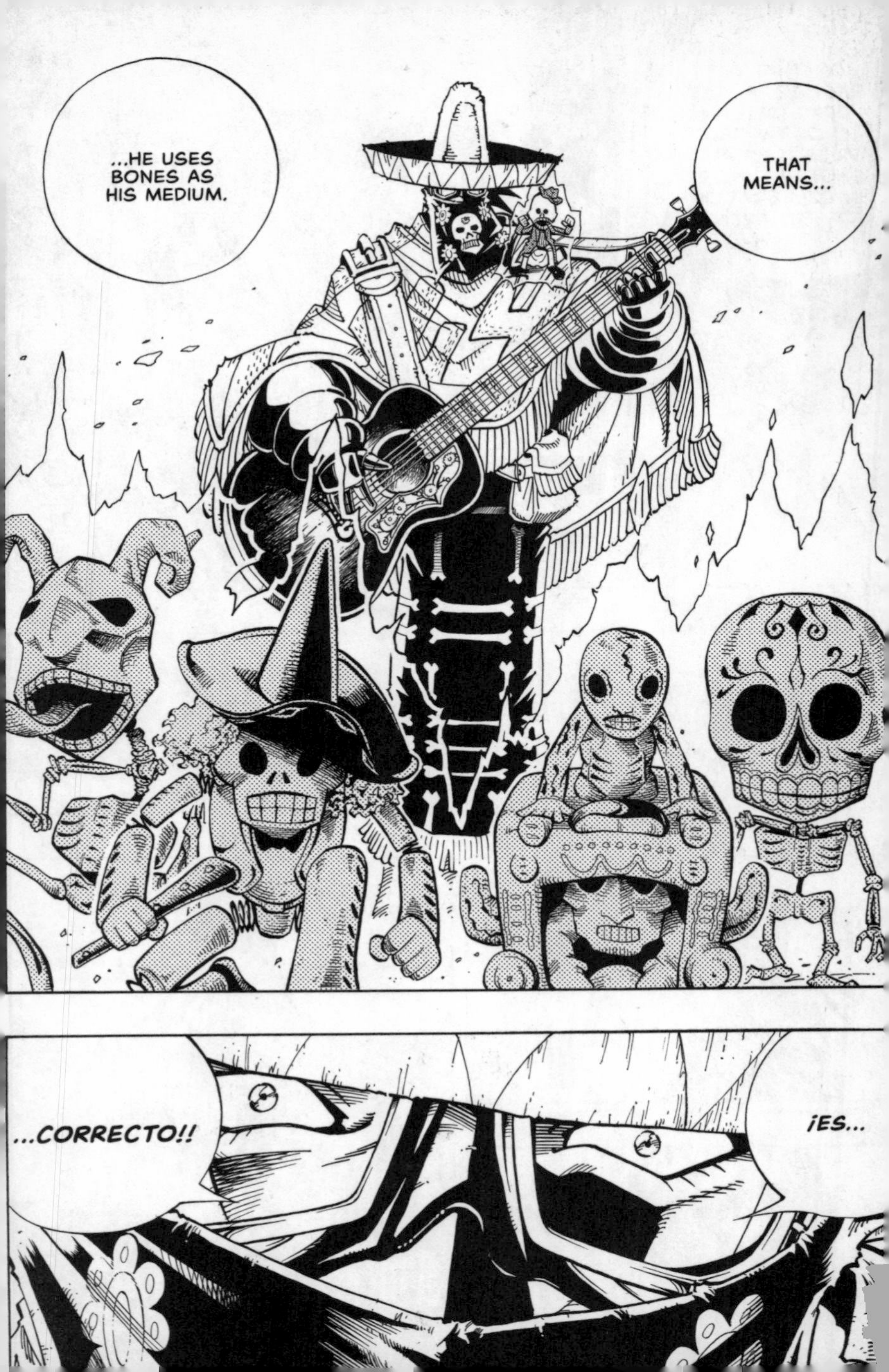
THAT MEANS...
...HE USES BONES AS HIS MEDIUM.
¡ES...
...CORRECTO!!

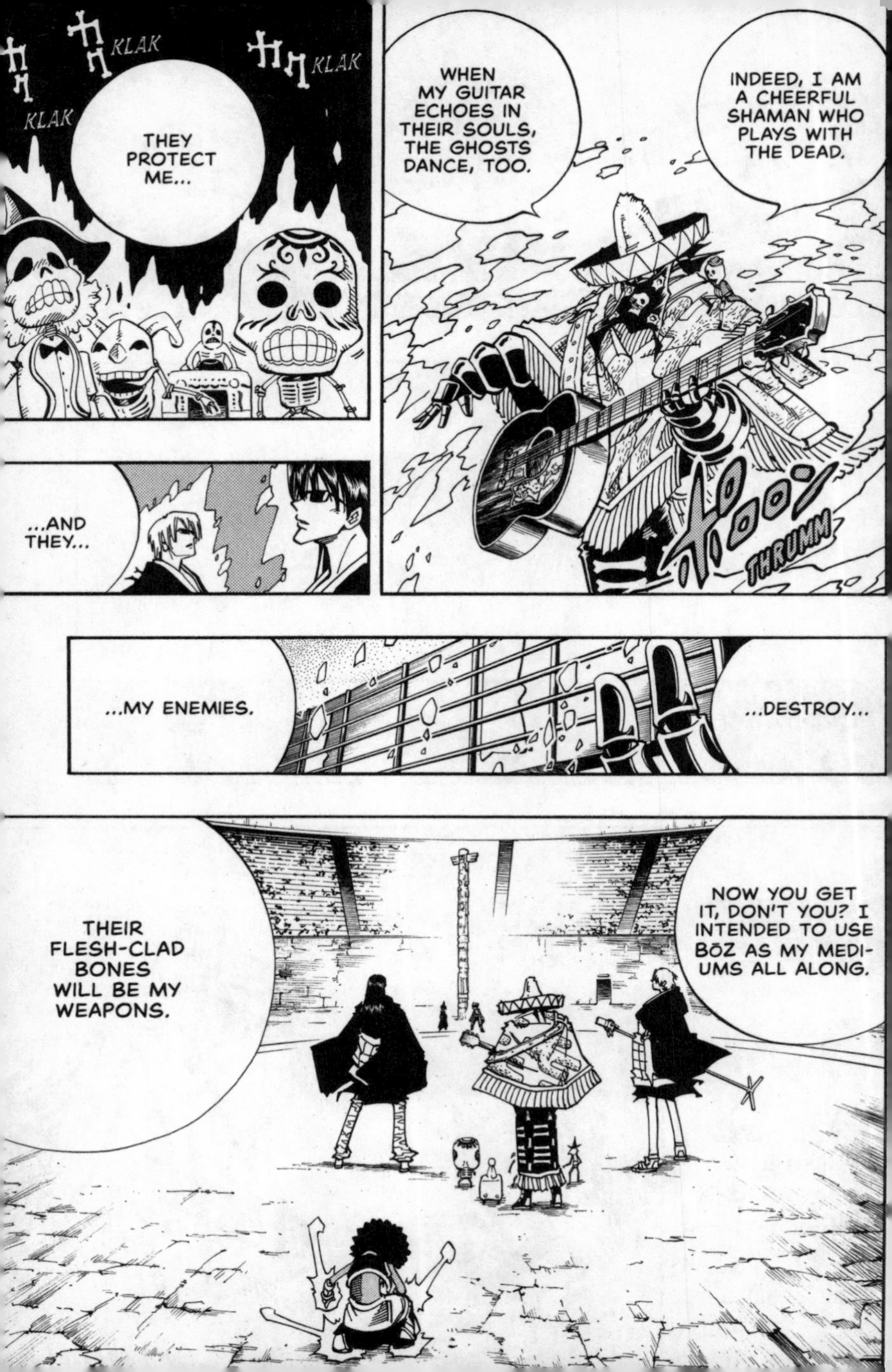
INDEED, I AM A CHEERFUL SHAMAN WHO PLAYS WITH THE DEAD.
WHEN MY GUITAR ECHOES IN THEIR SOULS, THE GHOSTS DANCE, TOO.
THRUMM
KLAK
KLAK
KLAK
THEY PROTECT ME...
...AND THEY...
...DESTROY...
...MY ENEMIES.
NOW YOU GET IT, DON'T YOU? I INTENDED TO USE BŌZ AS MY MEDIUMS ALL ALONG.
THEIR FLESH-CLAD BONES WILL BE MY WEAPONS.

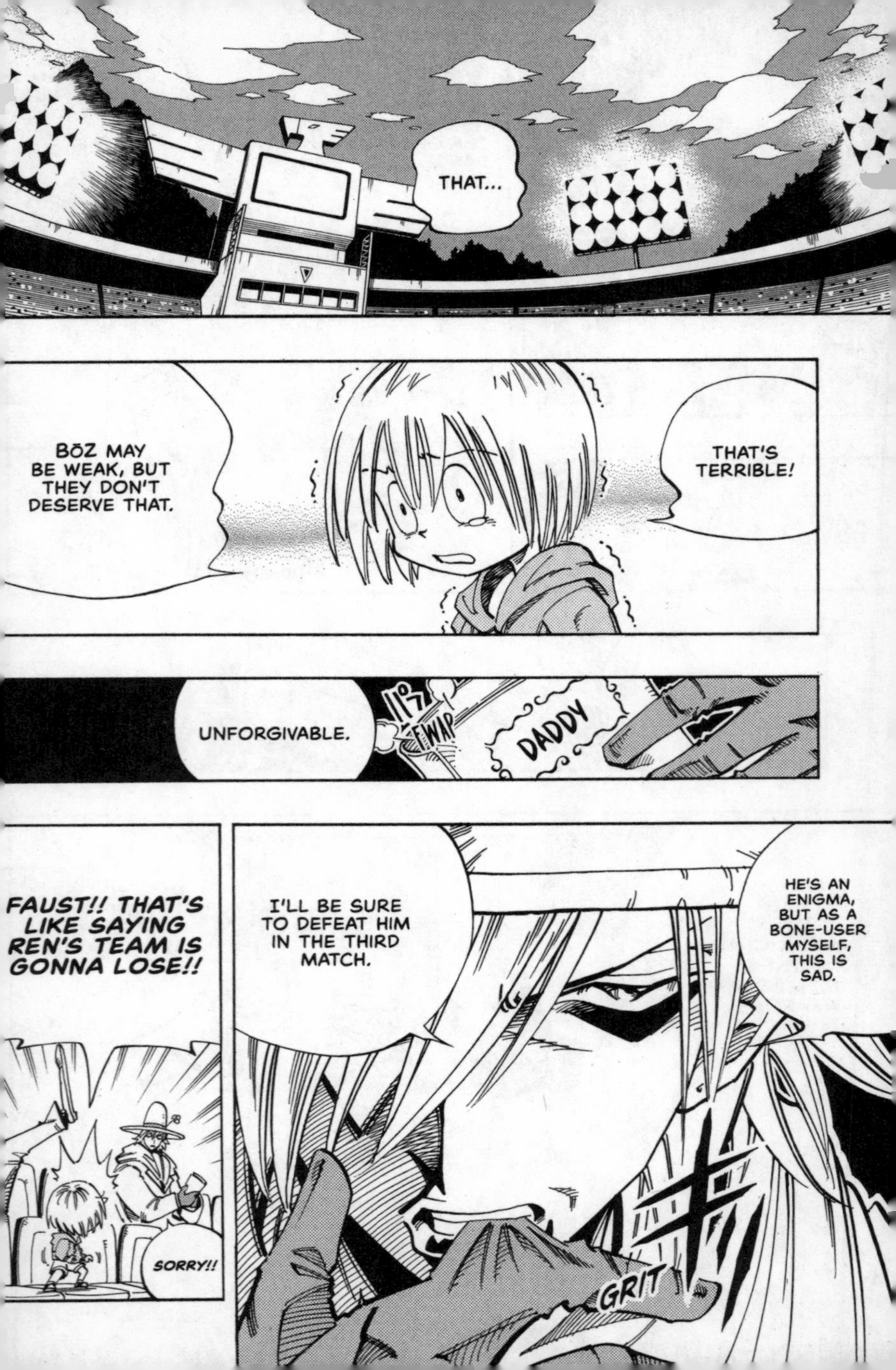
THAT...
THAT'S TERRIBLE!
BŌZ MAY BE WEAK, BUT THEY DON'T DESERVE THAT.
DADDY
FWAP
UNFORGIVABLE.
HE'S AN ENIGMA, BUT AS A BONE-USER MYSELF, THIS IS SAD.
I'LL BE SURE TO DEFEAT HIM IN THE THIRD MATCH.
GRIT
FAUST!! THAT'S LIKE SAYING REN'S TEAM IS GONNA LOSE!!
SORRY!!

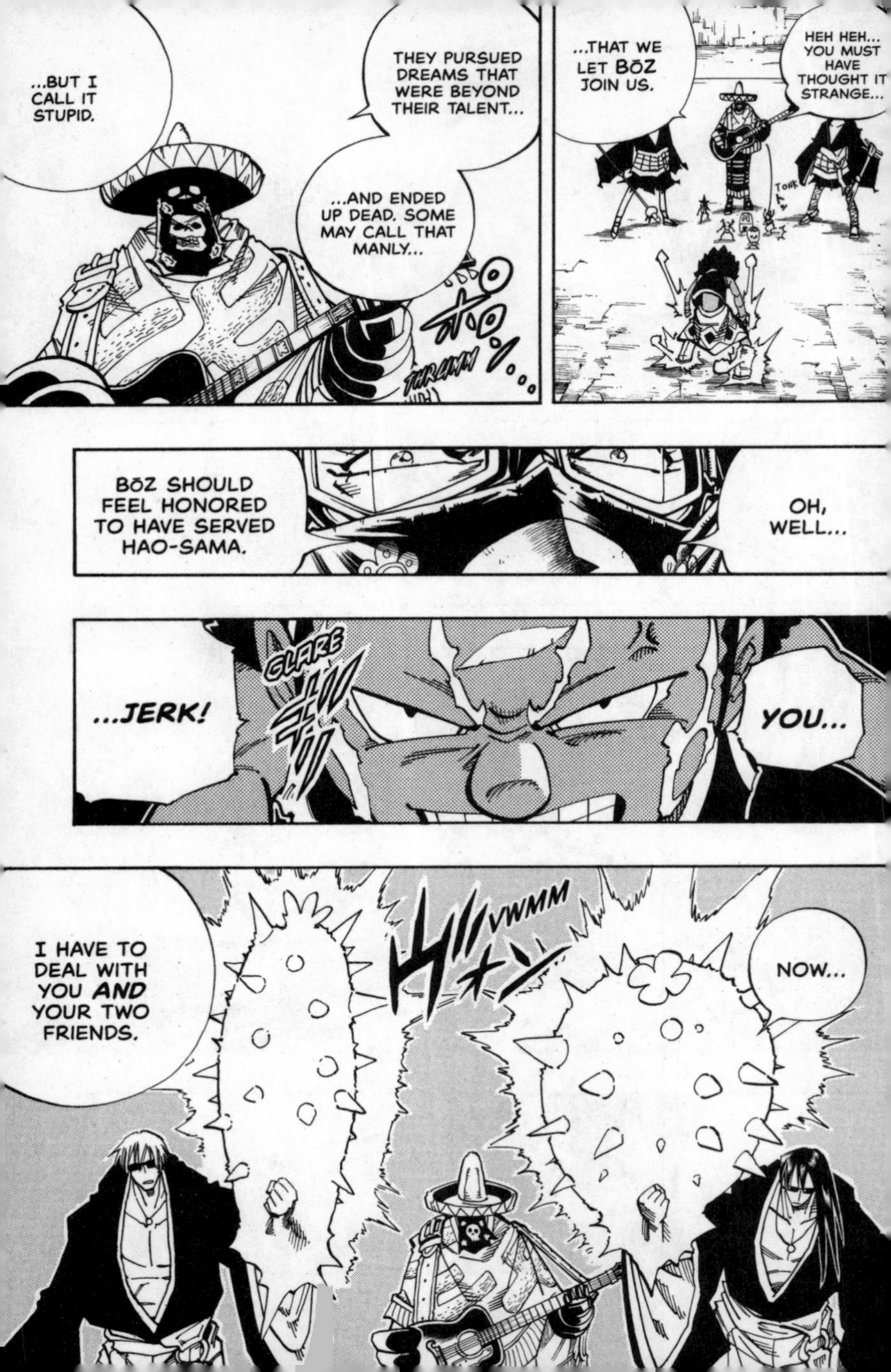
HEH HEH... YOU MUST HAVE THOUGHT IT STRANGE...
...THAT WE LET BŌZ JOIN US.
TONK
THEY PURSUED DREAMS THAT WERE BEYOND THEIR TALENT...
...AND ENDED UP DEAD. SOME MAY CALL THAT MANLY...
...BUT I CALL IT STUPID.
THRUMM
OH, WELL...
BŌZ SHOULD FEEL HONORED TO HAVE SERVED HAO-SAMA.
YOU...
GLARE
...JERK!
NOW...
VWMM
I HAVE TO DEAL WITH YOU *AND* YOUR TWO FRIENDS.

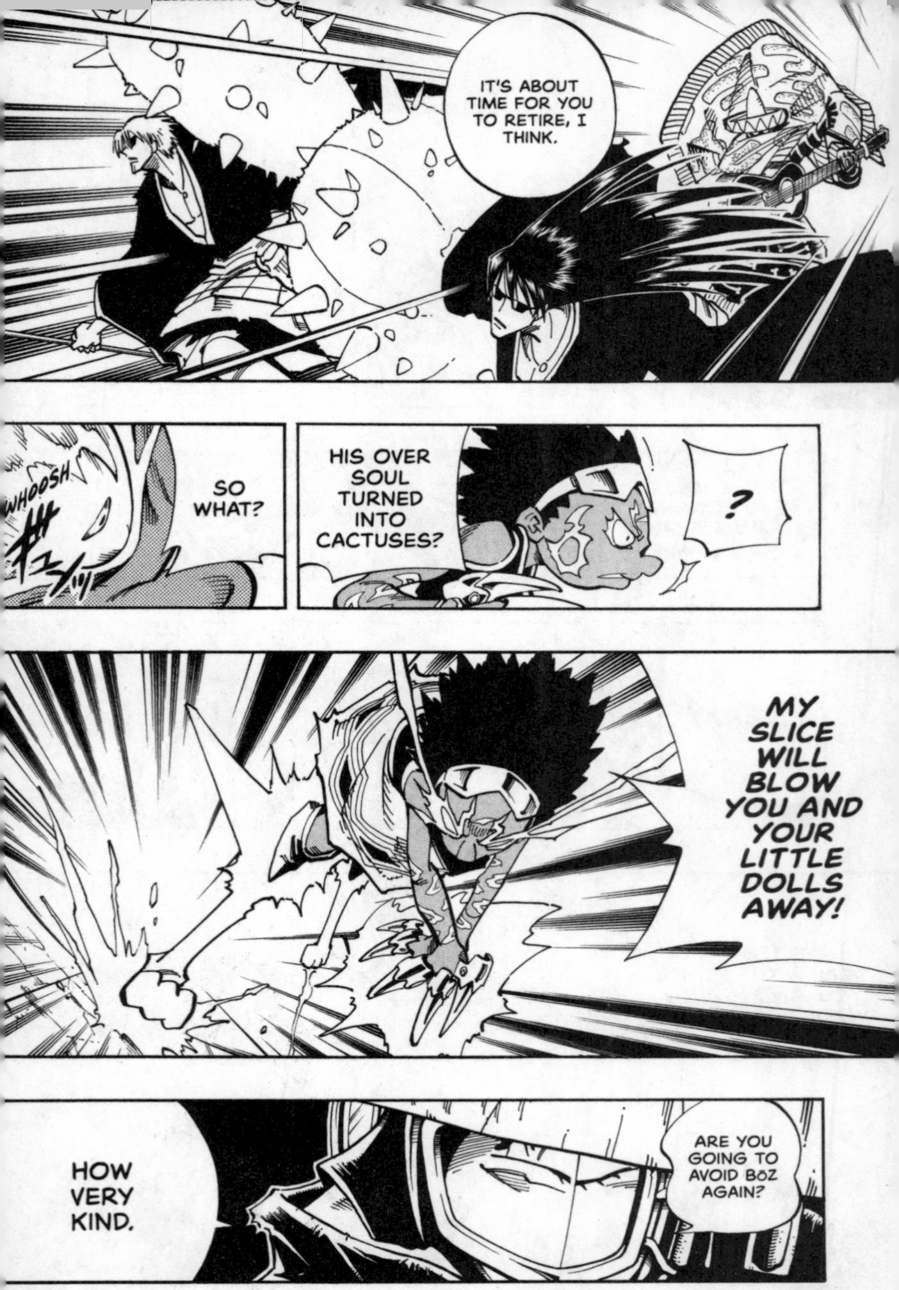
IT'S ABOUT TIME FOR YOU TO RETIRE, I THINK.
?
HIS OVER SOUL TURNED INTO CACTUSES?
SO WHAT?
WHOOSH
MY SLICE WILL BLOW YOU AND YOUR LITTLE DOLLS AWAY!
ARE YOU GOING TO AVOID BōZ AGAIN?
HOW VERY KIND.

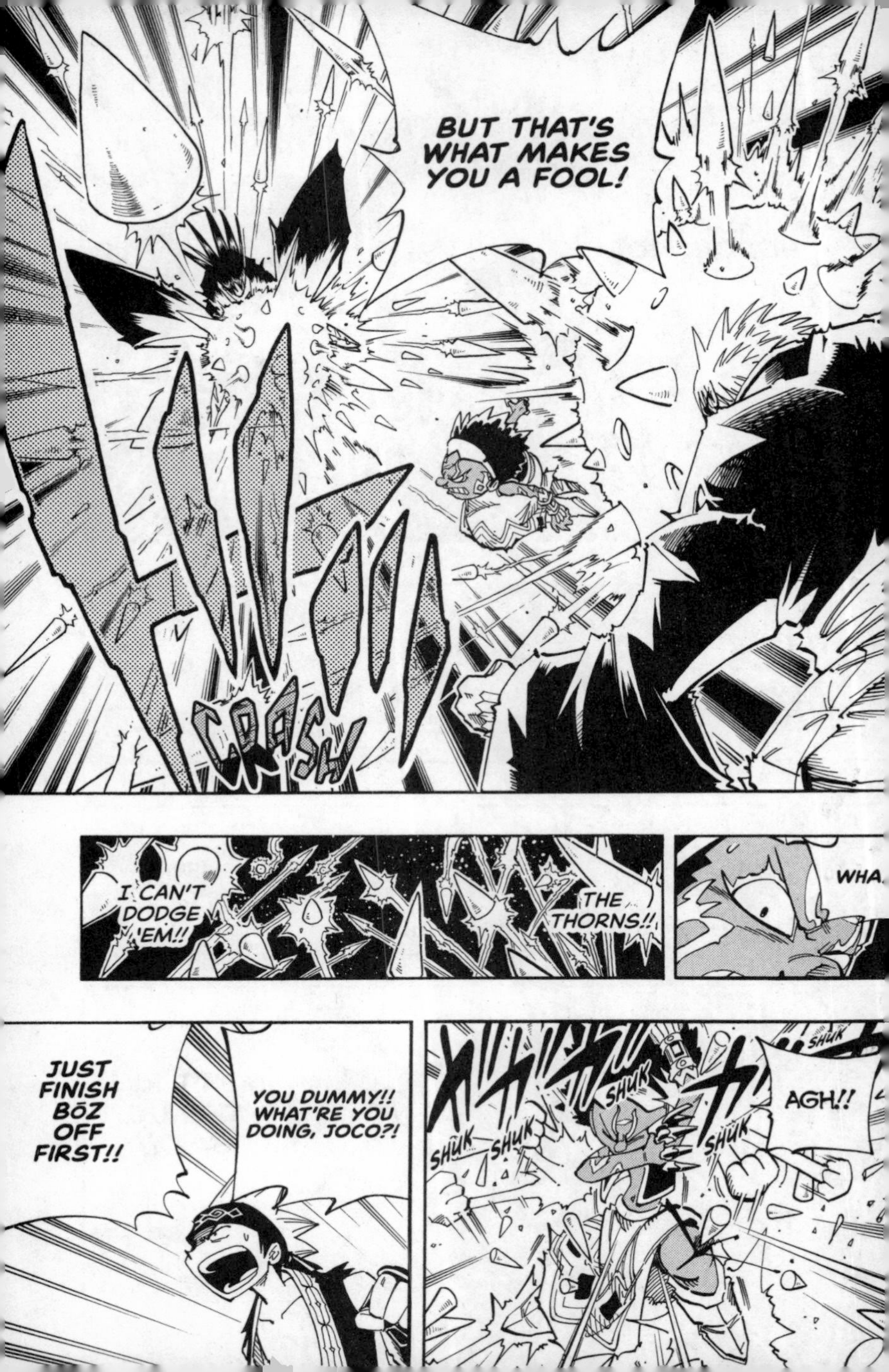
BUT THAT'S WHAT MAKES YOU A FOOL!
CRASH
WHA...
THE THORNS!!
I CAN'T DODGE 'EM!!
SHUK
AGH!!
SHUK
SHUK
SHUK
SHUK
YOU DUMMY!! WHAT'RE YOU DOING, JOCO?!
JUST FINISH BŌZ OFF FIRST!!

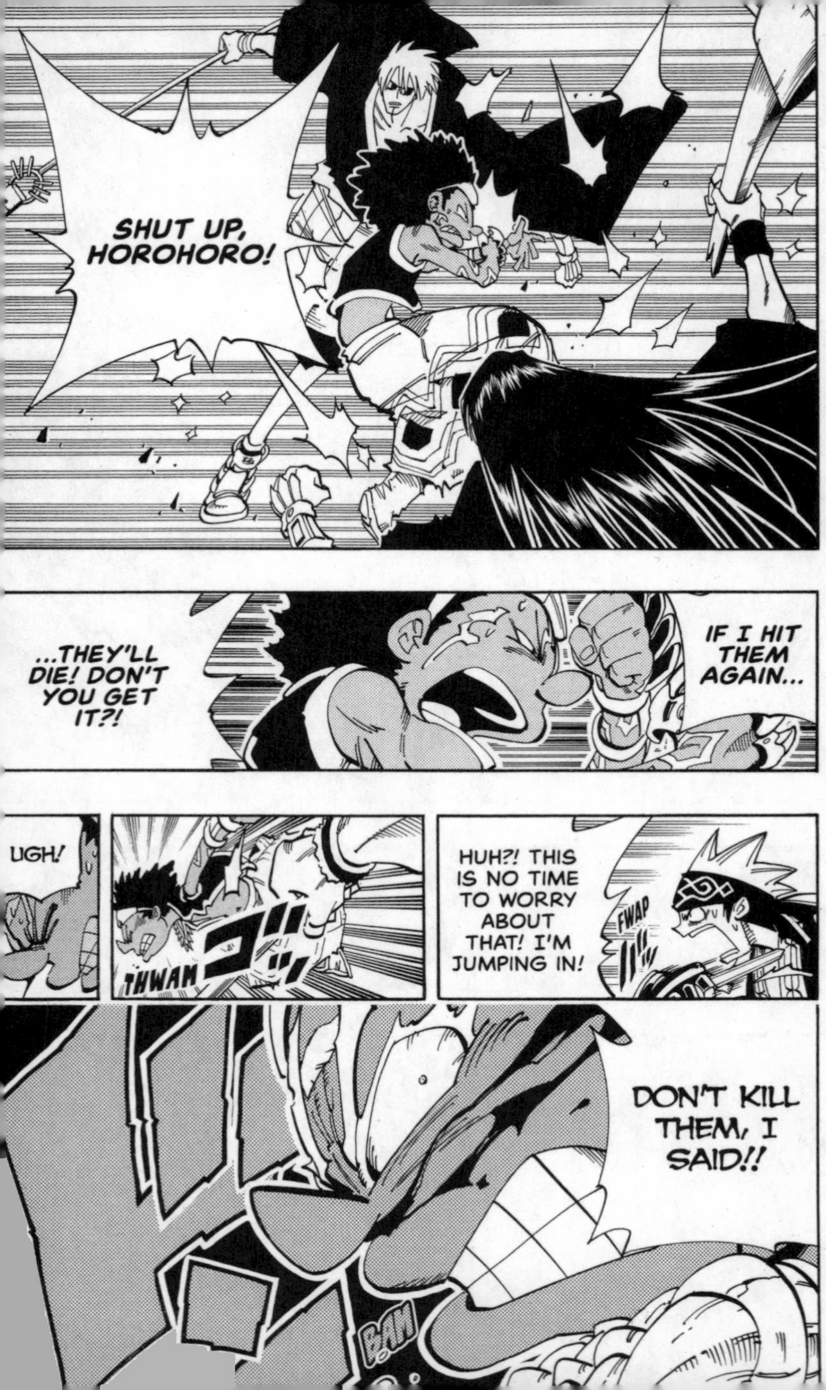
SHUT UP, HOROHORO!
IF I HIT THEM AGAIN...
...THEY'LL DIE! DON'T YOU GET IT?!
HUH?! THIS IS NO TIME TO WORRY ABOUT THAT! I'M JUMPING IN!
FWAP
THWAM
UGH!
DON'T KILL THEM, I SAID!!
BAM

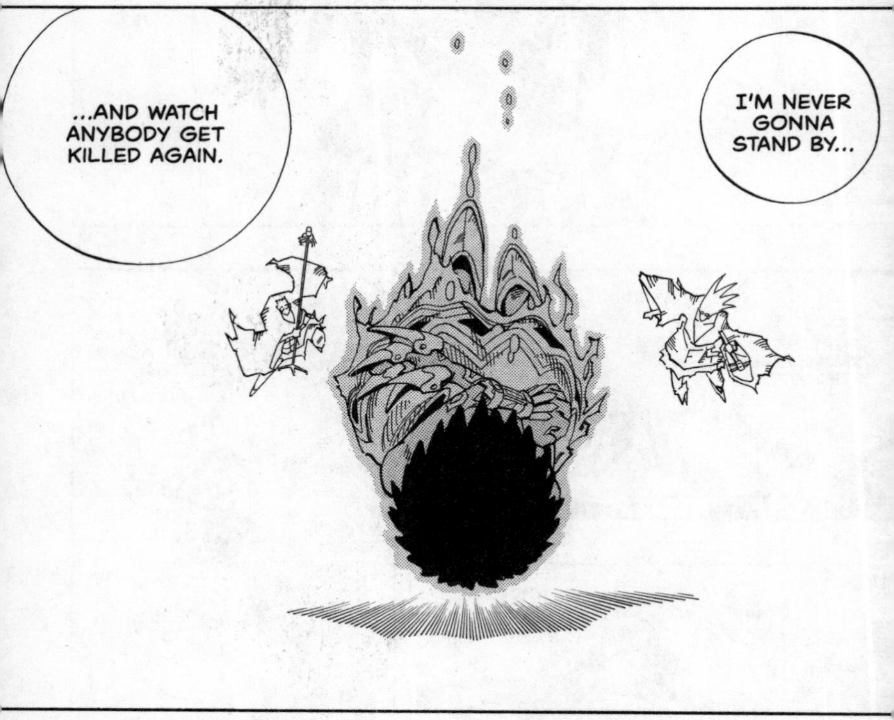
I'M NEVER GONNA STAND BY...
...AND WATCH ANYBODY GET KILLED AGAIN.
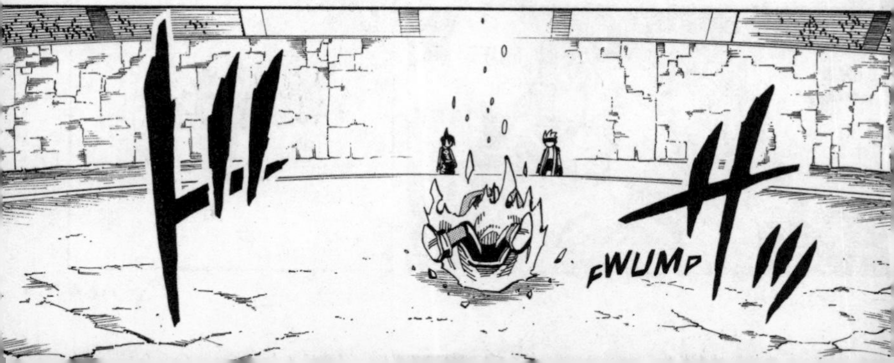
FWUMP

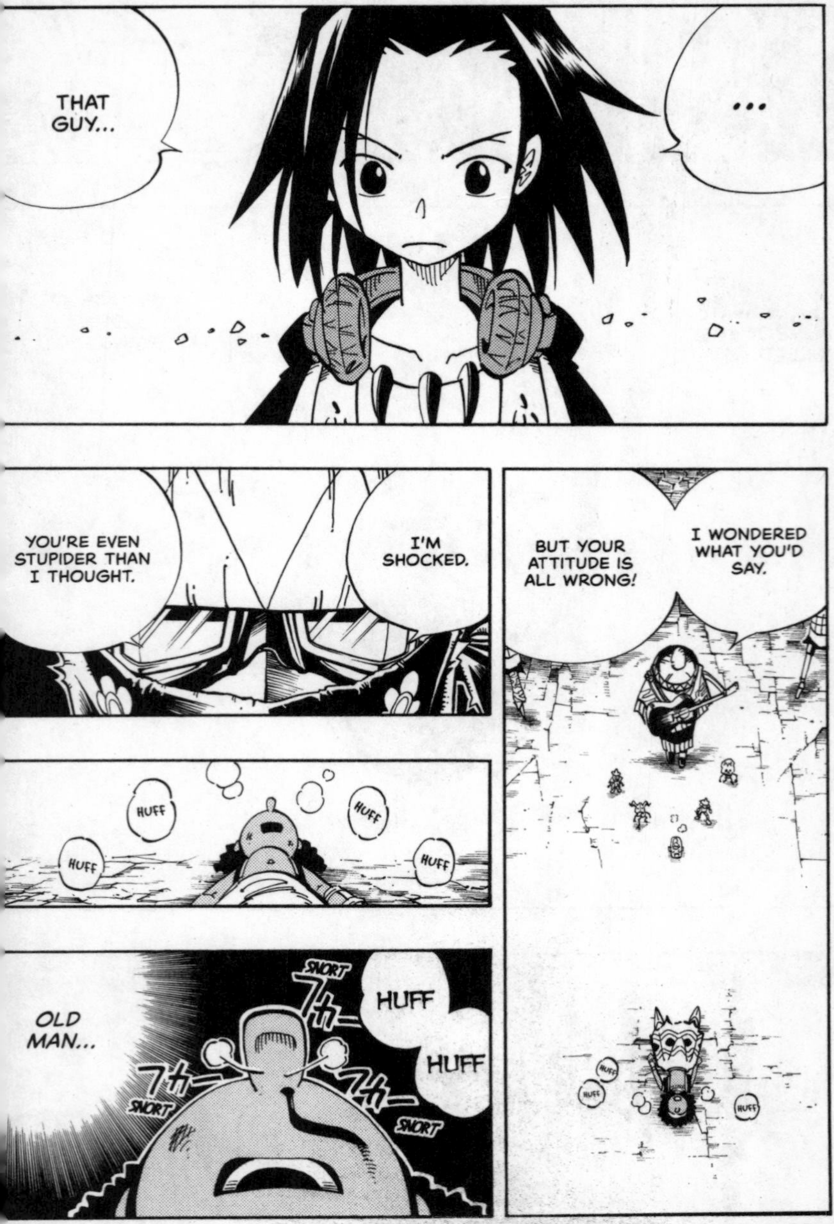
...
THAT GUY...
I WONDERED WHAT YOU'D SAY.
BUT YOUR ATTITUDE IS ALL WRONG!
HUFF
HUFF
HUFF
I'M SHOCKED.
YOU'RE EVEN STUPIDER THAN I THOUGHT.
HUFF
HUFF
HUFF
HUFF
HUFF
HUFF
SNORT
フカー
SNORT
フカー
SNORT
フカー
OLD MAN...

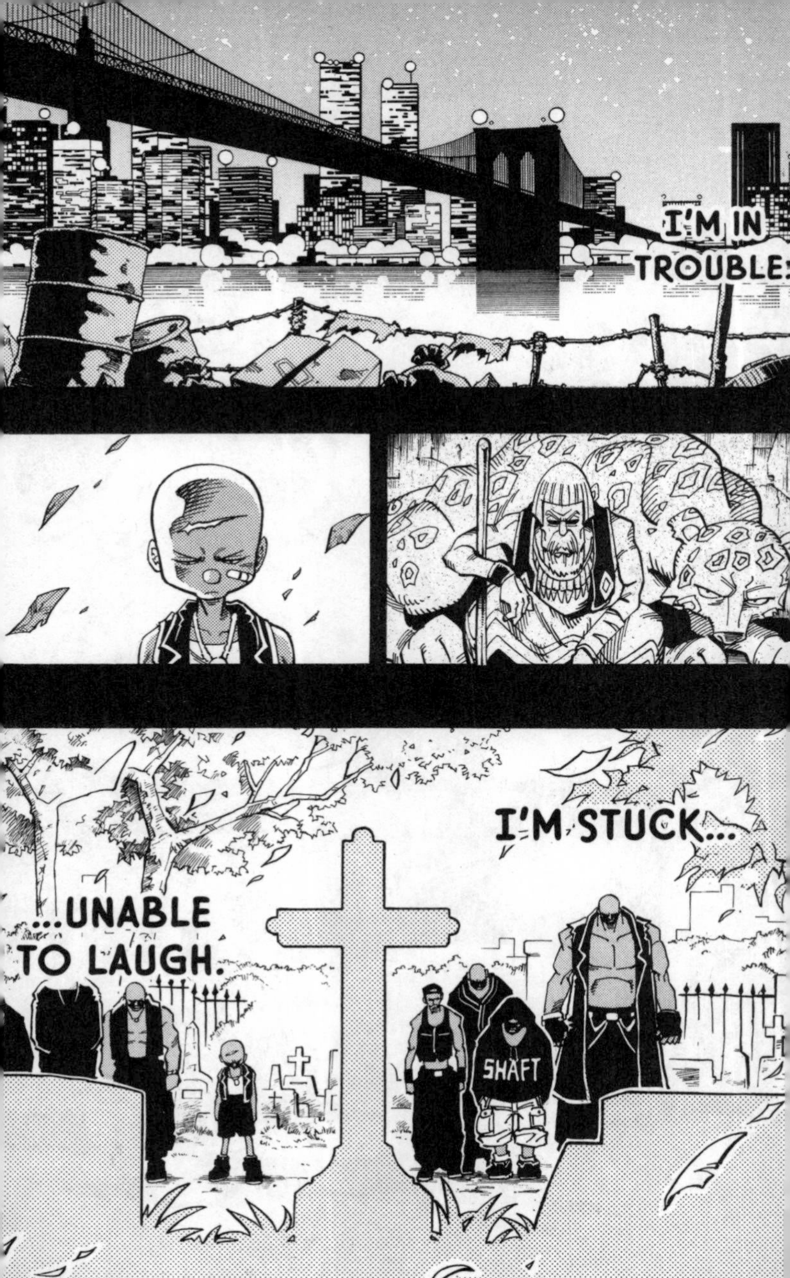
I'M IN TROUBLE.
I'M STUCK...
...UNABLE TO LAUGH.
SHAFT

SHAMAN KING CHARACTER FILE No.63

Calavera Dolls

March 2001

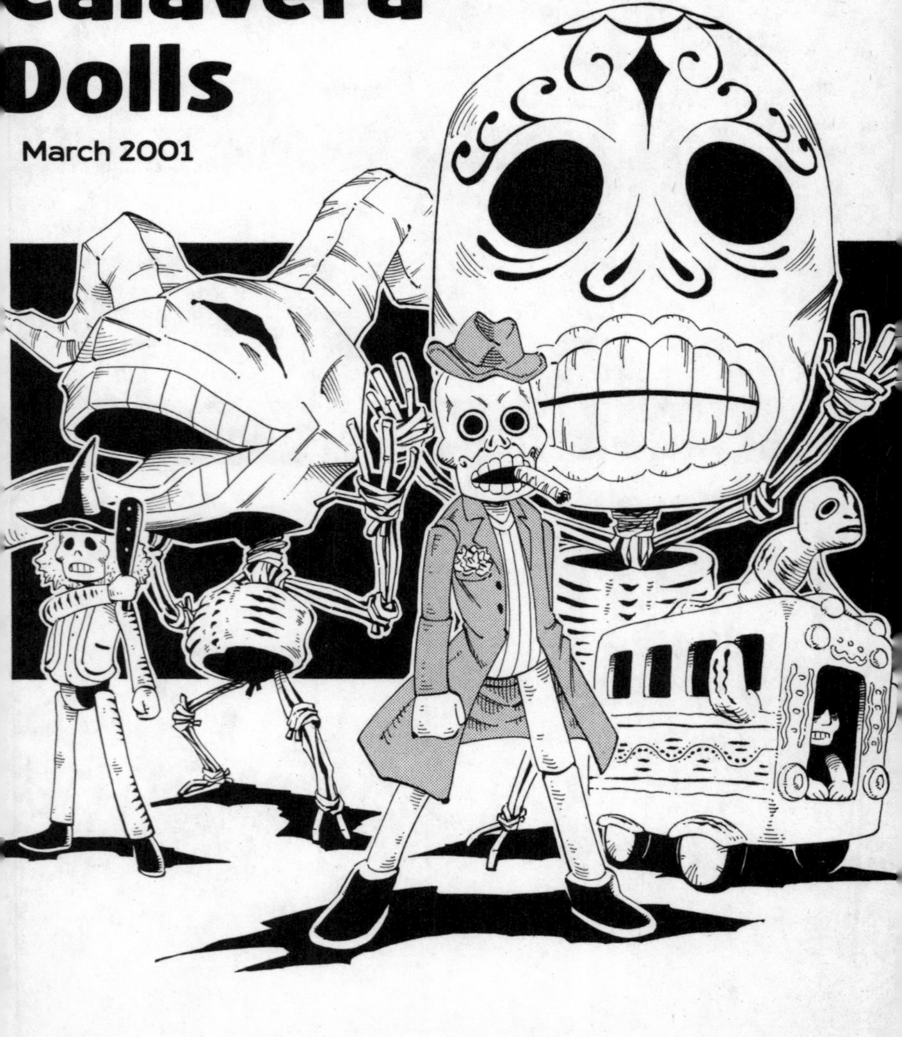

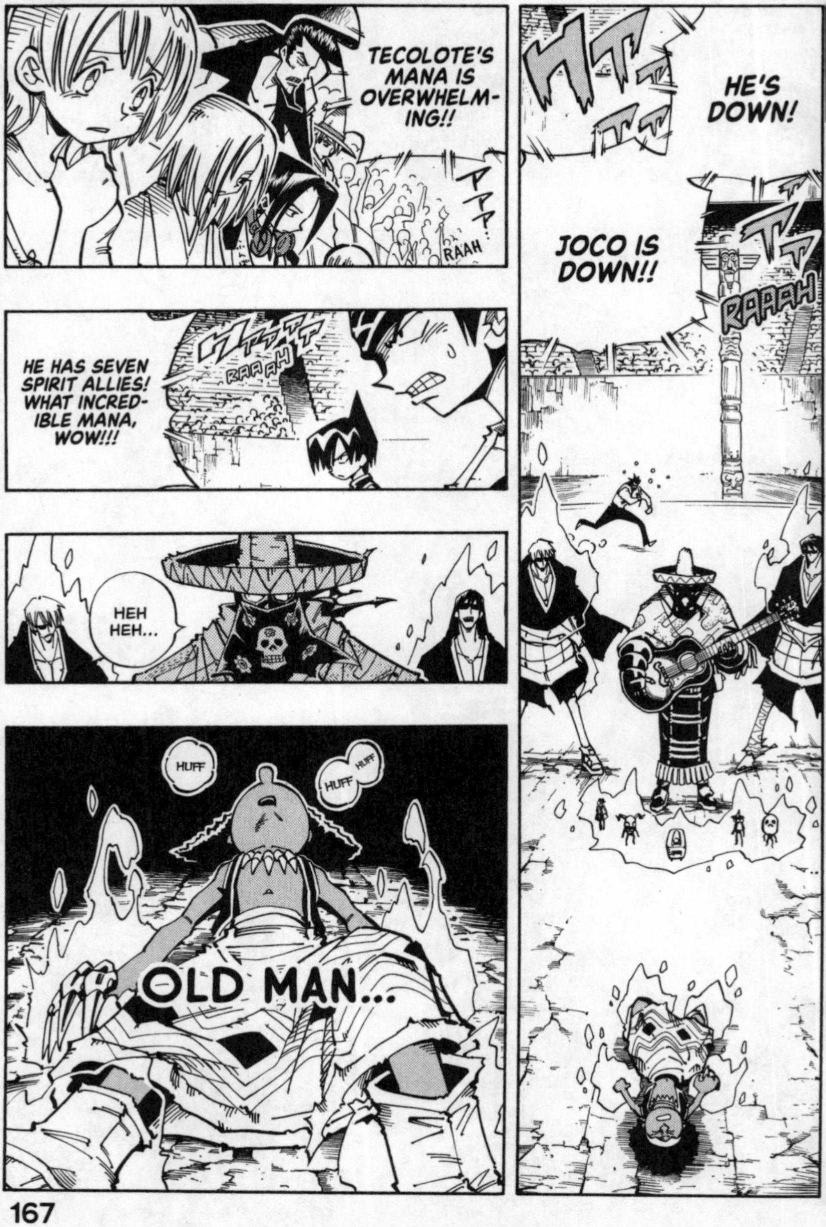
HE'S DOWN!
JOCO IS DOWN!!
RAAAH
TECOLOTE'S MANA IS OVERWHELMING!!
RAAH
HE HAS SEVEN SPIRIT ALLIES! WHAT INCREDIBLE MANA, WOW!!!
RAAAH
HEH HEH...
HUFF
HUFF HUFF
OLD MAN...

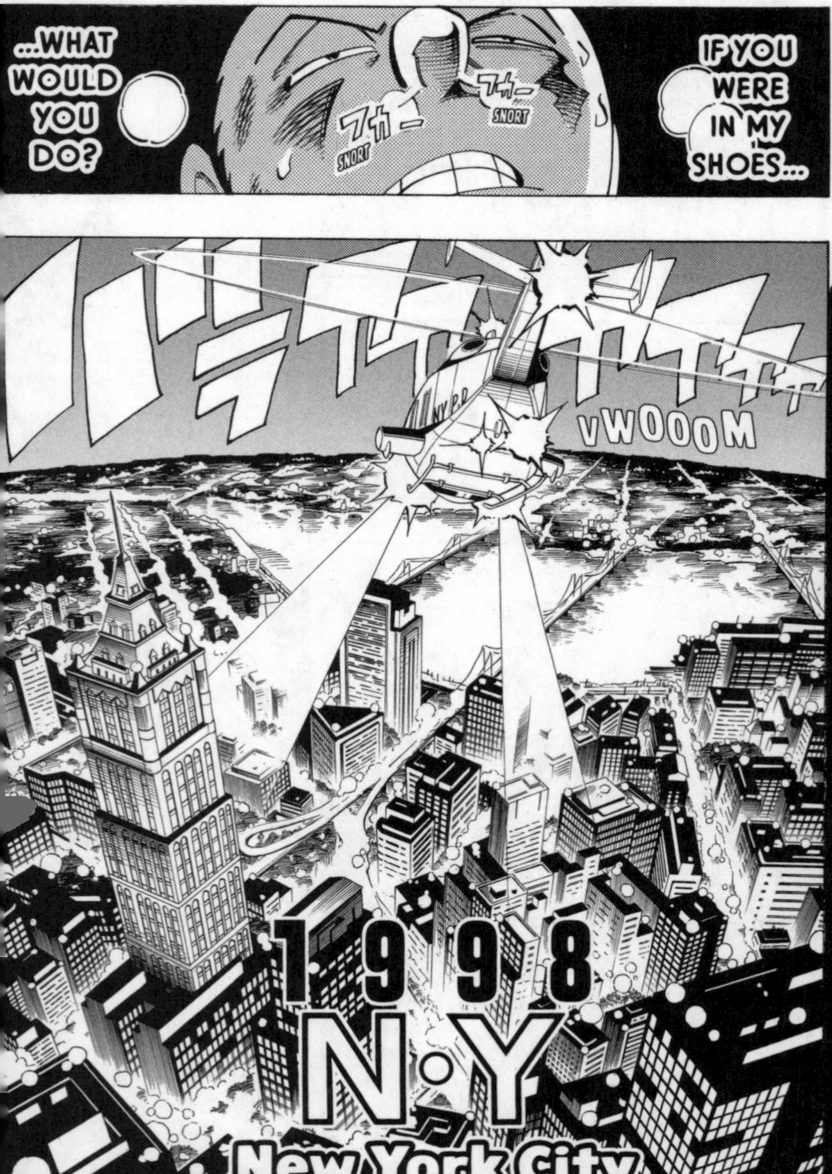
IF YOU WERE IN MY SHOES...
SNORT
SNORT
...WHAT WOULD YOU DO?
VWOOOM
1998
N·Y
New York City

Chapter 116:

Joco's Christmas

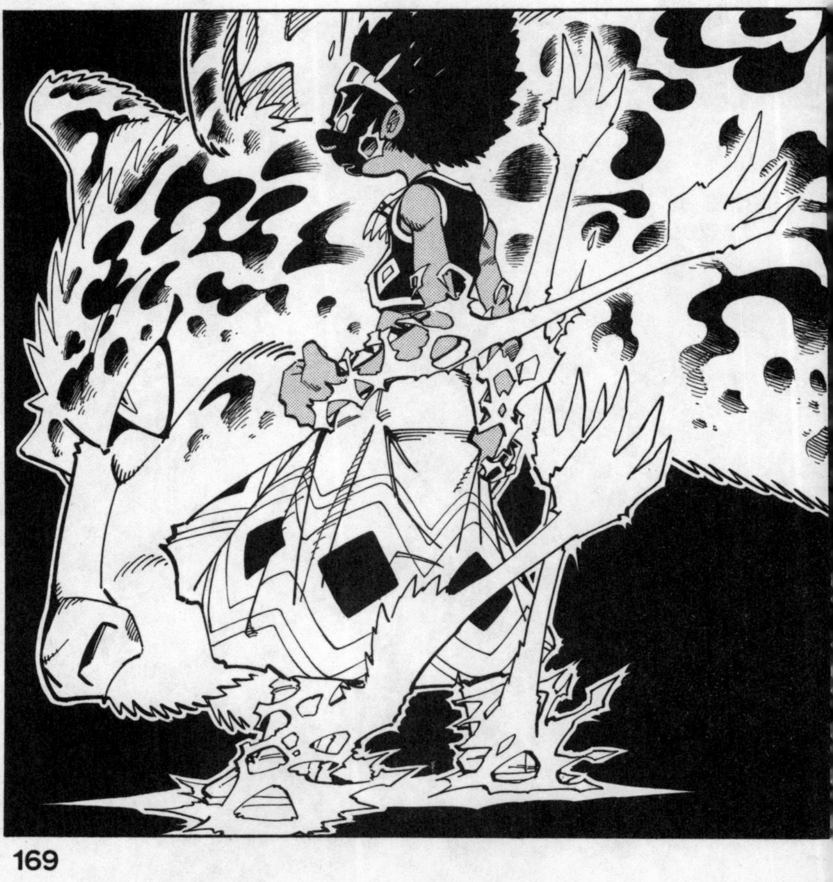

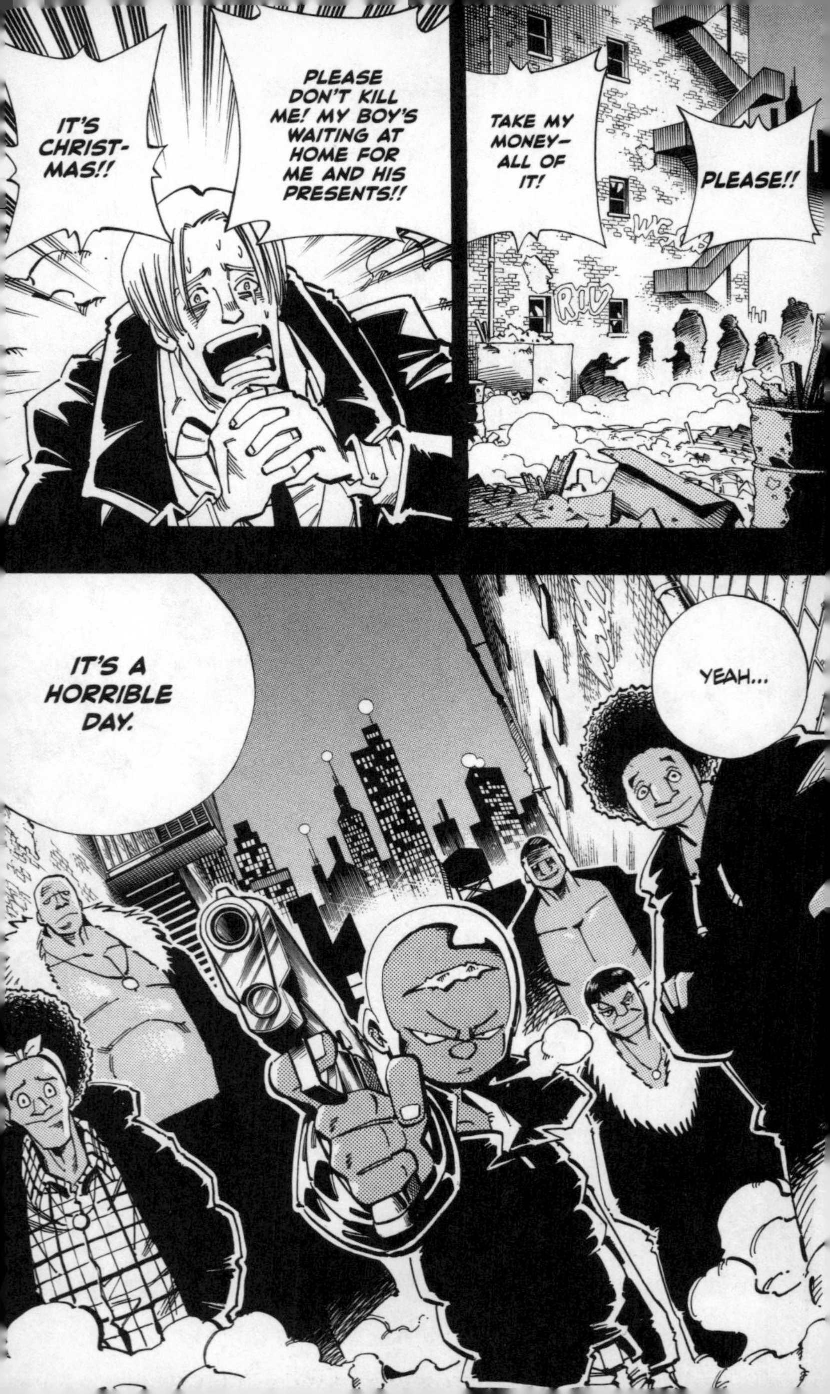
PLEASE!!
TAKE MY MONEY—ALL OF IT!
PLEASE DON'T KILL ME! MY BOY'S WAITING AT HOME FOR ME AND HIS PRESENTS!!
IT'S CHRISTMAS!!
YEAH...
IT'S A HORRIBLE DAY.

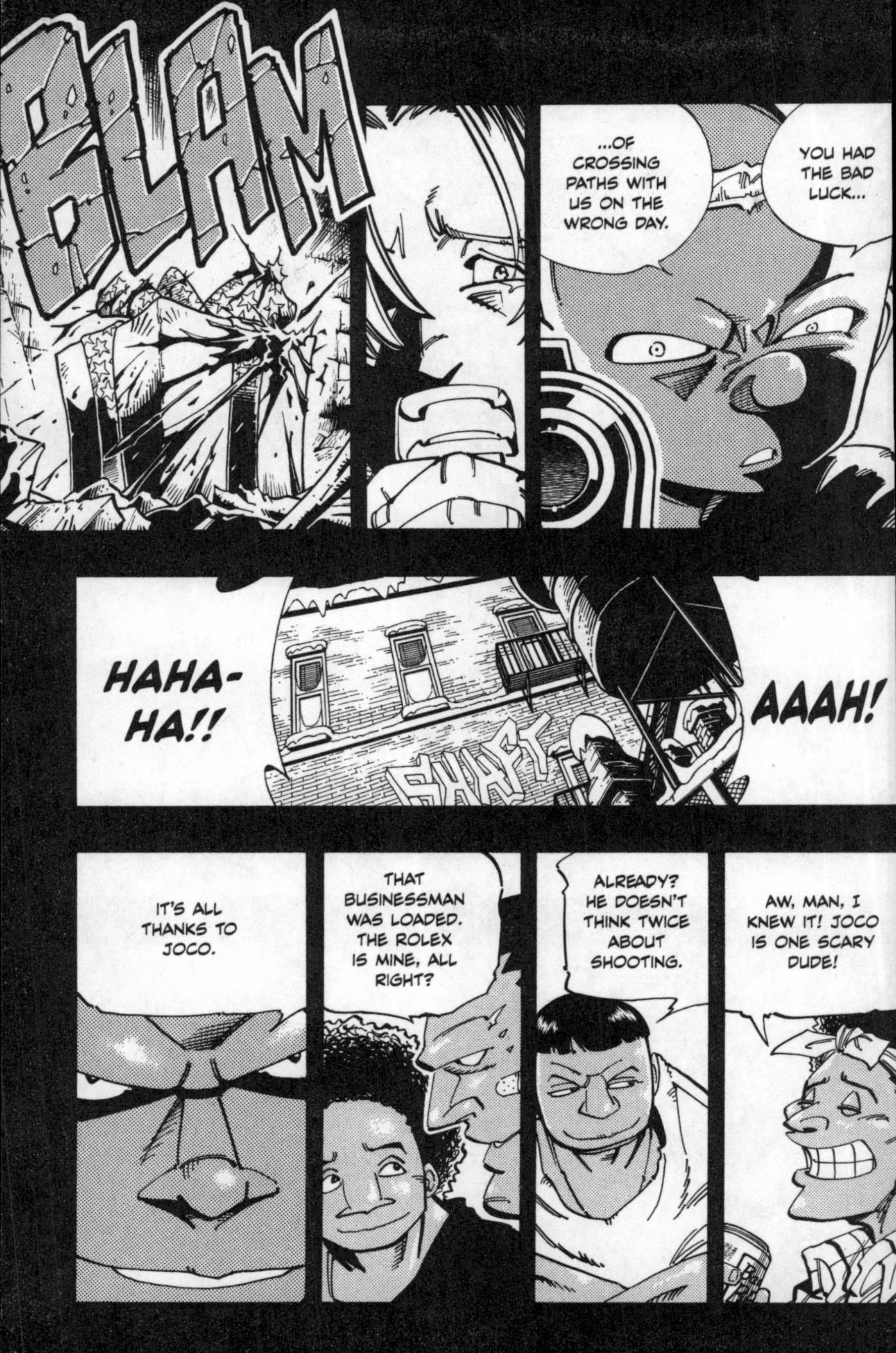
YOU HAD THE BAD LUCK...
...OF CROSSING PATHS WITH US ON THE WRONG DAY.
BLAM
AAAH!
HAHA-HA!!
AW, MAN, I KNEW IT! JOCO IS ONE SCARY DUDE!
ALREADY? HE DOESN'T THINK TWICE ABOUT SHOOTING.
THAT BUSINESSMAN WAS LOADED. THE ROLEX IS MINE, ALL RIGHT?
IT'S ALL THANKS TO JOCO.

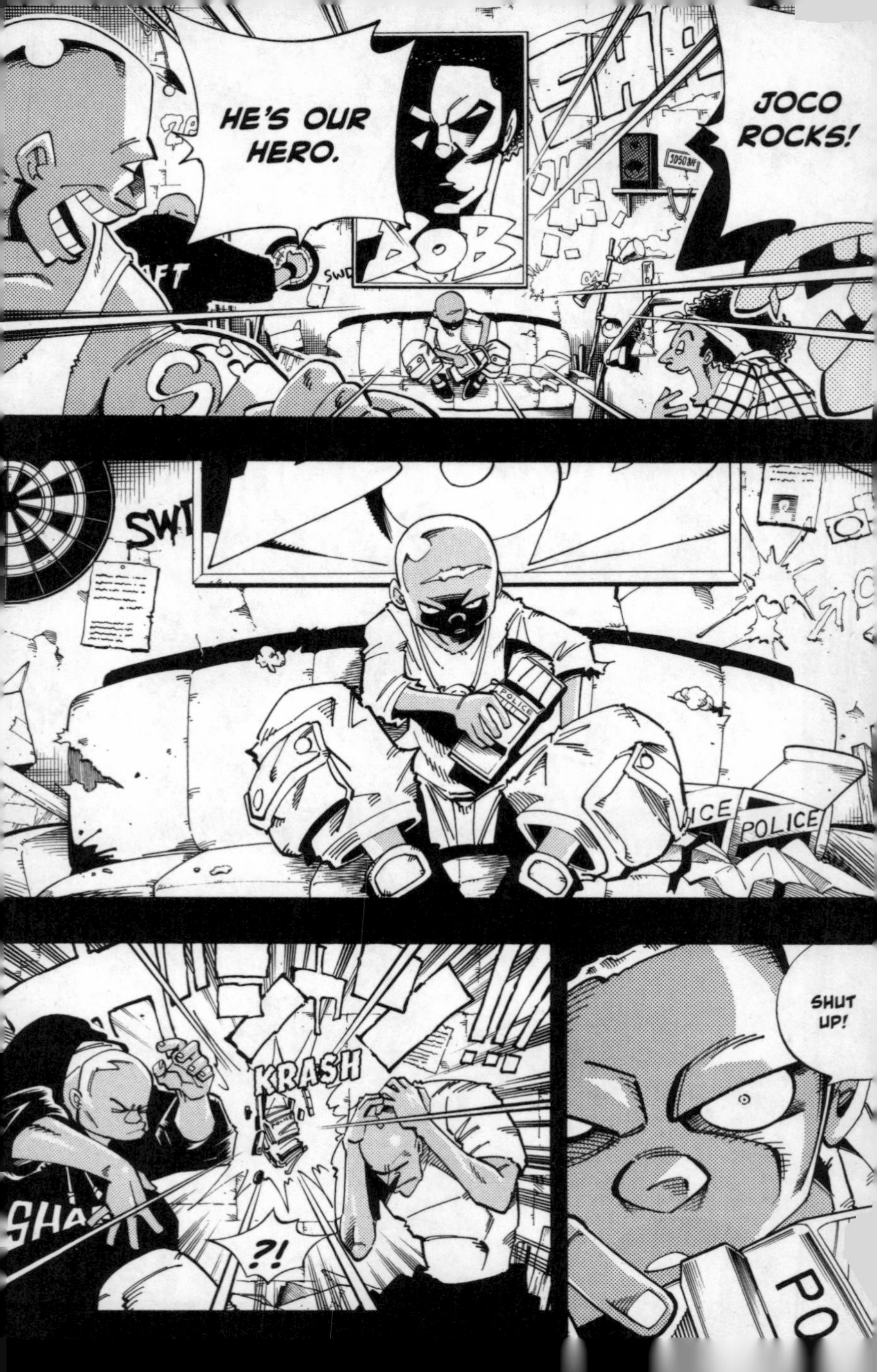
JOCO ROCKS!
HE'S OUR HERO.
BOB
POLICE
POLICE
SHUT UP!
KRASH
!!!
...
?!

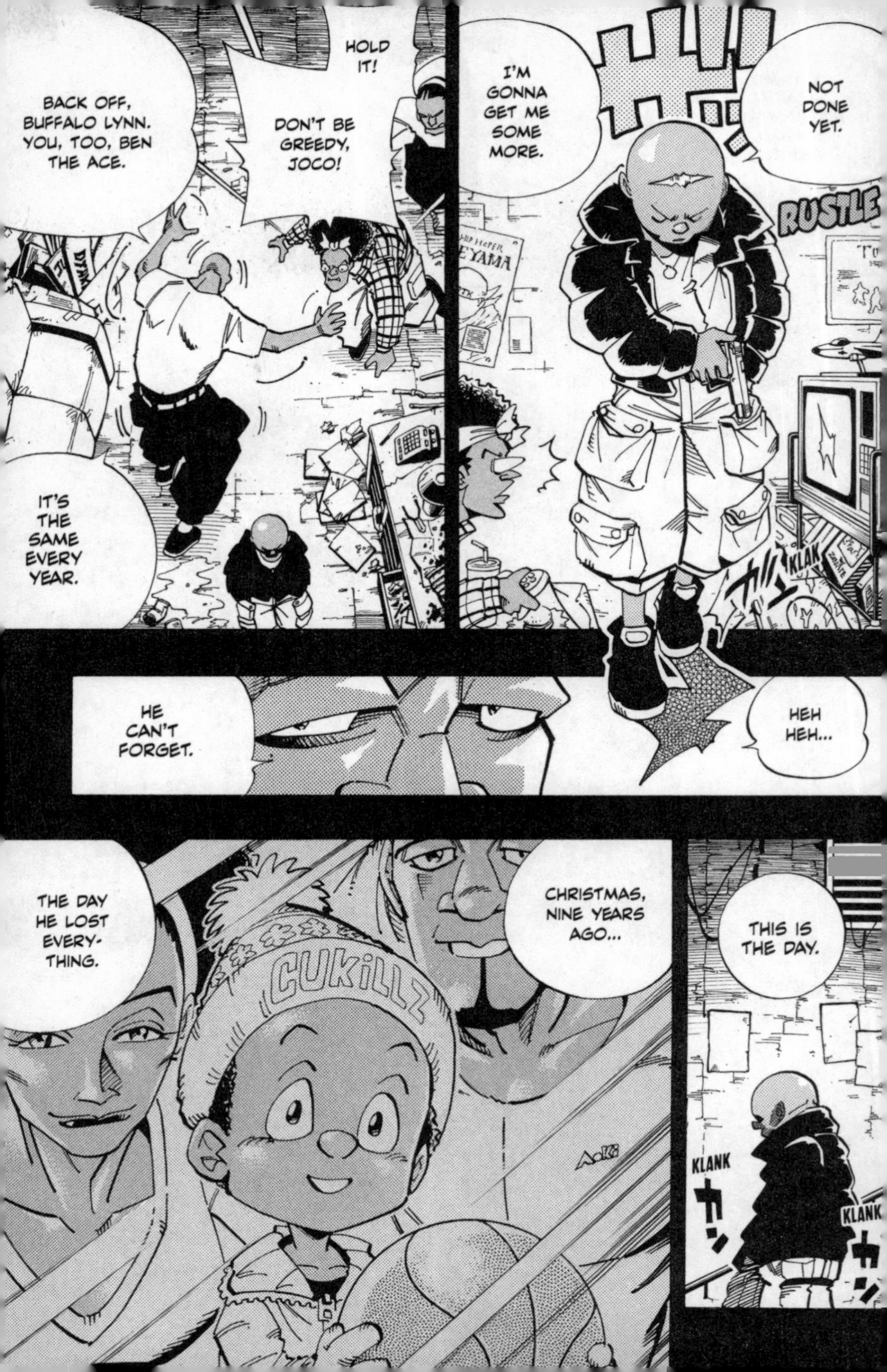

NOT DONE YET.
I'M GONNA GET ME SOME MORE.
RUSTLE
KLAK
HEH HEH...
HOLD IT!
BACK OFF, BUFFALO LYNN. YOU, TOO, BEN THE ACE.
DON'T BE GREEDY, JOCO!
IT'S THE SAME EVERY YEAR.
HE CAN'T FORGET.
THIS IS THE DAY.
KLANK
KLANK
CHRISTMAS, NINE YEARS AGO...
THE DAY HE LOST EVERY-THING.
CUKiLLZ

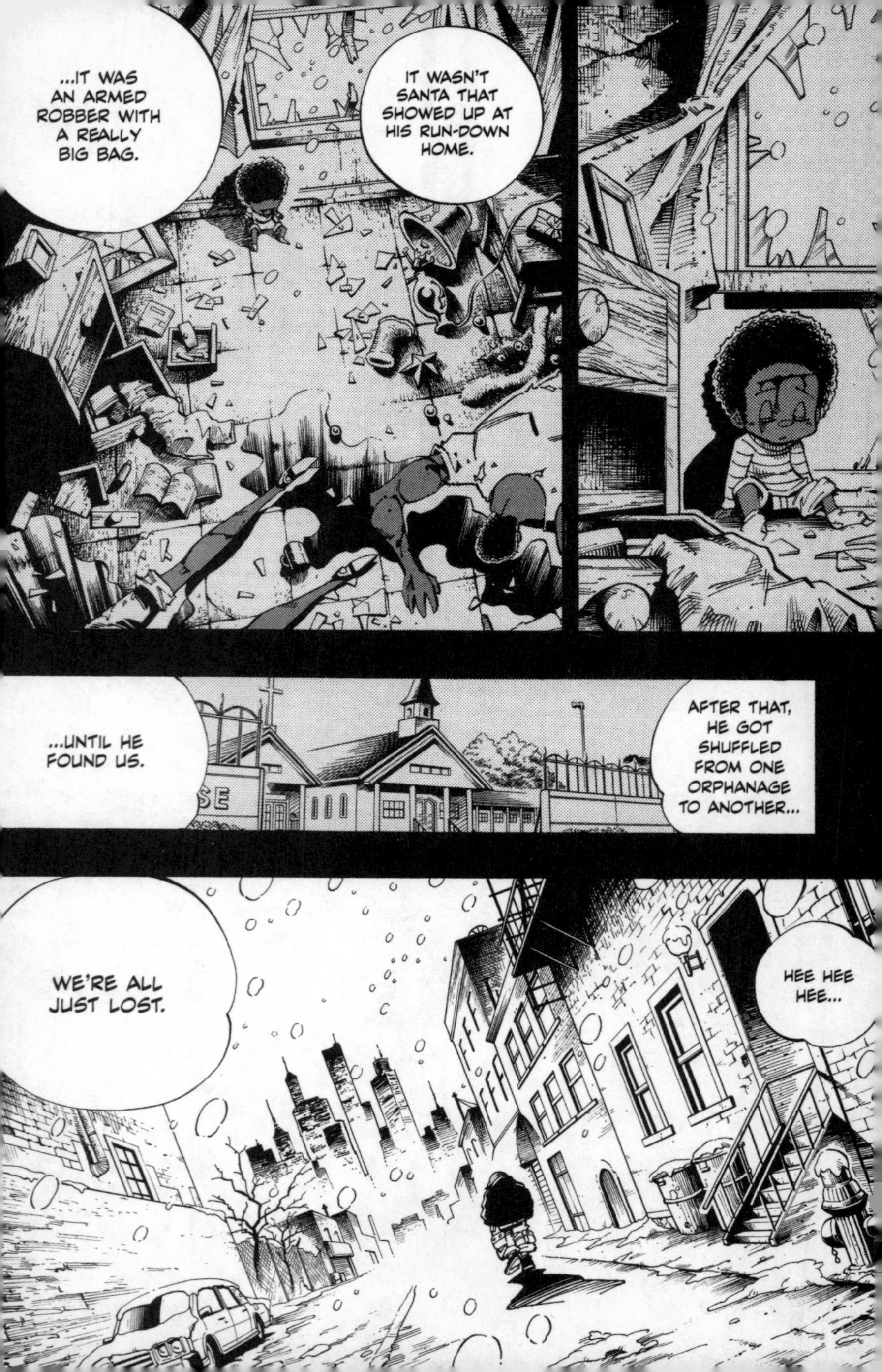
IT WASN'T SANTA THAT SHOWED UP AT HIS RUN-DOWN HOME.
...IT WAS AN ARMED ROBBER WITH A REALLY BIG BAG.
AFTER THAT, HE GOT SHUFFLED FROM ONE ORPHANAGE TO ANOTHER...
...UNTIL HE FOUND US.
HEE HEE HEE...
WE'RE ALL JUST LOST.

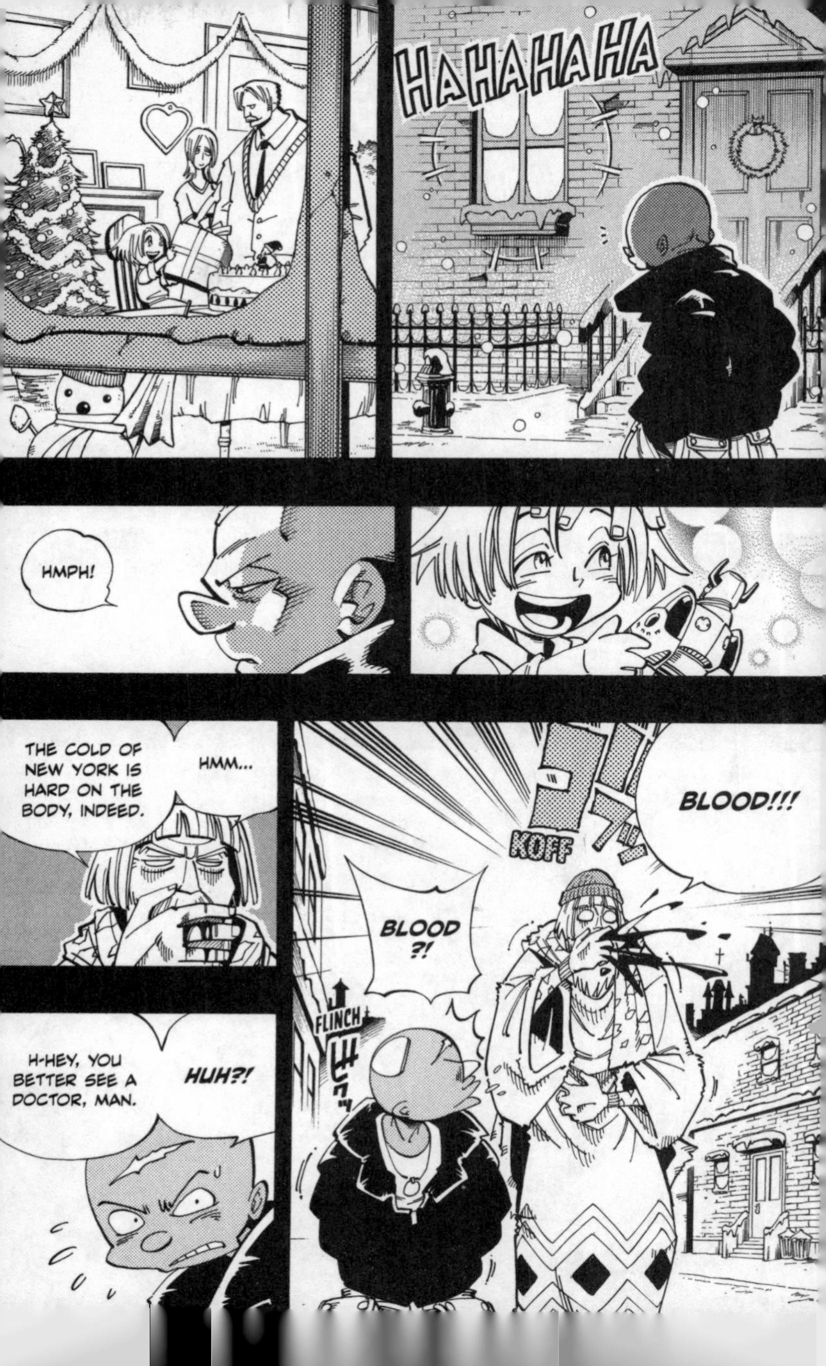
HAHAHAHA
HMPH!
KOFF
BLOOD!!!
BLOOD ?!
FLINCH
HMM...
THE COLD OF NEW YORK IS HARD ON THE BODY, INDEED.
HUH?!
H-HEY, YOU BETTER SEE A DOCTOR, MAN.

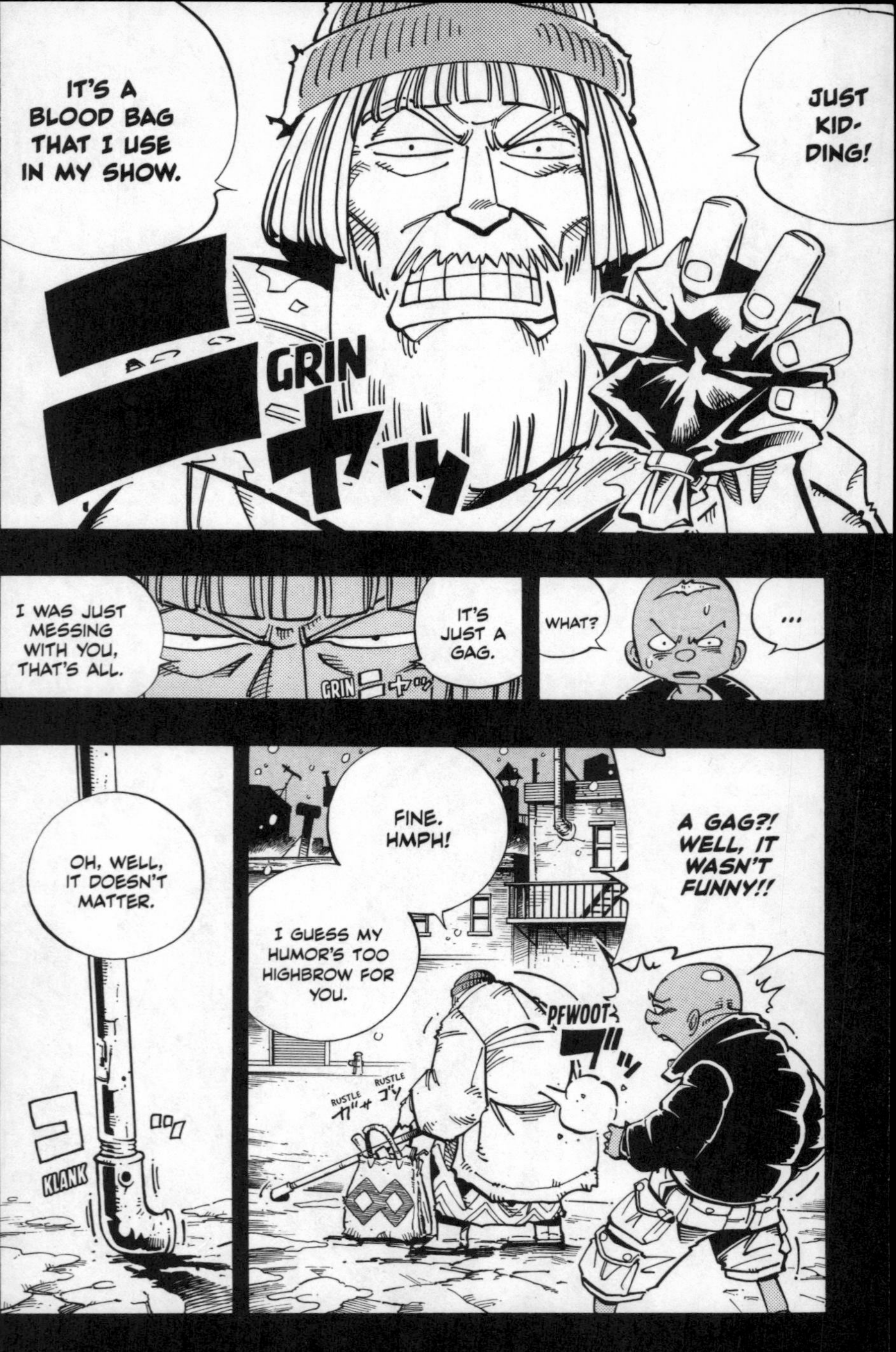
IT'S A BLOOD BAG THAT I USE IN MY SHOW.
JUST KID-DING!
GRIN
ニヤッ
...
WHAT?
IT'S JUST A GAG.
I WAS JUST MESSING WITH YOU, THAT'S ALL.
GRIN
A GAG?! WELL, IT WASN'T FUNNY!!
FINE. HMPH!
I GUESS MY HUMOR'S TOO HIGHBROW FOR YOU.
PFWOOT
RUSTLE
RUSTLE
OH, WELL, IT DOESN'T MATTER.
KLANK

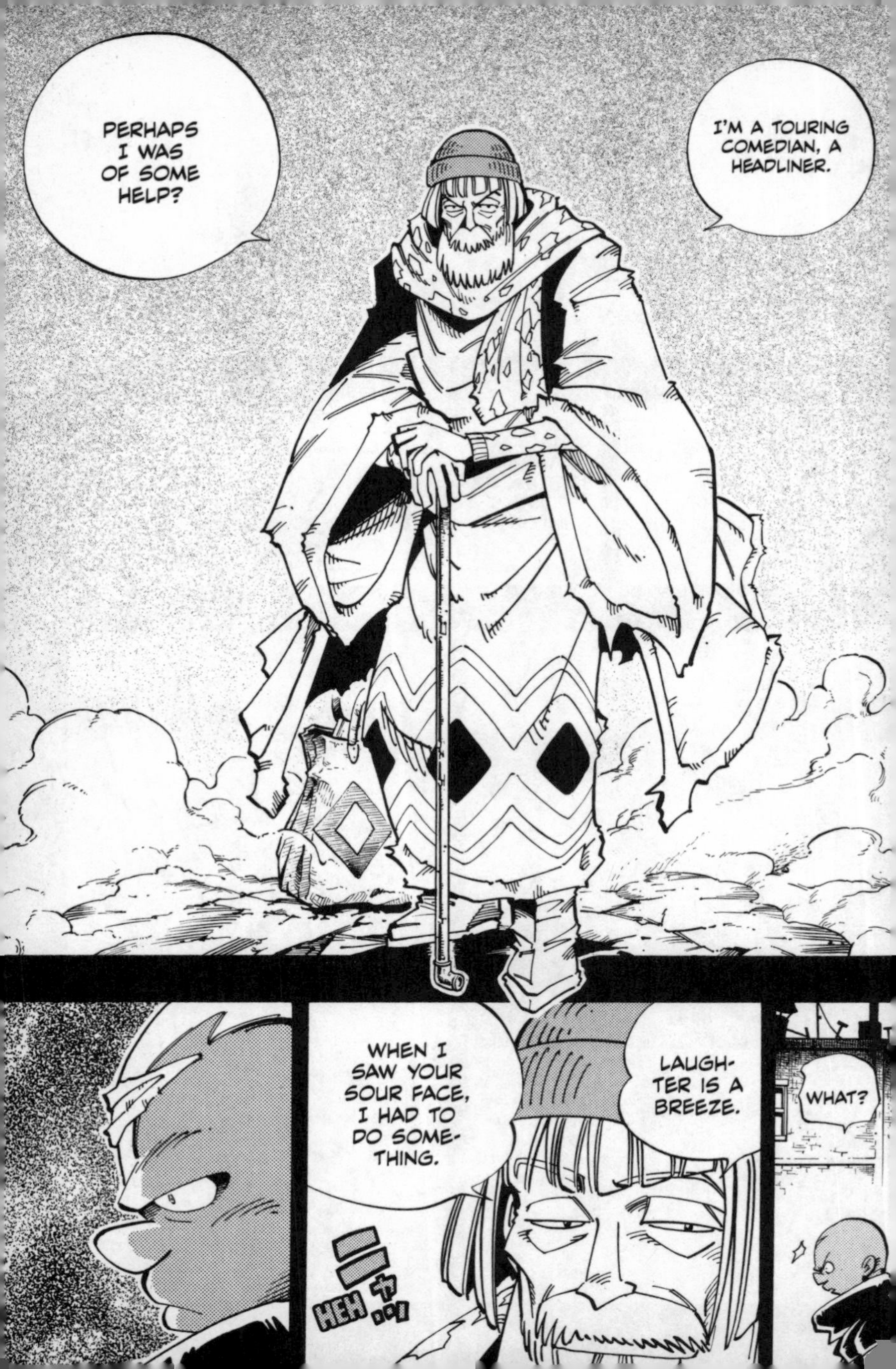

I'M A TOURING COMEDIAN, A HEADLINER.
PERHAPS I WAS OF SOME HELP?
WHAT?
LAUGHTER IS A BREEZE.
WHEN I SAW YOUR SOUR FACE, I HAD TO DO SOMETHING.
HEH

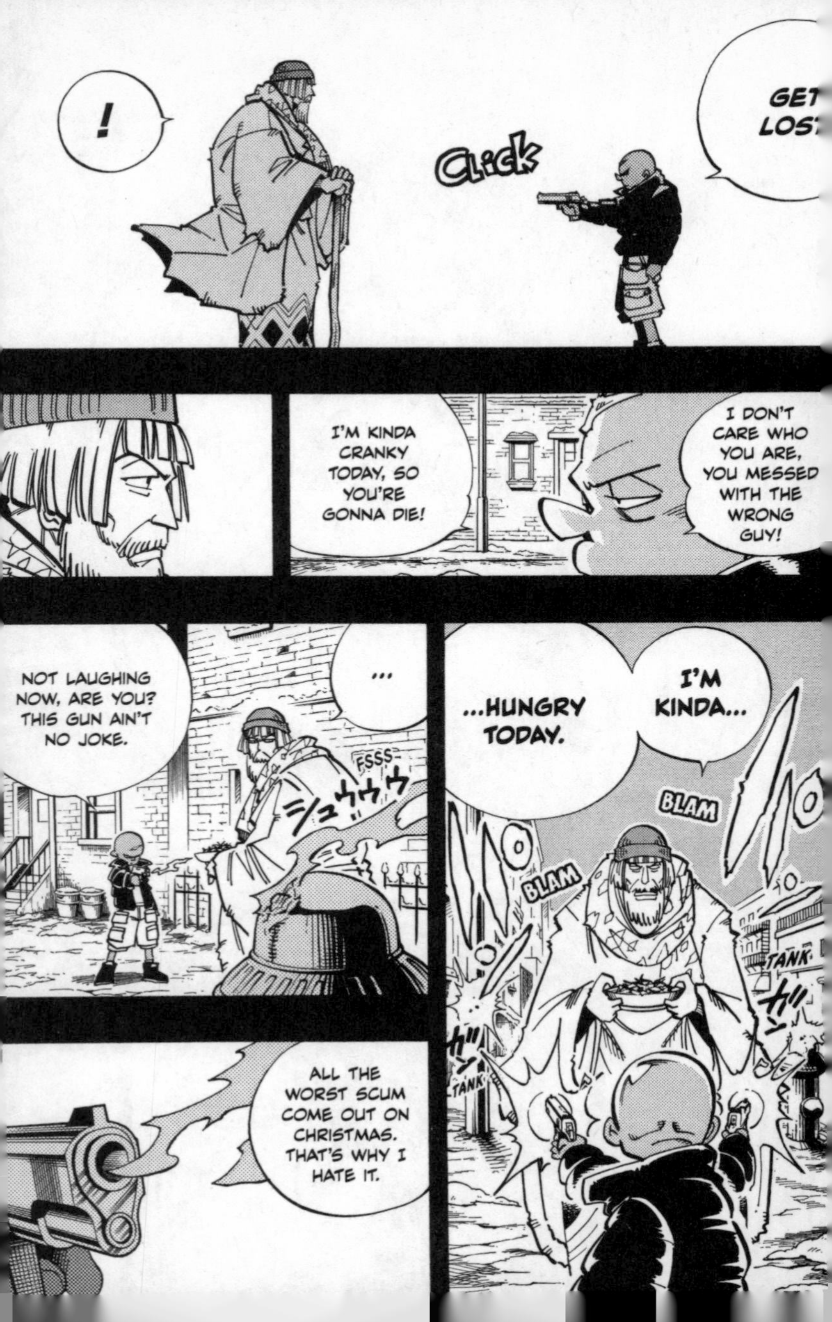
GET LOST
CLICK
!
I DON'T CARE WHO YOU ARE, YOU MESSED WITH THE WRONG GUY!
I'M KINDA CRANKY TODAY, SO YOU'RE GONNA DIE!
I'M KINDA...
...HUNGRY TODAY.
BLAM
BLAM
TANK
TANK
...
FSSS
NOT LAUGHING NOW, ARE YOU? THIS GUN AIN'T NO JOKE.
ALL THE WORST SCUM COME OUT ON CHRISTMAS. THAT'S WHY I HATE IT.

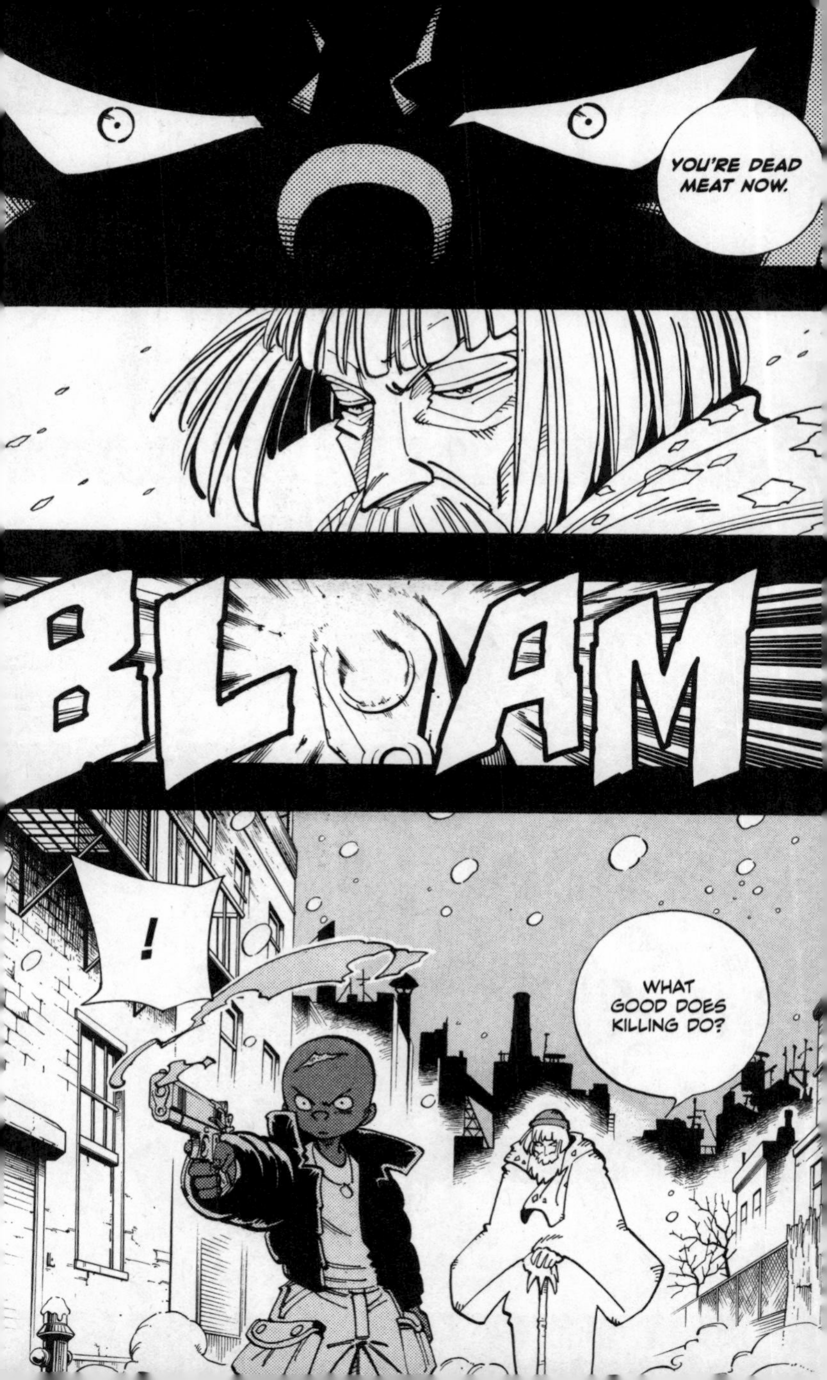
YOU'RE DEAD MEAT NOW.
BLAM
WHAT GOOD DOES KILLING DO?
!

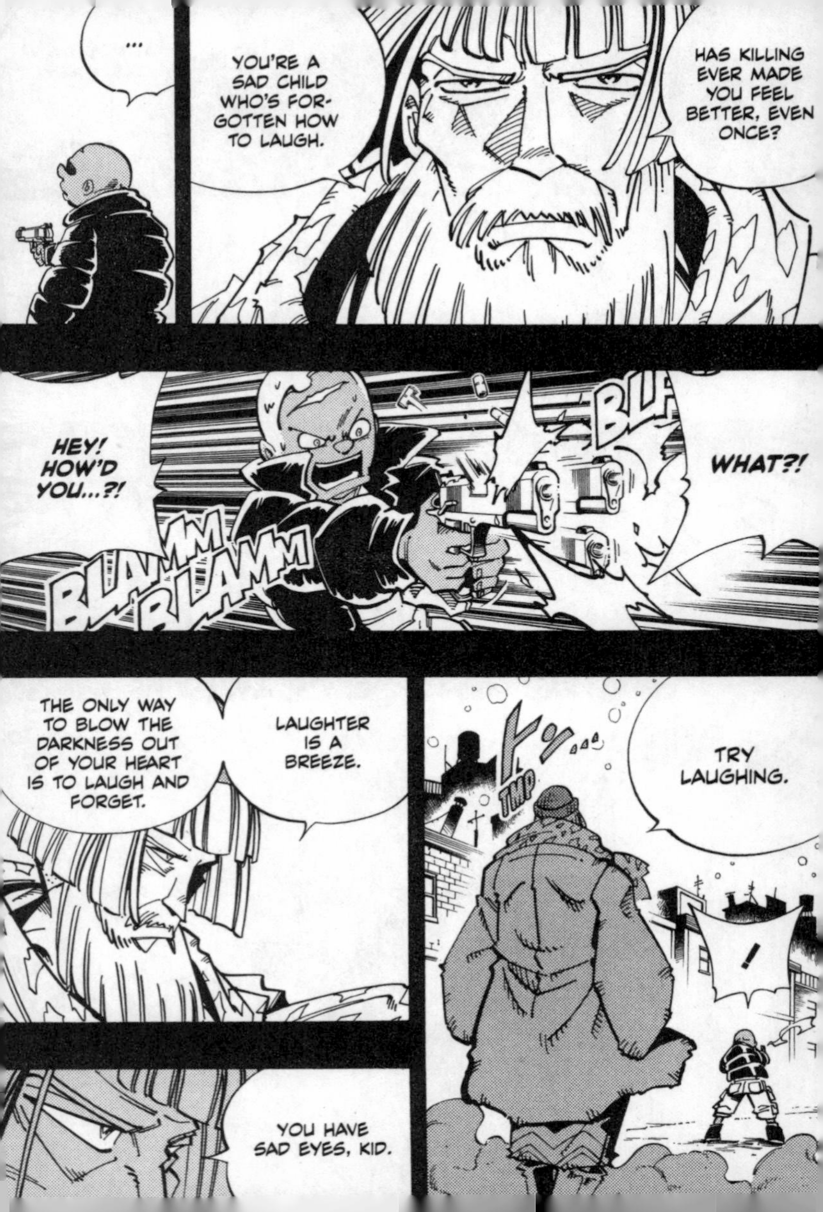
HAS KILLING EVER MADE YOU FEEL BETTER, EVEN ONCE?
YOU'RE A SAD CHILD WHO'S FOR-GOTTEN HOW TO LAUGH.
...
BLA
WHAT?!
HEY! HOW'D YOU...?!
BLAMM
BLAMM
TRY LAUGHING.
TMP
!
LAUGHTER IS A BREEZE.
THE ONLY WAY TO BLOW THE DARKNESS OUT OF YOUR HEART IS TO LAUGH AND FORGET.
YOU HAVE SAD EYES, KID.

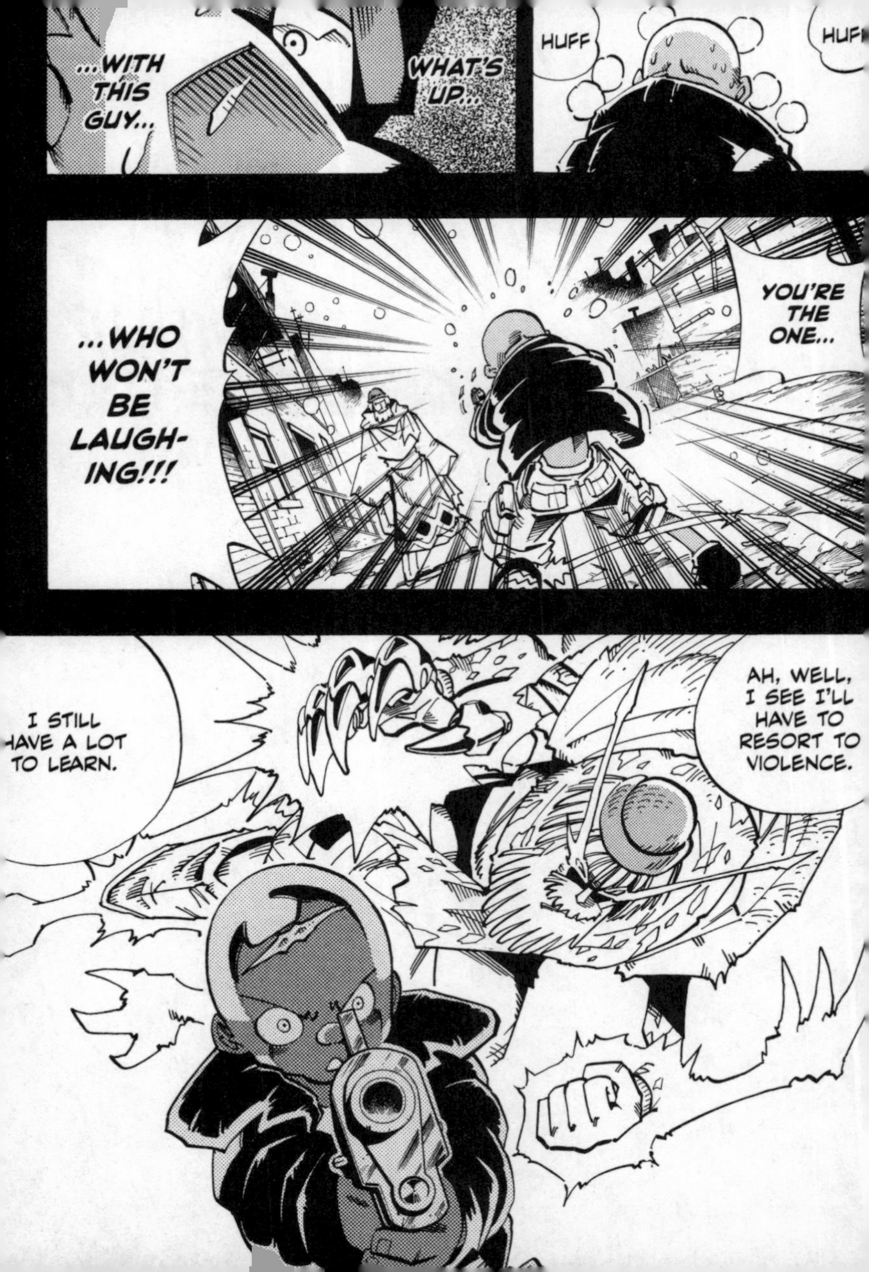
HUF
HUFF
WHAT'S UP...
...WITH THIS GUY...
YOU'RE THE ONE...
...WHO WON'T BE LAUGHING!!!
AH, WELL, I SEE I'LL HAVE TO RESORT TO VIOLENCE.
I STILL HAVE A LOT TO LEARN.

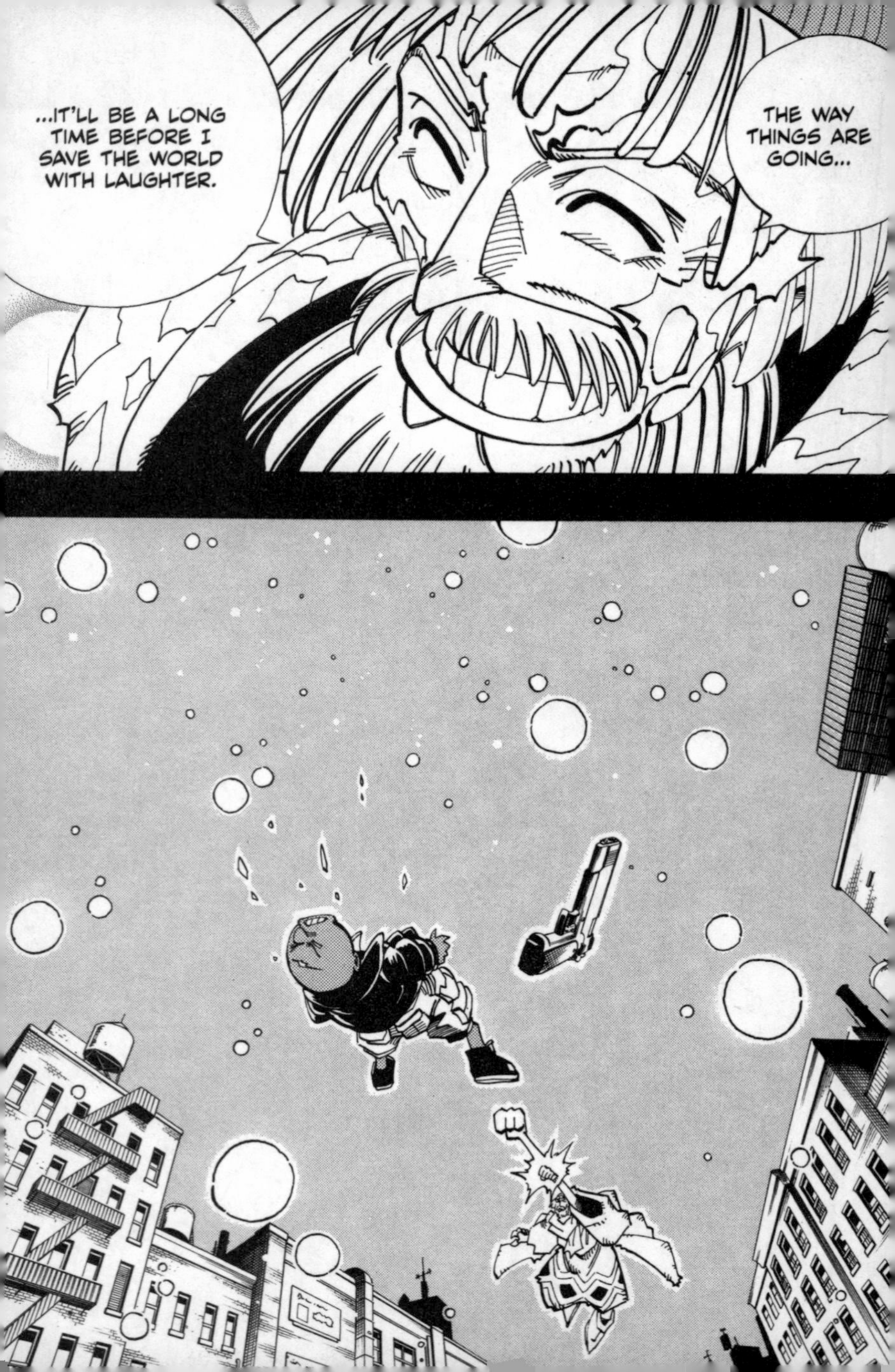
THE WAY THINGS ARE GOING...
...IT'LL BE A LONG TIME BEFORE I SAVE THE WORLD WITH LAUGHTER.

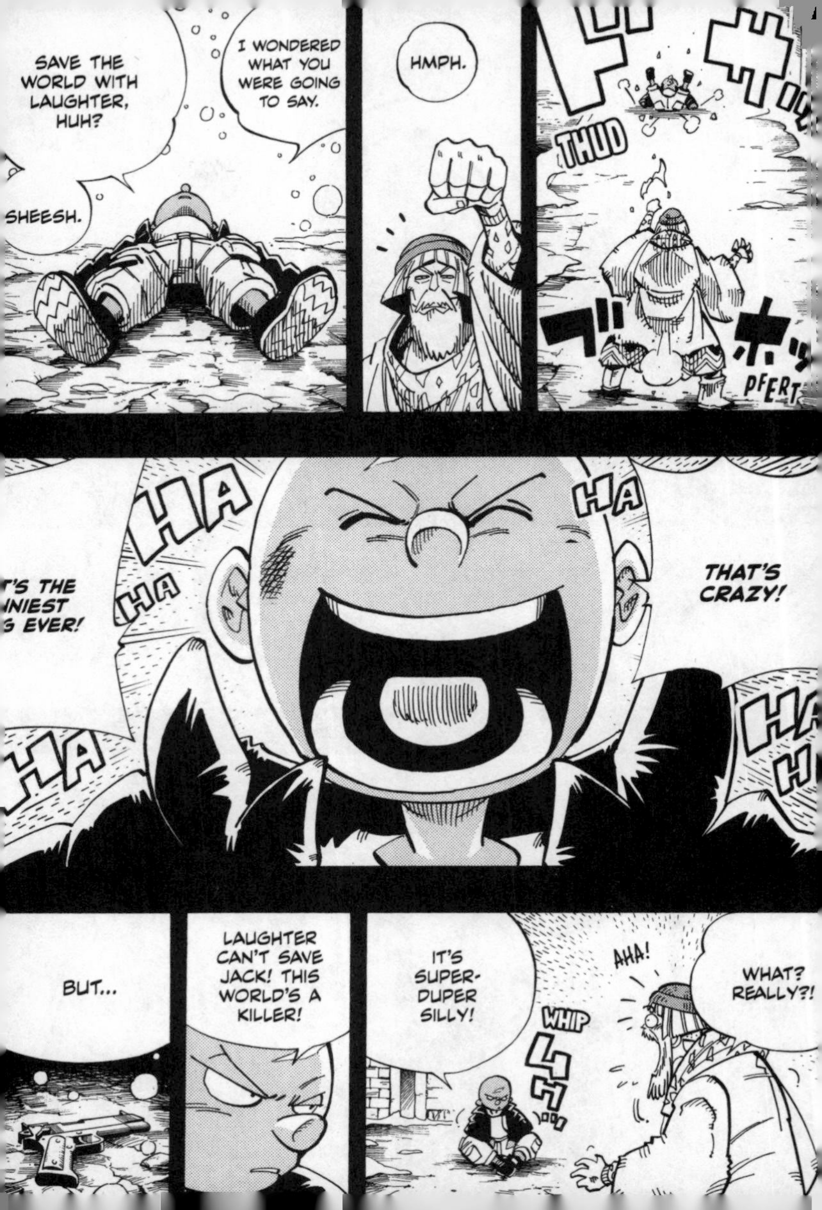
THUD
PFERT
HMPH.
I WONDERED WHAT YOU WERE GOING TO SAY.
SAVE THE WORLD WITH LAUGHTER, HUH?
SHEESH.
HA
THAT'S CRAZY!
HA
HA
'S THE NIEST G EVER!
HA
WHAT? REALLY?!
AHA!
IT'S SUPER-DUPER SILLY!
WHIP
LAUGHTER CAN'T SAVE JACK! THIS WORLD'S A KILLER!
BUT...

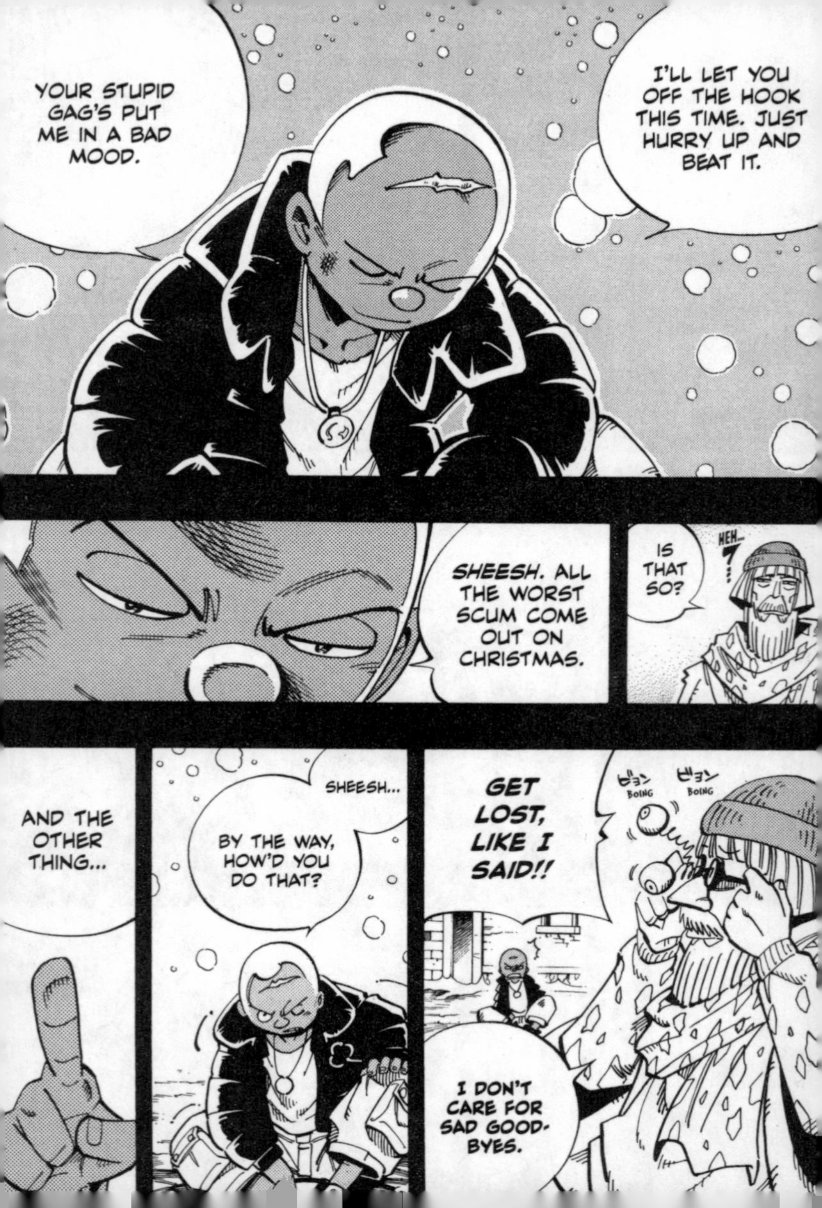
I'LL LET YOU OFF THE HOOK THIS TIME. JUST HURRY UP AND BEAT IT.
YOUR STUPID GAG'S PUT ME IN A BAD MOOD.
HEH...
IS THAT SO?
SHEESH. ALL THE WORST SCUM COME OUT ON CHRISTMAS.
ビヨン BOING
ビヨン BOING
GET LOST, LIKE I SAID!!
I DON'T CARE FOR SAD GOOD-BYES.
SHEESH...
BY THE WAY, HOW'D YOU DO THAT?
AND THE OTHER THING...

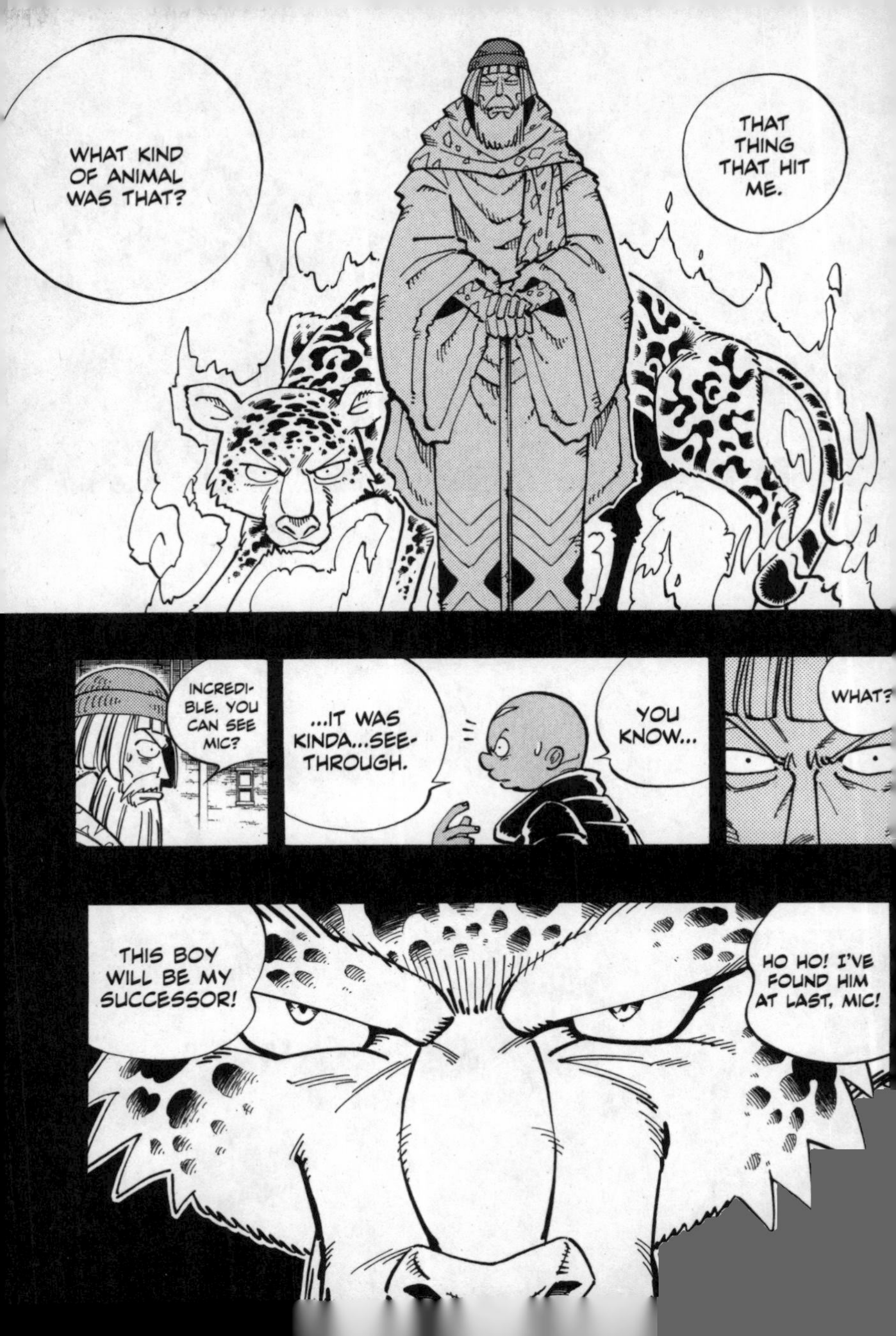
THAT THING THAT HIT ME.
WHAT KIND OF ANIMAL WAS THAT?
WHAT?
YOU KNOW...
...IT WAS KINDA...SEE-THROUGH.
INCREDI-BLE. YOU CAN SEE MIC?
HO HO! I'VE FOUND HIM AT LAST, MIC!
THIS BOY WILL BE MY SUCCESSOR!

SHAMAN
KING
13

The Old Man's Gift

Bonus four-panel comics

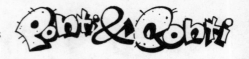

PONCHI AND CONCHI NO. 1

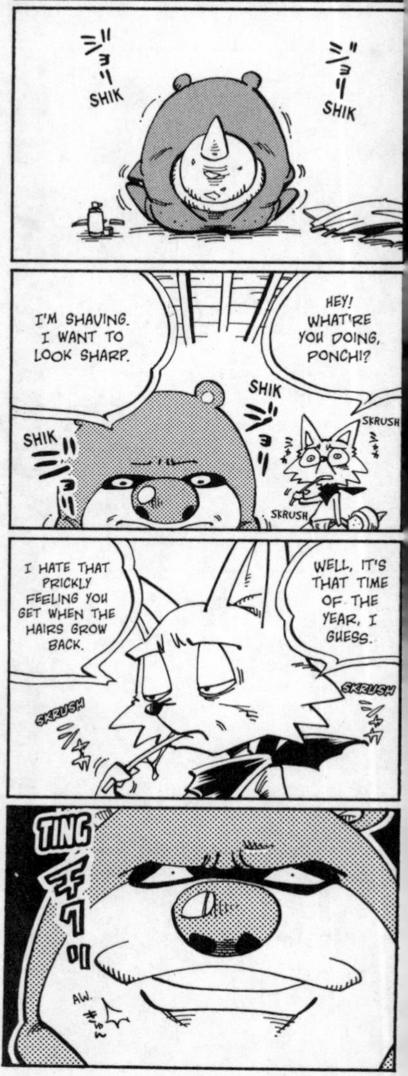

ジョリ
SHIK
ジョリ
SHIK
HEY! WHAT'RE YOU DOING, PONCHI?
I'M SHAVING. I WANT TO LOOK SHARP.
SHIK
SHIK
SKRUSH
SKRUSH
WELL, IT'S THAT TIME OF THE YEAR, I GUESS.
I HATE THAT PRICKLY FEELING YOU GET WHEN THE HAIRS GROW BACK.
SKRUSH
SKRUSH
TING
チクッ
AW.

PONCHI AND CONCHI NO. 2

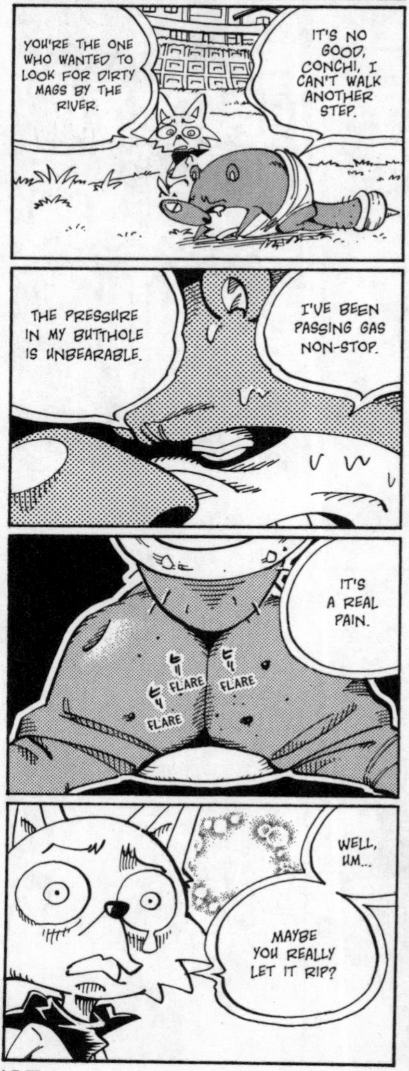

IT'S NO GOOD, CONCHI, I CAN'T WALK ANOTHER STEP.
YOU'RE THE ONE WHO WANTED TO LOOK FOR DIRTY MAGS BY THE RIVER.
I'VE BEEN PASSING GAS NON-STOP.
THE PRESSURE IN MY BUTTHOLE IS UNBEARABLE.
IT'S A REAL PAIN.
FLARE
FLARE
FLARE
WELL, UM...
MAYBE YOU REALLY LET IT RIP?

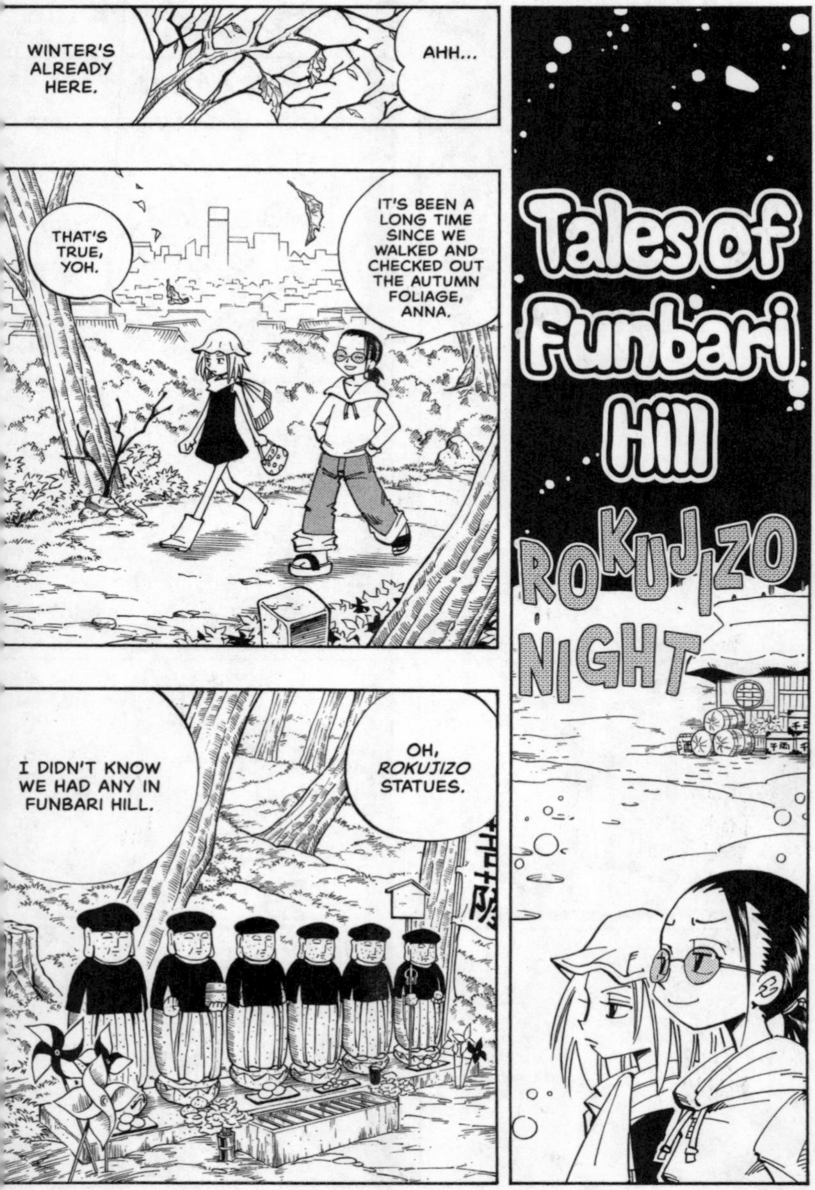

Tales of Funbari Hill
ROKUJIZO NIGHT
AHH...
WINTER'S ALREADY HERE.
IT'S BEEN A LONG TIME SINCE WE WALKED AND CHECKED OUT THE AUTUMN FOLIAGE, ANNA.
THAT'S TRUE, YOH.
OH, *ROKUJIZO* STATUES.
I DIDN'T KNOW WE HAD ANY IN FUNBARI HILL.

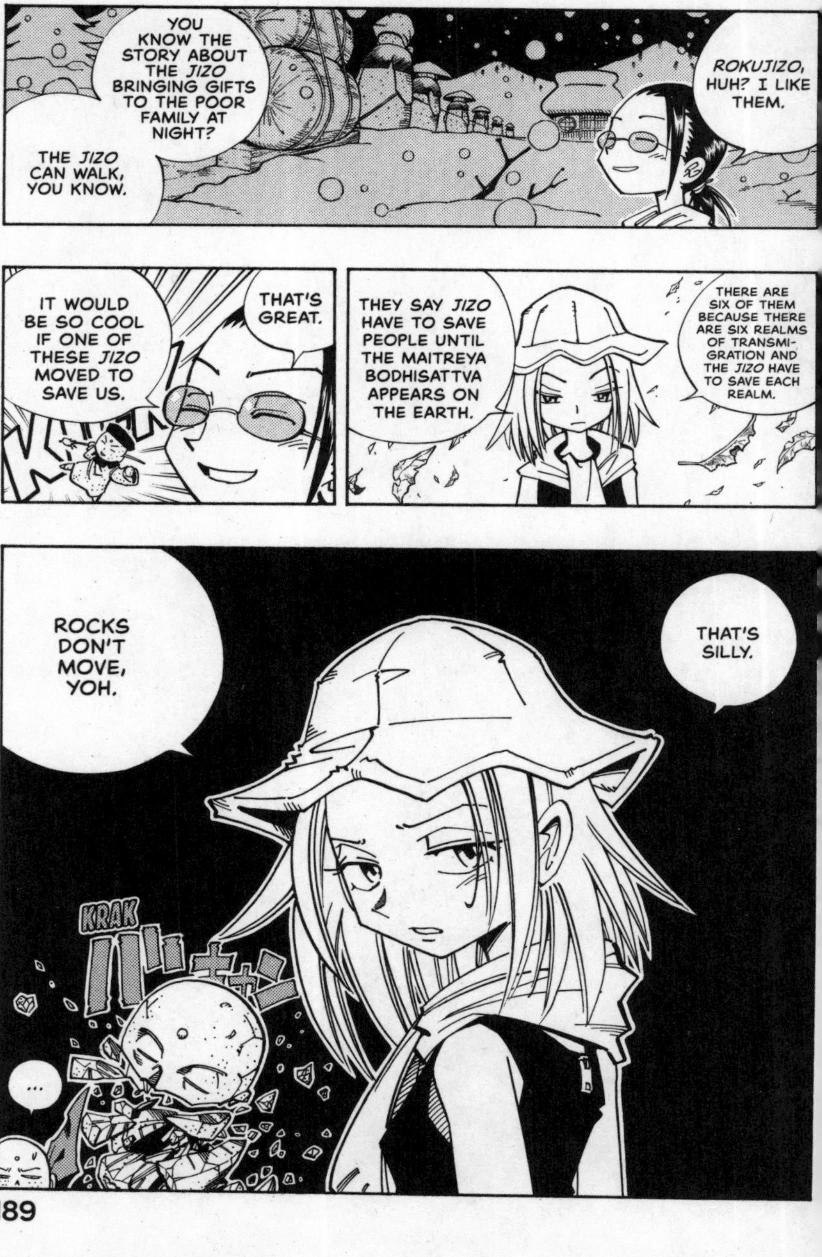
ROKUJIZO, HUH? I LIKE THEM.
YOU KNOW THE STORY ABOUT THE JIZO BRINGING GIFTS TO THE POOR FAMILY AT NIGHT?
THE JIZO CAN WALK, YOU KNOW.
THERE ARE SIX OF THEM BECAUSE THERE ARE SIX REALMS OF TRANSMI-GRATION AND THE JIZO HAVE TO SAVE EACH REALM.
THEY SAY JIZO HAVE TO SAVE PEOPLE UNTIL THE MAITREYA BODHISATTVA APPEARS ON THE EARTH.
THAT'S GREAT.
IT WOULD BE SO COOL IF ONE OF THESE JIZO MOVED TO SAVE US.
THAT'S SILLY.
ROCKS DON'T MOVE, YOH.
KRAK
...

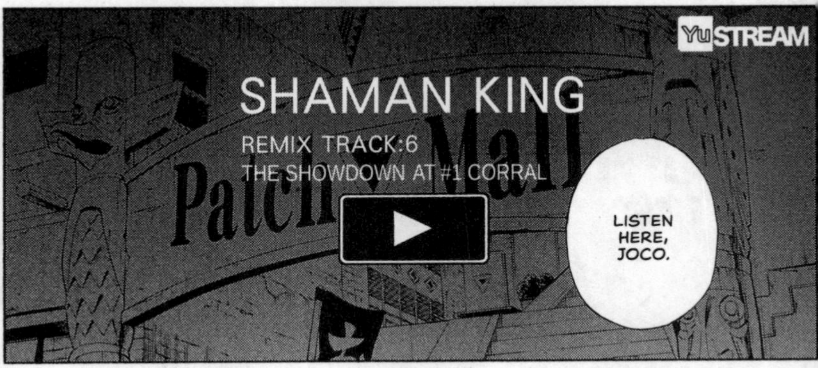
YuSTREAM
SHAMAN KING
REMIX TRACK:6
THE SHOWDOWN AT #1 CORRAL
Patch Mall
LISTEN HERE, JOCO.

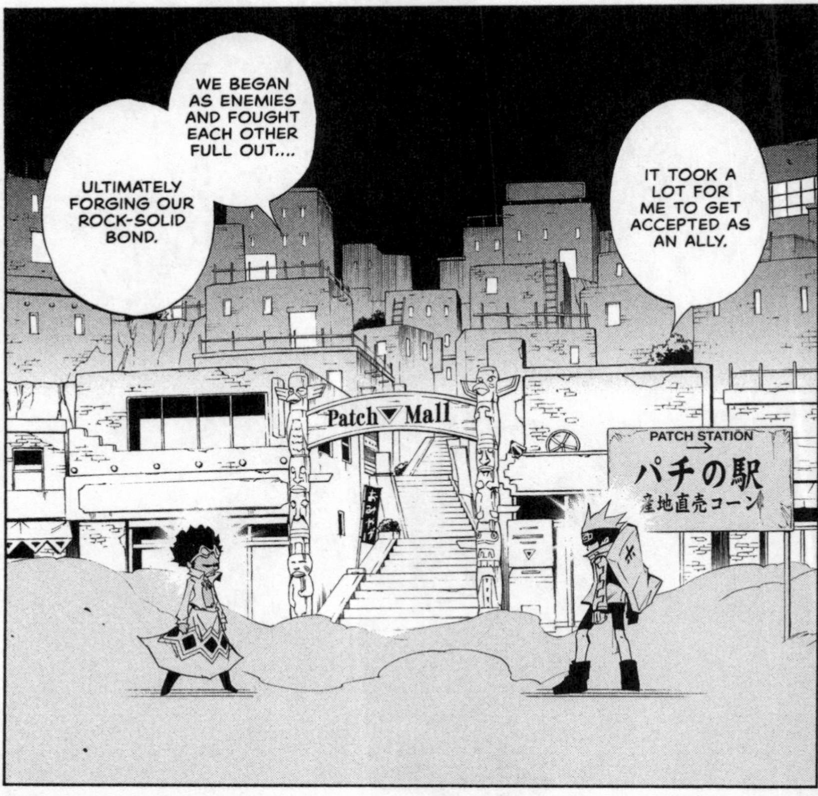
IT TOOK A LOT FOR ME TO GET ACCEPTED AS AN ALLY.
WE BEGAN AS ENEMIES AND FOUGHT EACH OTHER FULL OUT....
ULTIMATELY FORGING OUR ROCK-SOLID BOND.
PATCH STATION →
パチの駅
産地直売コーン
Patch Mall

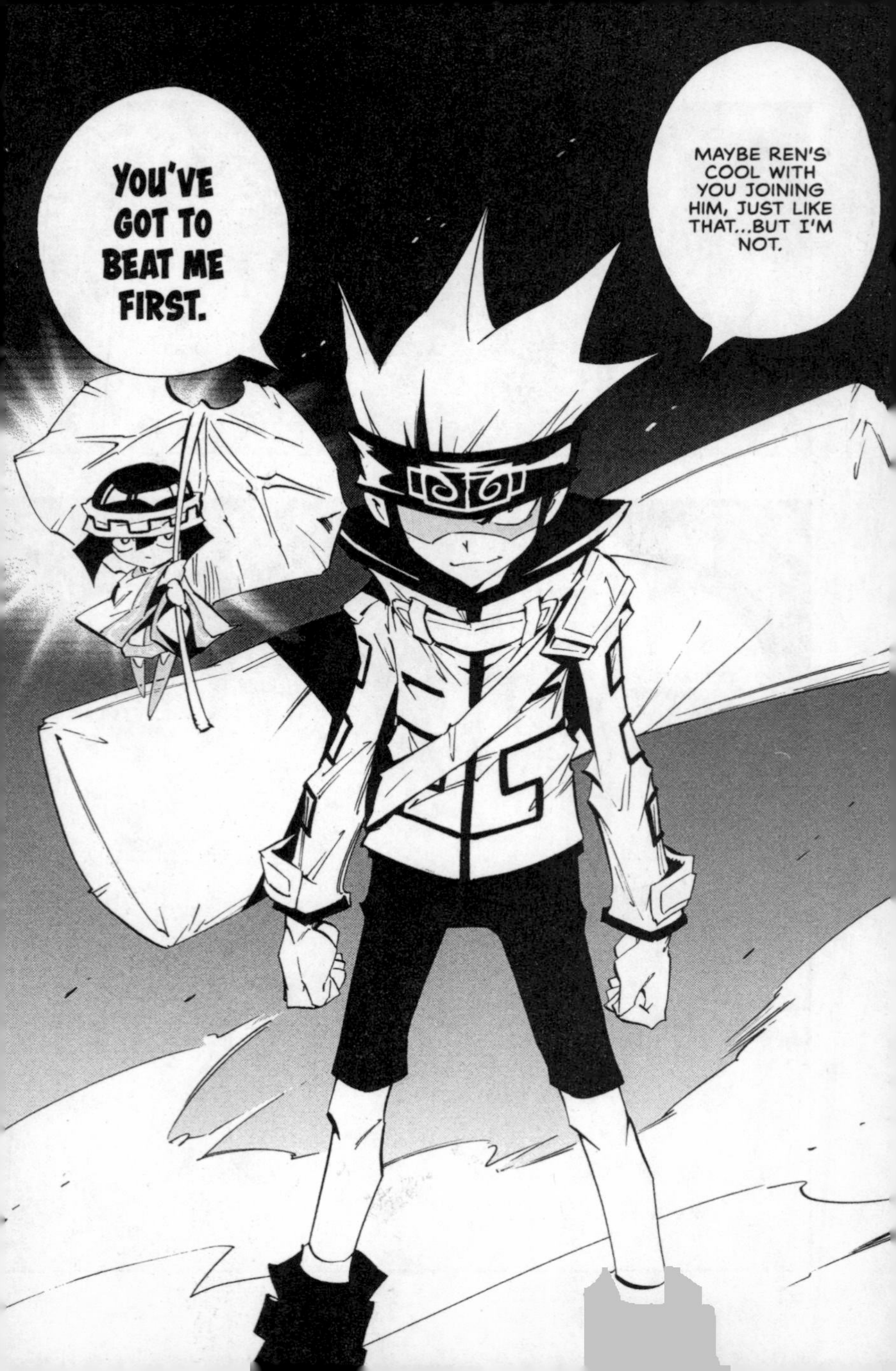
MAYBE REN'S COOL WITH YOU JOINING HIM, JUST LIKE THAT...BUT I'M NOT.
YOU'VE GOT TO BEAT ME FIRST.

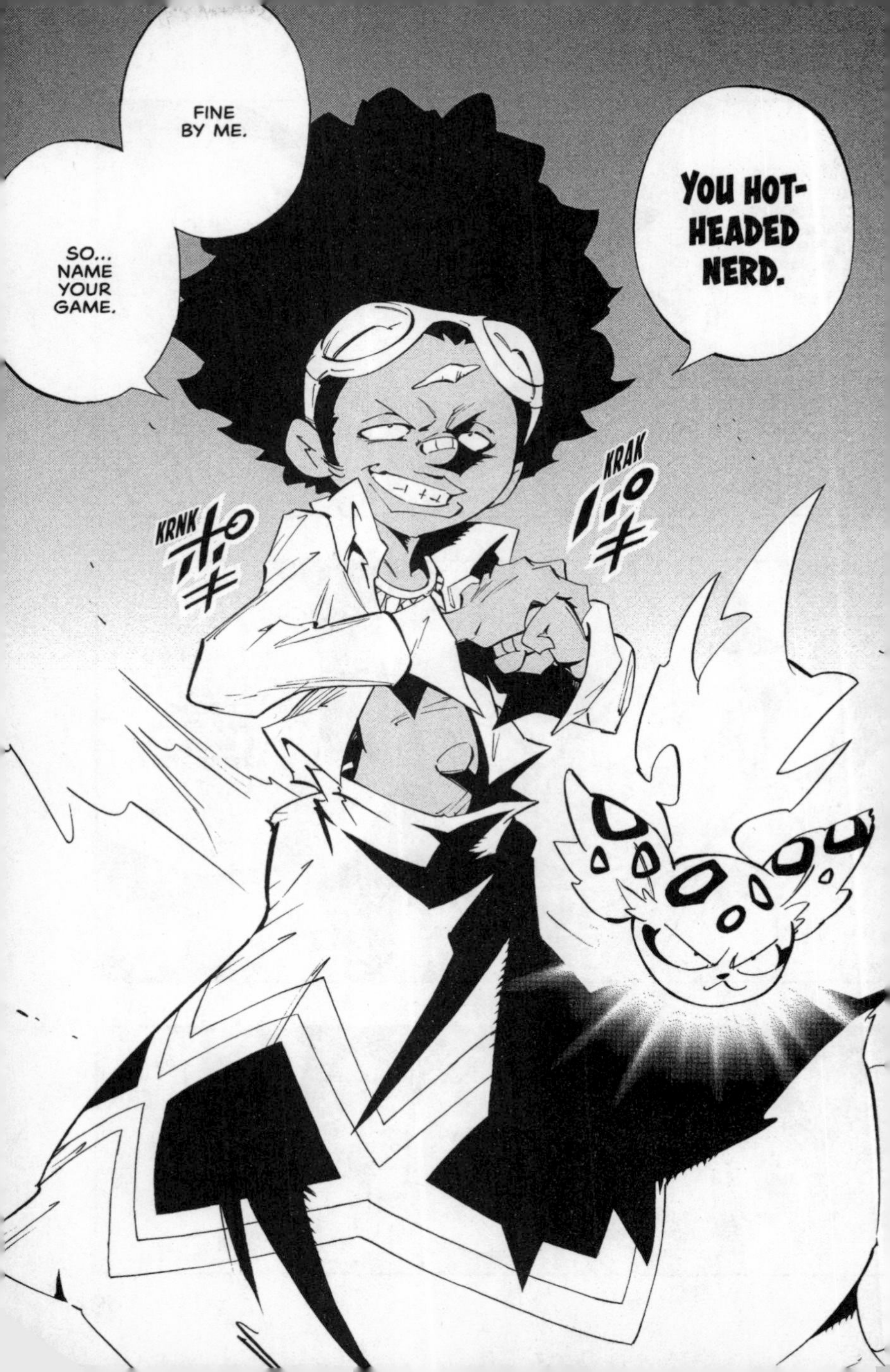
YOU HOT-HEADED NERD.
FINE BY ME.
SO... NAME YOUR GAME.
KRAK
KRNK

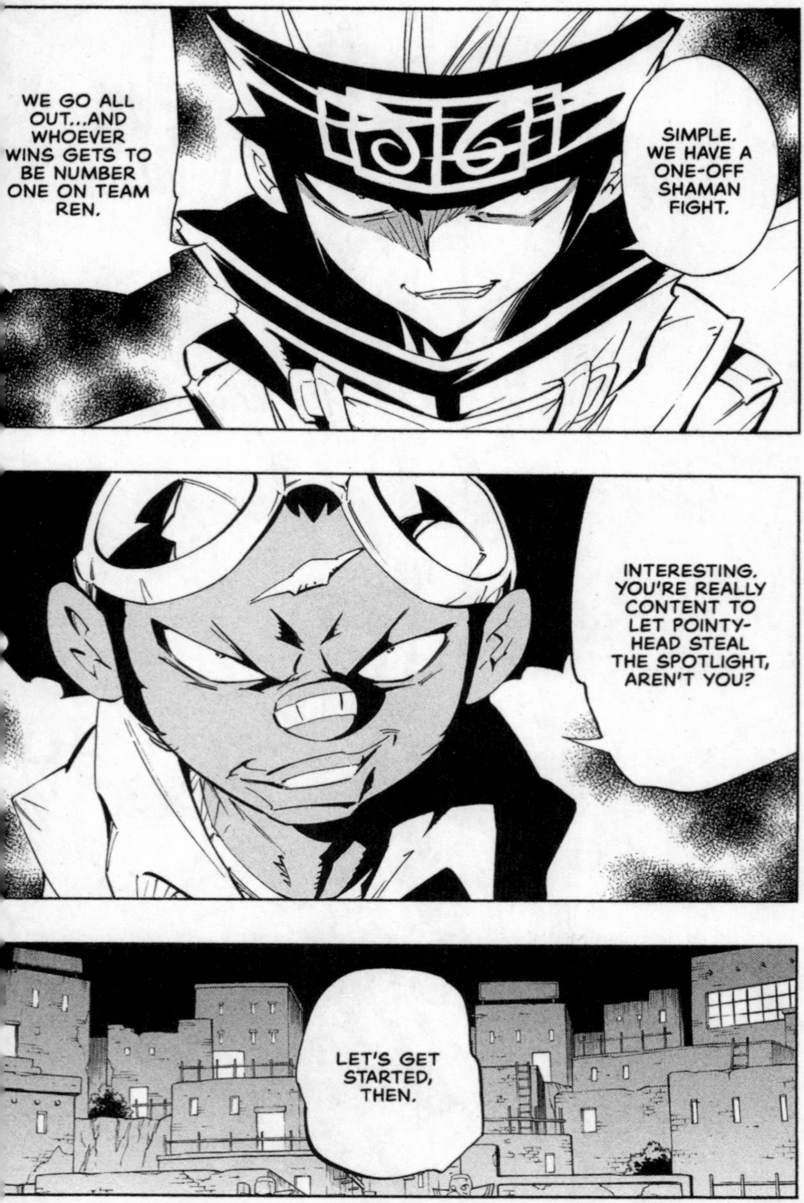
SIMPLE. WE HAVE A ONE-OFF SHAMAN FIGHT.
WE GO ALL OUT...AND WHOEVER WINS GETS TO BE NUMBER ONE ON TEAM REN.
INTERESTING. YOU'RE REALLY CONTENT TO LET POINTY-HEAD STEAL THE SPOTLIGHT, AREN'T YOU?
LET'S GET STARTED, THEN.

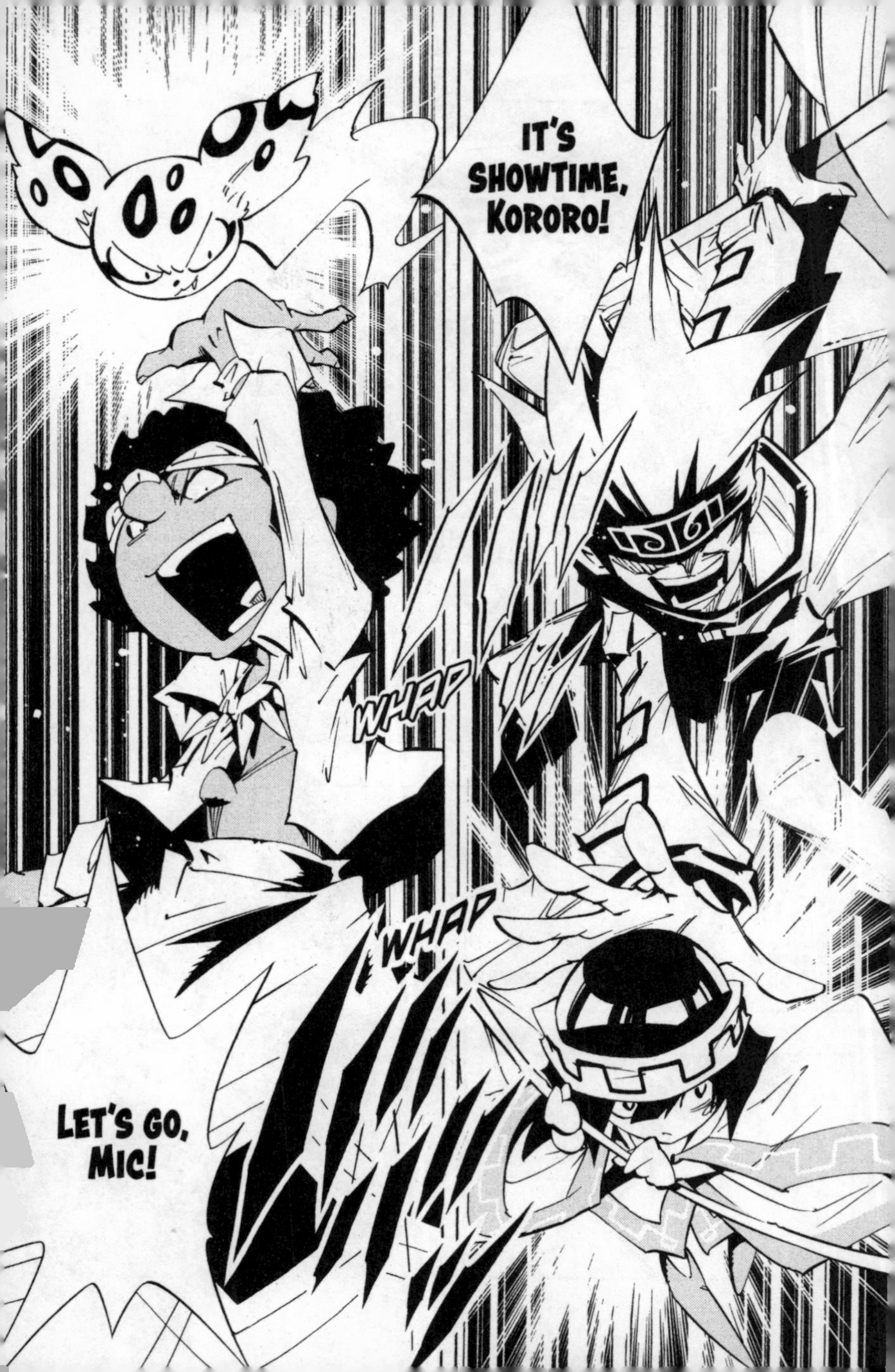
IT'S SHOWTIME, KORORO!
WHAP
WHAP
LET'S GO, MIC!

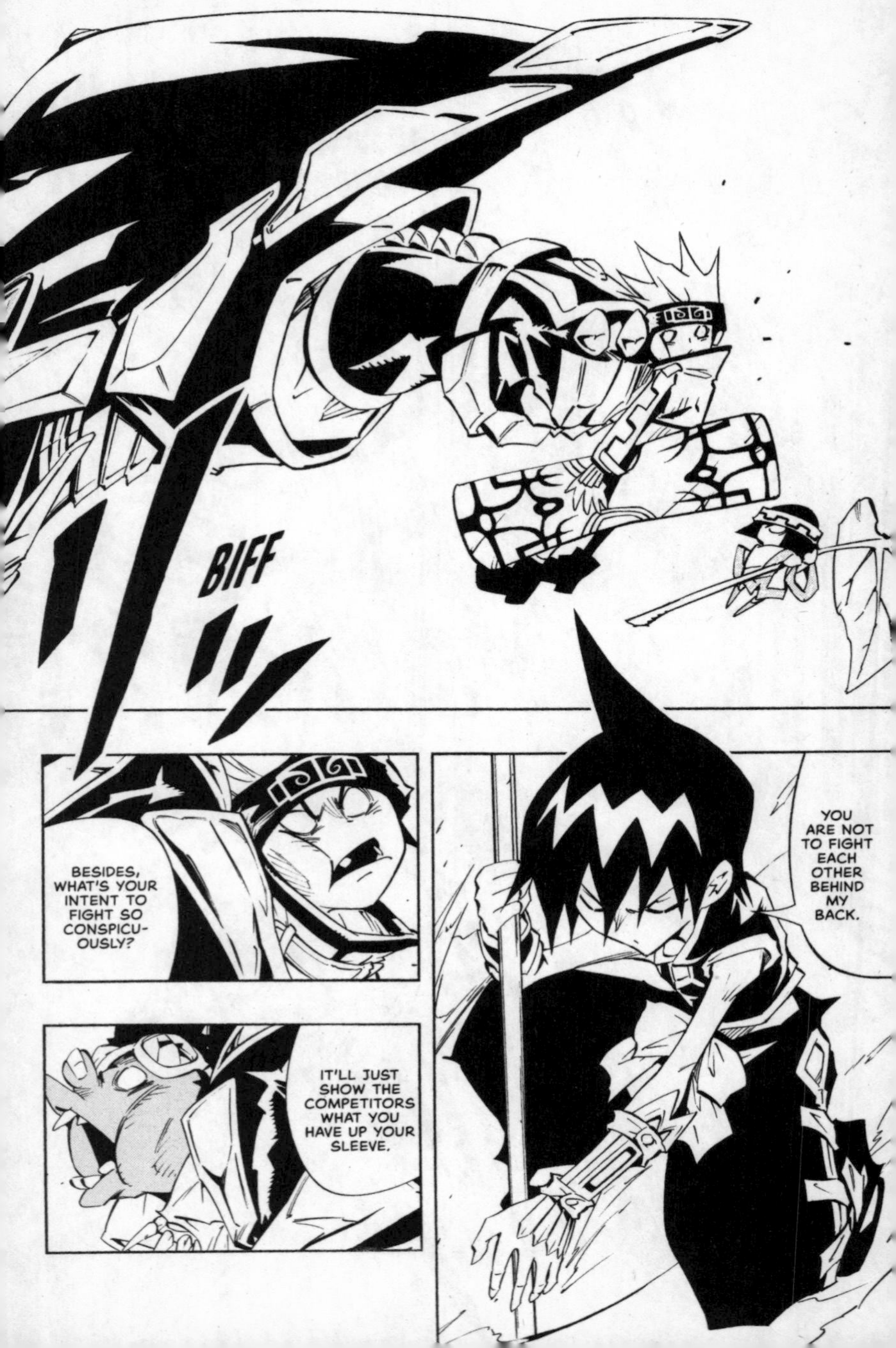
BIFF
YOU ARE NOT TO FIGHT EACH OTHER BEHIND MY BACK.
BESIDES, WHAT'S YOUR INTENT TO FIGHT SO CONSPICU-OUSLY?
IT'LL JUST SHOW THE COMPETITORS WHAT YOU HAVE UP YOUR SLEEVE.

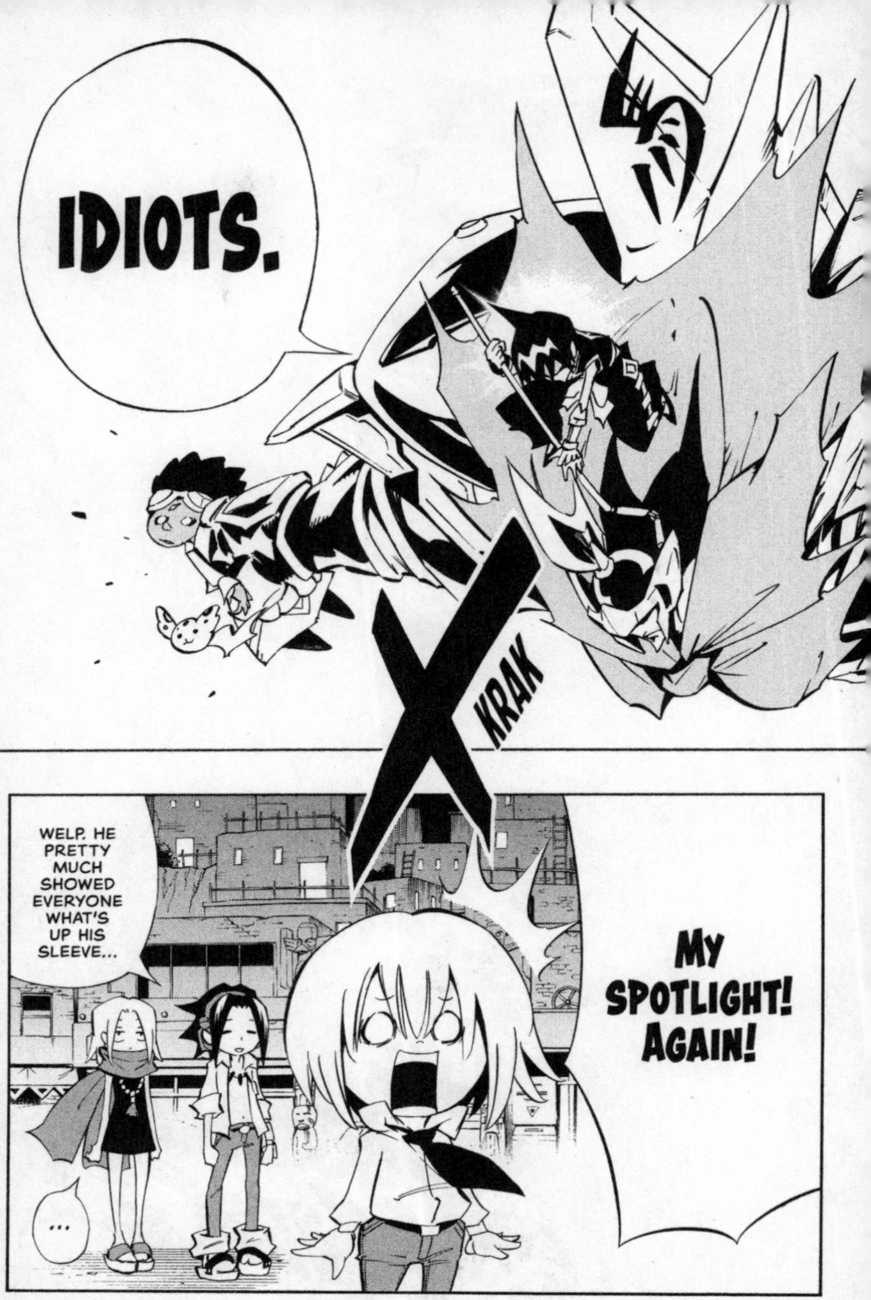
IDIOTS.
KRAK
MY SPOTLIGHT! AGAIN!
WELP. HE PRETTY MUCH SHOWED EVERYONE WHAT'S UP HIS SLEEVE...
...

SHAMAN KING

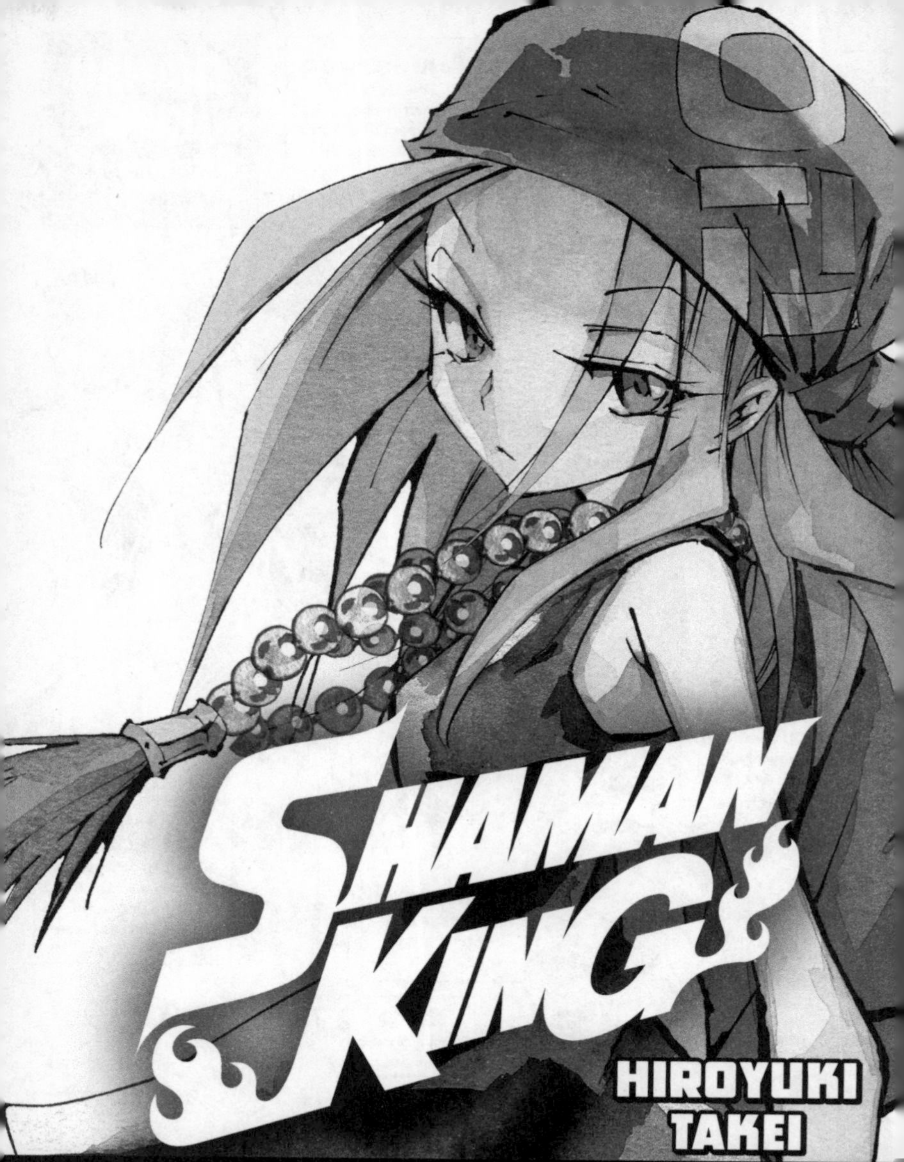
SHAMAN KING
HIROYUKI TAKEI

14

The Tortured Princess

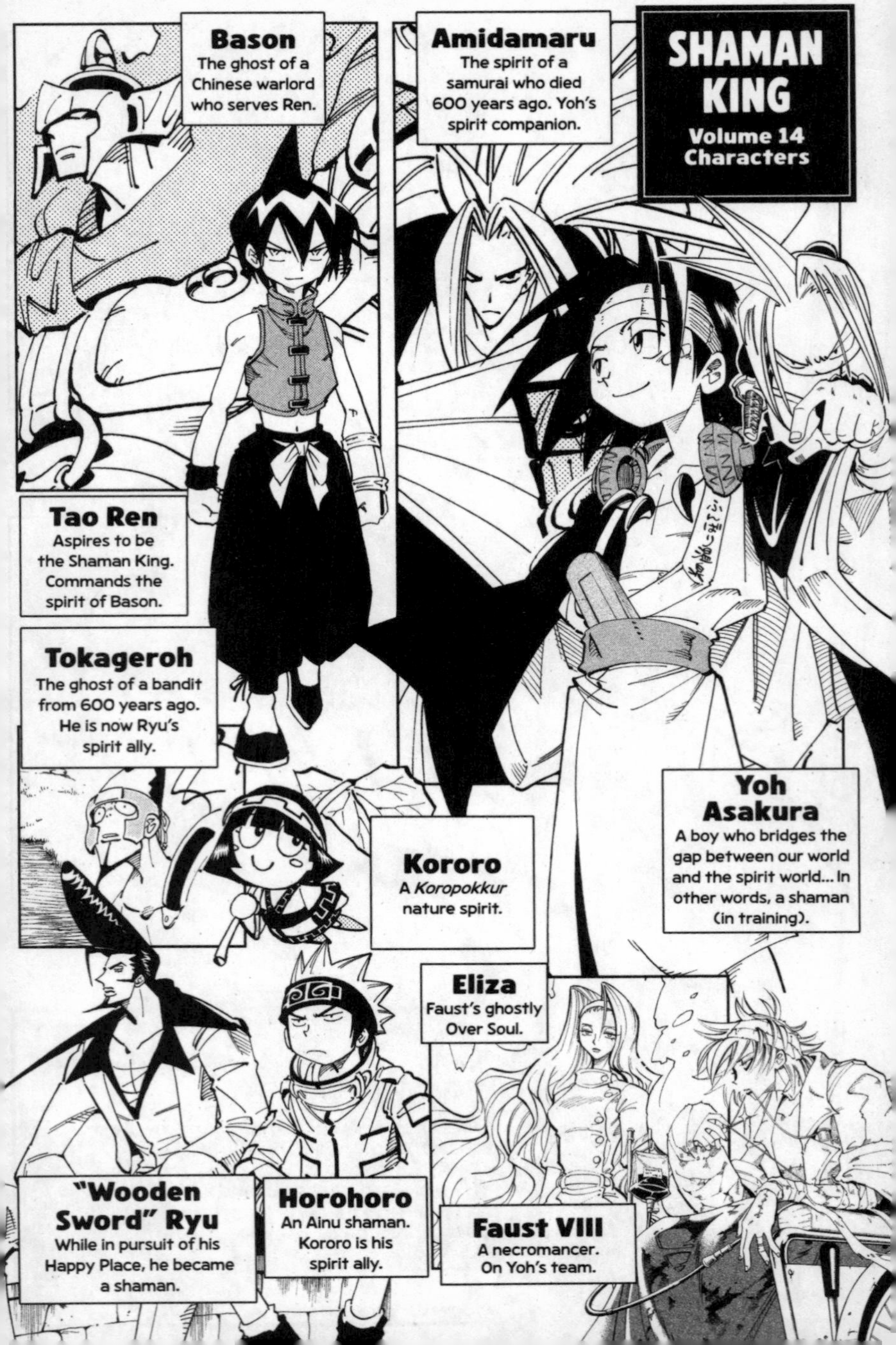
SHAMAN KING
Volume 14 Characters
Amidamaru
The spirit of a samurai who died 600 years ago. Yoh's spirit companion.
Bason
The ghost of a Chinese warlord who serves Ren.
Yoh Asakura
A boy who bridges the gap between our world and the spirit world... In other words, a shaman (in training).
Kororo
A *Koropokkur* nature spirit.
Tao Ren
Aspires to be the Shaman King. Commands the spirit of Bason.
Tokageroh
The ghost of a bandit from 600 years ago. He is now Ryu's spirit ally.
Eliza
Faust's ghostly Over Soul.
Faust VIII
A necromancer. On Yoh's team.
Horohoro
An Ainu shaman. Kororo is his spirit ally.
"Wooden Sword" Ryu
While in pursuit of his Happy Place, he became a shaman.

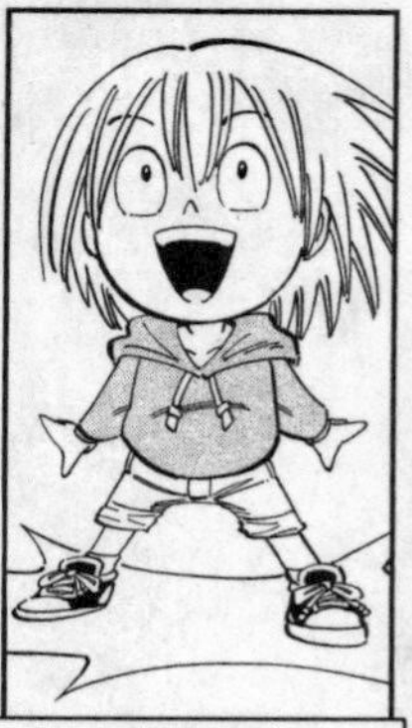

Manta Oyamada
Yoh's friend. Always carrying his trusty dictionary.

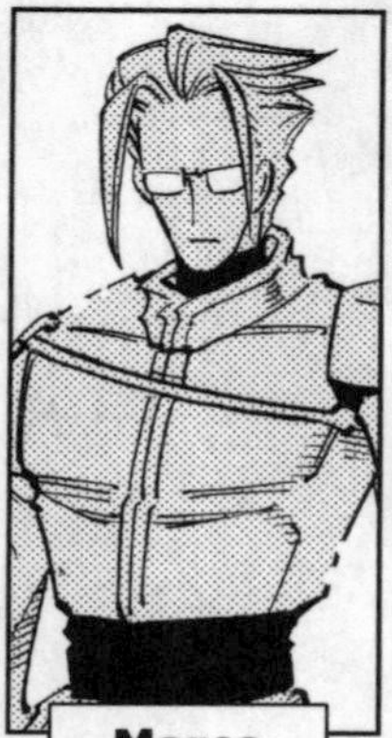

Marco
The leader of the X-Laws.

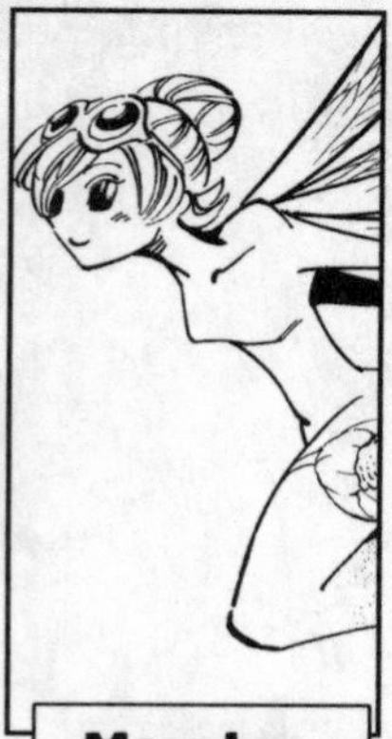

Morphea
Lyserg's spirit ally. A poppy flower fairy.

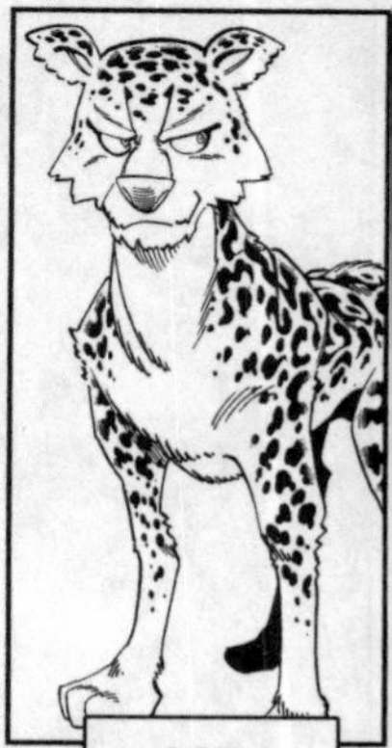

Mic
Joco's jaguar spirit ally.

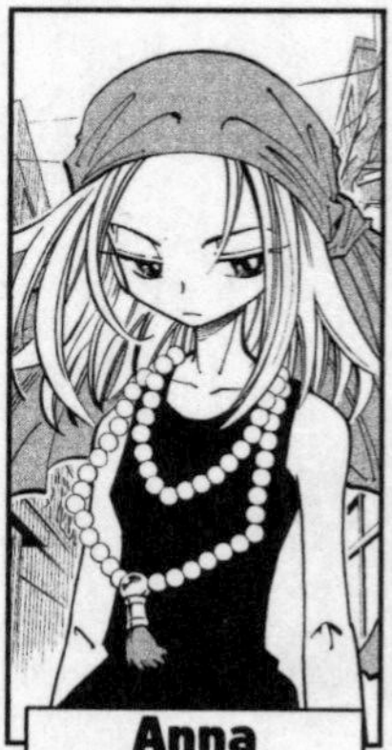

Anna Kyoyama
An *itako* from Mt. Osore. Yoh's arranged fiancée.

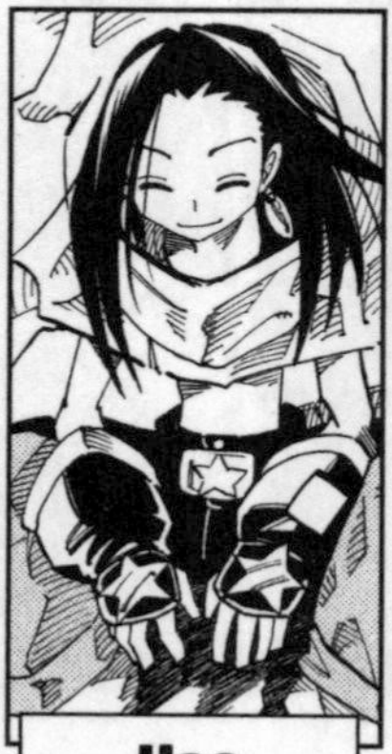

Hao
An enigmatic figure who calls himself the "Future King."

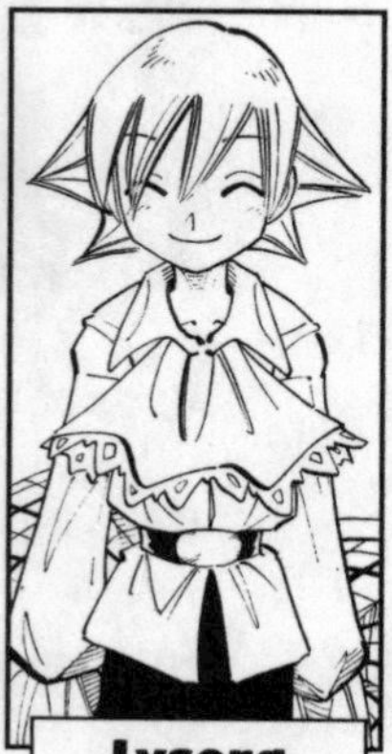

Lyserg
A boy who wants revenge against Hao.

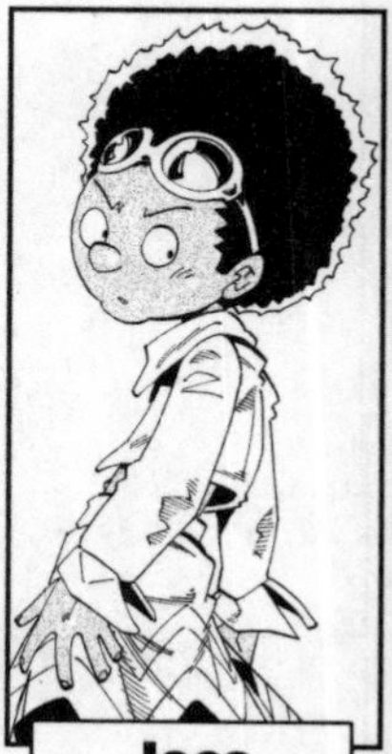

Joco
A shaman and an aspiring comedian.

THE STORY SO FAR

This kid named Yoh Asakura-kun transferred to my class from Izumo... and it turns out he's a shaman! The Shaman Fight, which takes place once every 500 years, has begun. Yoh-kun and friends arrived at Patch Village—and experienced the limitless power of the Great Spirit. They formed new teams for the tournament proper. Ryu and Faust joined Yoh-kun's team. Ren, Horohoro, and a new ally, Joco, formed another trio. It's war against Hao's minions from the get-go. Can Joco and team battle their way through?!

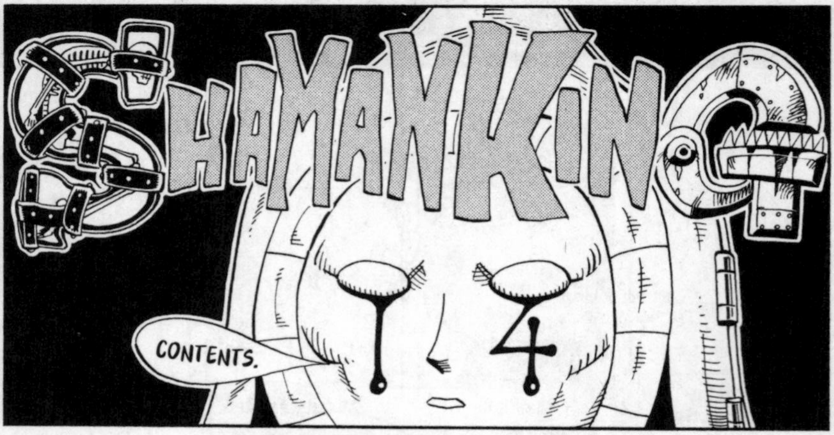
SHAMAN KING
CONTENTS.

The Tortured Princess

14

Chapter 117: His Name was Orona

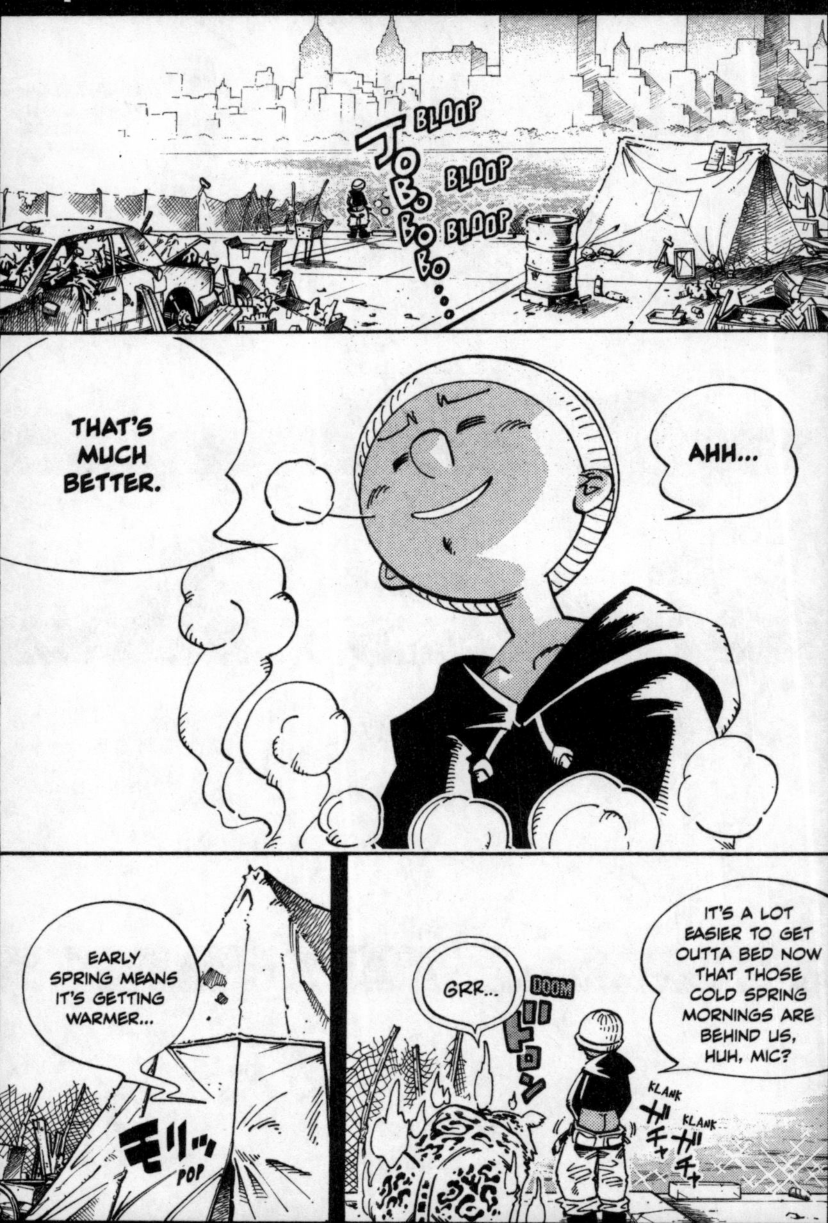

BLOOP
BLOOP
BLOOP
AHH...
THAT'S MUCH BETTER.
IT'S A LOT EASIER TO GET OUTTA BED NOW THAT THOSE COLD SPRING MORNINGS ARE BEHIND US, HUH, MIC?
KLANK
KLANK
GRR...
DOOM
EARLY SPRING MEANS IT'S GETTING WARMER...
POP

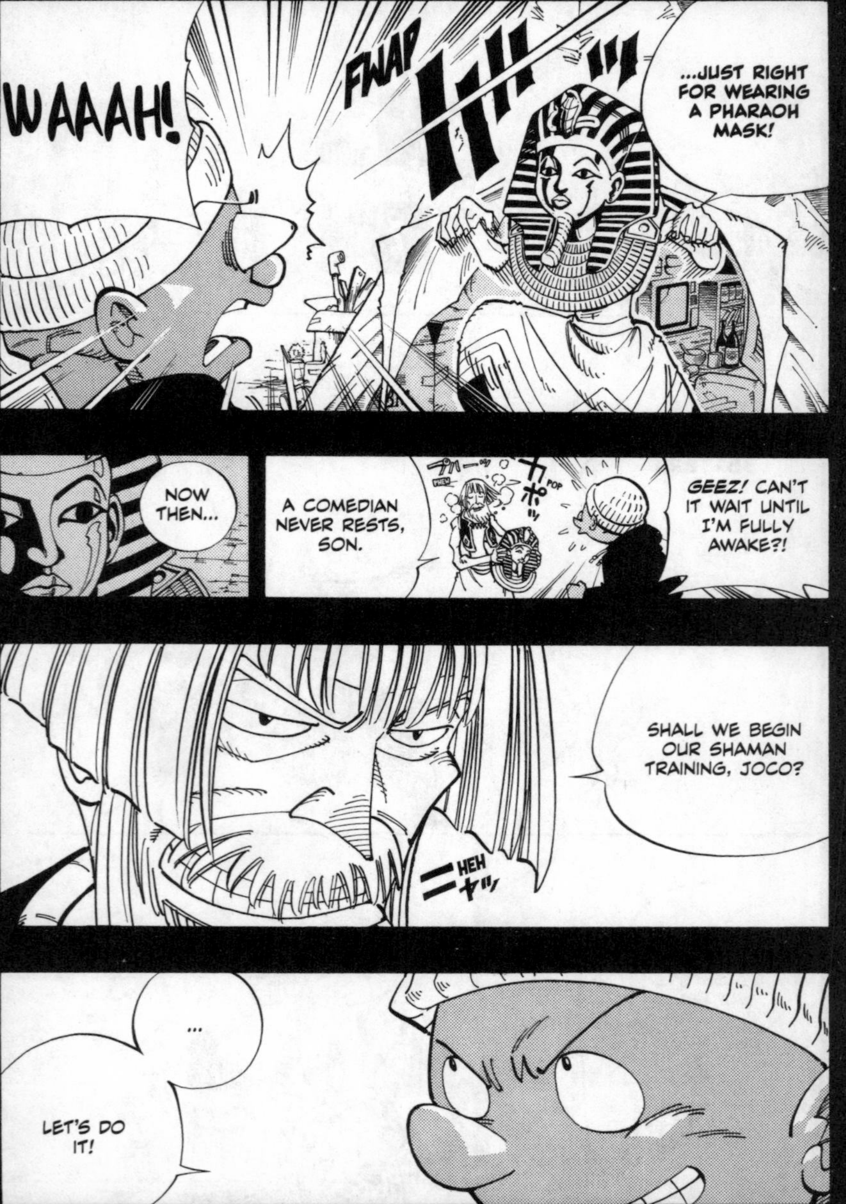
...JUST RIGHT FOR WEARING A PHARAOH MASK!
FWAP
WAAAH!
GEEZ! CAN'T IT WAIT UNTIL I'M FULLY AWAKE?!
POP
PHEW
A COMEDIAN NEVER RESTS, SON.
NOW THEN...
SHALL WE BEGIN OUR SHAMAN TRAINING, JOCO?
HEH
...
LET'S DO IT!

Chapter 117:

His Name Was Orona

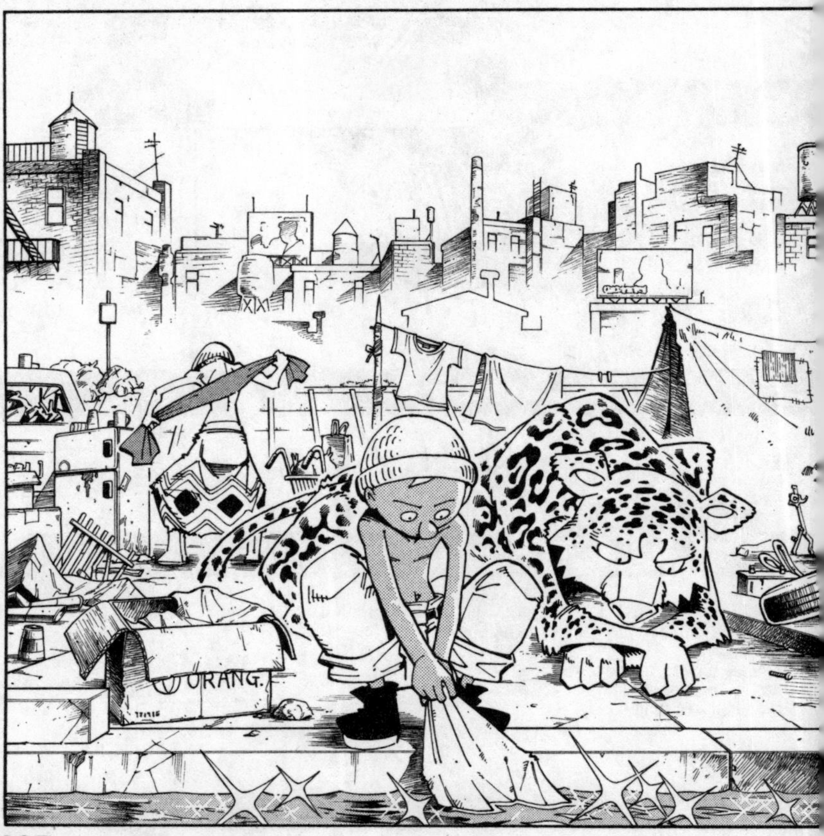

ORANG.

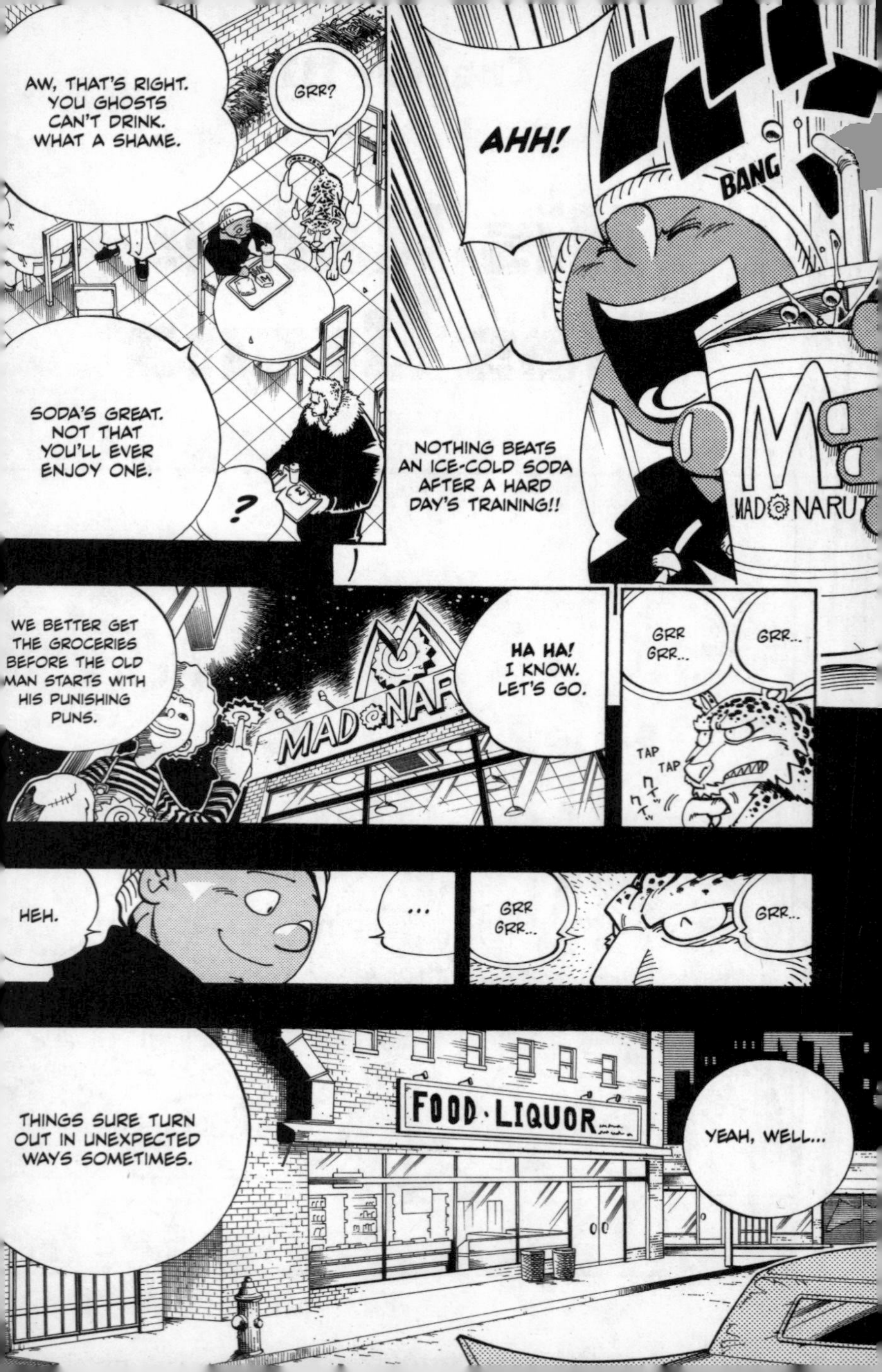
BANG
AHH!
NOTHING BEATS AN ICE-COLD SODA AFTER A HARD DAY'S TRAINING!!
MAD NARU
GRR?
AW, THAT'S RIGHT. YOU GHOSTS CAN'T DRINK. WHAT A SHAME.
SODA'S GREAT. NOT THAT YOU'LL EVER ENJOY ONE.
?
GRR...
GRR GRR...
TAP
TAP
HA HA! I KNOW. LET'S GO.
MAD NAR
WE BETTER GET THE GROCERIES BEFORE THE OLD MAN STARTS WITH HIS PUNISHING PUNS.
GRR...
GRR GRR...
...
HEH.
YEAH, WELL...
FOOD · LIQUOR
THINGS SURE TURN OUT IN UNEXPECTED WAYS SOMETIMES.

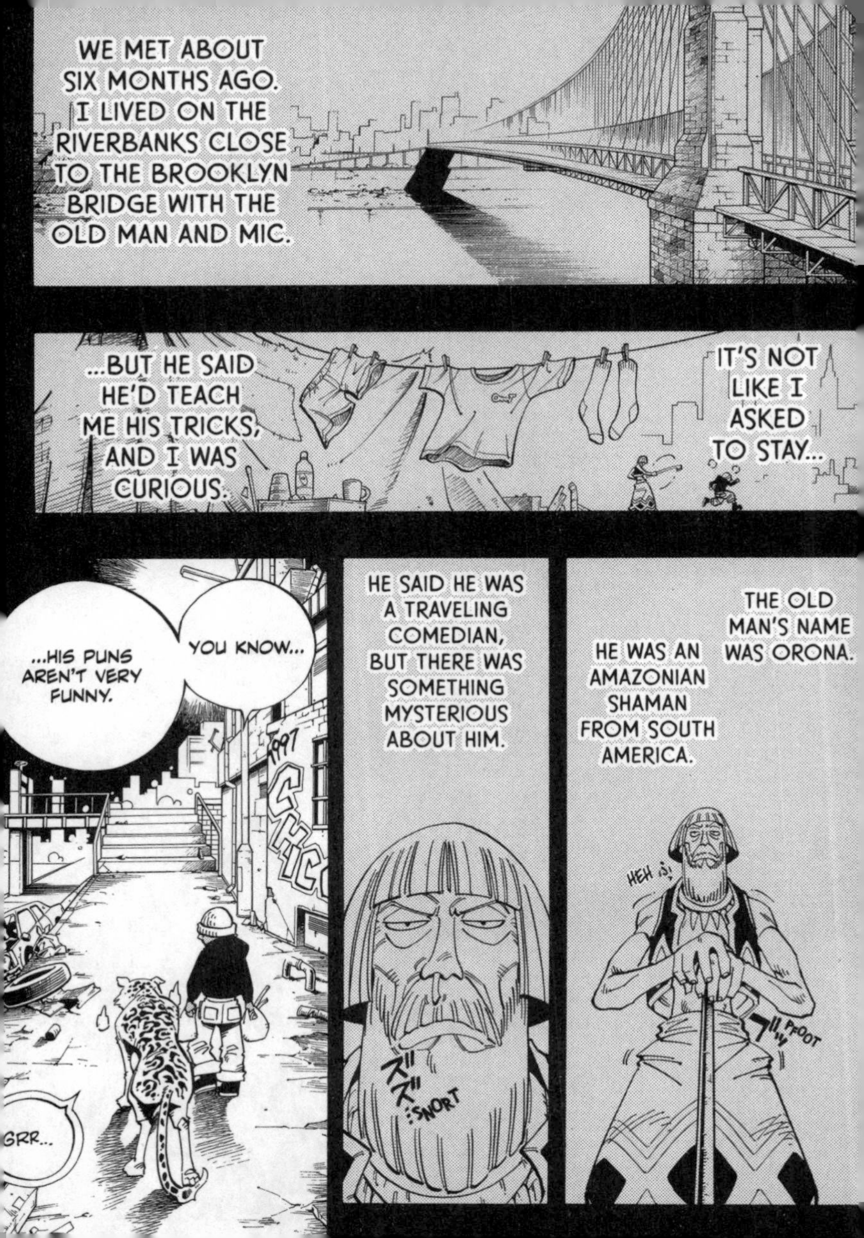
WE MET ABOUT SIX MONTHS AGO. I LIVED ON THE RIVERBANKS CLOSE TO THE BROOKLYN BRIDGE WITH THE OLD MAN AND MIC.
IT'S NOT LIKE I ASKED TO STAY...
...BUT HE SAID HE'D TEACH ME HIS TRICKS, AND I WAS CURIOUS.
THE OLD MAN'S NAME WAS ORONA.
HE WAS AN AMAZONIAN SHAMAN FROM SOUTH AMERICA.
HEH
PFOOT
HE SAID HE WAS A TRAVELING COMEDIAN, BUT THERE WAS SOMETHING MYSTERIOUS ABOUT HIM.
SNORT
YOU KNOW...
...HIS PUNS AREN'T VERY FUNNY.
GRR...

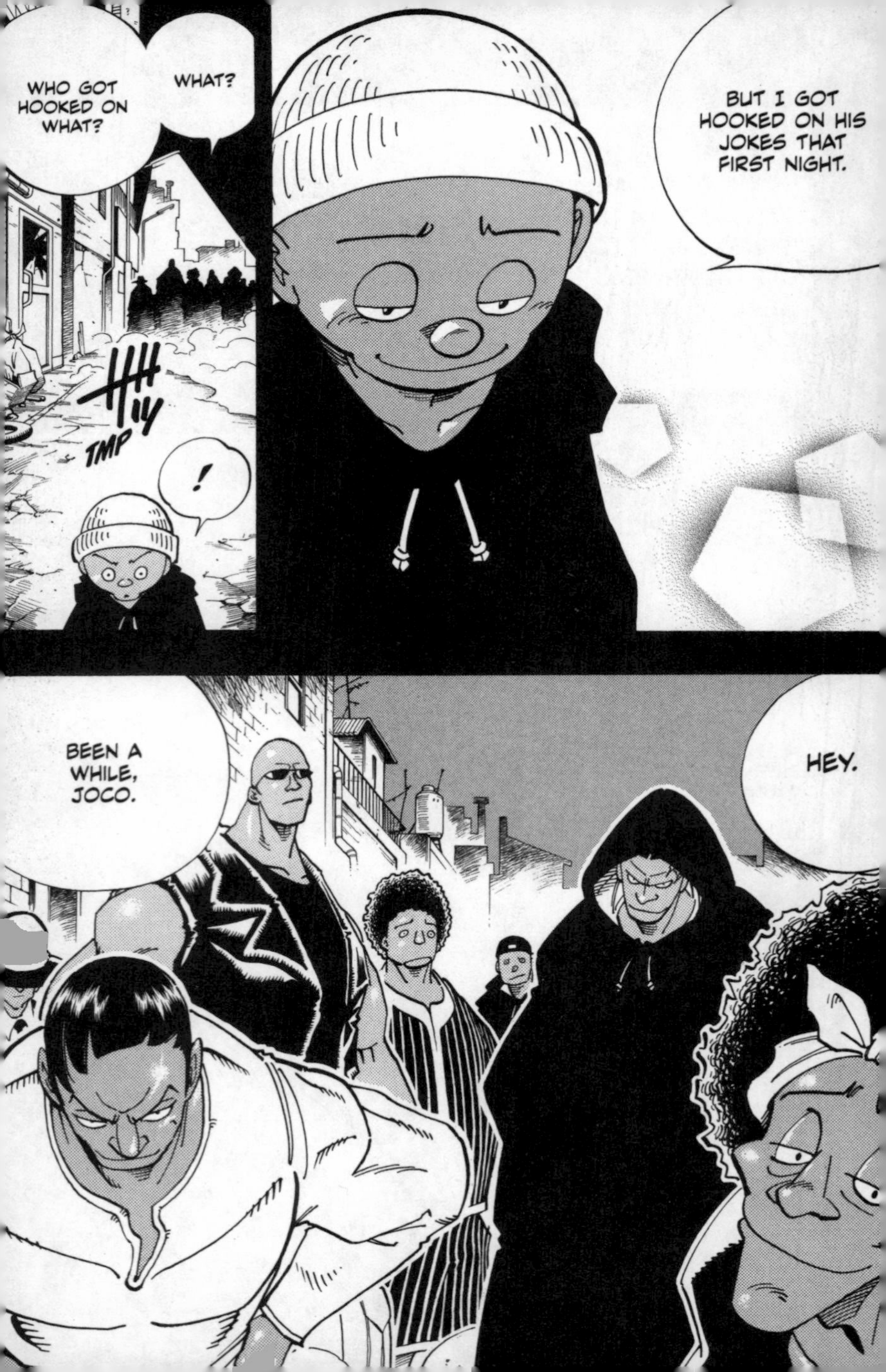
BUT I GOT HOOKED ON HIS JOKES THAT FIRST NIGHT.
WHAT?
WHO GOT HOOKED ON WHAT?
TMP
!
HEY.
BEEN A WHILE, JOCO.

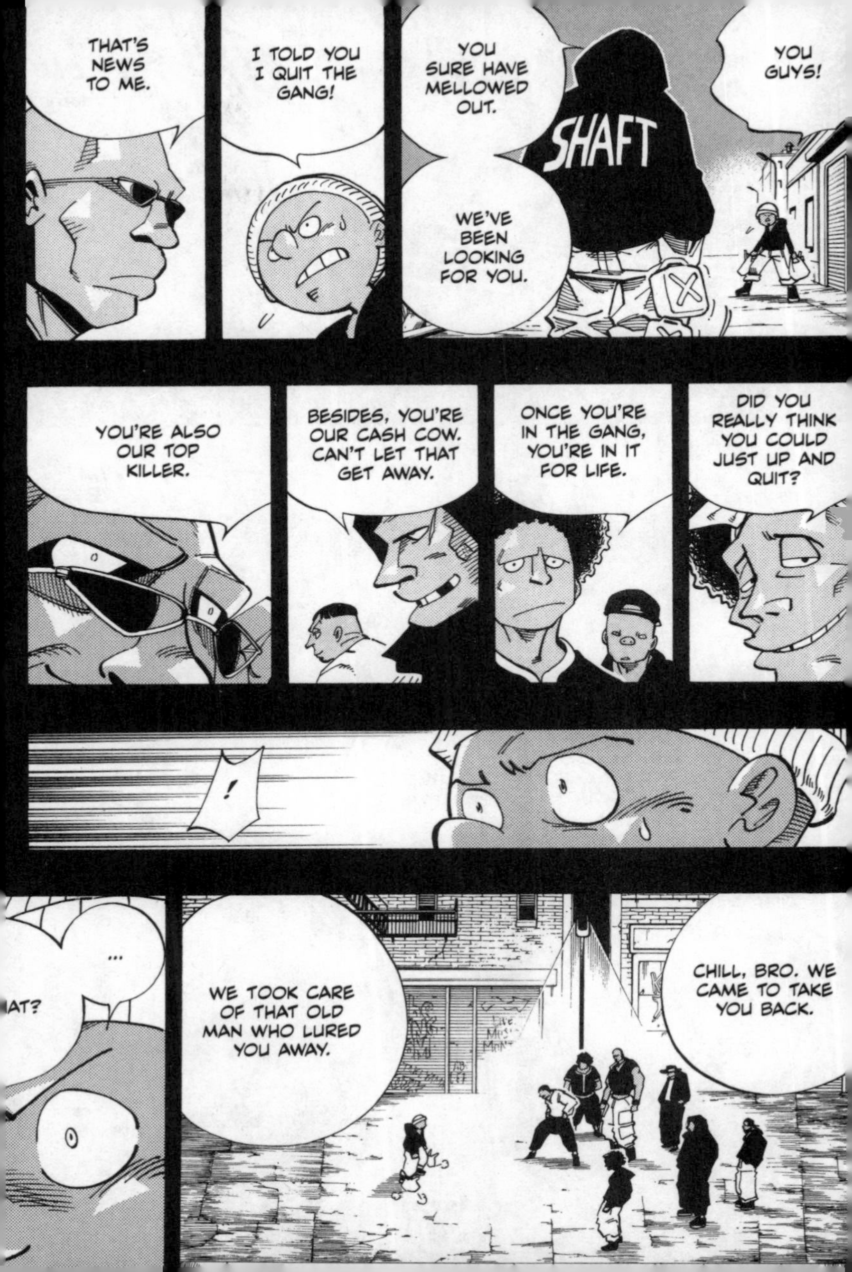
YOU GUYS!
YOU SURE HAVE MELLOWED OUT.
WE'VE BEEN LOOKING FOR YOU.
I TOLD YOU I QUIT THE GANG!
THAT'S NEWS TO ME.
DID YOU REALLY THINK YOU COULD JUST UP AND QUIT?
ONCE YOU'RE IN THE GANG, YOU'RE IN IT FOR LIFE.
BESIDES, YOU'RE OUR CASH COW. CAN'T LET THAT GET AWAY.
YOU'RE ALSO OUR TOP KILLER.
!
CHILL, BRO. WE CAME TO TAKE YOU BACK.
WE TOOK CARE OF THAT OLD MAN WHO LURED YOU AWAY.
...
AT?

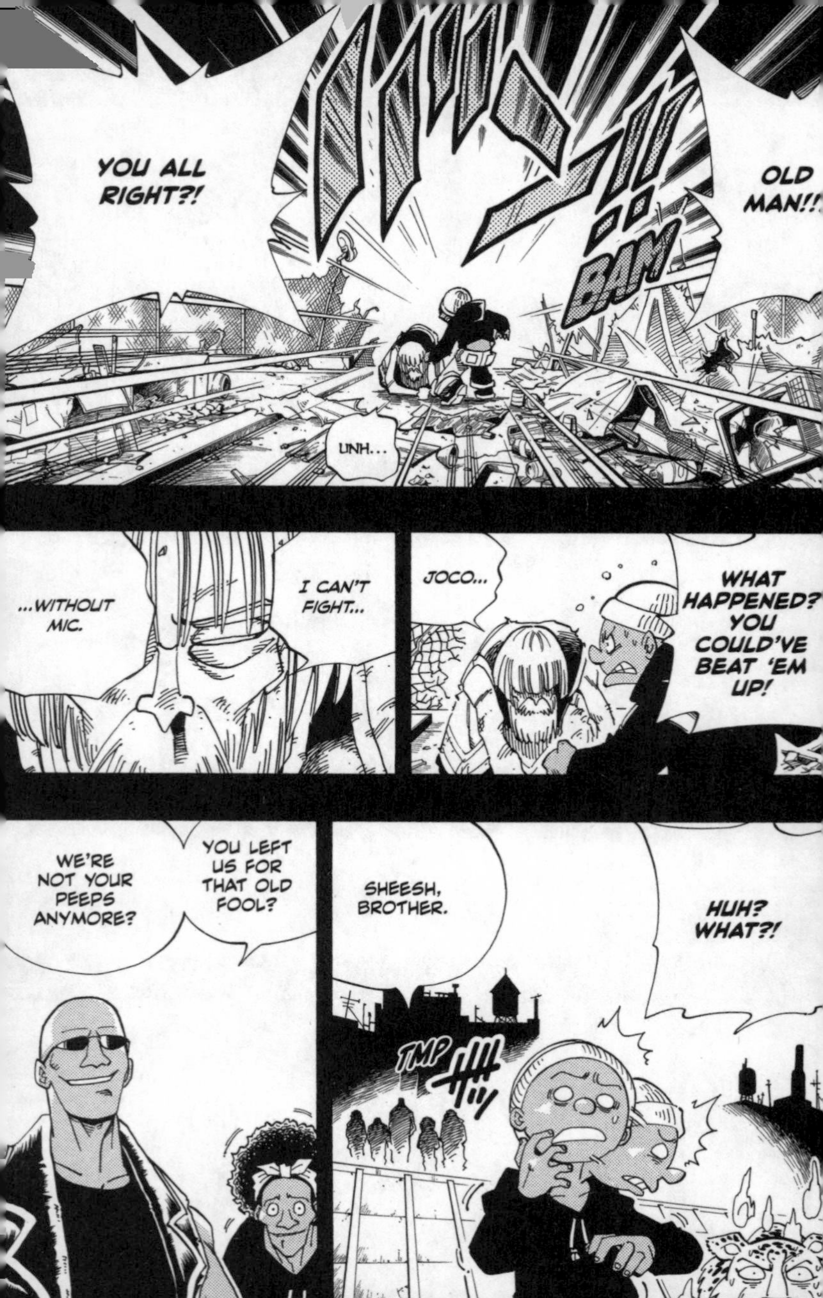
OLD MAN!!
BAM
YOU ALL RIGHT?!
UNH...
WHAT HAPPENED? YOU COULD'VE BEAT 'EM UP!
JOCO...
I CAN'T FIGHT...
...WITHOUT MIC.
HUH? WHAT?!
SHEESH, BROTHER.
TMP
YOU LEFT US FOR THAT OLD FOOL?
WE'RE NOT YOUR PEEPS ANYMORE?

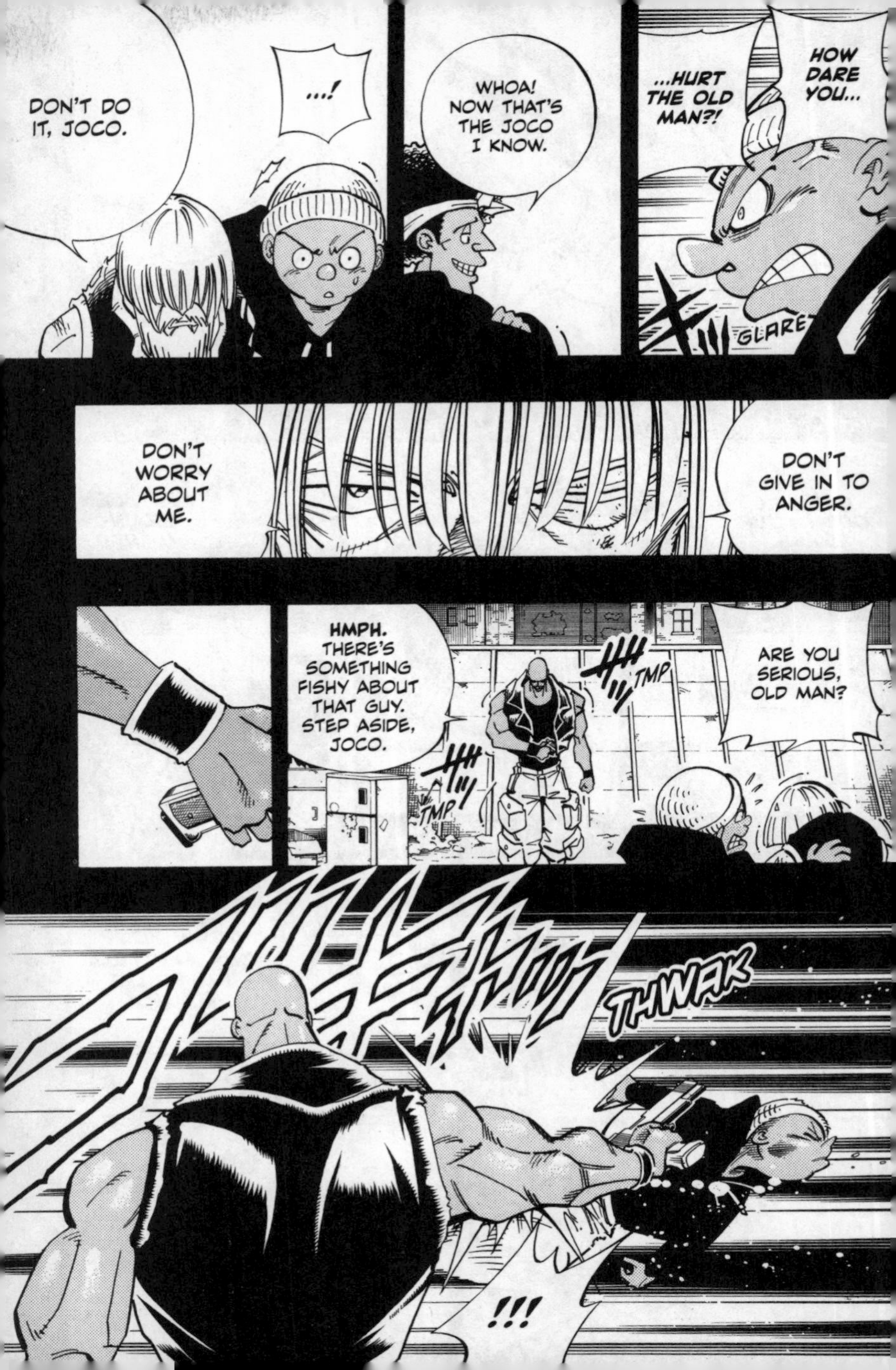
HOW DARE YOU...
...HURT THE OLD MAN?!
GLARE
WHOA! NOW THAT'S THE JOCO I KNOW.
...!
DON'T DO IT, JOCO.
DON'T GIVE IN TO ANGER.
DON'T WORRY ABOUT ME.
ARE YOU SERIOUS, OLD MAN?
TMP
HMPH. THERE'S SOMETHING FISHY ABOUT THAT GUY. STEP ASIDE, JOCO.
TMP
THWAK
!!!

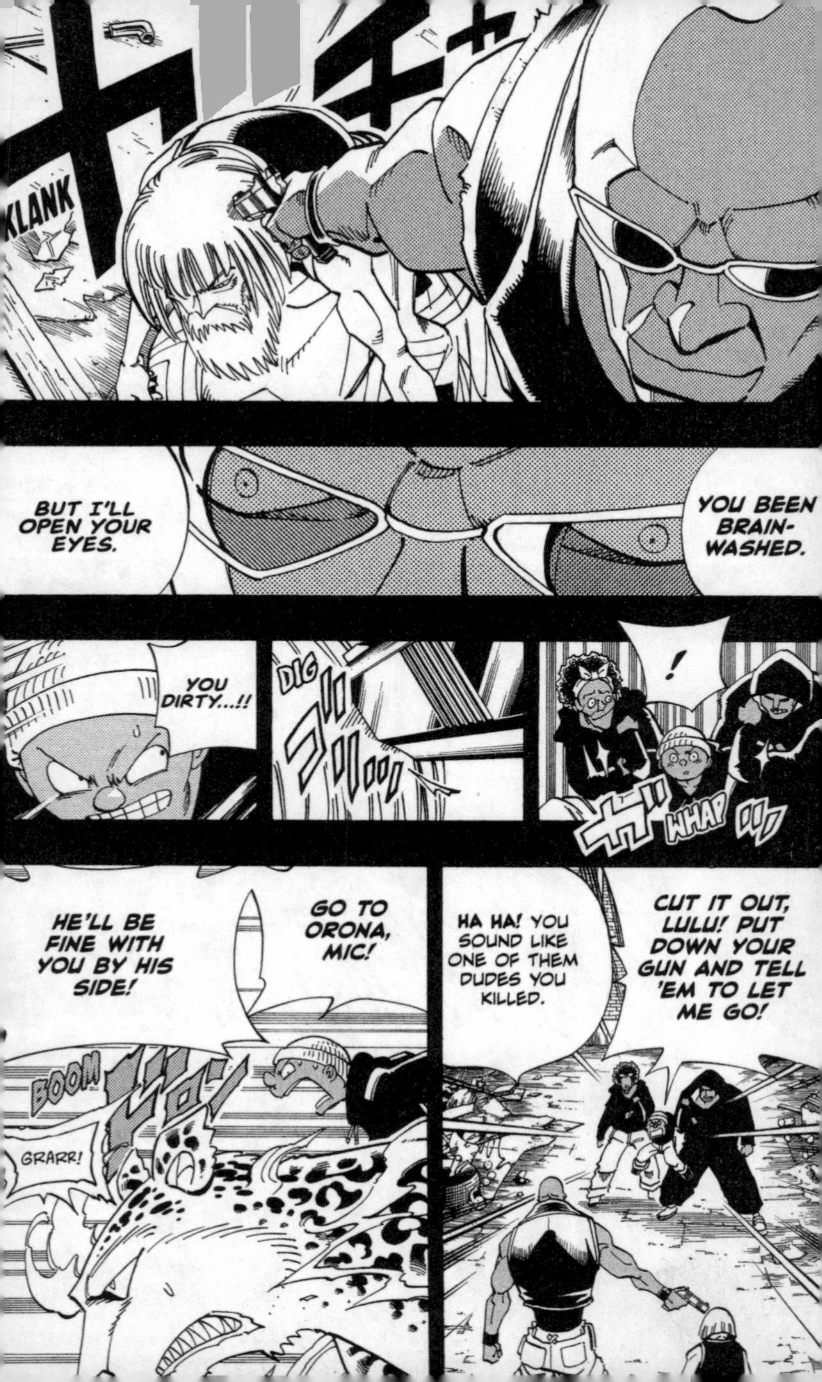
KLANK
YOU BEEN BRAIN-WASHED.
BUT I'LL OPEN YOUR EYES.
!
WHAP
DIG
YOU DIRTY...!!
CUT IT OUT, LULU! PUT DOWN YOUR GUN AND TELL 'EM TO LET ME GO!
HA HA! YOU SOUND LIKE ONE OF THEM DUDES YOU KILLED.
GO TO ORONA, MIC!
HE'LL BE FINE WITH YOU BY HIS SIDE!
BOOM
GRARR!

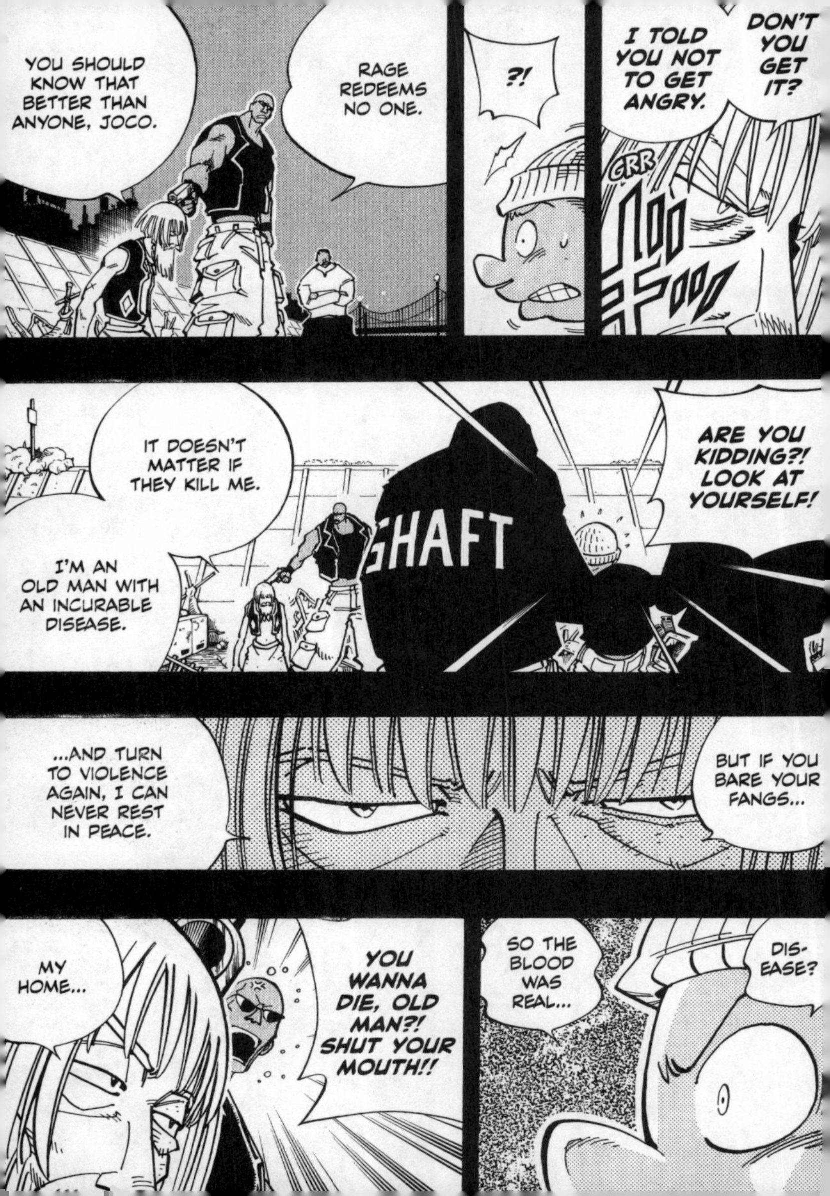
DON'T YOU GET IT?
I TOLD YOU NOT TO GET ANGRY.
GRR
?!
RAGE REDEEMS NO ONE.
YOU SHOULD KNOW THAT BETTER THAN ANYONE, JOCO.
ARE YOU KIDDING?! LOOK AT YOURSELF!
SHAFT
IT DOESN'T MATTER IF THEY KILL ME.
I'M AN OLD MAN WITH AN INCURABLE DISEASE.
BUT IF YOU BARE YOUR FANGS...
...AND TURN TO VIOLENCE AGAIN, I CAN NEVER REST IN PEACE.
DIS-EASE?
SO THE BLOOD WAS REAL...
YOU WANNA DIE, OLD MAN?! SHUT YOUR MOUTH!!
MY HOME...

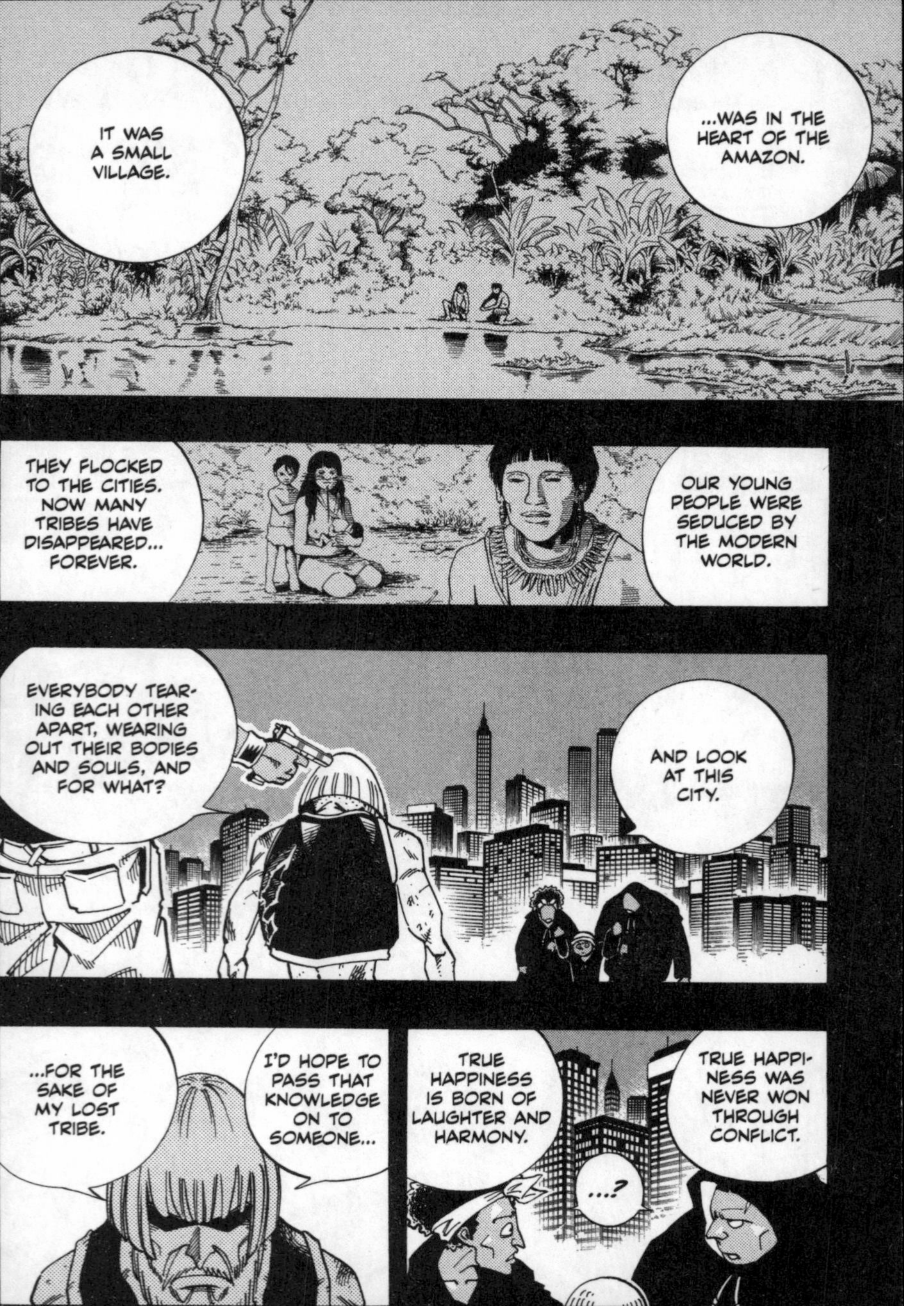
...WAS IN THE HEART OF THE AMAZON.
IT WAS A SMALL VILLAGE.
OUR YOUNG PEOPLE WERE SEDUCED BY THE MODERN WORLD.
THEY FLOCKED TO THE CITIES. NOW MANY TRIBES HAVE DISAPPEARED... FOREVER.
AND LOOK AT THIS CITY.
EVERYBODY TEAR-ING EACH OTHER APART, WEARING OUT THEIR BODIES AND SOULS, AND FOR WHAT?
TRUE HAPPI-NESS WAS NEVER WON THROUGH CONFLICT.
TRUE HAPPINESS IS BORN OF LAUGHTER AND HARMONY.
...?
I'D HOPE TO PASS THAT KNOWLEDGE ON TO SOMEONE...
...FOR THE SAKE OF MY LOST TRIBE.

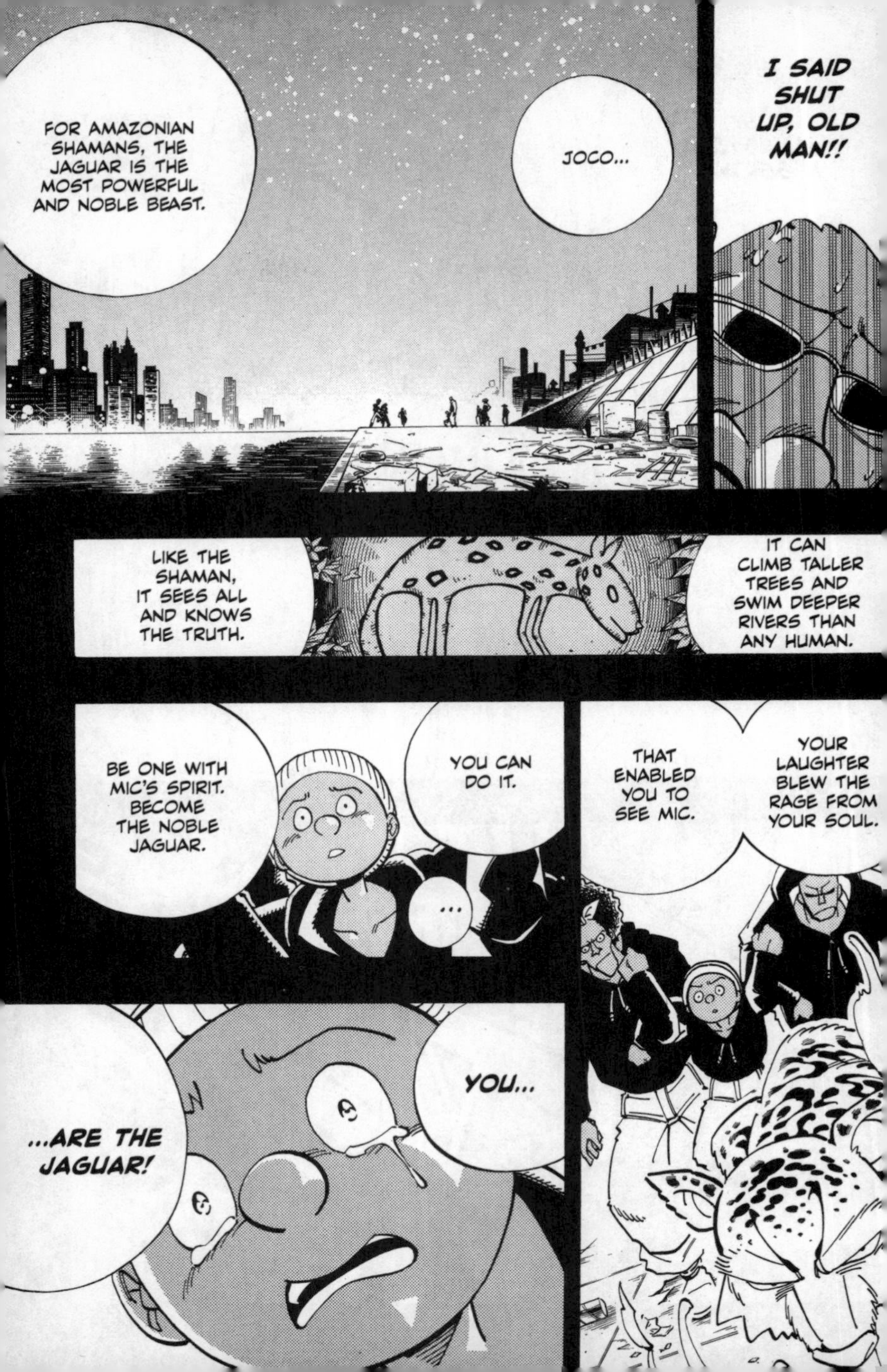
I SAID SHUT UP, OLD MAN!!
JOCO...
FOR AMAZONIAN SHAMANS, THE JAGUAR IS THE MOST POWERFUL AND NOBLE BEAST.
IT CAN CLIMB TALLER TREES AND SWIM DEEPER RIVERS THAN ANY HUMAN.
LIKE THE SHAMAN, IT SEES ALL AND KNOWS THE TRUTH.
YOUR LAUGHTER BLEW THE RAGE FROM YOUR SOUL.
THAT ENABLED YOU TO SEE MIC.
YOU CAN DO IT.
BE ONE WITH MIC'S SPIRIT. BECOME THE NOBLE JAGUAR.
...
YOU...
...ARE THE JAGUAR!

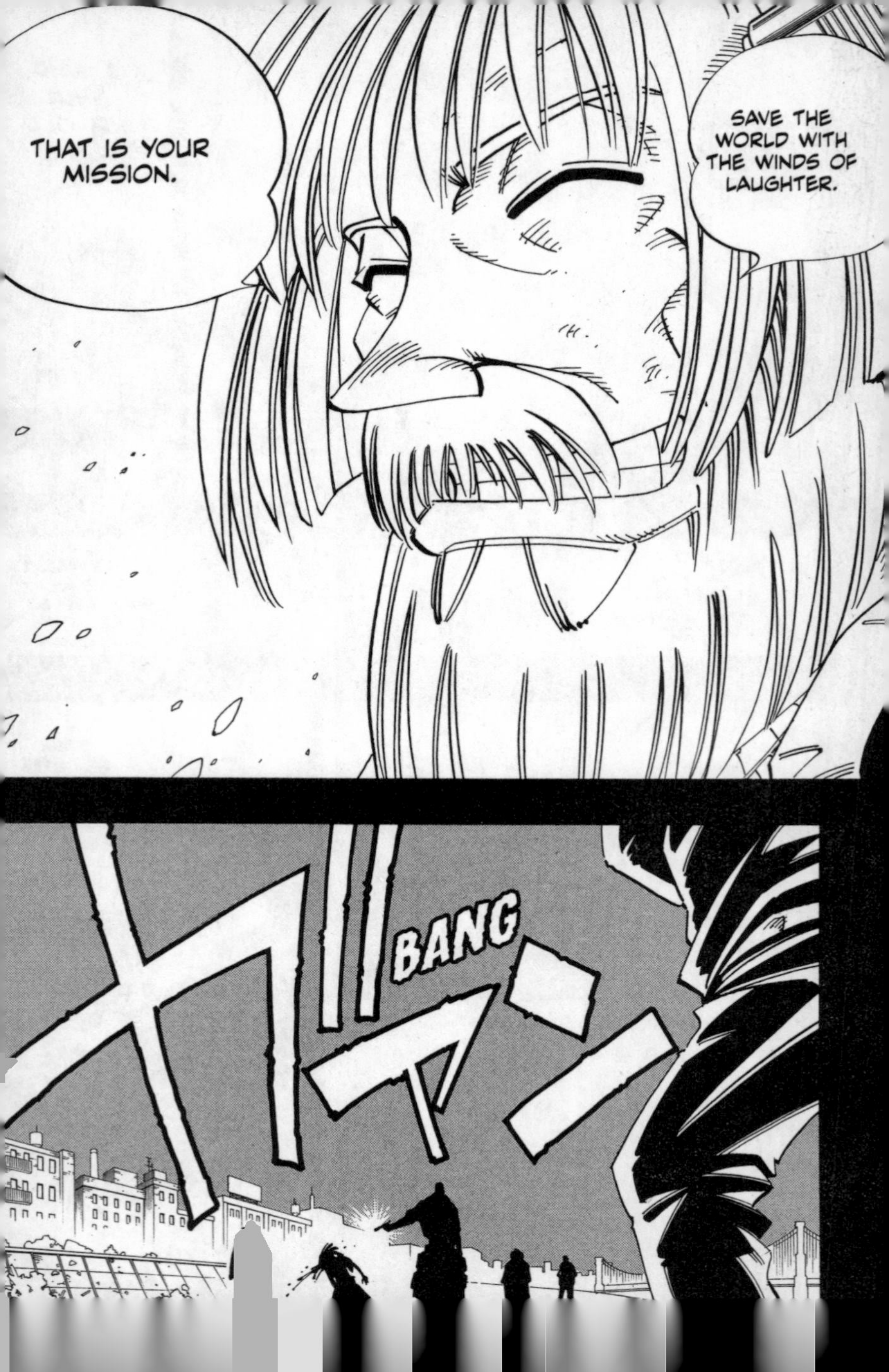
SAVE THE WORLD WITH THE WINDS OF LAUGHTER.
THAT IS YOUR MISSION.
BANG

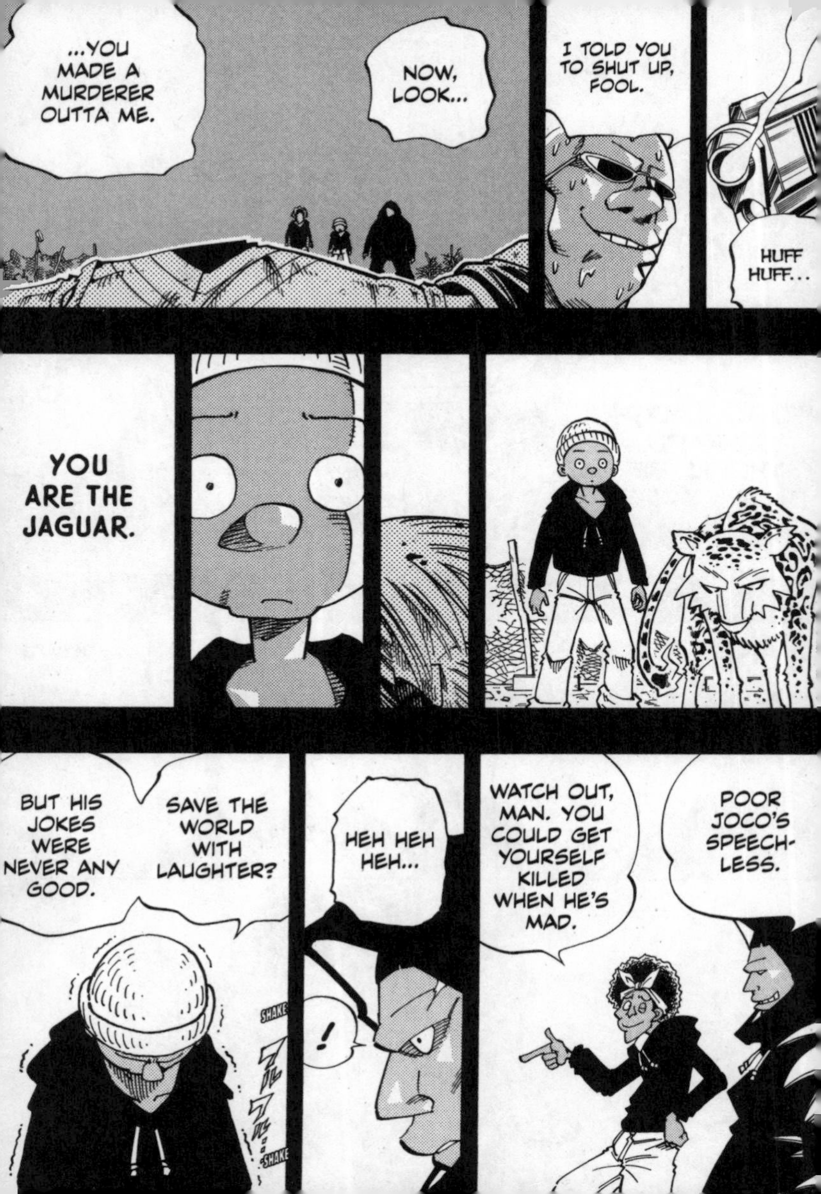
HUFF HUFF...
I TOLD YOU TO SHUT UP, FOOL.
NOW, LOOK...
...YOU MADE A MURDERER OUTTA ME.
YOU ARE THE JAGUAR.
POOR JOCO'S SPEECH-LESS.
WATCH OUT, MAN. YOU COULD GET YOURSELF KILLED WHEN HE'S MAD.
HEH HEH HEH...
!
SAVE THE WORLD WITH LAUGHTER?
BUT HIS JOKES WERE NEVER ANY GOOD.
SHAKE
SHAKE

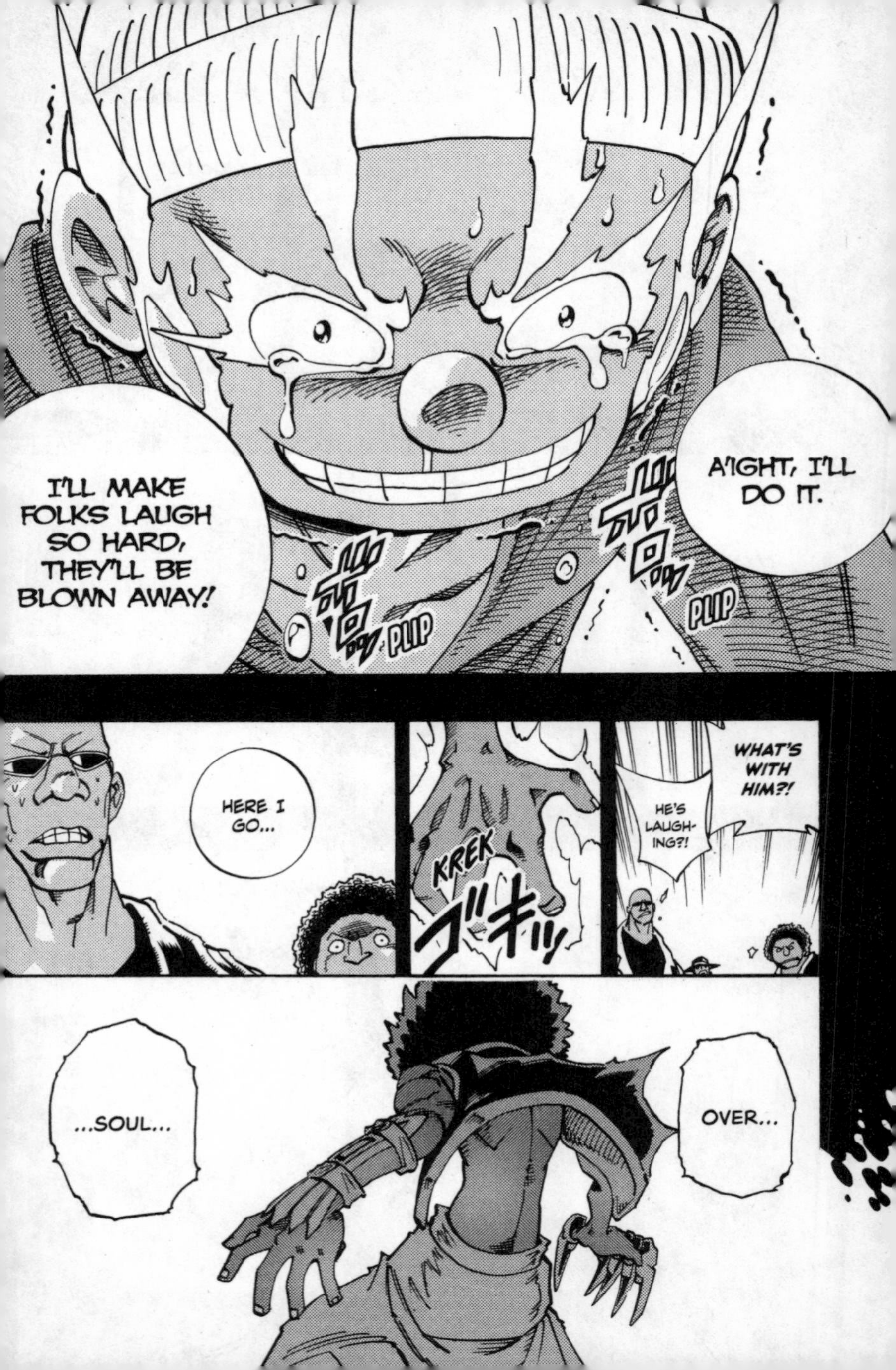

A'IGHT, I'LL DO IT.
PLIP
I'LL MAKE FOLKS LAUGH SO HARD, THEY'LL BE BLOWN AWAY!
PLIP
WHAT'S WITH HIM?!
HE'S LAUGH-ING?!
KREK
HERE I GO...
OVER...
...SOUL...

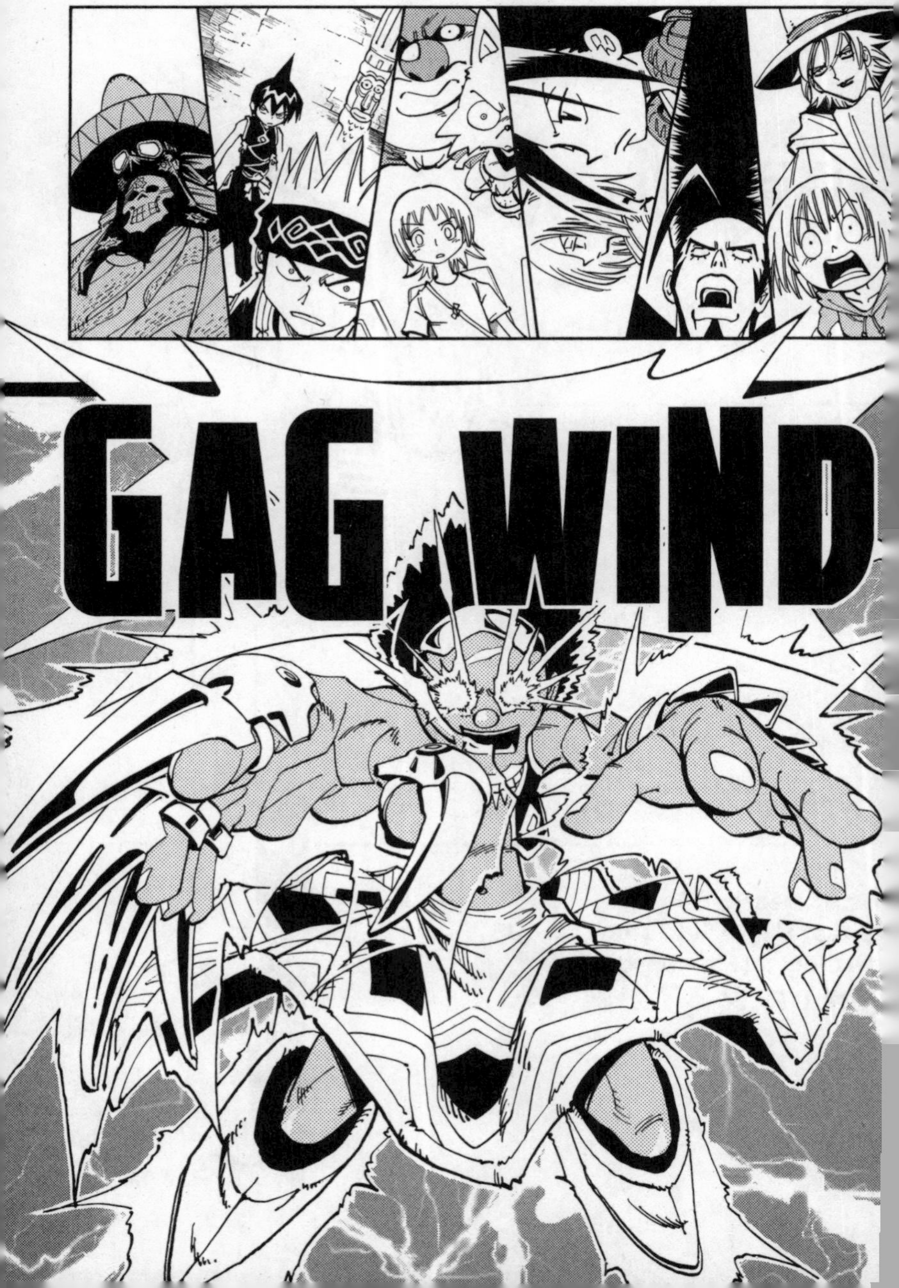
GAG WIND

SHAMAN KING CHARACTER FILE No.64

Anatel

June 2001

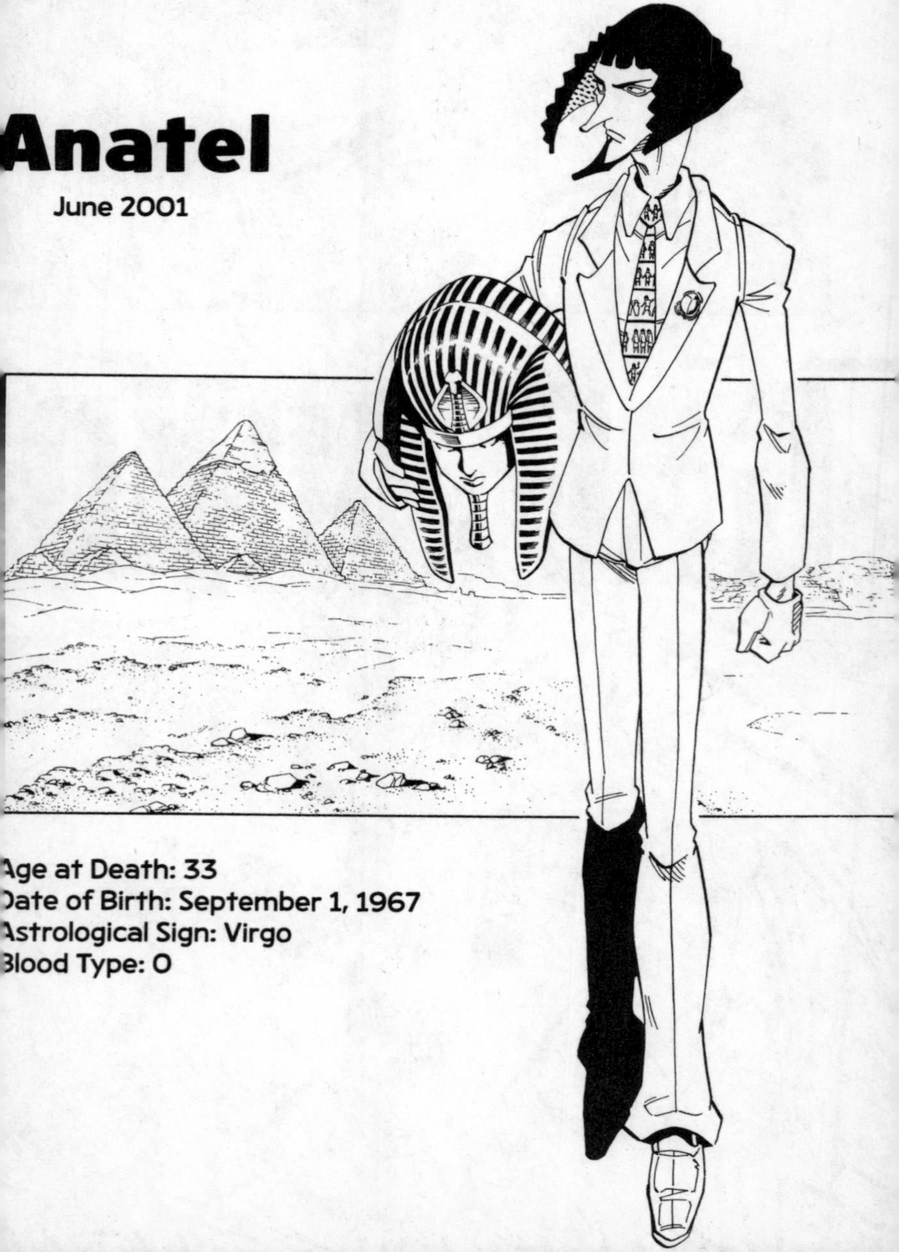

Age at Death: 33
Date of Birth: September 1, 1967
Astrological Sign: Virgo
Blood Type: O

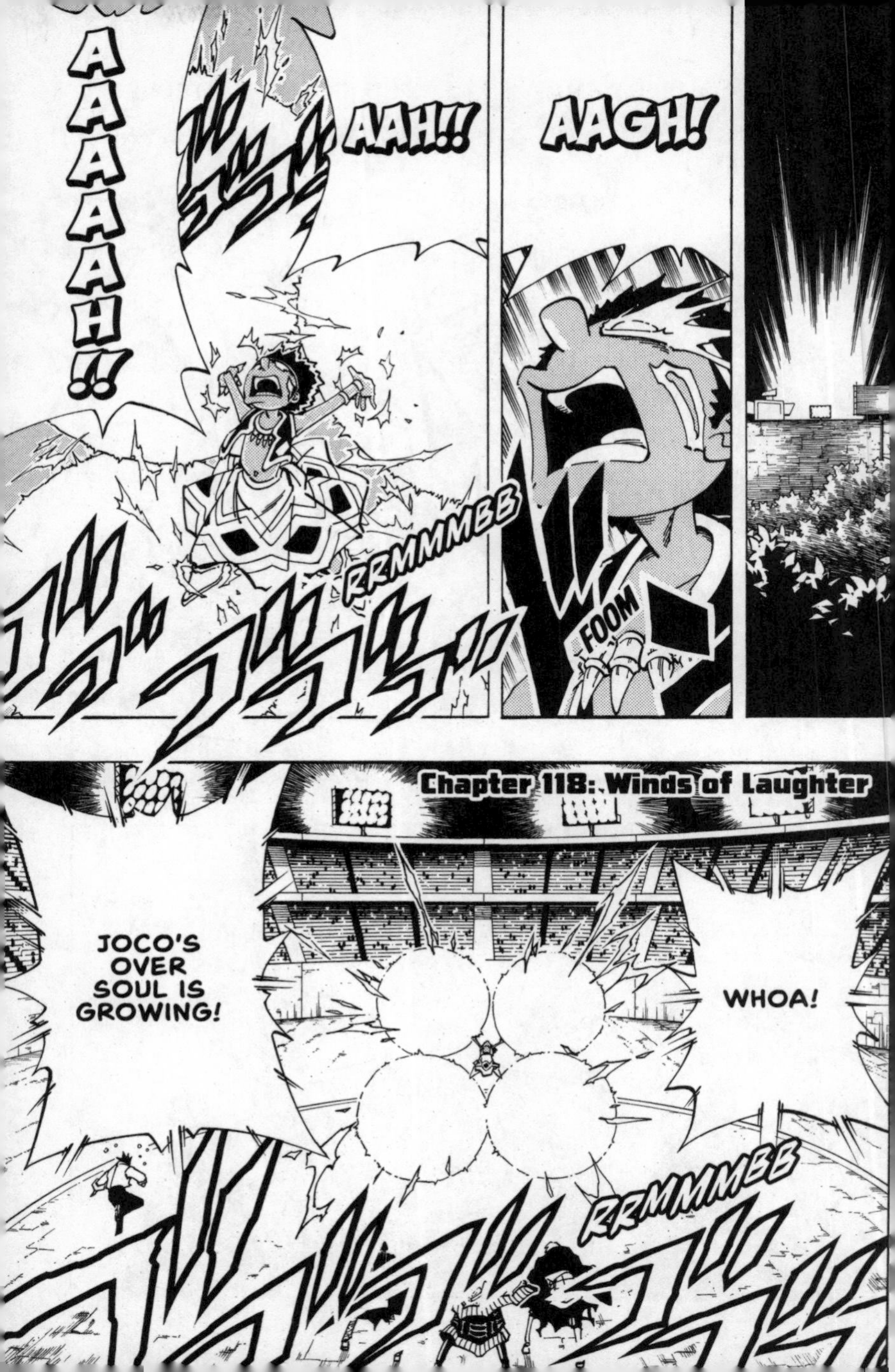
AAGH!
FOOM
AAH!!
AAAAAAH!!
RRMMMBB
Chapter 118: Winds of Laughter
WHOA!
JOCO'S OVER SOUL IS GROWING!
RRMMMBB

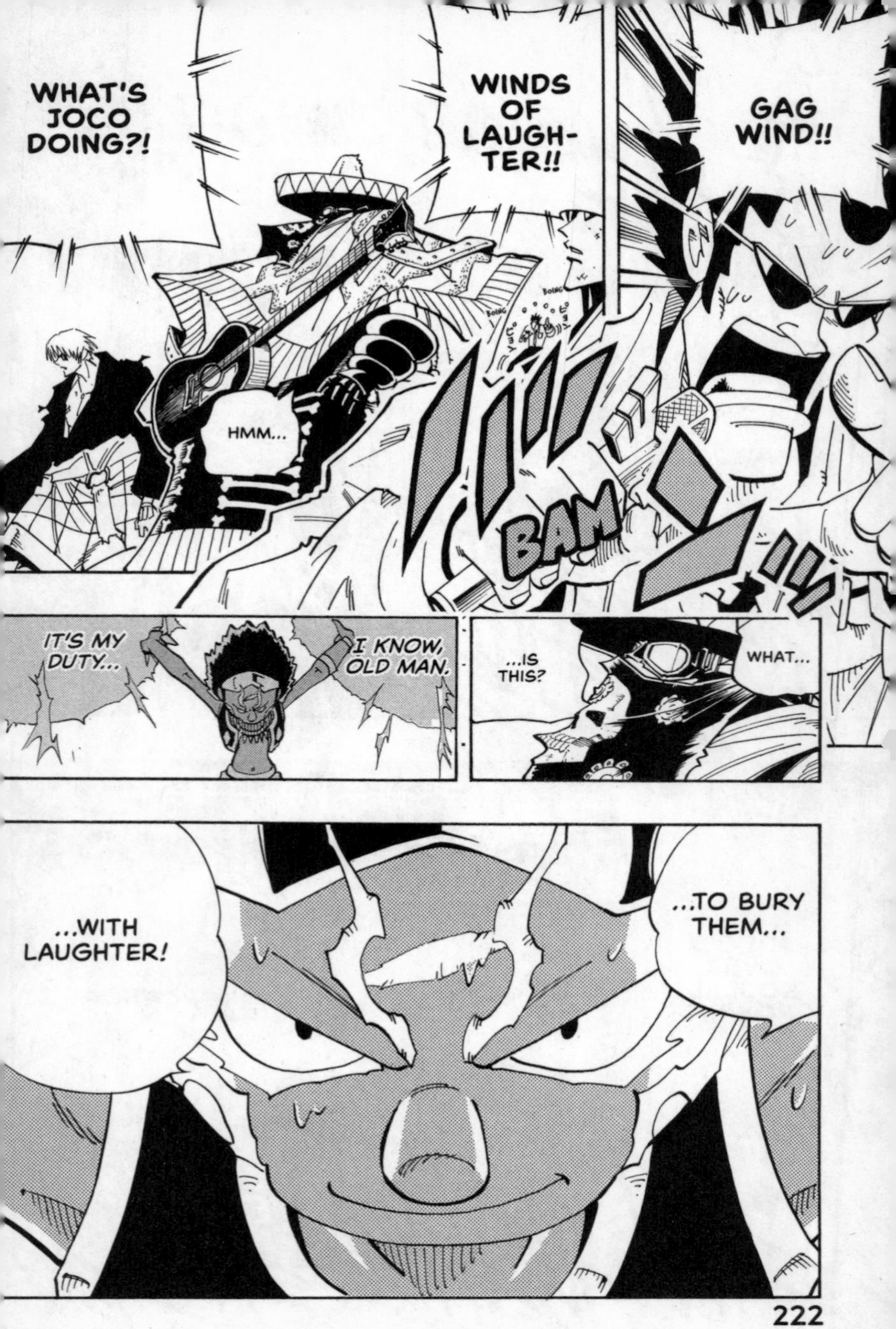
GAG WIND!!
WINDS OF LAUGHTER!!
BAM
WHAT'S JOCO DOING?!
HMM...
WHAT...
...IS THIS?
I KNOW, OLD MAN.
IT'S MY DUTY...
...TO BURY THEM...
...WITH LAUGHTER!

Chapter 118:

Winds of Laughter

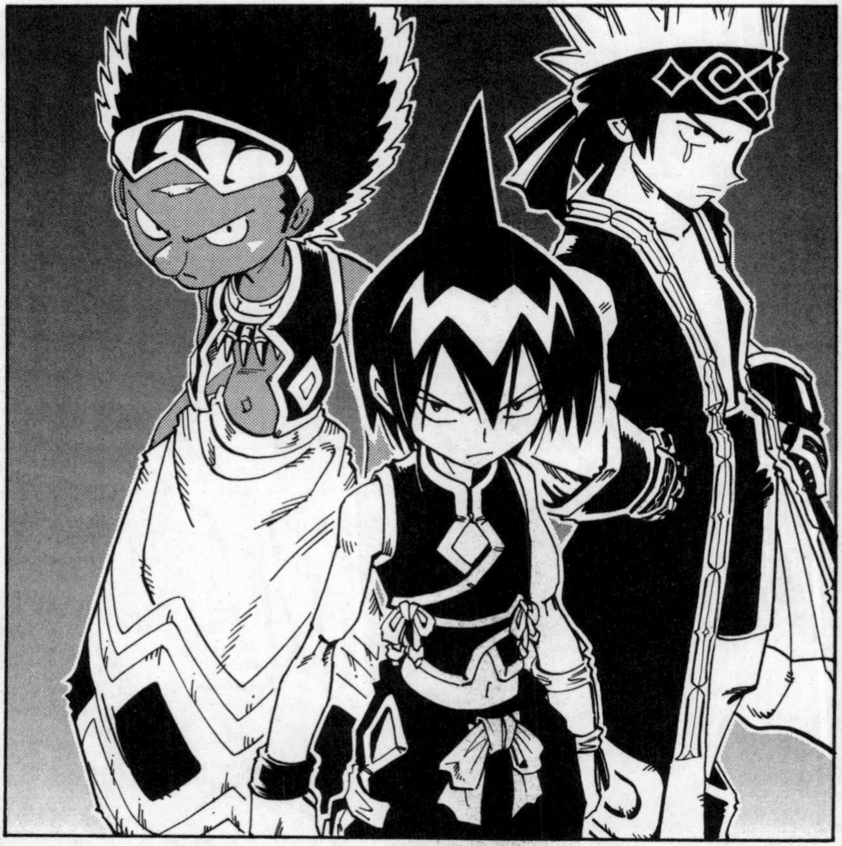

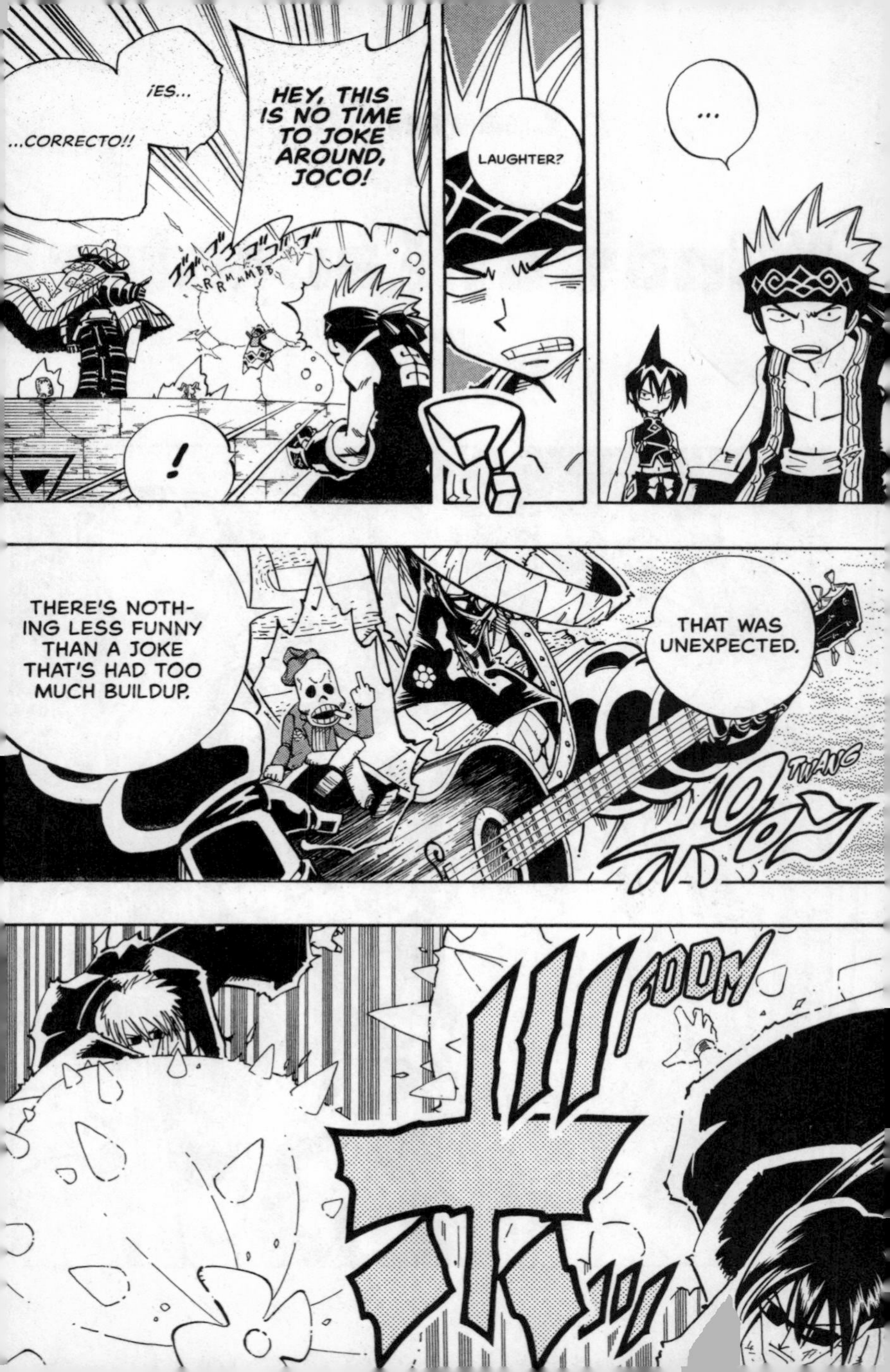
...
LAUGHTER?
HEY, THIS IS NO TIME TO JOKE AROUND, JOCO!
¡ES...
...CORRECTO!!
RRMMMBB
!
THAT WAS UNEXPECTED.
TWANG
THERE'S NOTH-ING LESS FUNNY THAN A JOKE THAT'S HAD TOO MUCH BUILDUP.
FOOM

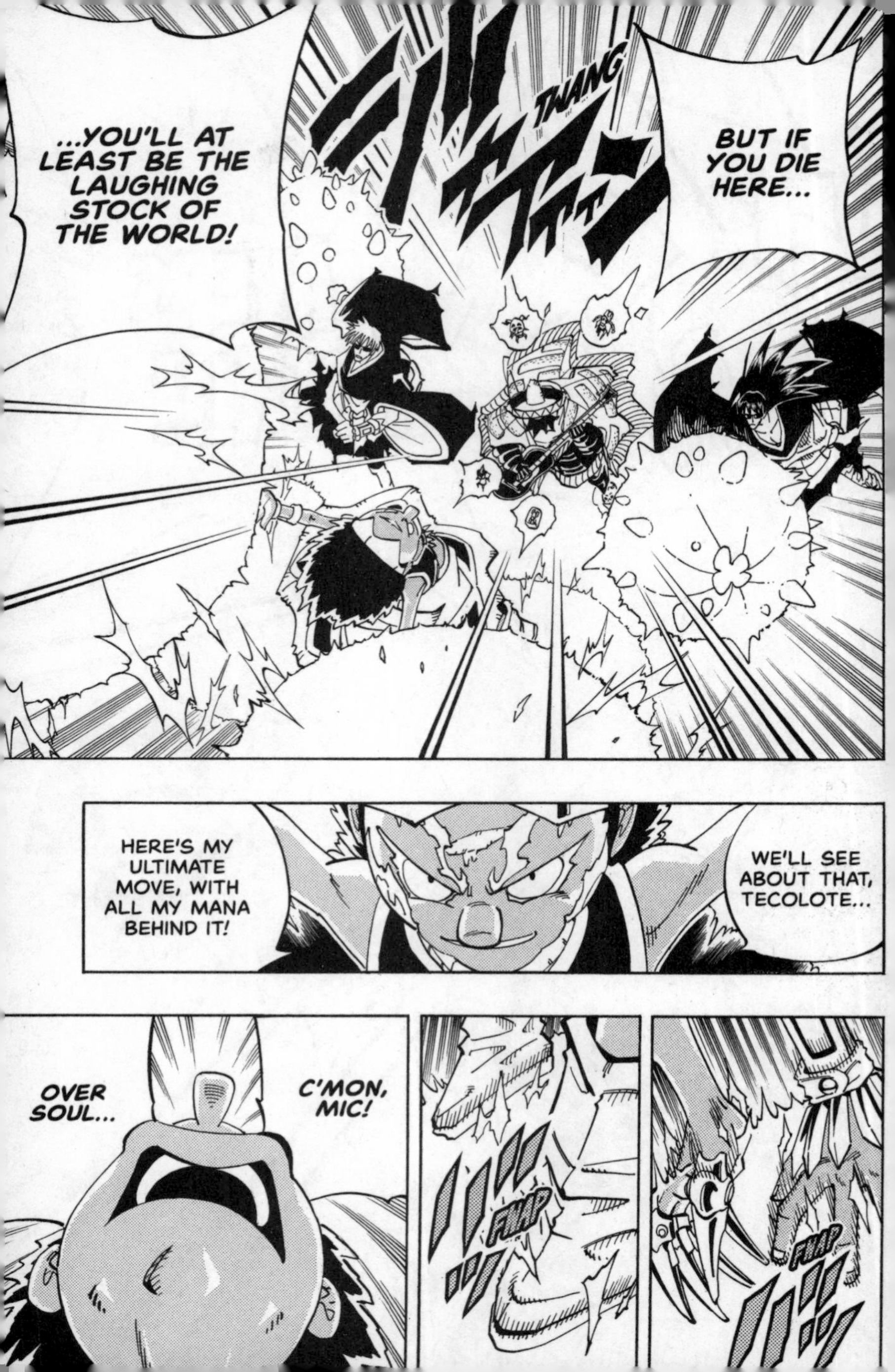
BUT IF YOU DIE HERE...
TWANG
...YOU'LL AT LEAST BE THE LAUGHING STOCK OF THE WORLD!
WE'LL SEE ABOUT THAT, TECOLOTE...
HERE'S MY ULTIMATE MOVE, WITH ALL MY MANA BEHIND IT!
FWIP
FWIP
C'MON, MIC!
OVER SOUL...

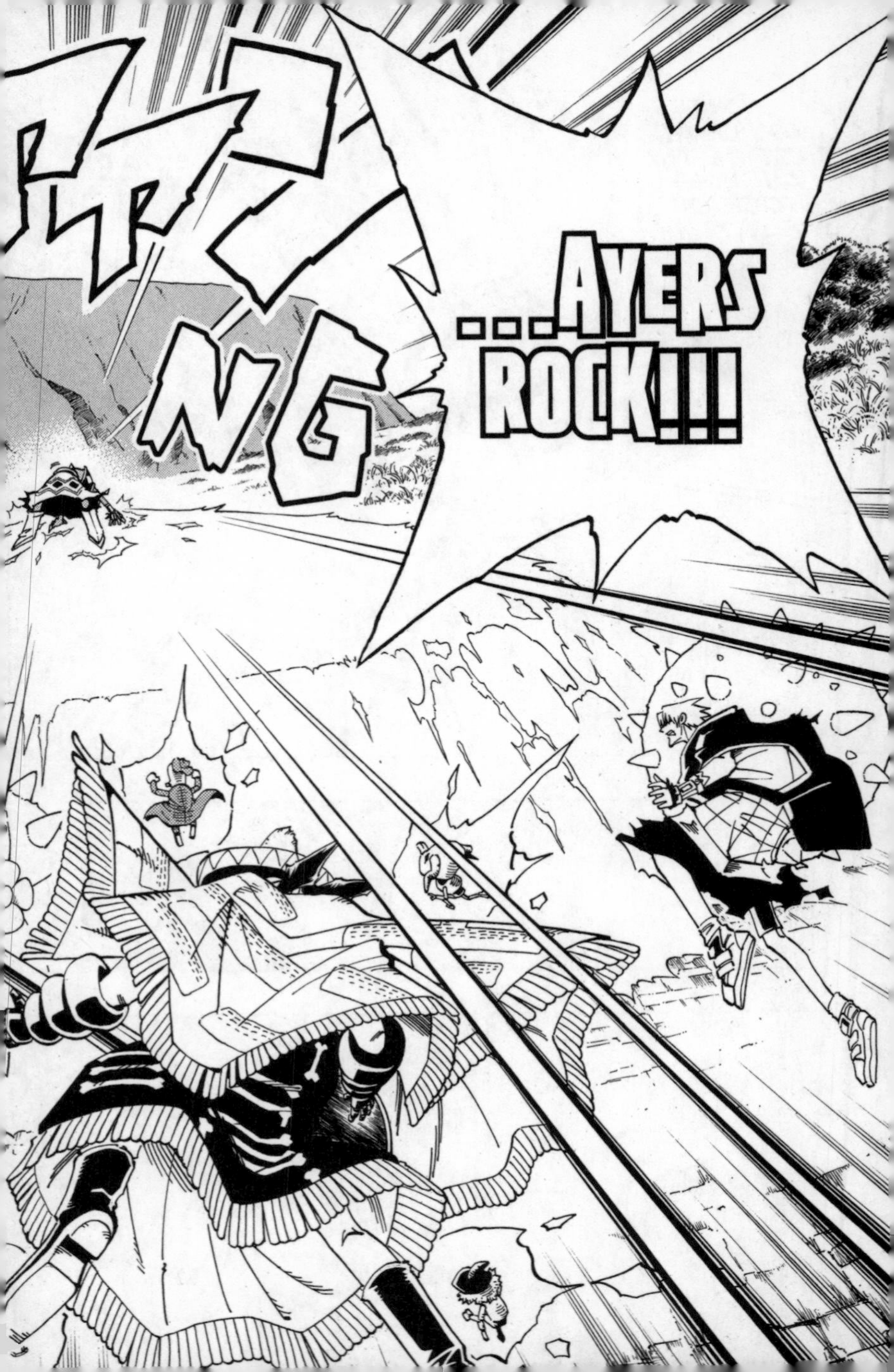
...AYERS ROCK!!!
NG

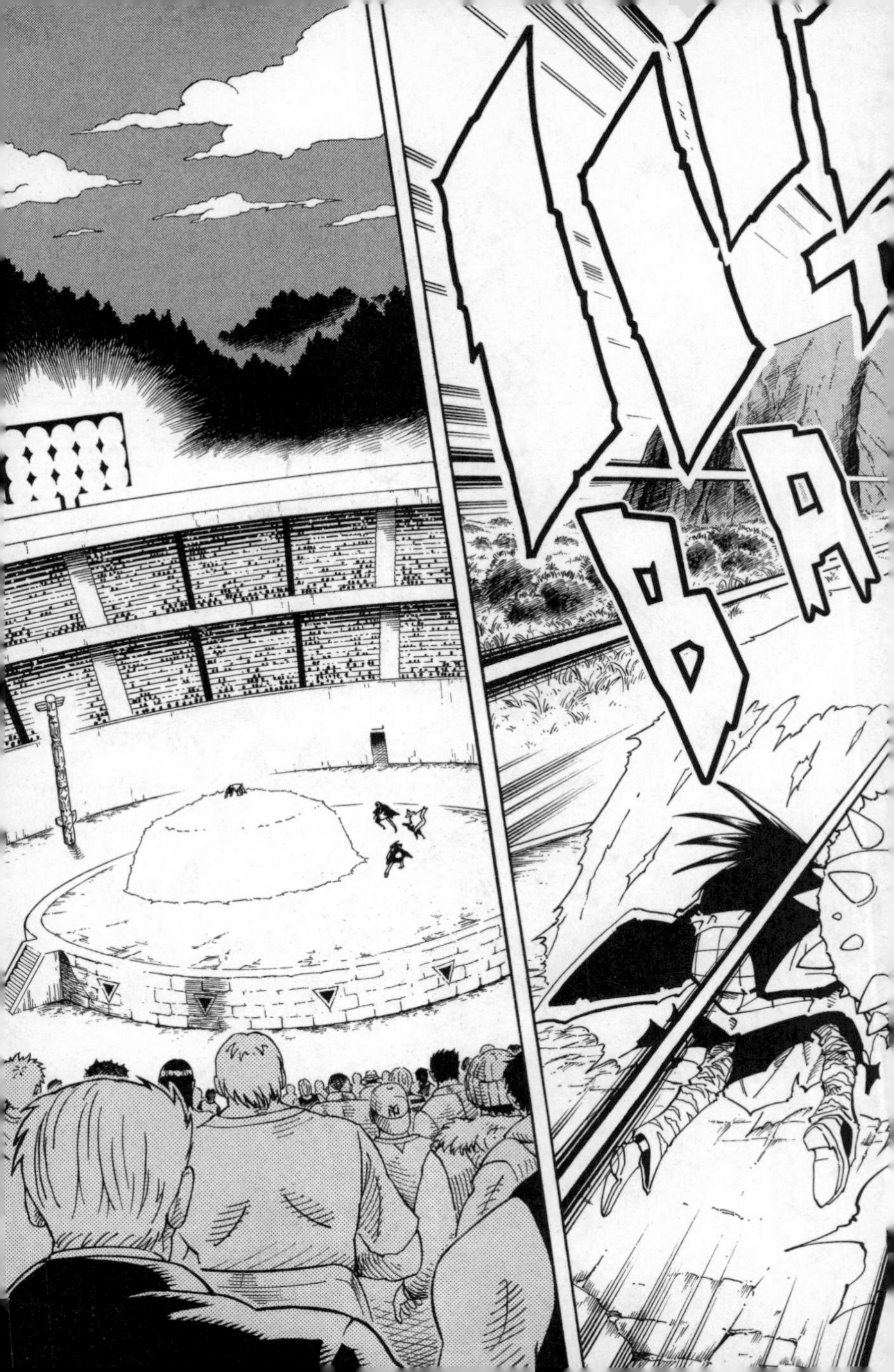

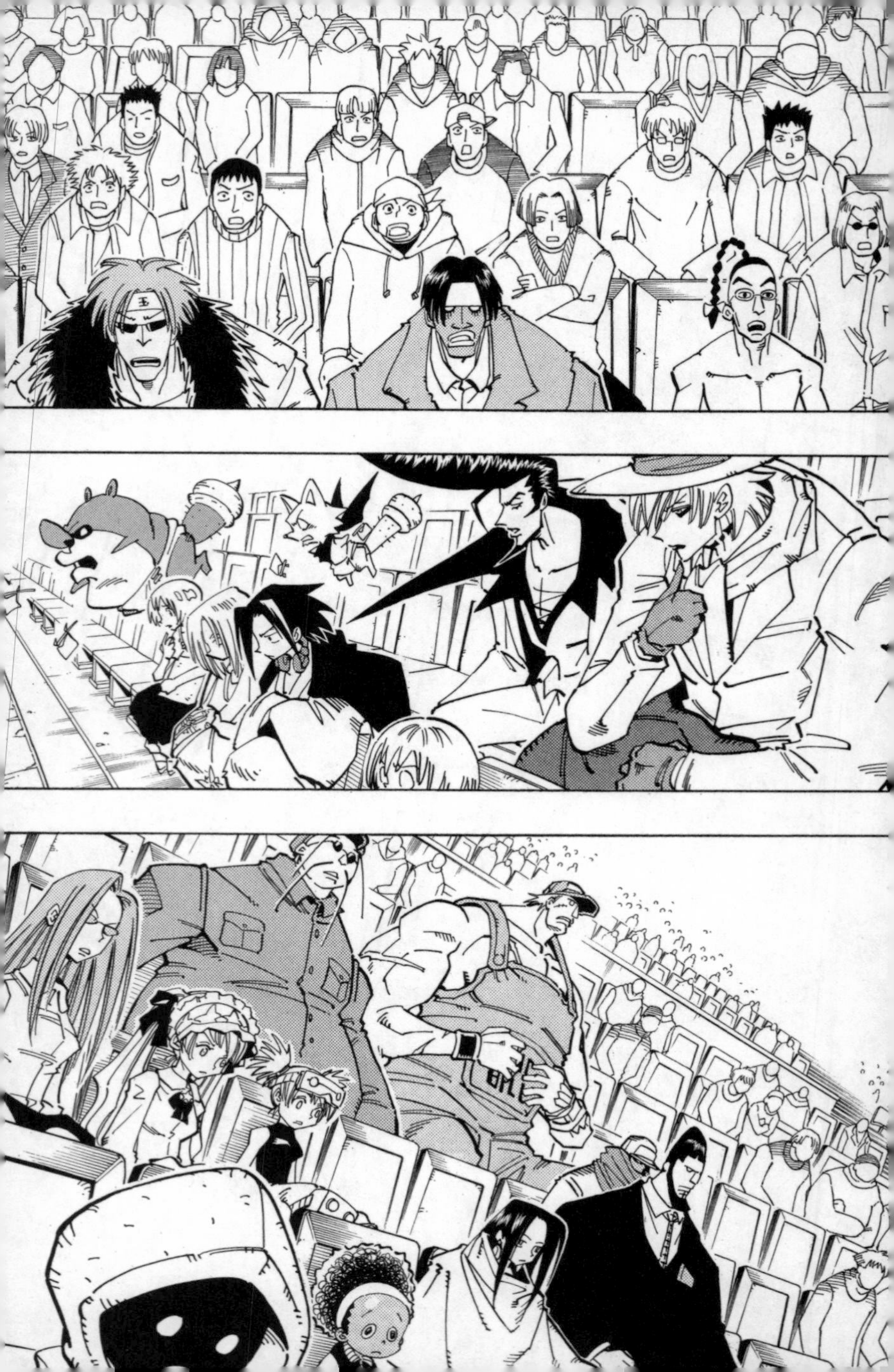

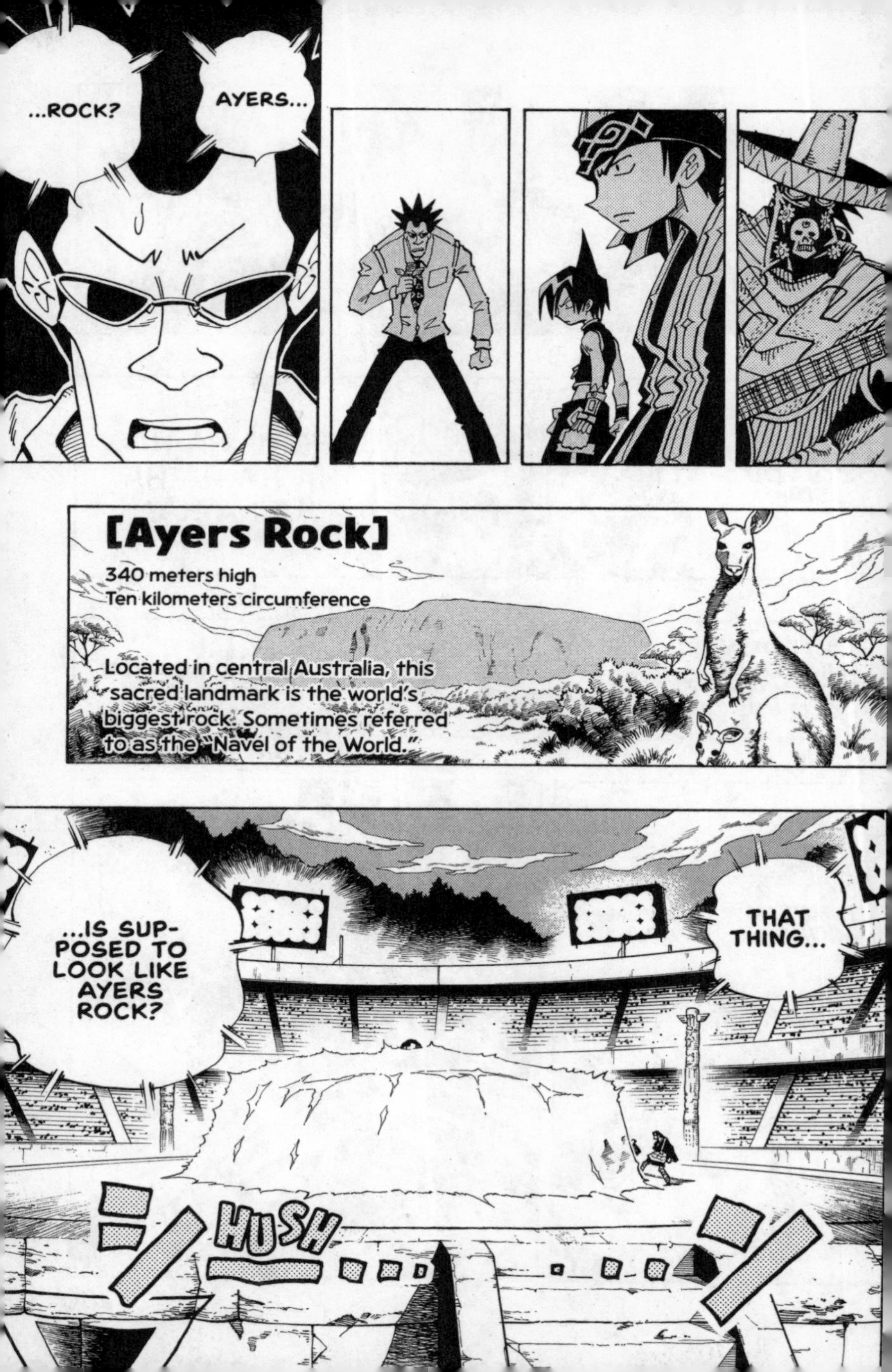
AYERS...
...ROCK?
[Ayers Rock]
340 meters high
Ten kilometers circumference
Located in central Australia, this sacred landmark is the world's biggest rock. Sometimes referred to as the "Navel of the World."
THAT THING...
...IS SUPPOSED TO LOOK LIKE AYERS ROCK?
HUSH

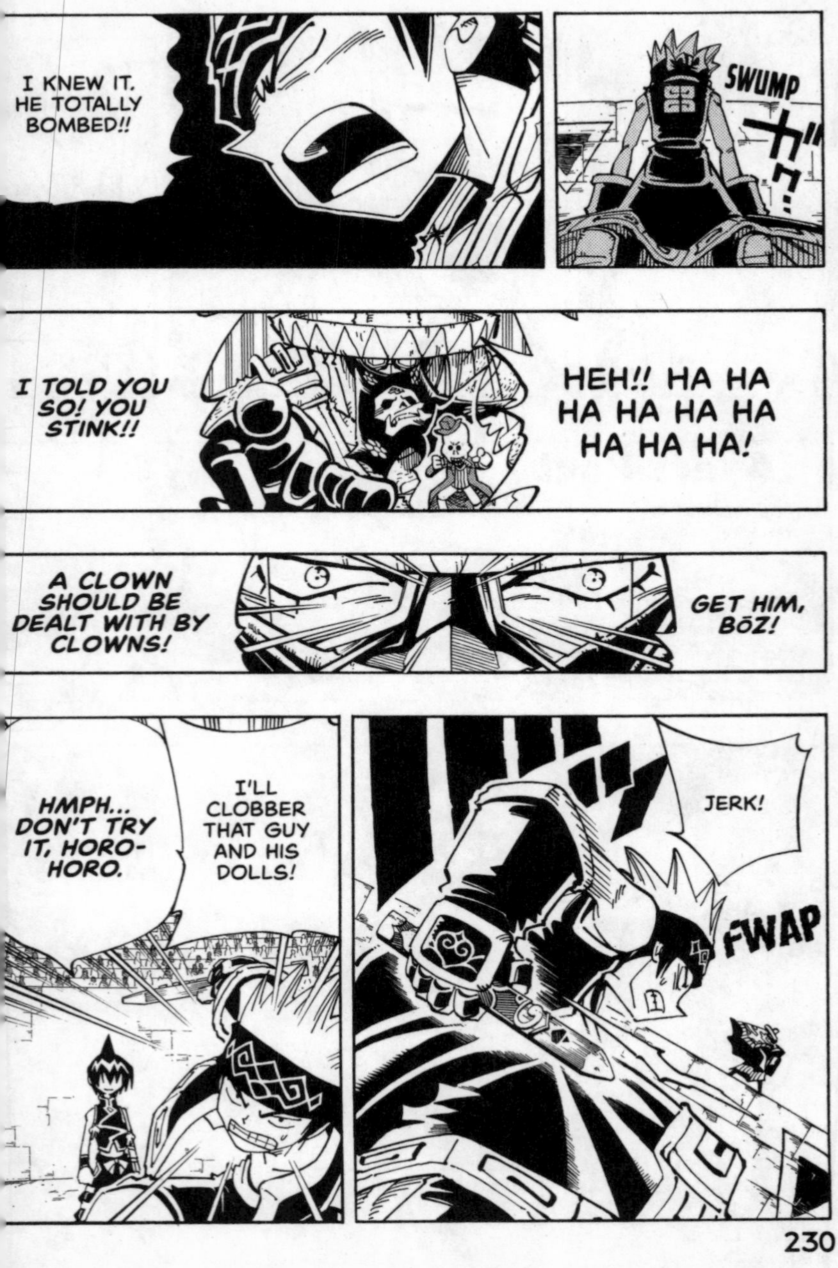
SWUMP
ガク!
I KNEW IT. HE TOTALLY BOMBED!!
HEH!! HA HA HA HA HA HA HA HA HA!
I TOLD YOU SO! YOU STINK!!
GET HIM, BŌZ!
A CLOWN SHOULD BE DEALT WITH BY CLOWNS!
JERK!
FWAP
I'LL CLOBBER THAT GUY AND HIS DOLLS!
HMPH... DON'T TRY IT, HORO-HORO.

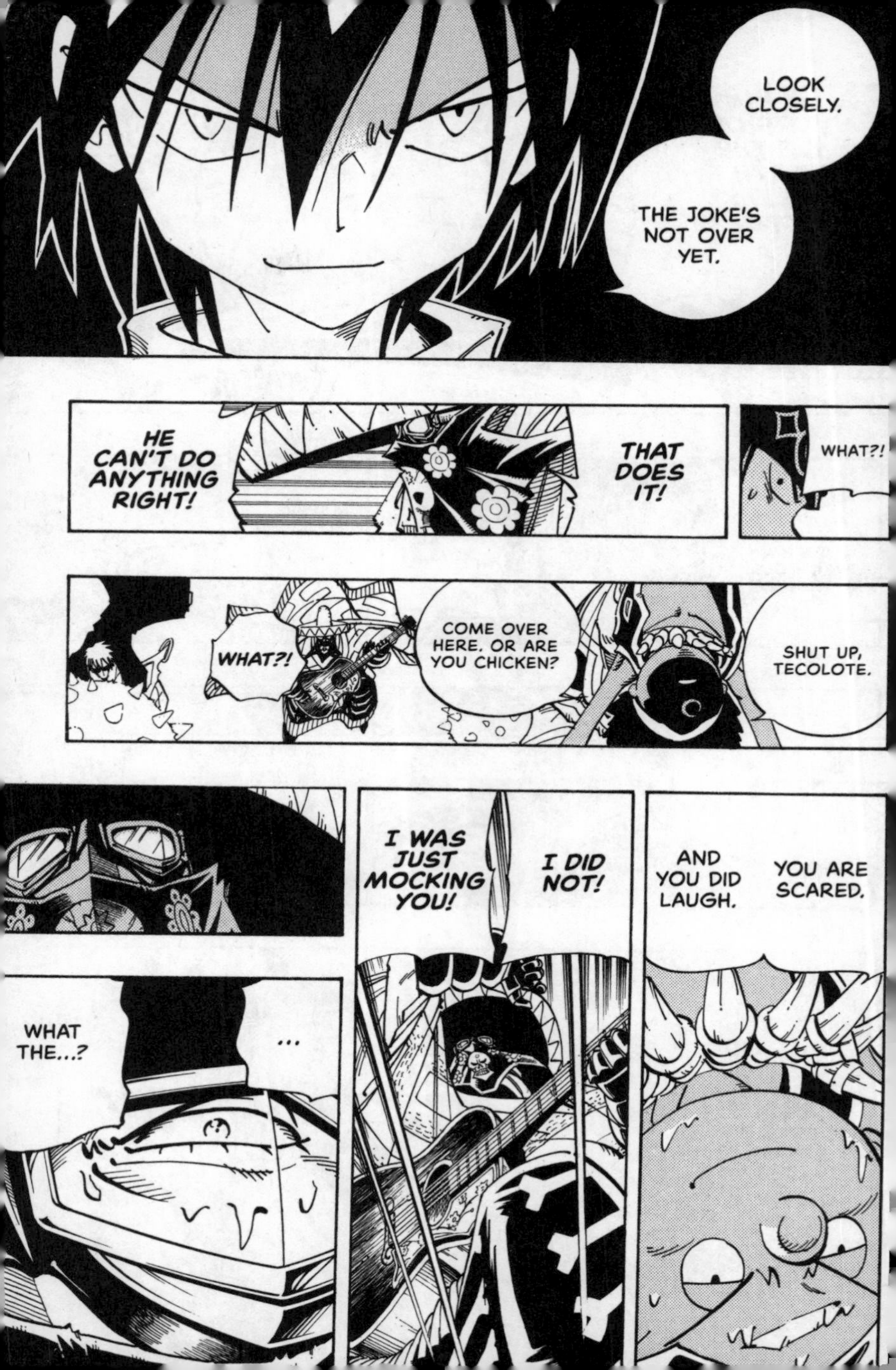

LOOK CLOSELY.
THE JOKE'S NOT OVER YET.
WHAT?!
THAT DOES IT!
HE CAN'T DO ANYTHING RIGHT!
SHUT UP, TECOLOTE.
COME OVER HERE. OR ARE YOU CHICKEN?
WHAT?!
YOU ARE SCARED.
AND YOU DID LAUGH.
I DID NOT!
I WAS JUST MOCKING YOU!
...
WHAT THE...?

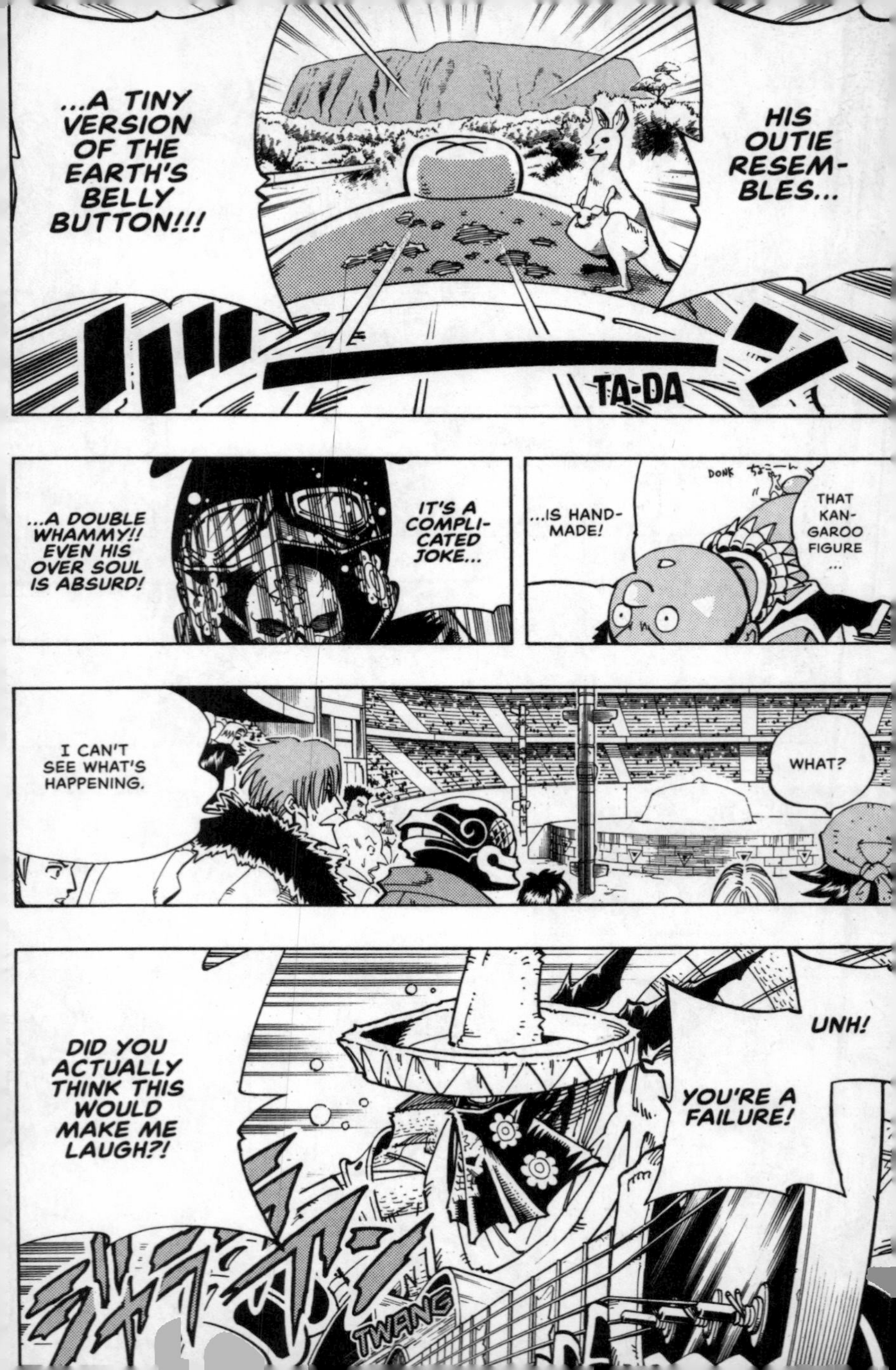
HIS OUTIE RESEMBLES...
...A TINY VERSION OF THE EARTH'S BELLY BUTTON!!!
TA-DA
DONK
THAT KANGAROO FIGURE ...
...IS HANDMADE!
IT'S A COMPLICATED JOKE...
...A DOUBLE WHAMMY!! EVEN HIS OVER SOUL IS ABSURD!
WHAT?
I CAN'T SEE WHAT'S HAPPENING.
UNH!
YOU'RE A FAILURE!
DID YOU ACTUALLY THINK THIS WOULD MAKE ME LAUGH?!
TWANG

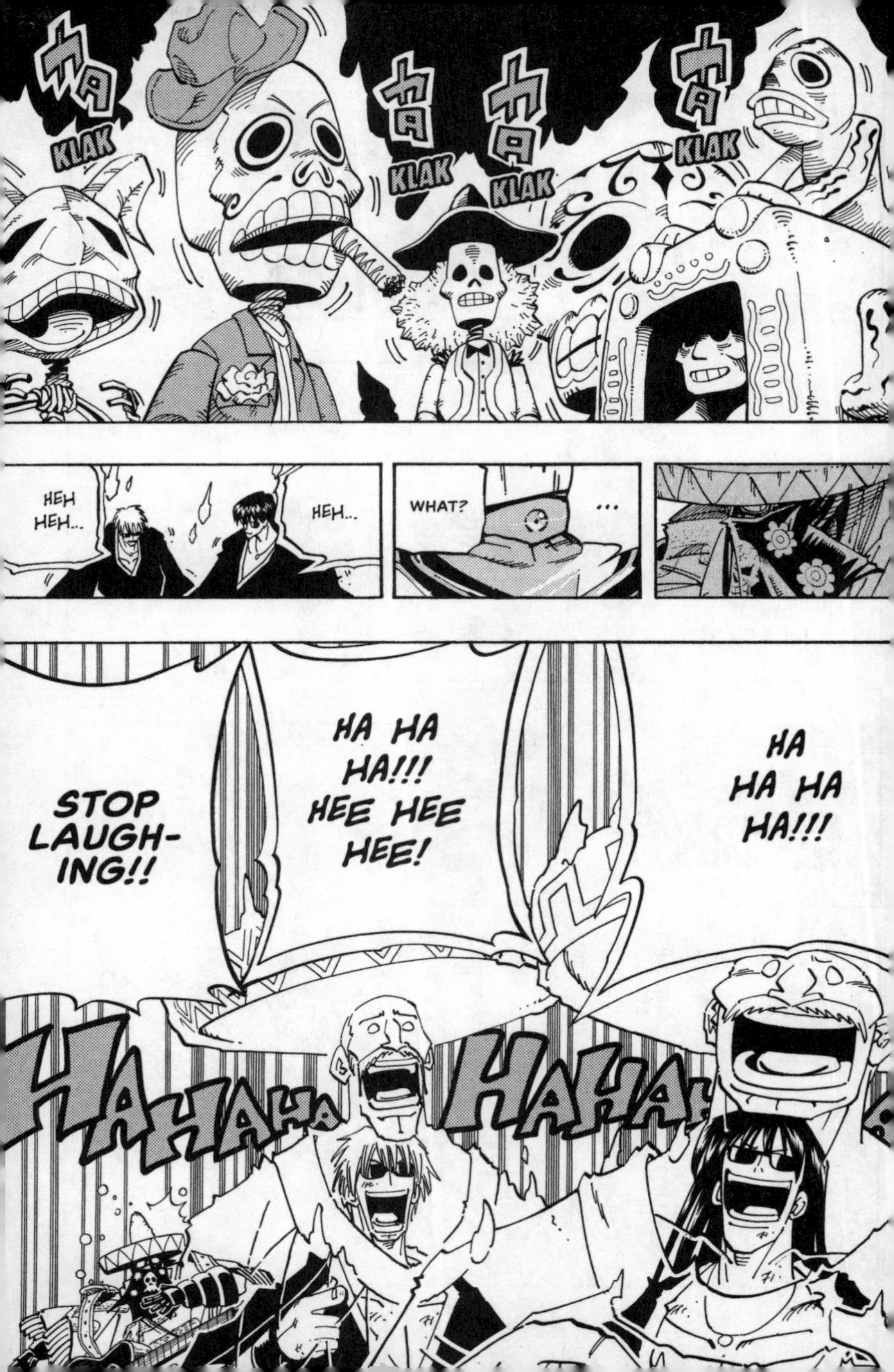

HA
KLAK
HA
KLAK
HA
KLAK
HA
KLAK
...
WHAT?
HEH...
HEH HEH...
HA HA HA HA!!!
HA HA HA!!! HEE HEE HEE!
STOP LAUGH-ING!!
HAHA
HAHAHA

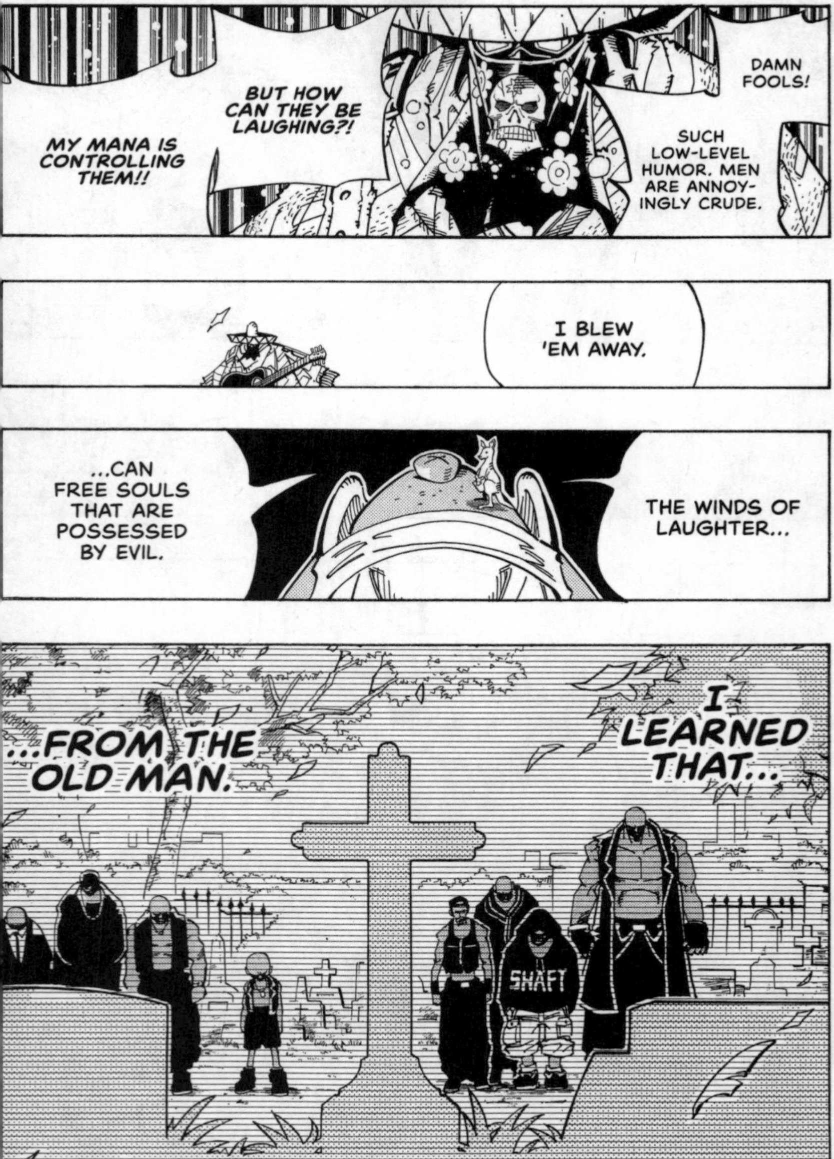
DAMN FOOLS!
SUCH LOW-LEVEL HUMOR. MEN ARE ANNOY-INGLY CRUDE.
BUT HOW CAN THEY BE LAUGHING?!
MY MANA IS CONTROLLING THEM!!
I BLEW 'EM AWAY.
THE WINDS OF LAUGHTER...
...CAN FREE SOULS THAT ARE POSSESSED BY EVIL.
I LEARNED THAT...
SHAFT
...FROM THE OLD MAN.

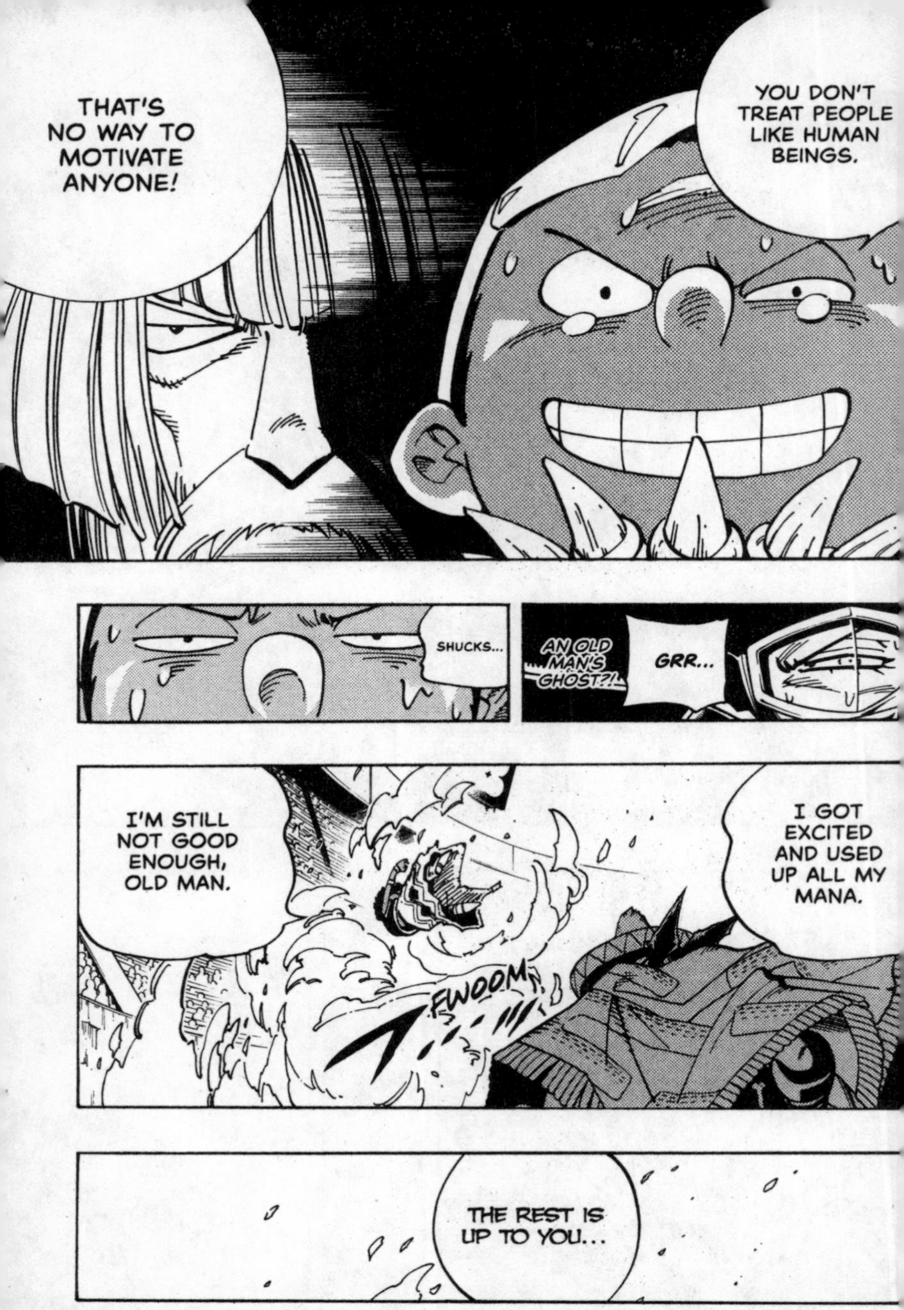
YOU DON'T TREAT PEOPLE LIKE HUMAN BEINGS.
THAT'S NO WAY TO MOTIVATE ANYONE!
GRR...
AN OLD MAN'S GHOST?!
SHUCKS...
I GOT EXCITED AND USED UP ALL MY MANA.
I'M STILL NOT GOOD ENOUGH, OLD MAN.
FWOOM
THE REST IS UP TO YOU...

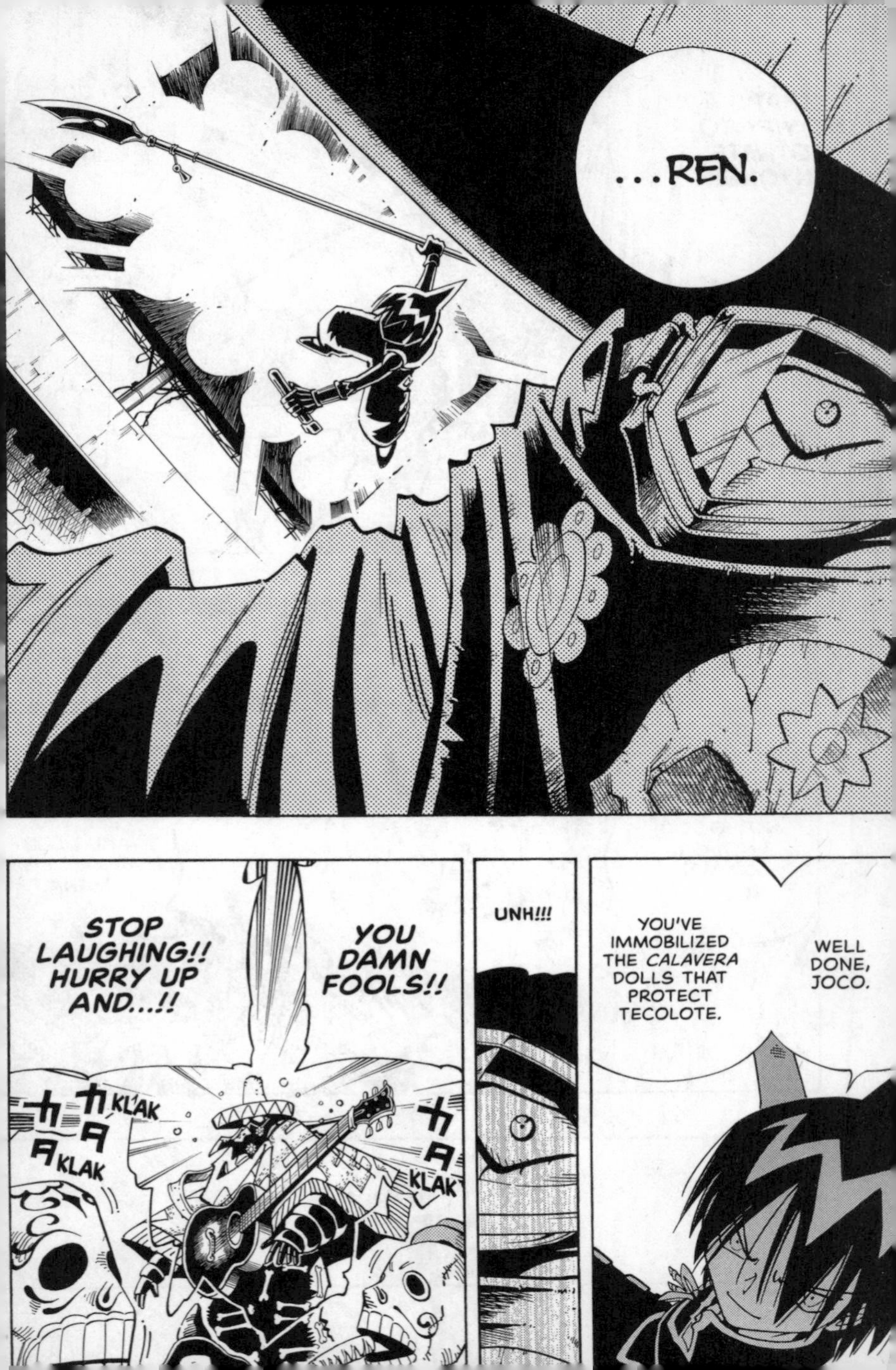
...REN.
WELL DONE, JOCO.
YOU'VE IMMOBILIZED THE *CALAVERA* DOLLS THAT PROTECT TECOLOTE.
UNH!!!
YOU DAMN FOOLS!!
STOP LAUGHING!! HURRY UP AND...!!
カタ KLAK
カタ KLAK
カタ KLAK

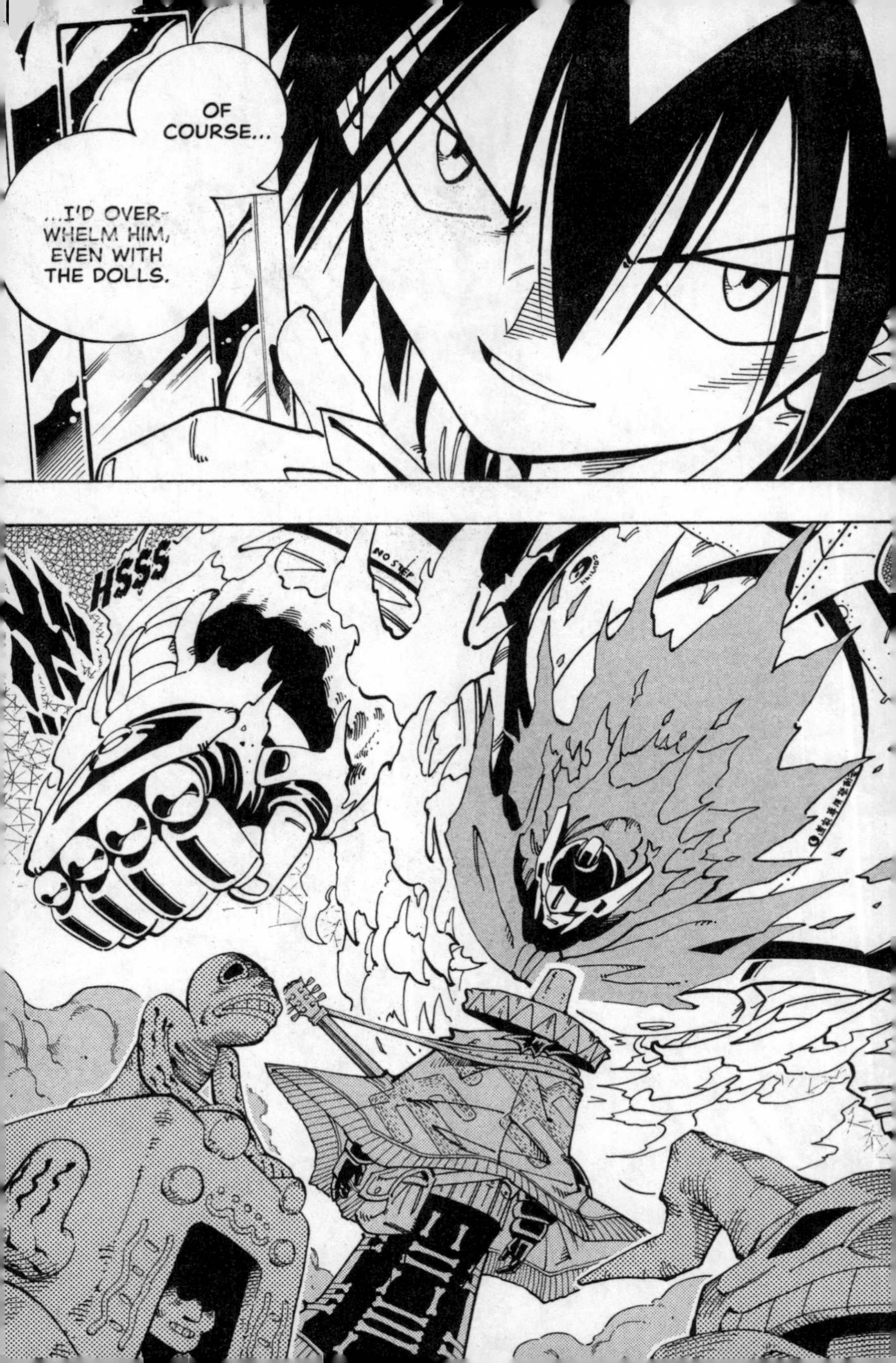
OF COURSE...
...I'D OVER-WHELM HIM, EVEN WITH THE DOLLS.
NO STEP
HSSS

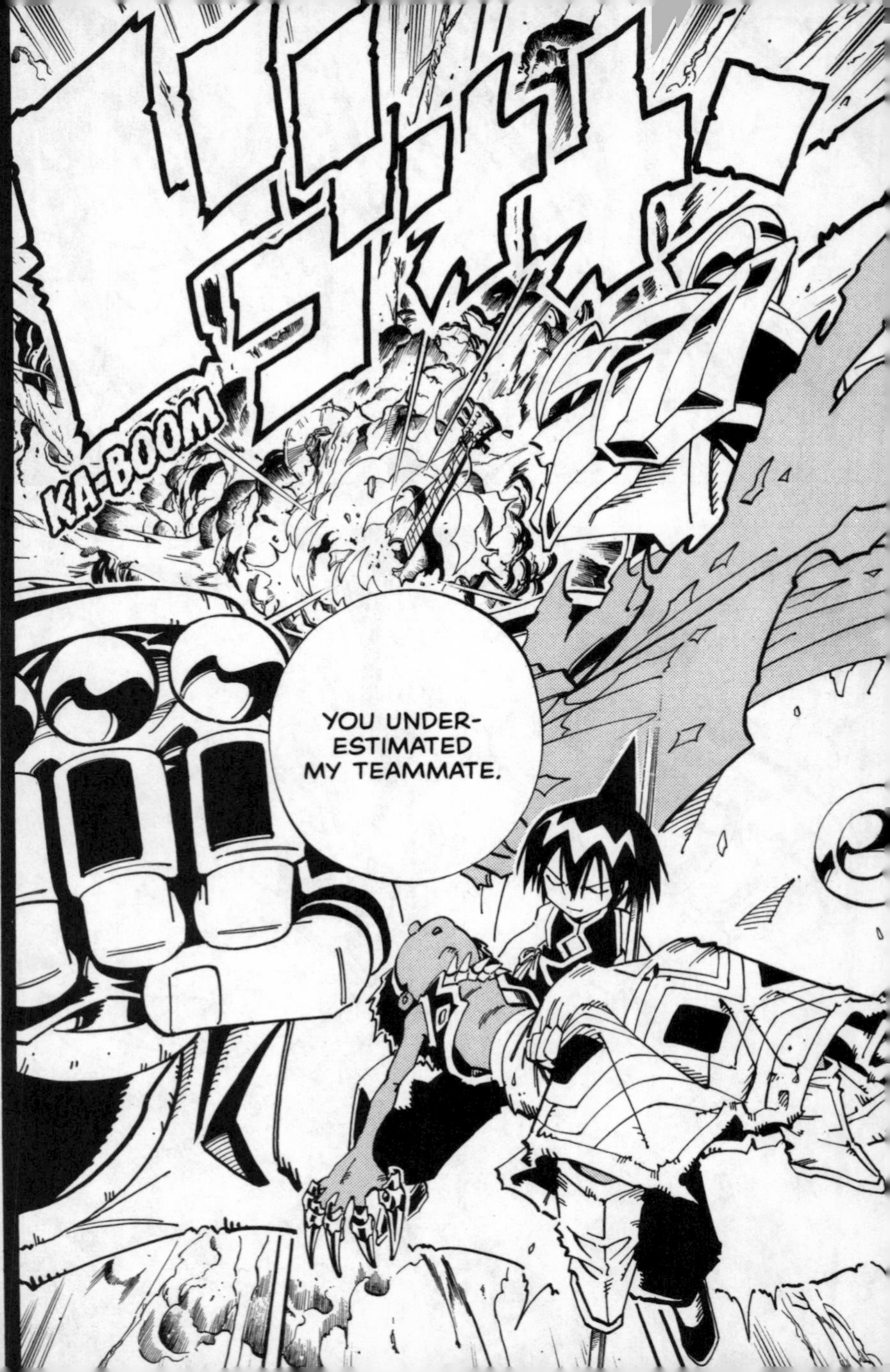
KA-BOOM
YOU UNDER-ESTIMATED MY TEAMMATE.

Nakht

June 2001

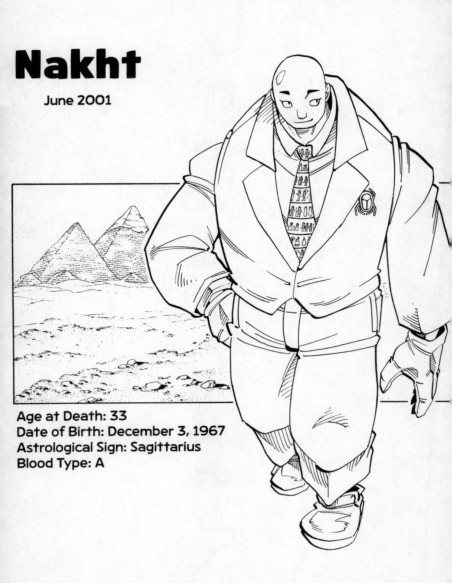

Age at Death: 33
Date of Birth: December 3, 1967
Astrological Sign: Sagittarius
Blood Type: A

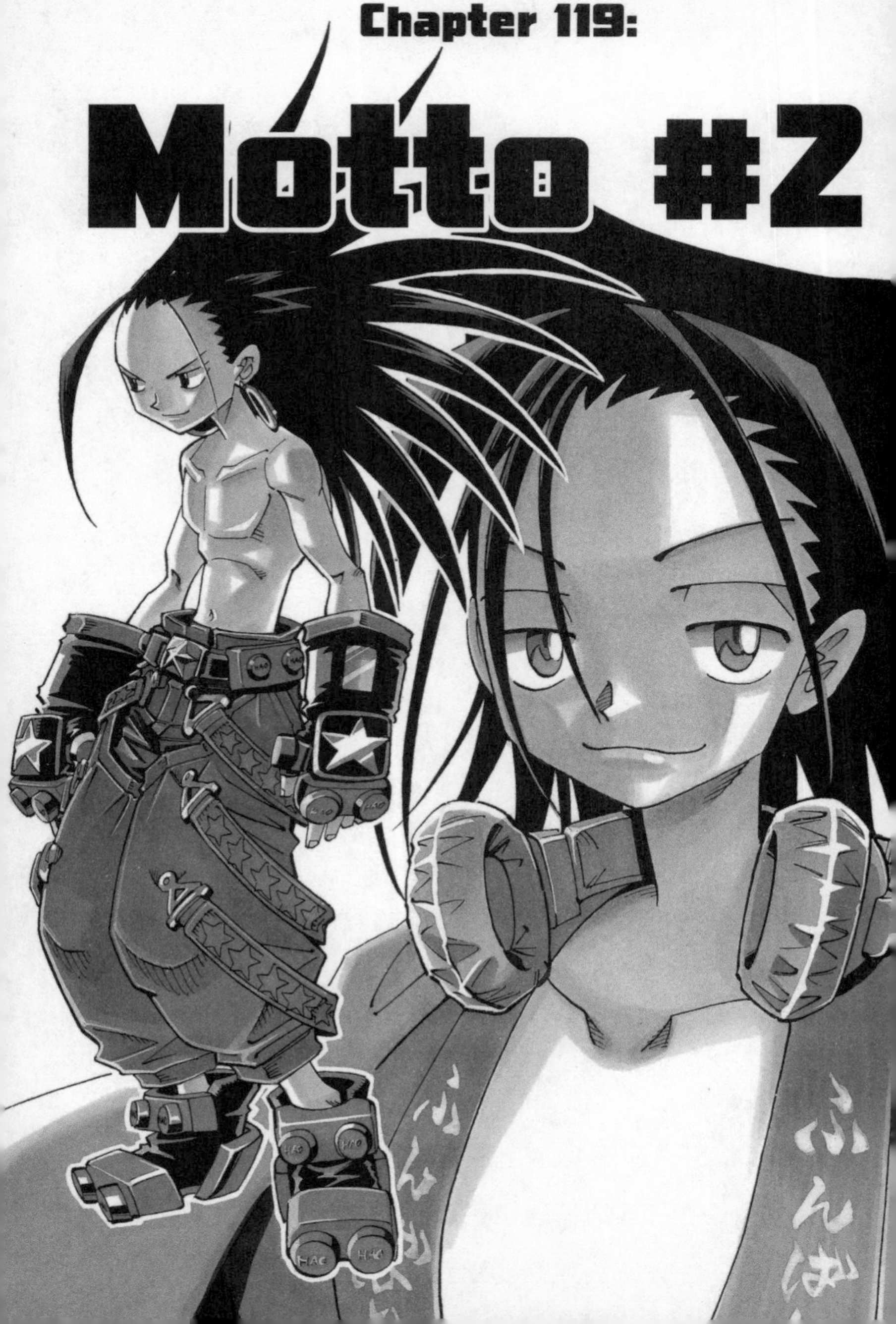
Chapter 119:
Motto #2

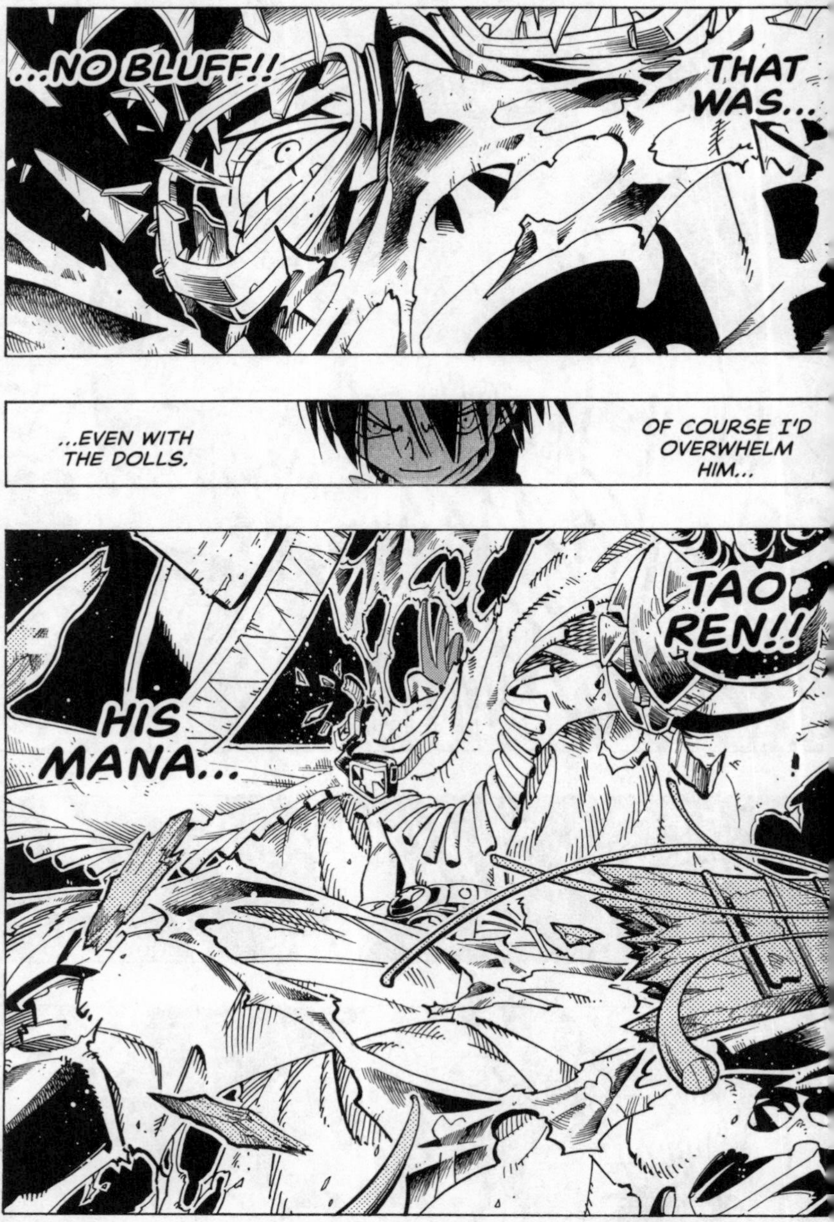
THAT WAS...
...NO BLUFF!!
OF COURSE I'D OVERWHELM HIM...
...EVEN WITH THE DOLLS.
TAO REN!!
HIS MANA...

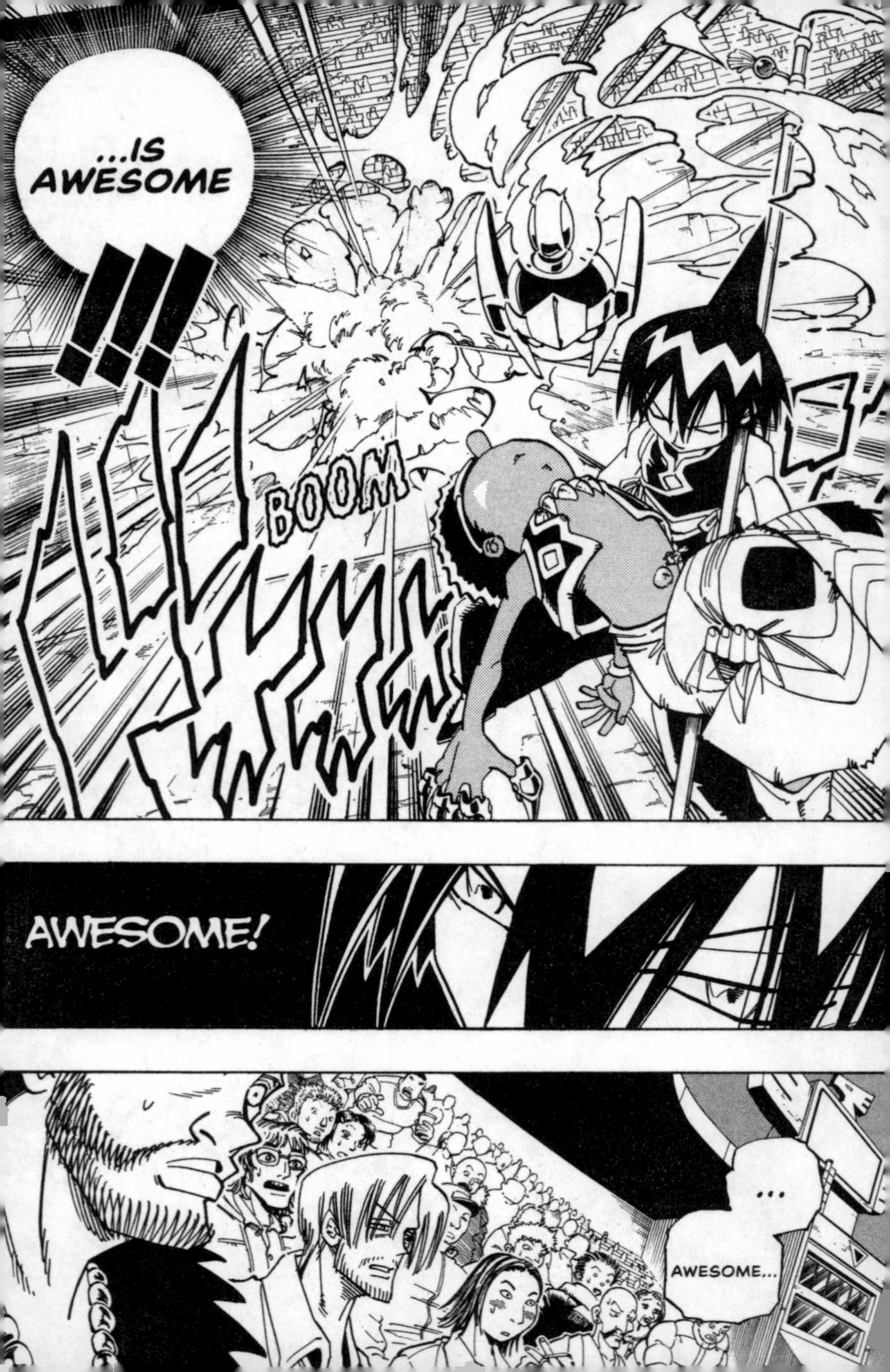

...IS AWESOME
!!!
BOOM
AWESOME!
...
AWESOME...

HE BLEW...
...THAT CACTUS GUY AWAY.
WOW.
THAT'S...
BA-BUMP
BA-BUMP
...REN'S POWER?
IMPOSSIBLE.
RIGHT NOW HIS MANA IS...
5,721.

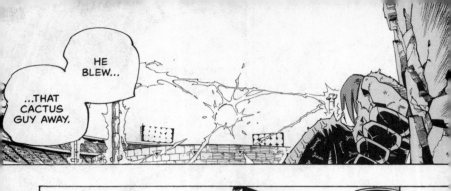

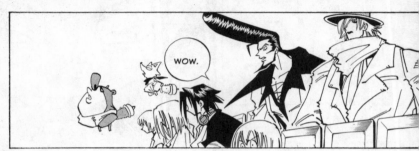

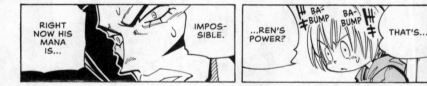

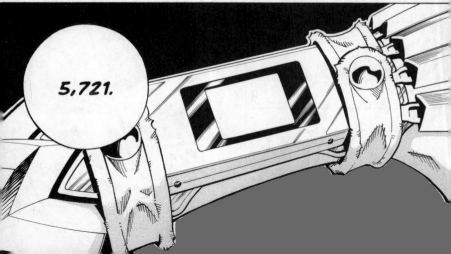

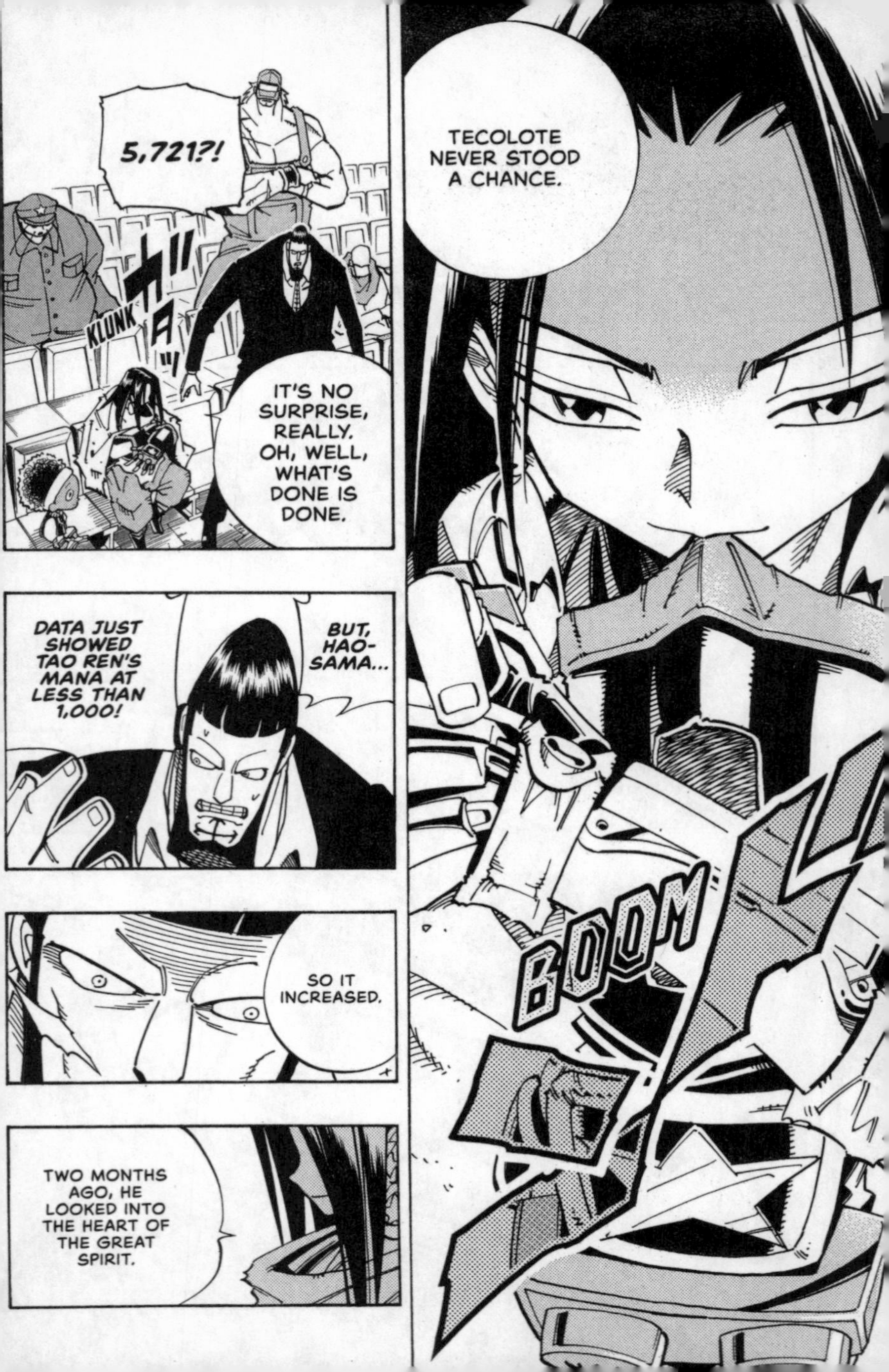
TECOLOTE NEVER STOOD A CHANCE.
BOOM
5,721?!
KLUNK
IT'S NO SURPRISE, REALLY. OH, WELL, WHAT'S DONE IS DONE.
BUT, HAO-SAMA...
DATA JUST SHOWED TAO REN'S MANA AT LESS THAN 1,000!
SO IT INCREASED.
TWO MONTHS AGO, HE LOOKED INTO THE HEART OF THE GREAT SPIRIT.

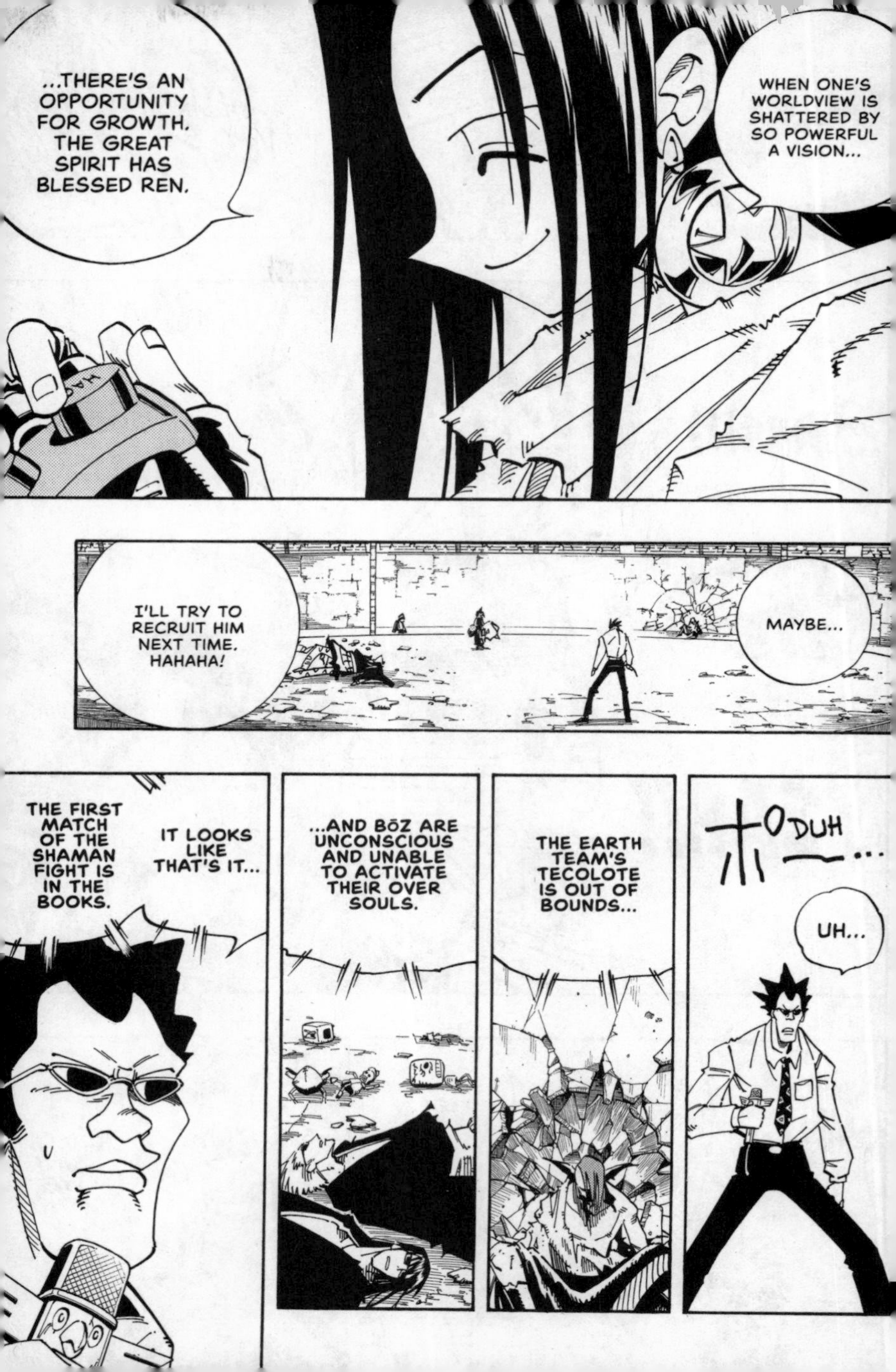
WHEN ONE'S WORLDVIEW IS SHATTERED BY SO POWERFUL A VISION...
...THERE'S AN OPPORTUNITY FOR GROWTH. THE GREAT SPIRIT HAS BLESSED REN.
MAYBE...
I'LL TRY TO RECRUIT HIM NEXT TIME. HAHAHA!
ODUH ...
UH...
THE EARTH TEAM'S TECOLOTE IS OUT OF BOUNDS...
...AND BŌZ ARE UNCONSCIOUS AND UNABLE TO ACTIVATE THEIR OVER SOULS.
IT LOOKS LIKE THAT'S IT...
THE FIRST MATCH OF THE SHAMAN FIGHT IS IN THE BOOKS.

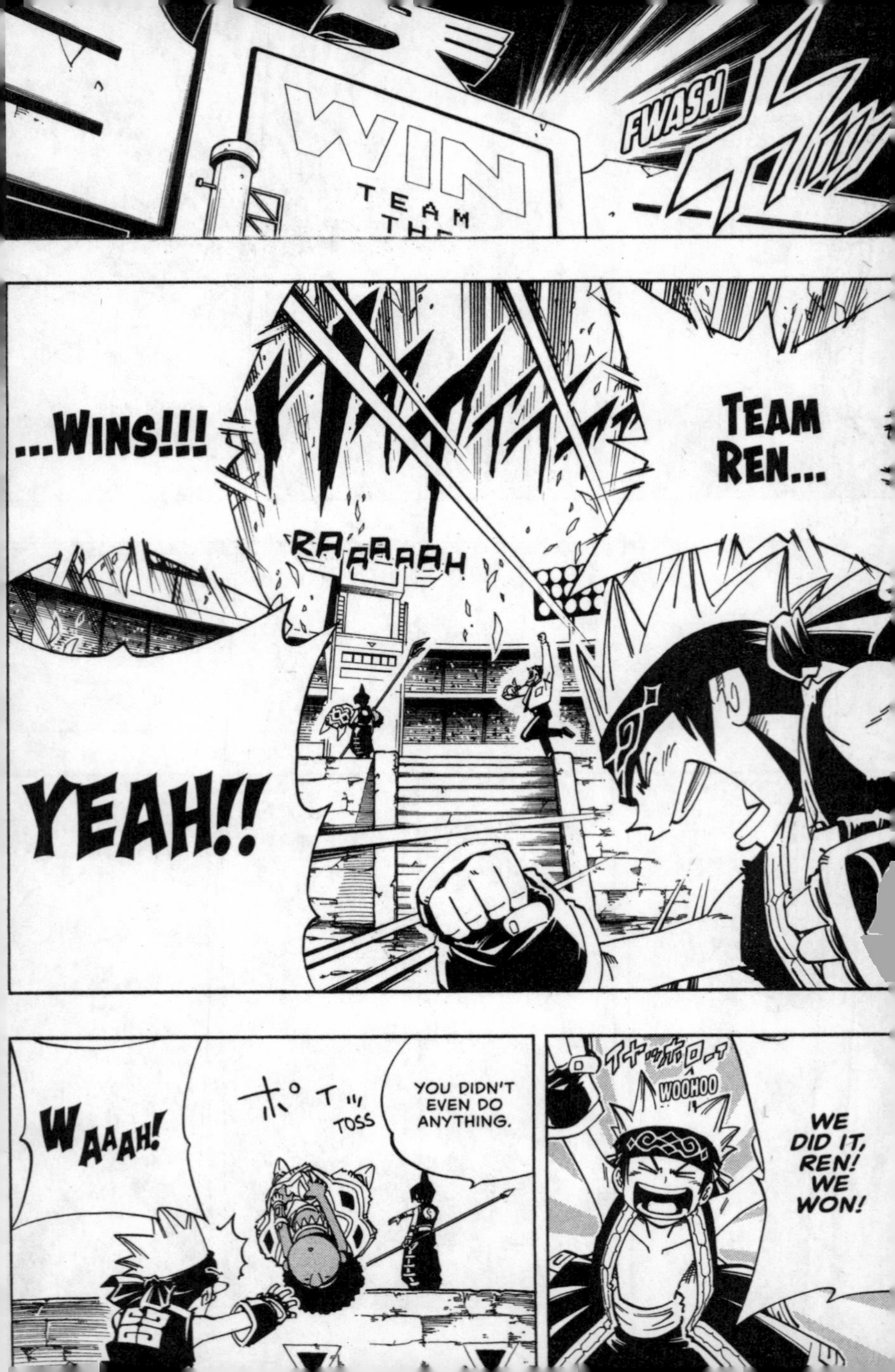
WIN
TEAM
FWASH
TEAM REN...
...WINS!!!
RAAAAAH
YEAH!!
イヤッホローィ
WOOHOO
WE DID IT, REN! WE WON!
YOU DIDN'T EVEN DO ANYTHING.
ポイッ
TOSS
WAAAH!

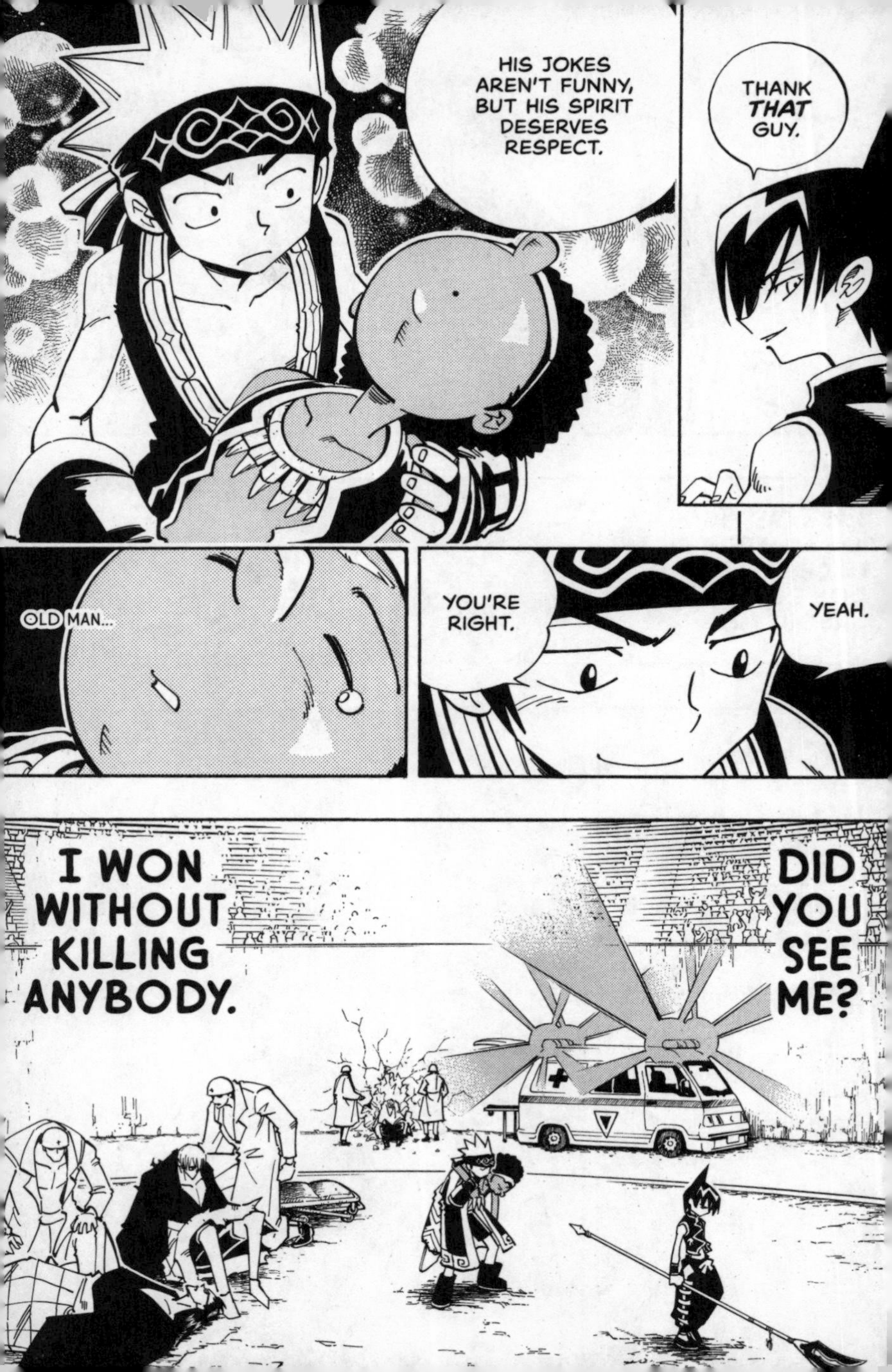
THANK THAT GUY.
HIS JOKES AREN'T FUNNY, BUT HIS SPIRIT DESERVES RESPECT.
YEAH.
YOU'RE RIGHT.
OLD MAN...
DID YOU SEE ME?
I WON WITHOUT KILLING ANYBODY.

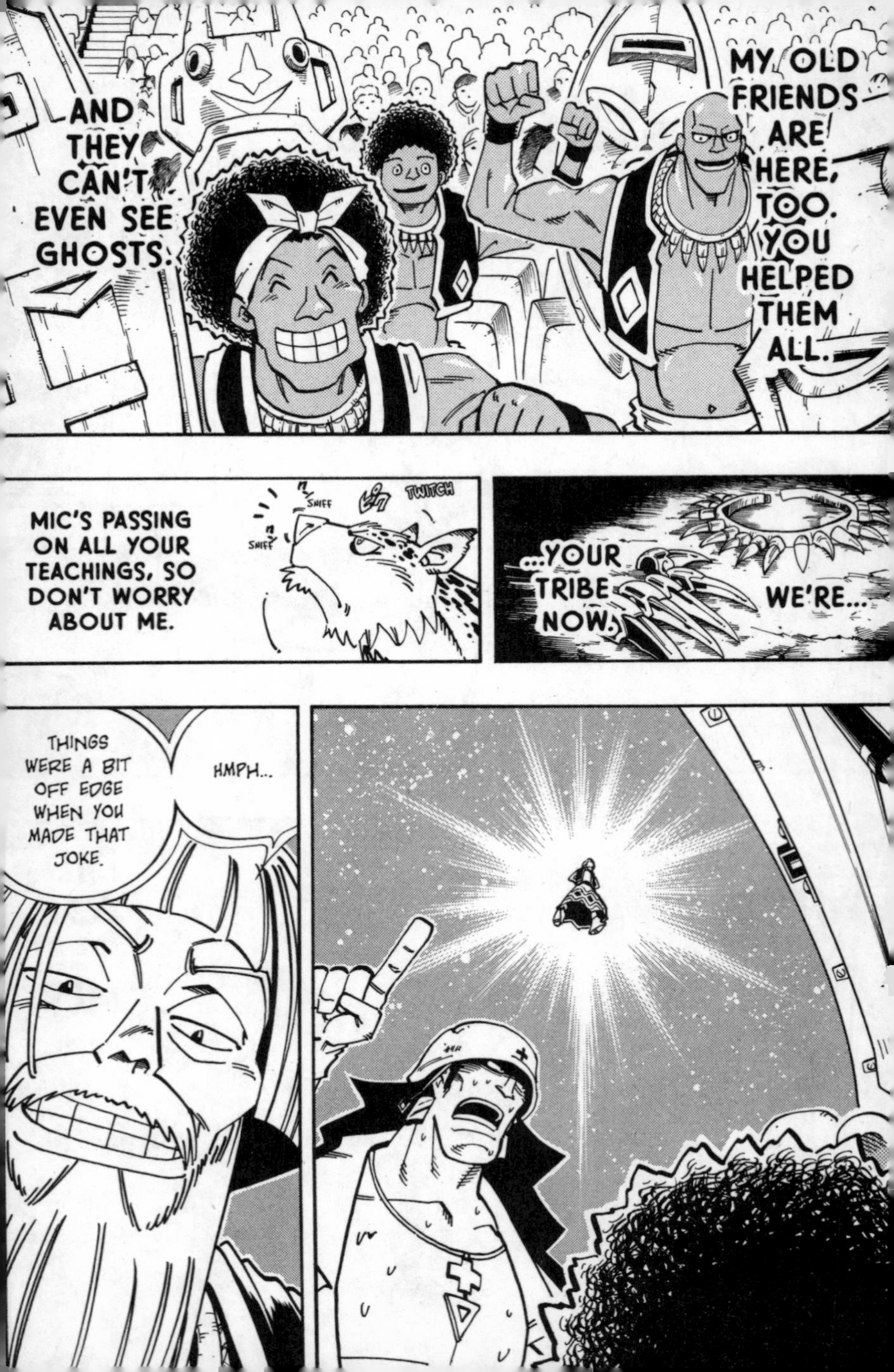
MY OLD FRIENDS ARE HERE, TOO. YOU HELPED THEM ALL.
AND THEY CAN'T EVEN SEE GHOSTS.
WE'RE...
...YOUR TRIBE NOW.
TWITCH
SNIFF
SNIFF
MIC'S PASSING ON ALL YOUR TEACHINGS, SO DON'T WORRY ABOUT ME.
HMPH...
THINGS WERE A BIT OFF EDGE WHEN YOU MADE THAT JOKE.

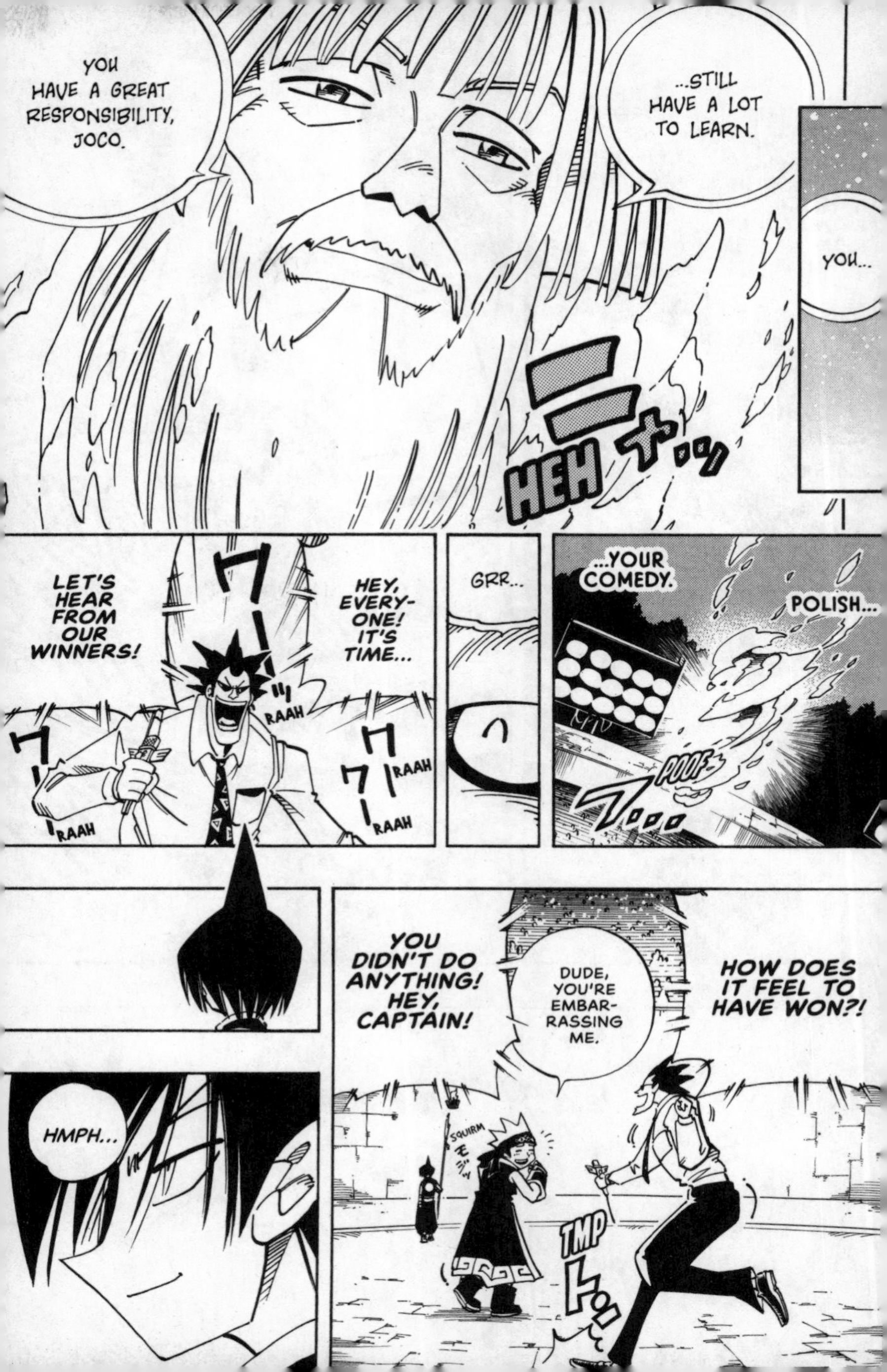
YOU...
...STILL HAVE A LOT TO LEARN.
YOU HAVE A GREAT RESPONSIBILITY, JOCO.
HEH
POLISH...
...YOUR COMEDY.
POOF
GRR...
HEY, EVERYONE! IT'S TIME...
LET'S HEAR FROM OUR WINNERS!
RAAH
RAAH
RAAH
RAAH
HOW DOES IT FEEL TO HAVE WON?!
DUDE, YOU'RE EMBAR-RASSING ME.
YOU DIDN'T DO ANYTHING! HEY, CAPTAIN!
SQUIRM
TMP
HMPH...

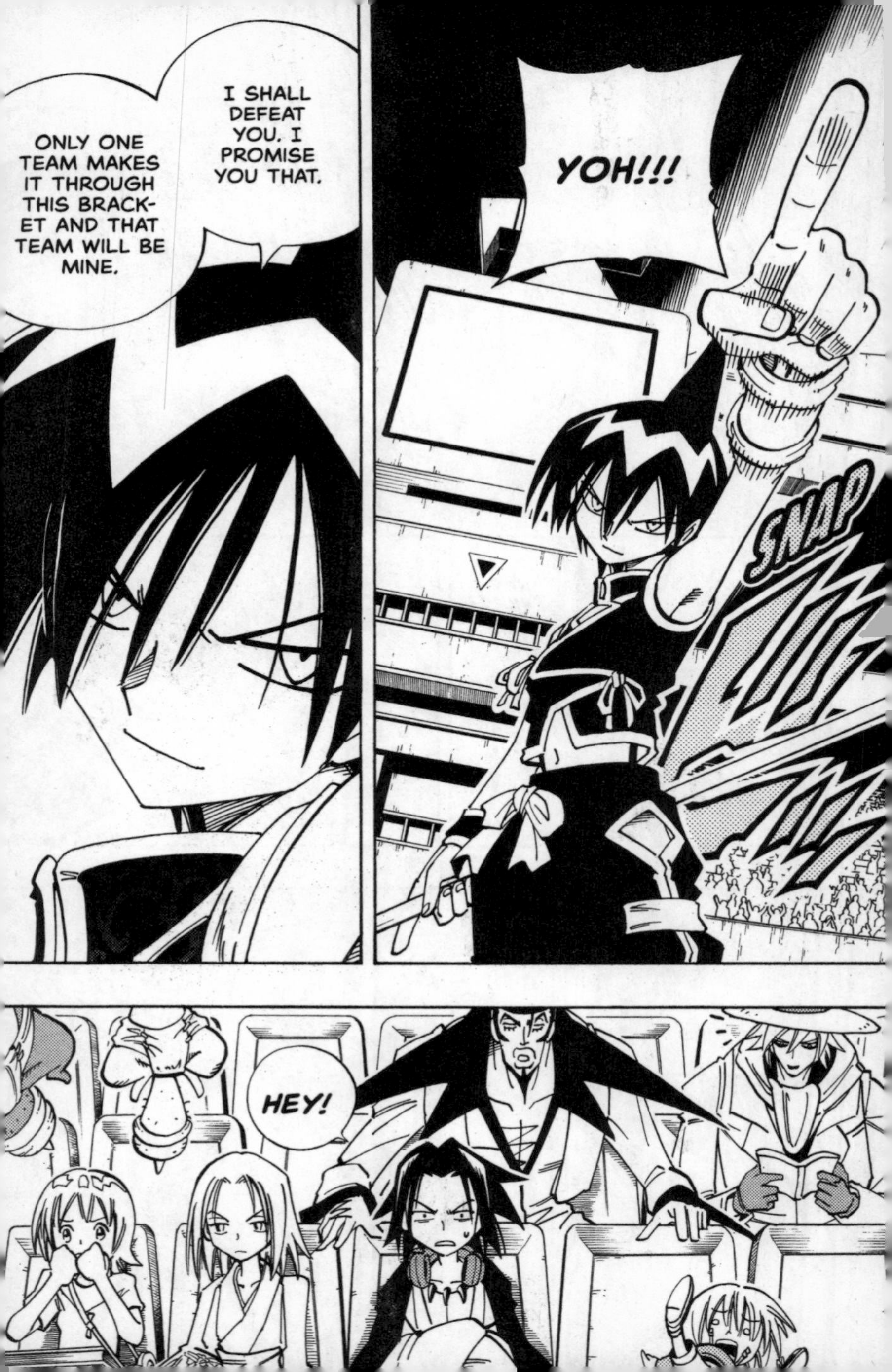
YOH!!!
SNAP
I SHALL DEFEAT YOU. I PROMISE YOU THAT.
ONLY ONE TEAM MAKES IT THROUGH THIS BRACK-ET AND THAT TEAM WILL BE MINE.
HEY!

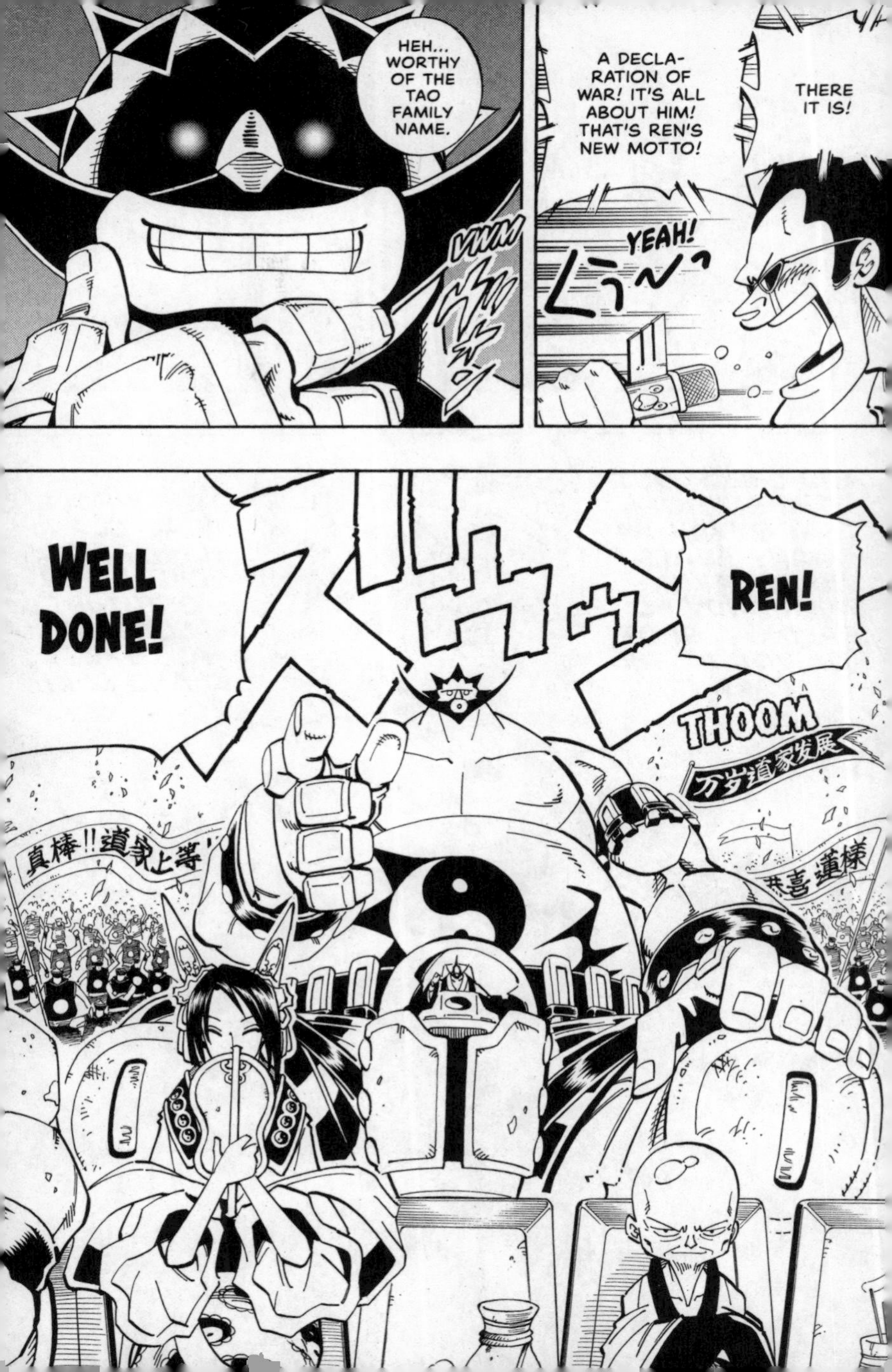
THERE IT IS!
A DECLARATION OF WAR! IT'S ALL ABOUT HIM! THAT'S REN'S NEW MOTTO!
YEAH!
HEH... WORTHY OF THE TAO FAMILY NAME.
VWM
REN!
THOOM
万岁道家发展
WELL DONE!
真棒!!道家上等!!

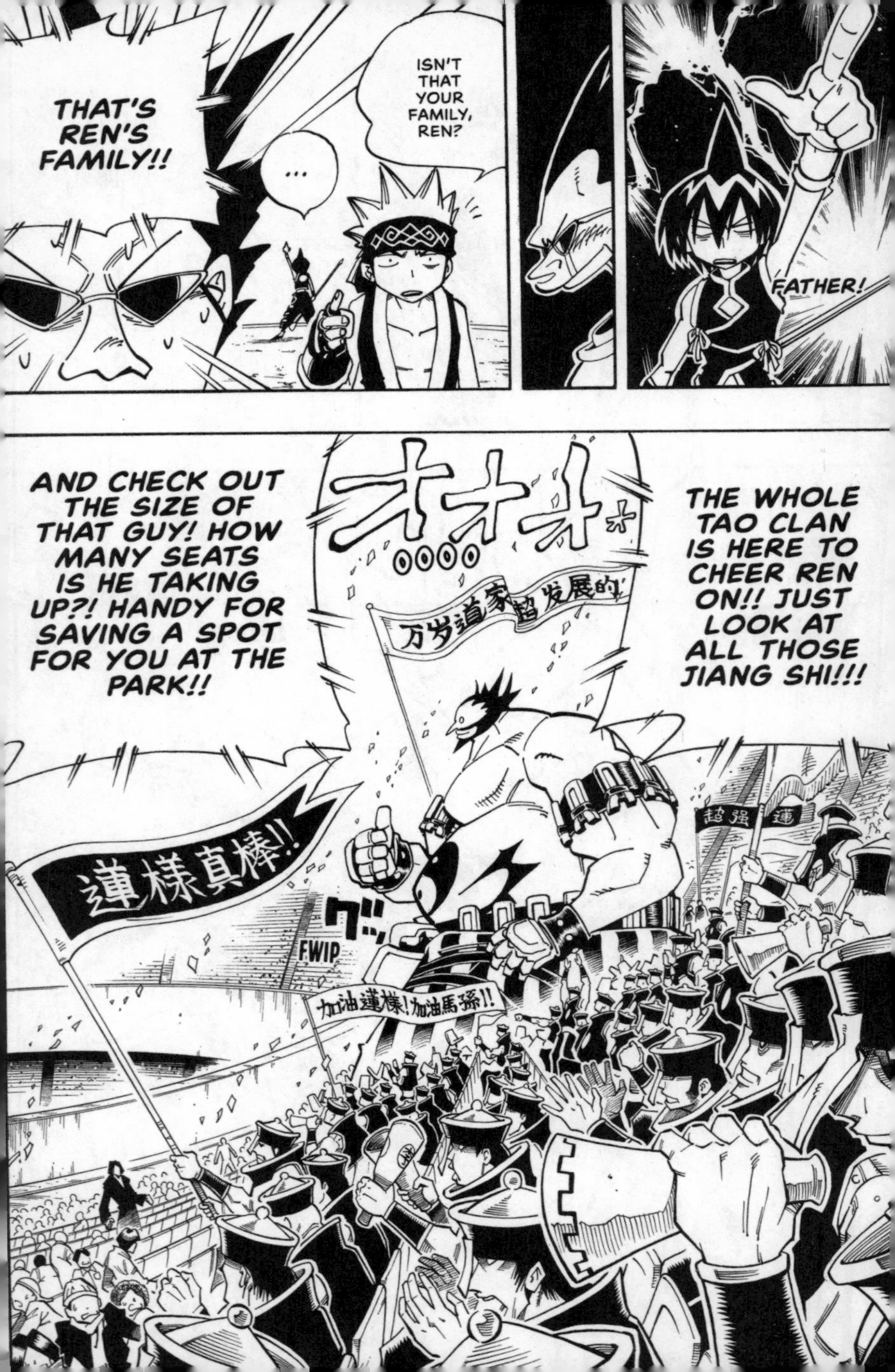
FATHER!
ISN'T THAT YOUR FAMILY, REN?
THAT'S REN'S FAMILY!!
...
THE WHOLE TAO CLAN IS HERE TO CHEER REN ON!! JUST LOOK AT ALL THOSE JIANG SHI!!!
オオオ。。。。
万岁道家超发展的
AND CHECK OUT THE SIZE OF THAT GUY! HOW MANY SEATS IS HE TAKING UP?! HANDY FOR SAVING A SPOT FOR YOU AT THE PARK!!
超强蓮
蓮様真棒!!
グッ
FWIP
加油蓮様!加油馬孫!!

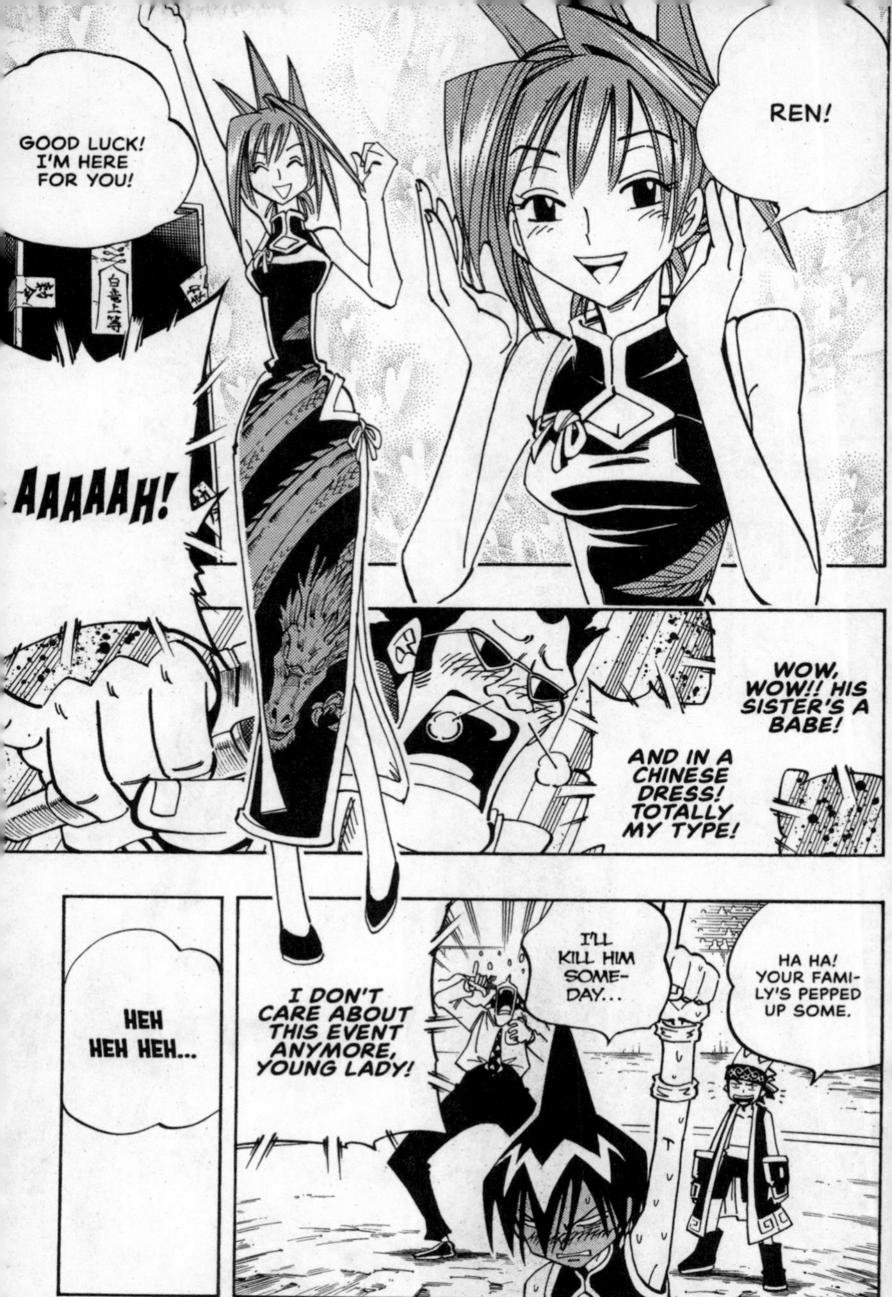
REN!
GOOD LUCK! I'M HERE FOR YOU!
AAAAAH!
WOW, WOW!! HIS SISTER'S A BABE!
AND IN A CHINESE DRESS! TOTALLY MY TYPE!
HA HA! YOUR FAMI-LY'S PEPPED UP SOME.
I'LL KILL HIM SOME-DAY...
I DON'T CARE ABOUT THIS EVENT ANYMORE, YOUNG LADY!
HEH HEH HEH...

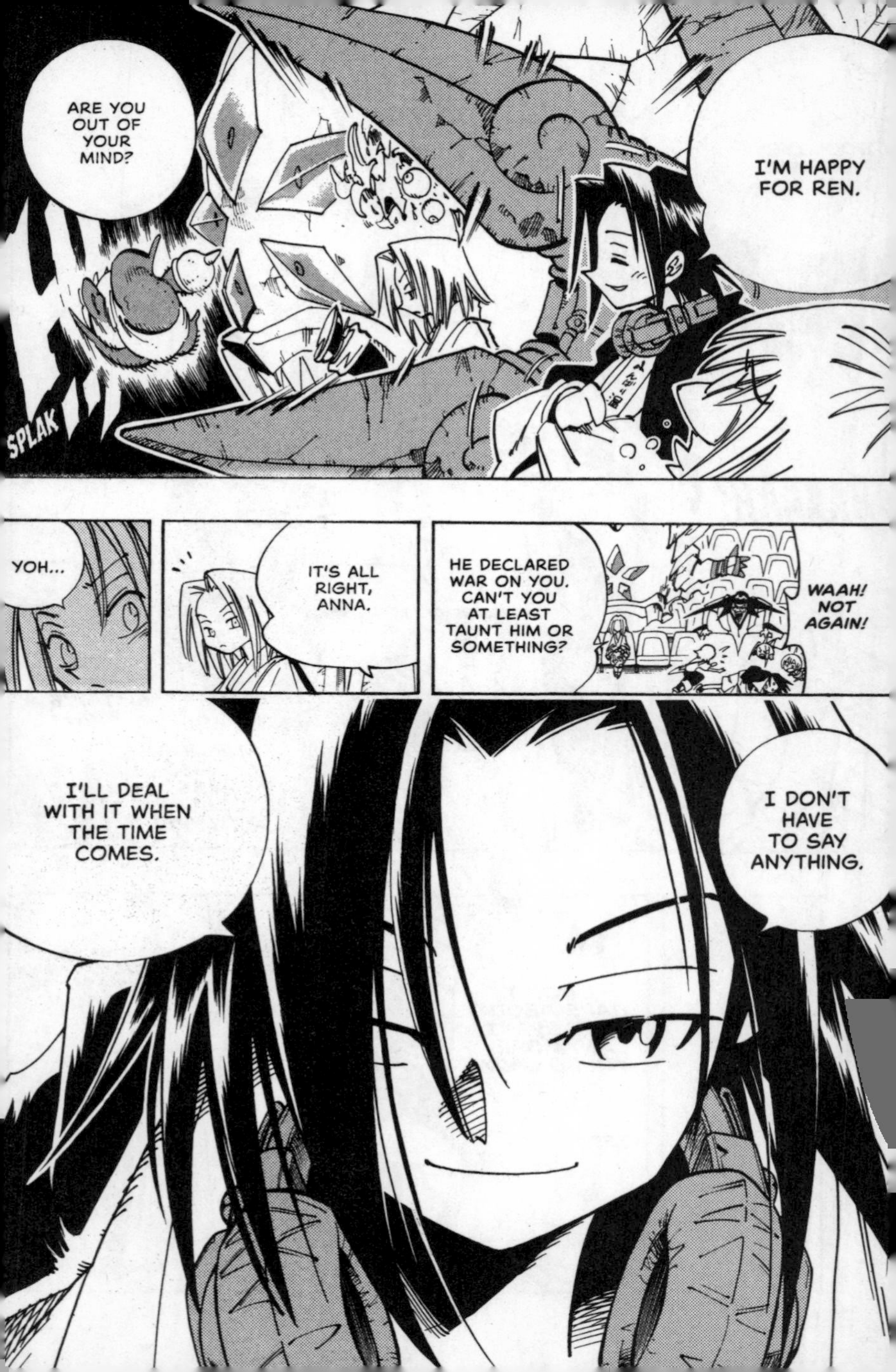
I'M HAPPY FOR REN.
ARE YOU OUT OF YOUR MIND?
SPLAK
HE DECLARED WAR ON YOU. CAN'T YOU AT LEAST TAUNT HIM OR SOMETHING?
WAAH! NOT AGAIN!
IT'S ALL RIGHT, ANNA.
YOH...
I DON'T HAVE TO SAY ANYTHING.
I'LL DEAL WITH IT WHEN THE TIME COMES.

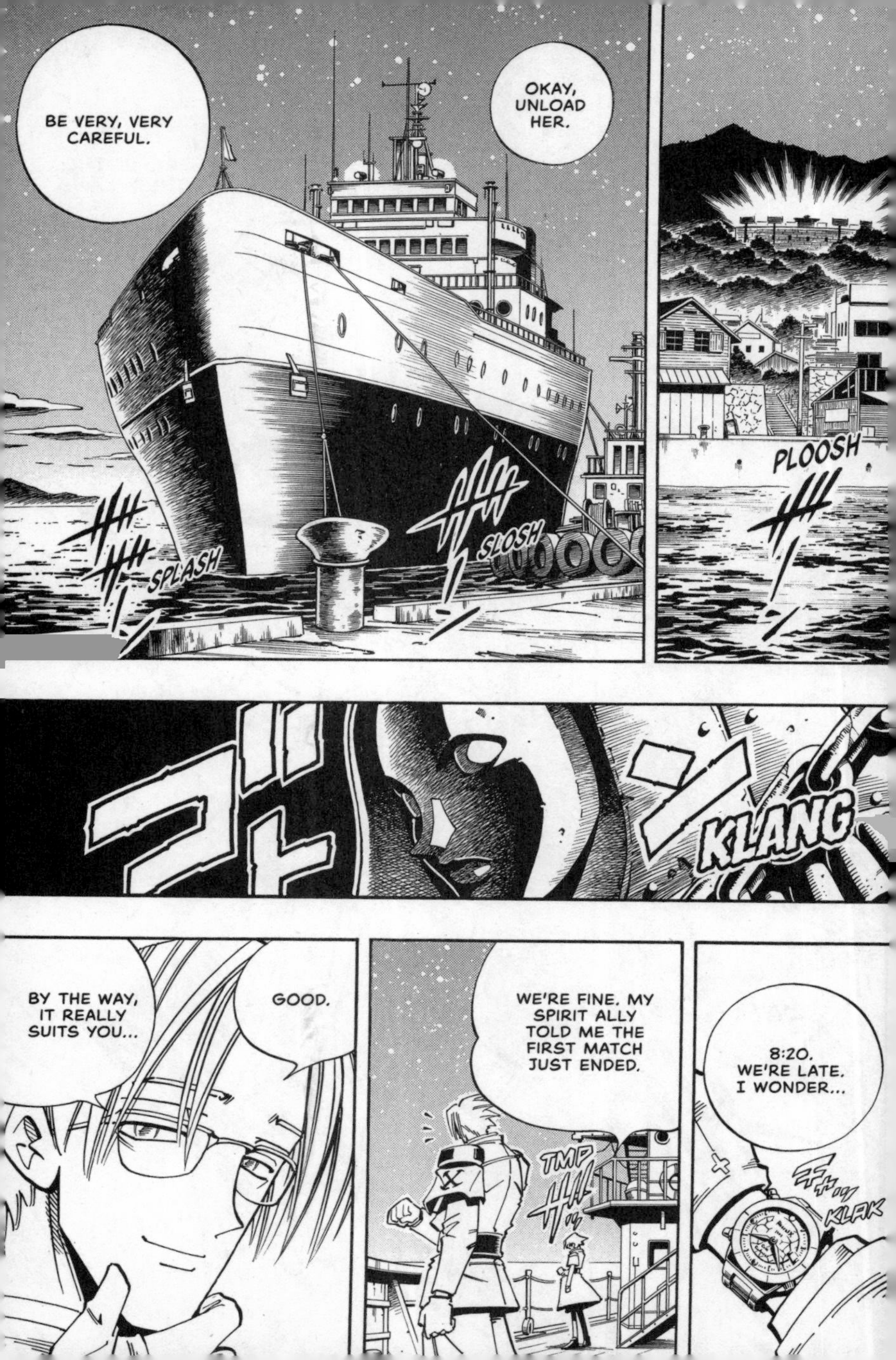
PLOOSH
OKAY, UNLOAD HER.
BE VERY, VERY CAREFUL.
SLOSH
SPLASH
KLANG
8:20. WE'RE LATE. I WONDER...
KLAK
WE'RE FINE. MY SPIRIT ALLY TOLD ME THE FIRST MATCH JUST ENDED.
TMP
GOOD.
BY THE WAY, IT REALLY SUITS YOU...

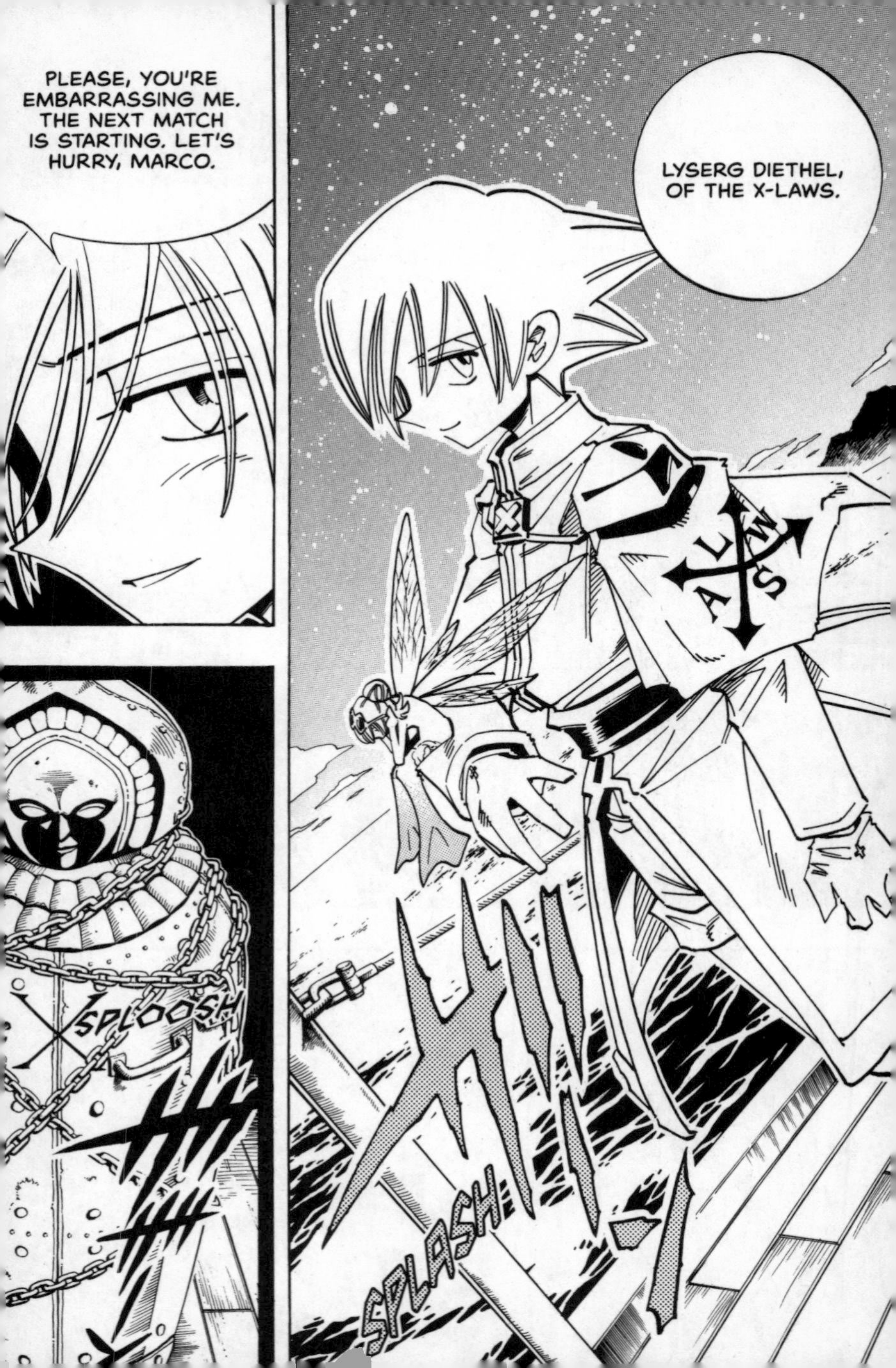
LYSERG DIETHEL, OF THE X-LAWS.
SPLASH
PLEASE, YOU'RE EMBARRASSING ME. THE NEXT MATCH IS STARTING. LET'S HURRY, MARCO.
SPLOOSH

SHAMAN KING CHARACTER FILE No.66

Khafre

June 2001

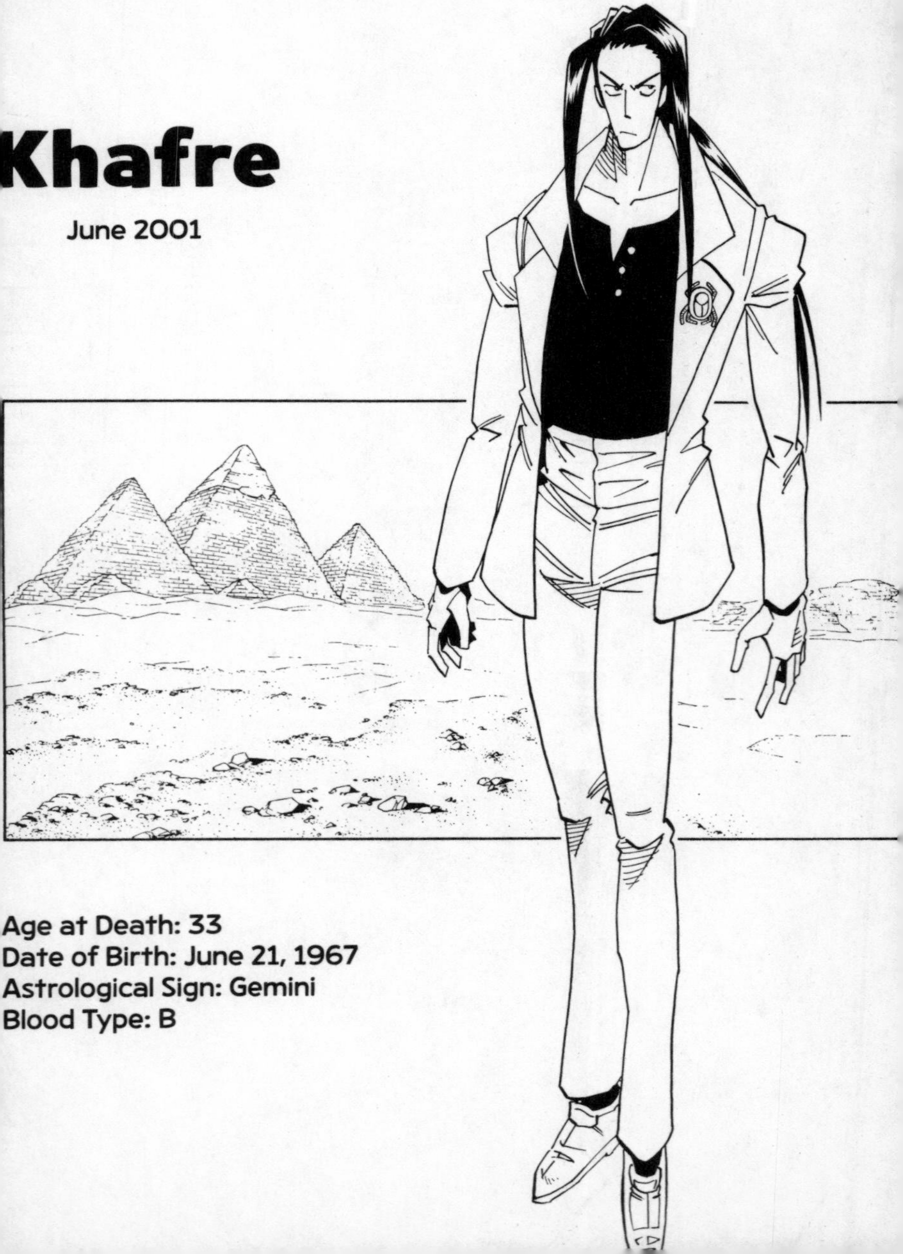

Age at Death: 33
Date of Birth: June 21, 1967
Astrological Sign: Gemini
Blood Type: B

Chapter 120: From Inn to Waiting Room

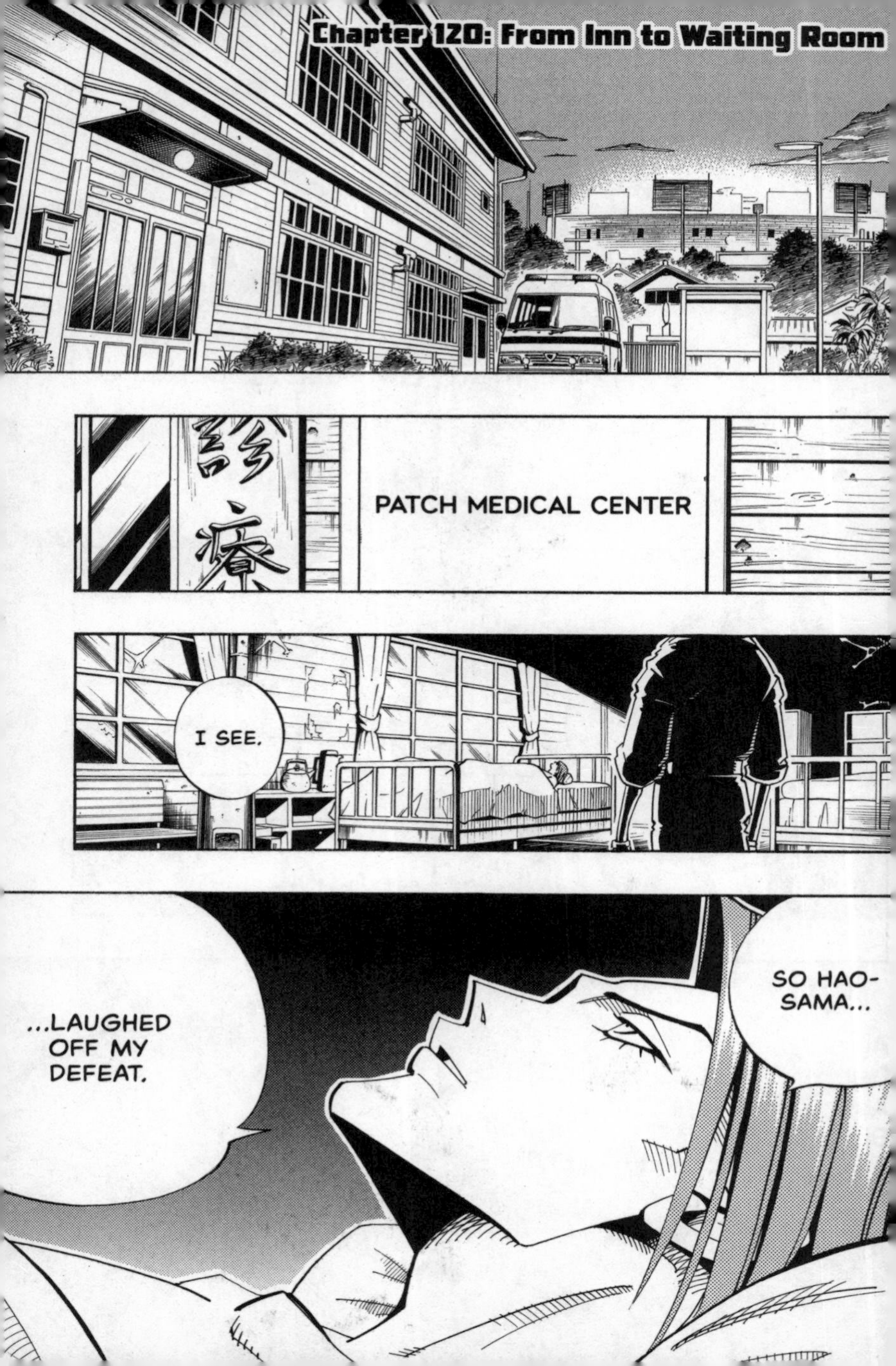

PATCH MEDICAL CENTER
I SEE.
SO HAO-SAMA...
...LAUGHED OFF MY DEFEAT.

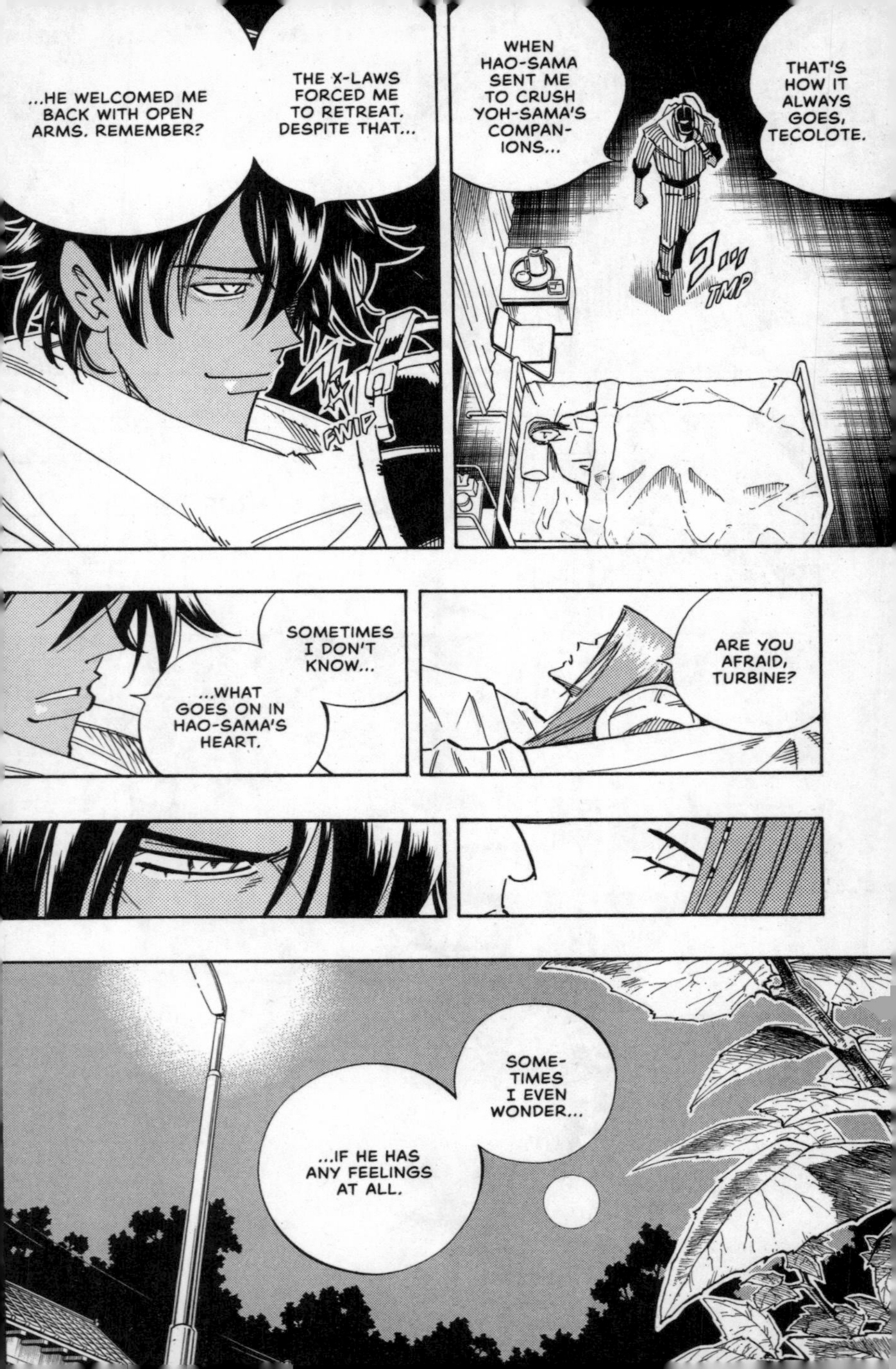
THAT'S HOW IT ALWAYS GOES, TECOLOTE.
WHEN HAO-SAMA SENT ME TO CRUSH YOH-SAMA'S COMPAN-IONS...
TMP
THE X-LAWS FORCED ME TO RETREAT. DESPITE THAT...
...HE WELCOMED ME BACK WITH OPEN ARMS. REMEMBER?
FWIP
ARE YOU AFRAID, TURBINE?
SOMETIMES I DON'T KNOW...
...WHAT GOES ON IN HAO-SAMA'S HEART.
SOME-TIMES I EVEN WONDER...
...IF HE HAS ANY FEELINGS AT ALL.

Chapter 120:

From Inn to Waiting Room

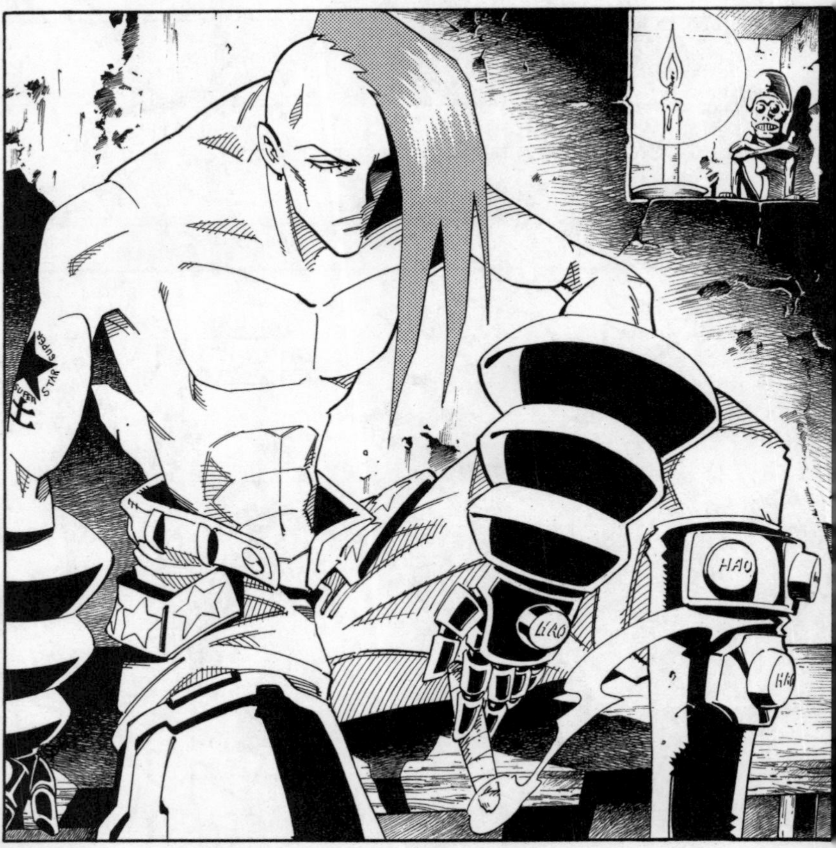

SUPER STAR SUPER
HAO
HAO
HAO

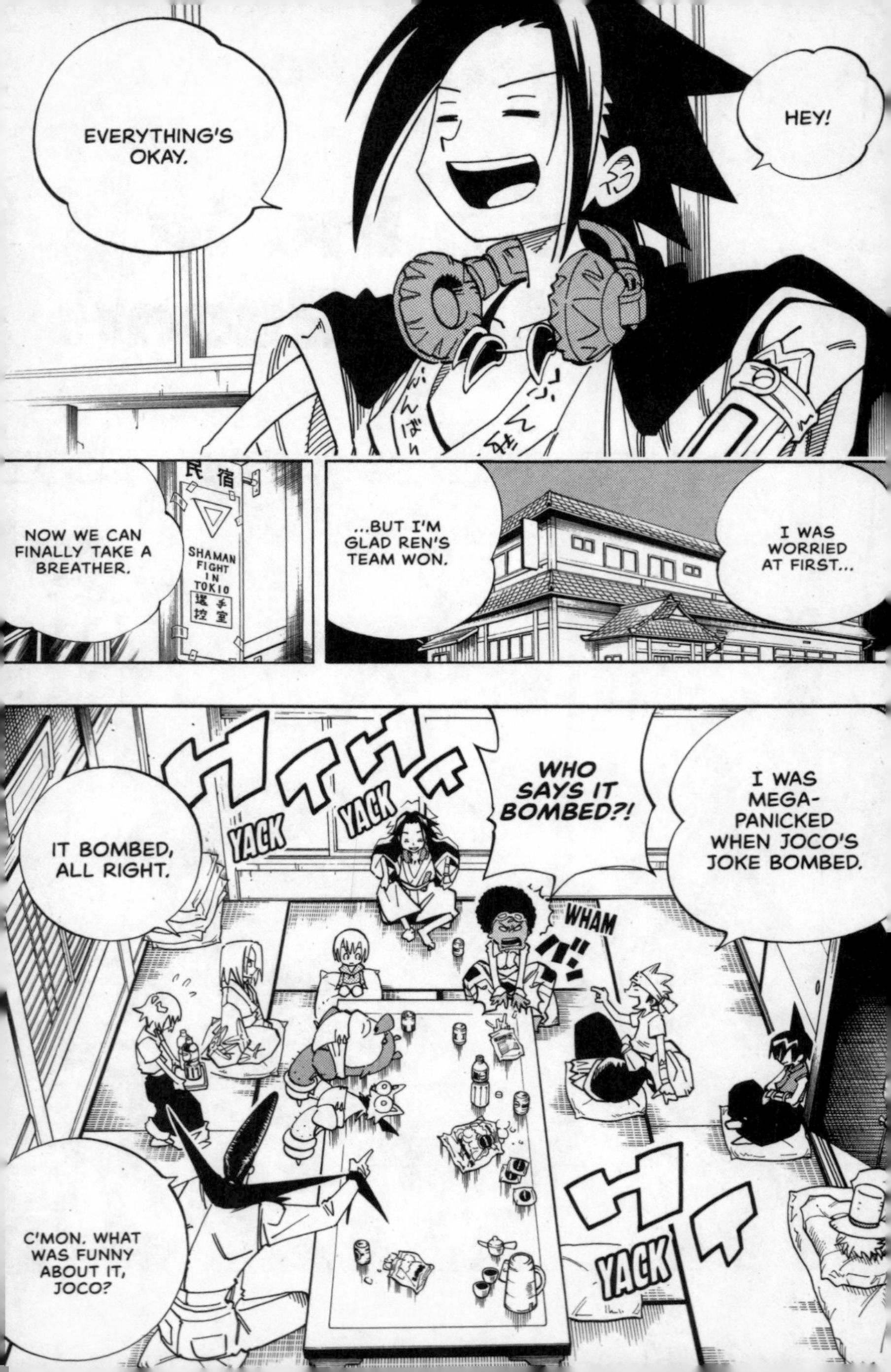
HEY!
EVERYTHING'S OKAY.
I WAS WORRIED AT FIRST...
...BUT I'M GLAD REN'S TEAM WON.
民宿
SHAMAN FIGHT IN TOKIO
選手控室
NOW WE CAN FINALLY TAKE A BREATHER.
I WAS MEGA-PANICKED WHEN JOCO'S JOKE BOMBED.
WHO SAYS IT BOMBED?!
WHAM
YACK
YACK
IT BOMBED, ALL RIGHT.
YACK
C'MON. WHAT WAS FUNNY ABOUT IT, JOCO?

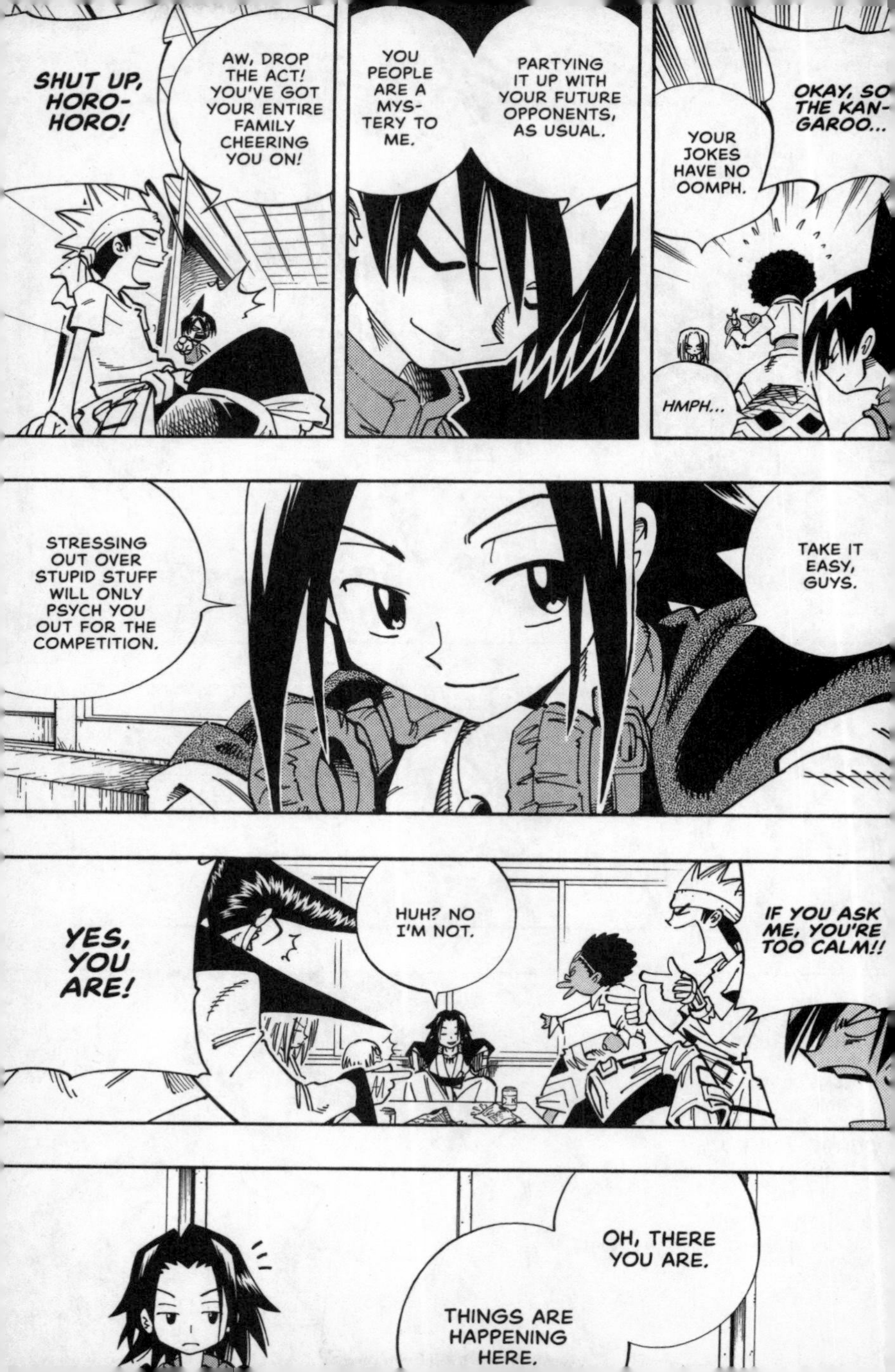
OKAY, SO THE KAN-GAROO...
YOUR JOKES HAVE NO OOMPH.
HMPH...
PARTYING IT UP WITH YOUR FUTURE OPPONENTS, AS USUAL.
YOU PEOPLE ARE A MYS-TERY TO ME.
AW, DROP THE ACT! YOU'VE GOT YOUR ENTIRE FAMILY CHEERING YOU ON!
SHUT UP, HORO-HORO!
TAKE IT EASY, GUYS.
STRESSING OUT OVER STUPID STUFF WILL ONLY PSYCH YOU OUT FOR THE COMPETITION.
IF YOU ASK ME, YOU'RE TOO CALM!!
HUH? NO I'M NOT.
YES, YOU ARE!
OH, THERE YOU ARE.
THINGS ARE HAPPENING HERE.

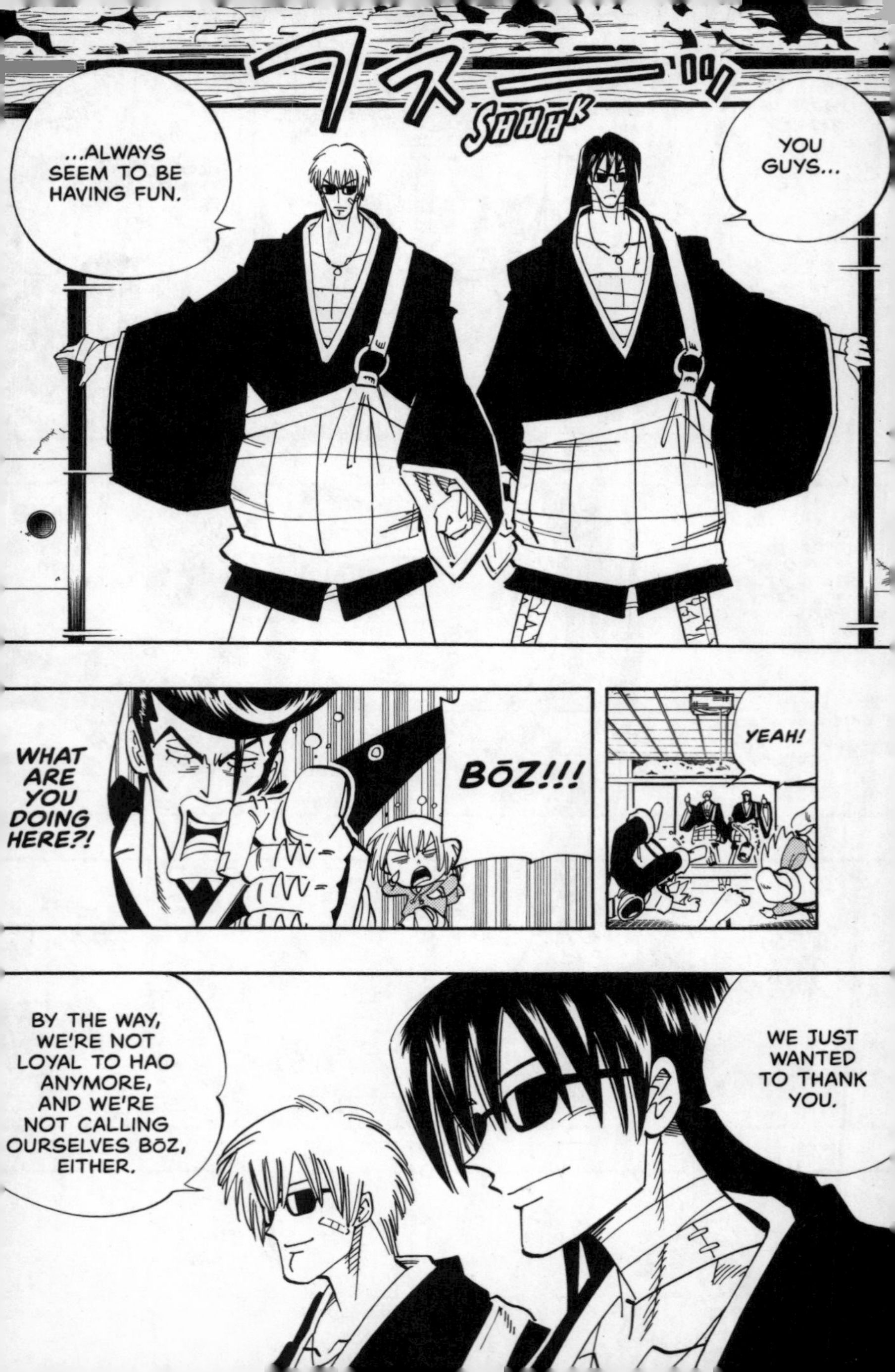
フスー
SHHHK
YOU GUYS...
...ALWAYS SEEM TO BE HAVING FUN.
YEAH!
BŌZ!!!
WHAT ARE YOU DOING HERE?!
WE JUST WANTED TO THANK YOU.
BY THE WAY, WE'RE NOT LOYAL TO HAO ANYMORE, AND WE'RE NOT CALLING OURSELVES BŌZ, EITHER.

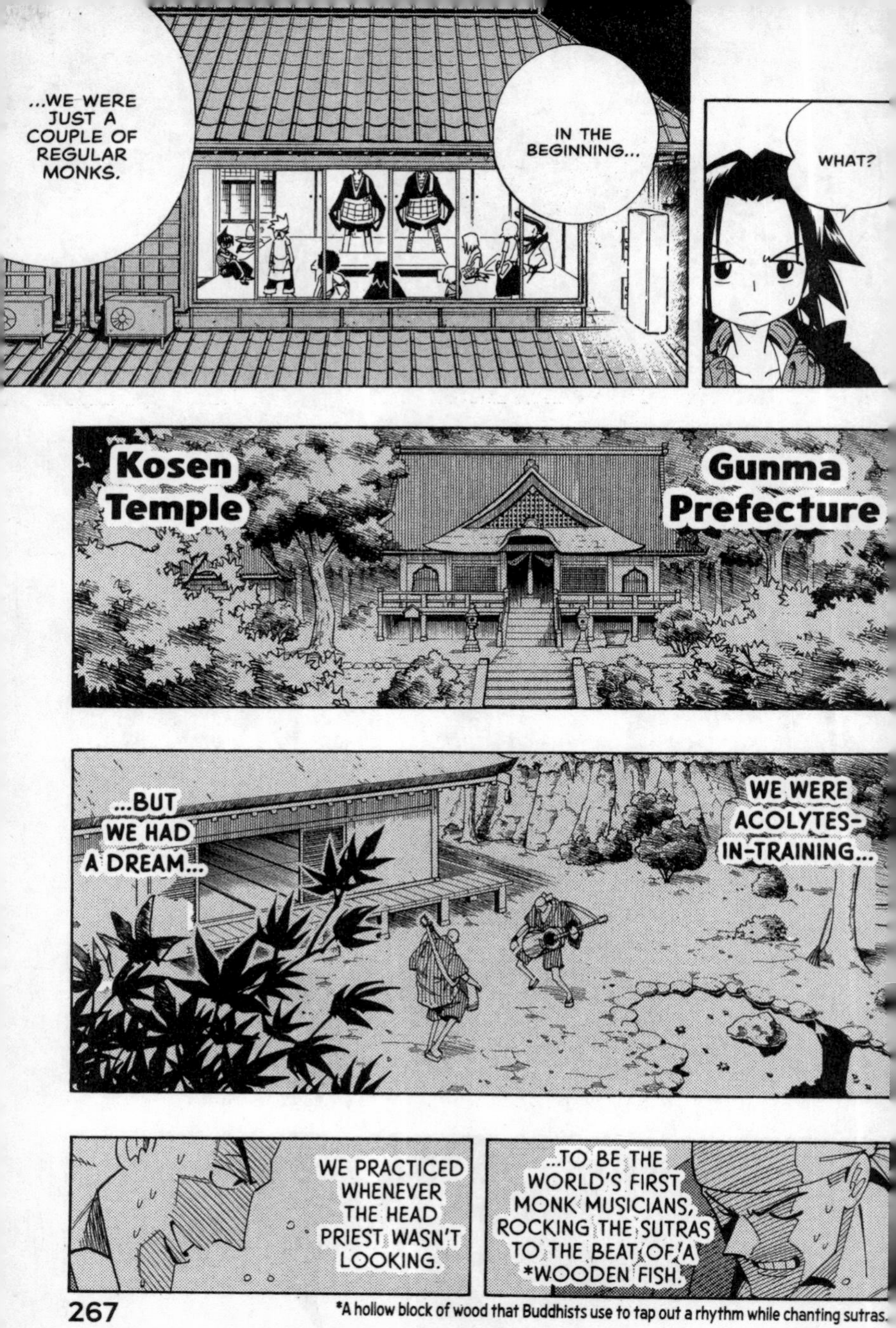
WHAT?
IN THE BEGINNING...
...WE WERE JUST A COUPLE OF REGULAR MONKS.
Gunma Prefecture
Kosen Temple
WE WERE ACOLYTES-IN-TRAINING...
...BUT WE HAD A DREAM...
...TO BE THE WORLD'S FIRST MONK MUSICIANS, ROCKING THE SUTRAS TO THE BEAT OF A *WOODEN FISH.
WE PRACTICED WHENEVER THE HEAD PRIEST WASN'T LOOKING.

*A hollow block of wood that Buddhists use to tap out a rhythm while chanting sutras.

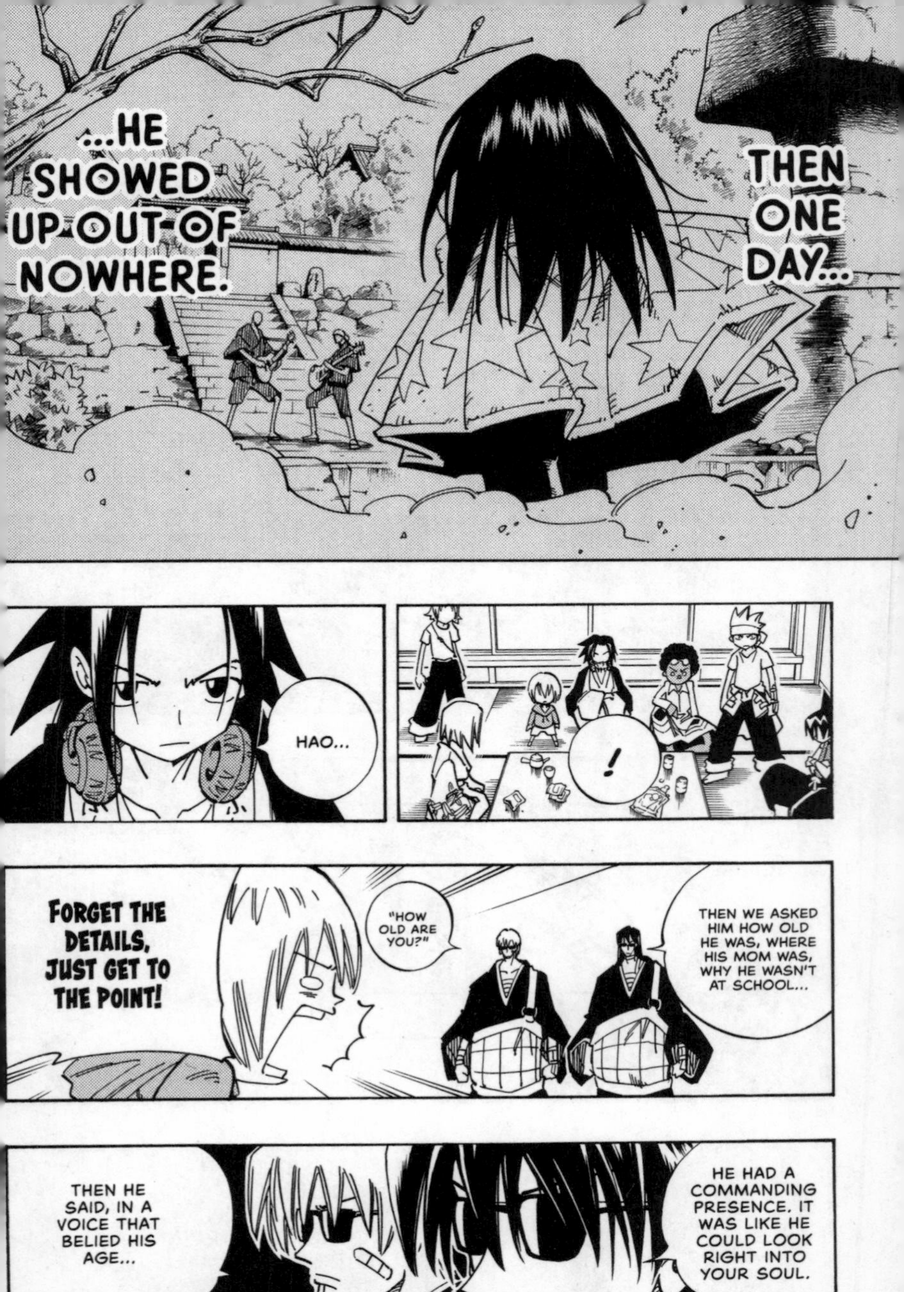
THEN ONE DAY...
...HE SHOWED UP OUT OF NOWHERE.
!
HAO...
THEN WE ASKED HIM HOW OLD HE WAS, WHERE HIS MOM WAS, WHY HE WASN'T AT SCHOOL...
"HOW OLD ARE YOU?"
FORGET THE DETAILS, JUST GET TO THE POINT!
HE HAD A COMMANDING PRESENCE. IT WAS LIKE HE COULD LOOK RIGHT INTO YOUR SOUL.
THEN HE SAID, IN A VOICE THAT BELIED HIS AGE...

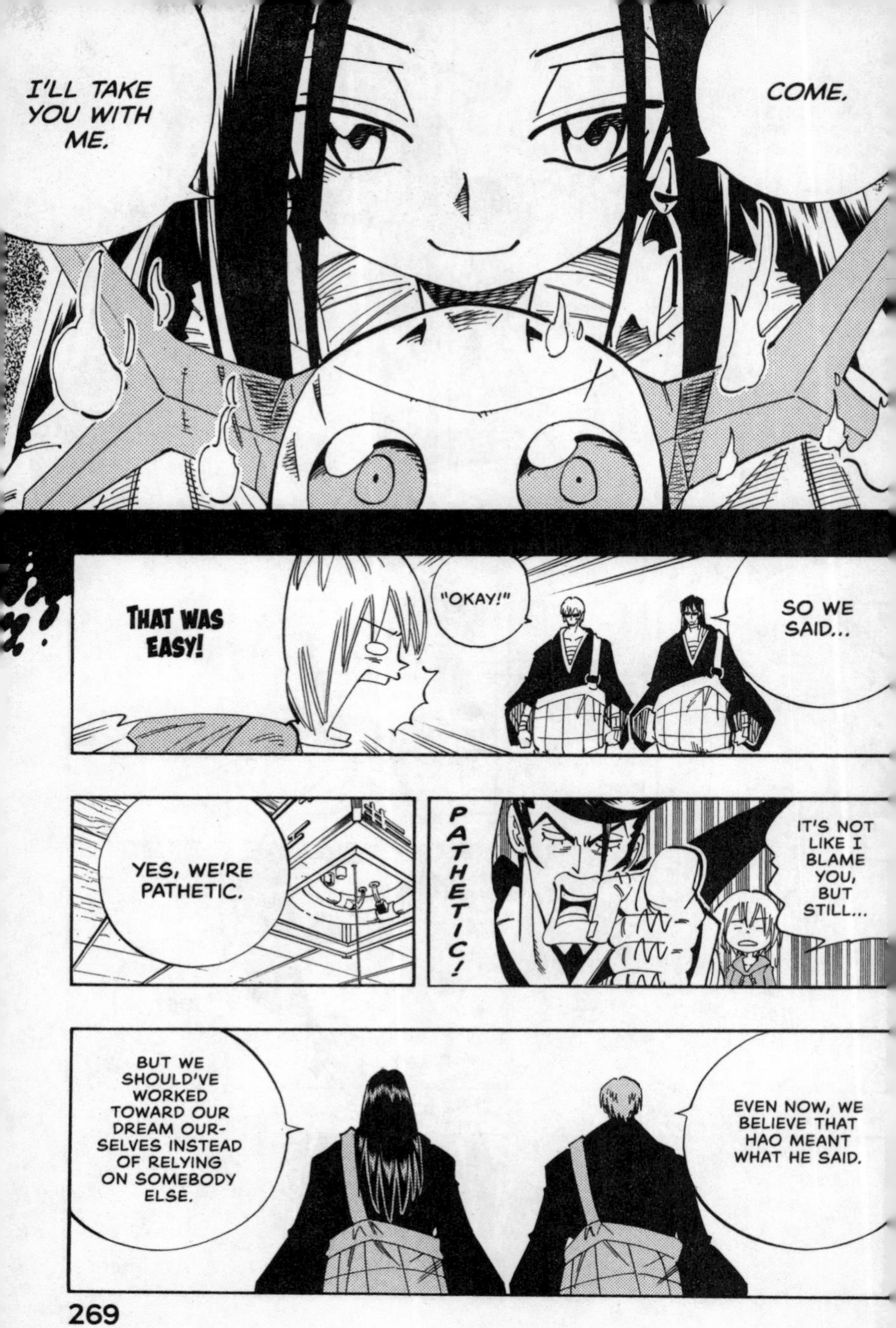
COME.
I'LL TAKE YOU WITH ME.
SO WE SAID...
"OKAY!"
THAT WAS EASY!
IT'S NOT LIKE I BLAME YOU, BUT STILL...
PATHETIC!
YES, WE'RE PATHETIC.
EVEN NOW, WE BELIEVE THAT HAO MEANT WHAT HE SAID.
BUT WE SHOULD'VE WORKED TOWARD OUR DREAM OUR-SELVES INSTEAD OF RELYING ON SOMEBODY ELSE.

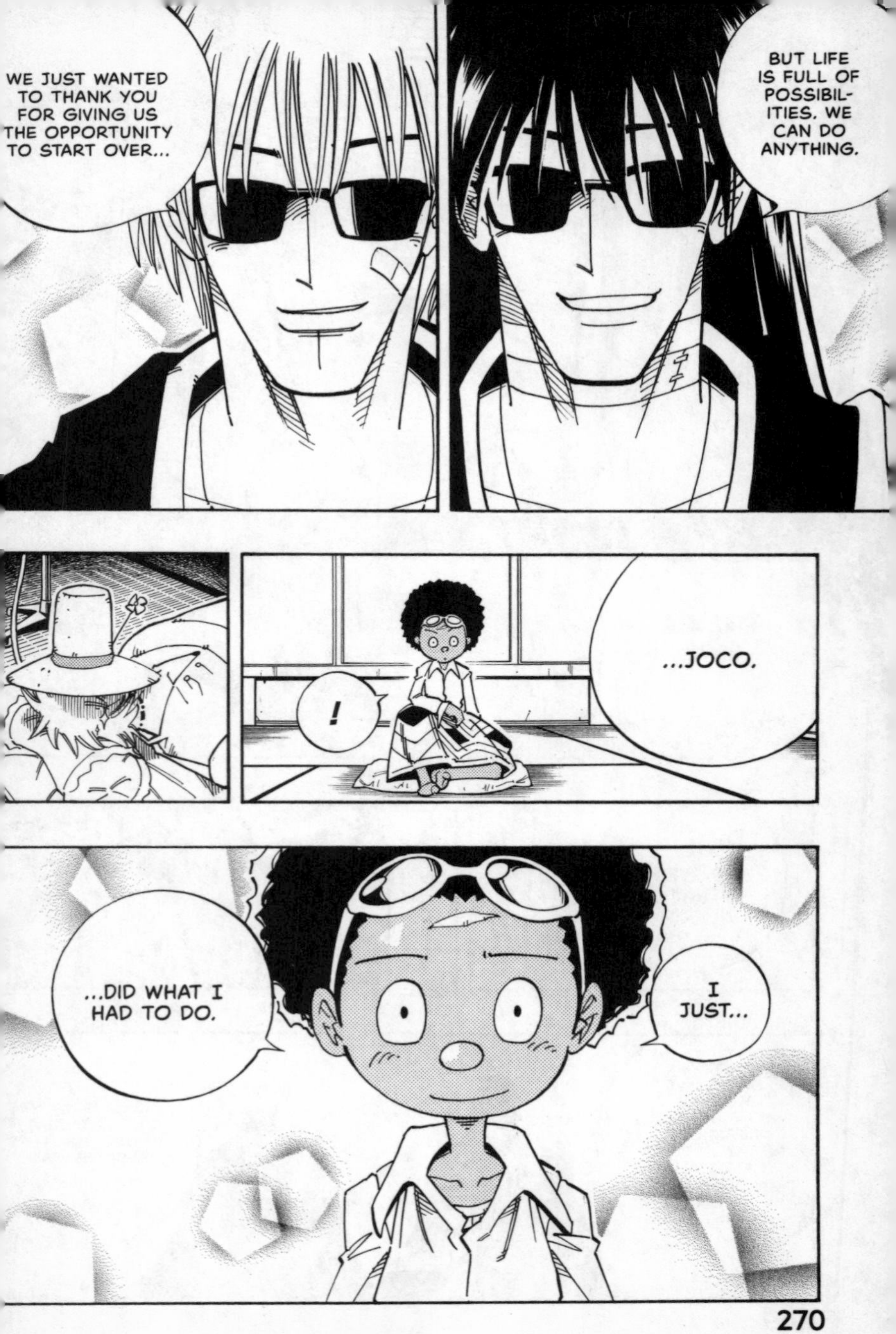
BUT LIFE IS FULL OF POSSIBIL-ITIES. WE CAN DO ANYTHING.
WE JUST WANTED TO THANK YOU FOR GIVING US THE OPPORTUNITY TO START OVER...
...JOCO.
!
I JUST...
...DID WHAT I HAD TO DO.

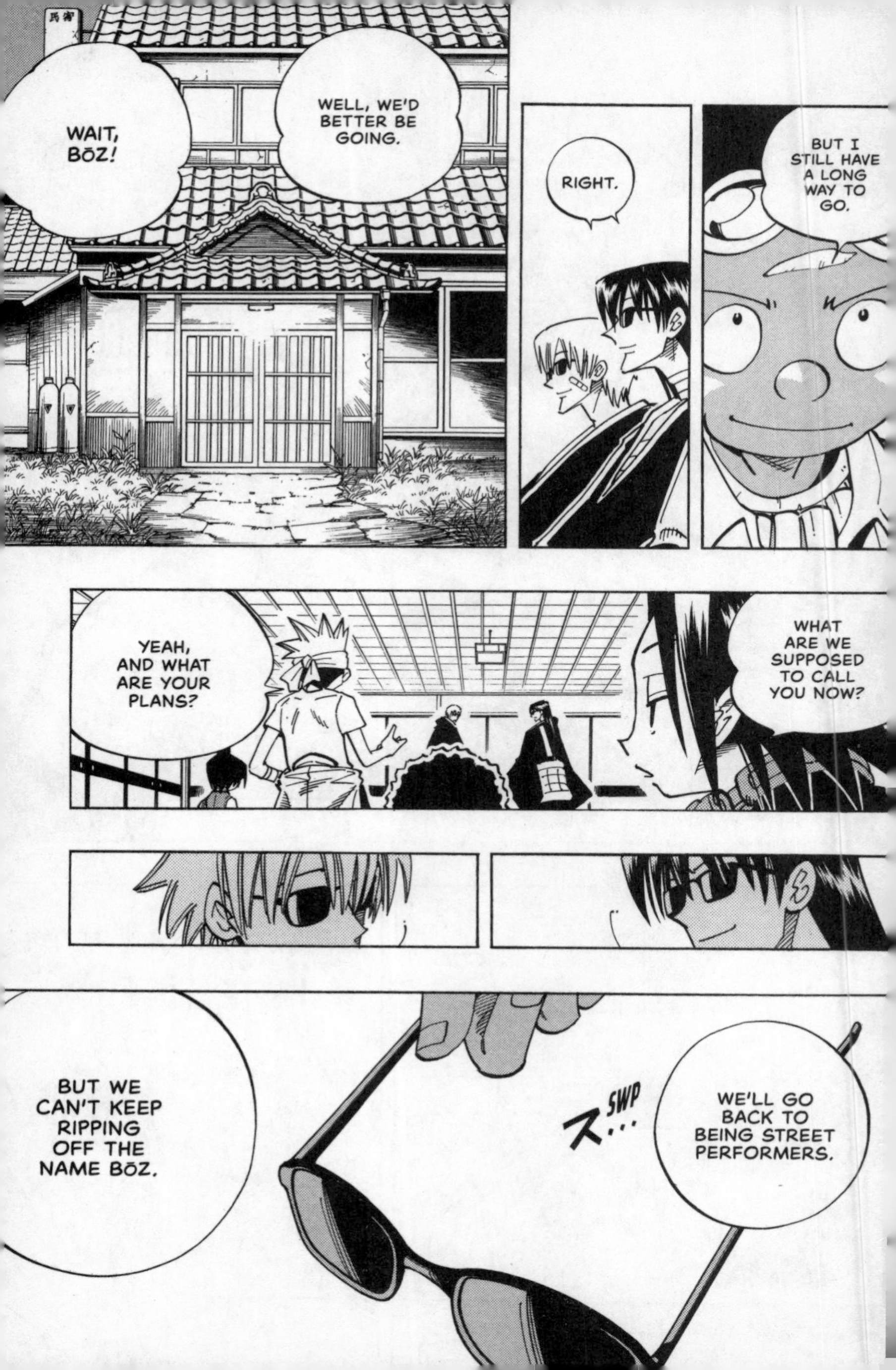
BUT I STILL HAVE A LONG WAY TO GO.
RIGHT.
WELL, WE'D BETTER BE GOING.
WAIT, BŌZ!
WHAT ARE WE SUPPOSED TO CALL YOU NOW?
YEAH, AND WHAT ARE YOUR PLANS?
WE'LL GO BACK TO BEING STREET PERFORMERS.
ス… SWP
BUT WE CAN'T KEEP RIPPING OFF THE NAME BŌZ.

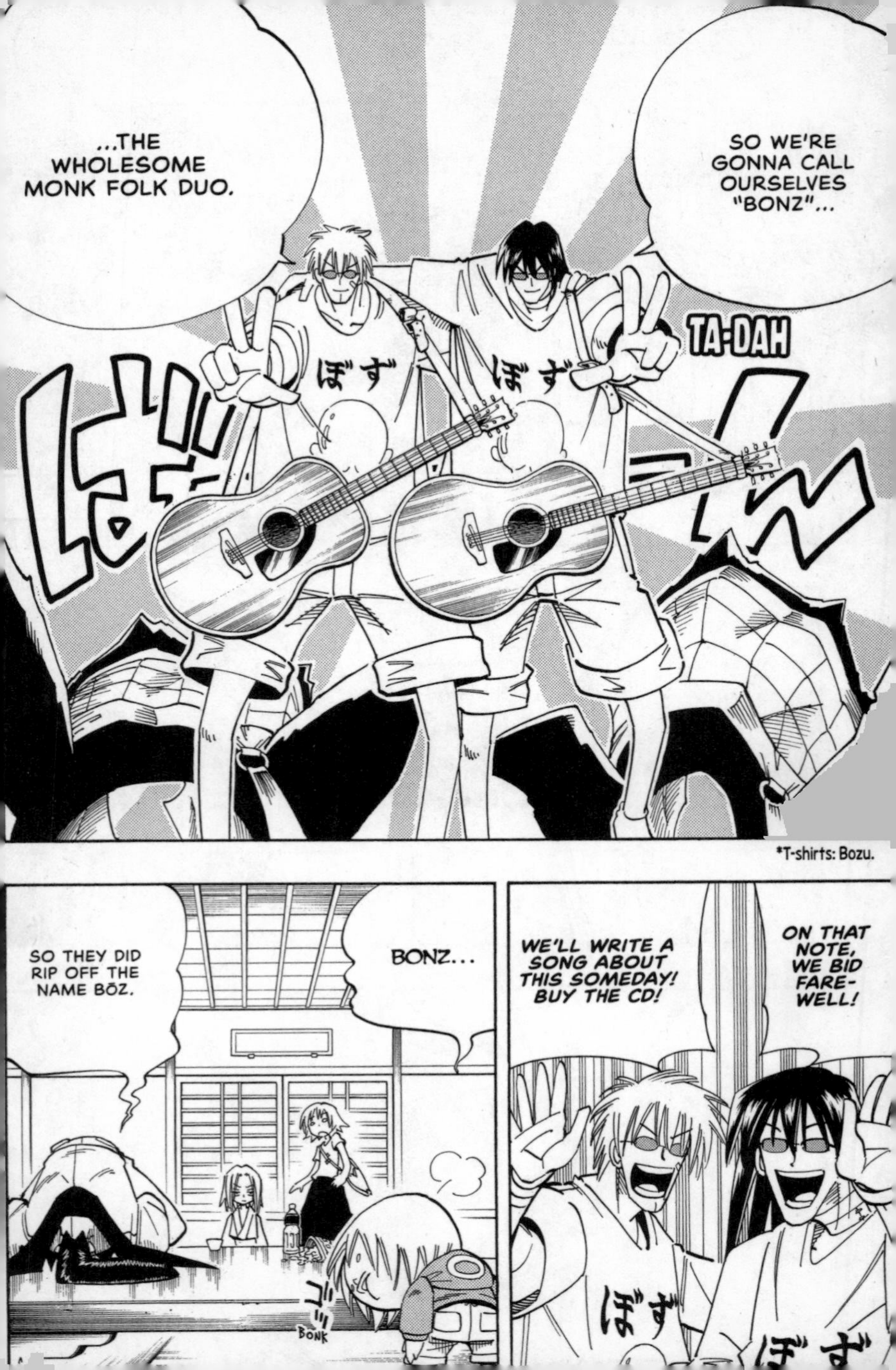
SO WE'RE GONNA CALL OURSELVES "BONZ"...
...THE WHOLESOME MONK FOLK DUO.
TA-DAH
ぼず
ぼず
*T-shirts: Bozu.
ON THAT NOTE, WE BID FARE-WELL!
WE'LL WRITE A SONG ABOUT THIS SOMEDAY! BUY THE CD!
ぼず
BONZ...
SO THEY DID RIP OFF THE NAME BÖZ.
BONK

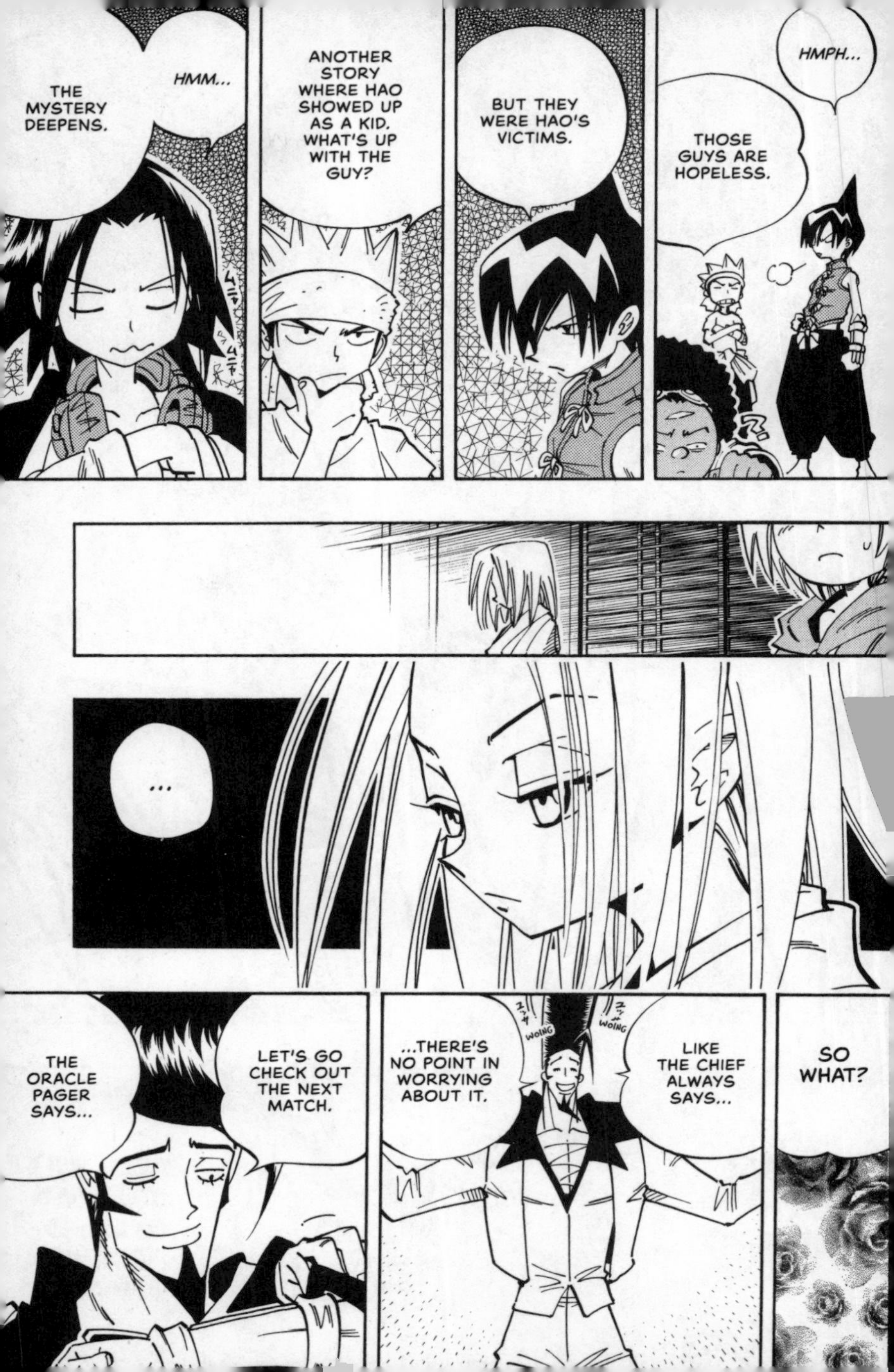
HMPH...
THOSE GUYS ARE HOPELESS.
BUT THEY WERE HAO'S VICTIMS.
ANOTHER STORY WHERE HAO SHOWED UP AS A KID. WHAT'S UP WITH THE GUY?
HMM...
THE MYSTERY DEEPENS.
...
SO WHAT?
WOING
LIKE THE CHIEF ALWAYS SAYS...
WOING
...THERE'S NO POINT IN WORRYING ABOUT IT.
LET'S GO CHECK OUT THE NEXT MATCH.
THE ORACLE PAGER SAYS...

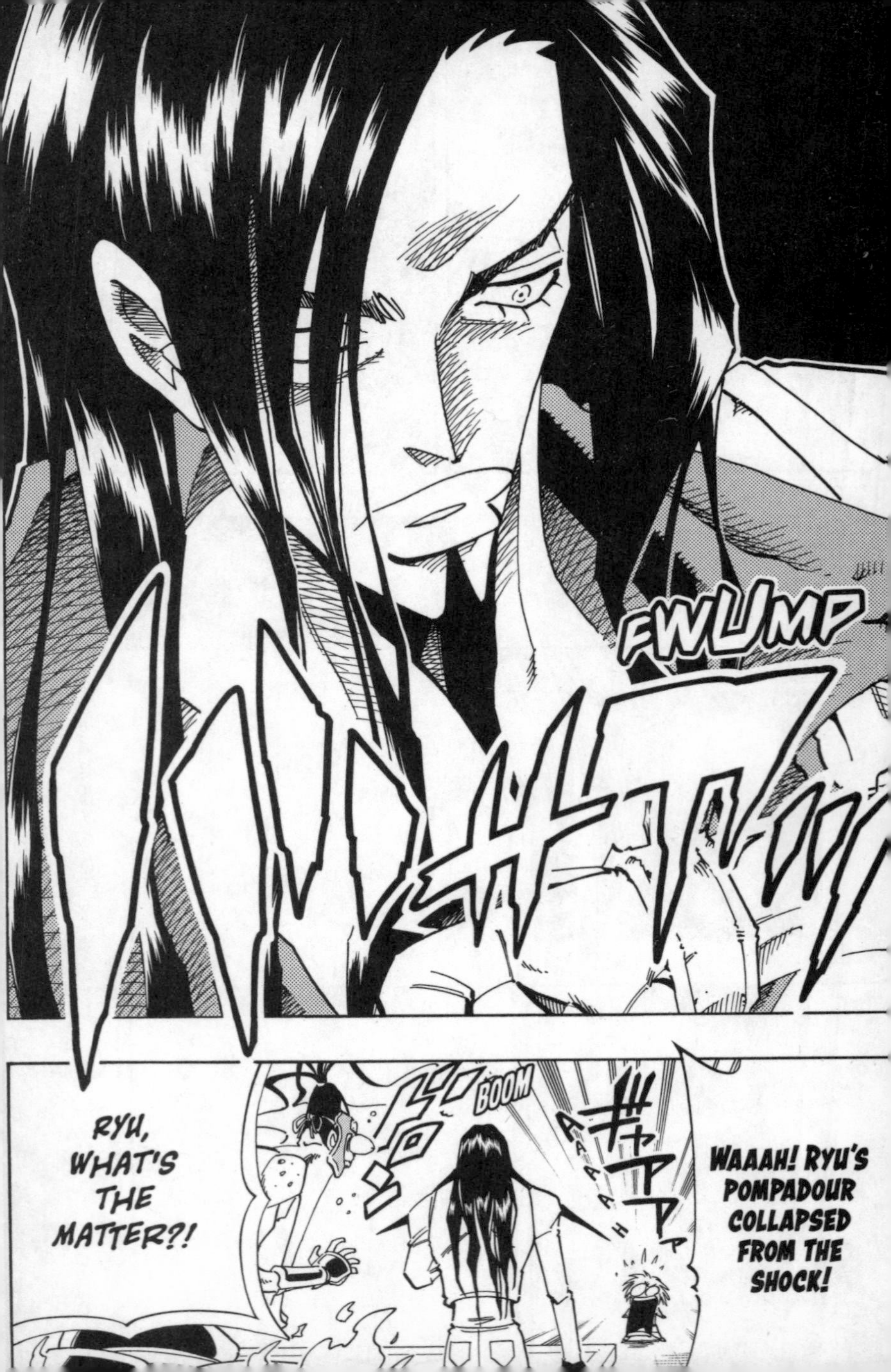
FWUMP
WAAAH! RYU'S POMPADOUR COLLAPSED FROM THE SHOCK!
BOOM
RYU, WHAT'S THE MATTER?!

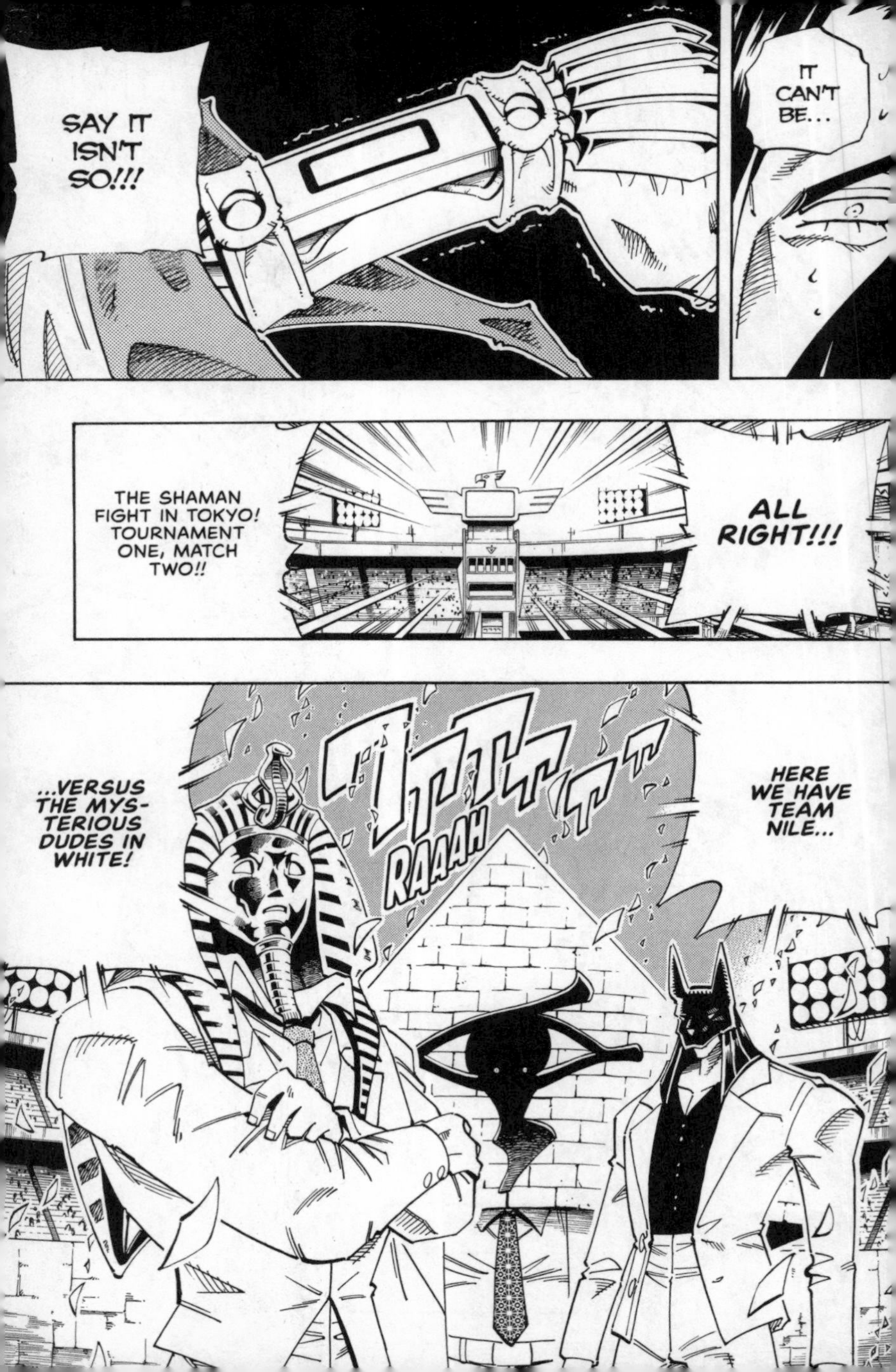
IT CAN'T BE...
SAY IT ISN'T SO!!!
ALL RIGHT!!!
THE SHAMAN FIGHT IN TOKYO! TOURNAMENT ONE, MATCH TWO!!
HERE WE HAVE TEAM NILE...
RAAAH
...VERSUS THE MYSTERIOUS DUDES IN WHITE!

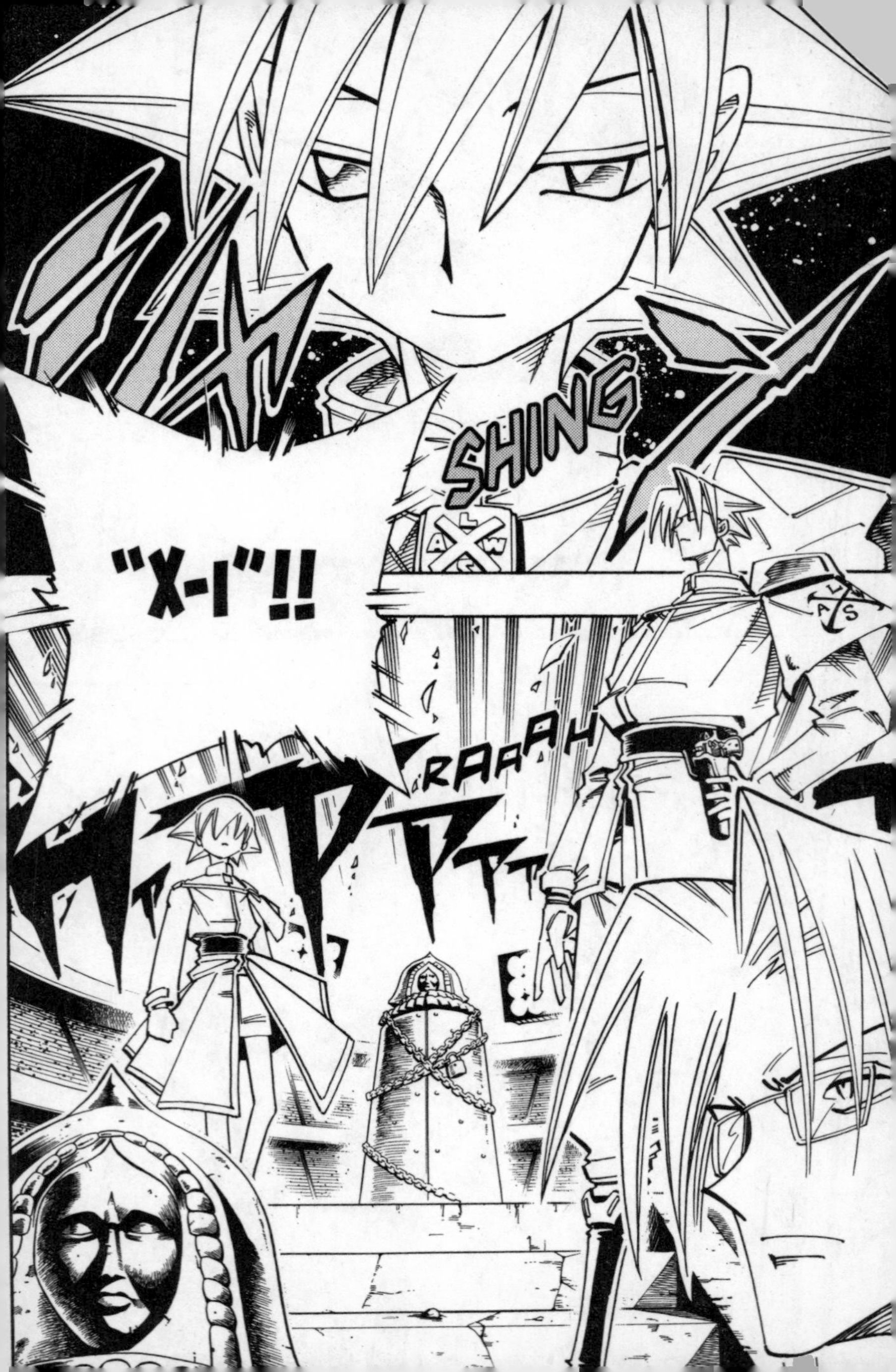
SHING
"X-I"!!
RAAAAH

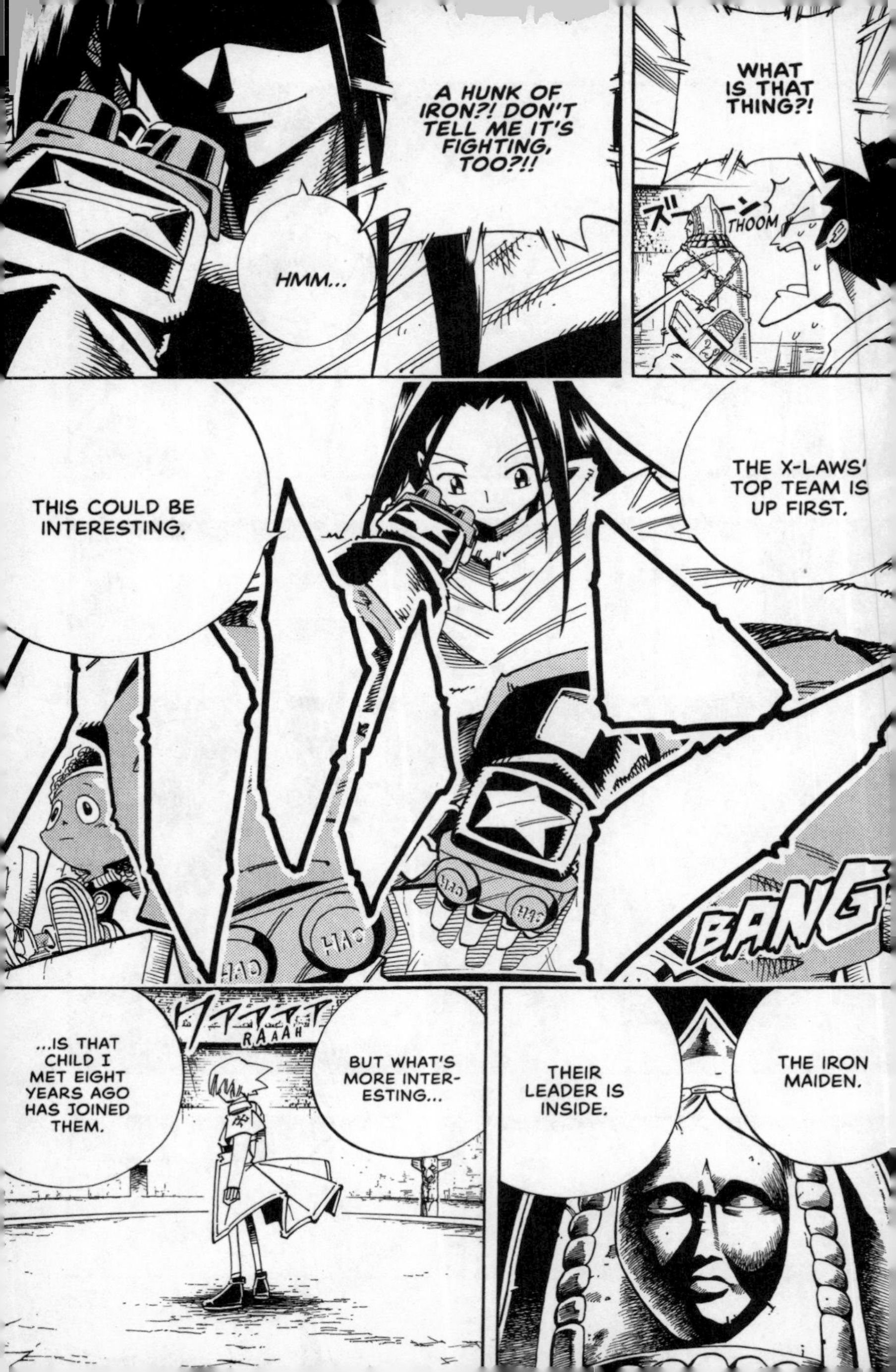
WHAT IS THAT THING?!
ズーン
THOOM
A HUNK OF IRON?! DON'T TELL ME IT'S FIGHTING, TOO?!!
HMM...
THE X-LAWS' TOP TEAM IS UP FIRST.
THIS COULD BE INTERESTING.
BANG
THE IRON MAIDEN.
THEIR LEADER IS INSIDE.
BUT WHAT'S MORE INTER-ESTING...
...IS THAT CHILD I MET EIGHT YEARS AGO HAS JOINED THEM.
RAAAH

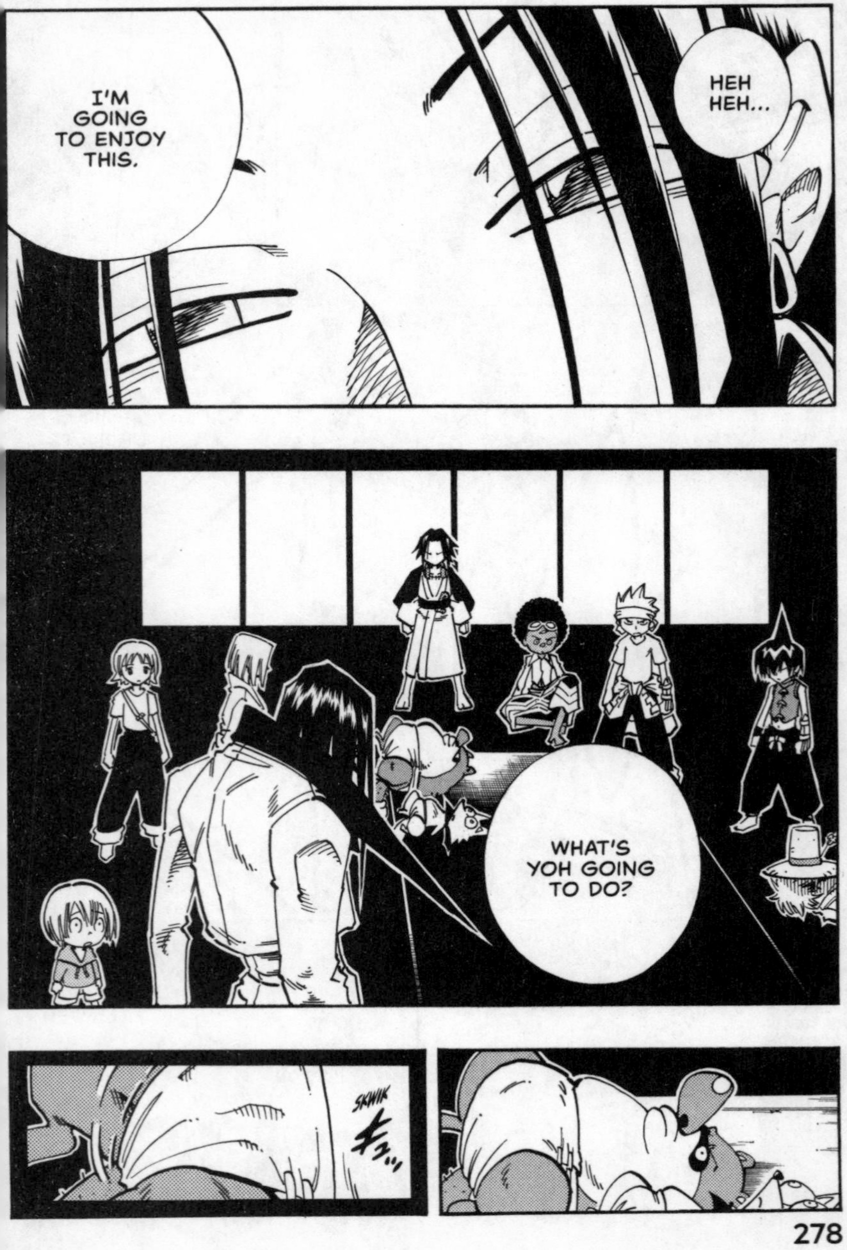
HEH HEH...
I'M GOING TO ENJOY THIS.
WHAT'S YOH GOING TO DO?
SKWIK

Team Nile's Spirit Media

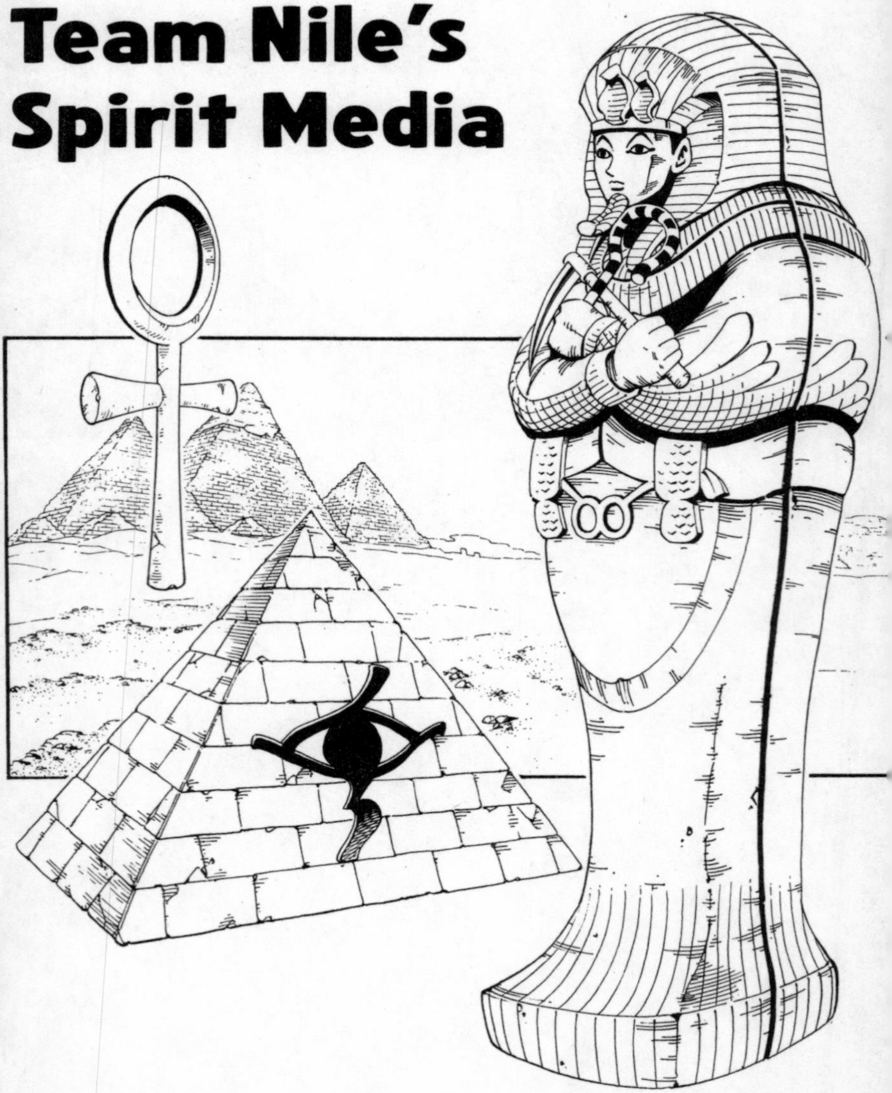

Chapter 121: Justice X

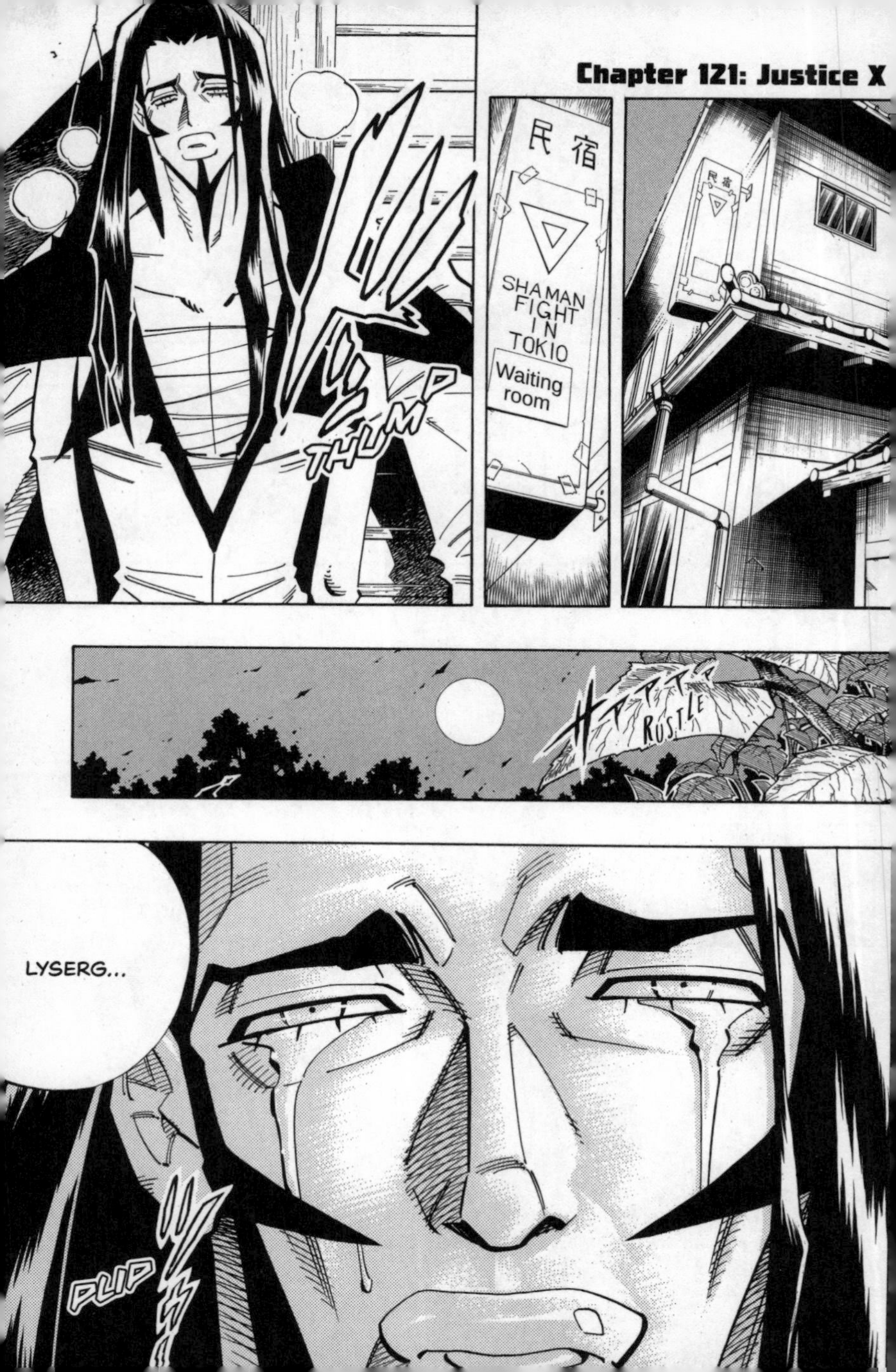
民宿
SHAMAN FIGHT IN TOKIO
Waiting room
THUMP
RUSTLE
LYSERG...
PLIP

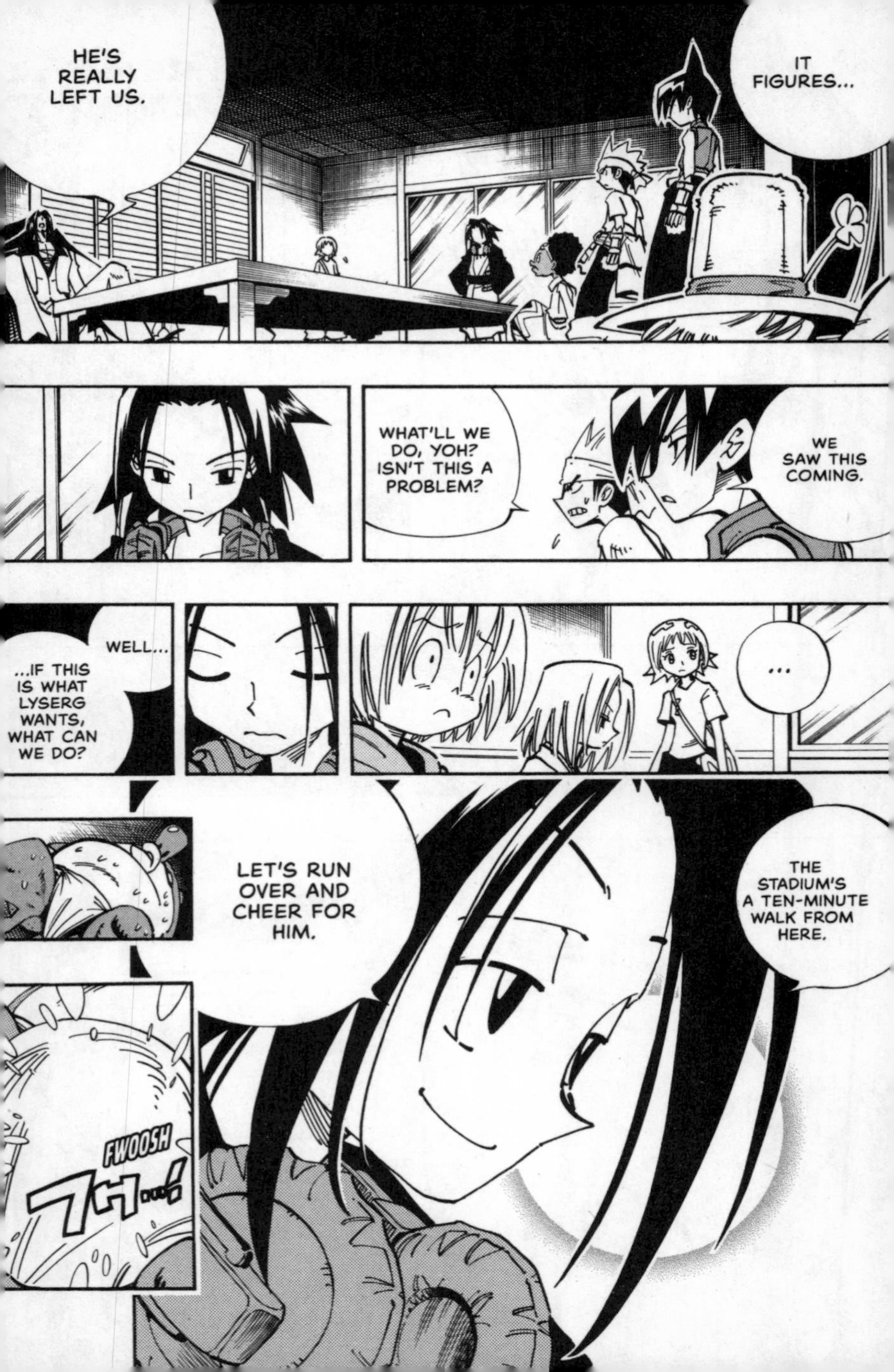
IT FIGURES...
HE'S REALLY LEFT US.
WHAT'LL WE DO, YOH? ISN'T THIS A PROBLEM?
WE SAW THIS COMING.
...
WELL...
...IF THIS IS WHAT LYSERG WANTS, WHAT CAN WE DO?
LET'S RUN OVER AND CHEER FOR HIM.
THE STADIUM'S A TEN-MINUTE WALK FROM HERE.
FWOOSH

Justice X

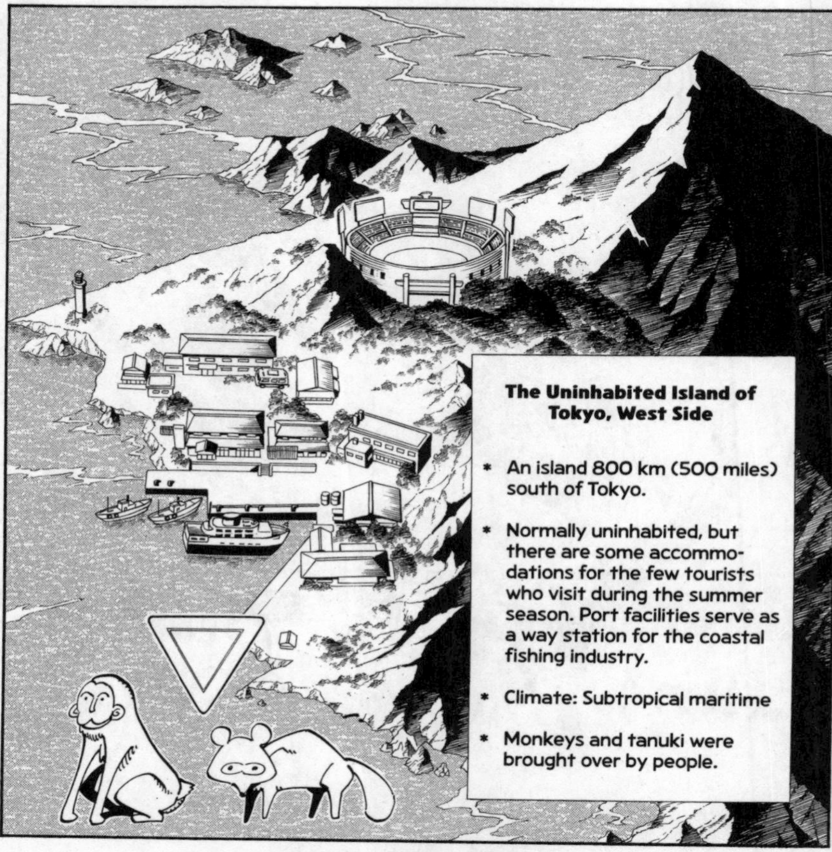
The Uninhabited Island of Tokyo, West Side
* An island 800 km (500 miles) south of Tokyo.
* Normally uninhabited, but there are some accommodations for the few tourists who visit during the summer season. Port facilities serve as a way station for the coastal fishing industry.
* Climate: Subtropical maritime
* Monkeys and tanuki were brought over by people.

Chapter 121:

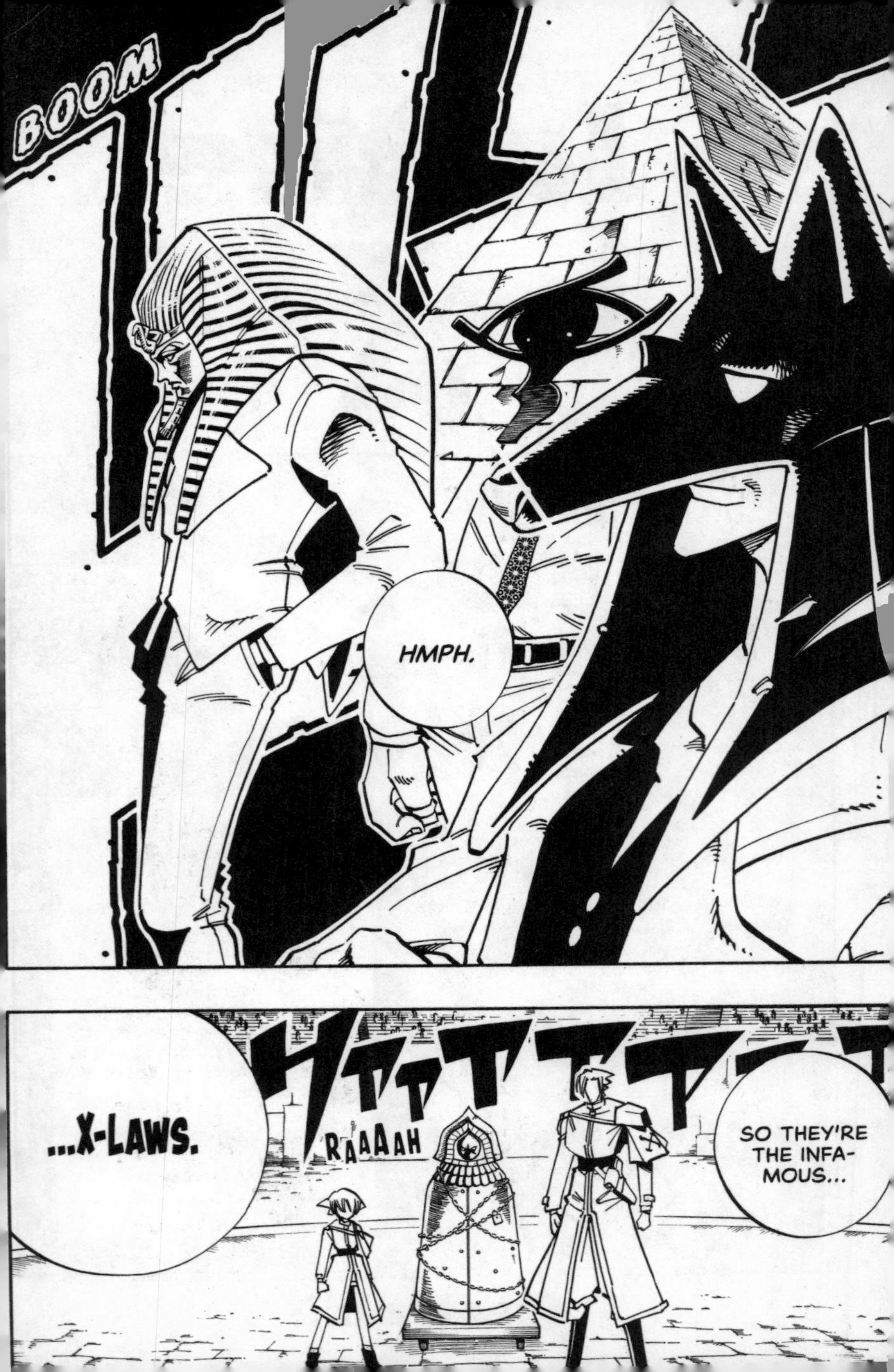
BOOM
HMPH.
SO THEY'RE THE INFAMOUS...
RAAAAH
...X-LAWS.

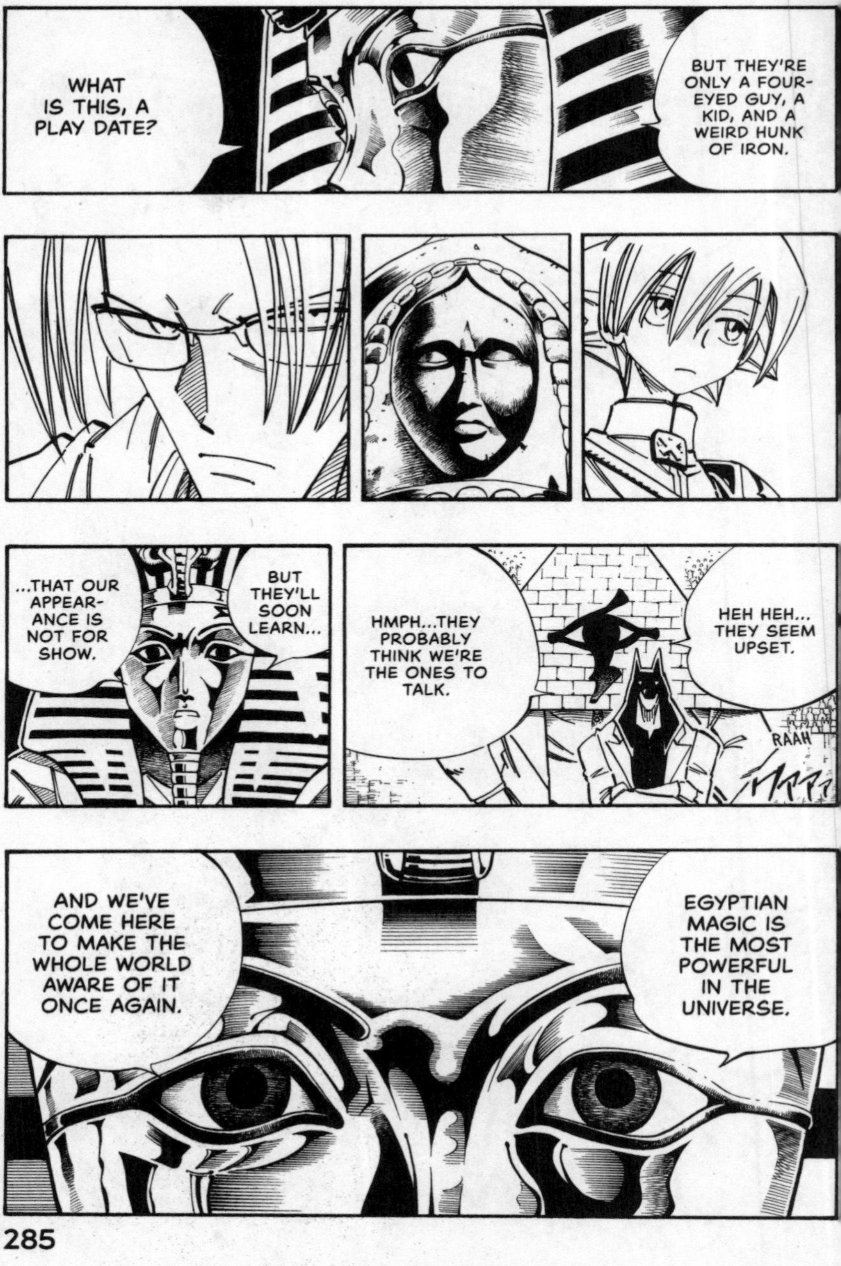
BUT THEY'RE ONLY A FOUR-EYED GUY, A KID, AND A WEIRD HUNK OF IRON.
WHAT IS THIS, A PLAY DATE?
HEH HEH... THEY SEEM UPSET.
RAAH
HMPH...THEY PROBABLY THINK WE'RE THE ONES TO TALK.
BUT THEY'LL SOON LEARN...
...THAT OUR APPEARANCE IS NOT FOR SHOW.
EGYPTIAN MAGIC IS THE MOST POWERFUL IN THE UNIVERSE.
AND WE'VE COME HERE TO MAKE THE WHOLE WORLD AWARE OF IT ONCE AGAIN.

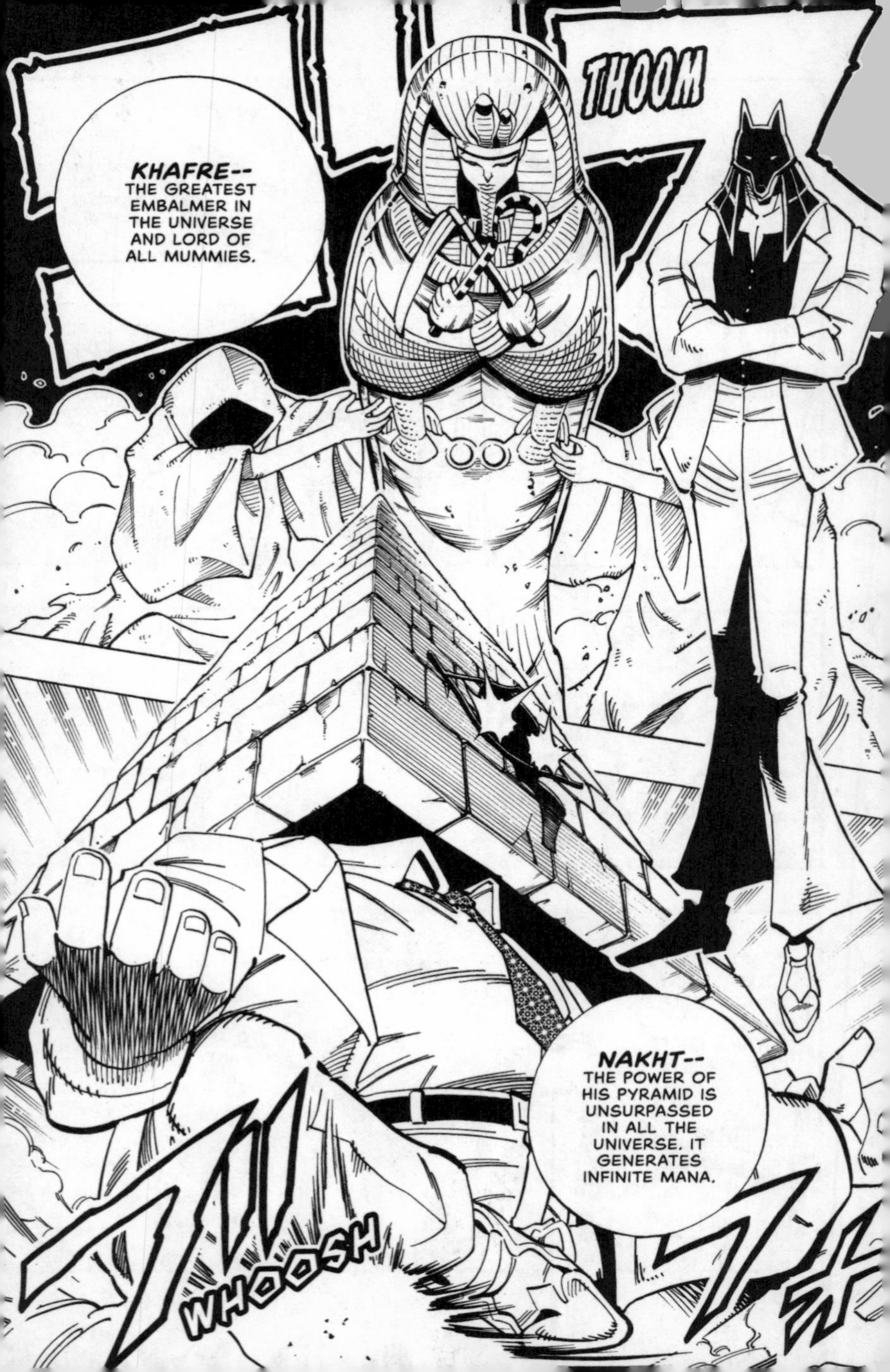
THOOM
KHAFRE-- THE GREATEST EMBALMER IN THE UNIVERSE AND LORD OF ALL MUMMIES.
NAKHT-- THE POWER OF HIS PYRAMID IS UNSURPASSED IN ALL THE UNIVERSE. IT GENERATES INFINITE MANA.
WHOOOSH

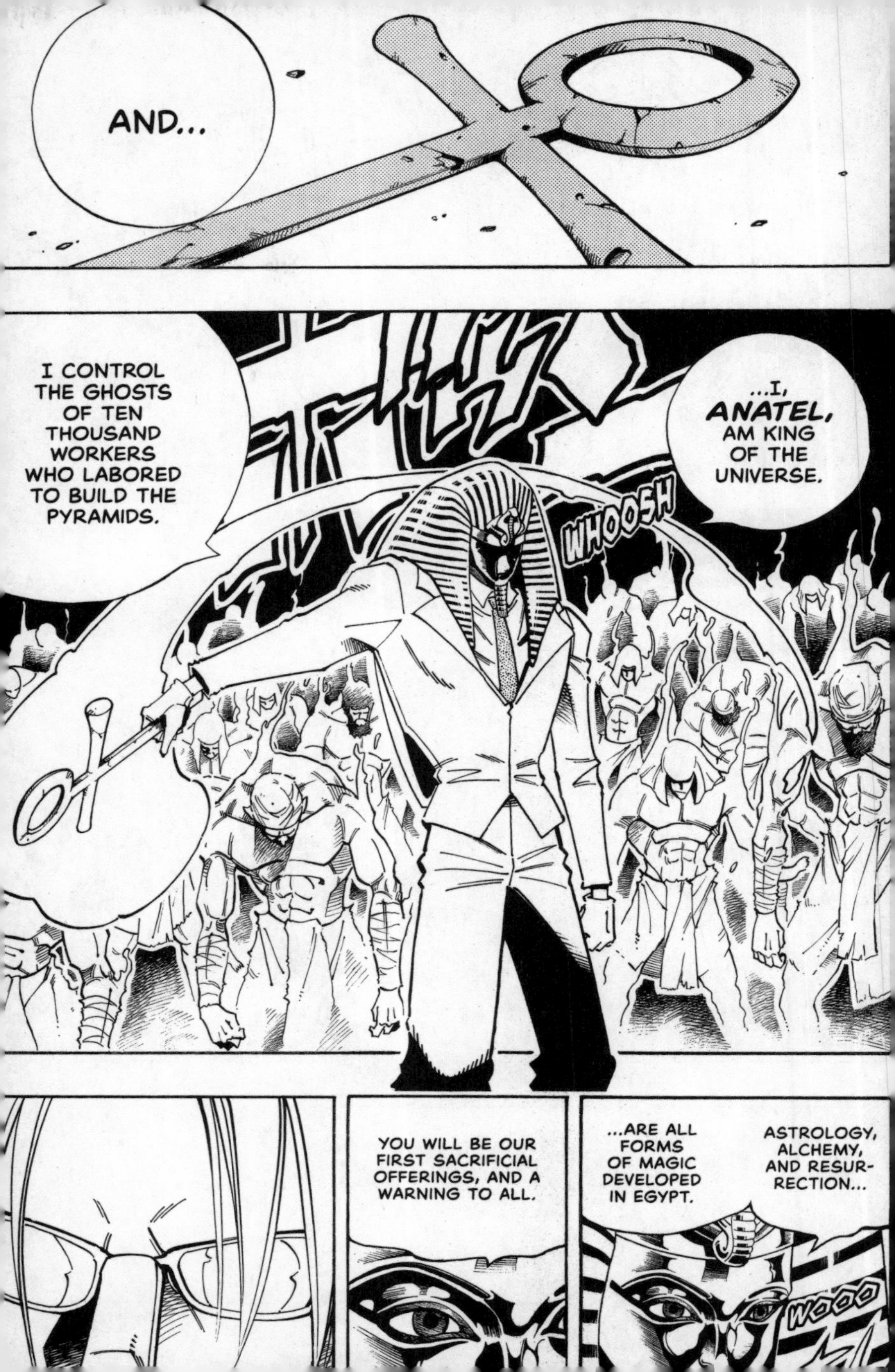
AND...
...I, ANATEL, AM KING OF THE UNIVERSE.
WHOOSH
I CONTROL THE GHOSTS OF TEN THOUSAND WORKERS WHO LABORED TO BUILD THE PYRAMIDS.
ASTROLOGY, ALCHEMY, AND RESURRECTION...
...ARE ALL FORMS OF MAGIC DEVELOPED IN EGYPT.
WOOO
YOU WILL BE OUR FIRST SACRIFICIAL OFFERINGS, AND A WARNING TO ALL.

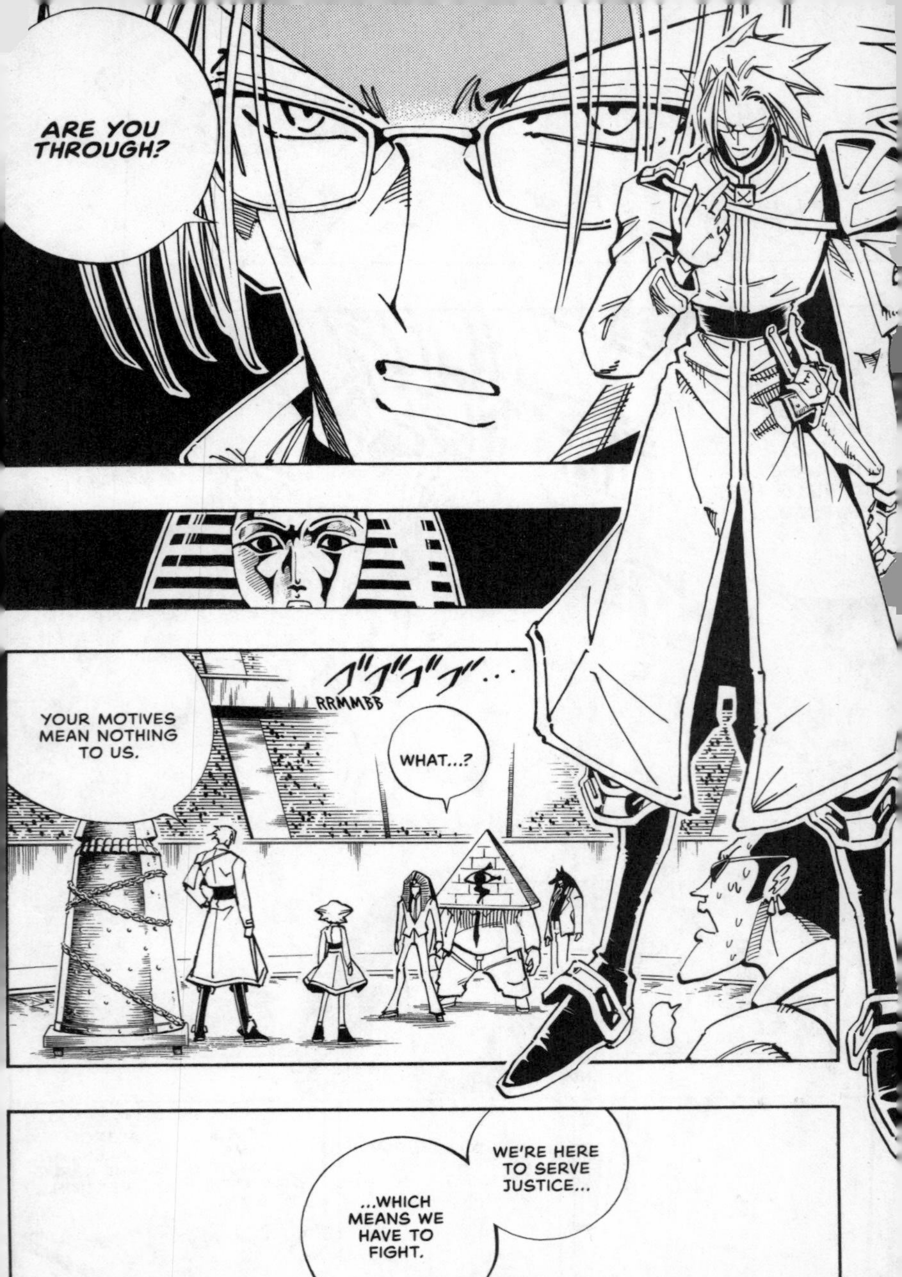

ARE YOU THROUGH?
ゴゴゴゴ…
RRMMBB
YOUR MOTIVES MEAN NOTHING TO US.
WHAT...?
WE'RE HERE TO SERVE JUSTICE...
...WHICH MEANS WE HAVE TO FIGHT.

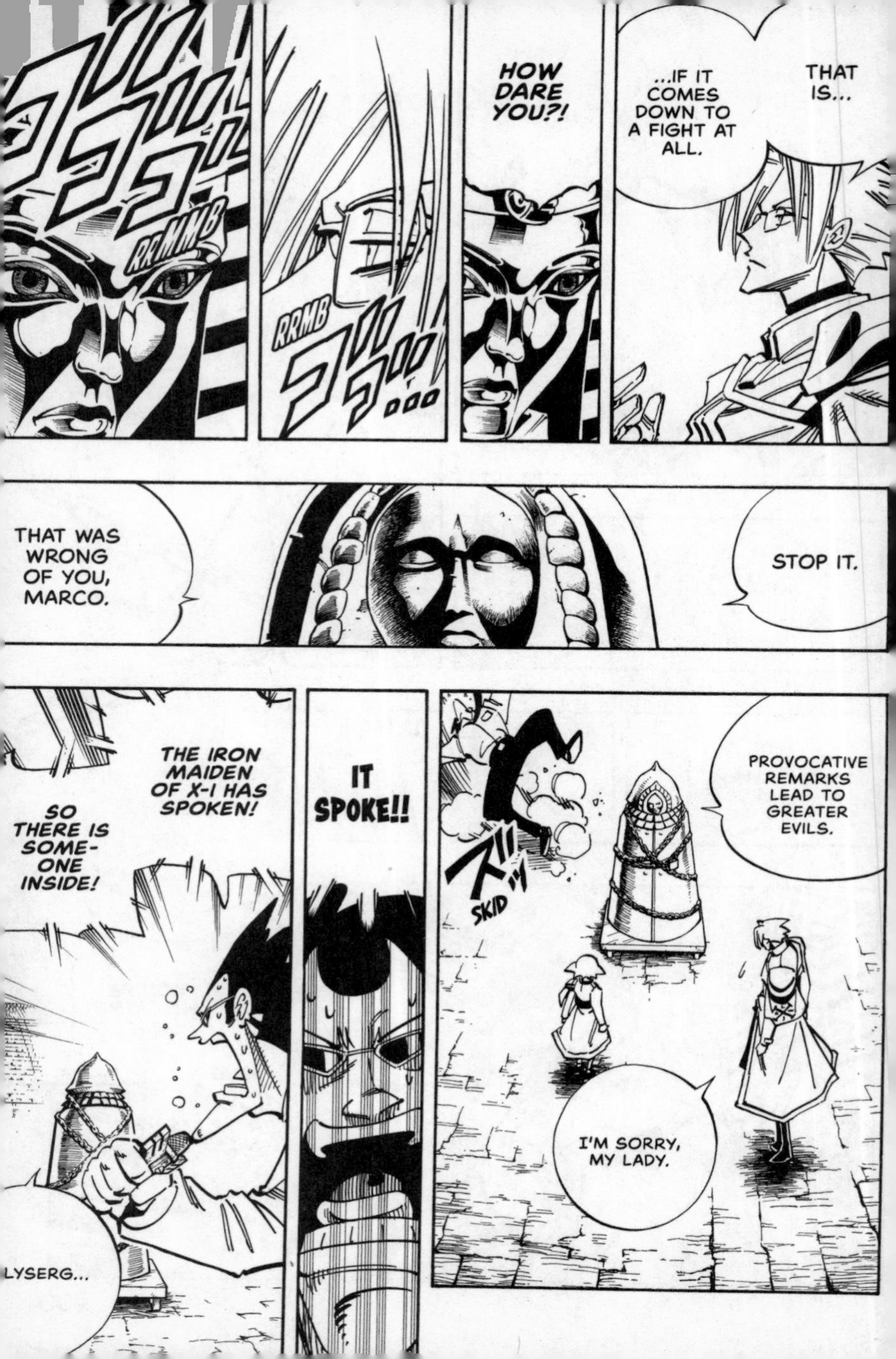
THAT IS...
...IF IT COMES DOWN TO A FIGHT AT ALL.
HOW DARE YOU?!
RRMB
RRMMB
STOP IT.
THAT WAS WRONG OF YOU, MARCO.
PROVOCATIVE REMARKS LEAD TO GREATER EVILS.
SKID
I'M SORRY, MY LADY.
IT SPOKE!!
THE IRON MAIDEN OF X-I HAS SPOKEN!
SO THERE IS SOME-ONE INSIDE!
LYSERG...

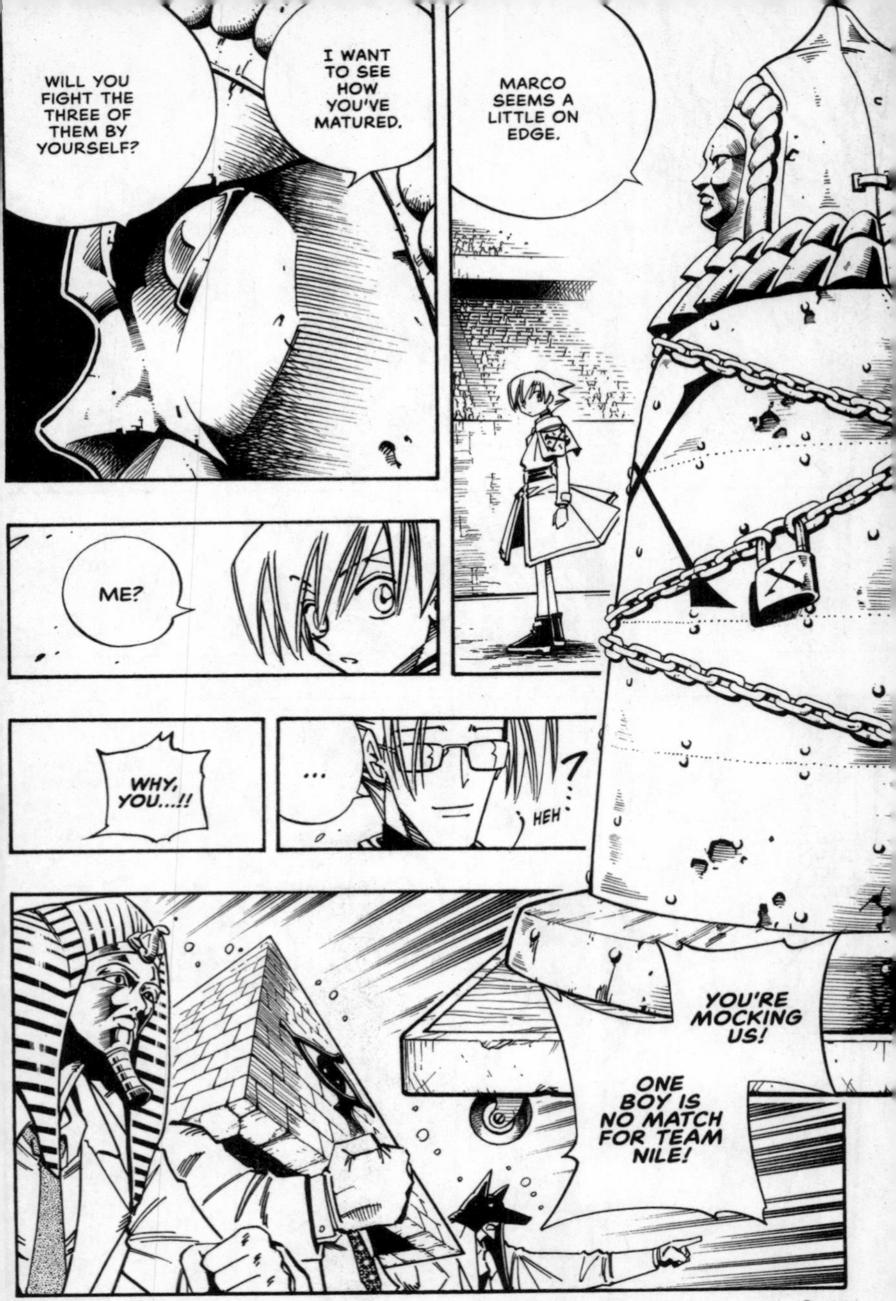
MARCO SEEMS A LITTLE ON EDGE.
I WANT TO SEE HOW YOU'VE MATURED.
WILL YOU FIGHT THE THREE OF THEM BY YOURSELF?
ME?
...
HEH
WHY, YOU...!!
YOU'RE MOCKING US!
ONE BOY IS NO MATCH FOR TEAM NILE!

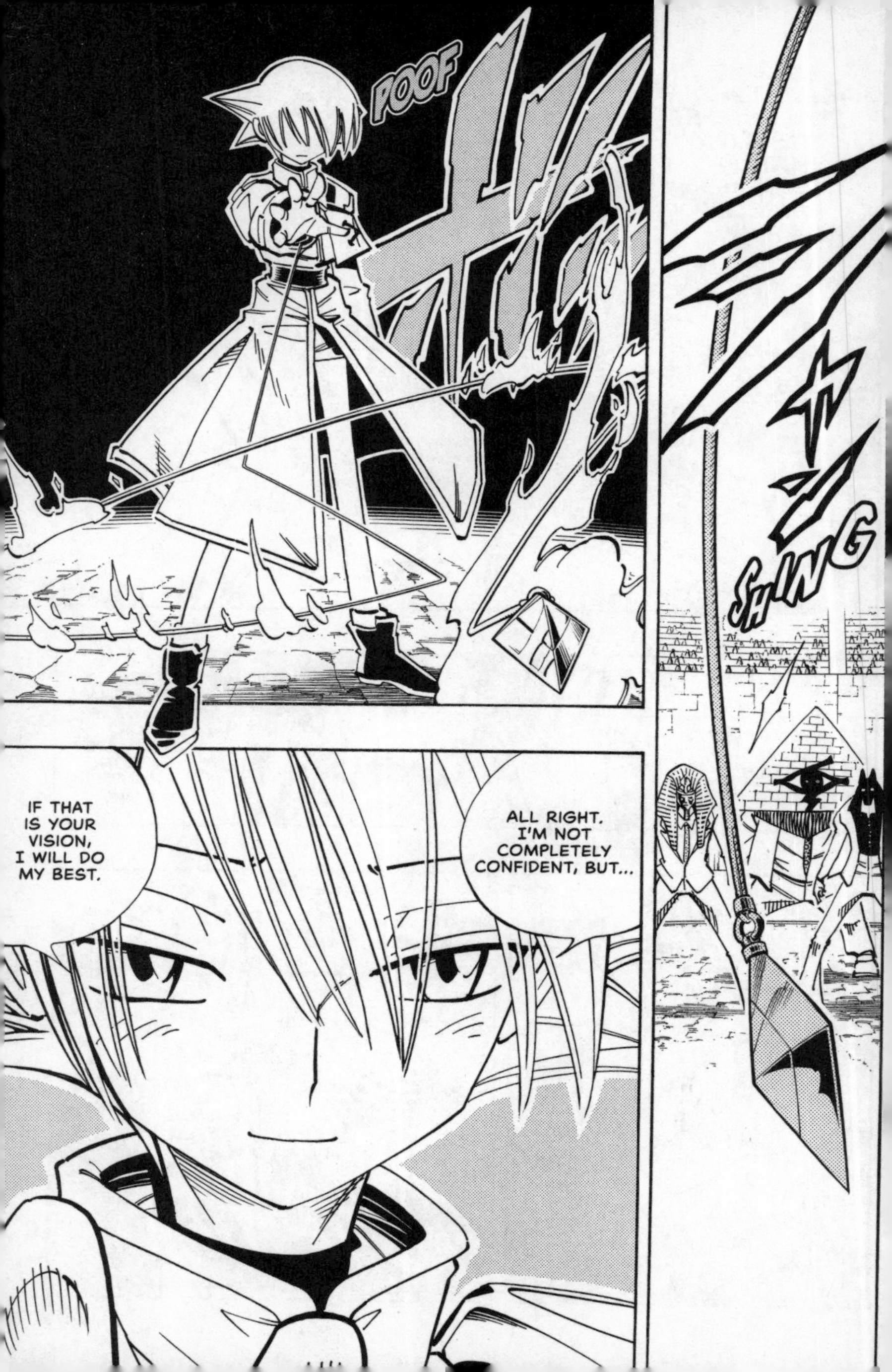
SHING
POOF
ALL RIGHT. I'M NOT COMPLETELY CONFIDENT, BUT...
IF THAT IS YOUR VISION, I WILL DO MY BEST.

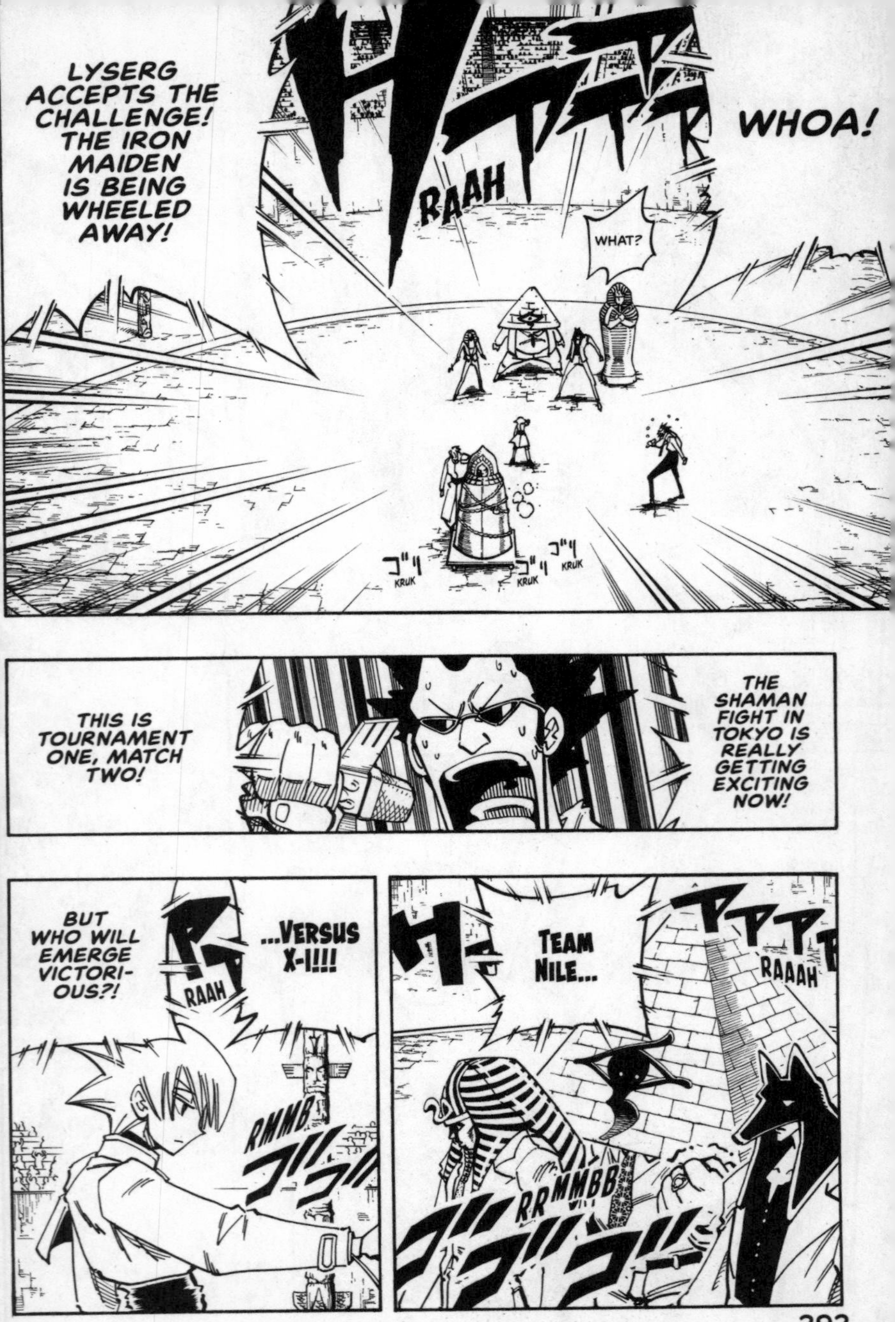
WHOA!
WHAT?
RAAH
LYSERG ACCEPTS THE CHALLENGE! THE IRON MAIDEN IS BEING WHEELED AWAY!
KRUK
KRUK
KRUK
THE SHAMAN FIGHT IN TOKYO IS REALLY GETTING EXCITING NOW!
THIS IS TOURNAMENT ONE, MATCH TWO!
RAAAH
TEAM NILE...
RRMMBB
...VERSUS X-I!!!
BUT WHO WILL EMERGE VICTORI-OUS?!
RAAH
RMMB

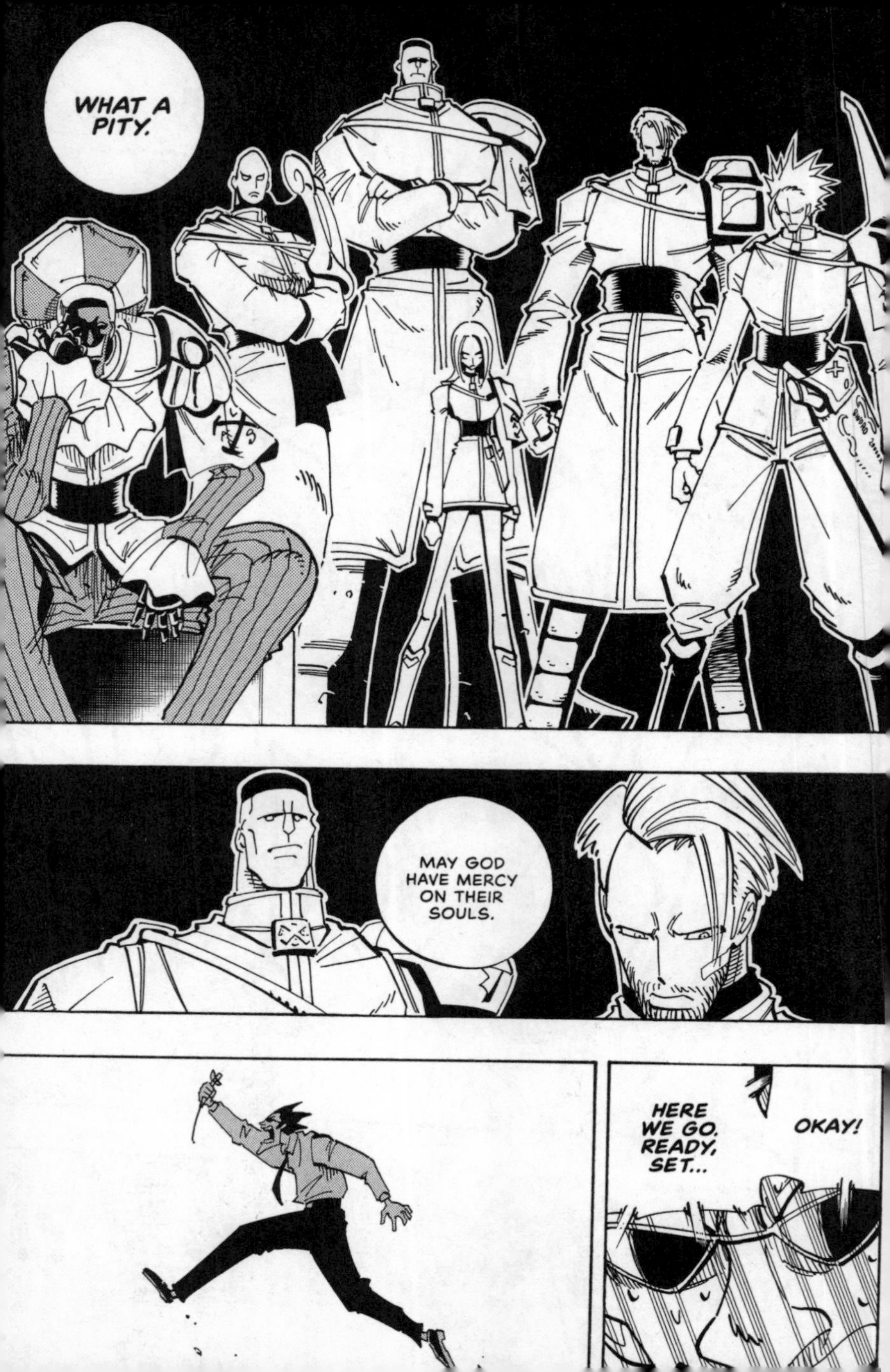
WHAT A PITY.
MAY GOD HAVE MERCY ON THEIR SOULS.
OKAY!
HERE WE GO. READY, SET...

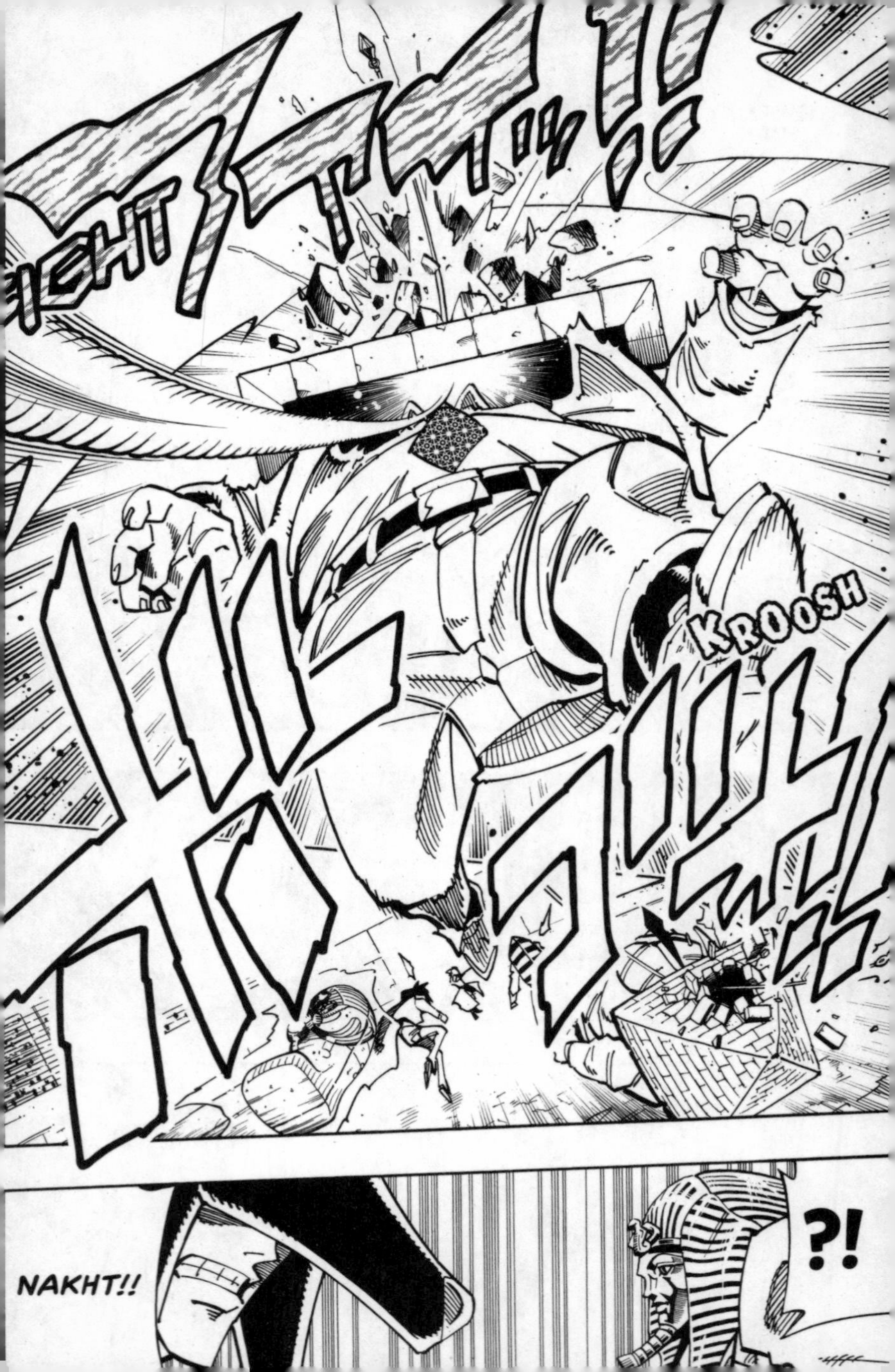
EIGHT
KROOSH
?!
NAKHT!!

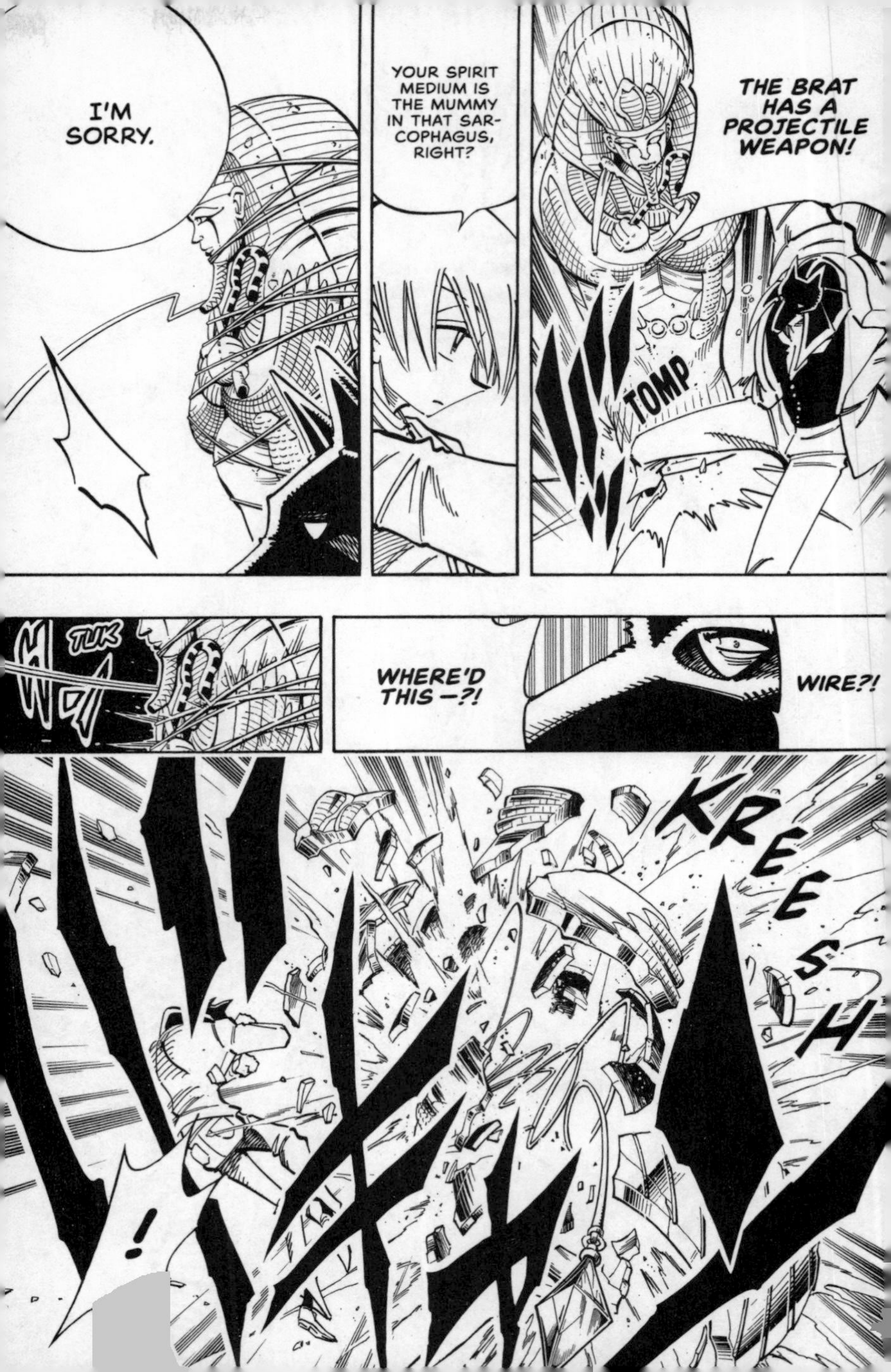
THE BRAT HAS A PROJECTILE WEAPON!
TOMP
YOUR SPIRIT MEDIUM IS THE MUMMY IN THAT SAR-COPHAGUS, RIGHT?
I'M SORRY.
WHERE'D THIS —?!
WIRE?!
TUK
KREESH
!

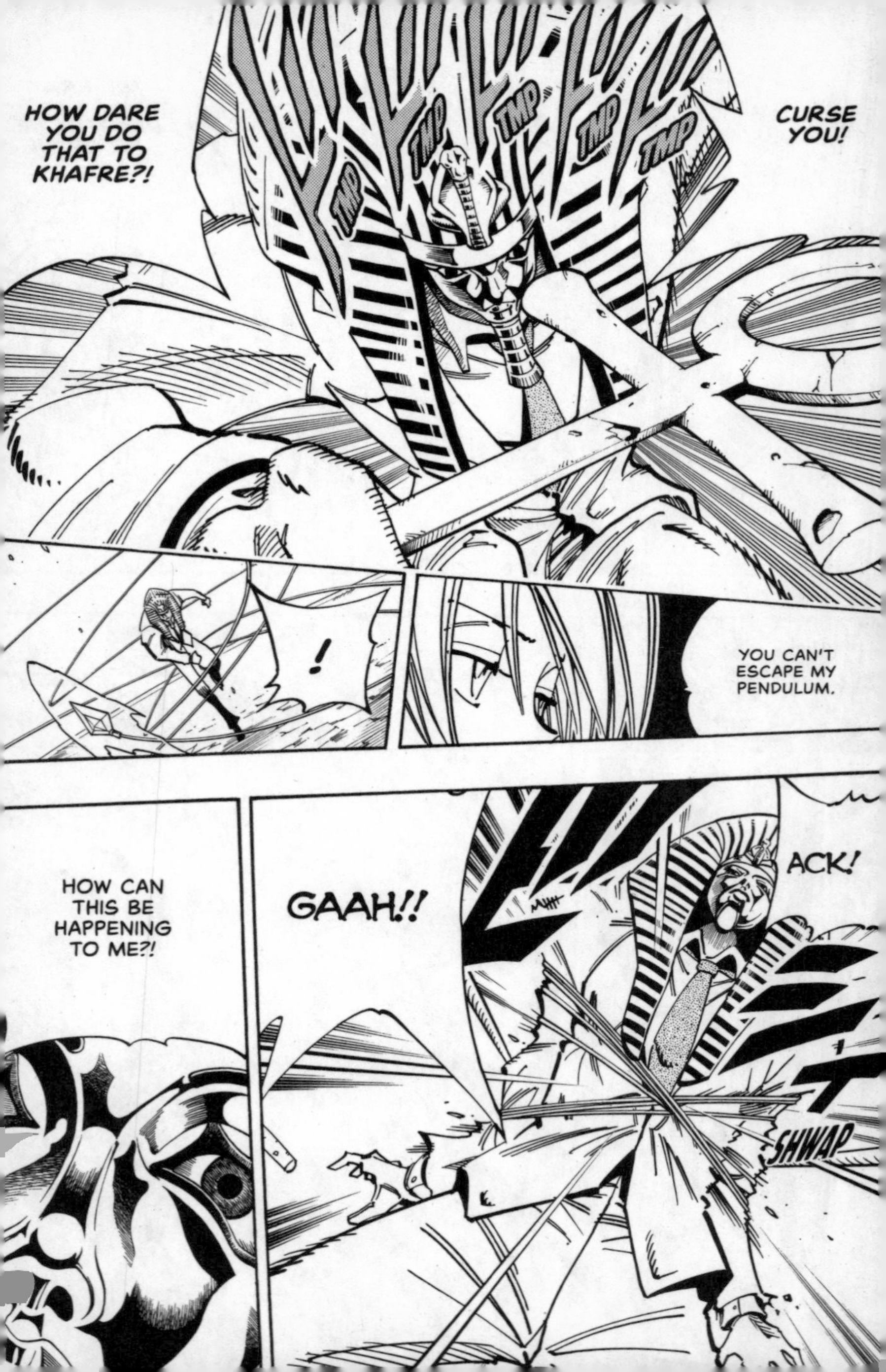
CURSE YOU!
TMP TMP TMP TMP TMP
HOW DARE YOU DO THAT TO KHAFRE?!
YOU CAN'T ESCAPE MY PENDULUM.
!
ACK!
GAAH!!
SHWAP
HOW CAN THIS BE HAPPENING TO ME?!

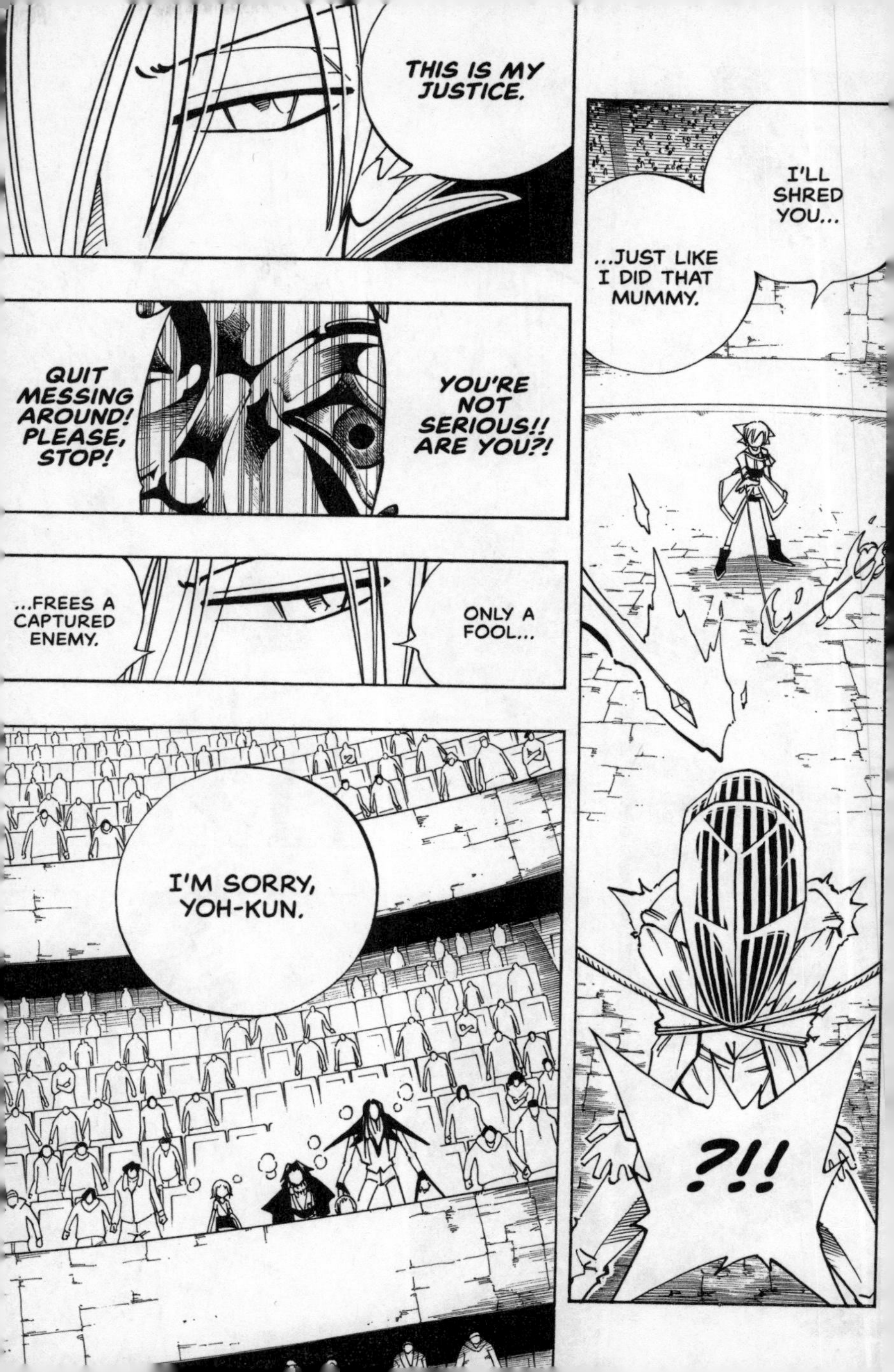
I'LL SHRED YOU...
...JUST LIKE I DID THAT MUMMY.
?!!
THIS IS MY JUSTICE.
YOU'RE NOT SERIOUS!! ARE YOU?!
QUIT MESSING AROUND! PLEASE, STOP!
ONLY A FOOL...
...FREES A CAPTURED ENEMY.
I'M SORRY, YOH-KUN.

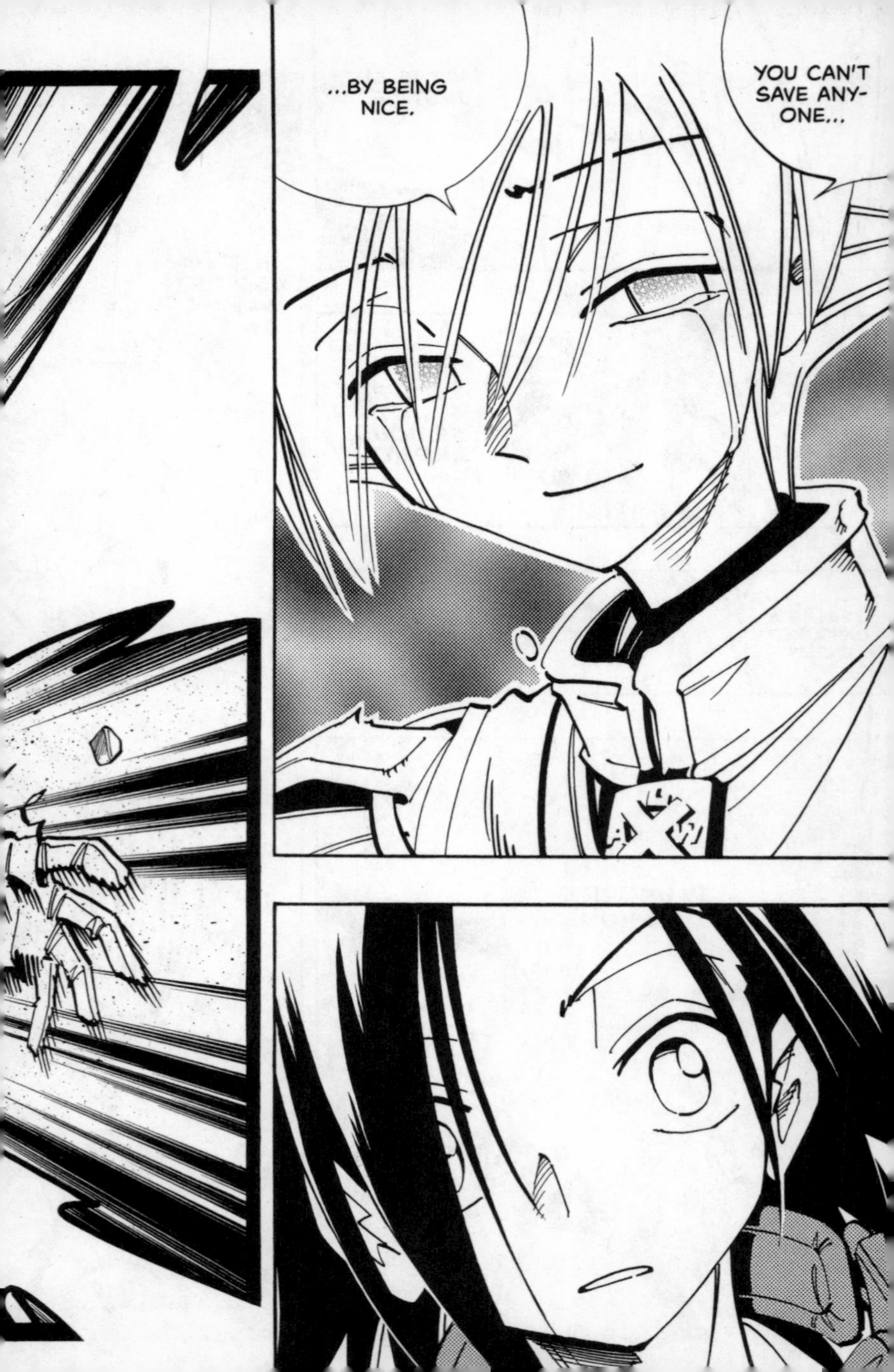
YOU CAN'T SAVE ANY-ONE...
...BY BEING NICE.

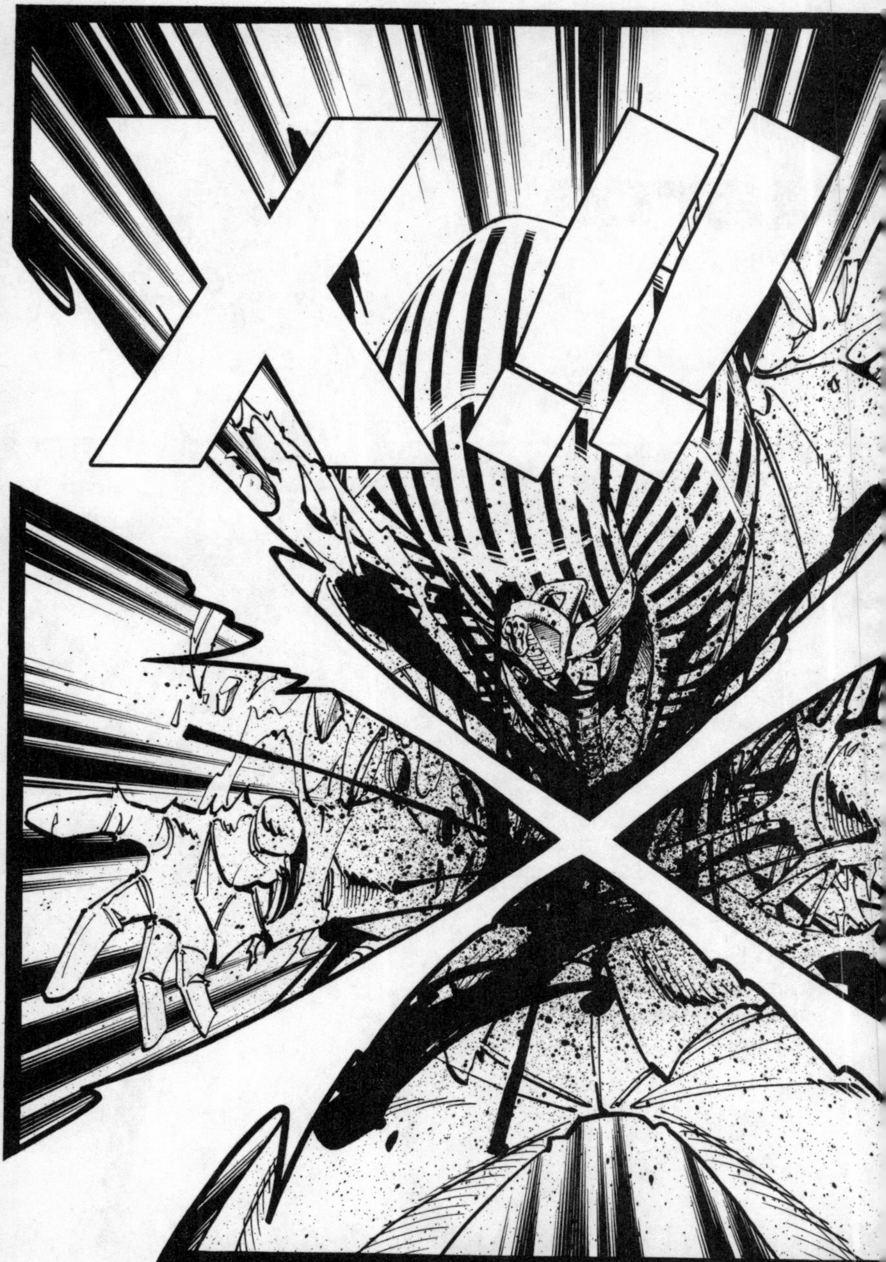
X!!

SHAMAN KING CHARACTER FILE No.67

Marco

June 2001

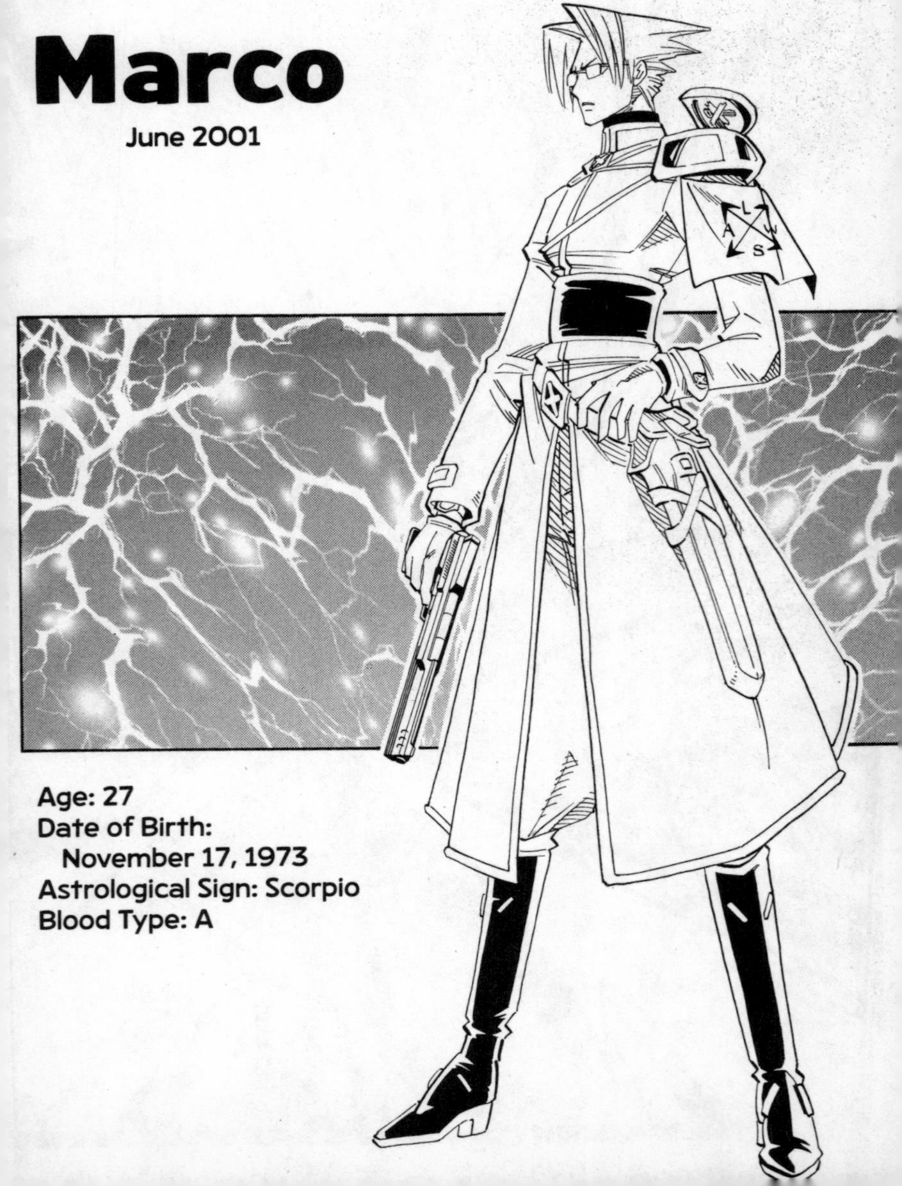

Age: 27
Date of Birth:
November 17, 1973
Astrological Sign: Scorpio
Blood Type: A

Chapter 122: A-Nile-Lation

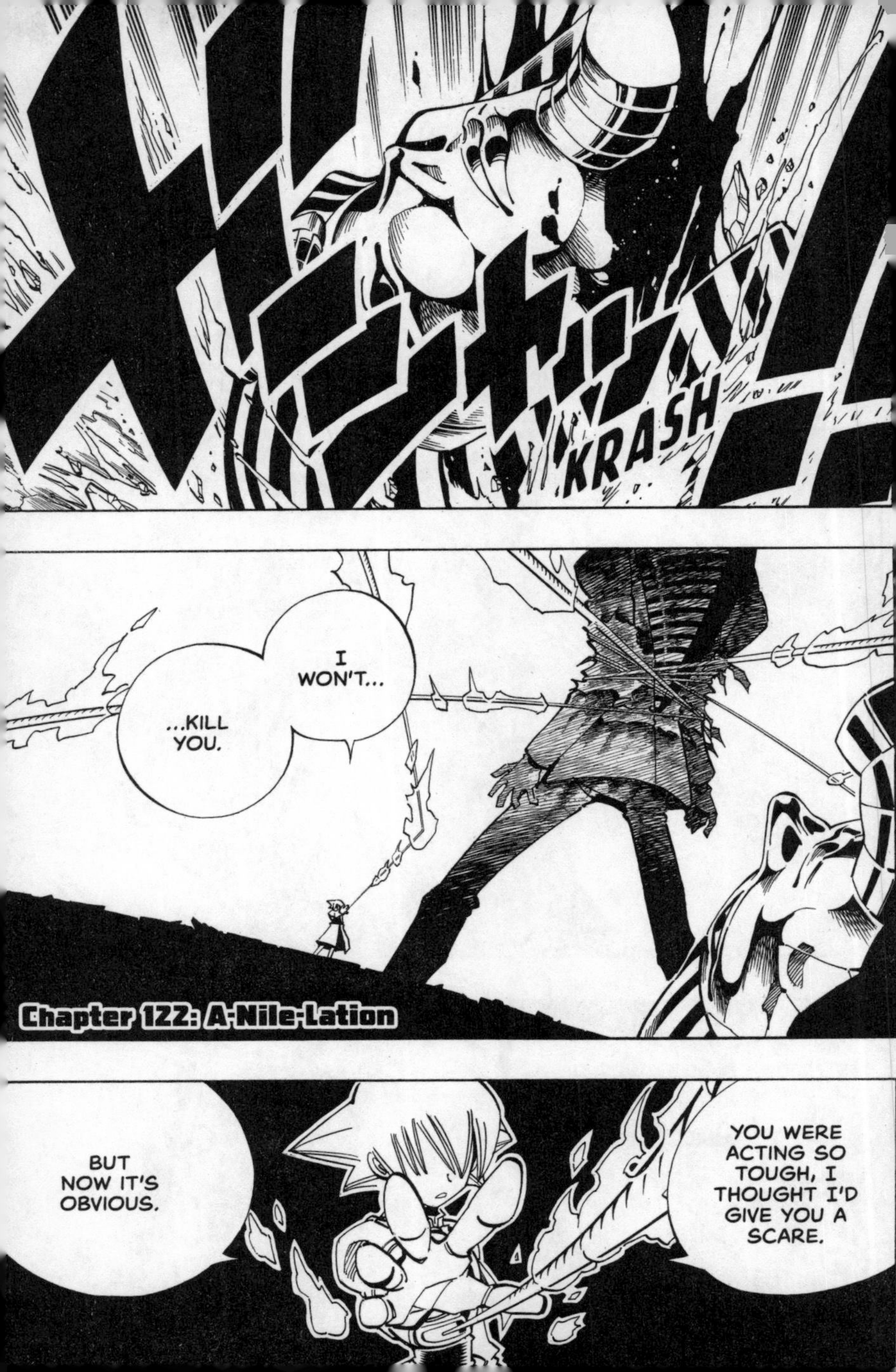
KRASH
I WON'T...
...KILL YOU.
YOU WERE ACTING SO TOUGH, I THOUGHT I'D GIVE YOU A SCARE.
BUT NOW IT'S OBVIOUS.

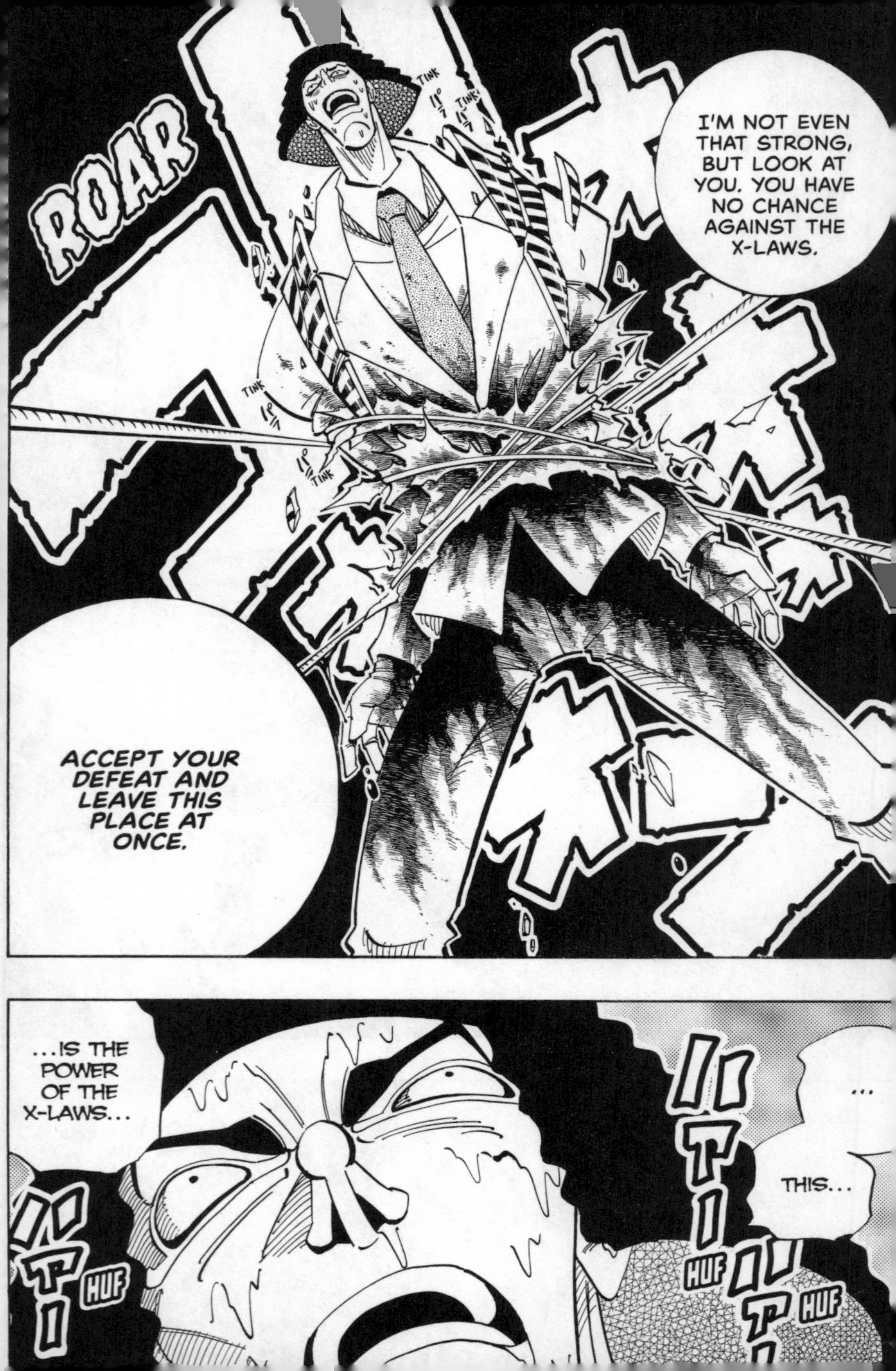
I'M NOT EVEN THAT STRONG, BUT LOOK AT YOU. YOU HAVE NO CHANCE AGAINST THE X-LAWS.
ROAR
TINK
TINK
TINK
TINK
ACCEPT YOUR DEFEAT AND LEAVE THIS PLACE AT ONCE.
...
THIS...
...IS THE POWER OF THE X-LAWS...
HUF
HUF
HUF

Chapter 122:

A-Nile-Lation

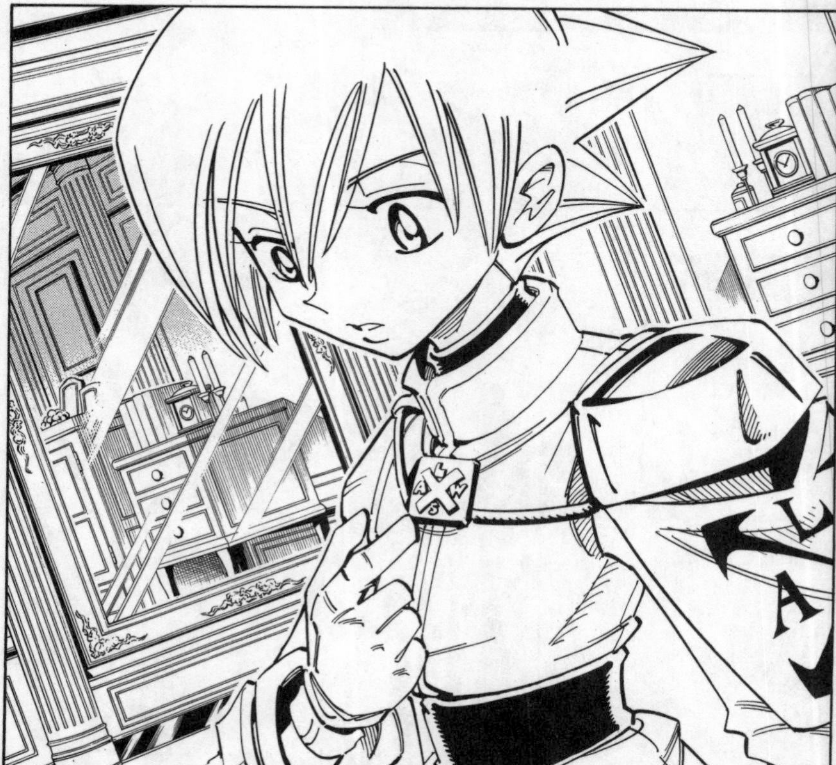

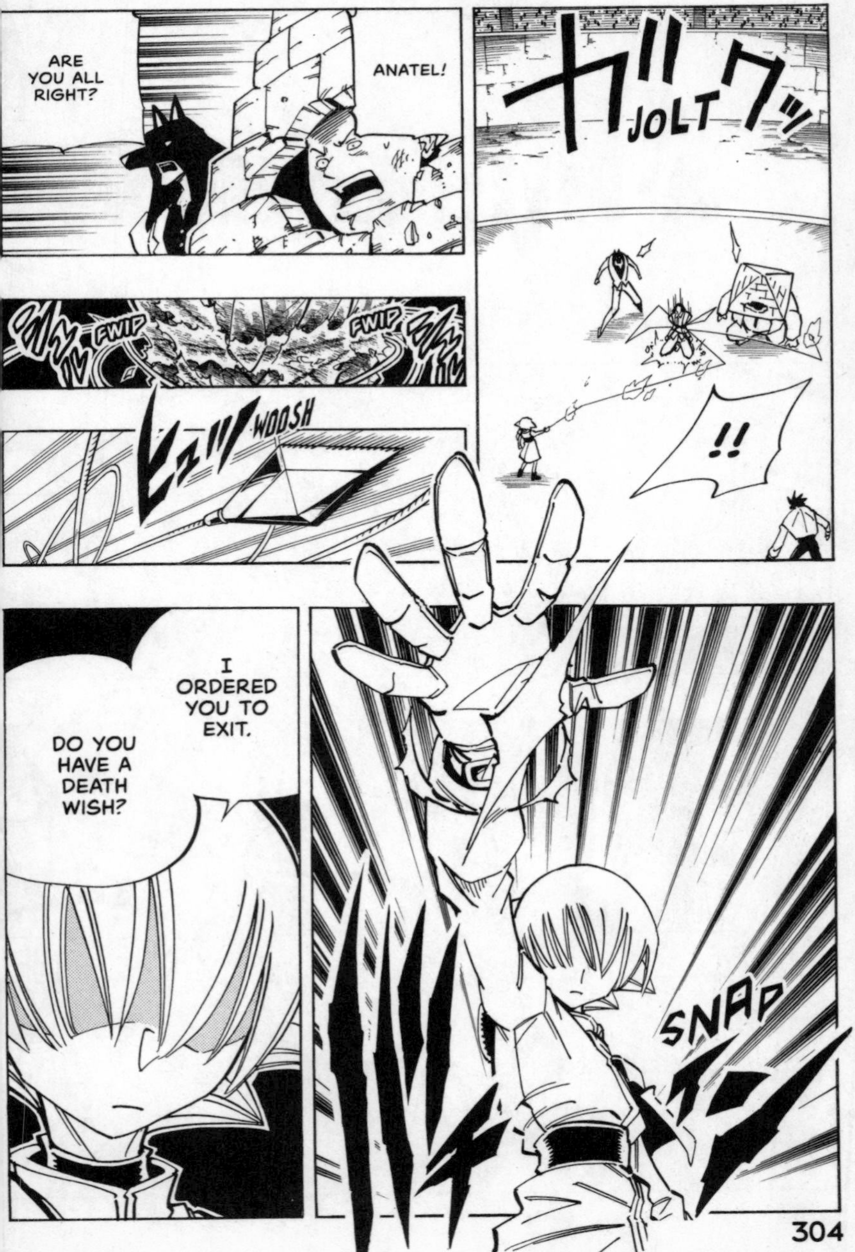
JOLT
!!
ANATEL!
ARE YOU ALL RIGHT?
FWIP
FWIP
WOOSH
SNAP
I ORDERED YOU TO EXIT.
DO YOU HAVE A DEATH WISH?

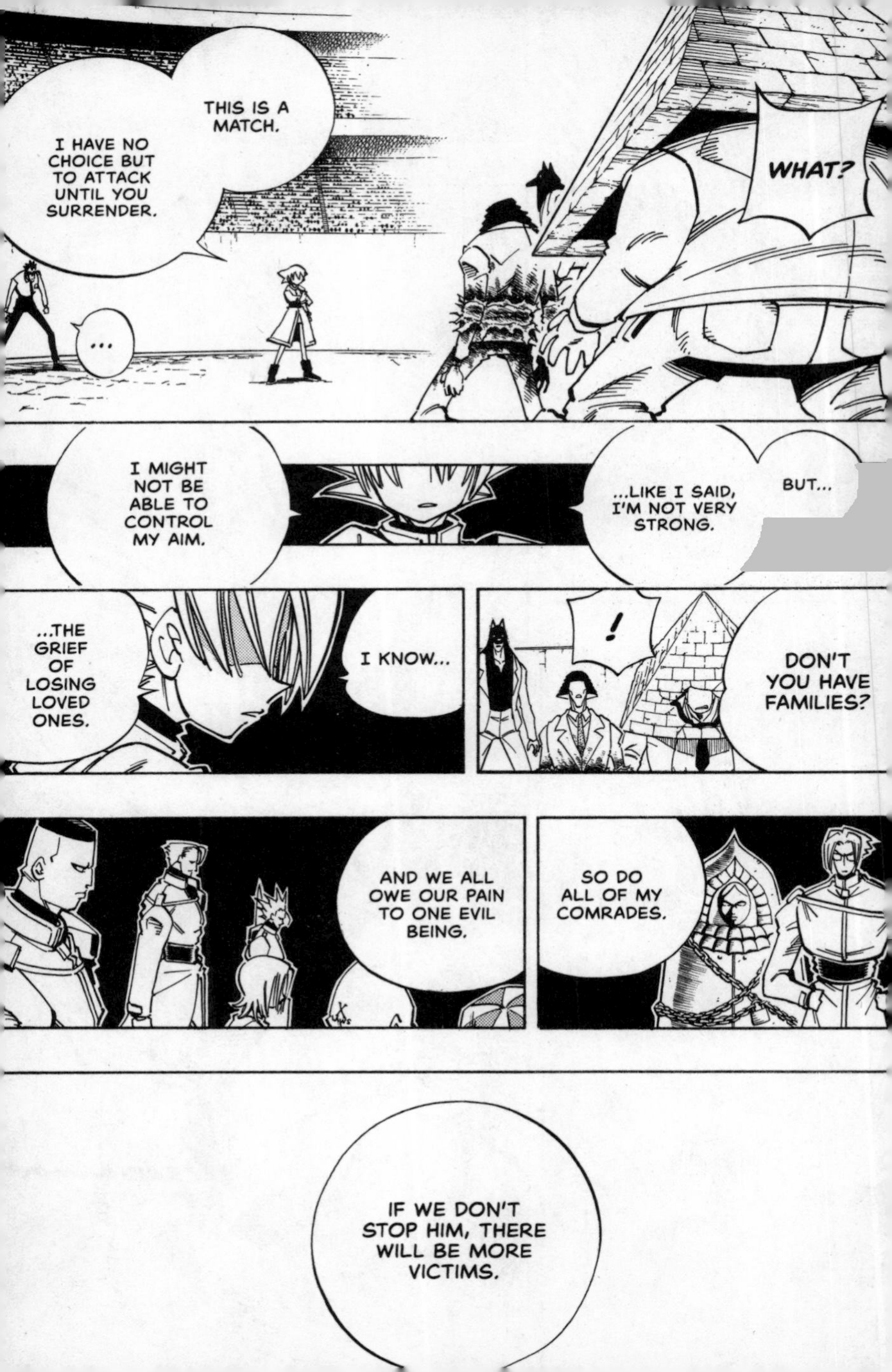
WHAT?
THIS IS A MATCH. I HAVE NO CHOICE BUT TO ATTACK UNTIL YOU SURRENDER.
...
BUT...
...LIKE I SAID, I'M NOT VERY STRONG.
I MIGHT NOT BE ABLE TO CONTROL MY AIM.
DON'T YOU HAVE FAMILIES?
!
I KNOW...
...THE GRIEF OF LOSING LOVED ONES.
SO DO ALL OF MY COMRADES.
AND WE ALL OWE OUR PAIN TO ONE EVIL BEING.
IF WE DON'T STOP HIM, THERE WILL BE MORE VICTIMS.

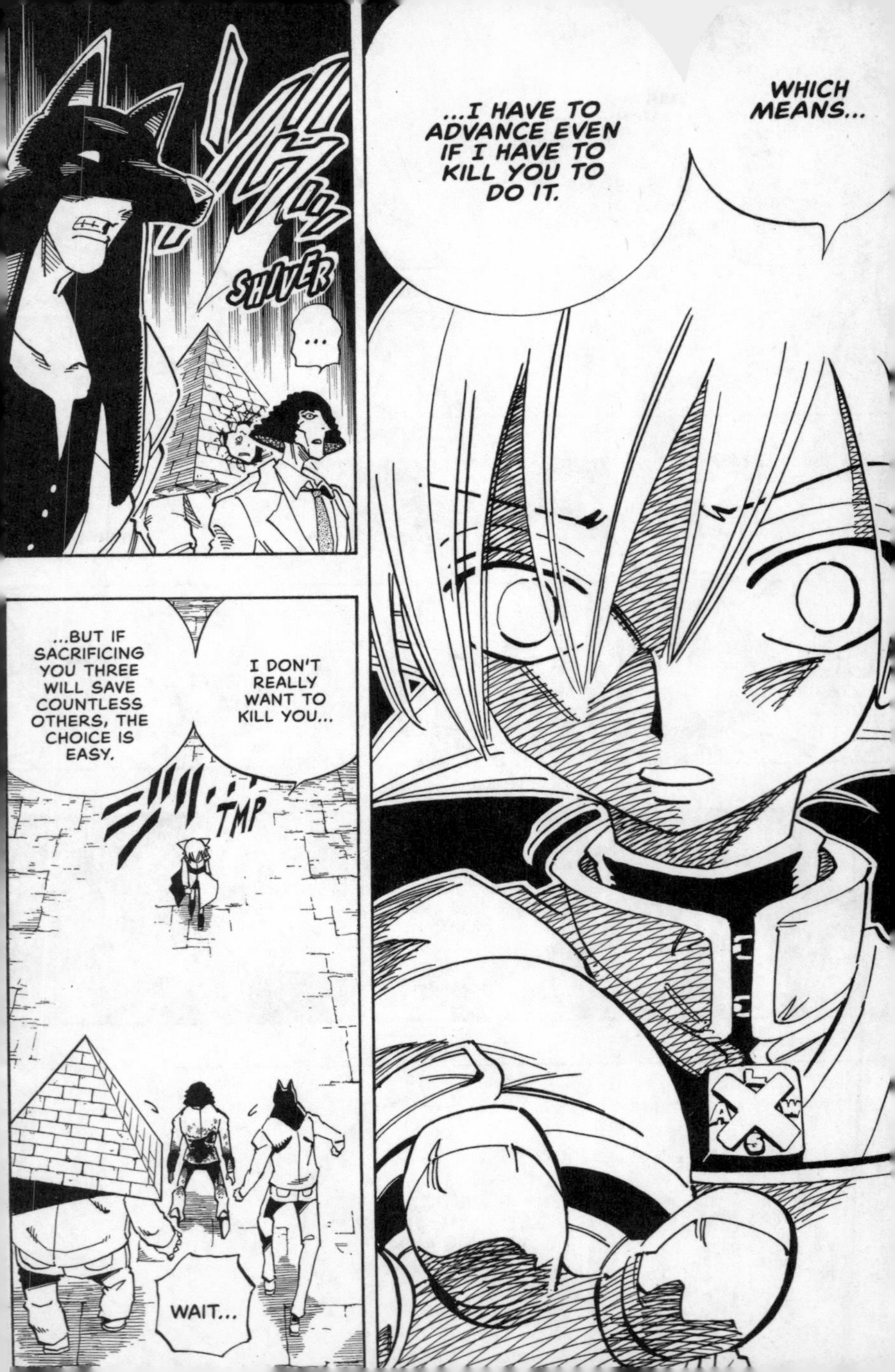
WHICH MEANS...
...I HAVE TO ADVANCE EVEN IF I HAVE TO KILL YOU TO DO IT.
SHIVER
...
I DON'T REALLY WANT TO KILL YOU...
...BUT IF SACRIFICING YOU THREE WILL SAVE COUNTLESS OTHERS, THE CHOICE IS EASY.
TMP
WAIT...

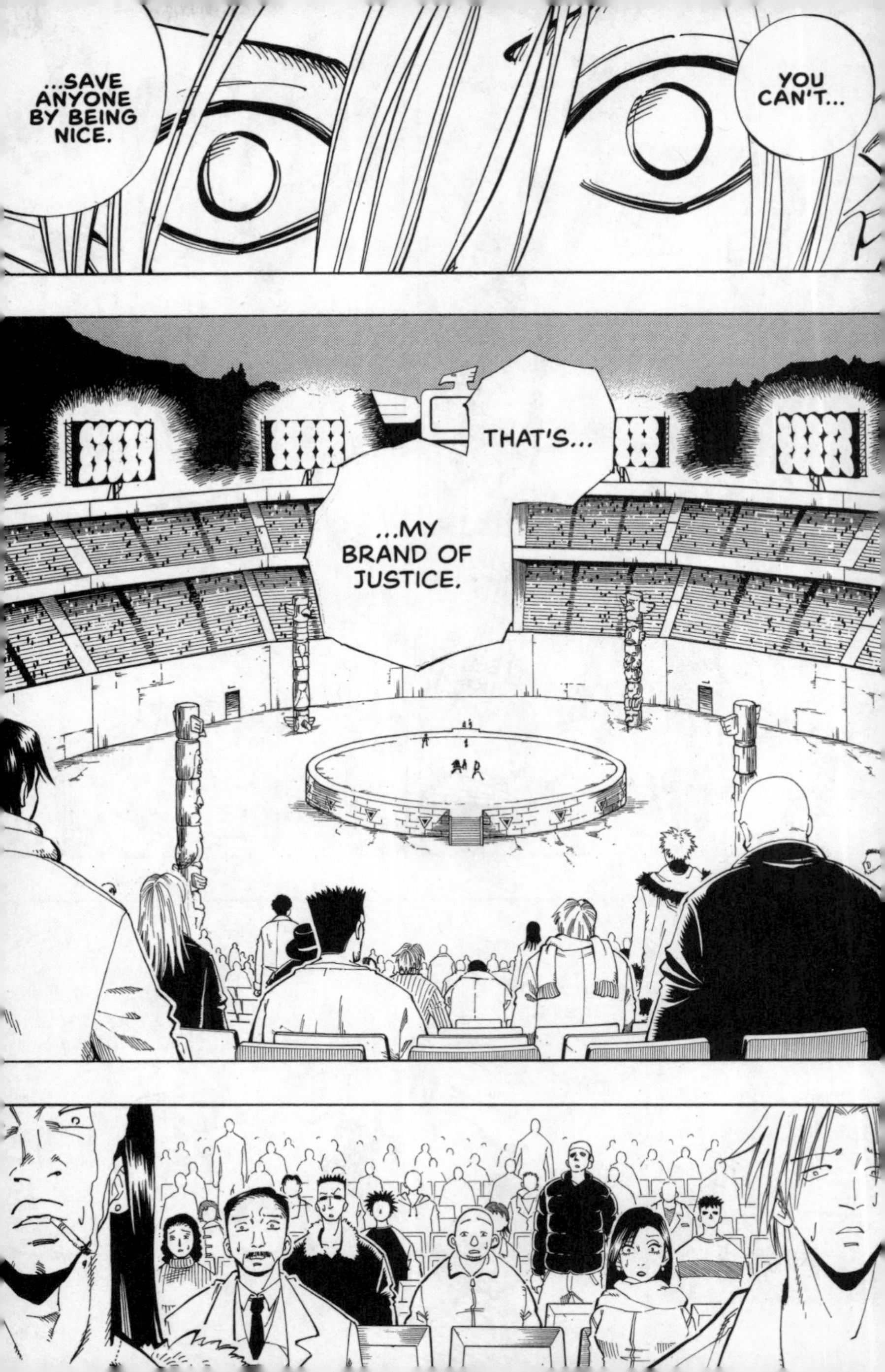
YOU CAN'T...
...SAVE ANYONE BY BEING NICE.
THAT'S...
...MY BRAND OF JUSTICE.

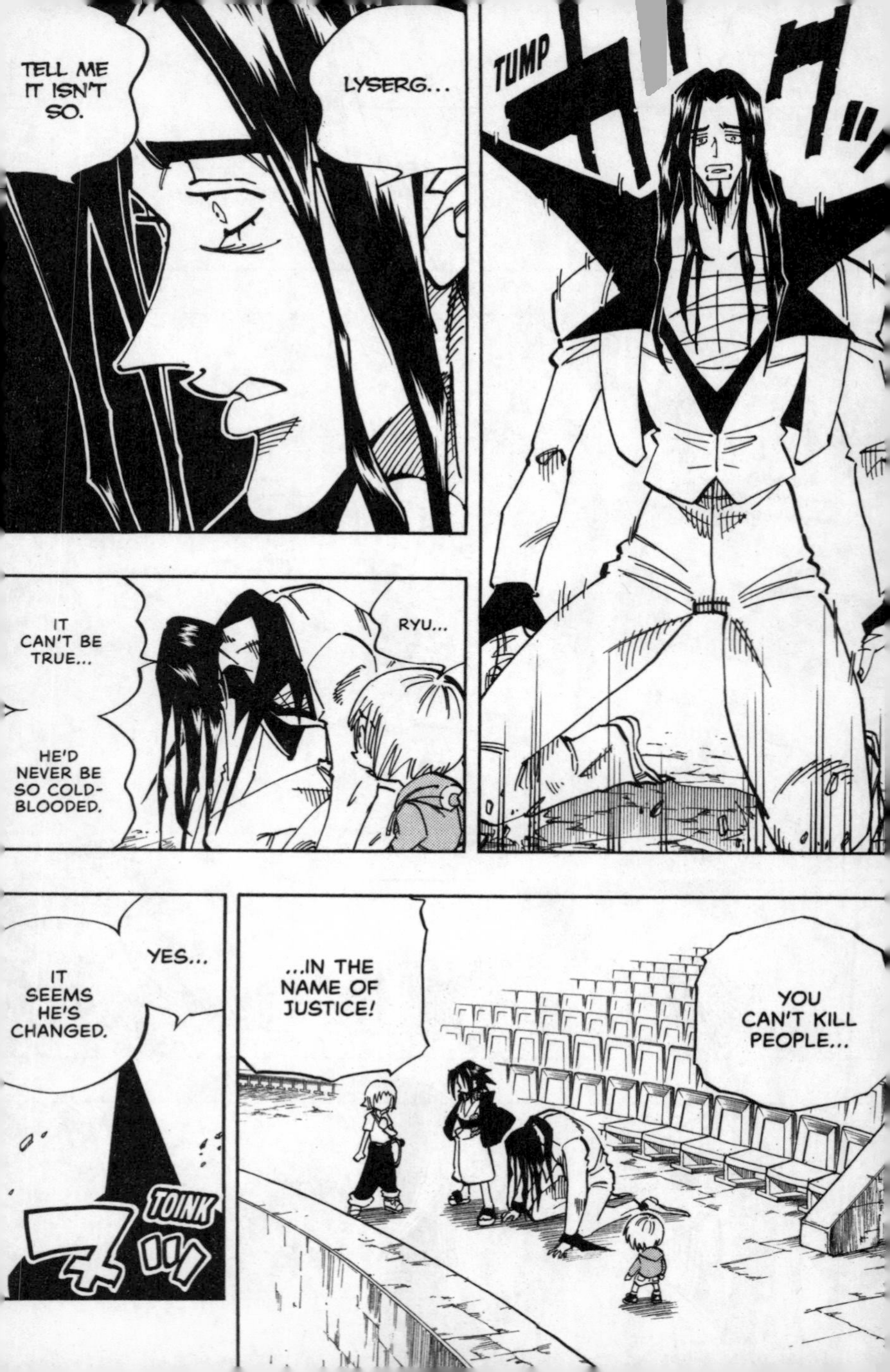
TUMP
LYSERG...
TELL ME IT ISN'T SO.
RYU...
IT CAN'T BE TRUE...
HE'D NEVER BE SO COLD-BLOODED.
YOU CAN'T KILL PEOPLE...
...IN THE NAME OF JUSTICE!
YES...
IT SEEMS HE'S CHANGED.
TOINK

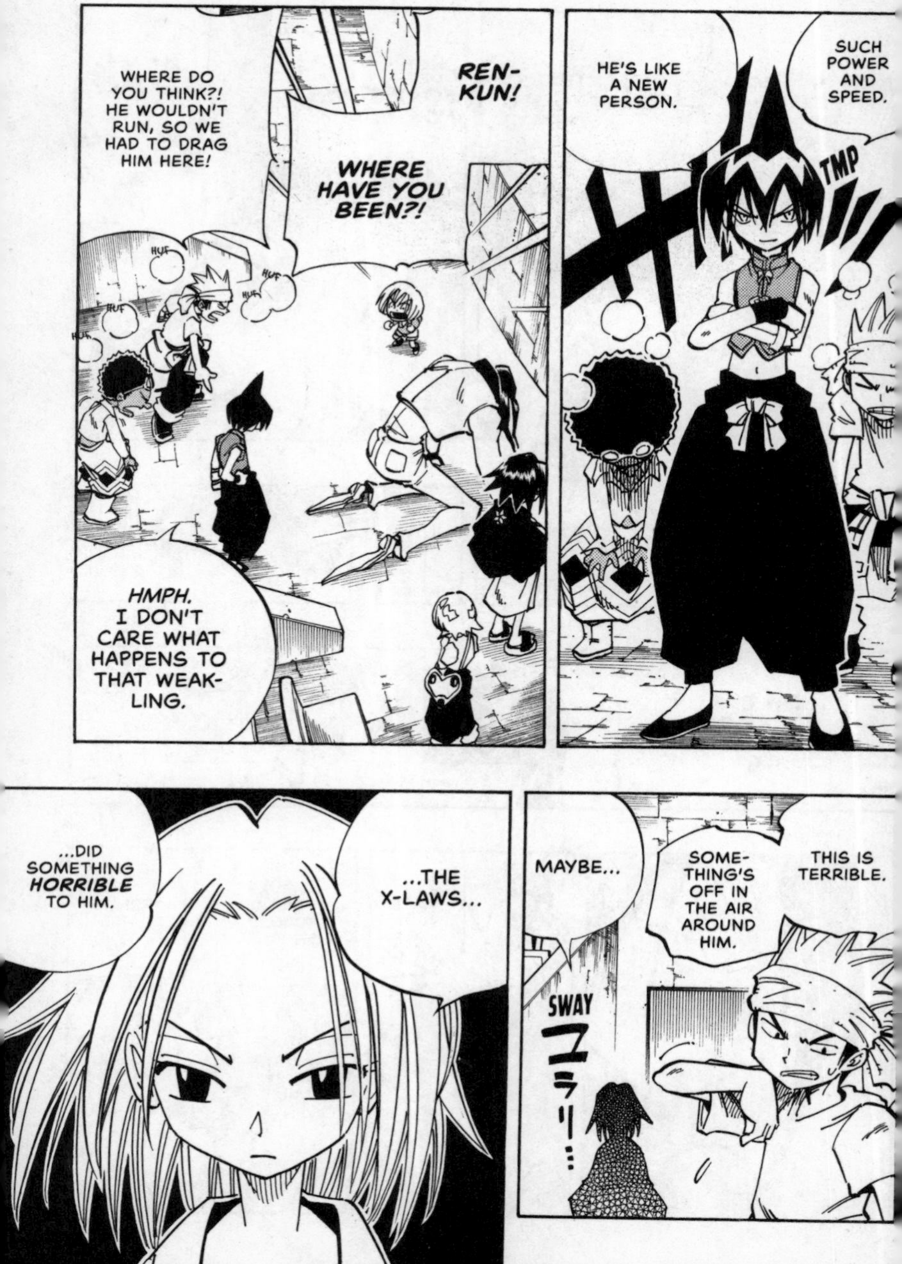

SUCH POWER AND SPEED.
HE'S LIKE A NEW PERSON.
TMP
REN-KUN!
WHERE HAVE YOU BEEN?!
WHERE DO YOU THINK?! HE WOULDN'T RUN, SO WE HAD TO DRAG HIM HERE!
HUF
HUF
HUF
HUF
HUF
HMPH. I DON'T CARE WHAT HAPPENS TO THAT WEAK-LING.
THIS IS TERRIBLE.
SOME-THING'S OFF IN THE AIR AROUND HIM.
MAYBE...
SWAY
ユラリ
...THE X-LAWS...
...DID SOMETHING HORRIBLE TO HIM.

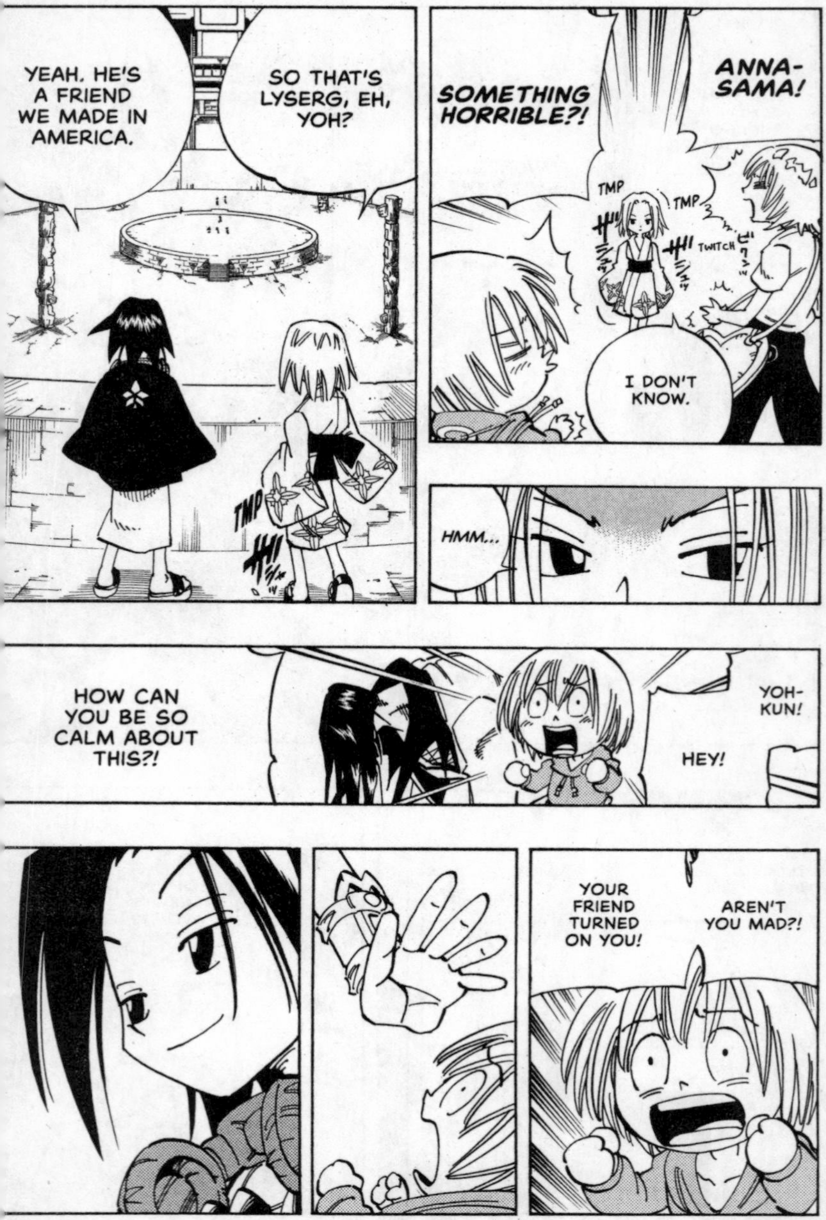
ANNA-SAMA!
SOMETHING HORRIBLE?!
TMP
TMP
TWITCH
I DON'T KNOW.
HMM...
SO THAT'S LYSERG, EH, YOH?
YEAH. HE'S A FRIEND WE MADE IN AMERICA.
TMP
YOH-KUN!
HEY!
HOW CAN YOU BE SO CALM ABOUT THIS?!
AREN'T YOU MAD?!
YOUR FRIEND TURNED ON YOU!

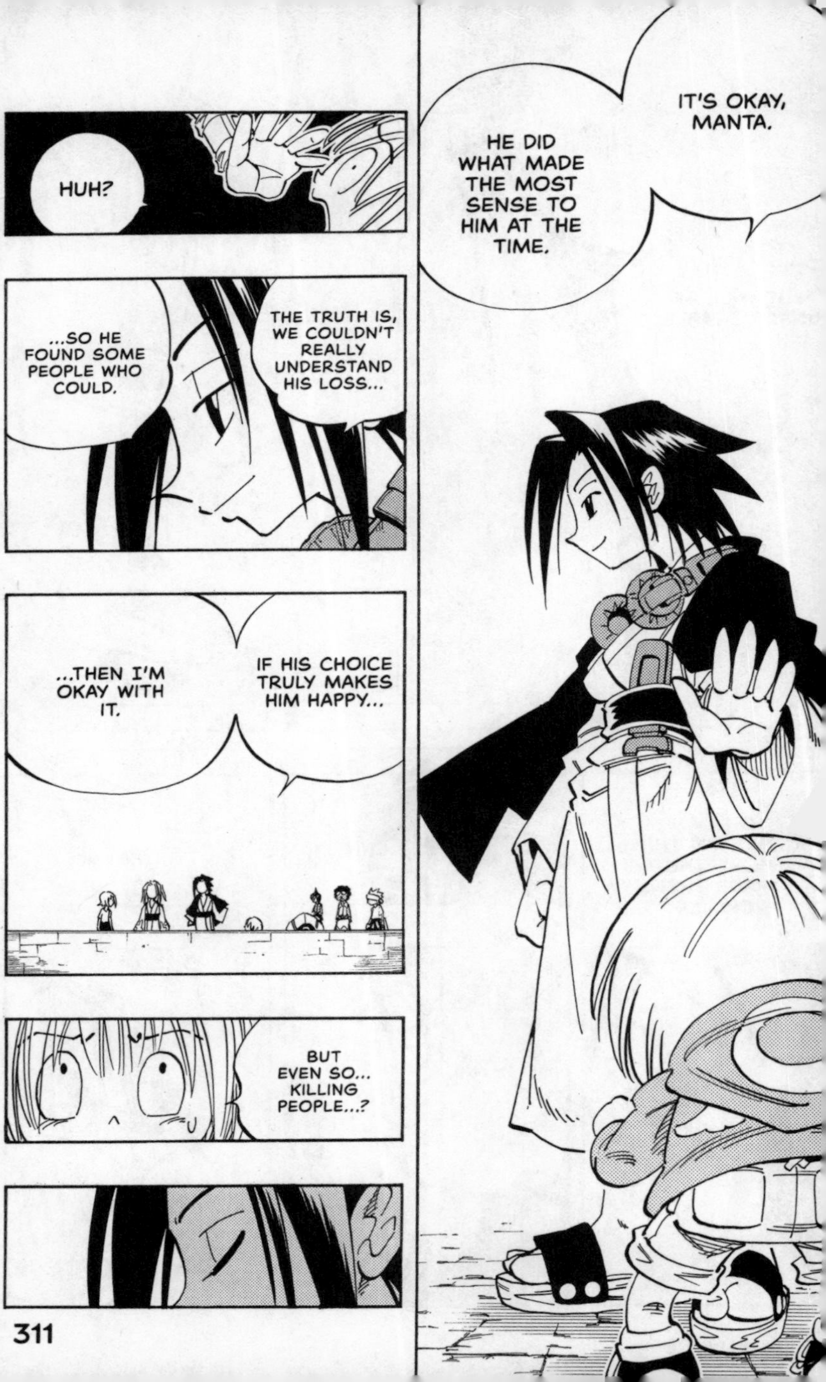
HUH?
THE TRUTH IS, WE COULDN'T REALLY UNDERSTAND HIS LOSS...
...SO HE FOUND SOME PEOPLE WHO COULD.
IF HIS CHOICE TRULY MAKES HIM HAPPY...
...THEN I'M OKAY WITH IT.
BUT EVEN SO... KILLING PEOPLE...?
IT'S OKAY, MANTA.
HE DID WHAT MADE THE MOST SENSE TO HIM AT THE TIME.

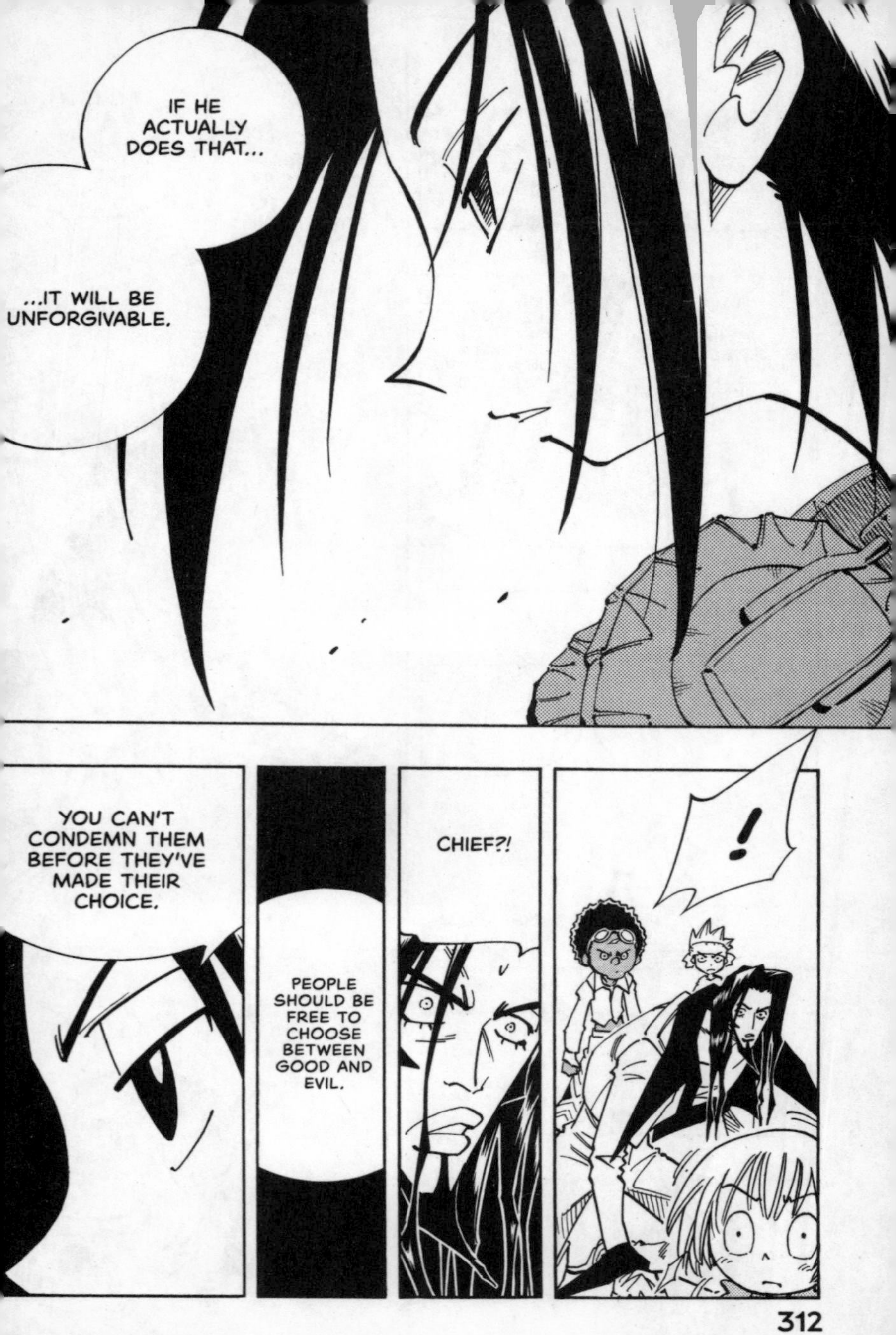
IF HE ACTUALLY DOES THAT...
...IT WILL BE UNFORGIVABLE.
!
CHIEF?!
PEOPLE SHOULD BE FREE TO CHOOSE BETWEEN GOOD AND EVIL.
YOU CAN'T CONDEMN THEM BEFORE THEY'VE MADE THEIR CHOICE.

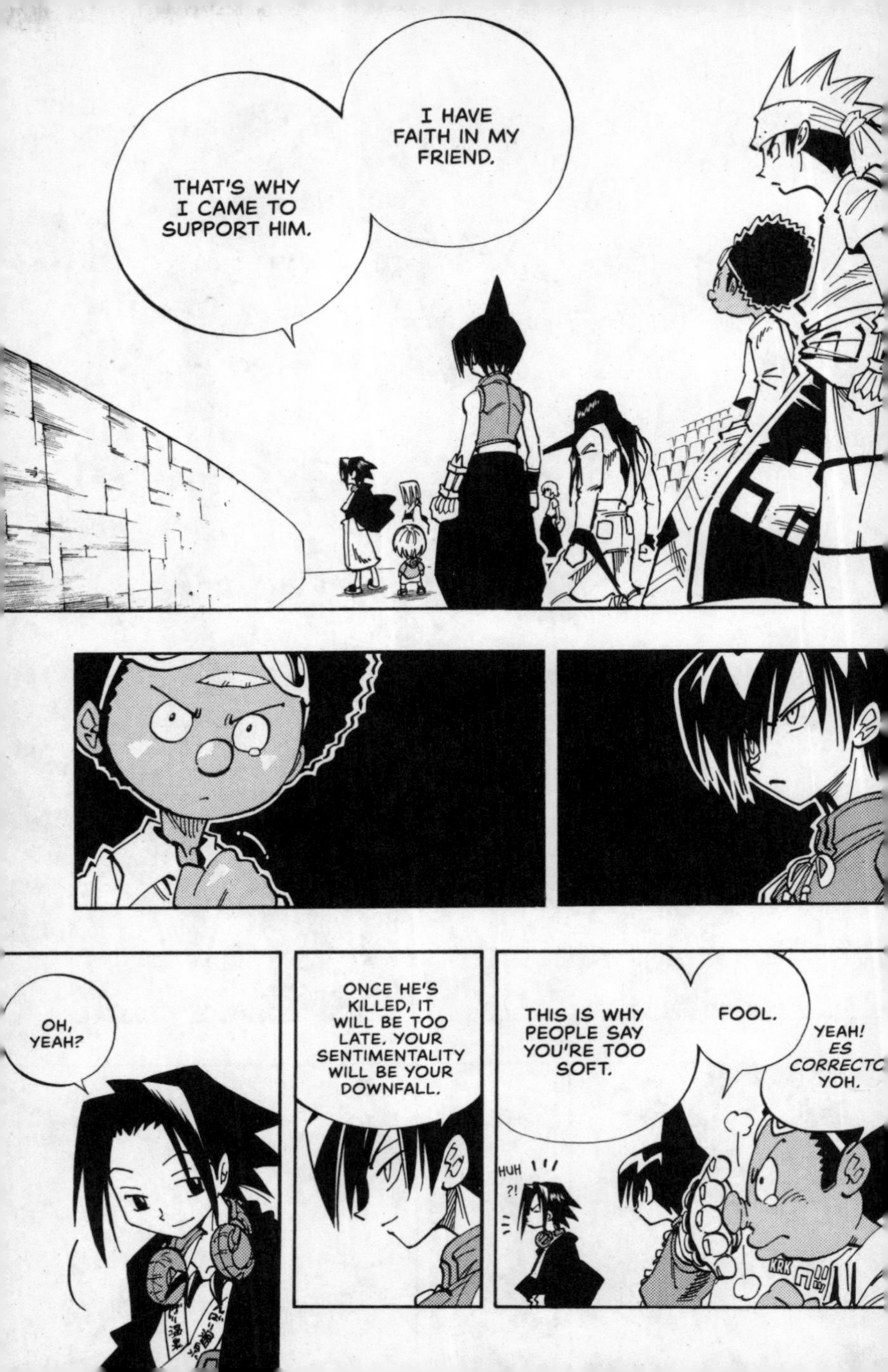
I HAVE FAITH IN MY FRIEND.
THAT'S WHY I CAME TO SUPPORT HIM.
YEAH! ES CORRECTO YOH.
FOOL.
THIS IS WHY PEOPLE SAY YOU'RE TOO SOFT.
KRK
HUH ?!
ONCE HE'S KILLED, IT WILL BE TOO LATE. YOUR SENTIMENTALITY WILL BE YOUR DOWNFALL.
OH, YEAH?

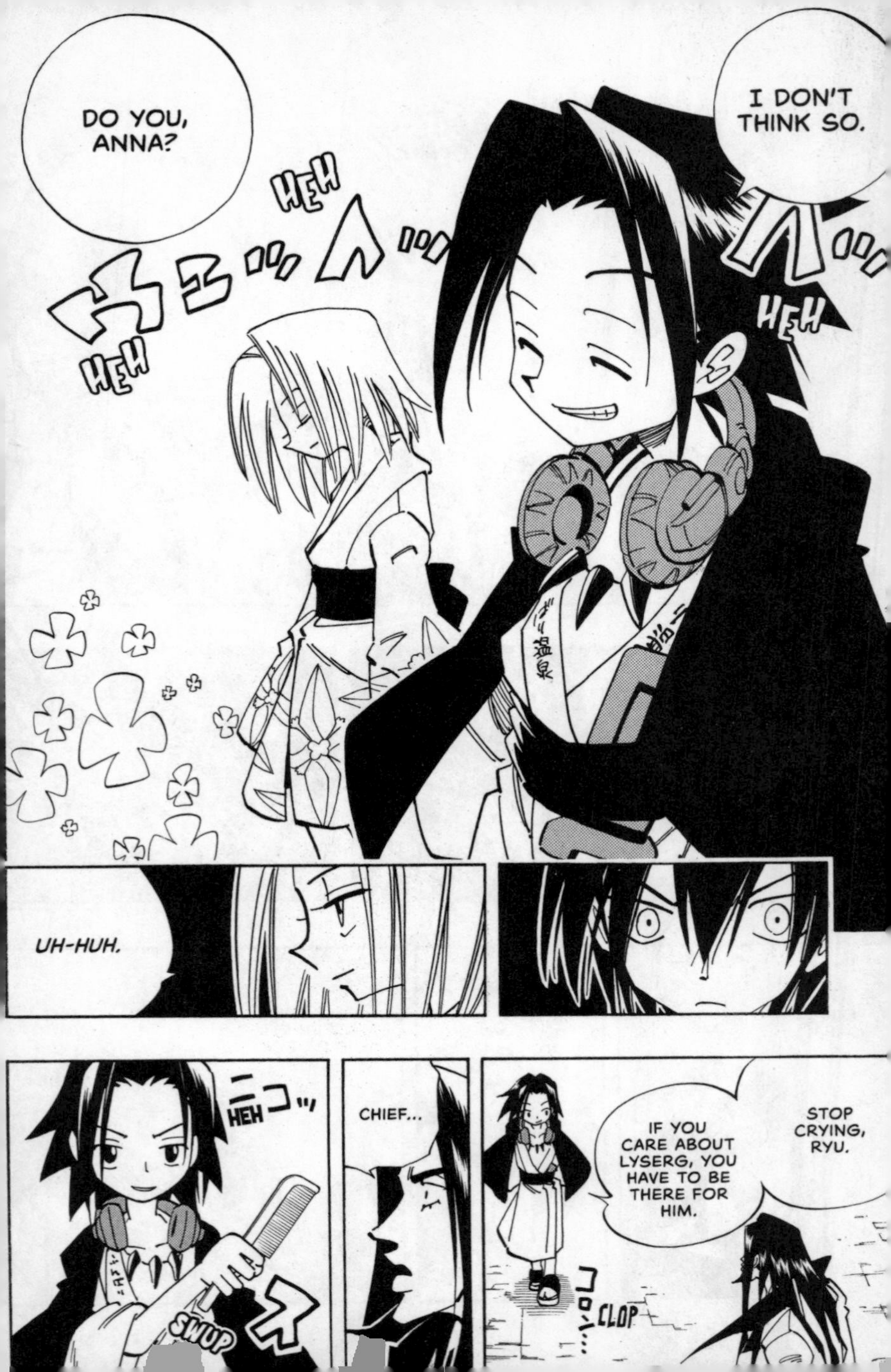
I DON'T THINK SO.
HEH
HEH
DO YOU, ANNA?
HEH
HEH
UH-HUH.
STOP CRYING, RYU.
IF YOU CARE ABOUT LYSERG, YOU HAVE TO BE THERE FOR HIM.
CLOP
CHIEF...
HEH
SWUP

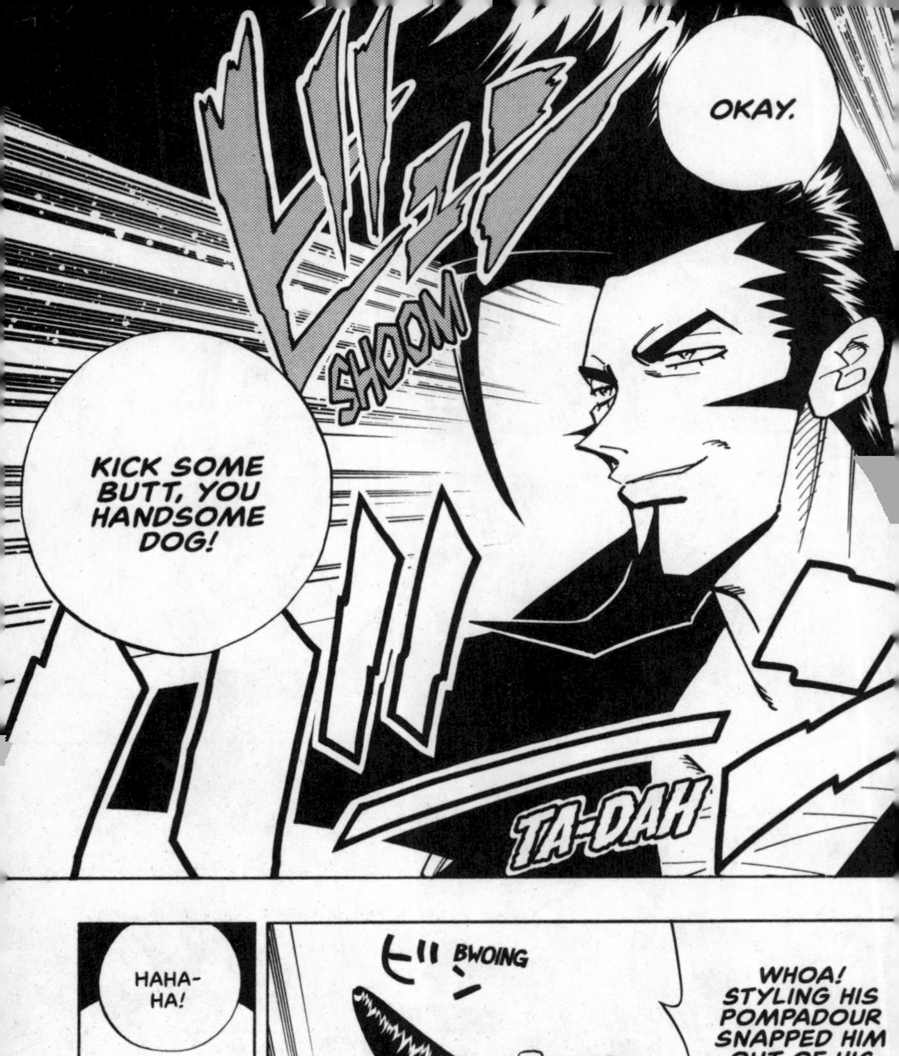
OKAY.
SHOOM
KICK SOME BUTT, YOU HANDSOME DOG!
TA-DAH

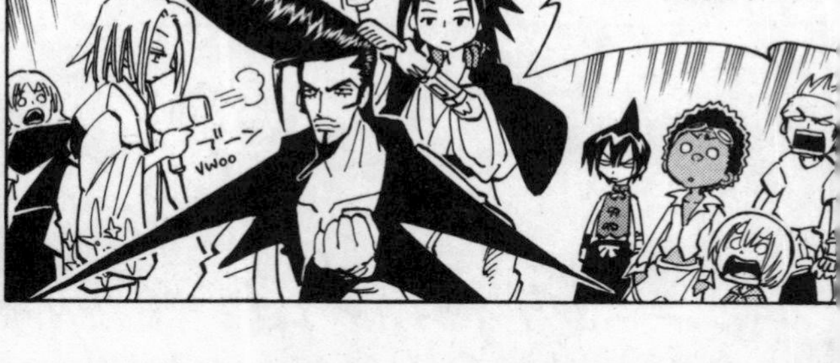
BWOING
WHOA! STYLING HIS POMPADOUR SNAPPED HIM OUT OF HIS FUNK!
VWOO

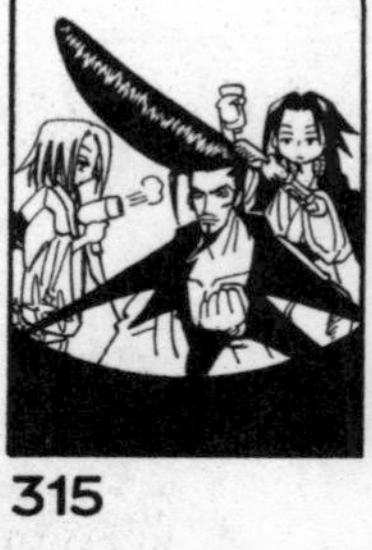
HAHA-HA!

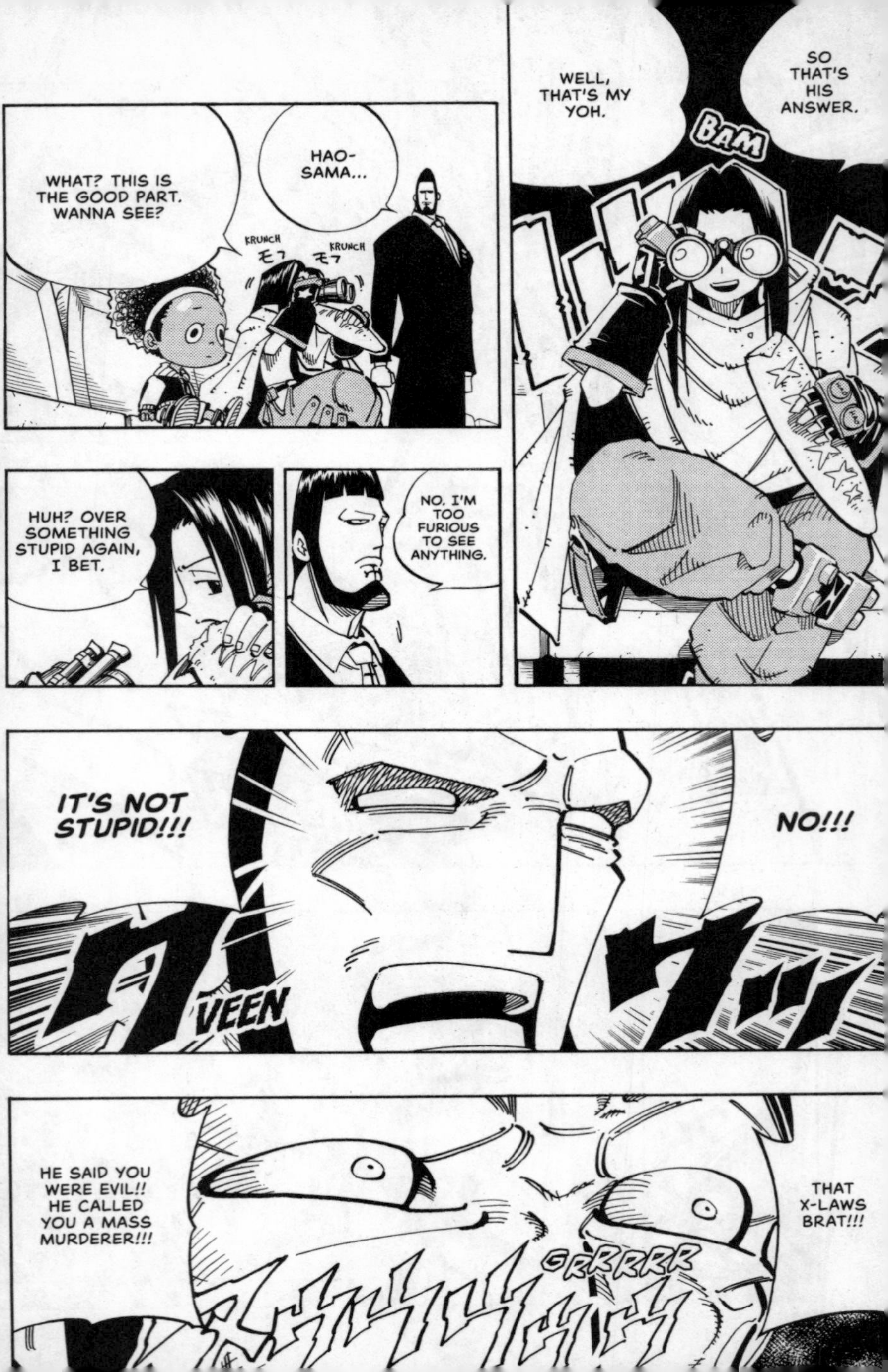
SO THAT'S HIS ANSWER.
WELL, THAT'S MY YOH.
BAM
HAO-SAMA...
WHAT? THIS IS THE GOOD PART. WANNA SEE?
KRUNCH
モフ
KRUNCH
モフ
NO. I'M TOO FURIOUS TO SEE ANYTHING.
HUH? OVER SOMETHING STUPID AGAIN, I BET.
NO!!!
IT'S NOT STUPID!!!
VEEN
THAT X-LAWS BRAT!!!
HE SAID YOU WERE EVIL!! HE CALLED YOU A MASS MURDERER!!!
GRRRRR

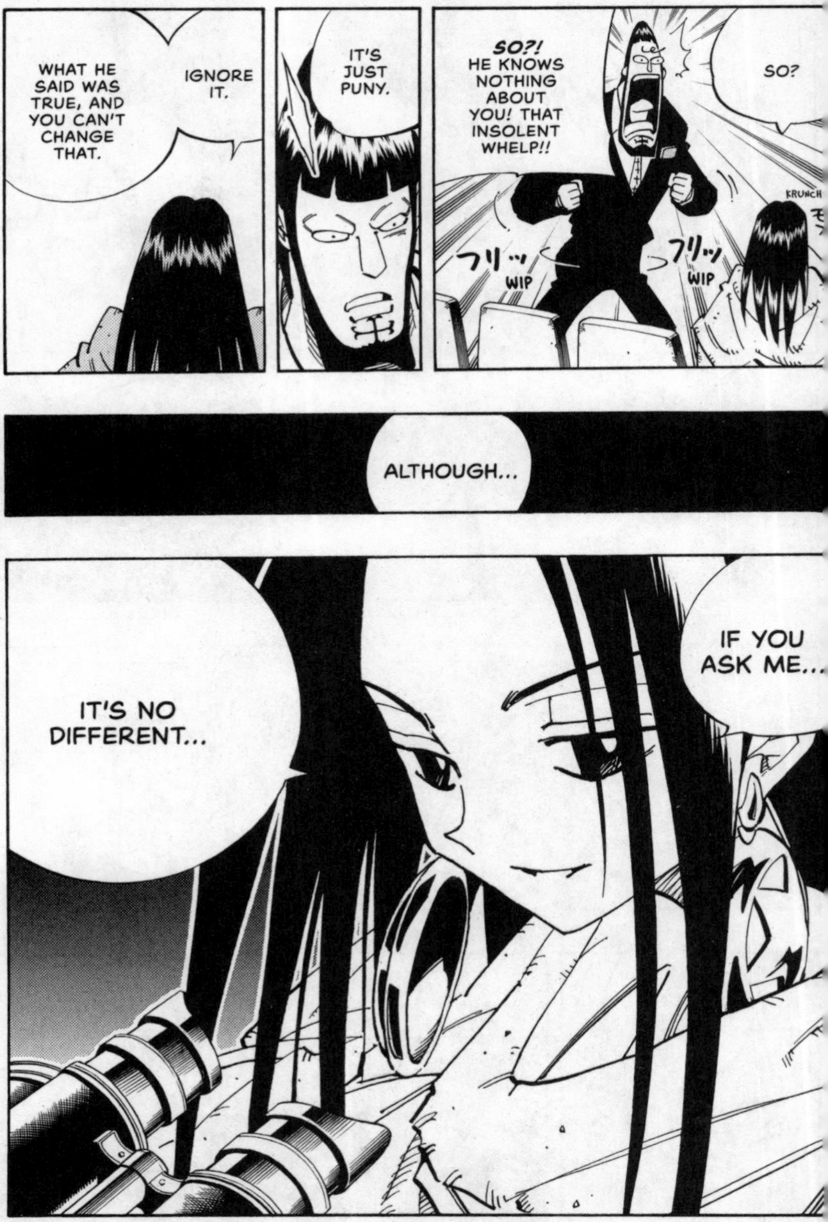
SO?
KRUNCH
SO?! HE KNOWS NOTHING ABOUT YOU! THAT INSOLENT WHELP!!
フリッ
WIP
フリッ
WIP
IT'S JUST PUNY.
IGNORE IT.
WHAT HE SAID WAS TRUE, AND YOU CAN'T CHANGE THAT.
ALTHOUGH...
IF YOU ASK ME...
IT'S NO DIFFERENT...

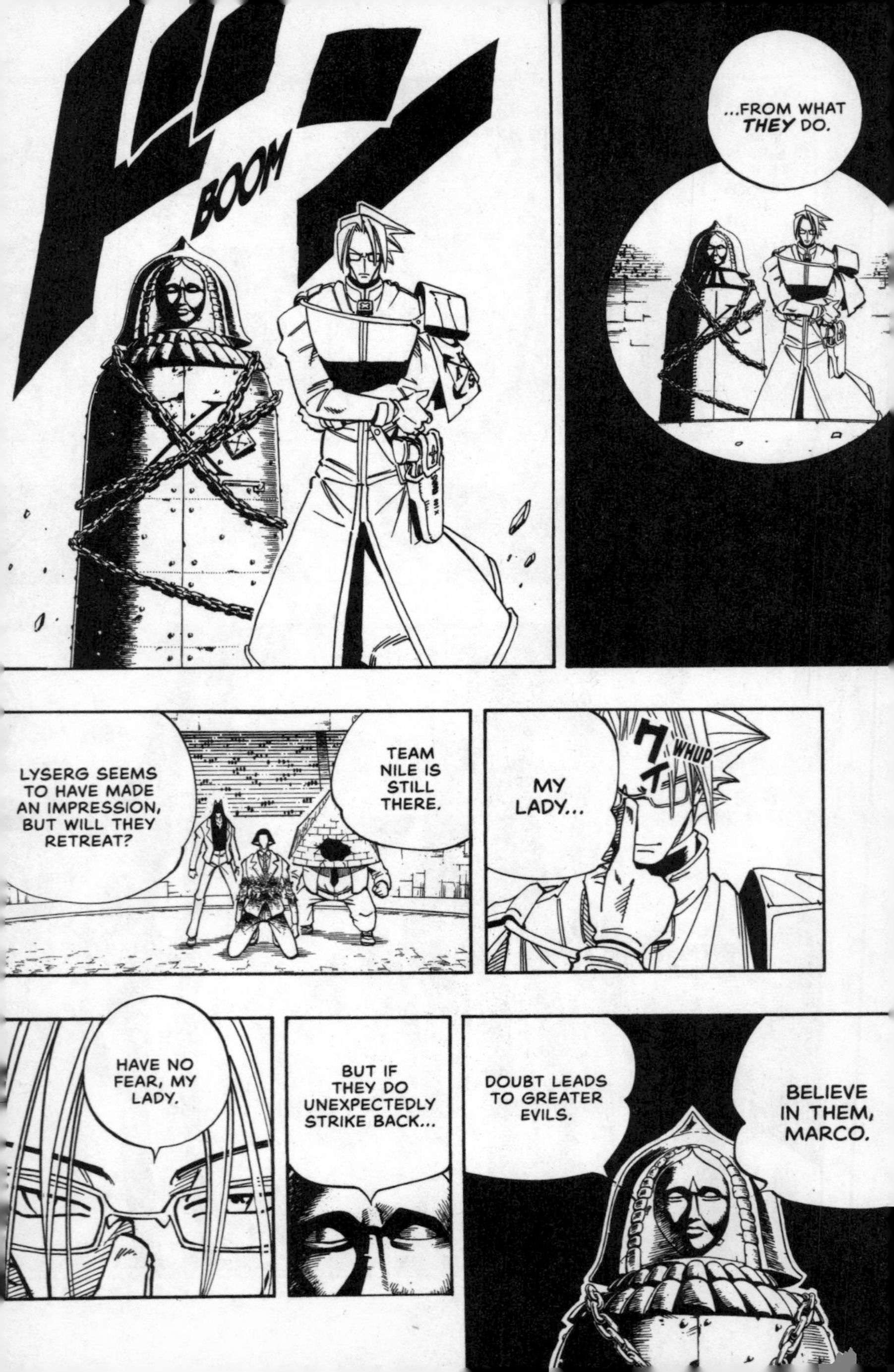
...FROM WHAT THEY DO.
BOOM
MY LADY...
WHUP
TEAM NILE IS STILL THERE.
LYSERG SEEMS TO HAVE MADE AN IMPRESSION, BUT WILL THEY RETREAT?
BELIEVE IN THEM, MARCO.
DOUBT LEADS TO GREATER EVILS.
BUT IF THEY DO UNEXPECTEDLY STRIKE BACK...
HAVE NO FEAR, MY LADY.

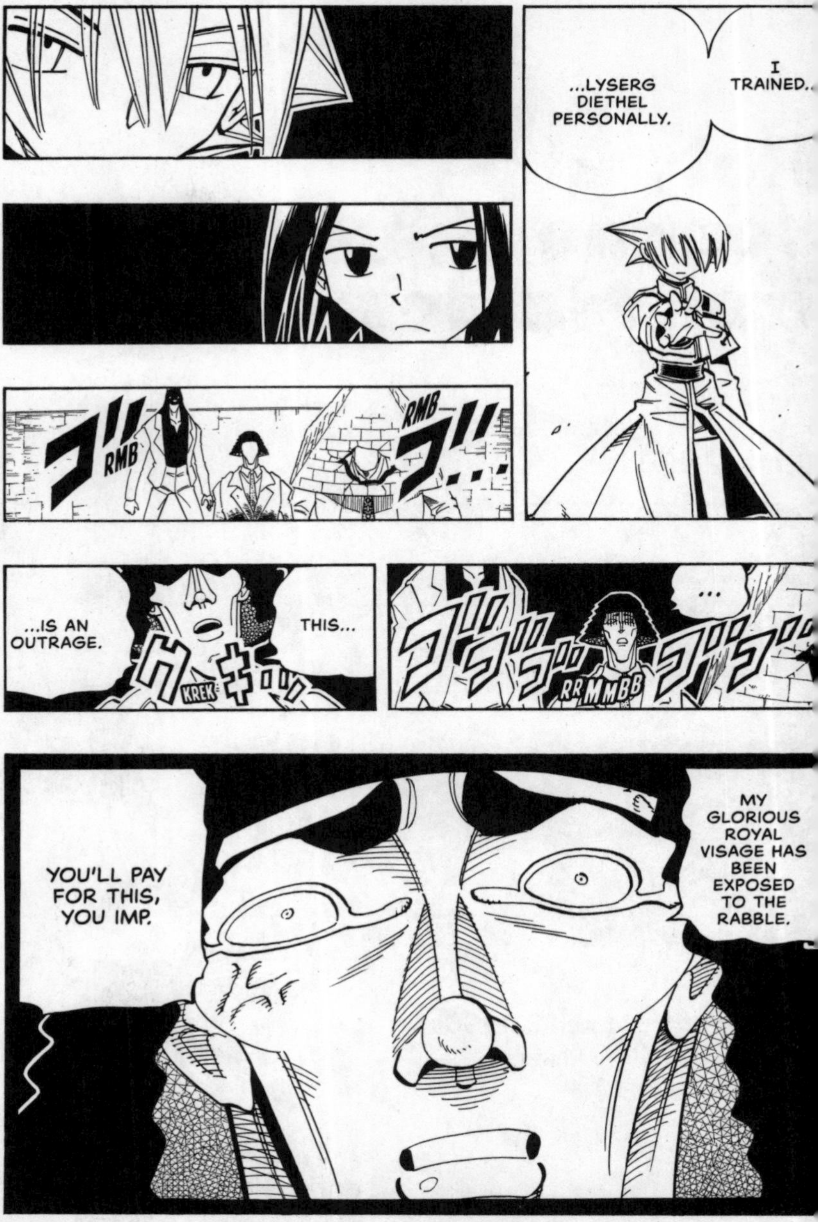
I TRAINED...
...LYSERG DIETHEL PERSONALLY.
RMB
RMB
...
RRMMBB
THIS...
KREK
...IS AN OUTRAGE.
MY GLORIOUS ROYAL VISAGE HAS BEEN EXPOSED TO THE RABBLE.
YOU'LL PAY FOR THIS, YOU IMP.

SHAMAN KING CHARACTER FILE No.68

Holy Girl Jeanne the Iron Maiden

June 2001

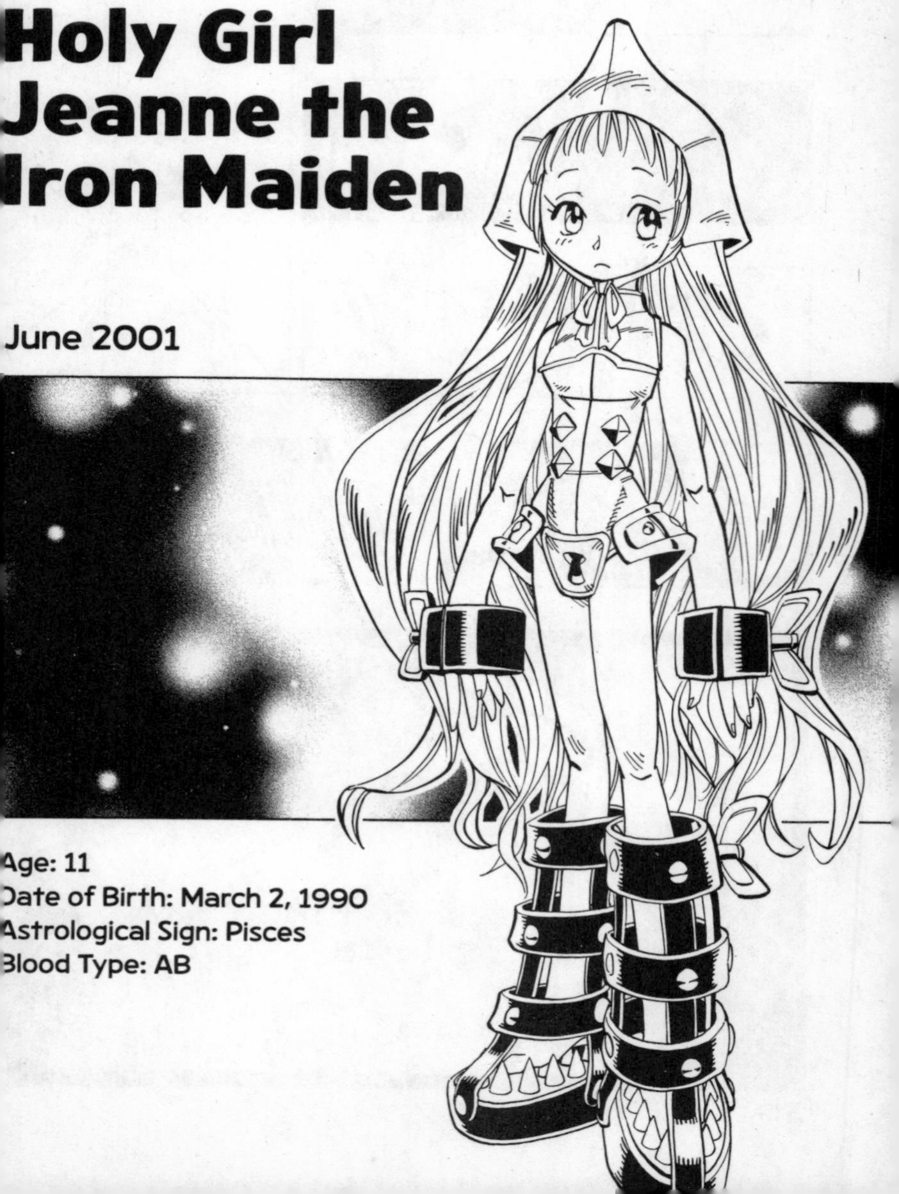

Age: 11
Date of Birth: March 2, 1990
Astrological Sign: Pisces
Blood Type: AB

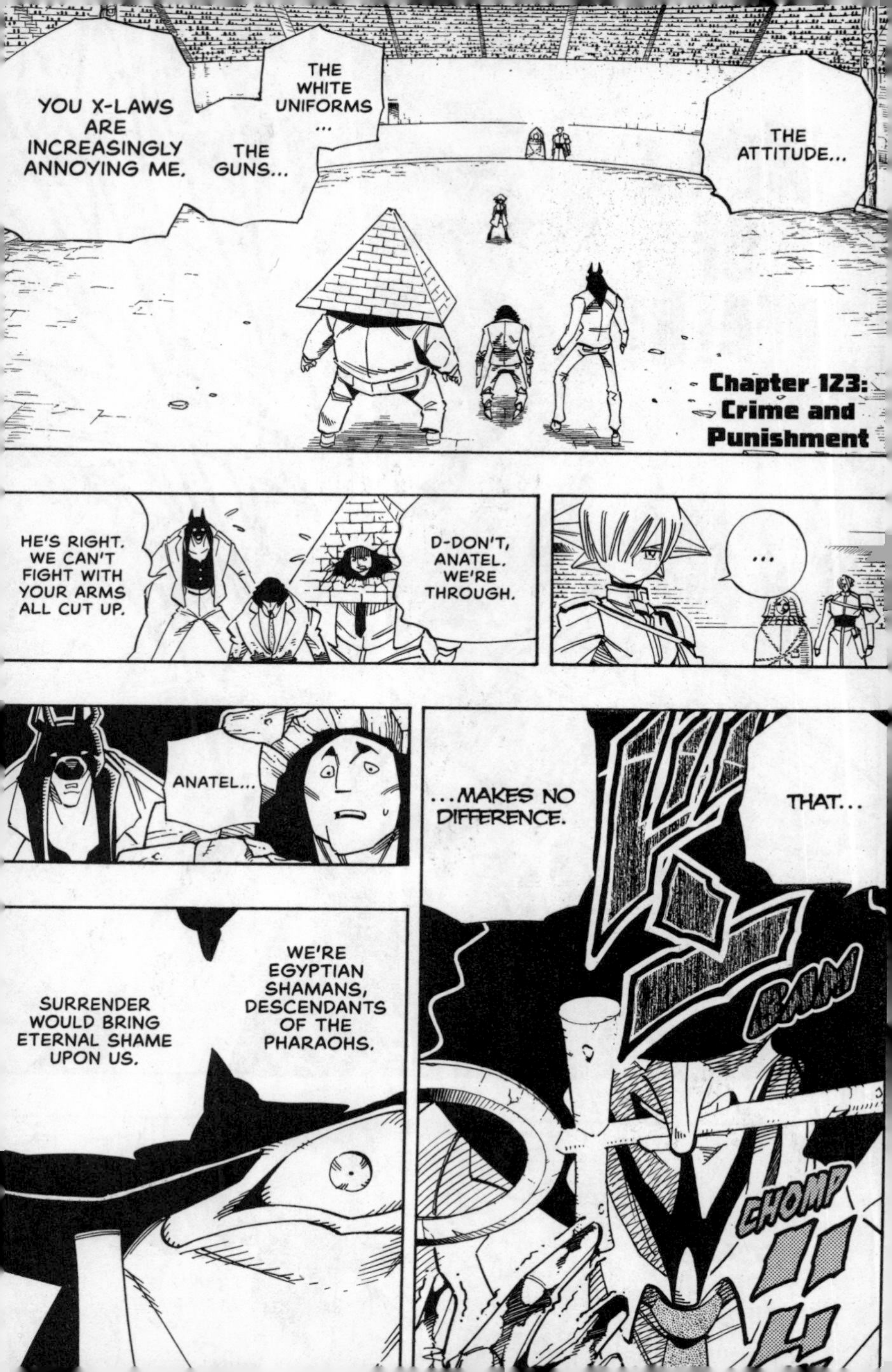
THE ATTITUDE...
THE WHITE UNIFORMS ...
THE GUNS...
YOU X-LAWS ARE INCREASINGLY ANNOYING ME.
Chapter 123: Crime and Punishment
...
D-DON'T, ANATEL. WE'RE THROUGH.
HE'S RIGHT. WE CAN'T FIGHT WITH YOUR ARMS ALL CUT UP.
THAT...
...MAKES NO DIFFERENCE.
BAM
CHOMP
ANATEL...
WE'RE EGYPTIAN SHAMANS, DESCENDANTS OF THE PHARAOHS.
SURRENDER WOULD BRING ETERNAL SHAME UPON US.

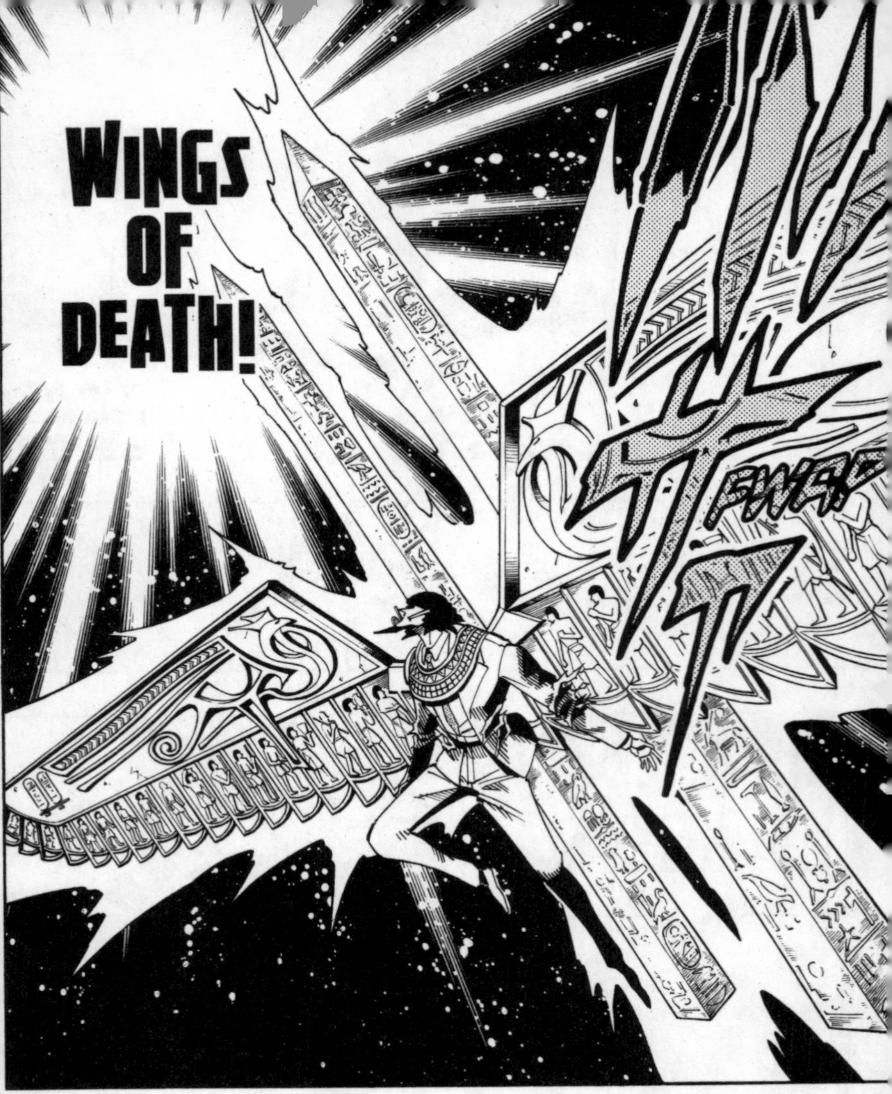
WINGS OF DEATH!
FWAP
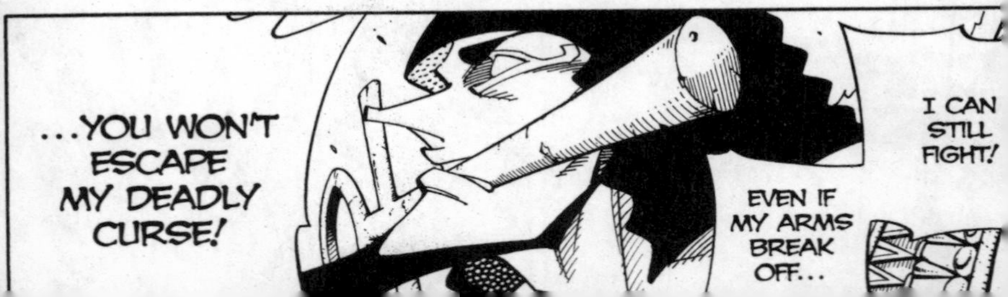
I CAN STILL FIGHT!
EVEN IF MY ARMS BREAK OFF...
...YOU WON'T ESCAPE MY DEADLY CURSE!

Chapter 123:

Crime and Punishment

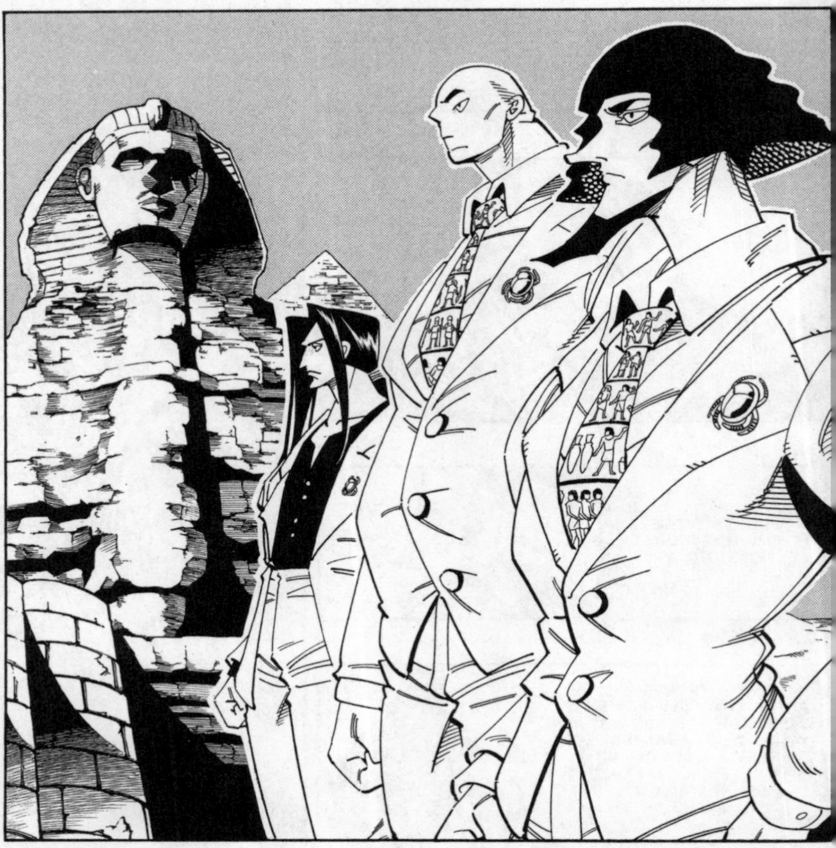

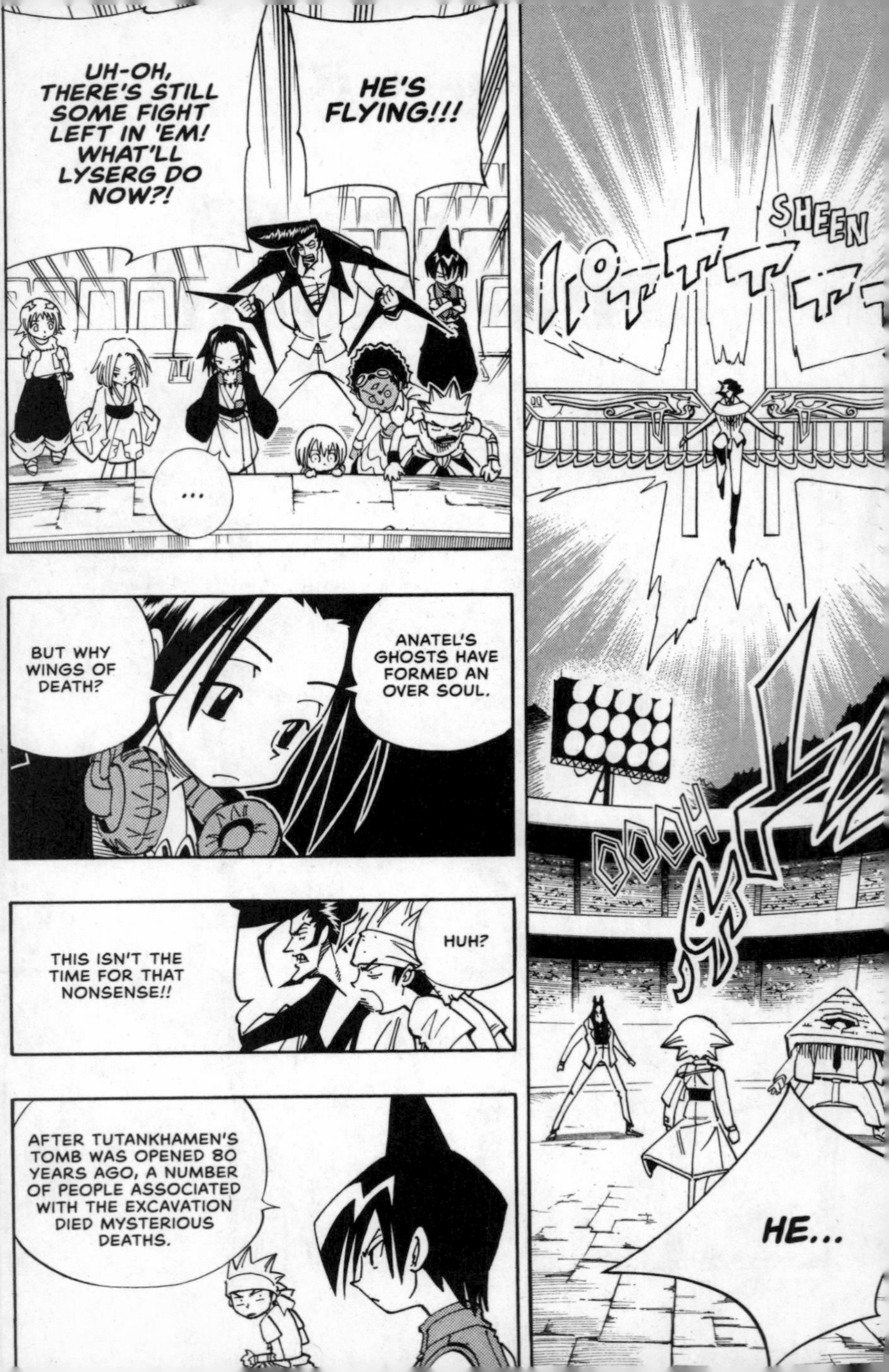
SHEEN
OOOH
HE...
HE'S FLYING!!!
UH-OH, THERE'S STILL SOME FIGHT LEFT IN 'EM! WHAT'LL LYSERG DO NOW?!
...
ANATEL'S GHOSTS HAVE FORMED AN OVER SOUL.
BUT WHY WINGS OF DEATH?
HUH?
THIS ISN'T THE TIME FOR THAT NONSENSE!!
AFTER TUTANKHAMEN'S TOMB WAS OPENED 80 YEARS AGO, A NUMBER OF PEOPLE ASSOCIATED WITH THE EXCAVATION DIED MYSTERIOUS DEATHS.

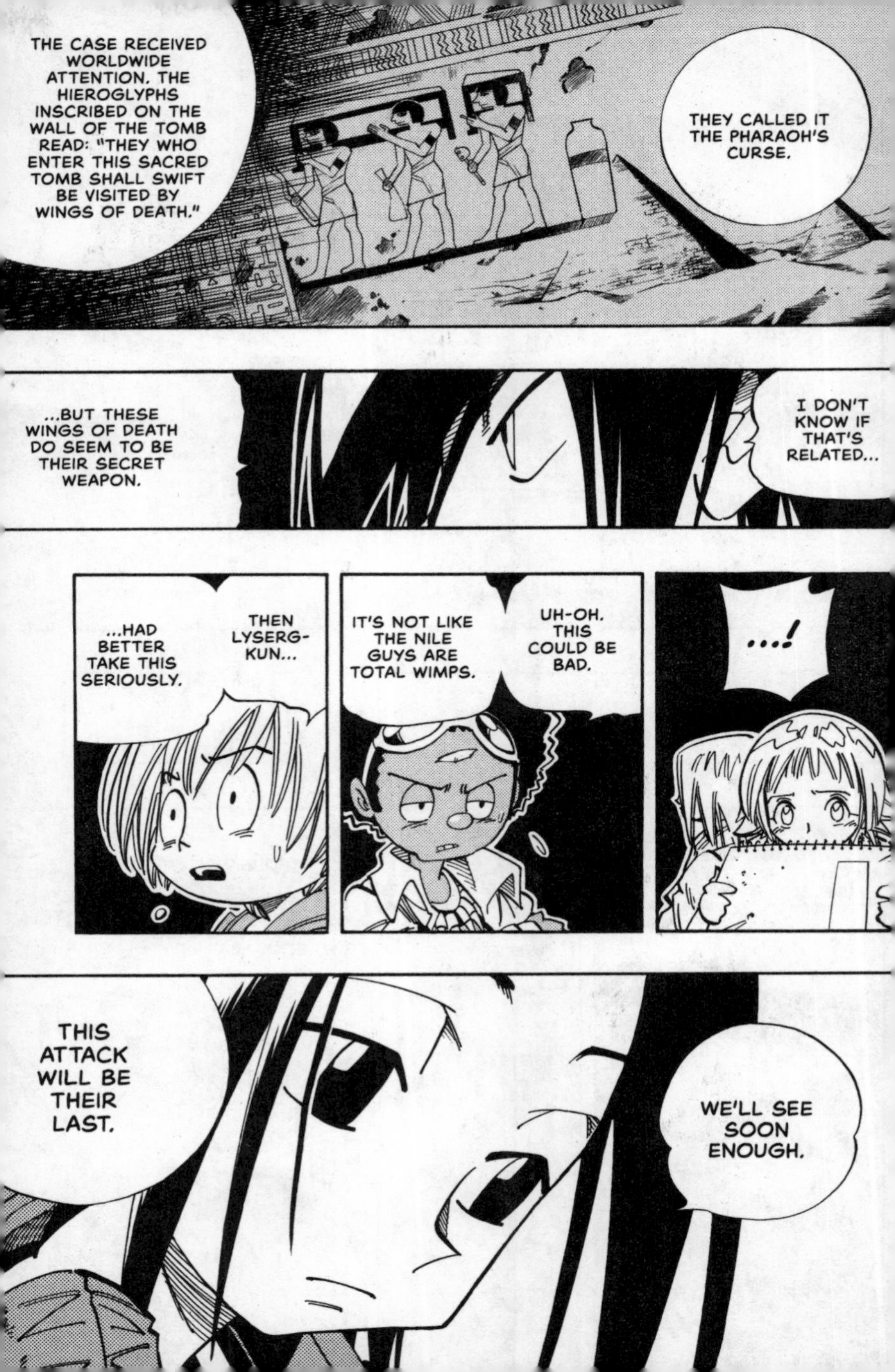
THE CASE RECEIVED WORLDWIDE ATTENTION. THE HIEROGLYPHS INSCRIBED ON THE WALL OF THE TOMB READ: "THEY WHO ENTER THIS SACRED TOMB SHALL SWIFT BE VISITED BY WINGS OF DEATH."
THEY CALLED IT THE PHARAOH'S CURSE.
I DON'T KNOW IF THAT'S RELATED...
...BUT THESE WINGS OF DEATH DO SEEM TO BE THEIR SECRET WEAPON.
...!
UH-OH. THIS COULD BE BAD.
IT'S NOT LIKE THE NILE GUYS ARE TOTAL WIMPS.
THEN LYSERG-KUN...
...HAD BETTER TAKE THIS SERIOUSLY.
THIS ATTACK WILL BE THEIR LAST.
WE'LL SEE SOON ENOUGH.

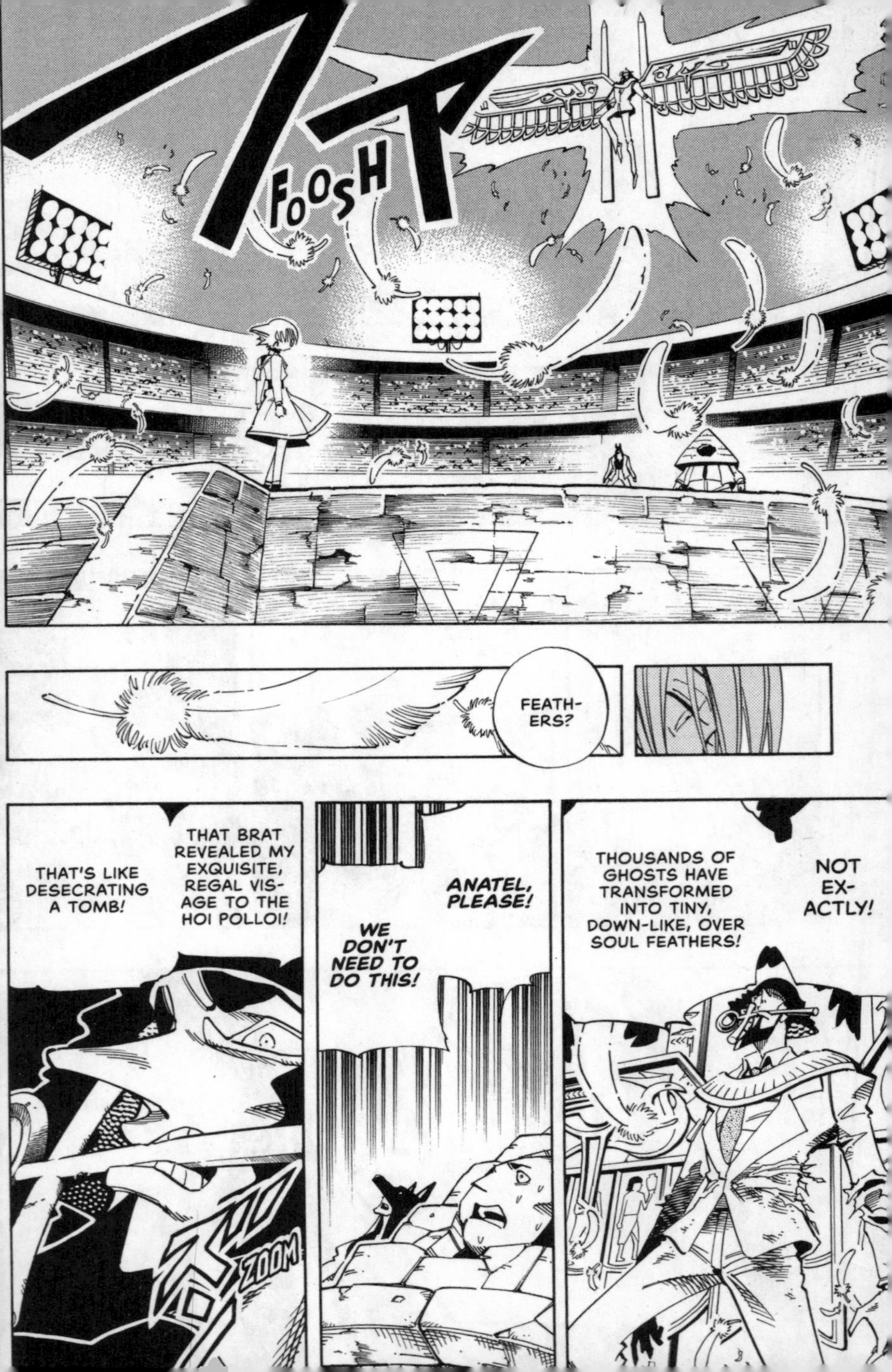
FOOSH
FEATHERS?
NOT EXACTLY!
THOUSANDS OF GHOSTS HAVE TRANSFORMED INTO TINY, DOWN-LIKE, OVER SOUL FEATHERS!
ANATEL, PLEASE!
WE DON'T NEED TO DO THIS!
THAT BRAT REVEALED MY EXQUISITE, REGAL VISAGE TO THE HOI POLLOI!
THAT'S LIKE DESECRATING A TOMB!
ZOOM

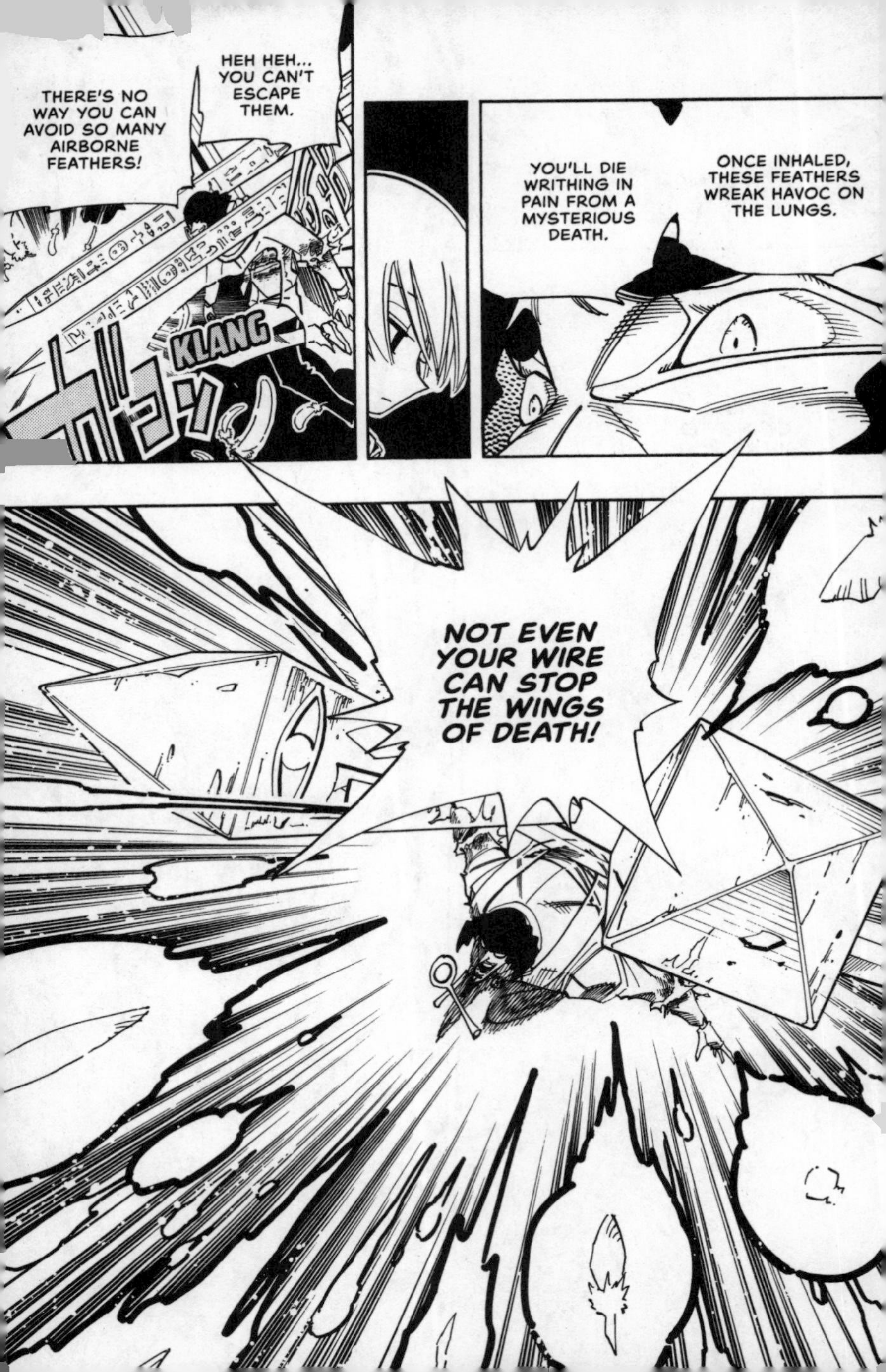
ONCE INHALED, THESE FEATHERS WREAK HAVOC ON THE LUNGS.
YOU'LL DIE WRITHING IN PAIN FROM A MYSTERIOUS DEATH.
HEH HEH... YOU CAN'T ESCAPE THEM.
THERE'S NO WAY YOU CAN AVOID SO MANY AIRBORNE FEATHERS!
KLANG
NOT EVEN YOUR WIRE CAN STOP THE WINGS OF DEATH!

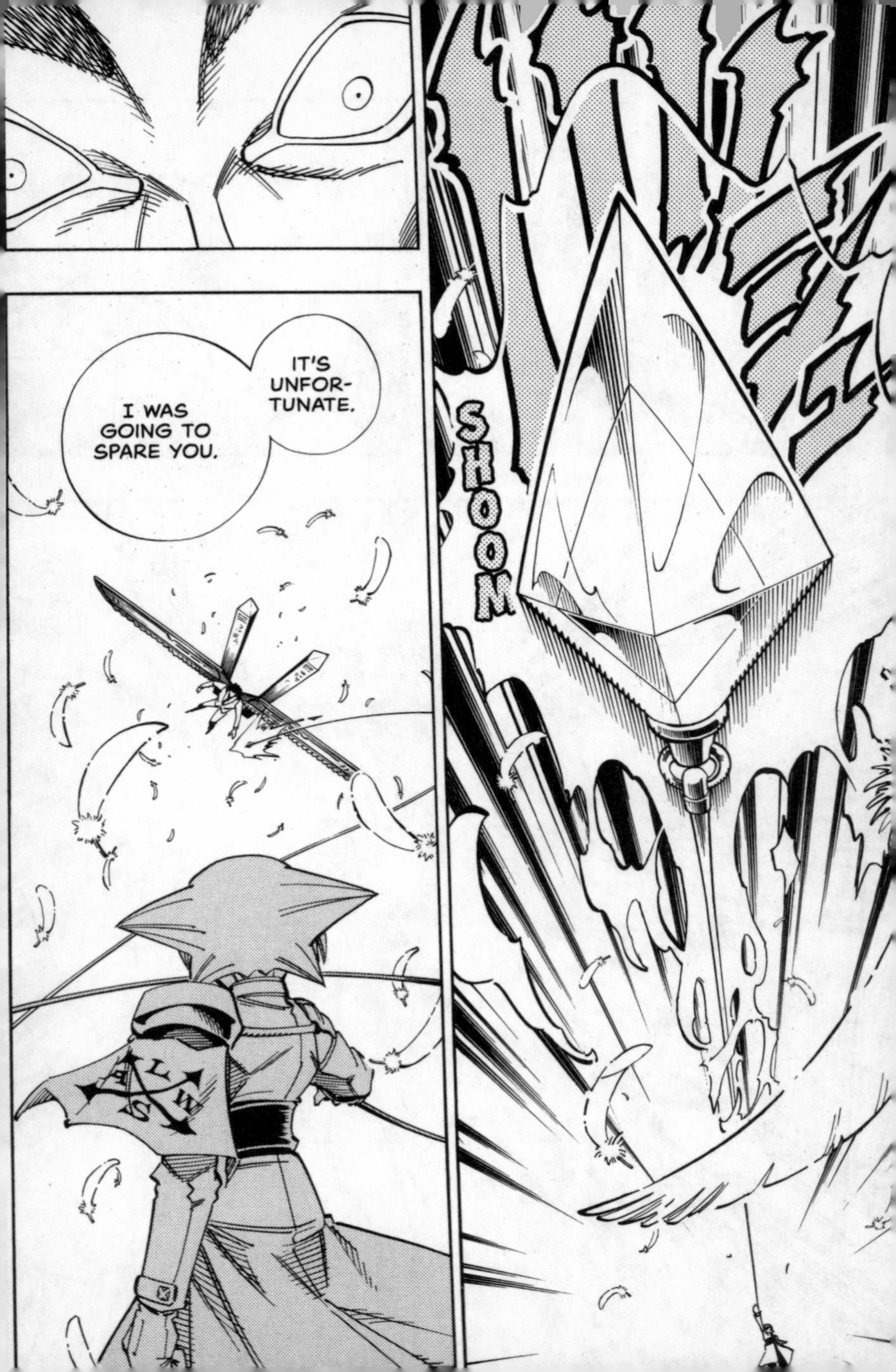
SHOOM
IT'S UNFORTUNATE.
I WAS GOING TO SPARE YOU.

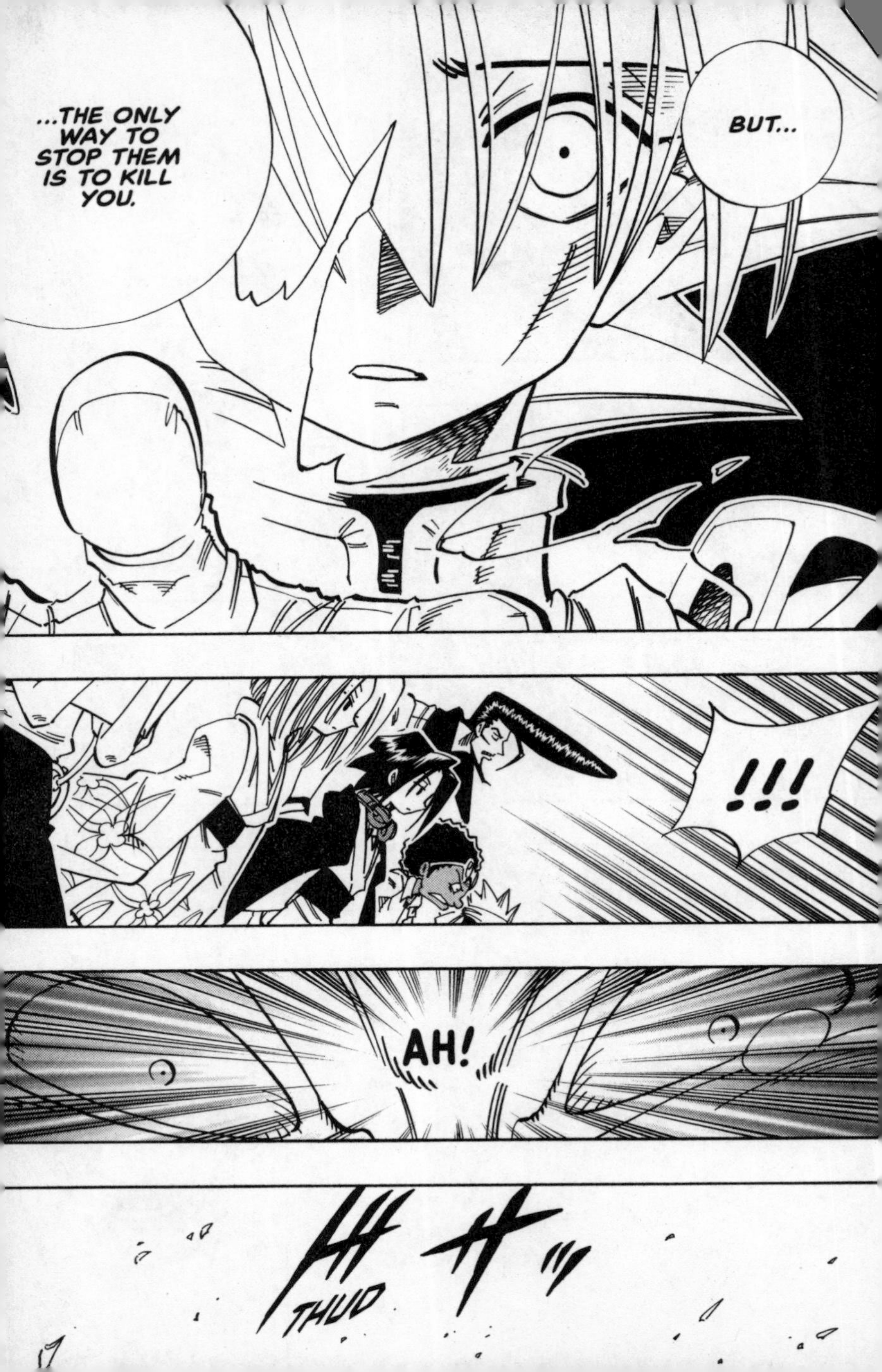
BUT...
...THE ONLY WAY TO STOP THEM IS TO KILL YOU.
!!!
AH!
THUD

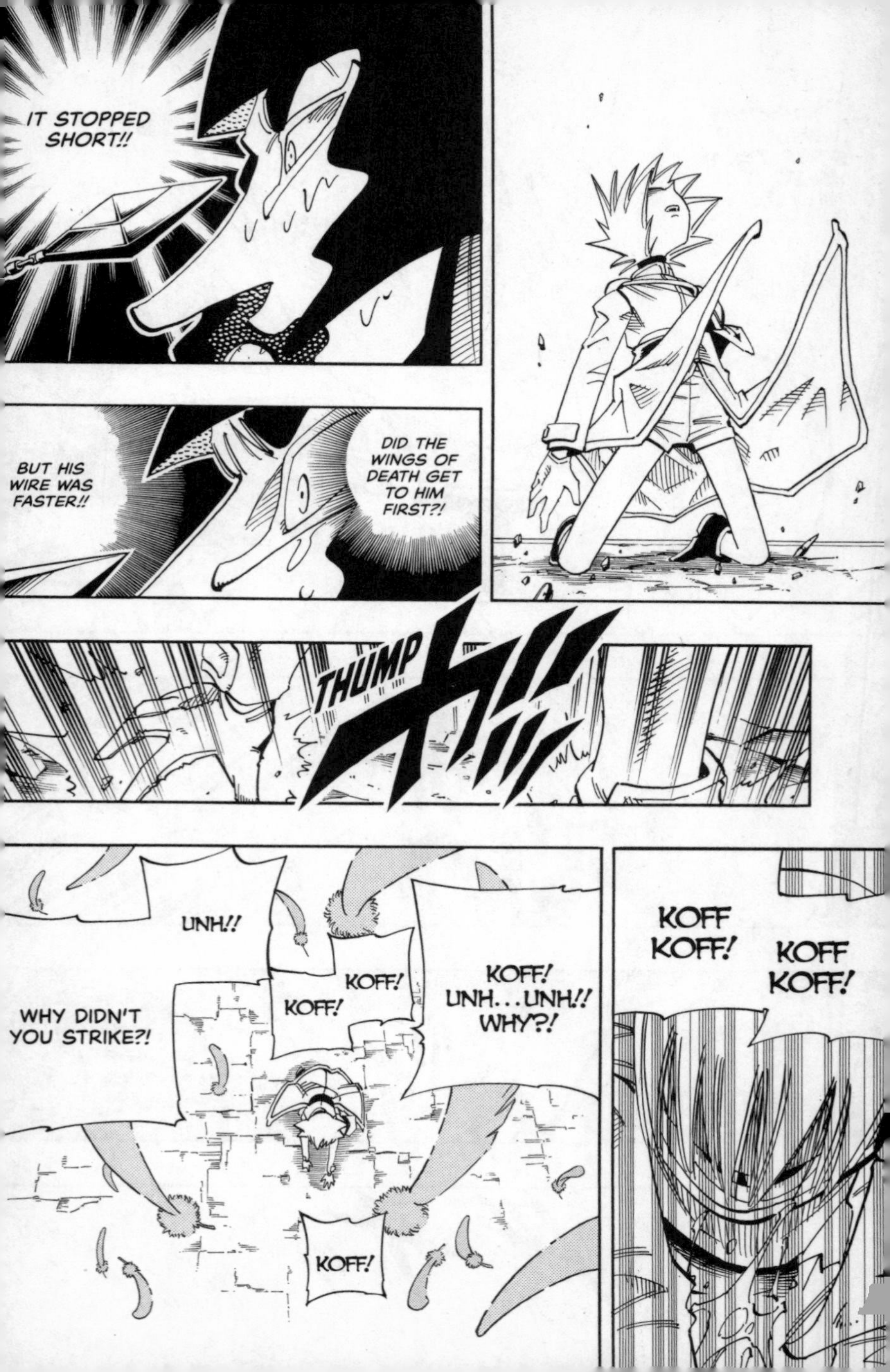
IT STOPPED SHORT!!
DID THE WINGS OF DEATH GET TO HIM FIRST?!
BUT HIS WIRE WAS FASTER!!
THUMP
KOFF KOFF!
KOFF KOFF!
KOFF! UNH...UNH!! WHY?!
UNH!!
KOFF!
KOFF!
WHY DIDN'T YOU STRIKE?!
KOFF!

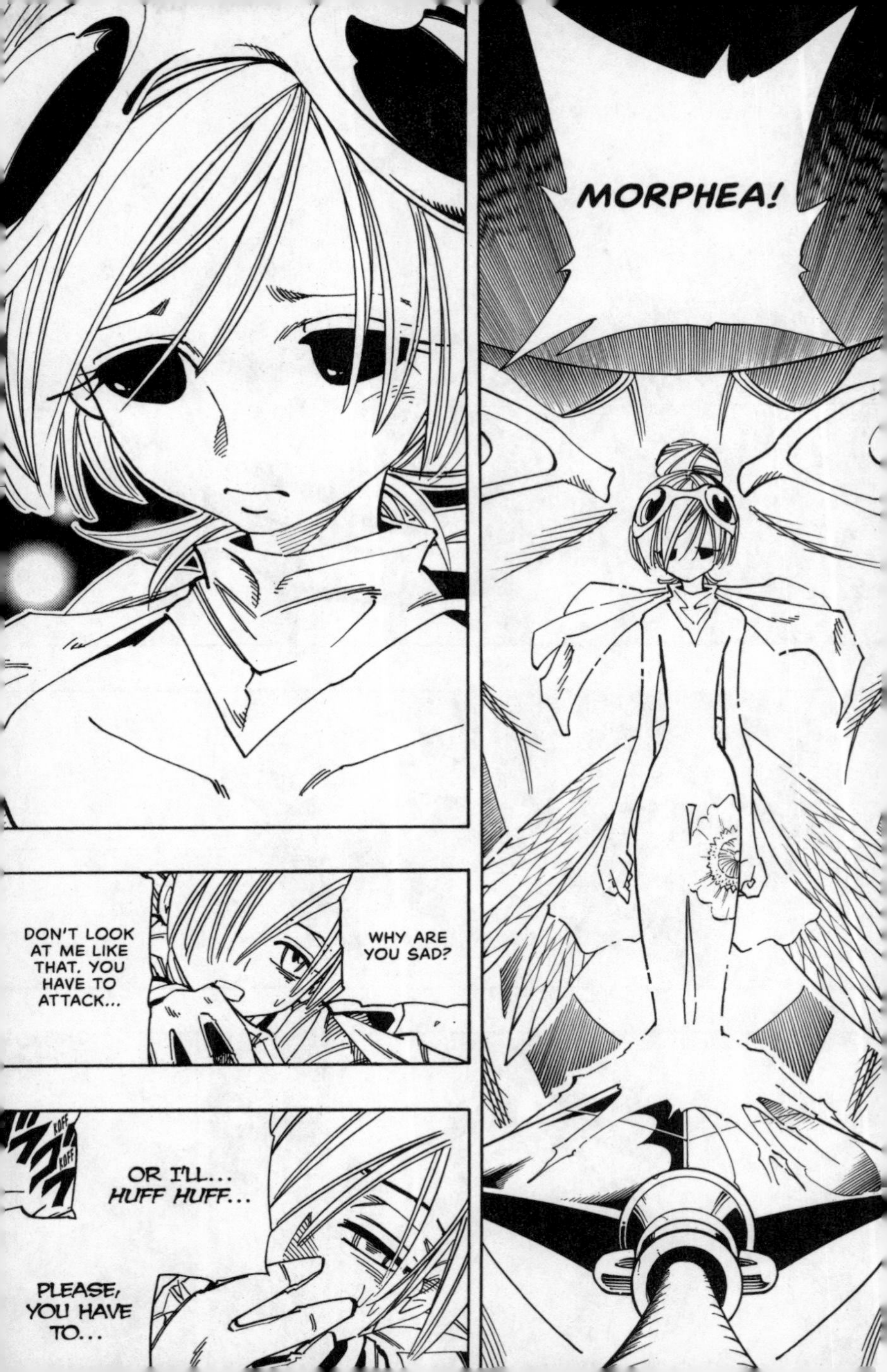

MORPHEA!
WHY ARE YOU SAD?
DON'T LOOK AT ME LIKE THAT. YOU HAVE TO ATTACK...
OR I'LL... *HUFF HUFF...*
KOFF KOFF
PLEASE, YOU HAVE TO...

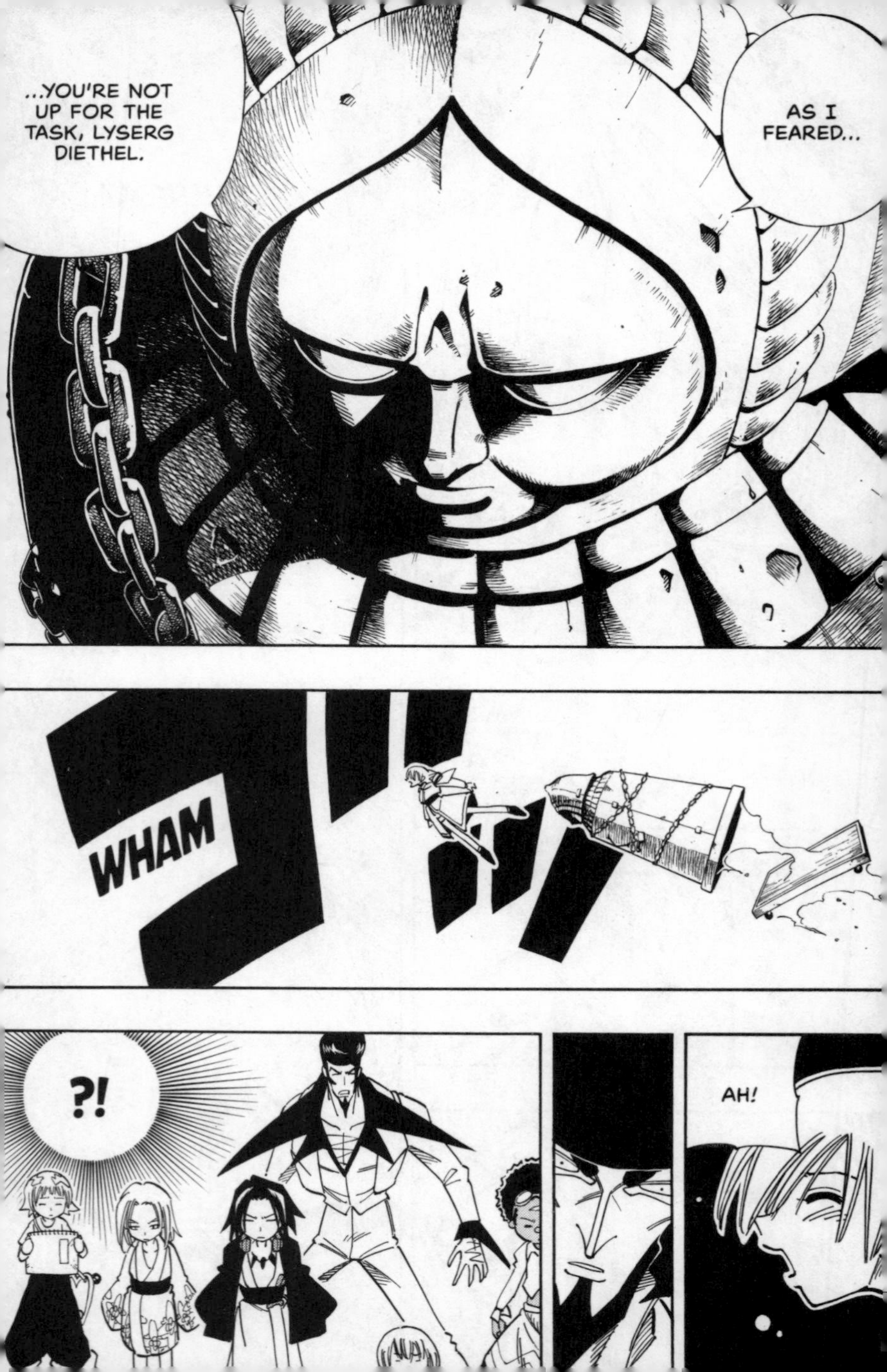
AS I FEARED...
...YOU'RE NOT UP FOR THE TASK, LYSERG DIETHEL.
WHAM
AH!
?!

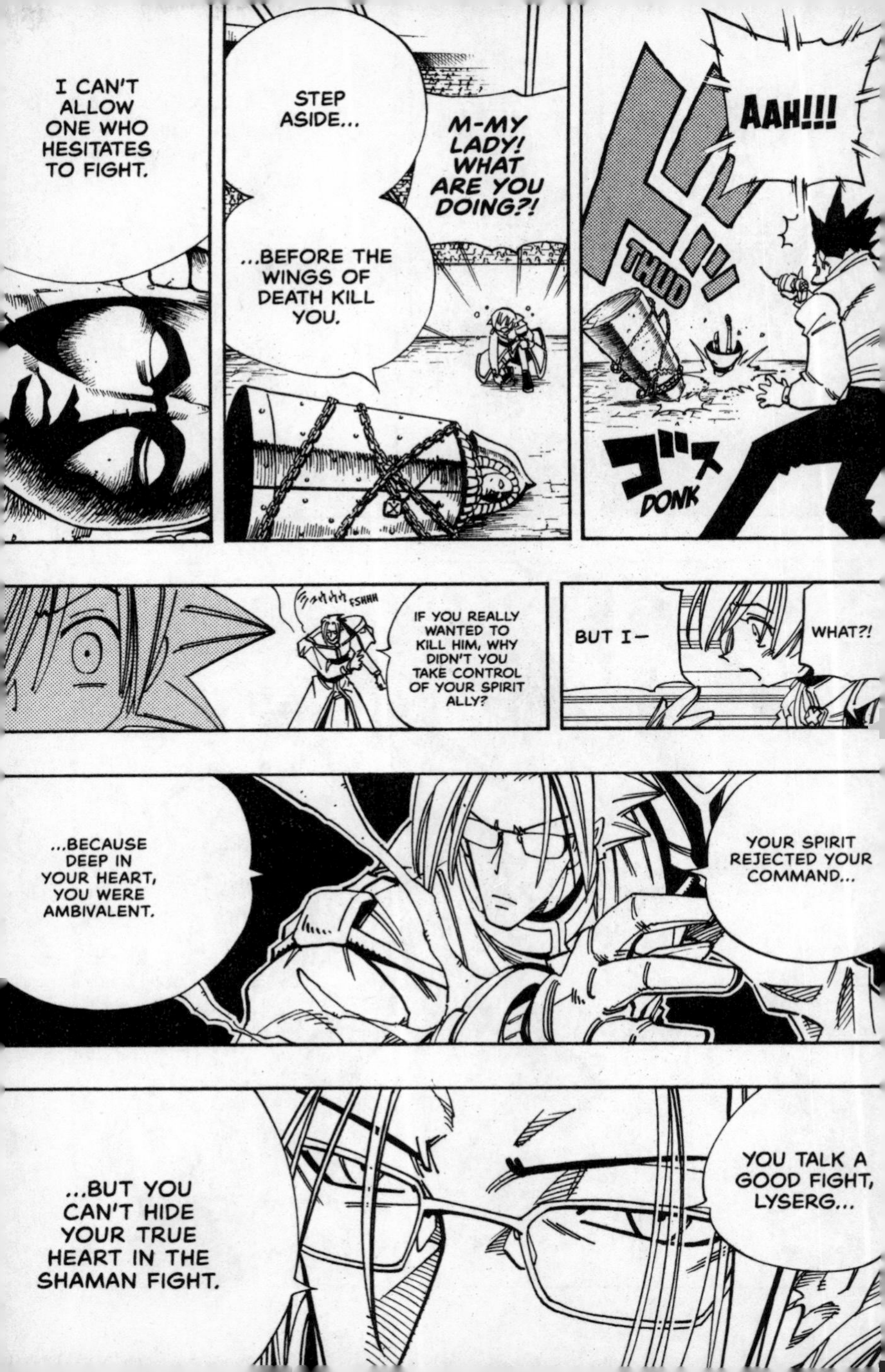
AAH!!!
THUD
DONK
M-MY LADY! WHAT ARE YOU DOING?!
STEP ASIDE...
...BEFORE THE WINGS OF DEATH KILL YOU.
I CAN'T ALLOW ONE WHO HESITATES TO FIGHT.
WHAT?!
BUT I—
FSHHH
IF YOU REALLY WANTED TO KILL HIM, WHY DIDN'T YOU TAKE CONTROL OF YOUR SPIRIT ALLY?
YOUR SPIRIT REJECTED YOUR COMMAND...
...BECAUSE DEEP IN YOUR HEART, YOU WERE AMBIVALENT.
YOU TALK A GOOD FIGHT, LYSERG...
...BUT YOU CAN'T HIDE YOUR TRUE HEART IN THE SHAMAN FIGHT.

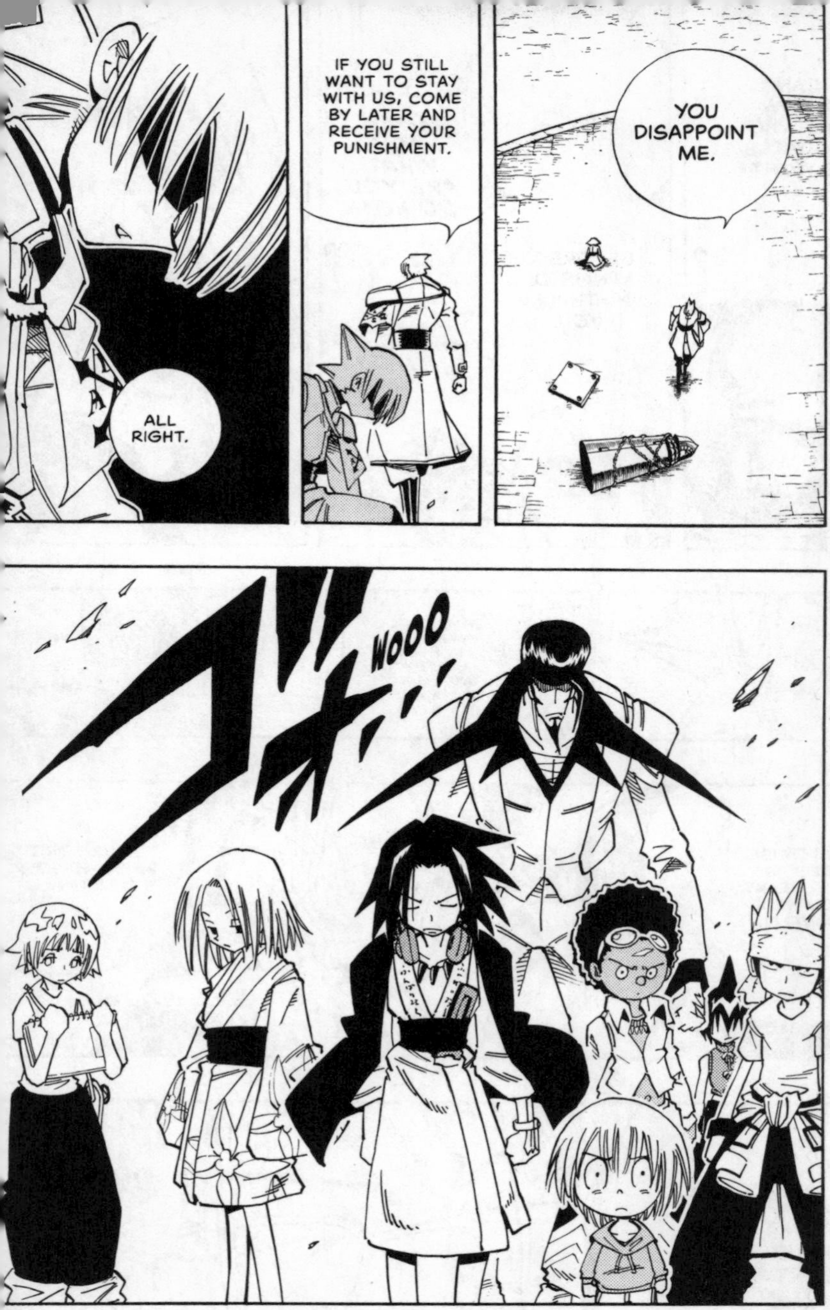
YOU DISAPPOINT ME.
IF YOU STILL WANT TO STAY WITH US, COME BY LATER AND RECEIVE YOUR PUNISHMENT.
ALL RIGHT.
WOOO

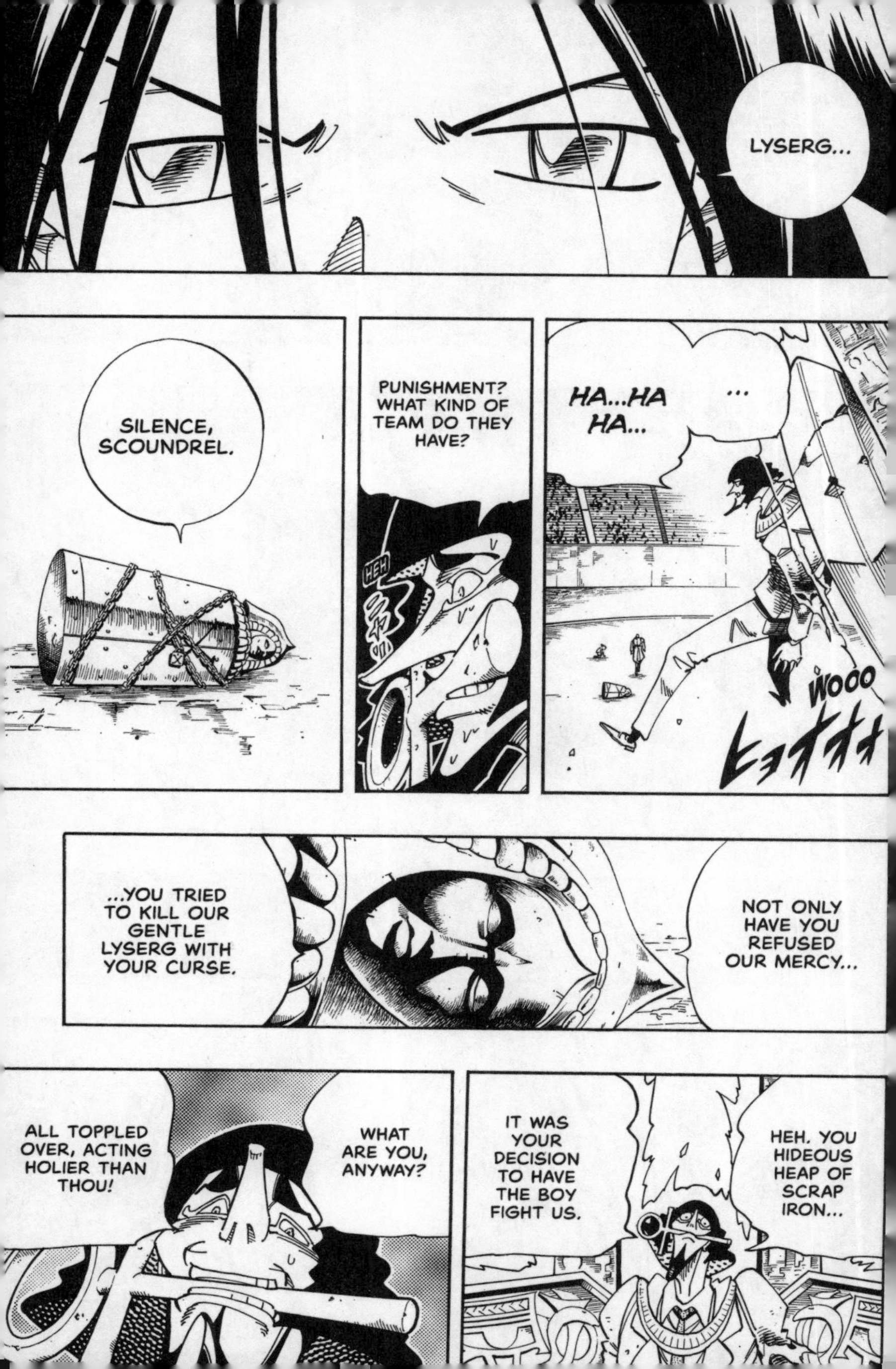
LYSERG...
HA...HA HA...
...
WOOO
ヒョオオオ
PUNISHMENT? WHAT KIND OF TEAM DO THEY HAVE?
HEH
ミキ
SILENCE, SCOUNDREL.
NOT ONLY HAVE YOU REFUSED OUR MERCY...
...YOU TRIED TO KILL OUR GENTLE LYSERG WITH YOUR CURSE.
HEH. YOU HIDEOUS HEAP OF SCRAP IRON...
IT WAS YOUR DECISION TO HAVE THE BOY FIGHT US.
WHAT ARE YOU, ANYWAY?
ALL TOPPLED OVER, ACTING HOLIER THAN THOU!

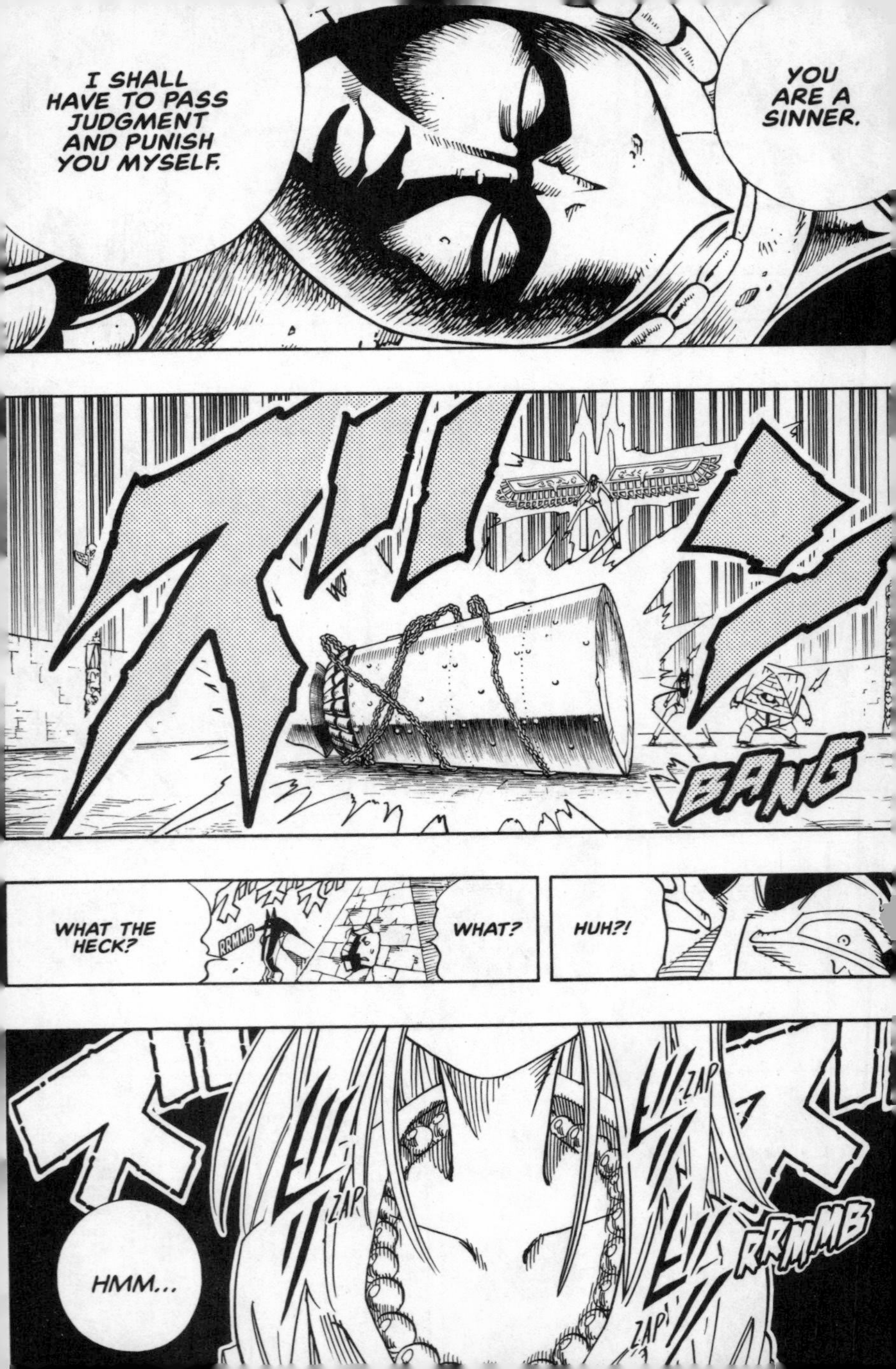
YOU ARE A SINNER.
I SHALL HAVE TO PASS JUDGMENT AND PUNISH YOU MYSELF.
BANG
HUH?!
WHAT?
RRMMB
WHAT THE HECK?
ZAP
RRMMB
ZAP
ZAP
HMM...

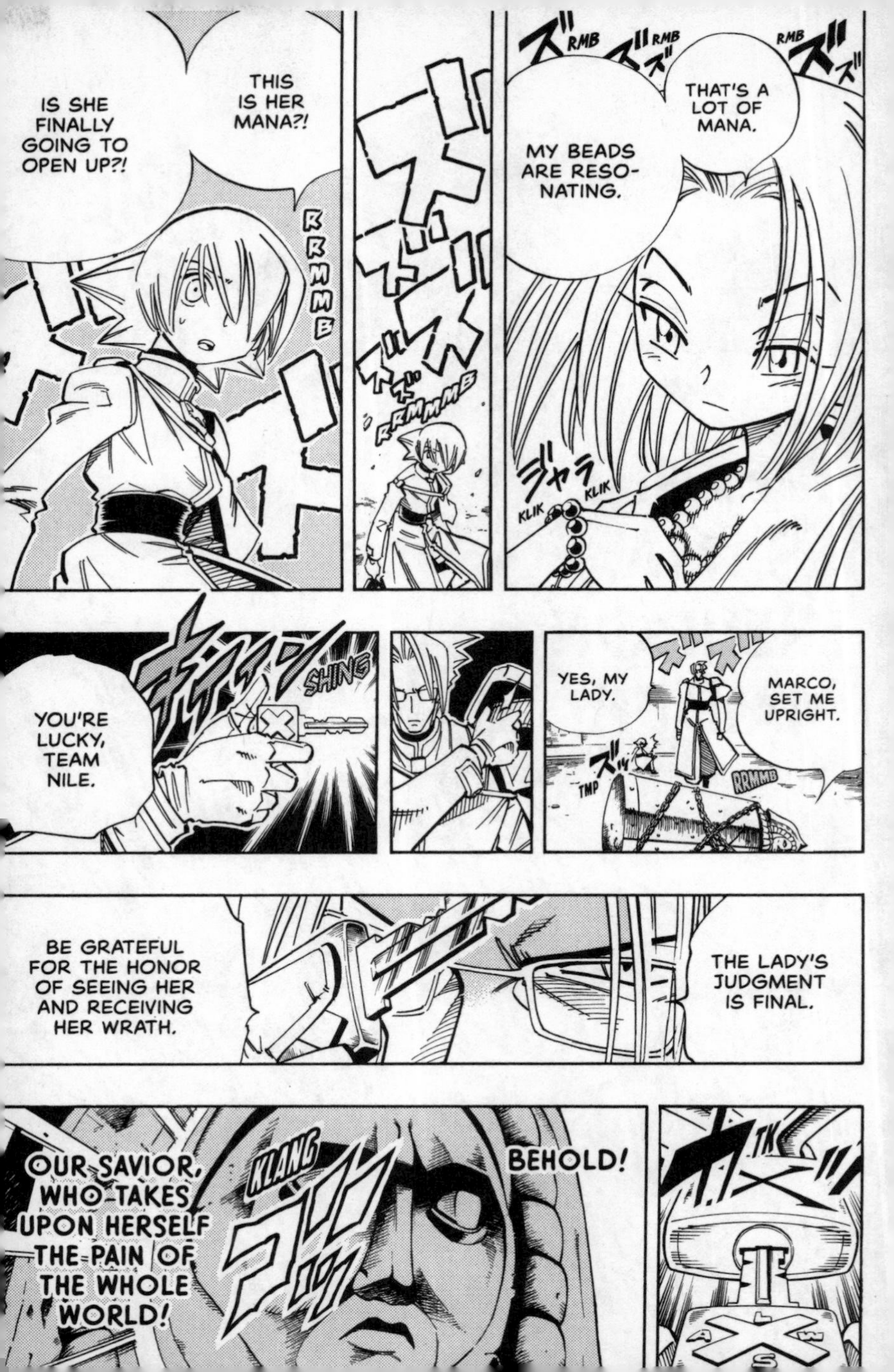
RMB
RMB
RMB
THAT'S A LOT OF MANA.
MY BEADS ARE RESO-NATING.
ジャラ
KLIK
KLIK
RRMMMB
THIS IS HER MANA?!
IS SHE FINALLY GOING TO OPEN UP?!
RRMMMB
MARCO, SET ME UPRIGHT.
YES, MY LADY.
RRMMB
TMP
SHING
YOU'RE LUCKY, TEAM NILE.
THE LADY'S JUDGMENT IS FINAL.
BE GRATEFUL FOR THE HONOR OF SEEING HER AND RECEIVING HER WRATH.
TK
BEHOLD!
KLANG
OUR SAVIOR, WHO TAKES UPON HERSELF THE PAIN OF THE WHOLE WORLD!

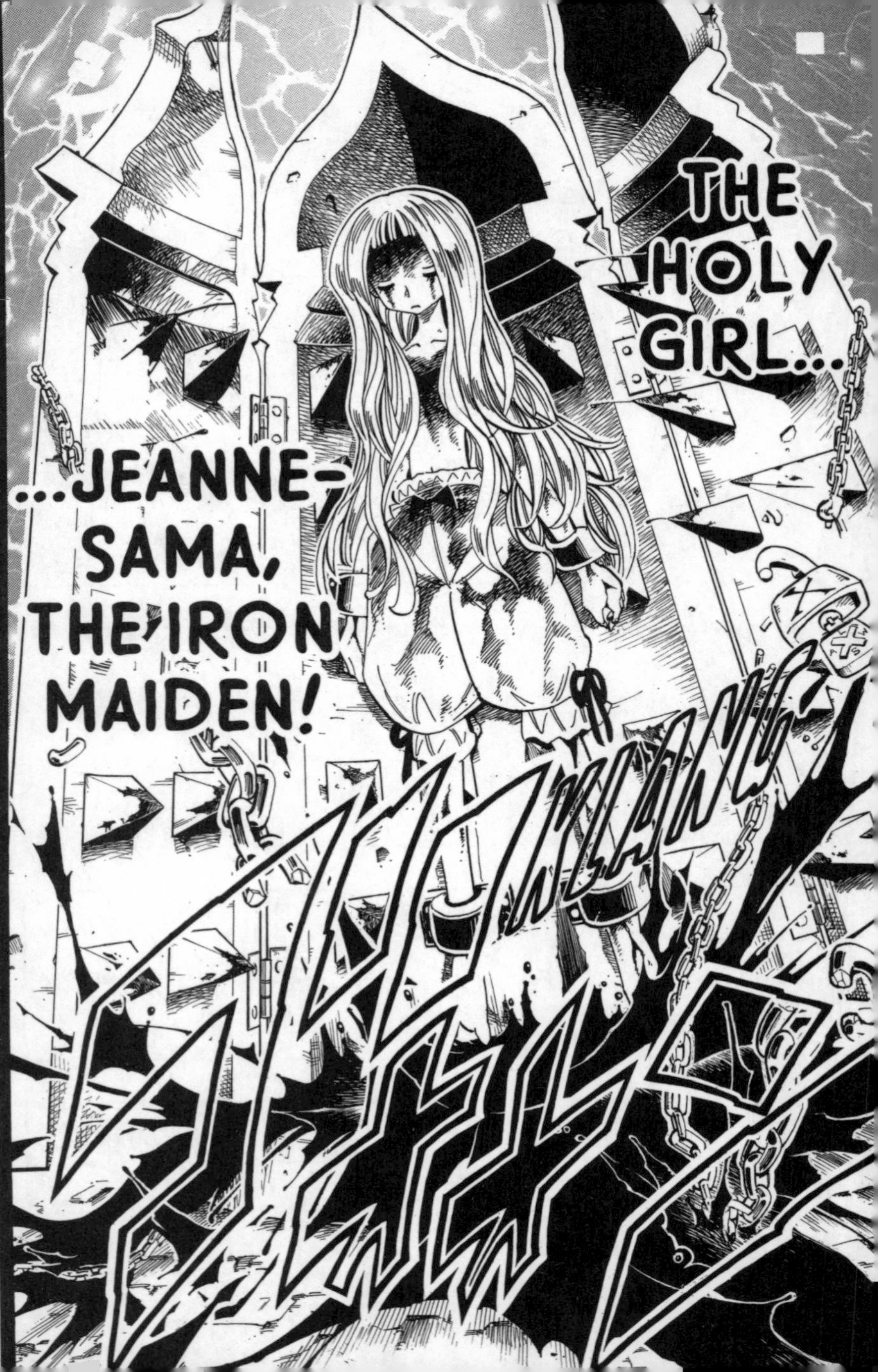
THE HOLY GIRL...
...JEANNE-SAMA, THE IRON MAIDEN!

Shamash

June 2001

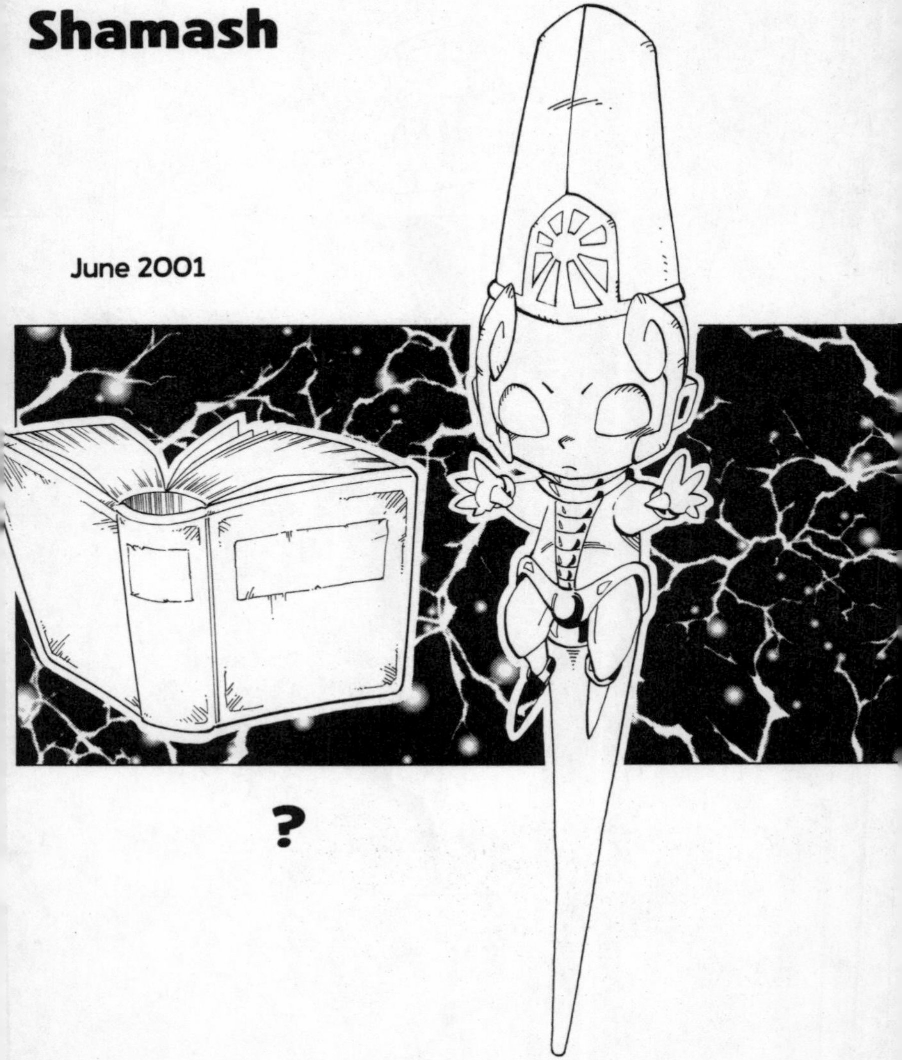

?

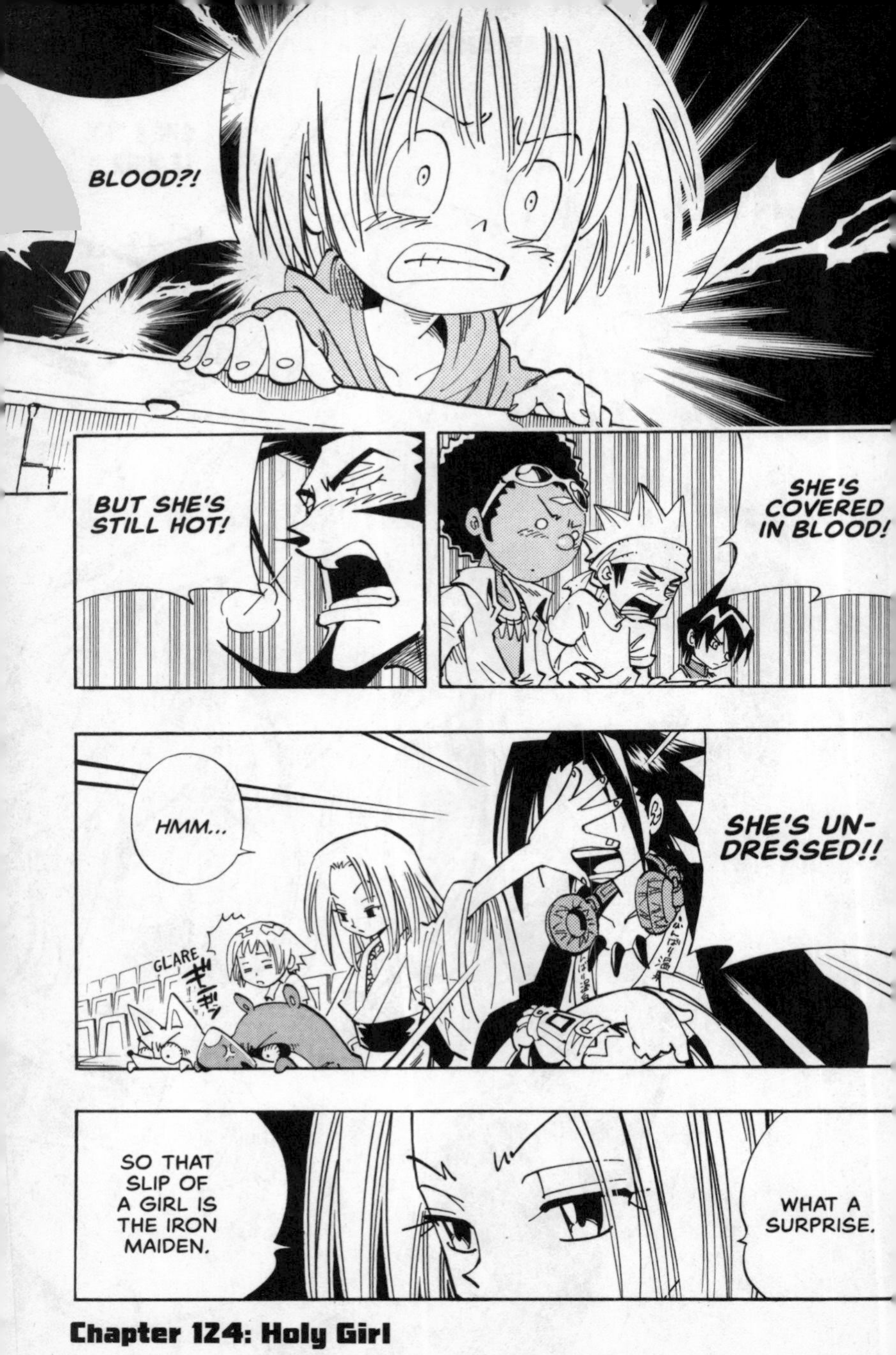
BLOOD?!
SHE'S COVERED IN BLOOD!
BUT SHE'S STILL HOT!
SHE'S UN-DRESSED!!
HMM...
GLARE
WHAT A SURPRISE.
SO THAT SLIP OF A GIRL IS THE IRON MAIDEN.

Chapter 124: Holy Girl

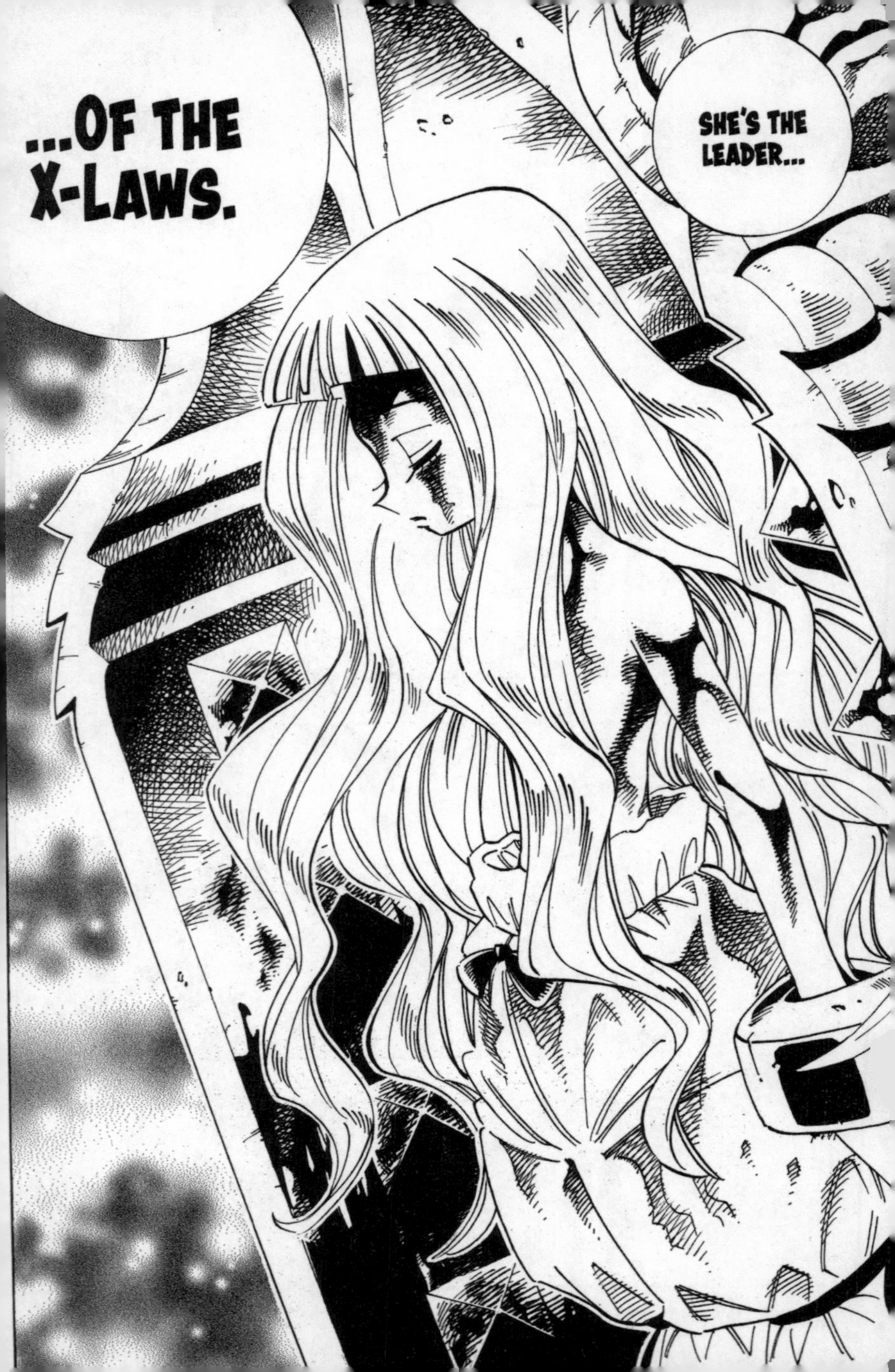
SHE'S THE LEADER...
...OF THE X-LAWS.

Chapter 124:

Holy Girl

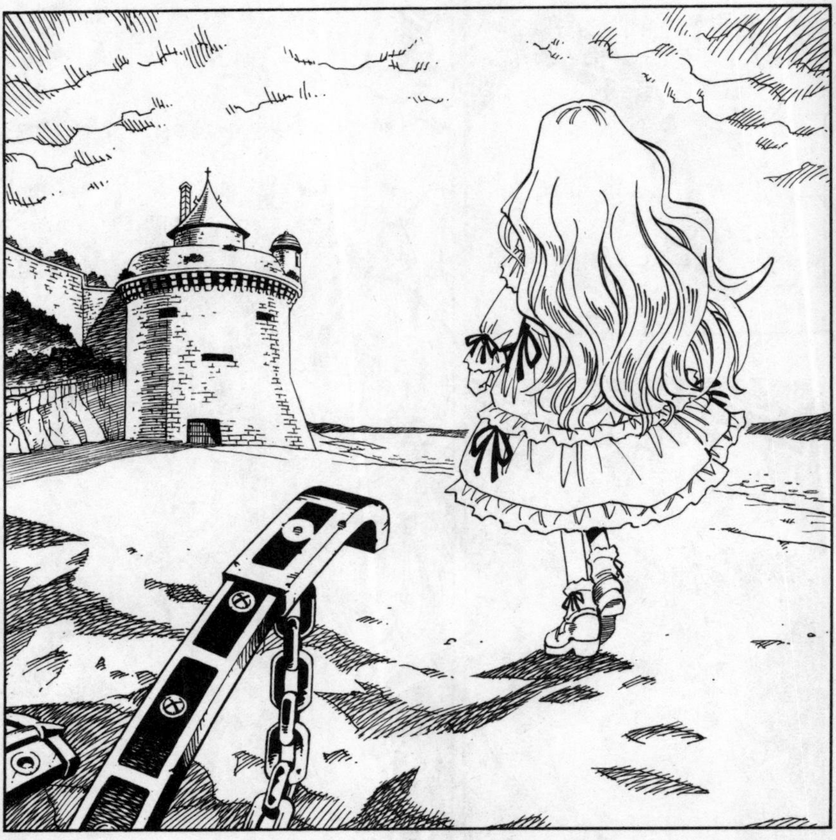

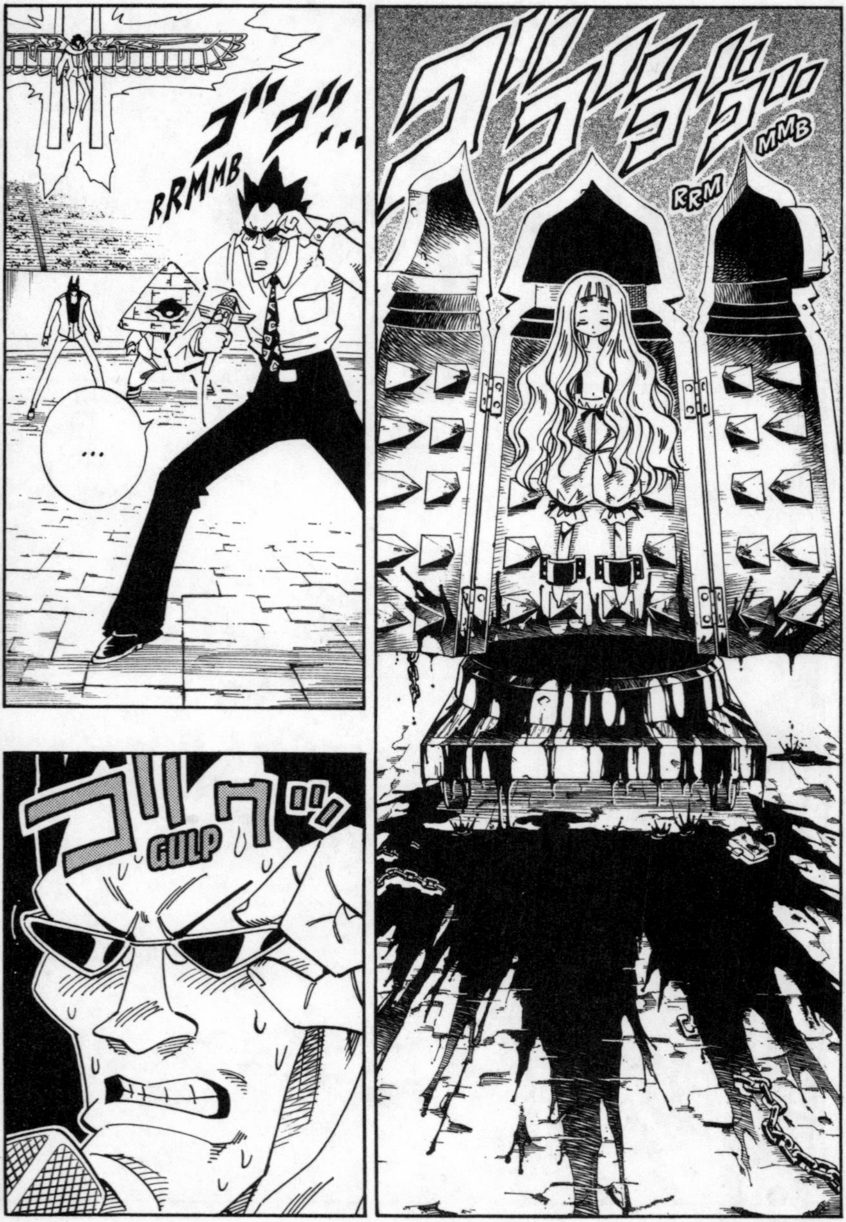
RRM
MMB
RRMMB
...
GULP

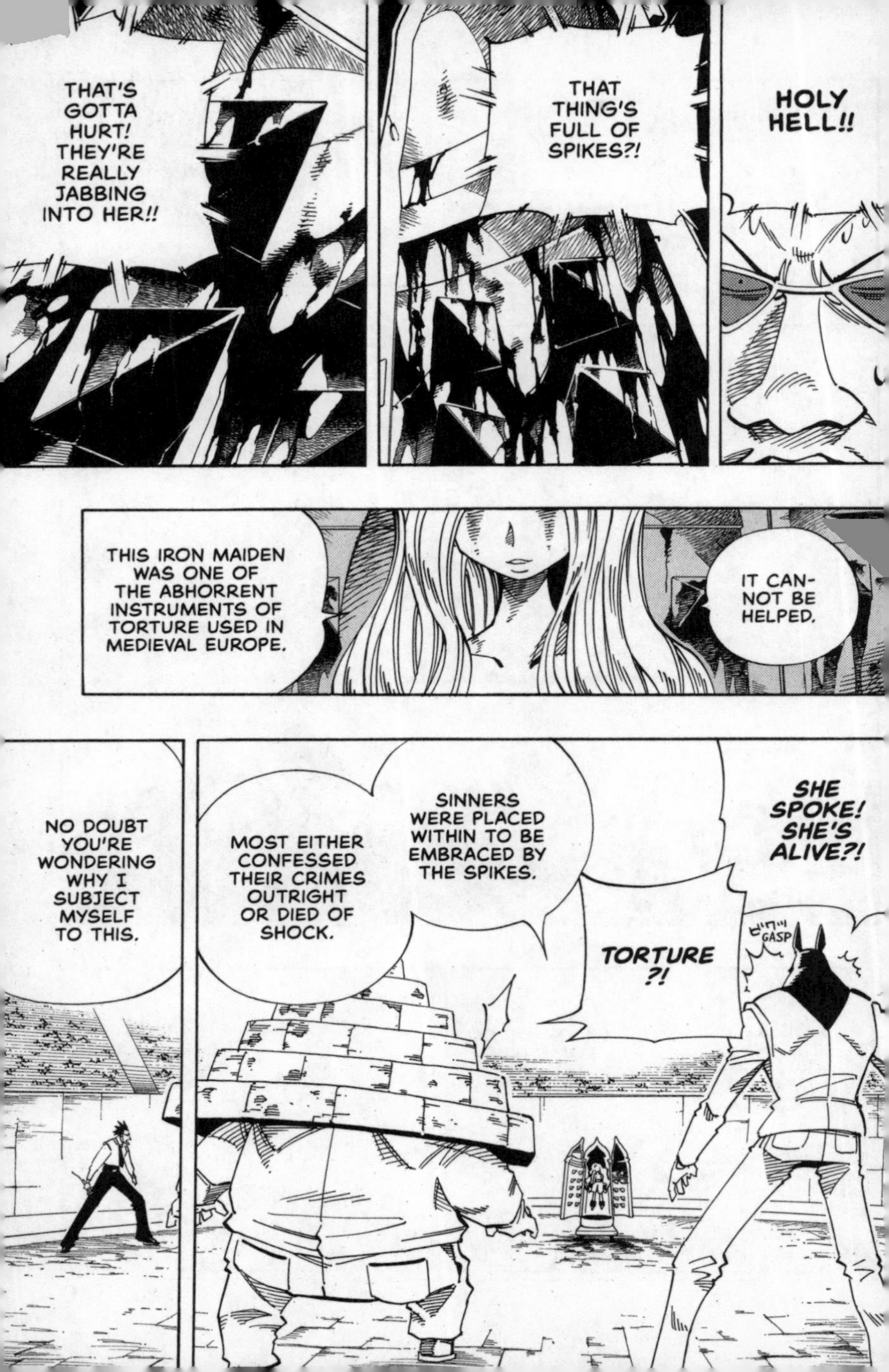

HOLY HELL!!
THAT THING'S FULL OF SPIKES?!
THAT'S GOTTA HURT! THEY'RE REALLY JABBING INTO HER!!
IT CAN-NOT BE HELPED.
THIS IRON MAIDEN WAS ONE OF THE ABHORRENT INSTRUMENTS OF TORTURE USED IN MEDIEVAL EUROPE.
SHE SPOKE! SHE'S ALIVE?!
ビクッ
GASP
TORTURE ?!
SINNERS WERE PLACED WITHIN TO BE EMBRACED BY THE SPIKES.
MOST EITHER CONFESSED THEIR CRIMES OUTRIGHT OR DIED OF SHOCK.
NO DOUBT YOU'RE WONDERING WHY I SUBJECT MYSELF TO THIS.

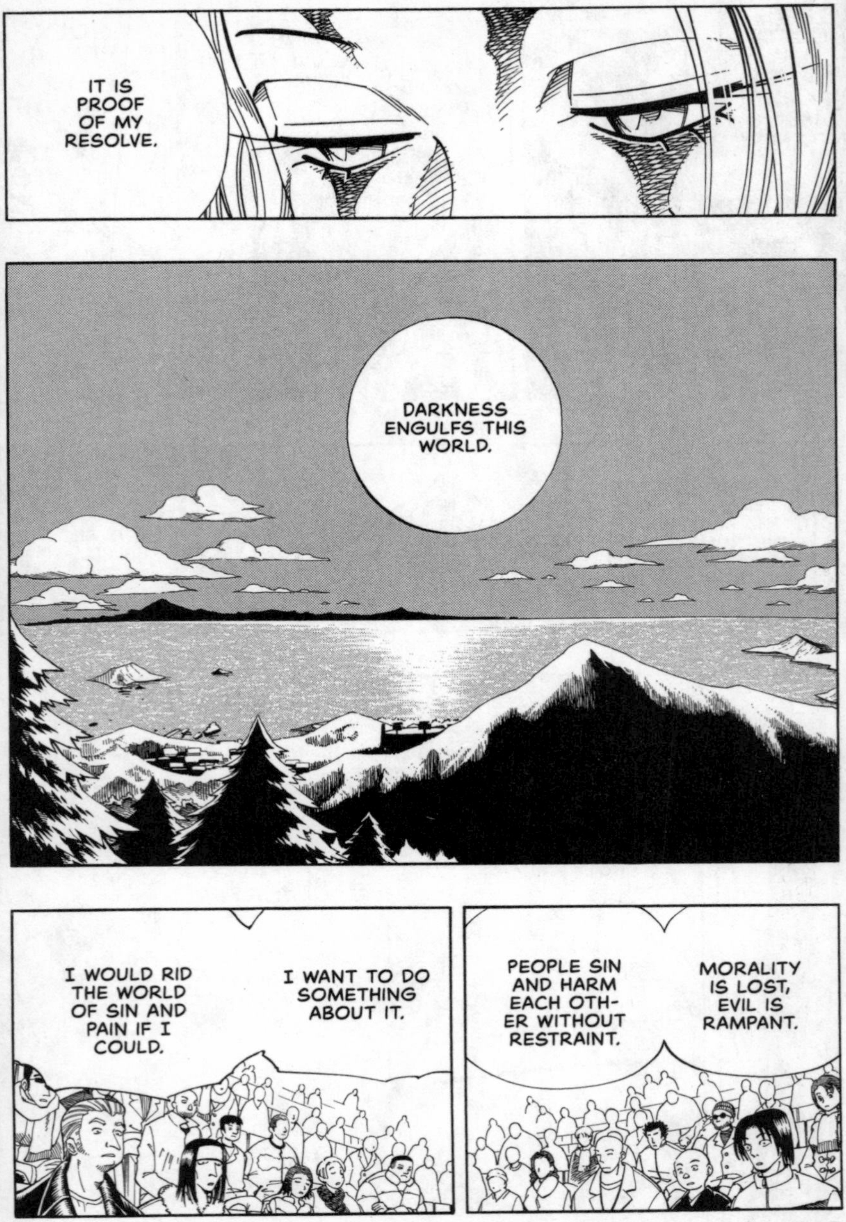
IT IS PROOF OF MY RESOLVE.
DARKNESS ENGULFS THIS WORLD.
MORALITY IS LOST, EVIL IS RAMPANT.
PEOPLE SIN AND HARM EACH OTH-ER WITHOUT RESTRAINT.
I WANT TO DO SOMETHING ABOUT IT.
I WOULD RID THE WORLD OF SIN AND PAIN IF I COULD.

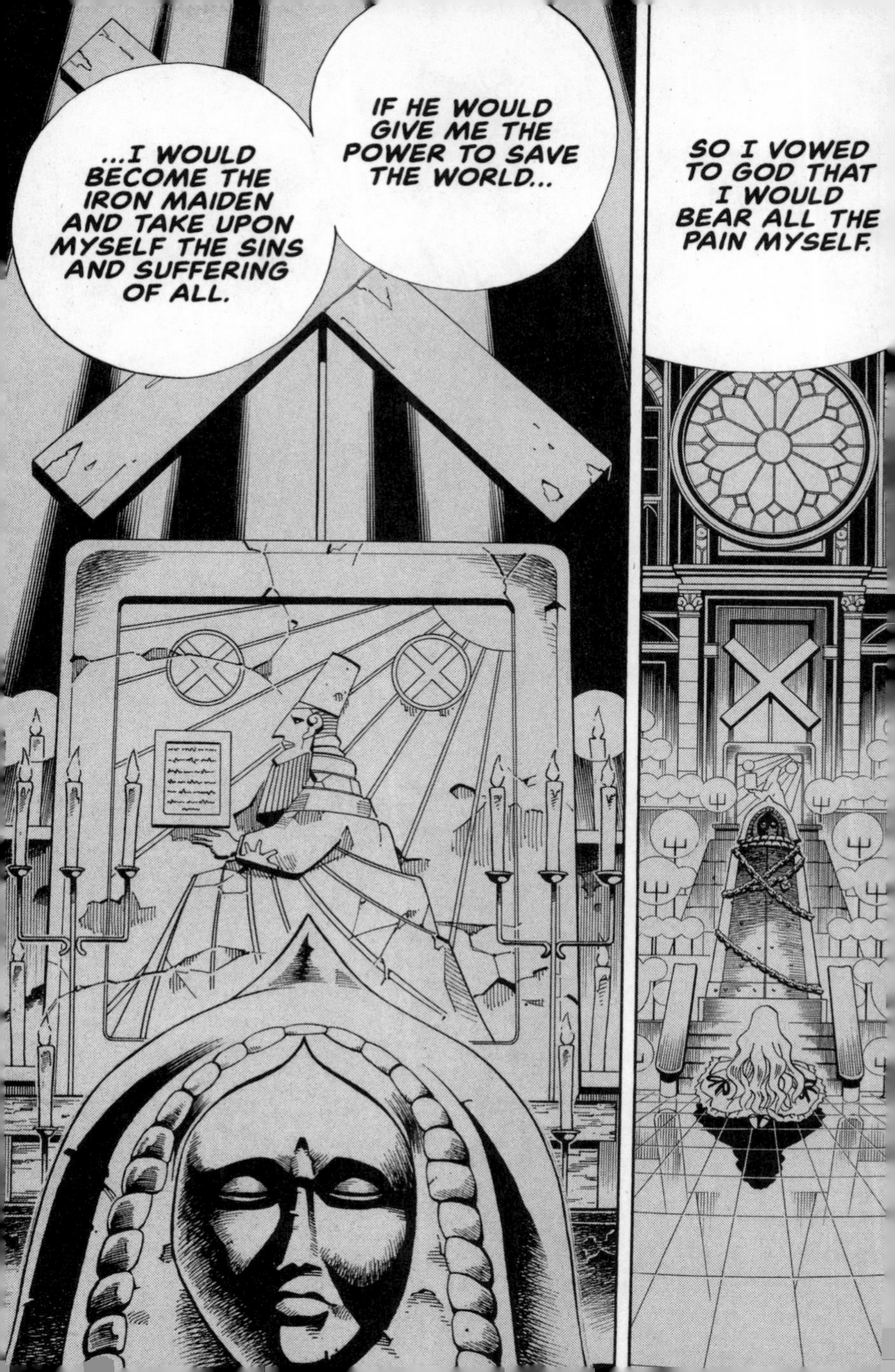
SO I VOWED TO GOD THAT I WOULD BEAR ALL THE PAIN MYSELF.
IF HE WOULD GIVE ME THE POWER TO SAVE THE WORLD...
...I WOULD BECOME THE IRON MAIDEN AND TAKE UPON MYSELF THE SINS AND SUFFERING OF ALL.

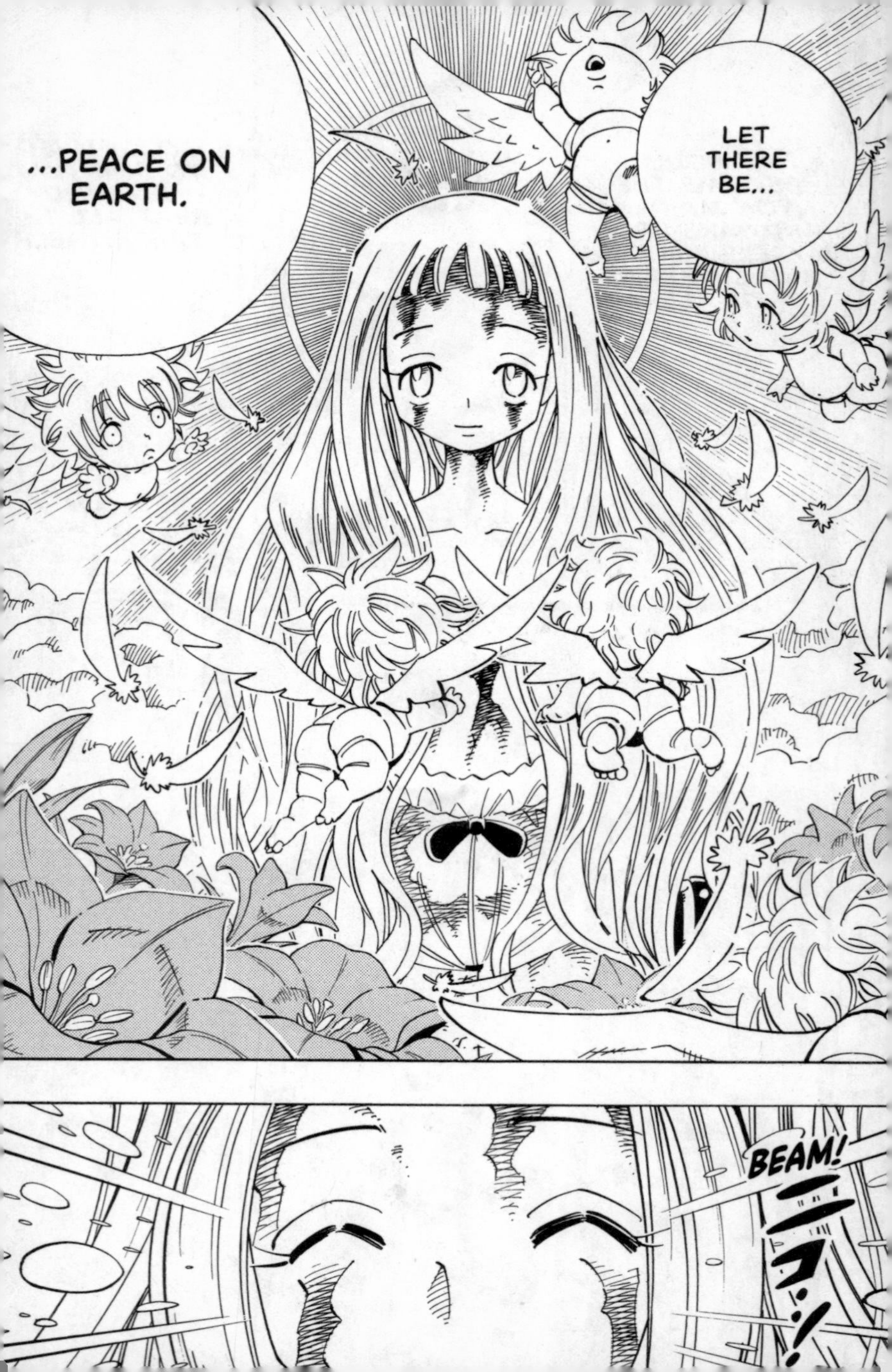
LET THERE BE...
...PEACE ON EARTH.
BEAM!

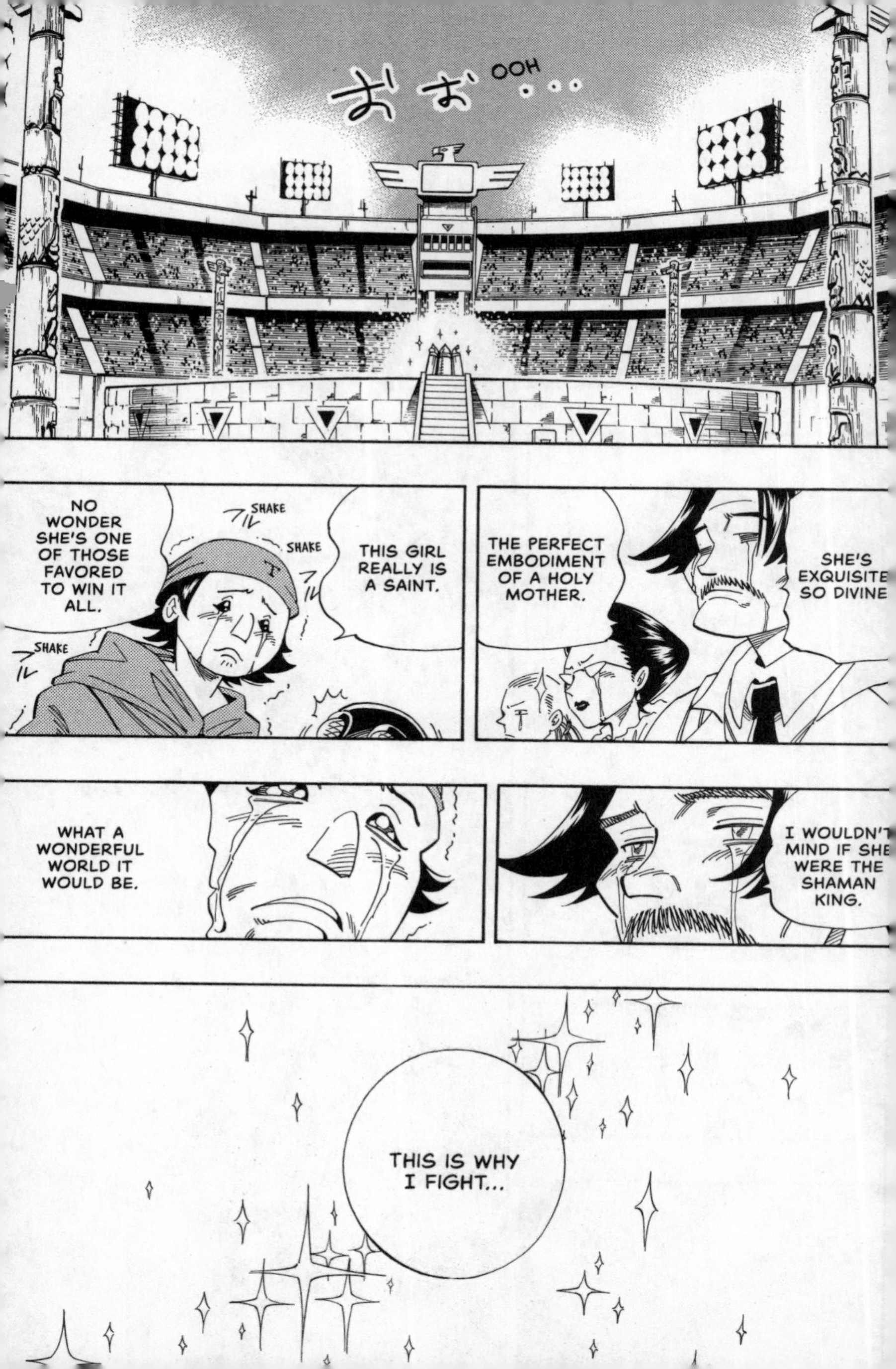
おお OOH...
SHE'S EXQUISITE SO DIVINE
THE PERFECT EMBODIMENT OF A HOLY MOTHER.
THIS GIRL REALLY IS A SAINT.
SHAKE
SHAKE
NO WONDER SHE'S ONE OF THOSE FAVORED TO WIN IT ALL.
SHAKE
I WOULDN'T MIND IF SHE WERE THE SHAMAN KING.
WHAT A WONDERFUL WORLD IT WOULD BE.
THIS IS WHY I FIGHT...

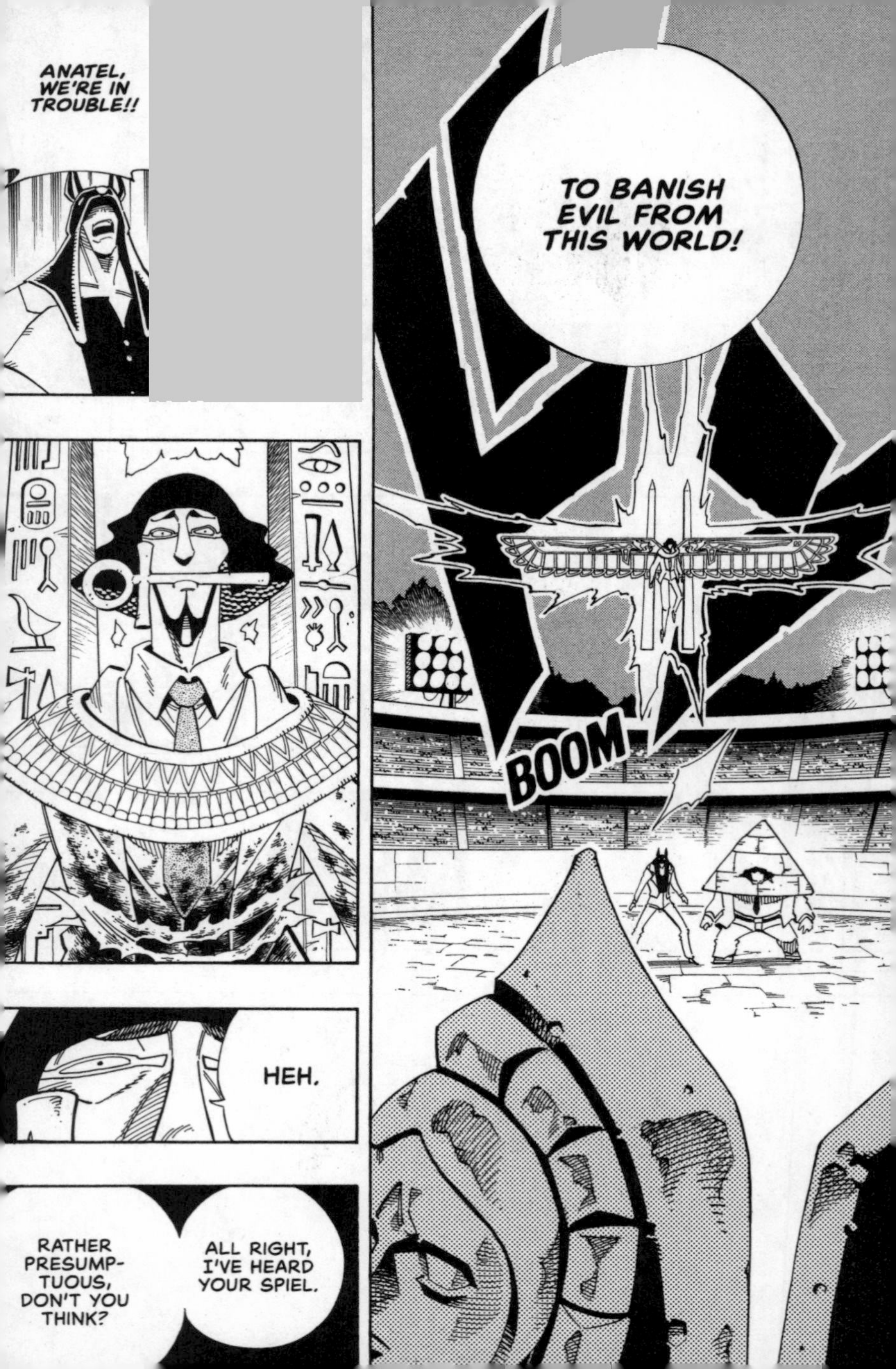
TO BANISH EVIL FROM THIS WORLD!
BOOM
ANATEL, WE'RE IN TROUBLE!!
HEH.
ALL RIGHT, I'VE HEARD YOUR SPIEL.
RATHER PRESUMP-TUOUS, DON'T YOU THINK?

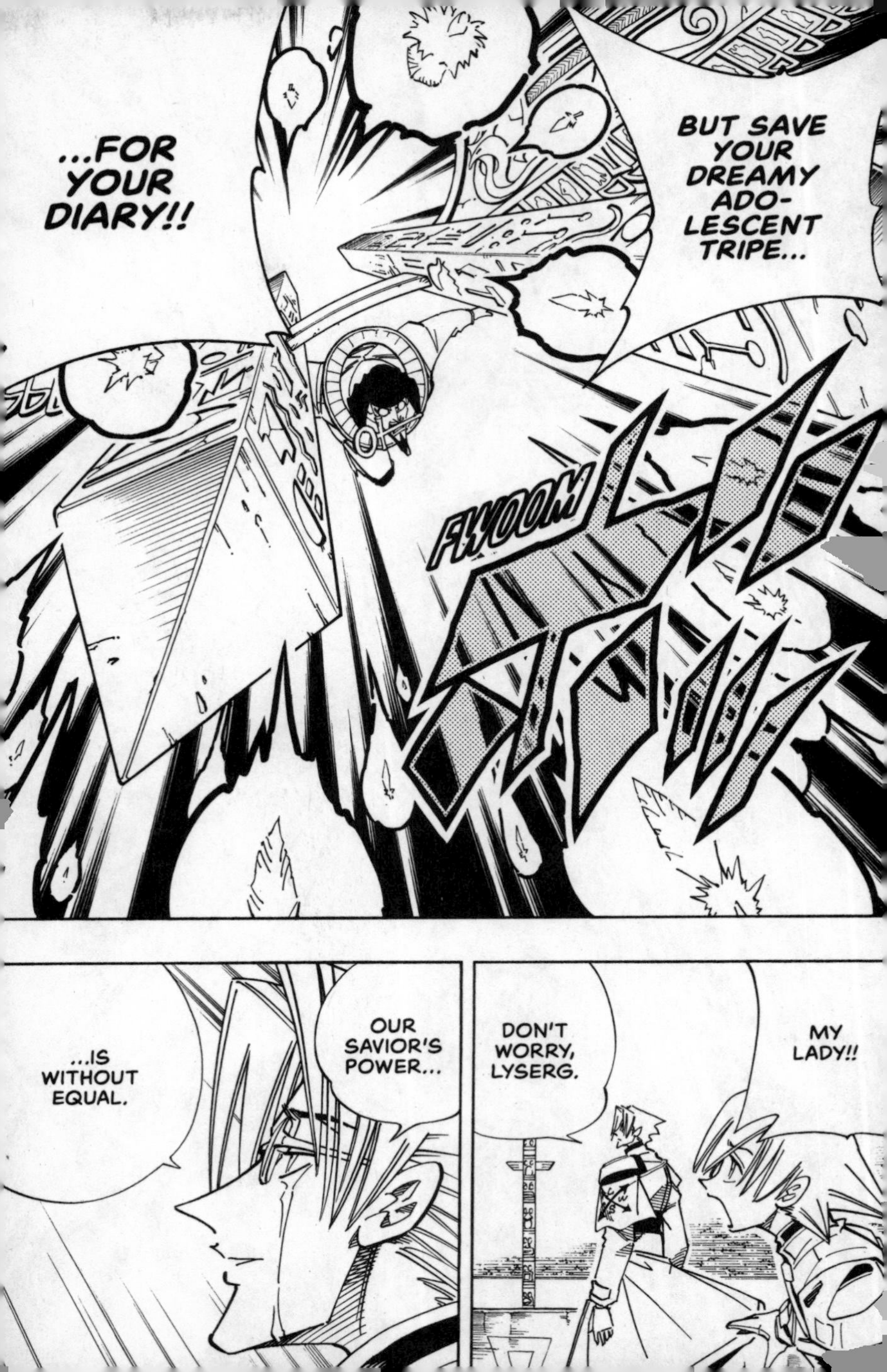
BUT SAVE YOUR DREAMY ADO-LESCENT TRIPE...
...FOR YOUR DIARY!!
FWOOM
MY LADY!!
DON'T WORRY, LYSERG.
OUR SAVIOR'S POWER...
...IS WITHOUT EQUAL.

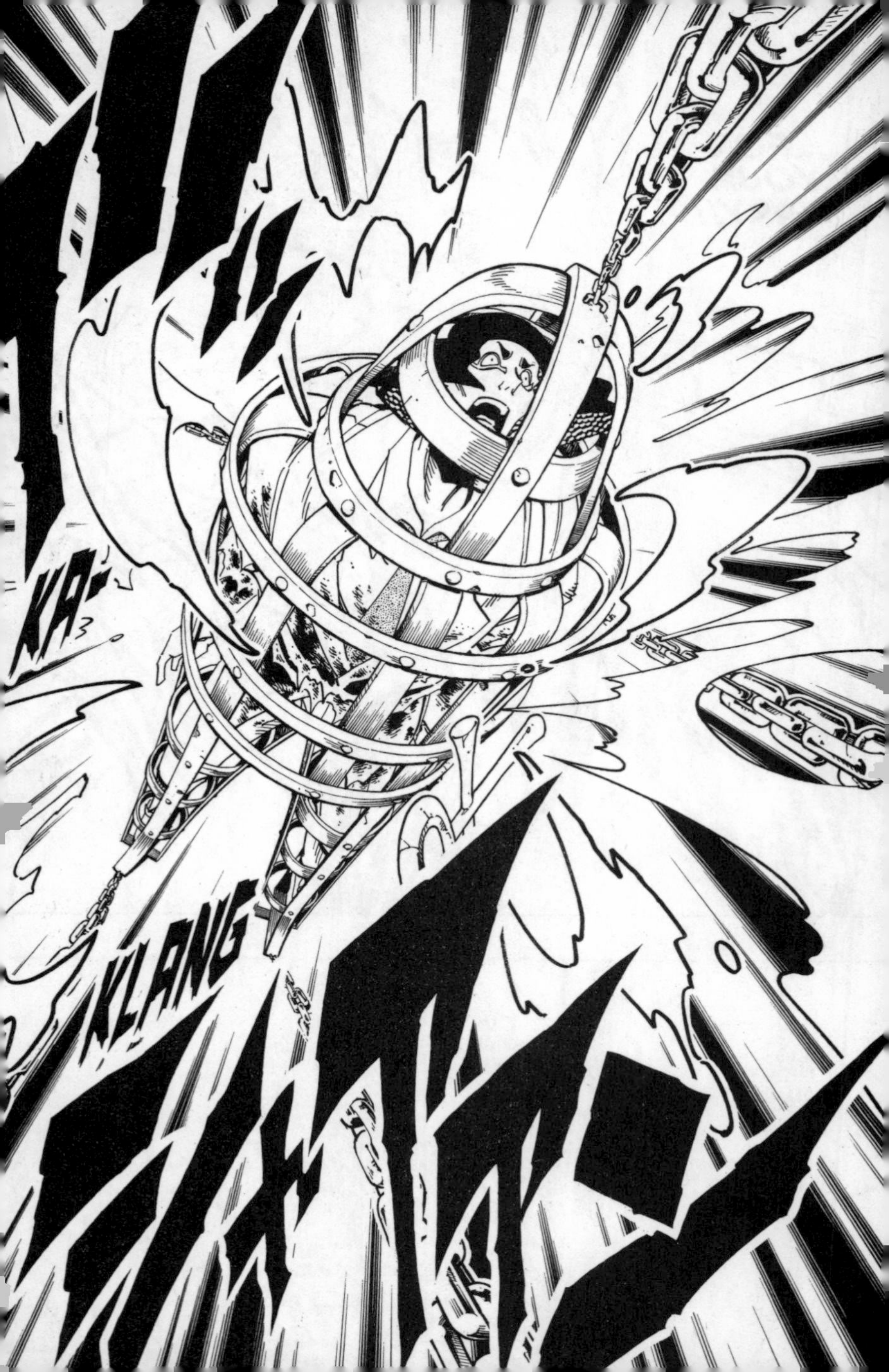
KA-
KLANG

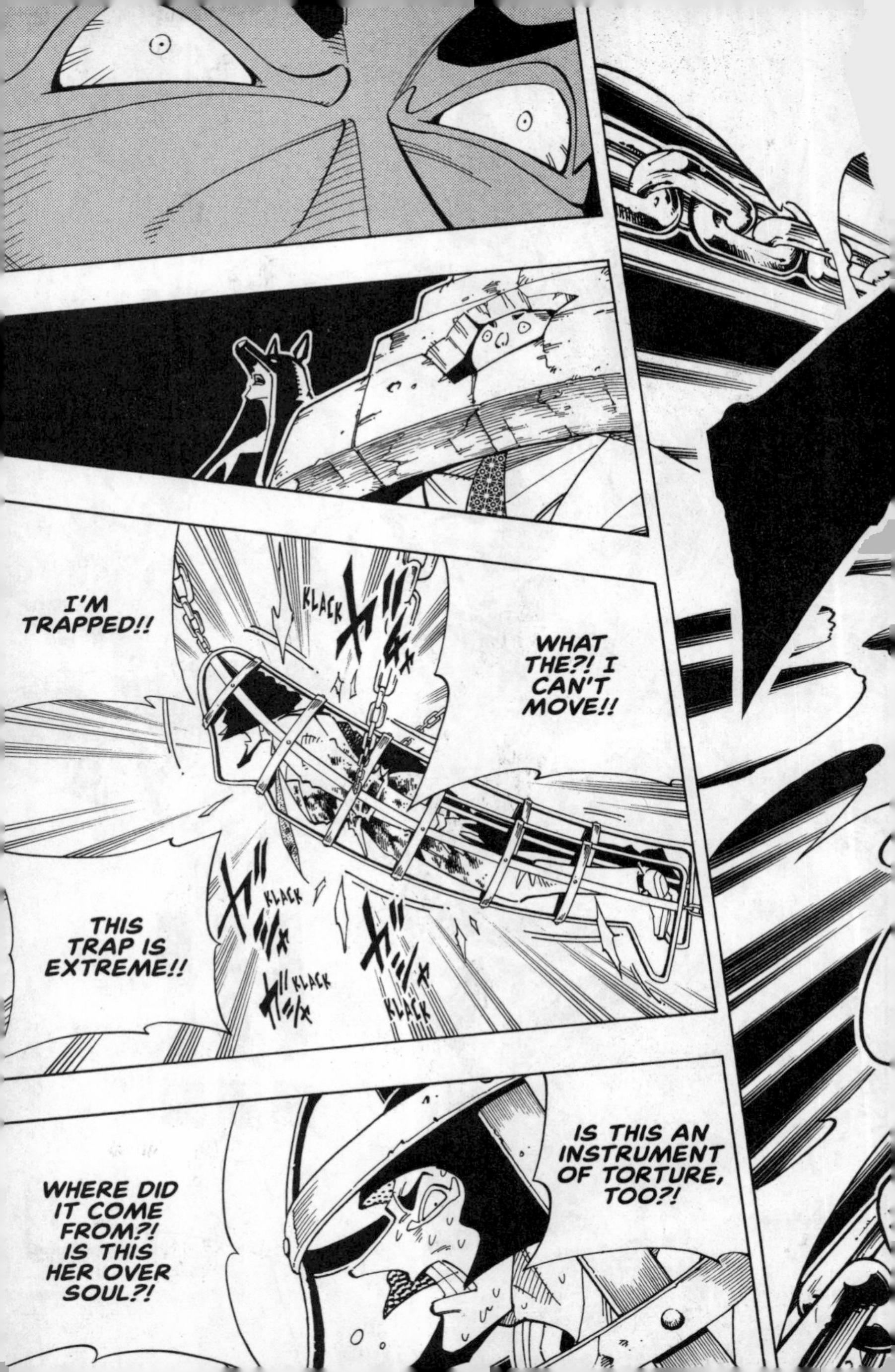
KLACK
WHAT THE?! I CAN'T MOVE!!
I'M TRAPPED!!
KLACK
KLACK
KLACK
THIS TRAP IS EXTREME!!
IS THIS AN INSTRUMENT OF TORTURE, TOO?!
WHERE DID IT COME FROM?! IS THIS HER OVER SOUL?!

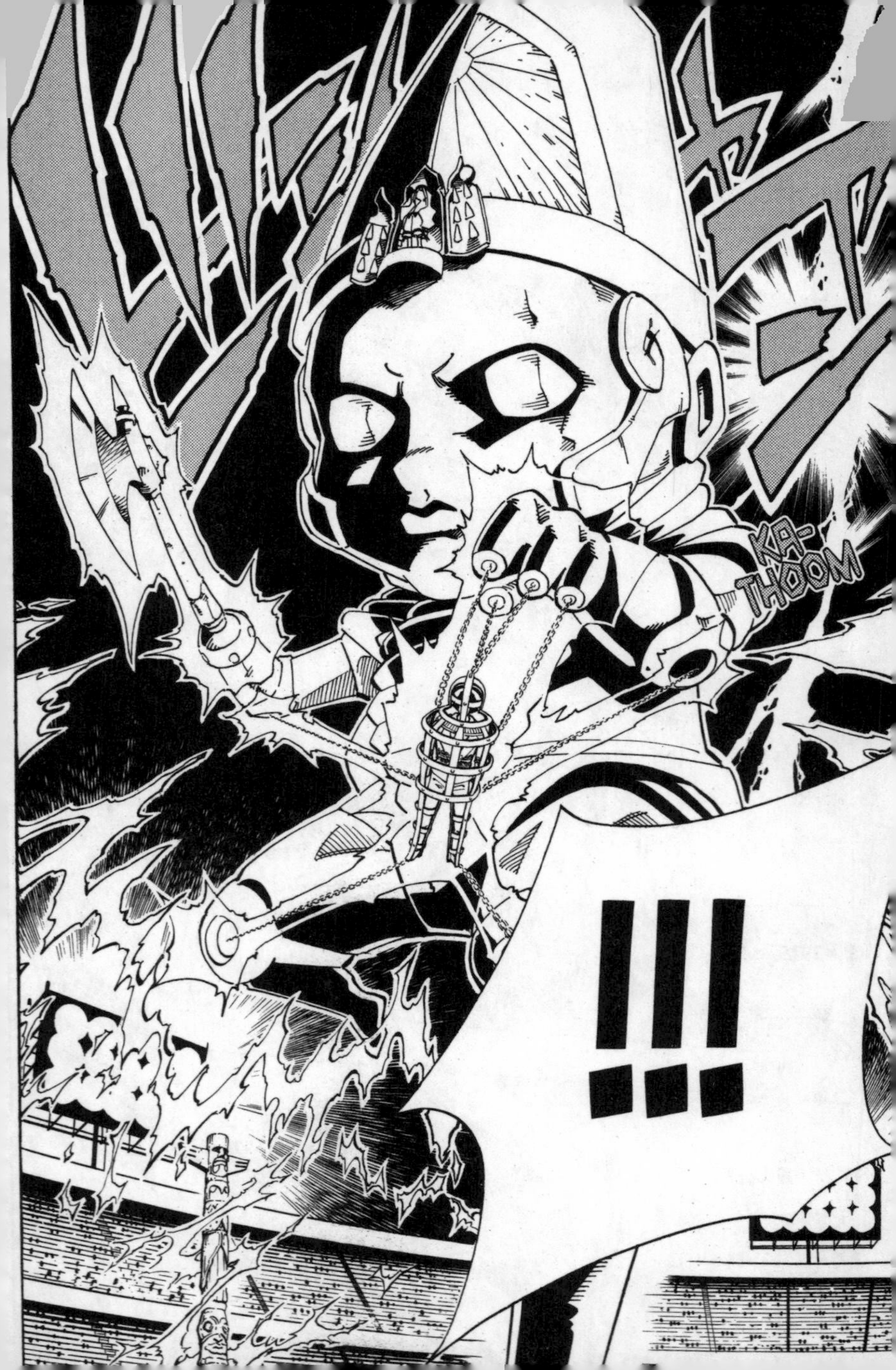
KA-THOOM
!!!

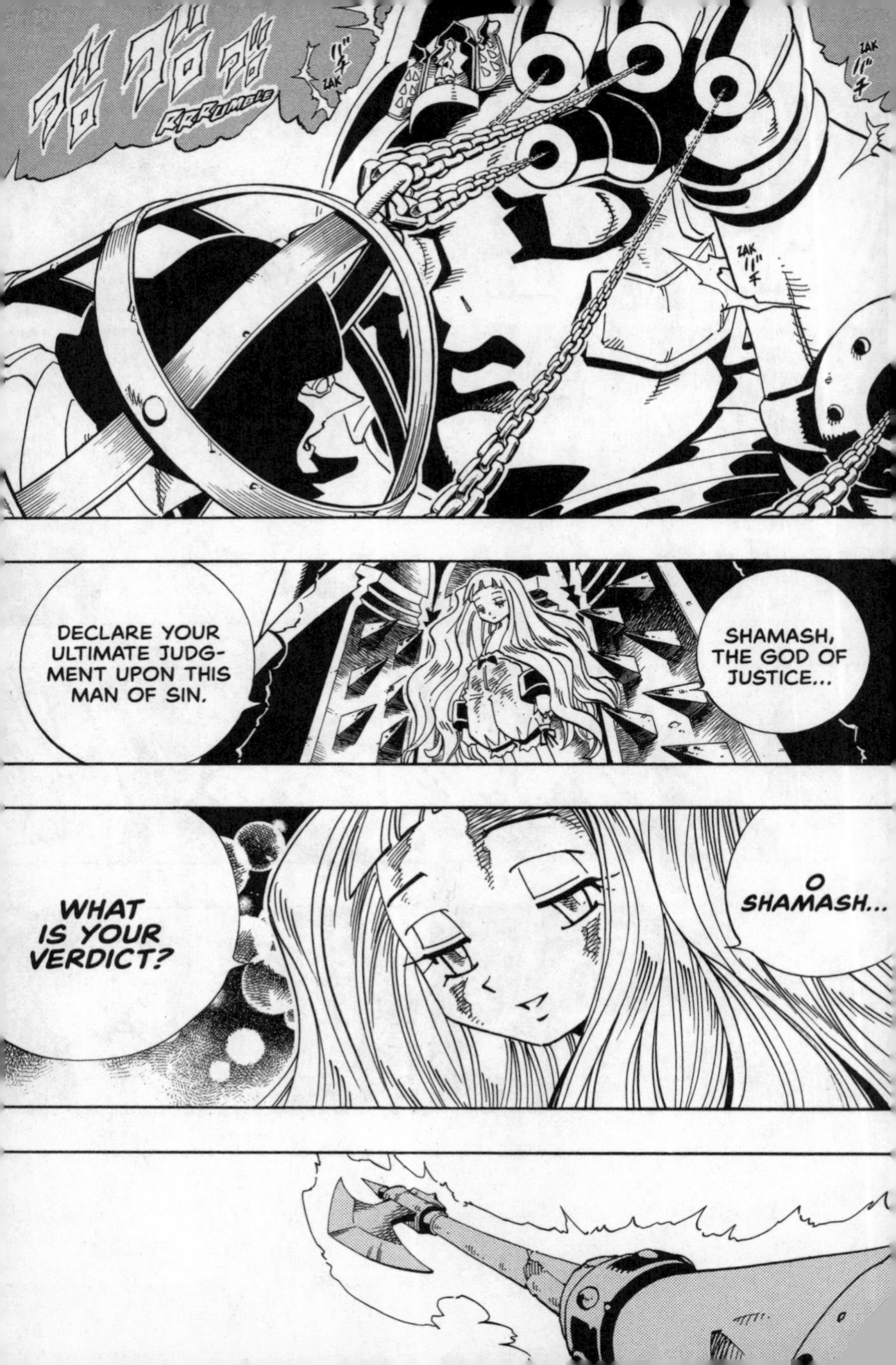
ZAK
ZAK
RRRUMBLE
ZAK
ZAK
SHAMASH, THE GOD OF JUSTICE...
DECLARE YOUR ULTIMATE JUDGMENT UPON THIS MAN OF SIN.
O SHAMASH...
WHAT IS YOUR VERDICT?

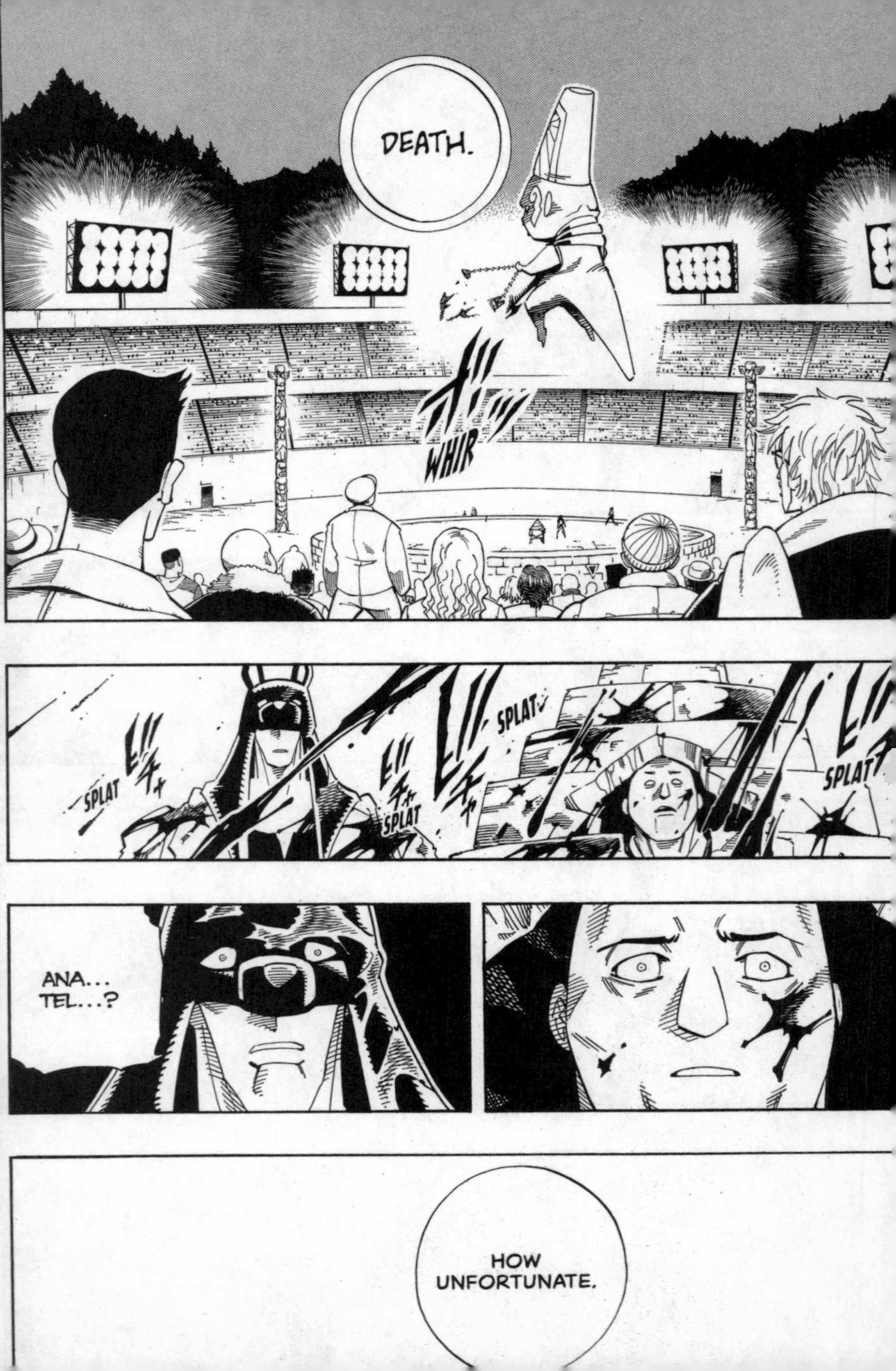
DEATH.
WHIR
SPLAT
SPLAT
SPLAT
SPLAT
ANA...
TEL...?
HOW
UNFORTUNATE.

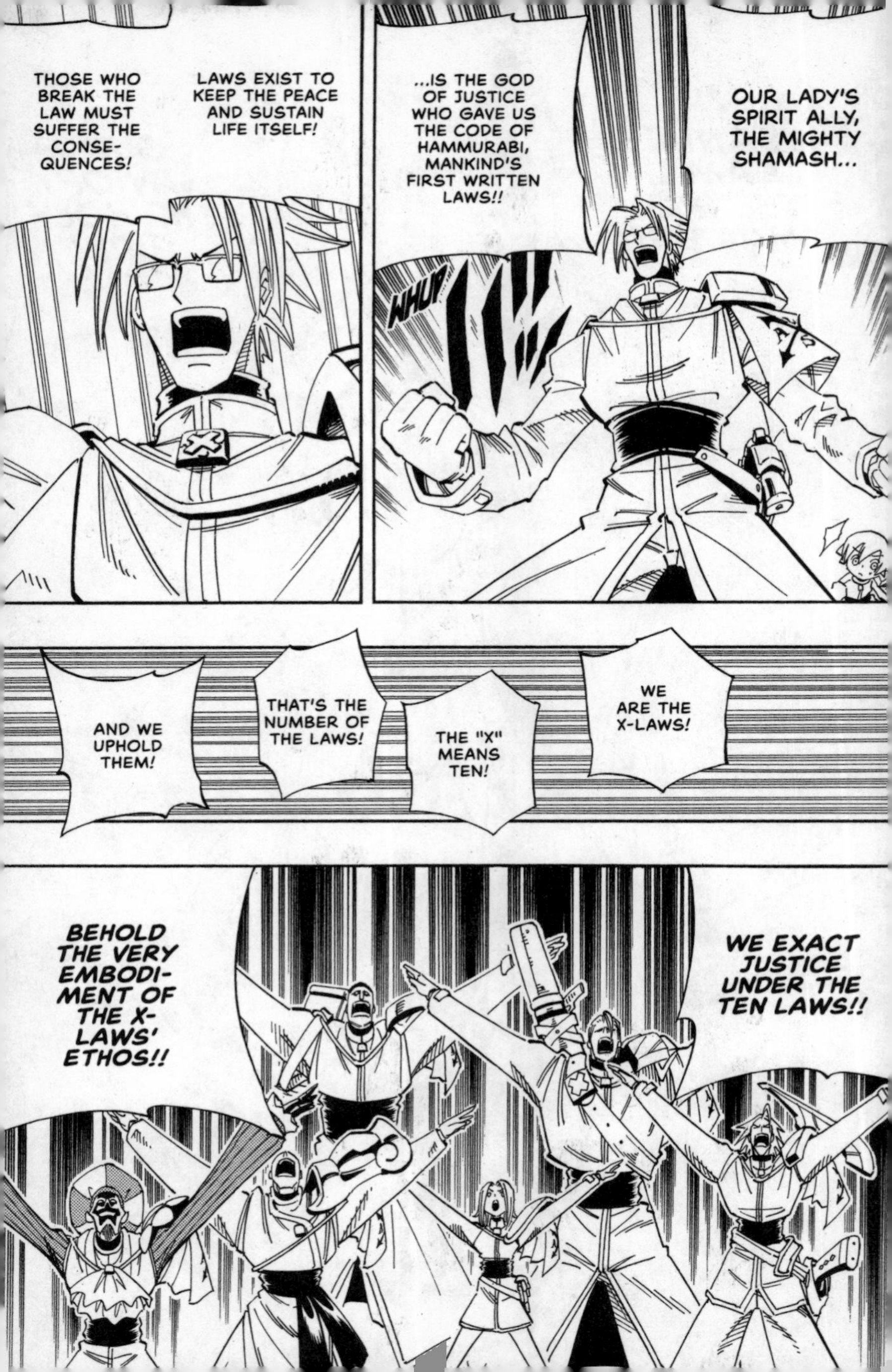
OUR LADY'S SPIRIT ALLY, THE MIGHTY SHAMASH...
...IS THE GOD OF JUSTICE WHO GAVE US THE CODE OF HAMMURABI, MANKIND'S FIRST WRITTEN LAWS!!
WHUP
LAWS EXIST TO KEEP THE PEACE AND SUSTAIN LIFE ITSELF!
THOSE WHO BREAK THE LAW MUST SUFFER THE CONSE-QUENCES!
WE ARE THE X-LAWS!
THE "X" MEANS TEN!
THAT'S THE NUMBER OF THE LAWS!
AND WE UPHOLD THEM!
WE EXACT JUSTICE UNDER THE TEN LAWS!!
BEHOLD THE VERY EMBODI-MENT OF THE X-LAWS' ETHOS!!

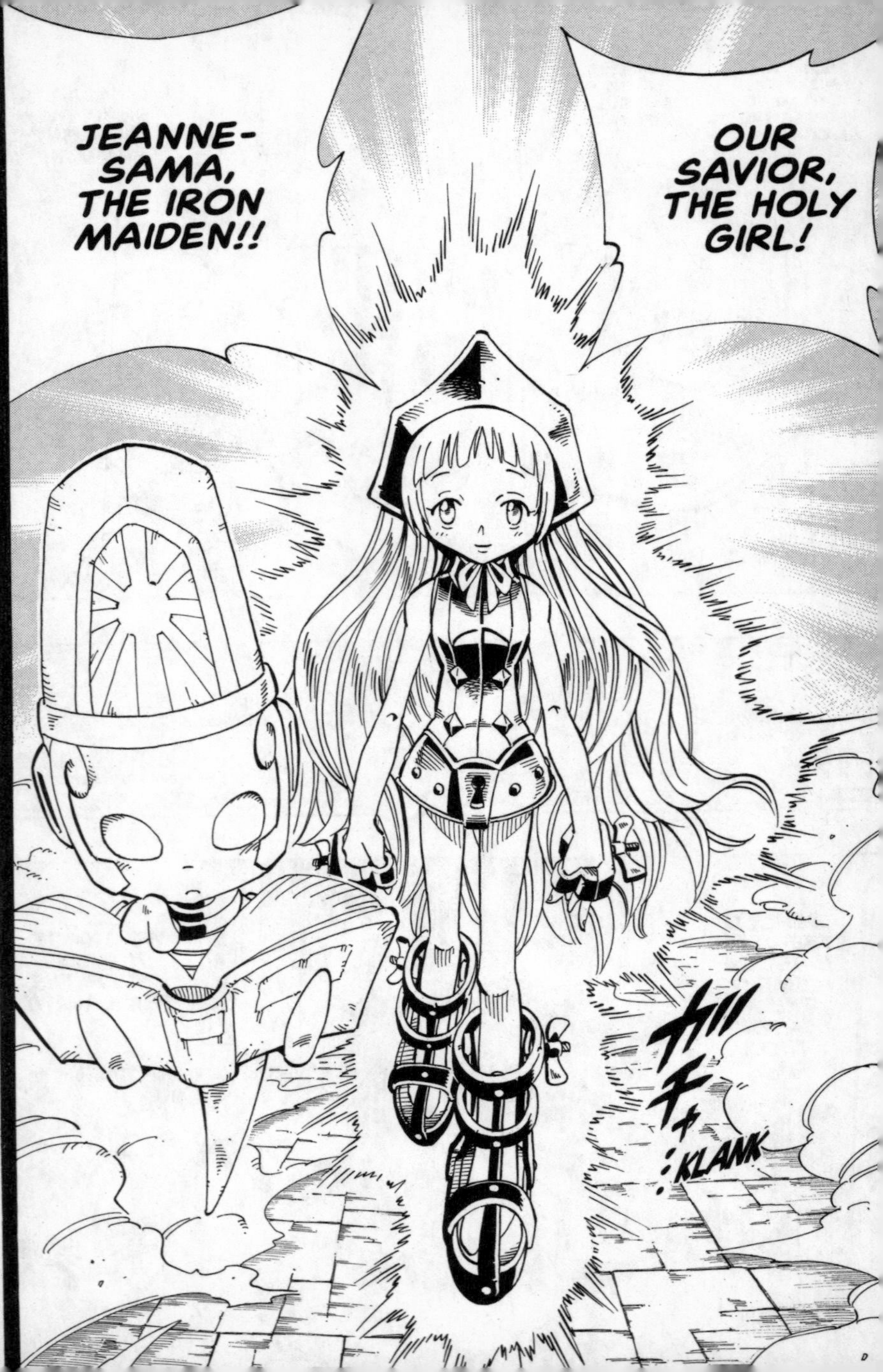
OUR SAVIOR, THE HOLY GIRL!
JEANNE-SAMA, THE IRON MAIDEN!!
ガチャ
KLANK

Instrument of Torture: The Iron Maiden

(For Jeanne's Private Use)

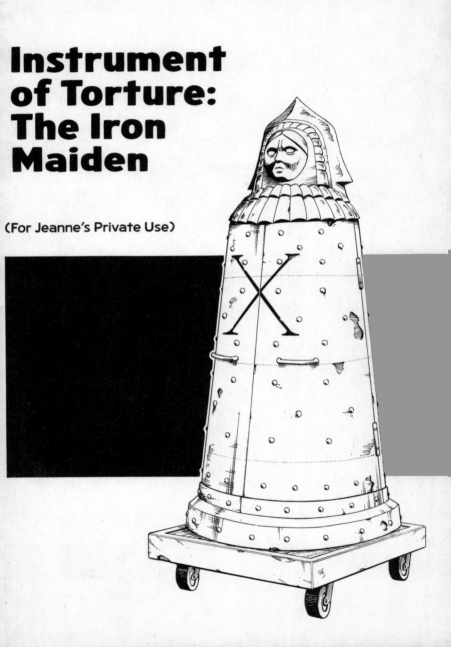

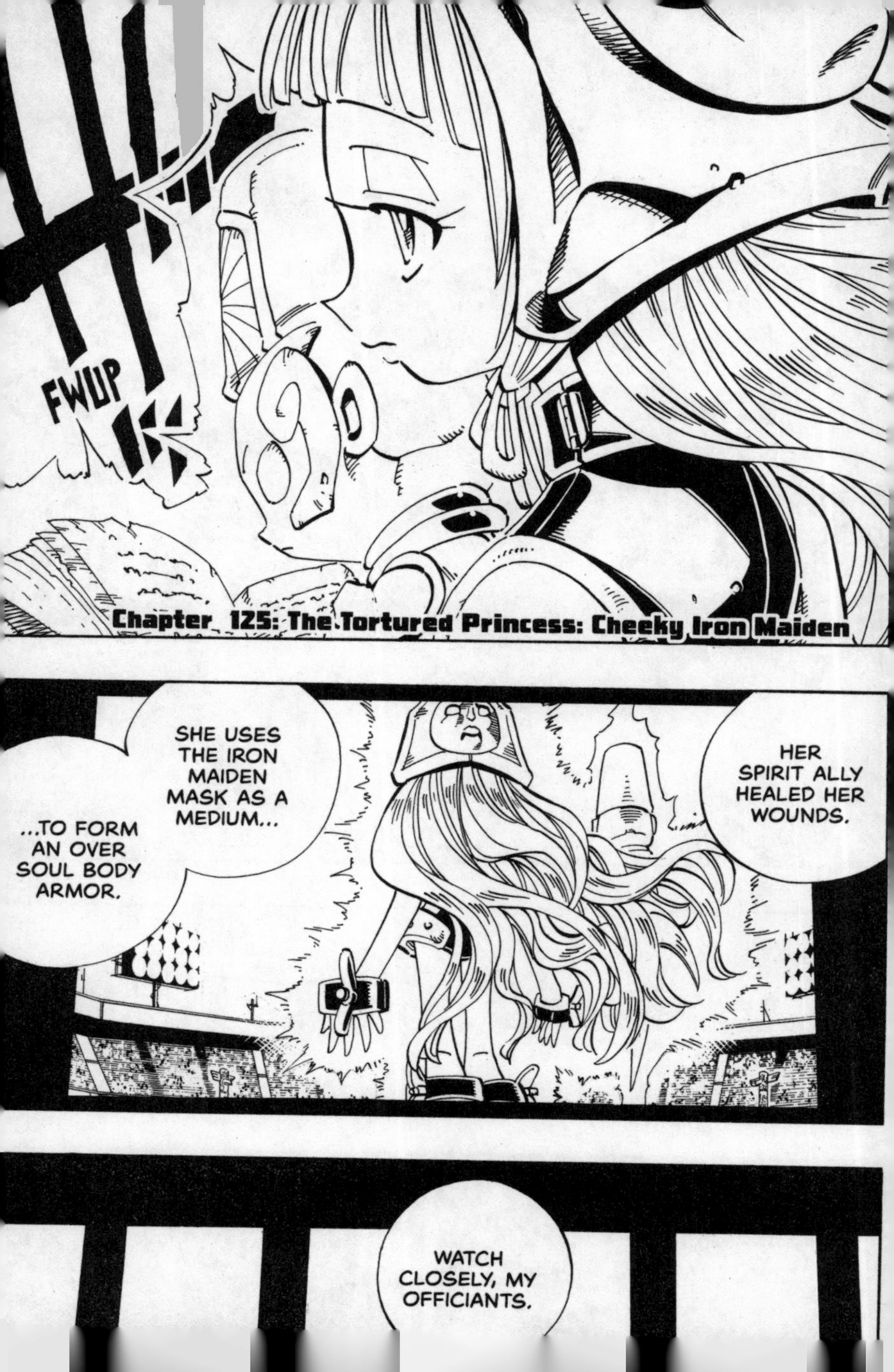
FWUP
Chapter 125: The Tortured Princess: Cheeky Iron Maiden
HER SPIRIT ALLY HEALED HER WOUNDS.
SHE USES THE IRON MAIDEN MASK AS A MEDIUM...
...TO FORM AN OVER SOUL BODY ARMOR.
WATCH CLOSELY, MY OFFICIANTS.

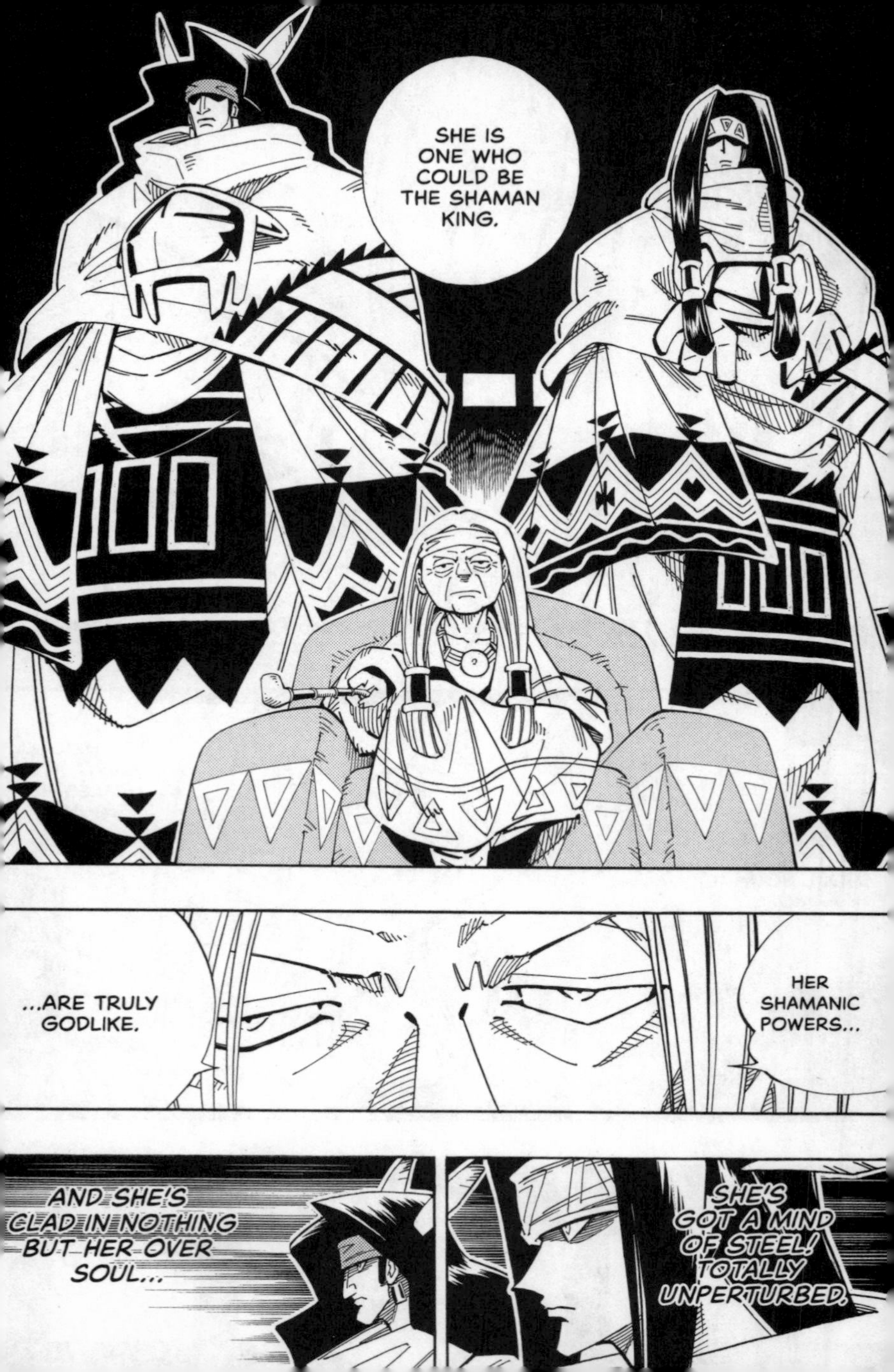
SHE IS ONE WHO COULD BE THE SHAMAN KING.
HER SHAMANIC POWERS...
...ARE TRULY GODLIKE.
SHE'S GOT A MIND OF STEEL! TOTALLY UNPERTURBED.
AND SHE'S CLAD IN NOTHING BUT HER OVER SOUL...

Chapter 125:

The Tortured Princess:

Cheeky Iron Maiden

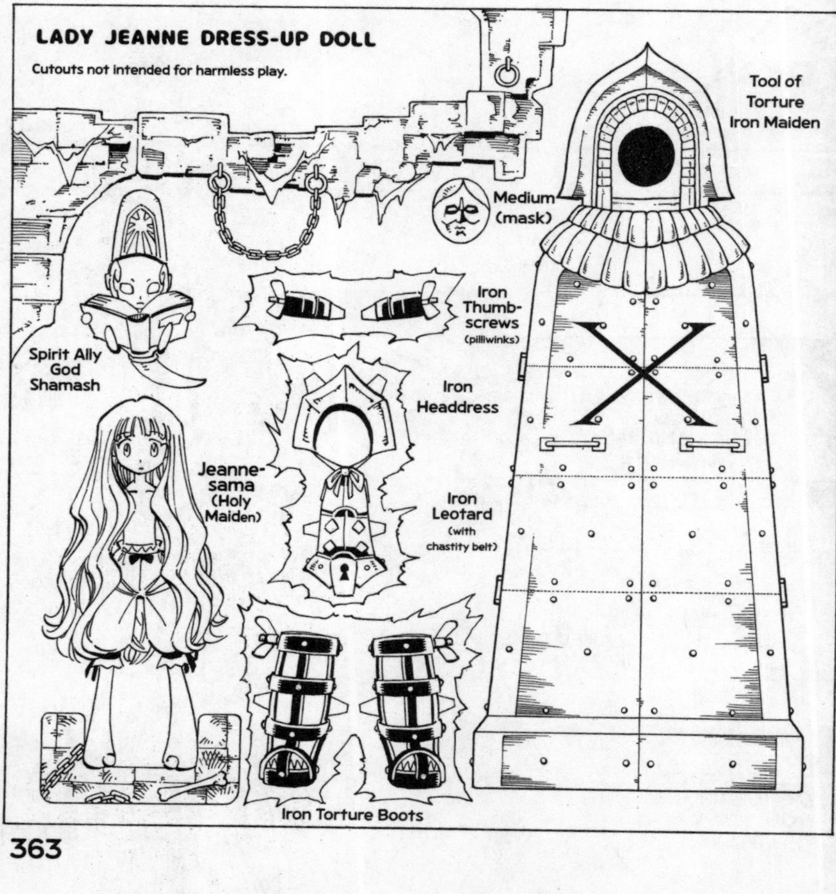

LADY JEANNE DRESS-UP DOLL
Cutouts not intended for harmless play.
Tool of Torture Iron Maiden
Medium (mask)
Iron Thumb-screws (pilliwinks)
Spirit Ally God Shamash
Iron Headdress
Jeanne-sama (Holy Maiden)
Iron Leotard (with chastity belt)
Iron Torture Boots

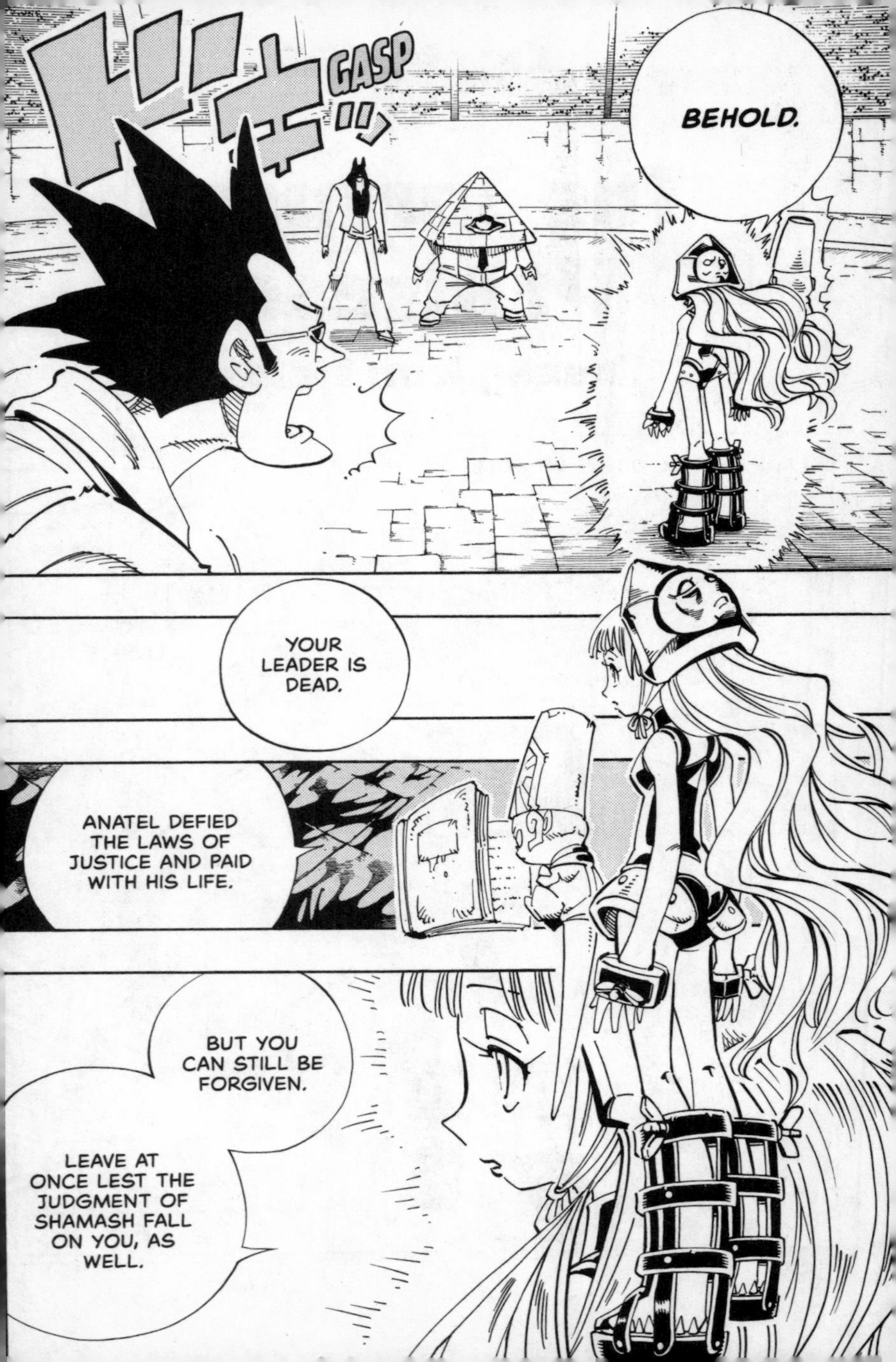
BEHOLD.
GASP
YOUR LEADER IS DEAD.
ANATEL DEFIED THE LAWS OF JUSTICE AND PAID WITH HIS LIFE.
BUT YOU CAN STILL BE FORGIVEN.
LEAVE AT ONCE LEST THE JUDGMENT OF SHAMASH FALL ON YOU, AS WELL.

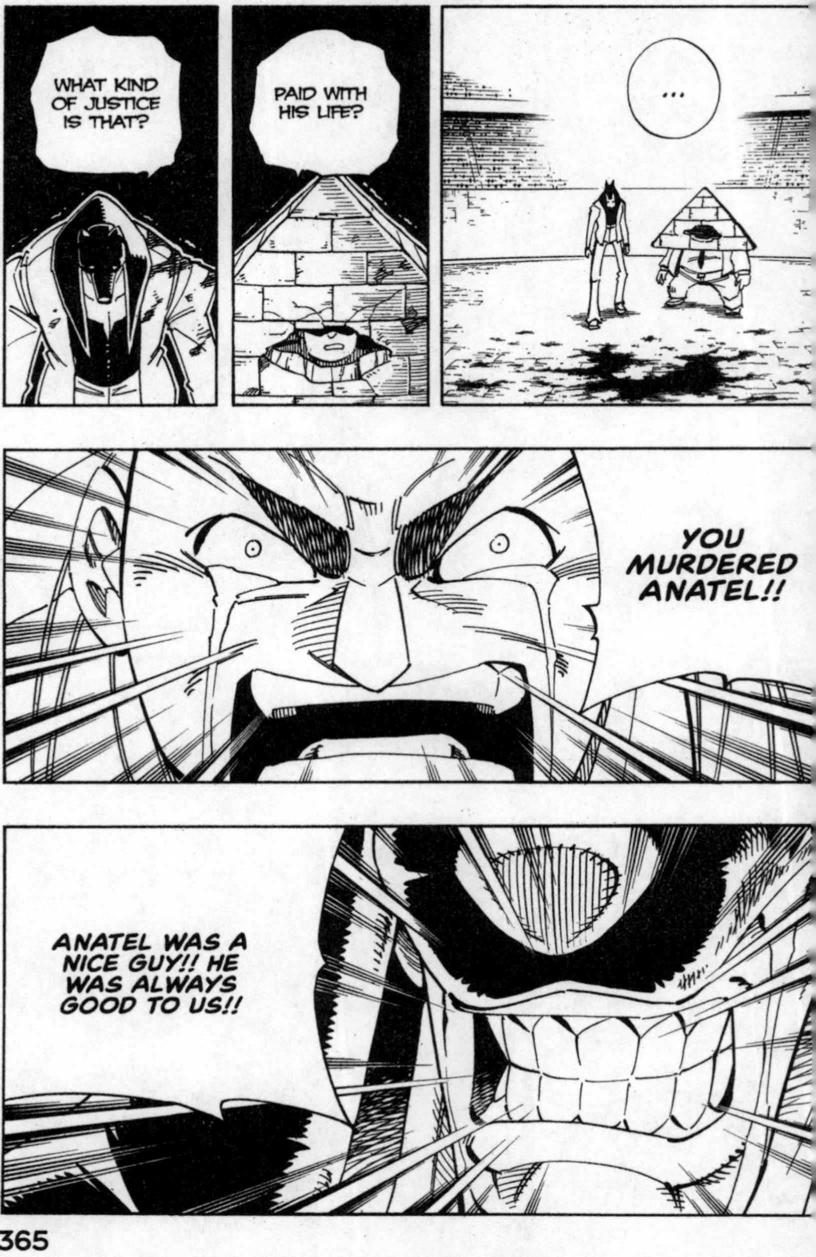
...
PAID WITH HIS LIFE?
WHAT KIND OF JUSTICE IS THAT?
YOU MURDERED ANATEL!!
ANATEL WAS A NICE GUY!! HE WAS ALWAYS GOOD TO US!!

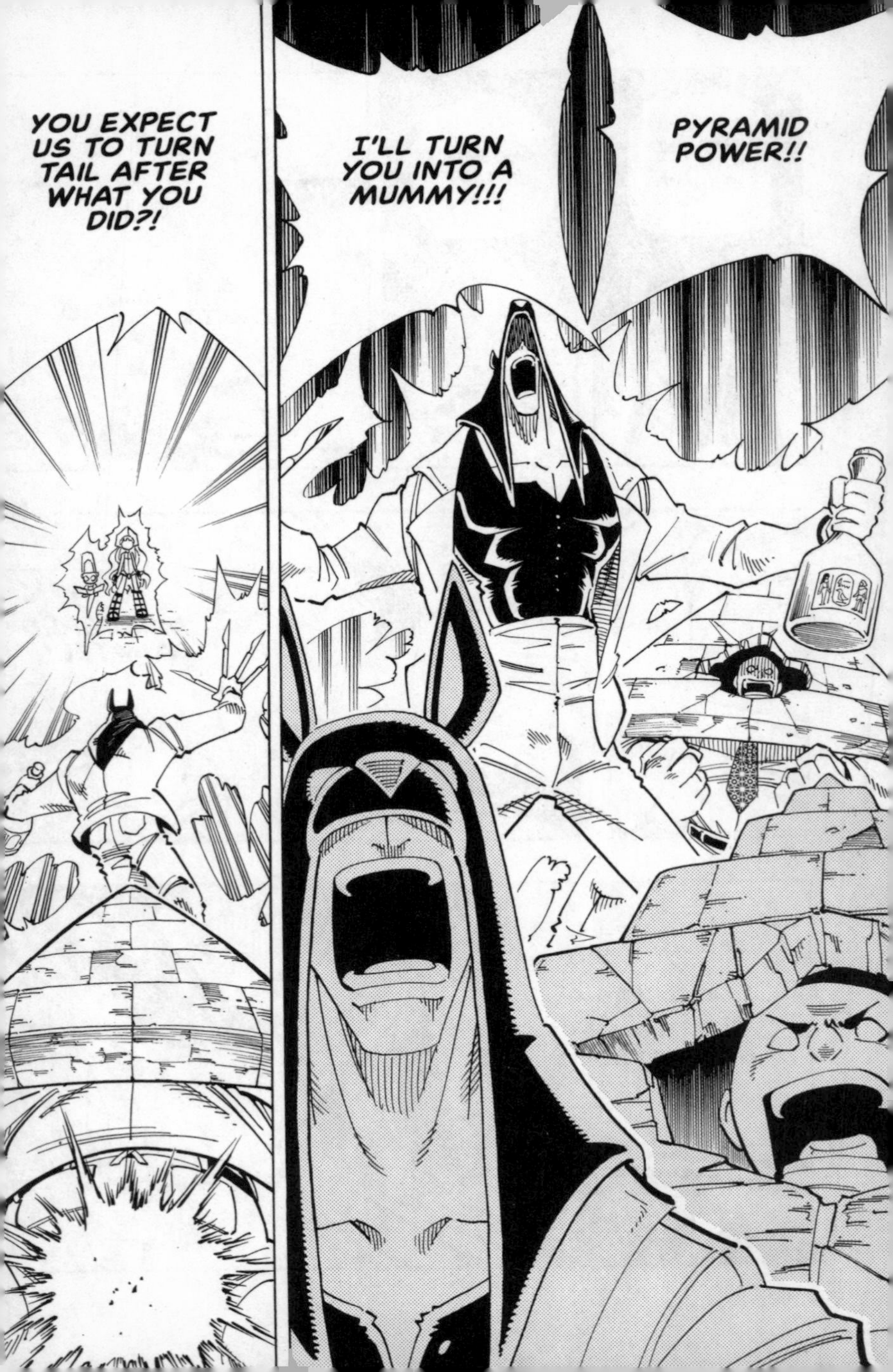
PYRAMID POWER!!
I'LL TURN YOU INTO A MUMMY!!!
YOU EXPECT US TO TURN TAIL AFTER WHAT YOU DID?!

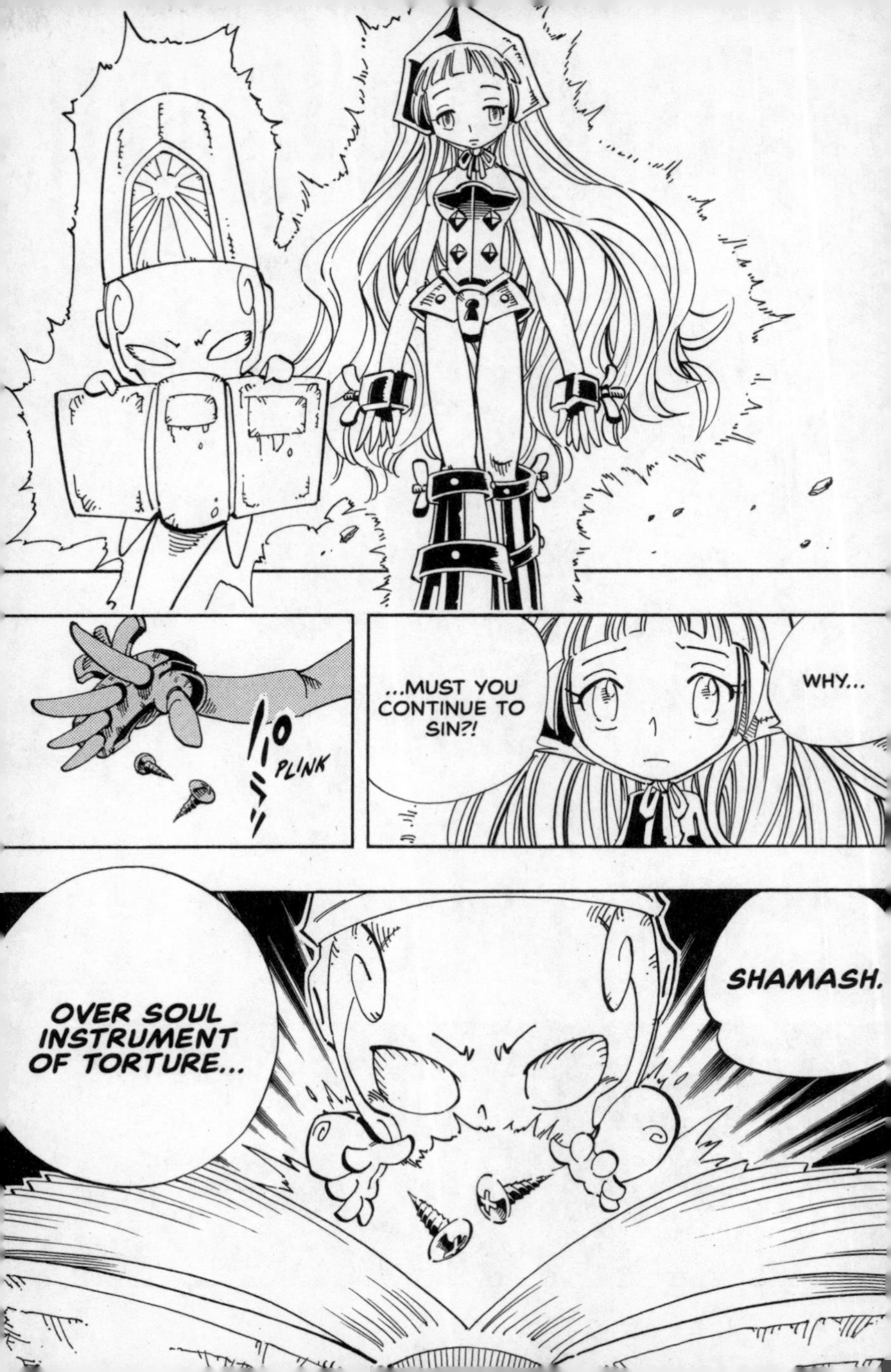

WHY...
...MUST YOU CONTINUE TO SIN?!
PLINK
SHAMASH.
OVER SOUL INSTRUMENT OF TORTURE...

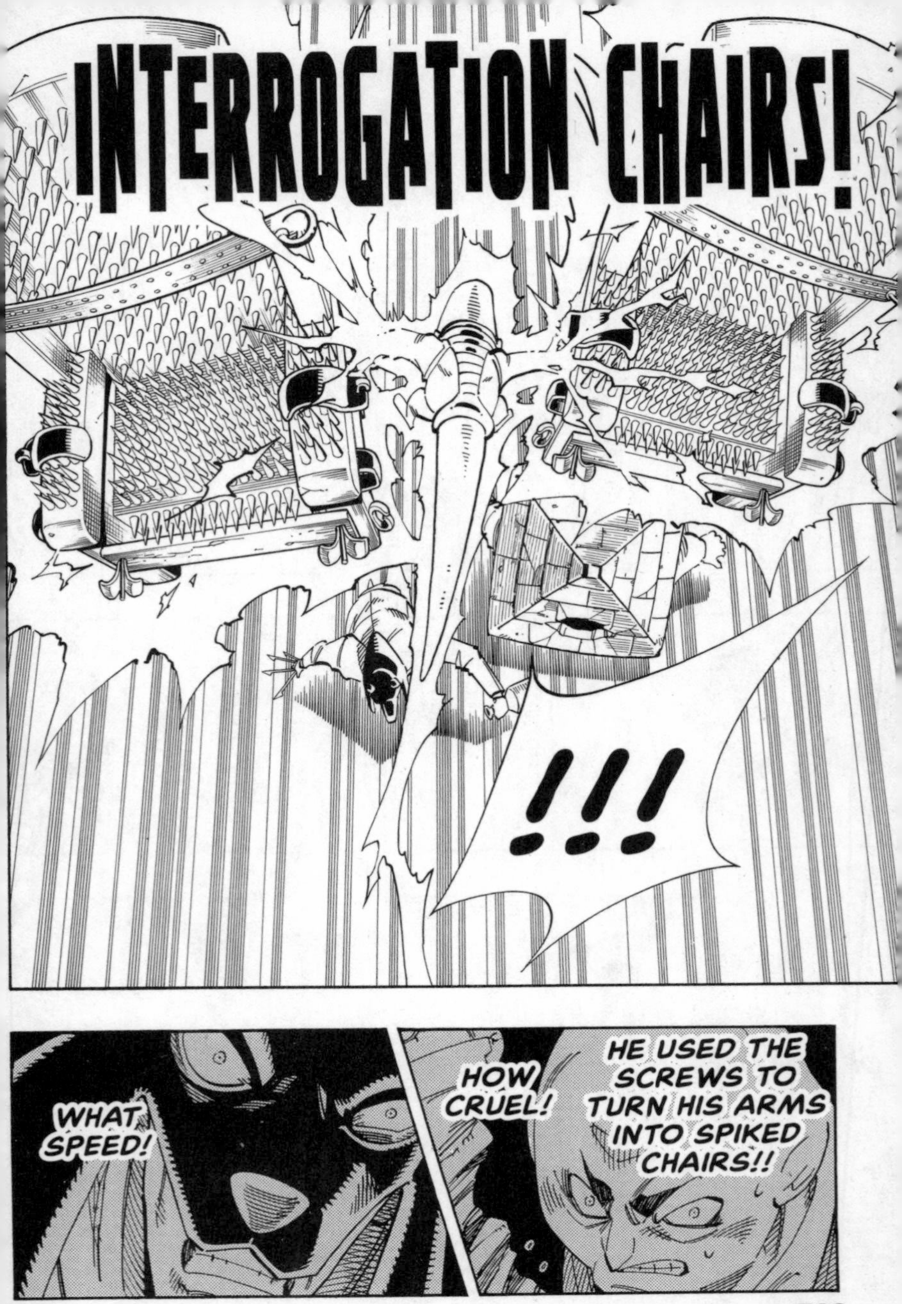
INTERROGATION CHAIRS!
!!!
HE USED THE SCREWS TO TURN HIS ARMS INTO SPIKED CHAIRS!!
HOW CRUEL!
WHAT SPEED!

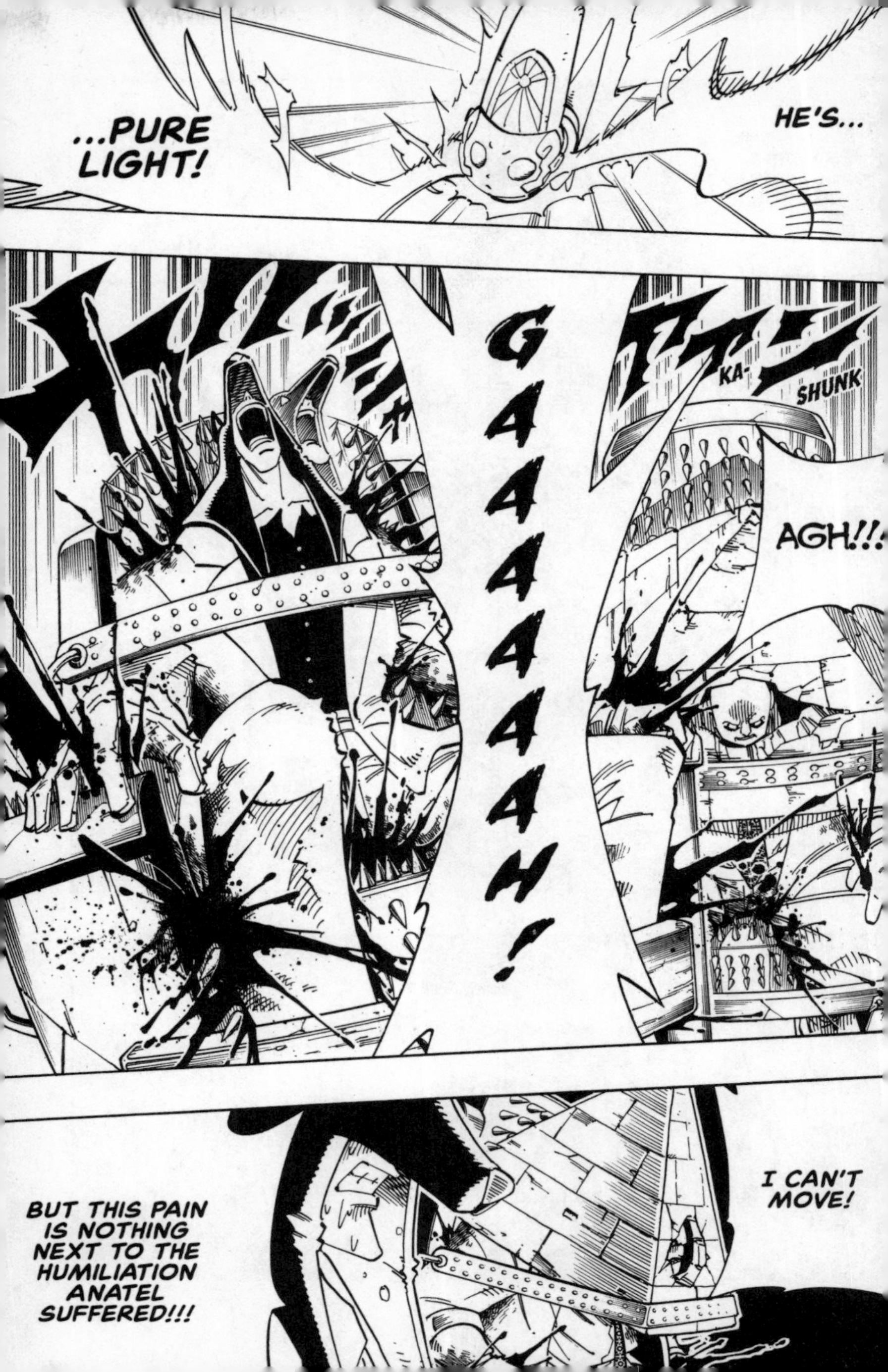

HE'S...
...PURE LIGHT!
KA-SHUNK
AGH!!!
GAAAAAAH!
I CAN'T MOVE!
BUT THIS PAIN IS NOTHING NEXT TO THE HUMILIATION ANATEL SUFFERED!!!

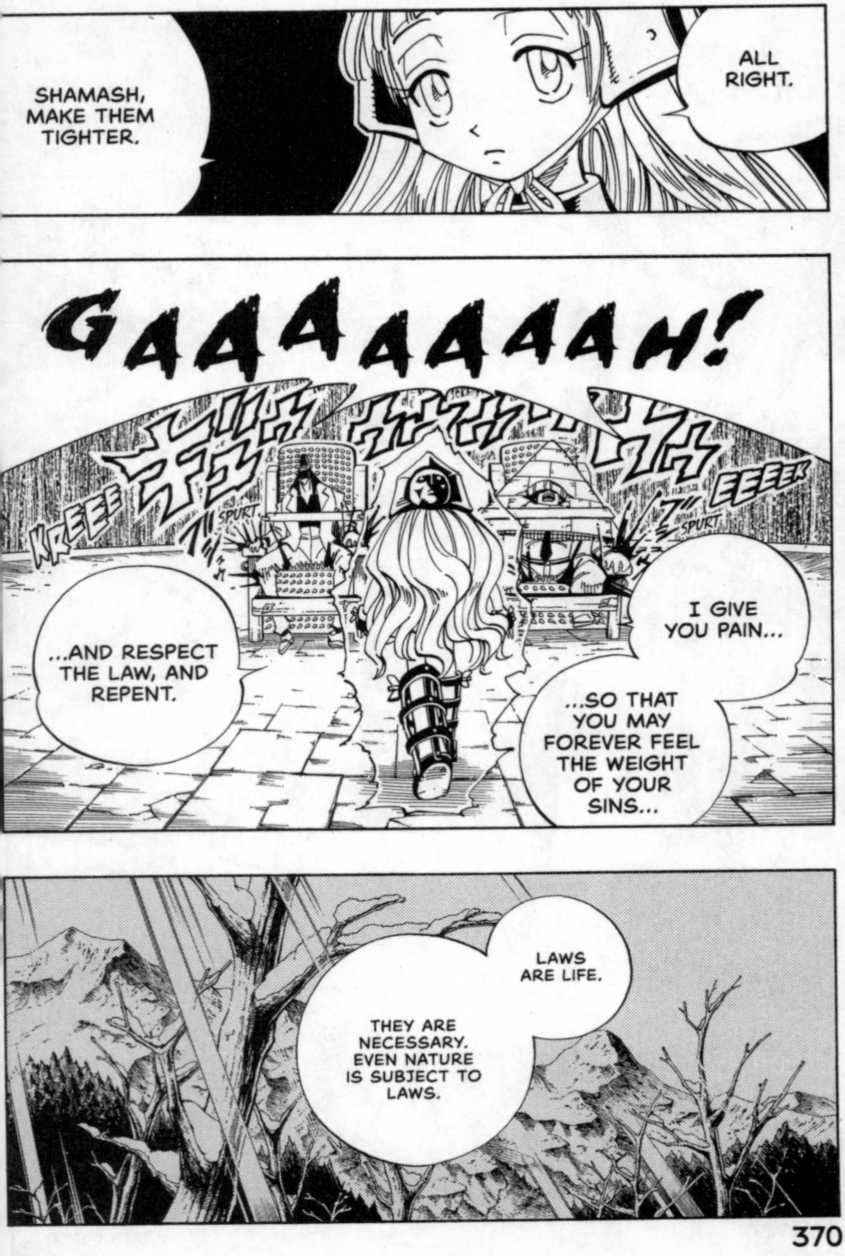
ALL RIGHT.
SHAMASH, MAKE THEM TIGHTER.
GAAAAAAH!
EEEEK
SPURT
I GIVE YOU PAIN...
...SO THAT YOU MAY FOREVER FEEL THE WEIGHT OF YOUR SINS...
KREEE
SPURT
...AND RESPECT THE LAW, AND REPENT.
LAWS ARE LIFE.
THEY ARE NECESSARY. EVEN NATURE IS SUBJECT TO LAWS.

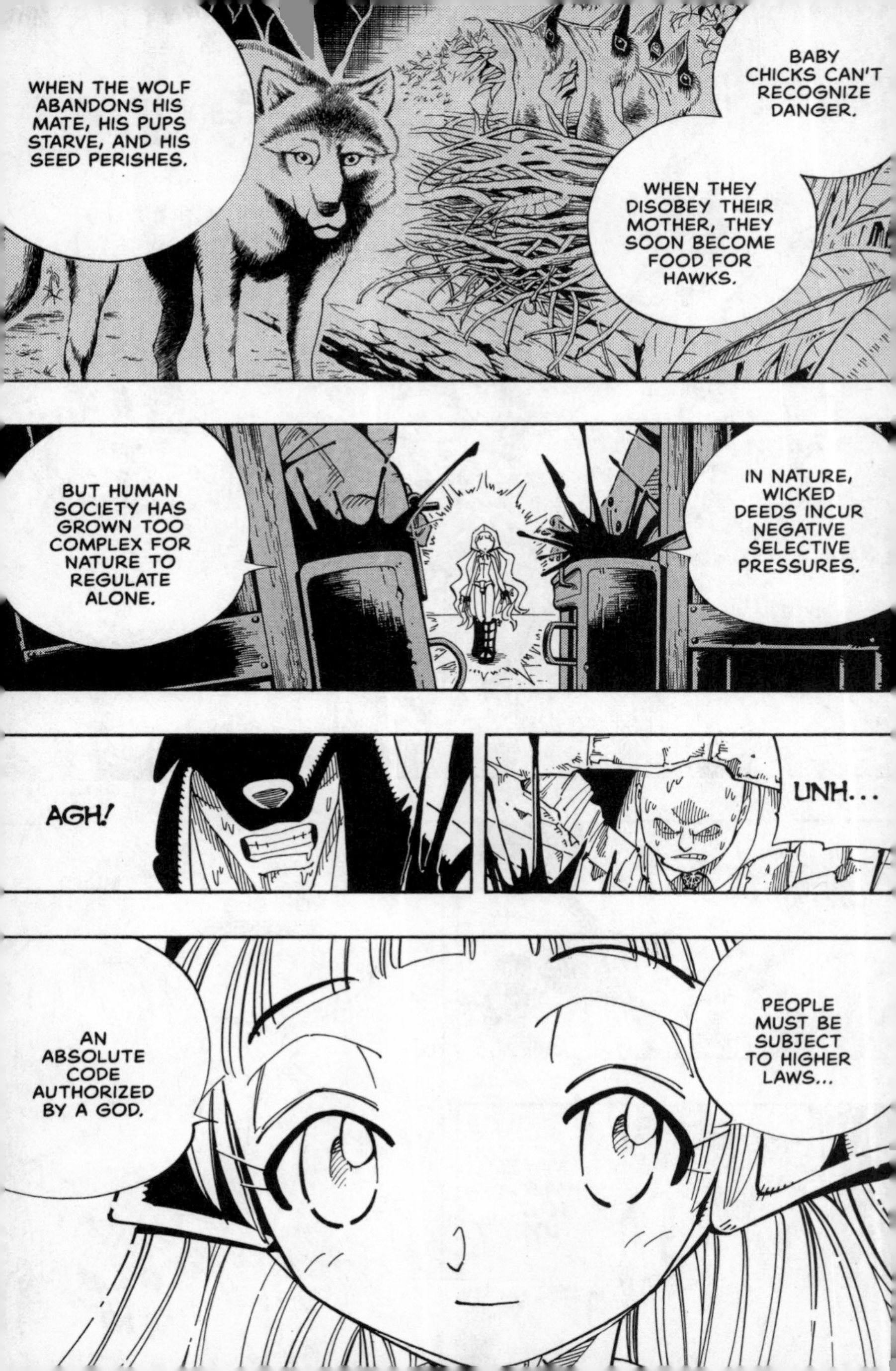
BABY CHICKS CAN'T RECOGNIZE DANGER.
WHEN THEY DISOBEY THEIR MOTHER, THEY SOON BECOME FOOD FOR HAWKS.
WHEN THE WOLF ABANDONS HIS MATE, HIS PUPS STARVE, AND HIS SEED PERISHES.
IN NATURE, WICKED DEEDS INCUR NEGATIVE SELECTIVE PRESSURES.
BUT HUMAN SOCIETY HAS GROWN TOO COMPLEX FOR NATURE TO REGULATE ALONE.
UNH...
AGH!
PEOPLE MUST BE SUBJECT TO HIGHER LAWS...
AN ABSOLUTE CODE AUTHORIZED BY A GOD.

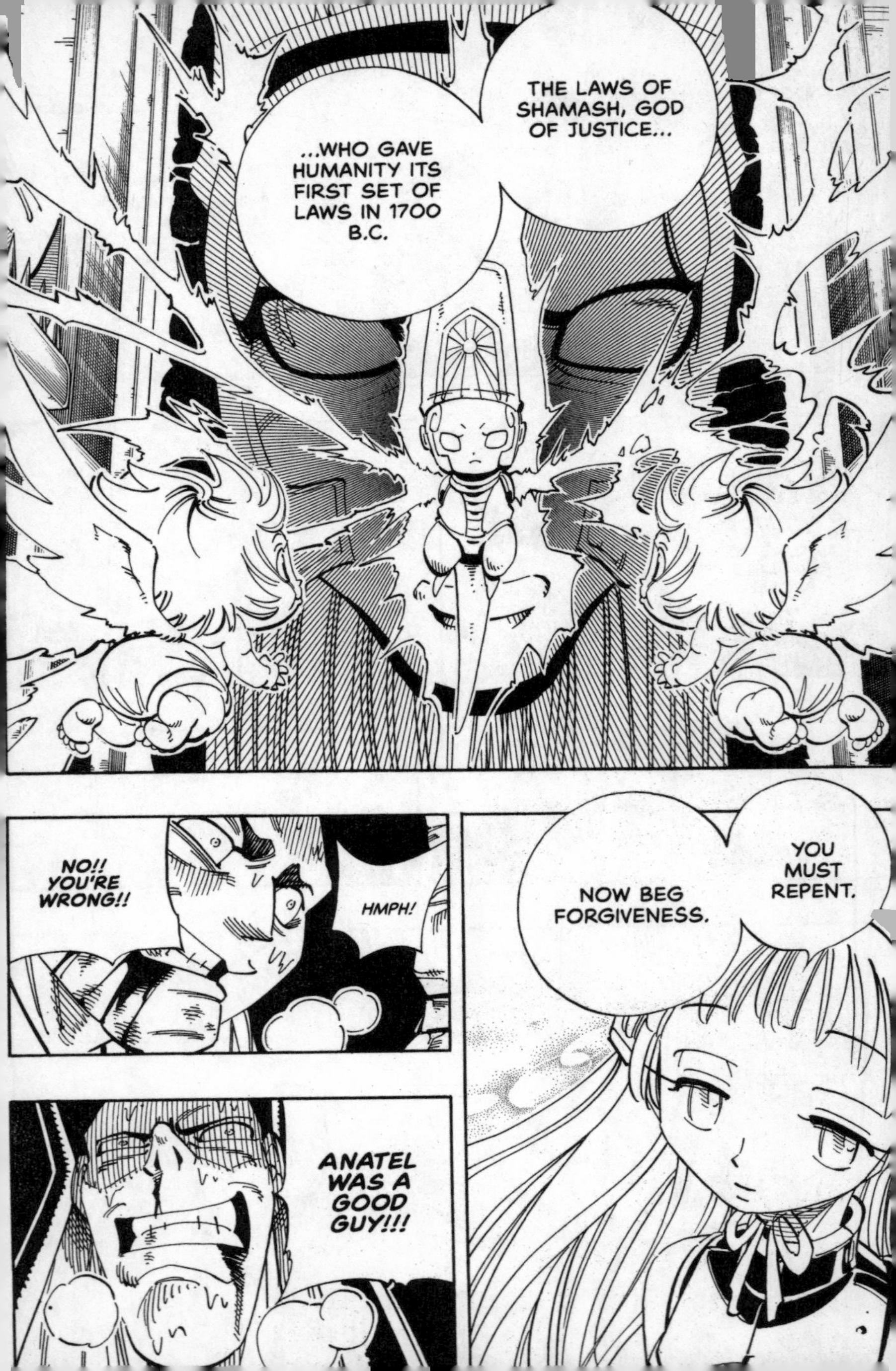
THE LAWS OF SHAMASH, GOD OF JUSTICE...
...WHO GAVE HUMANITY ITS FIRST SET OF LAWS IN 1700 B.C.
YOU MUST REPENT.
NOW BEG FORGIVENESS.
NO!! YOU'RE WRONG!!
HMPH!
ANATEL WAS A GOOD GUY!!!

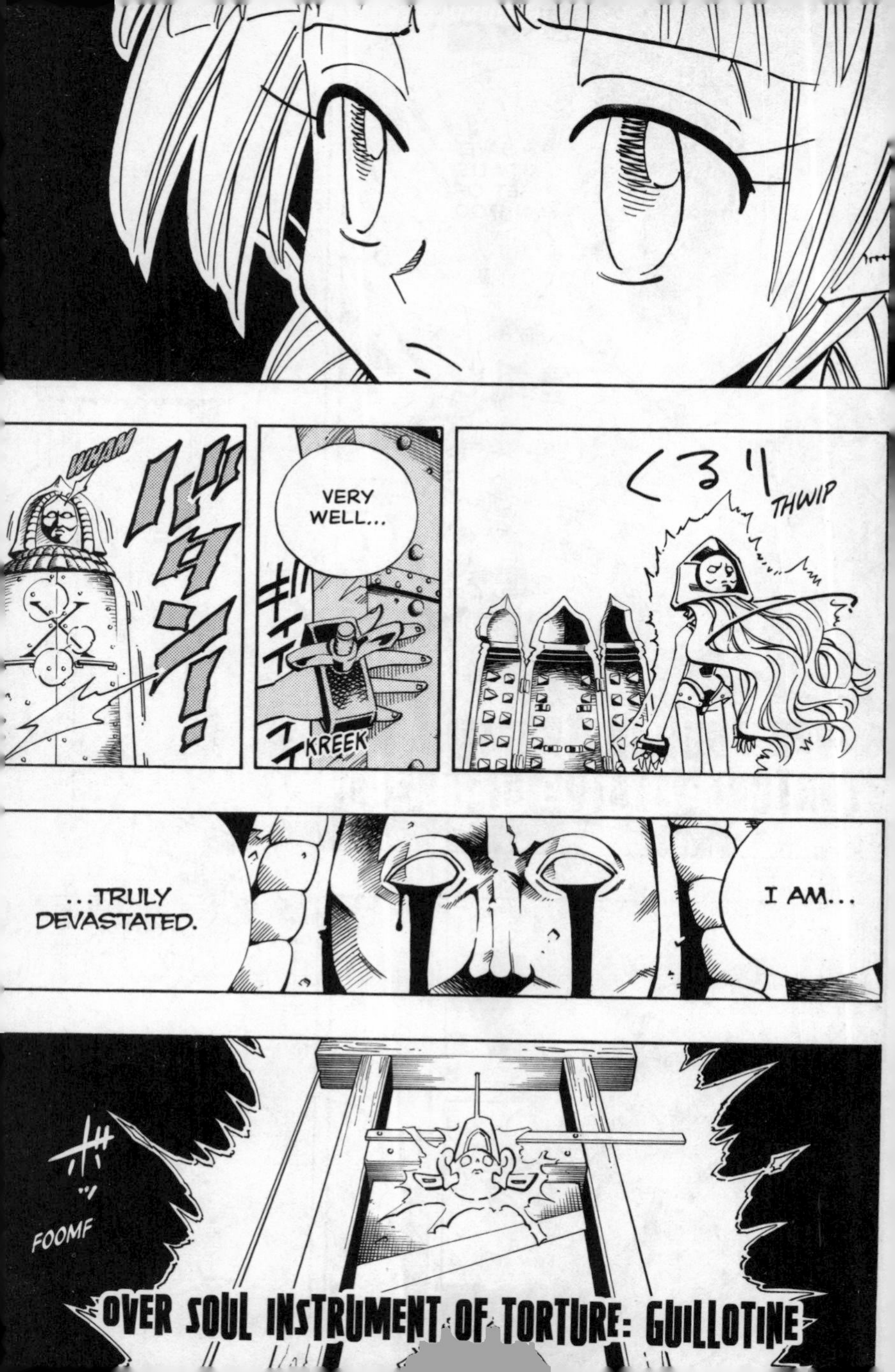

くるり
THWIP
VERY WELL...
KREEK
WHAM
バタン!
I AM...
...TRULY DEVASTATED.
FOOMF
OVER SOUL INSTRUMENT OF TORTURE: GUILLOTINE

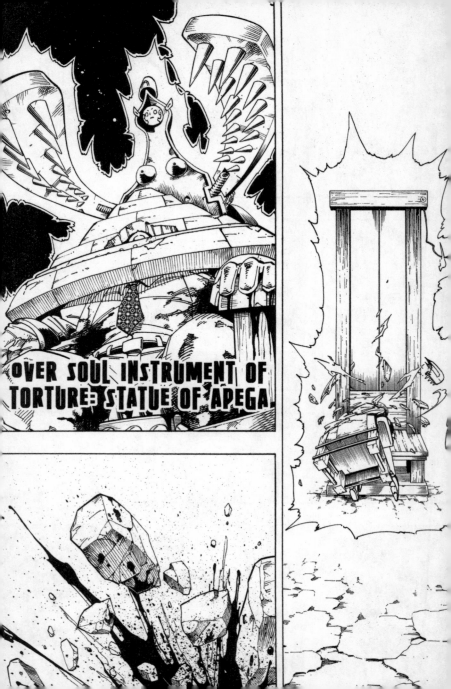

OVER SOUL INSTRUMENT OF TORTURE: STATUE OF APEGA

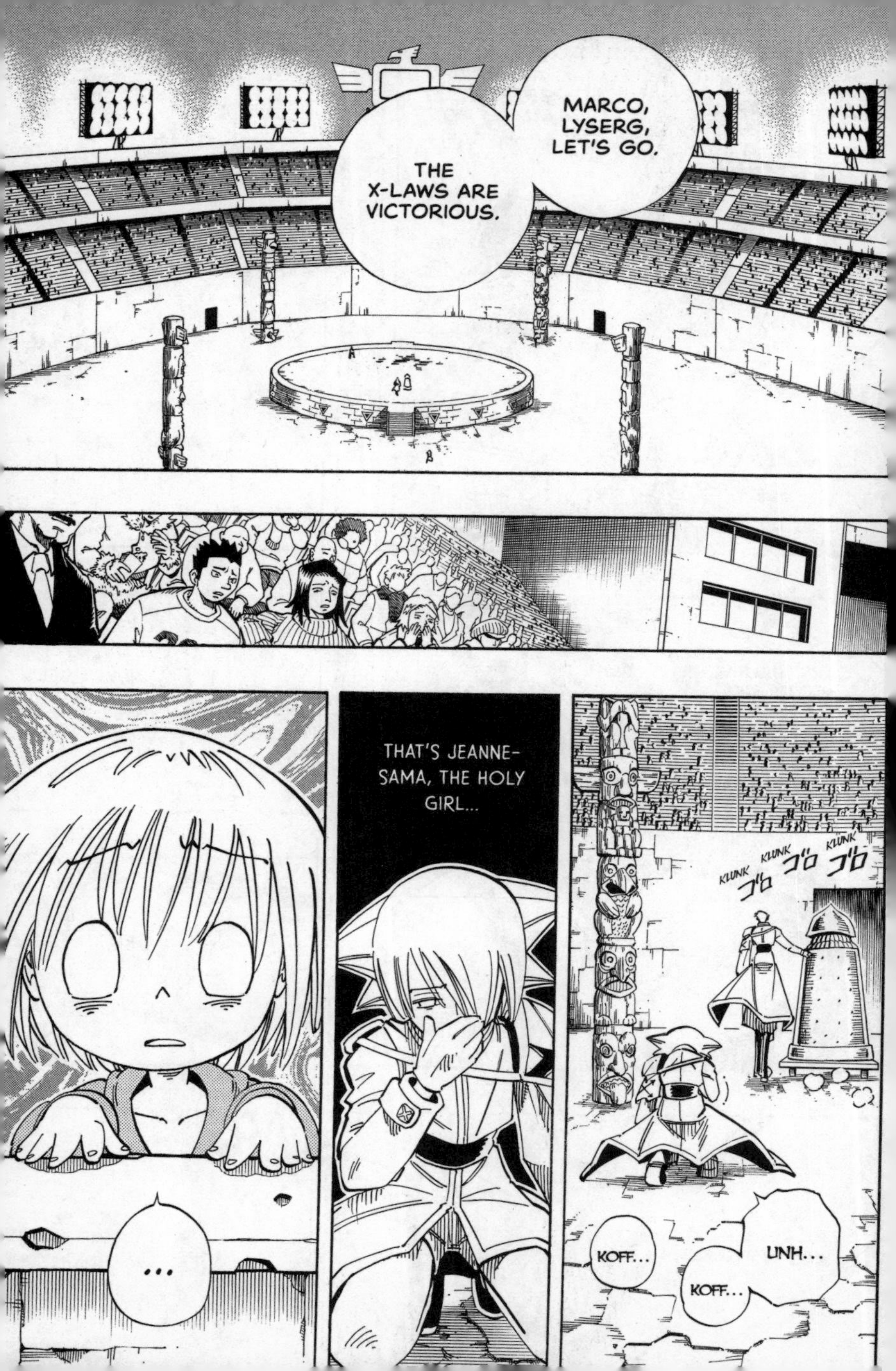

MARCO, LYSERG, LET'S GO.
THE X-LAWS ARE VICTORIOUS.
KLUNK ゴロ KLUNK ゴロ KLUNK ゴロ
UNH...
KOFF...
KOFF...
THAT'S JEANNE-SAMA, THE HOLY GIRL...
...

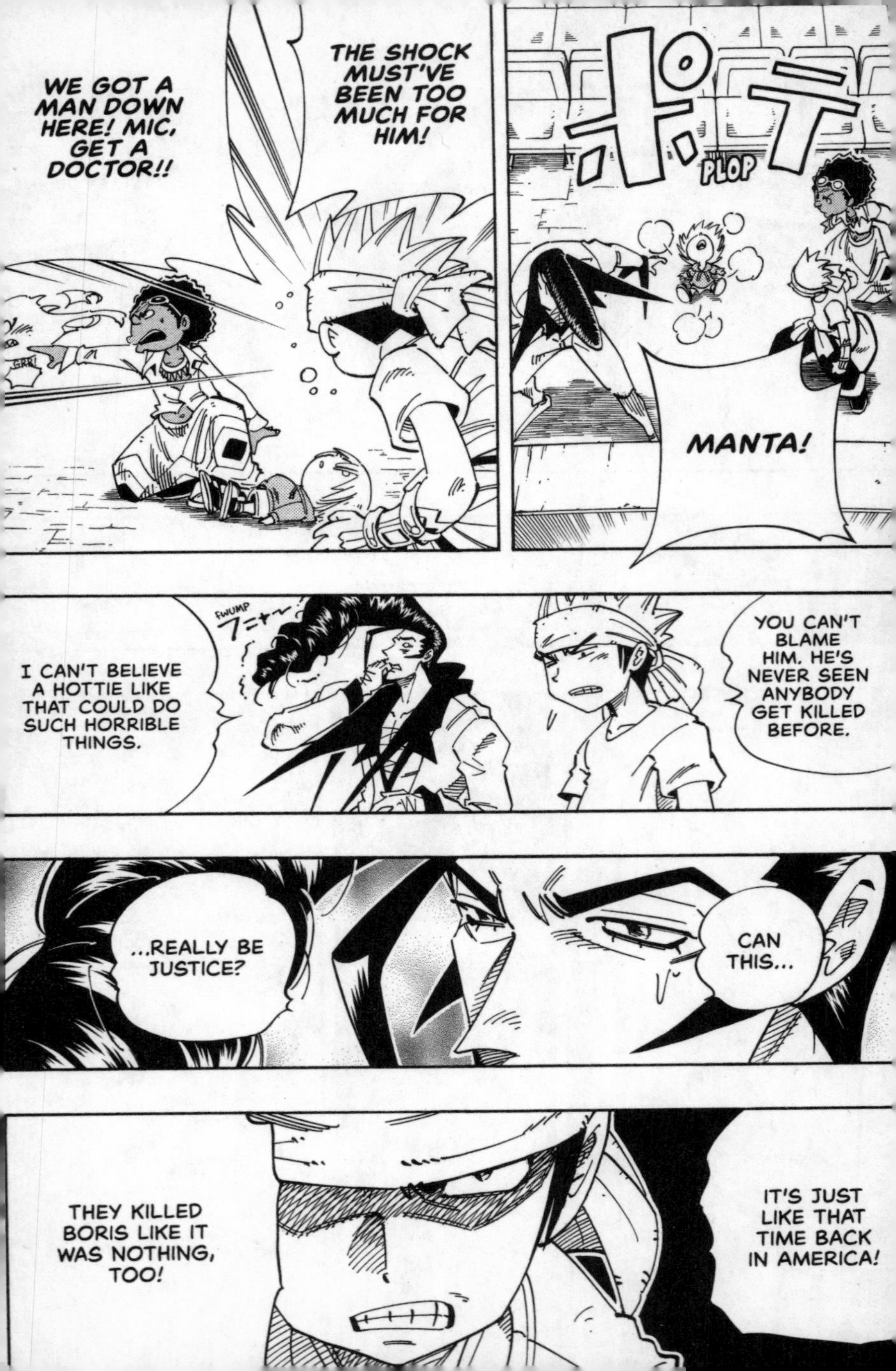
PLOP
MANTA!
THE SHOCK MUST'VE BEEN TOO MUCH FOR HIM!
WE GOT A MAN DOWN HERE! MIC, GET A DOCTOR!!
YOU CAN'T BLAME HIM. HE'S NEVER SEEN ANYBODY GET KILLED BEFORE.
FWUMP
I CAN'T BELIEVE A HOTTIE LIKE THAT COULD DO SUCH HORRIBLE THINGS.
CAN THIS...
...REALLY BE JUSTICE?
IT'S JUST LIKE THAT TIME BACK IN AMERICA!
THEY KILLED BORIS LIKE IT WAS NOTHING, TOO!

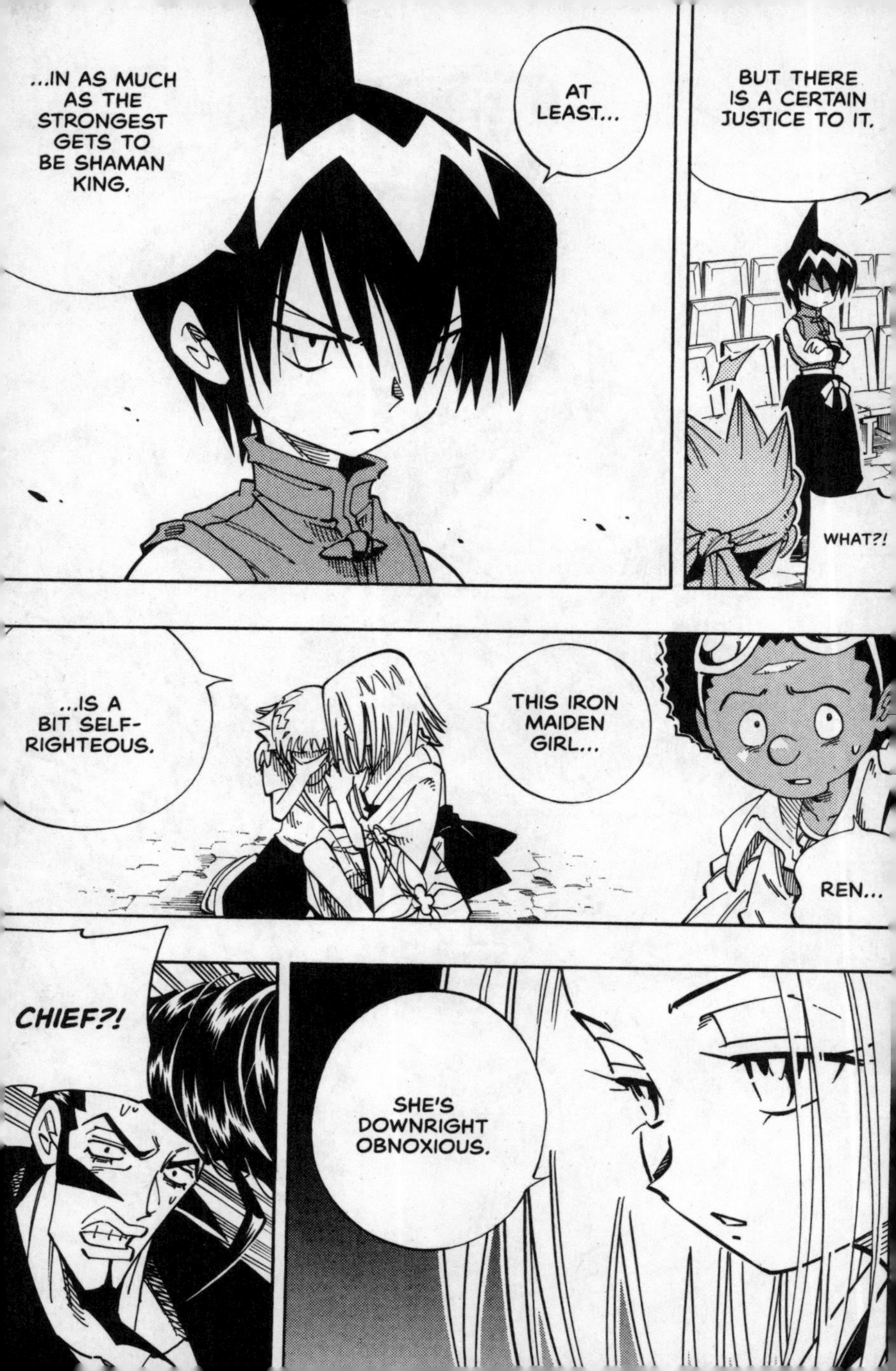
BUT THERE IS A CERTAIN JUSTICE TO IT.
WHAT?!
AT LEAST...
...IN AS MUCH AS THE STRONGEST GETS TO BE SHAMAN KING.
THIS IRON MAIDEN GIRL...
...IS A BIT SELF-RIGHTEOUS.
REN...
SHE'S DOWNRIGHT OBNOXIOUS.
CHIEF?!

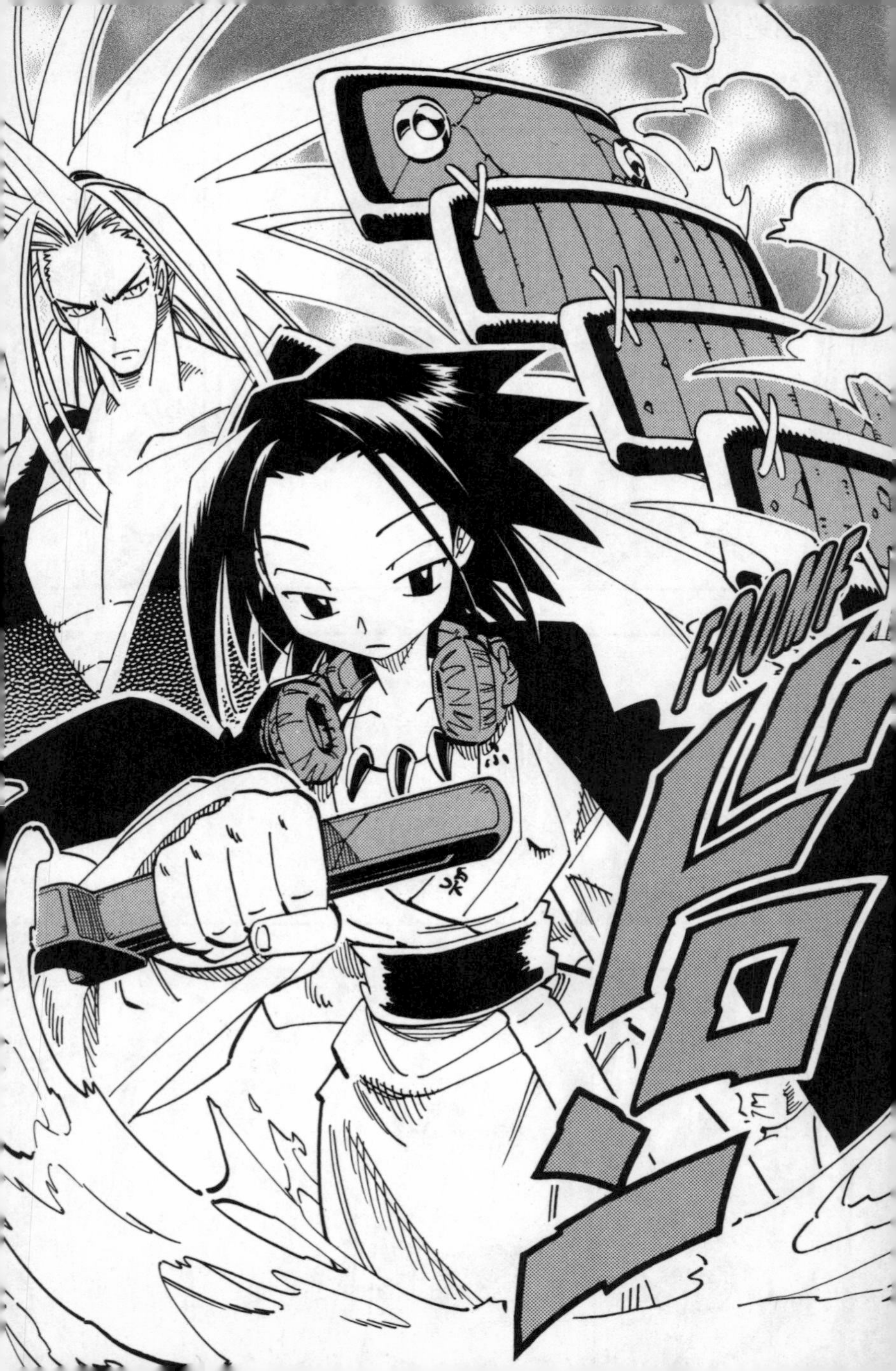
FOOMF

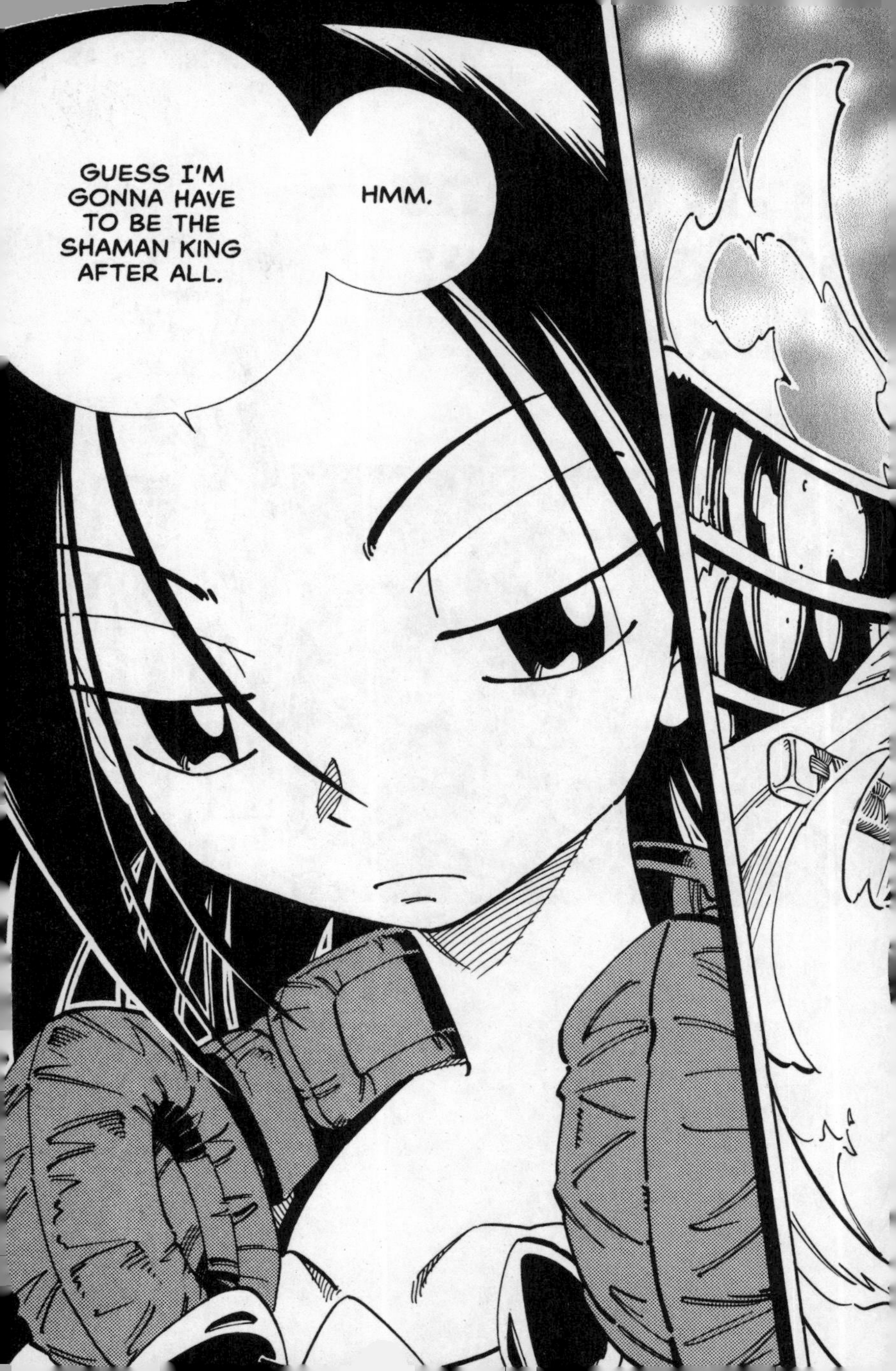
HMM.
GUESS I'M GONNA HAVE TO BE THE SHAMAN KING AFTER ALL.

SHAMAN KING ITEM FILE No.45

Instrument of Torture: Gibbet

[redacted]

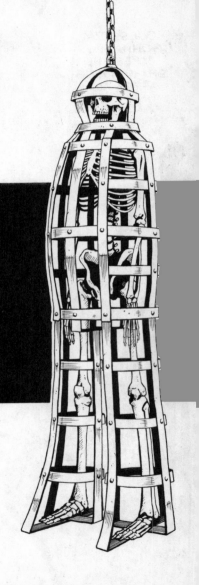

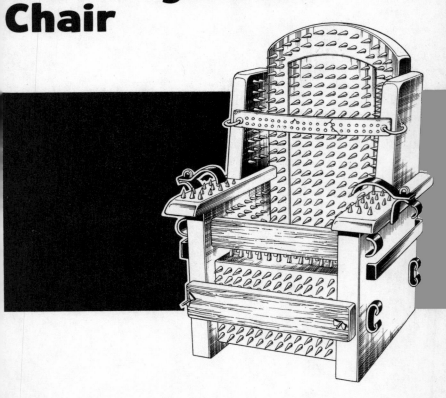

Instrument of Torture: Interrogation Chair

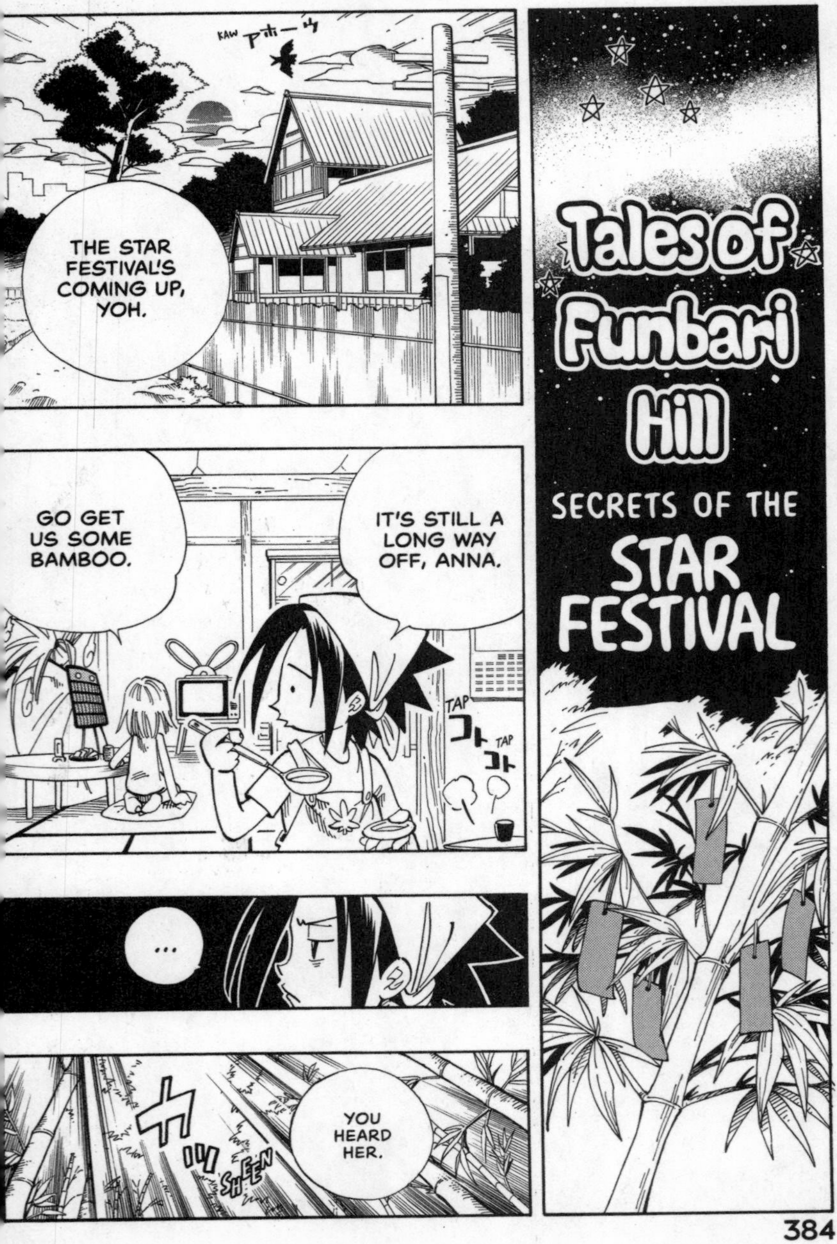
Tales of Funbari Hill
SECRETS OF THE STAR FESTIVAL
KAW
THE STAR FESTIVAL'S COMING UP, YOH.
IT'S STILL A LONG WAY OFF, ANNA.
GO GET US SOME BAMBOO.
TAP
TAP
...
YOU HEARD HER.
SHEEN

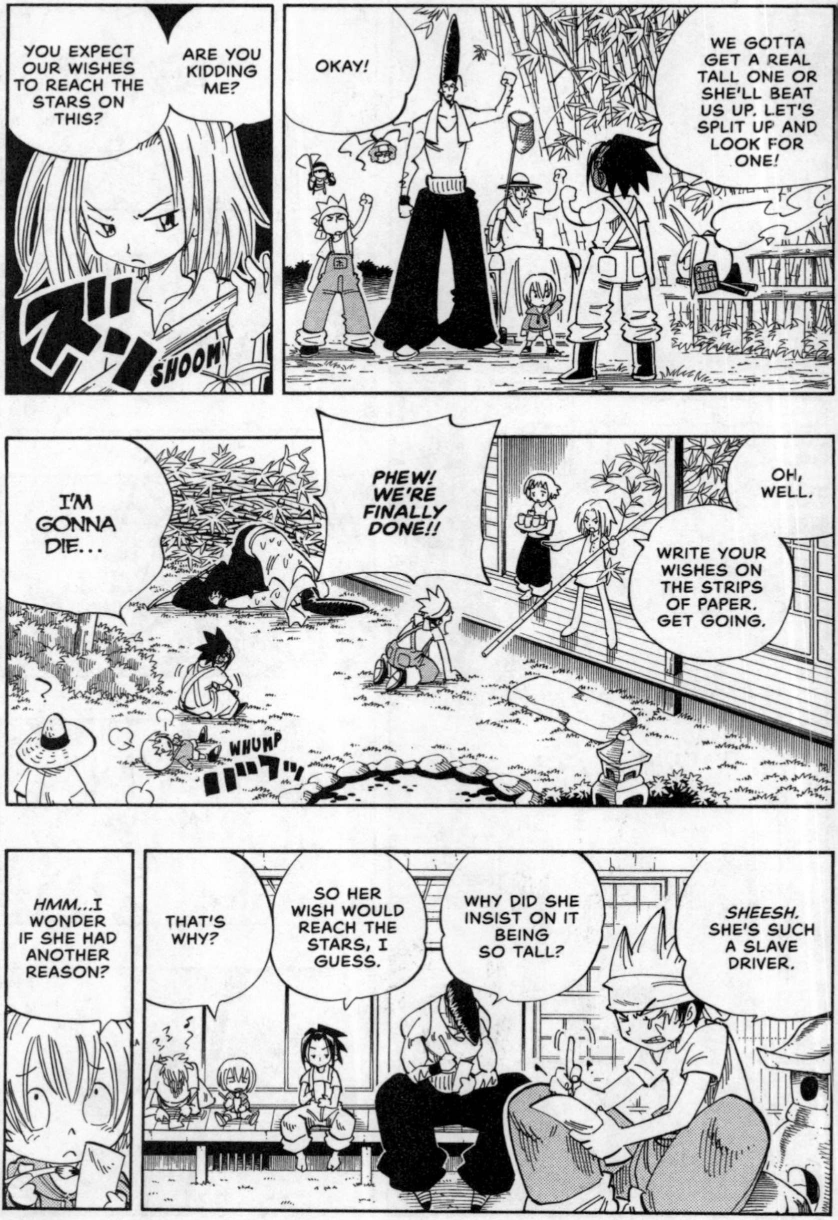

WE GOTTA GET A REAL TALL ONE OR SHE'LL BEAT US UP. LET'S SPLIT UP AND LOOK FOR ONE!
OKAY!
ARE YOU KIDDING ME?
YOU EXPECT OUR WISHES TO REACH THE STARS ON THIS?
SHOOM
OH, WELL.
WRITE YOUR WISHES ON THE STRIPS OF PAPER. GET GOING.
PHEW! WE'RE FINALLY DONE!!
I'M GONNA DIE...
WHUMP
SHEESH. SHE'S SUCH A SLAVE DRIVER.
WHY DID SHE INSIST ON IT BEING SO TALL?
SO HER WISH WOULD REACH THE STARS, I GUESS.
THAT'S WHY?
HMM...I WONDER IF SHE HAD ANOTHER REASON?

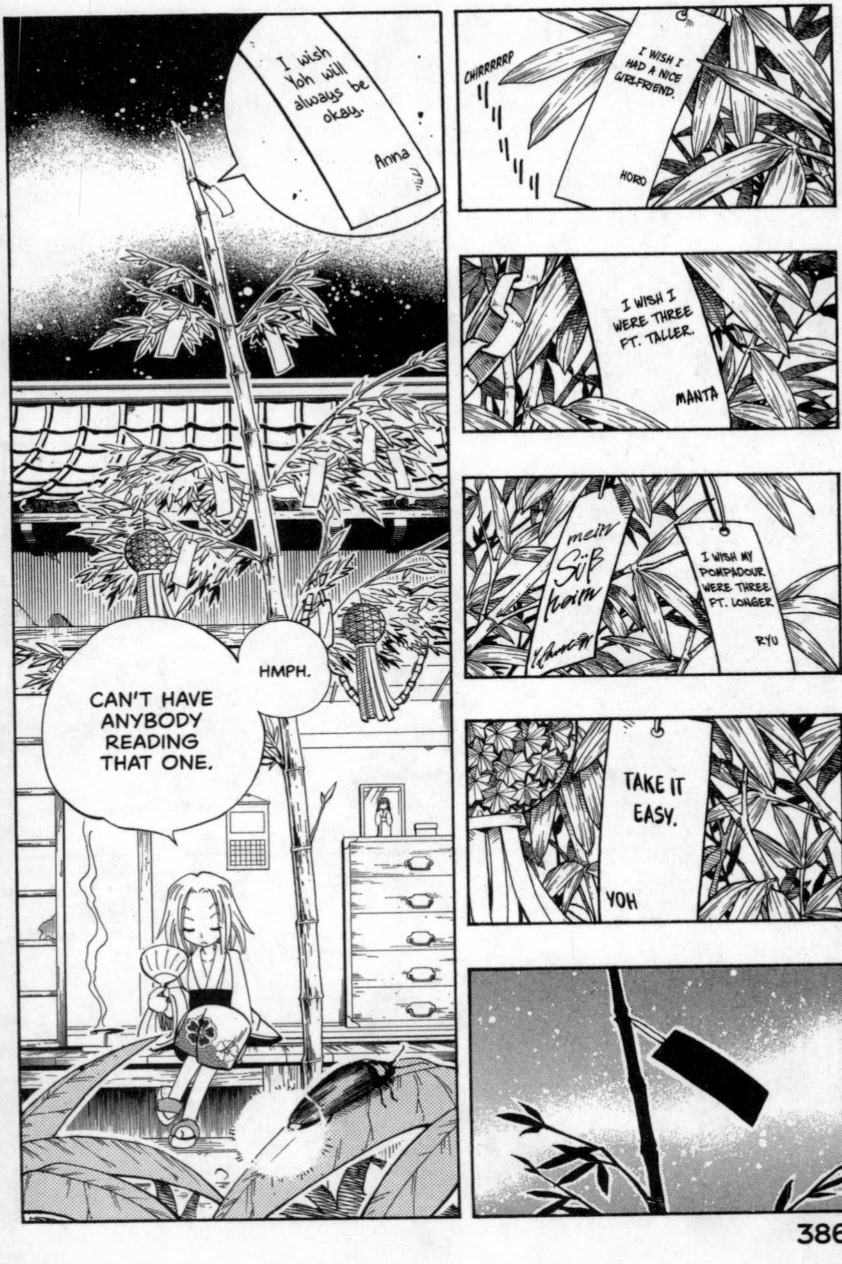
CHIRRRRRP
I WISH I HAD A NICE GIRLFRIEND.
HORO
I WISH I WERE THREE FT. TALLER.
MANTA
I WISH MY POMPADOUR WERE THREE FT. LONGER
RYU
mein Süß heim
TAKE IT EASY.
YOH
I wish Yoh will always be okay.
Anna
HMPH.
CAN'T HAVE ANYBODY READING THAT ONE.

SHAMAN KING

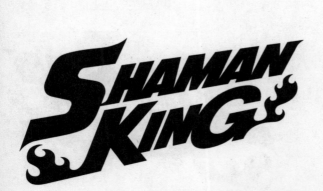

SHAMAN KING

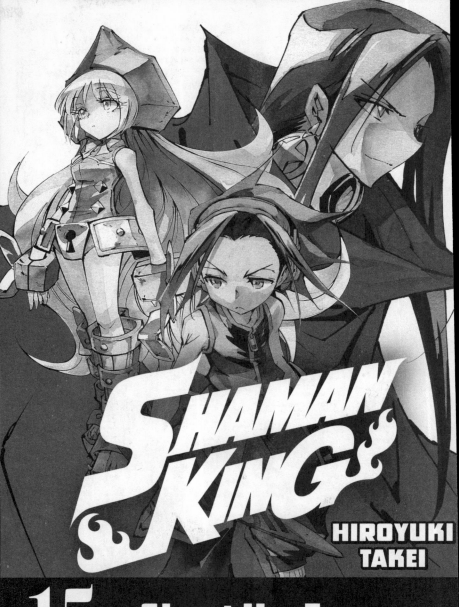

SHAMAN KING

HIROYUKI
TAKEI

15 Stand Up, Team
Funbari Hot Springs

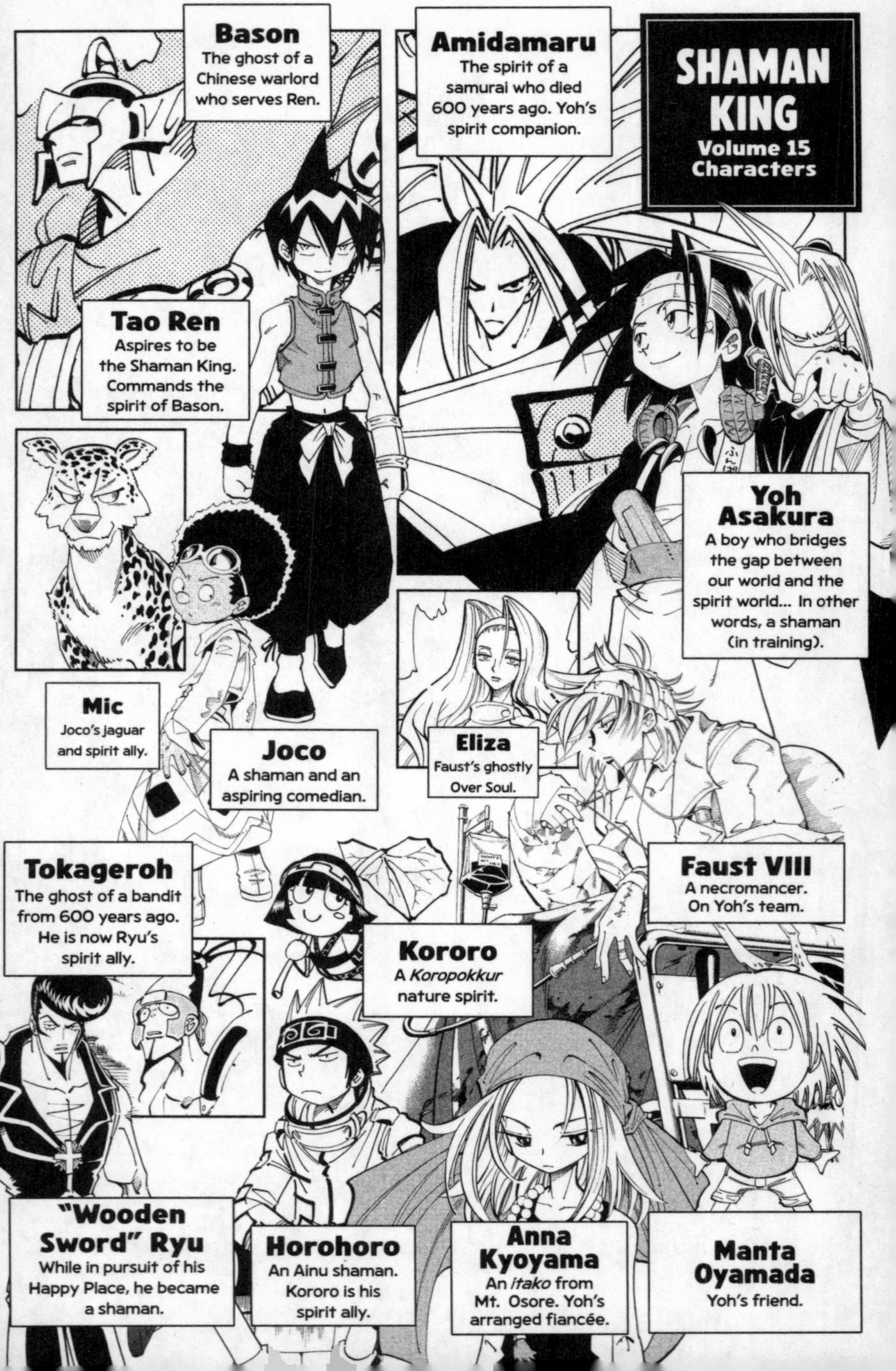

SHAMAN KING
Volume 15 Characters
Amidamaru
The spirit of a samurai who died 600 years ago. Yoh's spirit companion.
Bason
The ghost of a Chinese warlord who serves Ren.
Tao Ren
Aspires to be the Shaman King. Commands the spirit of Bason.
Yoh Asakura
A boy who bridges the gap between our world and the spirit world... In other words, a shaman (in training).
Eliza
Faust's ghostly Over Soul.
Joco
A shaman and an aspiring comedian.
Mic
Joco's jaguar and spirit ally.
Faust VIII
A necromancer. On Yoh's team.
Kororo
A *Koropokkur* nature spirit.
Tokageroh
The ghost of a bandit from 600 years ago. He is now Ryu's spirit ally.
Manta Oyamada
Yoh's friend.
Anna Kyoyama
An *itako* from Mt. Osore. Yoh's arranged fiancée.
Horohoro
An Ainu shaman. Kororo is his spirit ally.
"Wooden Sword" Ryu
While in pursuit of his Happy Place, he became a shaman.

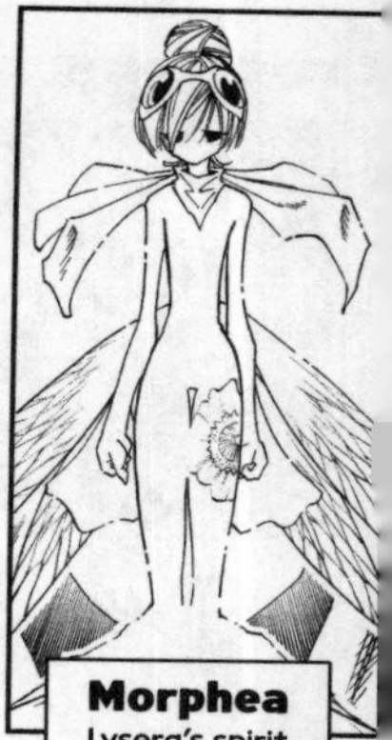

Morphea
Lyserg's spirit ally. A poppy flower fairy.

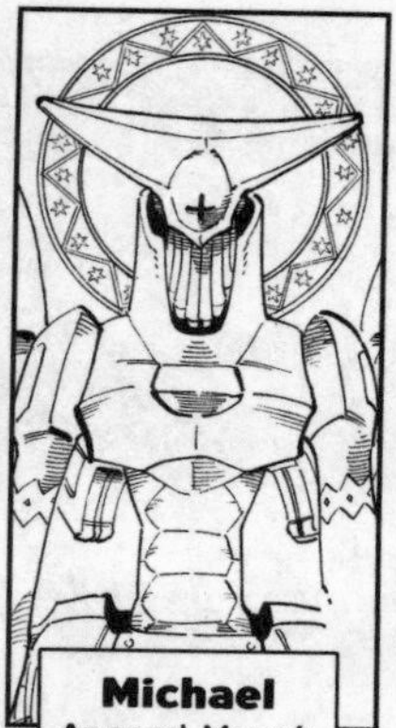

Michael
An angel. Marco's spirit ally.

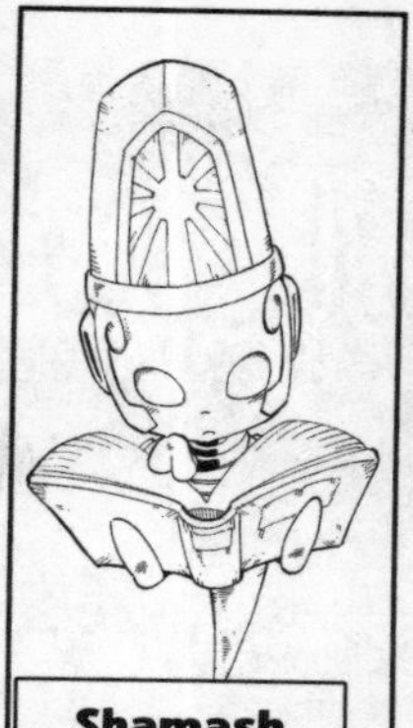

Shamash
Jeanne's spirit ally. *Kami* class.

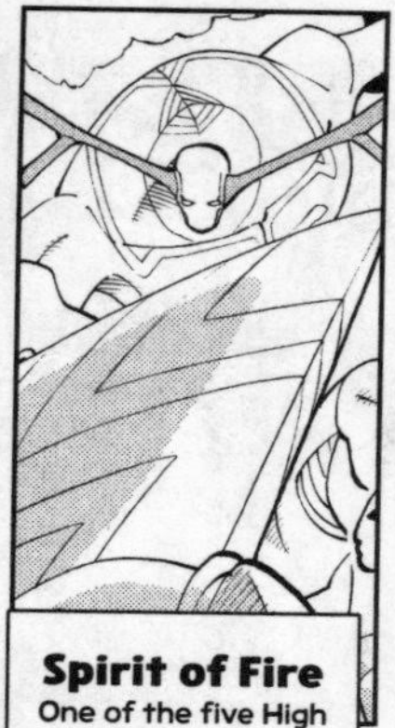

Spirit of Fire
One of the five High Spirits, and Hao's spirit ally.

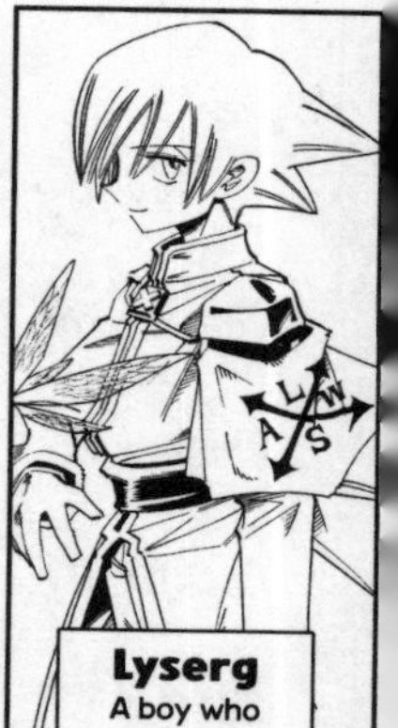

A L W
S

Lyserg
A boy who wants revenge against Hao.

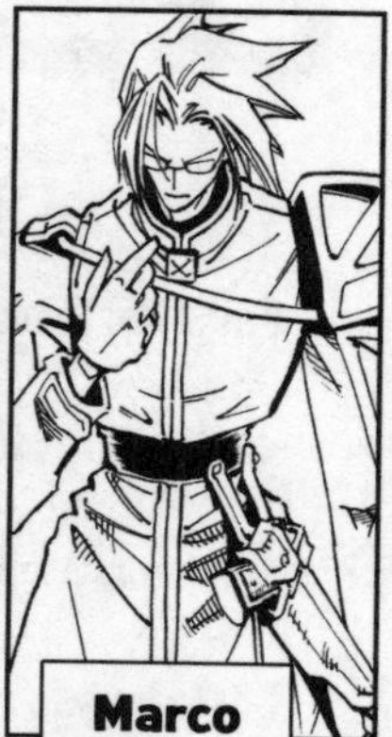

Marco
The leader of the X-Laws.

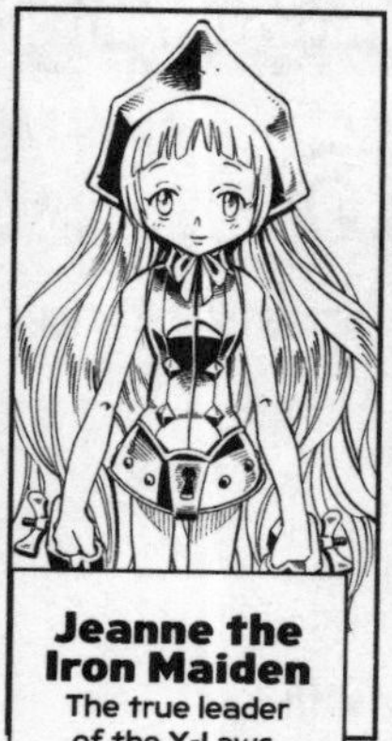

Jeanne the Iron Maiden
The true leader of the X-Laws. Mostly inside an iron maiden.

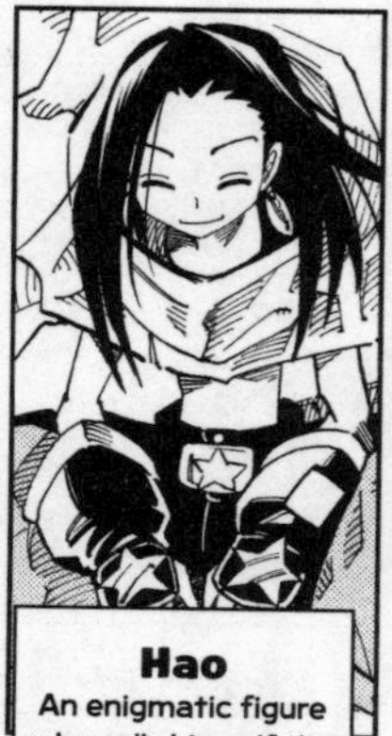

Hao
An enigmatic figure who calls himself the "Future King."

THE STORY SO FAR

This kid named Yoh Asakura-kun transferred to my class from Izumo... and it turns out he's a shaman! The Shaman Fight, which takes place once every 500 years, has begun. Yoh-kun and friends arrived at Patch Village—and experienced the limitless power of the Great Spirit. They formed new teams for the tournament proper. Along with their new ally, Joco, they divided into two teams. The third match of the tournament got underway—and it was Lyserg's shocking debut with the X-Laws. Their use of unethical tactics puts Yoh in a dilemma!

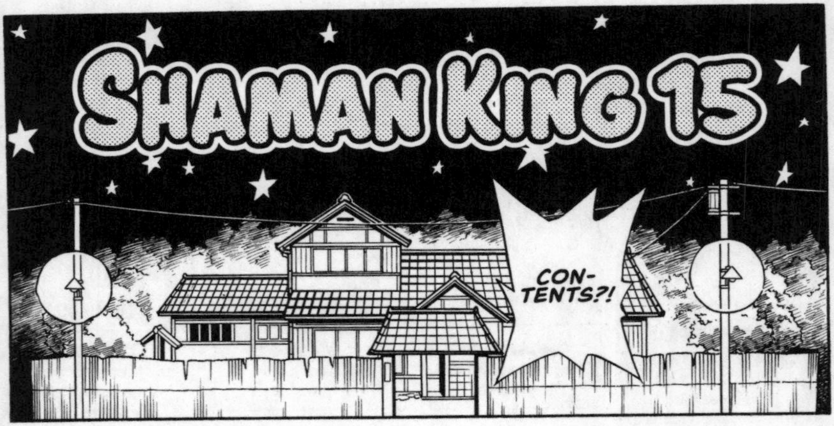
SHAMAN KING 15
CON-
TENTS?!

Stand Up, Team Funbari Hot Springs

15

Chapter 126: Stand Up, Team Funbari Hot Springs

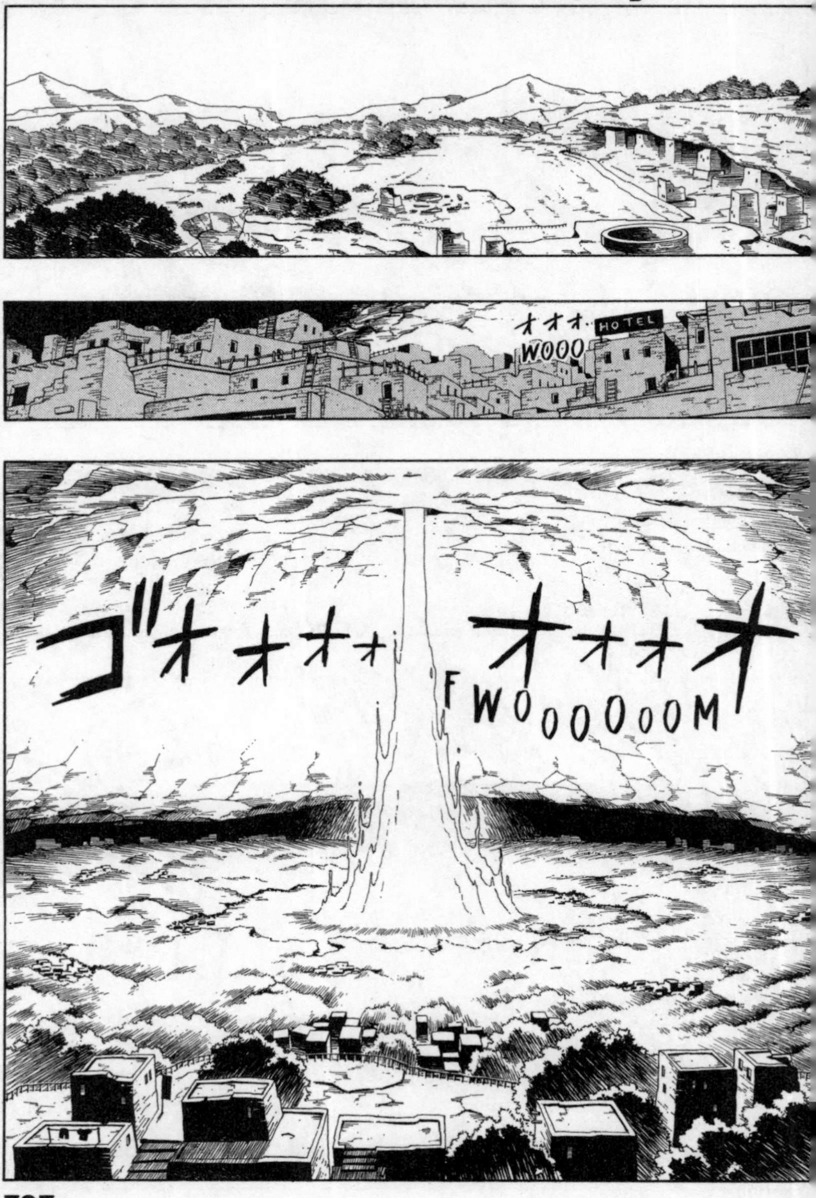
オオオ
WOOO
HOTEL
ゴオオオオオオオオオ
FWOOOOOOM

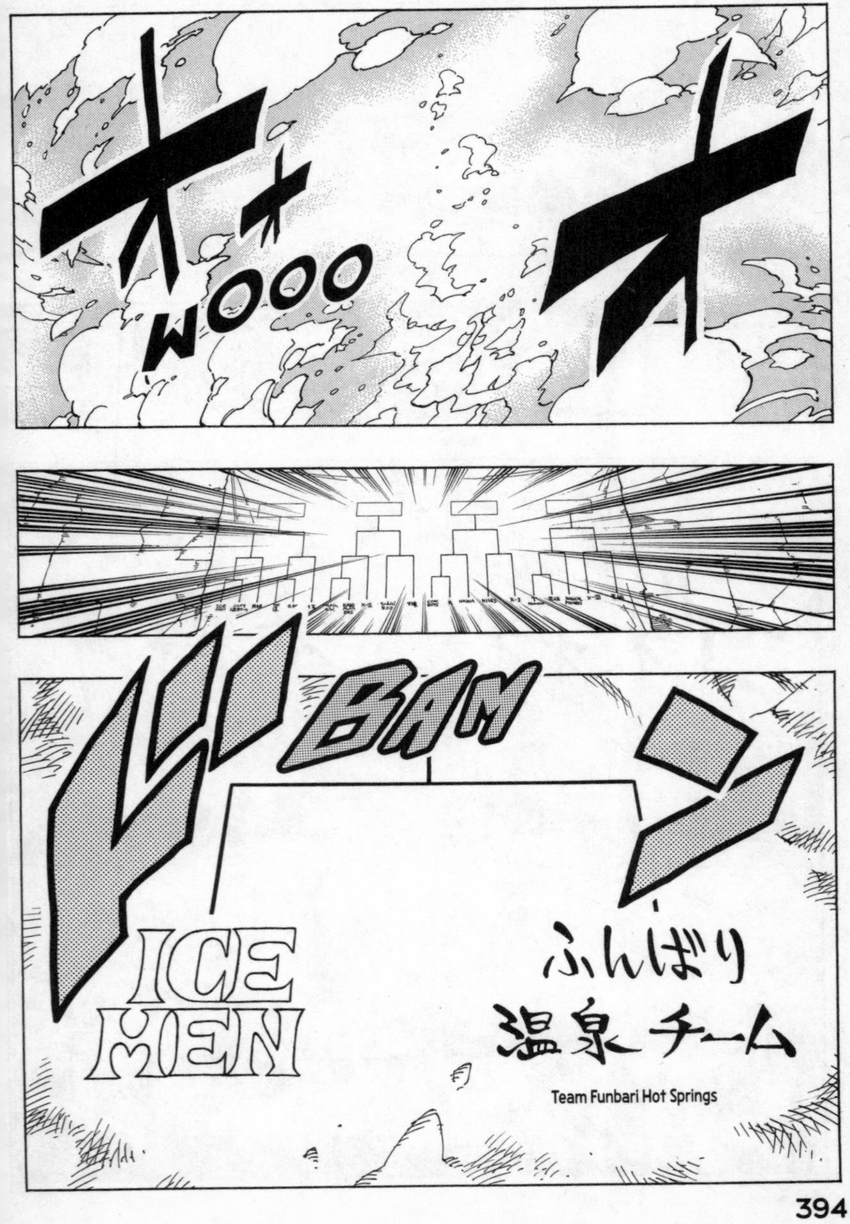
オォオ
WOOO
BAM
ふんばり温泉チーム
Team Funbari Hot Springs
ICE MEN

Chapter 126:

Stand Up, Team Funbari Hot Springs

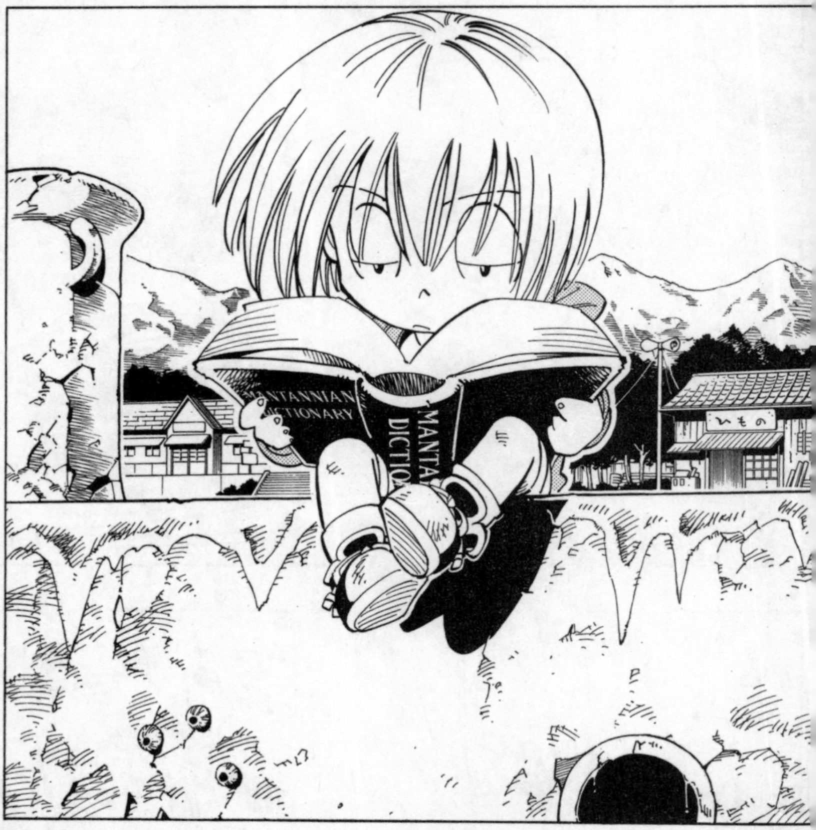
MANTANNIAN DICTIONARY
MANTA DICTIO
ひもの

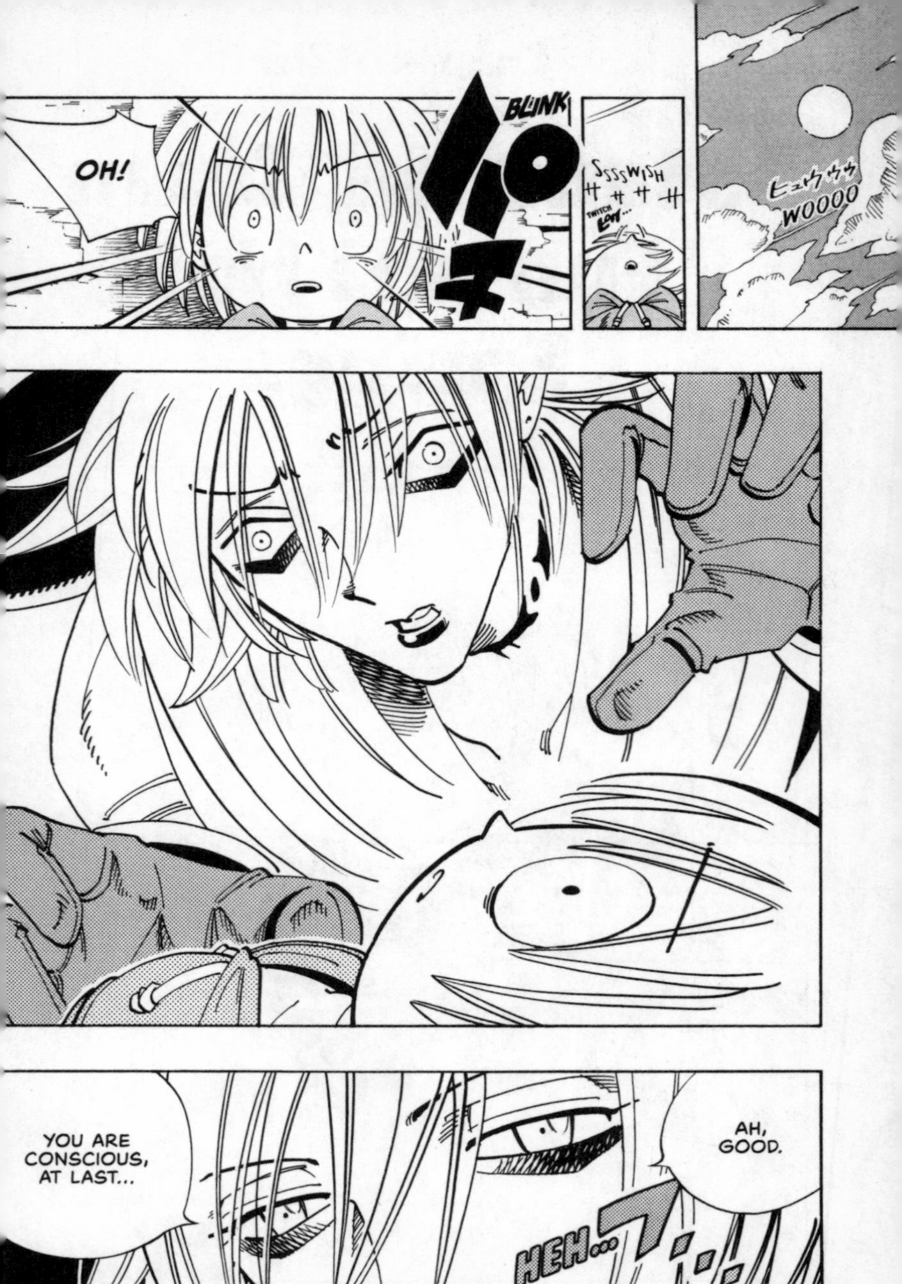
ヒュウゥゥ
WOOOO
SSSSWISH
TWITCH
BLINK
OH!
AH, GOOD.
HEH...
YOU ARE CONSCIOUS, AT LAST...

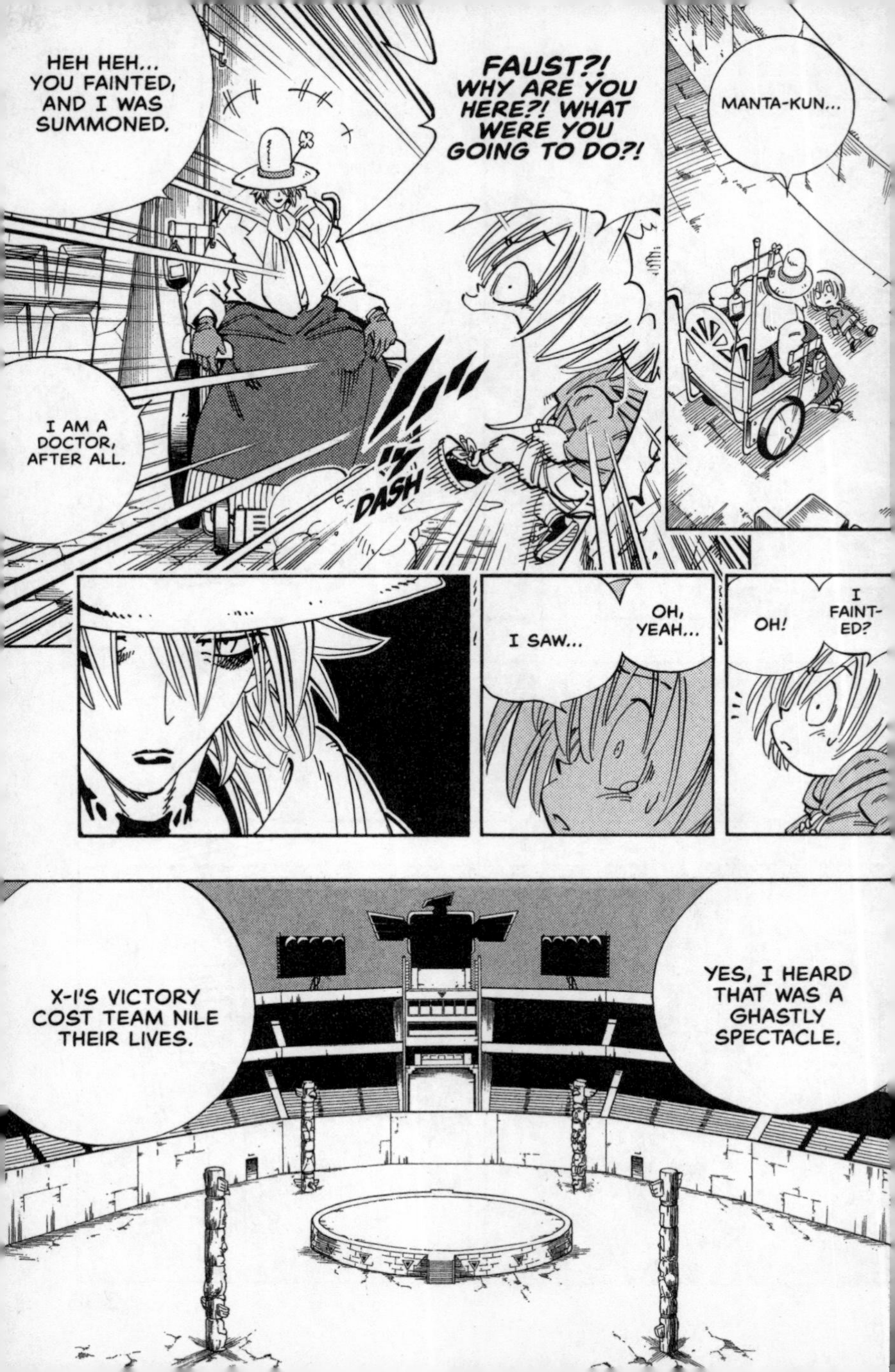
MANTA-KUN...
FAUST?! WHY ARE YOU HERE?! WHAT WERE YOU GOING TO DO?!
DASH
HEH HEH... YOU FAINTED, AND I WAS SUMMONED.
I AM A DOCTOR, AFTER ALL.
OH! I FAINT-ED?
OH, YEAH... I SAW...
YES, I HEARD THAT WAS A GHASTLY SPECTACLE.
X-I'S VICTORY COST TEAM NILE THEIR LIVES.

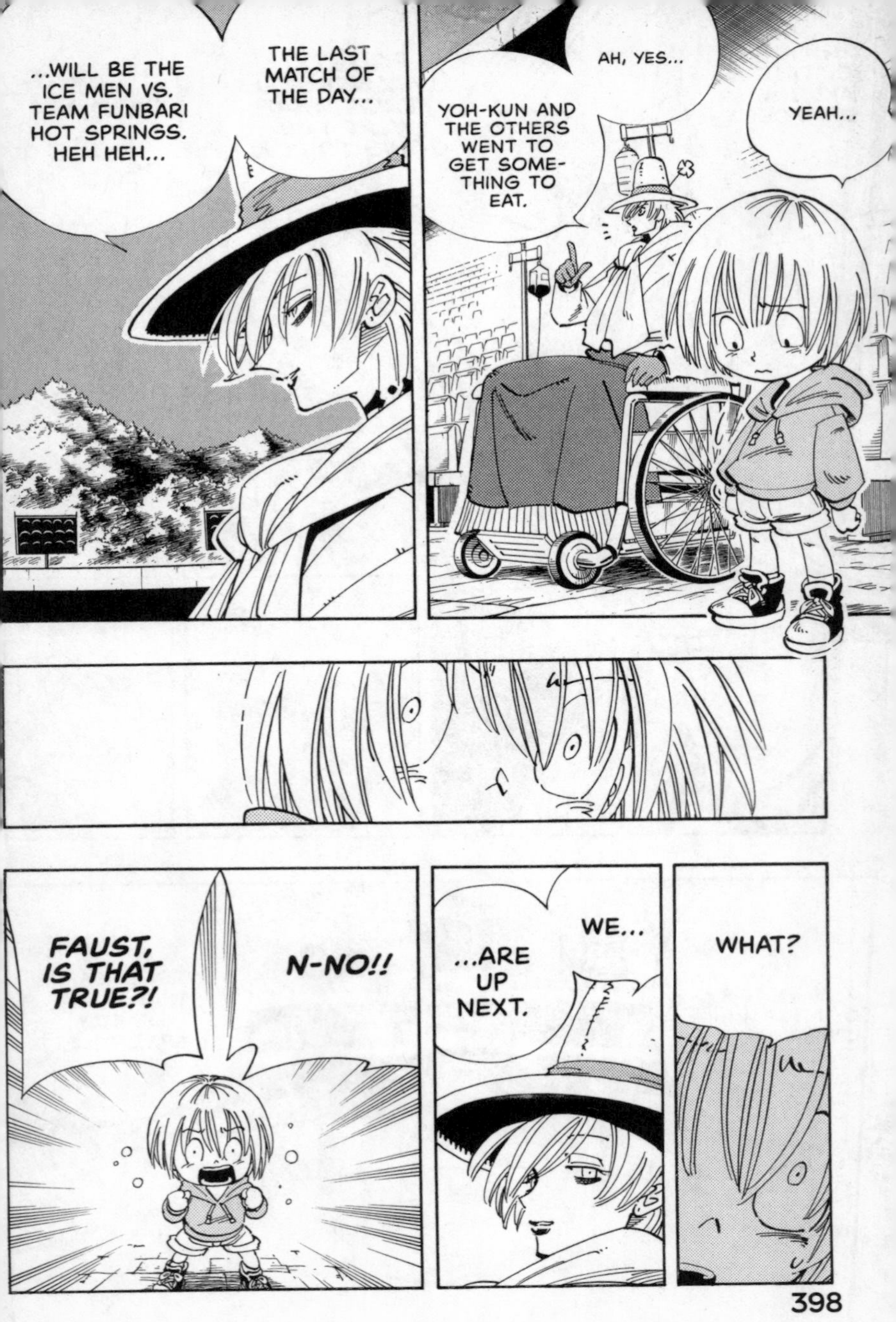
YEAH...
AH, YES...
YOH-KUN AND THE OTHERS WENT TO GET SOME-THING TO EAT.
THE LAST MATCH OF THE DAY...
...WILL BE THE ICE MEN VS. TEAM FUNBARI HOT SPRINGS. HEH HEH...
WHAT?
WE...
...ARE UP NEXT.
N-NO!!
FAUST, IS THAT TRUE?!

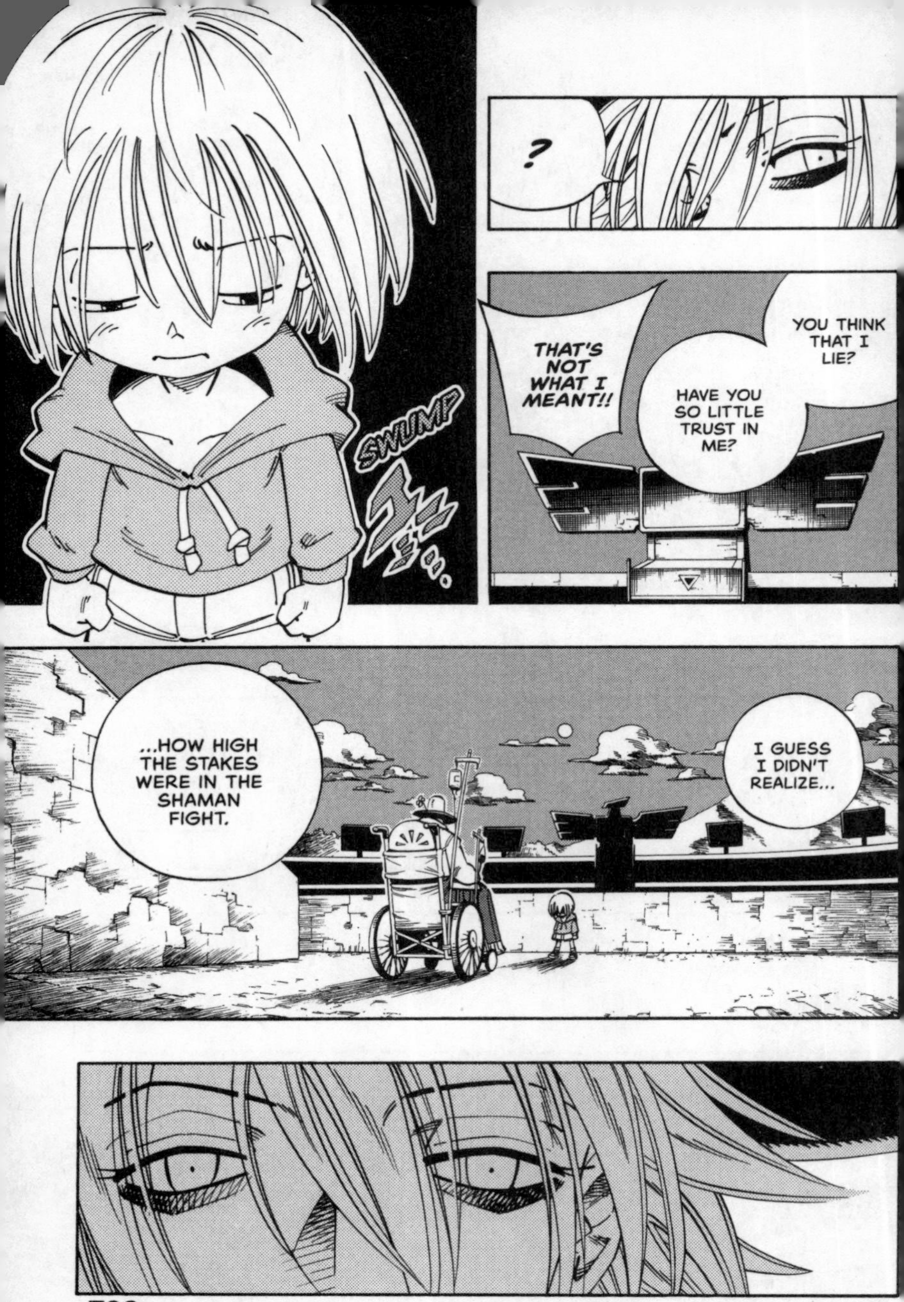
?
YOU THINK THAT I LIE?
HAVE YOU SO LITTLE TRUST IN ME?
THAT'S NOT WHAT I MEANT!!
SWUMP
I GUESS I DIDN'T REALIZE...
...HOW HIGH THE STAKES WERE IN THE SHAMAN FIGHT.

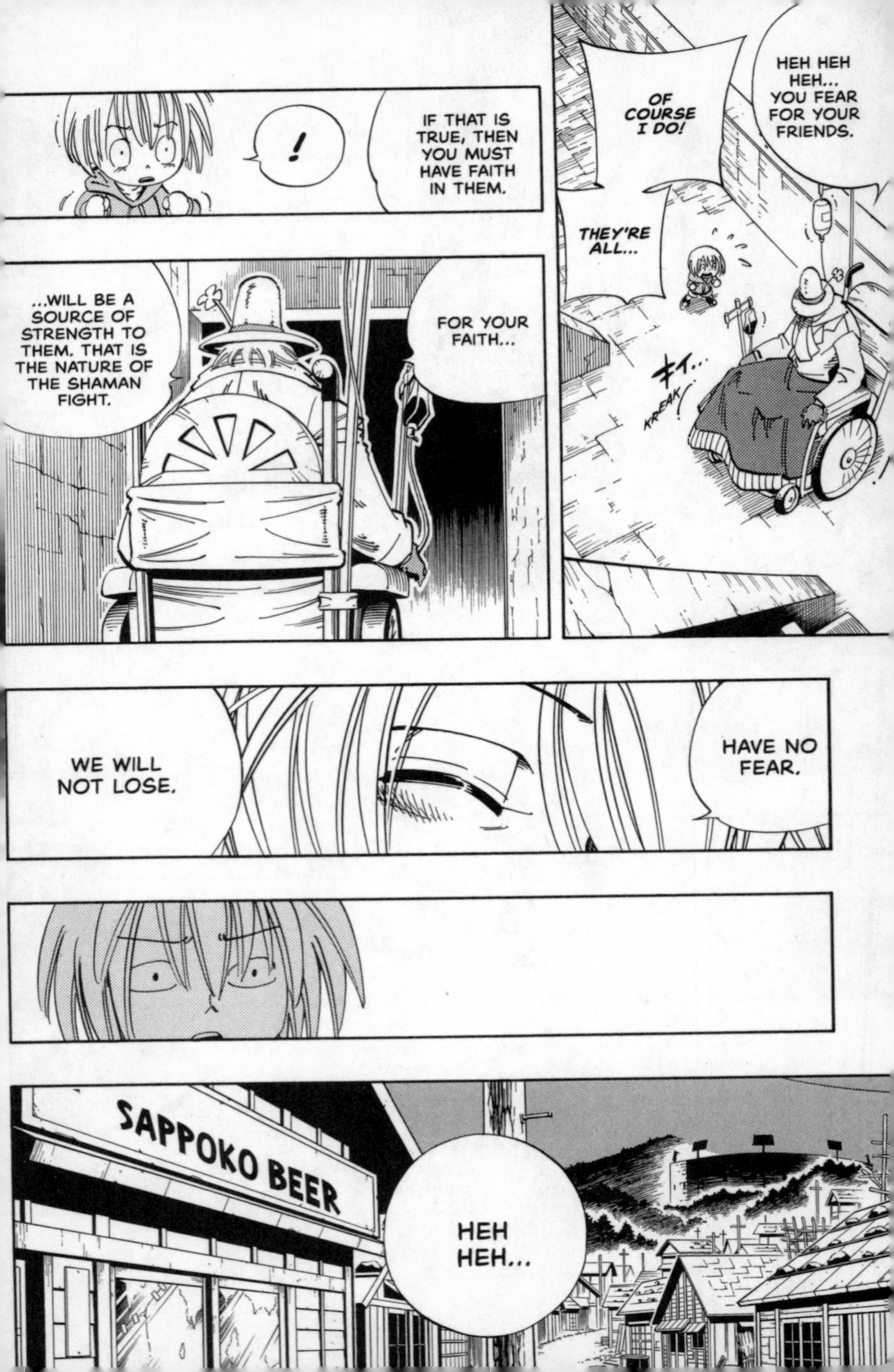
HEH HEH HEH... YOU FEAR FOR YOUR FRIENDS.
OF COURSE I DO!
THEY'RE ALL...
キイ…
KREAK
IF THAT IS TRUE, THEN YOU MUST HAVE FAITH IN THEM.
!
FOR YOUR FAITH...
...WILL BE A SOURCE OF STRENGTH TO THEM. THAT IS THE NATURE OF THE SHAMAN FIGHT.
HAVE NO FEAR.
WE WILL NOT LOSE.
SAPPOKO BEER
HEH HEH...

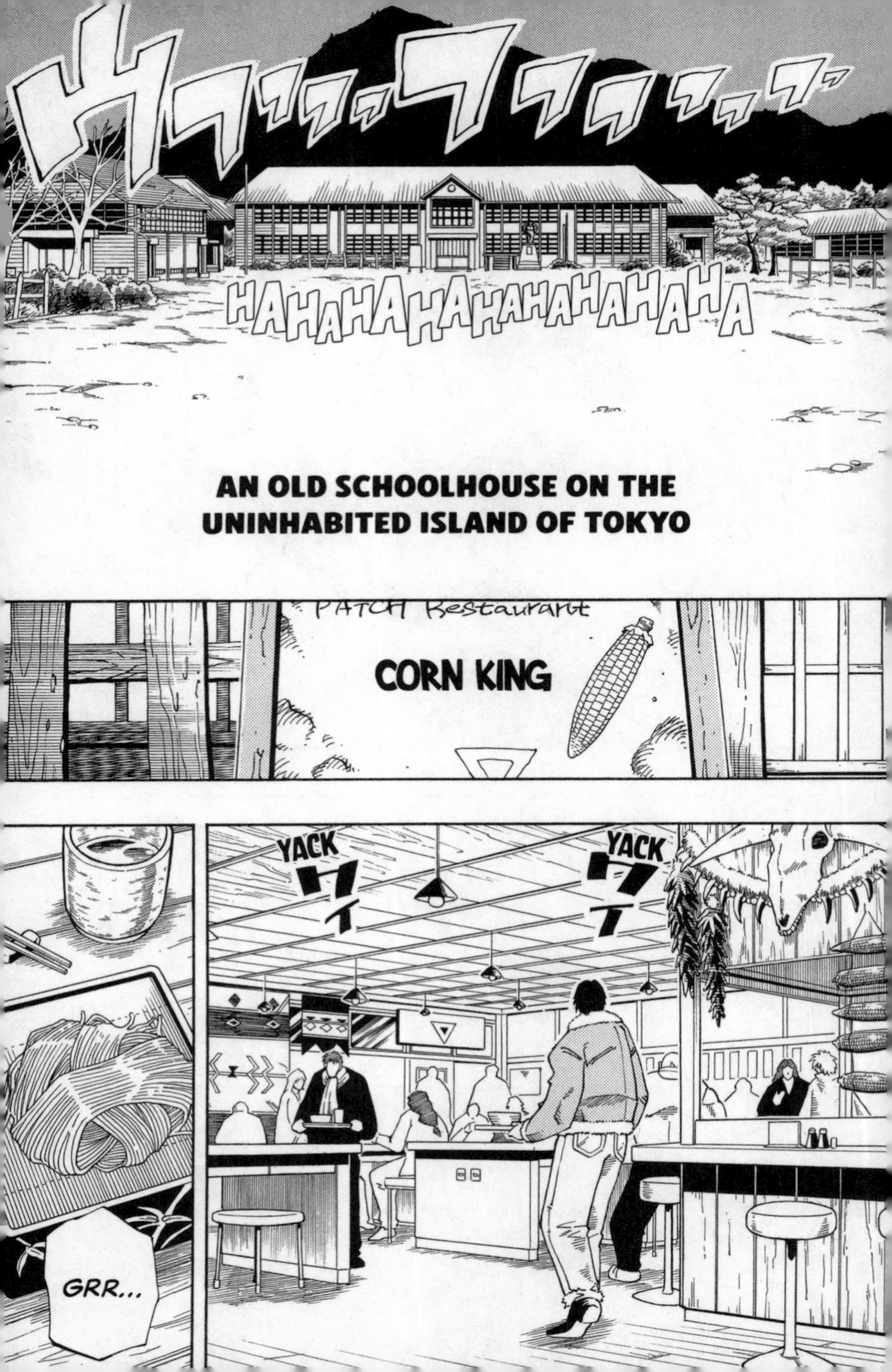
HAHAHAHAHAHAHAHAHA
AN OLD SCHOOLHOUSE ON THE UNINHABITED ISLAND OF TOKYO
PATCH Restaurant
CORN KING
YACK
YACK
GRR...

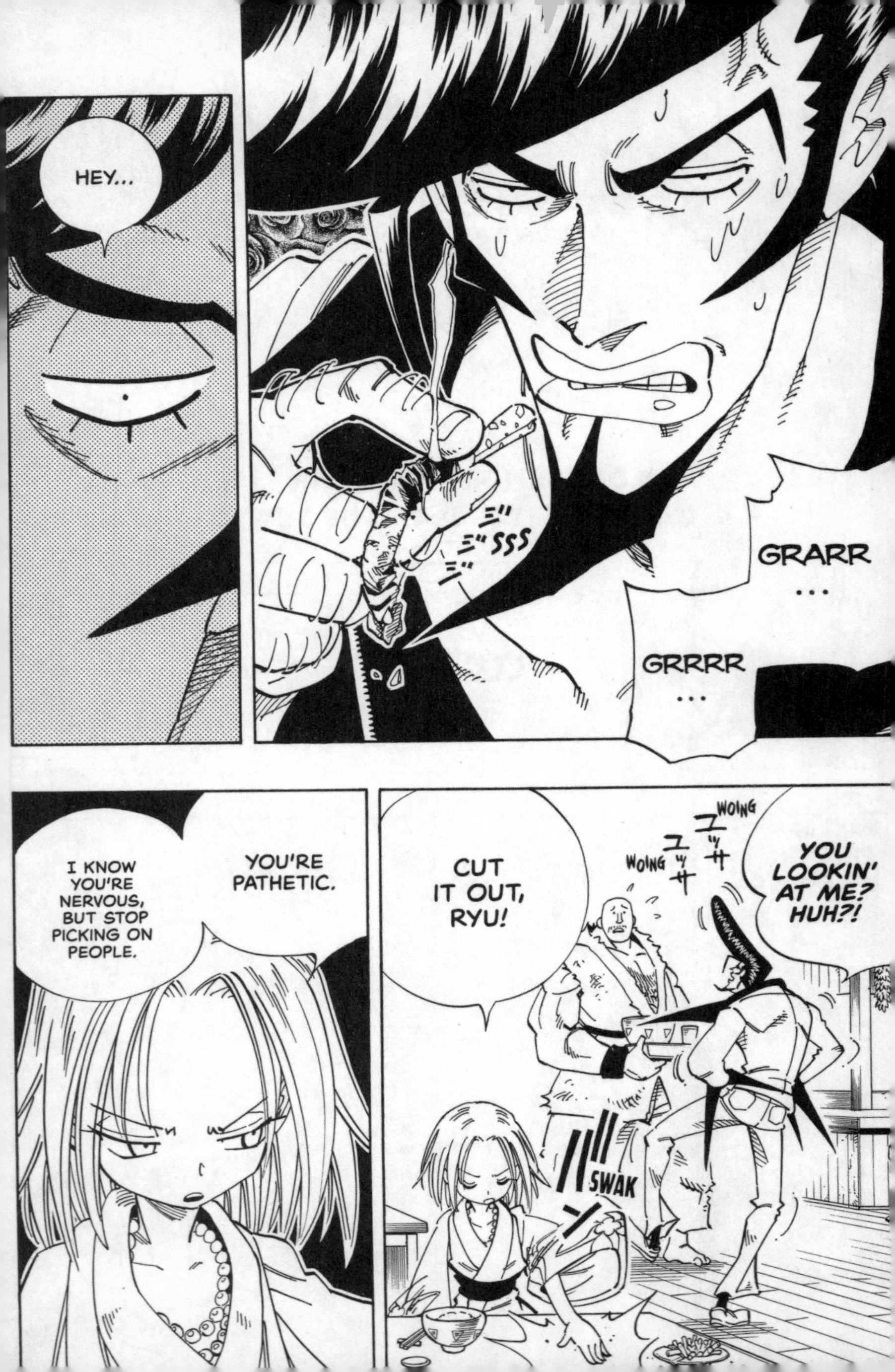

ジ
ジ SSS
ジ
GRARR ...
GRRRR ...
HEY...
YOU LOOKIN' AT ME? HUH?!
WOING
ユッサ
WOING
ユッサ
CUT IT OUT, RYU!
SWAK
YOU'RE PATHETIC.
I KNOW YOU'RE NERVOUS, BUT STOP PICKING ON PEOPLE.

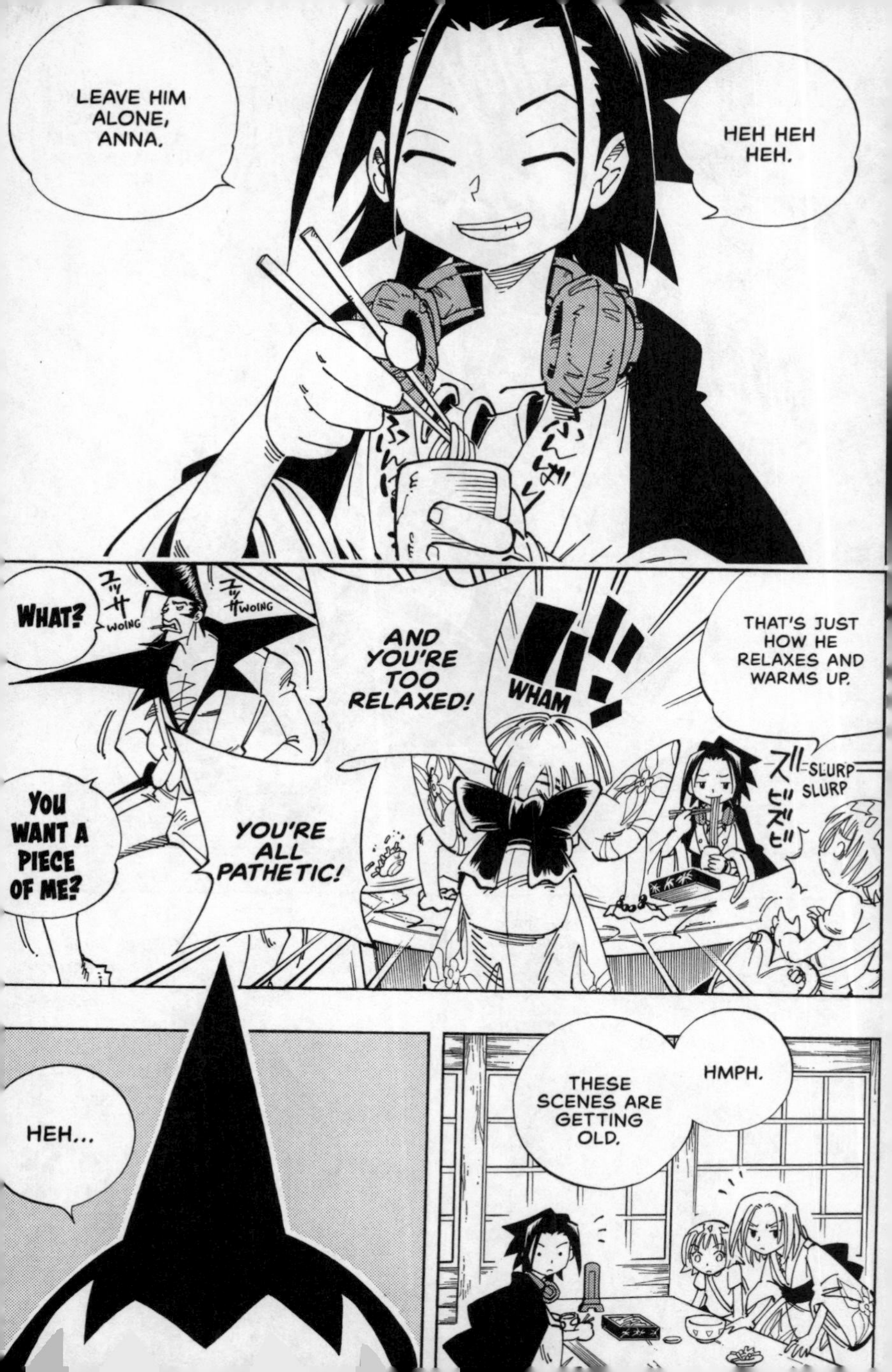
HEH HEH HEH.
LEAVE HIM ALONE, ANNA.
THAT'S JUST HOW HE RELAXES AND WARMS UP.
SLURP SLURP
WHAM
AND YOU'RE TOO RELAXED!
YOU'RE ALL PATHETIC!
WOING
WHAT?
WOING
YOU WANT A PIECE OF ME?
HMPH.
THESE SCENES ARE GETTING OLD.
HEH...

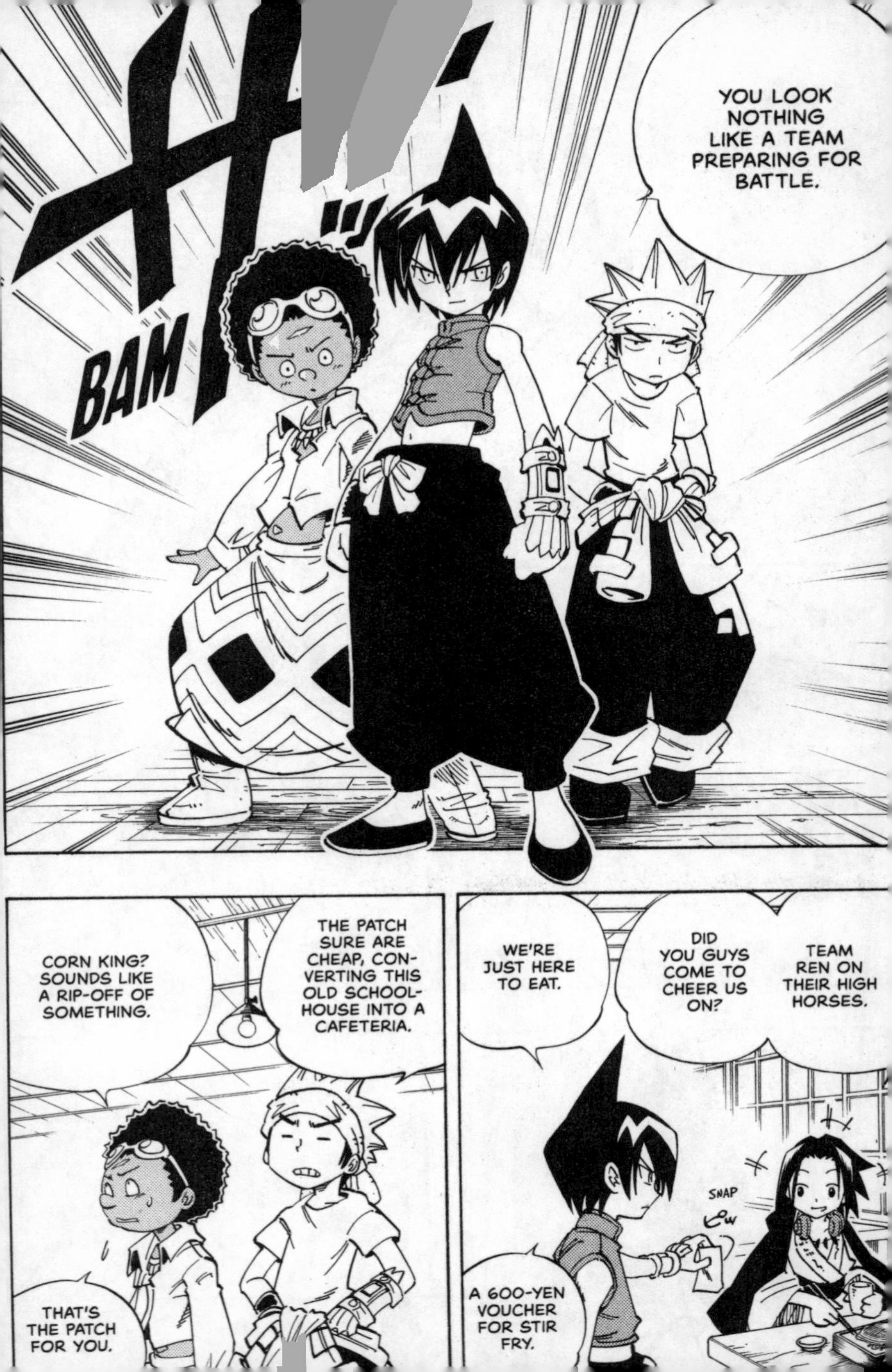
YOU LOOK NOTHING LIKE A TEAM PREPARING FOR BATTLE.
BAM
TEAM REN ON THEIR HIGH HORSES.
DID YOU GUYS COME TO CHEER US ON?
WE'RE JUST HERE TO EAT.
SNAP
A 600-YEN VOUCHER FOR STIR FRY.
THE PATCH SURE ARE CHEAP, CON-VERTING THIS OLD SCHOOL-HOUSE INTO A CAFETERIA.
CORN KING? SOUNDS LIKE A RIP-OFF OF SOMETHING.
THAT'S THE PATCH FOR YOU.

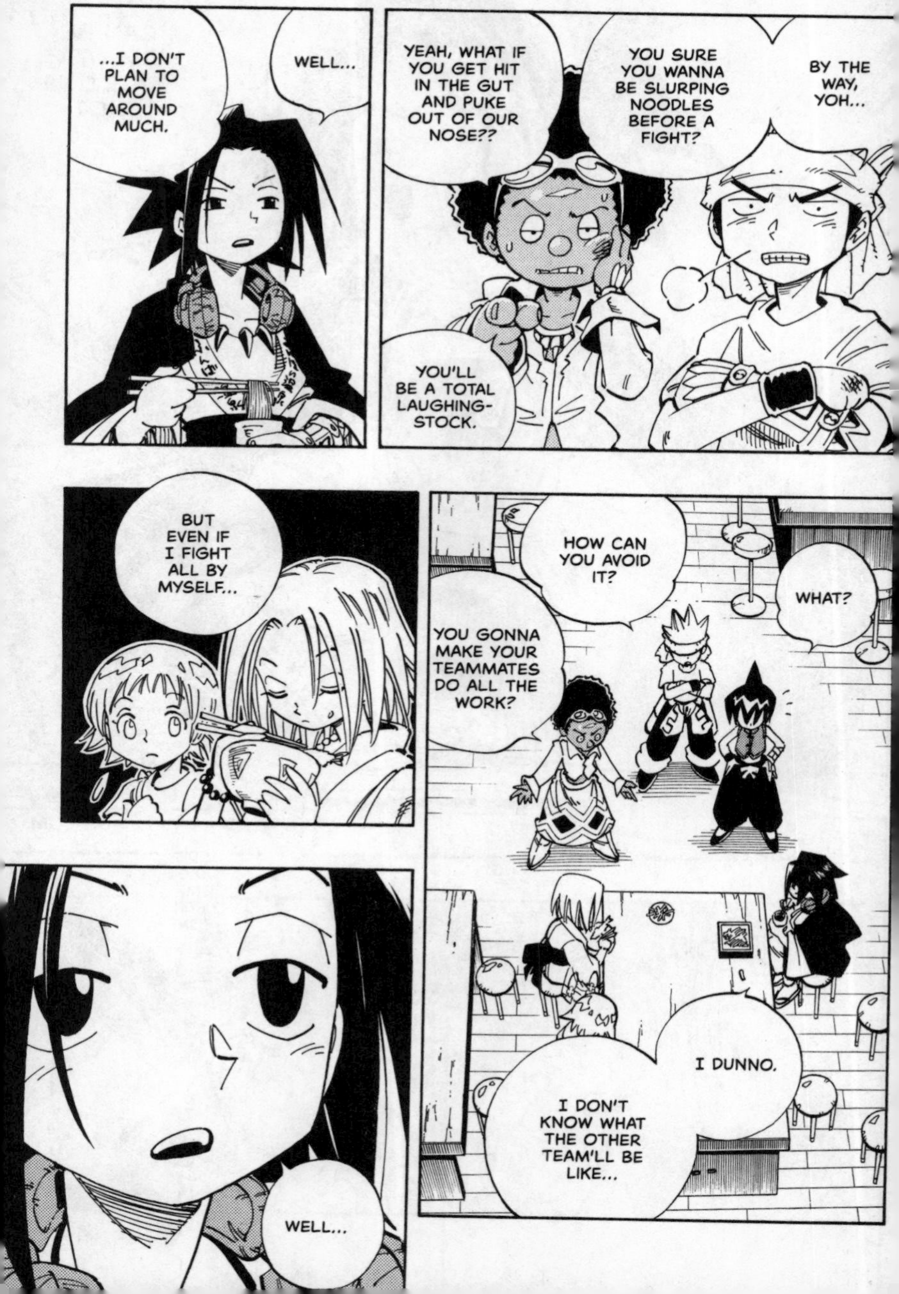
BY THE WAY, YOH...
YOU SURE YOU WANNA BE SLURPING NOODLES BEFORE A FIGHT?
YEAH, WHAT IF YOU GET HIT IN THE GUT AND PUKE OUT OF OUR NOSE??
YOU'LL BE A TOTAL LAUGHING-STOCK.
WELL...
...I DON'T PLAN TO MOVE AROUND MUCH.
WHAT?
HOW CAN YOU AVOID IT?
YOU GONNA MAKE YOUR TEAMMATES DO ALL THE WORK?
BUT EVEN IF I FIGHT ALL BY MYSELF...
I DUNNO.
I DON'T KNOW WHAT THE OTHER TEAM'LL BE LIKE...
WELL...

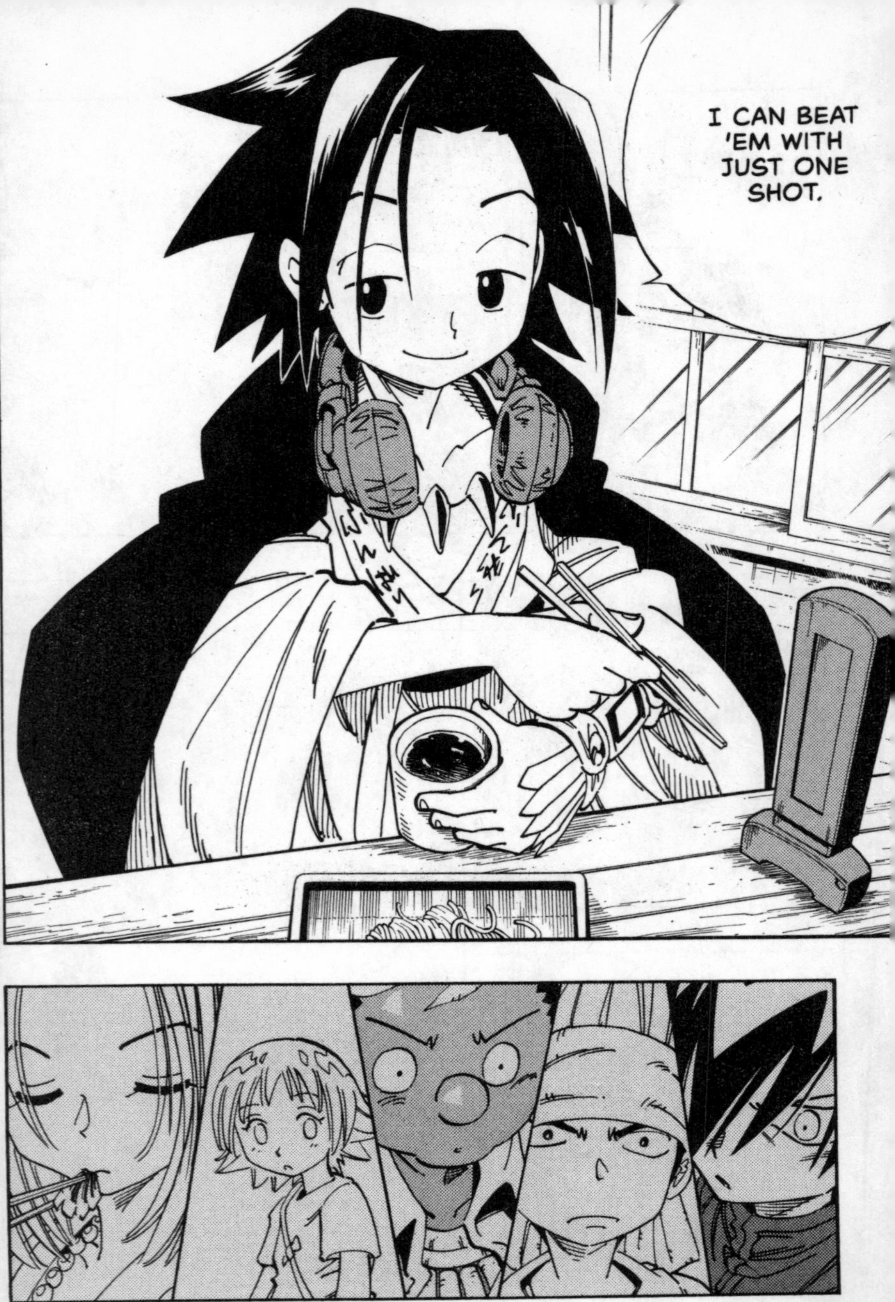
I CAN BEAT 'EM WITH JUST ONE SHOT.

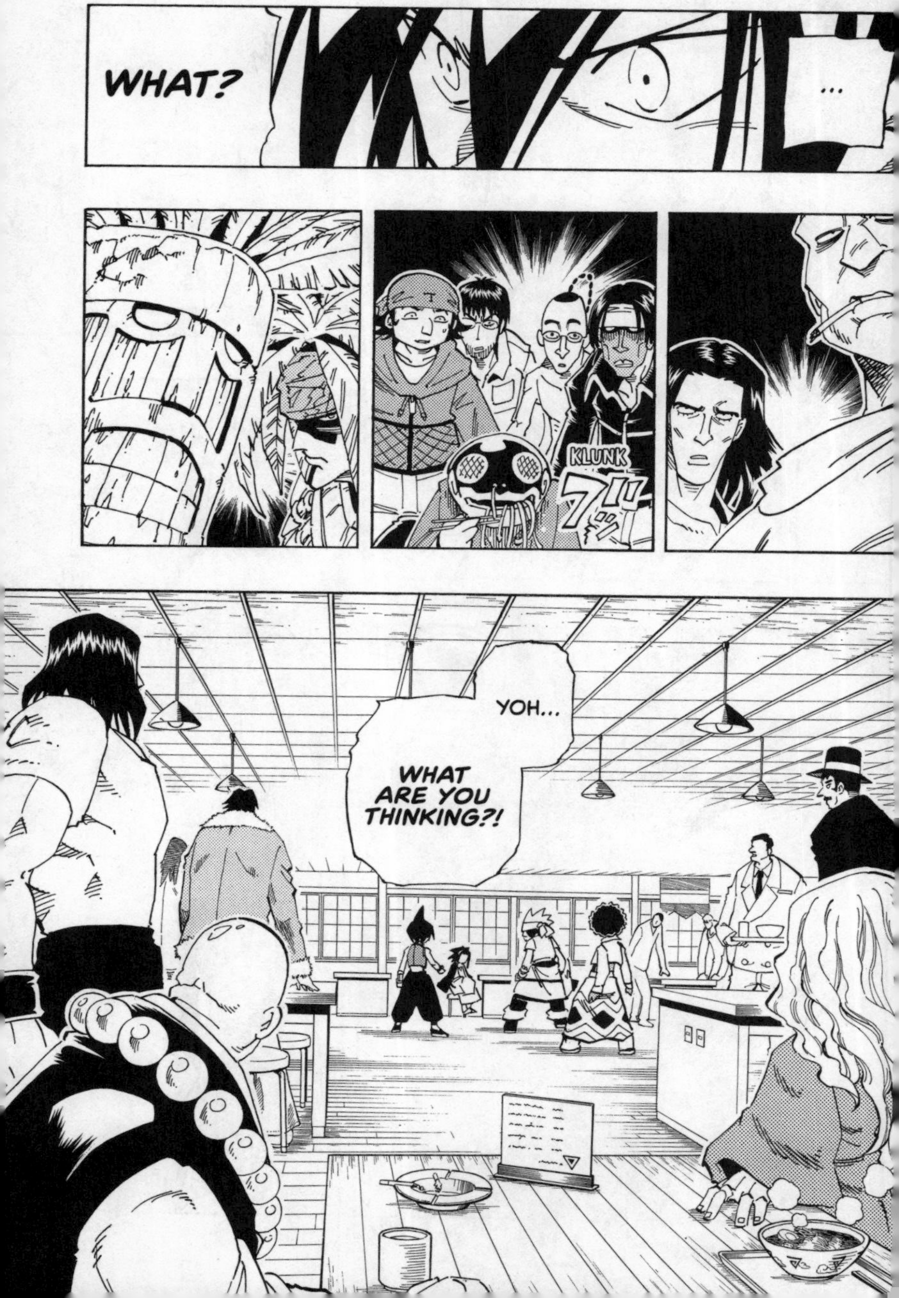
...
WHAT?
KLUNK
YOH...
WHAT ARE YOU THINKING?!

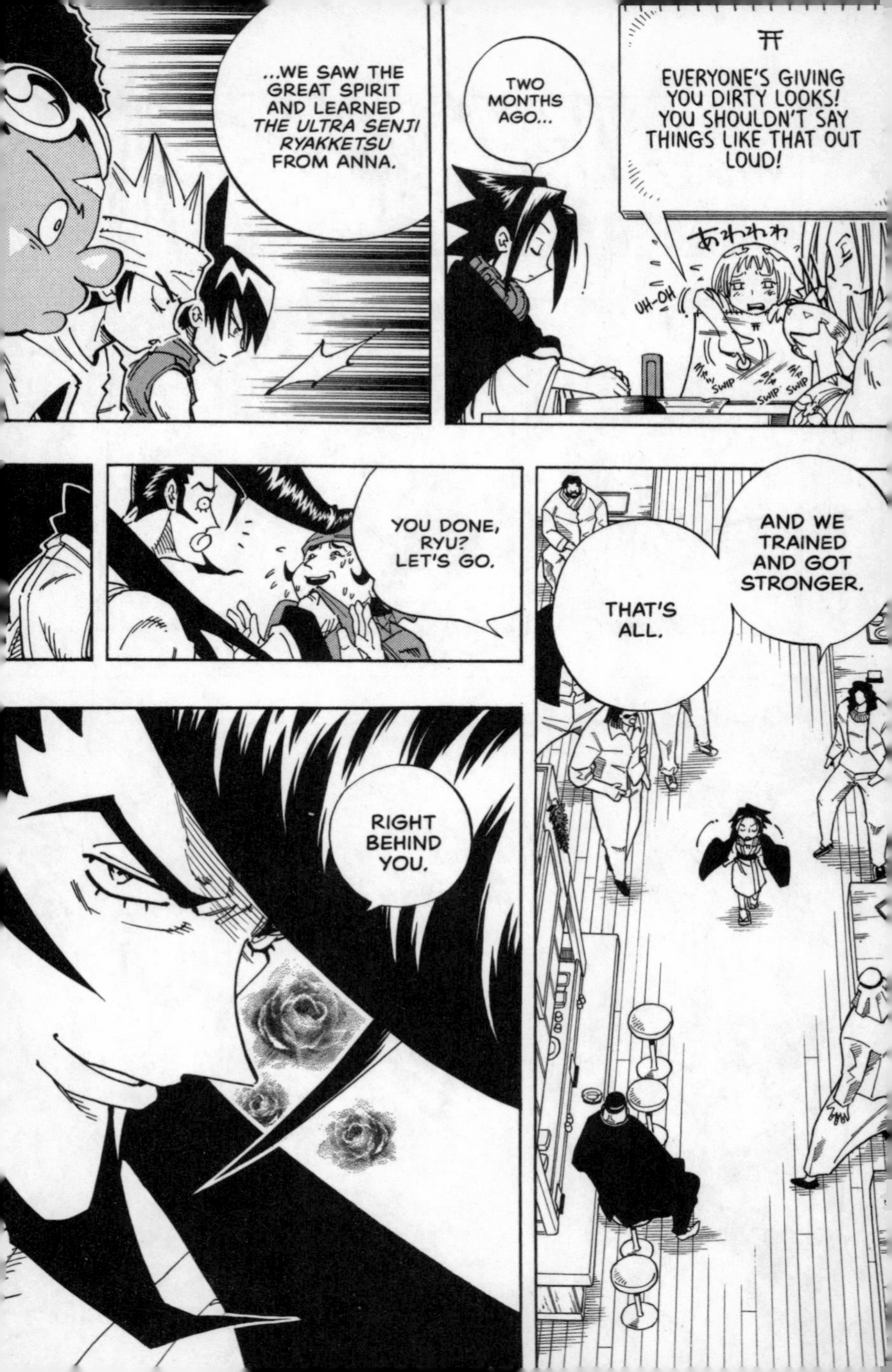
EVERYONE'S GIVING YOU DIRTY LOOKS! YOU SHOULDN'T SAY THINGS LIKE THAT OUT LOUD!
あわわわ
UH-OH
SWIP SWIP SWIP
TWO MONTHS AGO...
...WE SAW THE GREAT SPIRIT AND LEARNED *THE ULTRA SENJI RYAKKETSU* FROM ANNA.
AND WE TRAINED AND GOT STRONGER.
THAT'S ALL.
YOU DONE, RYU? LET'S GO.
RIGHT BEHIND YOU.

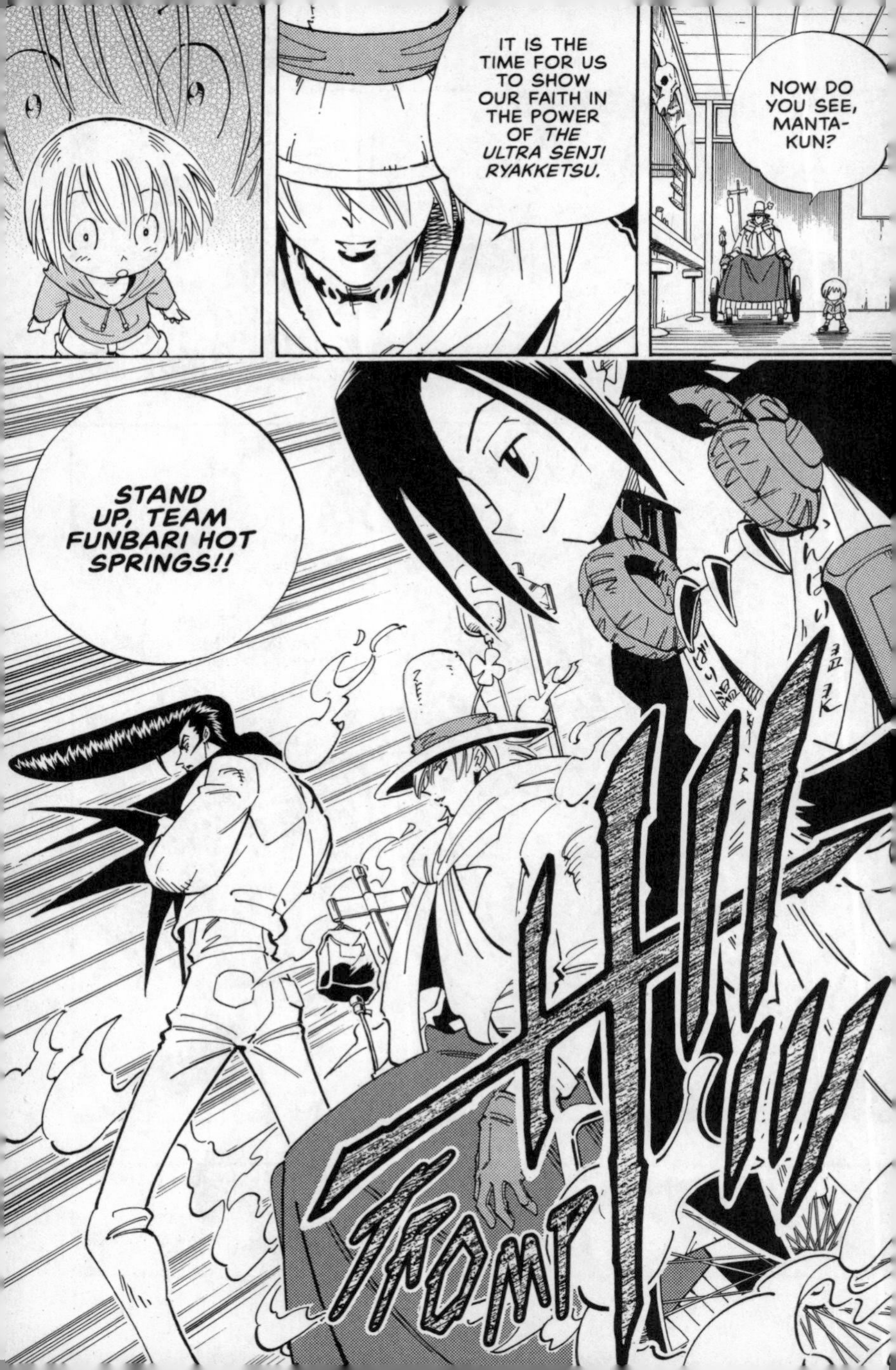
NOW DO YOU SEE, MANTA-KUN?
IT IS THE TIME FOR US TO SHOW OUR FAITH IN THE POWER OF THE ULTRA SENJI RYAKKETSU.
STAND UP, TEAM FUNBARI HOT SPRINGS!!
TROMP

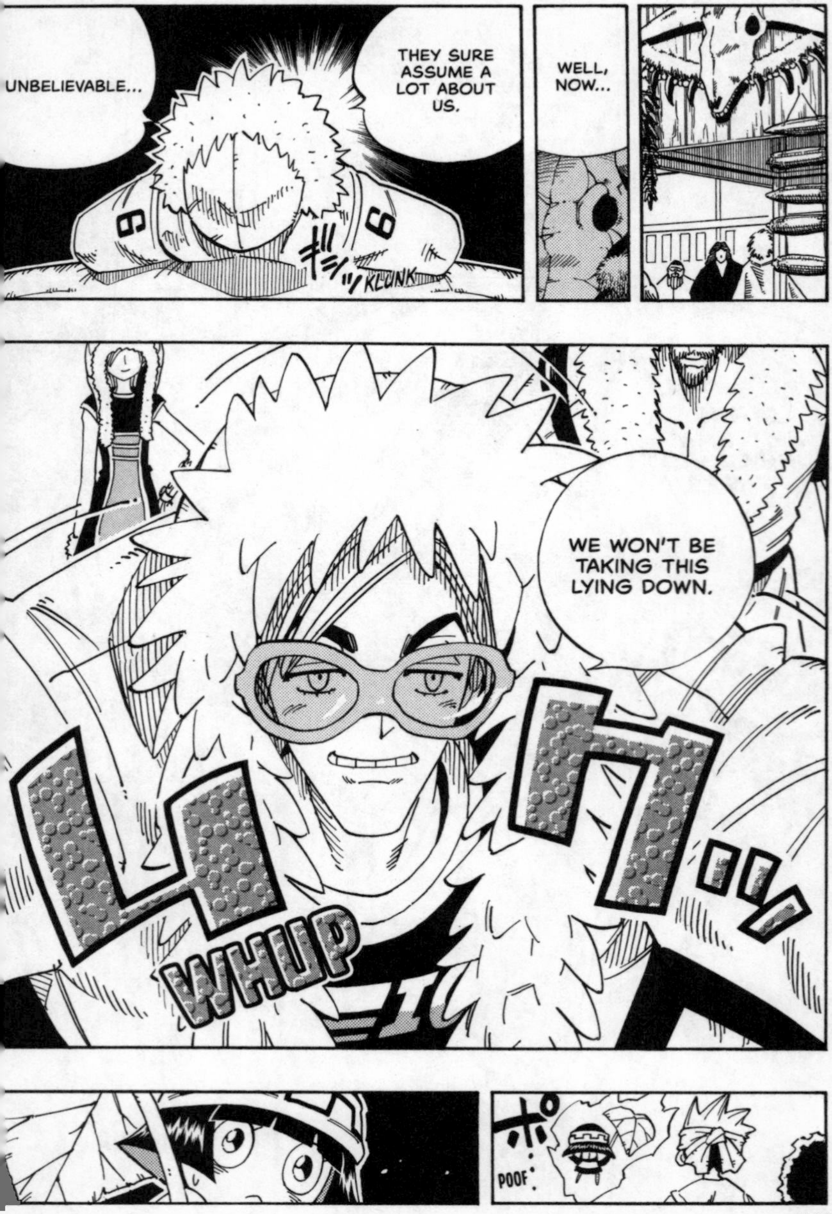
WELL, NOW...
THEY SURE ASSUME A LOT ABOUT US.
UNBELIEVABLE...
KLUNK
WE WON'T BE TAKING THIS LYING DOWN.
WHUP
POOF

Pino

July 2001

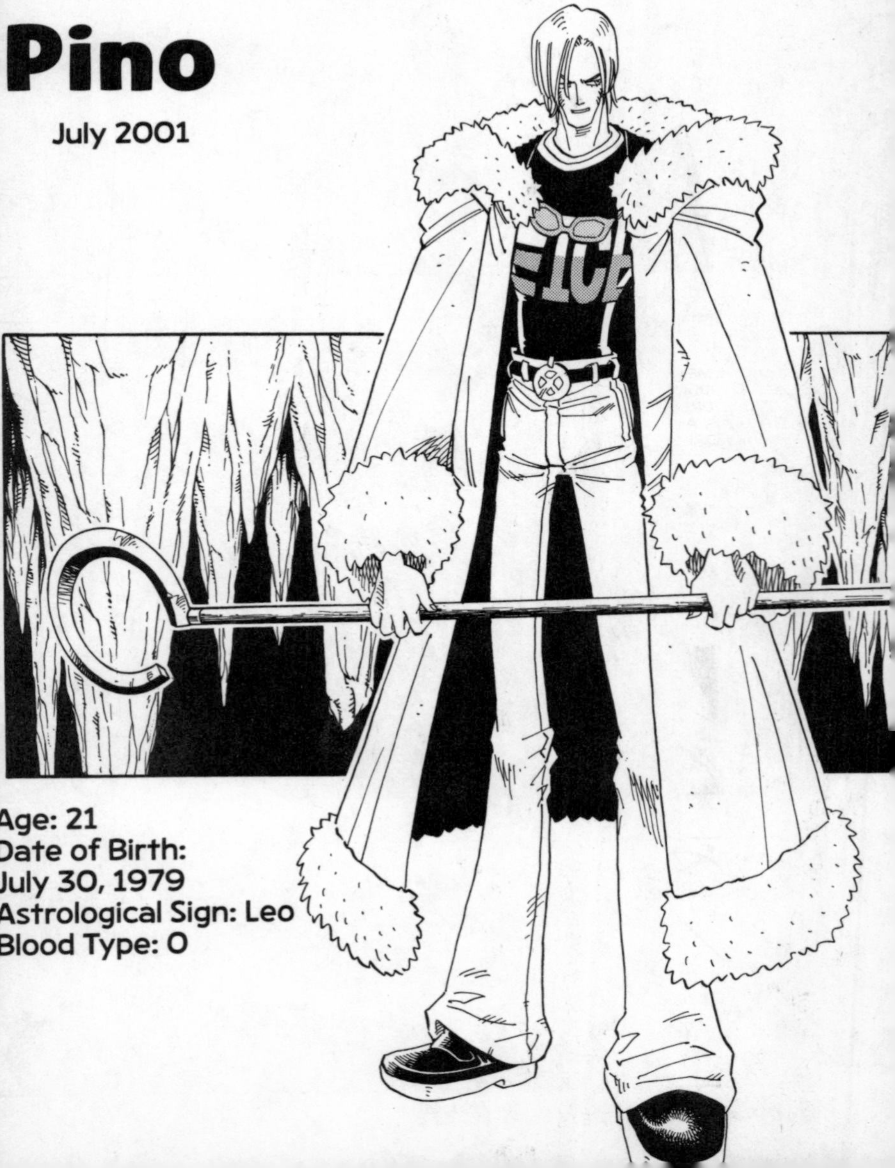
ICE

Age: 21
Date of Birth:
July 30, 1979
Astrological Sign: Leo
Blood Type: O

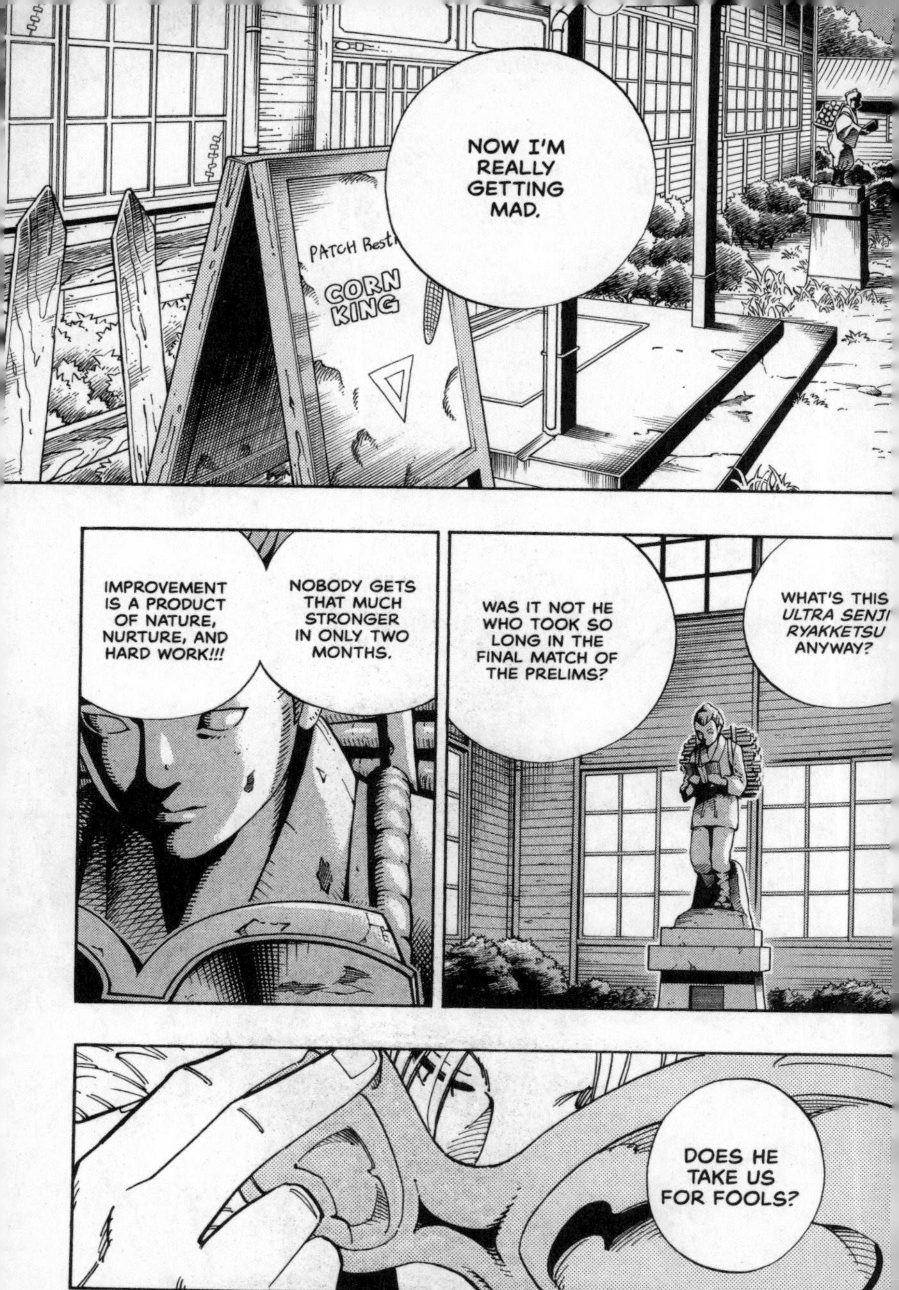

NOW I'M REALLY GETTING MAD.
CORN KING
WHAT'S THIS *ULTRA SENJI RYAKKETSU* ANYWAY?
WAS IT NOT HE WHO TOOK SO LONG IN THE FINAL MATCH OF THE PRELIMS?
NOBODY GETS THAT MUCH STRONGER IN ONLY TWO MONTHS.
IMPROVEMENT IS A PRODUCT OF NATURE, NURTURE, AND HARD WORK!!!
DOES HE TAKE US FOR FOOLS?

Chapter 127: Northern Pride

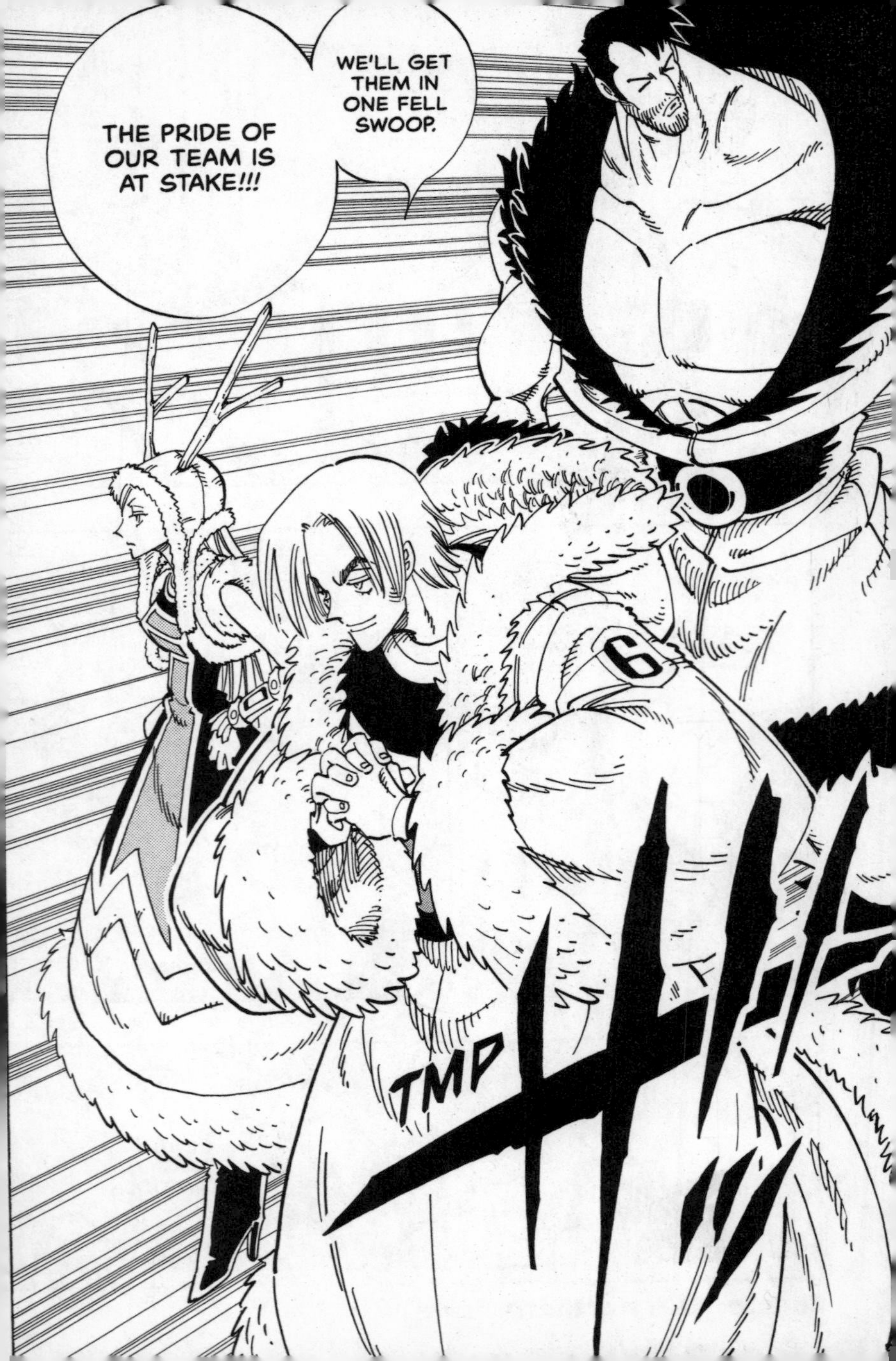
WE'LL GET THEM IN ONE FELL SWOOP.
THE PRIDE OF OUR TEAM IS AT STAKE!!!
TMP

Chapter 127:

Northern Pride

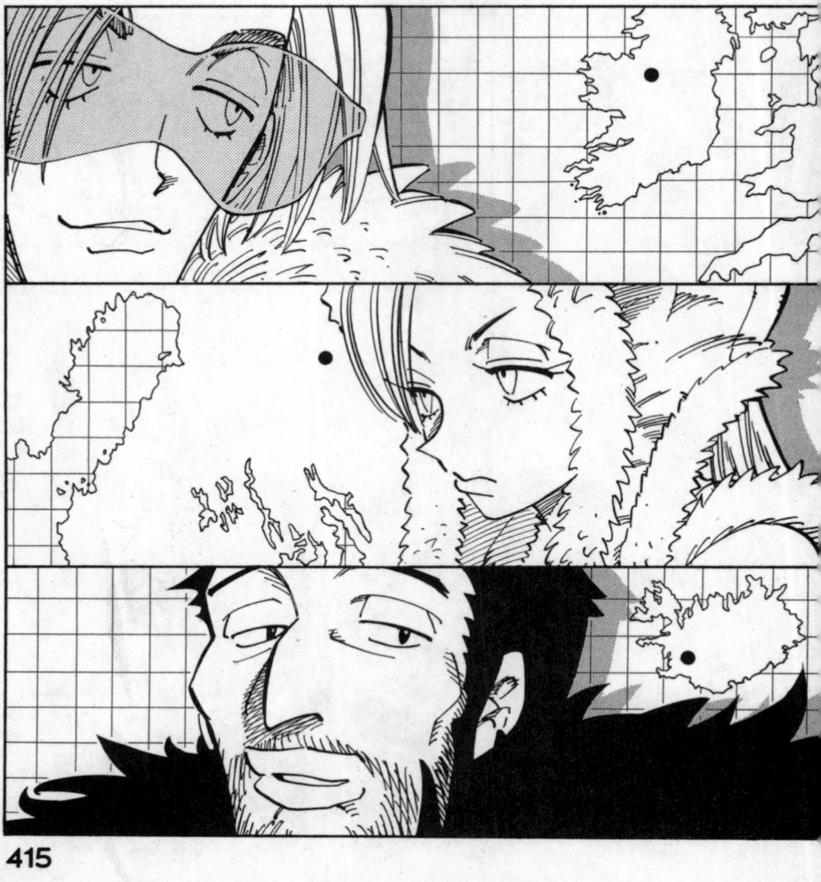

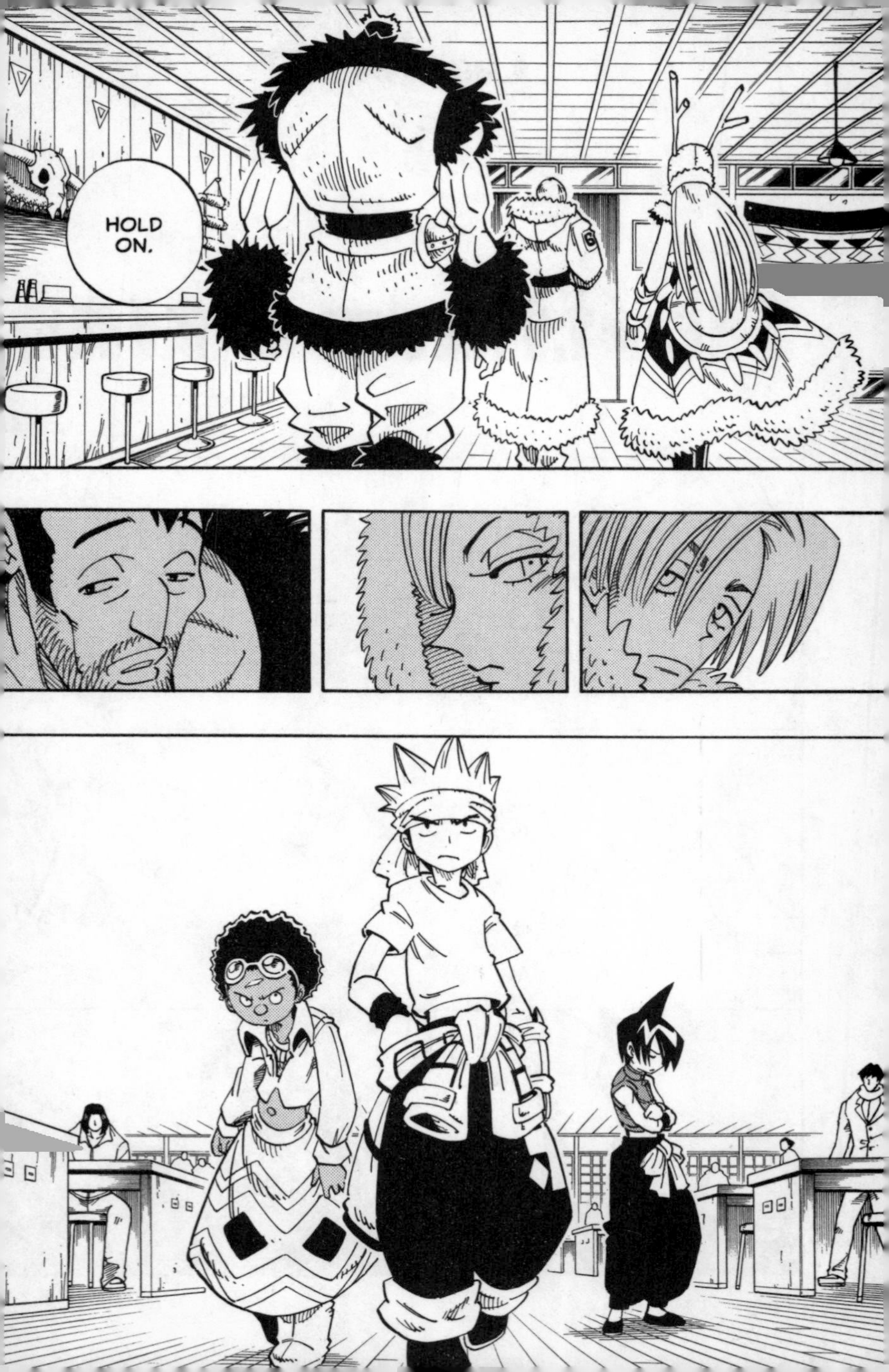
HOLD ON.

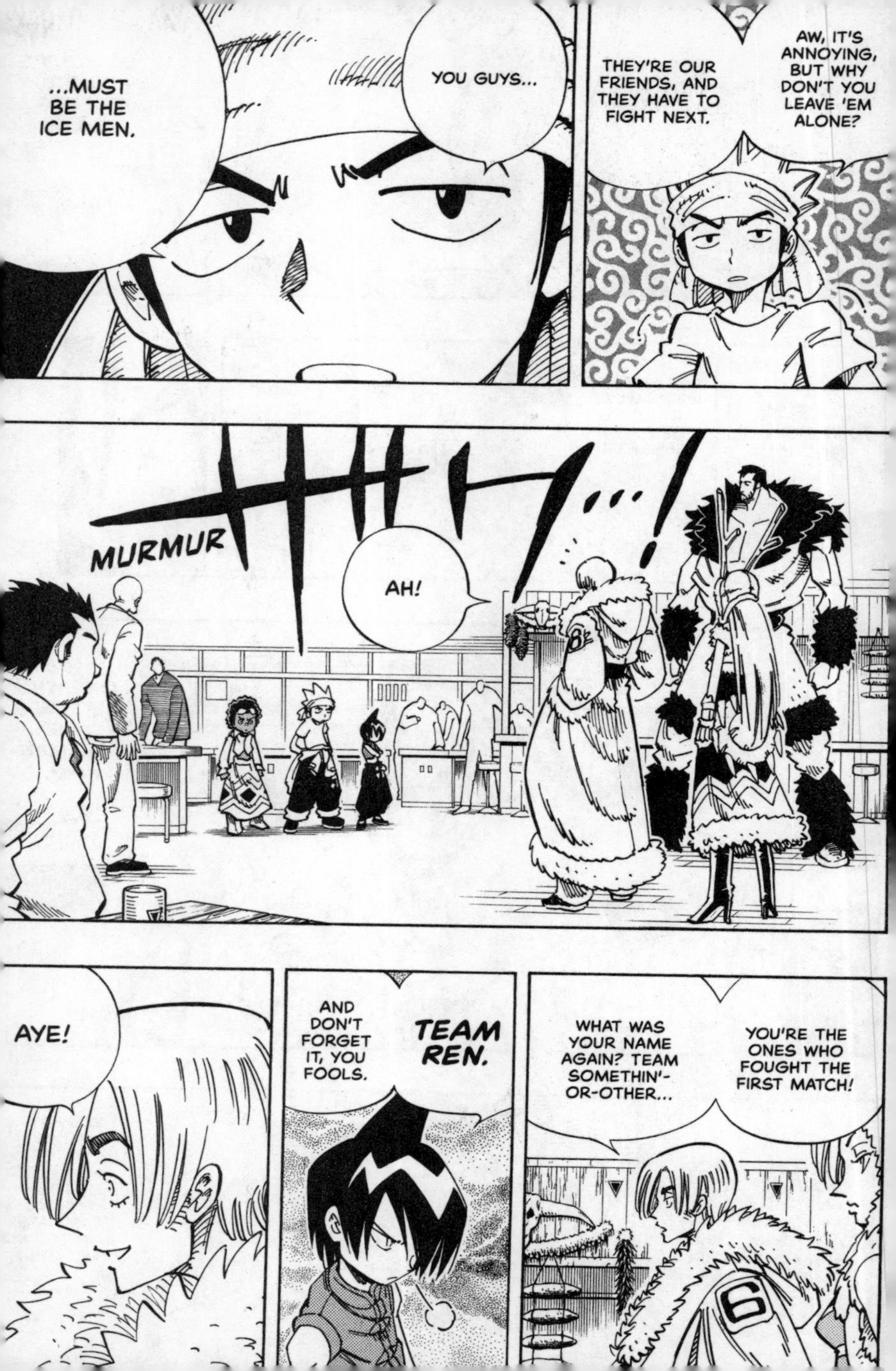

AW, IT'S ANNOYING, BUT WHY DON'T YOU LEAVE 'EM ALONE?
THEY'RE OUR FRIENDS, AND THEY HAVE TO FIGHT NEXT.
YOU GUYS...
...MUST BE THE ICE MEN.
AH!
MURMUR
YOU'RE THE ONES WHO FOUGHT THE FIRST MATCH!
WHAT WAS YOUR NAME AGAIN? TEAM SOMETHIN'-OR-OTHER...
TEAM REN.
AND DON'T FORGET IT, YOU FOOLS.
AYE!

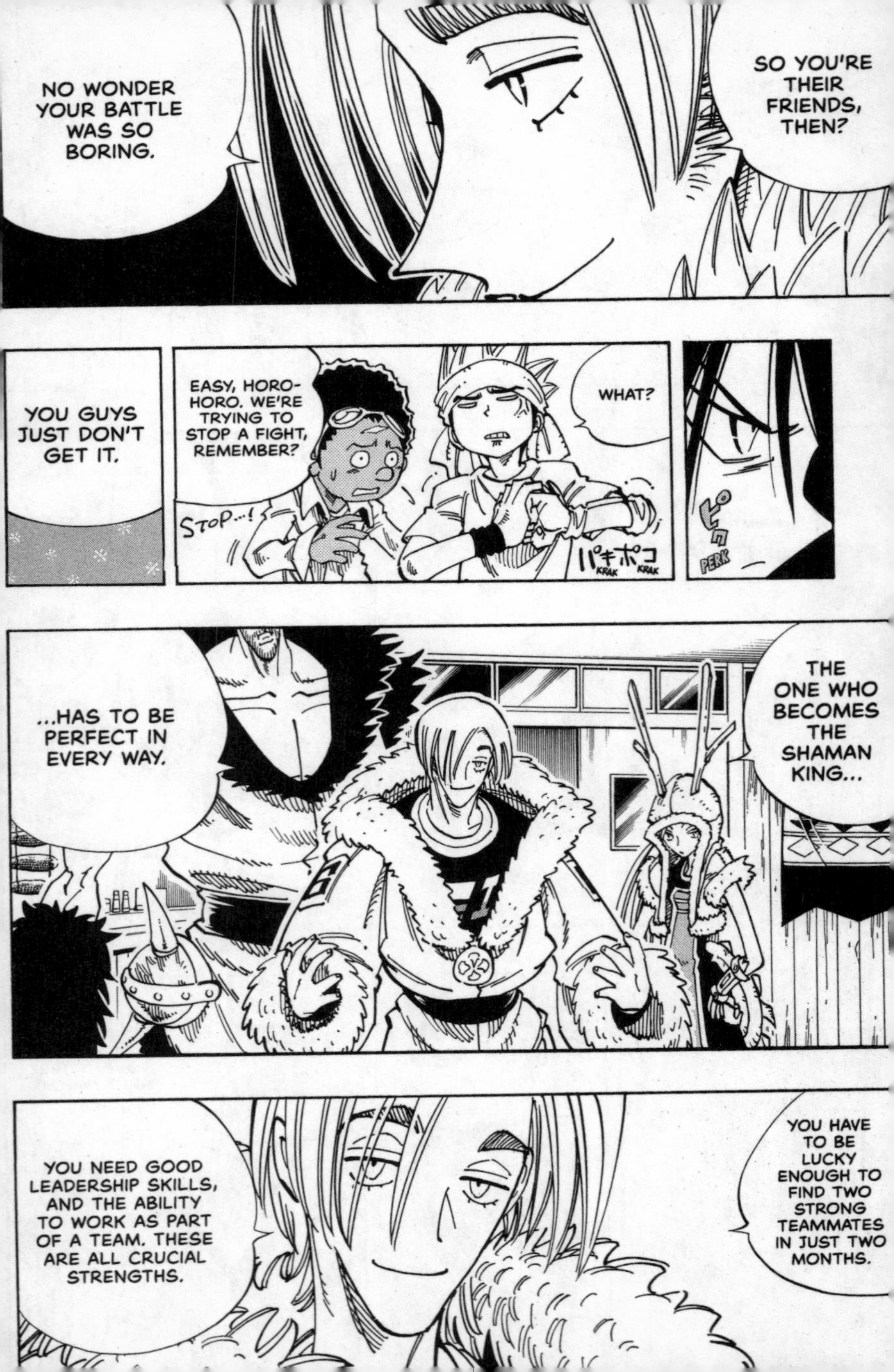
SO YOU'RE THEIR FRIENDS, THEN?
NO WONDER YOUR BATTLE WAS SO BORING.
ピク
PERK
WHAT?
EASY, HORO-HORO. WE'RE TRYING TO STOP A FIGHT, REMEMBER?
パキポコ
KRAK KRAK
STOP...!
YOU GUYS JUST DON'T GET IT.
THE ONE WHO BECOMES THE SHAMAN KING...
...HAS TO BE PERFECT IN EVERY WAY.
YOU HAVE TO BE LUCKY ENOUGH TO FIND TWO STRONG TEAMMATES IN JUST TWO MONTHS.
YOU NEED GOOD LEADERSHIP SKILLS, AND THE ABILITY TO WORK AS PART OF A TEAM. THESE ARE ALL CRUCIAL STRENGTHS.

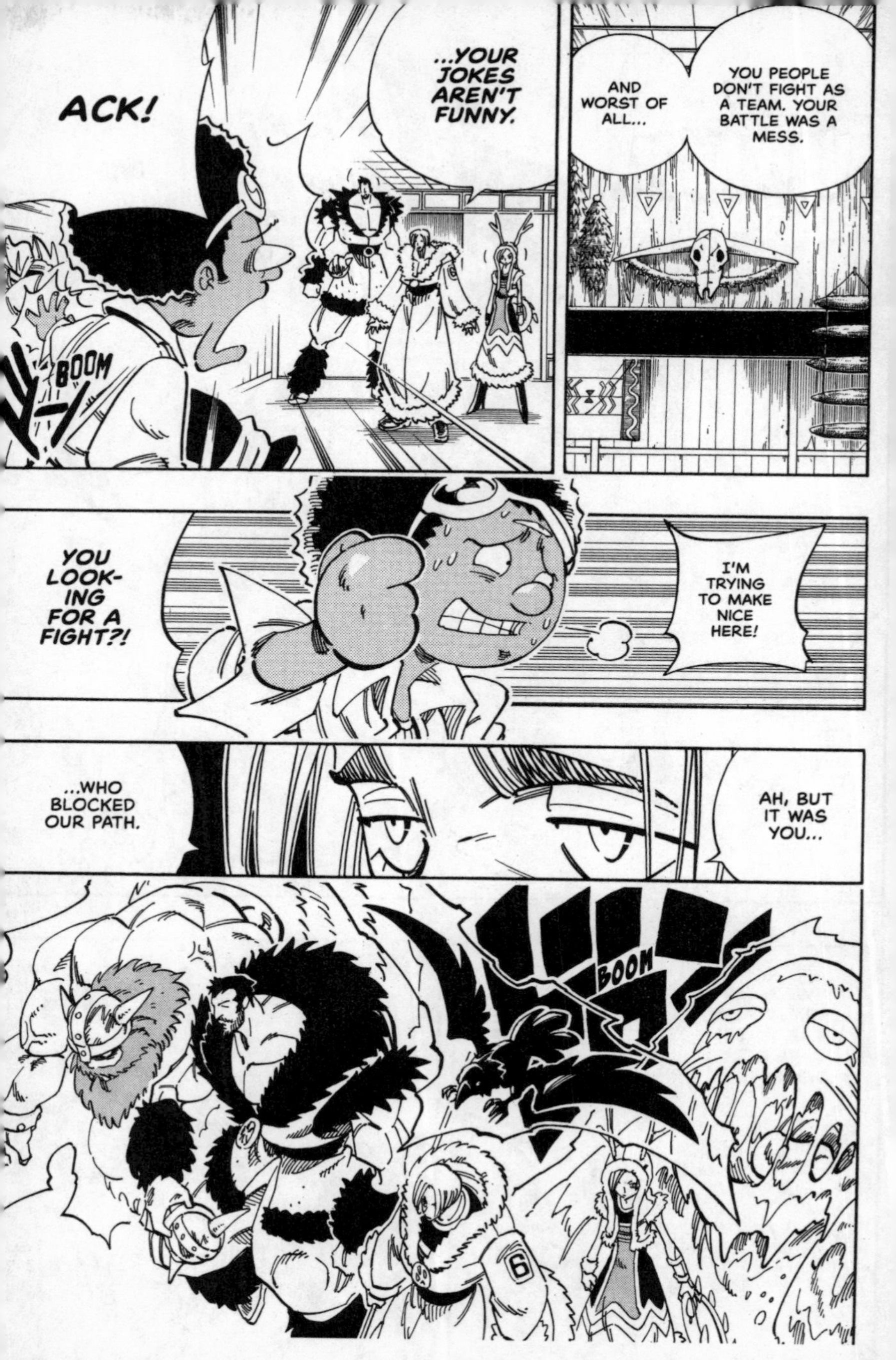
YOU PEOPLE DON'T FIGHT AS A TEAM. YOUR BATTLE WAS A MESS.
AND WORST OF ALL...
...YOUR JOKES AREN'T FUNNY.
ACK!
BOOM
I'M TRYING TO MAKE NICE HERE!
YOU LOOKING- ING FOR A FIGHT?!
AH, BUT IT WAS YOU...
...WHO BLOCKED OUR PATH.
BOOM

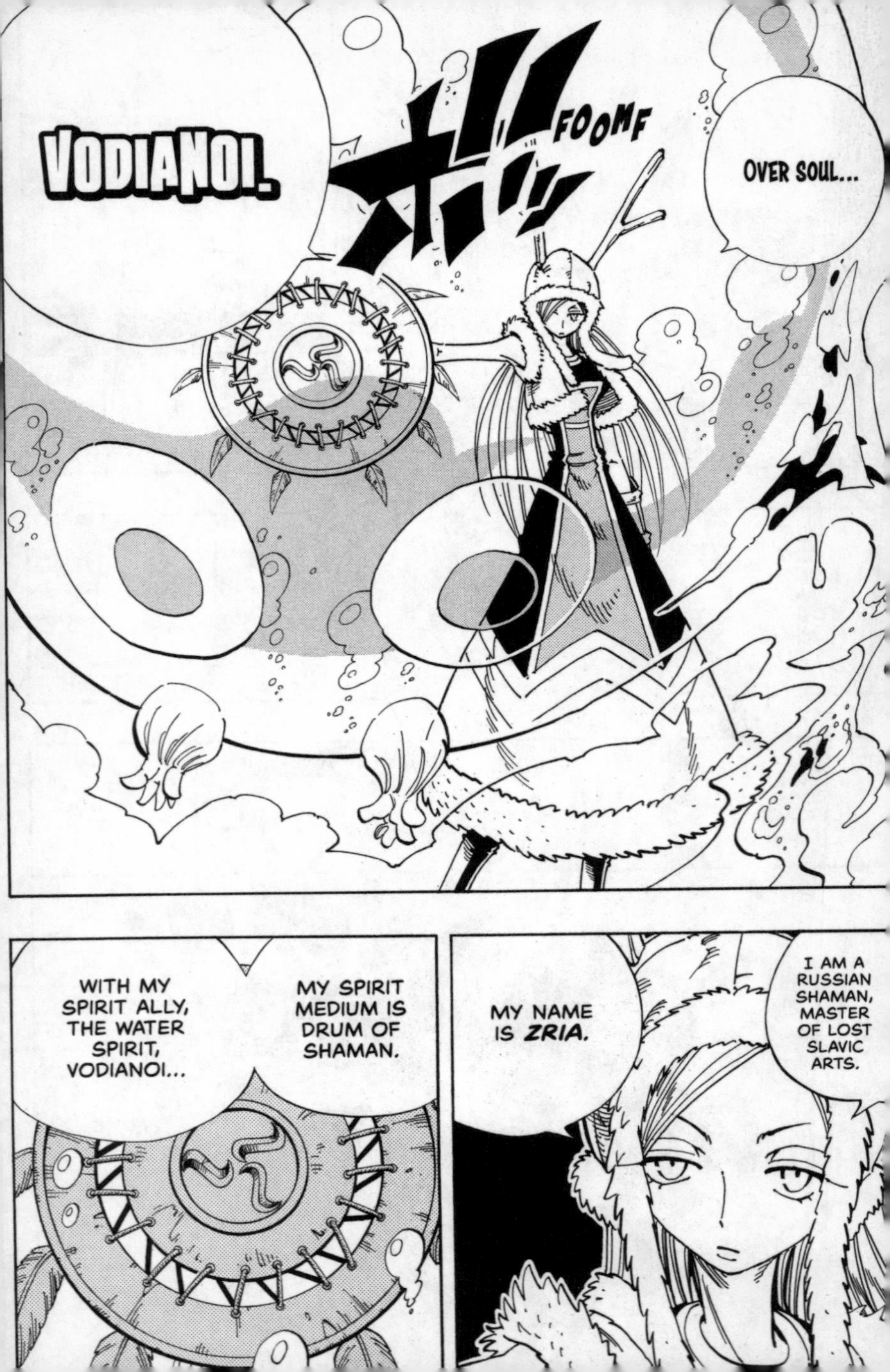
OVER SOUL...
FOOMF
VODIANOI.
I AM A RUSSIAN SHAMAN, MASTER OF LOST SLAVIC ARTS.
MY NAME IS *ZRIA.*
MY SPIRIT MEDIUM IS DRUM OF SHAMAN.
WITH MY SPIRIT ALLY, THE WATER SPIRIT, VODIANOI...

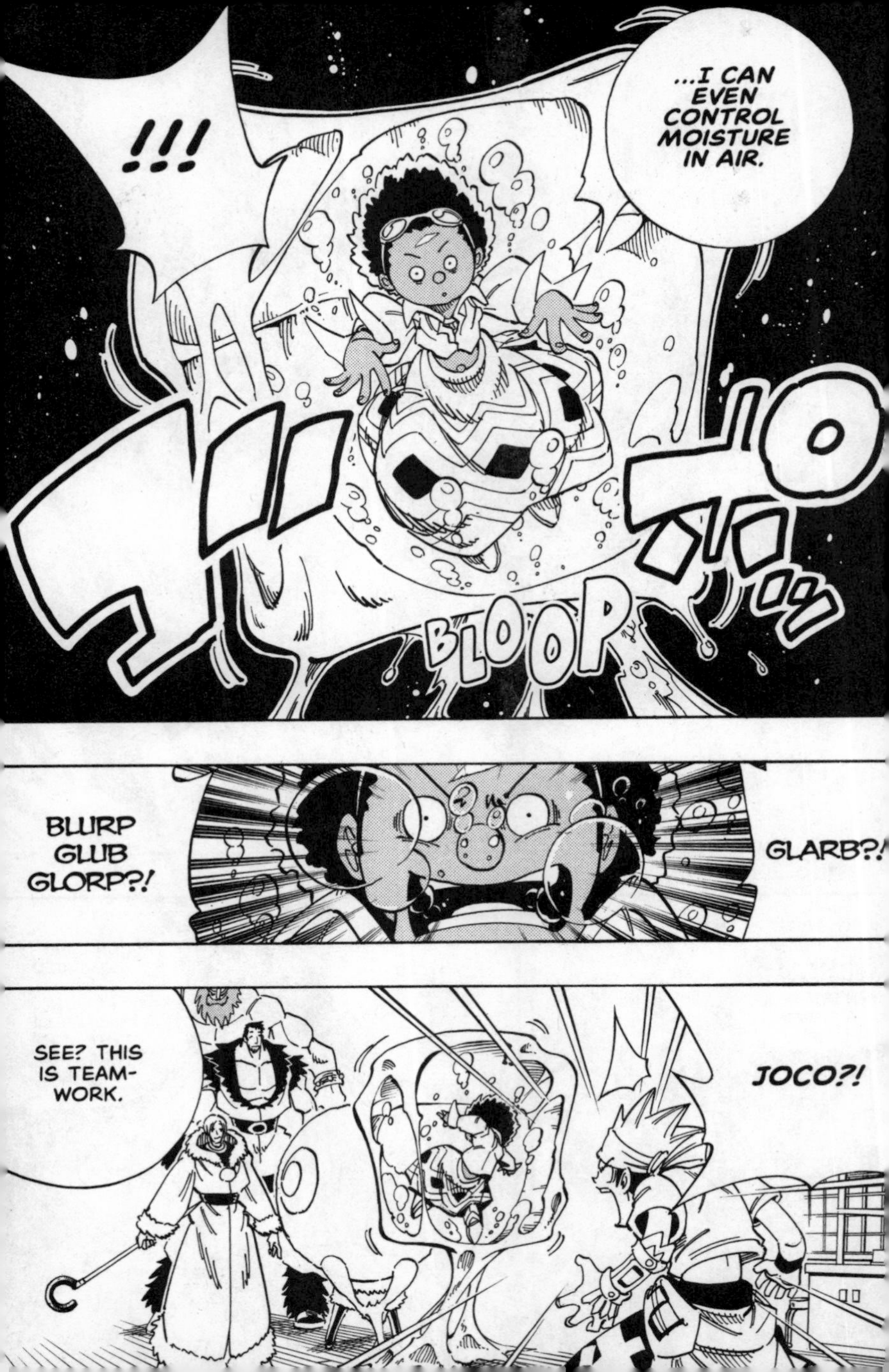
...I CAN EVEN CONTROL MOISTURE IN AIR.
!!!
BLOOP
GLARB?!
BLURP GLUB GLORP?!
JOCO?!
SEE? THIS IS TEAM-WORK.

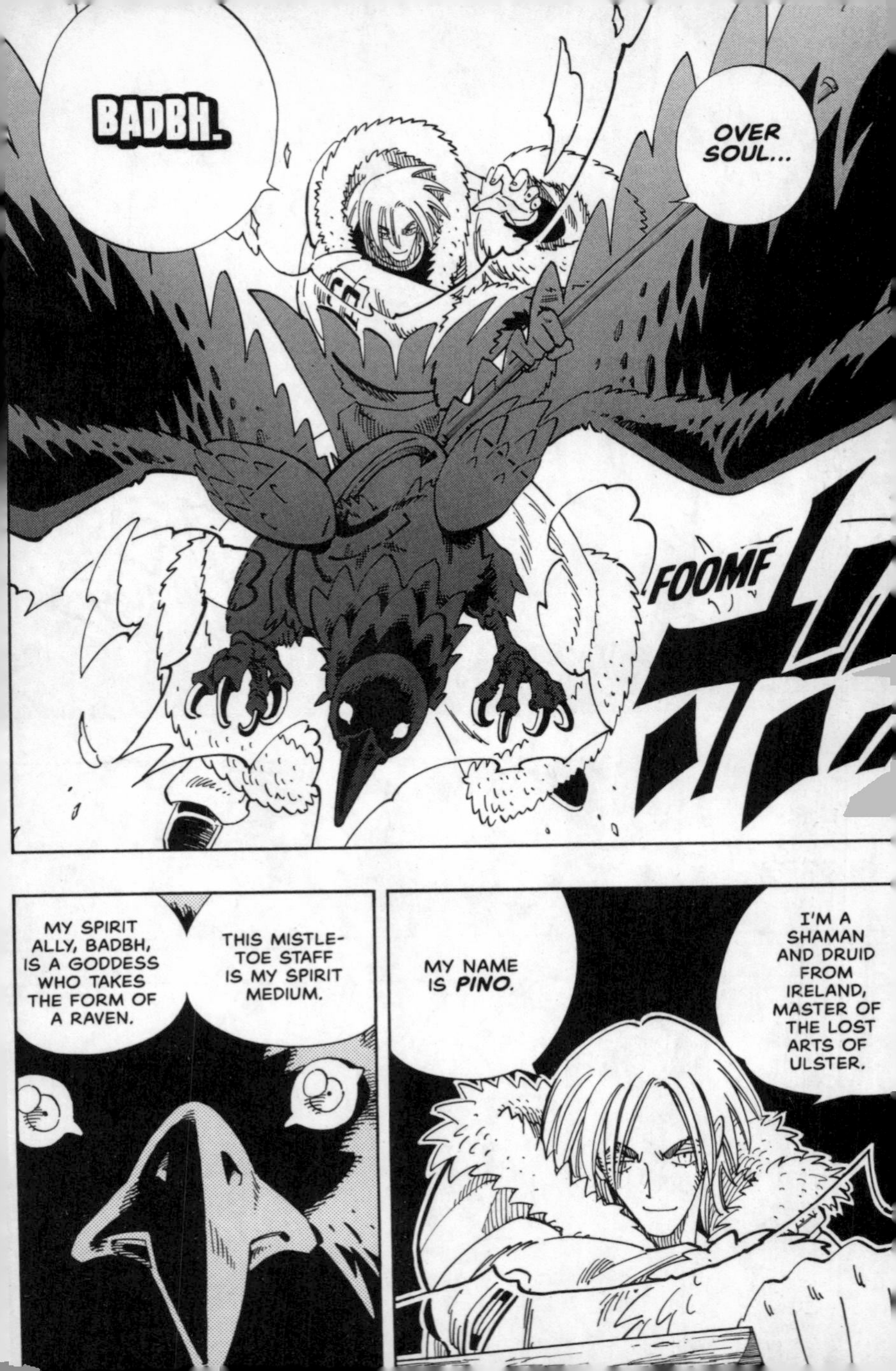
OVER SOUL...
BADBH.
FOOMF
I'M A SHAMAN AND DRUID FROM IRELAND, MASTER OF THE LOST ARTS OF ULSTER.
MY NAME IS *PINO.*
THIS MISTLETOE STAFF IS MY SPIRIT MEDIUM.
MY SPIRIT ALLY, BADBH, IS A GODDESS WHO TAKES THE FORM OF A RAVEN.

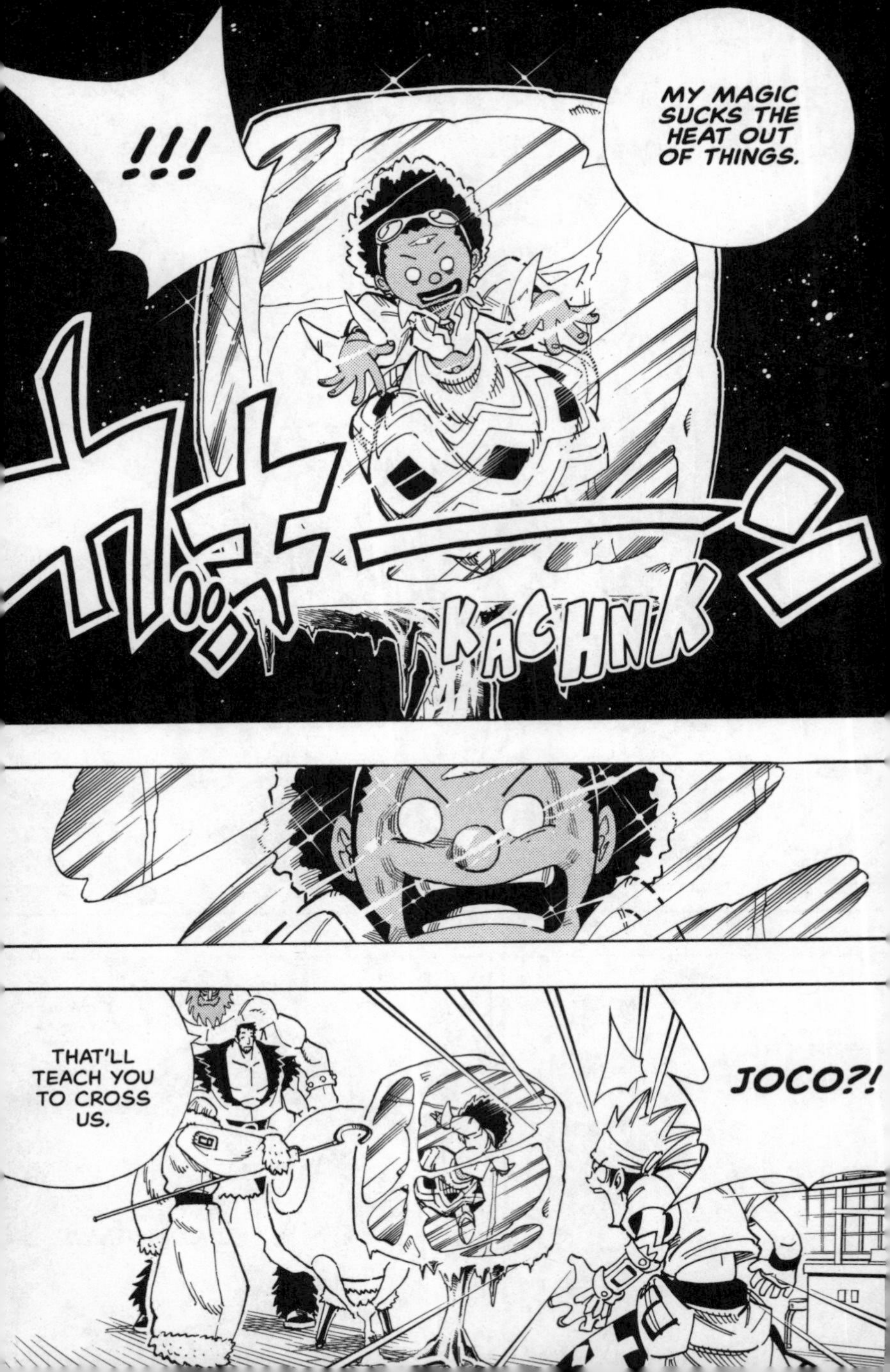
MY MAGIC SUCKS THE HEAT OUT OF THINGS.
!!!
KACHNK
JOCO?!
THAT'LL TEACH YOU TO CROSS US.

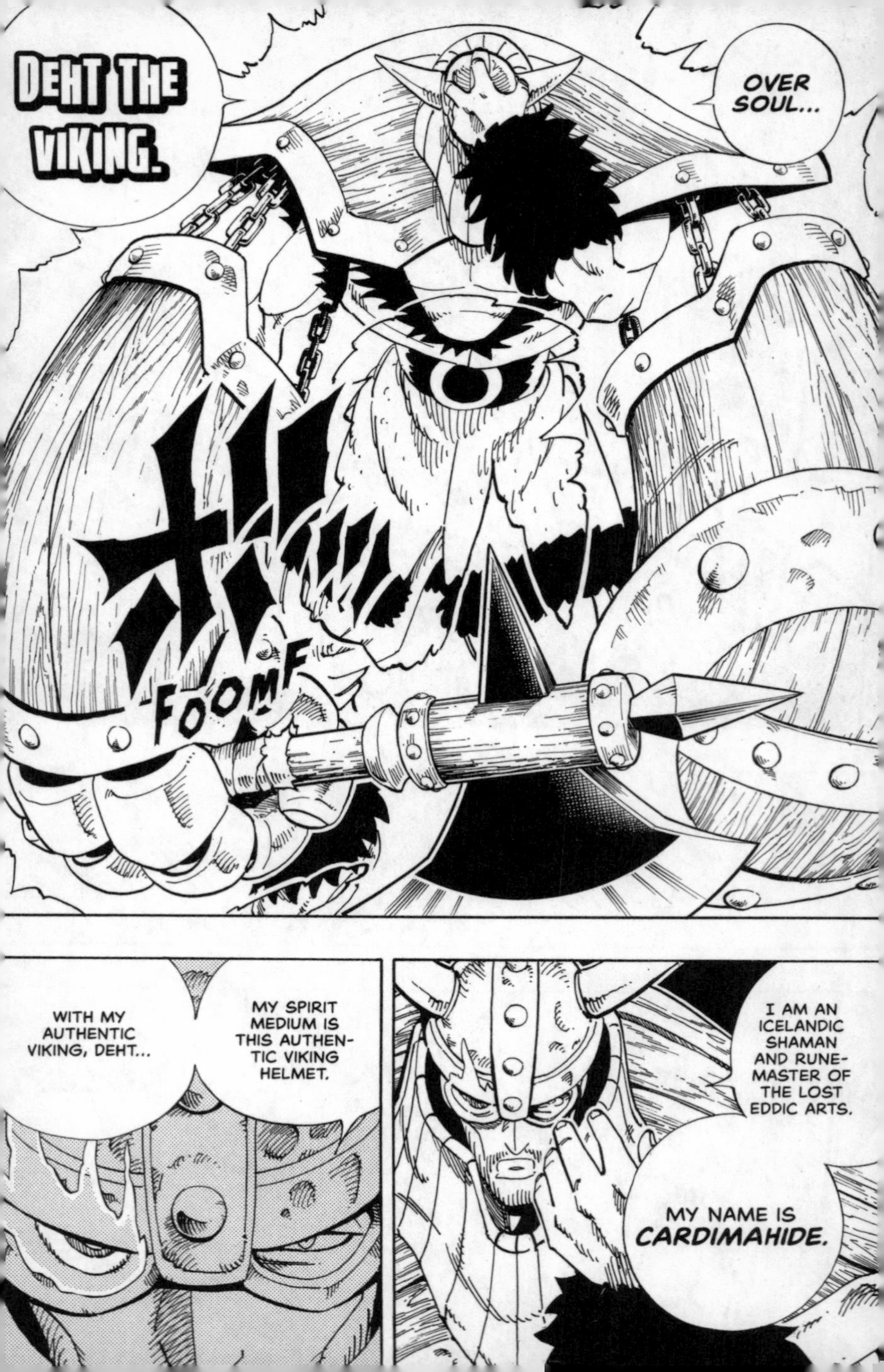
OVER SOUL...
DEHT THE VIKING.
FOOMF
I AM AN ICELANDIC SHAMAN AND RUNE-MASTER OF THE LOST EDDIC ARTS.
MY NAME IS CARDIMAHIDE.
MY SPIRIT MEDIUM IS THIS AUTHEN-TIC VIKING HELMET.
WITH MY AUTHENTIC VIKING, DEHT...

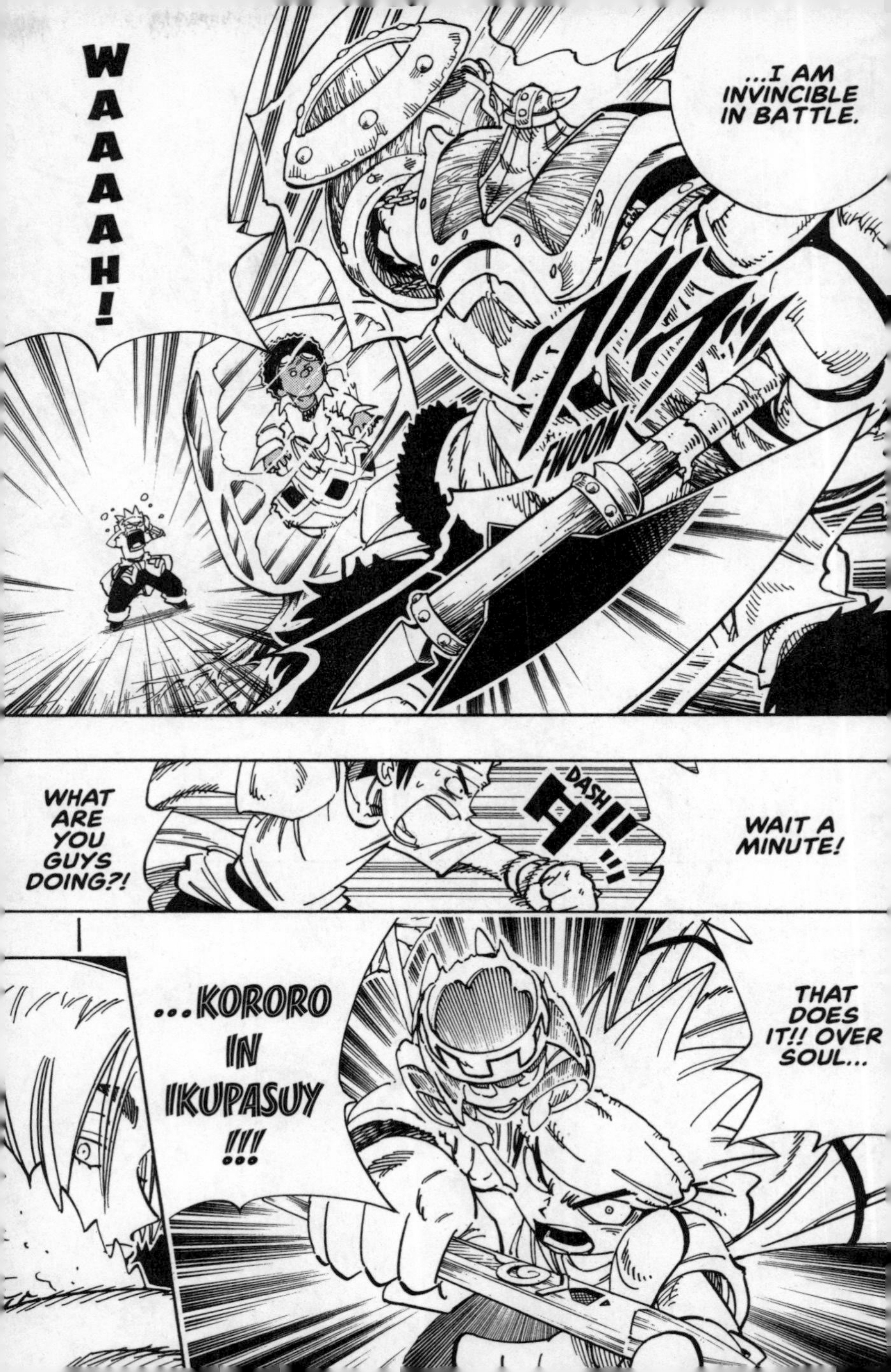
...I AM INVINCIBLE IN BATTLE.
FWOOM
WAAAAAH!
WAIT A MINUTE!
DASH
WHAT ARE YOU GUYS DOING?!
THAT DOES IT!! OVER SOUL...
...KORORO IN IKUPASUY!!!

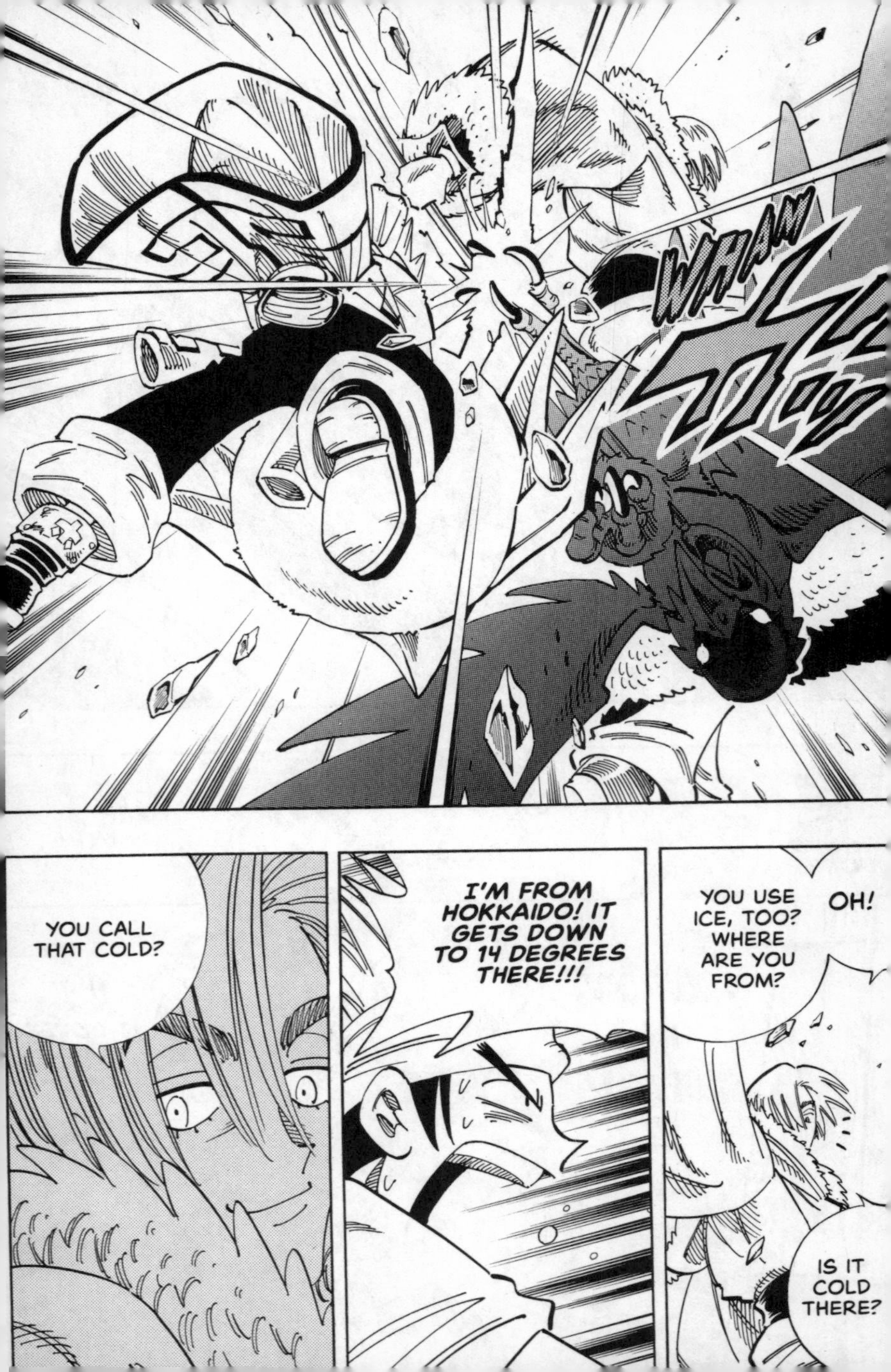
WHAM
OH!
YOU USE ICE, TOO? WHERE ARE YOU FROM?
IS IT COLD THERE?
I'M FROM HOKKAIDO! IT GETS DOWN TO 14 DEGREES THERE!!!
YOU CALL THAT COLD?

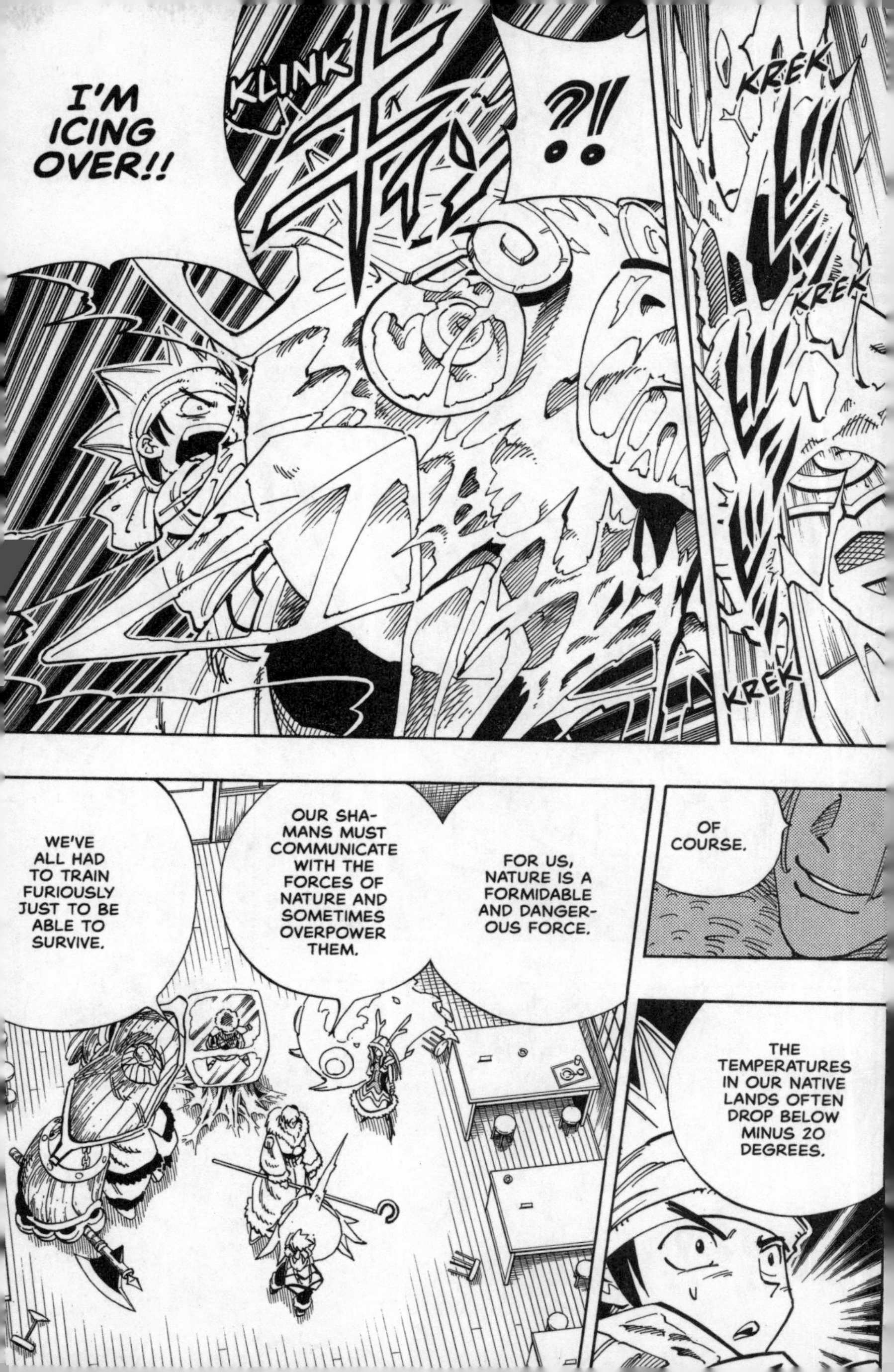
KREK
KREK
?!!
KLINK
I'M ICING OVER!!
KREK
OF COURSE.
THE TEMPERATURES IN OUR NATIVE LANDS OFTEN DROP BELOW MINUS 20 DEGREES.
FOR US, NATURE IS A FORMIDABLE AND DANGER-OUS FORCE.
OUR SHA-MANS MUST COMMUNICATE WITH THE FORCES OF NATURE AND SOMETIMES OVERPOWER THEM.
WE'VE ALL HAD TO TRAIN FURIOUSLY JUST TO BE ABLE TO SURVIVE.

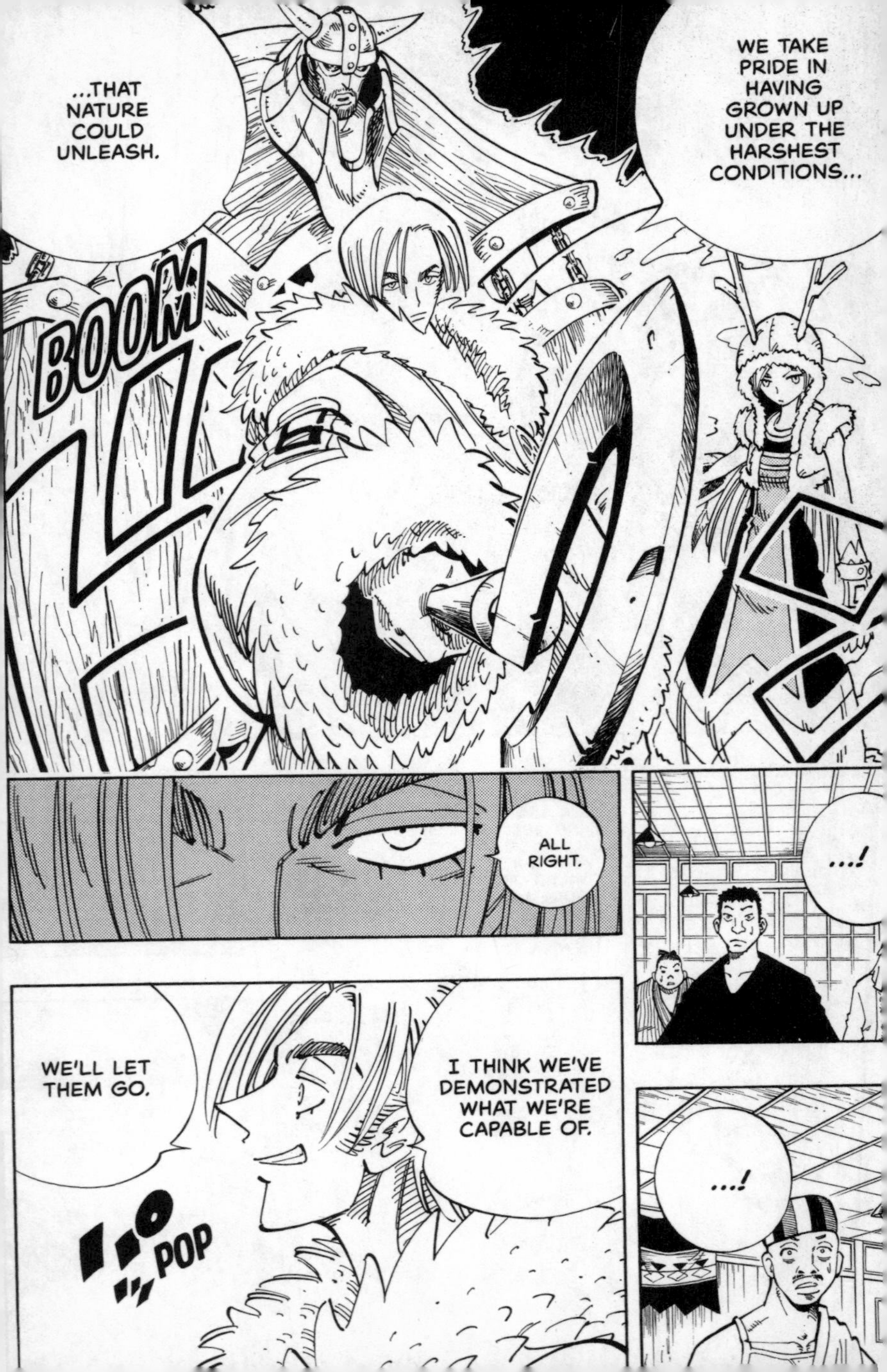

WE TAKE PRIDE IN HAVING GROWN UP UNDER THE HARSHEST CONDITIONS...
...THAT NATURE COULD UNLEASH.
BOOM
...!
...!
ALL RIGHT.
I THINK WE'VE DEMONSTRATED WHAT WE'RE CAPABLE OF.
WE'LL LET THEM GO.
POP

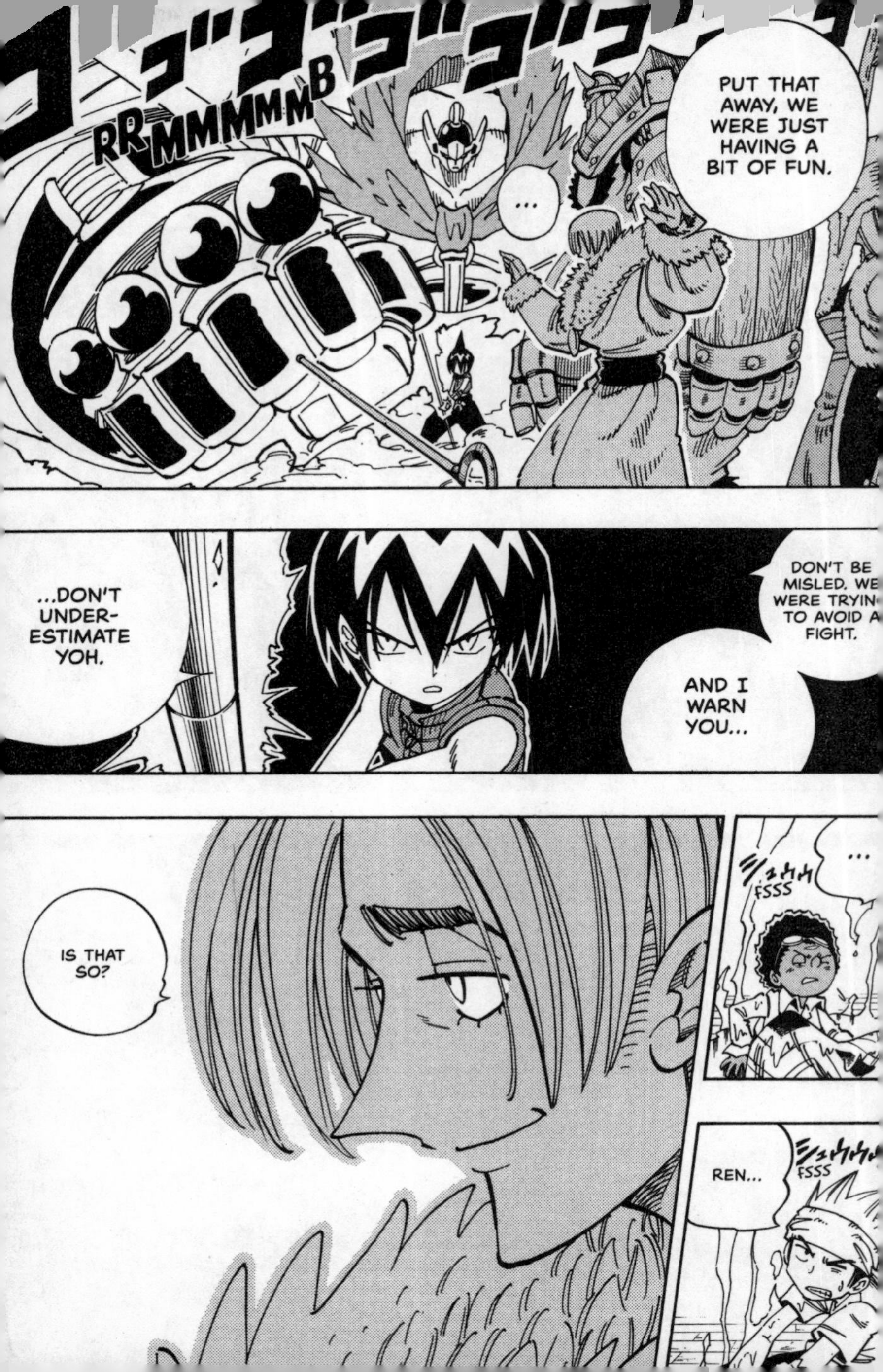
PUT THAT AWAY, WE WERE JUST HAVING A BIT OF FUN.
...
RRMMMMMMB
DON'T BE MISLED. WE WERE TRYIN TO AVOID A FIGHT.
AND I WARN YOU...
...DON'T UNDER-ESTIMATE YOH.
...
FSSS
REN...
FSSS
IS THAT SO?

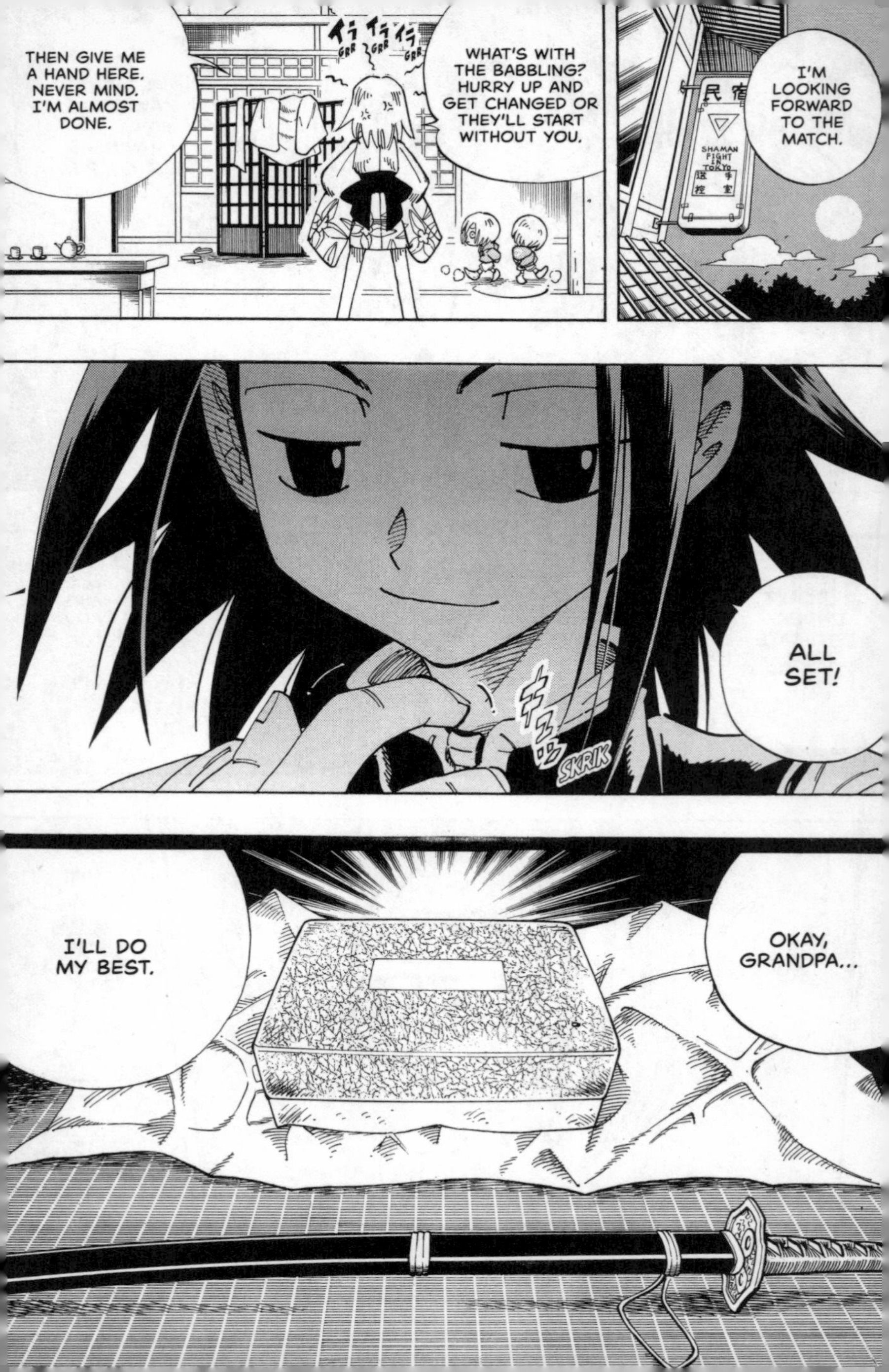

I'M LOOKING FORWARD TO THE MATCH.
民宿
SHAMAN FIGHT IN TOKYO
選手控室
イラ イラ イラ
GRR GRR GRR
WHAT'S WITH THE BABBLING? HURRY UP AND GET CHANGED OR THEY'LL START WITHOUT YOU.
THEN GIVE ME A HAND HERE. NEVER MIND. I'M ALMOST DONE.
ALL SET!
SKRIK
OKAY, GRANDPA...
I'LL DO MY BEST.

Badbh

July 2001

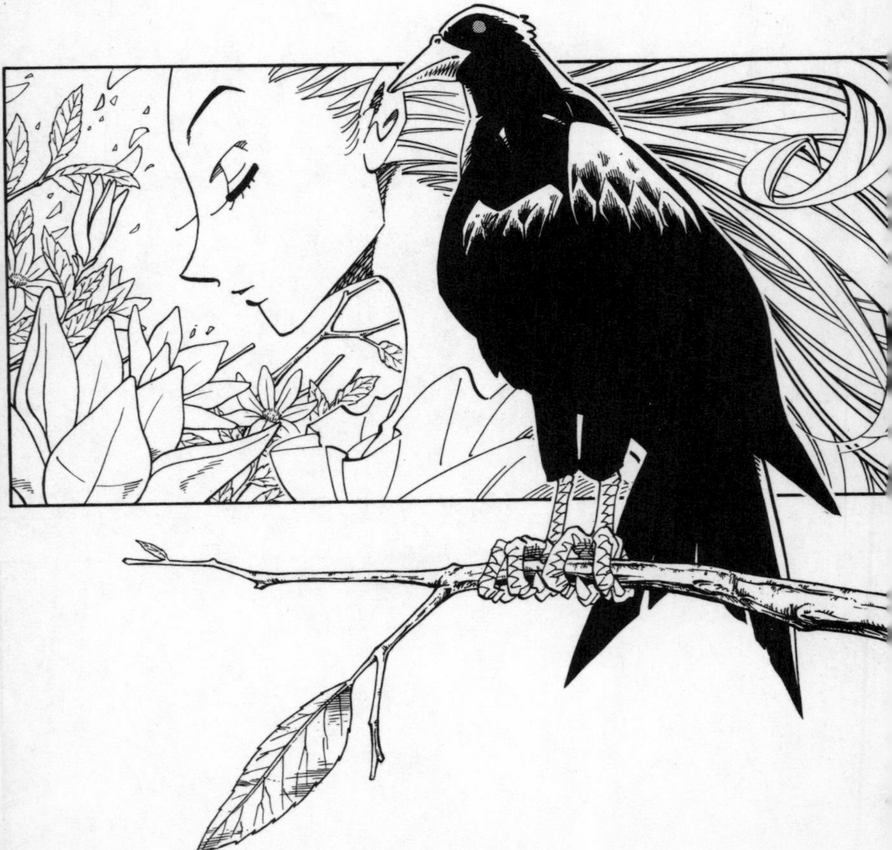

Chapter 128: Amidamaru's Album

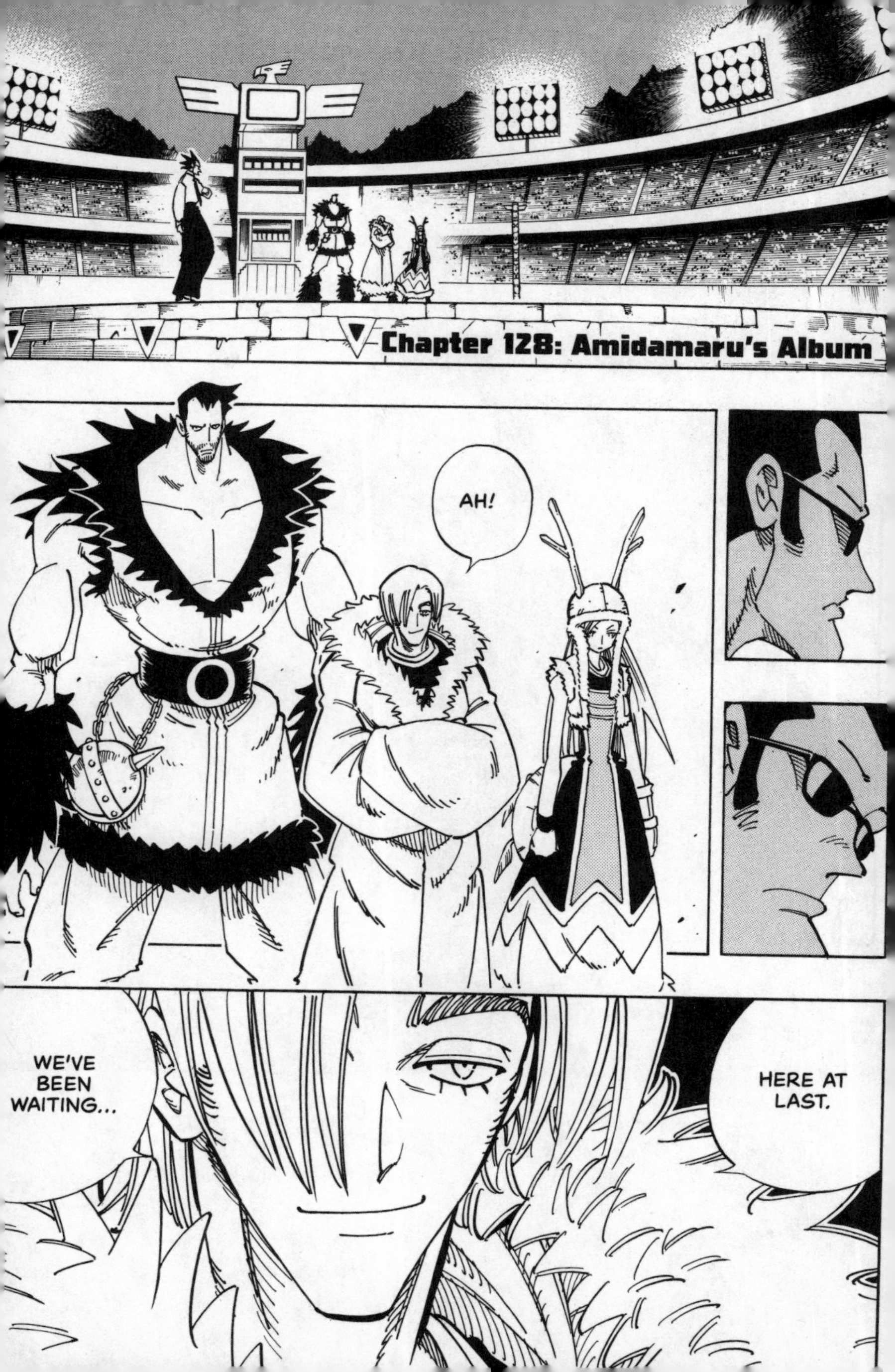
AH!
HERE AT LAST.
WE'VE BEEN WAITING...

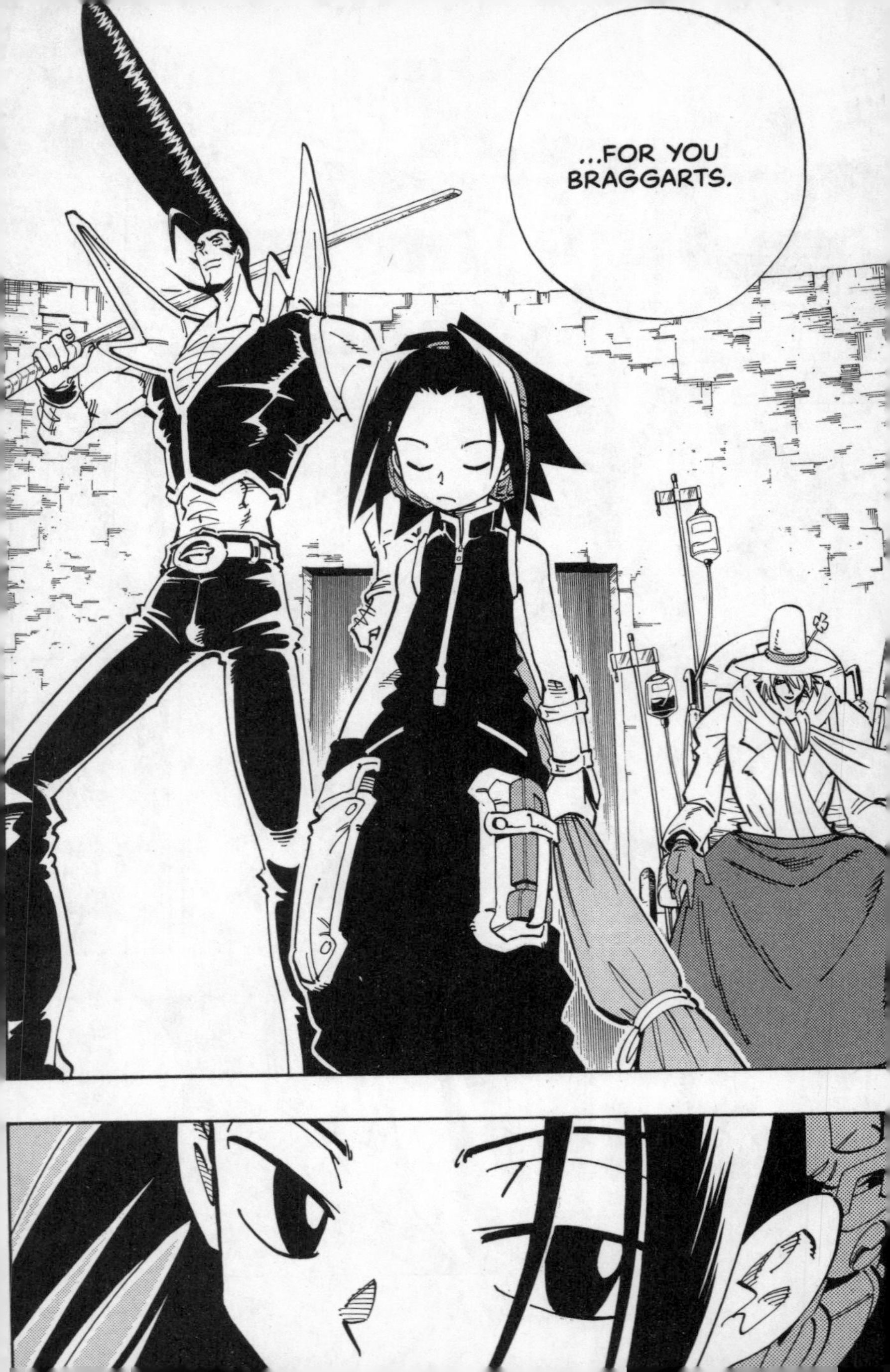
...FOR YOU BRAGGARTS.

Chapter 128:

Amidamaru's Album

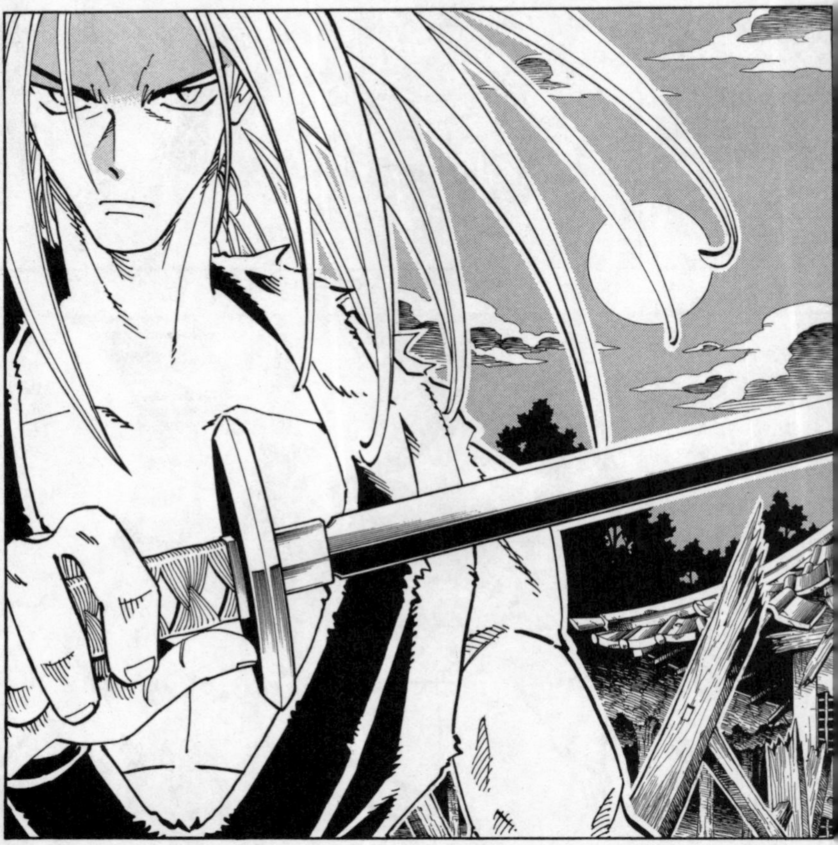

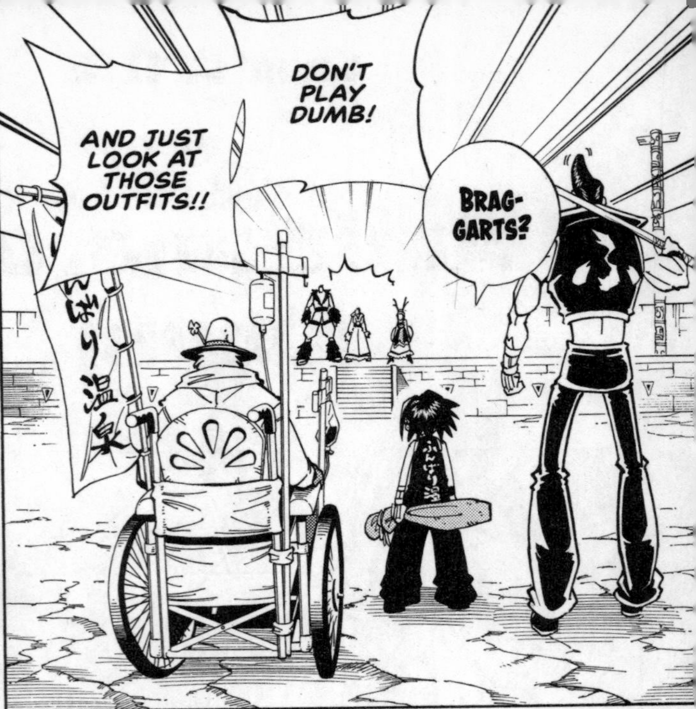

BRAG-GARTS?
DON'T PLAY DUMB!
AND JUST LOOK AT THOSE OUTFITS!!

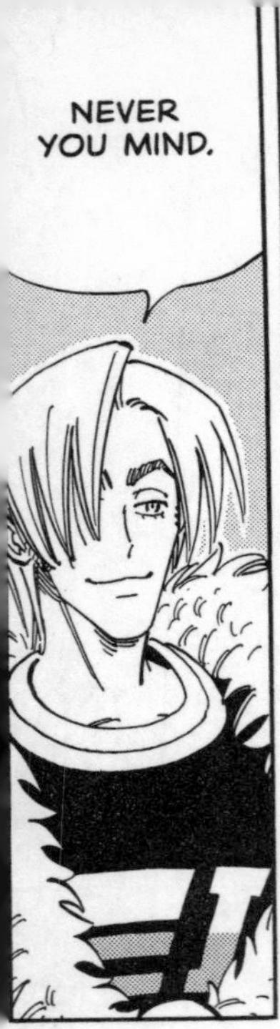

NEVER YOU MIND.

Flag: Funbari hot springs. Shirt: "fu" for Funbari

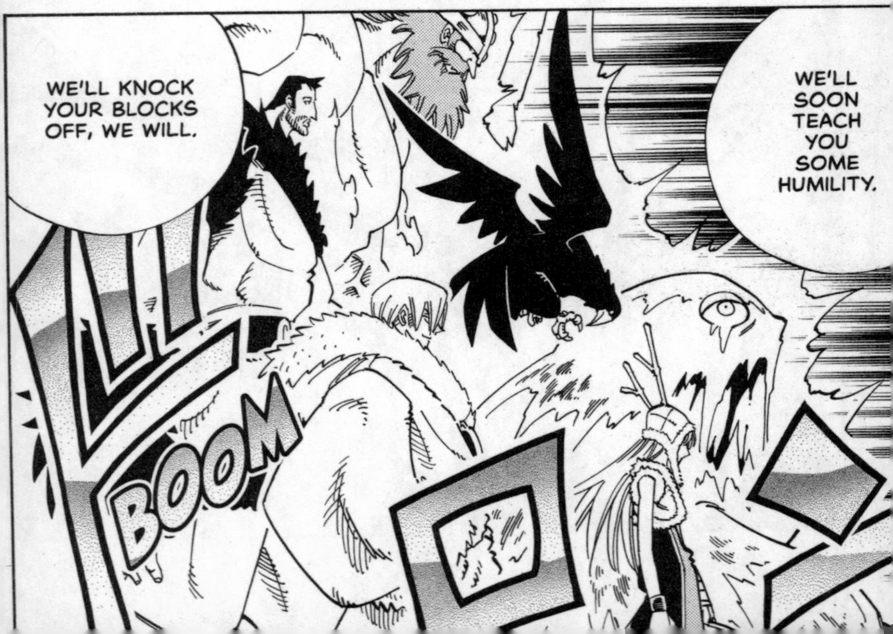

WE'LL SOON TEACH YOU SOME HUMILITY.
WE'LL KNOCK YOUR BLOCKS OFF, WE WILL.
BOOM

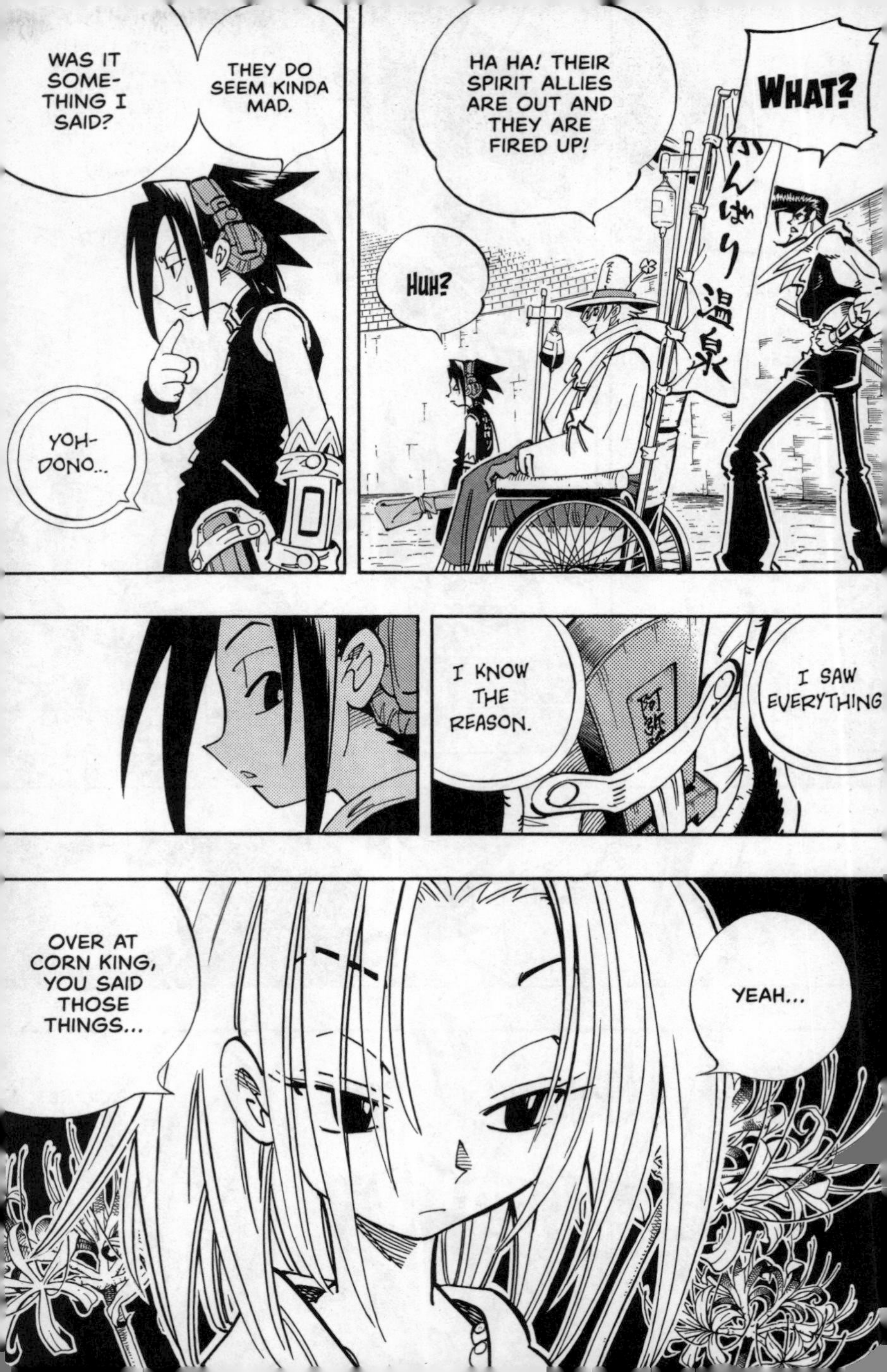
WHAT?
HA HA! THEIR SPIRIT ALLIES ARE OUT AND THEY ARE FIRED UP!
ふんばり温泉
HUH?
THEY DO SEEM KINDA MAD.
WAS IT SOME-THING I SAID?
YOH-DONO...
I SAW EVERYTHING
I KNOW THE REASON.
YEAH...
OVER AT CORN KING, YOU SAID THOSE THINGS...

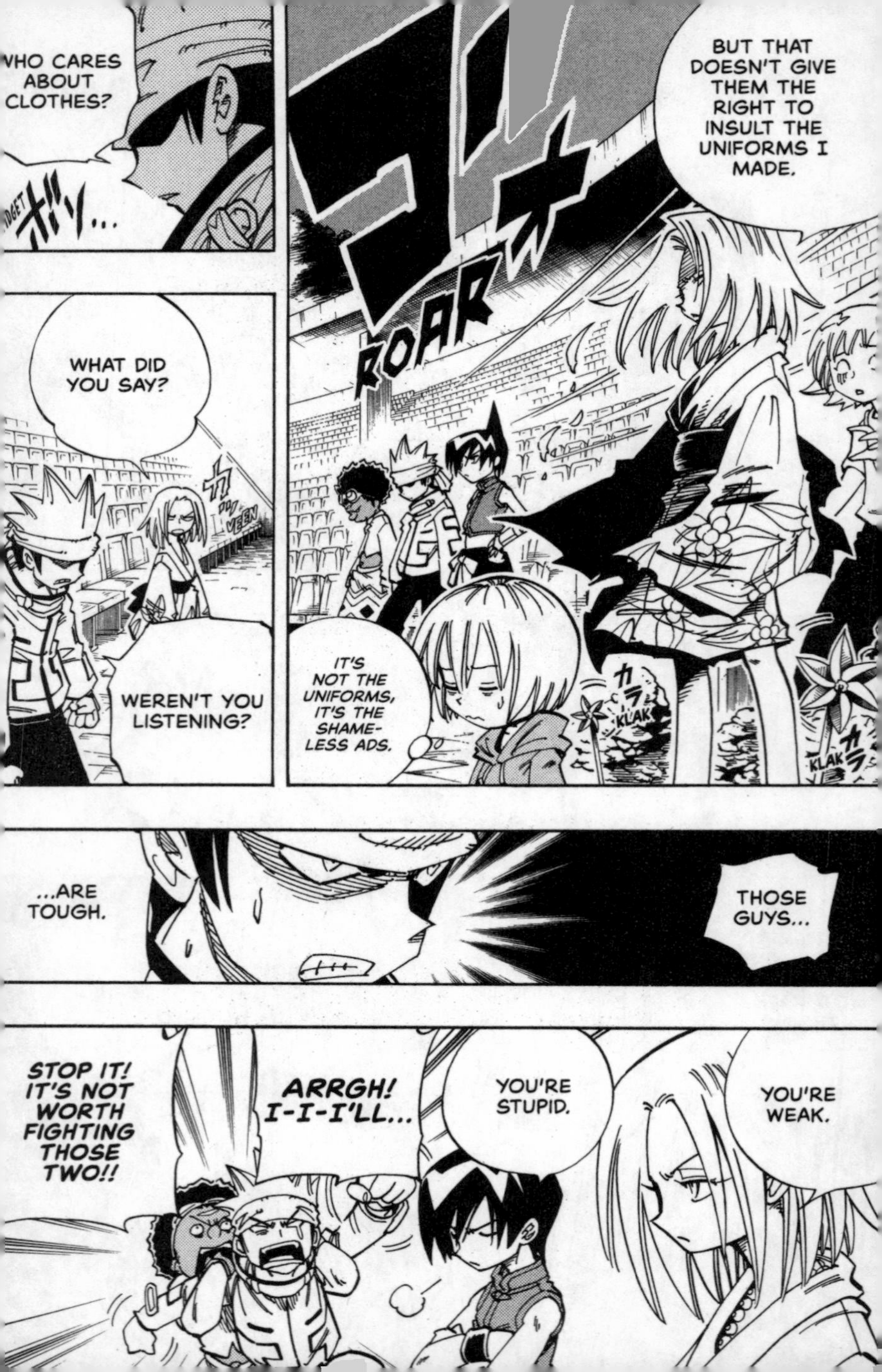
BUT THAT DOESN'T GIVE THEM THE RIGHT TO INSULT THE UNIFORMS I MADE.
ROAR
KLAK
KLAK
IT'S NOT THE UNIFORMS, IT'S THE SHAME-LESS ADS.
VHO CARES ABOUT CLOTHES?
...
WHAT DID YOU SAY?
VEEN
WEREN'T YOU LISTENING?
THOSE GUYS...
...ARE TOUGH.
YOU'RE WEAK.
YOU'RE STUPID.
ARRGH! I-I-I'LL...
STOP IT! IT'S NOT WORTH FIGHTING THOSE TWO!!

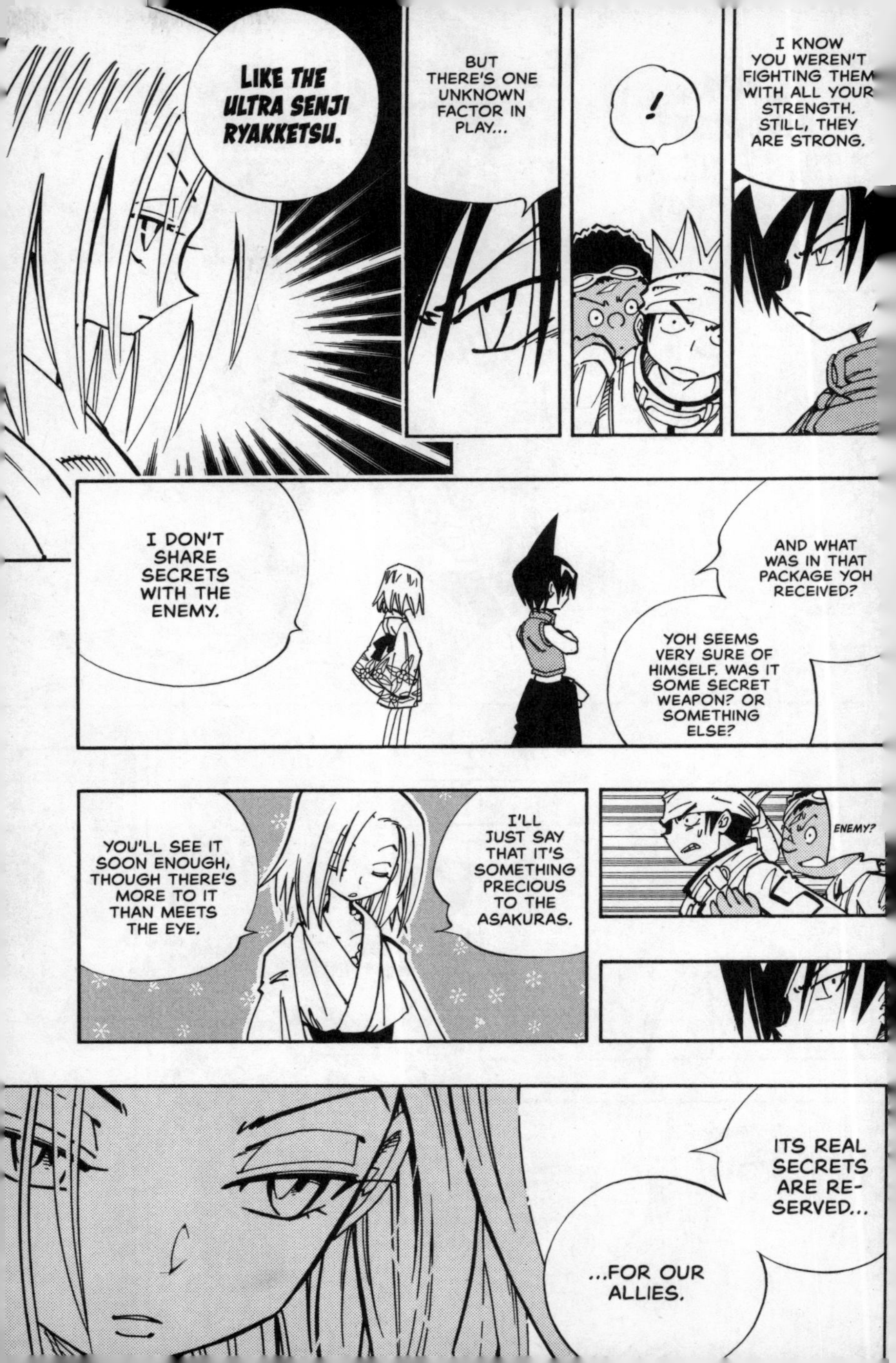
I KNOW YOU WEREN'T FIGHTING THEM WITH ALL YOUR STRENGTH. STILL, THEY ARE STRONG.
!
BUT THERE'S ONE UNKNOWN FACTOR IN PLAY...
LIKE THE ULTRA SENJI RYAKKETSU.
AND WHAT WAS IN THAT PACKAGE YOH RECEIVED?
YOH SEEMS VERY SURE OF HIMSELF. WAS IT SOME SECRET WEAPON? OR SOMETHING ELSE?
I DON'T SHARE SECRETS WITH THE ENEMY.
ENEMY?
I'LL JUST SAY THAT IT'S SOMETHING PRECIOUS TO THE ASAKURAS.
YOU'LL SEE IT SOON ENOUGH, THOUGH THERE'S MORE TO IT THAN MEETS THE EYE.
ITS REAL SECRETS ARE RE-SERVED...
...FOR OUR ALLIES.

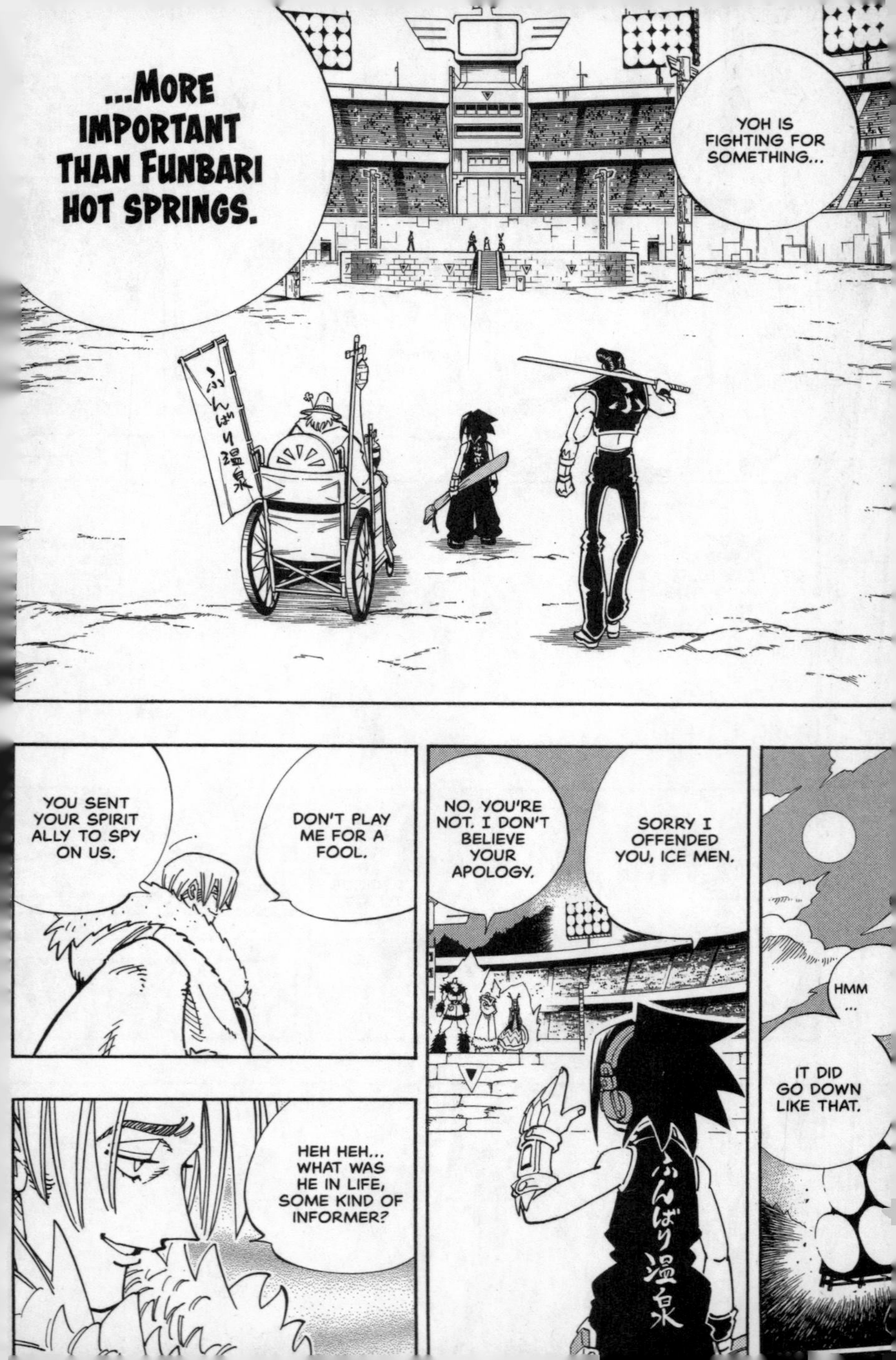
YOH IS FIGHTING FOR SOMETHING...
...MORE IMPORTANT THAN FUNBARI HOT SPRINGS.
ふんばり温泉
HMM...
IT DID GO DOWN LIKE THAT.
SORRY I OFFENDED YOU, ICE MEN.
NO, YOU'RE NOT. I DON'T BELIEVE YOUR APOLOGY.
DON'T PLAY ME FOR A FOOL.
YOU SENT YOUR SPIRIT ALLY TO SPY ON US.
HEH HEH... WHAT WAS HE IN LIFE, SOME KIND OF INFORMER?

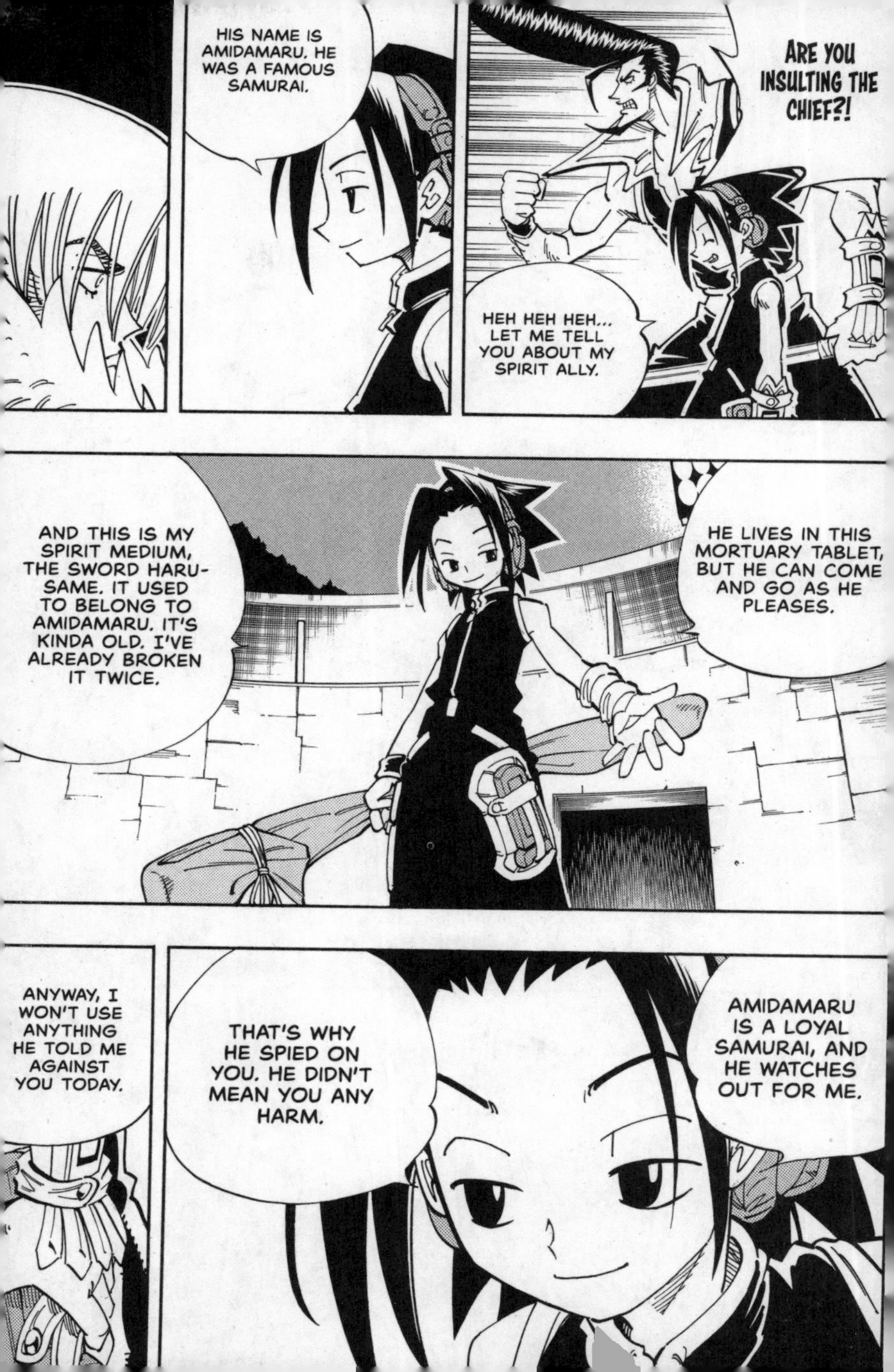
ARE YOU INSULTING THE CHIEF?!
HEH HEH HEH... LET ME TELL YOU ABOUT MY SPIRIT ALLY.
HIS NAME IS AMIDAMARU. HE WAS A FAMOUS SAMURAI.
HE LIVES IN THIS MORTUARY TABLET, BUT HE CAN COME AND GO AS HE PLEASES.
AND THIS IS MY SPIRIT MEDIUM, THE SWORD HARU-SAME. IT USED TO BELONG TO AMIDAMARU. IT'S KINDA OLD. I'VE ALREADY BROKEN IT TWICE.
AMIDAMARU IS A LOYAL SAMURAI, AND HE WATCHES OUT FOR ME.
THAT'S WHY HE SPIED ON YOU. HE DIDN'T MEAN YOU ANY HARM.
ANYWAY, I WON'T USE ANYTHING HE TOLD ME AGAINST YOU TODAY.

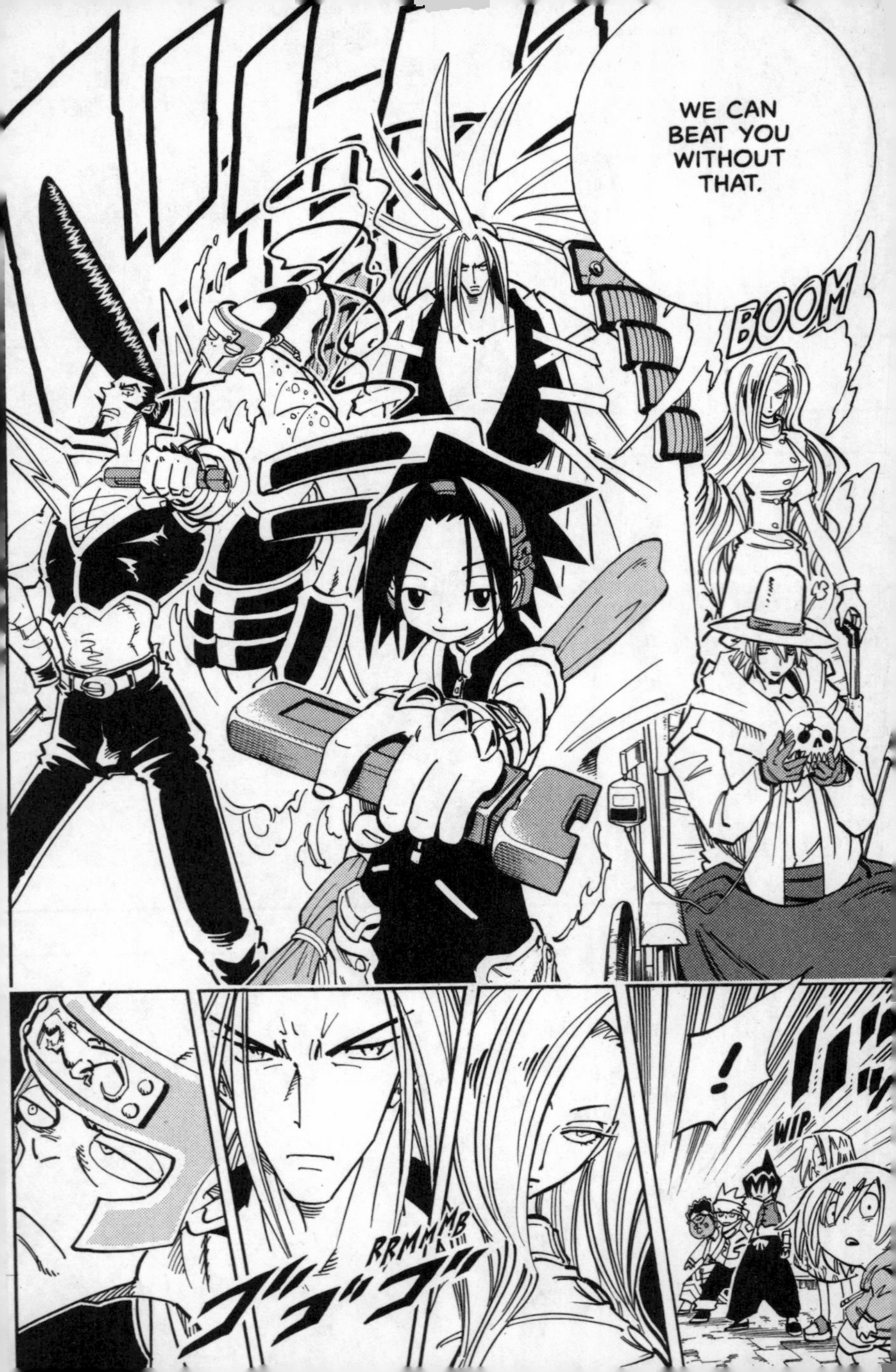
WE CAN BEAT YOU WITHOUT THAT.
BOOM
!
WIP
RRMMMB

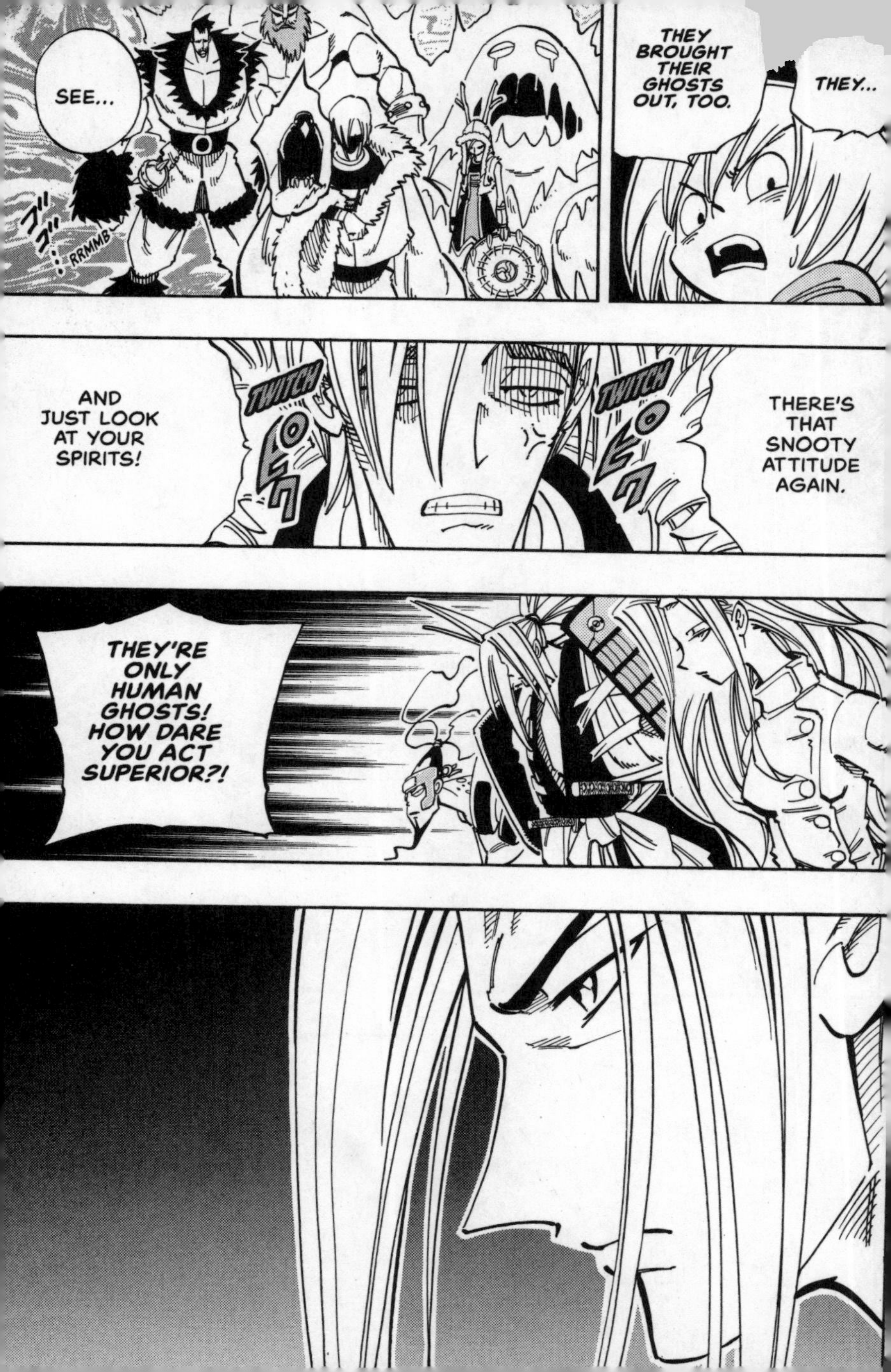

THEY...
THEY BROUGHT THEIR GHOSTS OUT, TOO.
SEE...
RRMMB
THERE'S THAT SNOOTY ATTITUDE AGAIN.
TWITCH
TWITCH
AND JUST LOOK AT YOUR SPIRITS!
THEY'RE ONLY HUMAN GHOSTS! HOW DARE YOU ACT SUPERIOR?!

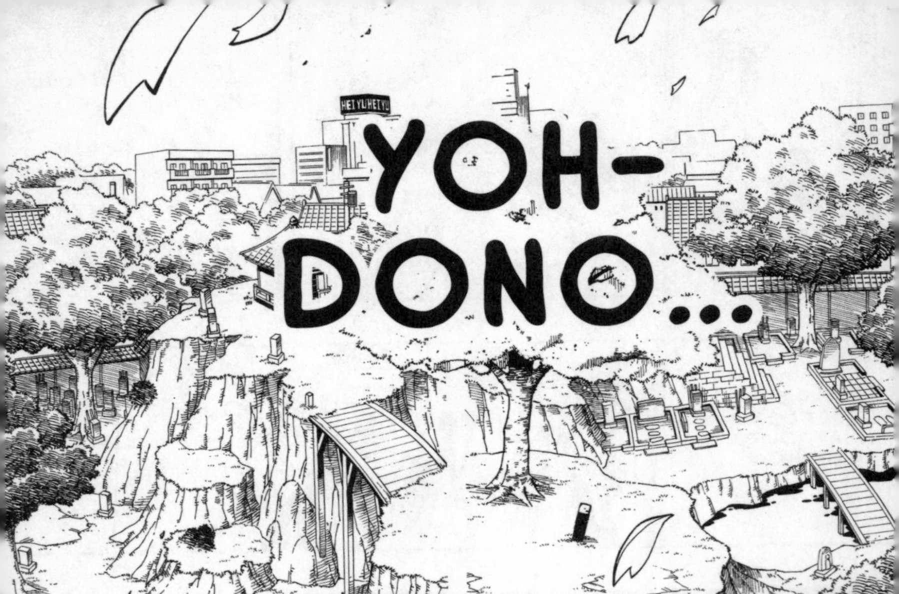
HEIYUHEIYU
YOH-DONO...

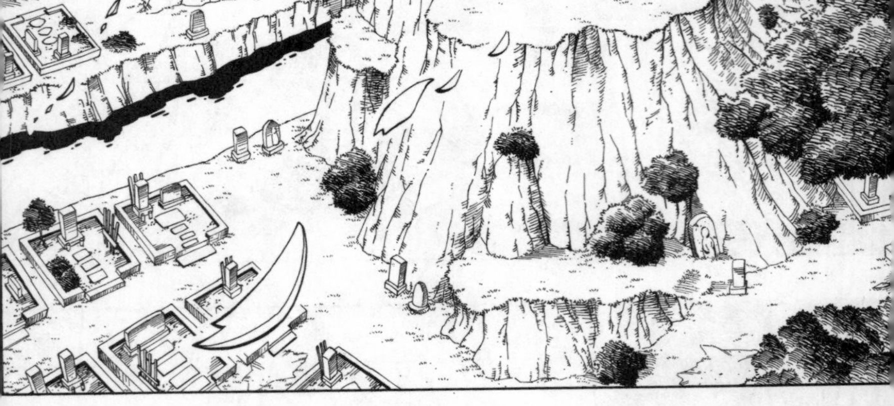
IT HAS BEEN THREE YEARS...
...SINCE YOU SAVED ME IN THAT CEMETERY...

Tombstone: Namu Amida Butsu

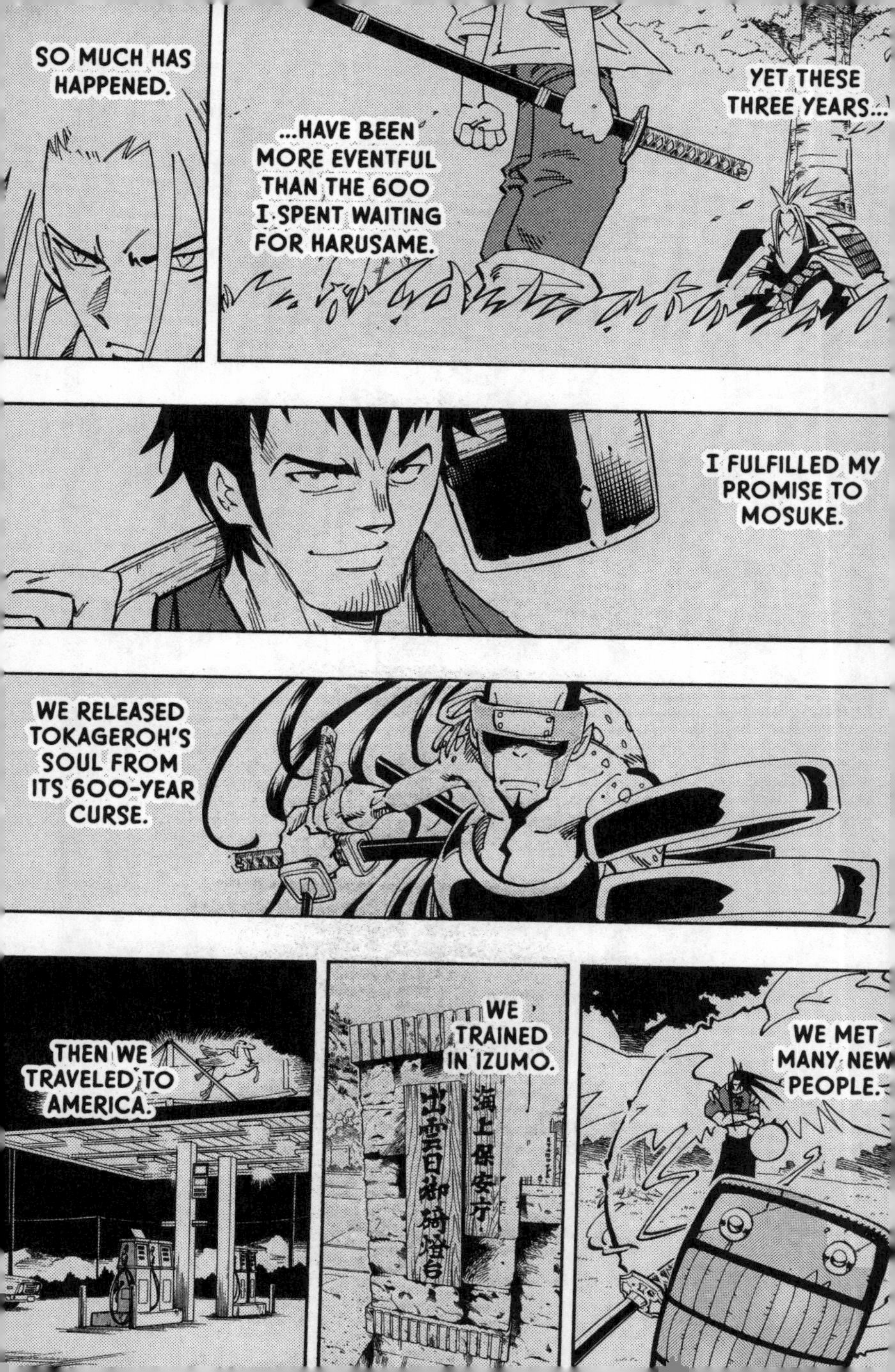
YET THESE THREE YEARS...
...HAVE BEEN MORE EVENTFUL THAN THE 600 I SPENT WAITING FOR HARUSAME.
SO MUCH HAS HAPPENED.
I FULFILLED MY PROMISE TO MOSUKE.
WE RELEASED TOKAGEROH'S SOUL FROM ITS 600-YEAR CURSE.
WE MET MANY NEW PEOPLE.
WE TRAINED IN IZUMO.
海上保安庁
出雲日御碕燈台
THEN WE TRAVELED TO AMERICA.

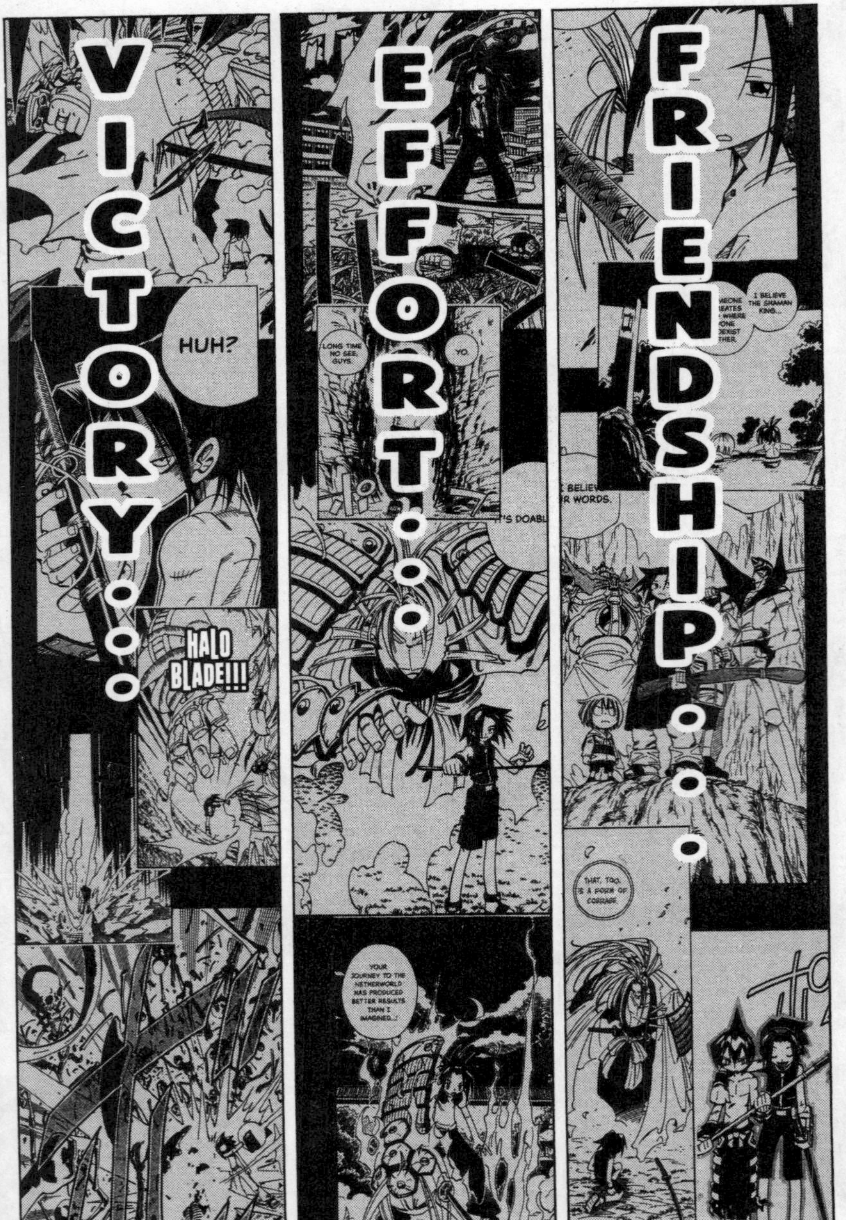
FRIENDSHIP...
I BELIEVE THE SHAMAN KING...
THAT, TOO, IS A FORM OF COURAGE.
EFFORT...
YO.
LONG TIME NO SEE, GUYS.
YOUR JOURNEY TO THE NETHERWORLD HAS PRODUCED BETTER RESULTS THAN I IMAGINED...!
VICTORY...
HUH?
HALO BLADE!!!

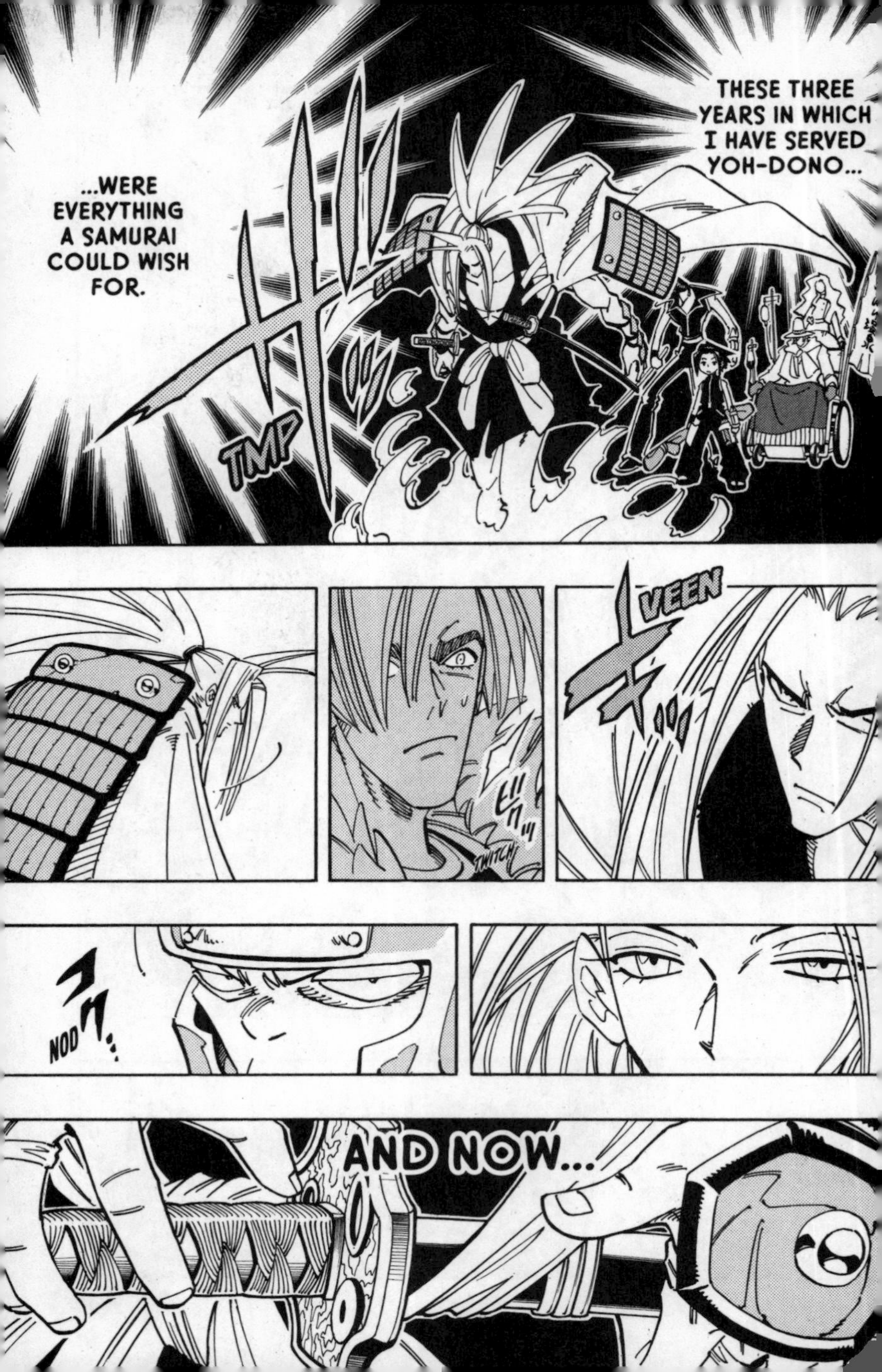
THESE THREE YEARS IN WHICH I HAVE SERVED YOH-DONO...
...WERE EVERYTHING A SAMURAI COULD WISH FOR.
TMP
VEEN
TWITCH
NOD
AND NOW...

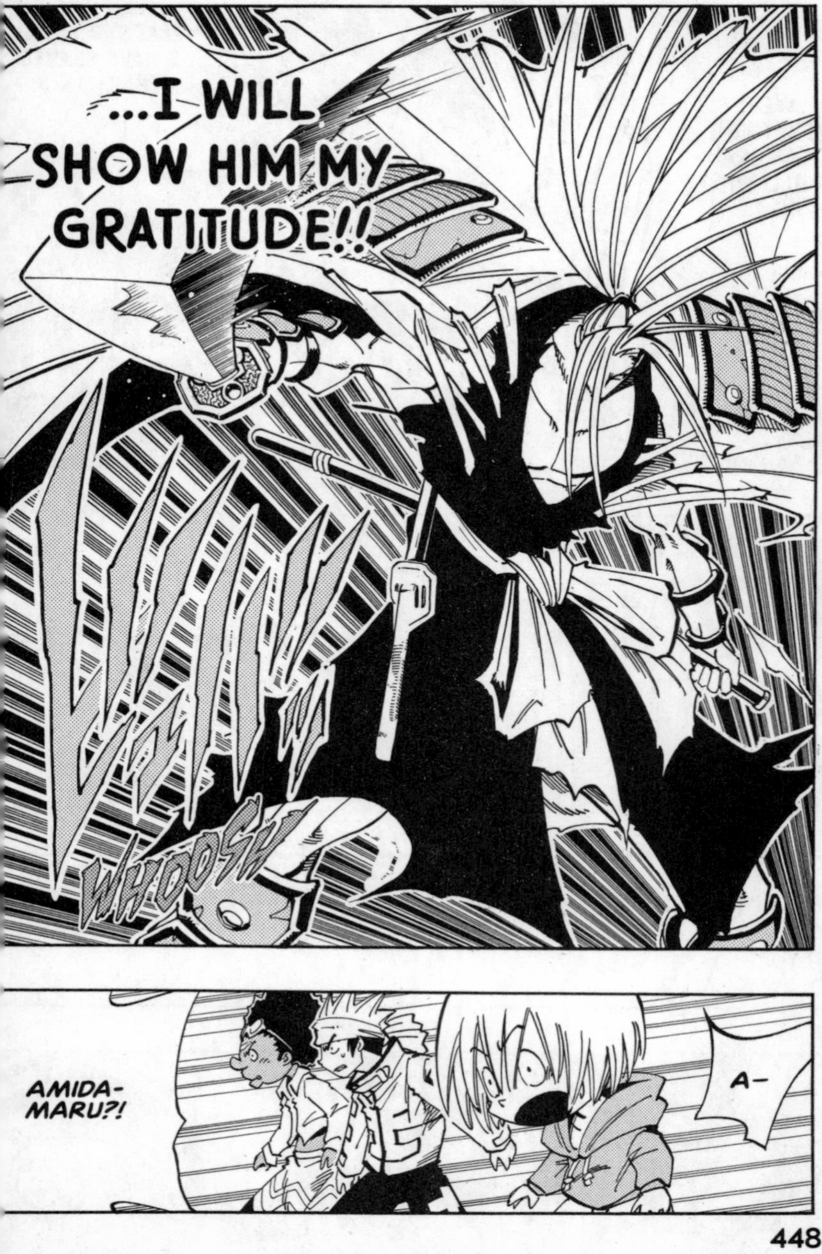
...I WILL SHOW HIM MY GRATITUDE!!
WHOOSH
A-
AMIDA-MARU?!

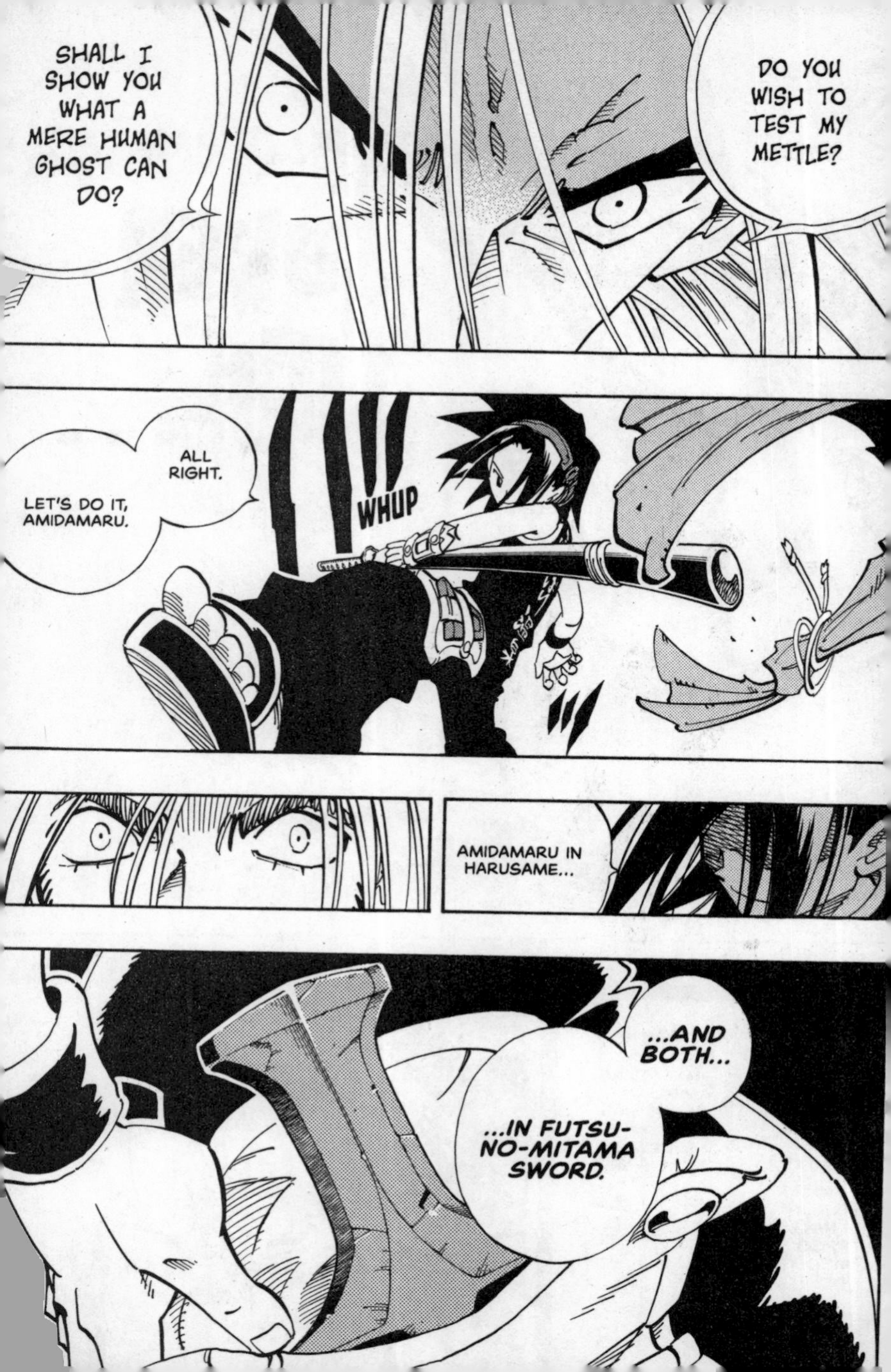
DO YOU WISH TO TEST MY METTLE?
SHALL I SHOW YOU WHAT A MERE HUMAN GHOST CAN DO?
WHUP
ALL RIGHT.
LET'S DO IT, AMIDAMARU.
AMIDAMARU IN HARUSAME...
...AND BOTH...
...IN FUTSU-NO-MITAMA SWORD.

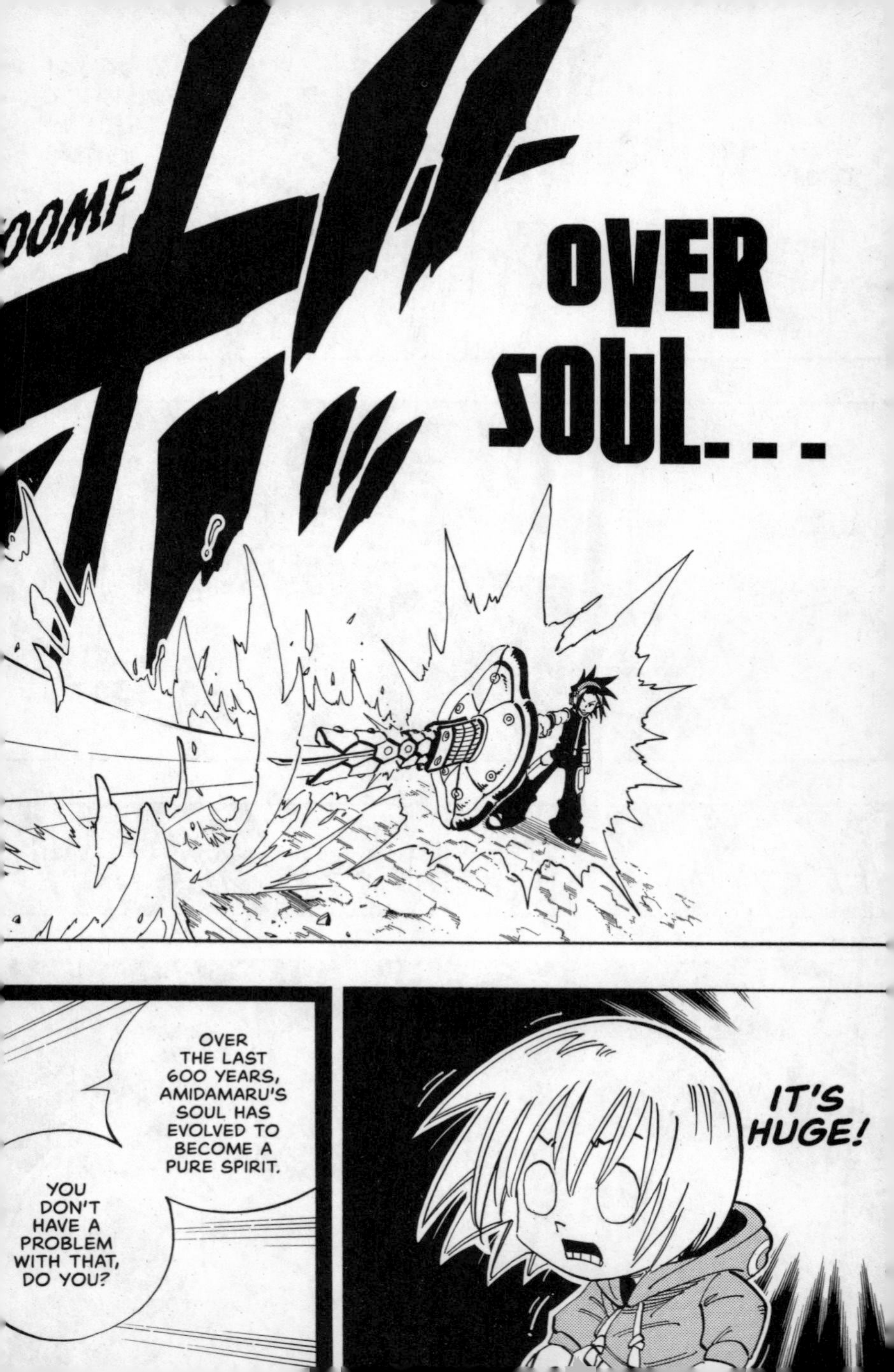

OVER SOUL...
OOMF
IT'S HUGE!
OVER THE LAST 600 YEARS, AMIDAMARU'S SOUL HAS EVOLVED TO BECOME A PURE SPIRIT.
YOU DON'T HAVE A PROBLEM WITH THAT, DO YOU?

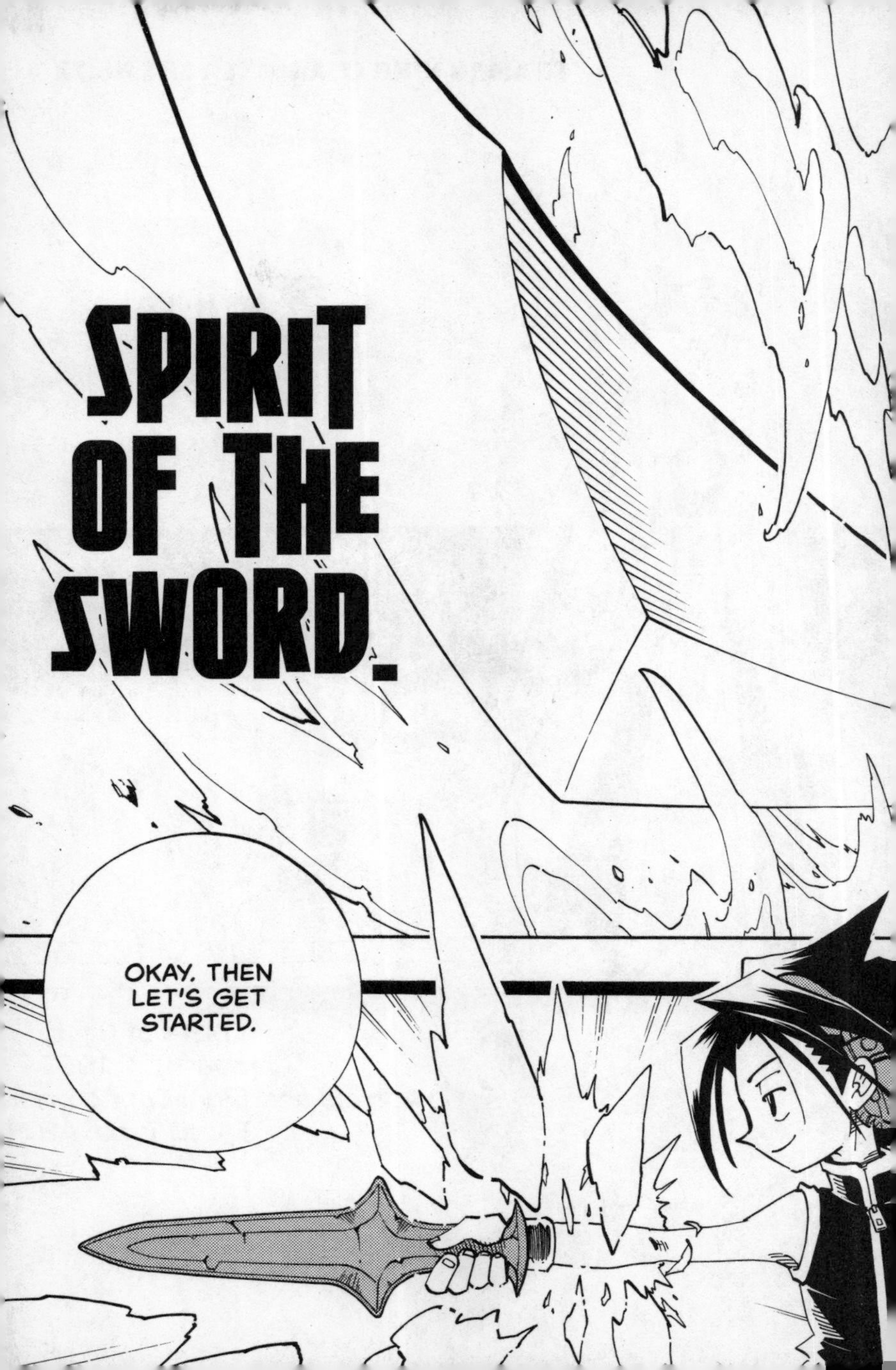
SPIRIT OF THE SWORD.
OKAY. THEN LET'S GET STARTED.

SHAMAN KING CHARACTER FILE No.72

Zria

July 2001

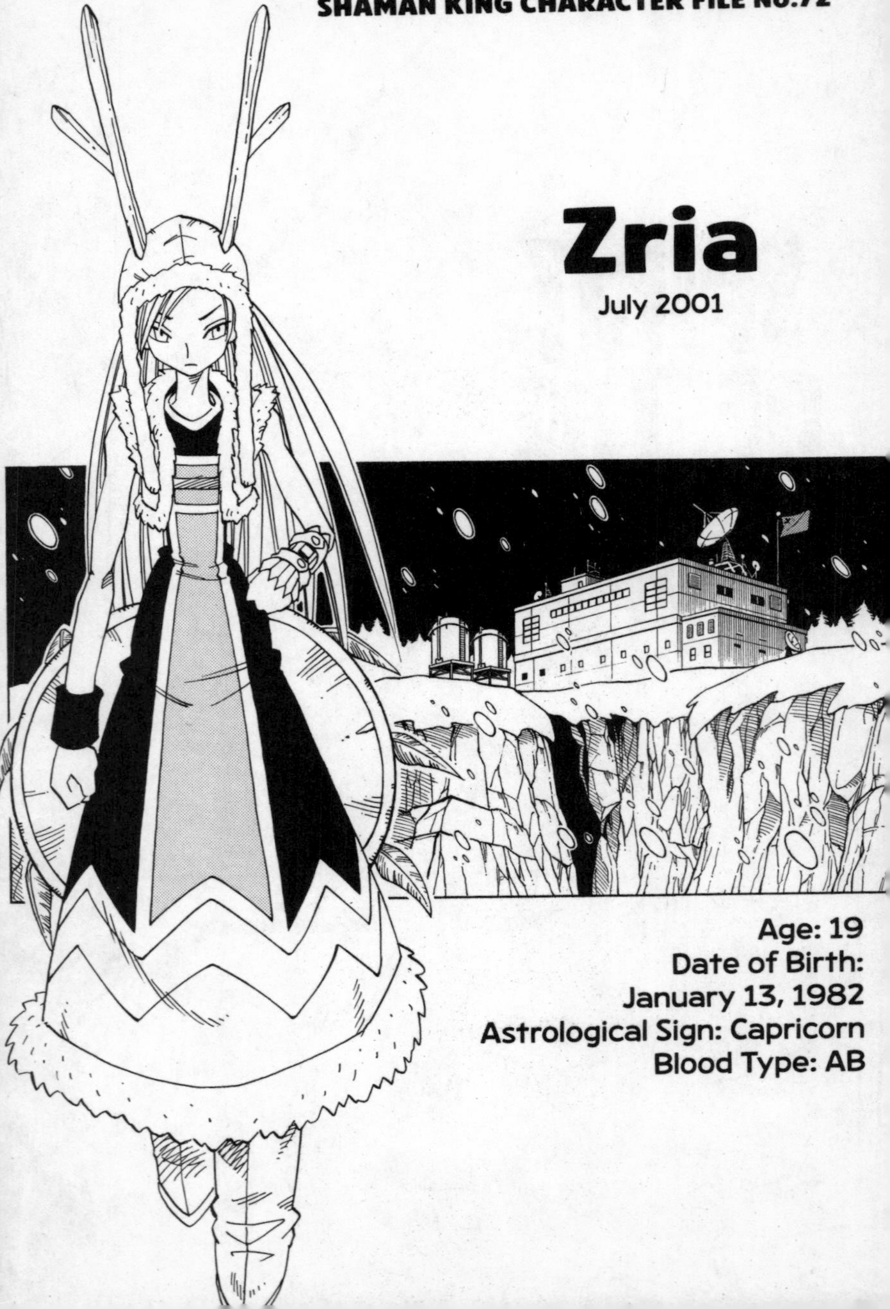

Age: 19
Date of Birth:
January 13, 1982
Astrological Sign: Capricorn
Blood Type: AB

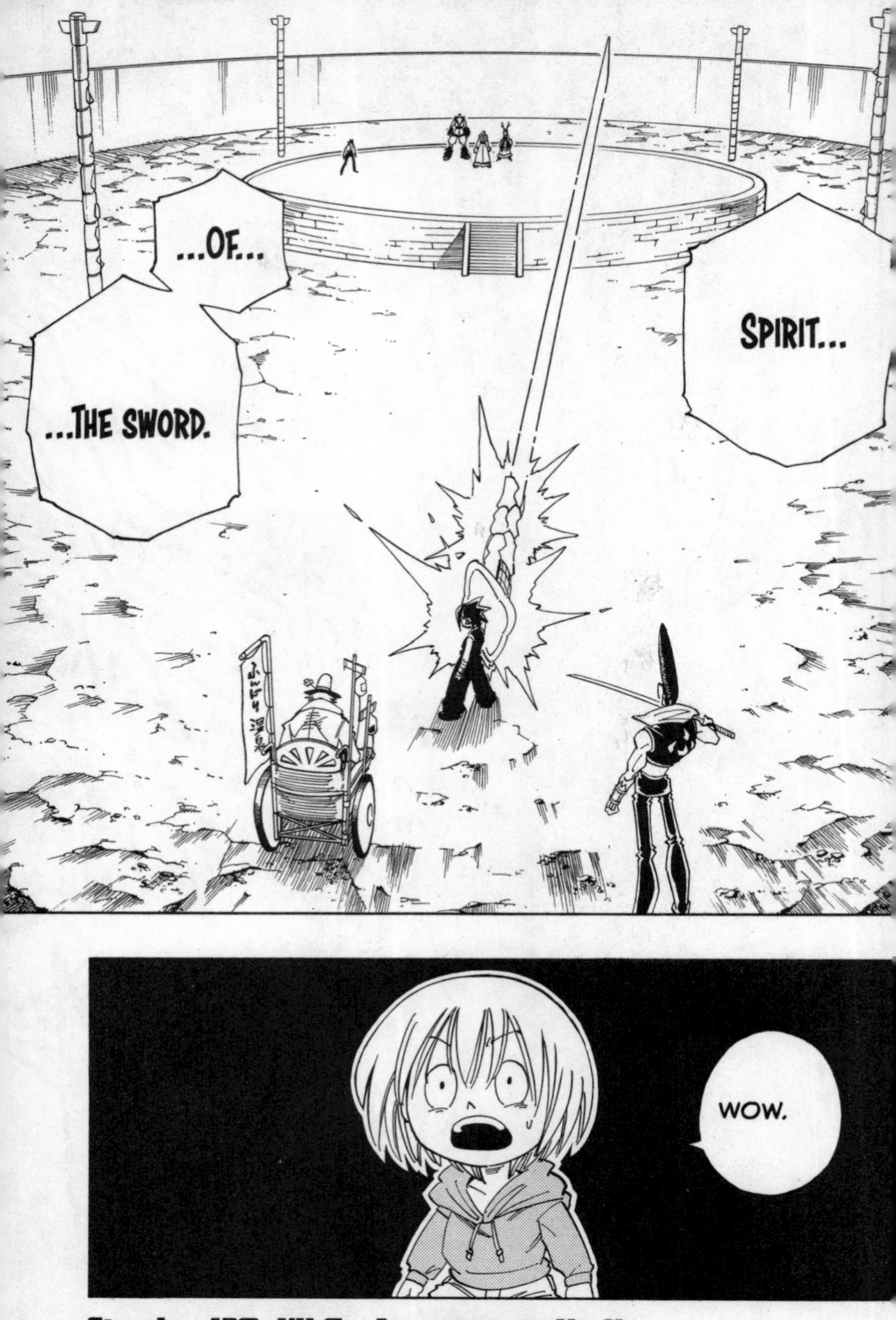
SPIRIT...
...OF...
...THE SWORD.
WOW.

Chapter 129: I'll Go Anywhere with You

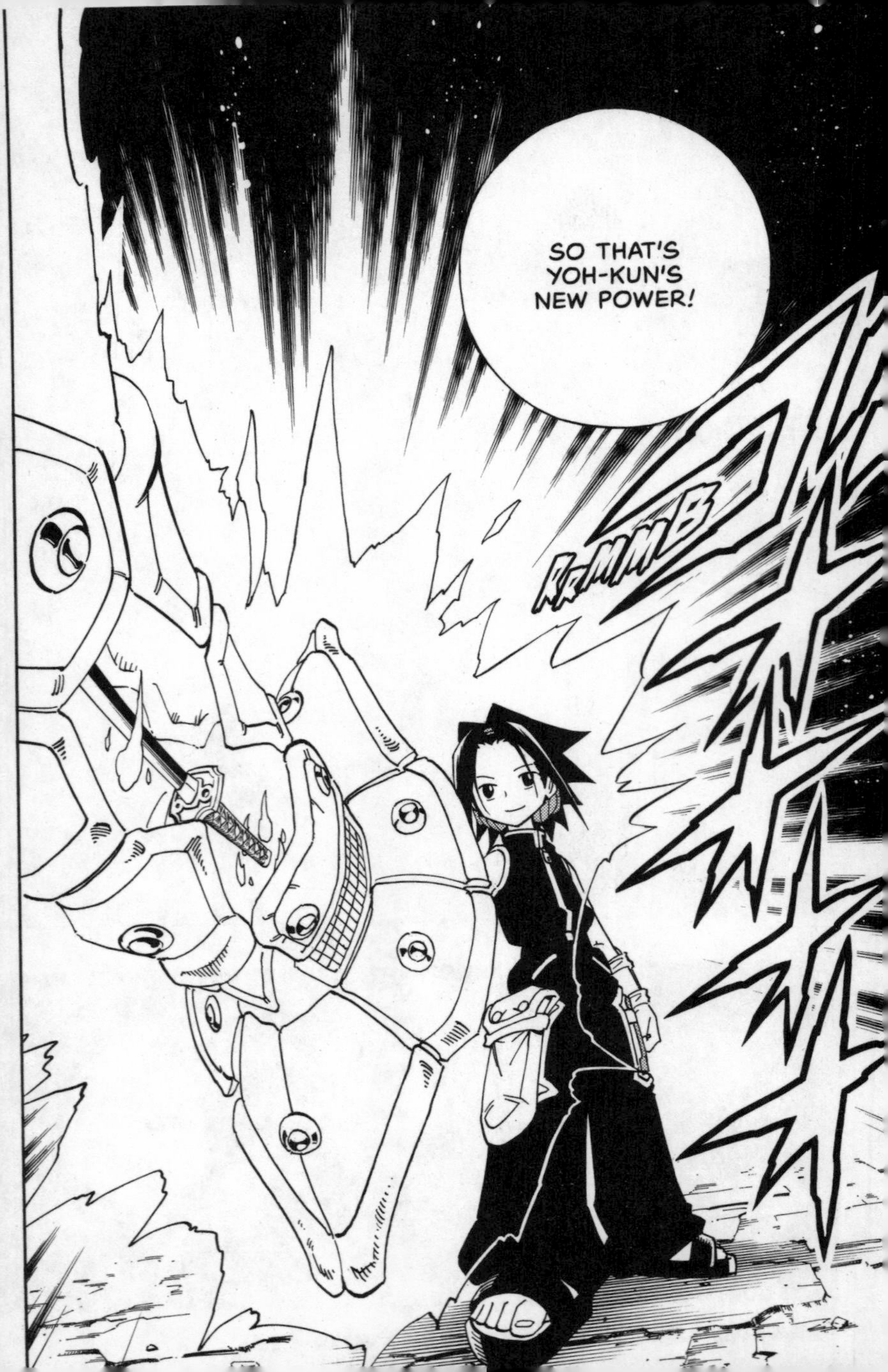
SO THAT'S YOH-KUN'S NEW POWER!

Chapter 129:

I'll Go Anywhere with You

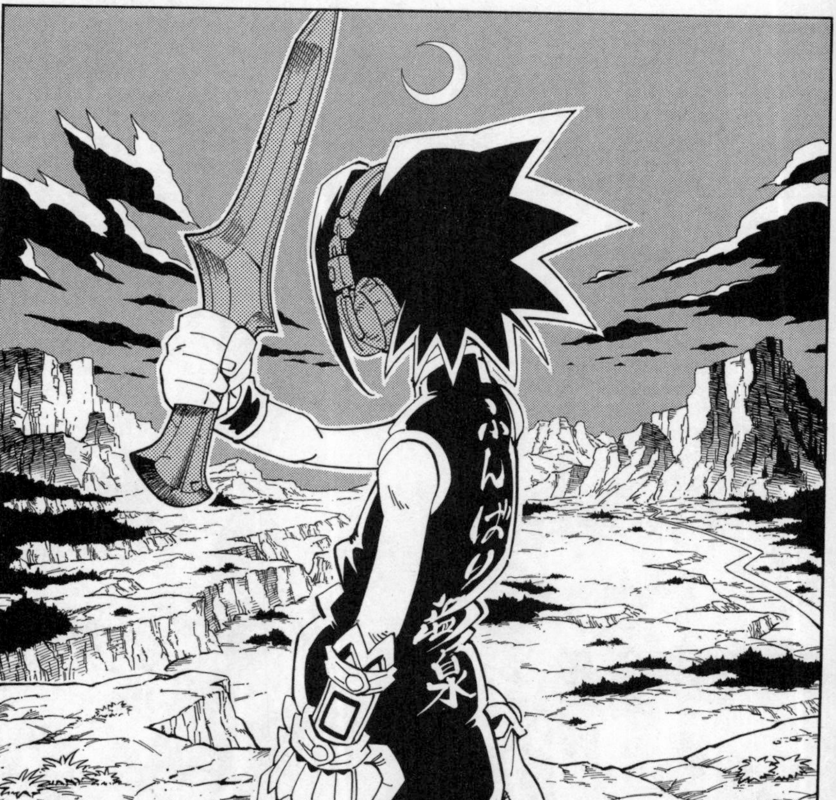
ふんばり温泉

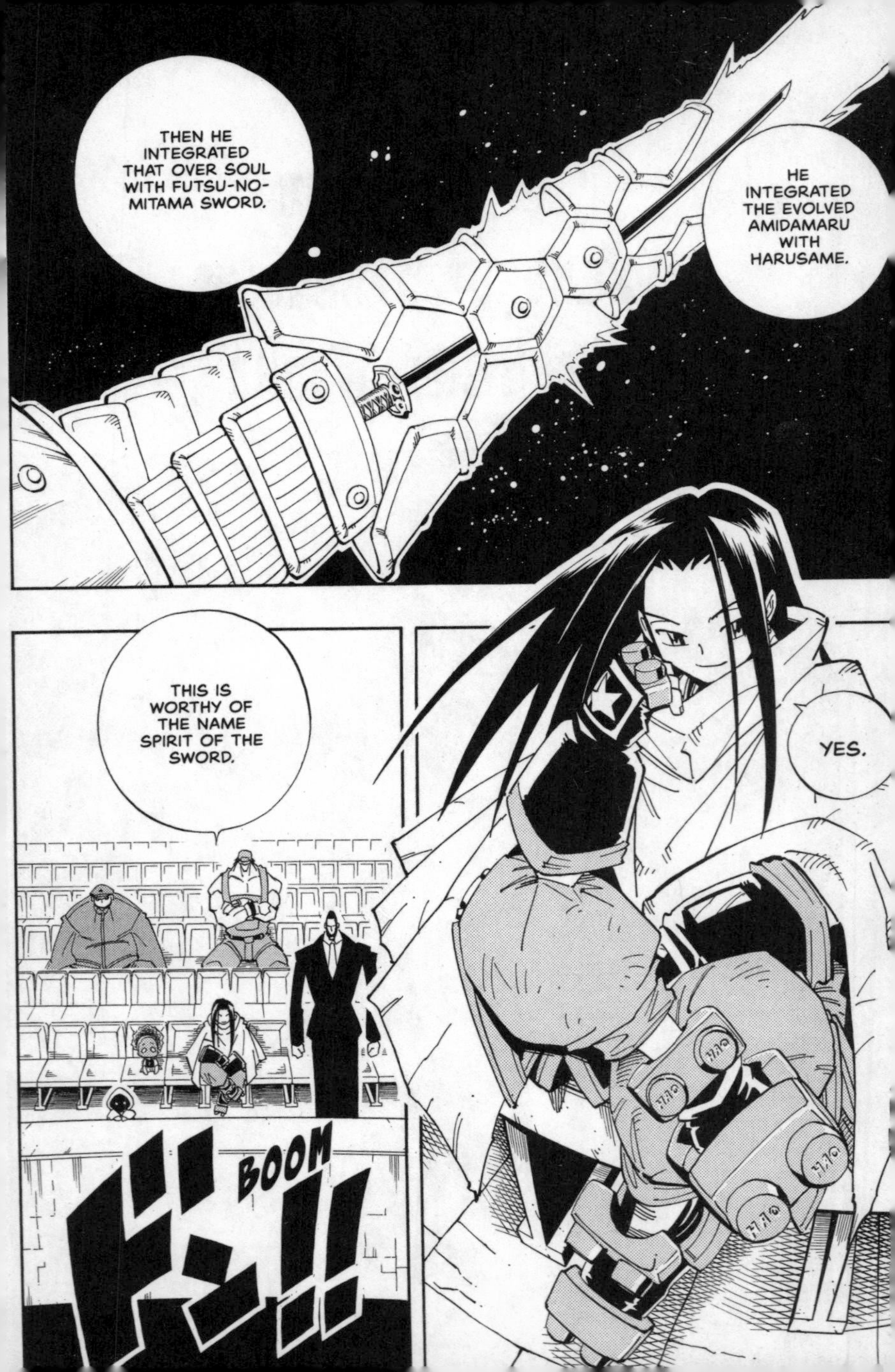
HE INTEGRATED THE EVOLVED AMIDAMARU WITH HARUSAME.
THEN HE INTEGRATED THAT OVER SOUL WITH FUTSU-NO-MITAMA SWORD.
YES.
THIS IS WORTHY OF THE NAME SPIRIT OF THE SWORD.
BOOM

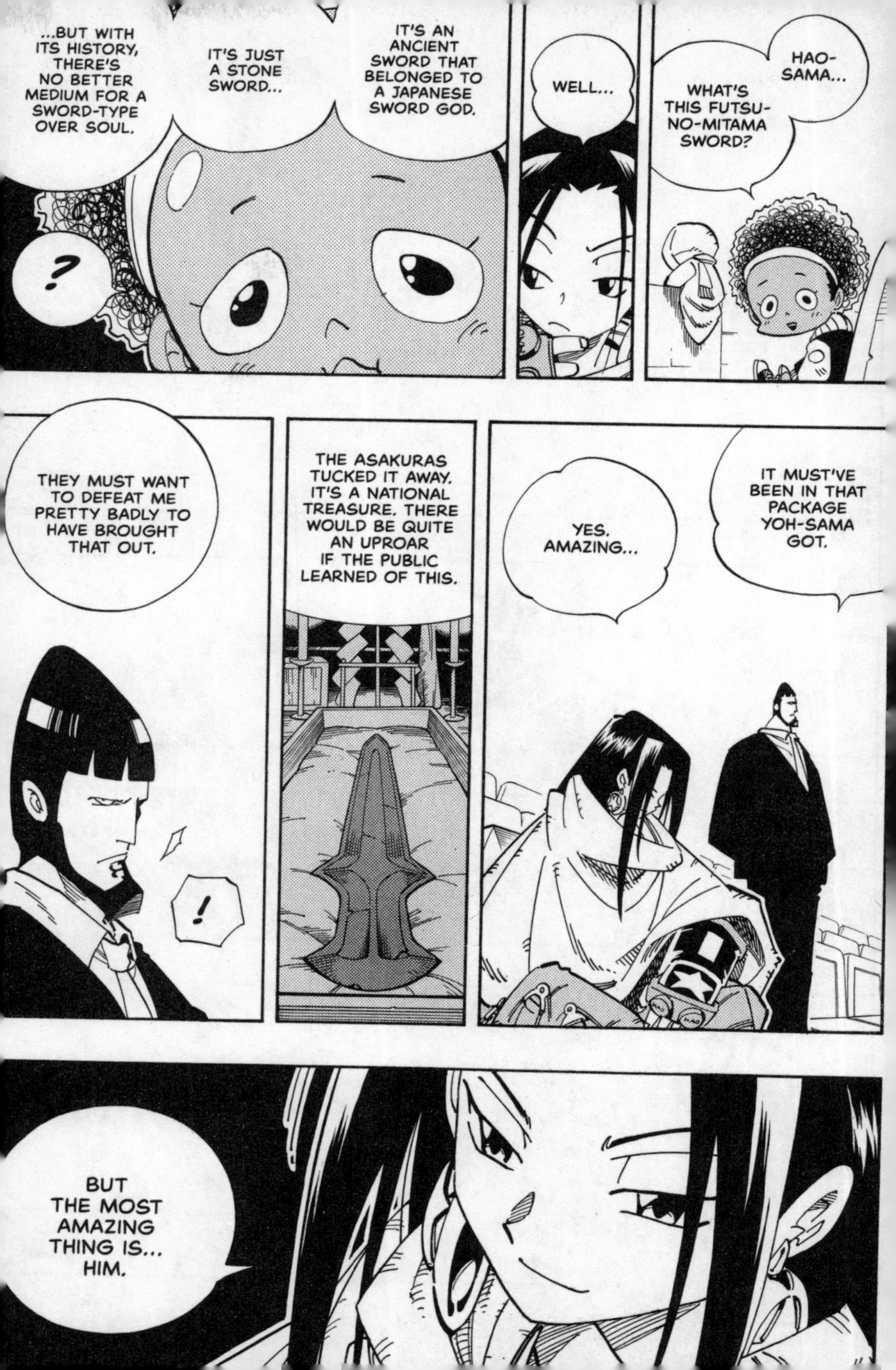
HAO-SAMA...
WHAT'S THIS FUTSU-NO-MITAMA SWORD?
WELL...
IT'S AN ANCIENT SWORD THAT BELONGED TO A JAPANESE SWORD GOD.
IT'S JUST A STONE SWORD...
...BUT WITH ITS HISTORY, THERE'S NO BETTER MEDIUM FOR A SWORD-TYPE OVER SOUL.
?
IT MUST'VE BEEN IN THAT PACKAGE YOH-SAMA GOT.
YES. AMAZING...
THE ASAKURAS TUCKED IT AWAY. IT'S A NATIONAL TREASURE. THERE WOULD BE QUITE AN UPROAR IF THE PUBLIC LEARNED OF THIS.
THEY MUST WANT TO DEFEAT ME PRETTY BADLY TO HAVE BROUGHT THAT OUT.
!
BUT THE MOST AMAZING THING IS... HIM.

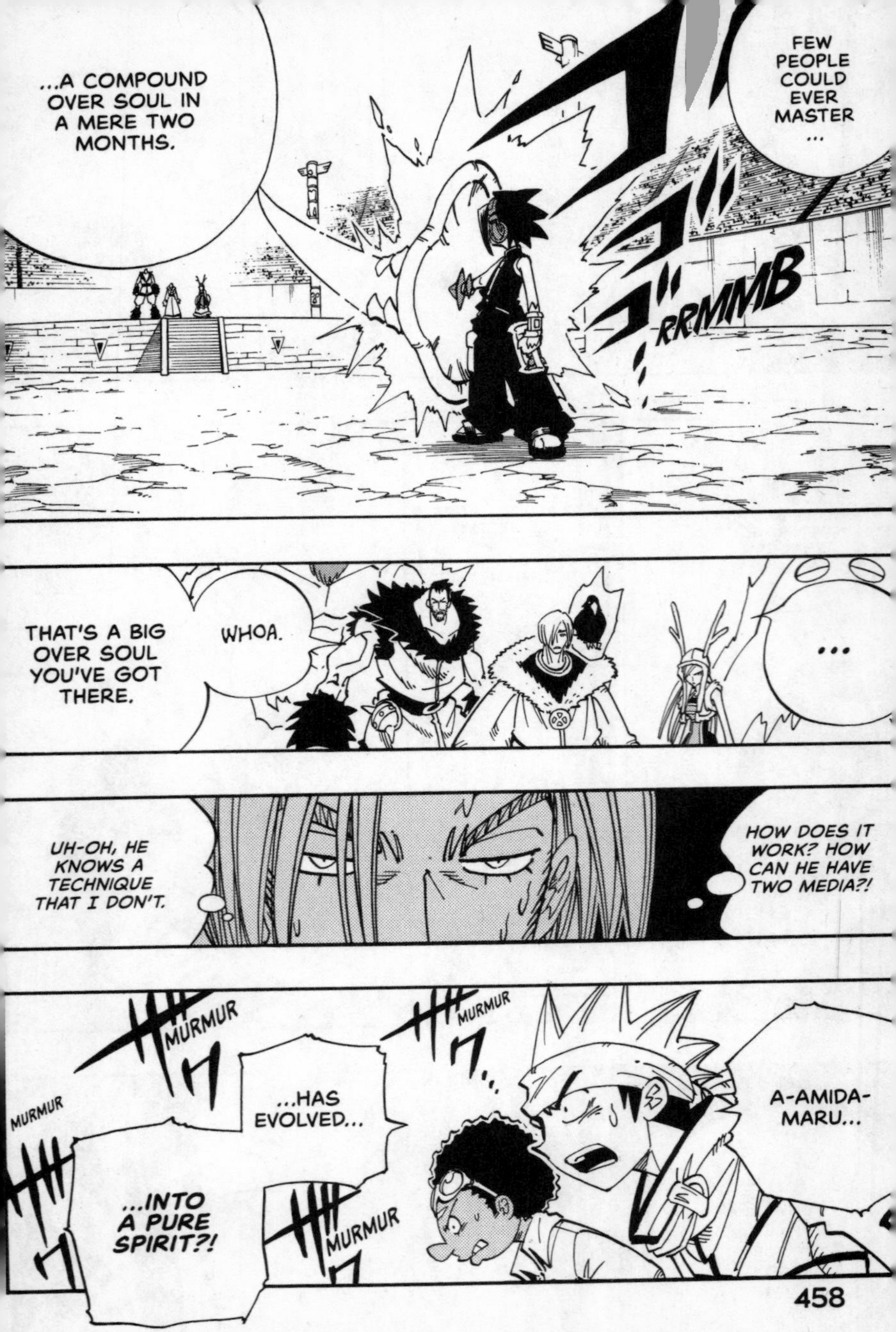
FEW PEOPLE COULD EVER MASTER ...
...A COMPOUND OVER SOUL IN A MERE TWO MONTHS.
RRMMB
...
WHOA.
THAT'S A BIG OVER SOUL YOU'VE GOT THERE.
HOW DOES IT WORK? HOW CAN HE HAVE TWO MEDIA?!
UH-OH, HE KNOWS A TECHNIQUE THAT I DON'T.
MURMUR
MURMUR
A-AMIDA-MARU...
...HAS EVOLVED...
MURMUR
...INTO A PURE SPIRIT?!
MURMUR

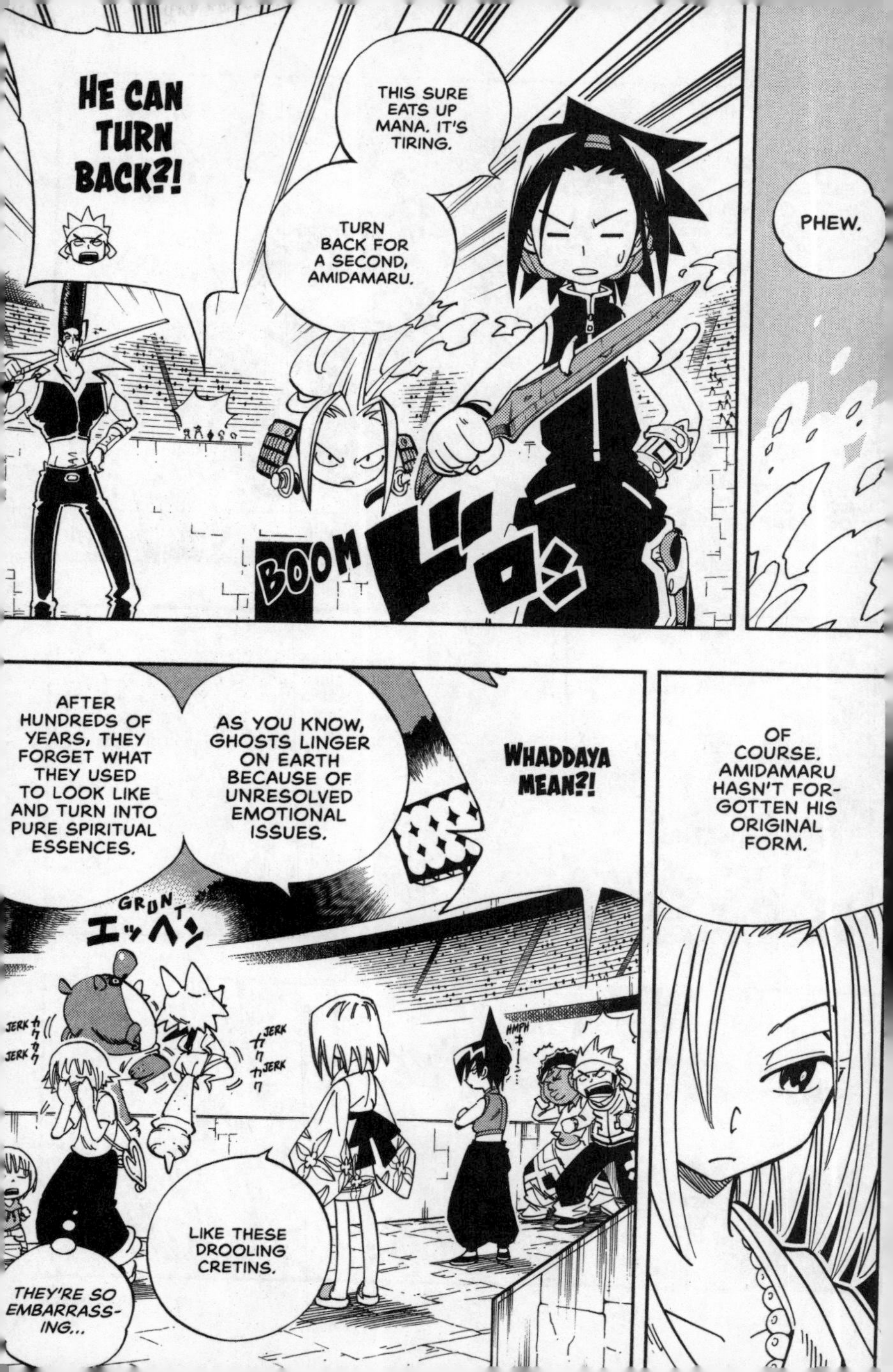
PHEW.
THIS SURE EATS UP MANA. IT'S TIRING.
TURN BACK FOR A SECOND, AMIDAMARU.
HE CAN TURN BACK?!
BOOM
OF COURSE. AMIDAMARU HASN'T FOR-GOTTEN HIS ORIGINAL FORM.
WHADDAYA MEAN?!
AS YOU KNOW, GHOSTS LINGER ON EARTH BECAUSE OF UNRESOLVED EMOTIONAL ISSUES.
AFTER HUNDREDS OF YEARS, THEY FORGET WHAT THEY USED TO LOOK LIKE AND TURN INTO PURE SPIRITUAL ESSENCES.
GRUNT
エッヘン
HMPH
JERK JERK
JERK JERK
LIKE THESE DROOLING CRETINS.
THEY'RE SO EMBARRASS-ING...

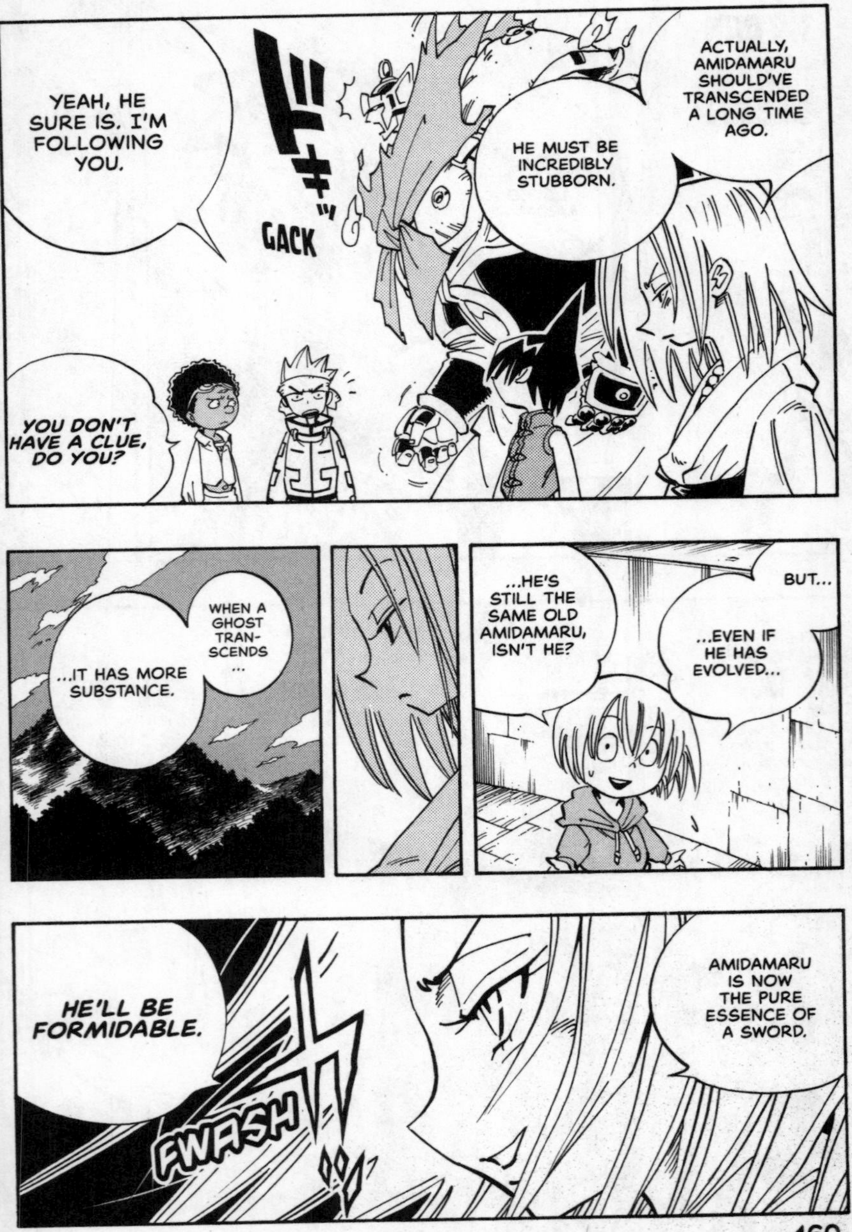
ACTUALLY, AMIDAMARU SHOULD'VE TRANSCENDED A LONG TIME AGO.
HE MUST BE INCREDIBLY STUBBORN.
GACK
YEAH, HE SURE IS. I'M FOLLOWING YOU.
YOU DON'T HAVE A CLUE, DO YOU?
BUT...
...EVEN IF HE HAS EVOLVED...
...HE'S STILL THE SAME OLD AMIDAMARU, ISN'T HE?
WHEN A GHOST TRAN-SCENDS...
...IT HAS MORE SUBSTANCE.
AMIDAMARU IS NOW THE PURE ESSENCE OF A SWORD.
FWASH
HE'LL BE FORMIDABLE.

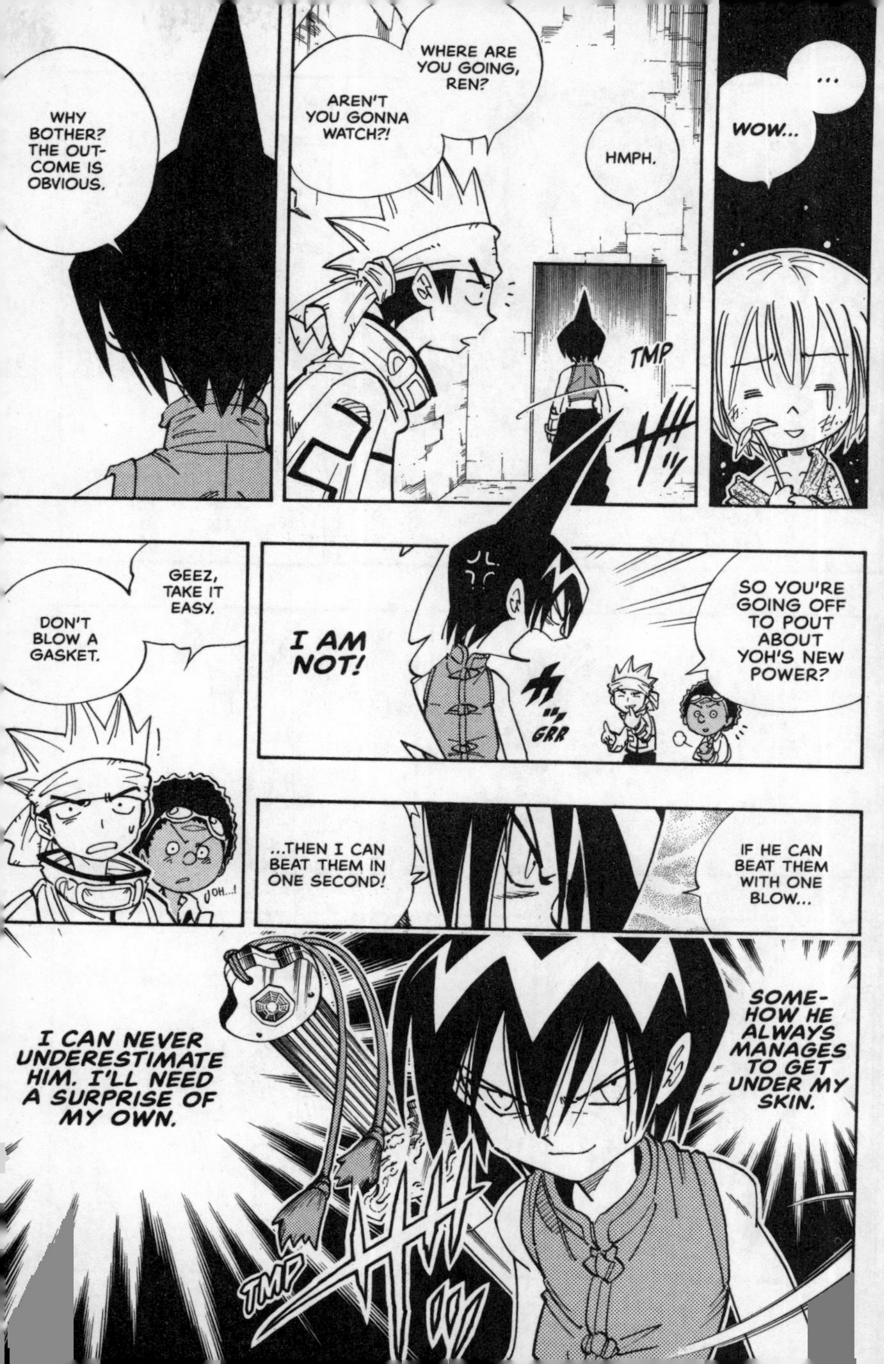
...
WOW...
WHERE ARE YOU GOING, REN?
AREN'T YOU GONNA WATCH?!
HMPH.
TMP
WHY BOTHER? THE OUT-COME IS OBVIOUS.
SO YOU'RE GOING OFF TO POUT ABOUT YOH'S NEW POWER?
I AM NOT!
GRR
GEEZ, TAKE IT EASY.
DON'T BLOW A GASKET.
OH...!
IF HE CAN BEAT THEM WITH ONE BLOW...
...THEN I CAN BEAT THEM IN ONE SECOND!
SOME-HOW HE ALWAYS MANAGES TO GET UNDER MY SKIN.
I CAN NEVER UNDERESTIMATE HIM. I'LL NEED A SURPRISE OF MY OWN.
TMP

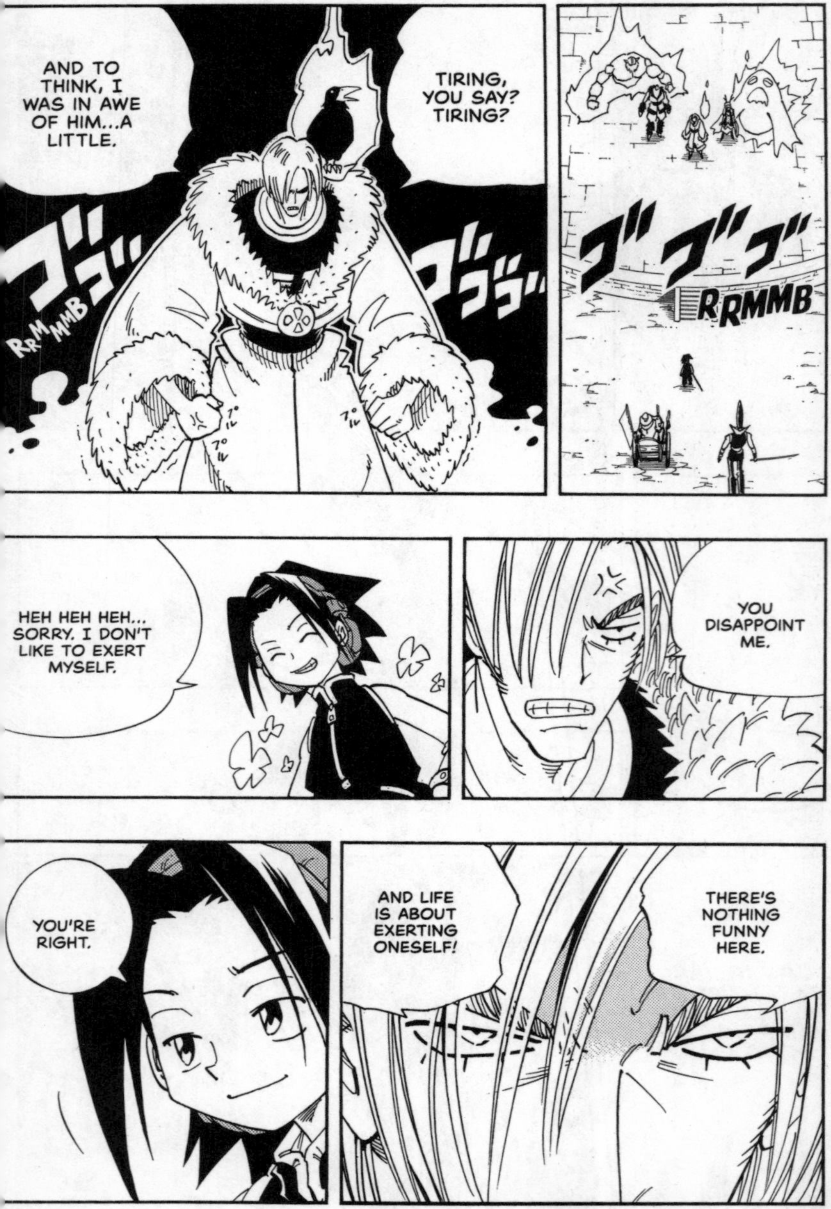
RRMMB
TIRING, YOU SAY? TIRING?
AND TO THINK, I WAS IN AWE OF HIM...A LITTLE.
RRMMMB
YOU DISAPPOINT ME.
HEH HEH HEH... SORRY. I DON'T LIKE TO EXERT MYSELF.
THERE'S NOTHING FUNNY HERE.
AND LIFE IS ABOUT EXERTING ONESELF!
YOU'RE RIGHT.

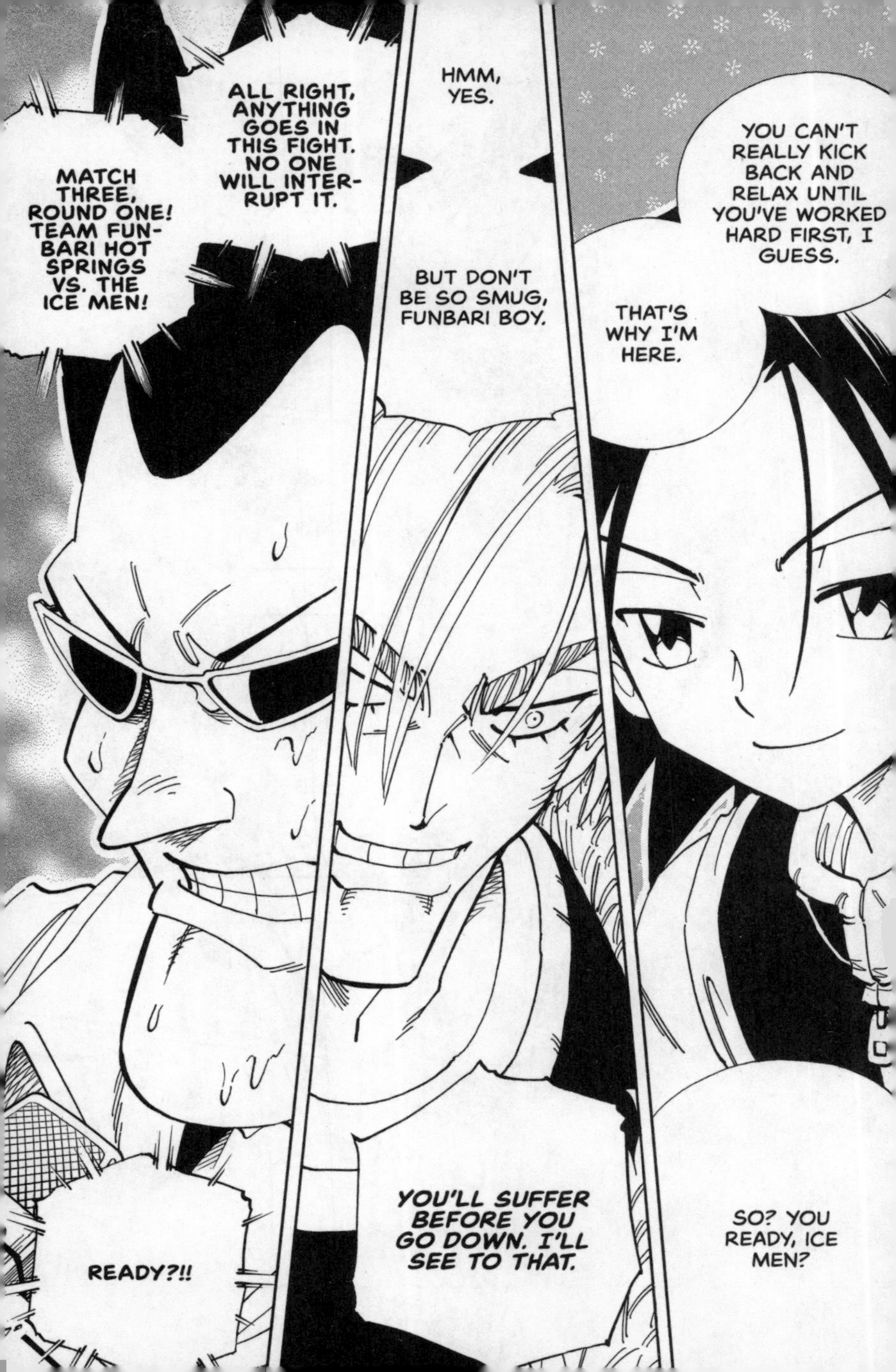
YOU CAN'T REALLY KICK BACK AND RELAX UNTIL YOU'VE WORKED HARD FIRST, I GUESS.
THAT'S WHY I'M HERE.
SO? YOU READY, ICE MEN?
HMM, YES.
BUT DON'T BE SO SMUG, FUNBARI BOY.
YOU'LL SUFFER BEFORE YOU GO DOWN. I'LL SEE TO THAT.
ALL RIGHT, ANYTHING GOES IN THIS FIGHT. NO ONE WILL INTER-RUPT IT.
MATCH THREE, ROUND ONE! TEAM FUN-BARI HOT SPRINGS VS. THE ICE MEN!
READY?!!

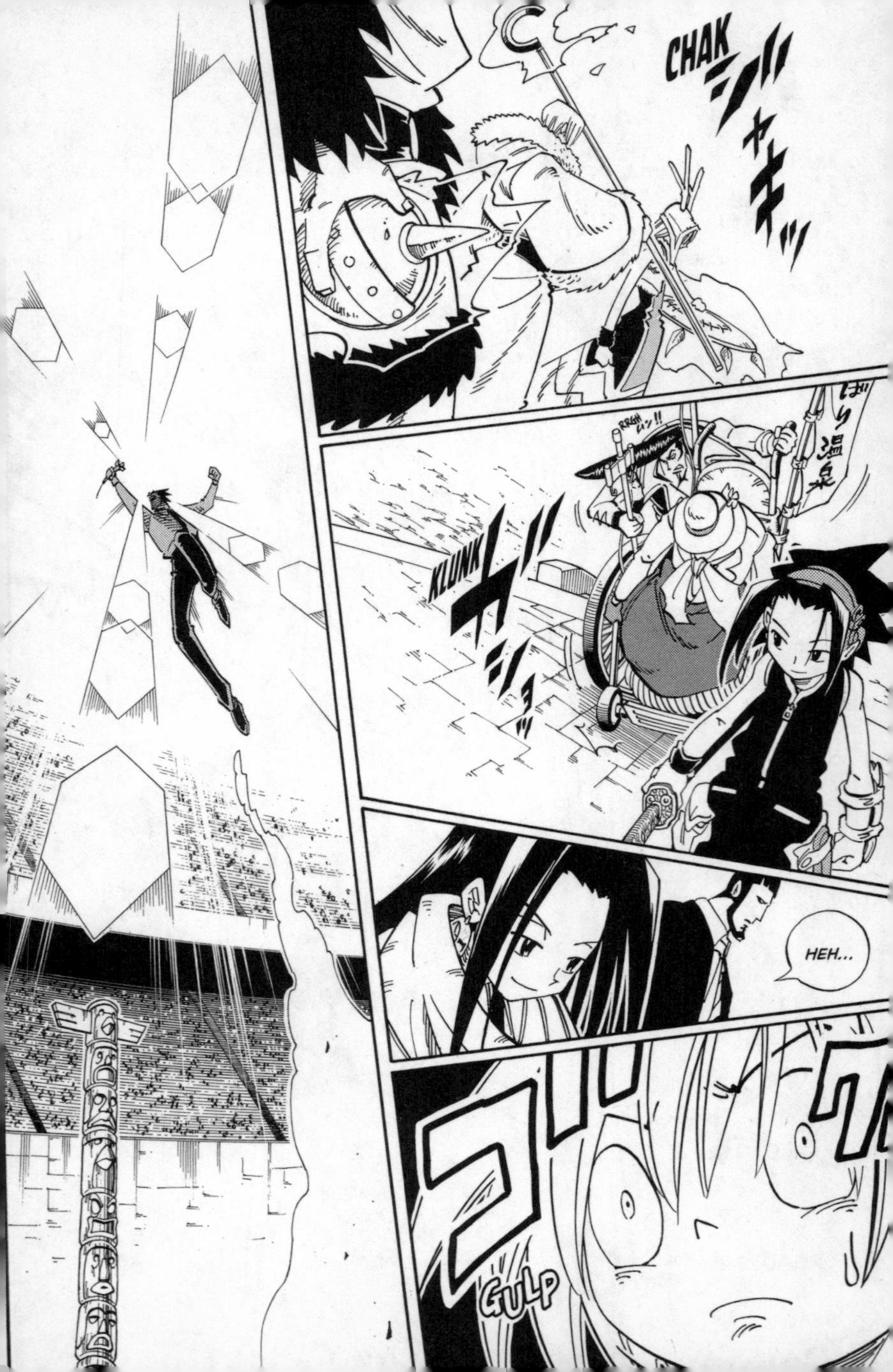

CHAK
シャキッ
RRGH
KLUNK
HEH...
GULP

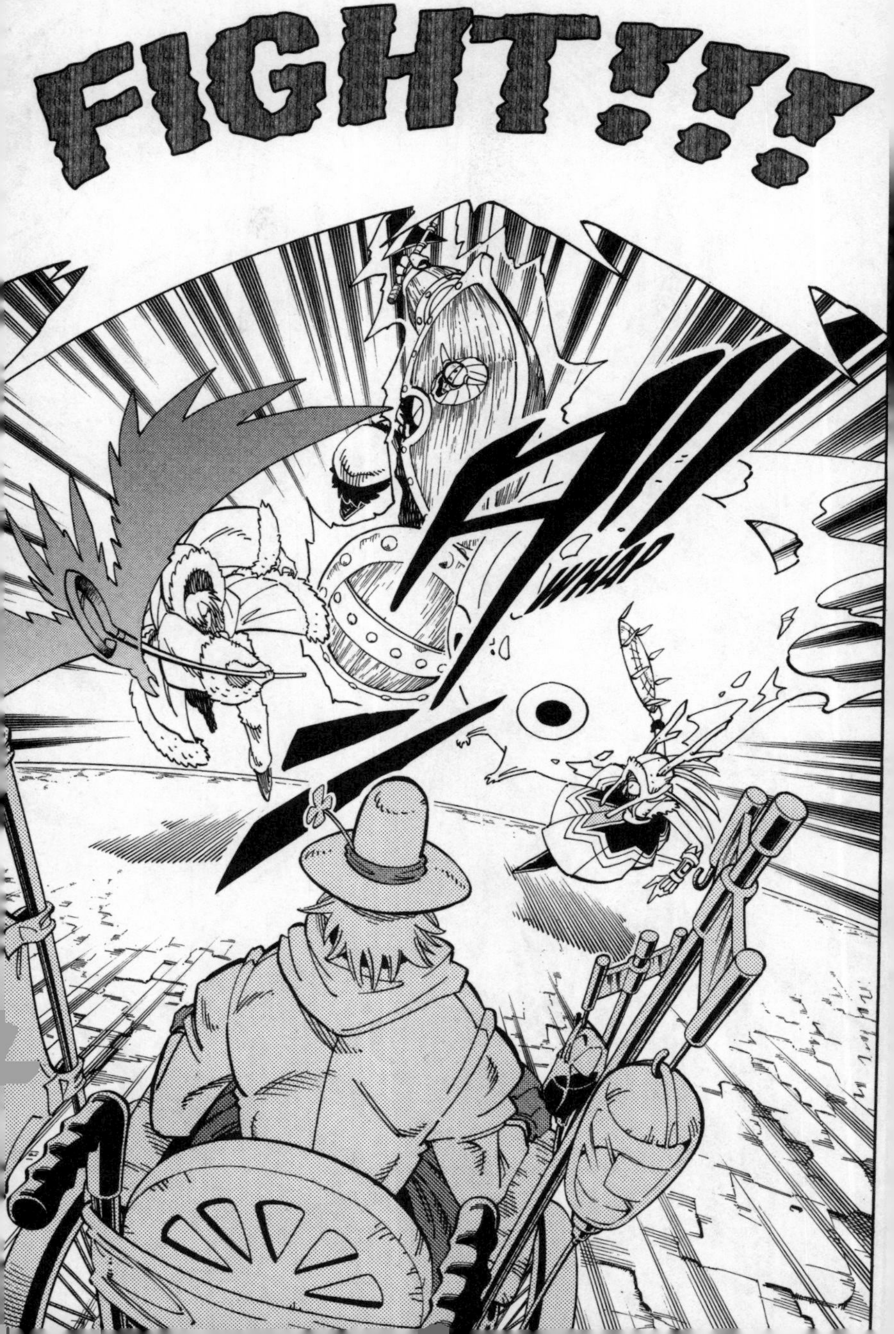
FIGHT!!!
WHAP

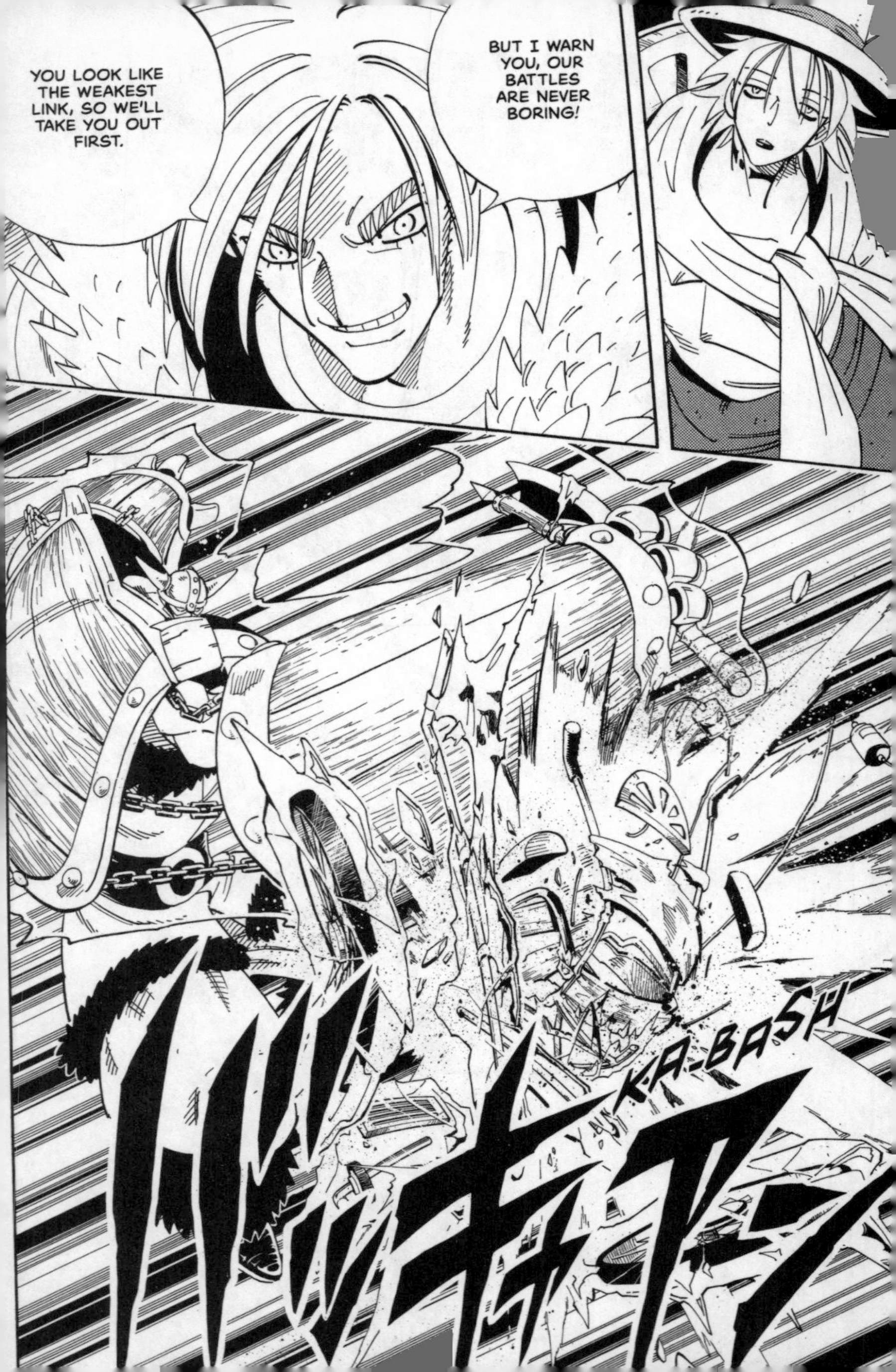
YOU LOOK LIKE THE WEAKEST LINK, SO WE'LL TAKE YOU OUT FIRST.
BUT I WARN YOU, OUR BATTLES ARE NEVER BORING!
KA-BASH

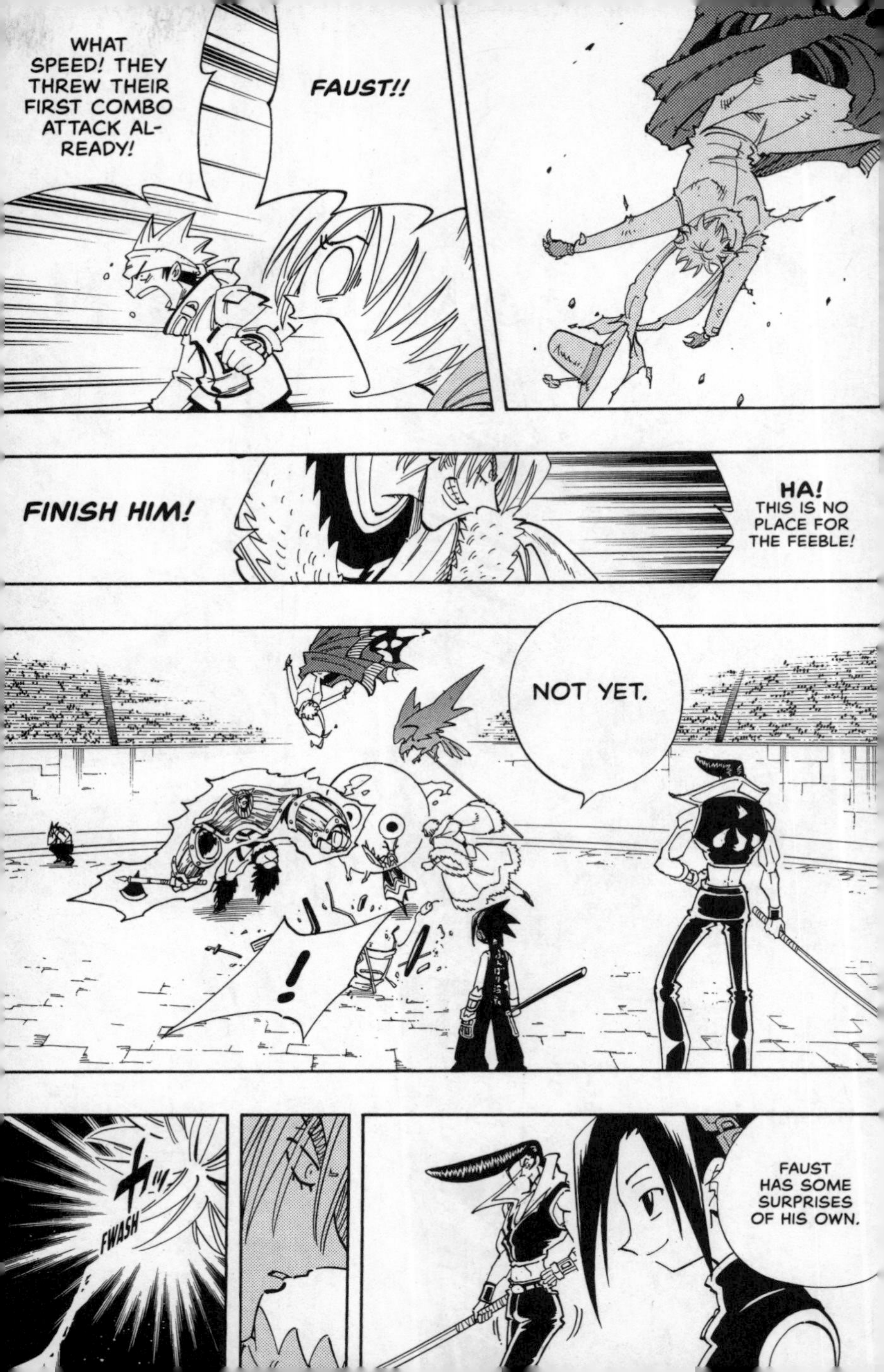
FAUST!!
WHAT SPEED! THEY THREW THEIR FIRST COMBO ATTACK AL-READY!
HA! THIS IS NO PLACE FOR THE FEEBLE!
FINISH HIM!
NOT YET.
FAUST HAS SOME SURPRISES OF HIS OWN.
FWASH

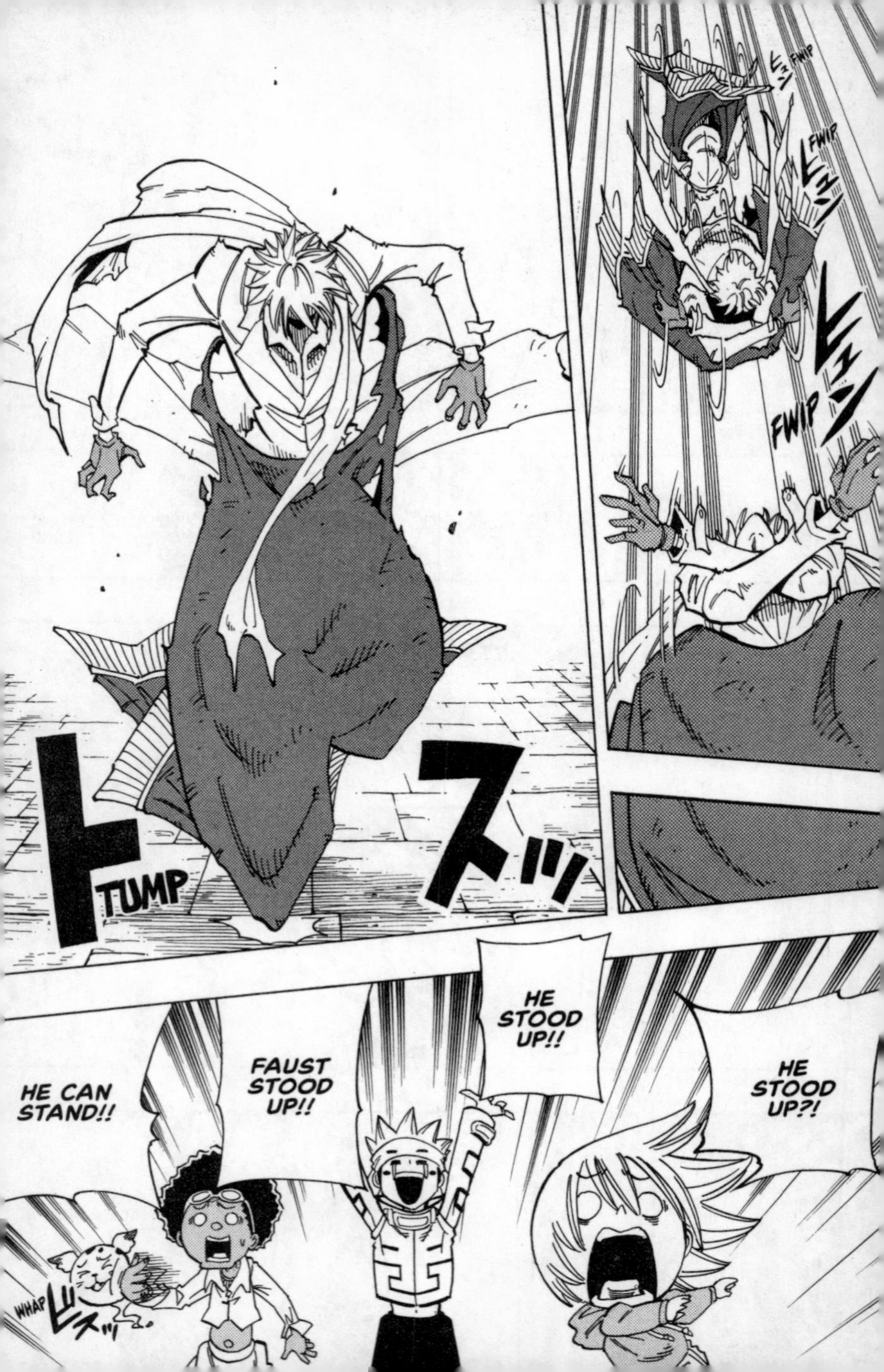
FWIP
FWIP
FWIP
TUMP
トスッ
HE STOOD UP?!
HE STOOD UP!!
FAUST STOOD UP!!
HE CAN STAND!!
WHAP

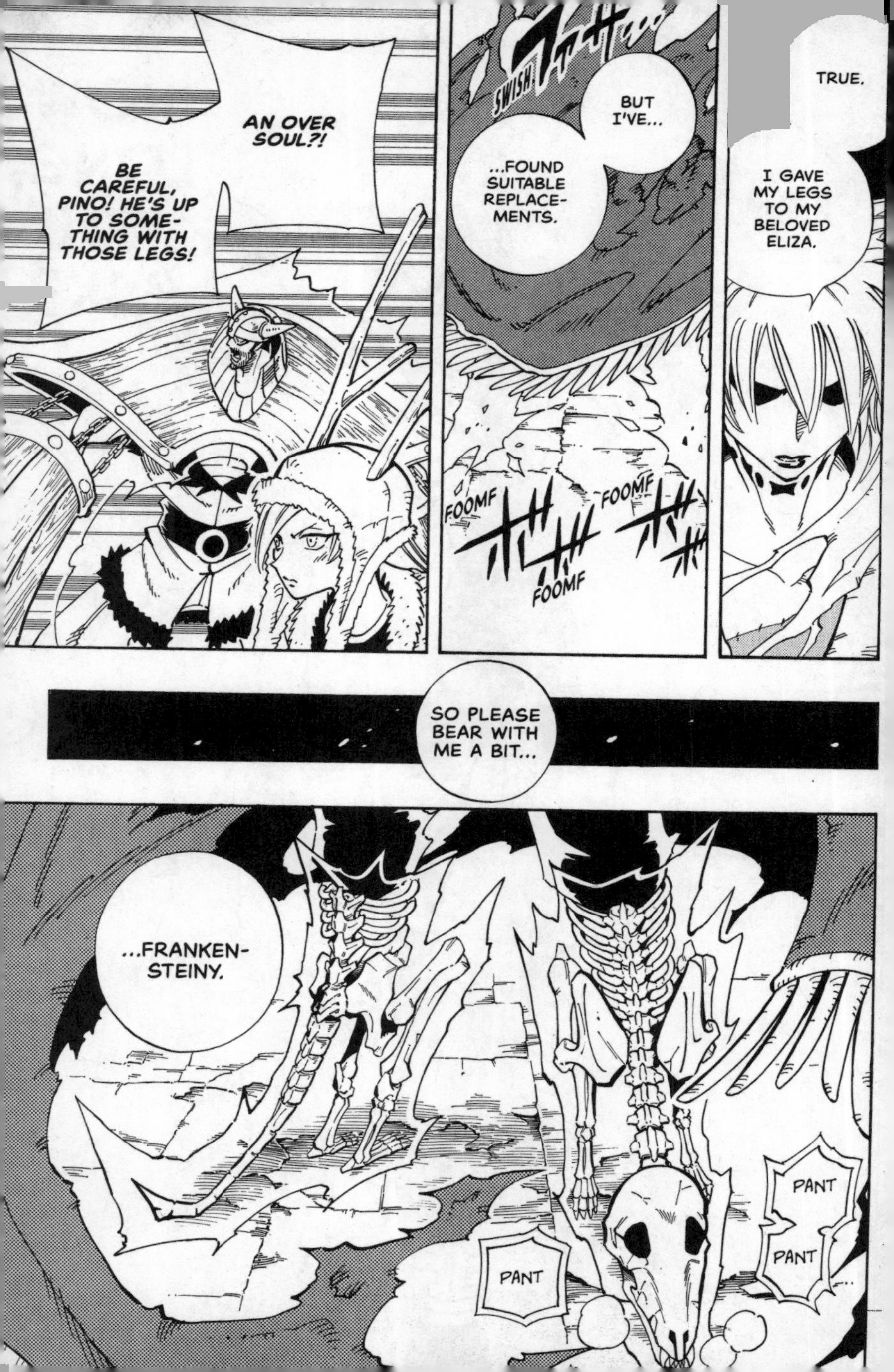
TRUE.
I GAVE MY LEGS TO MY BELOVED ELIZA.
SWISH
BUT I'VE...
...FOUND SUITABLE REPLACE-MENTS.
FOOMF
FOOMF
FOOMF
AN OVER SOUL?!
BE CAREFUL, PINO! HE'S UP TO SOME-THING WITH THOSE LEGS!
SO PLEASE BEAR WITH ME A BIT...
...FRANKEN-STEINY.
PANT
PANT
PANT

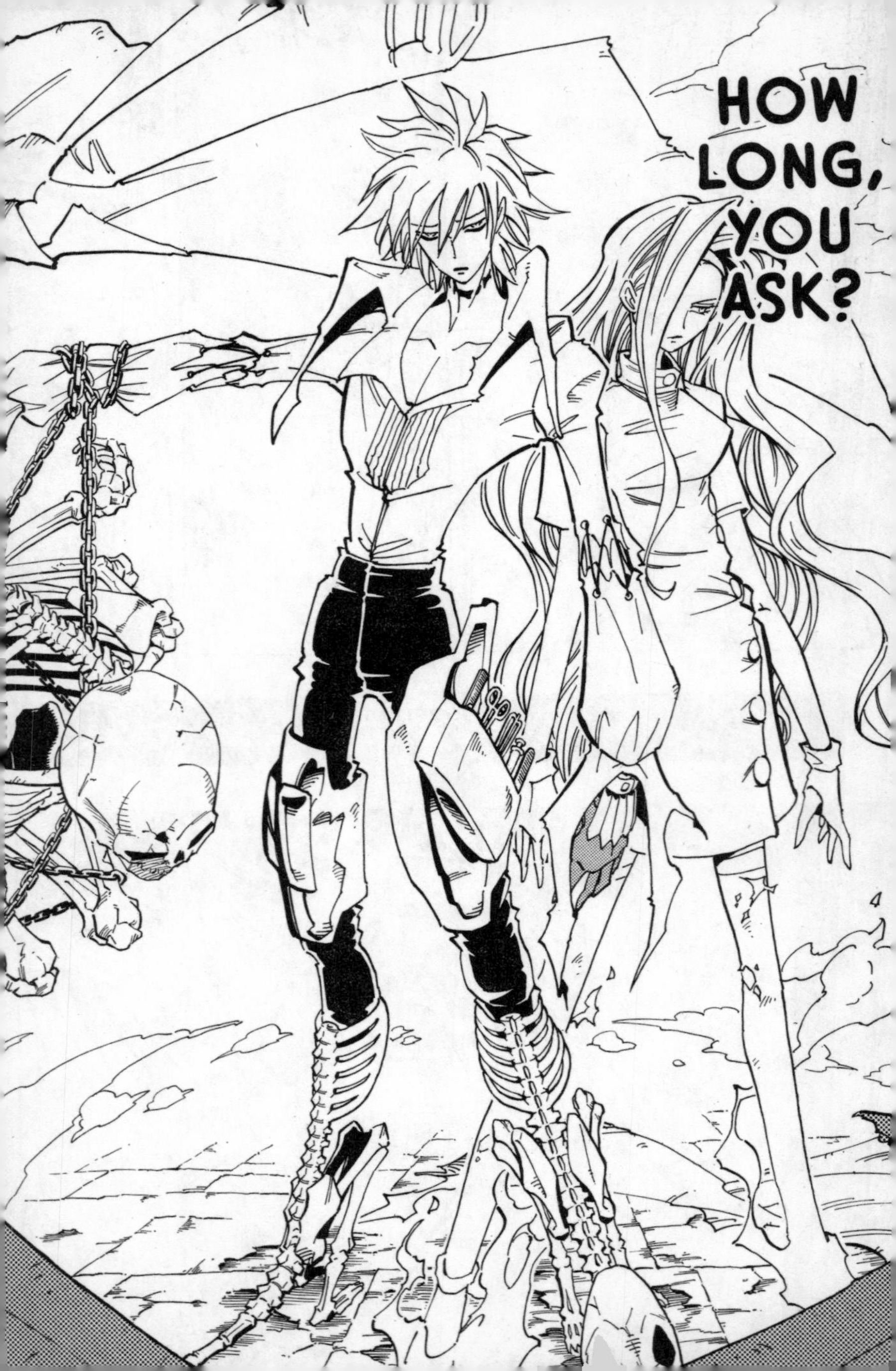
HOW LONG, YOU ASK?

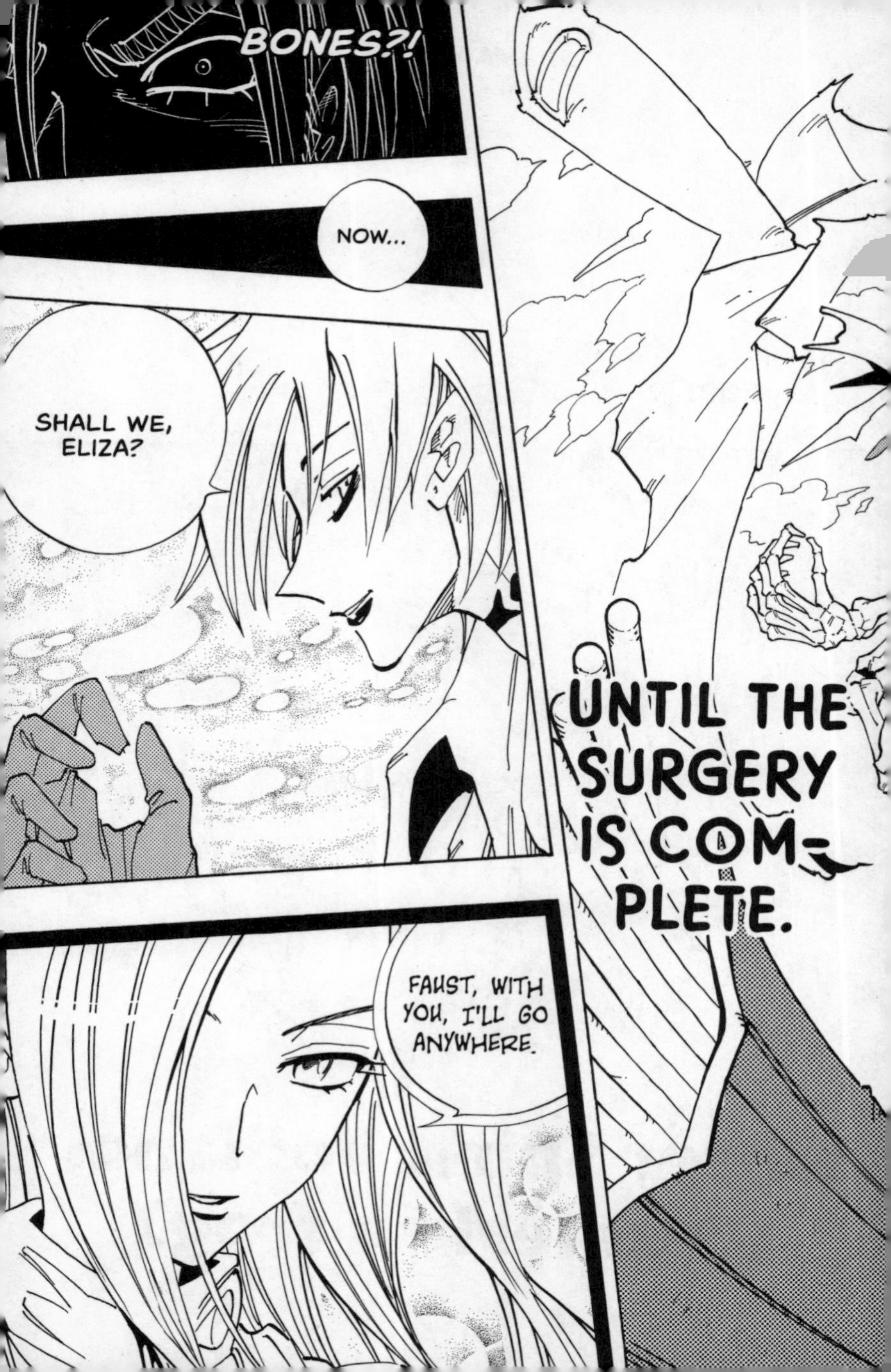
UNTIL THE SURGERY IS COM-PLETE.
BONES?!
NOW...
SHALL WE, ELIZA?
FAUST, WITH YOU, I'LL GO ANYWHERE.

SHAMAN KING CHARACTER FILE No.73

July 2001

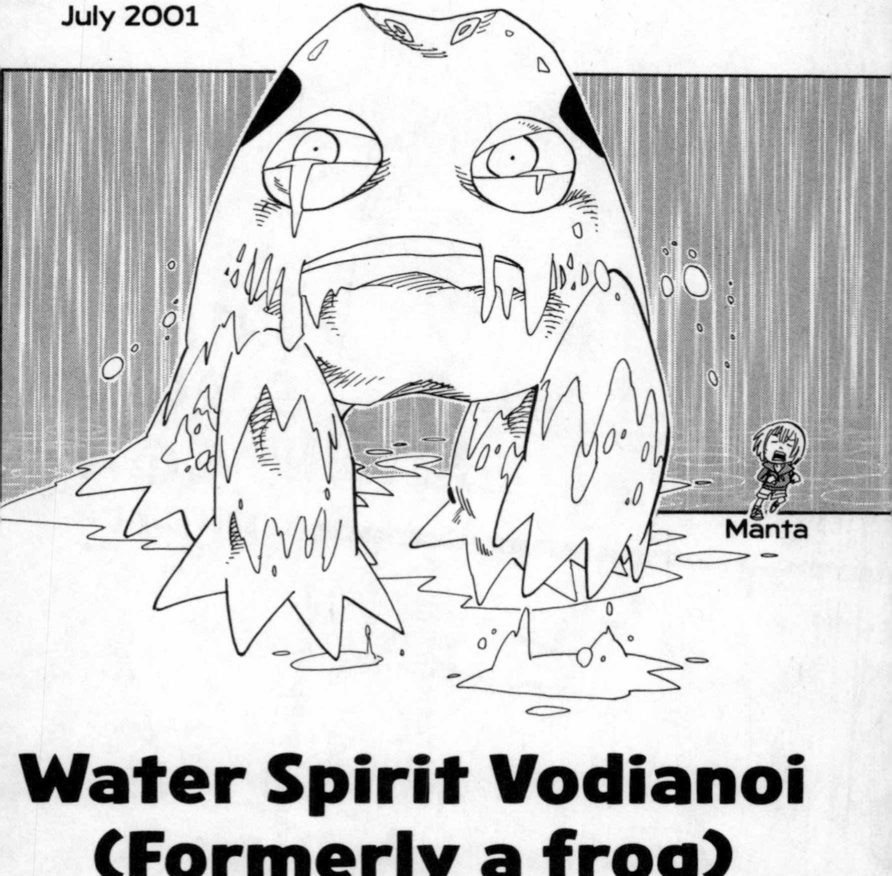
Manta

Water Spirit Vodianoi (Formerly a frog)

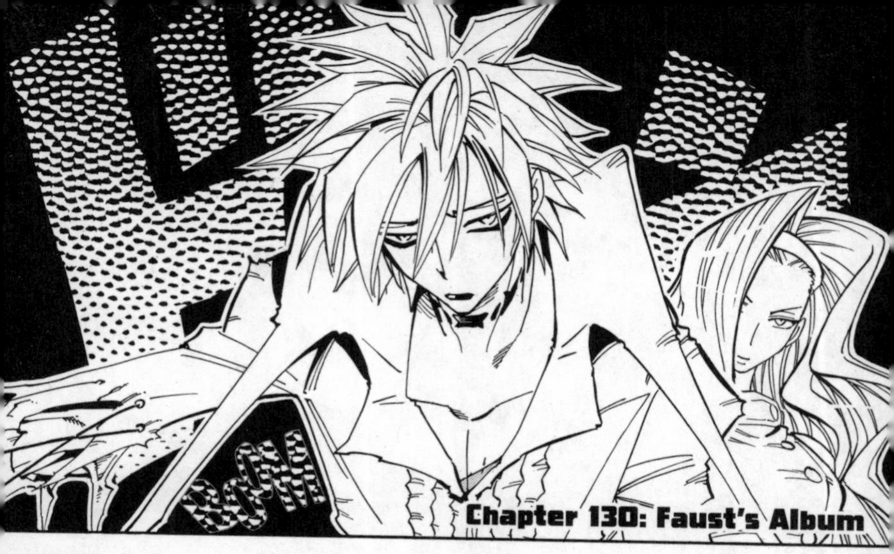
Chapter 130: Faust's Album
BOOM

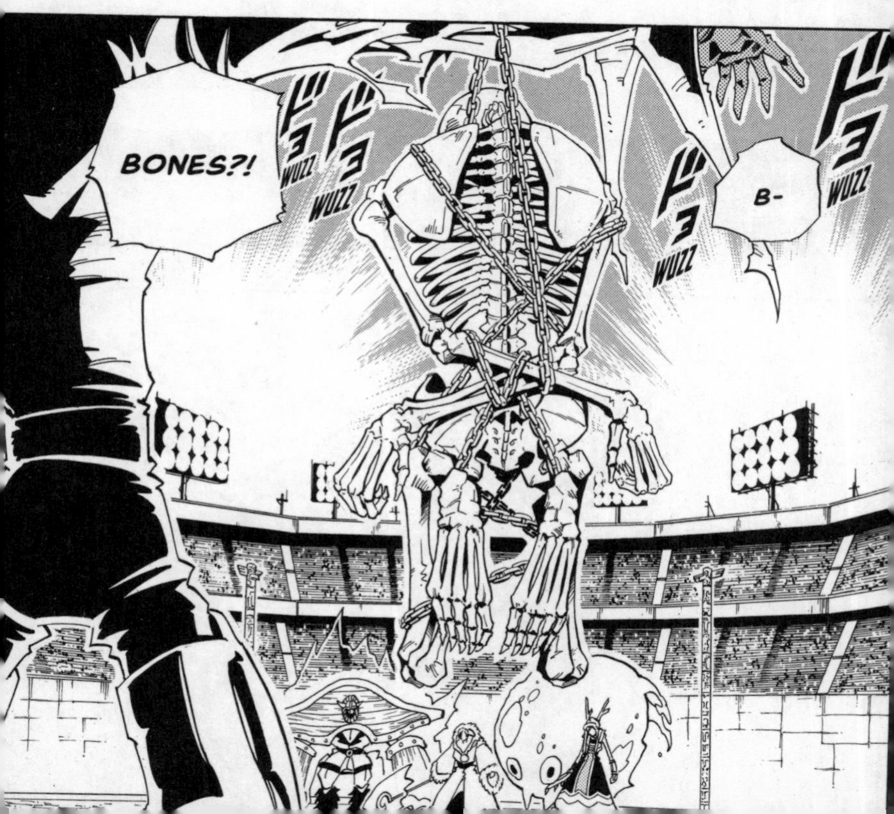
ドヨ
WUZZ
B-
ドヨ
WUZZ
ドヨ
WUZZ
ドヨ
WUZZ
BONES?!

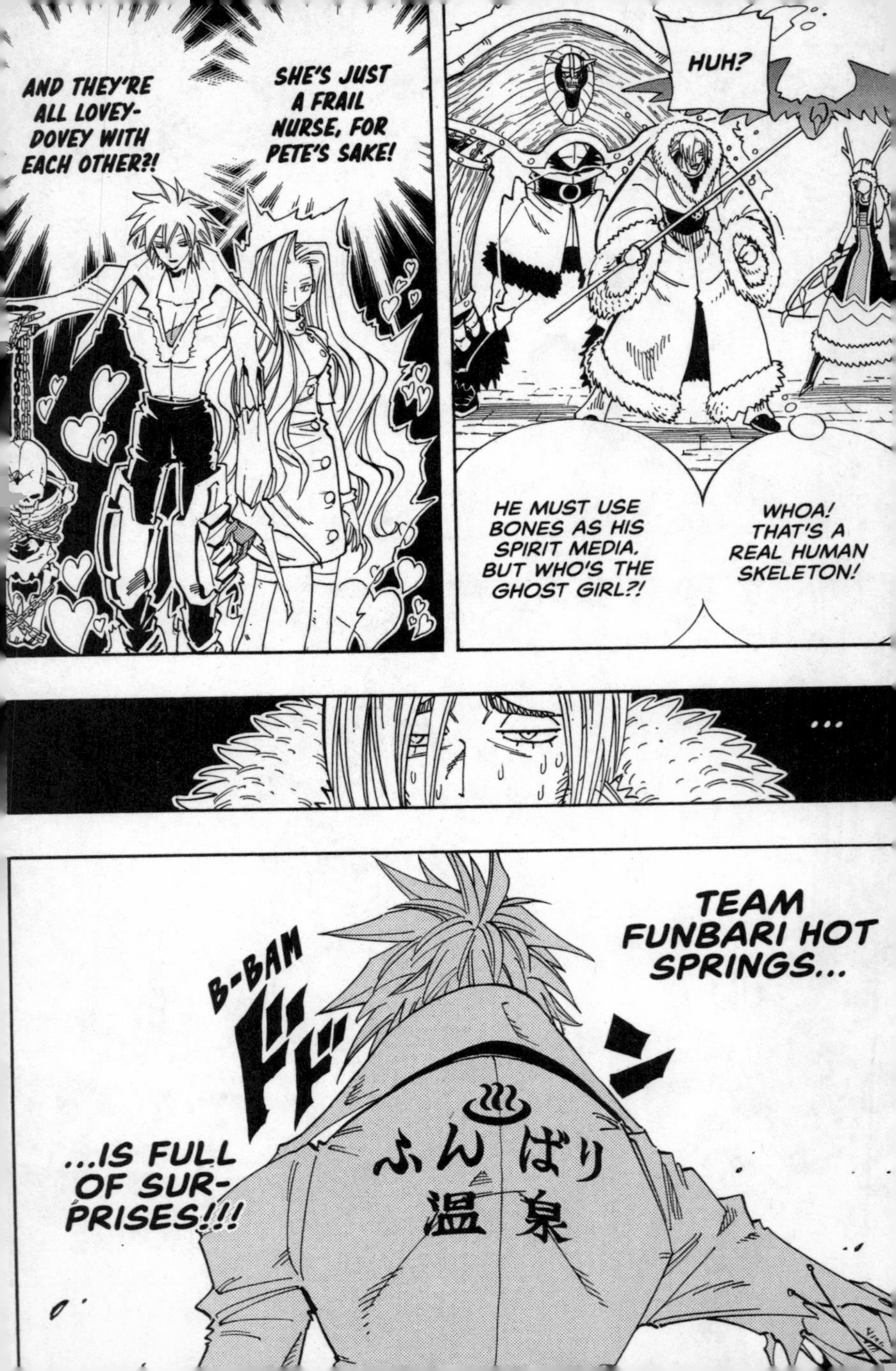
HUH?
WHOA! THAT'S A REAL HUMAN SKELETON!
HE MUST USE BONES AS HIS SPIRIT MEDIA. BUT WHO'S THE GHOST GIRL?!
SHE'S JUST A FRAIL NURSE, FOR PETE'S SAKE!
AND THEY'RE ALL LOVEY-DOVEY WITH EACH OTHER?!
...
TEAM FUNBARI HOT SPRINGS...
B-BAM
ふんばり温泉
...IS FULL OF SUR-PRISES!!!

Chapter 130:

Faust's Album

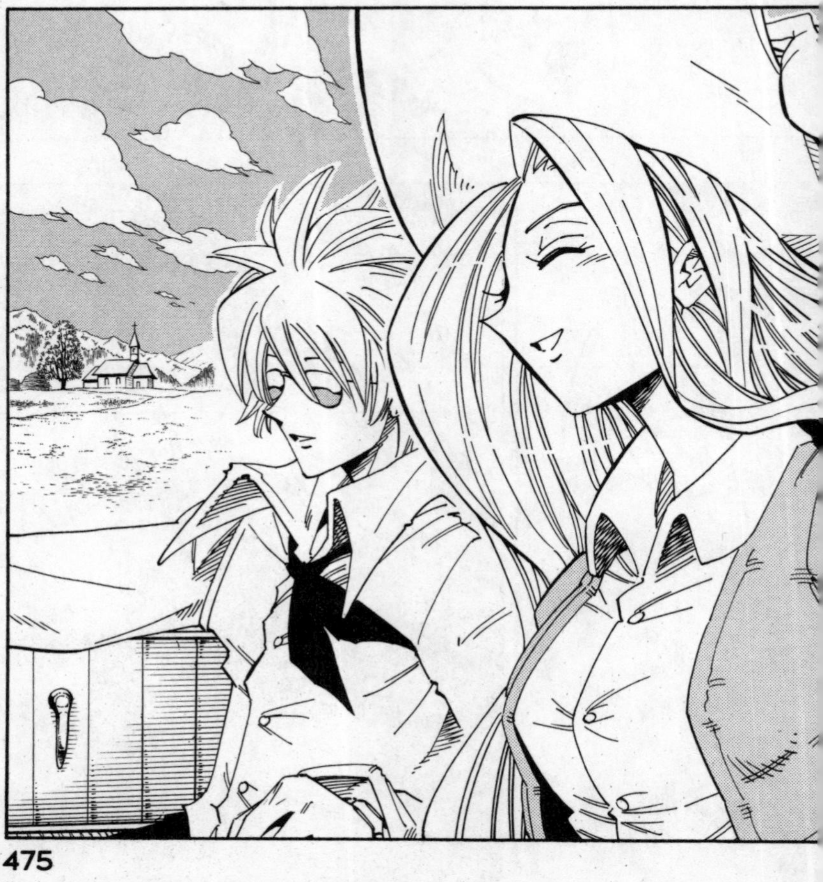

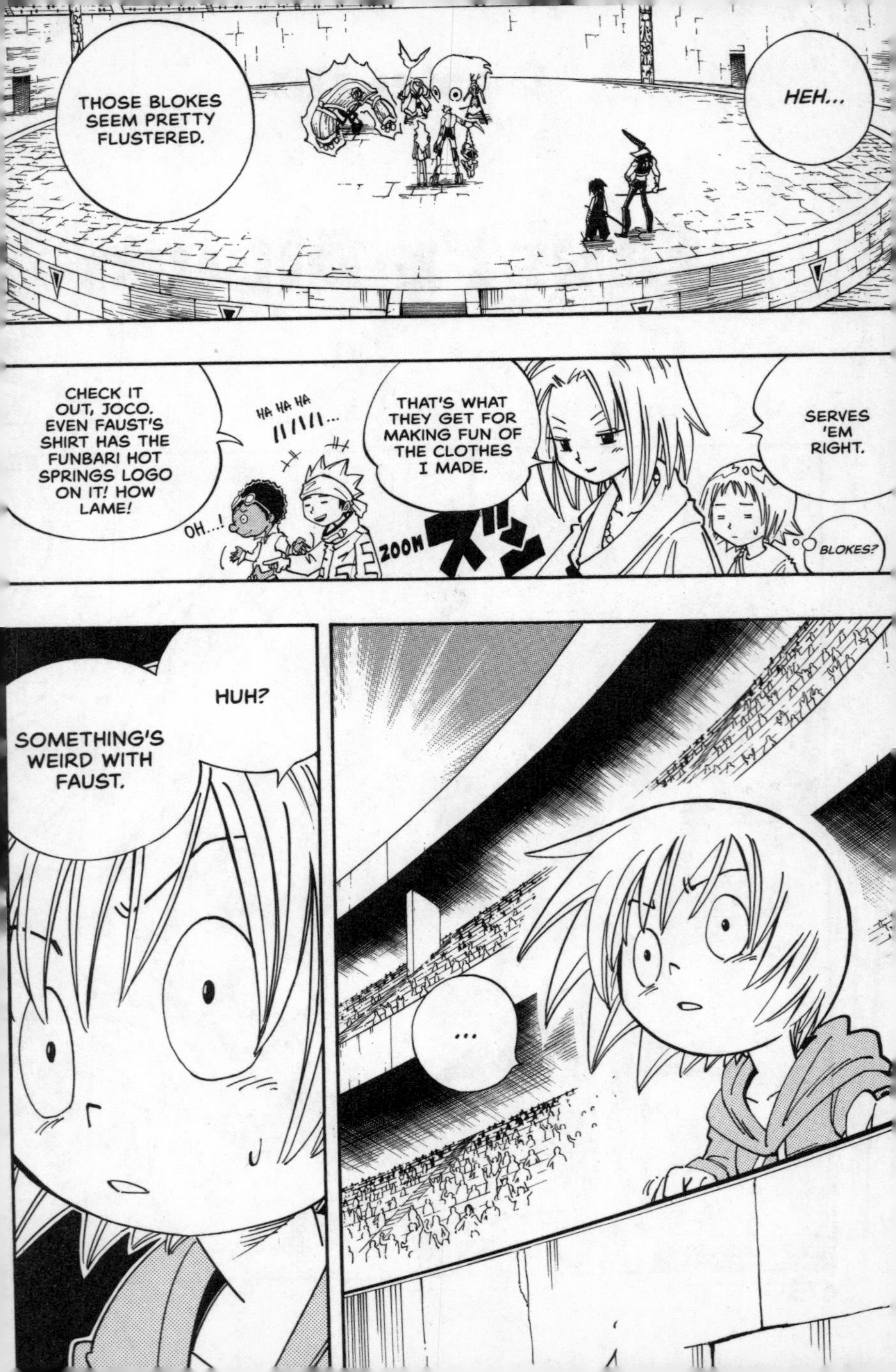
HEH...
THOSE BLOKES SEEM PRETTY FLUSTERED.
SERVES 'EM RIGHT.
BLOKES?
THAT'S WHAT THEY GET FOR MAKING FUN OF THE CLOTHES I MADE.
ZOOM
HA HA HA
CHECK IT OUT, JOCO. EVEN FAUST'S SHIRT HAS THE FUNBARI HOT SPRINGS LOGO ON IT! HOW LAME!
OH...!
...
HUH?
SOMETHING'S WEIRD WITH FAUST.

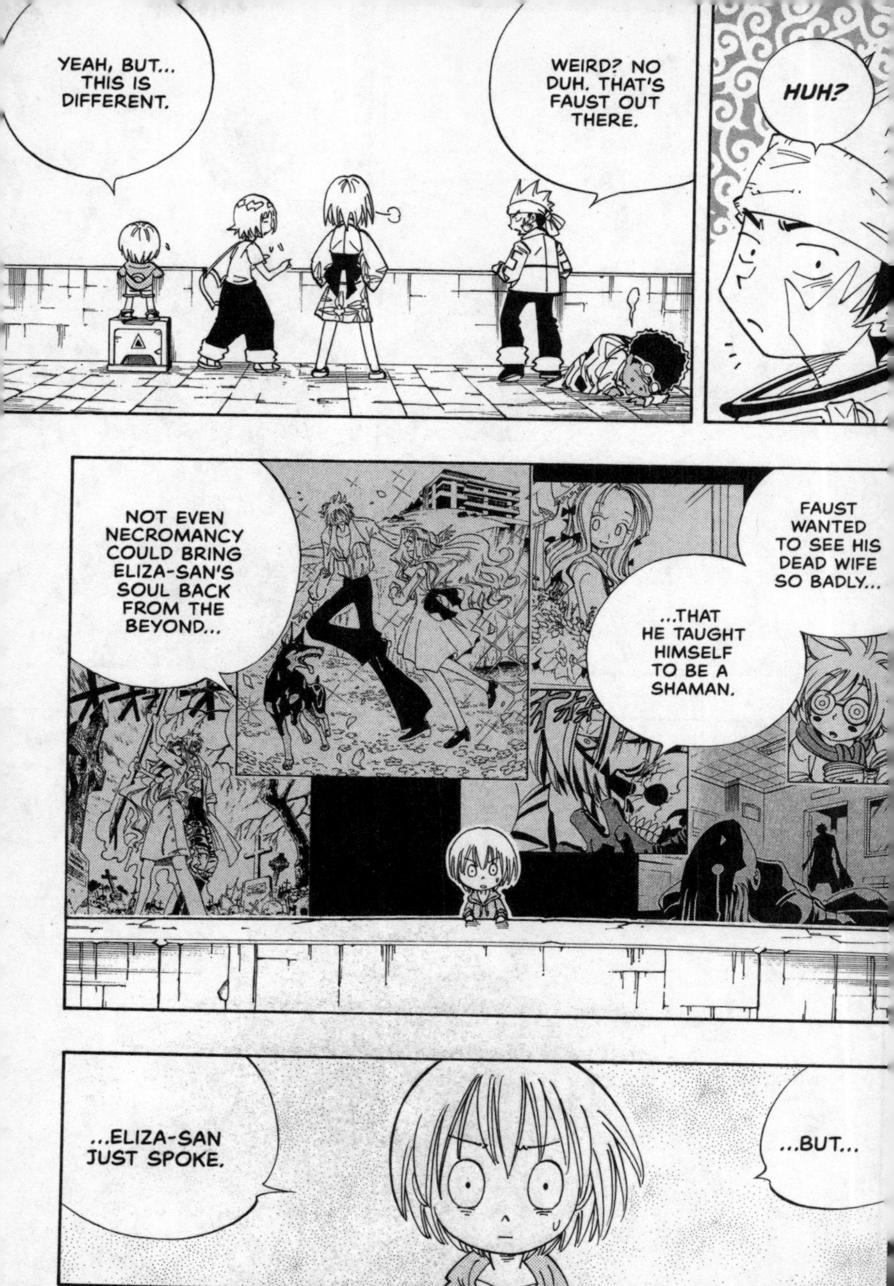
HUH?
WEIRD? NO DUH. THAT'S FAUST OUT THERE.
YEAH, BUT... THIS IS DIFFERENT.
FAUST WANTED TO SEE HIS DEAD WIFE SO BADLY...
...THAT HE TAUGHT HIMSELF TO BE A SHAMAN.
NOT EVEN NECROMANCY COULD BRING ELIZA-SAN'S SOUL BACK FROM THE BEYOND...
...BUT...
...ELIZA-SAN JUST SPOKE.

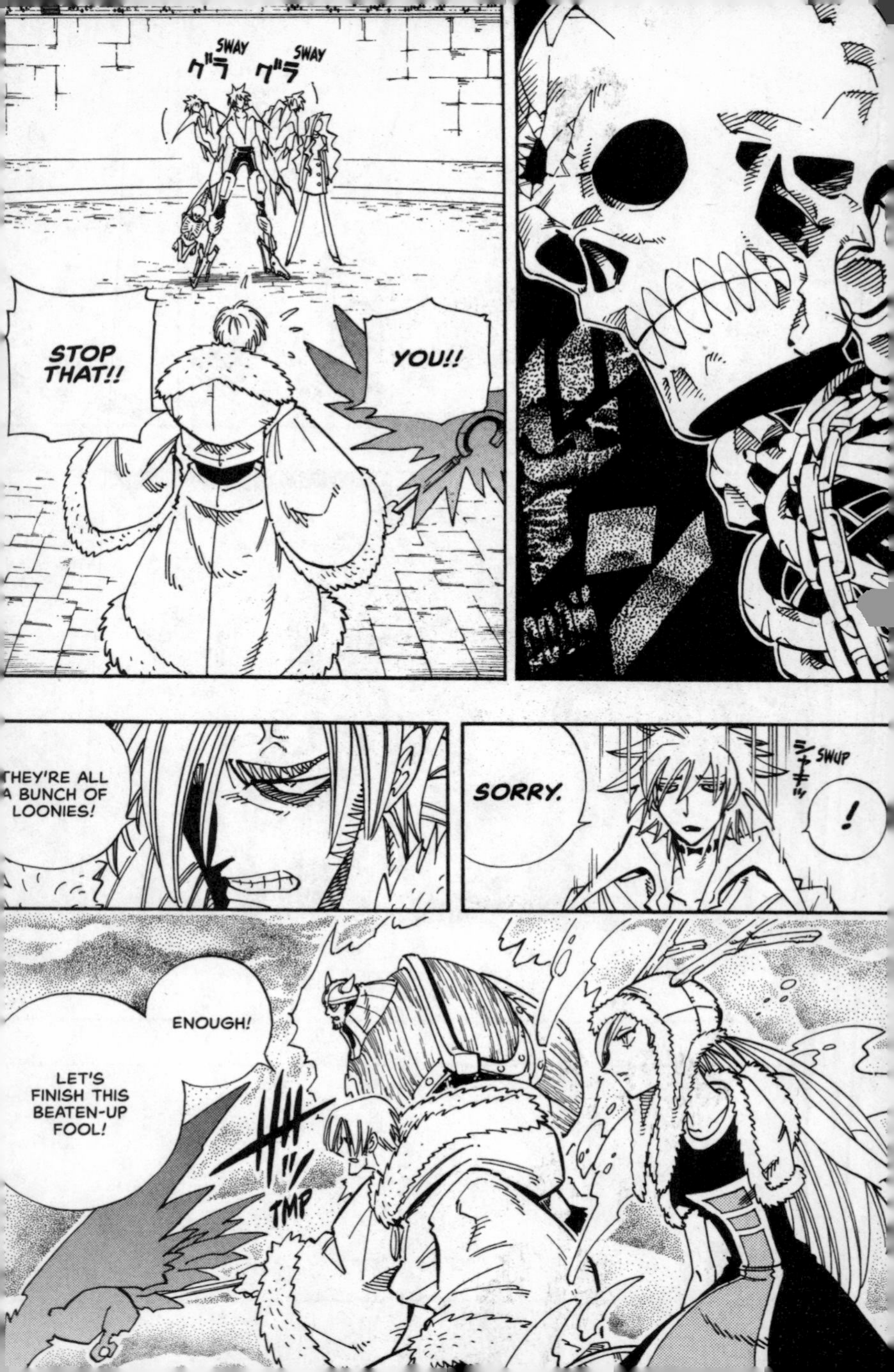

SWAY
グラ
SWAY
グラ
YOU!!
STOP THAT!!
SWUP
シャキッ
!
SORRY.
THEY'RE ALL A BUNCH OF LOONIES!
ENOUGH!
LET'S FINISH THIS BEATEN-UP FOOL!
TMP

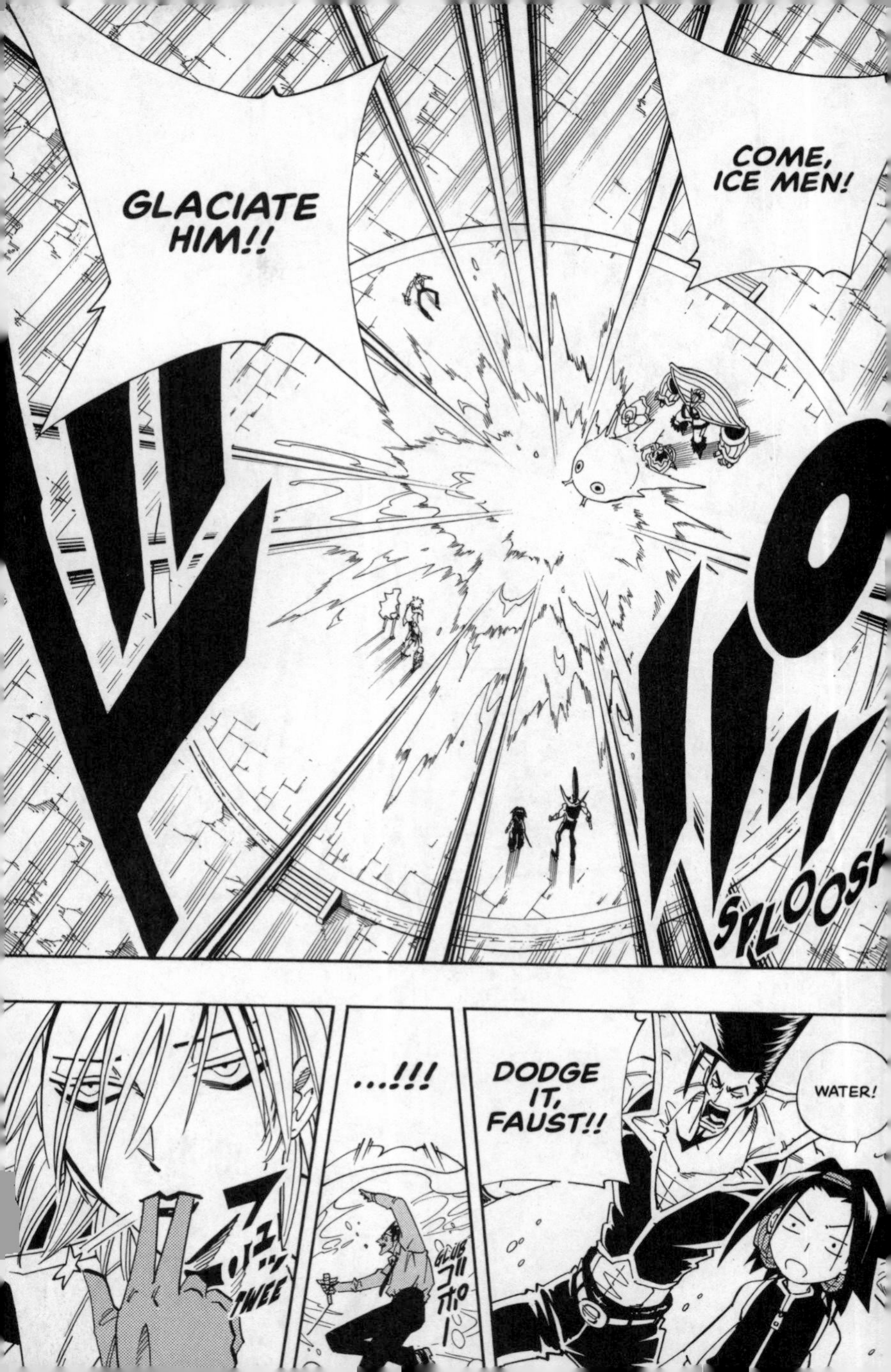
COME, ICE MEN!
GLACIATE HIM!!
SPLOOSH
WATER!
DODGE IT, FAUST!!
...!!!
GLUB
TWEE

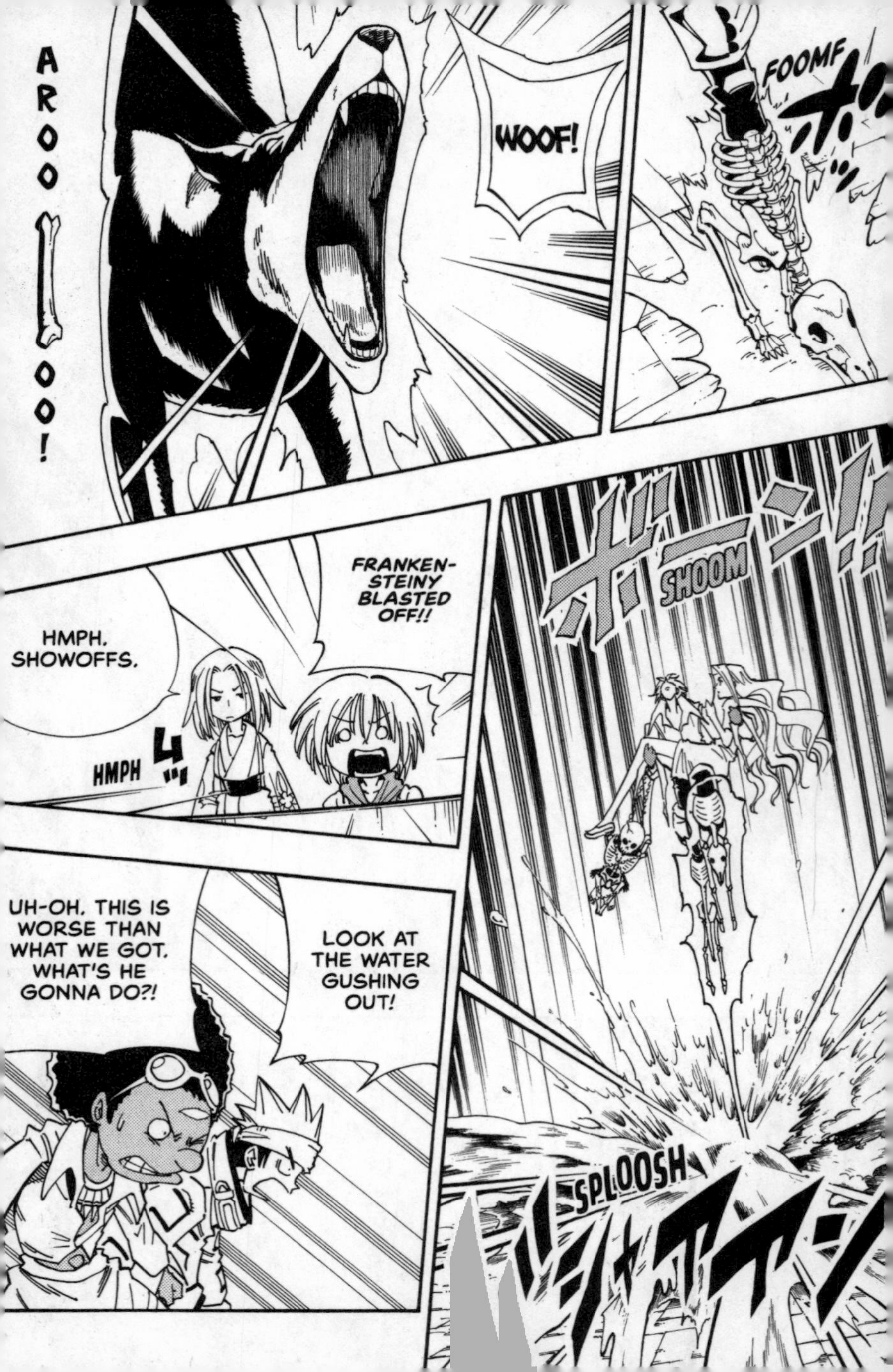
FOOMF
WOOF!
AROO—OOO!
SHOOM
SPLOOSH
FRANKEN-STEINY BLASTED OFF!!
HMPH. SHOWOFFS.
HMPH
LOOK AT THE WATER GUSHING OUT!
UH-OH. THIS IS WORSE THAN WHAT WE GOT. WHAT'S HE GONNA DO?!

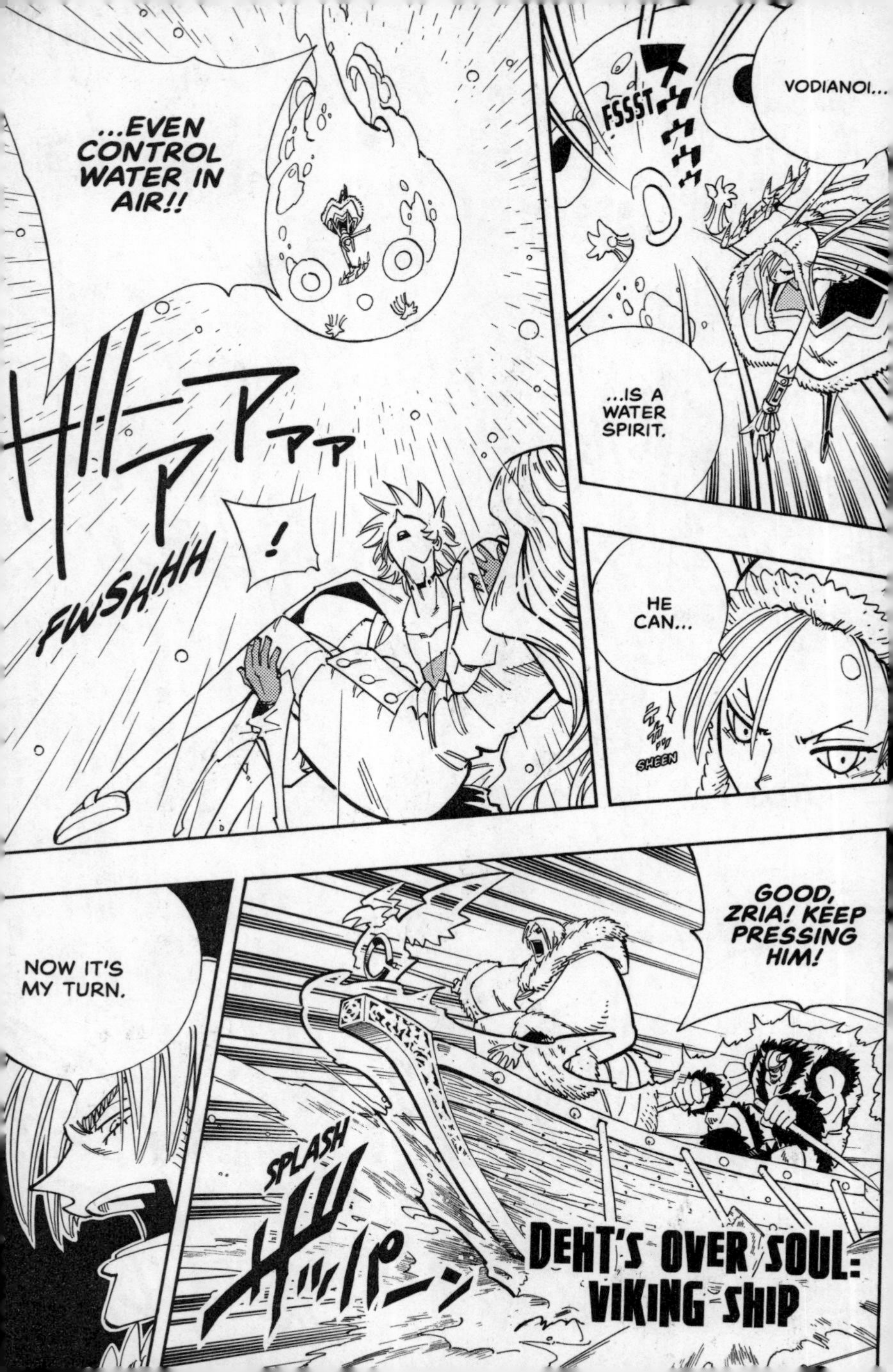

VODIANOI...
FSSST
...IS A WATER SPIRIT.
HE CAN...
SHEEN
...EVEN CONTROL WATER IN AIR!!
FWSHHH
!
GOOD, ZRIA! KEEP PRESSING HIM!
SPLASH
DEHT'S OVER SOUL: VIKING SHIP
NOW IT'S MY TURN.

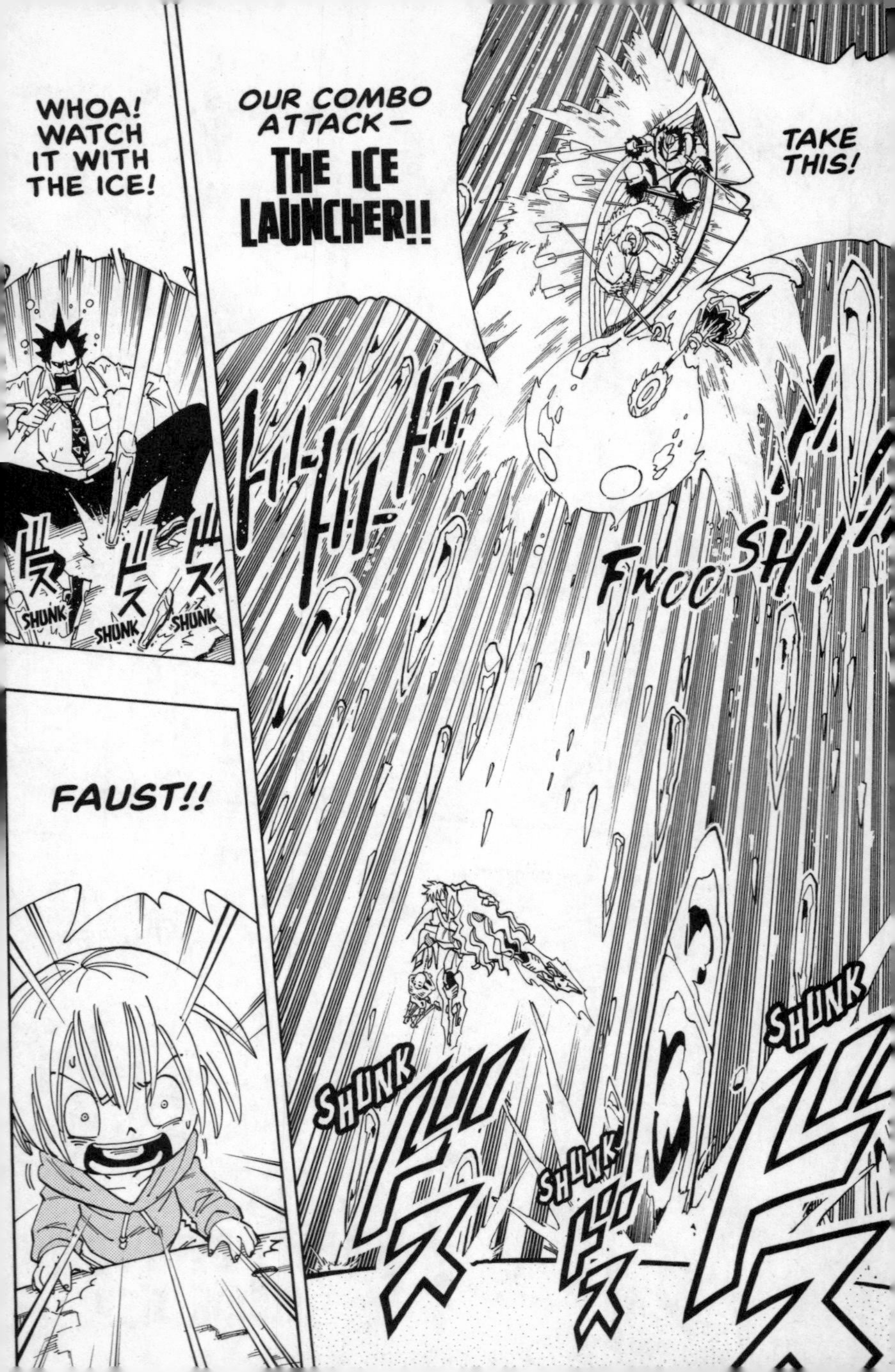
TAKE THIS!
OUR COMBO ATTACK—
THE ICE LAUNCHER!!
FWOOSH
SHUNK
SHUNK
SHUNK
WHOA! WATCH IT WITH THE ICE!
SHUNK
SHUNK
SHUNK
FAUST!!

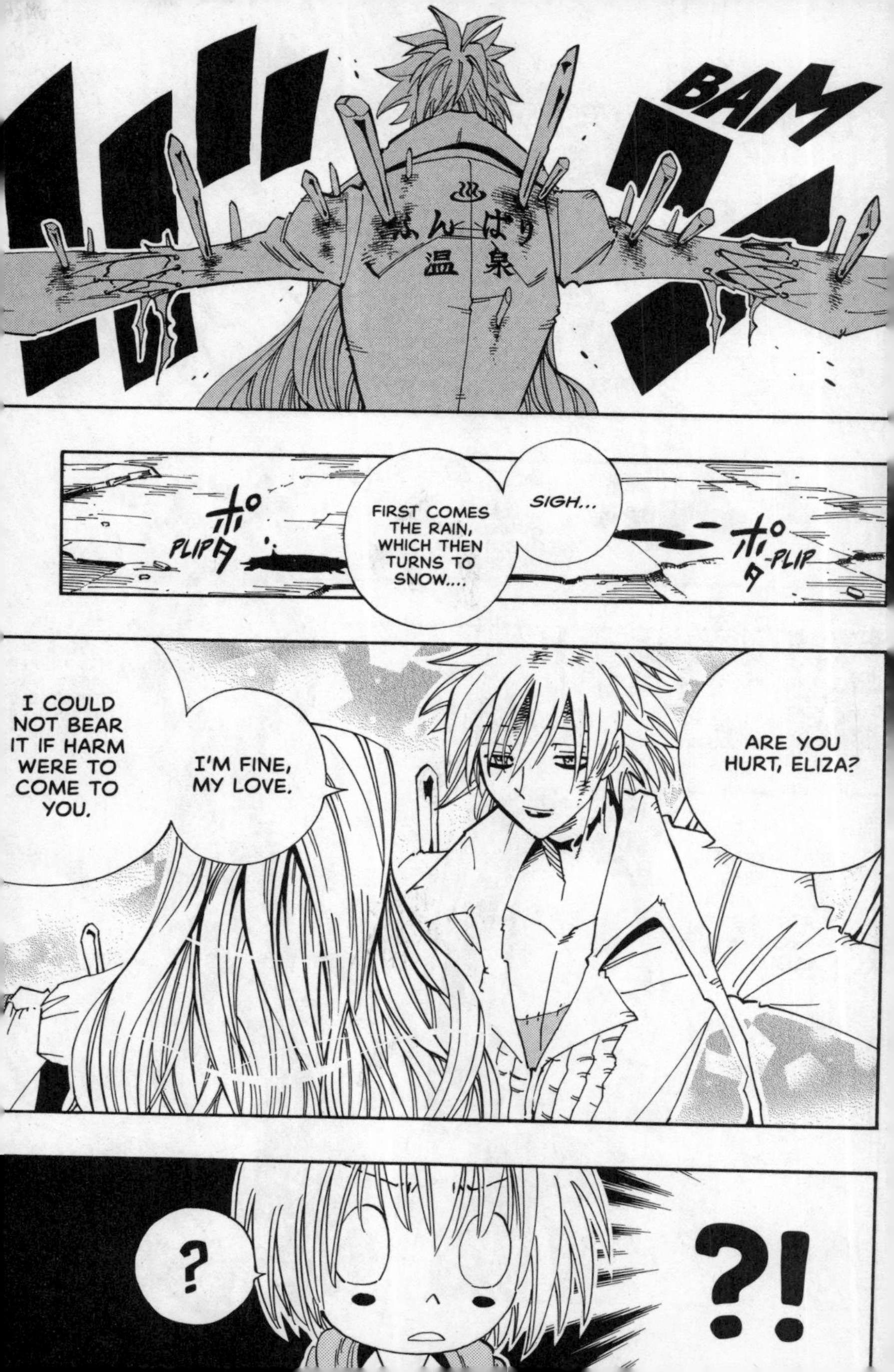
BAM
ふんばり
温泉
ポタ PLIP
SIGH...
FIRST COMES THE RAIN, WHICH THEN TURNS TO SNOW....
ポタ PLIP
ARE YOU HURT, ELIZA?
I'M FINE, MY LOVE.
I COULD NOT BEAR IT IF HARM WERE TO COME TO YOU.
?!
?

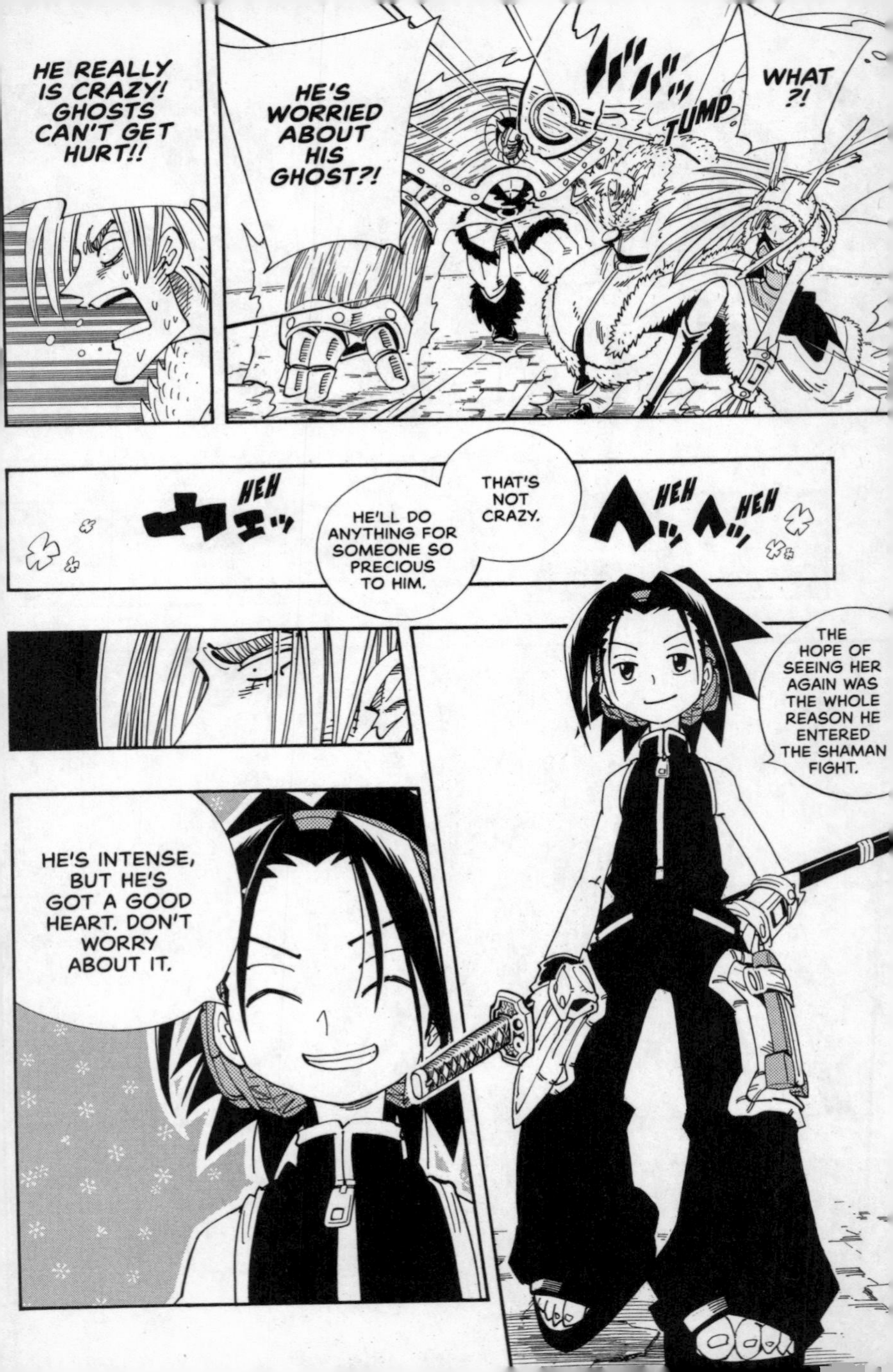
WHAT?!
TUMP
HE'S WORRIED ABOUT HIS GHOST?!
HE REALLY IS CRAZY! GHOSTS CAN'T GET HURT!!
HEH HEH
THAT'S NOT CRAZY.
HE'LL DO ANYTHING FOR SOMEONE SO PRECIOUS TO HIM.
HEH
THE HOPE OF SEEING HER AGAIN WAS THE WHOLE REASON HE ENTERED THE SHAMAN FIGHT.
HE'S INTENSE, BUT HE'S GOT A GOOD HEART. DON'T WORRY ABOUT IT.

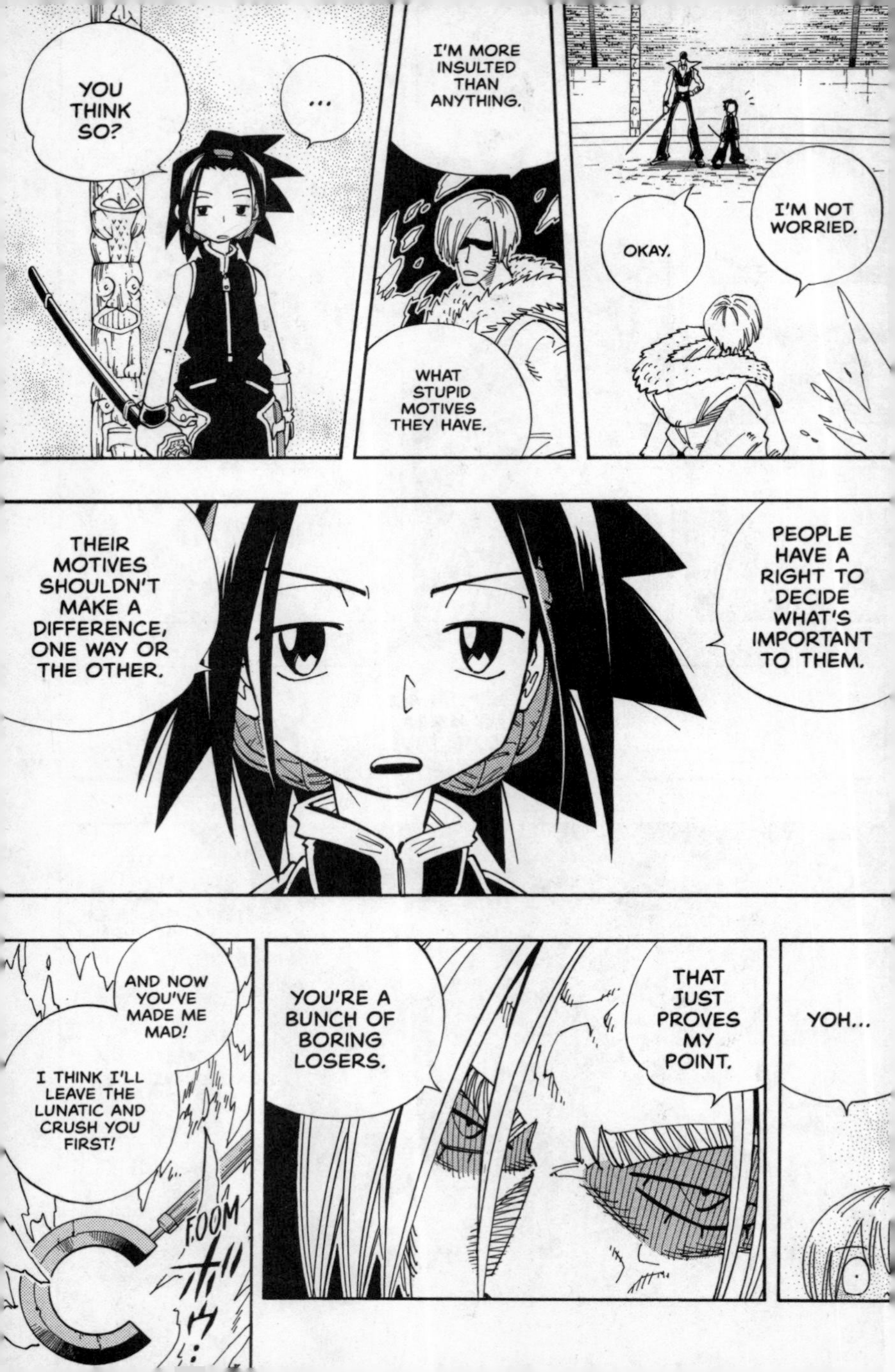
I'M NOT WORRIED.
OKAY.
I'M MORE INSULTED THAN ANYTHING.
WHAT STUPID MOTIVES THEY HAVE.
...
YOU THINK SO?
PEOPLE HAVE A RIGHT TO DECIDE WHAT'S IMPORTANT TO THEM.
THEIR MOTIVES SHOULDN'T MAKE A DIFFERENCE, ONE WAY OR THE OTHER.
YOH...
THAT JUST PROVES MY POINT.
YOU'RE A BUNCH OF BORING LOSERS.
AND NOW YOU'VE MADE ME MAD!
I THINK I'LL LEAVE THE LUNATIC AND CRUSH YOU FIRST!
FOOM

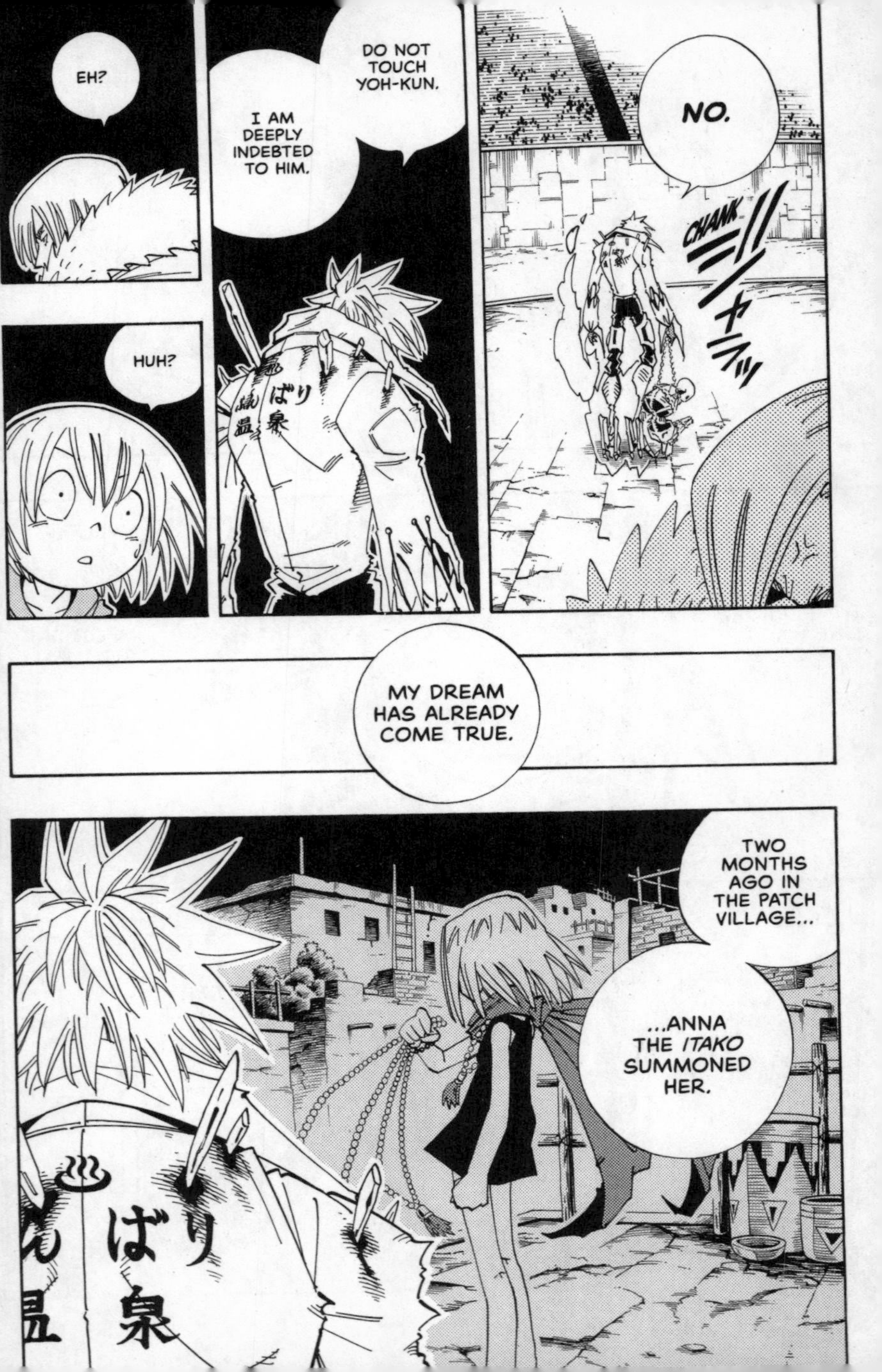
NO.
CHANK
DO NOT TOUCH YOH-KUN.
I AM DEEPLY INDEBTED TO HIM.
EH?
HUH?
MY DREAM HAS ALREADY COME TRUE.
TWO MONTHS AGO IN THE PATCH VILLAGE...
...ANNA THE *ITAKO* SUMMONED HER.

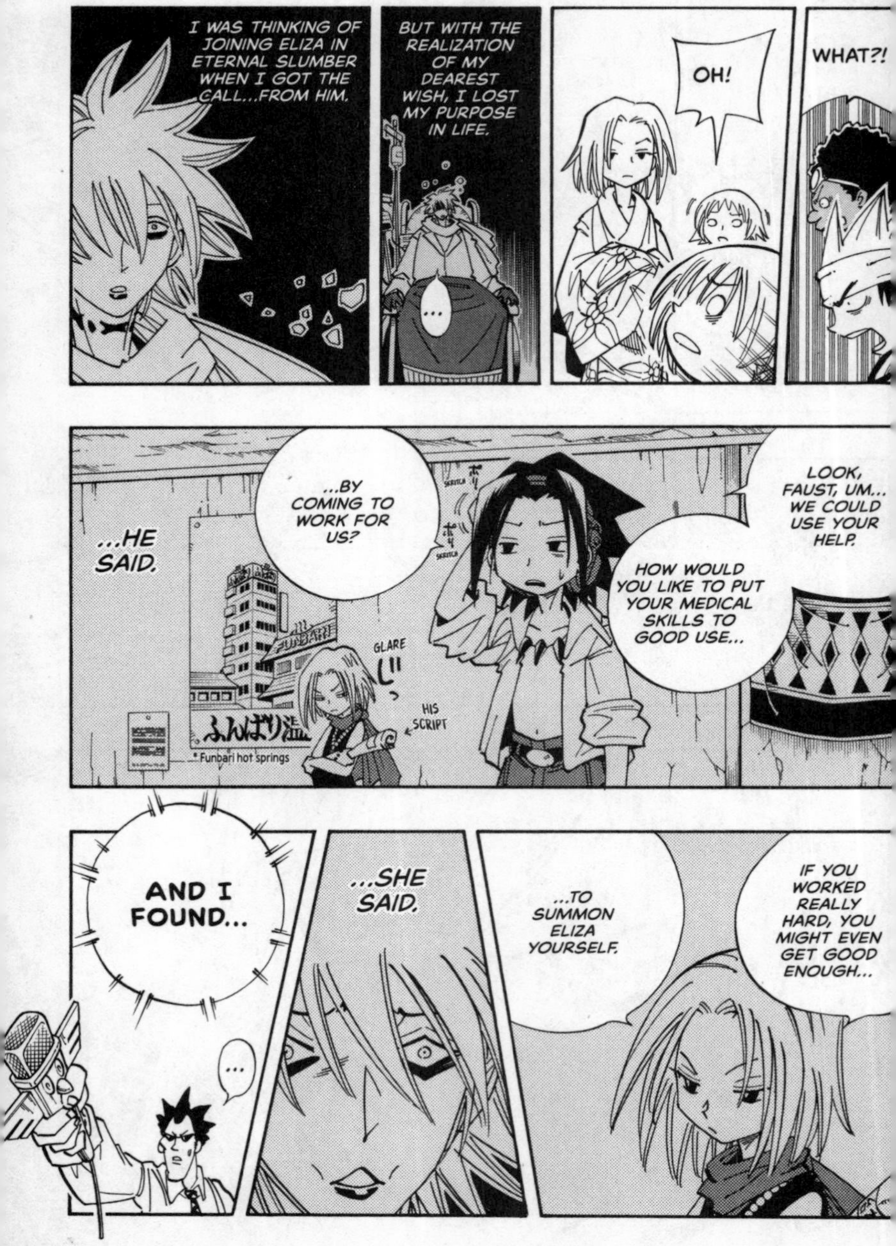
WHAT?!
OH!
BUT WITH THE REALIZATION OF MY DEAREST WISH, I LOST MY PURPOSE IN LIFE.
...
I WAS THINKING OF JOINING ELIZA IN ETERNAL SLUMBER WHEN I GOT THE CALL...FROM HIM.
LOOK, FAUST, UM... WE COULD USE YOUR HELP.
HOW WOULD YOU LIKE TO PUT YOUR MEDICAL SKILLS TO GOOD USE...
SCRITCH
SCRITCH
...BY COMING TO WORK FOR US?
GLARE
HIS SCRIPT
FUNBARI
* Funbari hot springs
...HE SAID.
IF YOU WORKED REALLY HARD, YOU MIGHT EVEN GET GOOD ENOUGH...
...TO SUMMON ELIZA YOURSELF.
...SHE SAID.
AND I FOUND...
...

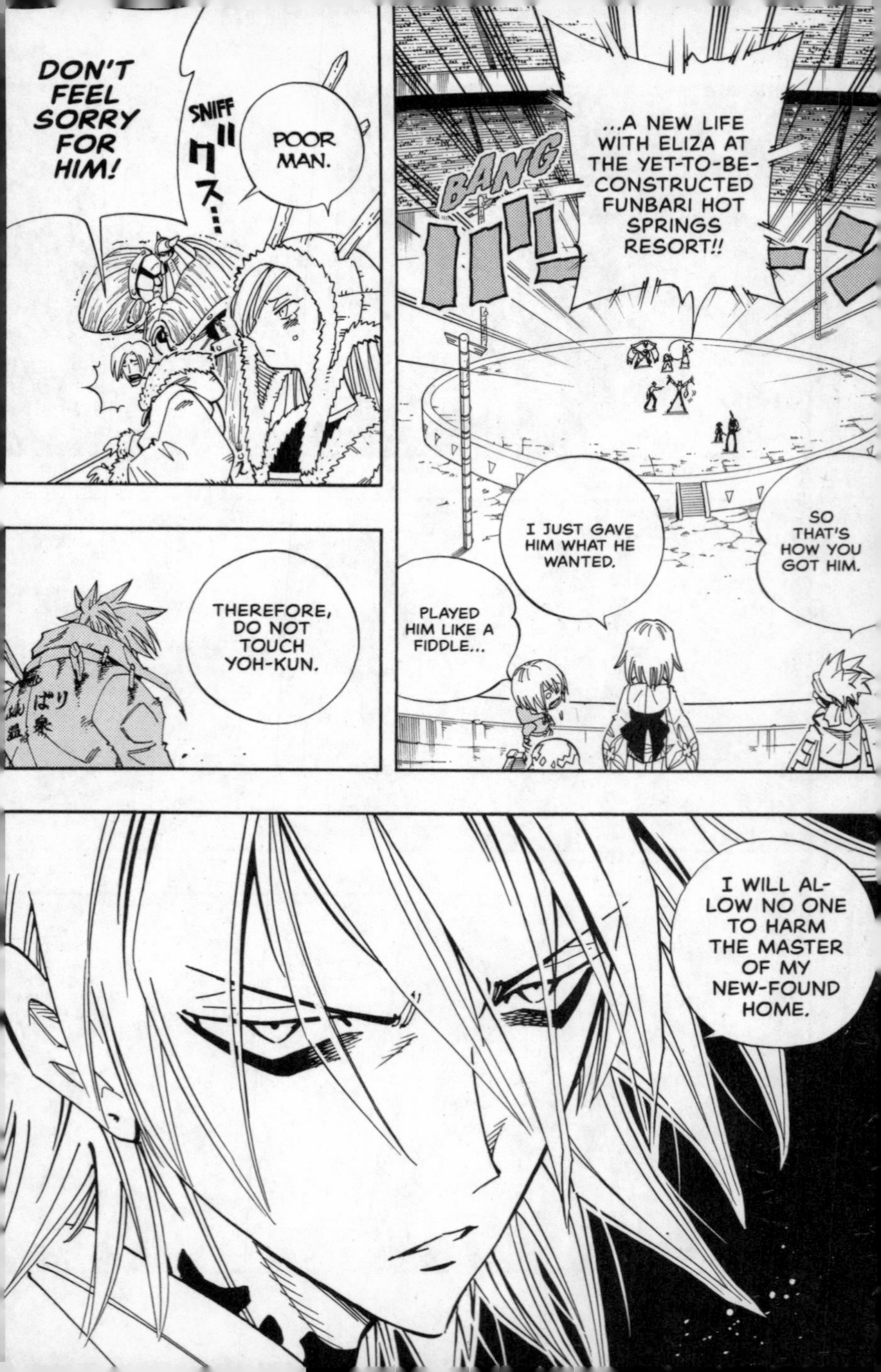
...A NEW LIFE WITH ELIZA AT THE YET-TO-BE-CONSTRUCTED FUNBARI HOT SPRINGS RESORT!!
BANG
SO THAT'S HOW YOU GOT HIM.
I JUST GAVE HIM WHAT HE WANTED.
PLAYED HIM LIKE A FIDDLE...
POOR MAN.
SNIFF
グス…
DON'T FEEL SORRY FOR HIM!
THEREFORE, DO NOT TOUCH YOH-KUN.
I WILL AL-LOW NO ONE TO HARM THE MASTER OF MY NEW-FOUND HOME.

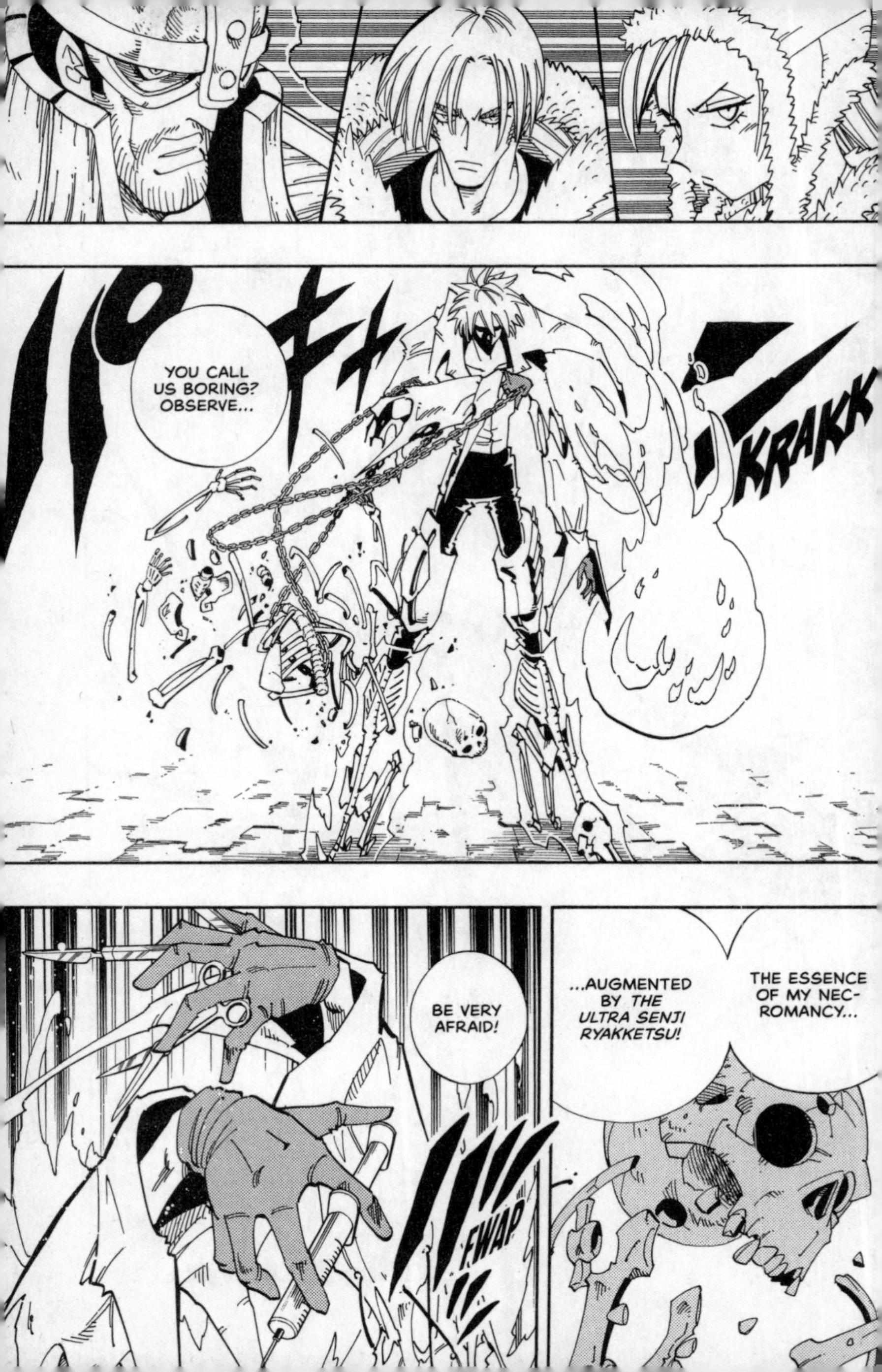
KRAKK
YOU CALL US BORING? OBSERVE...
THE ESSENCE OF MY NECROMANCY...
...AUGMENTED BY *THE* ULTRA SENJI RYAKKETSU!
BE VERY AFRAID!
FWAP

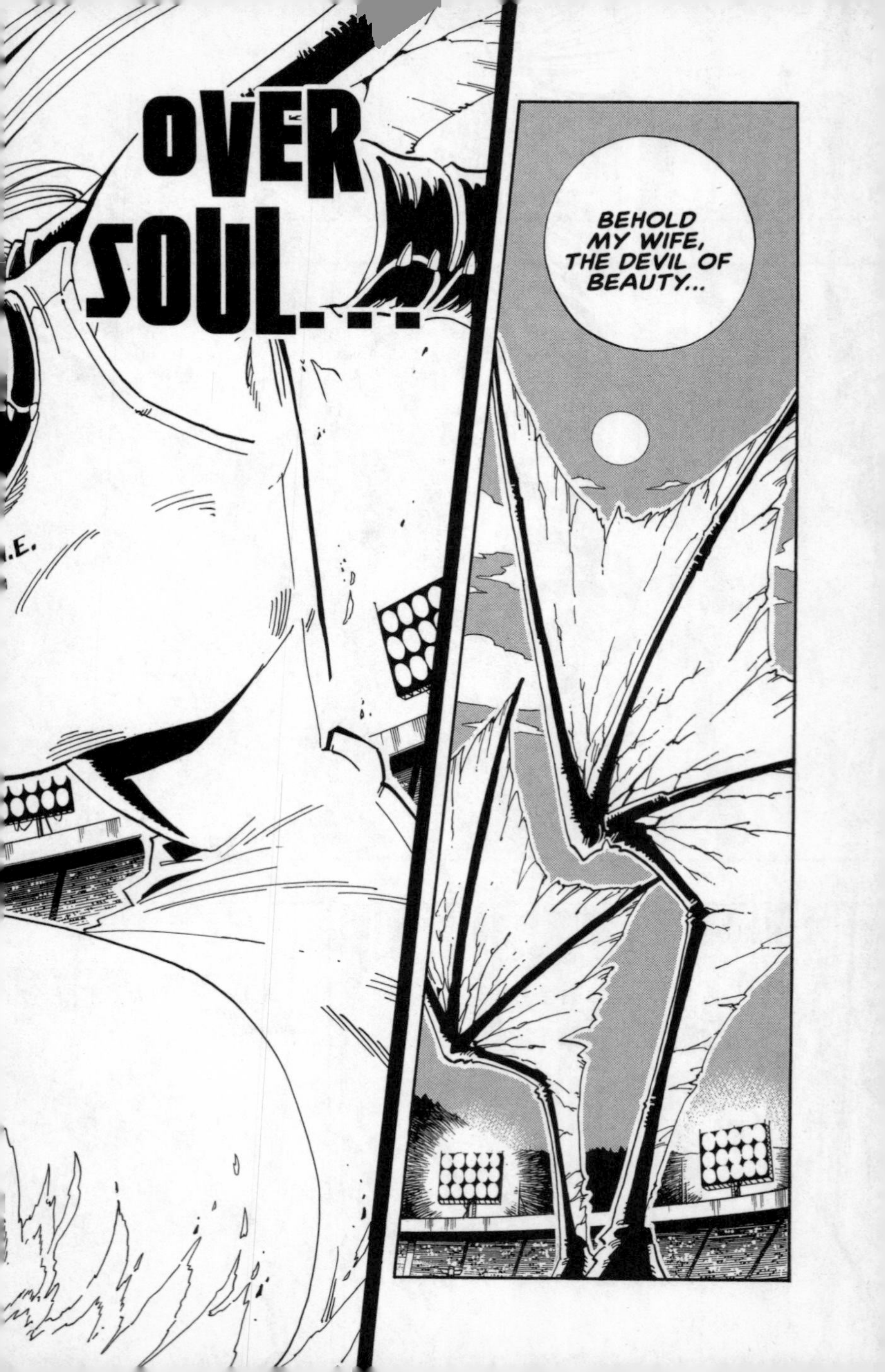
BEHOLD MY WIFE, THE DEVIL OF BEAUTY...
OVER SOUL...

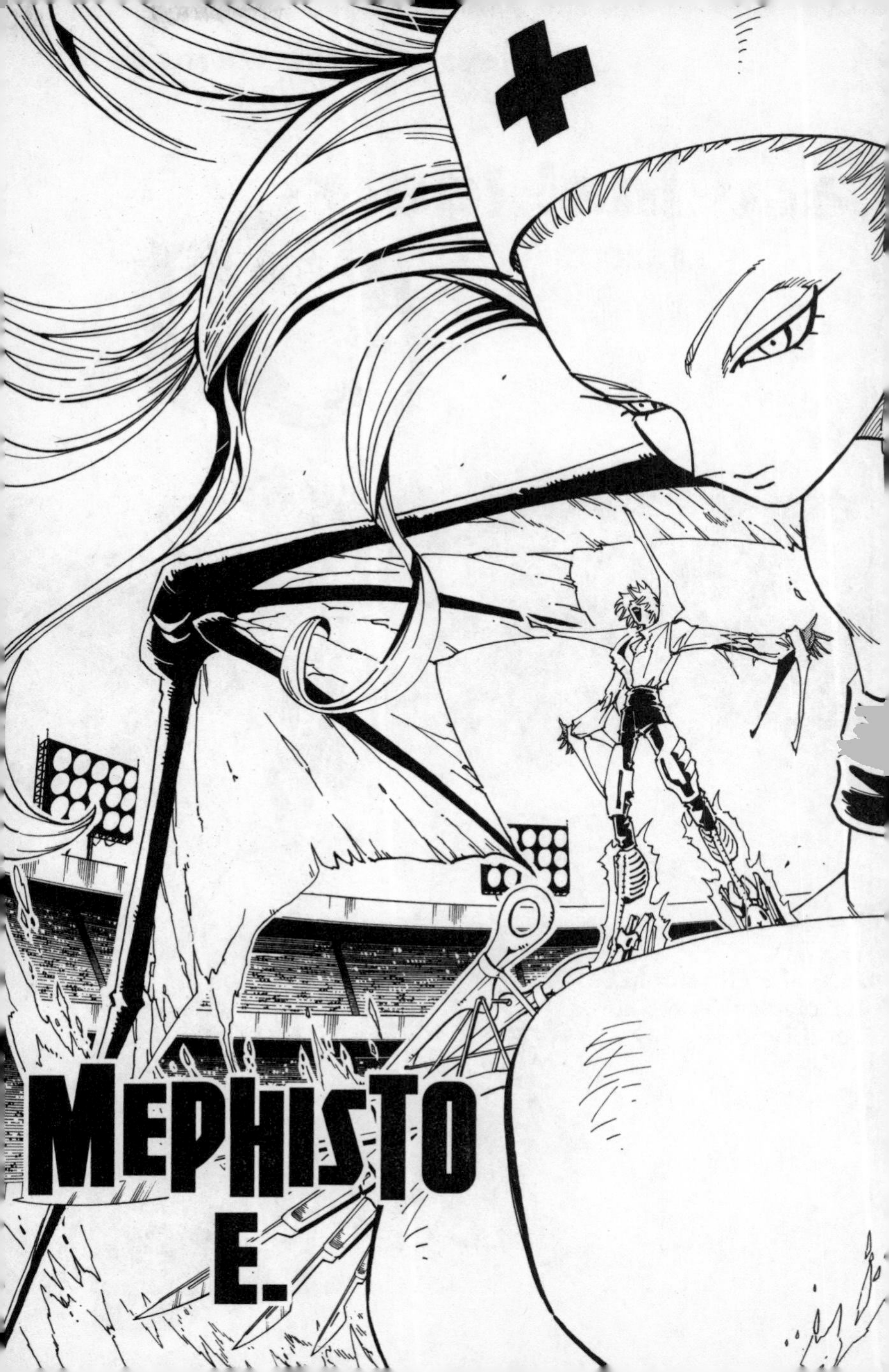
MEPHISTO
E.

ardimahide

July 2001

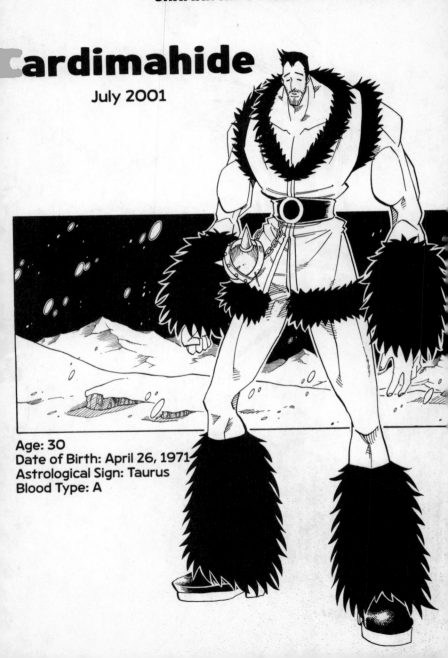

Age: 30
Date of Birth: April 26, 1971
Astrological Sign: Taurus
Blood Type: A

Chapter 131:

Bedeviled

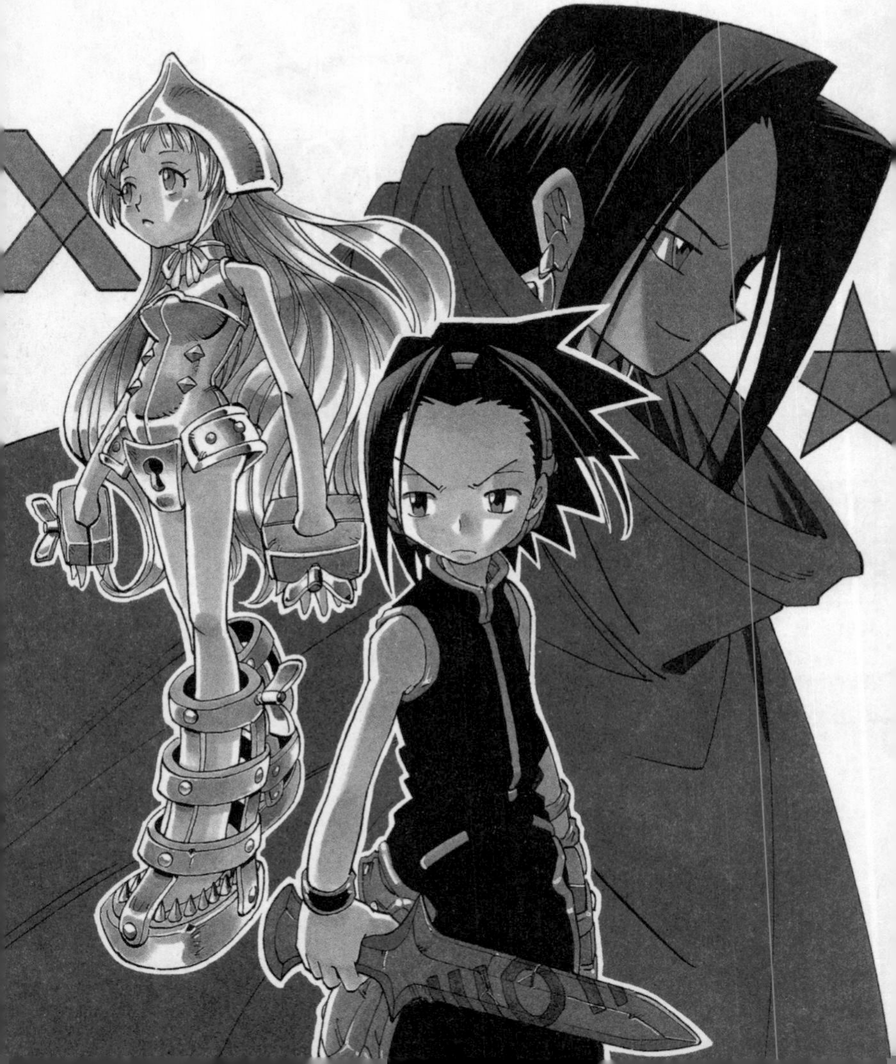

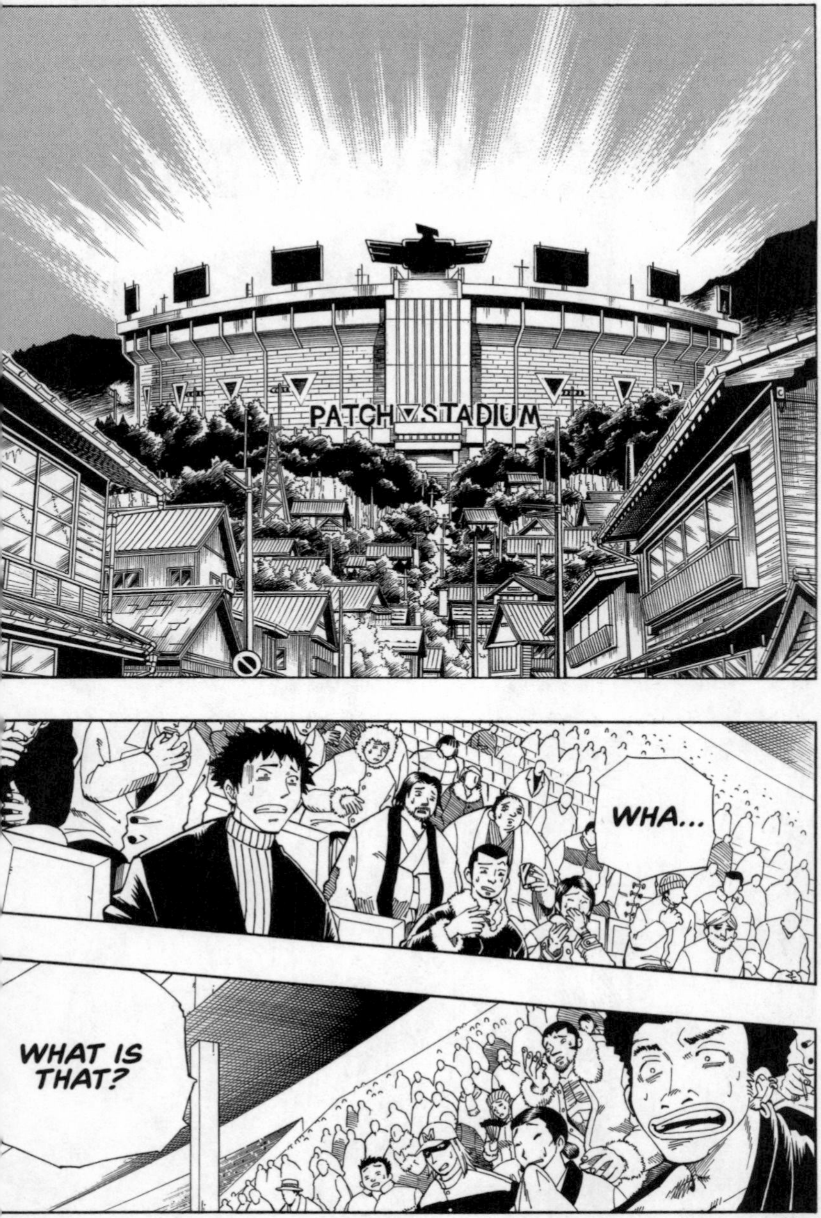
PATCH▽STADIUM
WHA...
WHAT IS THAT?

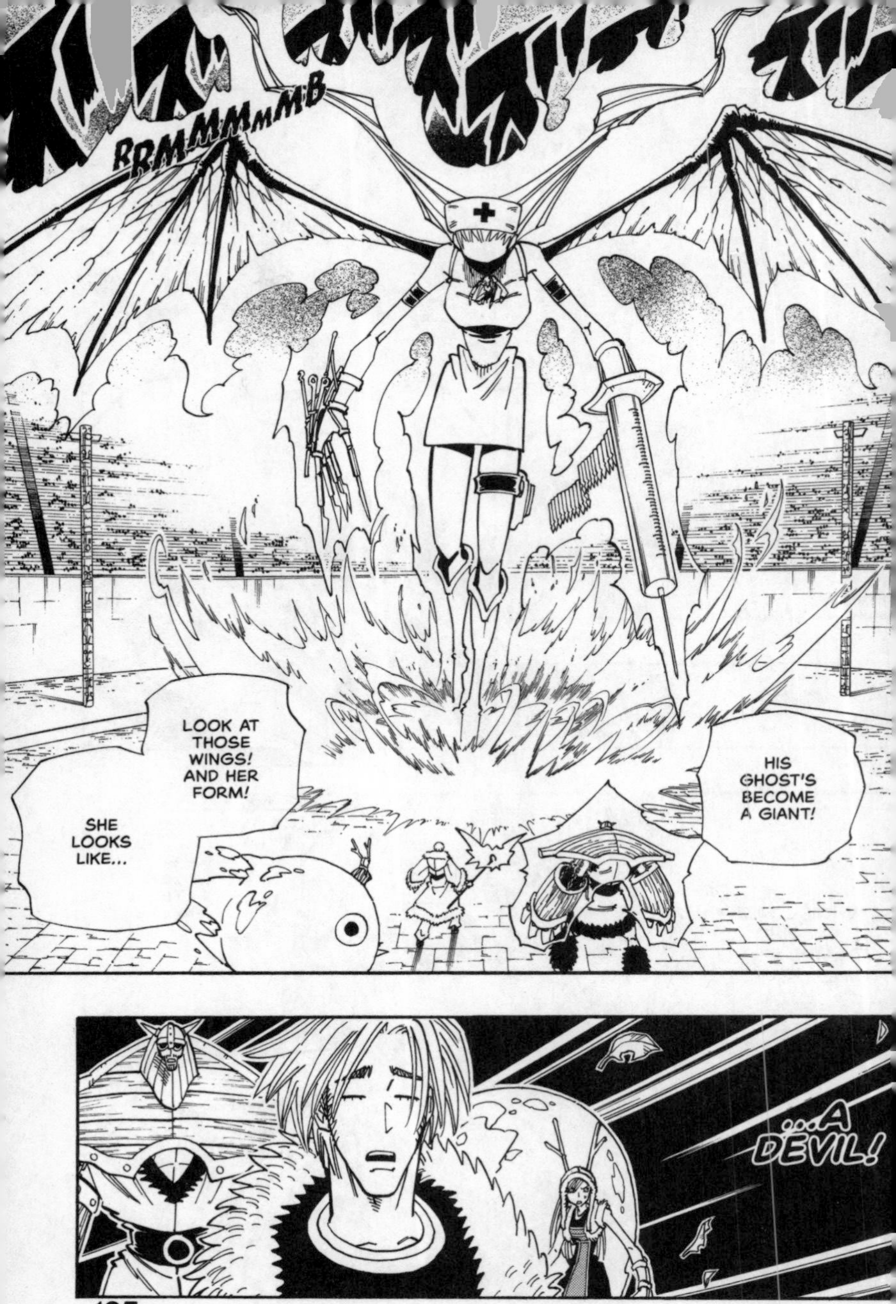
BRMMMMMMB
HIS GHOST'S BECOME A GIANT!
LOOK AT THOSE WINGS! AND HER FORM!
SHE LOOKS LIKE...
...A DEVIL!

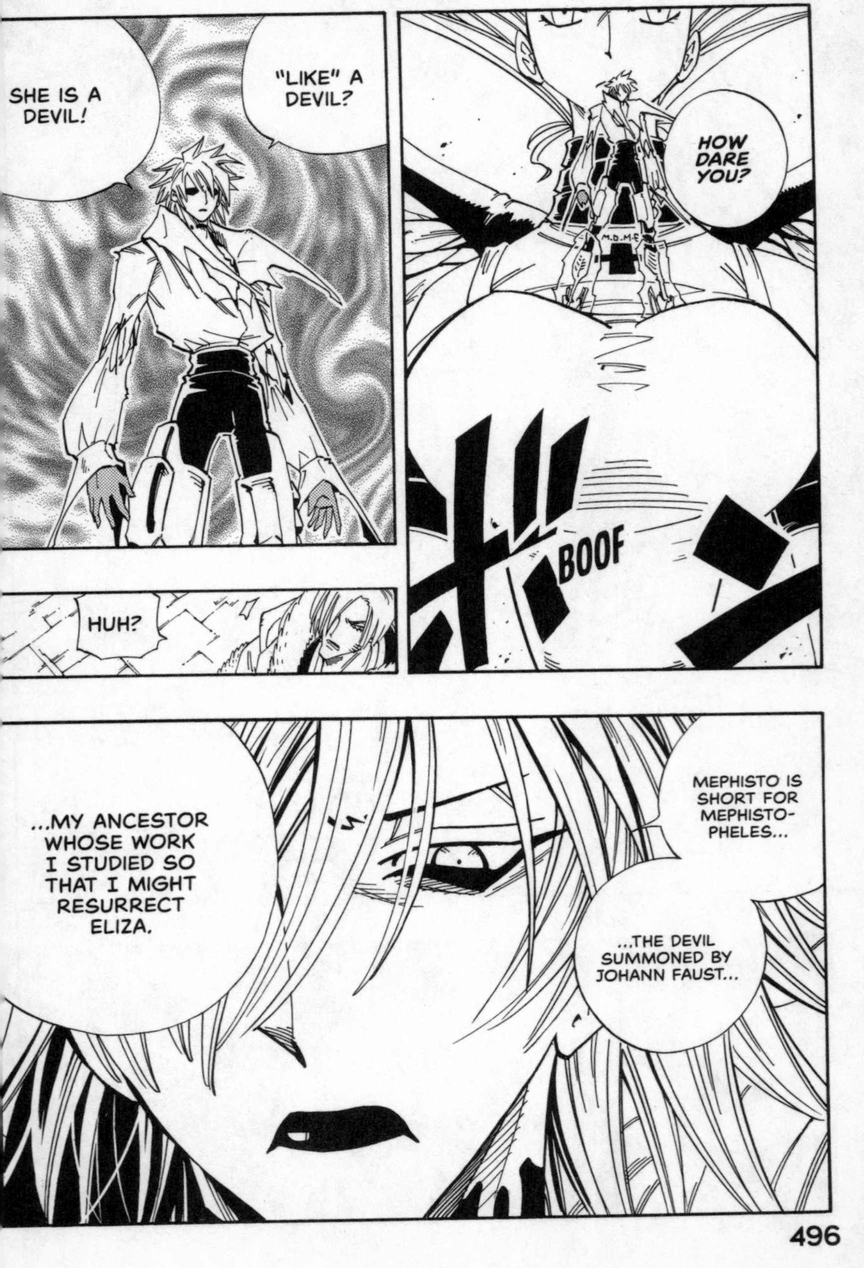
HOW DARE YOU?
BOOF
"LIKE" A DEVIL?
SHE IS A DEVIL!
HUH?
MEPHISTO IS SHORT FOR MEPHISTO-PHELES...
...THE DEVIL SUMMONED BY JOHANN FAUST...
...MY ANCESTOR WHOSE WORK I STUDIED SO THAT I MIGHT RESURRECT ELIZA.

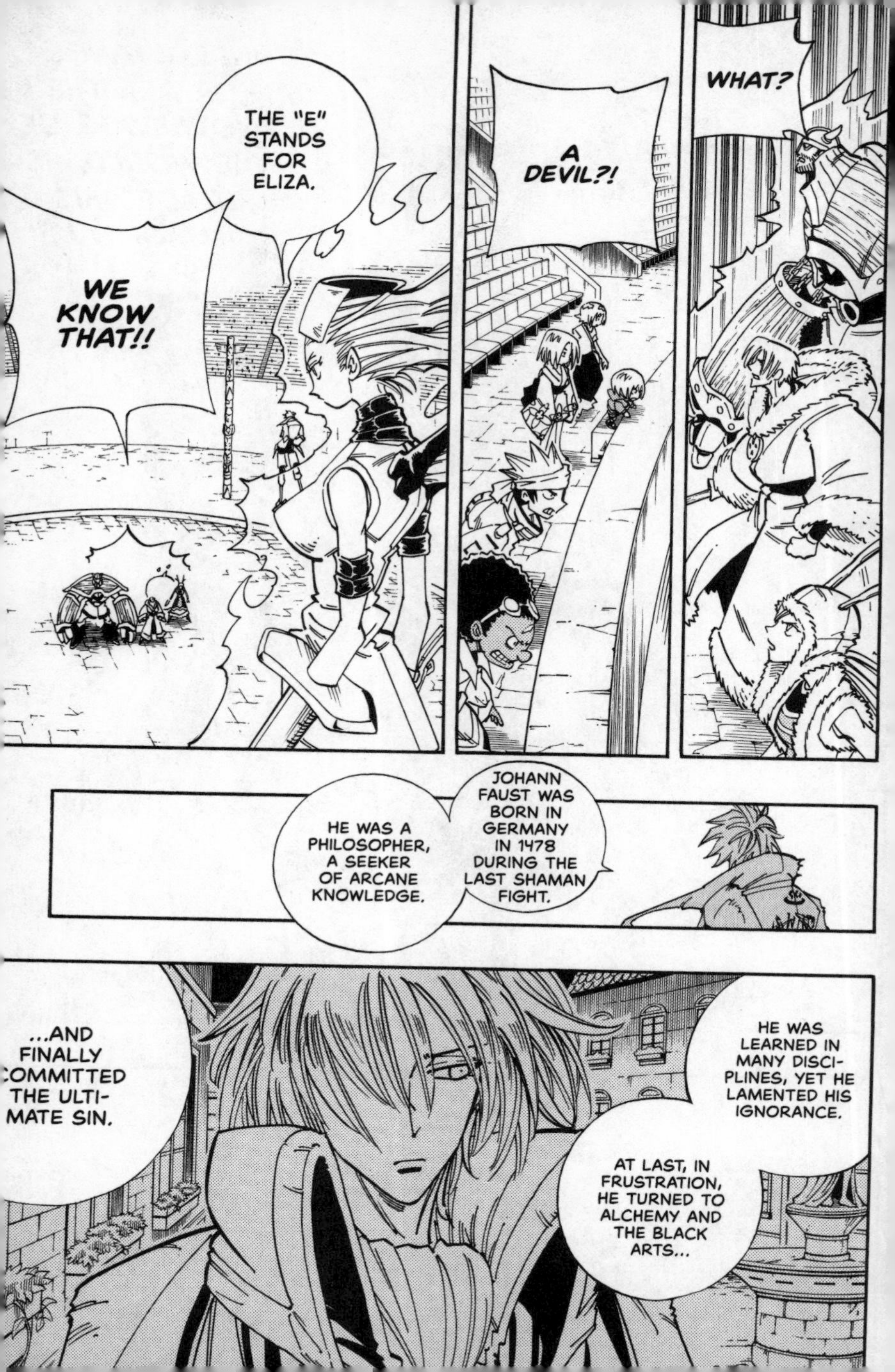

WHAT?
A DEVIL?!
THE "E" STANDS FOR ELIZA.
WE KNOW THAT!!
JOHANN FAUST WAS BORN IN GERMANY IN 1478 DURING THE LAST SHAMAN FIGHT.
HE WAS A PHILOSOPHER, A SEEKER OF ARCANE KNOWLEDGE.
HE WAS LEARNED IN MANY DISCI- PLINES, YET HE LAMENTED HIS IGNORANCE.
AT LAST, IN FRUSTRATION, HE TURNED TO ALCHEMY AND THE BLACK ARTS...
...AND FINALLY COMMITTED THE ULTI- MATE SIN.

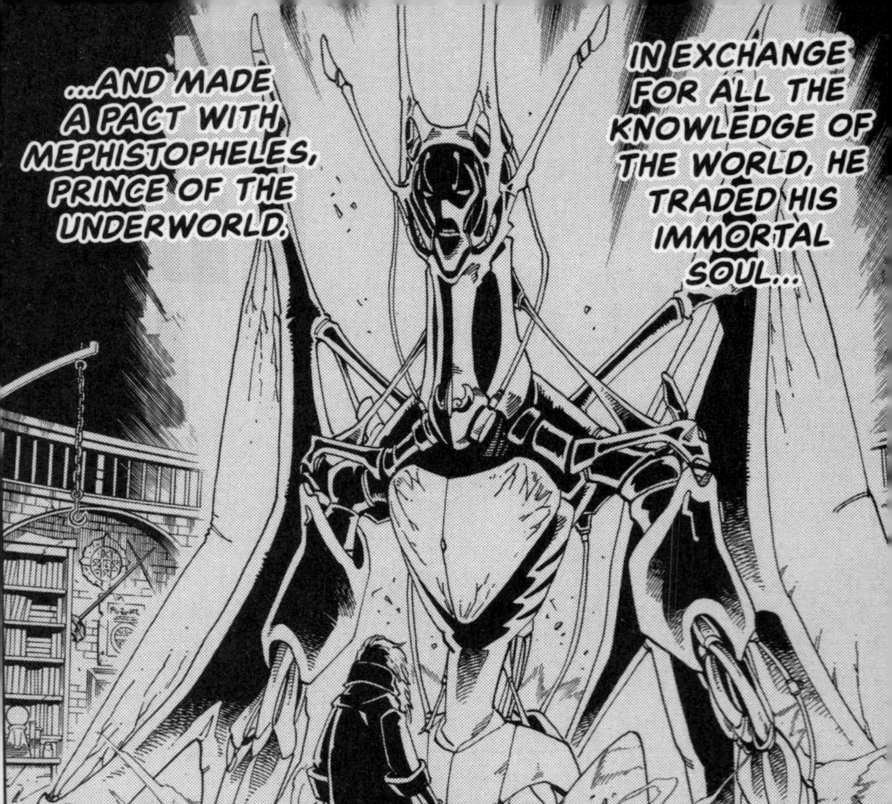
...AND MADE A PACT WITH MEPHISTOPHELES, PRINCE OF THE UNDERWORLD.
IN EXCHANGE FOR ALL THE KNOWLEDGE OF THE WORLD, HE TRADED HIS IMMORTAL SOUL...

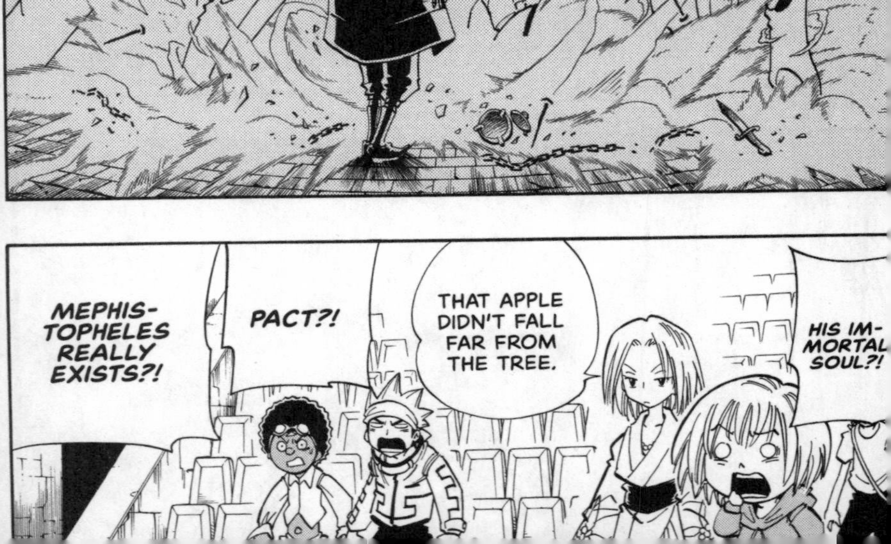
MEPHIS-TOPHELES REALLY EXISTS?!
PACT?!
THAT APPLE DIDN'T FALL FAR FROM THE TREE.
HIS IM-MORTAL SOUL?!

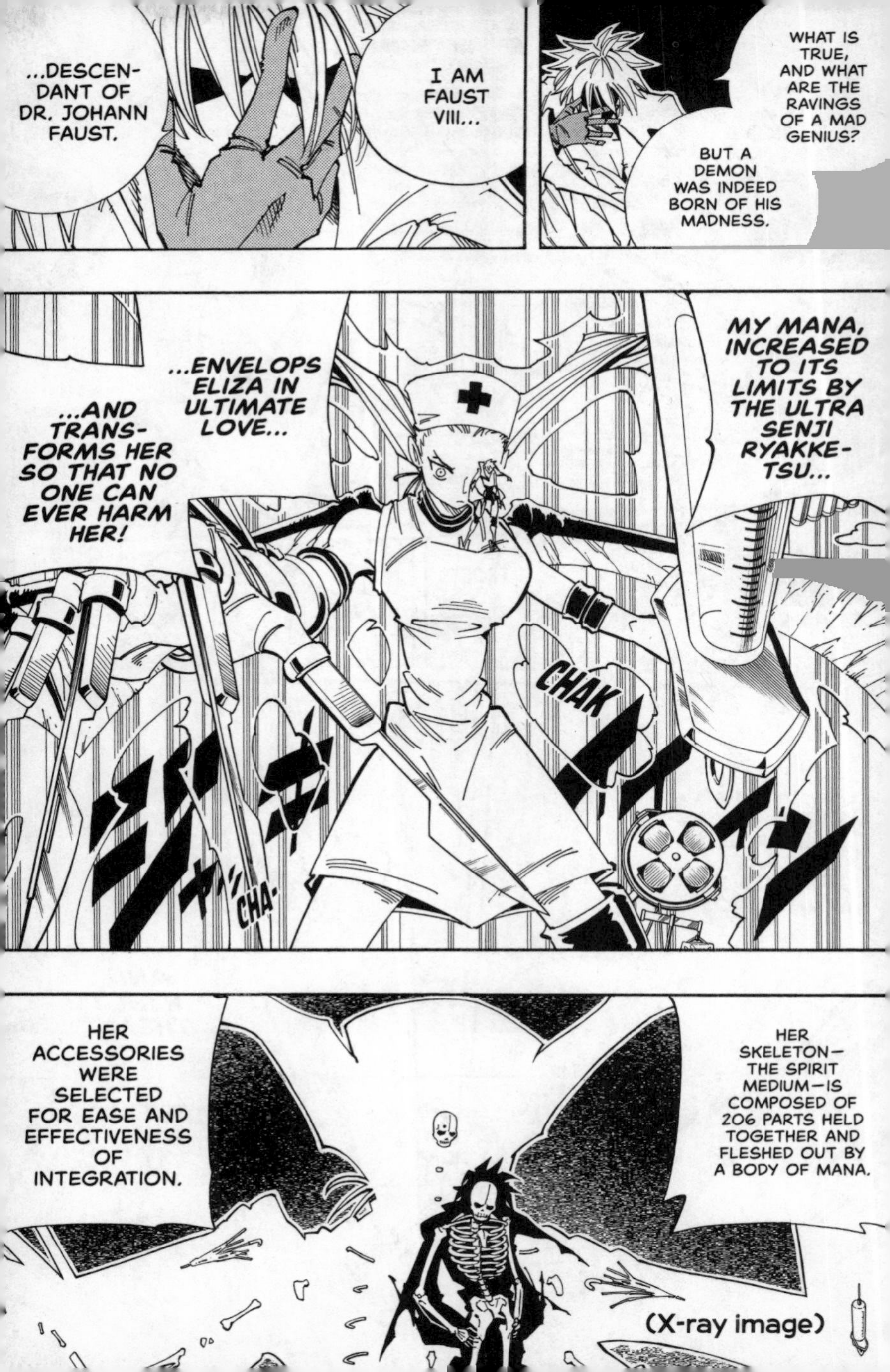

WHAT IS TRUE, AND WHAT ARE THE RAVINGS OF A MAD GENIUS?
BUT A DEMON WAS INDEED BORN OF HIS MADNESS.
I AM FAUST VIII...
...DESCENDANT OF DR. JOHANN FAUST.
MY MANA, INCREASED TO ITS LIMITS BY THE ULTRA SENJI RYAKKETSU...
...ENVELOPS ELIZA IN ULTIMATE LOVE...
...AND TRANSFORMS HER SO THAT NO ONE CAN EVER HARM HER!
CHAK
CHA-
HER SKELETON—THE SPIRIT MEDIUM—IS COMPOSED OF 206 PARTS HELD TOGETHER AND FLESHED OUT BY A BODY OF MANA.
HER ACCESSORIES WERE SELECTED FOR EASE AND EFFECTIVENESS OF INTEGRATION.
(X-ray image)

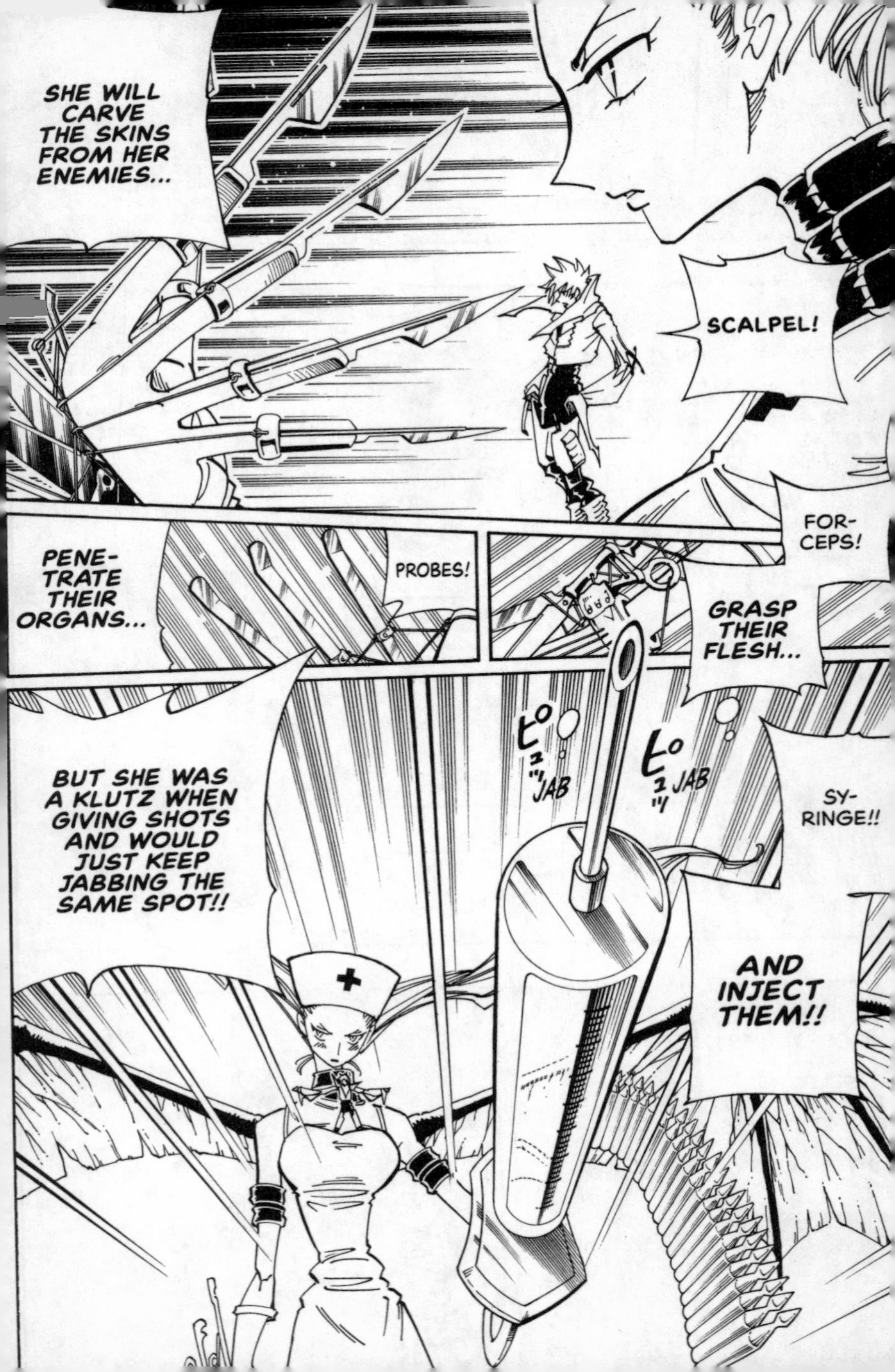

SCALPEL!
SHE WILL CARVE THE SKINS FROM HER ENEMIES...
FOR-CEPS!
GRASP THEIR FLESH...
PROBES!
PENE-TRATE THEIR ORGANS...
SY-RINGE!!
AND INJECT THEM!!
ピュッ JAB
ピュッ JAB
BUT SHE WAS A KLUTZ WHEN GIVING SHOTS AND WOULD JUST KEEP JABBING THE SAME SPOT!!

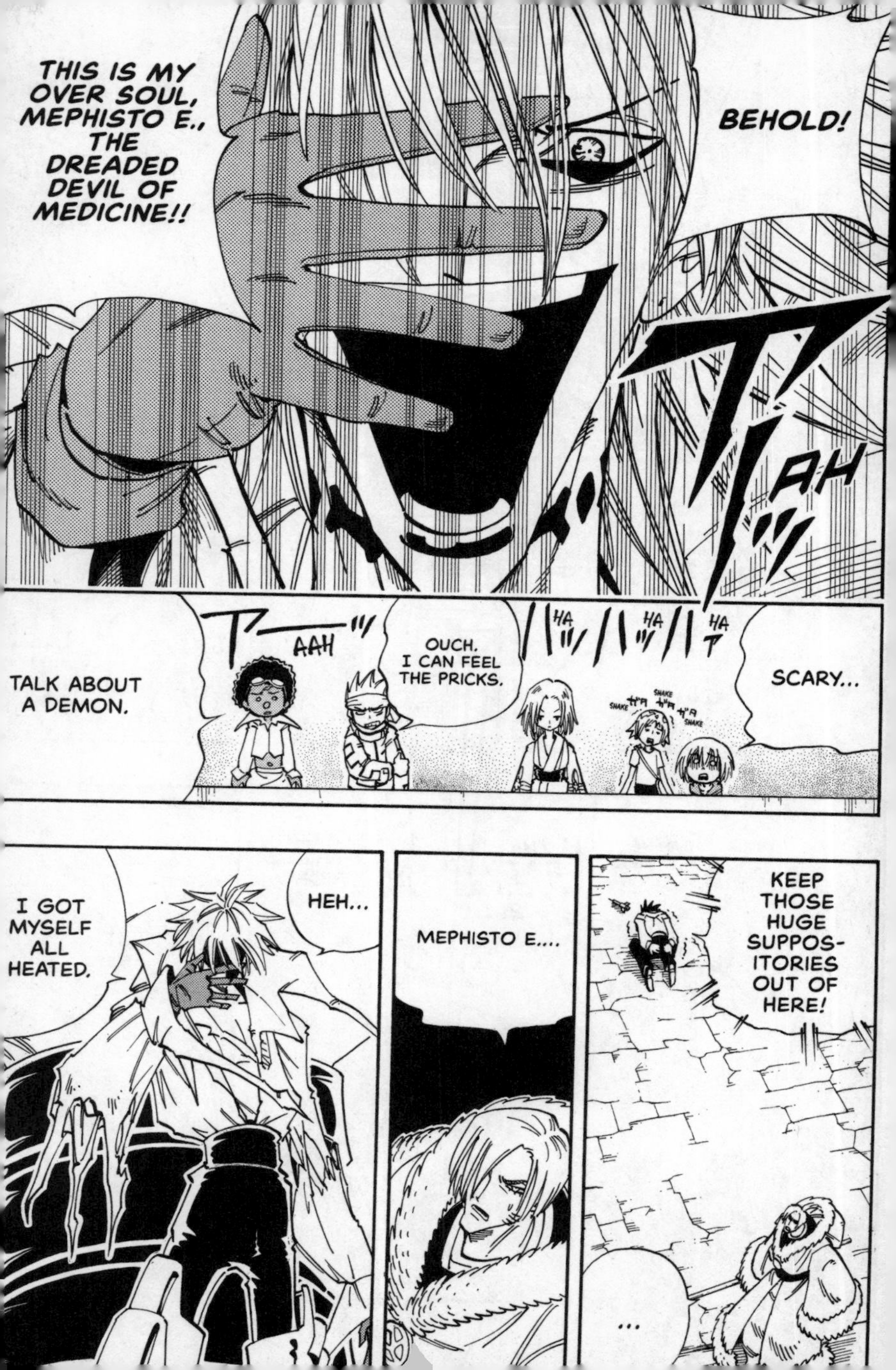

BEHOLD!
THIS IS MY OVER SOUL, MEPHISTO E., THE DREADED DEVIL OF MEDICINE!!
AH
SCARY...
SHAKE SHAKE SHAKE
HA HA HA
OUCH. I CAN FEEL THE PRICKS.
AAH
TALK ABOUT A DEMON.
KEEP THOSE HUGE SUPPOS-ITORIES OUT OF HERE!
...
MEPHISTO E....
HEH...
I GOT MYSELF ALL HEATED.

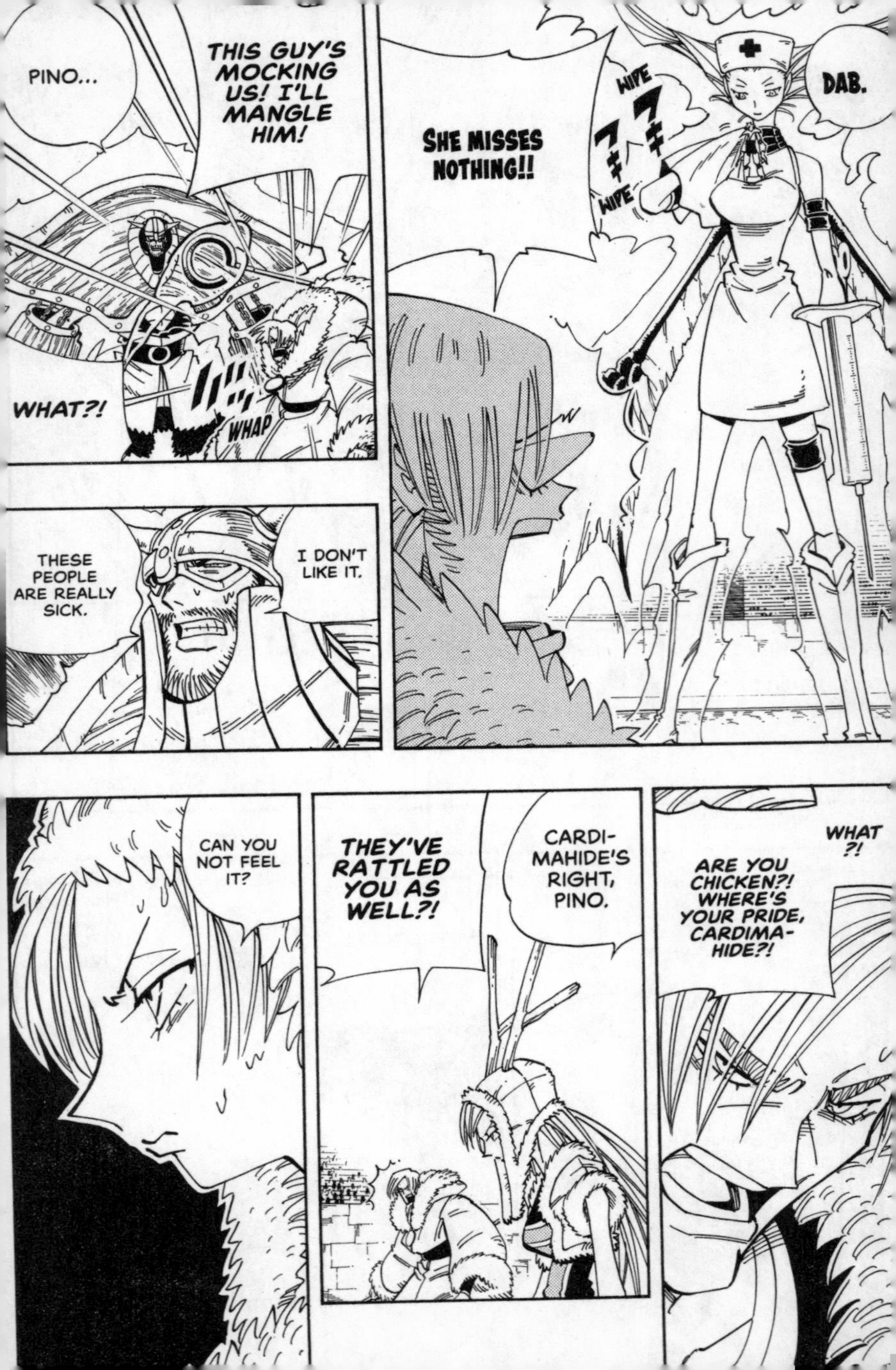
DAB.
WIPE
WIPE
SHE MISSES NOTHING!!
THIS GUY'S MOCKING US! I'LL MANGLE HIM!
PINO...
WHAT?!
WHAP
I DON'T LIKE IT.
THESE PEOPLE ARE REALLY SICK.
WHAT?!
ARE YOU CHICKEN?! WHERE'S YOUR PRIDE, CARDIMA-HIDE?!
CARDI-MAHIDE'S RIGHT, PINO.
THEY'VE RATTLED YOU AS WELL?!
CAN YOU NOT FEEL IT?

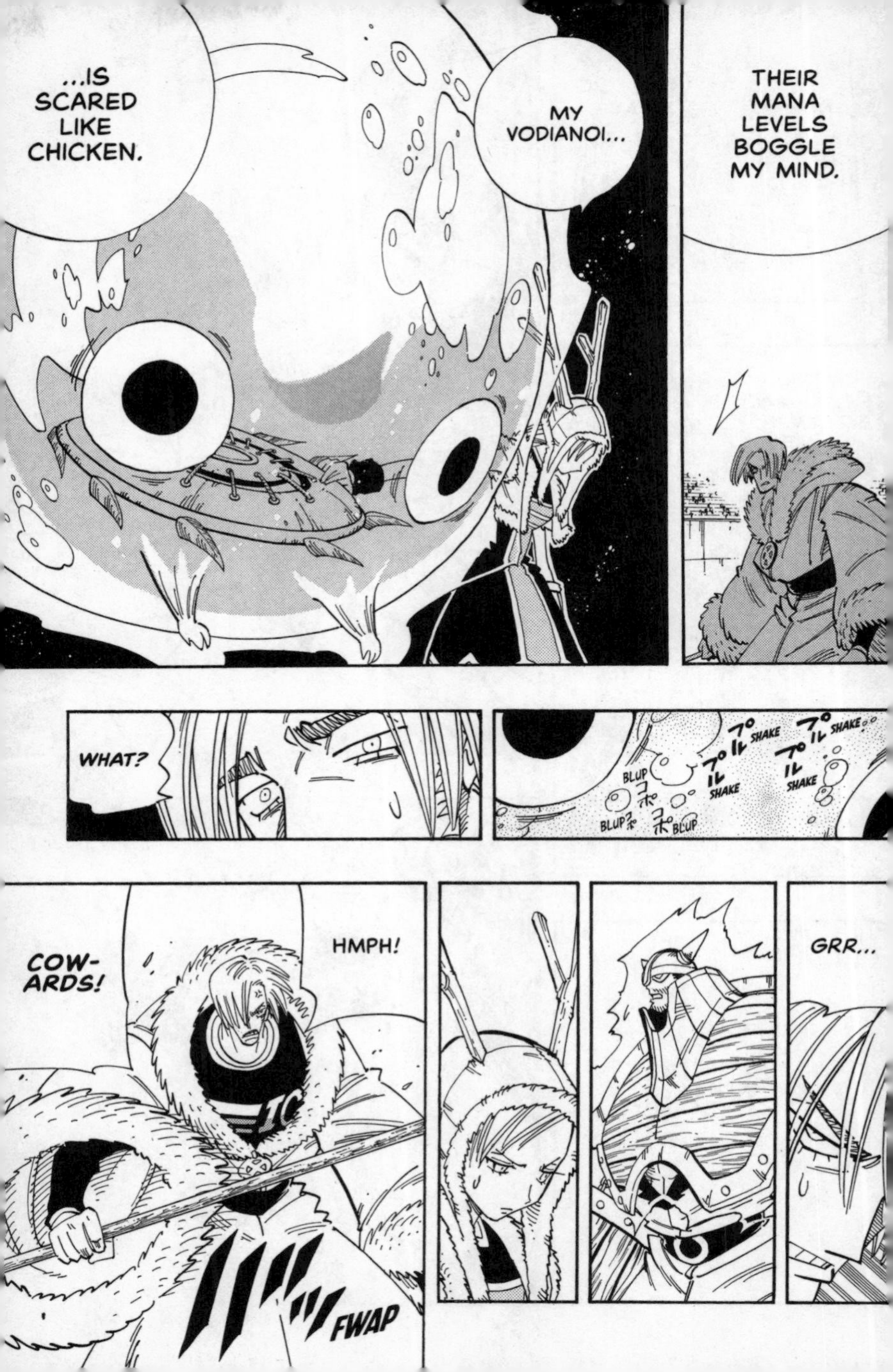
THEIR MANA LEVELS BOGGLE MY MIND.
MY VODIANOI...
...IS SCARED LIKE CHICKEN.
SHAKE SHAKE SHAKE SHAKE
BLUP BLUP BLUP
WHAT?
GRR...
HMPH!
COW-ARDS!
FWAP

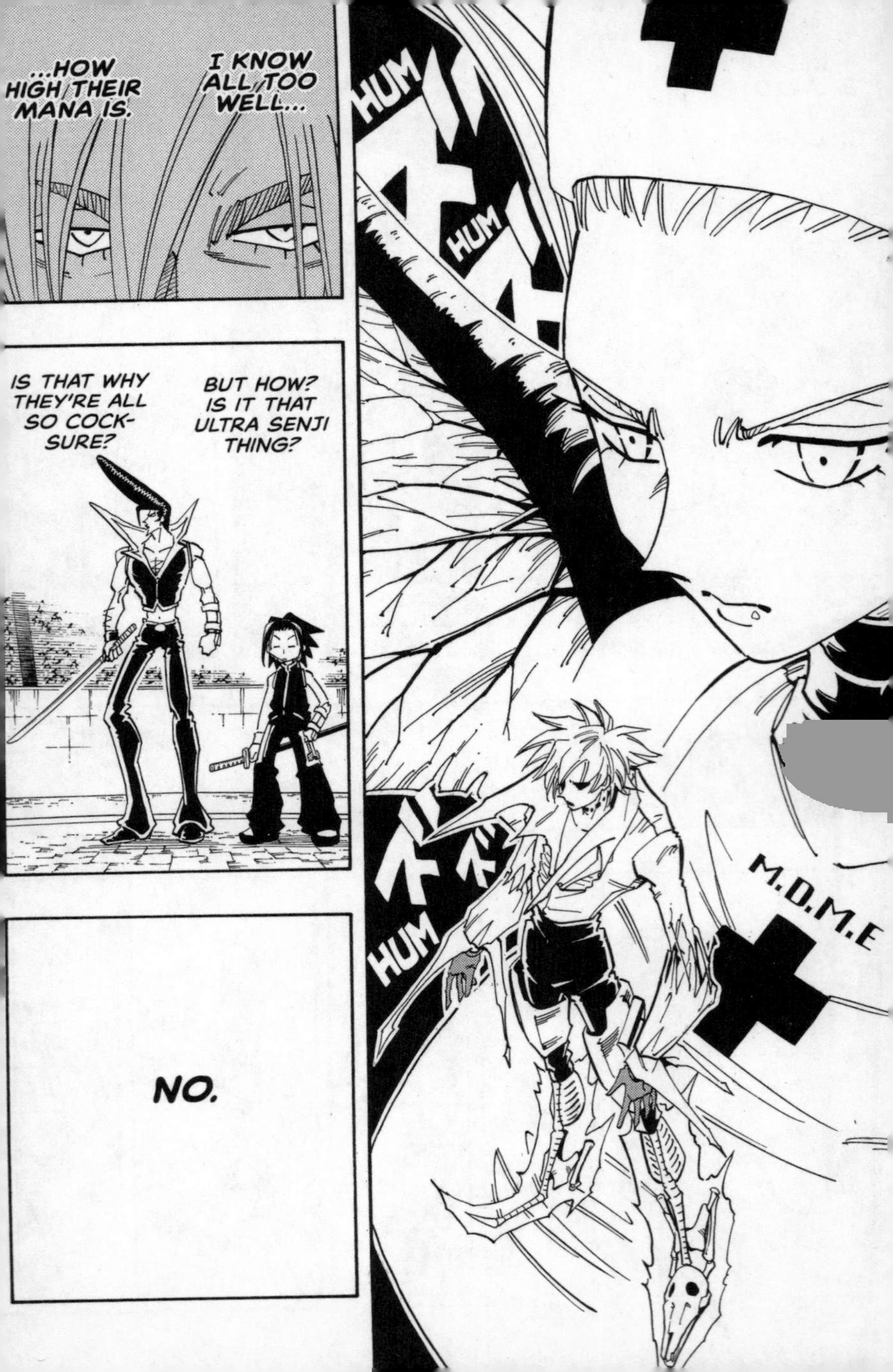
HUM
HUM
HUM
M.D.M.E
I KNOW ALL TOO WELL...
...HOW HIGH THEIR MANA IS.
BUT HOW? IS IT THAT ULTRA SENJI THING?
IS THAT WHY THEY'RE ALL SO COCK-SURE?
NO.

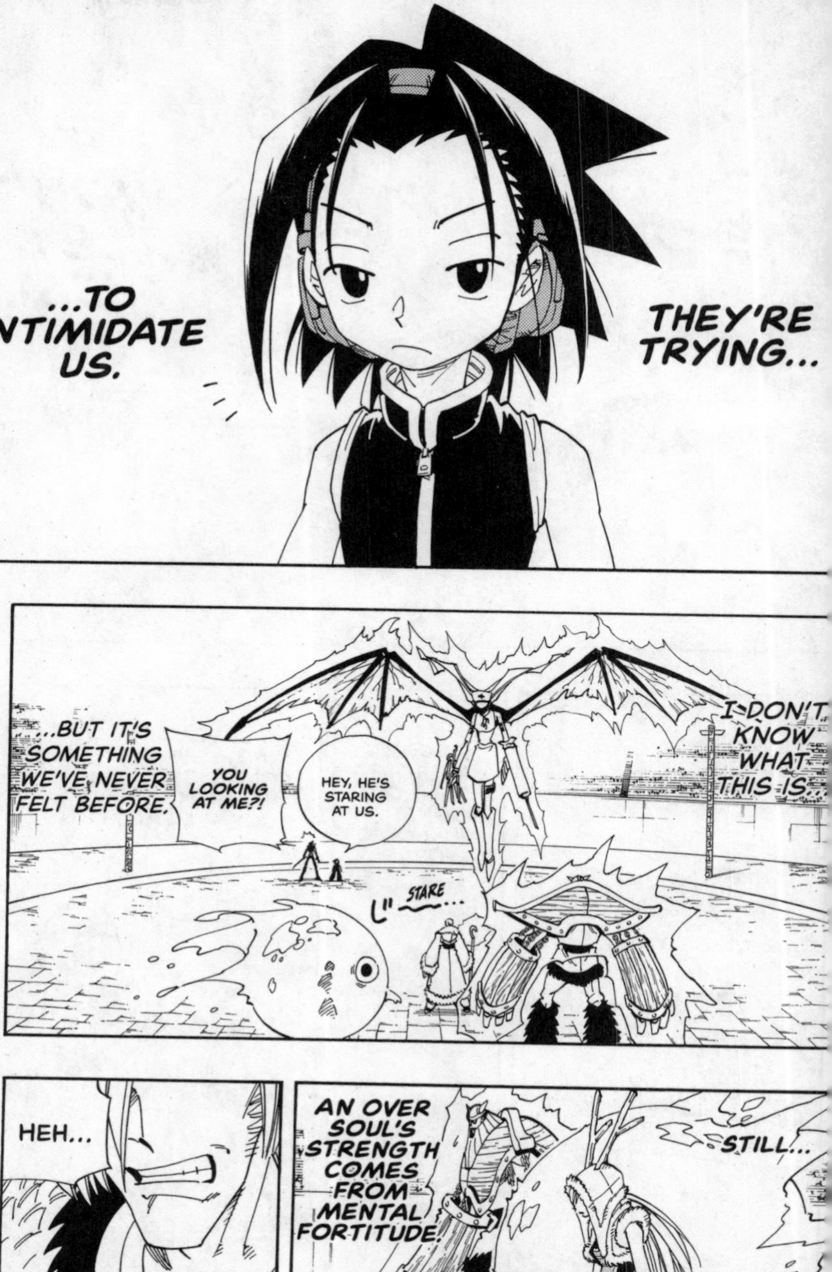
THEY'RE TRYING...
...TO INTIMIDATE US.
I DON'T KNOW WHAT THIS IS...
HEY, HE'S STARING AT US.
YOU LOOKING AT ME?!
...BUT IT'S SOMETHING WE'VE NEVER FELT BEFORE.
STARE...
STILL...
AN OVER SOUL'S STRENGTH COMES FROM MENTAL FORTITUDE.
HEH...

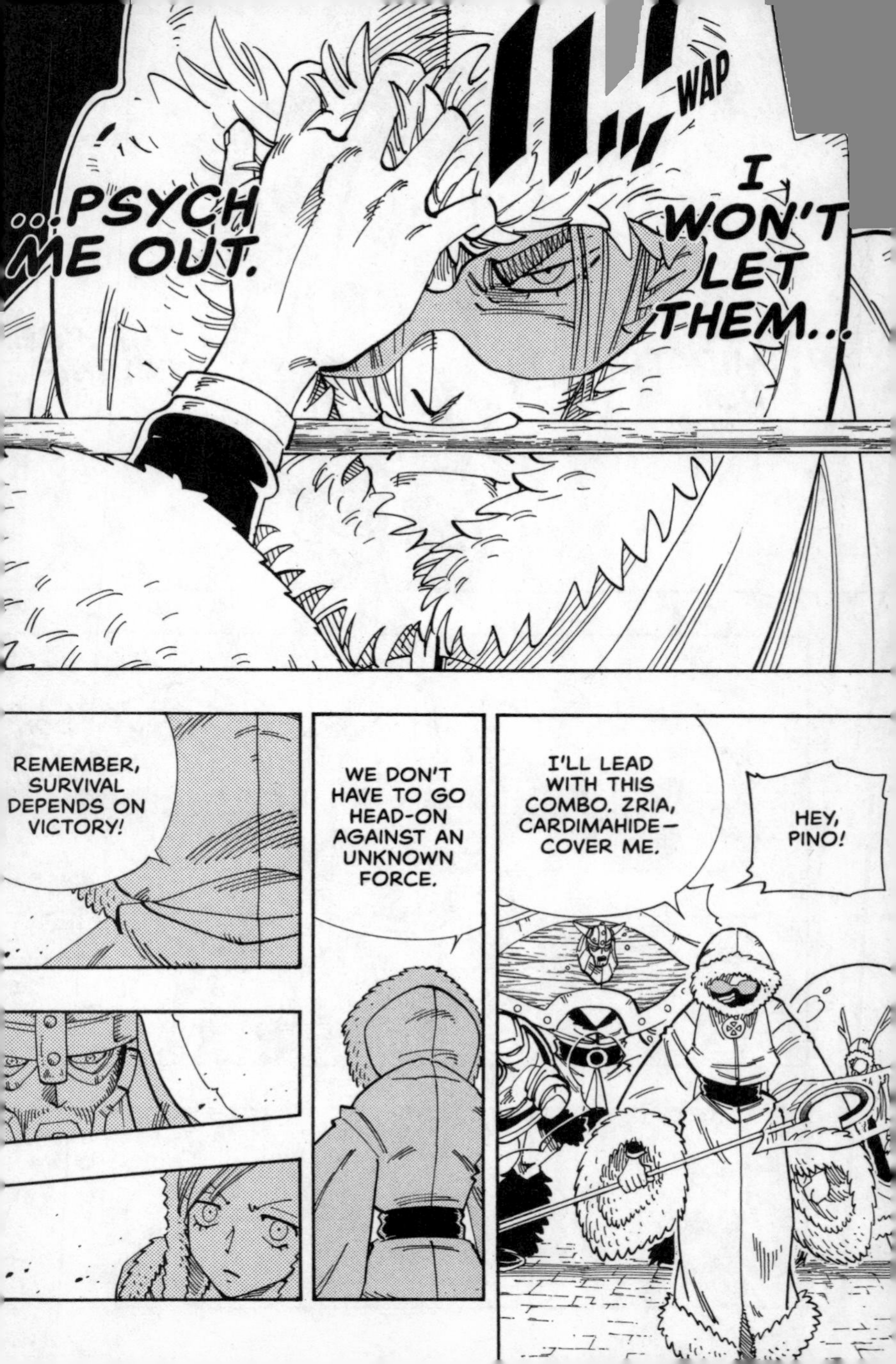
WAP
I WON'T LET THEM...
...PSYCH ME OUT.
HEY, PINO!
I'LL LEAD WITH THIS COMBO. ZRIA, CARDIMAHIDE— COVER ME.
WE DON'T HAVE TO GO HEAD-ON AGAINST AN UNKNOWN FORCE.
REMEMBER, SURVIVAL DEPENDS ON VICTORY!

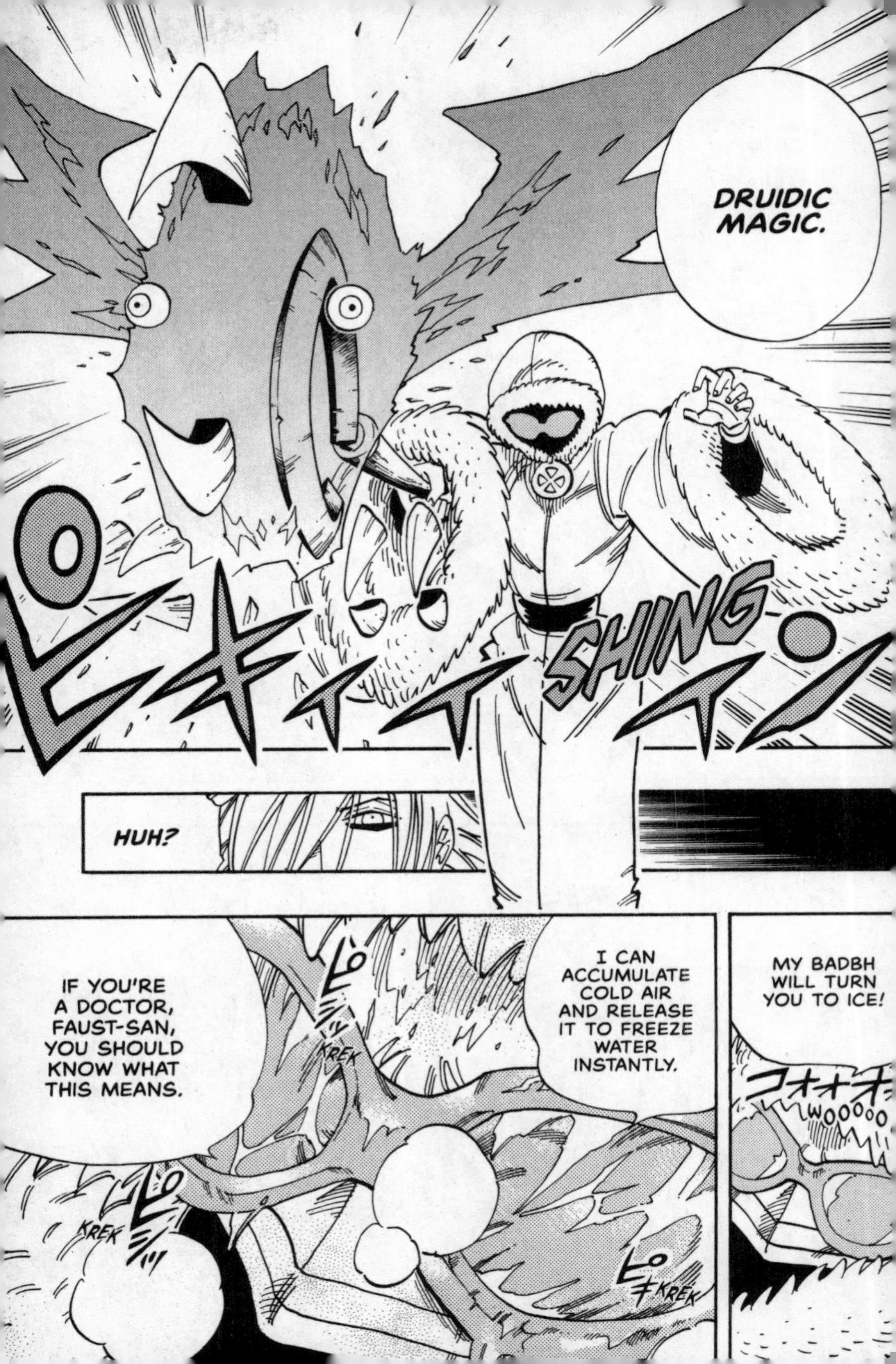
DRUIDIC MAGIC.
SHING
HUH?
MY BADBH WILL TURN YOU TO ICE!
WOOOOO
I CAN ACCUMULATE COLD AIR AND RELEASE IT TO FREEZE WATER INSTANTLY.
IF YOU'RE A DOCTOR, FAUST-SAN, YOU SHOULD KNOW WHAT THIS MEANS.
KREK
KREK
KREK

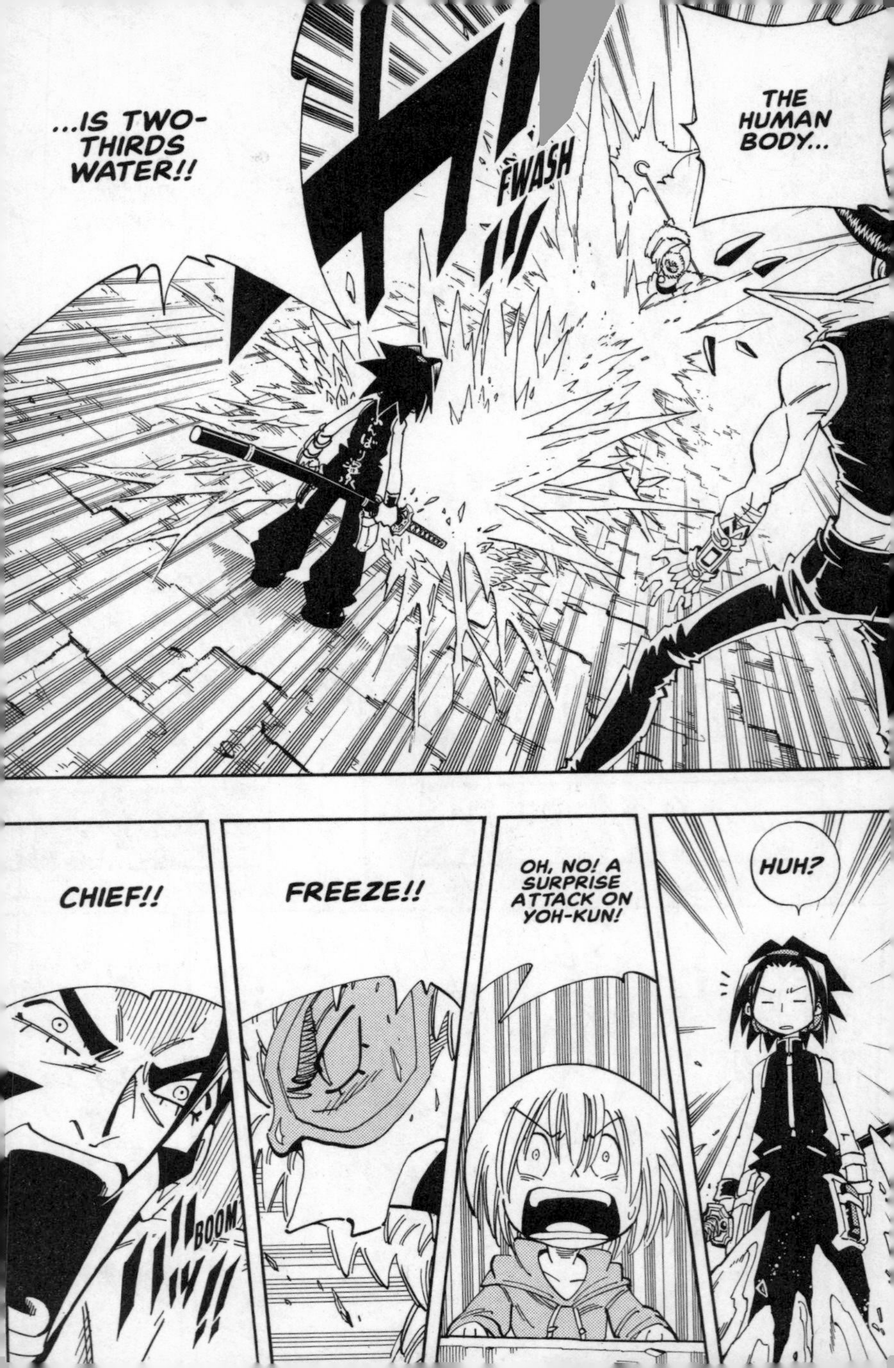
THE HUMAN BODY...
FWASH
...IS TWO-THIRDS WATER!!
HUH?
OH, NO! A SURPRISE ATTACK ON YOH-KUN!
FREEZE!!
CHIEF!!
BOOM

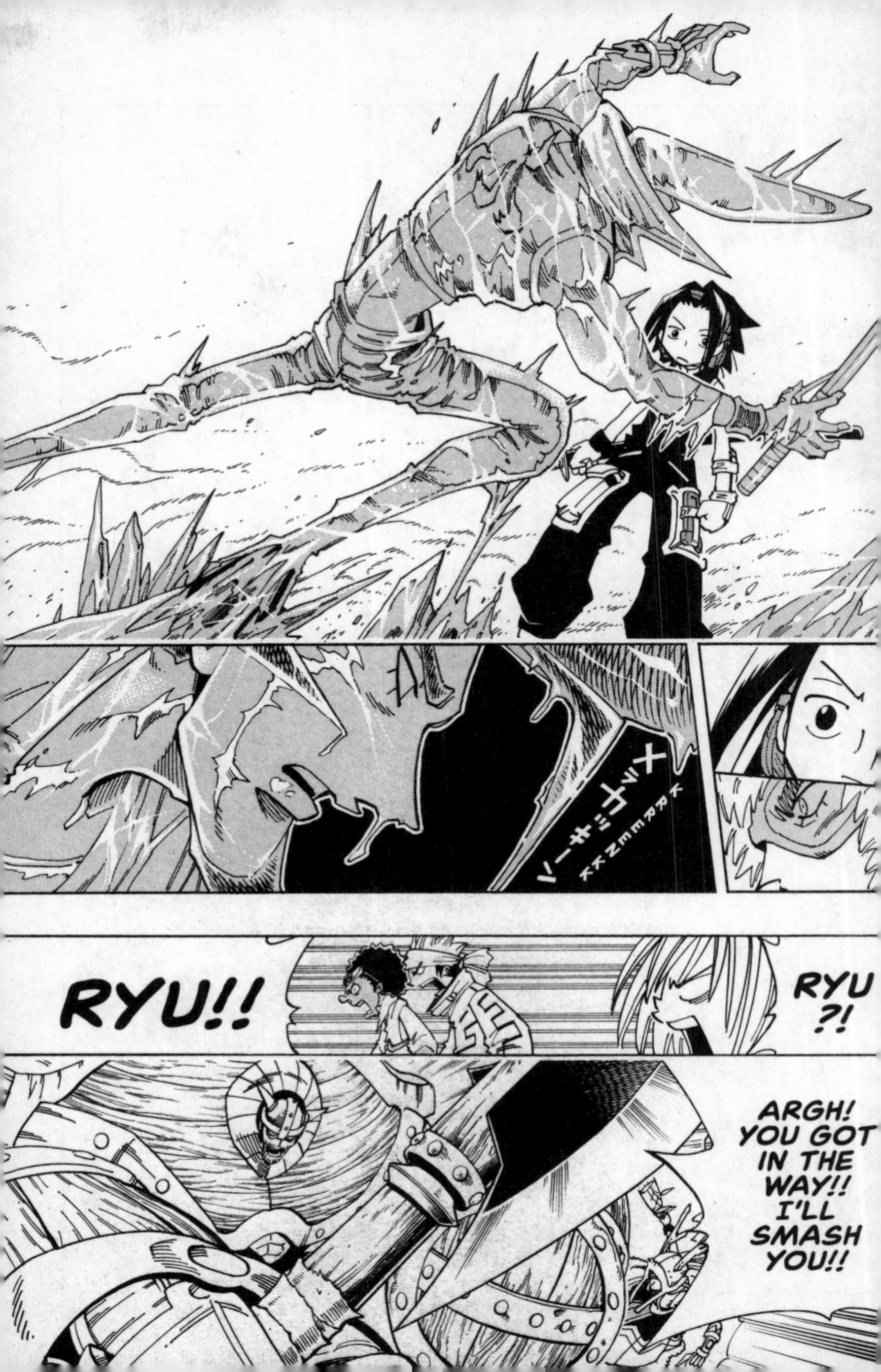
KRREEZKK
RYU ?!
RYU!!
ARGH! YOU GOT IN THE WAY!! I'LL SMASH YOU!!

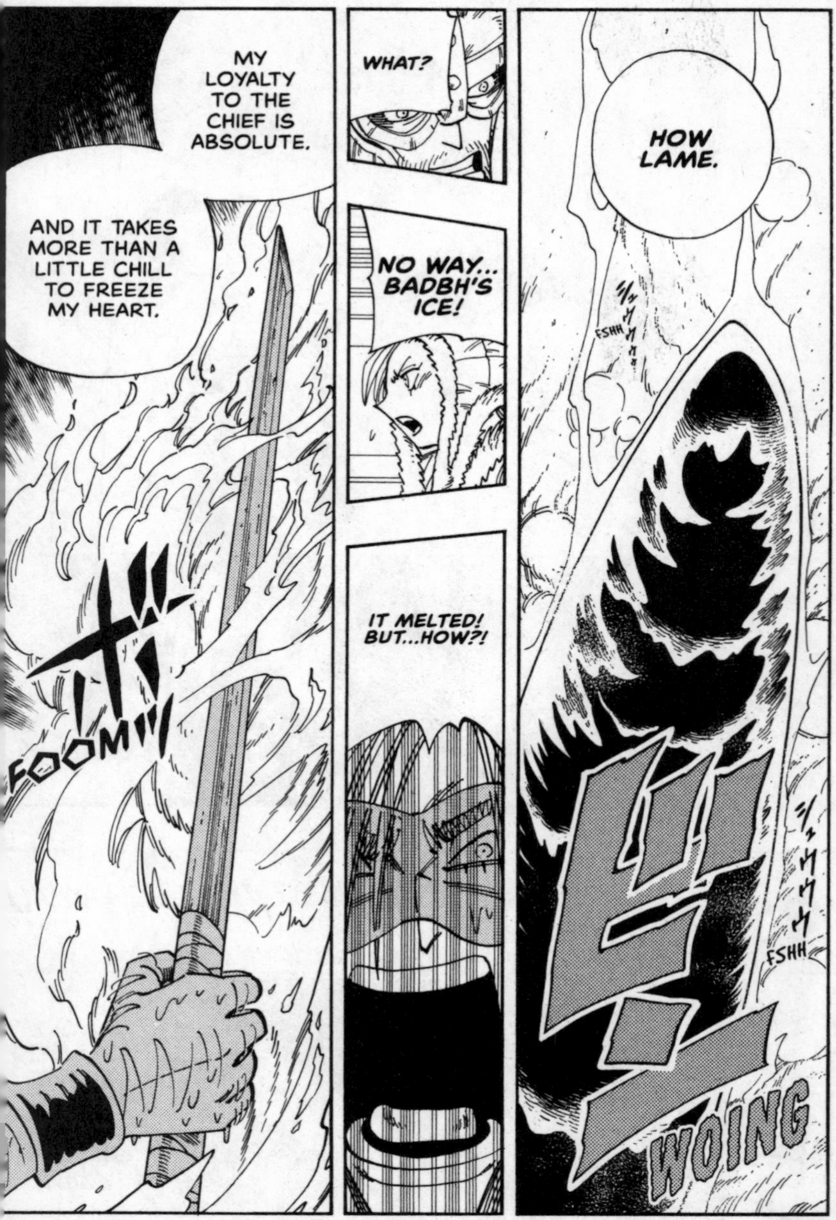
HOW LAME.
FSHH
WOING
FSHH
WHAT?
NO WAY... BADBH'S ICE!
IT MELTED! BUT...HOW?!
MY LOYALTY TO THE CHIEF IS ABSOLUTE.
AND IT TAKES MORE THAN A LITTLE CHILL TO FREEZE MY HEART.
FOOM!!

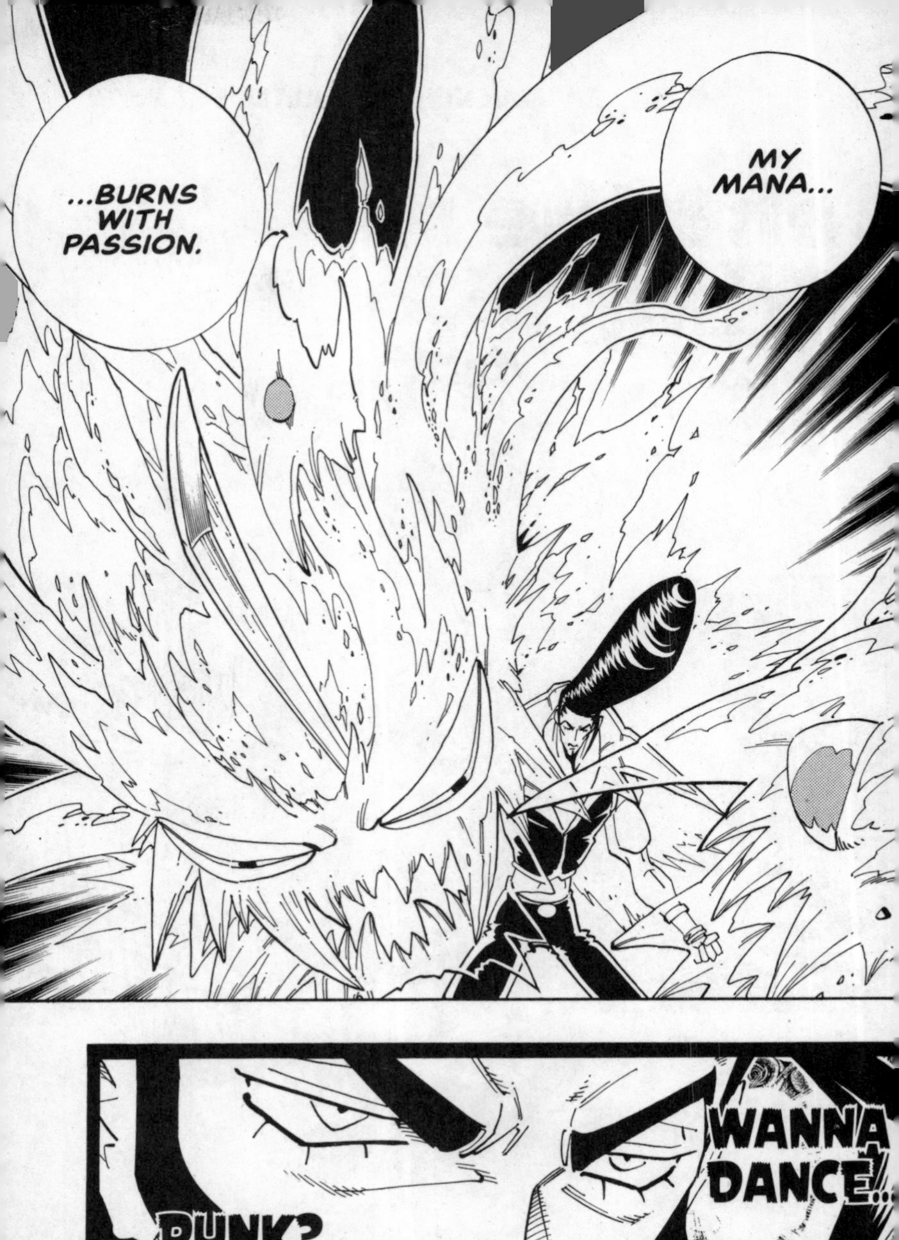
MY MANA...
...BURNS WITH PASSION.
WANNA DANCE...
...PUNK?

SHAMAN KING CHARACTER FILE No.75

Deht the Viking

July 2001

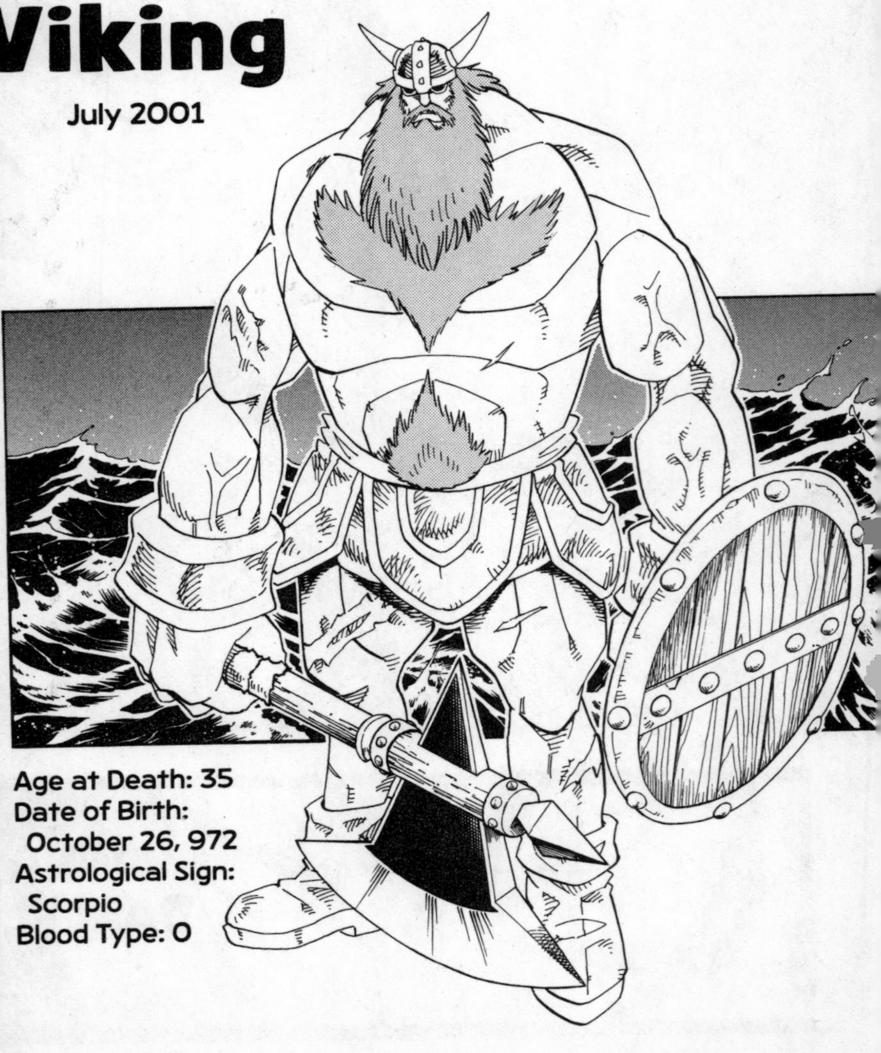

Age at Death: 35
Date of Birth:
October 26, 972
Astrological Sign:
Scorpio
Blood Type: O

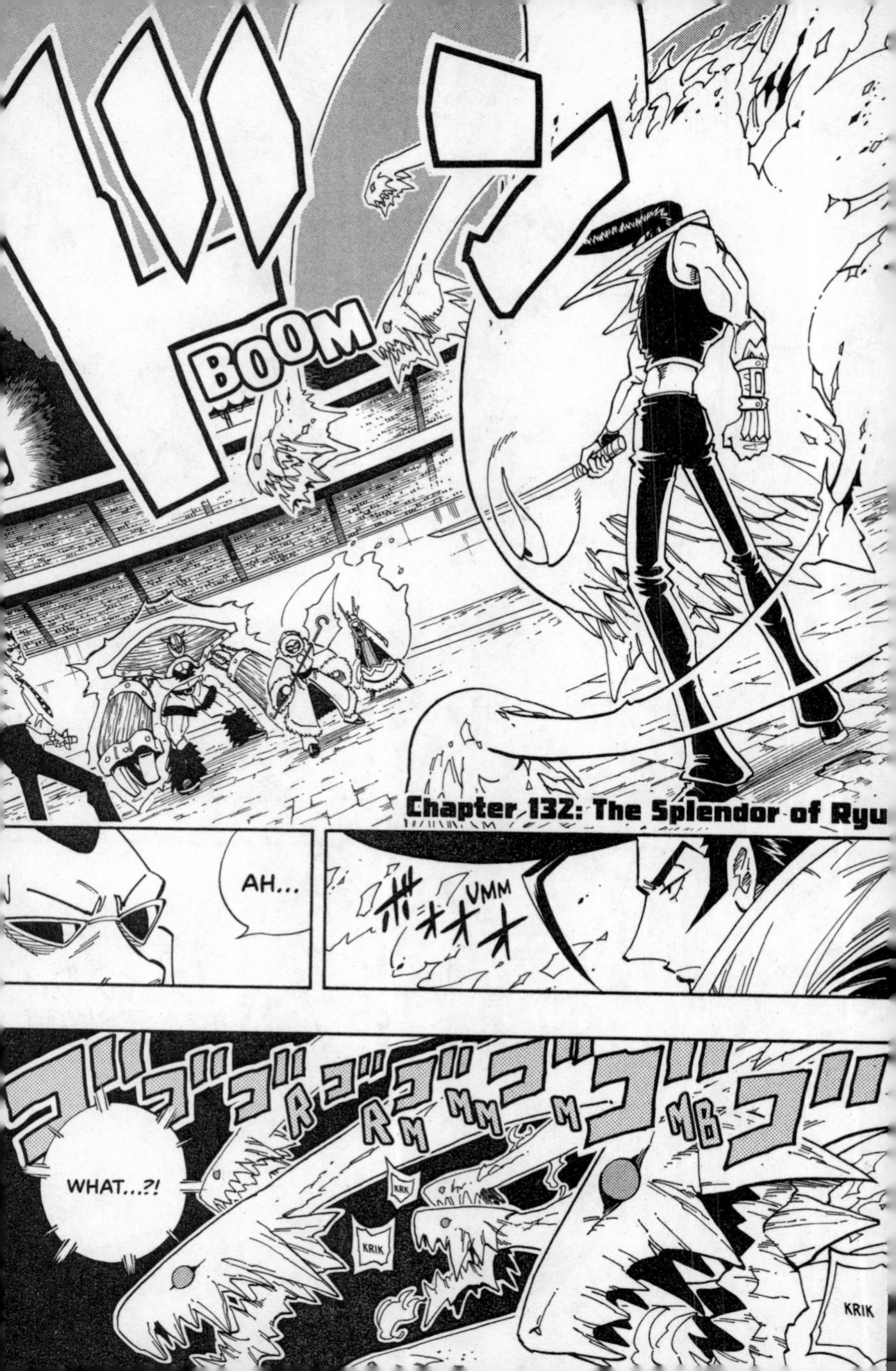
BOOM
Chapter 132: The Splendor of Ryu
VMM
AH...
KRIK
KRIK
KRIK
WHAT...?!

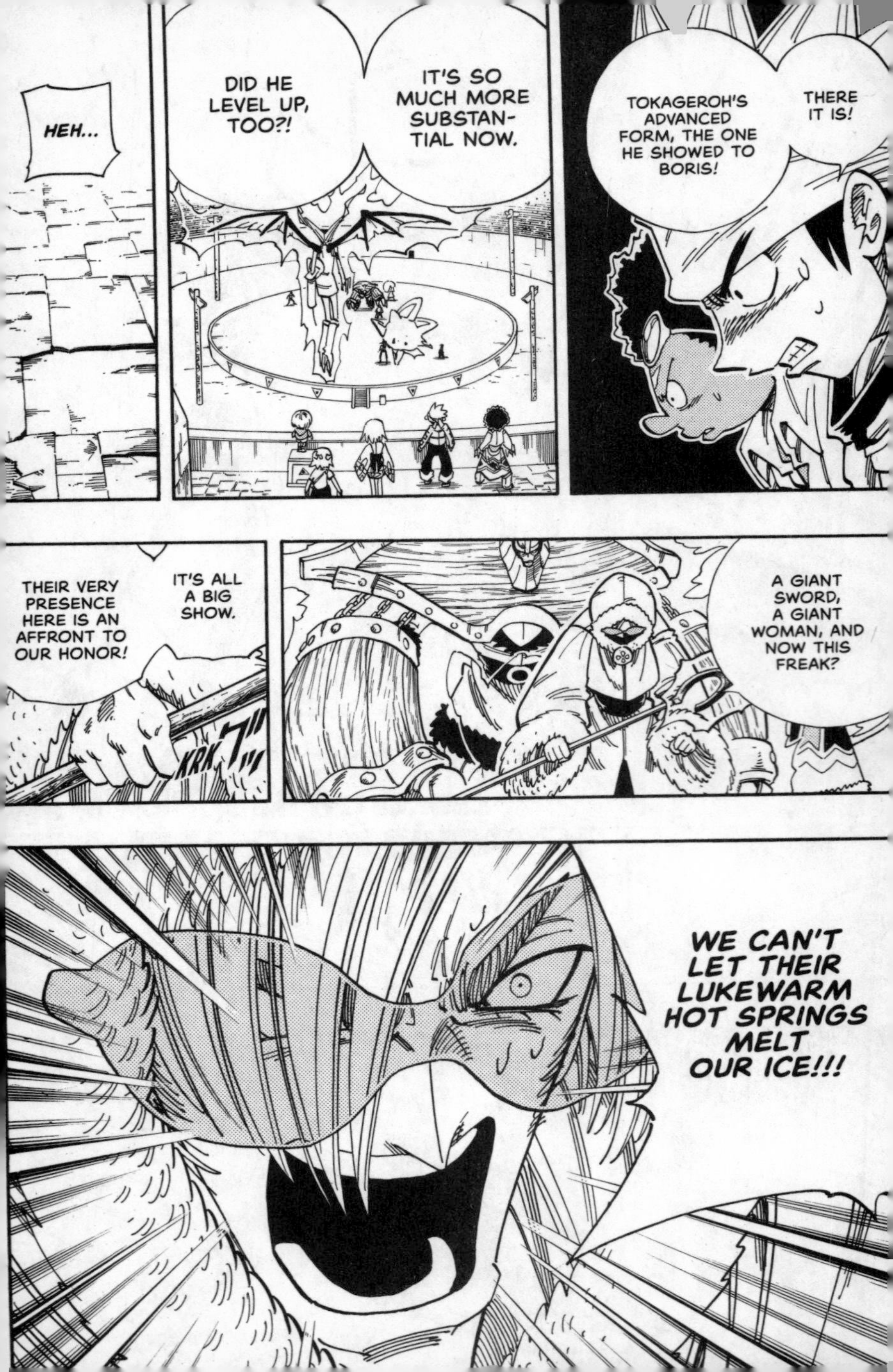
THERE IT IS!
TOKAGEROH'S ADVANCED FORM, THE ONE HE SHOWED TO BORIS!
IT'S SO MUCH MORE SUBSTAN-TIAL NOW.
DID HE LEVEL UP, TOO?!
HEH...
A GIANT SWORD, A GIANT WOMAN, AND NOW THIS FREAK?
IT'S ALL A BIG SHOW.
THEIR VERY PRESENCE HERE IS AN AFFRONT TO OUR HONOR!
KRK
WE CAN'T LET THEIR LUKEWARM HOT SPRINGS MELT OUR ICE!!!

Chapter 132:

The Splendor of Ryu

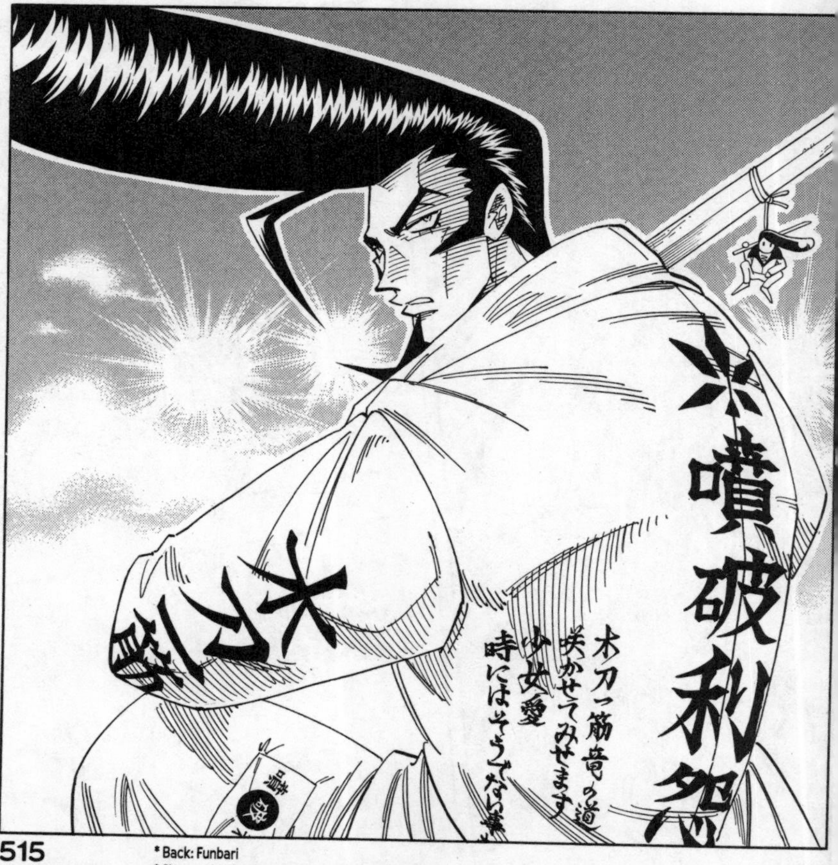
噴破利
木刀一筋竜の道
咲かせてみせます
少女愛
時にはそうでない

* Back: Funbari
* Sleeve: My life is devoted to the wooden sword.
* Bottom: My life is devoted to the wooden sword. I will make love happen, though it may not take the form I wish for.
* Leg: Funbari

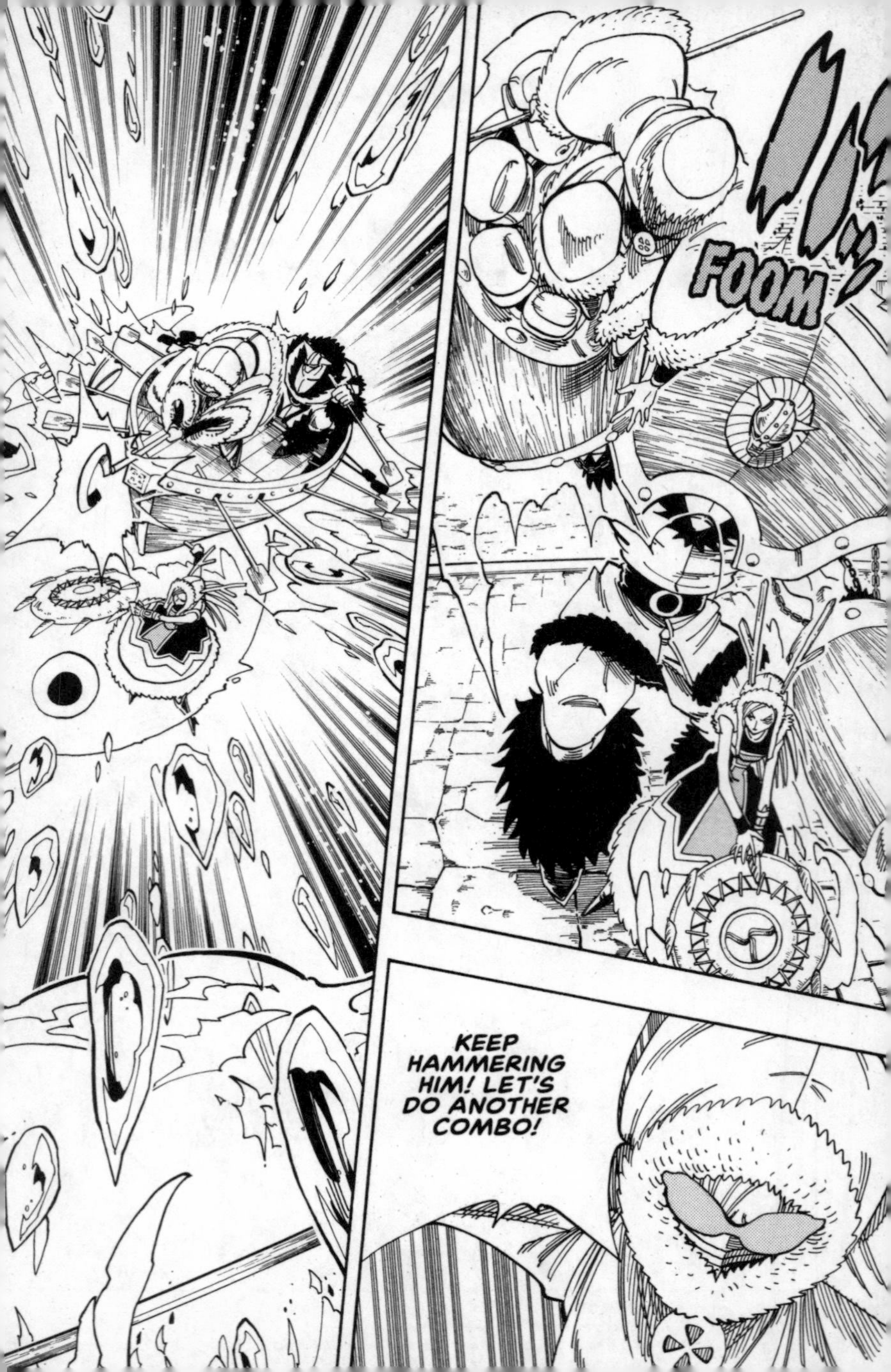
FOOM!
KEEP HAMMERING HIM! LET'S DO ANOTHER COMBO!

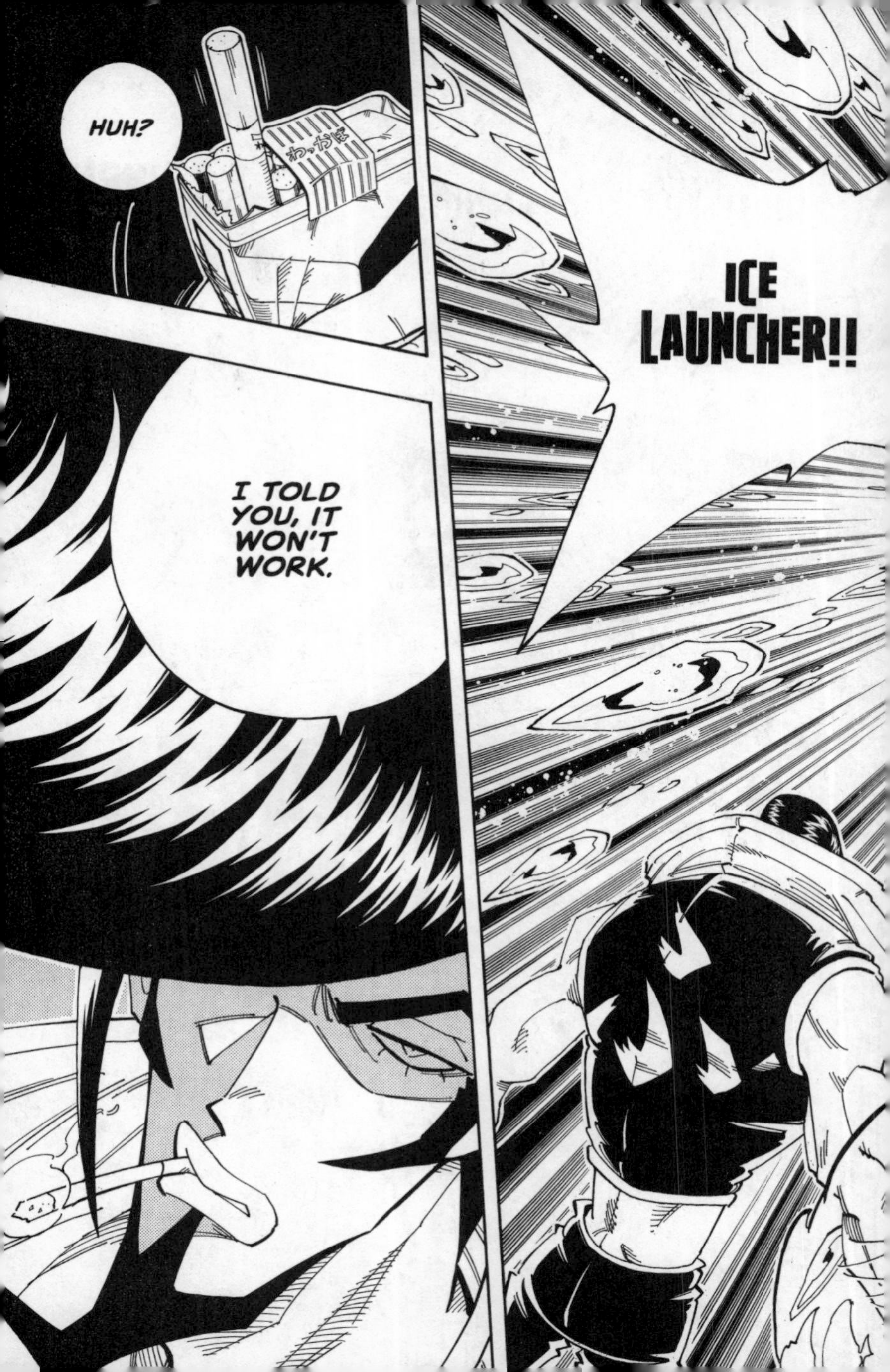
ICE LAUNCHER!!
HUH?
I TOLD YOU, IT WON'T WORK.

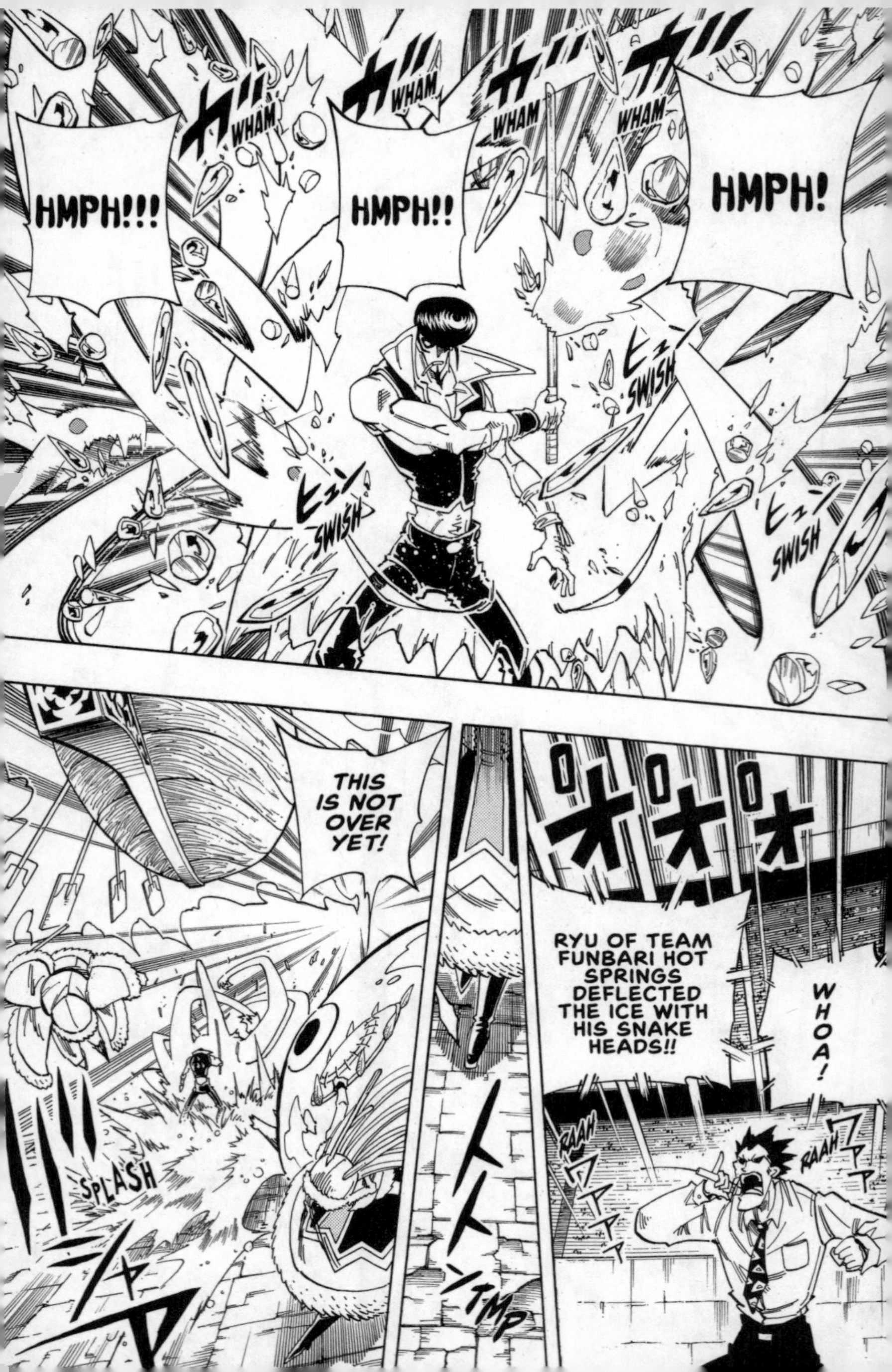

WHAM
HMPH!
WHAM
WHAM
HMPH!!
WHAM
HMPH!!!
SWISH
SWISH
SWISH
O O O
オオオ
RYU OF TEAM FUNBARI HOT SPRINGS DEFLECTED THE ICE WITH HIS SNAKE HEADS!!
WHOA!
RAAH
RAAH
TMP
THIS IS NOT OVER YET!
SPLASH

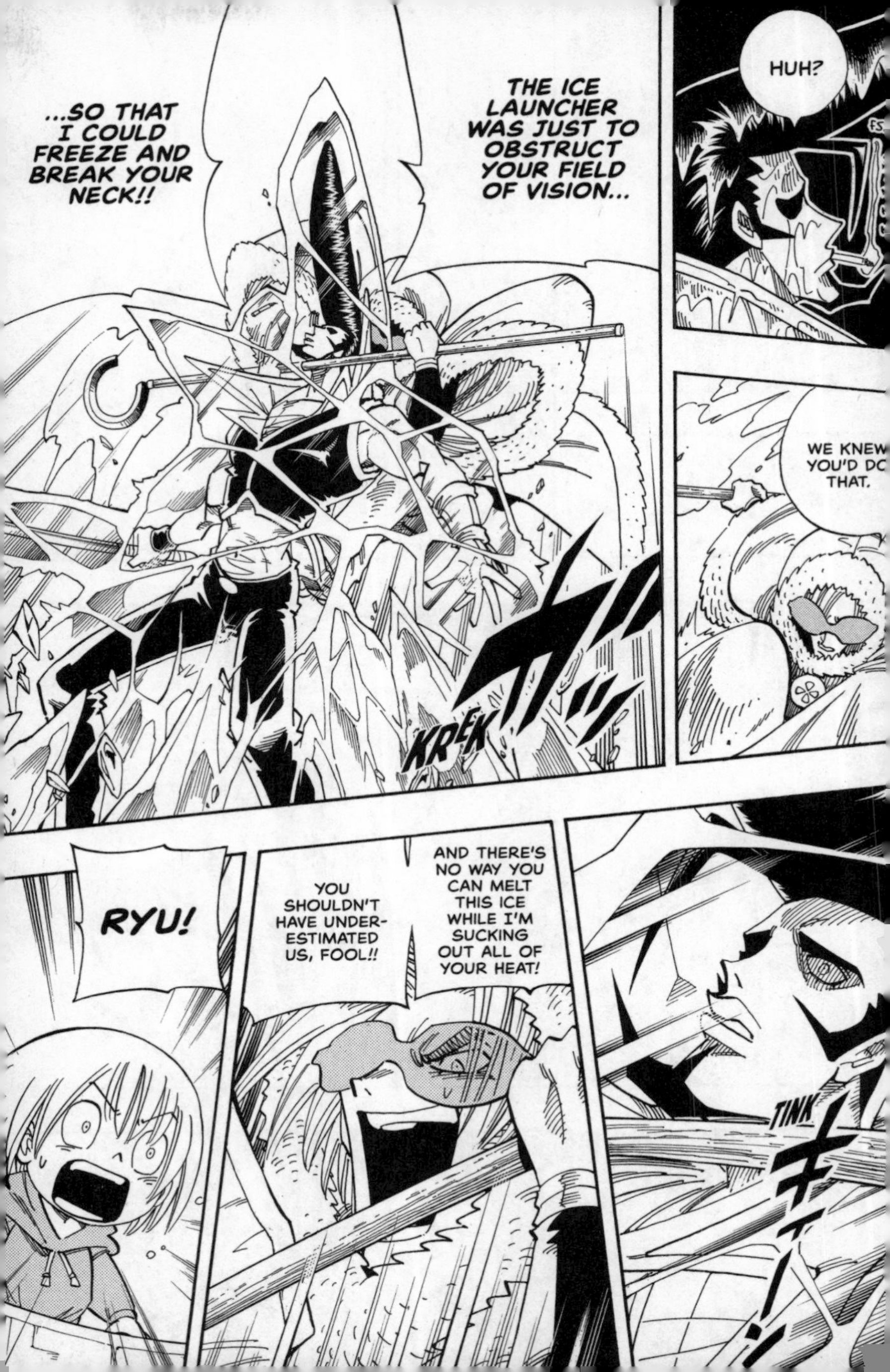
HUH?
WE KNEW YOU'D DO THAT.
THE ICE LAUNCHER WAS JUST TO OBSTRUCT YOUR FIELD OF VISION...
...SO THAT I COULD FREEZE AND BREAK YOUR NECK!!
KREK
TINK
AND THERE'S NO WAY YOU CAN MELT THIS ICE WHILE I'M SUCKING OUT ALL OF YOUR HEAT!
YOU SHOULDN'T HAVE UNDER-ESTIMATED US, FOOL!!
RYU!

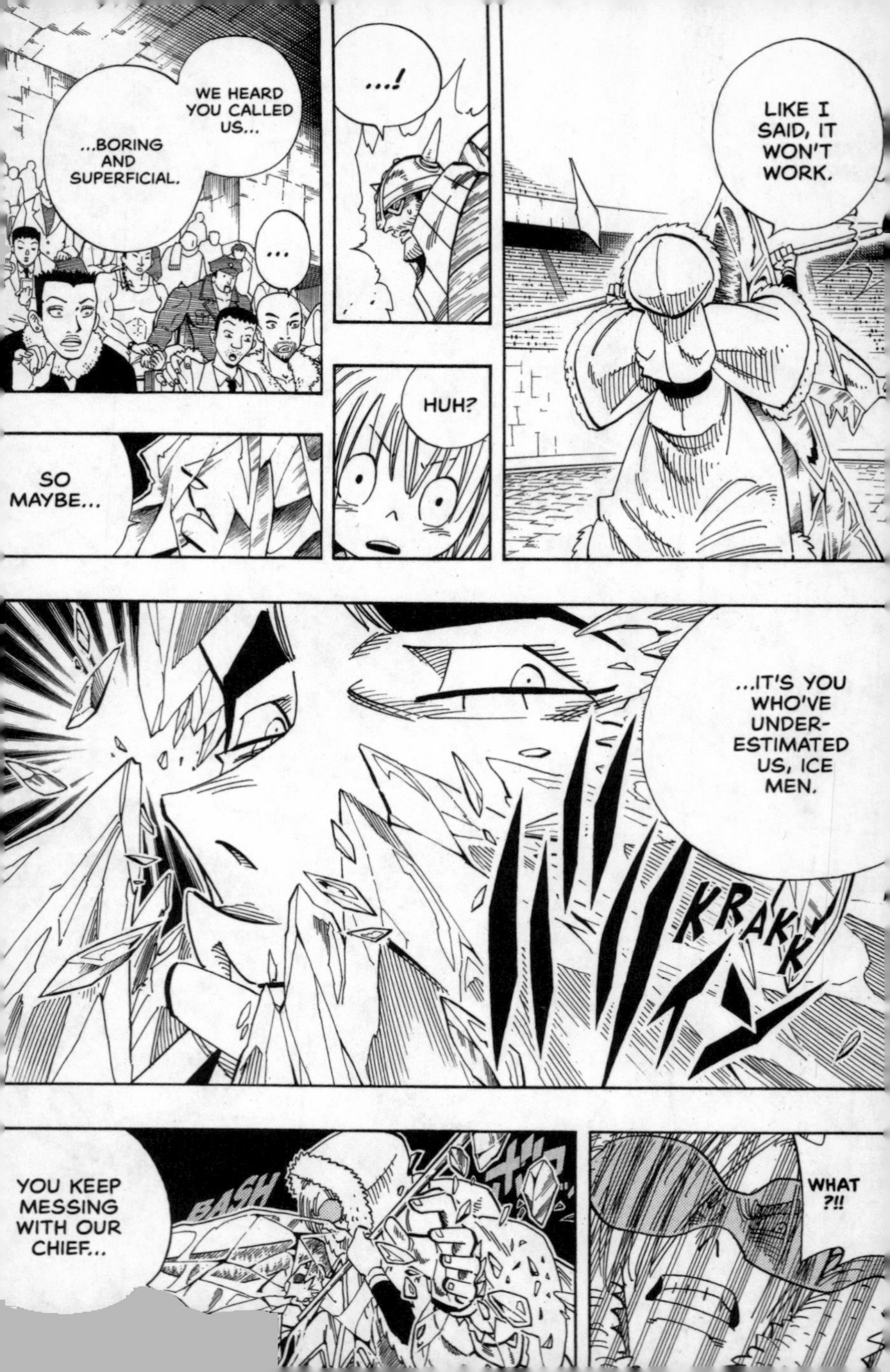
LIKE I SAID, IT WON'T WORK.
...!
HUH?
WE HEARD YOU CALLED US...
...BORING AND SUPERFICIAL.
...
SO MAYBE...
...IT'S YOU WHO'VE UNDER-ESTIMATED US, ICE MEN.
KRAKK
WHAT ?!!
BASH
YOU KEEP MESSING WITH OUR CHIEF...

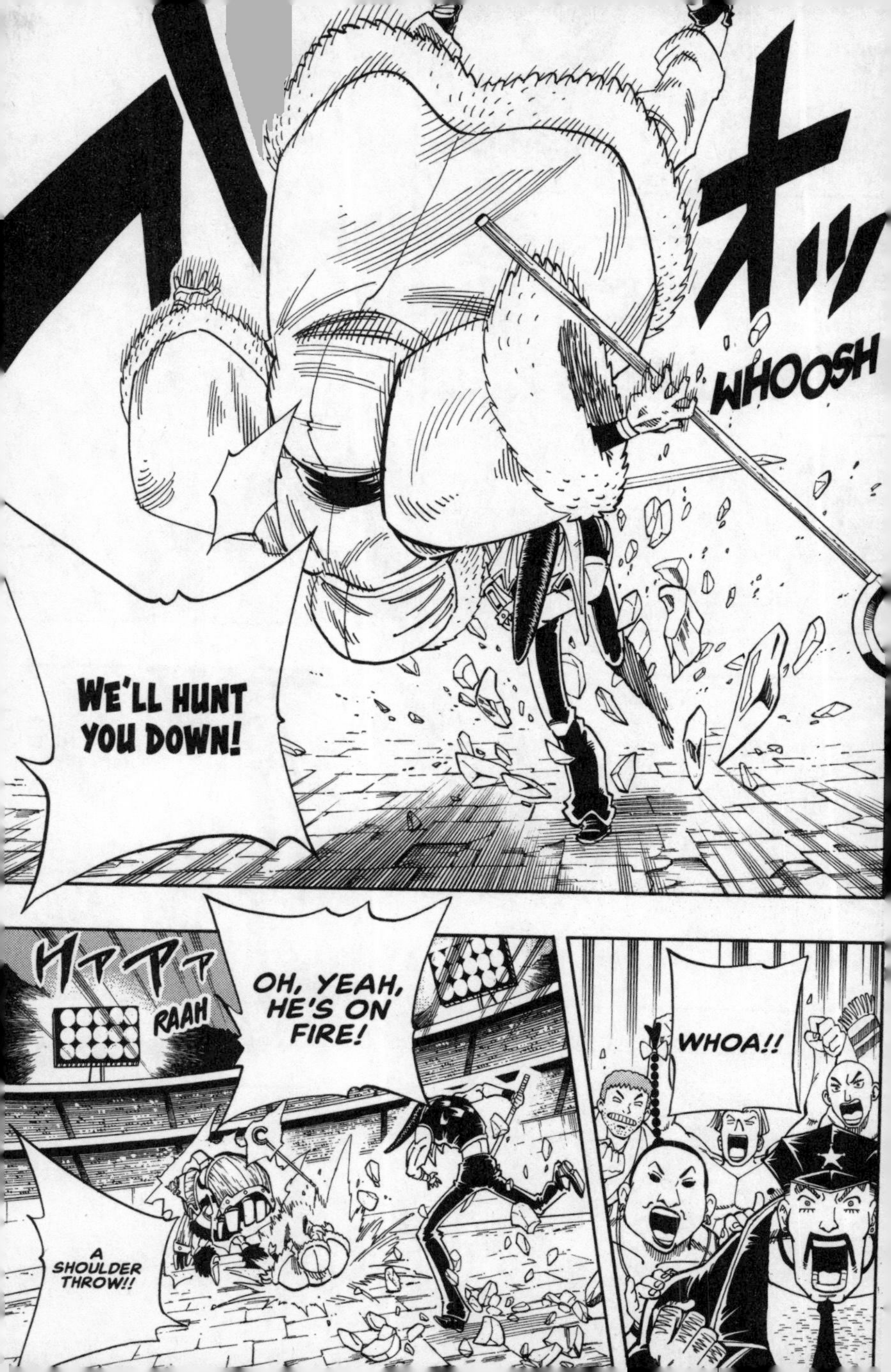
WHOOSH
WE'LL HUNT YOU DOWN!
WHOA!!
OH, YEAH, HE'S ON FIRE!
RAAH
A SHOULDER THROW!!

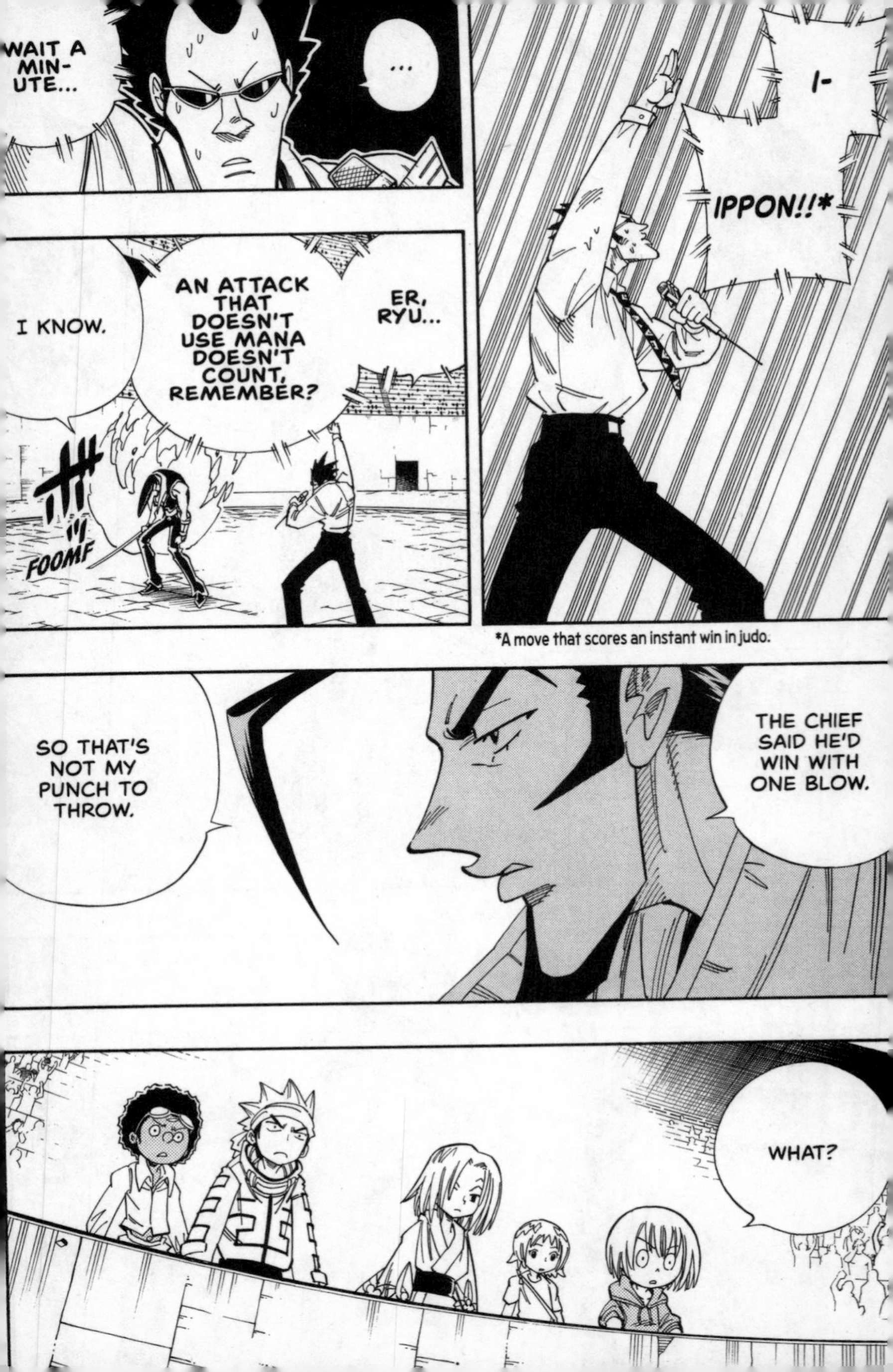
I-
IPPON!!*
...
WAIT A MINUTE...
ER, RYU...
AN ATTACK THAT DOESN'T USE MANA DOESN'T COUNT, REMEMBER?
I KNOW.
FOOMF
THE CHIEF SAID HE'D WIN WITH ONE BLOW.
SO THAT'S NOT MY PUNCH TO THROW.
WHAT?

*A move that scores an instant win in judo.

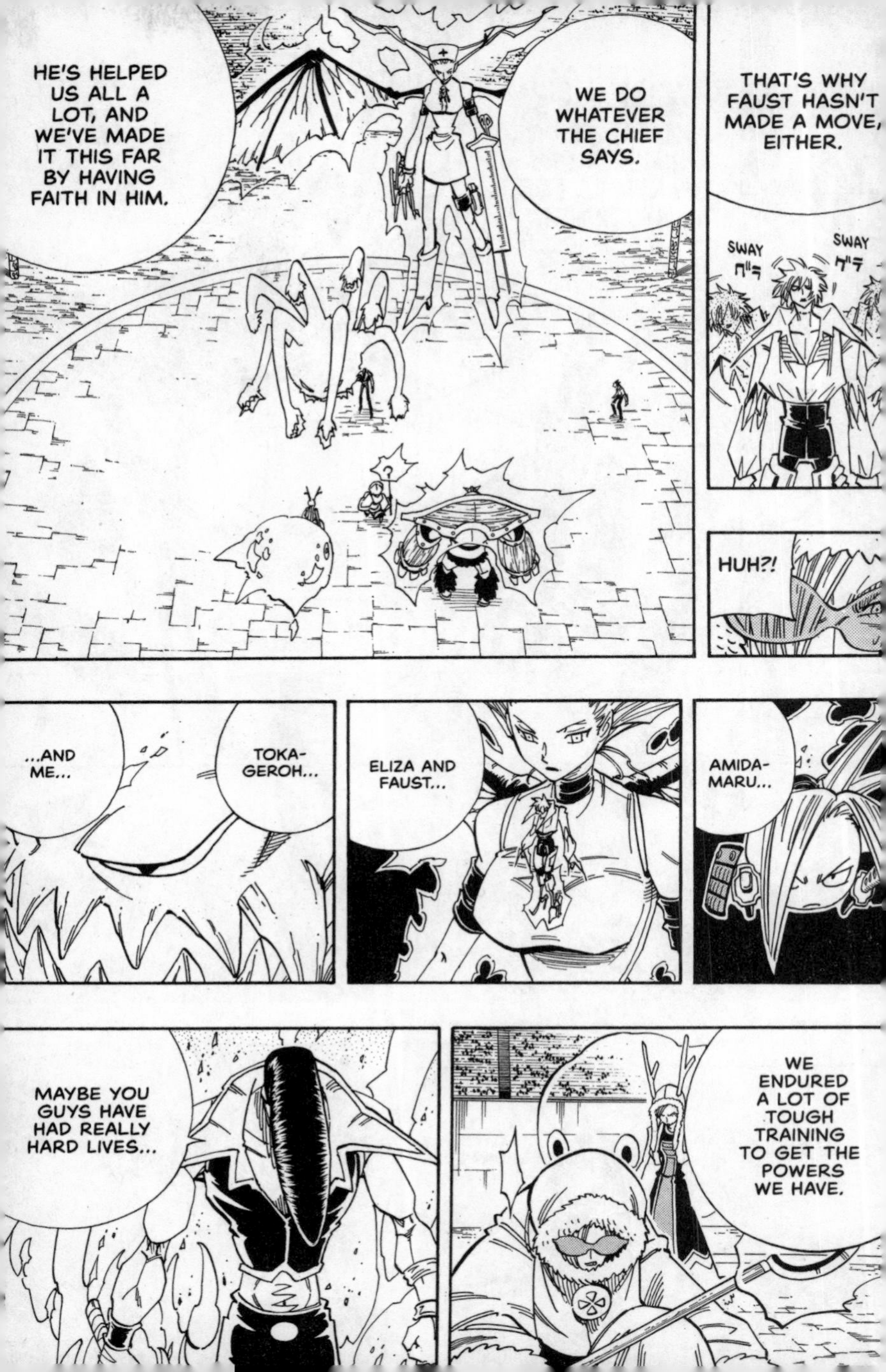
THAT'S WHY FAUST HASN'T MADE A MOVE, EITHER.
SWAY
SWAY
HUH?!
WE DO WHATEVER THE CHIEF SAYS.
HE'S HELPED US ALL A LOT, AND WE'VE MADE IT THIS FAR BY HAVING FAITH IN HIM.
AMIDA-MARU...
ELIZA AND FAUST...
TOKA-GEROH...
...AND ME...
WE ENDURED A LOT OF TOUGH TRAINING TO GET THE POWERS WE HAVE.
MAYBE YOU GUYS HAVE HAD REALLY HARD LIVES...

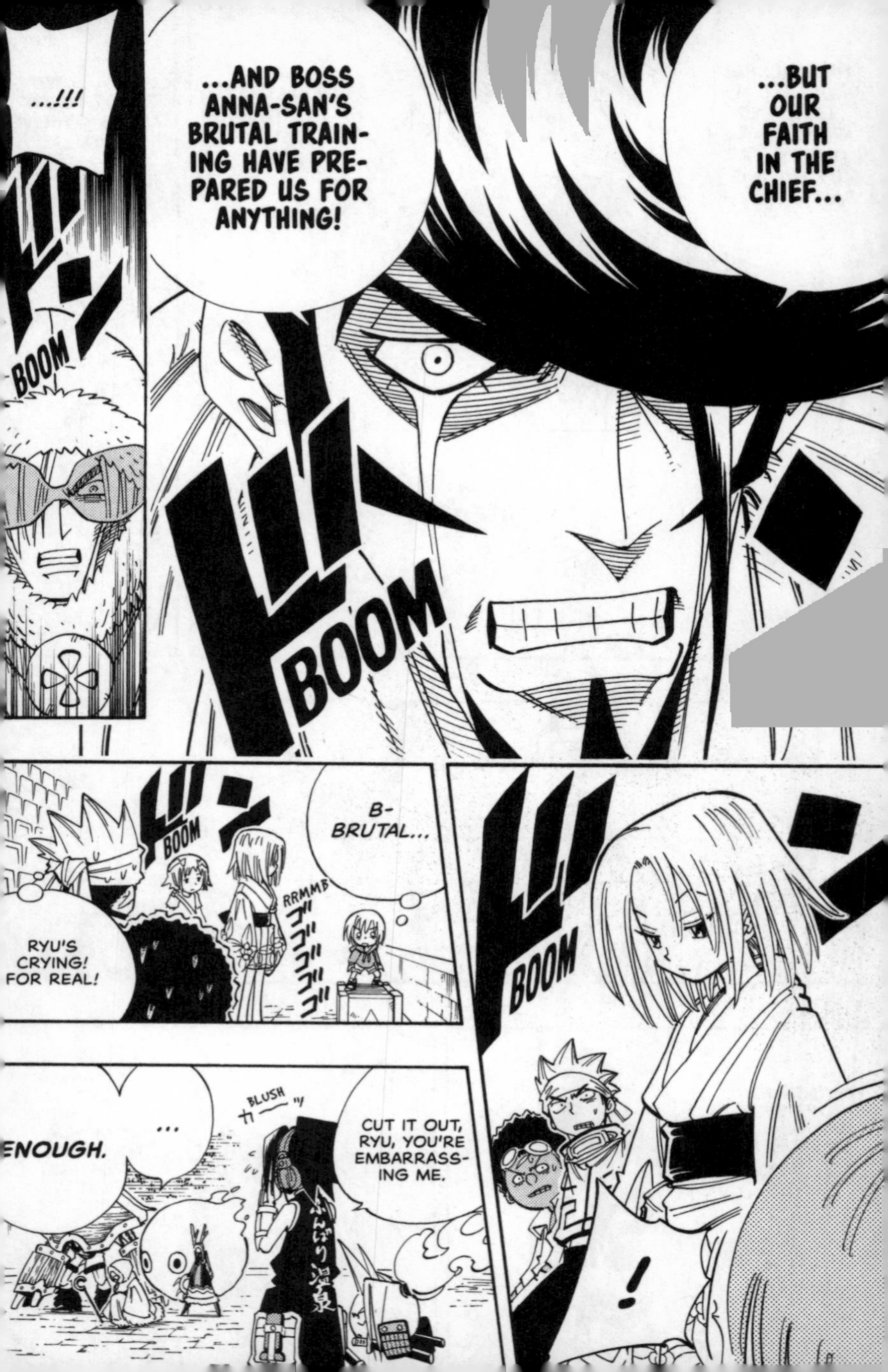
...BUT OUR FAITH IN THE CHIEF...
...AND BOSS ANNA-SAN'S BRUTAL TRAINING HAVE PREPARED US FOR ANYTHING!
BOOM
...!!!
BOOM
BOOM
!
B-BRUTAL...
RRMMB
ゴゴゴゴゴ
BOOM
RYU'S CRYING! FOR REAL!
CUT IT OUT, RYU, YOU'RE EMBARRASSING ME.
BLUSH
...
ENOUGH.

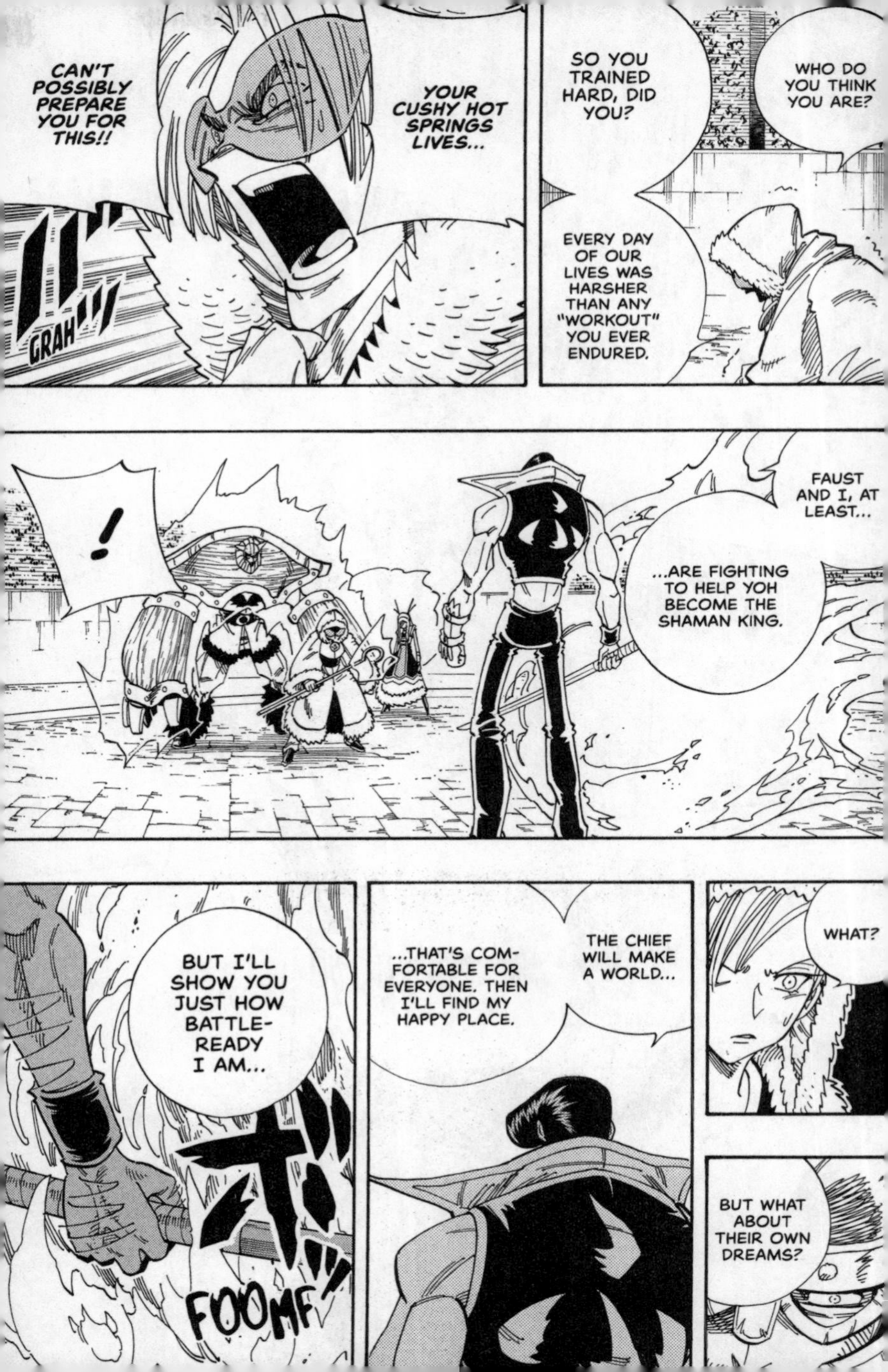
WHO DO YOU THINK YOU ARE?
SO YOU TRAINED HARD, DID YOU?
EVERY DAY OF OUR LIVES WAS HARSHER THAN ANY "WORKOUT" YOU EVER ENDURED.
YOUR CUSHY HOT SPRINGS LIVES...
CAN'T POSSIBLY PREPARE YOU FOR THIS!!
GRAH!!
FAUST AND I, AT LEAST...
...ARE FIGHTING TO HELP YOH BECOME THE SHAMAN KING.
!
WHAT?
BUT WHAT ABOUT THEIR OWN DREAMS?
THE CHIEF WILL MAKE A WORLD...
...THAT'S COM-FORTABLE FOR EVERYONE. THEN I'LL FIND MY HAPPY PLACE.
BUT I'LL SHOW YOU JUST HOW BATTLE-READY I AM...
FOOMF

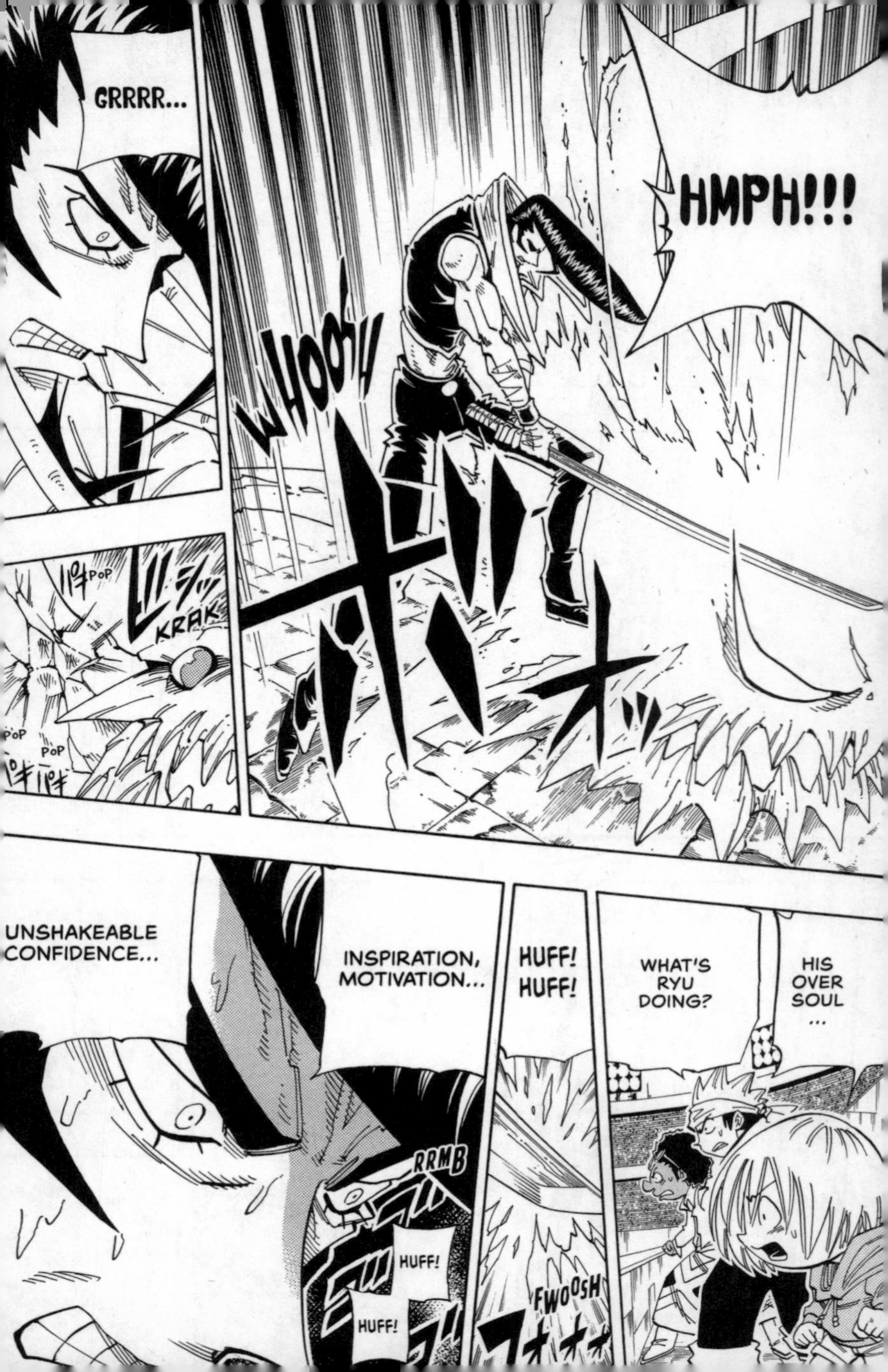
HMPH!!!
WHOOSH
GRRRR...
POP
KRAK
POP
POP
HIS OVER SOUL ...
WHAT'S RYU DOING?
HUFF! HUFF!
FWOOSH
INSPIRATION, MOTIVATION...
RRMB
HUFF!
HUFF!
UNSHAKEABLE CONFIDENCE...

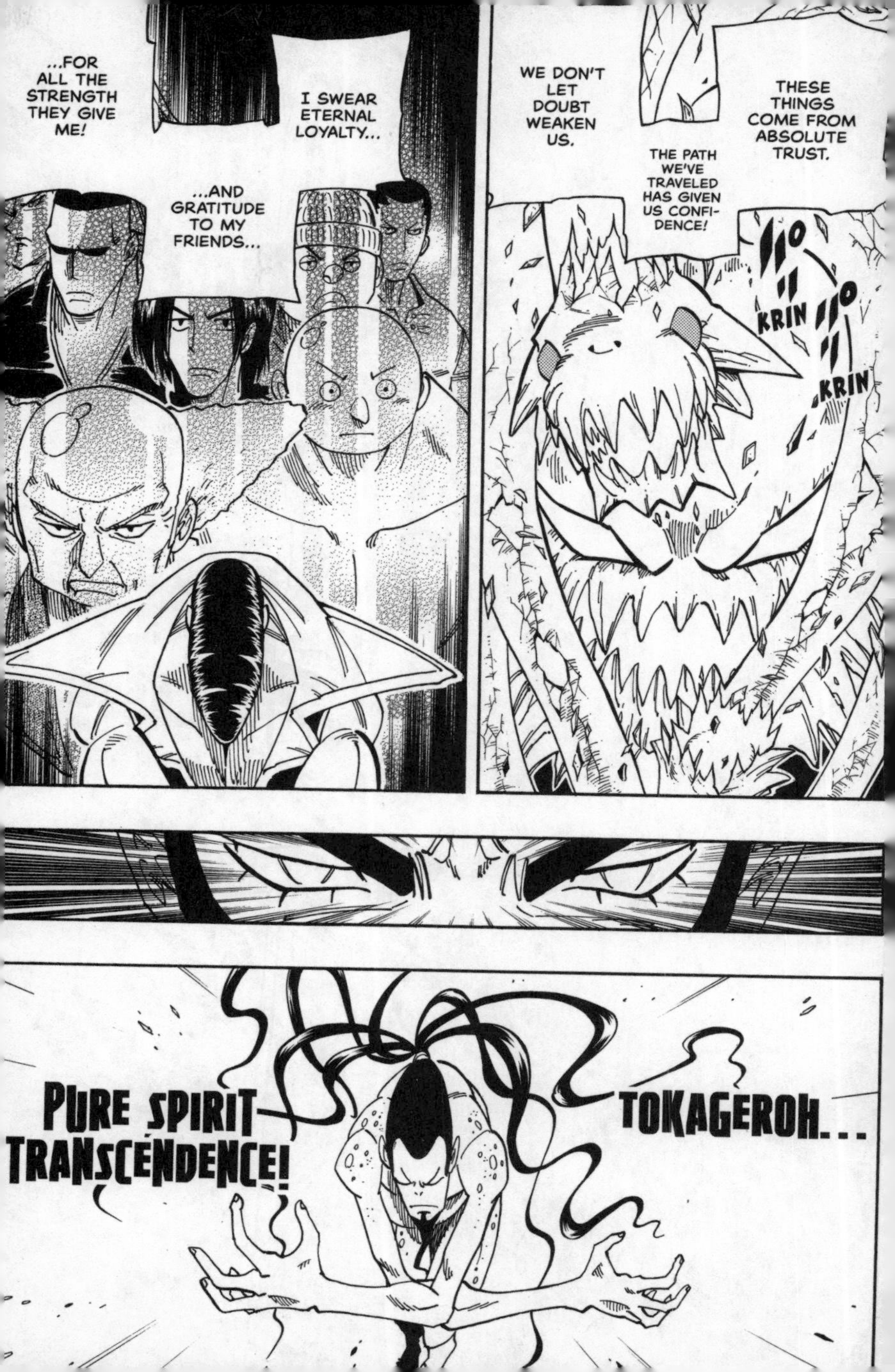
THESE THINGS COME FROM ABSOLUTE TRUST.
WE DON'T LET DOUBT WEAKEN US.
THE PATH WE'VE TRAVELED HAS GIVEN US CONFIDENCE!
KRIN
KRIN
I SWEAR ETERNAL LOYALTY...
...FOR ALL THE STRENGTH THEY GIVE ME!
...AND GRATITUDE TO MY FRIENDS...
TOKAGEROH...
PURE SPIRIT TRANSCÉNDENCE!

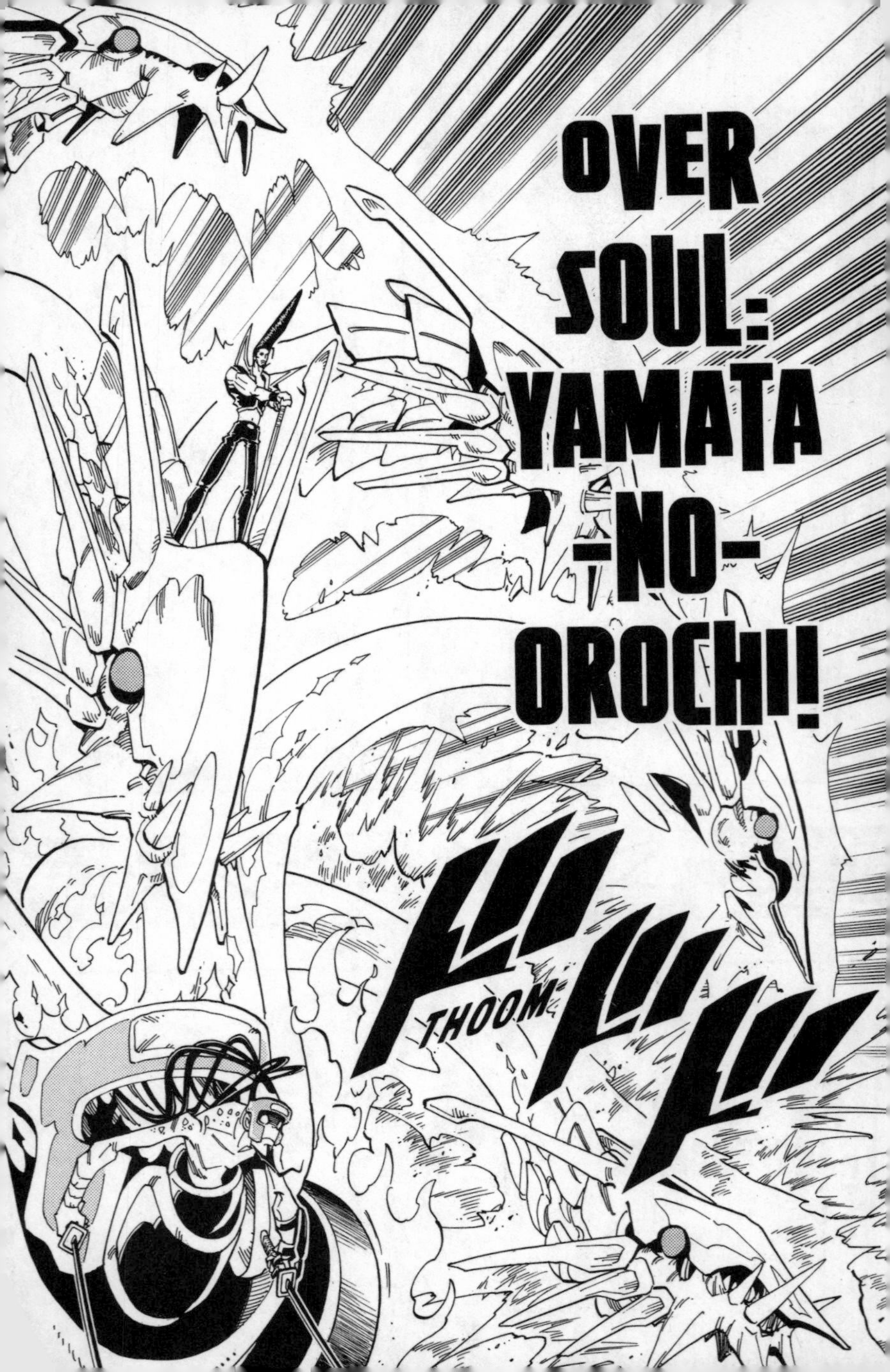
OVER SOUL: YAMATA-NO-OROCHI!
THOOM

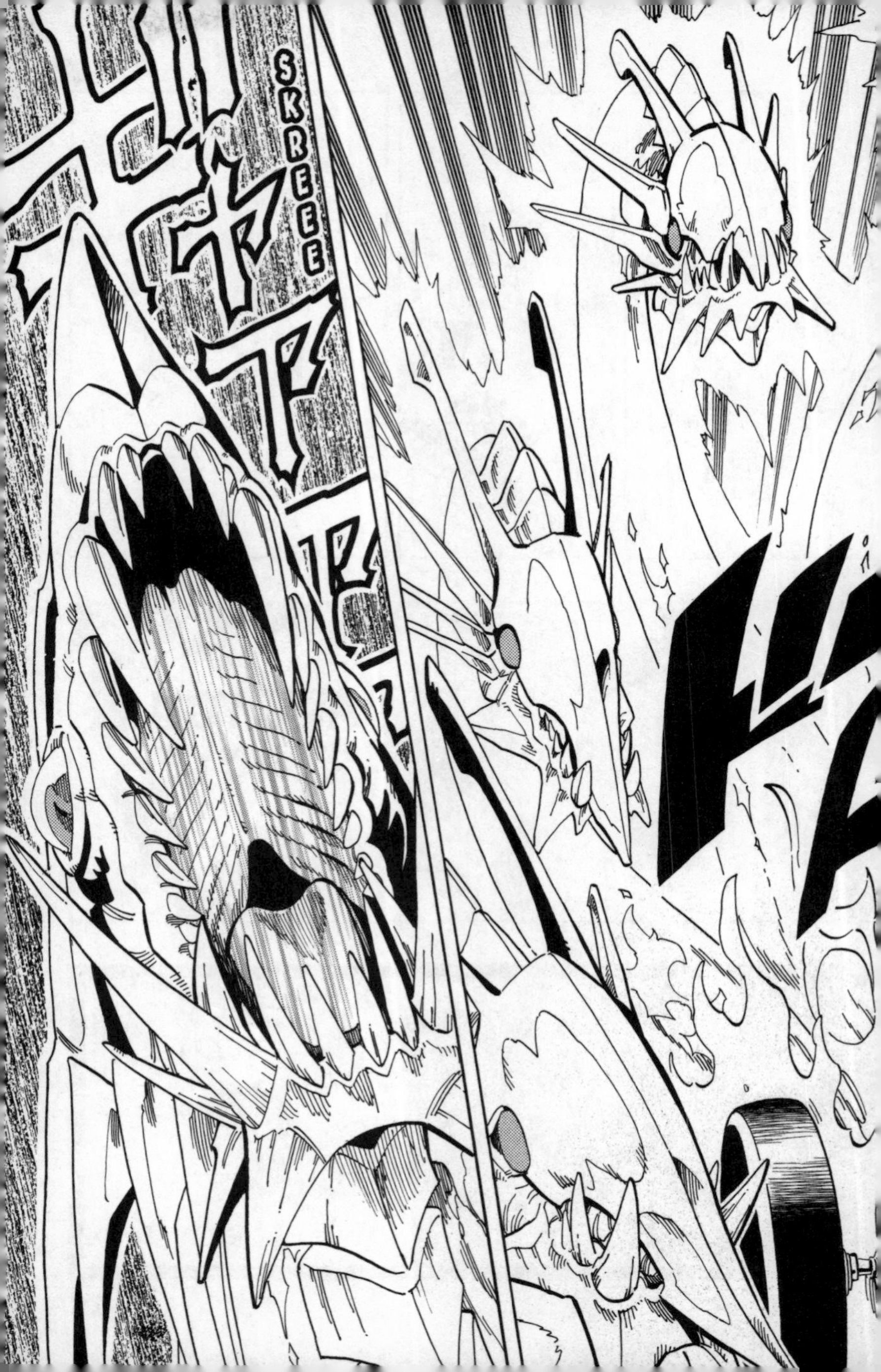
SKREEE

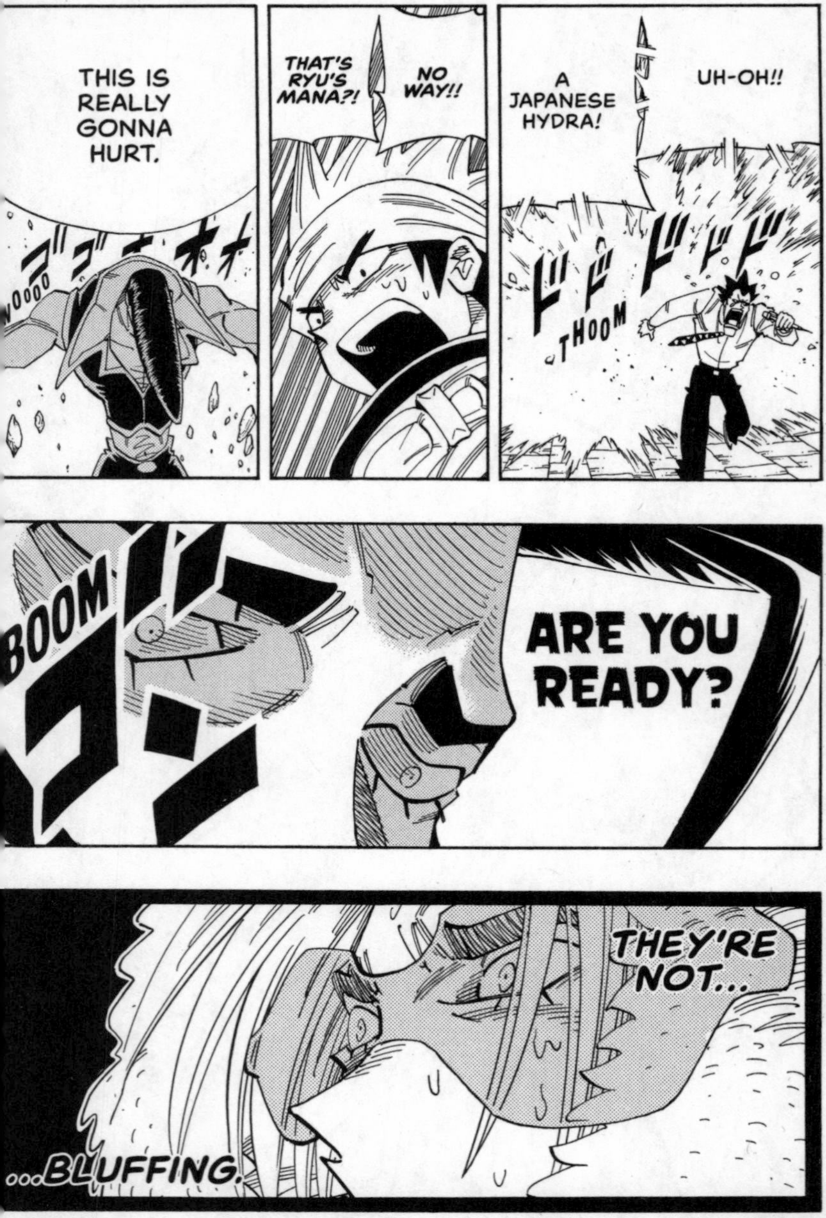
UH-OH!!
A JAPANESE HYDRA!
THOOM
NO WAY!!
THAT'S RYU'S MANA?!
THIS IS REALLY GONNA HURT.
VOOOO
ARE YOU READY?
BOOM
THEY'RE NOT...
...BLUFFING.

SHAMAN KING CHARACTER FILE No.76

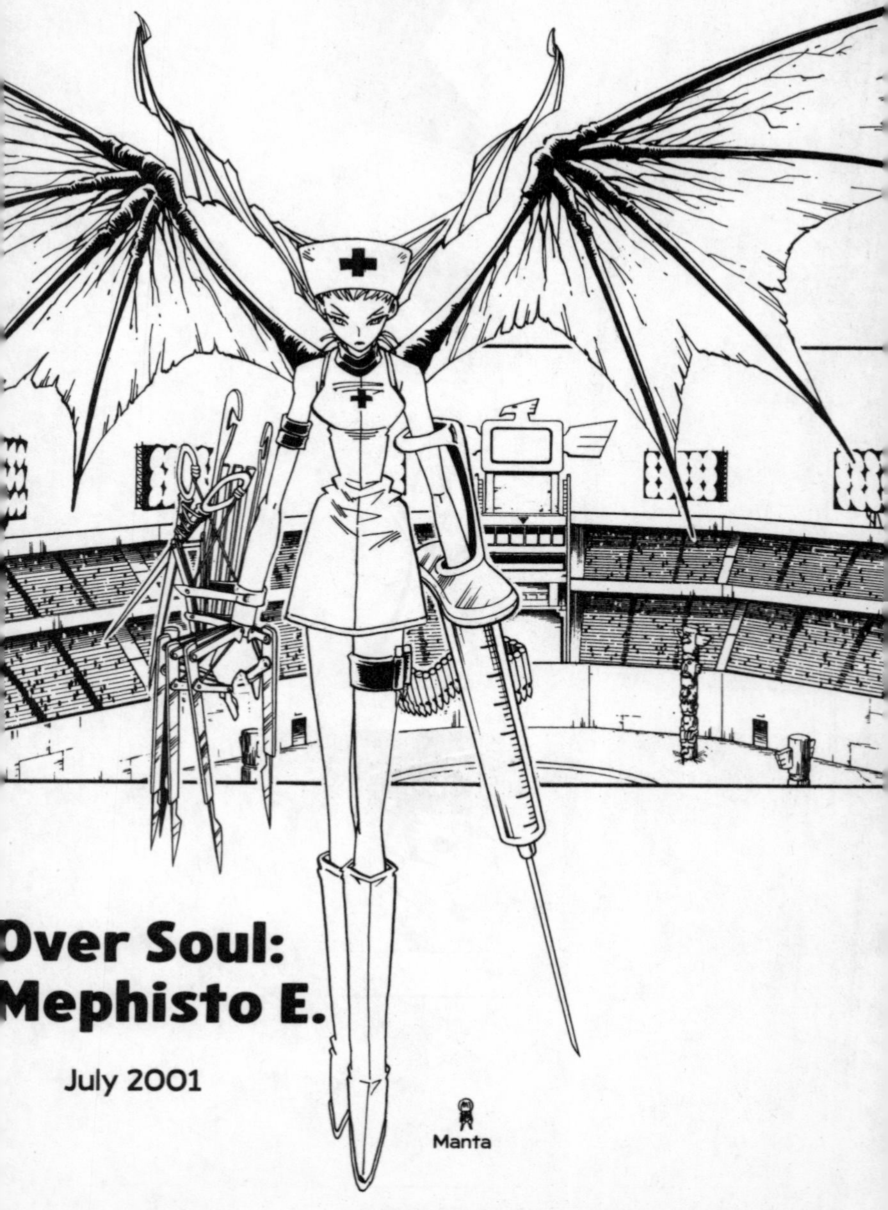
Over Soul:
Mephisto E.
July 2001
Manta

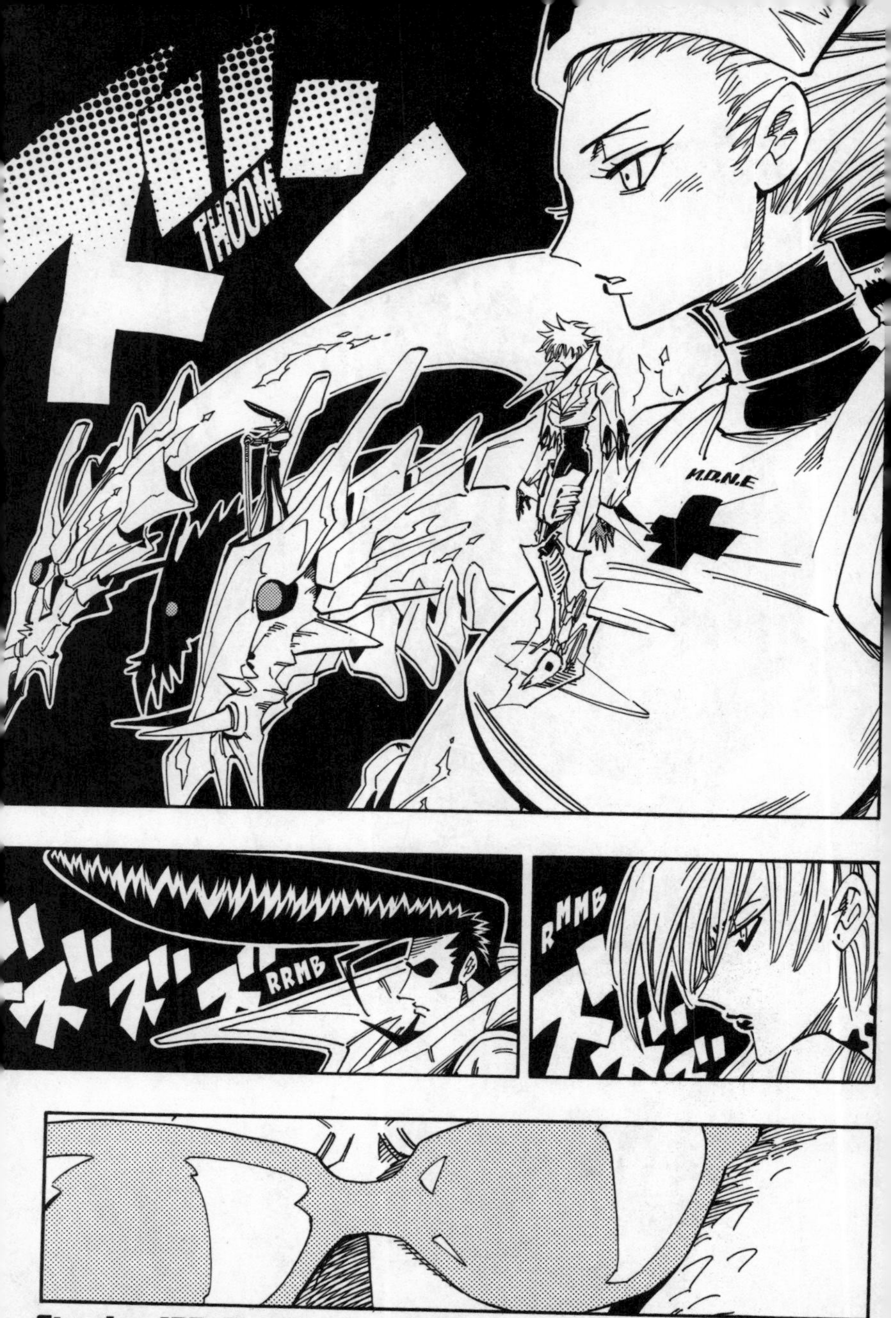
THOOM
M.D.N.E
RMMB
RRMB

Chapter 133: The Power of Yoh

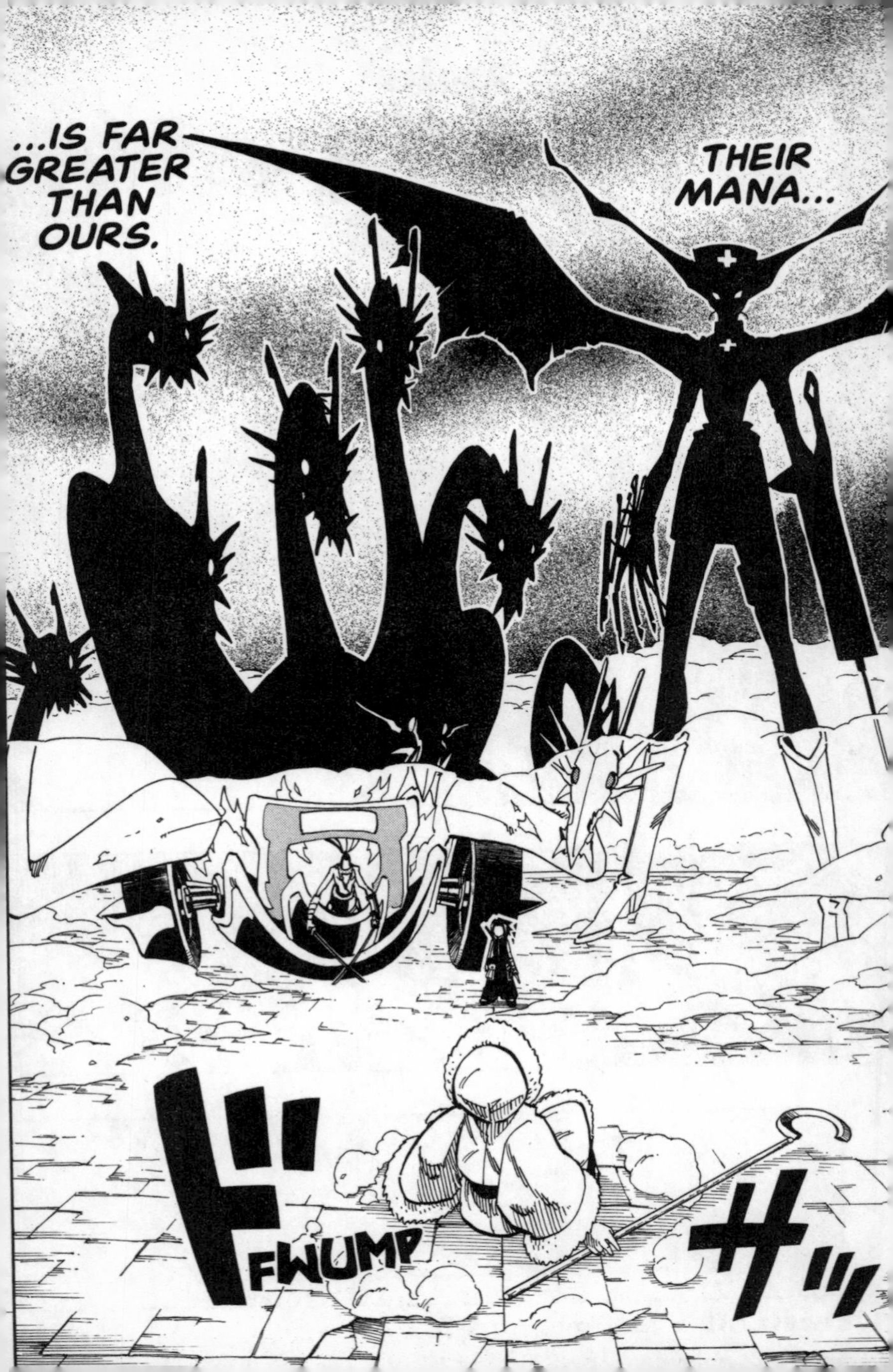
THEIR MANA...
...IS FAR GREATER THAN OURS.
FWUMP

Chapter 133:

The Power of Yoh

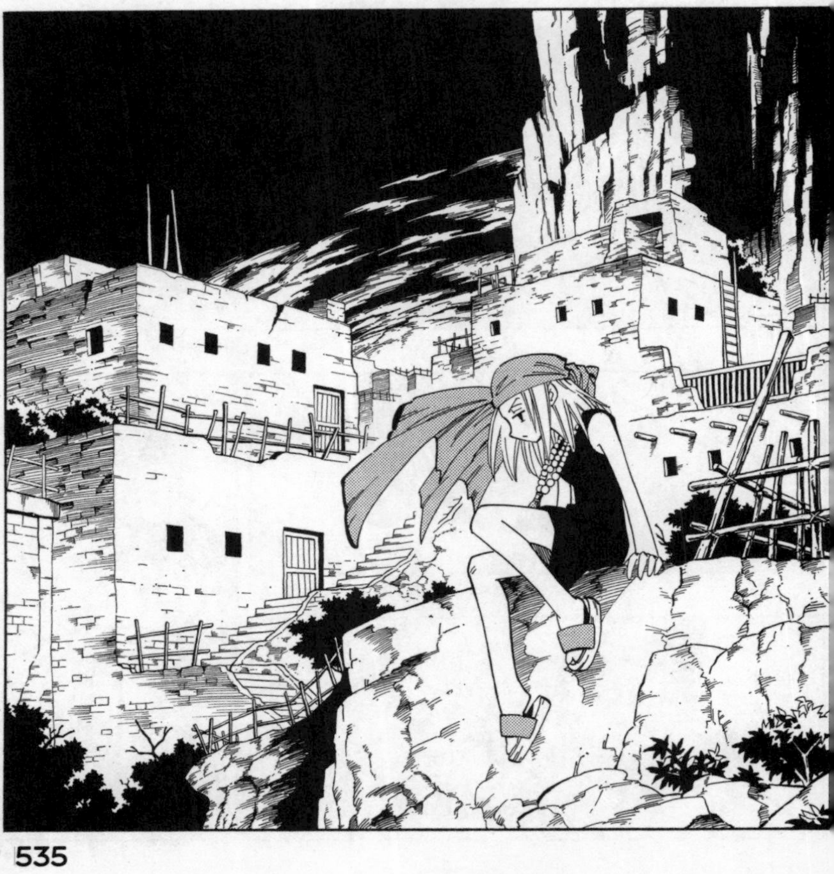

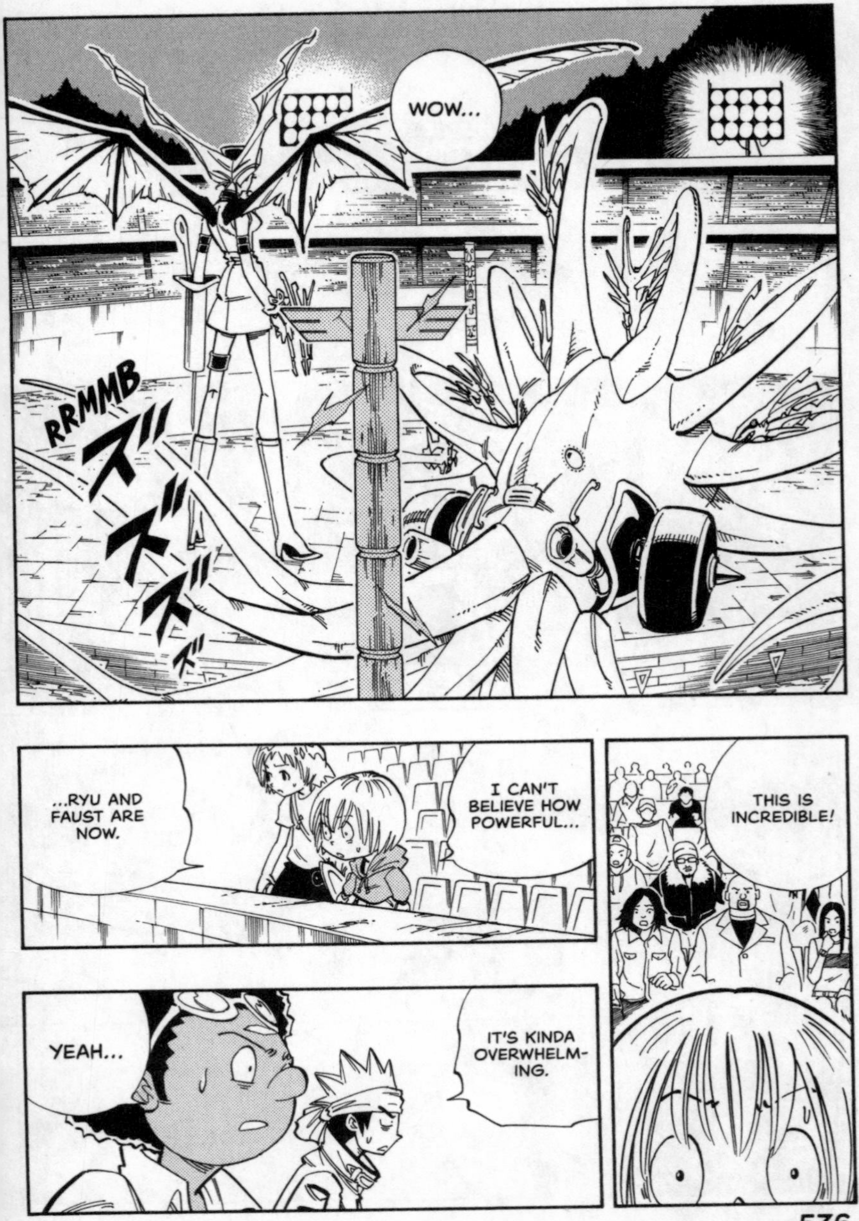

WOW...
RRMMB
THIS IS INCREDIBLE!
I CAN'T BELIEVE HOW POWERFUL...
...RYU AND FAUST ARE NOW.
IT'S KINDA OVERWHELMING.
YEAH...

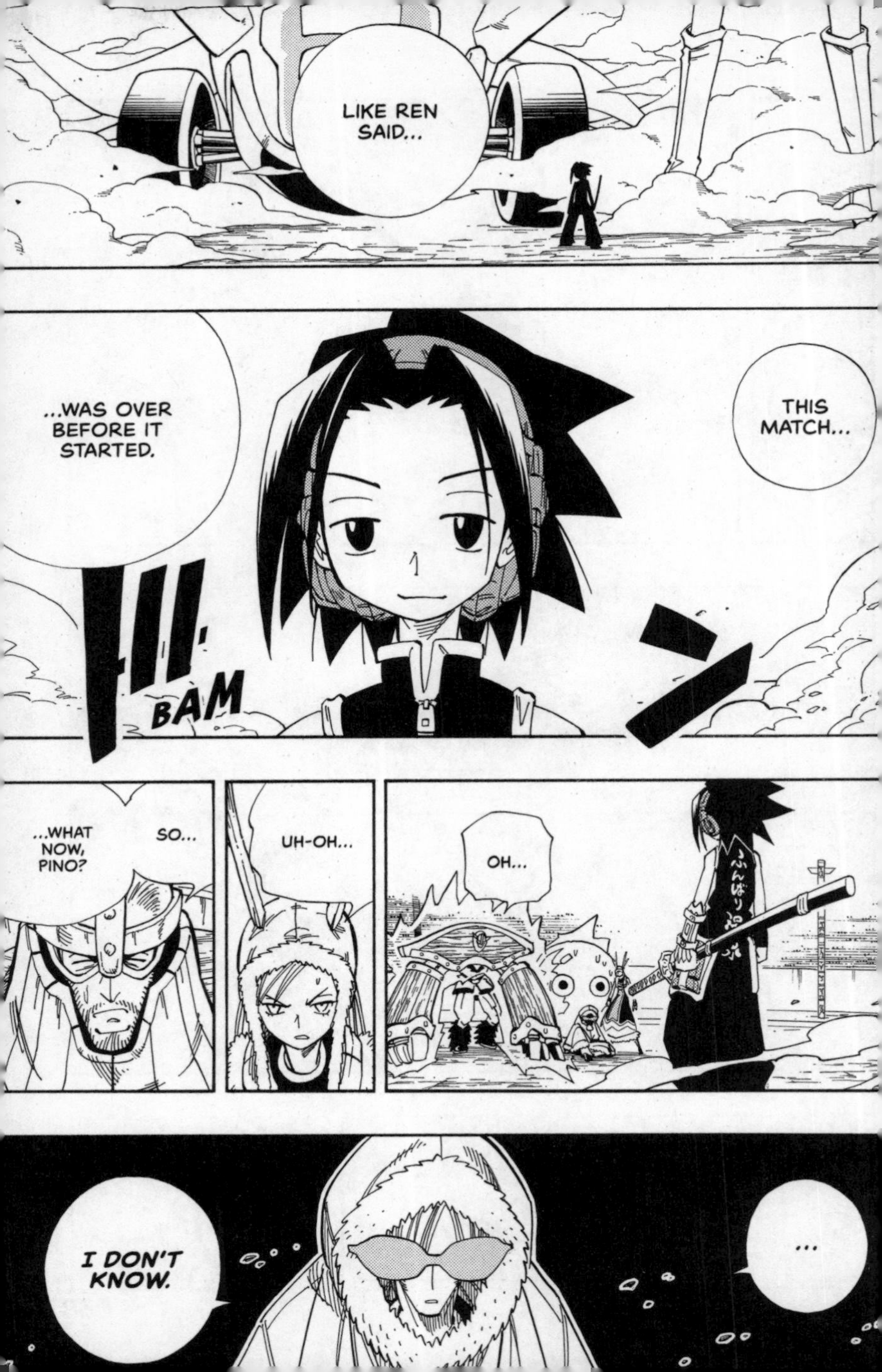
LIKE REN SAID...
THIS MATCH...
...WAS OVER BEFORE IT STARTED.
BAM
OH...
UH-OH...
SO...
...WHAT NOW, PINO?
...
I DON'T KNOW.

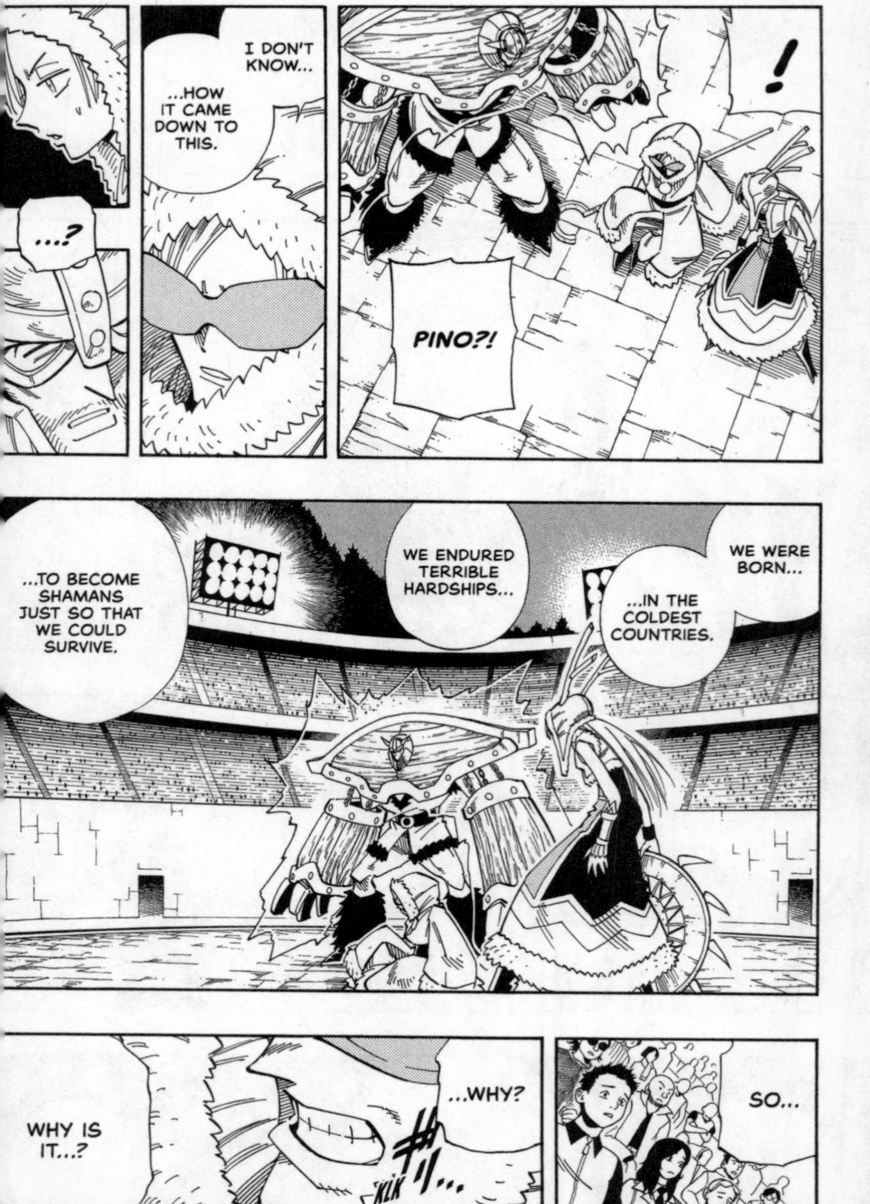
!
PINO?!
I DON'T KNOW...
...HOW IT CAME DOWN TO THIS.
...?
WE WERE BORN...
...IN THE COLDEST COUNTRIES.
WE ENDURED TERRIBLE HARDSHIPS...
...TO BECOME SHAMANS JUST SO THAT WE COULD SURVIVE.
SO...
...WHY?
WHY IS IT...?
KLIK

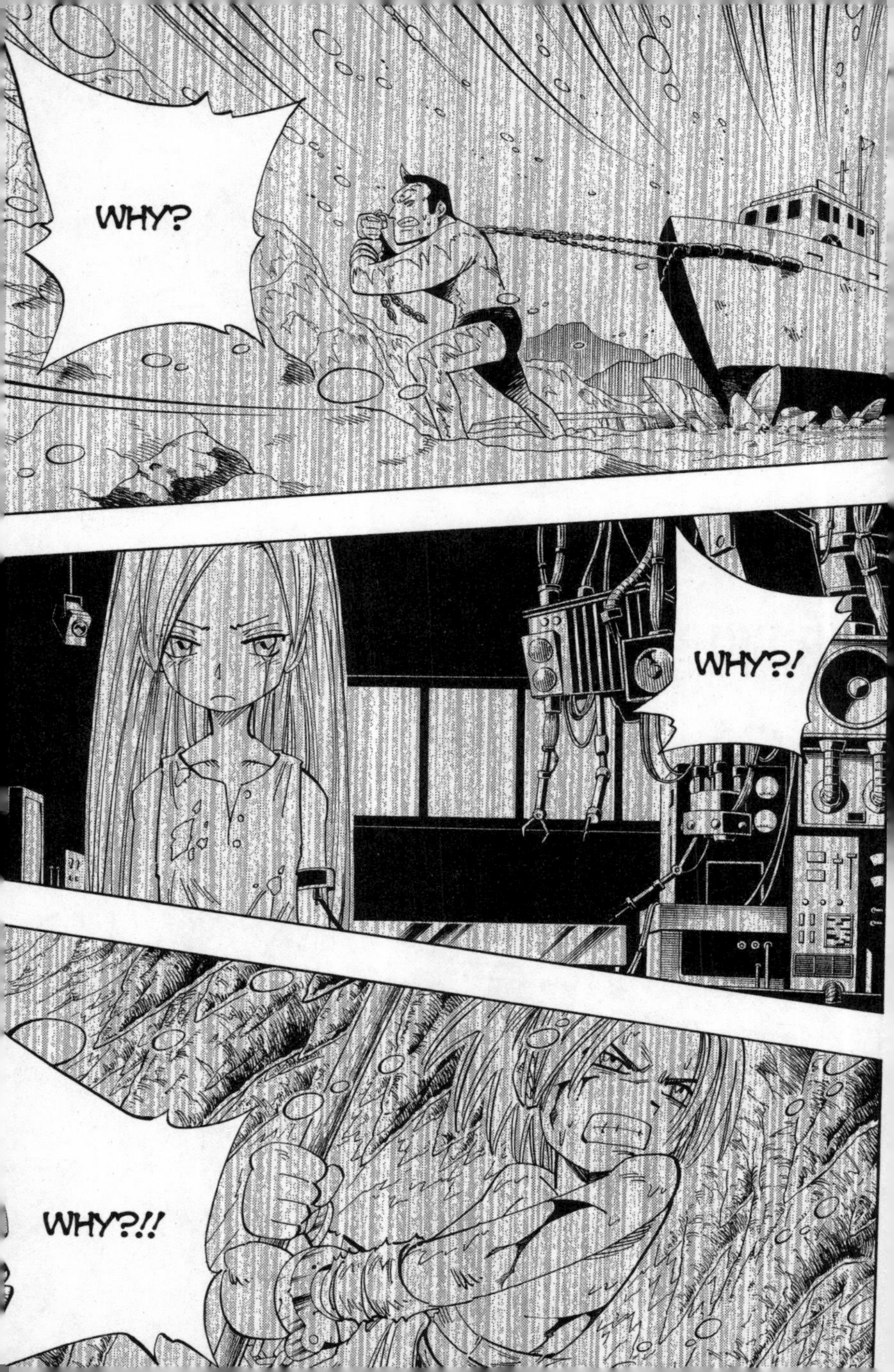
WHY?
WHY?!
WHY?!!

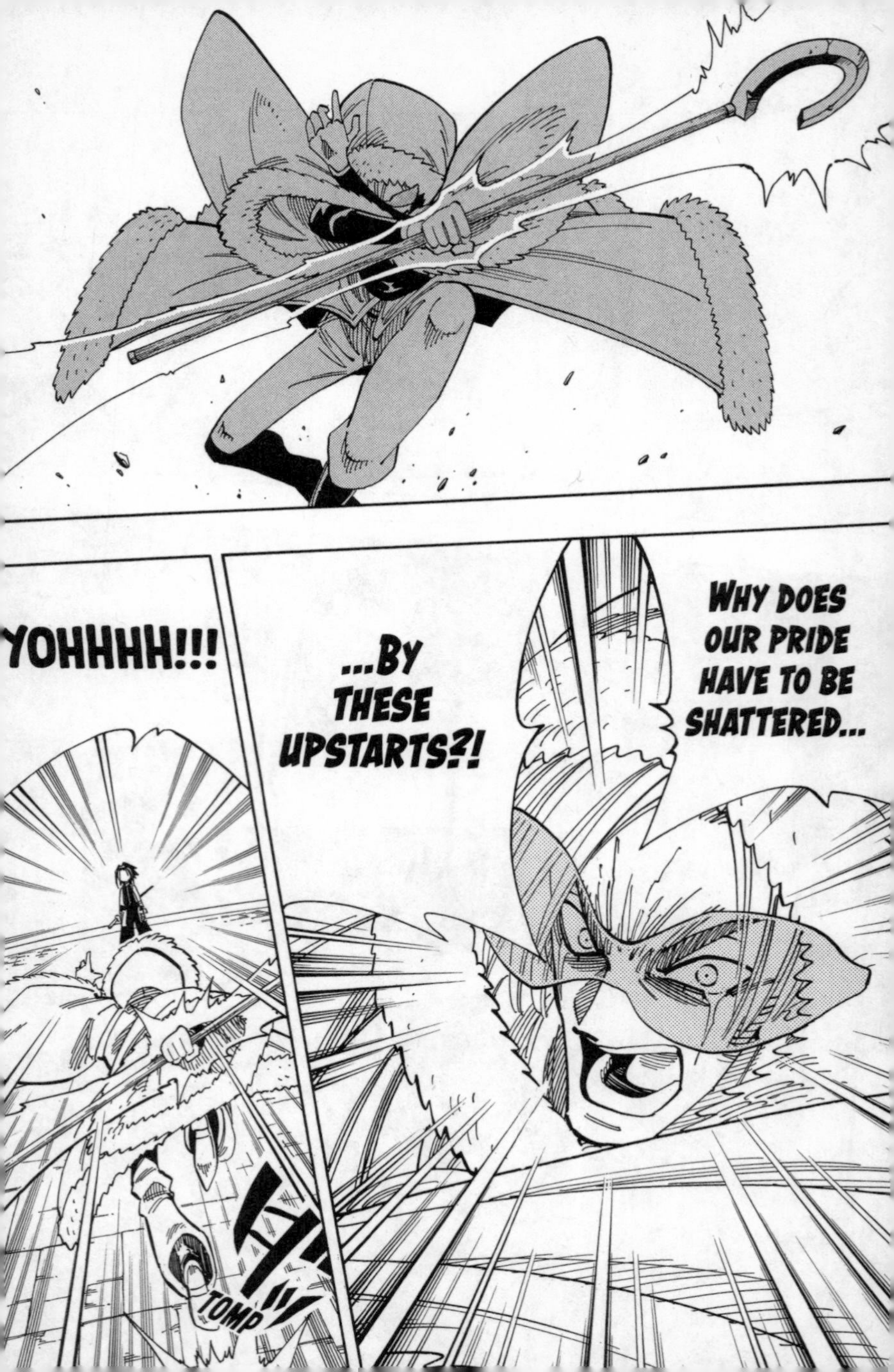
WHY DOES OUR PRIDE HAVE TO BE SHATTERED...
...BY THESE UPSTARTS?!
YOHHHH!!!
TOMP

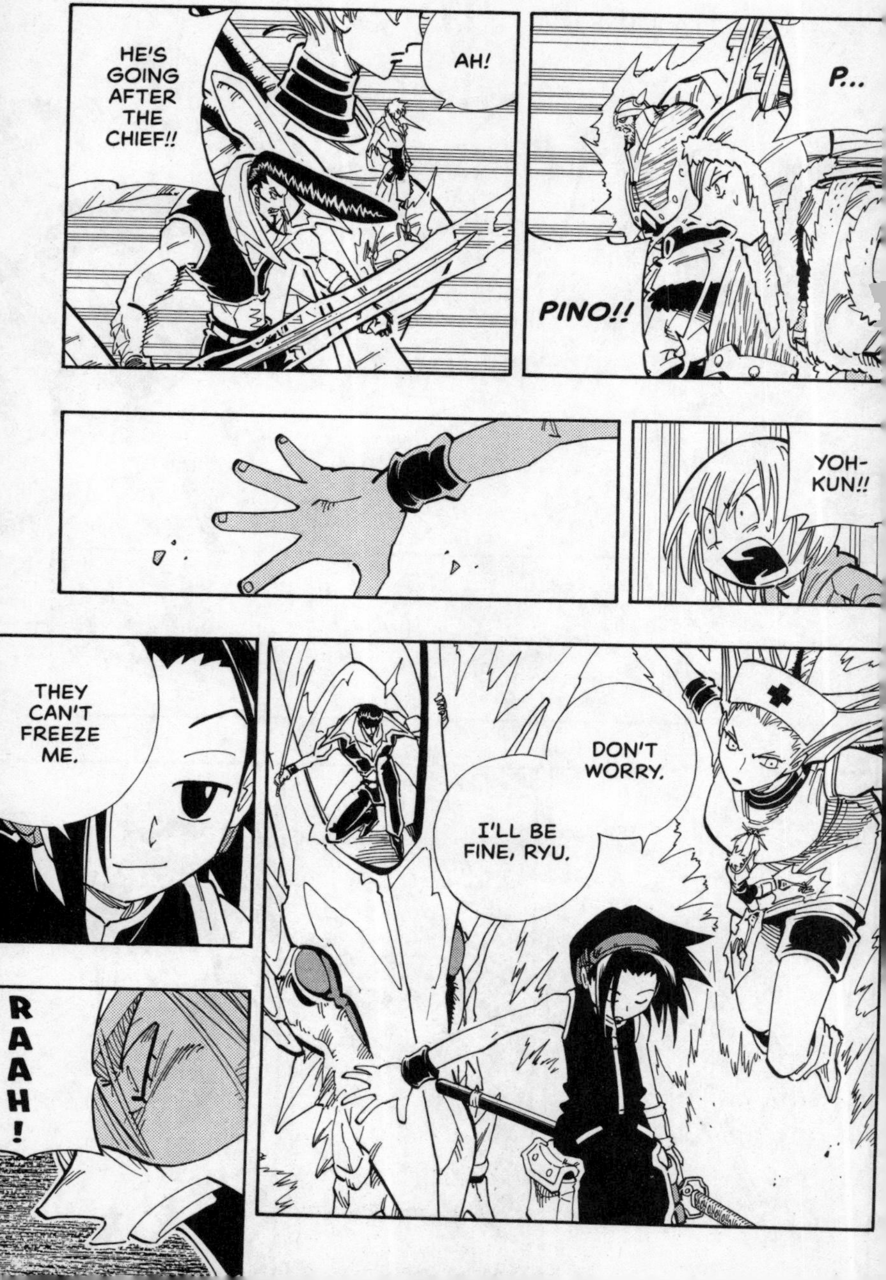
P...
PINO!!
AH!
HE'S GOING AFTER THE CHIEF!!
YOH-KUN!!
DON'T WORRY.
I'LL BE FINE, RYU.
THEY CAN'T FREEZE ME.
RAAH!

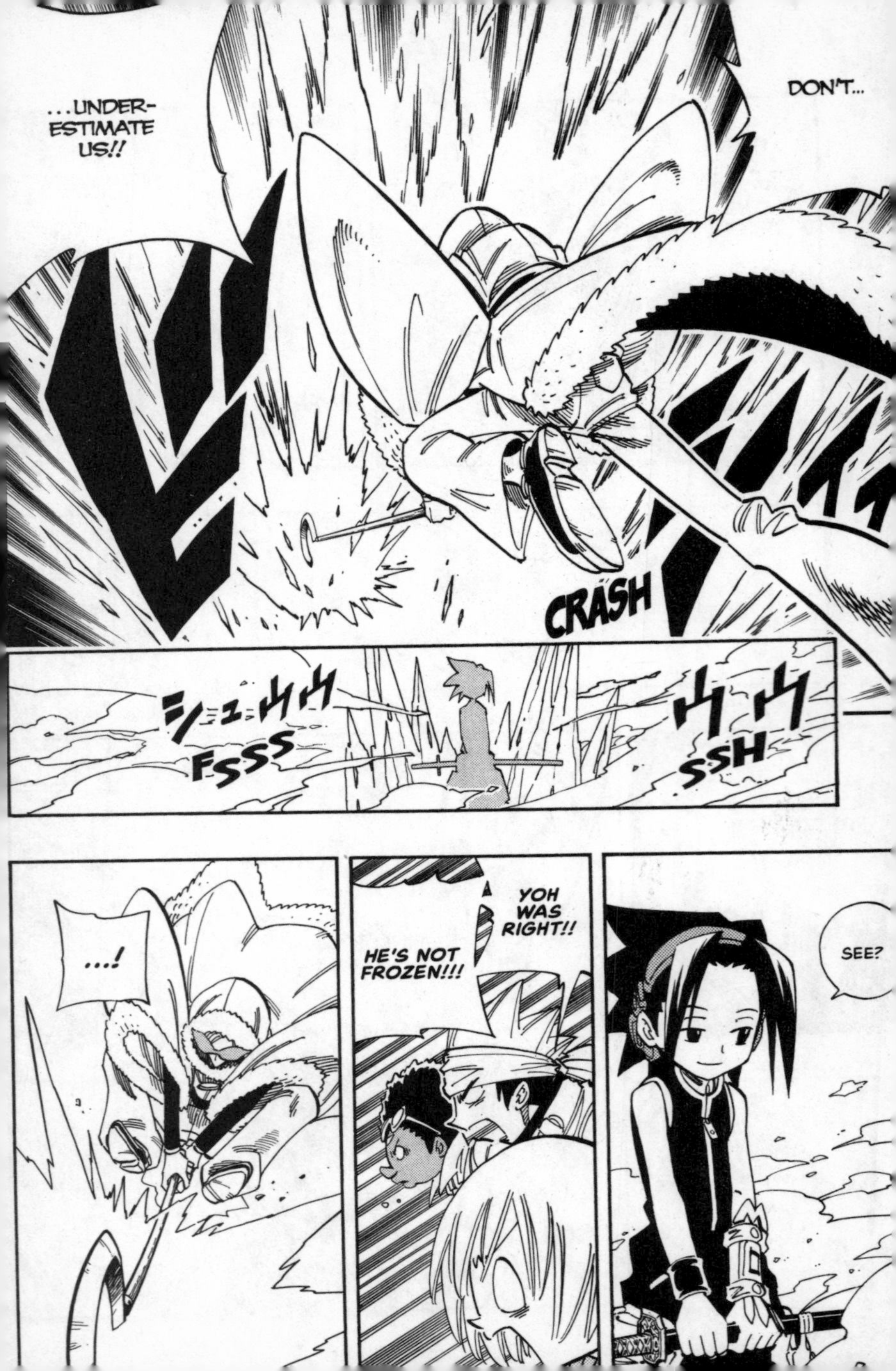
DON'T...
...UNDER-ESTIMATE US!!
CRASH
SSH
FSSS
SEE?
YOH WAS RIGHT!!
HE'S NOT FROZEN!!!
...!

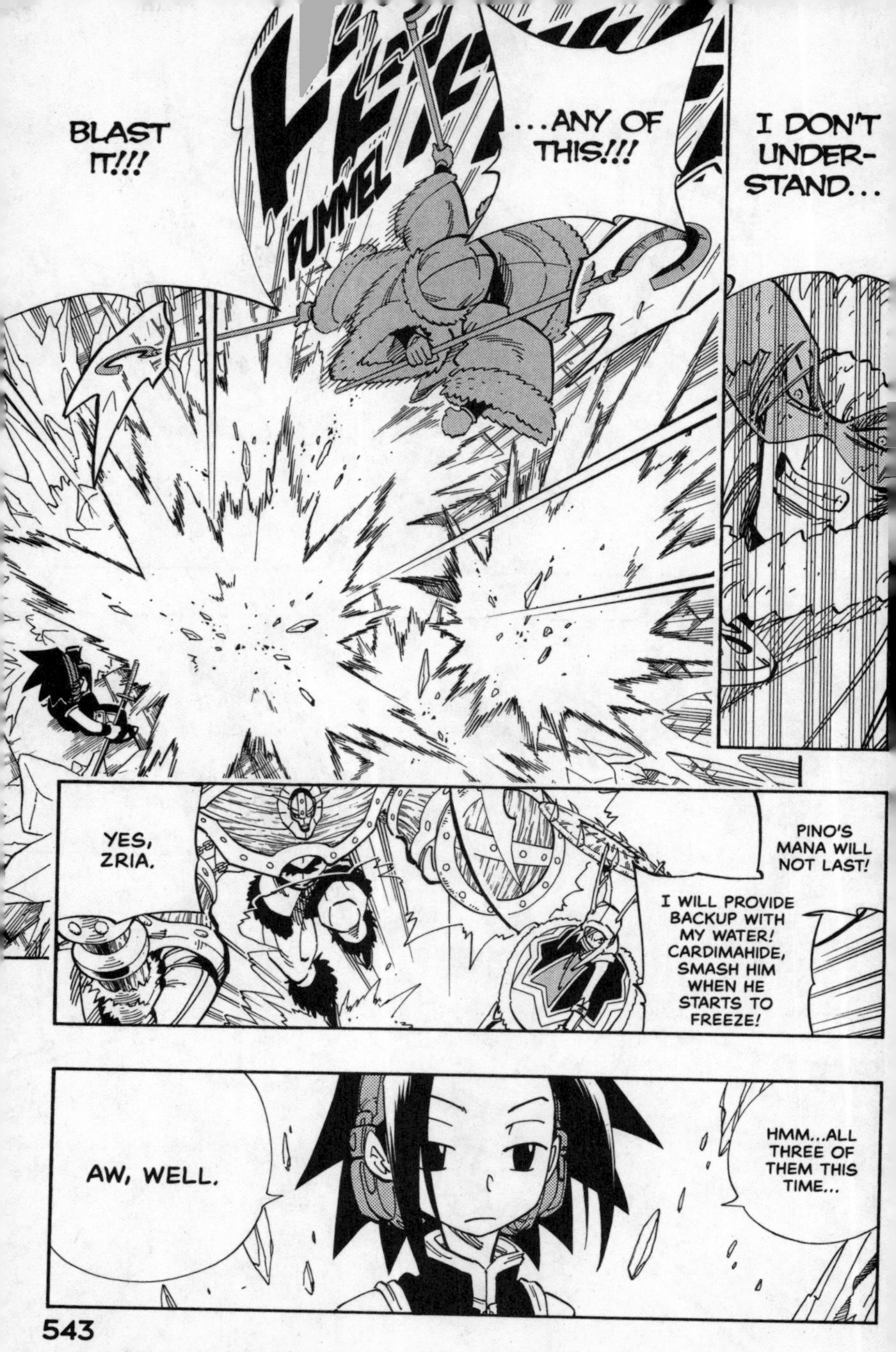
I DON'T UNDERSTAND...
...ANY OF THIS!!!
PUMMEL
BLAST IT!!!
PINO'S MANA WILL NOT LAST!
I WILL PROVIDE BACKUP WITH MY WATER! CARDIMAHIDE, SMASH HIM WHEN HE STARTS TO FREEZE!
YES, ZRIA.
HMM...ALL THREE OF THEM THIS TIME...
AW, WELL.

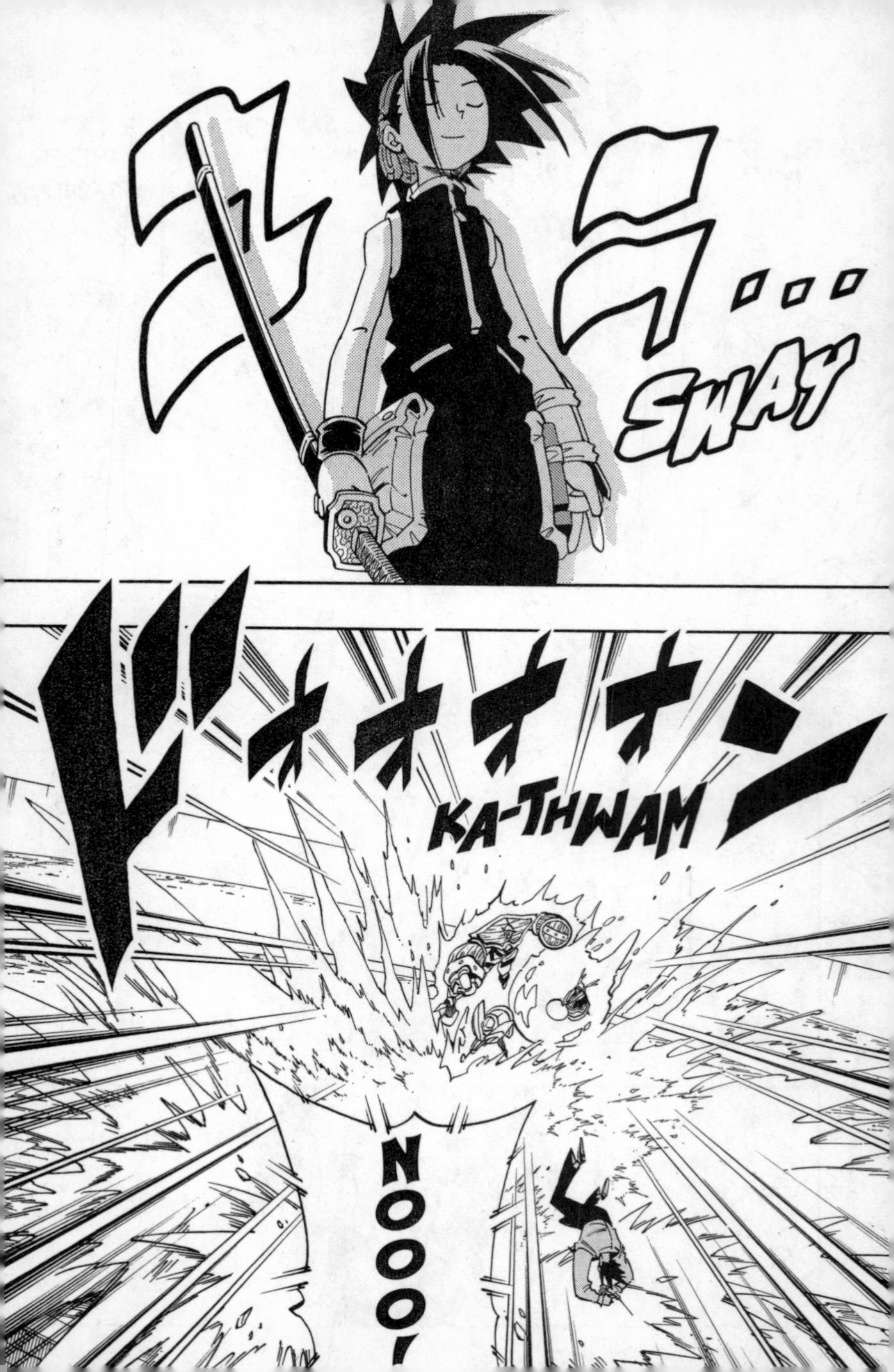
SWAY
KA-THWAM
NOOO!

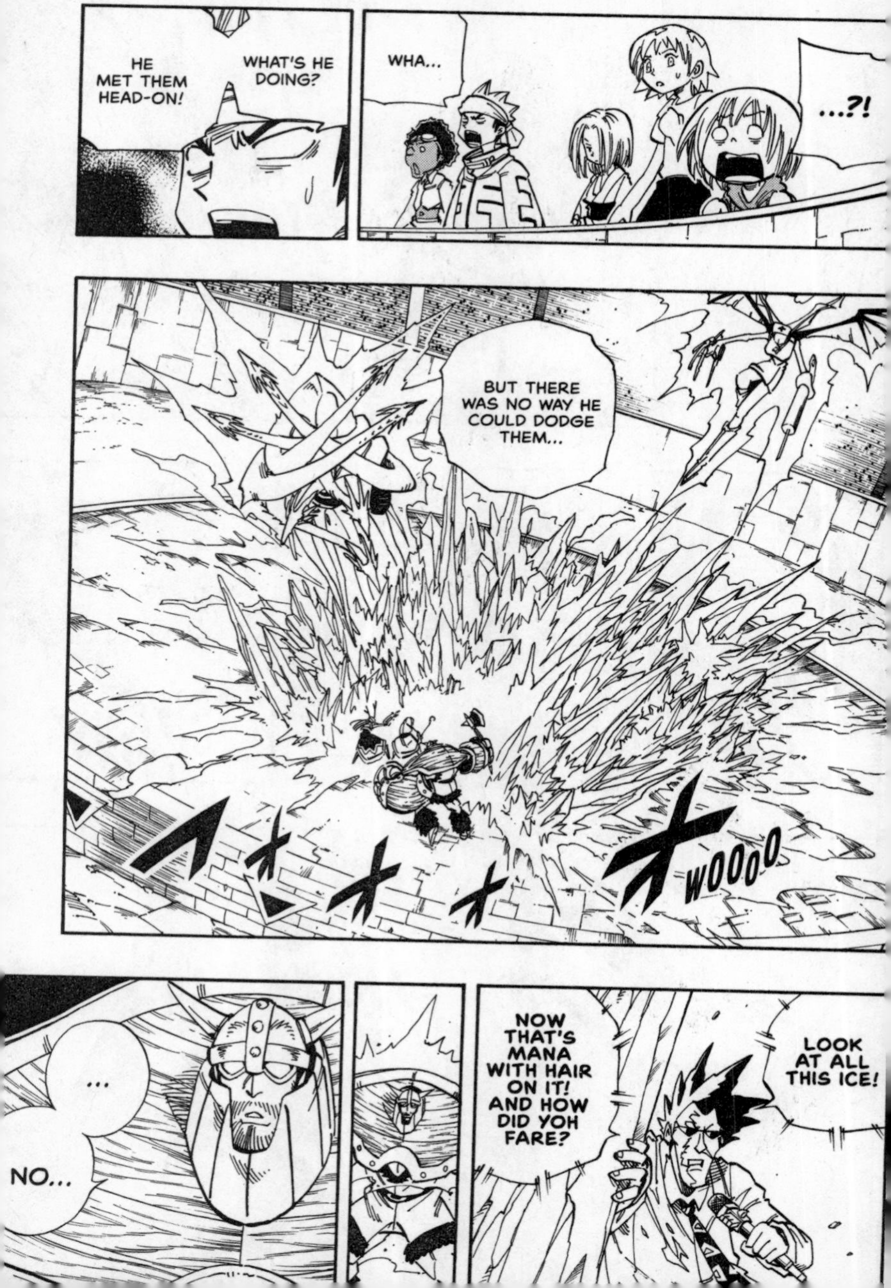
...?!
WHA...
WHAT'S HE DOING?
HE MET THEM HEAD-ON!
BUT THERE WAS NO WAY HE COULD DODGE THEM...
WOOOO
LOOK AT ALL THIS ICE!
NOW THAT'S MANA WITH HAIR ON IT! AND HOW DID YOH FARE?
...
NO...

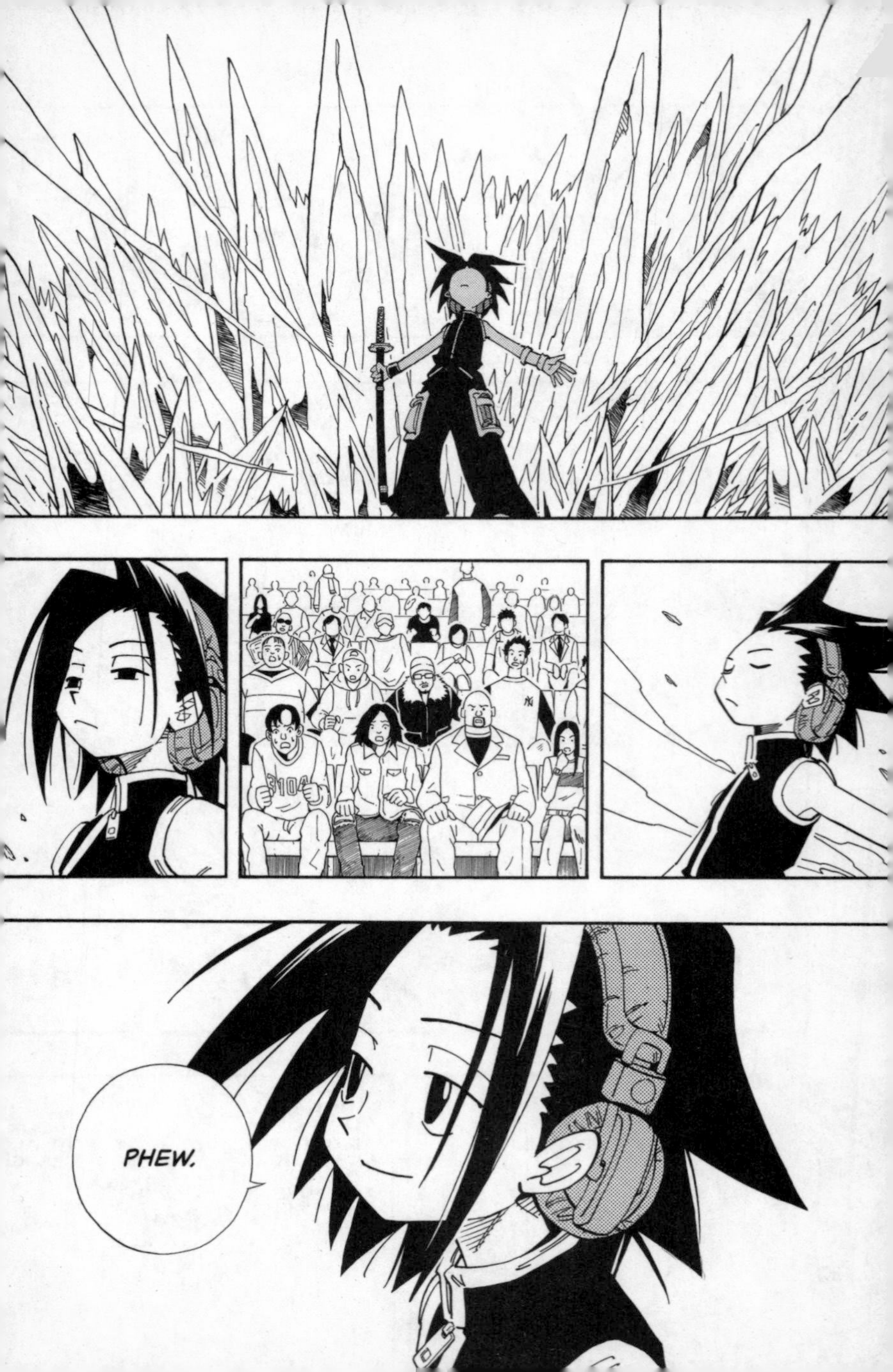
PHEW.

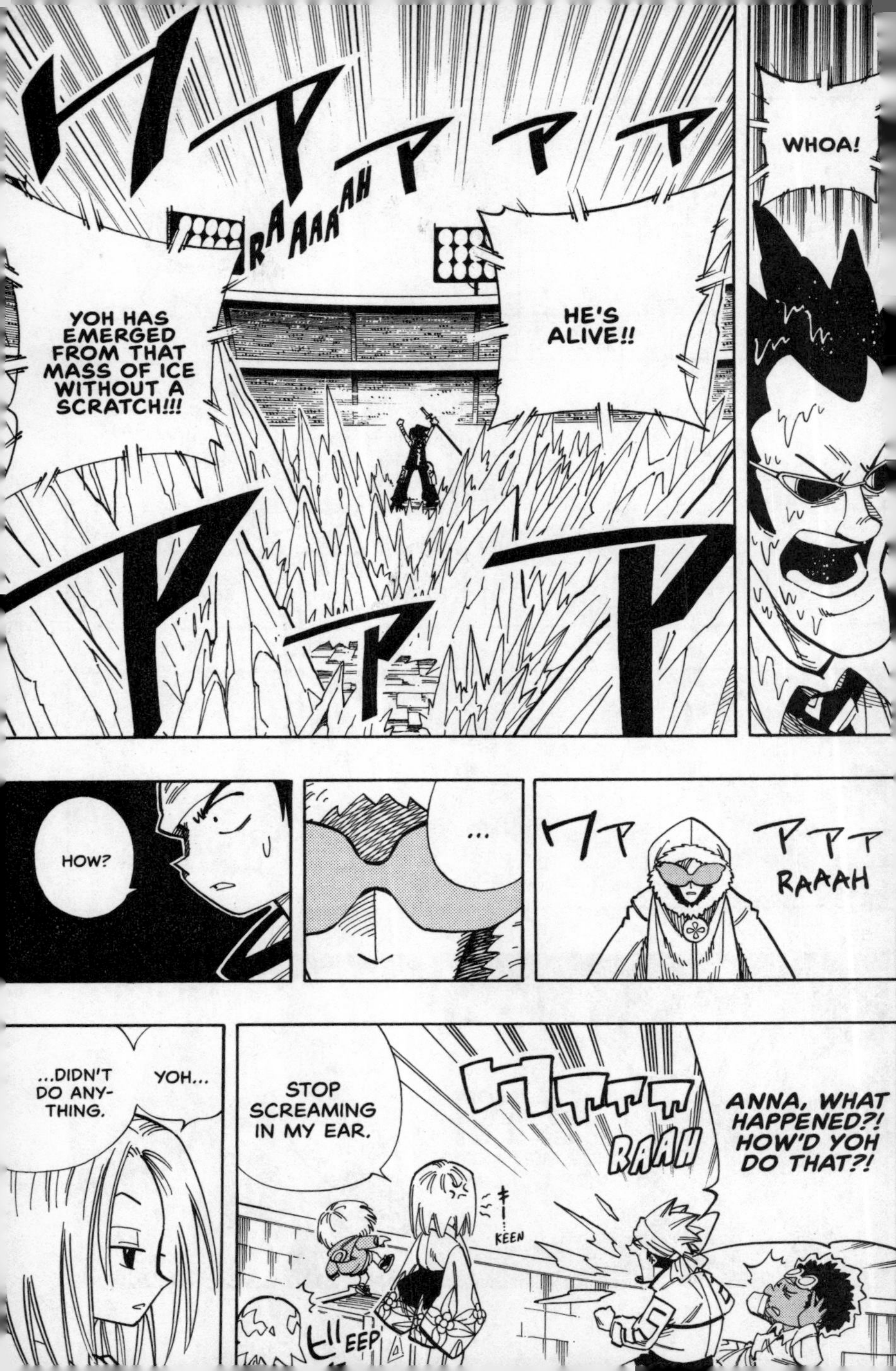

WHOA!
RAAAAAH
HE'S ALIVE!!
YOH HAS EMERGED FROM THAT MASS OF ICE WITHOUT A SCRATCH!!!
RAAAH
...
HOW?
ANNA, WHAT HAPPENED?! HOW'D YOH DO THAT?!
RAAH
STOP SCREAMING IN MY EAR.
KEEN
EEP
YOH...
...DIDN'T DO ANY-THING.

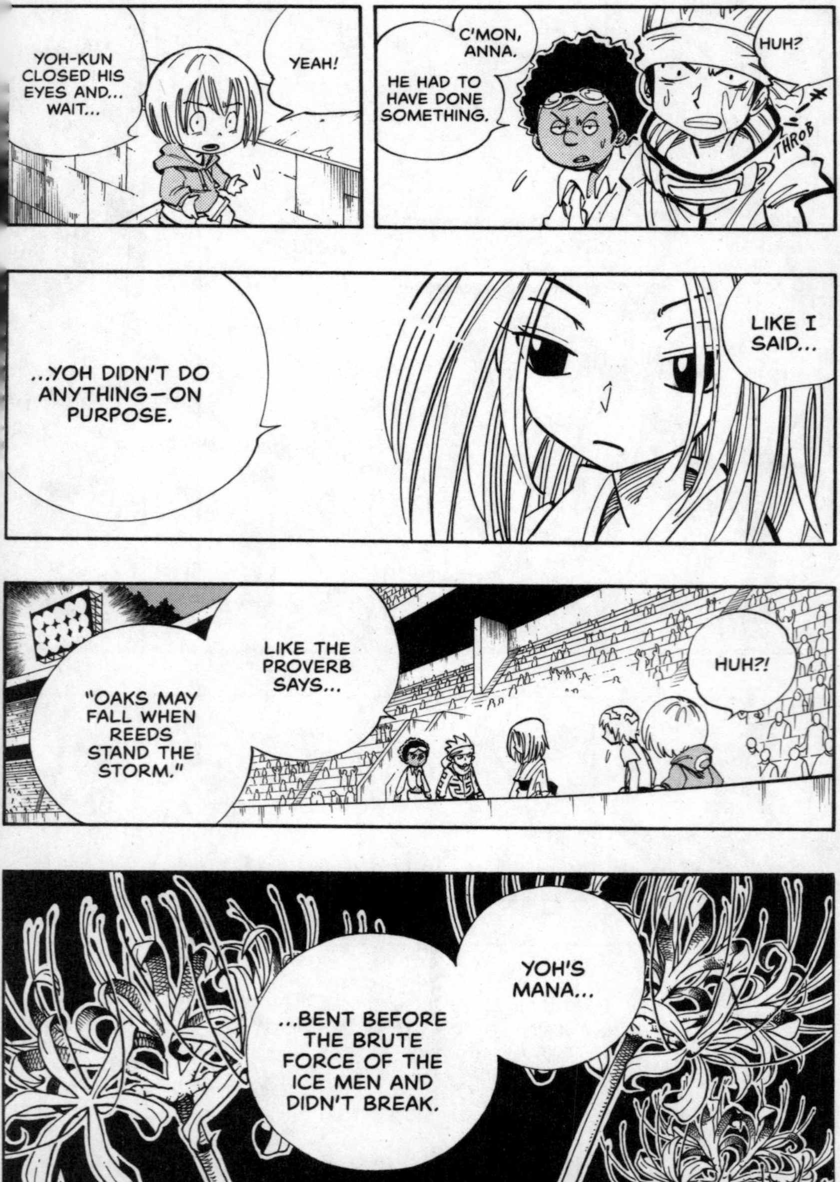

C'MON, ANNA.
HE HAD TO HAVE DONE SOMETHING.
HUH?
THROB
YEAH!
YOH-KUN CLOSED HIS EYES AND... WAIT...
LIKE I SAID...
...YOH DIDN'T DO ANYTHING—ON PURPOSE.
HUH?!
LIKE THE PROVERB SAYS...
"OAKS MAY FALL WHEN REEDS STAND THE STORM."
YOH'S MANA...
...BENT BEFORE THE BRUTE FORCE OF THE ICE MEN AND DIDN'T BREAK.

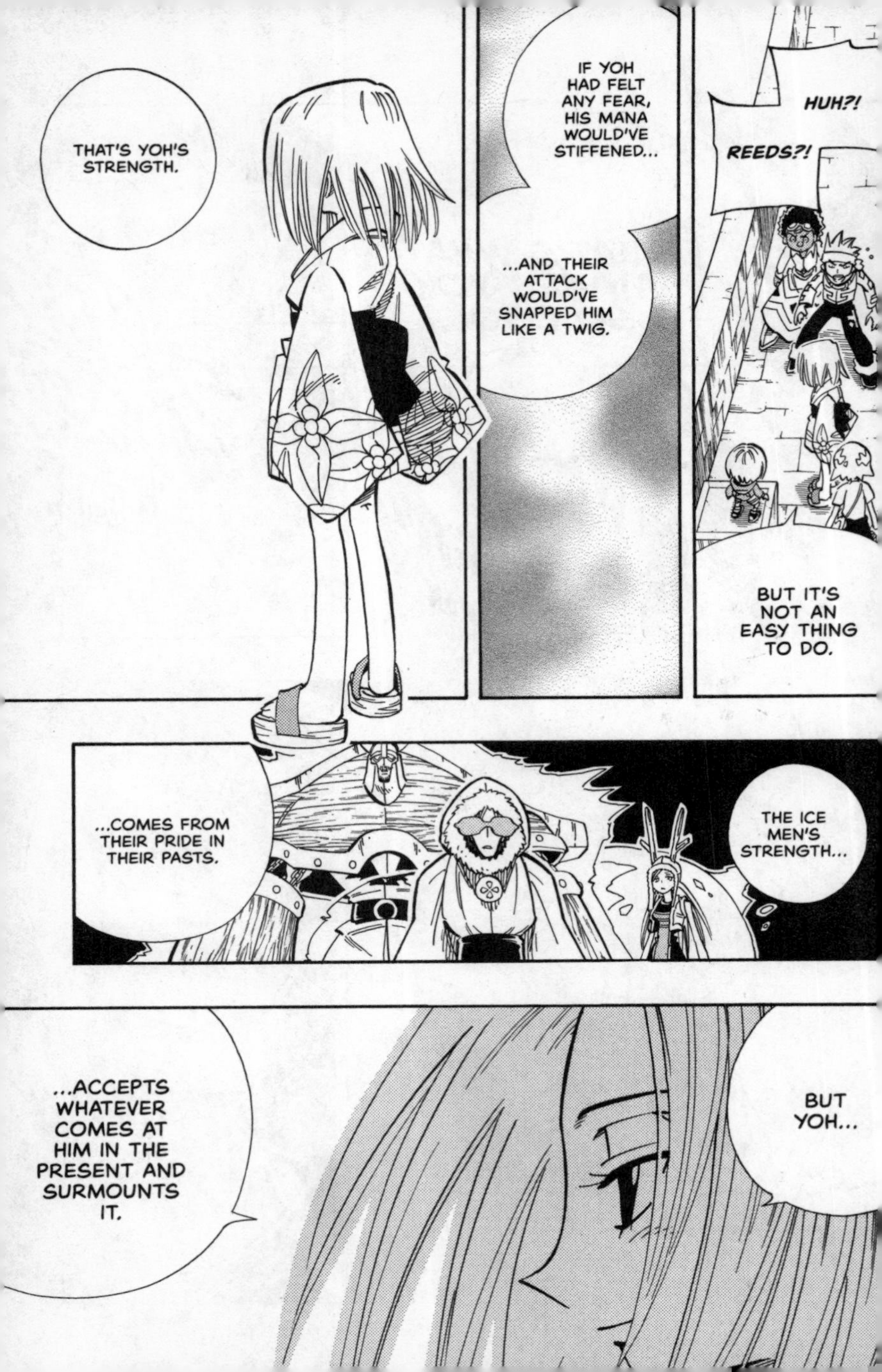
HUH?!
REEDS?!
BUT IT'S NOT AN EASY THING TO DO.
IF YOH HAD FELT ANY FEAR, HIS MANA WOULD'VE STIFFENED...
...AND THEIR ATTACK WOULD'VE SNAPPED HIM LIKE A TWIG.
THAT'S YOH'S STRENGTH.
THE ICE MEN'S STRENGTH...
...COMES FROM THEIR PRIDE IN THEIR PASTS.
BUT YOH...
...ACCEPTS WHATEVER COMES AT HIM IN THE PRESENT AND SURMOUNTS IT.

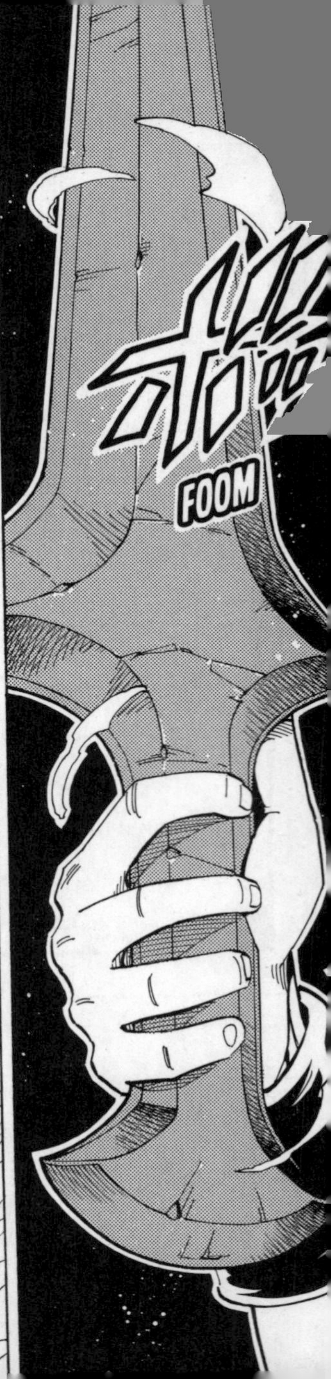
FOOM

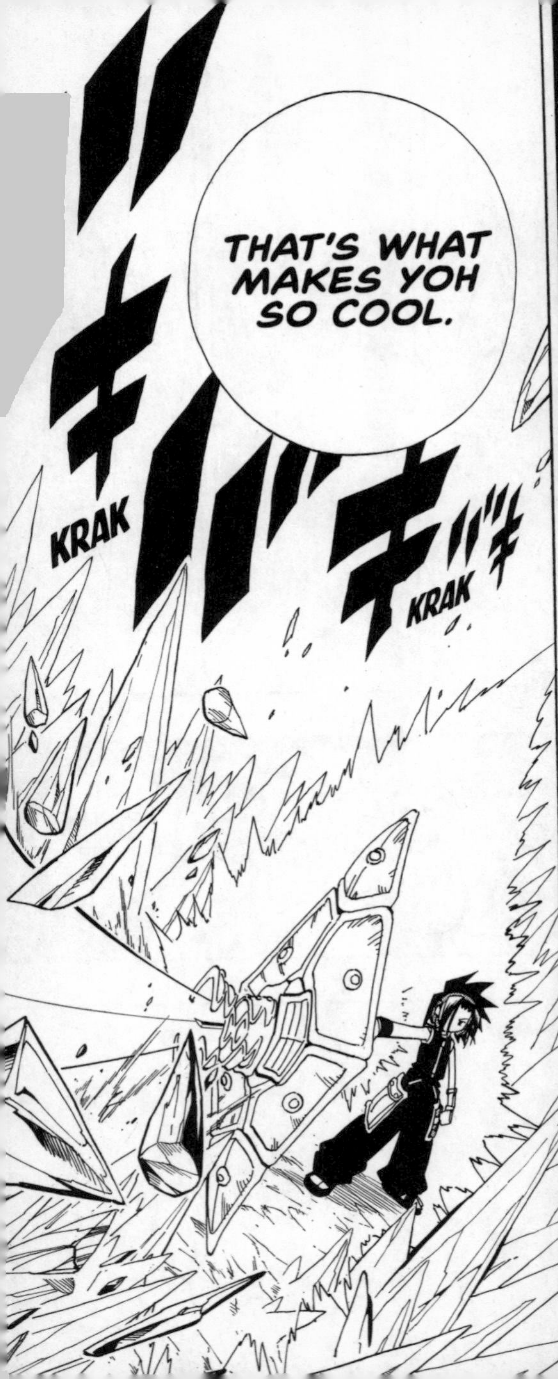
THAT'S WHAT MAKES YOH SO COOL.
KRAK
KRAK

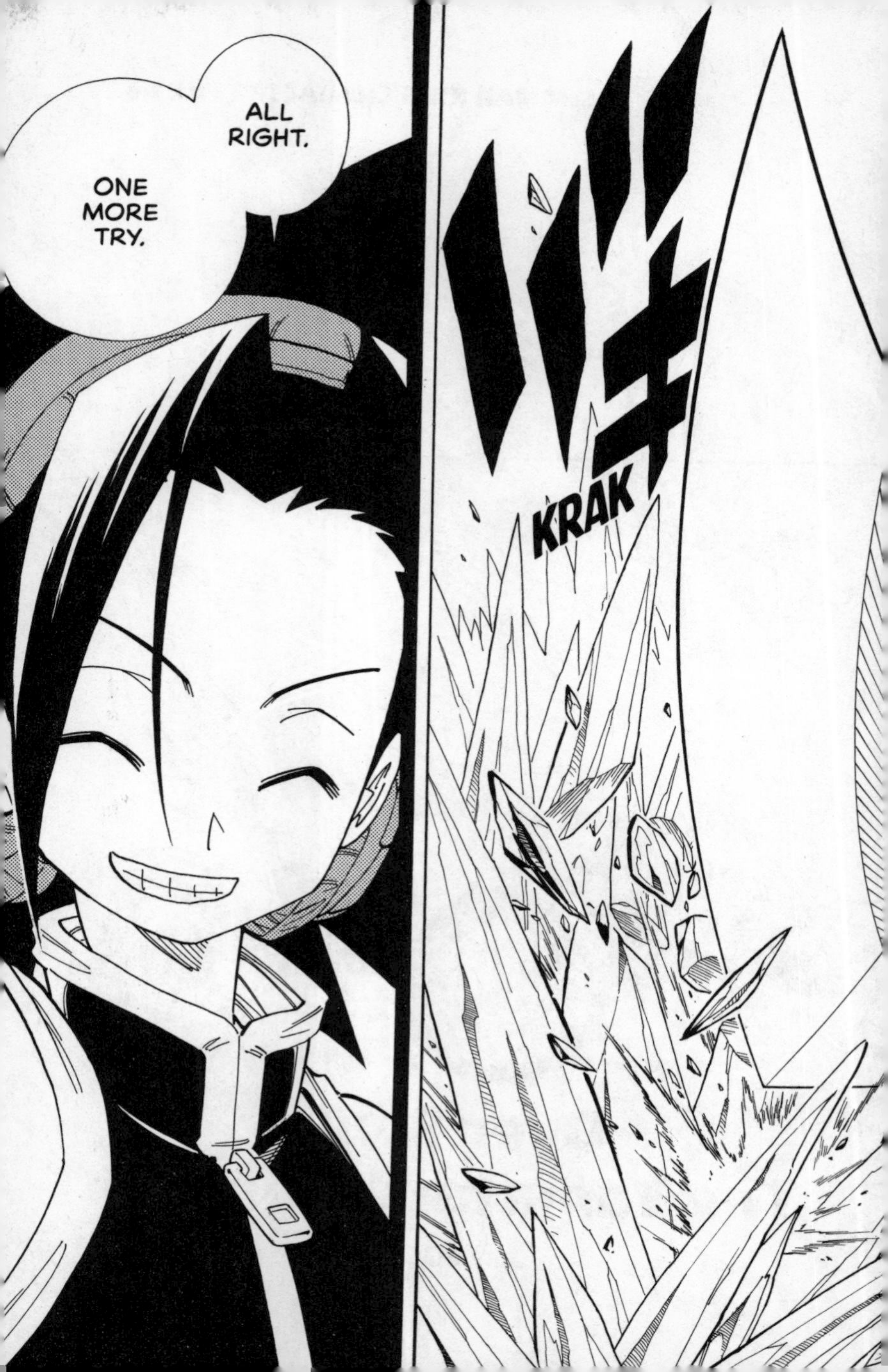
バキ
KRAK
ALL RIGHT. ONE MORE TRY.

SHAMAN KING CHARACTER FILE No.77

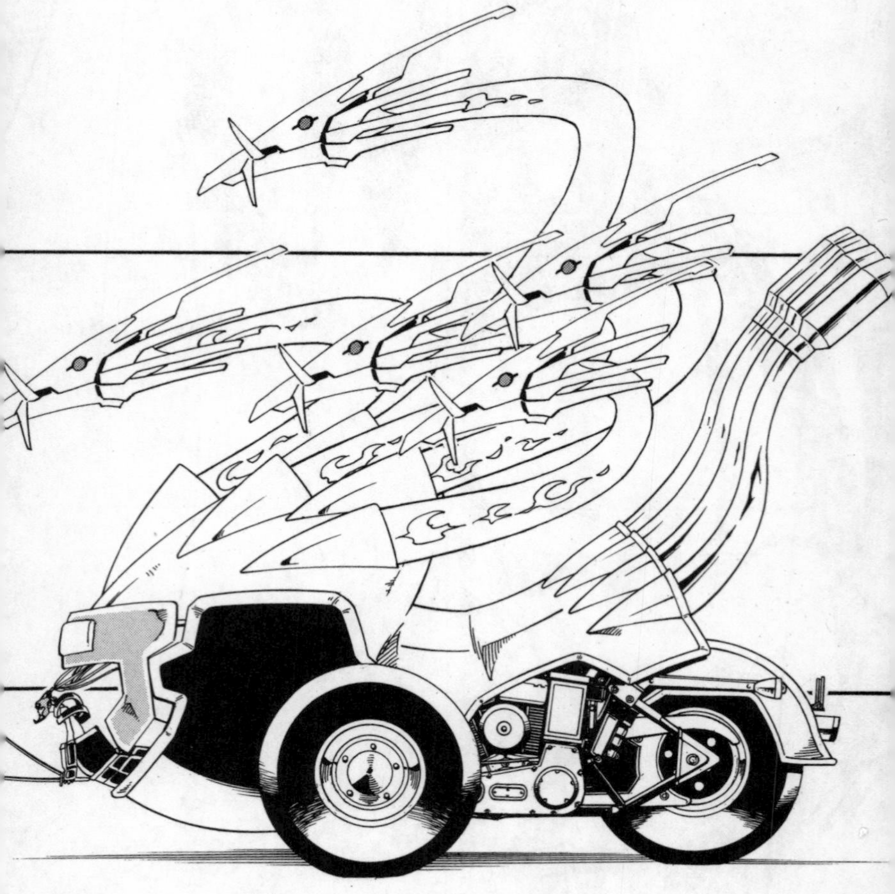

Over Soul:
The Yamata-No-Orochi

July 2001

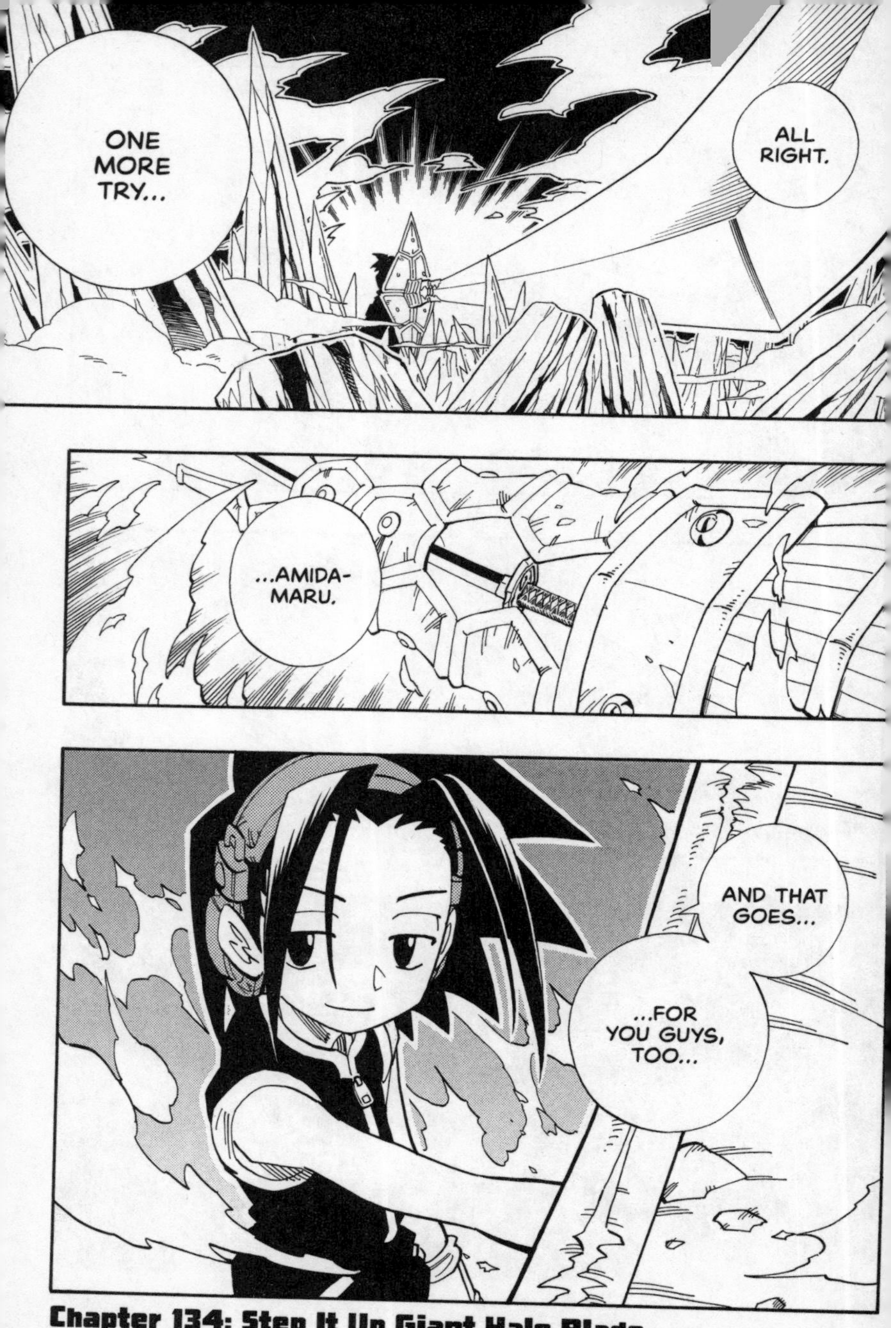
ALL RIGHT.
ONE MORE TRY...
...AMIDA-MARU.
AND THAT GOES...
...FOR YOU GUYS, TOO...

Chapter 134: Step It Up Giant Halo Blade

...ICE MEN.

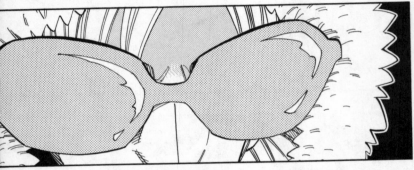

STEP IT UP.

Chapter 134:

Step It Up Giant Halo Blade

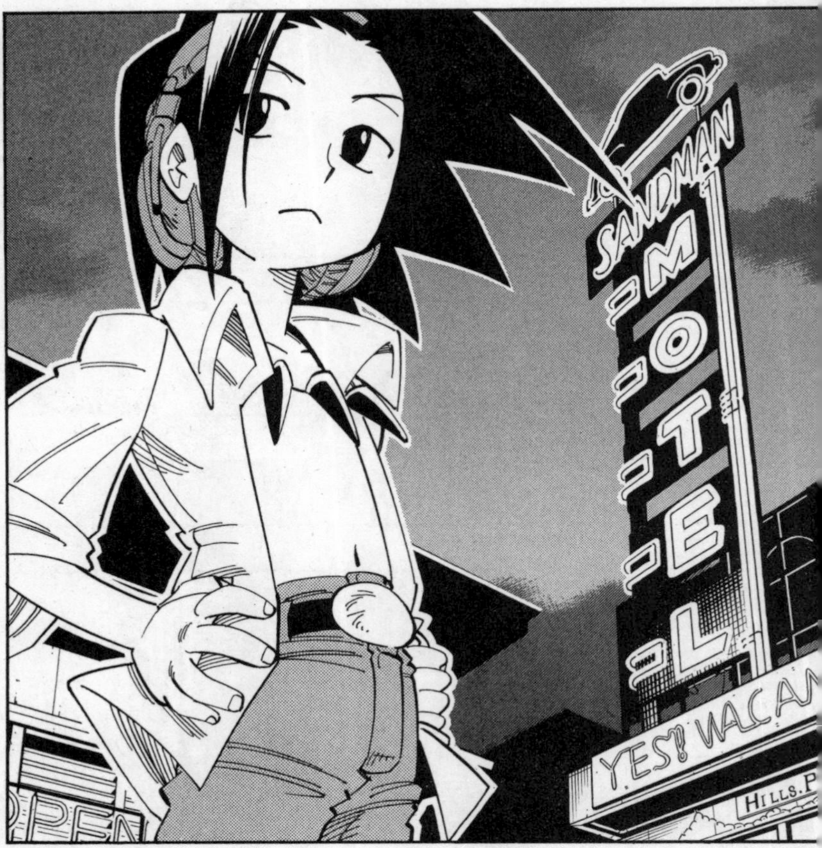
SANDMAN
MOTEL
YES! VACAN
HILLS.P
OPEN

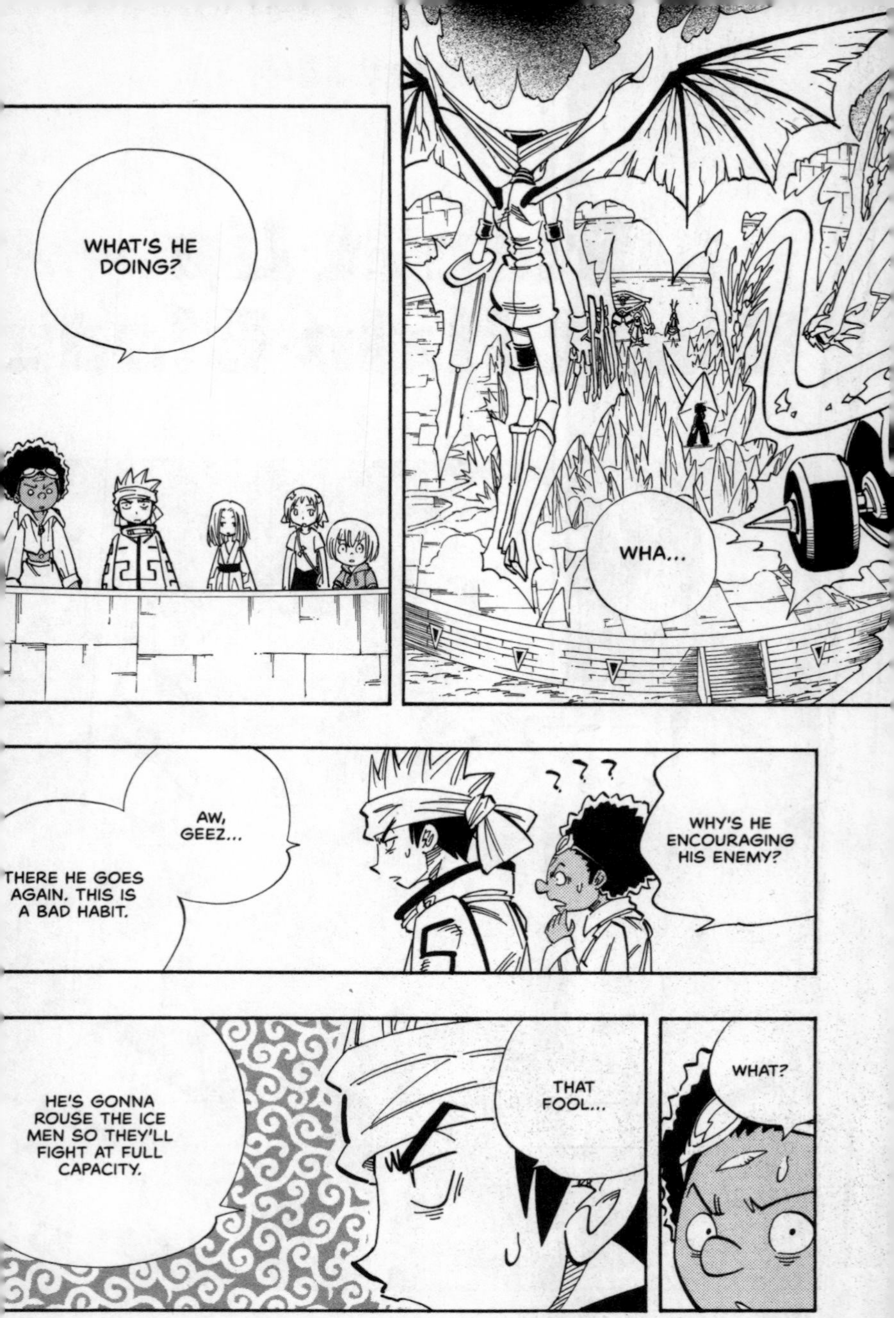
WHA...
WHAT'S HE DOING?
WHY'S HE ENCOURAGING HIS ENEMY?
AW, GEEZ...
THERE HE GOES AGAIN. THIS IS A BAD HABIT.
WHAT?
THAT FOOL...
HE'S GONNA ROUSE THE ICE MEN SO THEY'LL FIGHT AT FULL CAPACITY.

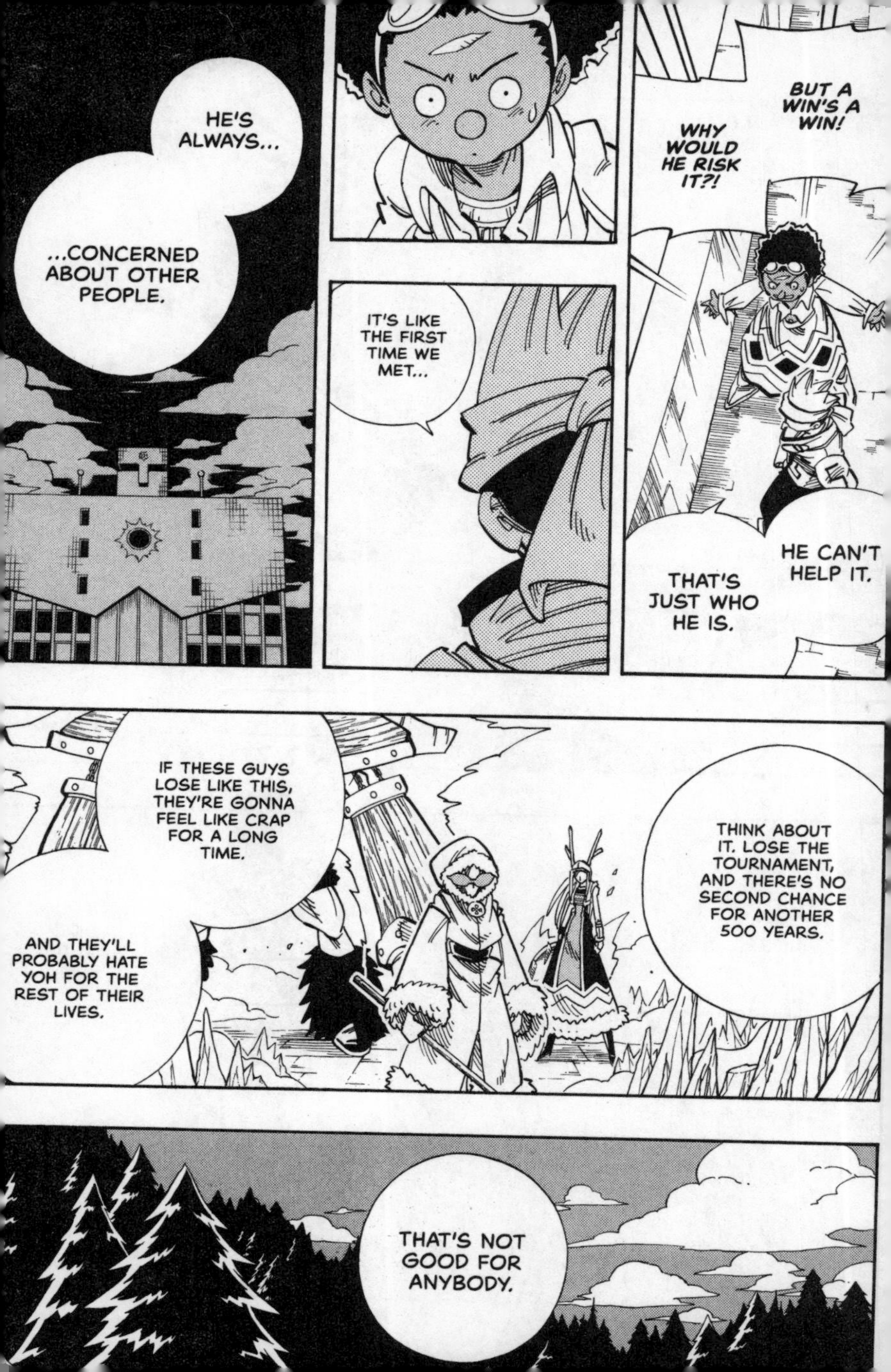
BUT A WIN'S A WIN!
WHY WOULD HE RISK IT?!
HE CAN'T HELP IT.
THAT'S JUST WHO HE IS.
IT'S LIKE THE FIRST TIME WE MET...
HE'S ALWAYS...
...CONCERNED ABOUT OTHER PEOPLE.
THINK ABOUT IT. LOSE THE TOURNAMENT, AND THERE'S NO SECOND CHANCE FOR ANOTHER 500 YEARS.
IF THESE GUYS LOSE LIKE THIS, THEY'RE GONNA FEEL LIKE CRAP FOR A LONG TIME.
AND THEY'LL PROBABLY HATE YOH FOR THE REST OF THEIR LIVES.
THAT'S NOT GOOD FOR ANYBODY.

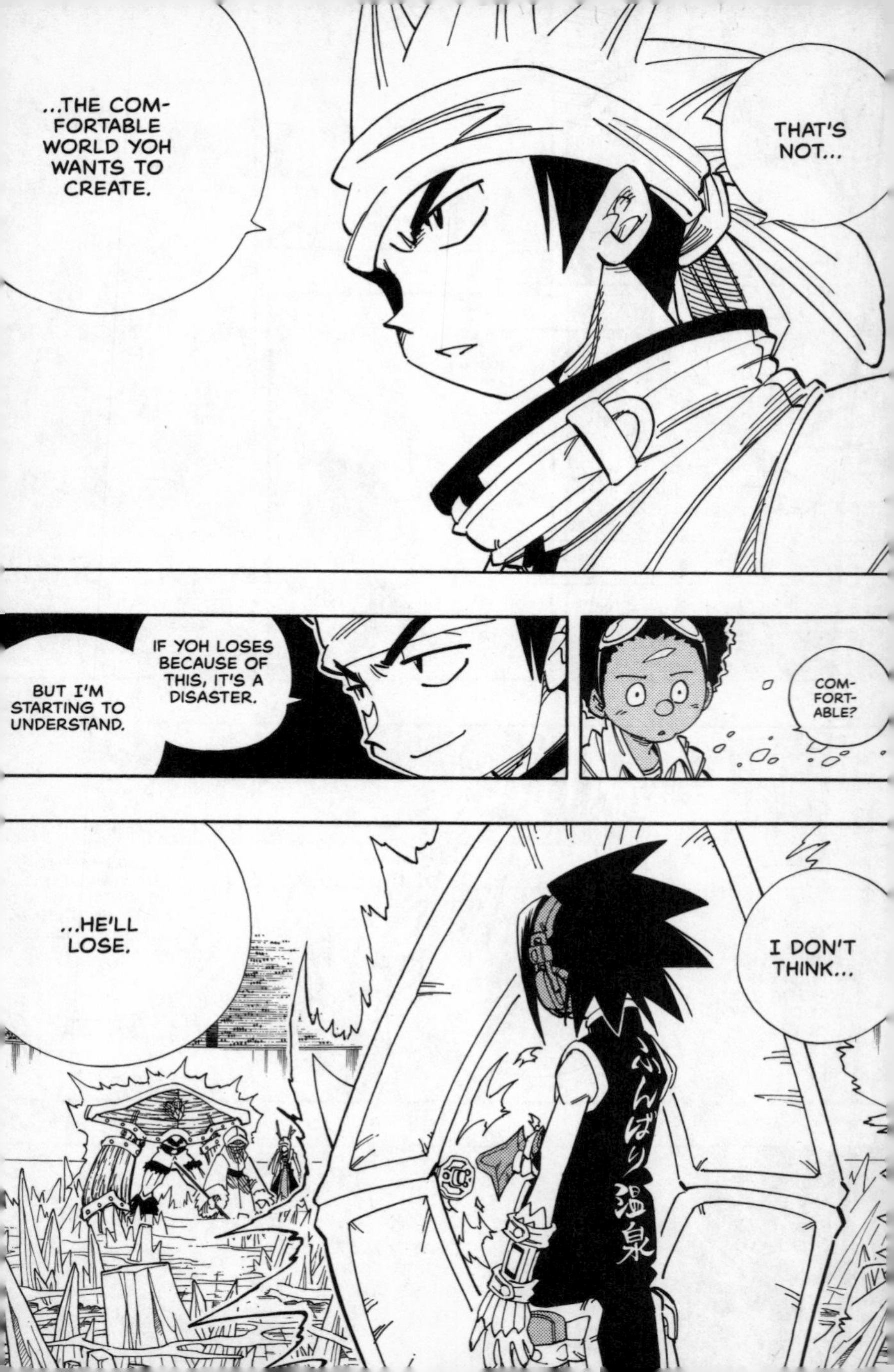
THAT'S NOT...
...THE COM-FORTABLE WORLD YOH WANTS TO CREATE.
COM-FORT-ABLE?
IF YOH LOSES BECAUSE OF THIS, IT'S A DISASTER.
BUT I'M STARTING TO UNDERSTAND.
I DON'T THINK...
...HE'LL LOSE.
ふんばり温泉

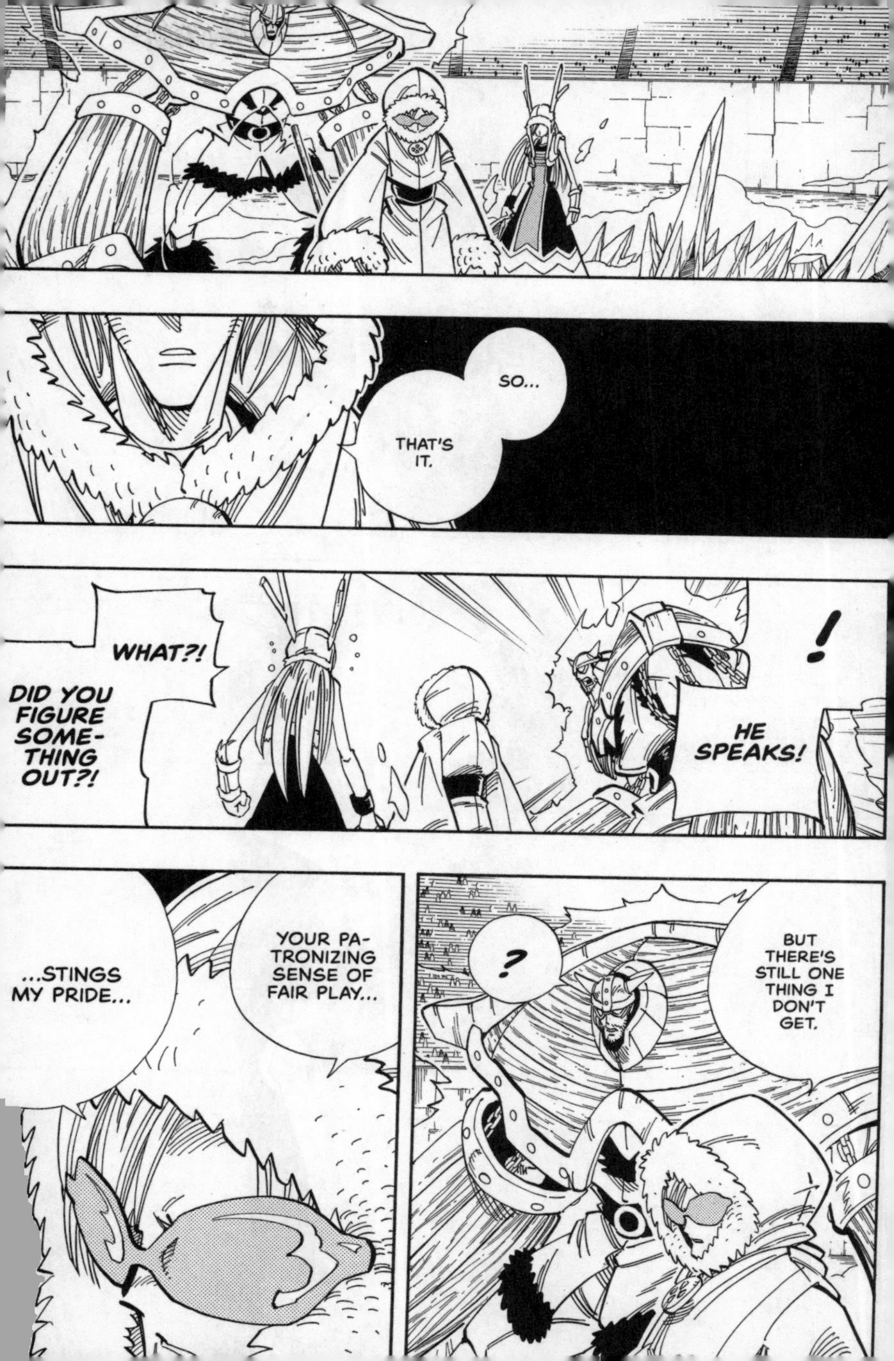
SO...
THAT'S IT.
!
HE SPEAKS!
WHAT?!
DID YOU FIGURE SOME-THING OUT?!
BUT THERE'S STILL ONE THING I DON'T GET.
?
YOUR PA-TRONIZING SENSE OF FAIR PLAY...
...STINGS MY PRIDE...

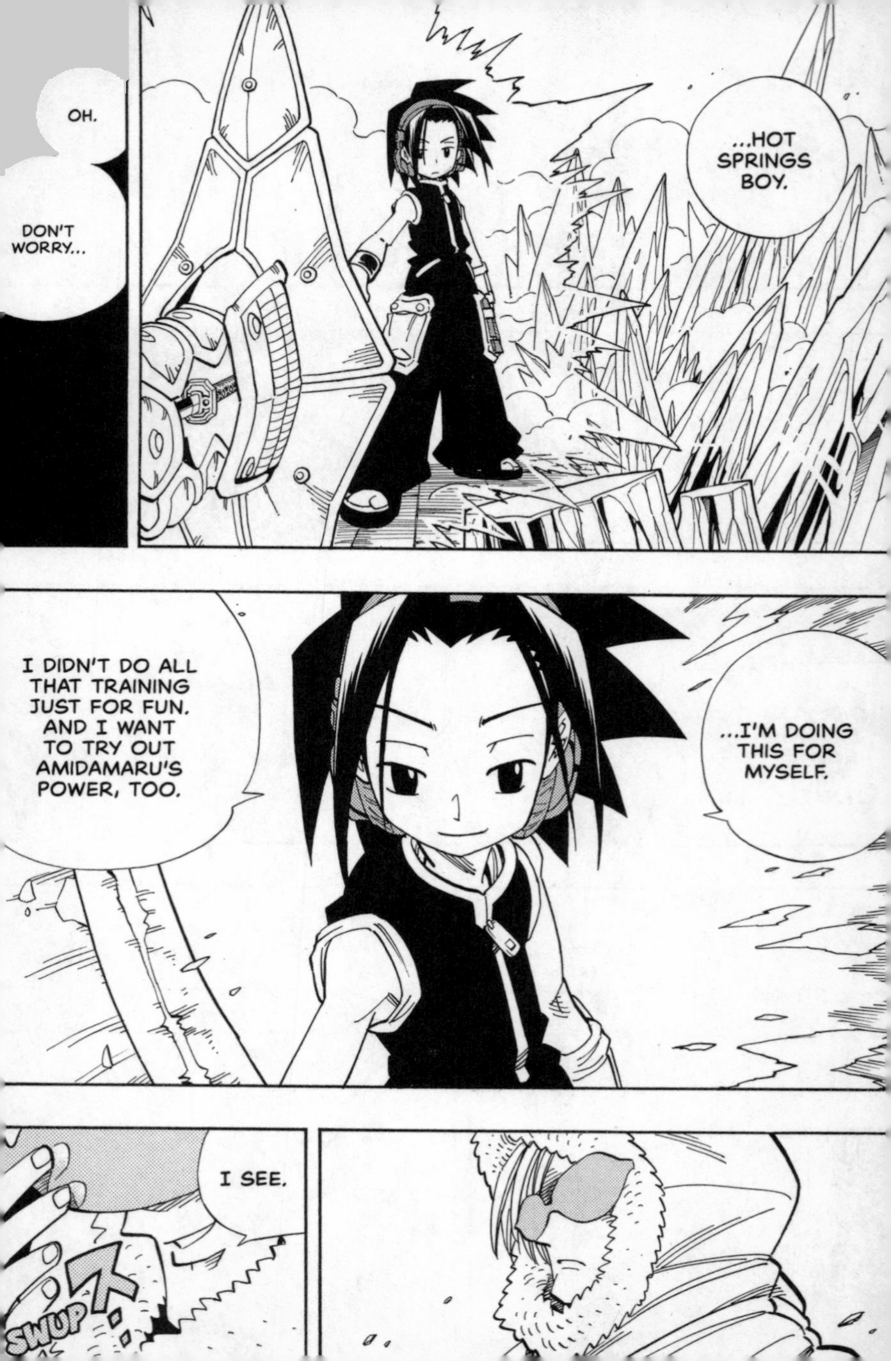
...HOT SPRINGS BOY.
OH.
DON'T WORRY...
...I'M DOING THIS FOR MYSELF.
I DIDN'T DO ALL THAT TRAINING JUST FOR FUN. AND I WANT TO TRY OUT AMIDAMARU'S POWER, TOO.
I SEE.
SWUP

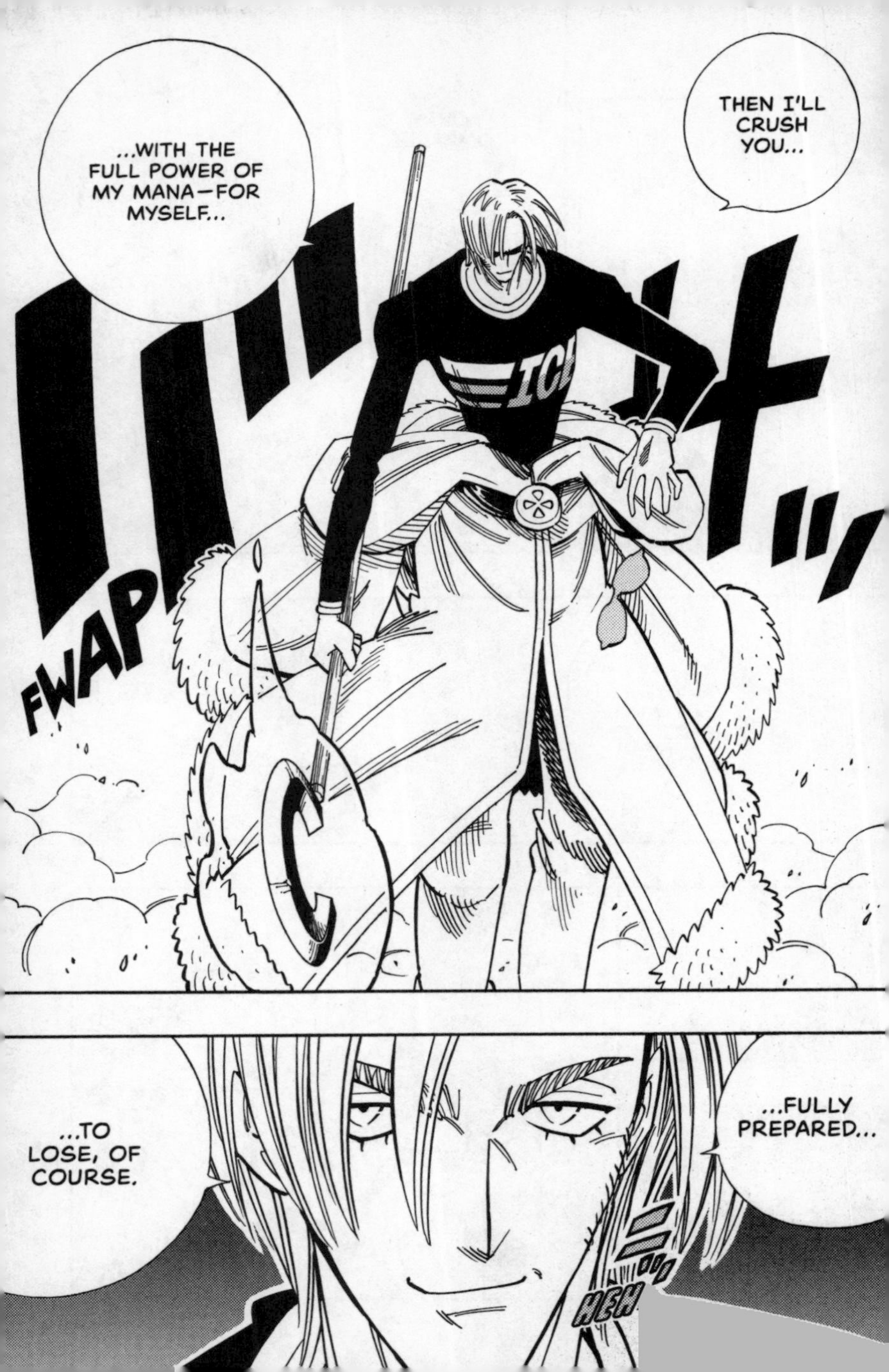
THEN I'LL CRUSH YOU...
...WITH THE FULL POWER OF MY MANA—FOR MYSELF...
FWAP
...FULLY PREPARED...
...TO LOSE, OF COURSE.
HEH

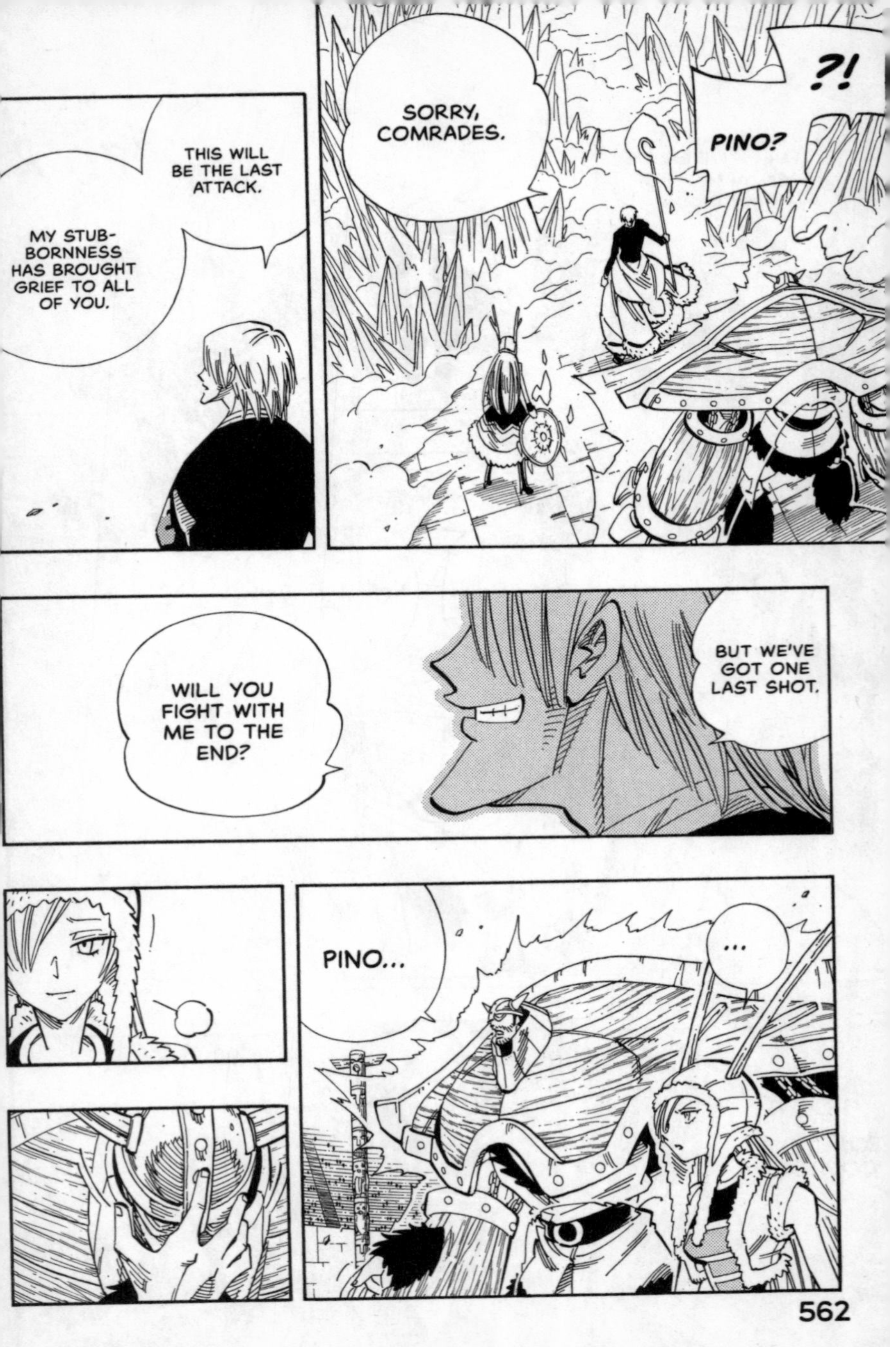
?!
PINO?
SORRY, COMRADES.
THIS WILL BE THE LAST ATTACK.
MY STUB-BORNNESS HAS BROUGHT GRIEF TO ALL OF YOU.
BUT WE'VE GOT ONE LAST SHOT.
WILL YOU FIGHT WITH ME TO THE END?
...
PINO...
!

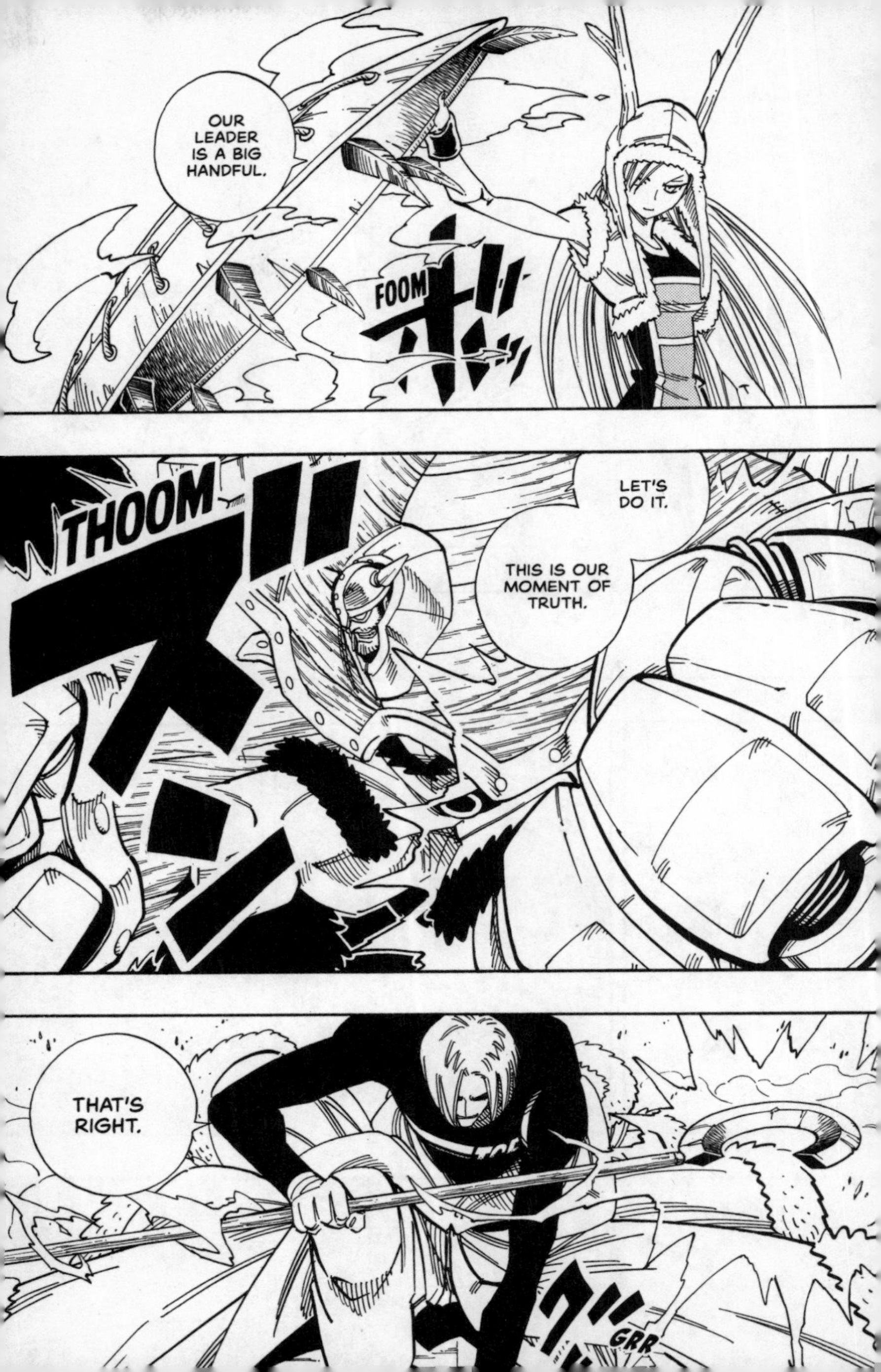
OUR LEADER IS A BIG HANDFUL.
FOOM
LET'S DO IT.
THIS IS OUR MOMENT OF TRUTH.
THOOM
THAT'S RIGHT.
GRR

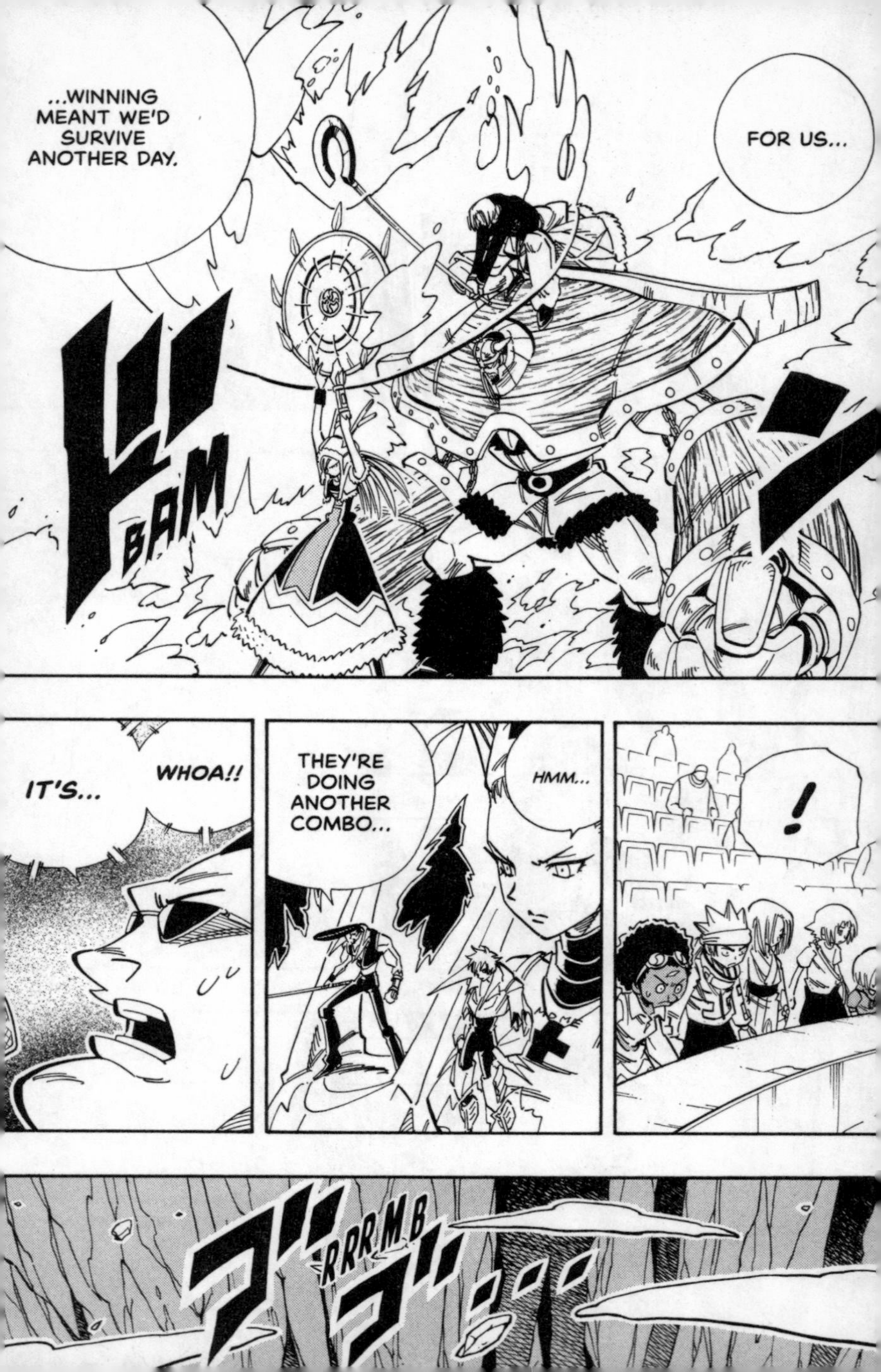
FOR US...
...WINNING MEANT WE'D SURVIVE ANOTHER DAY.
BAM
!
HMM...
THEY'RE DOING ANOTHER COMBO...
WHOA!!
IT'S...
RRRMB

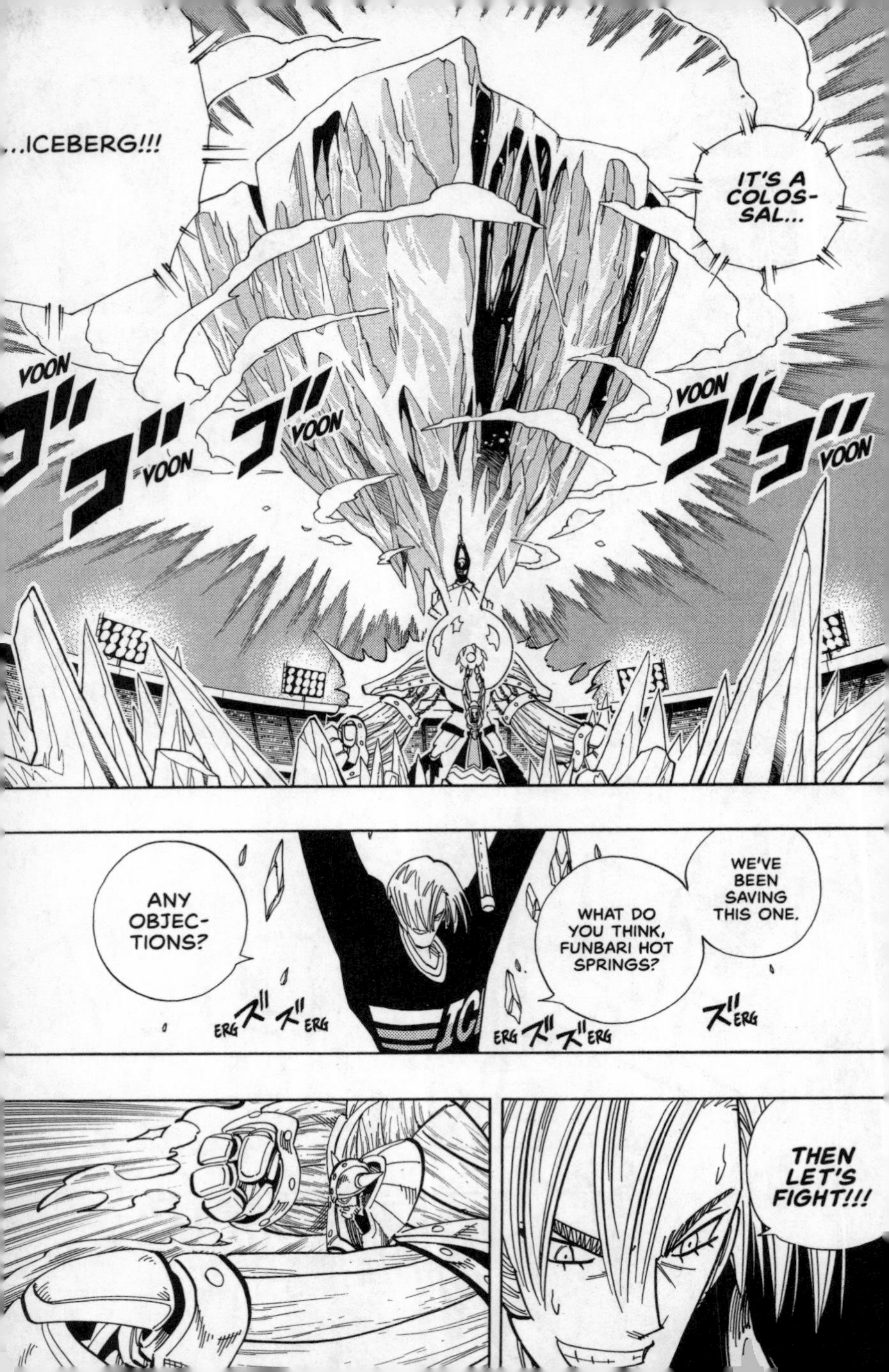
IT'S A COLOSSAL...
...ICEBERG!!!
VOON ゴゴ VOON
VOON ゴゴ VOON
VOON ゴゴ VOON
VOON
WE'VE BEEN SAVING THIS ONE.
WHAT DO YOU THINK, FUNBARI HOT SPRINGS?
ANY OBJECTIONS?
ズ ERG
ERG ズズ ERG
ERG ズズ ERG
THEN LET'S FIGHT!!!

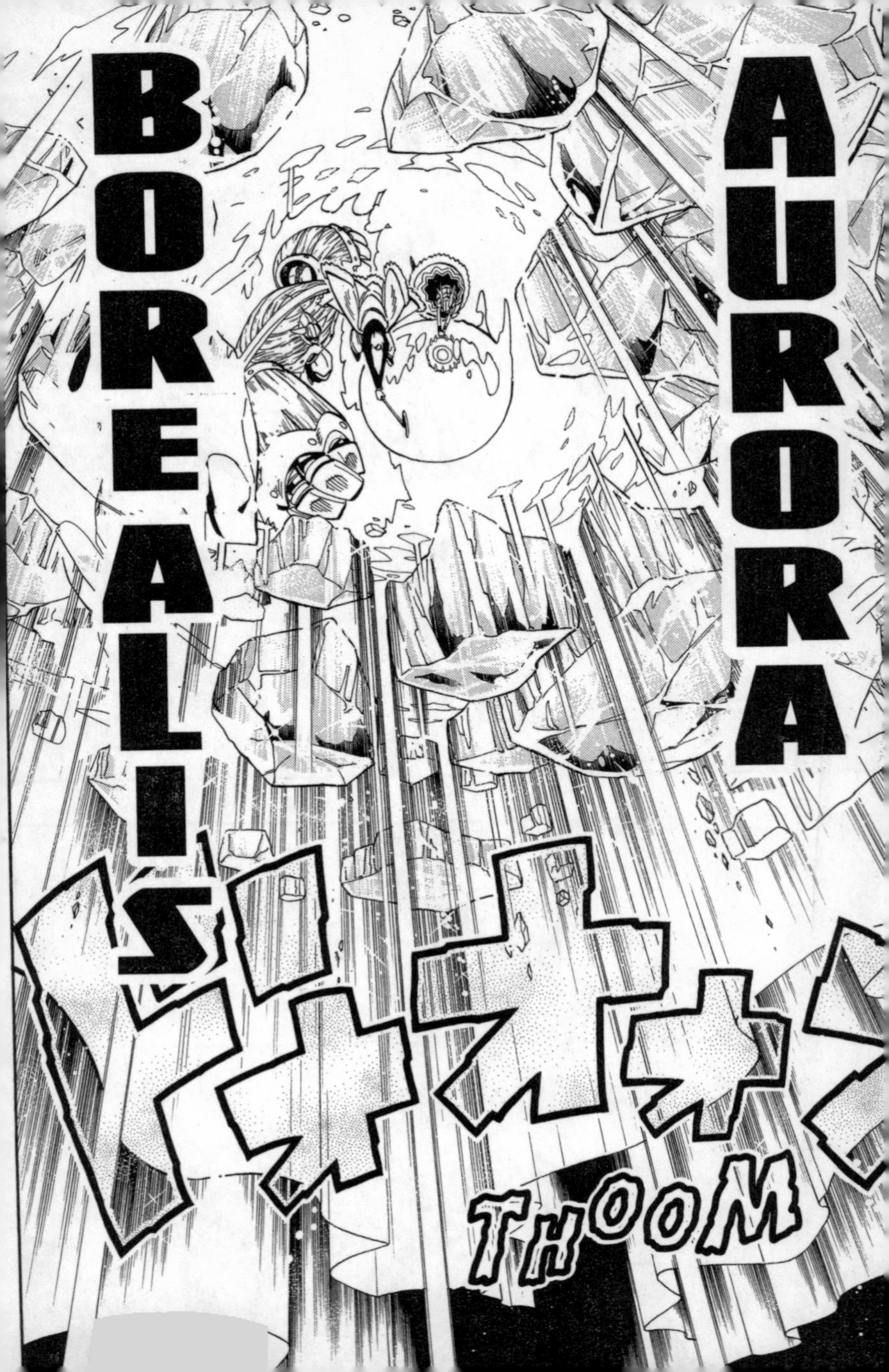
AURORA
BOREALIS
THOOM

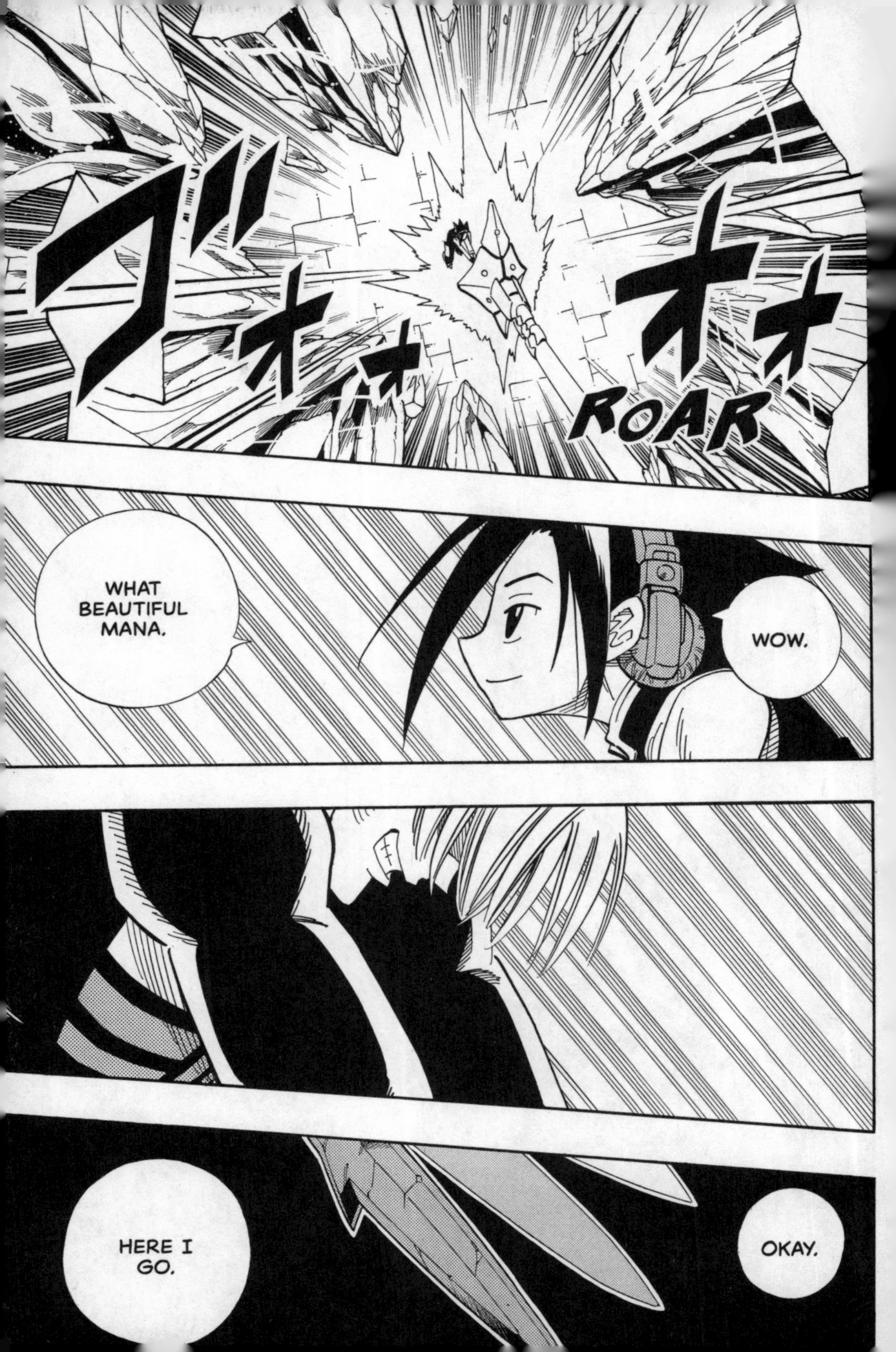
ゴオォオォ
ROAR
WOW.
WHAT BEAUTIFUL MANA.
OKAY.
HERE I GO.

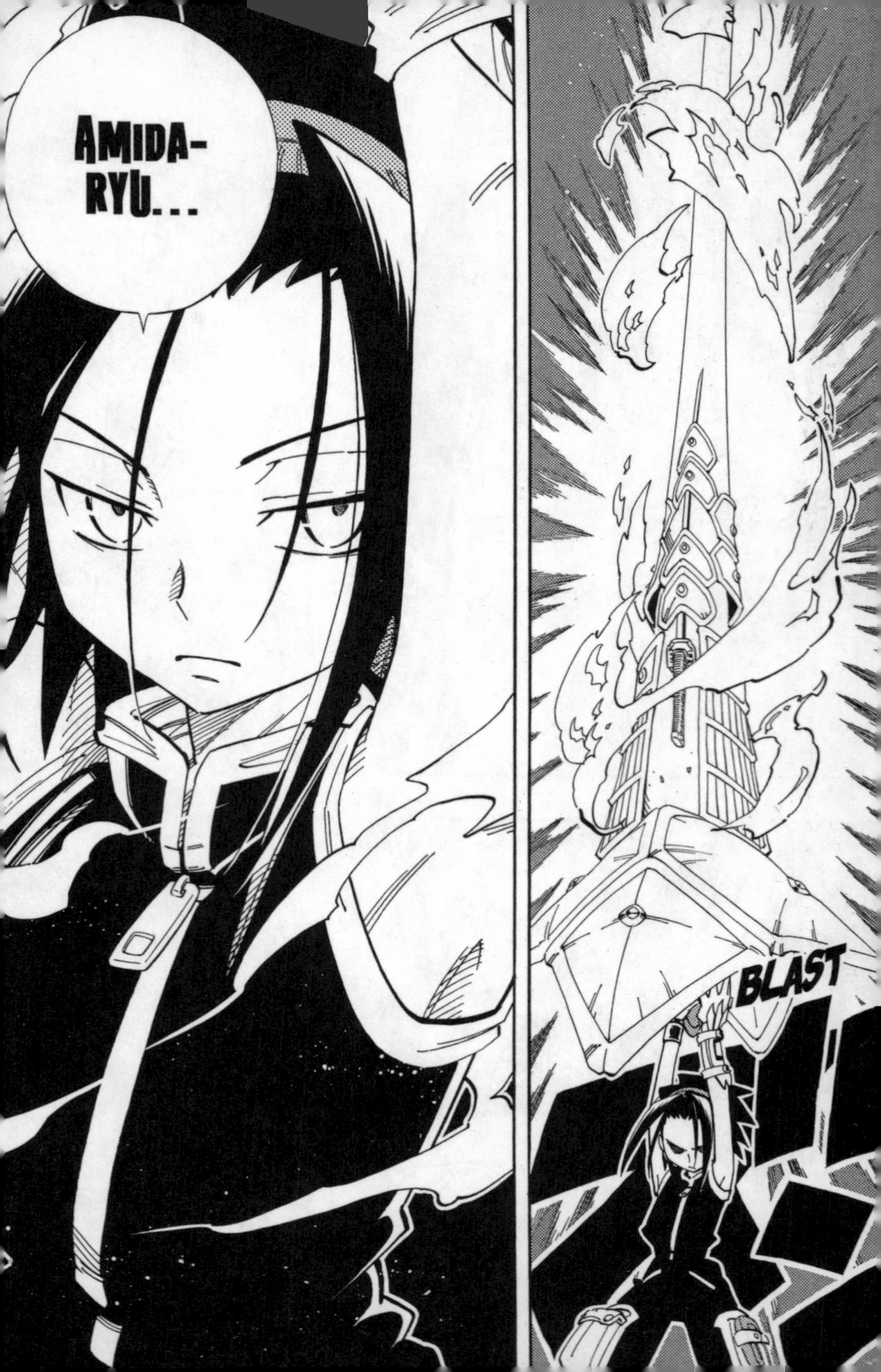
BLAST
AMIDA-RYU...

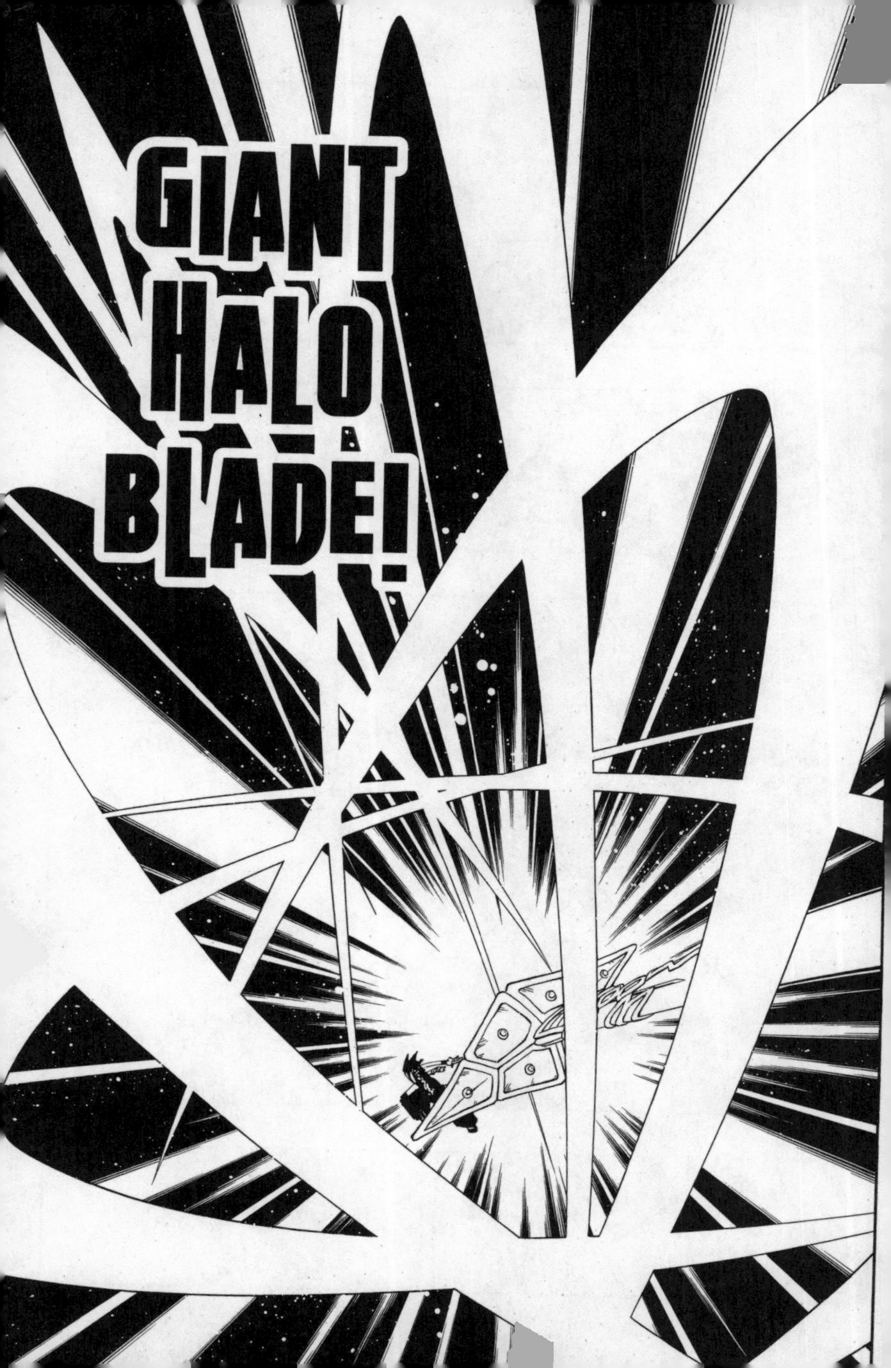
GIANT HALO BLADE!

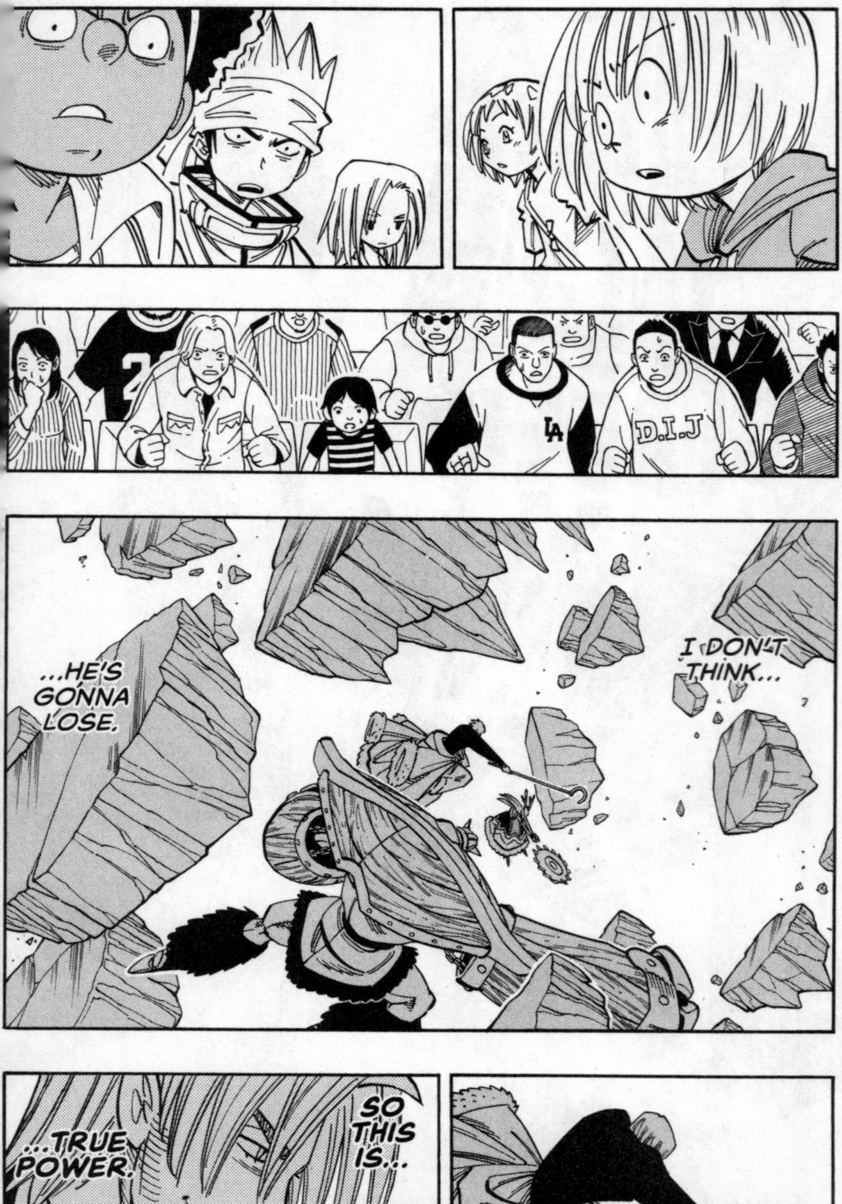
I DON'T THINK...
...HE'S GONNA LOSE.
SO THIS IS...
...TRUE POWER.

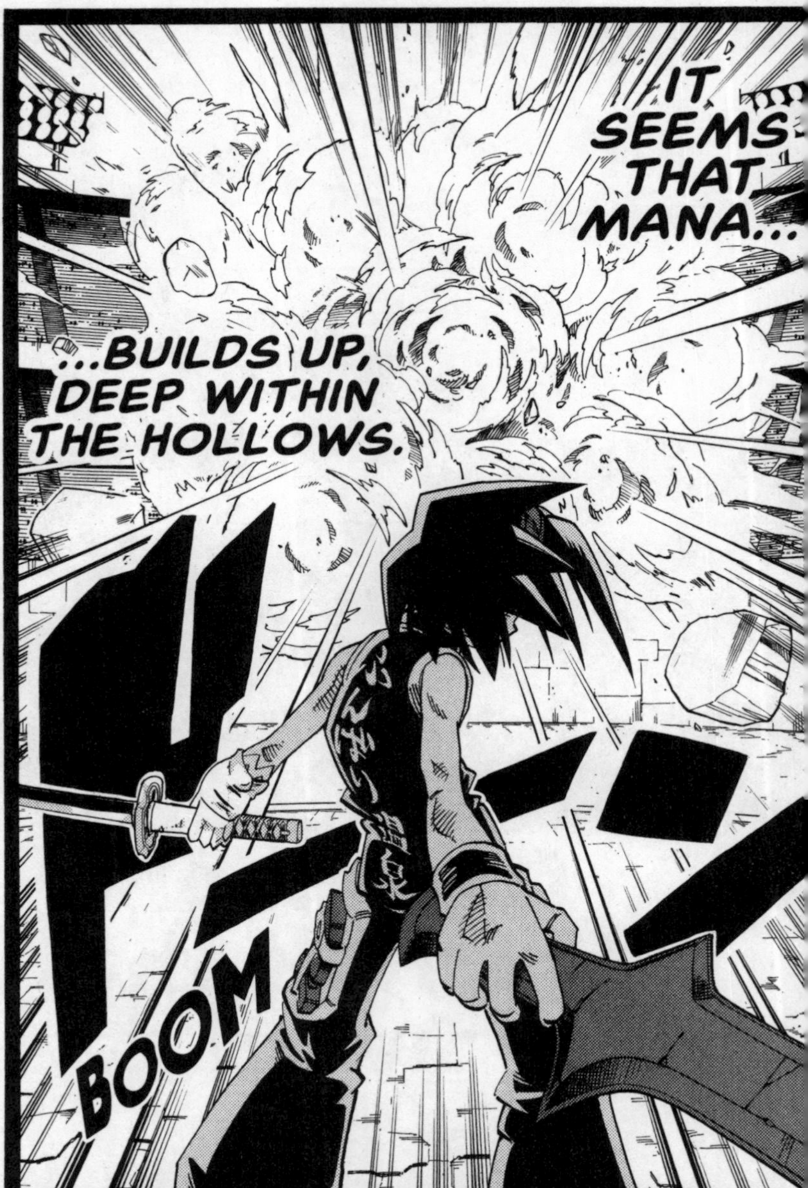
IT SEEMS THAT MANA...
...BUILDS UP, DEEP WITHIN THE HOLLOWS.
BOOM

To be continued in Shaman King Omnibus 6!

SHAMAN KING CHARACTER FILE No.78

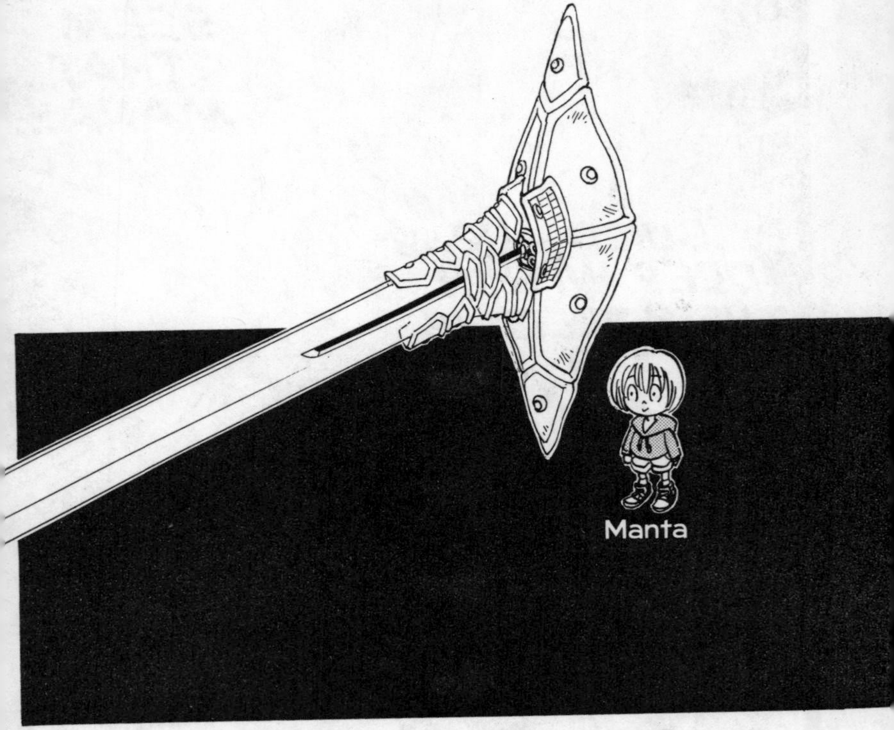
Manta

Over Soul: Spirit of the Sword

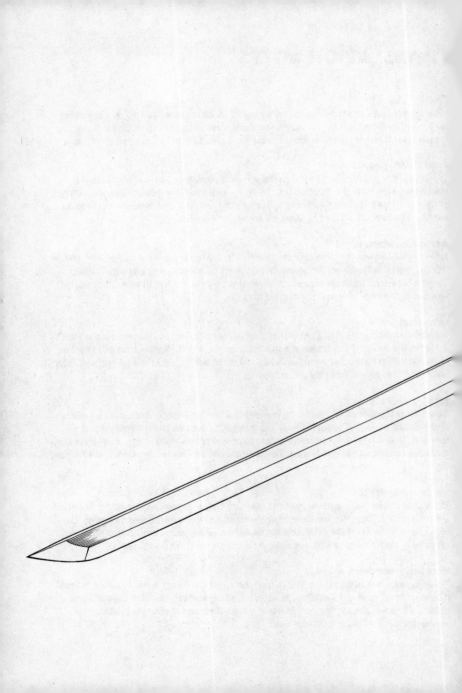

TRANSLATION NOTES

"Horses", page 52
In the original Japanese, Joco made a pun using the word *seifuku*, meaning "uniform," as a play on the word *seiryoku*, meaning "forces." The black, high-collared jacket with round buttons that Joco wears in the joke scene is part of the typical school uniform, called *gakuran*, worn by high school boys in Japan.

Zenki and Goki, page 91
The pair guarding Hao's *The Ultra Senji Ryakettsu* are *oni*, or ogres, from Japanese folklore. Zenki is the male, representing the bright characteristics of the yang, while Goki is the female counterpart with dark qualities of the ying. They are traditionally associated with En no Gyōja, considered the founder of the ascetic art of *shugendō*, practiced by Tamao and her mentor, Mikihisa.

Amazonian shaman, page 127
In the original Japanese, the katakana of the term *indio* is used to describe Joco's mentor. *Indio*, literally meaning "Indian" in Spanish and Portuguese, typically refers to indigenous people in South America. The term has become less commonly accepted in recent years, hence the translation has been adapted according to Orona's origins revealed later in the story.

Calavera, page 154
Tecolote's Over Souls are portrayed and referred to as *calavera* dolls. The term *calavera*, meaning "skull" in Spanish, is a distinctive visualization of a skull and associated with the Mexican tradition of the Day of the Dead. Often made out of sugar, the shape is just of the skull, instead of as a full-body doll. These "sugar skulls" are popular during the celebrations.

Rokujizo, page 188
These statues of *jizō*, or *bodhisattvas*, are frequently found in public spaces in Japan. *Jizō* are protectors of children and providers of comfort to those who are suffering. Anna explains the significance of the number six (*roku* means "six" in Japanese), as they correspond to each of the realms. Some believe that the statues, which are often next to cemeteries, symbolize a border between the worlds of the living and the dead.

Star Festival, page 384
Tanabata, or Star Festival, is a summer tradition filled with lively gatherings, brightly colored decorations, and fireworks. It is famous for the custom of writing wishes on paper and tying them to bamboo. The celebration is rooted in the story of Orihime and Hikoboshi, two star-crossed lovers in the heavens separated by the Milky Way who can only meet on the seventh day of the seventh month.

Futsu-no-Mitama sword, page 449
The divine sword in possession of the Asakura family has roots in mythology as well as history. In legend, it belonged to the sword god, Takemikazuchi. Later, it is said to have been owned by Emperor Jimmu, considered by some to be the first imperial leader of Japan. The sword continues to be an object of worship and is at the Isonokami Shrine in Nara.